Women's Health

Readings on Social, Economic, and Political Issues

Third Edition

Edited by

Nancy Worcester and Mariamne H. Whatley

Women's Studies Program
University of Wisconsin—Madison

KENDALL/HUNT PUBLISHING COMPANY
4050 Westmark Drive   Dubuque, Iowa 52002

Contents

Chapter 3 • Images and Gender Roles   141

Chapter 4 • Mental Health   189

Chapter 5 • Drugs, Alcohol, and Smoking   223

Chapter 6 • Menstruation   269

Chapter 7 • Aging, Ageism, Mid-life and Older Women's Health Issues   305

Chapter 8 • Sexuality   345

Chapter 9 • Fertility, Infertility and Reproductive Rights/Freedom   381

Chapter 10 • Childbearing   429

🏛 = "classic" articles = key older articles

Acknowledgments

*E*ach woman who has worked as a part of the Women's Studies 103 teaching team of the University of Wisconsin-Madison has made her own contributions to the course. This book reflects the input of all the women who have worked as Teaching Assistants for WS103 since the course was first taught in 1978. We especially wish to thank Carol McKinley for the many hours she spent making phone calls and photocopying to help us prepare this book and check resource information.

Book Introduction

Women cannot have control over our own lives until we have control over our bodies; thus, understanding and gaining control over our bodies and our health is essential to taking control of our lives. Consequently, activism around women's health issues has been a central part of the struggles, by women and men, for improving the role of women in society.

The readings in this book are a representation of the exciting range of excellent resources now available on women's health issues. The resource information at the end of the book summarizes many of the sources for the material used in this book and thus serves as a partial list of the periodicals and magazines which regularly feature women's health topics. These articles are examples of the amazing range of women's health writing and organizing being done throughout the world by individuals and groups actively striving for health care systems more appropriate to women's needs.

This collection of readings is designed specifically for use as a part of the women's health course, *Women Studies 103: Women and Their Bodies in Health and Disease,* which is taught to 320-400 students each semester, in the Women's Studies Program at the University of Wisconsin-Madison. (We are delighted to hear that the book is also being used in many other women's health courses throughout the country!) Readings and worksheets are particularly chosen or written to stimulate thought and analysis in preparation for discussion sections. Selections have been made to complement, rather than overlap, material covered in the other books which are required for the course: *Biology of Women* by Ethel Sloane, published by Wiley, *The Black Women's Health Book* edited by Evelyn C. White, published by Seal Press, and *Our Bodies, Ourselves for the New Century* by the Boston Women's Health Book Collective, published by Simon and Schuster.

This is the third edition of this book. Reflecting the rapidly changing area of women's health, the tremendous interest shown in women's health in recent years by both health care providers and consumers, and the new national debates, this book contains a very different range of articles than was available for the first two editions. In an effort to provide an historical context to many present debates, we have deliberately added not only new articles but also those with an historical perspective, as well as older articles which we mark as "classics." A goal for this book is to have students learn to value and use women's health "classics" as a part of studying present day issues and developing their own analysis. Often in the field of women's health, earliest articles written on a topic do an excellent job of identifying the crucial issues. Once that basic analysis has been written, other women's health writers are more likely to write an article which serves to update the information rather than writing an article very similar to the first one. When researching a women's health topic, students are encouraged to read both the "classics" and the most recent information to get the clearest overview of both the fundamental issues and which aspects of the area have and have not changed.

This collection will be regularly updated. We work towards having an anti-racist, cross-cultural perspective on topics, and are eager to find articles which make the connections between social, economic, scientific and political issues and women's mental and physical health. We hope our next book will be even better in looking at health issues related to poverty, ageism, racism, anti-semitism, heterosexism, fatphobia, and what it means to be differently abled. Readers' suggestions or reactions to articles are welcome and valued.

CHAPTER 1

Women and the Health Care System

The role of women in the health care system reflects the role of women in society. Men tend to be "at the top", having status and power, and making decisions which greatly influence others' lives. Women have less status and little role in decision-making, but carry the responsibility for daily servicing and caring. Mirroring the family, we see the doctor as father, the nurse as mother, and the patient often treated as a child. Since the late 1960's, modern women's health movements have critiqued curative medical systems based on the values of the male medical establishment, organized for fundamental changes in the system, and worked for the empowerment of women, as consumers and as health care providers, to be more involved in health care decisions for themselves and the system.

The classic 1979 article "Sexism in Women's Medical Care" sets the scene for the important ongoing discussion of how sexism in medical practice is rooted in the socialization of women to be passive patients and the socialization of doctors (men and women) to have a lack of respect for women and their right to information about their own bodies. The question of how much this has changed (or stayed the same) since 1979 will be a theme addressed throughout many specific topics in this book. Mary Halas emphasizes why it is essential for women to take a more involved role in their own health care. Adriane Fugh-Berman's more recent "Tales Out of Medical School" vividly describes some of the traumas still facing women trying to become doctors today and reminds us that simply getting more women into medicine will do little to make the health system more appropriate for women (or men) until the medical school socialization of doctors is changed.

The writing and debates of the 70's and 80's focused largely on why the health system was not adequately serving women and *why* women's health needed to be taken seriously. Now that the medical system has "discovered" women's health, the debate has changed to *how* it should take women's health seriously.

Increasingly, many women's health activists like Adriane Fugh-Berman are simultaneously critiquing the delivery of health care both from outside, as consumers, and from inside the health system as health care workers. The next two papers represent an important debate which is taking place as health care practitioners/activists work to make the system more appropriate for women.

Although both doctors Karen Johnson ("PRO: Women's Health: Developing a New Interdisciplinary Specialty") and Michelle Harrison ("CON: Women's Health as a Specialty: A Deceptive Solution") agree that there need to be fundamental changes in the health system for it to better serve women, they do not agree on what strategy will be most effective.

Readers will want to read articles in this book carefully and monitor the health system's changing (or non-changing) response to the issues of women's health. For the most part, the medical establishment does not deserve congratulations for how it has listened and responded to the issues raised by women's health movements. A clear pattern has emerged. When possible, the medical establishment has ignored women's health movements. When a demand could not be ignored, the medical response has been to coopt the move for change without making fundamental changes. For example, converting hospital-run services into a "women's health center" by painting the walls pink, buying several paintings by women artists, ordering a few women's health books, hiring a couple women doctors, and only superficially imitating the feminist women's health centers run by women, for women, did little to transform the dynamics of the doctor-patient relationship. Health institutions are now acting on what the drug companies have known for years—marketing products or services to normal, healthy women opens up huge markets ready to be exploited. There is enormous potential for what the medical "discovery" of women's health can mean, but activists need to remain diligent in making certain that women's health is no longer simply medically defined nor merely identified as issues related to gynecology but is redefined as encompassing all aspects of women's bodies and the social, economic factors (including our interactions with the health system) which impact upon our health. But, in asking for wider definitions of women's health, we also have to be careful that we are not encouraging yet more aspects of women's lives to become medicalized!

Ruzek and Becker's "The Women's Health Movement in the United States: From Grass-Roots Activism to Professional Agendas" gives us the tools to look at both the key issues and forms of women's activism of the last 30 years which brought us to this new stage at which women's health is taken seriously and helps us see that increased interest and investment in women's health provides both new opportunities and challenges for women's health activists. Their analysis of the impact of electronic communication on women's health is particularly thought provoking.

In "Women and Health: In Search of a Paradigm," Margaret Chesney and Elizabeth Ozer propose a framework for how to organize themes and approaches in the complex, dynamic, multidisciplinary field of women's health. Readers will gain two different kinds of information from this article. The overriding theme of the article helps the reader to think about what it means to be a pioneer helping to establish the framework for how a new field will be approached in future decades and whether there is a "feminist" way of doing this: "The traditional scientific strategy would be to debate, to be reductionistic, and to select a 'winner.' We would like to recommend that the field of women's health choose a different path characterized by inclusiveness and collaboration." Additionally, this comprehensive article is rich in content to introduce readers to specific details of many women's health topics.

The next articles in this chapter represent a range of ways that women as consumers and health care practitioners have been working to help women individually and collectively be more informed, active patients and to get the health system ready for consumers who expect a more respectful relationship with their health care providers. The classic, "How to Tell Your Doctor a Thing or Two," published by Bread and Roses Women's Health Center (a feminist health center, *by* women, *for* women) is representative of how women's health movements have encouraged women to be a different kind of patient. In this article, Morton Hunt identifies changes in medical practices which have caused a deterioration in doctor–patient relationships and proposes a seven-point program for becoming a more active patient. In an article reminiscent of women's researching topics for the original *Our Bodies, Ourselves*, Louise Marsden's "More than One Womb" shares what she learned about the wide range of "normal" variations in female anatomy as she pored over medical books to figure out her own anatomy. Building on a key women's health issue, "the politics of information" (who does and does not have access to information and who benefits and who loses when women do not have the information they need for health care decision-making?), this article questions whether women are not told about possible variations in female reproductive anatomy because the mystification prevents them from having control over their bodies and their lives, and she goes on to ask for a healthier definition of "normal" for women's bodies (and women's lives.)

From the other end of the speculum, Judy Schmidt's "The Gynecologic Exam and the Training of Medical Students: An Opportunity for Health Education" gives an example of a training program which consciously aims to educate physicians to be "patient-orientated" so they can communicate with their patients. In a more theoretical approach to the same issues, Terri Kapsalis, in "Cadavers, Dolls, and Prostitutes: Medical Pedagogy and the Pelvic Rehearsal," explores how "the types of practice performances adopted reveal and promote specific ideas about female bodies and sexuality held by the medical institution."

At the core of discussions on women's health is the question of who does and does not have access to the health system. Any debate on health issues (although seldom focusing on women and too often leaving out women's voices) is basically a women's health debate because women are overwhelmingly the health care providers and consumers who have the most to gain by meaningful change. The next two articles provide the type of information people need in order to appreciate and participate in decisions about how to move out of our present health care crisis. This issue is too important to leave to politicians and lobbyists! Recurring resistance to meaningful health care reform often is framed, always by people who presently have decent health insurance coverage, as the fear of having health care rationed in this country. Adriane Fugh-Berman's "Health Care Rationing" clarifies the situation and the question which must be asked. Health care is already rationed in this country. Do we want to keep our present system (which uses income and access to health insurance as the rationing determinant) or is it time to move to a fairer, more health-promoting system which establishes a standard of care to which everyone is entitled?

"Towards Universal Coverage" briefly outlines that all health care "reform" in the last few years has been piecemeal legislation which only served to patch up one very specific broken piece or address one abuse of the present system. Politicians and even activists have often been clever in organizing around legislative issues which give them visibility and with which absolutely no one would disagree. Who could be against legislation which requires birthing mothers to have the choice to stay in hospital for two days after delivery or requires that health insurance pay for mastectomies and emergency room visits? But such legislation does absolutely nothing to address the more fundamental issue that many birthing mothers, many women needing mastectomies, and a huge percentage of people who go to emergency rooms have *NO* health insurance. In the U.S., the only industrialized with no basic access to health services for everyone, health care has indeed become a privilege, not a right. More than 43 million people living in the U.S. (almost 1 in 6 of the population) have *no* health insurance. "Towards Universal Coverage" reminds us that we could be doing something about this.

The "Scientific Terms Explained" information is from Adriane Fugh-Berman's excellent *Alternative Medicine What Works* (A Comprehensive Easy-to-Read Review of the Scientific Evidence, Pro and Con). It demystifies many of the terms involved in describing scientific studies and helps the consumer become a better judge of which studies to take seriously and which should be critiqued. Diana Zuckerman's briefing paper on silicone breast implants demonstrates exactly why activists and policy makers need to have a much better understanding of "good" science vs. "poorly done" science. The author illustrates that even though a number of silicone breast implant studies have been reported (and have sometimes received much media attention), no one really knows how safe these implants are because studies needed to answer that have not been done.

Where would *you* put "The Safety of Silicone Breast Implants" if you were organizing this book or designing a woman's health course? Our dilemma about where to put this particular article is symbolic of the interrelationship of all the issues and topics in this book, especially when trying to analyze each specific issue within the broadest context of all the social, economic and political factors which impact on women's health, women's roles in societies, and women's relationship with the health care system. Silicone breast implants could be included in any discussion of images and gender roles or body image issues because approximately 80% of breast implants are used to enlarge healthy breasts. Twenty percent of breast implants are used for reconstruction after mastectomy for cancer or other trauma or illness, so it might be suitable to include it with the articles on breast cancer and it certainly provides a contrast to Audre Lorde's provocative "Breast Cancer: Power vs. Prosthesis". More than 400,000 women have filed lawsuits against manufacturers of silicone breast implants because they feel their illnesses were caused by their breast implants, so it is also tempting to place this article clearly under the title of politics of disease.

Sexism in Women's Medical Care

by Mary A. Halas

A twenty-seven-year old woman complained that her health had taken a sudden unexplained change for the worse. She had a diffuse sense of not being well, with pains in various parts of her body, weakness, and fatigue. Her gynecologist gave her a physical exam and pronounced her fine. As the symptoms continued, she returned to her physician and also went to several other doctors—meeting reactions of disbelief and even ridicule with increasing frequency. Eventually one specialist recommended she see a counselor, because she obviously had no real physical problems.

That recommendation turned out to be a good one. After a few sessions the counselor concluded that the woman was in good mental health and concentrated on supporting her to continue seeking medical attention to evaluate the sudden change in her physical health.

Finally, months after her symptoms appeared and weeks after her last visit to her gynecologist, the woman had an appointment with a female physician who listened to an exhaustive list of her symptoms and concerns, and gave her an extremely thorough physical examination.

The results: the woman had a large lump in her left breast; after surgery two days later the lump was diagnosed as cancer. No one will ever know whether the lump was already there during her gynecologist's hurried and skeptical exam, but it is certain that the woman might have had a better chance of finding the lump herself if her doctor had ever taught her how to examine her own breasts. According to the woman's oncologist, there is a 70 percent chance that the cancer will recur, because of its type and size at the time of discovery.

Fortunately, the woman's counselor knew that sexism in the medical care system poses particular problems for women. Many physicians see women's physical complaints as trivial, neurotic disorders best treated with placebos or symptomatic therapy. A therapist who had conducted a prolonged analysis of the possible psycho-logical causes of this woman's complaints or had considered the symptoms to be evidence of emotional disturbance would have put her life in even further jeopardy.

The medical needs of women and their problems in getting good health care are key issues. First, many women have psychosomatic illnesses, and counselors get many legitimate referrals from doctors who recognize that there needs to be a psychological as well as medical component to healing women's medical problems. Second, therapists get *too many* referrals from doctors, as the case of the woman with undetected breast cancer illustrates. Serious, treatable problems often progress to irreversible damage or death while a woman is trying to convince her doctor that her problems are not all in her head.

Before the advent of modern medical technology and the professionalization of medicine, women were the primary healers as "witches" and herbalists, and female midwives were the sole practitioners of physical care for women's special concerns—childbirth and gynecology. Now, however, the situation is radically reversed. Although women are the largest single group of health care consumers, 93 percent of all doctors are male, and 97 percent of all gynecologists are male.[1]

Women's experience in obtaining health care is different from men's in that women almost always are putting their bodies in the hands of someone of the opposite sex for medical care. In addition, women make 25 percent more visits to the doctors than men. They also take 50 percent more prescribed drugs than men and are admitted to hospitals more frequently.[2]

Sex-role stereotyping in the socialization of women has skewed the kind of medical care they seek. Women learn to identify themselves in terms of their reproductive potential, and the medical system reinforces this behavior. For example, a majority of women turn to the specialist obstetrician/ gynecologist, not as a source of care for specialized problems, but as a first-line source

Reprinted with permission from *Frontiers: A Journal of Women's Studies*, Vol. IV, No. 2, 1979. Copyright © 1979 by Frontiers Editorial Collective.

for all medical care—rather than choosing a general practitioner or internist for routine care. A study which Helen Marieskind presented at a 1974 meeting of the American Association of Obstetricians and Gynecologists found that 86 percent of the women in the study saw no doctor other than an obstetrician/gynecologist on a regular, periodic basis.

Socialization of Women as Patients

The socialization of women to be passive recipients of medical care—especially from men—militates against their receiving adequate care. The attitude with which women seek medical care within the male-dominated system is one of subservient dependence on all-knowing authority. This dependence on all-powerful doctors and women's relinquishing of responsibility for their health to male doctors is the result of physician behavior that reduces the patient's sense of autonomy.

For example, a woman having a routine gynecological exam is ushered into the examining room without meeting the physician first in his office and is instructed to take off her clothes. Vulnerable, naked, and draped with a white sheet, she waits an indeterminate period for the doctor to enter. Once he arrives and her feet are in the examining table stirrups, she is literally helpless in his hands and feels this way—naked, supine, being manipulated with fingers and tools in her body by a male hidden behind a sheet. This dependence on male doctors works against women patients' interests. A patient's stereotyped respect for a doctor's wisdom and competence does not make a poor doctor into a good one.

Dependence on doctors also eliminates the woman's own desires and needs from decision-making about her care. Most medical care involves various levels of benefits and risks and choices about them, even when doctors do not allow patients to make those choices. Lack of information about their bodies, plus the dependent, fearful relationship with their physicians, make it difficult for women to find out what is really wrong with them physically and what methods of treatment are possible. In a study on doctor-patient communication, Barbara Korsch and Vida Negrete found that the use of medical jargon which is unintelligible to patients, plus doctors' frequent disregard for patients' concerns and perspectives, were obstacles to effective care.[3]

A logical result of this confusion and failure in doctor-patient communication is that only 42 percent of the women in this study carried out all the medical advice they received; 38 percent complied in part; and 11 percent did not follow instructions at all.

In gynecology and obstetrics the level of communication can be even poorer, because of an attitude generated by the fact that many of the visits are from healthy women. The attitude is that if there is nothing wrong, then there is nothing to tell. In 1970 hearings before the U.S. Senate, a physician who did research on oral contraceptives opposed labeling for these drugs which would inform women of the risks. He said, "A misguided effort to inform such women leads only to anxiety on their part and loss of confidence in the physician. . . . They want him [the doctor] to tell them what to do, not to confuse them by asking them to make decisions beyond their comprehension. . . . The idea of informing such a woman is not possible."[4]

One would hope that this individual doctor's attitude represents an extreme case. However, in general many doctors neglect to give women information they do not ask for, and treat them as if they are not capable of understanding the basis of decisions and treatment. In the view of much of the medical profession, women cannot even be trusted with information about their own conditions or medication.

A graphic illustration of this point is the years-old controversy still raging over the government's proposal to require patient education leaflets on all prescription drugs. In response to tremendous pressure from Congressional advocates and the Food and Drug Administration, the major medical associations reluctantly have endorsed the abstract concept of such leaflets but continue to oppose specific applications.

The specter the medical associations raise in their congressional testimony on patient package inserts for drugs is that if patients are told all that can go wrong with a drug, a disease, or an operation, their hypochondriacal minds will ensure that all these things do go wrong. It is significant that it was a consumer group, the Center for Law and Social Policy, which sparked the government initiative on patient package inserts through a petition—and not the medical profession.

An example in which doctors have not given women information that can have life and death consequences for themselves and their children involves the hormone diethylstilbestrol (DES). During the 1950's many thousands of pregnant women received DES without being informed what the medication was. No one knew until fifteen years later that this drug greatly increased the risk of cancer in their children.

In October 1978, after years of press coverage of DES-caused cancer, the government issued a special letter and bulletin to the country's doctors because of the finding that some doctors were still prescribing DES for pregnant women and many others still were not informing their patients who had taken the drug of possible risks.[5]

Socialization of Doctors

Where do doctors get this lack of respect for a woman's right to information about health care and for her ability to participate intelligently in her medical care? Mary Howell describes the process of professionalization of doctors in medical school—where they learn attitudes about work and patients—as strongly colored by a demeaning regard for women.[6] Medical schools teach discrimination against women as patients, Howell says, through lack of focus on diseases specific to women, in misogynic comparisons made between male and female patients with similar health problems, and in instructions regarding the appropriate behavior of doctors toward women patients.

In their classes, medical students learn both implicitly and explicitly that women patients have uninteresting illnesses, are unreliable historians of their health, and are beset by such emotionality that their symptoms are unlikely to reflect real disease.

Pauline Bart and Diana Scully reviewed twenty-seven gynecology textbooks published between 1943 and 1972 and found that at least half of the writers stated women are inherently frigid, have less sex drive than men, or are interested in sex only for procreation.[7] Two authors urged physicians to encourage women to simulate orgasm to please their husbands. The core of the female personality as described in these textbooks is narcissistic, masochistic, and passive.

Another much-used vehicle for the socialization of doctors in their attitudes toward women is drug advertisements in medical journals. Many of these ads serve to reinforce the prejudices against women. They teach doctors that women's physical complaints are trivial; their illnesses are irritating to others; and that women are emotional, have psychosomatic illnesses, and are bothersome to doctors.

Many ads for tranquilizers and antidepressants in particular suggest these products as treatment of choice before psychotherapy or social action for life situations and problems beyond the traditional concepts of illness and disease.

In a 1971 review of medical journals, Seidenberg found that misogynic statements in drug advertisements resonate with the bias of the intended observer—the male doctor. He targeted in particular advertisements that recommended doctors use drugs to adjust women to their lot when they are discontented with a humdrum environment. One caption accompanying a portrayal of a woman behind the bars of broom and mop handles read, "you can't set her free, but you can help her feel less anxious."[8]

In 1979 men are beginning to appear more frequently in drug advertisements as patients, but the difference in portrayal of men and women is still striking. Men on antidepressant medications are depicted as, "Alert on the job," and "functioning effectively in daily activities" (Pamelor). Women needing antidepressant medications, however, appear in drug ads as helpless patients under a doctor's care because, "Everything I saw was negative" (Norpramin).

The insidious effects of the sexist bias doctors learn in medical school, the professional literature they read, and the drug advertising they are exposed to are broad-ranging. The bias affects decision-making about individual patients and perpetuates misinformation about women's psychic and physiological processes. Negative consequences of these medical myths about women include the justification of limited opportunities for education, employment, and participation in the political process.

The following three specific issues are examples of sexism in medical care. All pose particular threats to women's well-being and as such are illustrations of medical care delivery to women.

Contraceptive Methods. Every woman has a right to make a free and informed choice about birth control for herself. The information about methods and the freedom of choice are key, because there is no completely satisfactory method of birth control. Each method has a unique range of benefits and risks which will differ for women of various medical histories, personal preferences, income, and health habits.

There are widespread misunderstandings about the risks and failure rates of various methods of contraception.[9] Some of this is caused by unethical advertising by pharmaceutical firms. In addition, the biases of clinics or individual doctors frequently deprive women of complete information on which to base their choices. Planned Parenthood prides itself on giving women unbiased information so they can make choices, but many women have already made up their minds about a method before they come into the clinics. According to the Washington, D.C. Public Interest Research Group, the popularity of the Pill is based on its convenience, and fewer women would expose themselves to its many risks if they took these into account in making their choices. Much of the pro-Pill reasoning is fallacious, especially the comparison of risks of the Pill with risks of pregnancy. Such comparisons assume that women not taking oral contraceptives will become pregnant, whereas they could use other safer contraceptive methods; furthermore, many of the necessary studies on the Pill's long-term safety have not been done, and many complications are never reported, so that valid comparisons between the risks of pregnancy and oral contraceptives cannot be made.

Estrogen Use in Menopause. Uterine cancer used to be rare—about one in 1,000 postmenopausal women who had not had their uteruses surgically removed. Since 1970, however, the incidence of uterine cancer in women over fifty years of age increased dramatically—by 50 percent for invasive cancer and by 100 percent for localized cancer.[10] It is not a coincidence that in the last ten to fifteen years the use of estrogen has at least tripled, and recent studies have concluded that there is a causal connection, and that the major cause of the increasing rate of uterine cancer in the United States is estrogen therapy. The sharpest rise in uterine cancer rates is among white upper- and middle-class women, who are most likely to take estrogens. Fifty percent of all postmenopausal women have taken estrogens, and approximately half of these women have taken estrogen for more than ten years. The longer the estrogen treatment and the higher the dose, the higher the incidence of uterine cancer. There are strong social pressures causing the high use of estrogen. Unsupported claims that estrogen will retard the aging process, plus the sexism that devalues older women, combine to create strong consumer demand for the drug. This demand reinforces physicians' entrenched prescribing habits, despite new scientific findings.

Six million women are using estrogens, many of them in hopes that the drug will keep them "feminine forever." This attitude, created in large part by irresponsible drug company advertising, is not going to evaporate soon. Also resistant to change are the time-hallowed doctors' attitudes toward menopause as a disease rather than as a normal physiological process.

Psychoactive Drugs. Use of legitimate psychoactive drugs among women is an important issue. An estimated one to two million people in the U.S. from all walks of life and social strata have abuse problems with prescription drugs, according to the National Institute of Drug Abuse's February and April 1978 *Capsules* press releases.

Almost twice as many women as men have had tranquilizers, sedatives, and stimulants prescribed for them. In many cases, there is no medical reason for use of the drugs, but they become a chemical support system to adjust a woman to a frustrating or unfulfilling marriage, divorce, lifestyle, or work situation. Psychoactive drugs become both a substitute and a barrier to use of counseling or other measures to combat or alter the distressing situation or the individual's response to it.

Chemical crutches for women are nothing new. In the 1800's it was common medical custom to prescribe then-legal opium for "female troubles."[11] A wide spread pattern of opium abuse grew among women-outnumbering male opium-eaters three to one in the late nineteenth and early twentieth centuries. In the drug pattern of the 1970's, general practitioners write most of the tranquilizer prescriptions for Valium alone, there were fifty-seven million prescriptions between May 1976 and April 1977.[12]

Doctors get their education about psychoactive drugs primarily from drug companies. A survey of seventy-two medical schools found that only 20 percent had any course in psychopharmacology, and the average time on the subject was seventeen hours in four years.[13] Medical advertising for drugs typically portrays women as frustrated, anxious, neurotic, and depressed.

Tranquilizers, sedatives, and stimulants are addictive, and in conjunction with alcohol they can be deadly. Persons who take excessive doses of either sedatives or certain tranquilizers for extended periods of time will experience dramatic withdrawal symptoms including convulsions, tremor, abdominal and muscle cramps, vomiting, and sweating.[14]

Alarming information that only recently has come to light is that some patients will experience withdrawal from such drugs as Librium and Valium when they have been taking normal therapeutic doses, with no abuse.[15] These symptoms include tremors, agitation, fear and anxiety, stomach cramps, and sweating. Since these symptoms of withdrawal so closely resemble the anxiety manifestations for which women in particular originally receive these drugs, and since so many millions of women are taking these drugs, they represent a complex problem for counselors.

Sexism in medical practice is rooted in the socialization of women to be passive recipients of care from authoritarian male doctors, plus doctors' socialization which trivializes women's medical problems and fosters attitudes that demean women patients. The results are that many women suffer needlessly from treatable organic problems labeled as psychogenic, experience irreparable damage or death because of ignored symptoms, or unwittingly fall into drug dependence due to doctors' attempts to "help" women adjust through drugs to an uncomfortable sex-typed role.

The implications are clear—it is vital for women to become informed partners in their own medical care. This will involve learning about key medical issues concerning women and developing skills to assert their rights in the sexist dynamics that pervade the health care of women. Useful tools in this task will be information sharing and assertiveness training to assist women in getting information on their own and getting responses they want from professionals. Some authors suggest limiting the practice of women's medicine (obstetrics/gynecology) to women practitioners. At some future date that may be thinkable or possible; at present, however, since 97 percent of all obstetrician/gynecologists are male, women are faced with the art of the possible in dealing with sexism in their medical care.

NOTES

1. Linda Bakiel, Susan Daily, and Carolyn Kott Washburne, ed., *Women in Transition: A Feminist Handbook on Separation and Divorce* (New York: Scribners, 1975), p. 392.

2. Boston Women's Health Collective, *Our Bodies Ourselves* (New York: Simon and Schuster, 1976), p. 337.

3. Barbara H. Korsch and Vida F. Negrete, "Doctor-Patient Communication." *Scientific American,* 227 (1972), 66–72.

4. Gena Corea, *The Hidden Malpractice* (New York: Marron Co., 1977), p. 77

5. Food and Drug Administration, "Alert on DES," *FDA Drug Bulletin,* 8, (1978), p. 3

6. Mary Howell, "What Medical Schools Teach About Women, *New England Journal of Medicine,* 291 (1974), 304–07.

7. Pauline Bart and Diana Scully, "A Funny Think Happened on the Way to the Orifice," *American Journal of Sociology,* 28 (1973), 1045–50.

8. R. Seidenberg, "Drug Advertising and Perceptions of Mental Illness," *Mental Hygiene,* 55 (1971), 21–31.

9. *Our Bodies Ourselves,* p. 185.

10. Food and Drug Administration, "Estrogens and Endometrial Cancer," *FDA Drug Bulletin,* 6 (1976), 2–3.

11. Annabel Hecht, "Women and Drugs," *FDA Consumer,.* October 1978, pp. 7–12.

12. Jody Forman-Sher and Jonica Homiler, "An Overview of the Problem of Combined Drug/Alcohol Dependencies Among Women," paper presented at the International Conference on Alcoholism and Addictions, Zurich, Switzerland, June 1978.

13. Ann H. Clark, *National Consumers League Position on Minor Tranquilizers,* paper presented at the public hearing before the Food and Drug Administration, Rockville, Maryland, March 1978.

14. David Haskell, "Withdrawal of Diazepam," *Journal of the American Medical Association,* 233 (1975), 135.

15. Arthur Rifkin, Frederick Quitkin, and Donald Klein, "Withdrawal Reactions to Diazepam," *Journal of the American Medical Association,* 236 (1976), 2173.

Tales Out of Medical School

by Adriane Fugh-Berman, M.D.

With the growth of the women's health movement and the influx of women into medical school, there has been abundant talk of a new enlightenment among physicians. Last summer, many Americans were shocked when Frances Conley, a neurosurgeon on the faculty of Stanford University's medical school, resigned her position, citing "pervasive sexism." Conley's is a particularly elite and male-dominated subspecialty, but her story is not an isolated one. I graduated from the Georgetown University School of Medicine in 1988, and while medical training is a sexist process anywhere, Georgetown built disrespect for women into its curriculum.

A Jesuit school, most recently in the news as the alma mater of William Kennedy Smith, Georgetown has an overwhelmingly white, male and conservative faculty. At a time when women made up one-third of all medical students in the United States, and as many as one-half at some schools, my class was 73 percent male and more than 90 percent white.

Adriane Fugh-Berman, M.D., is on the board of the National Women's Health Network. She practices general medicine in Washington, D.C.

The prevailing attitude toward women was demonstrated on the first day of classes by my anatomy instructor, who remarked that our elderly cadaver "must have been a Playboy bunny" before instructing us to cut off her large breasts and toss them into the thirty-gallon trash can marked "cadaver waste." Barely hours into our training, we were already being taught that there was nothing to be learned from examining breasts. Given the fact that one out of nine American women will develop breast cancer in her lifetime, to treat breasts as extraneous tissue seemed an appalling waste of an educational opportunity, as well as a not-so-subtle message about the relative importance of body parts. How many of my classmates now in practice, I wonder, regularly examine the breasts of their female patients?

My classmates learned their lesson of disrespect well. Later in the year one carved a tick-tack-toe on a female cadaver and challenged others to play. Another gave a languorous sigh after dissecting female genitalia, as if he had just had sex. "Guess I should have a cigarette now," he said.

Ghoulish humor is often regarded as a means by which med students overcome fear and anxiety. But it serves a darker purpose as well: Depersonalizing our cadaver was good preparation for depersonalizing our patients later. Further on in my training an ophthalmologist would yell at me when I hesitated to place a small instrument meant to measure eye pressure on a fellow student's cornea because I was afraid it would hurt. "You have to learn to treat patients as lab animals," he snarled at me.

On the first day of an emergency medicine rotation in our senior year, students were asked who had had experience placing a central line (an intravenous line placed into a major vein under the clavicle or in the neck). Most of the male students raised their hands. None of the women did. For me, it was graphic proof of inequity in teaching; the men had had the procedure taught to them, but the women had not. Teaching rounds were often, for women, a spectator sport. One friend told me how she craned her neck to watch a physician teach a minor surgical procedure to a male student; when they were done the physician handed her his dirty gloves to discard. I have seen a male attending physician demonstrate an exam on a patient and then wade through several female medical students to drag forth a male in order to teach it to him. This sort of discrimination was common and quite unconscious: The women just didn't register as medical students to some of the doctors. Female students, for their part, tended (like male ones) to gloss over issues that might divert attention, energy or focus from the all-important goal of getting through their training. "Oh, they're just of the old school," a female classmate remarked to me as if being ignored by our teachers was really rather charming, like having one's hand kissed.

A woman resident was giving a radiology presentation and I felt mesmerized. Why did I feel so connected and involved? It suddenly occurred to me that the female physician was regularly meeting my eyes; most of the male residents and attendings made eye contact only with the men.

"Why are women's brains smaller than men's!" asked a surgeon of a group of male medical students in the doctors' lounge (I was in the room as well, but was apparently invisible). "Because they're missing logic!" Guffaws all around.

Such instances of casual sexism are hardly unique to Georgetown, or indeed to medical schools. But at Georgetown female students also had to contend with outright discrimination of a sort most Americans probably think no longer exists in education. There was one course women were not allowed to take. The elective in sexually transmitted diseases required an interview with the head of the urology department, who was teaching the course. Those applicants with the appropriate genitalia competed for invitations to join the course (a computer was supposed to assign us electives, which we had ranked in order of preference, but that process had been circumvented for this course). Three women who requested an interview were told that the predominantly gay male clinic where the elective was held did not allow women to work there. This was news to the clinic's executive director, who stated that women were employed in all capacities.

The women who wanted to take the course repeatedly tried to meet with the urologist, but he did not return our phone calls. (I had not applied for the course, but became involved as an advocate for the women who wanted to take it.) We figured out his schedule, waylaid him in the hall and insisted that a meeting be set up.

At this meeting, clinic representatives disclosed that a survey had been circulated years before to the clientele in order to ascertain whether women workers would be accepted; 95 percent of the clients voted to welcome women. They were also asked whether it was acceptable to have medical students working at the clinic; more than 90 percent approved. We were then told that these results could not be construed to indicate that clients did not mind women medical students; the clients would naturally have assumed that "medical student" meant "male medical student." Even if that were true, we asked, if 90 percent of clients did not mind medical students and 95 percent did not mind women, couldn't a reasonable person assume that female medical students would be acceptable? No, we were informed. Another study would have to be done.

We raised formal objections to the school. Meanwhile, however, the entire elective process had been postponed by the dispute, and the blame for the delay and confusion was placed on us. The hardest part of the struggle, indeed, was dealing with the indifference of most of our classmates—out of 206, maybe a dozen actively supported us—and with the intense anger of the ten men who had been promised places in the course.

"Just because you can't take this course,"one of the men said to me, "why do you want to ruin it for the rest of us?" It seemed incredible to me that I had to argue that women should be allowed to take the same courses as men. The second or third time someone asked me the same question, I suggested that if women were not allowed to participate in the same curriculum as the men, then in the interest of fairness we should get a 50 percent break on our $22,500 annual tuition. My colleague thought that highly unreasonable.

Eventually someone in administration realized that not only were we going to sue the school for discrimination but that we had an open-and-shut case. The elective in sexually transmitted diseases was canceled, and from its ashes arose a new course, taught by the same man, titled "Introduction to Urology." Two women were admitted. When the urologist invited students to take turns working with him in his office, he scheduled the two female students for the same day—one on which only women patients were to be seen (a nifty feat in a urology practice).

The same professor who so valiantly tried to prevent women from learning anything unseemly about sexually transmitted diseases was also in charge of the required course in human sexuality (or, as I liked to call it, he-man sexuality). Only two of the eleven lectures focused on women; of the two lectures on homosexuality, neither mentioned lesbians. The psychiatrist who co-taught the class treated us to one lecture that amounted to an apology for rape: Aggression, even hostility, is normal in sexual relations between a man and a woman, he said, and inhibition of aggression in men can lead to impotence.

We were taught that women do not need orgasms for a satisfactory sex life, although men, of course, do; and that inability to reach orgasm is only a problem for women with "unrealistic expectations." I had heard that particular lecture before in the backseat of a car during high school. The urologist told us of couples who came to him for sex counseling because the woman was not having orgasms; he would reassure them that this is normal and the couple would be relieved. (I would gamble that the female half of the couple was anything but relieved.) We learned that oral sex is primarily a homosexual practice, and that sexual dysfunction in women is often caused by "working." In the women-as-idiots department, we learned that when impotent men are implanted with permanently rigid penile prostheses, four out of five wives can't tell that their husbands have had the surgery.

When dealing with sexually transmitted diseases in which both partners must be treated, we were advised to vary our notification strategy according to marital status. If the patient is a single man, the doctor should write the diagnosis down on a prescription for his partner to bring to her doctor. If the patient is a married man, however, the doctor should contact the wife's gynecologist and arrange to have her treated without knowledge of what she is being treated for. How to notify the male partner of a female patient, married or single, was never revealed.

To be fair, women were not the only subjects of out-moded concepts of sexuality. We also received anachronistic information about men. Premature ejaculation, defined as fewer than ten thrusts(!) was to be treated by having the man think about something unpleasant, or by having the woman painfully squeeze, prick or pinch the penis. Aversive therapies such as these have long been discredited.

Misinformation about sexuality and women's health peppered almost every course (I can't recall any egregious wrongs in biochemistry). Although vasectomy and abortion are among the safest of all surgical procedures, in our lectures vasectomy was presented as fraught with long-term complications and abortion was never mentioned without the words "peritonitis" and "death" in the same sentence. These distortions represented Georgetown's Catholic bent as it worst. (We were not allowed to perform, or even watch abortion procedures in our affiliated hospitals.) On a lighter note, one obstetrician assisting us in the anatomy lab told us that women shouldn't lift heavy weights because their pelvic organs will fall out between their legs.

In our second year, several women in our class started a women's group, which held potlucks and offered presentations and performances: A former midwife talked about her profession, a student demonstrated belly dancing, another discussed dance therapy and one sang selections from *A Chorus Line*. This heavy radical feminist activity created great hostility among our male classmates. Announcements of our meetings were defaced and women in the group began receiving threatening calls at home from someone who claimed to be watching the listener and who would then accurately describe what she was wearing. One woman received obscene notes in her school mailbox, including one that contained a rape threat. I received insulting cards in typed envelopes at my home address; my mother received similar cards at hers.

We took the matter to the dean of student affairs, who told us it was "probably a dental student" and suggested we buy loud whistles to blow into the phone when we received unwanted calls. We demanded that the school attempt to find the perpetrator and expel him.

We were told that the school would not expel the student but that counseling would be advised.

The women's group spread the word that we were collecting our own information on possible suspects and that any information on bizarre, aggressive, antisocial or misogynous behavior among the male medical students should be reported to our designated representative. She was inundated with a list of classmates who fit the bill. Finally, angered at the school's indifference, we solicited the help of a prominent woman faculty member. Although she shamed the dean into installing a hidden camera across from the school mailboxes to monitor unusual behavior, no one was ever apprehended.

Georgetown University School of Medicine churns out about 200 physicians a year. Some become good doctors despite their training, but many will pass on the misinformation and demeaning attitudes handed down to them. It is a shame that Georgetown chooses to perpetuate stereotypes and reinforce prejudices rather than help students acquire the up-to-date information and sensitivity that are vital in dealing with AIDS, breast cancer, teen pregnancy and other contemporary epidemics. Female medical students go through an ordeal, but at least it ends with graduation. It is the patients who ultimately suffer the effects of sexist medical education.

Is Medical School the right choice for *you?*
A SELF-EVALUATION TEST FOR THE PRE-MEDICAL STUDENT
Answer true or false

T   F

☐   ☐   1. Mothers often overreact to the most trivial symptoms in their children.

☐   ☐   2. Mothers are often guilty of denial followed by neglect in not bringing a symptomatic child to the doctor.

☐   ☐   3. Women often imagine breast lumps.

☐   ☐   4. Women should examine their breasts often enough, but not too often*

☐   ☐   5. Informing patients of the side effects of the drugs prescribed for them will cause the patients to experience these side effects in their most virulent form.

☐   ☐   6. Women are sexually excited by gynecological examinations.

☐   ☐   7. Patients never ask the really interesting questions.

☐   ☐   8. A certain amount of physical discomfort is to be expected in anyone over 35, and old people should keep their symptoms to themselves.

☐   ☐   9. No doctor can ever really be guilty of malpractice.

☐   ☐   10. Most people when asked to describe your personality would say, "He's not real warm."

Too often if the lump disappears in a few months; *not often* enough if the lump turns out to be malignant.
ANSWERS: You know who you are.

PRO
Women's Health
Developing a New Interdisciplinary Specialty

by Karen Johnson, M.D.

Abstract. This paper argues that medicine is based on a male paradigm that does not permit high-quality comprehensive care for women within existing medical specialities. Suggestions are made to alleviate the shortcomings of the current paradigm by including women. A call for the development of a specialty in women's health is made. Types of resistance to this proposal, stemming from sexism, economics, and alliances to existing specialties, are also discussed. Finally, it is argued that bringing the study and practice of women's health to parity with the understanding and treatment of men must be achieved rapidly and comprehensively using an active and multifaceted approach.

Introduction

*N*o existing medical specialty is devoted exclusively to the comprehensive care of women. Many of us providing health care for women in a variety of existing specialties believe that the absence of such a comprehensively trained specialist is a significant problem in the health care services offered to women.[1] This problem could be solved through the development of an interdisciplinary specialty in women's health.

Medicine as a Paradigm Based upon Experiences with Men

With the exception of physicians in one surgical specialty, obstetrics-gynecology, physicians caring for women base the majority of their diagnoses and interventions on clinical trials and studies with men, often unknowingly.[2] However benevolent the original intentions in excluding women from drug trials and clinical studies, their absence has led to unnecessary morbidity and premature mortality. For example, the Baltimore Longitudinal Study on Aging started in 1958 and did not include women for the first 20 years. This omission delayed the discovery of the link among osteoporosis, calcium, estrogen, and progesterone, resulting in the needless suffering and death of hundreds of thousands of women.

More recently the AIDS epidemic has highlighted the serious consequences of assuming that diseases in women manifest with exactly the same signs and symptoms as diseases in men. Until 1991 the Center for Disease Control (CDC) criteria for AIDS was based on men. HIV positive women presenting with cervical cancer, pelvic inflammatory disease, and vaginal thrush were diagnosed much later in the disease process. Not only did these uniquely female diagnoses delay treatment and thus shorten life expectancy compared with men, they often caused undue economic hardship because meeting the CDC criteria was a prerequisite to receiving public assistance available to patients with AIDS.

Other problems are created by the assumption that our experience with men is transferable to women. Although cardiovascular disease is the leading cause of death in women, we would hardly know it based on most of the research in this field.[3] The initial study affirming that aspirin could be used as preventive therapy for coronary disease included more than 22,000 subjects, all male. The Mr. FIT study (Multiple Risk Factor Intervention Trials) identified coronary disease risk factors in 15,000 subjects, again all men. Even when women's risk of cardiovascular disease is assessed, clinical experience and interventions with men may not be applicable to women. Women may present with different symptoms in the office; they often arrive further in the progression of a myocardial infarction in the emergency room; they are more likely to die in the operating room.

Many diseases common in both men and women have a substantially higher incidence in women. It is not entirely clear why. Diseases of the gastrointestinal tract are just one example. Gallstones occur earlier in women and women continue to have a greater prevalence of them throughout their lives. Biliary dyskinesia occurs more often in women. Irritable bowel syndrome and gastroparesis are three times more common in women than men. Women are more susceptible to the hepatotoxic effects of alcohol than men. However, as is often the case in diseases that occur in both genders, clinical investigations have been carried out mostly in men. As a result in caring for women we cannot be confident that our diagnostic techniques and medical interventions are sound.

Health matters that occur exclusively (or primarily) in women such as menstruation, premenstrual symptoms, uterine fibroids, menopause, and breast cancer have received less attention than the patient population (52% of adults) would warrant. This has hindered our ability to offer advice with confidence.

Sometimes relying on the male paradigm is nothing short of ludicrous. Consider the study at Rockefeller University in which researchers were analyzing the effects of obesity on estrogen activity and the tendency to develop breast and uterine cancer. All the subjects were male.[4] Although it is finally a widely held belief that women and men are equal they are not the same—physiologically or psychologically.[5,6] Using men as the medical standard from which women diverge is unpardonable.[7]

Crossing Boundaries

Now that the consciousness of medicine has been raised, it has been suggested that improving women's health care can be achieved by making adjustments in the education of physicians within existing specialties.[8] This plan on its own would not address the numerous health concerns experienced by women that do not easily fit into any existing specialty. Consider the woman whose abdominal pain is finally diagnosed as endometriosis. Lacking an interdisciplinary-trained women's health specialist, the recommended interventions are likely to be biased by the specialty training of her provider. A primary care physician may be inclined to prescribe analgesics for pain, whereas a gynecologist leans more toward hormonal or surgical interventions. A psychiatrist or other mental health provider may need to be included to assist with corollary emotional distress or sexual dysfunction. Two or more physicians are required to provide complete care, an inefficient and expensive process.

Many medical problems experienced by women present similar dilemmas. Two additional examples are premenstrual symptoms and domestic violence. Premenstrual symptoms are inadequately defined within the existing paradigm, but they are certainly experienced by many women. Lacking agreement about diagnosis and treatment, specialists tend to interpret symptoms through their own frame of reference. Domestic violence is a major health hazard for American women, but it is overlooked by many physicians.[9] Untrained in a broader understanding of women's health, physicians' impressions are biased by the perspective of their own specialty. When presented with only a small part of the clinical problem, they often fail to piece together the larger diagnostic picture. A woman complaining of insomnia or suffering with a fracture may be treated in an emergency room or family practice center, but never asked directly about physical abuse. Although the lack of a unified approach to premenstrual symptoms can lead to discomfort and distress, the failure to accurately diagnose domestic violence can be life threatening. What is called for in these and many other situations experienced by women is an interdisciplinary approach.

Correcting the Paradigm

Most physicians until recently have been unaware that the practice of medicine is based on a male paradigm.[10] Many of the problems that have arisen because of this have been identified. There is now relative agreement within the medical profession that these problems must be addressed, but we are by no means in agreement as to the method.

Some believe that we have crossed the barriers to the full inclusion of women's health care needs and that we can correct the existing medical paradigm by alterations within current specialties. This belief is at odds with the limited achievements women have made in other areas when analogous omissions were brought to light, as noted in Faludi's *Backlash*.[11]

Representatives from at least three specialties—internal medicine, obstetrics-gynecology, and family practice—have argued that these specialties can adequately meet the comprehensive needs of women patients. I question their assertions. Unless practitioners of these specialties have taken it upon themselves to round out their standard residency training, few are qualified to call themselves women's health specialists in the manner I am arguing is required.

At present most internists have inadequate knowledge of women's reproductive health, extremely limited experience with the psychosocial aspects of women's health care, and a discipline that is built entirely on a male paradigm. Although obstetrics-gynecology training is based upon experiences with women, it is arguable whether it can genuinely be considered a primary care specialty. The training is fundamentally surgical, and the inclusion of a psychosocial perspective is also limited.

Family physicians argue that they are in the best position to offer high-quality comprehensive care for women. This is true within the context of the current medical paradigm. Their interdisciplinary training serves them well in approaching the multiplicity of women's health care concerns. However, the training and practice of family medicine require these physicians to divide their attention among women, men, and children.

Certainly family physicians treat the young as well as the elderly and more than other specialists gain a psychosocial perspective in their training. Nevertheless, this has not negated the need for the specialty of pediatrics or the subspecialty of geriatrics. Pediatricians' focused attention on children and geriatricians' focused attention on the elderly have led to improved health care for the youngest and the oldest of patients. Specialists in women's health will bring similar benefits to all our woman patients—no matter what specialty we practice.

I do agree with colleagues who caution that a specialty in women's health must not be viewed as alleviating the imperative that every existing medical specialty revise its content to include the accurate and respectful treatment of women.[12] However, I do not believe that these efforts will be adequate. Nor do I think that these improvements and the development of a new interdisciplinary specialty are mutually exclusive. They would be complementary.

Placing Women's Health in the Larger Context

The idea of a specialty in women's health is a logical extension of the women's health movement that began in the 1960s.[13] Physicians influenced by this movement began to articulate the need for a specialty in women's health by the 1980s.[14,15] The recent increased interest in women's health at all levels is gratifying; however, attention to the concerns of women has been inconsistent during this century. It would be a mistake to assume the current flurry of activity in women's health will continue without formalizing the specialty.

Having a medical specialty in women's health could be viewed much like having a room of one's own.[16] Just as departments of women's studies have been instrumental in assuring that women's experiences are accurately represented in the academic community, a specialty in women's health would serve a similar purpose in medicine.

Those who believe it will be sufficient to simply add women's health to existing specialties would be wise to study the history of science, the sociology of knowledge, and the role of values in science if the missed opportunities of other pioneers are to be avoided. Nineteenth century scientists argued that the rigors of a university education would drain energy from women's reproductive organs. These and other socially expedient biases were used to justify the exclusion of women from positions of authority and decision making. Unless health issues are approached from a solid interdisciplinary, pro-woman perspective, I am not confident that current or future physicians will serve women significantly better than their earlier counterparts. We have already seen a great deal of the money targeted for new research in women's health funneled into the existing "old boys" research network.[17] This is worrisome and disappointing to those of us who had hoped for more adventuresome funding and innovative projects. Rest assured, the age-old debate of autonomy versus integration will wage on as we struggle with how to include women's health in medical training. Common sense and experience suggest that we must do both. It is from the power base of a residency in women's health that efforts to mainstream are most likely to be successful. Furthermore, women's health is a separate body of knowledge and deserves to be treated as a legitimate area of inquity.

Positioning a Women's Health Specialty

There are several possible routes to specialization. Women's health could be a primary care specialty like pediatrics or subspeciality like geriatrics. Alternatively, much like toxicology, it could be a field of study. Entry from any number of specialties would be possible. The positioning of the specialty is less critical than its content. Women's health must be based on research and experience with women, not men.

Those of us interested in fostering the development of an interdisciplinary specialty in women's health have many resources to turn for valuable advice and information. Nursing, a female-dominated profession, has had training programs in women's health for over a decade. Feminist scholars in health psychology and women's studies also have much to offer.

There are already many interesting and active steps being taken within medicine to assure a better response to women's health care needs. Since 1982, hospital-affiliated multidisciplinary women's health centers have offered a closer approximation of an interdisciplinary approach than more conventional group practices.[18] This summer Harvard Medical School held their fifth annual conference on women's health, combining internal medicine, obstetrics-gynecology, and psychiatry. The American

Medical Women's Association is preparing a multidisciplinary postgraduate course on the health care needs of women. Fellowships in women's medicine have started to appear at several institutions, and a number of medical schools offer electives in women's health.[19] Nevertheless, a growing number of medical students longing to specialize in women's health express frustration at the lack of a residency program anywhere in the United States. For now, highly motivated trainees are left to customize existing residencies to achieve their goal of specializing in women's health (D. Moran, personal communication).

Resistance

The resistance to this proposal has been intense and is no doubt determined by many factors. Change is almost always anxiety provoking. In this case the anxiety is fueled by forces as divergent as sexism, economics, and alliances to existing specialties.

Treating women with knowledge drawn from research on men is enough of a problem without being compounded by pervasive sexism.[20] This is an issue in patient care that we have hardly begun to address.[21] Sexist behavior ranges from simple patronizing[22] to explicit harassment and abuse.[23] One male obstetrician has suggested that unless male physicians correct their sexist attitudes and behavior, they should not be allowed to provide health care for women.[2,24]

Unfortunately, sexism is not unique to male physicians. It is embedded in the professionalization of almost every medical student. How else can we interpret the disturbing revelation this year of a graduating medical student that in the anatomy lab female breasts were designated as "waste" and tossed in the trash without careful dissection and examination?[25] This behavior is unconscionable when one in nine American women can expect to develop breast cancer within her lifetime.

Arguments that a specialty in women's health will lead to costly fragmentation and overspecialization do not make sense. It is the current arrangement that causes these problems. Divisions in medicine are arbitrary and based on any number of factors including physician interest, expanding scientific knowledge, and political agendas. Siphoning funds from other critical areas such as AIDS and cancer research will undoubtedly be used as economic scarecrows. At a less conscious level some will be concerned that specialists in women's health will compete more favorably for women patients. Women are the greatest users of health care. Yet another potential financial loss is hard to swallow when physicians are already feeling under siege.

Those of us specializing in the care of women have been cautioned against proposing the development of a new specialty just as medicine is being forced to tighten its belt. The proposal of a new specialty at this time may seem to burden a crumbling system. But it is in this climate that attending to the health care needs of women is even more urgent. Unless we are vigilant about the quality and availability of care for women, it is likely with any of the insurance reforms currently under consideration that health care services for women will be the first to suffer.[26]

Even many well-meaning physicians are unconvinced that a specialty is needed. They believe that theirs is either providing perfectly adequate care for women or that with only modest efforts the quality of care can be raised to acceptable levels. Their identification with their own training interferes with an accurate understanding of the problem.

Framing the Solution

What most opponents fail to appreciate is that women's health is a unique body of knowledge and skills based upon experience with women that cross the boundaries of existing specialties. Women's health care needs are not being met, and cannot be met, within the existing medical paradigm.

The criterion of the American Board of Medical Specialists for a new specialty is that it must "represent a distinct and well-defined field of medical practice" such as "special concerns with problems of patients according to age, sex, organ systems or interaction between patients and their environment." With practice specialties ranging from addiction medicine to undersea medicine,[27] I am hard pressed to understand why a specialty embracing 52% of the adult population is unreasonable or unnecessary.

Conclusion

When it comes to women's health, there are far more questions than answers. Specialists devoted to women's health care in a number of fields are beginning to provide some answers, but the information is fragmented and unknown to physicians who have no particular interest in the field.

It is not only discriminatory, but truly dangerous to fail to bring the study and practice of women's medicine to parity with the understanding and treatment of men rapidly and comprehensively. This can and must be achieved through an active and multifaceted approach. This includes physicians examining their practices and attitudes for social or cultural biases that affect medical care, funding medical research in women's health, and increasing the number of women in positions of authority in teaching, research, and the practice of medicine.[28] The Women's Health Initiative,[29] a multidisciplinary, multiinstitute intervention study to address the major causes of death, disability, and frailty among middle-aged and older women, is an important step, as is the creation of the Office of Research on Women's Health. However, as valuable as these efforts are, they are insufficient. Women deserve no less than children who have specialists in pediatrics and the elderly who have specialists in geriatrics. A new interdisciplinary specialty in women's health is required.

REFERENCES

1. Johnson K, Dawson L. Women's health as a multidisciplinary specialty: An exploratory proposal. J Am Med Wom Assoc 1990;45:222–224.
2. Rodin J., Ickovics J. Women's health: Review and research agendas we approach the 21st century. Am Psychol 1990;45:1018–1034.
3. National Women's Health Resource Center. Cardiovascular disease. In: forging a women's health research agenda, 1990;1–20.
4. Flynn T. Female trouble: Imagine a study about uterine cancer that only examines men. Chicago Tribune 1986 Oct 29; Sec 7:26.
5. Miller JB. Toward a new psychology of women (2nd ed.) Boston: Beacon Press, 1986.
6. Johnson K. Trusting ourselves. New York: Atlantic Monthly Press, 1991.
7. Toward a women's health research agenda: Findings of the scientific advisory meeting. Society for the Advancement of Women's Health Research. Washington, DC: Bass and Howes, Inc. 1991:1–16.
8. Your opinion: Women's health specialty. Internal Medicine World Report 1990; Sept 15–30:30.
9. Novello A. Cited in: Fore J. Doctors urged to ask about abuse. San Francisco Examiner 1992 June 17:A–10.
10. Liebert MA. From the publisher. J Wom Health 1992;1:xix.
11. Faludi S. Backlash. New York: Crown, 1990.
12. Harrison M. Women as other: The premise of medicine. J. Am Med Wom Assoc 1990;45:225–226.
13. Ruzek S. The women's health movement: Feminist alternatives to medical control. New York: Praeger, 1979.
14. Johnson K. Seminar presented at the Center for Educational Development, University of Illinois, Chicago, April 1981.
15. Wallis L. Presentation to the National Association of Women Health Professionals. Chicago, Oct 1989.
16. Woolf V. A room of one's own. New York: Harcourt Brace Jovanovich, 1929.
17. Hamilton JA. Women's health research: Public policy issues. Presented at Second Annual Syntex Women's Health Roundtable, Washington, DC, Feb 1992.
18. Johnson K. Women's health care: An innovative model. Wom Ther 1987;6:305–311.
19. Montgomery K, Moulton A. Undergraduate medical education in women's health. Wom Health Forum. 1992;1:1–2.
20. Novello A. Cited in: Surgeon general says sexism is a problem. San Francisco Examiner 1992 May 13: A–15.
21. Eichler M, Reisman A, Borins E. Gender bias in medical research. Paper presented at Conference on Gender, Science and Medicine, Toronto, November 1988.
22. Wallis LA, Klass P. Toward improving women's health care. J. Am Med Wom Assoc 1990;45:219–221.
23. Gartrell N, Milliken N, Goodson W., Thiemann S. Physician patient sexual contact: Prevalence and problems. Western J Med. In Press.
24. Smith, JH. Women and doctors. New York: Atlantic Monthly Press, 1992.
25. Fugh-Berman A. Tales out of medical school. The Nation 1992 January 20; 1:54–56.
26. Jecker NS. Age-based rationing and women JAMA. 1991;226:3012–3015.
27. List of self-designated practice specialty codes. Chicago: American Medical Association, 1992.
28. Council on Ethical and Judicial Affairs. Gender disparities in clinical decision making. JAMA 1991;266:559–562.
29. Healy B. The Yentl syndrome. N Engl J Med 1991:325:274–275.

CON
Women's Health as a Specialty
A Deceptive Solution

by Michelle Harrison, M.D.

Abstract. A proposed call for a new specialty in women's health is an attempt to rectify current inadequacies in the care of women. This paper discusses nineteenth century origins of the current organization of medical specialties in which the male body is the norm and woman becomes "other." Nineteenth century attitudes toward women, with the belief in the biological inferiority of women due to their sexual organs, and the replacement of midwives by physicians, became the basis of this bifurcated system of care in which women require two physicians for their ongoing care. A reorganization of medical specialties is proposed in which: (1) Internal medicine incorporates the primary care aspect of gynecology, as does family medicine; (2) Obstetrics and gynecology remains the surgical and referral specialty that it is; (3) Interdisciplinary research addresses gaps in understanding the role of reproductive events, hormones, and cycles to normal and pathological functioning; (4) Medical students are taught to identify across gender lines; (5) All specialties are examined for the purpose of making them "user friendly" to women; and (6) The medical profession addresses and rectifies past inequities in the conceptual framework about women and their subsequent denial of leadership opportunities. The need for education in women's health is acknowledged, but with the goal of making that need obsolete. A new specialty has the potential to further isolate women's issues from mainstream medicine and to marginalize its practitioners.

The proposition that women's health become a separate specialty derives from the failure of the established medical system to address adequately the health care needs of women. These inadequacies exist in the social, medical, educational, and research aspects of women's health. Even though women consume proportionally more medical services than do men, the basic organization of medical specialization has been based upon a male standard to which woman is the eternal exception. Although the establishment of a separate specialty of women's health may initially seem appealing, it has the potential of further isolating the women's perspective in delivery of health care, while simultaneously marginalizing those practitioners who commit themselves to its practice.

This paper discusses the history of the development of the current system of medicine with its adaptation toward the male body and psyche. A model of health care in which women's bodies are the norm, not the exception, is developed.

Nineteenth Century Attitudes

The current treatment of women has its roots in the history of medicine in America, which in turn reflected the prevailing cultural attitudes toward women. Dr. Charles D. Meigs, Professor of Midwifery and the Diseases of Women and Children at Jefferson Medical College in Philadelphia, in 1838 translated the following from the French physician Velpeau:

> Puberty, or the marriageable age, is announced in girls, as it is in boys, by numerous changes. . . . The young girl becomes more timid and reserved; her form becomes more rounded. . . . Her eyes, which are at once brilliant and languishing, express commingled desires, fears, and tenderness; the sensations she experiences and the sense of her own weakness, are the causes why she no longer dares to approach the companions of her childhood but with a downcast look.[1]

From *Journal of Women's Health*, Vol. 1, No. 2, 1992. Copyright © 1992 by Mary Ann Liebert, Inc. Reprinted by permission.

The biological transition from girl to young woman was seen as the causative factor in her change in personality. Biology was deemed destiny, and hers was to be one of fear and weakness.

The nineteenth century saw the development of a sizable population of women who, because of industrialization and urbanization, became part of a middle class in which women's employment outside the home was unnecessary. So, while the vast majority of women throughout the world toiled in fields and factories, bore child after child, then aged and died early, Western Europe and America were creating a new version of woman expressive of new political and economic times. The new version conveniently placed women out of competition with men and created a biological basis for that exclusion. Meigs, in an 1859 collection of his own lectures, wrote, "The sexuality of the woman does in its essence consist in the possession of that peculiar structure called ovarian stroma—her heart, brain, lungs, all her viscera, all indeed that she is, would not make her a female without the primordial central essence—stroma."[2] He continues, "She demands a treatment adapted to the very specialties of her own constitution, as a moral, a sexual, germiferous, gestative, or parturient creature."[2,3] Women's sexuality then became the heart of the justification of difference, and difference invariably meant lesser.

Laqueur, in *Making Sex: Body and Gender from the Greeks to Freud*, describes the Greek model in which the genders were measured by metaphysical perfection in hierarchical relation to each other. This early model of "one sex" in various states of perfection and imperfection was replaced in the nineteenth century with a model of biological divergence based upon anatomical and physiological incommensurability.[3] What had previously been a variation on a single human body became two distinct sexes, believed to be different in every aspect. The shift had been one of changing from comparing grades of apples to comparing apples and oranges, male and female.

Laqueur argues that the polarities of gender can be understood as polarities of power and that "the competition for power generates new ways of constituting the subject and the social realities within which humans dwell."[3] As if to illustrate Laqueur's point, Dr. Alfred Stille in his presidential address to the American Medical Association in 1871 stated, "If, then, woman is unfitted by nature to become a physician, we should, when we oppose her pretensions, be acquitted of any malicious or even unkindly spirit."[4] Woman had been discovered to be a new species, one conveniently unsuited to compete with men in the profession of medicine.

Nineteenth century medicine developed along two lines simultaneously. The body of medicine treated men and the nonreproductive aspects of women's health. Childbirth and common gynecologic problems were usually left to midwives, in part because of prohibitions against male physicians examining female sexual organs. Women's genitals began to be "observed" by physicians in the mid nineteenth century.[5] With the development of gynecologic surgery, which established gynecology as a recognized field, and the successful effort on the part of medicine to define childbirth as a surgical procedure, female midwives were replaced by male obstetricians and gynecologists.

The lifting of cultural prohibitions against the gynecological examination of women by men opened the way for increasing male knowledge about female reproductive anatomy and physiology. If not for the pursuit of economic and professional power on the part of physicians, there might have been a partnership with the midwives, with benefit to both professions and especially to women as patients. Instead there was the destruction of midwifery and a loss of the ways in which women had for centuries attended to the needs of other women. The midwives' care of women exclusively meant that for midwifery, the female body was the standard, the normal, the regular. With the transfer of care to a male medical profession, in which the standard was the male body, the body without female parts, woman's body became "other."[6] With the destruction of midwifery and the paucity of women physicians, the woman's body with its sexual organs was now a foreign body to the overwhelmingly male medical profession and the exclusively male gynecologic surgeons.

The stage was thus set for the current organization of medicine in which internal medicine attends to the nonreproductive aspects of women's health and the generative-related conditions are relegated to the obstetrician-gynecologist. The woman's body with its sexual and generative functions had been medicalized, even in those processes that can be viewed as normal functions. Because medicine was organized around a male body and because physicians were male, nothing about a woman's menstrual cycle or reproduction was "normal." It was all new. She had to be "managed," an approach to women that has not significantly changed.[7]

Nineteenth century medicine attributed the state of women's mental health to the health of their ovaries. Mental illness (at times defined as the inability to accept culturally defined roles, with symptoms including a desire to run away from home, dislike of a husband, or a refusal to sleep with him[8]) was attributed to the dysfunction of sexual organs. The reproductive organs became the seat of not just sexual passions but were seen as the cause of insanity. Clitoridectomy was the first operation performed to check woman's mental disorder.[9] Proponents of castration described the benefits of removal of the ovaries: "the moral sense of the patient is elevated . . . she becomes tractable, orderly, industrious, and cleanly."[9] There was apparently some recognition that castration could lead to postoperative insanity, in which case further surgery was recommended, namely removal of the uterus and Fallopian tubes. Clitoridectomy, castration, and hysterectomy were the nineteenth century treatment of uncontrolled female emotions.[9] The operation was successful if the woman "was restored to a placid contentment with her domestic functions."[10]

Normality was defined as male, with sanity therefore being closer to male function than to female function. Barker-Benfield suggests that the identification of female sexuality with madness was a result of the assumption that "man's madness" was the norm within the society and therefore woman's was easier to cure.[11] Female "madness" was also easier to see because to the extent it expressed resistance to stereotypic roles, it stood in sharp contrast to the social and political prohibitions of the society.

Such practices as the nineteenth century surgical treatments to return women to their acceptable "passivity" may seem shocking by contemporary standards. Less obvious are the current ways in which society accommodates male behavior and male "madness." For example, although the current diagnosis of postraumatic stress disorder describes the woman's reaction to rape, and adequate framework to describe the causative behavior on the part of the male aggressor is lacking. The psychological effects of sexual harassment on the part of the victim can be described, but the language and understanding of perpetrators is wanting.

The long delay in recognizing wife battering and marital rape may be traced to the nineteenth century when, "throughout much of the bourgeois century, all across the Western world, women remained virtual chattels in the hands of their fathers, and later, of their husbands."[12] For the last two centuries it was the women victims of battering and marital rape who were brought for mental health services. Society's acceptance of, and possibly hopelessness about, male violence may prevent perception of these acts as deviant and destructive.

Sex role stereotyping within the mental health field was aptly described by Broverman et al., who described sex biases in interpretation of behavior by clinicians. In their 1970 study, a healthy adult (nonspecified sex) had attributes more like a healthy male than a healthy woman. They found that "clinicians are more likely to suggest that healthy women differ from healthy men by being more submissive, less independent, less adventurous, more easily influenced, less aggressive, less competitive, more excitable in minor crises. . . ."[13]

These findings from 1970 are not unlike the descriptions of Velpeau (quoted above) in 1838 or those describing results of castration. In those intervening 130 years, a civil war was fought, women organized and fought for the right to vote, they organized against alcohol, they entered the professions of medicine and law against great odds, they joined the military for two world wars, and yet the stereotypes prove more resilient than reality. Women's sex and sexuality continued to be perceived as the basis for her inferiority. Physicians had, "turned the stereotype of feminine frailty into a medical principle."[14]

The diagnosis of late luteal phrase dysphoric disorder was added to the *Diagnostic and Statistical Manual* of the American Psychiatric Association in 1987.[15] This diagnosis describes a mental disorder whose etiology is the menstrual cycle and whose language includes anger as a symptom of mental illness. Although few would dispute that the menstrual cycle may affect how some women feel, including anger, there is an important distinction between influencing and causing symptoms and behavior.

Men and women are influenced in mood by weather, light, diet, general health, and day of the week, but few would designate those as the determinants of mental illness. However, old beliefs persist, in practitioners and in women. When a contemporary woman visits her gynecologist because she is irritable with her children premenstrually, she is the "medical" expression of the nineteenth century view of women's mental state being controlled by her ovaries. Likewise, her gynecologist is supporting this premise when ovariectomy is the treatment recommended for the woman's mood or behavioral problems. Chemical and surgical castration remain accepted treatments for disorders of mood.[16–18]

Educating for Women's Health

The establishment of training programs in women's health is a separate issue from the creation of a new specialty. There is an enormous job to be done in educating the medical profession and institutions. Ideally, this would be a task undertaken with the aim of eventual obsolescence. Fellowships are needed in order to teach and to create meaningful research. However, to create a new specialty, to certify those physicians trained to take care of women, would allow the rest of those in medicine to feel absolved of responsibility for addressing the needs of women, and more inclined to leave the sensitive care of women to those few practitioners who are now the "experts." In reality, only a very small percentage of women (and of a given social class) would have access to this care, and the vast majority of women would continue as they do now with their bifurcated care.

The Call for a Specialty

The problems in contemporary medicine that have brought forth the call for a new specialty in women's health are related to: (1) unexplored and unanswered questions in research and education related to women's health; (2) the ways in which women's health needs are not met; and (3) the bifurcation of routine medical care of women.

Given the shortcomings of the present medical system, the call for a separate specialty is understandable. It comes out of frustration, disappointment, and mistrust. The presence of increasing numbers of women physicians has led to a reassessment as to whether medicine could do a better job in addressing needs of women patients. However, there is no aspect of this new proposed specialty that should not be an integral part of the education and practice of every physician, male or female. Rather, the solutions lie in a reorganization of current medical specialization and a demand for the provision of services that more adequately address the needs of women patients.

QUESTIONS FOR RESEARCH AND EDUCATION

Major gaps exist in the understanding of differences in female physiology and pathology, related, but not restricted, to the menstrual cycle. Because of the "foreign nature" of female bodies to a male medical profession, the menstrual cycle and its effects were for a long time ignored, stigmatized, or left strictly to gynecology. Were all males to menstruate, the interrelated effects of the menstrual cycle on other aspects of a person's health would have been considered essential, even fascinating, areas of study, worthy of the best research and funding. In fact, the vast majority of physicians have never experienced menstruation, looked at sanitary pads, handled tampons, or had cramps. Though it may not be necessary to experience illness in order to understand or treat them, the lack of understanding or familiarity with what is normal may result in a tendency to pathologize the entire process. That deficiency in personal experience may limit one's ability to be comfortable with integrating menstruation into a "normal" body.

On the other side, the fact that women are not defined by their menstrual cycles does not mean that this process is irrelevant. It is clear that many medications react differently over the course of the menstrual cycle, yet this area remains largely unexplored. Pharmacologic research has been done on males in part because the menstrual cycle becomes a confounding factor in analysis of results. However, the drugs are then used on women and those confounding effects become clinical

effects—poorly understood because of a paucity of research. The research that is needed is not necessarily on the menstrual cycle itself, but rather interdisciplinary research that looks at the menstrual cycle in relation to heart disease, asthma, seizures, and lupus, areas where it is already clear that gender is relevant.[19-25] Interdisciplinary and gender-conscious research is needed to look at osteoporosis in relation to nutrition, exercise, vitamins, *and* the menstrual cycle. Current research and understanding of substance abuse lacks any systematic or "systems" study of the effects of the menstrual cycle or of menopause.

The designation of obstetrics and gynecology as *the* women's specialty may have actually isolated the understanding of interrelations between menstruation, pregnancy, and other metabolic processes. And, because of the bifurcation in treatment and approach to women's health, the rest of medicine has tended to leave these questions to obstetrics and gynecology.

There is a consistency to the problems identified in the care of women. The common thread is the lack of integration of women's physiologic and metabolic processes into the body of medicine. As a result, the female body remains somewhat "foreign," something a bit more alien to (primarily male) physicians than a regular (male) body.

THE PROBLEM OF SHORTCOMINGS IN THE SYSTEM

The differential attention paid to male versus female patients has been documented. Armitage, Schneiderman and Bass, in a study of physician response to complaints in men and women, speculate that "they might be responding to current stereotypes that regard the male as typically stoic and the female as typically 'hypochondriacal.'"[26] Recent literature has addressed differences in referral patterns for male and female cardiac patients[27] and in their selection for coronary angiography and coronary revascularization.[28] This research attempts to discriminate between bias in the care of women and their different needs because of different courses of specific illness. If there is bias in the care of women cardiac patients, it must be addressed, but it does not warrant the development of separate surgery based upon the "female" heart as opposed to a "male" heart. Whatever differences exist in severity of illness, circulation of coronary arteries, or innervation of conducting muscle, they are all within overlapping variations of both male and female hearts. With the exception of those organs involved in reproduction, the vast majority of human organs are truly androgynous.

THE BIFURCATION OF MEDICAL CARE OF WOMEN

Internal medicine is founded on the model of a male body, with women as "other."[29] That specialty attends to the medical illnesses of the entire male body and part of the female body, whereas obstetrics and gynecology treats those parts of the body related to reproductive health. The result is that most women during their reproductive years must go to two physicians to get their whole body attended to, or use one and forgo the services of the other.

The archaic nature of this arrangement is nowhere more evident than in the assessment of abdominal disorders. The partitioning of the abdominal cavity into the domain of two specialties reflects the dual origins of internists descending from the regular physicians and ob-gyns replacing midwives. No clear anatomical distinction exists, however, between abdomen and pelvis in a female. The area is a continuous cavity divided by imaginary lines that delineate the boundaries of the specialist's territory rather than anatomical structures. The gastrointestinal tract passes through the pelvis and may adhere to the ovaries; endometrial tissue may migrate to the diaphragm, and yet the woman with abdominal pain must visit two doctors, each of whom only partially examines her and then communicates findings with the other by phone or written report, or through the patient. In a male it would be akin to having initial chest pain evaluated by two different doctors, one for the heart and one for the lungs. One doctor would only listen to heartbeats, the other only to breath sounds. Each would then write reports back to the other as to whether the shortness of breath and pain on deep inspiration were of cardiac or pulmonary origin. The need for two physicians to evaluate abdominal pain in a woman is equally absurd.

It is the organization of medical knowledge and practice that are the problem, not the female body. Whereas internal medicine and ob-gyn fall short of addressing the whole woman, family medicine takes care of the whole woman, but in the context of her family, a social role not a medical condition. The one specialty that teaches care of the whole woman also includes children and men. In other words, either a specialty treats only parts of the woman, or it treats all of her and her family.

Rather than the establishment of a new specialty based upon the care of more than half of all adult patients, the current system, in both its structure and content, must address the needs of women as an integral and legitimate aspect of the practice of medicine within every specialty. There simply is no special training for an orthopedist treating women or a radiologist reading women's films or a cardiologist listening to a woman's heart. There is rather the necessity for all orthopedists, all radiologists, and all cardiologists—indeed, all physicians—to look beyond bias and sex stereotyping, and to view being female as only one aspect of the biological, social, and psychological person.

If all human bodies were female and social structure was based upon some other factor than gender, the thorough knowledge of the body would be the medical standard. For instance, anatomically, the physician would examine the whole body because vaginas would not be alien anatomical parts but rather within the norm. If men had large breasts, they would be included in the routine examination of a person. The same physician who examines for spleens and prostrates would be expected to feel for breast lumps. The internist examining for abdominal pain would also do a pelvic exam as part of the assessment, and at the same time, would also do a Pap if needed. In other words, the female reproductive and sexual parts would be part of the everyday practice of an everyday physician.

Even though childbirth has become a surgical procedure,[30] pregnancy remains a metabolic process with the major risk factors being related to the medical health of the woman. Hypertension and diabetes, normally the domain of internists, in pregnancy becomes the domain of the obstetrician-gynecologist, a highly trained surgeon. The major difficulties of the postpartum period are likewise not surgical. Bleeding may occasionally be a problem, but the physician is more likely to encounter thyroid disease, depression, and questions about medications that might pass into breast milk. These are areas more appropriately addressed by an internist or family physician than by a surgeon.

Marginalization of "Women's Health" Specialists

The entrance of women and minorities into male-dominated fields has more commonly led to what the anthropologists term "ritual contamination" of a field than to an increase in the prestige of the women who enter the profession. A field created for the nonsurgical routine care of women, whose practitioners would invariably be mostly female, would likely become a relatively low-paid, low-status field with little or no opportunities for advancement or access to power within universities or specialty societies. Just recently in this century women have entered into medicine in significant numbers. However, their continued inability to achieve positions of power makes it likely that "women's health" would become a marginalized area for a few dedicated (probably most female) physicians. Meanwhile, the rest of medicine would continue as it is, with both the male body and male psyche the standard of normality and health. And, as long as the standard is male, "other" invariably will mean less.

Women do not need special practitioners. Except for diseases of the male reproductive tract and some rare genetic diseases, there are no illnesses restricted to men only. The basic diseases of man are the diseases of woman. The surgical care of women's reproductive organs would rightfully remain the domain of the obstetrician/gynecologist. Although ob-gyns would like to be designated as the primary care physicians of women, it is more likely that internists or family physicians will retain expertise in pelvis exams rather than ob-gyns adding to their training the routine management of diabetes, hypertension, heart disease, gastric ulcers, pneumonia, and all the other diseases encountered in the routine primary care of women.

Necessary Changes

The changes needed to rectify current shortcomings are broad in scope but necessary if anything except cosmetic changes are to be made. Hospital facilities can be dressed up in pink colors and new labeling, but unless the need for fundamental changes in the structure of medicine are acknowledged and implemented, health for the vast majority of women will go unaltered. The basic deficiencies and biases that exist in the conceptual framework of woman—as a biological, psychological, and social person—will continue to undermine any attempt to put women on an equal medical and professional footing with men. The changes needed are as follows.

1.   The current specialty of internal medicine must incorporate the menstrual cycle and reproduction into its conceptual framework. The routine gynecologic care of women must be a part of the practice of internal medicine. Family medicine, while continuing to provide primary care for a woman, must recognize her individual existence separate from the family.

2.   Obstetrics and gynecology should remain the specialty for referral of obstetric and gynecologic difficulties.

3.   Interdisciplinary research must address gaps in the understanding of female functions and their relationship to normal and pathological conditions.

4.   Medical students must be taught to identify with patients across gender lines.

5.   All medical specialties must be examined for ways in which they are or are not "user friendly" to women.

6.   Organized medicine, including medical schools and professional societies, must begin to actively address and rectify those unfounded assumptions about the biological inferiority of women that have been the basis for exclusion of women from medicine and from positions of leadership and power within medicine.

It is not clear what medicine would look like without the standard of the male body and the concomitant underlying assumptions of a biological basis for female passivity and weakness. However, we have the opportunity to find out. Women as patients and as professionals should not settle for a small corner of medicine as a women's health specialty, however appealing that might be. Women instead need to establish their rightful place and perspective within the body of medicine, a body that has been entirely too male in its conceptual framework as well as its membership. There is no medical imperative for a new specialty. Instead, there is an urgent social and economic imperative to restructure medical specialization and to create a nonadversarial body of knowledge and code of practice, in which gender may represent difference but not "other," and certainly not less.

References

1.   Velpeau ALM. An elementary treatise on midwifery (CD Meigs, trans.; 2nd Am. ed). Philadelphia: Grigg & Elliot, 1838:83.

2.   Meigs CD. Woman: Her diseases and remedies. Philadelphia: Blanchard and Lea, 1859:51, 55.

3.   Laqueur T. Making sex: Body and gender from the Greeks to Freud. Cambridge, MA: Harvard University Press, 1990:5–8, 11.

4.   Fishbein M. A history of the American Medical Association 1847 to 1947. Philadelphia: WB. Saunders, 1947:83.

5.   Barker-Benfield GJ. The horrors of the half-known life. New York: Harper Colophon Books, 1976:85.

6.   Harrison M. Woman as other: The premise of medicine. J Am Med Wom Assoc 1990;45:225–226.

7.   Harrison M. A woman in residence. New York: Random House, 1982:199.

8.   Corea G. The hidden malpractice (updated ed.). New York: Harper Colophon Books, 1985:102–103.

9.   Barker-Benfield GJ. The horrors of the half-known life. New York: Harper Colophon Books, 1976:120–126.

10.   Ehrenreich B, English D. For her own good. Garden City NY: Anchor Books, 1979:124.

11.   Barker-Benfield GJ. The horrors of the half-known life. New York: Harper Colophon Books, 1976:84.

12.   Gay P. The bourgeois experience. Vol. 1: Education of the senses. New York: Oxford University Press, 1984:174.

13.   Broverman IK, Broverman DM, Clarkson FE, Rosenkrantz PS, Vogel SR. Sex-role stereotypes and clinical judgments of mental health. J Consult Clin Psychol 1970;34:1–7.

14.   Corea G. The hidden malpractice (updated ed.). New York: Harper Colophon Books, 1985:96.

15.   American Psychiatric Association. Diagnostic and statistical manual of mental disorders (3rd ed., rev.). Washington, DC: American Psychiatric Press, 1987.

16.   Casper RF, Heart MT. The effect of hysterectomy and bilateral oophorectomy in women with severe premenstrual syndrome. Am J Obstet Gynecol 1990;162;105–109.

17. Casson P, Hahn PM, Van Vugt DA, Reid RL. Lasting response to ovariectomy in severe intractable premenstrual syndrome. Am J. Obstet Gynecol 1990; 162:99–105.

18. Muse KN, Cetel NS, Futterman LA, Yen SSC. The premenstrual syndrome: Effects of a "medical ovariectomy." N Engl J Med 1984; 311:1345–1349.

19. Stampfer MJ, Willett WC, Colditz GA, Rosner B, Speizer FE, Hennekens CH. A prospective study of postmenopausal estrogen therapy and coronary heart disease. N Engl J Med 1985;313:1044–1049.

20. Wilson PWF, Garrison RJ, Castelli WP. Postmenopausal estrogen use, cigarette smoking, and cardiovascular morbidity in women over 50. N Engl J Med 1985;313:1038–1043.

21. Wolf PW, Madans JH, Finucane FF, Higgins M, Kleinman JC. Reduction of cardiovascular disease-related mortality among post-menopausal women who use hormones: Evidence from a national cohort. Am J Obstet Gynecol 1991;164:489–494.

22. Eliasson OK, Scherzer HH, DeGraff Jr. AC. Morbidity in asthma in relation to the menstrual cycle. J Allergy Clin Immunol 1986;77:87–94.

23. Lenoir RJ. Severe acute asthma and the menstrual cycle. Anesthesia 1987;42:1287–1290.

24. Price TRP. Temporal lobe epilepsy as a premenstrual behavioral syndrome. Biol Psychiatry 1980;15:957–963.

25. Steinberg AD, Steinberg BJ. Lupus disease activity associated with the menstrual cycle. J Rheumatol 1985;12:816–817.

26. Armitage KJ, Schneiderman LJ, Bass RA. Response of physicians to medical complaints in men and women. JAMA, 1979; 241:2186–2187.

27. Bickell NA, Pieper KS, Lee KL, et al. Referral patterns for coronary artery disease treatment: Gender bias or good clinical judgment? Ann Int Med 1992;116:791–797.

28. Krumholz HM, Douglass PS, Lauer MS, Pasternak RC. Selection of patients for coronary angiography and coronary revascularization early after myocardial infarction: Is there evidence for a gender bias? Ann Int Med 1992;116:785–790.

29. Harrison M. Woman as other: The premise of medicine. J Am Med Wom Assoc 1990;4:225–226.

30. Harrison M. A woman in residence. New York: Random House, 1982:93.

The Women's Health Movement in the United States
From Grass-Roots Activism to Professional Agendas

by Sheryl Burt Ruzek, PHD, MPH · Julie Becker, MA, MPH

The grass-roots women's health movement grew rapidly during the 1970s and 1980s, but contracted by the end of that decade. Surviving organizations must now negotiate roles and relationships with newer women's health organizations that burgeoned in the 1990s and that are typically professionalized and disease specific. They differ from grass-roots groups through: 1) their relationships to broader movements for social change; 2) leadership; 3) attitudes toward biomedicine; 4) relationships to corporate sponsors; 5) educational goals; and 6) lay versus professional authority. There is little overlap between women's health advocacy organizations identified by the National Women's Health Network and two Internet search engines. The proliferation of newer organizations dilutes the role of grass-roots groups as information brokers for women in the United States and raises questions about who will speak for women in the electronic age. (JAMWA. 1999;54:4–8)

From *Journal of the American Medical Women's Association*, January 30, 1998. Copyright © 1998 American Medical Women's Association, Inc. All rights reserved. Reprinted with permission.

Dr. Ruzek is professor and Ms. Becker is a doctoral candidate, both in the Department of Health Studies. Temple University in Philadelphia, Pennsylvania.

Women's health activists have generated public debate and spearheaded social action in a number of waves throughout US history, waves that Carol Weisman views as part of a women's health "megamovement" that has spanned two centuries.[1(p37–93)] The US women's health movement grew rapidly through the 1970s; broadened its base with women of color and others in the early 1980s; and contracted, was co-opted, and became institutionalized during the late 1980s and 1990s. Surviving grass-roots organizations are now negotiating roles and relationships with newer, more professional women's health support and advocacy organizations. While both older and newer women's health organizations seek improvements in women's health care, their focus and priorities vary.

In this article, we analyze the historical development of the grass-roots women's health movement in the United States, note key contributions, and differentiate surviving movement organizations from the newer, professionalized women's health advocacy groups. Distinguishing between grass-roots and more professional women's health groups becomes particularly important as we move into the global "information age." Because public trust of mainstream medical institutions is eroding, as evidenced by the growth of alternative and complementary medical practices[2–4] and the increasing distrust of managed care organizations,[5] both grass-roots and professionalized health advocacy groups are likely to play key roles in defining the quality and trustworthiness of health information.[6–8] Growing calls for accountability and improved patient satisfaction create windows of opportunity for health advocates to use their influence and authority to shape how the quality of health information and services will be defined.[9]

Social Movements and Social Change

The women's health movement's very success makes differentiating surviving grass-roots movement organizations from professionalized ones that are historically, ideologically, and strategically aligned with this episode of activism particularly challenging. For conceptual clarity, it is important to note that social scientists have long distinguished between general social movements and specific social movements. Theorists of social movements are particularly careful to differentiate between grass-roots movements and professionalized movements that emerge from within established institutions.[10–13] General social movements affect the public's consciousness of many issues and bring about social change in many arenas. The general feminist movement of the 1960s and 1970s spawned dozens of specific

movements and hundreds of movement organizations.[14–17] As specific social movements gain momentum, they, like general social movements, shape public consciousness beyond the smaller world of movement organizations.

It is also crucial not to confuse formally constituted movement organizations with social movements themselves, although these groups represent the active components of a movement.[18] As health activists differentiated themselves within the broader feminist movement and developed an identity as a specific grass-roots feminist movement, they founded organizations such as the Boston Women's Health Book Collective, the Federation of Feminist Women's Health Centers, DES Action, and the National Women's Health Network.[19–21]

Rise and Development of the Women's Health Movement

More than three decades ago, when access to medical information was restricted almost exclusively to physicians (who were mostly men), laywomen's insistence on access to medical research was truly "revolutionary." Few books on women's health could be found in bookstores, except for books on childbirth. The assumption was simply that physicians were the experts and women were to do as instructed. Breaking open this closed system, laywomen asserted that personal, subjective knowledge of one's own body was a valid source of information and deserved recognition, not scorn.[22–23]

The women's health movement grew rapidly through the leadership of several grass-roots groups with strong ties to other social change movements, particularly the abortion rights, prepared childbirth, and consumer health movements. As the general feminist movement of the 1960s and 1970s sought equal rights and the full participation of women in all public spheres, many believed that without control over reproduction, all other rights were in jeopardy. Thus in the early years, reproductive issues defined many branches of the movement and shaped group consciousness and social action.[16,24] Reproductive rights remain central to feminist health agendas worldwide.[25]

Feminist health writers such as Barbara Seaman,[26] Barbara Ehreinreich and Deirdre English,[27] Ellen Frankfort,[28] Gena Corea,[29] Claudia Dreifus,[30] and columnists for prominent feminist newspapers galvanized women to explore their own health, providing critical momentum for the emerging grass-roots movement. The Boston Women's Health Book Collective produced the enormously popular *Our Bodies, Ourselves*, which has gone through numerous US and many other language editions worldwide.[31] The Federation of Feminist Women's

Health Centers "invented" and championed gynecological self-help and woman-centered reproductive health services.[23] The National Women's Health Network (NWHN) linked a wide array of local groups to provide a voice for women in Washington. Monitoring legislation, Food and Drug Administration actions, and informing the public about women's health issues continue to be central to this organization's mission.[32] A few nationally prominent groups focused on specific diseases or condition (eg, DES Action, the Endometriosis Association). Members of pivotal groups and other health activists traveled, spoke, and published widely, and used contacts with the media effectively, becoming spokespeople for the rapidly growing movement.

An important achievement of the women's health movement was transferring women's health from the domain of largely male experts to women themselves. Developing in parallel with self-help medical care movements, consciousness-raising and gynecological self-help became strategies for empowering women to define their own health and create alternative services. Local movement groups in all 50 states were providing gynecological self-help, women-controlled reproductive health clinics, clearinghouses for health information, and referral services and producing their own health educational materials. Advocacy ranged from accompanying individual women seeking medical care to advising and influencing state and local health departments. By the mid-1970s, more than 250 formally identifiable groups provided education, advocacy, and direct service in the United States.[19(p.245-265)] Nearly 2,000 informal self-help groups and projects provided additional momentum to the movement (B. Seaman, unpublished data, 1998). Although ideologically committed to being inclusive, the leadership of the women's health movement remained largely white and middle class in North America during the early years. Sterilization abuse mobilized women of color to seek government protection during the 1970s, and groups such as the Committee to End Sterilization Abuse (CESA) were founded.[33]

The women's health movement grew increasingly visible globally, with groups such as ISIS in Geneva creating opportunities for worldwide feminist health activism.[34,35] By the mid-1970s, there were more than 70 feminist health groups in Canada, Europe, and Australia.[19(p 241-245)] Today, there are growing efforts to make connections with feminist health activists worldwide, both in industrialized and developing countries.[36-38]

As the women's health movement evolved in the United States, the distinct health needs of diverse women emerged, and women of color formed their own movement organizations such as the National Black Women's Health Project, the National Latina Women's Health Organization, the Native American Women's Health Education and Resource Center, and the National Asian Women's Health Organization. Women of color health organizations gained national recognition and developed agendas to protect women against racist sterilization and contraceptive practices; to widen access to medical care for low-income women, including abortions no longer covered by Medicaid; and to focus on diseases and conditions affecting women of color such as lupus, fetal alcohol syndrome, hypertension, obesity, drug addiction, and stress related to racism and poverty that were ignored or misunderstood by largely white movement groups.[39] By the late 1980s, the National Black Women's Health Project had established local chapters with more than 150 self-help groups for African-American women.[40]

Other women added distinct health agendas. Lesbians, rural women, and women with disabilities joined older women's groups and women with specific health concerns to direct attention to their particular needs. Groups such as the Dis-Abled Women's Network, the Older Women's League, and the Lesbian Health Agenda broadened constituencies and issues. With the rise of environmental health concerns, groups such as the Women's Environmental Development Organization (WEDO) built bridges between feminist health activism and other movements for social change.

Like other social movements, the women's health movement has gone through periods of emergence, rapid growth, decline, and institutionalization. Grass-roots feminist health organizations declined in the 1980s, apparently as a result of changes in movement adherents and the social context in which movement groups operated. For example, many founders of movement organizations returned to school, began families, or entered the paid labor force, as have the next generation of women who increasingly juggle careers and families, thus reducing the traditional volunteer labor pool. Much of organized feminism as it evolved both in media imagery and academe, came to be seen as distant or disconnected from ordinary women's lives.[41-43] The success of single-issue groups, particularly acquired immune deficiency syndrome (AIDS) organizations, to secure funding for direct services, education, and research presented new models for health activism.[44-46] And the discovery of mainstream health institutions that "marketing to women" could increase profits[47] led to the designation of a wide array of clinical services as "women's health clinics." By the 1990s, women's health services were widespread, although most were now part of larger medical institutions. In a recent national survey of women's health services, most centers founded in the 1960s and 1970s claimed a commitment to a feminist ideology; those founded later or sponsored by hospitals were significantly less likely to report this commitment.[48]

By the end of the 1980s, most alternative feminist health clinics had ceased to exist, and the survivors had broadened their range of services and affiliated with larger health systems.[49] Gynecological self-help has virtually disappeared. The surviving grass-roots movement advocacy and education groups such as the NWHN face declining support from both individuals and foundations as they compete with newer organizations for members and resources. Thus, grass-roots groups contracted internally as they were diluted externally by the growing prominence of both mainstream women's support groups (on a wide array of health issues ranging from alcohol problems to breast cancer) and disease-focused health advocacy groups whose efforts supported the growing federal initiatives for greater equity in women's health research (S.B. Ruzek, unpublished data, 1998).

From Grass-Roots Ideologies to Professional Institutional Agendas

The success of the women's health movement is reflected in the extent to which mainstream organizations and institutions, particularly federal agencies, have incorporated or adopted core ideas and created new opportunities for women's health advocates. By the 1990s, the reform wings of feminism had made significant claims for gender equity in all social institutions. With a growing number of women in Congress, in the biomedical professions, and in health advocacy communities, organizations that had pursued very different paths to improving women's health coalesced around the 1989 General Accounting Office (GAO) report showing that the National Institutes of Health (NIH) had failed to implement its policy of including women in study populations. The GAO report proved to be a catalyst for pressuring Congress and the NIH to take action, and by the end of 1990, the Women's Health Equity Act was passed, and the NIH established the Office of Research on Women's Health. In 1991, the NIH undertook the Women's Health Initiative, the largest project of its kind, seeking data on prevention and treatment of cancer, cardiovascular disease, and osteoporosis.[1(p.77–89)] Although grass-roots women's health groups have criticized many aspects of the research and have attempted to rectify perceived problems in consent procedures and inclusion criteria, they have largely supported greater federal funding of biomedical research into women's health.[50] Thus the women's health movement critique of biomedicine and the call for demedicalizing women's health care[51] was reframed into a bipartisan agenda for equity. Scientific and professional interest in women's health burgeoned in the early 1990s. Spurred by growing federal investment in women's health and by the "cold-war dividend" funding of women's research through the Department of Defense, health activists saw

opportunities to collaborate with scientists and professionals who were eager to take advantage of these new research priorities.

To maximize the likelihood of obtaining federal funding for research on women's health, scientists and their consumer allies focused on specific diseases. This narrowing of focus was critical for navigating federal funding streams that are tied to specific diseases and organ systems. The new "disease-oriented" organizations reflect the interests of women who expect a high level of professionalism. Facing dual roles as workers outside the home and traditional caretakers inside the home, the highly educated women who support the new single-issue groups may find that their interests lie in organizations that dispense professionally endorsed information, solicit donations, and carry out advocacy efforts on behalf of women. Thus the success of women's entry into the labor force, changes in cultural ethos, and women's own commitment to specialization and professionalism may explain why the narrower, highly professionalized women's health equity organizations attract women who do not identify either with broader movements for social change or with feminism per se.

AIDS advocacy groups also raised a new standard of effectiveness for health activists. They not only successfully increased funding for education and research, but gained a voice in how these added appropriations from government and foundations would be spent. Thereafter, breast cancer advocates[52,53] and others (ovarian cancer advocates, Parkinson patients and their families, etc) adopted many of the AIDS organizations' strategies, albeit with a more professional and less confrontational style. A growing willingness to own illness and become "poster people" for cancer, as people with AIDS has done effectively, put a face on diseases that women privately and pervasively feared. Creating strong alliances between consumers, medical professionals, and researchers, breast cancer advocates rallied behind a specific cause that affected many of them directly or through family and friends. Many local support and advocacy organizations joined larger, well-funded organizations such as the National Breast Cancer Coalition, leaving behind older-style support groups and feminist health organizations with broader agendas.

Using well-established letter-writing and advocacy strategies, breast cancer activists testified at hearings, held press conferences, and took their case to the NIH. In collaboration with growing bipartisan support in Congress and the scientific community, advocates succeeded in increasing federal funding for breast cancer research from $84 million to more than $400 million in 1993.[53(p315–325)] Breast cancer advocates also insisted that survivors be involved in shaping research agendas and educational efforts and aligned themselves more consistently and collaboratively with scientists than some AIDS activists or earlier grass-roots movement leaders had.

The success of breast cancer advocacy quickly created a "disease du jour" climate, where professionals rallied people directly or indirectly affected by particular diseases to lobby for increased funding. Ovarian cancer was the next women's disease to achieve national prominence. While this approach secures more resources for particular groups in the short run, it pits diseases against each other, turning research funding into a "popularity contest" or war of each against all—to be won by the group that can make the most noise or wield the greatest political pressure. A result may be overfunding some diseases without regard for their prevalence, contribution to overall population health, or likelihood of scientific value. In this environment, orphan diseases will join orphan drugs as the unfortunate, but unavoidable downsides of market-driven research and medicine.

Differences of Grass-Roots and Professionalized Women's Health Organizations

In a market-focused society, identifying differences is important for establishing a niche, and like other organizations, movement groups emphasize their unique features. Grass-roots women's health movement groups see themselves as different from what they perceive the more professional, mainstream organizations to be, although these differences are not always clearly articulated. After observing a wide range of groups for three decades, we have found that surviving grass-roots advocacy groups are differentiated from most professionalized, disease-focused groups in the following six ways.

Social Movement Orientation. The founders of many grass-roots feminist groups had ties to progressive or radical social movements that emphasized social justice and social change, to which many remain committed. In contrast, the newer professionalized support and advocacy organizations are typically more narrowly focused on a single disease or health issue, and except for environmentally focused groups such as WEDO, few are integral to broader social movements for social change (although some individual members may have such commitments).

Leadership. Although some women physicians who were critical of medical education, training, and practice were leaders of the grass-roots women's health movement, lay leadership was the norm. The role of physicians relative to others remains a point of contention.[55-56] In contrast, the professionalized support and

advocacy groups formed in the 1990s had a growing pool of women physicians, scientists, and other highly trained professionals to turn to for leadership.

Attitude Toward Biomedicine. A recurring theme in the grass-roots women's health movement has been the demand for "evidence-based medicine," long before this term came into vogue. Major feminist advocacy groups aligned themselves with scientists and physicians who sought to put medical practice on a more scientific basis at a time when it was resisted by many clinicians. Grass-roots health activists were critical of the side effects of inadequately tested drugs and devices, particularly early high-dose oral contraceptives, diethylstilbestrol, and the intrauterine device.[5] They also questioned the number of unnecessary hysterectomies and radical mastectomies performed. In short, consumer groups sought to protect women from unsafe or unnecessary biomedical interventions.[21,57] The professionalized advocacy groups founded in the 1990s focus more on ensuring women an equitable share of biopsychosocial science and treatment. The growing number of women physicians and scientists also facilitates alliances with women consumers because perceived interests in safety and effectiveness make these relationships seem mutually beneficial.

Relationships with Corporate Sponsors. Older grass-roots advocacy groups remain deeply concerned about the effects of drug and device manufacturers sponsoring journals and organizational activities. In fact, this issue is a pivotal source of strain between grass-roots groups and professionalized women's health organizations. While organizations of women physicians and professionalized advocacy groups rely heavily on corporate sponsorships, older grass-roots groups avoid such relationships on grounds that financial ties affect the willingness of groups to criticize sponsors, promote competitors' products, or address alternative or complementary therapies that might undermine conventional prescribing patterns. Refusing support from corporate sponsors remains a hallmark of grass-roots movement groups, but they struggle financially as a result. Because professionalized groups accept corporate support, they have more resources for education and advocacy.

Goals of Education. Both older and newer women's health organizations share the goal of educating women to improve their own health and make decisions about their own care. A central feature of grass-roots feminst groups, particularly through the 1970s was to demystify medicine and to encourage women to trust their subjective experience of their own health. Having access to larger numbers of women physicians may have reduced the perceived need to demystify medicine, and professionalized organizations appear largely concerned with making their highly educated constituencies aware of medical and scientific information.

Lay Versus Professional Authority. Grass-roots health groups remain committed to substantial lay control over health and healing and to expanding the roles of such nonphysician healers as midwives, nurses, and counseling professionals. They would involve consumers in all aspects of health policy making, not simply transfer legitimate authority from male to female physicians. In professionalized organizations, women physicians become the primary societal experts on women's health matters.

The grass-roots women's health movement organizations leave a legacy of making health an important social concern and educating women to take responsibility for their own health and health care decision making. The movement as a whole has made substantial efforts to influence powerful social institutions—organized medicine, the pharmaceutical industry, and regulatory agencies. In partnership with newer, professionalized equity organizations, health movement activists have taken up mainstream reform efforts that will become increasingly important as medical care is dominated by market forces. Thus the current episode of women's health activism overlaps with, but is, in many ways, different from the activism of the 1960s and 1970s. These distinct episodes of women's health activism need to be differentiated and understood in the specific historical contexts in which they emerged, recognizing the distinct roles that their history may lead them to play in the future.

The Next Challenge: Who Will Speak for Women in the Electronic Age?

The electronic communication technologies foster a climate in which researchers and consumers expect to find information instantaneously and effortlessly. The reliability of information in electronic media is often questionable, however. Until data can be transformed into usable knowledge that can shape human action, the information age will not fulfill its promise.[58] Neither grass-roots women's health movement organizations nor newer professionalized disease agenda groups have adequately grappled with how to communicate with their constituencies effectively. Both types of groups as well as government and mainstream health organizations will have to assess, manage, and distribute what each sees as "reliable" health information. Organizational survival may depend increasingly on teaching both "customers" and staff how to use reliable information effectively.[58]

Because the role of advocacy groups in health policy making in the United States,[1] how they present themselves and are perceived are important. As electronic media provide all-comers the opportunity to claim organizational status in an increasingly "virtual" world, and the number of groups claiming to speak for women increases, how will the public differentiate among them? As we navigate the uncharted "information age," the ability of the grass-roots women's health movement to remain viable appears somewhat precarious because the technology allows anyone with a computer and minimal skill to "create" an organization with worldwide visibility. Most movement organizations have not moved beyond hard copy resource centers and clearinghouses, in part because they have well-established communication networks that have served them well in the past (S.B. Ruzek, J. Becker, unpublished data, 1998). Newer professionalized advocacy groups are better funded and more attuned to technological advancements. As electronic communications gain prominence, those who position themselves in this media will be perceived as speaking for women. In an effort to address the complexity of electronic media, the Boston Women's Health Book Collective is including a section on how to assess the adequacy of electronic sources of information in the 1998 edition of *Our Bodies, Ourselves.*[59]

To assess the complexity of the environment in which grass-roots activist groups find themselves at the close of this century, and to determine the array of groups that present themselves as speaking for women, we compared the number of national women's health advocacy organizations easily identified through two worldwide web search strategies with those identified by the National Women's Health Network in 1994 as meeting their criteria: national, women-controlled or a women-controlled project of a larger organization, feminist outlook, mostly consumer controlled, and primarily advocacy, not just engaged in service or education. In an effort to identify organizations that might easily be identified by the public, Yahoo, a common Internet search engine, was used along with Healthfinders, the electronic database that the Department of Health and Human Services unveiled for public use in May 1997. Using the term "women's health organizations," 339 groups were located on the two Internet sources. After coding them for meeting two of the five NWHN criteria (being national and having an advocacy agenda beyond service or education), and removing duplications, 223 women's health advocacy organizations were identified, 46 by the NWHN, 53 by Healthfinders, and 124 by Yahoo.

When we cross-tabulated the data, it became clear that there is little overlap in the women's health advocacy organizations identified by these three sources. Only the

Society for the Advancement of Women's Health Research was identified by all three. Six organizations were identified by both the NWHN and DHHS Healthfinders; 9 were identified by both DHHS and Yahoo; and 13 were identified by both NWHN and Yahoo. Thus, "who speaks for women's health" in the electronic age very much depends on where one looks—and how willing one is to sort through hundreds of self-characterized "women's health organizations." In this environment it is unclear how the women's health movement will continue to be perceived as a key information broker in an increasingly complex sea of women's health information.

Grass-roots health movement groups remain important forces for increasing awareness of women's health issues and are viewed as trustworthy sources of information by feminist groups in the United States and worldwide. Newer, professionalized equity organizations, too, face competition from a growing array of institutions that claim expertise in matters of women's health. The challenge for both types of women's health groups will be to differentiate themselves from others whose interests lie more in marketing than in meeting diverse women's health needs. Both types of groups need to be allies for widening access and equity in health care for all women,[60,61] not just some women, in the next century.

REFERENCES

1. Weisman C. *Women's Health Care. Activist Traditions and Institutional Change.* Baltimore, Md: The Johns Hopkins University Press; 1998.
2. Fugh-Berman A. *Alternative Medicine: What Works. A Comprehensive, Easy-to-read Review of the Scientific Evidence, Pro and Con.* Tucson, Ariz: Odonian Press; 1996.
3. Northrup C. *Women's Bodies, Women's Wisdom.* New York, NY: Bantam Books; 1994.
4. Weil A. *Spontaneous Healing.* New York, NY: Knopf; 1995.
5. Anders G. *Health Against Wealth, HMOs and the Breakdown of Medical Trust.* Boston, Mass: Houghton Mifflin; 1996.
6. Ruzek SB. Communicating with patients: Linking managed care and women's health advocacy organizations. In: *Proceedings of the Conference on Healthcare Technology Choices under Managed Care: Communicating Directly with Patients and Their Clinicians.* Plymouth Meeting, PA: ECRI/WHO Collaborating Center for Technology Transfer; 1997:81–85.
7. Parrot RL, Condit CM, eds. *Evaluating Women's Health Messages. A Resource Book.* Thousand Oaks, Calif: Sage; 1996.
8. Proctor RN. *Cancer Wars,* New York, NY: Basic Books; 1995.
9. Stabiner K. *To Dance with the Devil.* New York, NY: Delacorte Press; 1997.
10. McCarthy JD, Zald MN. Resource mobilization and social movements: A partial theory. *American Journal of Sociology.* 1977;82:1212–1241.
11. Zald MN. The trajectory of social movements in America. *Research in Social Movements, Conflicts and Change.* 1988;10:19–41.
12. Ash R. *Social Movements in America.* Chicago, Ill: Markham; 1972.
13. Tarrow S. *Power in Movement: Social Movements, Collective Action and Politics.* Cambridge: Cambridge University Press; 1994.
14. Buechler SM. *Women's Movements in the United States.* New Brunswick, NJ: Rutgers University Press; 1990.
15. Freeman J. *Social Movements of the Sixties and Seventies.* New York, NY: Longman; 1983.
16. Staggenborg S. *The Pro-Choice Movement.* New York, NY: Oxford University Press; 1991.
17. Ferree MM, Hess BB. *Controversy and Coalition: The New Feminist Movement Across Three Decades of Change.* Boston, Mass: Twayne; 1994.
18. Zald MN, Ash R. Social movement organizations. *Soc Forces,* 1966;44:327–41.
19. Ruzek SB. *The Women's Health Movement Feminist Alternatives to Medical Control.* New York, NY: Praeger; 1978.
20. Rodriguez-Trias H. The women's health movement: Women take power. In Sidel VW, Sidel R, eds. *Reforming Medicine: Lessons for the Last Quarter Century.* New York, NY: Pantheon; 1984:107–126.
21. Zimmerman M. The Women's health movement: A critique of medical enterprise and the position of women. In: Hess B, Ferree MM, eds. *Analyzing Gender: Social Science Perspectives.* Beverly Hills, Calif: Sage; 1987.
22. The Boston Women's Health Book Collective. *Our Bodies, Ourselves—A Book By and For Women.* New York, NY: Simon and Schuster; 1973.
23. Federation of Feminist Women's Health Centers. *A New View of a Woman's Body.* New York, NY: Simon and Schuster; 1981.
24. Gordon L. *Woman's Body, Woman's Right: Birth Control in America.* New York, NY: Penguin; 1990.
25. Cottingham J, Norsigian J, Guzman C, et al. The personal is political: Beginnings and endings in an ongoing history. *Reproductive Health Matters.* November 10, 1997: 9–28.
26. Seaman B. *The Doctors' Case Against the Pill.* New York, NY: Avon; 1969.
27. Ehreinreich B, English D. *Complaints and Disorders. The Sexual Politics of Sickness.* Old Westbury, New York, NY: The Feminist Press; 1972.
28. Frankfort E. *Vaginal Politics.* New York, NY: Quadrangle Books; 1972.
29. Corea G. *The Hidden Malpractice. How American Medicine Mistreats Women.* New York, NY: Harper & Row; 1985.
30. Dreifus C, ed. *Seizing Our Bodies.* New York, NY: Vintage Books; 1978.
31. The Boston Women's Health Book Collective. *The New Our Bodies, Ourselves, Updated and Expanded for the '90s.* New York, NY: Simon & Schuster; 1992.

32. The National Women's Health Network. *1997 Annual Report*. Washington, DC: National Women's Health Network; 1997.

33. Rodriguez-Trias H. Sterilization abuse. In: Hubbard R, Henifin MS, Fried B, eds. *Biological Woman: The Convenient Myth*. Cambridge, Mass: Schenkman; 1982:147–160.

34. The Boston Women's Health Book Collective and ISIS. *International Women and Health Resource Guide*. Boston, Mass: Boston Women's Health Book Collective; 1980.

35. Ruzek SB. Feminist visions of health: An international perspective. In: Mitchell J, Oakley A, eds. *What is Feminism: A Re-examination*. New York, NY: Pantheon; 1996:184–207.

36. Guzman C. Planting the seeds of a Latina women's health movement. *Reproductive Health Matters*. November 10, 1997:13–16.

37. Berer M. Editorial. The international women's health movement. *Reproductive Health Matters*. November 10, 1997:6–8.

38. Doyal L. Campaigning for women's health rights worldwide. *Nurs Times*. 1995;91:27–30.

39. Ruzek SB, Clarke AE, Olesen VL. What are the dynamics of differences? In: Ruzek SB, Olesen VE, Clarke AE. eds. *Women's Health: Complexities and Differences,* Columbus Ohio: The Ohio State University Press; 1997:51–95.

40. Avery BY. Breathing life into ourselves: The evolution of the National Black Women's Health Project. In: White EC, ed. *The Black Women's Health Book*. Seattle, Wash: Seal Press; 1994:4–10.

41. Sommers CH. *Who Stole Feminism?* New York, NY: Touchstone; 1994.

42. Wolf N. *Fire with Fire. The New Female Power and How to Use It*. New York, NY: Fawcett Columbine; 1994.

43. Fox-Genovese E. *Feminism Without Illusion: A Critique of Individualism*. Chapel Hill, NC: University of North Carolina Press; 1991.

44. Epstein S. *Impure Science: Aids, Activism, and the Politics of Knowledge*. Berkeley, Calif: University of California Press; 1996.

45. Shilts R. *And the Band Played On*. New York, NY: Penguin Books; 1987.

46. Schneider BE, Stoller NE. *Women Resisting AIDS*. Philadelphia, Pa: Temple University Press; 1995.

47. Alpern BB. *Reaching Women: The Way to Go in Marketing Healthcare Services*. Chicago, Ill: Pluribus Press; 1987.

48. Weisman CS, Curbow B, Khoury AJ. The national survey of women's health centers: Current models of women-centered care. *Women's Health Issues*. 1995;5:103–117.

49. Weisman CS, Curbow B, Khoury AJ. *Case Studies of Women's Health Centers: Innovations and Issues in Women-Centered Care*. New York, NY: Commonwealth Fund; 1997.

50. Narrigan D, Zones JS, Worcester N, Grad MJ. Research to improve women's health: An agenda for equity. In: Ruzek SB, Olesen VE, Clarke AE, eds. *Women's Health: Complexities and Differences*. Columbus, Ohio: The Ohio State University Press; 1997:551–579.

51. Reissman CK. Women and medicalization: A new perspective. *Soc Policy*. 1983;14:3–18.

52. Batt S. *Patient No More*. Charlottetown, Canada: Best Gagne; 1994.

53. Altman R. *Waking Up/Fighting Back. The Politics of Breast Cancer*. Boston, Mass: Little, Brown; 1996.

54. Wentz AC. Editorial. *Women's Health*. 1994; 3:249–50.

55. Wallis LA, Donoghue GD, Fourcroy JL. Editorial. Feminists and women physicians. *Women's Health*. 1994;3:6.

56. Cousins O, Fugh-Berman A, Kasper A, et al. Letter to the editor. *Women's Health*. 1994;3:6.

57. Ruzek SB. Technology and perceptions of risks: Clinical, scientific and consumer perspectives in breast cancer treatment. In: *Executive Briefings. Health Technology Assessment Information Service*. Plymouth Meeting, Pa: ECRI-WHO Collaborating Center for Technology Transfer; 1995:1–6.

58. Davis S, Botkin J. *The Monster Under the Bed. How Business is Mastering the Opportunity of Knowledge for Profit*. New York, NY: Touchstone Books; 1995.

59. The Boston Women's Health Collective. *Our Bodies, Ourselves for the New Century: A Book by and for Women*. New York, NY: Simon & Schuster. In press.

60. Ruzek SB. Rethinking feminist ideologies and actions: Thoughts on the past and future of health reform. In: Olesen VL, Clarke AE, eds. *Revisioning Women's Health and Healing*. New York, NY: Routledge. In press.

61. Kasper AS. *The Making of Women's Health Public Policy*. Chicago, Ill: University of Illinois Center for Research on Women and Gender; Spring 1996.

Women and Health
In Search of a Paradigm

Margaret A. Chesney
Department of Epidemiology and Biostatistics
School of Medicine University of California, San Francisco
Elizabeth M. Ozer
Division of Adolescent Medicine, Department of Pediatrics
School of Medicine University of California, San Fransciso

The growing interest in women and health is resulting in an expanding number of important issues and invested disciplines. In this article, we propose a framework to serve as a guide for organizing themes and integrating competing approaches to the field of women's health. Our framework is illustrated through a multilevel circular model that graphically represents the evolving nature of the field. We first describe key content areas in women's health, including topics that have traditionally been considered, as well as those that have only more recently received attention. We then discuss research processes and methods that are important in the field and call for the use of approaches often excluded from traditional scientific procedures. Finally, we address the conceptual models that various disciplines provide and the advantage of a multidisciplinary perspective to advancing the field of women's health.

Over the past decade, there has been an increased focus on women and health. This is reflected by the striking growth in the number of specialized conferences, monographs, and journal issues dedicated to the topic (Gallant, Coons, & Morokoff, 1994). This scholarship has spanned disciplines, content areas, methodologies, and conceptual models. A current search through the psychological literature alone revealed 5,266 citations under the category of women and health.

Although the phrase "women's health" is now widely used, it remains ill defined and subject to debate. Through our attempts to define a framework for the field of women's health, we realized that no single conceptual model or paradigm would be sufficient. Rather than contrasting competing models that differ in terms of content, research process, and conceptual orientation, we propose a framework that may serve as a guide to organize and integrate competing approaches to the field of women's health.

Our model presents the content areas in women's health in a circular pattern to graphically represent the evolving nature of the field. This evolution will certainly continue as the content areas grow and further differentiate with time. We include topics in the model that have traditionally been considered the focus of women's health as well as those that have only more recently received attention—and sometimes—legitimization as women's health concerns.

A framework for women's health is comprised of more than content. The process and the methods by which

Margaret Chesney and Elizabeth Ozer worked jointly on this article.

Correspondence concerning this article should be sent to either Margaret A. Chesney, UCSF Prevention Sciences Group, 74 New Montgomery, Suite 600, San Francisco, CA 94105 or to Elizabeth M. Ozer, Division of Adolescent Medicine, Department of Pediatrics, UCSF School of Medicine, 400 Parnassus Avenue, San Francisco, CA 94143-0374.

we study the health of women also extend beyond what have been considered the "traditional" methods of research. Our definition calls for the participation of communities and perspectives often excluded from traditional scientific approaches. Finally, we address the different conceptual models brought to the field through the multidisciplinary contribution of anthropologists, sociologists, psychologists, nurses, physicians, and other social, behavioral, and health scientists within the field of women's health.

Content

In this section, we describe the set of key content areas of women's health that we include in the model, which is presented in Figure 1. We do not presume to be exhaustive in this overview, but rather to be illustrative of the range of content areas that exists and to highlight current concerns within each of these areas. We also recognize that there is overlap between content areas, but present them separately because each is an area of study that receives independent attention from dedicated scholars. Because women's health is a dynamic field, we chose a circular model to permit the addition of an infinite number of new areas of study.

REPRODUCTIVE HEALTH

Early work in women's health focused on the reproductive system, where gender differences are most pronounced. Until recently, for many in medicine, women's health appears to have been viewed as synonymous with reproductive health. It is not unusual to find medical texts in use today with chapters on women's health that concentrate almost exclusively on reproductive topics with descriptions of menstrual cycles, fertility issues, childbearing, and menopause. The broader scope of women's health is not reflected in these texts, and it is not covered in the curricula at many medical schools. To address these problems, legislation has been introduced in the U.S. Congress to direct the Department of Health and Human Services to conduct an evaluation of the extent to which medical school curricula include a comprehensive appreciation of gender differences in health and disease. This legislation also seeks to address the teaching of

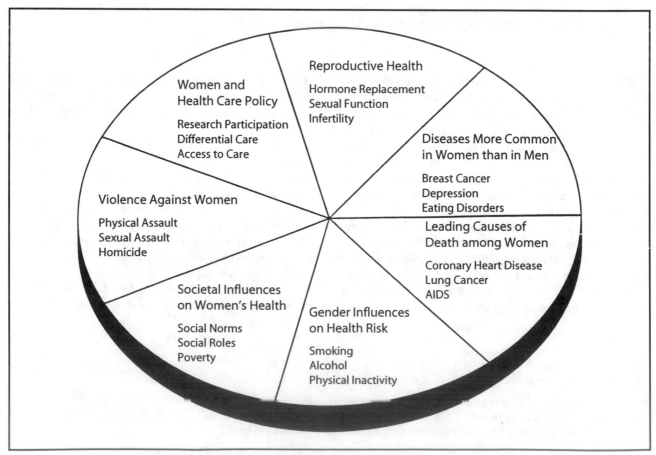

Figure 1 · Content areas in the study of women's health.

women's health in school accreditation standards, residency accreditation standards, and medical licensing examinations (Lowey, 1994).

As awareness of the diversity and far-reaching scope of women's health grows, reproductive health continues to be an active field of inquiry with new topics that raise important social, psychological, and behavioral research questions. These include controversies surrounding the use of estrogen for contraception or hormone replacement and factors associated with sexual functioning and infertility. For example, the decision to use estrogen replacement during menopause involves a risk-appraisal process that will be better informed when the psychological and physiological effects of estrogen, including effects on mood and cancer risk, are better understood (Matthews, 1992; Rodin & Ickovics, 1990).

Sexual functioning is another current issue in reproductive health that is important to women's health. Sexual functioning is associated with developmental stage, interpersonal relations, emotional states, and the incidence and prevalence of sexually-transmitted diseases (Chesney, 1994b; Morokoff & Calderone, 1994). Although these correlates and outcomes of sexual functioning represent long-standing issues, new areas of reproductive health that require psychological, behavioral, and social expertise are beginning to be investigated. These new areas, which include the use of reproductive technologies to enhance fertility and genetic screening for birth defects, are candidates for studies involving ethics, decision making, and stress and coping (Morokoff & Calderone, 1994).

DISEASES MORE COMMON IN WOMEN THAN IN MEN

Another traditional content area in women's health centers on disorders that are more common in women than men. These include breast cancer, lupus, depression, and eating disorders. Each of these conditions is subject to social, psychological, and behavioral influences. For example, there are studies of factors that predispose women to engage in breast self-examination (Mayer & Solomon, 1992) or adhere to recommendations for mammography (Aiken, West, Woodward, & Reno, 1994; Rimer, 1992). The National Institutes of Health recently published guidelines calling for routine mammography for women over 50 (Fletcher, Black, Harris, Rimer, & Shapiro, 1993; Shapiro, 1994), whereas others, including the American Cancer Society, recommended this test for women over 40 (Sickles & Kopans, 1993). These contradictory recommendations present an important opportunity to weigh the influence of conflicting public health messages on health attitudes and preventive practices. The impact of such conflicting recommendations is likely to be significant given that breast cancer is cited by American women as their leading health concern (Gallup Organization, 1994).

The prevalence of depression and other emotional disorders among women has been recognized for centuries. At the turn of the 17th century, Ralph Napier wrote that two thirds of patients seeking help for mental disorders were women (Leventhal, 1994). The situation has not changed significantly over the past 300 years. At least 70% of psychotropic prescriptions are written for women (Biener, 1987; Cafferata, Kasper, & Bernstein, 1983; Ogur, 1986). Women are more likely than men to be diagnosed with certain psychological disorders, particularly depression and anxiety related disorders (e.g., Belle, 1980; Kaplan, 1983; Rothblum, 1983; Russo, 1990; Weissman & Klerman, 1977). In 1990, the American Psychological Association (APA) Task Force on Women and Depression (McGrath, Keita, Strickland, & Russo, 1990) concluded that women are twice as likely as men to be suffering from depression. Efforts to determine the source of these differences have pointed to biases by health care professionals in diagnosing women (Russo, 1990), as well as life experiences of women that include poverty and physical and sexual abuse (McGrath et al., 1990).

Gender differences in psychological characteristics have also been considered as a possible explanation for the differences between women and men in distress. Perceived control or self-efficacy, coping strategies, and attributional styles are examples of important psychological factors that are related to health behavior, stress, depression, and anxiety (Bandura, 1988; Beck, 1976; Beck & Lund, 1981; Lazarus & Folkman, 1984; Miller, 1979; O'Leary, 1985; Ozer & Bandura, 1990; Seligman, 1975). The question remains, however, as to whether or not there are gender differences in these characteristics. Although early studies found evidence of gender differences in attributional styles among children (Dweck & Goetz, 1977; Parsons, Ruble, Hodges, & Small, 1976), overall, the research on causal attributions and perceptions of control has not found consistent differences between males and females (see Miller & Kirsch, 1987, for a review).

Gender differences in coping strategies have also been studied. For example, men have been reported to be more likely than women to engage in coping strategies that alter a stressful situation (Folkman & Lazarus, 1980; Stone & Neale, 1984; Viney & Westbrook, 1982). Pearlin and Schooler (1978) suggested that men more often than women possess psychological attributes, such as self-esteem and mastery, that influence their coping responses and inhibit stressful outcomes (Pearlin & Schooler, 1978). However, as Pearlin and others (Aneshensel & Pearlin, 1987; Bandura, 1986) pointed out, gender differences in mastery or a related characteristic, self-efficacy, are likely to be linked to differences in social experiences. Specifically, a consistently unresponsive or negative environment has been found to affect a person's sense of self-efficacy, which in turn leads to anxiety and depression (Bandura, 1986). Studies of gender differences in psychological characteristics have also drawn attention to the fact that traditional models of stress and coping were developed without specific consideration of women's experiences and roles and may not encompass aspects of coping that are of particular importance to women, such as relationship-focused coping (Gallant et al., 1994).

Eating disorders, yet another condition more common in women than men, are thought to be related to a cultural obsession with thinness for women. Among individuals suffering from anorexia and bulimia, 90% to 95% are women (Bushnell, Wells, Hornblow, Oakley-Browne, & Joyce, 1990). Efforts to understand and treat these disorders emphasize complex interactions between physiological and behavioral factors that regulate eating behavior (Fallon, 1994).

LEADING CAUSES OF DEATH AMONG WOMEN

Although attention is often drawn to diseases that disproportionately affect women, another critically important and distinct content area consists of the diseases that take the greatest toll in terms of morbidity and mortality among women. Although American women are most concerned about breast cancer, the leading cause of death among women is coronary heart disease (CHD), and the leading cause of cancer death is lung cancer, not breast cancer. For younger women who reside in major urban centers, the leading cause of death is HIV disease. In 1989, the American Heart Association launched a campaign to inform the health care community and the public that heart disease is the leading cause of death among adult women, accounting for approximately 250,000 deaths annually (Wenger, Speroff, & Packard, 1993). The role of heart disease in women's lives was in distinct contrast to the lack of women as participants in research on heart disease (Gallant et al., 1994). Efforts to address this inequality are underway, in large part because of the Women's Health Initiative, a large scale clinical trial of dietary and hormonal interventions on CHD and cancer being conducted by the National Institutes of Health. A comprehensive battery of psychological, social, and behavioral information being collected as part of this trial will undoubtedly lead to important advances in women's health.

Although CHD impacts women late in life, HIV disease is the leading cause of death among women between the ages of 25 and 44 in many urban centers (Chesney,1994b). In the United States, cases of AIDS among women accounted for 13% of all cumulative AIDS cases by 1993 (Centers for Disease Control and Prevention,

1994). By the end of that year, 44,357 women had been diagnosed with AIDS. Like CHD and lung cancer, a central focus in AIDS programs for women is on changing lifestyle. Thus, the diseases that are the leading causes of death among women can be prevented by effective programs designed to change behaviors that place women at risk, such as smoking and unprotected sex.

GENDER INFLUENCES ON HEALTH RISK

The study of gender differences in behaviors that confer risk, such as cigarette smoking, physical inactivity, and alcohol consumption, is another content area in women's health. For example, studies have shown that the number of women who smoke has increased in recent years, whereas the incidence of smoking among men has decreased (Fiore, Novotny, Hatziandreu, Patel, & Davis, 1989). Social, psychological, and behavioral research is examining this and related questions, including why there has been a slower rate of decline in smoking prevalence for women compared to men over the last 2 decades, why women are more likely than men to return to smoking after stopping, and why as many, if not more, adolescent girls than boys initiate smoking. This research is yielding valuable information for the design of programs tailored to assist women in smoking cessation and to prevent the initiation of smoking among girls (Chesney, 1991; S. M. Hall, 1994).

The importance of smoking to women's health cannot be overemphasized. It touches on most of the foregoing content areas in women's health. As a result of the prevalence of smoking among women, in 1985, lung cancer surpassed breast cancer as the leading cause of cancer death among women (Gritz, 1986). Smoking is also a major risk factor for CHD. It is estimated that in the absence of other CHD risk factors, 70% of myocardial infarctions among women under 50 are attributable to smoking (Slone et al., 1978). Smoking is also associated with coronary occlusion in female heart disease patients, early mortality in women patients who have undergone coronary artery bypass surgery, and earlier onset of menopause, an additional factor associated with increased heart disease risk (Chesney, 1991).

Although alcohol is still used more often and more heavily by men than women (Biener, 1987; Fillmore, 1984), drinking has become increasingly socially acceptable for women (Rodin & Ickovics, 1990). This change in the social norm has not been accompanied by dramatic increases in drinking among women in general (Wilsnack, Wilsnack, & Klessen, 1984). However, there has been an increase in drinking among adolescent girls (Biener, 1987), as well as some evidence that problem drinking among women is more prevalent (Wilsnack et al., 1984). In addition to the health problems associated with heavy drinking in both men and women (e.g., chronic gastritis, alcoholic hepatitis or cirrhosis, and increased risk of many cancers), abuse of alcohol may be more dangerous for women than for men (S. M. Hall, 1994). The specific risks for women include gynecological and obstetric problems (Mello, 1986) and more rapid development of liver disease than in men (S. M. Hall, 1994). In addition, even moderate alcohol consumption has been associated with up to a 50% elevation in the risk of breast cancer (Schatzkin et al., 1987).

SOCIETAL INFLUENCES ON WOMEN'S HEALTH

Social explanations for gender differences in health assert that stressors or illnesses that regularly occur more often in one sex or another are likely to be linked to the position of women and men in society (e.g., Aneshensel & Pearlin, 1987). Examples include differences in societal pressures, social roles, and economic status.

Societal Norms That Impact Women's Health. North American culture's preoccupation with thinness as the ideal for feminine beauty is one example of how societal pressures affect the health risks of girls and women. Being thin is often regarded as desirable for all women, rather than as a response to powerful cultural influences (Attic & Brooks-Gunn, 1987). Attempting to document a shift in cultural attitudes, Garner, Garfinkel, Schwartz, and Thompson (1980) found that between 1959 and 1978, women selected as models in Playboy Magazine and winners of the Miss America contest became progressively thinner. These women were thinner than the actuarial norms for comparable women in the general population (where the average weight for young women has actually steadily increased). During these same years, there was increased attention to dieting in the popular media (Attic & Brooks-Gunn, 1987).

Adolescent girls and women are more likely than males to link their sense of self to beliefs about their appearance (Fallon, 1994; Wadden, Brown, Foster, & Linowitz, 1991). Teenage and adult women also consistently report greater concern with being overweight than do males (e.g., Freedman, 1986; Rozin & Fallon, 1988; Stunkard, 1975). This concern increases health risks in a number of domains by providing an impetus for cigarette smoking (Chesney, 1994a) and, as noted previously, increasing the likelihood of eating disorders. It is not unexpected that anorexia nervosa and bulimia occur predominantly in females (Bushnell et al., 1990). Although good epidemiological data is rare, available evidence suggests that the prevalence of both anorexia and bulimia has risen over recent decades (Garner, Rockert, Olmsted, Johnson, & Coscina, 1985; Lucas, Beard, Kranz, & Kurland, 1983).

Women's Social Roles. The social and economic structure of the family has undergone a dramatic shift in recent decades. Less that 7% of all American families fit the traditional model of a father working full-time outside the home and a mother working full-time within the home (Sitterly & Duke, 1988). In 1986, two thirds of all women between the ages of 20 and 64 were in the labor force (Matthews & Rodin, 1989). This increase in the number of working women has led to much debate about the health effects of women's employment.

It was initially assumed that incorporating the additional role of employment would lead to an increase in psychological distress (see Barnett & Baruch, 1985, for a review) as well as possible physical health risks, such as cardiovascular disease (e.g., Frankenhauser, 1994). Although it is often difficult to determine causality, current research suggests that employed women are physically and psychologically healthier than women who are not employed (Aneshensel & Pearlin, 1987; LaCroix & Haynes, 1987; Verbrugge, 1989). Despite the difficulties of managing the demands of both family and work roles, and evidence that women still assume primary responsibility for the care of children (e.g., Biernat & Wortman, 1991; Hochschild, 1989; Ozer, 1993), employment has positive physical and psychological consequences for women who also engage in the roles of mother and wife (Barnett & Baruch, 1985; Crosby, 1984; Kessler & McRae, 1981; Repetti, Matthews, & Waldron, 1989; Rodin & Ickovics, 1990; Verbrugge, 1982).

Although employment does not appear to be detrimental to the health of women, it has been suggested that the poorer mental health of women compared to men may be linked to women's traditional role as the person primarily responsible for the care of others, particularly children (Barnett & Baruch, 1987; Rosenfield, 1989; Veroff, Douvan, & Kulka, 1981), but also ill spouses and elderly parents (Brody, 1981; Horowitz, 1985; Johnson & Catalano, 1983). For example, mothers who do not work outside the home have been found to experience higher rates of depression than mothers who do work outside the home (Ross & Mirowsky, 1988).

Poverty and Women's Health. Considering that more than 75% of the poor in the United States consist of women and children, poverty cannot be ignored as a significant women's health issue (U.S. Department of Health and Human Services, 1984). Further, minority women are disproportionately represented within this group (Ozer, 1986; Pearce, 1993). Living in poverty affects women's health in many different ways. For instance, lack of money for decent food and shelter is related to malnutrition and increased susceptibility to disease (Litt, 1993). Poverty is also related to lack of preventive care, higher infant mortality rates, more disability from chronic illness, more accidents, greater exposure to violence (Litt, 1993), and risk of depression (McGrath et al., 1990). In addition to the health risks that have traditionally been associated with poverty, the AIDS epidemic is growing most rapidly among minority, low-income women (O'Leary, Jemmott, Suarez-Al-Adam, Alroy, & Fernandez, 1993).

The number of homeless women has also increased rapidly, with mothers and their children now making up more than 30% of the homeless population in U.S. cities (U.S. Conference of Mayors, 1987). Homeless women have less access to health care and report more acute illness and chronic health problems than do poor women who are not homeless (Robertson & Cousineau, 1986, cited in Milburn & D'Ercole, 1991).

Engaging in safe health practices to prevent the spread of AIDS and avoiding risk behaviors such as smoking and alcohol use requires a sense of control over one's life that is more difficult under conditions of poverty. Pessimism about life opportunities not only discourages women from investing in preventive health but also hinders future alternatives to poverty. More than half the mothers on welfare had their first child in adolescence, with many of these mothers lacking compelling reasons to delay parenthood. In fact, some studies suggest that many teenage mothers would be out of school and unemployed at age 18 even if parenthood had not occurred (Children's Defense Fund, 1986).

VIOLENCE AGAINST WOMEN

A major public health issue for women in the United States is the prevalence of violence by men against women.[1] Domestic violence is the leading cause of injuries to women aged 15 to 44 (Novello, Rosenberg, Saltzman, & Shosky, 1992). Between 21% and 34% of adult women will be physically assaulted by a male partner in their lifetime (Browne, 1993); partner homicides accounted for 52% of the women murdered during the early 1980s; and 14% to 25% of adult women have been raped (M. P. Koss, 1993, cited in Goodman, M. P. Koss, Fitzgerald, Russo, & Keita, 1993). It is estimated that 50% of working women will experience sexual harassment at some point during their working lives (Fitzgerald, 1993).

Women who have been victims of sexual assault are more likely to receive psychiatric diagnoses such as major depression, alcohol and drug dependence, obsessive-compulsive disorder, and post-traumatic stress disorder (Burnam et al., 1988; Kilpatrick et al., 1985; Winfield, George, Schwartz, & Blazer, 1990). They are also more likely to report negative health behaviors such as smoking and alcohol use, to view their health less favorably, and to be diagnosed with gastrointestinal disorders,

chronic pelvic pain, headaches, general pain, psychogenic seizures, and premenstrual symptoms (Goodman et al., 1993; M. P. Koss, 1993; M. P. Koss & Heslet, 1992; M. P. Koss, P. G. Koss, & Woodruff, 1991).

Treatment for health problems associated with victimization may be jeopardized by incomplete clinical history. Medical and mental health professionals typically do not inquire about current or past victimization experiences. The failure to gather this history undermines accurate diagnoses, treatment planning, and interventions for these women (Browne, 1993; Council on Scientific Affairs, 1992; M. P. Koss, 1988).

WOMEN AND HEALTH CARE POLICY

Policy decisions have a significant impact on women's health. Until very recently, policy decisions have resulted in limited participation by women in research, inadequate training of health care professionals, differential care with less aggressive diagnosis and treatment of women, and guidelines for primary prevention and public and private reimbursement that restrict women's access to health care (Edmunds, 1995). With such influence, it is crucial to include policy as a content area for women and health.

First, it is important that existing research be well utilized in the formulation of public policy. For instance, the APA's Committee on Women in Psychology established a task force on male violence against women (see Goodman et al., 1993), and the APA convened a panel of experts to review the best scientific studies of abortion outcomes (see Adler et al., 1992). Both task forces were instrumental in providing policy makers with relevant psychological research that could guide the enactment of well-informed legislation.

Second, it has been well documented that although women are more likely to receive both medical and psychological care, they have been underrepresented in all aspects of research (Fee, 1983; Levey, 1991; Low, Jolicoeur, Stone, & Fleisher, 1994; Tavris, 1992). There is an even greater dearth of information on the health of minority women. As a result, we lack sufficient knowledge about many important aspects of women's health, ranging from the potential role of behavioral factors in the prevention of breast cancer morbidity and mortality, to the effect of various cardiovascular treatments on the quality of life of women with heart disease. Ironically, physicians and women may even lack the knowledge to adequately address common health problems.

Despite the fact that heart disease is the leading cause of death for women in the United States, cardiac therapies have typically been designed and tested on male subjects (Gurwitz, Col, & Avorn, 1992). As a result, it is not known whether aspirin has prophylactic effects on cardiac outcomes in women (Levey, 1991). Further, because women and their physicians have not been adequately informed about the risk of heart disease in women, there is evidence that heart disease has been treated less aggressively in women than in men (Ayanian & Epstein, 1991; Steingart et al., 1991, cited in Low et al., 1994), and women are more likely than men to delay seeking emergency help when they have signs of a heart attack (Meischke, Eisenberg, & Larsen, 1993).

Women in poverty and women in minority groups are less likely than women at higher socioeconomic levels to have access to adequate health care. This differential access has adverse impacts on health outcomes. The long-term survival rate of minority women with breast cancer is significantly lower than other women, a finding attributed, at least in part, to delays in reporting symptoms and diagnosis (Gallant et al., 1994). As health policies increase or decrease access to care, by either providing child care for patient visits or refusing to hold clinics open in evenings and weekends, they influence health decision making and health status. Other health policies, such as decisions to cover treatments for certain conditions and not others (such as in-vitro fertilization for infertility or certain cardiac procedures for women past a given age), limit access to health care options for those women not in a position to purchase the care they seek.

Health policy makers play a pivotal role in women's health. Although some set the limits on procedures covered by public or private insurance, others determine the agenda for women in health research. Given this level of influence, it is important that health care policy be included as the final content area in our model.

Process

Having noted some of the content domains within the field of women's health, we now turn our attention to the processes and methods by which we conduct our research. Our goal is to begin a discussion that moves beyond the content areas of women's health to highlight issues that span each content area. For instance, there has recently been increased attention on the need for including diverse populations of women in health research. We applaud this progress but think that the process of diversity implies more than simply making numbers more equitable: It also involves closely examining assumptions behind our empirical variables and measures, research questions, and methodologies. These issues apply to each content area. As such, they are integrated into the model as a layer underlying the content areas, as shown in Figure 2.

PARTICIPANTS

Women are not a homogeneous group: Participants of different socioeconomic and racial ethnic groups, ages, cultures, and sexual orientations must be represented across content areas. This involves the inclusion of participants from diverse groups in research, attention to diseases that disproportionately affect one population more than others, recognition that different sociocultural groups may vary in their perception of health and illness (Landrine & Klonoff, 1992), and a focus on how being a member of one of these groups interacts with other factors to affect health. One example is recognizing the interaction of gender and ethnicity (Comas-Díaz & Greene, 1994; LaFromboise, Heyle, & Ozer, 1990; Mays & Comas-Díaz, 1988; Olmedo & Parron, 1981) and gender and sexual orientation (Greene, 1994). Another example is a focus on disease prevention that considers racial, socioeconomic, and ethnic diversity (Anderson, 1991; Gallant et al., 1994). Researchers in women's health have considered these factors in the study of mammography utilization (Fox & Stein, 1991), prevention of HIV infection (e.g., Amaro, 1988; Worth, 1990), eating disorders (Osvold & Sodowaky, 1993; Thompson, 1994), barriers to health care (Leigh, 1994), the aging process (Padgett, 1988), and satisfaction with childcare roles (Uttal, 1994).

VARIABLES AND MEASURES

Both the variables that we use and the measurement of those variables need reconsideration. For instance, the traditional definition of *work* has reflected hours of employment or paid work outside the home. Although there is ample evidence that women work more hours per week than their husbands in combined employment and household tasks (Pleck, 1984; Rexroat & Shehan, 1987; Scarr, Phillips, & McCartney, 1989; Tavris & Wade, 1984), these "additional" work hours for women have often been ignored when evaluating issues such as workload or stress.

Models of job stress have been based almost exclusively on male subjects (e.g., Karasek et al., 1982). This research indicates that the stress associated with low levels of job control and highly demanding tasks is related to negative health outcomes such as elevated risk for heart disease and ulcers. Interestingly, recent research on dual-career couples suggests the need for an expansion of the traditional job stress model to reflect characteristics important to women and to full-time employed men and women in dual-earner couples (Barrett, Sayer, & Marshall, 1994).

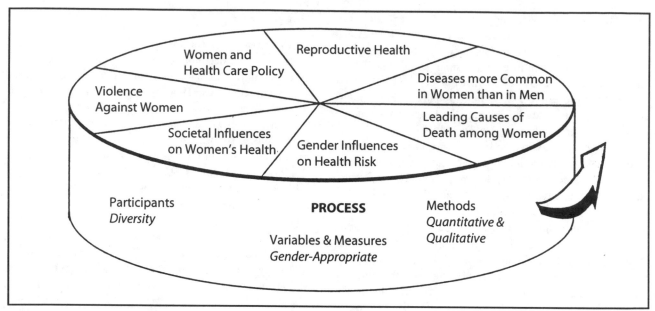

Figure 2 · Process and methods in the study of women's health.

As a final example, the links between cardiovascular disease and the Type A Behavior Pattern—a style characterized by time urgency, hostility, and competitiveness—has received considerable attention. However, the measure most frequently used to assess Type A Behavior, The Structured Interview, was developed on a male sample and was unsatisfactory in tapping coronary prone behavior in women (Chesney, 1988; Thoresen & Low, 1990). By shifting the focus to behaviors in women, the importance of depression in coronary prone behavior has emerged (Chesney, 1993). Thus, using measures conceptually appropriate to women's experience not only contributes to the field of women's health but also sheds light on new variables and measures beneficial to research on men.

METHODOLOGICAL APPROACHES

We believe that there is room for a wide variety of methodological approaches in the field of women's health. This includes traditional scientific approaches as well as alternative perspectives often excluded from mainstream social science research.

Critics from different disciplines have articulated the inadequacies of traditional research methods for addressing complex health problems (e.g., Hellman & Hellman, 1991; Kandrack, Grant, & Segall, 1991). In particular, feminist scholars have questioned analyses of women's health that ignore gender inequality and societal forces (e.g., Denmark, 1994; Fine, 1992; Lott & Maluso, 1993; Marecek & Hare-Mustin, 1991; Riger, 1992).

Feminist researchers (e.g., Reinharz, 1992), along with community psychologists (Kelly, 1966; Vincent & Trickett, 1983) and popular educators (e.g., Freire, 1973; B. Hall, 1975), have also long argued that the participation of "subjects" in the development of research questions, construction of assessment measures, and interpretation of results creates a more culturally relevant knowledge base than the traditional scientific methods.

The use of less structured research instruments and qualitative data collection and analysis also promotes the inclusion of the study populations' own concepts and words to define problems or concerns (e.g., the grounded theory technique developed by Glaser & Strauss, 1967). Qualitative, ideographic processes such as narration or storytelling are receiving more attention in the psychological literature as meaningful and valid ways of describing phenomena (e.g., Brown & Gilligan, 1991; J. Hall, Stevens, & Meleis, 1992; Howard, 1991; Uichol & Berry, 1993; White & Epston, 1990). Researchers in women's health have utilized these concepts (J. Hall et al., 1992; Henderson, Sampselle, Mayes, & Oakley, 1992; Morse, 1992) as well as articulated the need for attention to race, culture, and class in this type of methodology (e.g., Cannon, Higgenbotham, & Leung, 1988).

Given the complexity of the phenomena of women's health, we recommend that investigators draw from the full complement of methods, including both quantitative and qualitative methods of description and data collection. We do not believe that the field of women's health will benefit from reductionism or defense of a single perspective but will flourish with diversity of approaches.

Conceptual Models

In addition to the range of content domains and the processes and methods by which these areas are explored, a variety of conceptual models contribute to the field of women and health. As with the Process level of our overall model, the conceptual models of different scholars determine how they approach each content area. As such, these conceptual models or perspectives are integrated into our model as another layer underlying the Process level, as shown in Figure 3.

We believe that women's health can best be advanced by the involvement of a wide variety of disciplines and perspectives. Because both authors are trained in the field of psychology, this article reflects that orientation. Other disciplines, including medicine, anthropology, and sociology, bring their own unique strengths. In particular, each conceptual model and perspective sheds light on issues and adds to the knowledge base of women and health. Using the problem of CHD, we will illustrate the complementary contributions that a number of disciplines can make to the prevention and treatment of the leading cause of death among adult women.

Medicine seeks to isolate specific biologic mechanisms underlying disease and develop treatment strategies to address them. For heart disease in women, for ex-

ample, medicine is investigating the effect of menopause on risk, conducting trials to determine whether hormone replacement decreases or increases risk, and prescribing nicotine replacement drugs to aid women in smoking cessation. Although these efforts are worthwhile, they can be enhanced by the involvement of other disciplines, as discussed later.

Psychology concentrates on identifying individual, behavioral factors that contribute to psychological and physical health. In an effort to reduce the incidence of heart disease in women, psychologists are investigating the causal role of behavioral factors on cardiovascular morbidity and mortality. As a result of this research, psychologists work with women to prevent disease by increasing physical activity and stopping cigarette smoking. For example, psychologists have developed cognitive-behavioral strategies for smoking cessation, which can be used to enhance the effectiveness of nicotine replacement prescribed by physicians.

Sociology and anthropology contribute knowledge about how social and cultural contexts influence women's health (Landrine & Klonoff, 1992). Societal factors influence women's cardiovascular health in profound ways. Examples range from the social pressure on adolescent women to initiate cigarette smoking, to barriers to receiving adequate health care created by women's

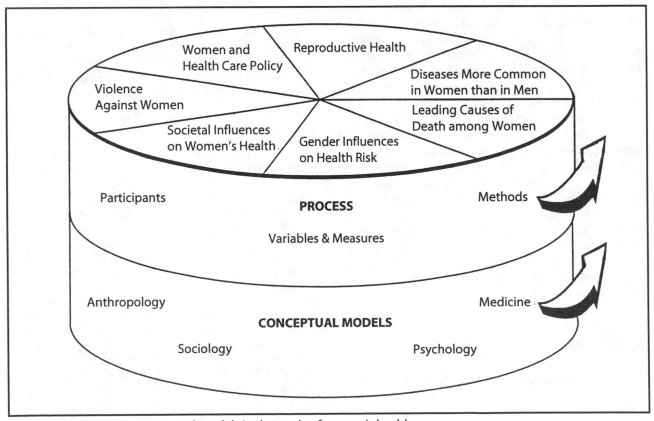

Figure 3 · Integrating conceptual models in the study of women's health.

greater likelihood to be among the poor and uninsured. The perspective of anthropology would be helpful in the deeply held sociocultural belief that heart disease is a problem that affects White, middle-aged men. This distortion of the public health reality and women's presumed invulnerability to heart disease are thought to be reasons that women do not engage in preventive behavior and delay in seeking care.

As previously discussed, the acknowledgment of the importance of a culture's own concepts, as well as the qualitative methodology utilized at times in sociology but most often associated with anthropology, has resulted in increased knowledge about what is meaningful for a specific group of people. Prevention programs, behavioral interventions, and medical treatment have often been ineffective due to lack of this knowledge and insensitivity to the needs of many ethnic-cultural minority groups in the United States. Recent mandates to address issues of central importance to women's health are beginning to shed light on these biases and barriers. Despite this progress, anthropological and sociological perspectives will continue to offer important insights into the influence that cultural and social contexts exert on the health of the widely diverse groups of women in our society.

We encourage researchers to enrich their work by considering integrating perspectives and/or methodologies that may have historically been considered the domain of different disciplines. This integration of perspectives is a strategy that is already pursued by professionals in such fields as public health, nursing, medical sociology, and behavioral medicine. In addition to integrating perspectives, it may also be fruitful to establish interdisciplinary research teams that would help reduce the fragmented approach to addressing complex women's health issues (Landrine & Klonoff, 1992).

The model we propose, including diverse conceptual models, presents a challenge for communication and collaboration. There is likely to be a climate of competitiveness, with debates about which perspective is optimal or correct. We hope that the field of women's health can transcend these divisive debates, while learning from active discussion and constructive criticism. The model, like the field, is dynamic. It allows the addition of new content areas in the first level as well as adding new cross-cutting themes at the underlying levels. Examples of such themes might be life-span, multicultural, and international perspectives.

Conclusion

As we search for a paradigm, it is evident that traditional models are inadequate. We have proposed a model that we hope will serve as a guide or framework for the dynamic field of women's health. We believe that other paradigms will and should be proposed. We hope that alternative paradigms will not only encompass a broad range of content domains but also consider a range of processes that are capable of capturing the experiences of women. In addition, we hope that alternative paradigms will accommodate different conceptual models. The traditional scientific strategy would be to debate, to be reductionistic, and to select a "winner." We would like to recommend that the field of women's health choose a different path characterized by inclusiveness and collaboration.

Acknowledgments

We thank Nancy Adler, Helen Coons, Marci Lobel, Kathryn Graff Low, Emily Ozer, Tracey A. Revenson, Ashley Wilder Smith, and Lynet Uttal for their insightful suggestions. In addition, we thank Derek Aspacher for his work on graphics.

Preparation of this article was supported by an NIMH Grant supporting the Center for AIDS Prevention Studies (MH42459) and an NIMH Training Grant entitled Psychology and Medicine: An Integrated Approach (MH19391).

Notes

1. Although partner violence in lesbian relationships is receiving more attention and is clearly of concern, the majority of physical and sexual violence experienced by women is perpetrated by men. For this reason, we focus on male violence against women.

References

Adler, N. E., David, H. P., Major, B. N., Roth, S. H., Russo, N. F., & Wyatt, G. E. (1992). Psychological factors in abortion. *American Psychologist, 47,* 1194–1204.

Aiken, L. S., West, S. G., Woodward, C. K., & Reno, R. R. (1994). Health beliefs and compliance with mammography-screening: Recommendations in asymptomatic women. *Health Psychology, 13,* 122–129.

Amaro, H. (1988). Considerations for prevention of HIV infection among Hispanic women. *Psychology of Women Quarterly, 12,* 429–443.

Anderson, N. B. (1991, March). *Addressing ethnic minority health issues: Behavioral medicine at the forefront of research and practice.* Paper presented at the Annual Meeting of the Society of Behavioral Medicine, Washington, DC.

Aneshensel, C., & Pearlin, L.1. (1987). Structural contexts of sex differences. In R. C. Barnett, L. Biener, & G. K. Baruch (Eds.), *Gender and stress* (pp. 75–95). New York: Free Press.

Attie, I., & Brooks-Gunn, J. (1987). Weight concerns as chronic stressors in women. In R. C. Barnett, L. Biener, & G. K. Baruch (Eds.), *Gender and stress* (pp. 218–254). New York: Free Press.

Ayanian, J. Z., & Epstein, A. M. (1991). Differences in the use of procedures between women and men hospitalized for coronary heart disease. *New England Journal of Medicine, 325,* 221–225.

Bandura, A. (1986). *Social foundations of thought and action: A social cognitive theory.* Englewood Cliffs, NJ: Prentice-Hall.

Bandura, A. (Ed.). (1988). *Self-efficacy mechanism in physiological activation and health promoting behavior.* New York: Raven Press.

Barnett, R., & Baruch, G. (1985). Women's involvement in multiple roles and psychological distress. *Journal of Personality and Social Psychology, 49,* 135–145.

Barnett, R., & Baruch, G. (1987). Social roles, gender, and psychological distress. In R. Barnett, L. Biener, & G. Baruch (Eds.), *Gender and stress* (pp. 112–143). New York: Frec Press.

Barnen, R., Sayer, A., & Marshall, N. (1994). *Gender, job rewards, job concerns and psychological distress: A study of dual-earner couples.* Working paper, Wellesley College, Center for Research on Women.

Beck, A. T. (1976). *Cognitive therapy and the emotional disorders.* New York: International Universities Press.

Beck, K. H., & Lund, A. K. (1981). The effects of health threat seriousness and personal efficacy upon intentions and behavior. *Journal of Applied Social Psychology, 11,* 401–415.

Belle, D. (1980). Who uses mental health facilities? In M. Guttentag, S. Salasin, & D. Belle (Eds.), *The mental health of women* (pp. 1–20). New York: Academic.

Biener, L. (1987). Gender differences in the use of substances for coping. In R. C. Barnett, L. Biener, & G. K. Baruch (Eds.), *Gender and stress* (pp. 330–349). New York: Free Press.

Biernat, M., & Wortman, C. (1991). Sharing of home responsibilities between professionally employed women and their husbands. *Journal of Personality and Social Psychology, 35,* 351–363.

Brody, E. M. (1981). "Women in the middle" and family help to older people. *The Gerontologist, 21,* 471–480.

Brown, L. M., & Gilligan, C. (1991). Listening for voice in narratives of relationship. In M. B. Tappan & M. J. Packer (Eds.), *Narrative and storytelling: Implications for understanding moral development. New directions for child development* (pp. 43–62). San Francisco: Jossey Bass.

Browne, A. (1993). Violence against women by male partners: Prevalence, outcomes, and policy implications. *American Psychologist, 48,* 1077–1087.

Burnam, M. A., Stein, J. A., Golding, J. M., Siegel, J. M., Sorenson, S. B., Forsythe, A. B., & Telles, C. A. (1988). Sexual assault and mental disorders in a community population. *Journal of Consulting and Clinical Psychology, 56,* 843–850.

Bushnell, J. A., Wells, E., Hornblow, A., Oakley-Browne, M., & Joyce, P. (1990). Prevalence of three bulimia syndromes in the general population. *Psychological Medicine, 20,* 671–690.

Cafferata, G. L., Kasper, J., & Bernstein, A. (1983). Family roles, structure, and stressors in relation to sex differences in obtaining psychotropic drugs. *Journal of Health and Social Behavior, 24,* 132–143.

Cannon, L. W., Higgenbotham, E., & Leung, M. L. (1988). Race and class bias in qualitative research on women. *Gender and Society, 2,* 449–462.

Centers for Disease Control and Prevention. (1994). *HIV/AIDS Surveillance Report, 5*(4), 1–33.

Chesney, M. A. (1988). The evolution of coronary-prone behavior. *Annals of Behavioral Medicine, 10,* 43–45.

Chesney, M. A. (1991). Women, work-related stress and smoking. In M. Frankenhauser, U. Lundberg, & M. A. Chesney (Eds.), *Women, work, stress and health* (pp. 139–155). Ncw York: Plenum.

Chesney, M. A. (1993). Social isolation, depression, and heart disease: Research on women broadens the agenda. *Psychosomatic Medicine, 55,* 426–433.

Chesney, M. A. (1994a). Behavioral barriers to cardiovascular disease in women. In N. K. Wenger, L. Speroff, & B. Packard (Eds.), *Cardiovascular health and disease in women* (pp. 55–60). Greenwich, CT: Le Jacq Communications.

Chesney, M. A. (1994b). Prevention of HIV and STD infections. *Preventive Medicine, 23,* 655–660.

Children's Defense Fund. (1986). *Adolescent pregnancy—Whose problem is it?* Washington, DC: Pregnancy Prevention Clearinghouse.

Comas-Díaz, L., & Greene, B. (1994). *Women of color: Integrating ethnic and gender identities in psychotherapy.* New York: Guilford.

Council on Scientific Affairs. (1992). Violence against women: Relevance for medical practitioners. *Journal of the American Medical Association, 257,* 3184–3189.

Crosby, F. (1984). Job satisfaction and domestic life. ln M. D. Lee & R. N. Kanugo (Eds.), *Management of work and personal life* (pp. 168–193). New York: Praeger.

Denmark, F.I. (1994). Engendering psychology. *American Psychologist, 49,* 329–334.

Dweck, C. S., & Goetz, T. E. (1977). Attributions and learned helplessness. In J. H. Harvey, W. Ickes, & R. F. Kidd (Eds.), *New directions in attribution research* (Vol. 2, pp. 157–179). Hillsdale, Nl: Lawrence Erlbaum Associates, Inc.

Edmunds, M. (1995). Policy research: Balancing rigor with relevance. *Women's Health: Research on Gender, Behavior, and Policy, 1,* 97–119.

Fallon, A. E. (1994). Body image and the regulation of weight. ln V.I. Adesso, D. M. Reddy, & R. Fleming (Eds.), *Psychological perspectives on women's health* (pp. 127–180). Milwaukee: Taylor and Francis.

Fee, E. (1983). Women and healthcare: A comparison of theories. ln E. Fee (Ed.), *Women in health: The politics of sex in medicine* (pp. 17–35). Farmingdale, NY: Baywood.

Fillmore, K. M. (1984). "When angels fall": Women's drinking as cultural preoccupation and as reality. ln S. C. Wilsnack & L. J. Beckman (Eds.), *Alcohol problems in women* (pp. 7–36). New York: Guilford.

Fine, M. (1992). *Disruptive voices: The possibilities of feminist research.* Ann Arbor: University of Michigan Press.

Fiore, M. C., Novotny, T. E., Hatziandreu, E. J., Patel, K. M., & Davis, R. M. (1989). Trends in cigarette smoking in the United States. *Journal of the American Medical Association, 261,* 49–55.

Fitzgerald, L. F. (1993). Sexual harassment: Violence against women in the workplace. *American Psychologist, 48,* 1070–1076.

Fletcher; S. W., Black, W., Harris, R., Rimer, B. K., & Shapiro, S. (1993). Report of the international workshop on screening for breast cancer. *Journal of the National Cancer Institute, 85,* 1644–1656.

Folkman, S., & Lazarus, R. S. (1980). An analysis of coping in a middle-aged community sample. *Journal of Health and Social Behavior, 21,* 219–239.

Fox, S., & Stein, J. A. (1991). The effect of physician-patient communication on mammography utilization by different ethnic groups. *Medical Care, 29,* 1065–1082.

Frankenhauser, M. (1994). A biopsychosocial approach to stress in women and men. In V. J. Adesso, D. M. Reddy, & R. Fleming (Eds.), *Psychological perspectives on women's health* (pp. 39–56). Milwaukee: Taylor and Francis.

Freedman, R. (1986). *Beauty bound.* Lexington, MA: Lexington Books.

Freire, P. (1973). *Research methods, studies in adult education, #7.* Dar es Salaam, Tanzania: Institute of Adult Education.

Gallant, S. J., Coons, H. L., & Morokoff, P. J. (1994). Psychology and women's health: Some reflections and future directions. In V. J. Adesso, D. M. Reddy, & R. Fleming (Eds.), *Psychological perspectives on women's health* (pp. 315–346). Milwaukee: Taylor and Francis.

Gallup Organization. (1994). *1993 Ortho women's health research poll; a national survey.* Raritan, NJ: Ortho.

Garner, D. M., Garfinkel, P. E., Schwartz, D., & Thompson, M. (1980). Cultural expectations of thinness in women. *Psychological Reports, 47,* 483–491.

Garner, D. M., Rocken, W., Olmsted, M. P., Johnson, C., & Coscina, D. V. (1985). Psychoeducational principles in the treatment of bulimia and anorexia nervosa. In D. M. Garner & P. E. Garfinkel (Eds.), *Handbook of psychotherapy for anorexia nervosa and bulimia* (pp. 513–572). New York: Guilford.

Glaser, B. G., & Strauss, A. L. (1967). *The discovery of grounded theory.* Chicago: Aldine.

Goodman, L. A., Koss, M. P., Fitzgerald, L. F., Russo, N. F., & Keita, G. P. (1993). Male violence against women. *American Psychologist, 48,* 1054–1058.

Greene, E. B. (1994). Ethnic-minority lesbians and gay men: Mental health and treatment issues. *Journal of Consulting and Clinical Psychology, 62,* 243–251.

Gritz, E. R. (Ed.). (1986). *Gender and the teenage smoker* (DHHS Publication No. ADM 87-1447). Rockville, MD: National Institute on Drug Abuse.

Gurwitz, J. H., Col, N. F., & Avorn, J. (1992). The exclusion of the elderly and women from clinical trials in acute myocardial infarction. *Journal of the American Medical Association, 268,* 1417–1422.

Hall, B. (1975). Participatory research: An approach for change. *Convergence, 8,* 24–31.

Hall, J., Stevens, P. E., & Meleis, A. I. (1992). Developing the construct of role integration: A narrative analysis of women clerical workers' daily lives. *Research in Nursing Health, 15,* 447–457.

Hall, S. M. (1994). Women and drugs. In V. J. Adesso, D. M. Reddy, & R. Fleming (Eds.), *Psychological perspectives on women's health* (pp. 101–126). Milwaukee: Taylor and Francis.

Hellman, S., & Hellman, D. S. (1991). Of mice but not men: Problems of the randomized clinical trial. *New England Journal of Medicine, 324,* 1585–1589.

Henderson, D., Sampselle, C., Mayes, F., & Oakley, D. (1992). Toward culturally sensitive research in a multicultural society. *Healthcare for Women International, 13,* 339–350.

Hochschild, A. (1989). *The second shift.* New York: Viking Penguin.

Horowitz, A. (1985). Sons and daughters as caregivers to older parents: Differences in role performance and consequence. *The Gerontologist, 25,* 612–617.

Howard, G. S. (1991). Culture tales: A narrative approach to thinking. *Cross Cultural Psychology and Psychotherapy, 46,* 187–197.

Johnson, C. L., & Catalano, D. J. (1983). A longitudinal study of family supports to impaired elderly. *The Gerontologist, 23,* 612–618.

Kandrack, M. A., Grant, K. R., & Segall, A. (1991). Gender differences in health related behavior: Some unanswered questions. *Social Science Medicine, 5,* 579–590.

Kaplan, M. (1983). A woman's view of DSM-III. *American Psychologist, 38,* 786–792.

Karasek, R. A., Schwartz, J., Theorell, T., Pieper, C., Russell, B. S., & Michela, J. (1982). *Final report: Job characteristics, occupation and coronary heart disease.* New York: Columbia University, Dept. of Industrial Engineering and Operations Research.

Kelly, J. G. (1966). Ecological constraints on mental health services. *American Psychologist, 32,* 535–539.

Kessler, R. C., & McRae, J. (1981). Trends in the relationship between sex and psychological distress. *American Sociological Review, 46,* 443–452.

Kilpatrick, D. G., Best, C. L., Veronen, L. J., Amick, A. E., Villeponteaux, L. A., & Ruff, G. A. (1985). Mental health correlates of criminal victimization: A random community survey. *Journal of Consulting and Clinical Psychology, 53,* 866–873.

Koss, M. P. (1988). *Women's mental health research agenda: Violence against women.* Washington, DC: National Institute of Mental Health.

Koss, M. P. (1993). Rape: Scope, impact, intervention and public policy response. *American Psychologist, 48,* 1062–1069.

Koss, M. P., & Heslet, L. (1992). Somatic consequences of violence against women. *Archives of Family Medicine, 1,* 53–59.

Koss, M. P., Koss, P. G., & Woodruff, W. J. (1991). Deleterious effects of criminal victimization of women's health and medical utilization. *Archives of Internal Medicine, 151,* 342–347.

LaCroix, A. Z., & Haynes, S. G. (1987). Gender differences in the health effects of workplace roles. In R. C. Barnett, L. Biener, & G. K. Baruch (Eds.), *Gender and stress* (pp. 96–121). New York: Free Press.

LaFromboise, T. D., Heyle, A. M., & Ozer, E. J. (1990). Changing and diverse roles. *Sex Roles, 22,* 455–476.

Landrine, H., & Klonoff, E. (1992). Culture and health related schemas: A review and proposal for interdisciplinary integration. *Health Psychology, 11,* 267–276.

Lazarus, R. S., & Folkman, S. (1984). *Stress, appraisal, and coping.* New York: Springer.

Leigh, W. (1994). The health status of women of color. In C. Costello & A. Stone (Eds.), *The American woman 1994-95: Where we stand, women and health* (pp. 154–196). New York: Norton.

Leventhal, E. (1994). Gender and aging: Women and their aging. In V. J. Adesso, D. M. Reddy, & R. Fleming (Eds.), *Psychological perspectives on women's health* (pp. 11–35). Milwaukee: Taylor and Francis.

Levey. B. A. (1991). Bridging the gap in gender research. *Clinical Pharmacology and Therapeutics, 50,* 641–646.

Litt, I. F. (1993). Health issues for women in the 1990s. In S. Matteo (Ed.), *American women in the nineties. Today's critical issues* (pp. 139–157). Boston: Northeastern University Press.

Lott, B., & Maluso, D. (1993). The social learning of gender. In A. E. Beall & R. J. Sternberg (Eds.), *The psychology of gender* (pp. 99–123). New York: Guilford.

Low, K. G.. Jolicoeur, M. R., Stone, L. E., & Fleisher, C. L. (1994). Women participants in research: Assessing the progress. *Women and Health, 22,* 81–100.

Lowey, N. M. (1994). Women's health and medical school curricula. *Academic Medicine, 69*(4), 280–281.

Lucas, A. R., Beard, C. M., Kranz, J. S., & Kurland, L. T. (1983). Epidemiology of anorexia nervosa and bulimia. *International Journal of Eating Disorders, 2,* 85–91.

Marecek, J., & Hare-Mustin, R. T. (1991). A short history of the future: Feminism and clinical psychology. *Psychology of Women Quarterly, 15,* 521–536.

Matthews, K. A. (1992). Myths and realities of menopause. *Psychosomatic Medicine, 54,* 1–9.

Matthews, K. A., & Rodin, J. (1989). Women's changing work roles: Impact on health, family, and public policy. *American Psychologist, 44,* 1389–1393.

Mayer, J. A., & Solomon, L. J. (1992). Breast self-examination skill and frequency: A review. *Annals of Behavioral Medicine, 14,* 189–196.

Mays, V. M., & Comas-Díaz, L. (1988). Feminist therapy with ethnic minority populations: A closer look at Blacks and Hispanics. In M. Dutton-Douglass & L. E. A. Walker (Eds.), *Feminist psychotherapies: Integration of therapeutic and feminist systems. Developments in clinical psychology* (pp. 228–251). Norwood, NJ: Ablex.

McGrath, E., Keita, G. P., Strickland, B. R., & Russo, N. F. (Eds.). (1990). *Women and depression: Risk factors and treatment issues.* Washington, DC: American Psychological Association.

Meischke, H., Eisenberg, M. S., & Larsen, M. P. (1993). Prehospital delay interval for patients who use emergency medical services: The effect of heart-related medical conditions and demographic variables. *Annals of Emergency Medicine, 22,* 1597–1601.

Mello, N. K. (1986). Drug use patterns and premenstrual dysphoria. In B. A. Ray & M. C. Braude (Eds.), *Women and drugs: A new era for research* (Research Monograph 65; pp. 31–48). Rockville, MD: National Institute on Drug Abuse.

Milburne, N., & D'Ercole, A. (1991). Homeless women: Moving toward a comprehensive model. *American Psychologist, 46,* 1161–1169.

Miller, S. M. (1979). Controllability and human stress: Method, evidence and theory. *Behavior, Research and Therapy, 17,* 287–304.

Miller, S. M., & Kirsch, N. (1987). Sex differences in cognitive coping with stress. In R. C. Barnett, L. Biener, & G. K. Baruch (Eds.), *Gender and stress* (pp. 278–307). New York: Free Press.

Morokoff, P. J., & Calderone, K. L. (1994). Sexuality and infertility. In V. J. Adesso, D. M. Reddy, & R. Fleming (Eds.), *Psychological perspectives on women's health* (pp. 251–284). Milwaukee: Taylor and Francis.

Morse, J. (Ed.). (1992). *Qualitative health research.* Newbury Park, CA: Sage.

Novello, A., Rosenberg, M., Saltzman, L., & Shosky, J. (1992). From the surgeon general, U.S. public health service. *The Journal of the American Medical Association, 267,* 3132.

Ogur, B. (1986). Long day's journey into night: Women and prescription drug abuse. *Women and Health, 11,* 99–115.

O'Leary, A. (1985). Self-efficacy and health. *Behavior Research and Therapy, 23,* 437–451.

O'Leary, A., Jemmott, L. S., Suarez-Al-Adam, M., Alroy, C., & Fernandez, M. I. (1993). Women and AIDS. In S. Matteo (Ed.), *American women in the nineties. Today's critical issues* (pp. 173–192). Boston: Northeastern University Press.

Olmedo, E. L., & Parron, D. L. (1981). Mental health of minority women: Some special issues. *Professional Psychology, 12,* 103–111.

Osvold, L. L., & Sodowaky, G. R. (1993). Eating disorders of White American, racial and ethnic minority American, and international women. *Journal of Multicultural Counseling and Development, 21,* 143–154.

Ozer, E. M. (1986). *Health status of minority women.* Washington, DC: Office of Ethnic Minority Affairs, American Psychological Association.

Ozer, E. M. (1993). *Division of childcare between mother and father: How does it affect full-time working mothers?* Paper presented at the Meeting of the American Psychological Association, Toronto, Canada.

Ozer, E. M., & Bandura, A. (1990). Mechanisms governing empowerment effects: A self-efficacy analysis. *Journal of Personality and Social Psychology, 58,* 472–486.

Padgett, D. (1988). Aging and minority women: Issues in research and health policy. *Women and Health, 14,* 213–225.

Parsons, J. E., Ruble, D., Hodges, K. L., & Small, A. W. (1976). Cognitive developmental factors in emerging sex differences in achievement related expectancies. *Journal of Social Issues, 32,* 47–62.

Pearce, D. M. (1993). Something old, something new: Women's poverty in the 1990s. In S. Matteo (Ed.), *American women in the nineties. Today's critical issues* (pp. 79–97). Boston: Northeastern University Press.

Pearlin, L. I., & Schooler, C. (1978). The structure of coping. *Journal of Health and Social Behavior, 19,* 2–21.

Pleck, J. H. (1984). The work-family role system. In P. Voydanoff (Ed.), *Work and family: Changing roles of men and women* (pp. 8–19). Palo Alto: Mayfield.

Reinharz, S. (1992). *Feminist methods in social research.* New York: Oxford University Press.

Repetti, R. L., Matthews, K. A., & Waldron, I. (1989). Employment and women's health: Effects of paid employment on women's mental and physical health. *American Psychologist, 44,* 1394–1401.

Rexroat, C., & Shehan, C. (1987). The family life cycle and spouses' time in housework. *Journal of Marriage and the Family, 49,* 737–750.

Riger, S. (1992). Epistomological debates, feminist voices: Science, social values, and the study of women. *American Psychologist, 47,* 730–740.

Rimer, B. K. (1992). Understanding the acceptance of mammography by women. *Annals of Behavioral Medicine, 14,* 197–203.

Robertson, M. J., & Cousineau, M. R. (1986). Health status and access to health services among the urban homeless. *American Journal of Public Health, 76,* 561–563.

Rodin, J., & Ickovics, J. R. (1990). Women's health: Review and research agenda as we approach the 21st century. *American Psychologist, 45,* 1018–1034.

Rosenfield, S. (1989). The effects of women's employment: Personal control and sex differences in mental health. *Journal of Health and Social Behavior, 30,* 77–91.

Ross, C. E., & Mirowsky, J. (1988). Childcare and emotional adjustment to wives' employment. *Journal of Health and Social Behavior, 29,* 127–138.

Rothblum, E. D. (1983). Sex role stereotypes and depression in women. In V. Franks & E. D. Rothblum (Eds.), *The stereotyping of women: Its effects on mental health* (pp. 3–11). New York: Springer.

Rozin, P., & Fallon, A. E. (1988). Body image, attitudes to weight and misperceptions of figure preferences of the opposite sex: A comparison of men and women in two generations. *Journal of Abnormal Psychology, 97,* 342–345.

Russo, N. F. (1990). Overview: Forging research priorities for women's health. *American Psychologist. 45,* 368–373.

Scarr, S., Phillips, D., & McCartney, K. (1989). Working mothers and their families. *American Psychologist, 44,* 1402–1409.

Schatzkin, A., Jones, D. Y., Hoover, R. N., Taylor, P. R., Brinton, L. A., Ziegler, R. G., Harvey, E. B., Carter, C. L., Licitra, L. M., Dufour, M. C., & Larson, D. B. (1987). Alcohol consumption and breast cancer in the epidemiologic follow-up study of the first national health and nutrition examination survey. *The New England Journal of Medicine, 316,* 1169–1173.

Seligman, M. E. P. (1975). *Helplessness: On depression. development and death.* San Francisco: Freeman.

Shapiro, S. (1994). The call for breast cancer screening guidelines. *American Journal of Public Health, 84,* 10–11.

Sickles, E. A., & Kopans, D. B. (1993). Deficiencies in the analysis of breast cancer screening data. *Journal of the National Cancer Institute, 85*(20), 1621–1625.

Sitterly, C., & Duke, B. (1988). *A woman's place: Management.* Englewood Cliffs, NJ: Prentice-Hall.

Slone, D., Shapiro, S., Rosenberg, L., Kaufman, D. W., Hartz, S. C., Rossi, A. C., Stolley, P. D., & Miettinen, O. S. (1978). Relation of cigarette smoking to myocardial infarction in young women. *The New England Journal of Medicine, 298,* 1273–1276.

Steingart, R. M., Packer, M., Hamm, P., Coglianese, M. E., Geesh, B., Geltman, E. M., Sollano, O. J., Katz, S., Moye, L., Basta, L. L., Lewis, S. J., Gottlieb, S. S., Bernstein, V., McEwan. P., Jacobson, K., Brown, E. J., Kukin, M. L., Kantrowitz, N. E., & Pfeffer, M. A. (1991). Sex differences in the management of coronary artery disease. *The New England Journal of Medicine, 325,* 226–230.

Stone, A. A., & Neale, J. M. (1984). New measure of daily coping: Development and preliminary results. *Journal of Personality and Social Psychology, 46,* 892–906.

Stunkard, A. J. (1975). From explanation to action in psychosomatic medicine: The case of obesity. *Psychosomatic Medicine, 37,* 195–236.

Tavris, C. (1992). *The mismeasure of woman.* New York: Simon & Schuster.

Tavris, C., & Wade, C. (1984). *The longest war: Sex differences in perspective.* New York: Harcourt Brace.

Thompson, B. W. (1994). *A hunger so wide and so deep: American women speak out on eating problems.* Minneapolis: University of Minnesota Press.

Thoresen, C. E., & Low, K. G. (1990). Women and the Type A behavior pattern: Review and commentary. *Journal of Social Behavior and Personality, 5,* 117–133.

Uichol, K., &: Berry, J. W. (Eds.). (1993). *Indigenous psychologies: Research and experience in cultural context.* Newbury Park, CA: Sage.

U.S. Conference of Mayors. (1987). The continuing growth of hunger, homelessness, and poverty in America's cities: 1987, a 26-city survey. *U.S. Conference of Mayors.* Washington, DC: Author.

U.S. Department of Health and Human Services. (1984). *Report of the public health service task force on women's health issues.* Washington, DC: U.S. Public Health Services.

Uttal, L. (1994). *Racial safety, cultural competence, and cultural maintenance: The child care concerns of employed mothers.* Memphis: Center for Research on Women, The University of Memphis.

Verbrugge, L. M. (1982). Women's social roles and health. In P. Berman & E. Ramey (Eds.), *Women: A developmental perspective* (National Institutes of Health Publication No. 82–2298). Washington, DC: U.S. Government Printing Office.

Verbrugge, L. M. (1989). The twain meet: Empirical explanations of sex differences in health and mortality. *Journal of Health and Social Behavior, 30,* 282–304.

Veroff, J., Douvan, E., & Kulka, R. A. (1981). *The inner American.* New York: Basic Books.

Vincent, T. A., & Trickett, E. J. (1983). Preventive interventions and the human context: Ecological approaches to environmental assessment and change. In R. D. Felner, L. A. Jason, M. J., & S. S. Farber (Eds.), *Preventive psychology: Theory, research and practice in community intervention* (pp. 67–86). New York: Pergamon.

Viney, L. L., & Westbrook, M. T. (1982). Coping with chronic illness: The mediating role of biographic and illness-related factors. *Journal of Psychosomatic Research, 26,* 595–605.

Wadden, T. A., Brown, G., Foster, G. D., & Linowitz, J. R. (1991). Salience of weight related worries in adolescent males and females. *International Journal of Eating Disorders, 10,* 407–414.

Weissman, M. M., & Klerman, G. L. (1977). Sex differences and the epidemiology of depression. *Archives of General Psychiatry, 34,* 98–111.

Wenger, N. K., Speroff, L., & Packard, B. (1993). Cardiovascular health and disease in women. *The New England Journal of Medicine, 329,* 247–256.

White, M., & Epston, D. (1990). *Narrative means to therapeutic ends.* New York: Norton.

Wilsnack, R. W., Wilsnack, S. C., & Klessen, A. D. (1984). Women's drinking and drinking problems: Patterns from a 1981 national survey. *American Journal of Public Health, 74,* 1231–1238.

Winfield, I., George, L. K., Schwartz, M., & Blazer, D. G. (1990). Sexual assault and psychiatric disorders among a community sample of women. *American Journal of Psychiatry, 147,* 335–341.

Worth, D. (1990). Minority women and AIDS: Culture, race, and gender. In D. A. Feldman (Ed.), *Culture and AIDS* (pp. 111–135). New York: Praeger.

How to Tell Your Doctor a Thing or Two

by Morton Hunt

If you're like most Americans, you've lost a lot of faith in doctors in recent years. In 1966 the Louis Harris survey organization reported that 73 percent of Americans had a great deal of confidence in the medical profession: by 1977 the figure had dropped to 43 percent.

As a result a new kind of patient has appeared—a patient who is questioning and even argumentative, sometimes mistrustful, often balky. This patient goes doctor-shopping, files complaints with medical societies, sues for malpractice. She may join one of the hundreds of new medical-consumer (patient) organizations that defend patients against their own doctors. She—or he—no longer silently listens to the doctor with awe but speaks up, wants to be told everything and to be convinced, and reserves the right to reject the doctor's advice or to ask for a second opinion.

I've been talking to leaders of the medical profession and of medical-consumer groups, and both sides agree on one thing: Doctors throughout America are seeing the new kind of patient increasingly often in their offices. Although some doctors—including my own—look approvingly on patients of this new breed, the majority view them with disapproval and even hostility. By training, position and tradition, doctors tend to play the role of Wise Patriarch Whose Word is Law, and they expect their patients to be Good Children Who Obey Without Argument. They consider the new breed "difficult," "troublemakers" and—above all—"bad" patients.

But there is growing evidence that nowadays the "bad" patient is a better one, in terms of medical results, than the "good" patient. According to a number of recent research studies, the passive, uncomplaining, unquestioning patient is less likely to get well quickly than the new kind. Or as Eli Glogow, director of the graduate program in health administration at the University of Southern California, succinctly puts it, "the 'bad patient' gets better quicker."

Why? Not because the "bad" patient—whom I'll call the "active" patient— refuses to follow instructions. Indeed, medical journals report that the independent patient is apt to carry out doctors' orders faithfully, once he or she accepts them, while the passive patient is more likely to forget or quietly disobey.

But following instructions is only part of it. What gives the active patient better odds at regaining health quickly or staying healthy is a whole new concept of the patient's role. Essentially it consists of taking responsibility for one's own health care—becoming an adult rather than a child in the doctor-patient relationship. That means finding the best doctor available but getting another opinion if doubtful about a major recommendation; defending one-self against overmedication and unnecessary surgery; and in general acting as the doctor's partner, collaborator and equal.

It is out of necessity that such patients are becoming ever more numerous for there has been a revolution in the nature of medical practice. In recent years the doctor-patient relationship has become coldly impersonal, and not very reassuring to the patient. Here are some of the reasons:

- The number of drugs, tests and special technological procedures has vastly increased. As a result, patients spend more time with nurses and technicians, less time with the doctor himself. Diseases get treated but treatment becomes an assembly-line affair.
- The new technology makes for greater specialization. Specialization makes for higher fees—and so more doctors want to specialize (more than four out of five now do so). In consequence there are fewer general practitioners, and the patient has to wait longer and settle for less time with a G.P. than ever before.
- Specialization also means that the patient is subdivided and parceled out among doctors—the gynecologist, the allergist, and so on—and is to each not a person but a symptom in some part of the body. Many patients get medical care from several doctors but have no one doctor who *cares*. There's the rub. Dr. W. Walter Menninger of the Menninger Foundation, a center of psychiatric research, says that most of the grievances patients have against doctors involve breakdown in the *caring* aspect of the physician-patient relationship, not in the quality of technical care.

    One young woman I know worried about menstrual spotting and went to a busy gynecologist who,

with little explanation, did a suction extraction of the endometrium (the mucus lining of the uterus). Unprepared for the invasive and painful procedure, she left the office shaken and burst into tears on the sidewalk. Months later she said to him as casually as she could, "Doctor, that last visit was so unpleasant I thought I might never come back"—to which he replied just as casually, "If you ever feel that way again, I think you *shouldn't* come back." Caring? He'd sneer at the word.

- We Americans move about more than ever. We become separated from the doctor who knows us best, and what he or she knows about us is, in most cases, lost or forgotten. Yet you, the patient, have no legal right in most states to make the doctor turn over his records to you. (If you ask, he'll send them to another doctor—but few patients ask.)
- Group practice, growing by leaps and bounds, gives the busy doctor much-needed relief and free time and assures you that someone will be on hand when needed. But the substitute doctor rarely knows your medical history or has time to read through your folder. Unless you can fill in the gaps in this stranger's knowledge of you—and have the courage to do so—you may get indifferent or even hurtful treatment.

    One 30-year-old woman went to her medical group when a rash spread over her arms and chest. An overworked doctor who had never seen her before asked her a few questions and concluded—correctly—that it was an allergic reaction; summer sunshine and an antibiotic she'd been taking didn't go well together. He prescribed a form of cortisone to be taken by mouth, and a week later she was in the hospital with a bleeding ulcer. Buried in her folder and unread by the doctor had been notes about a tendency on her part toward ulcers: cortisone treatment brought the condition to an acute state.

- The profit motive has altered the patient-doctor relationship. Profitmaking is an old, respectable incentive to businessmen and professionals alike, but it can easily lead to exploitative and unfair practices. That's why watchdog agencies protect consumers from impersonal big business. But medicine, though it too is now impersonal and big business—doctor's fees total over $26 billion a year—remains virtually unregulated except by itself.

Exploitation by doctors takes many forms. In a study of one group of internists, researchers found that some of the doctors ordered patients to come back for follow-up visits twice as often as others did, even though all were treating the same kinds of patients. Three of four doctors polled by the American Medical Association this year admit that they now order anywhere from one to several extra tests per patient—not for the patient's benefit but for their own, as protection from potential malpractice suits. But it is the patient who pays—and who is exposed to extra risks.

The most serious conflict between the patient's best interest and the profit motive occurs when the doctor stands to gain the most. A surgeon who will earn many hundreds of dollars from performing an operation is likely to be less objective, when deciding whether to recommend it, than a surgeon who is not involved and therefore impartial. A recent Congressional study indicates that one of every six operations is unnecessary: that's more than 3 million needless operations per year, costing $4 billion and leading to nearly 12,000 postoperative deaths. In some specialties the figures are even higher; various research teams have termed anywhere from a quarter to a half of the 800,000 hysterectomies performed each year "unjustified" or "unnecessary."

Reaction to all this was inevitable. Liberal doctors and medical administrators drafted "bills of rights" for patients, and a few legislators tried to get some of them enacted into state law. Labor unions and veterans' organizations began to fight for "patients' advocates" in clinics and hospitals, to listen to patients' grievances and take their complaints to the authorities. Everywhere the new breed of patient began to appear.

And perhaps most important, medical-consumer organizations sprang up, most of them offshoots of the 1960s consumer movement. Public Citizen, the national organization headed by Ralph Nader, set up the Health Research Group in Washington, D.C. Headed by Sidney M. Wolfe, a dynamic young doctor, it gathers research data and uses them to lobby for stronger Government controls over drug advertising, prescription writing, the use of x-rays; for the patient's right to obtain personal medical records; and for controls over cost and quality of health care in general.

In recent years other medical-consumer groups have been started in many cities by churches, by campus organizations and by women's groups. Some of them, chiefly educational, publish pamphlets, newsletters or books on medical matters, or operate Tel-Med libraries. (You phone, ask to hear a tape on a medical matter that concerns you and get plugged in to a four-to-seven minute cassette at no charge.) Others also offer counseling and advice and make referrals to doctors or clinics. Still others, like Nader's health group, are interested chiefly in bringing pressure to bear on city and state officials to control medical costs and practices and in getting consumer-minded representatives onto the governing boards of hospitals, medical-insurance plans and relevant state agencies.

In the long run it will be these collective efforts that will rebuild the patient-doctor relationship in a new, democratic form. Meanwhile what can you, the individual, do for yourself? A good deal. From my conversations with medical-consumer leaders I have put together a seven-point program for the new-style patient:

1. *Care for yourself as far as possible.* Save the doctor's time and your own—and your money—by doing at home certain things you can learn through community-health projects and self-care courses taught by medical-consumer groups. You can learn to take and record your own blood pressure and that of your husband and children (these days *everyone's* blood pressure is considered important information; the equipment costs as little as $20). You can learn to adjust the dosage of your own or your children's medication, within limits set by the doctor. You can give yourself or others in your family regular injections (allergy shots, for instance), when needed. Professor Lowell S. Levin, of the Yale University School of Medicine, a specialist in public health, says that the time has come for the "rediscovery of the lay function in health," and maintains that the informed patient can become the most important practitioner in the medical-care system.

2. *Keep your own medical records.* Since in most states you can't gain access to doctors' records, ask your doctor for his findings every time you visit him—your pulse, blood pressure, hemoglobin and white-cell count—whatever he checks; and don't settle for "It's fine." You have a moral if not a legal right to precise information. So start a notebook. Keep track of whatever the doctor tells you, plus the dates of illnesses, their symptoms and duration, diagnoses, medications taken and their effects.

    Also ask your doctor for the results of all tests and lab reports. A few doctors already provide such information; others do not but will if you ask; and many others will refuse. If your doctor refuses, you can either accept defeat or look for another doctor. You also can ask any medical-consumer group what the law is in your state; it may support your claims, and if it does, tell the doctor so.

3. *Come to the doctor prepared.* Before your visit, jot down everything you want to tell the doctor. Include the questions you want to ask. It's amazing how things will slip your mind when you're talking to a hurried doctor or when you're spraddled out on an examination table with some unseen gadget making its way into you. Many feminist groups urge patients to take along a friend to hold the list of questions and remind you of things you forget. Most doctors will ask a third party to leave before an examination, but this is only custom: A.M.A. spokesmen and consumer-group leaders agree that doctors should, and for the most part will, allow a third party to remain if the patient asks them to.

4. *Exercise your right to choose and refuse.* Even with a doctor you believe in—and all the more with one who is new to you—you should take an active part in decisions affecting you. Ask for a detailed explanation of the possible side effects of any recommended drug or procedure. Ask if there are alternate ways to treat your problem. Give due weight to the doctor's preference, but also to your own. It's your body and your life.

If the doctor calls for tests, ask how necessary they are; it's quite in order for you to say you'd like to keep costs down. And ask about risks; it's quite proper for you to say you'd like to avoid any x-rays that are of only marginal value, since it's not the individual exposure that endangers you but an excessive lifetime total of exposures. And it's also your right to say that you prefer to live with your medical problem—or even die of it—rather than submit to a painful, risky treatment if the outcome is highly uncertain.

But if you question the doctor's advice or decline to follow any of his recommendations, won't he be angered? It depends in part on how you put it—and on what kind of person he is. Says Dr. Wolfe, of the Health Research Group, "The doctor who gets huffy when you ask questions or express preferences is a doctor to stay away from. The doctor you should look for is the one who realizes that you have a right to ask questions and to decide what you want to do with your life."

Do you really have a right to refuse any of the doctor's orders? Medical-consumer leaders and A.M.A. officials agree that unless your disease endangers the public welfare, you do have such a right—but that if you exercise it, the doctor may exercise a corresponding right to stop treating you. If you're pregnant or seriously ill or worried, you may be afraid to risk it; you may choke back your questions or objections and play the part of the "good" patient.

But speaking up needn't mean confrontation. Denise Fuge, coordinator of the Women and Health Committee of the New York Chapter of NOW, says patients shouldn't *confront* the doctor, but should seek to *communicate* their fears; wishes and personal values openly and honestly. "Most doctors," she says, "don't know what women are thinking, and they'd like to. They'd respond to the patient much more sensitively if they did."

5. *Get a second opinion.* Before you agree to surgery or any other major procedure, or when some ailment isn't getting better under your doctor's management, tell him that you'd like a second opinion and that you feel sure he wouldn't mind your getting one. He probably will mind, but won't say so or threaten to stop treating you; publicly, most doctors are opposed only to mandatory (legally required) second opinions. Privately, though, many of them feel like Dr. James Sammons, executive vice-president of the A.M.A., who is against them in general.

"I'm opposed to them," he told me, "because the patient's right of choice is lost—he tends to assume the second opinion is more intelligent than the first one." What Dr. Sammons ignores is that the second opinion, though not necessarily more intelligent than the first, is disinterested and hence less subject to unconscious bias. Not all doctors, incidentally, are against second opinions; one quarter of a sample of doctors polled by the magazine *Medical World News* favored them, and the trend is in that direction.

6. *Ask for enough time.* Don't let yourself be rushed. "You're paying for an expensive service," says Maryann Napoli, of New York's Center for Medical Consumers and Health Care Information, "and consultation is part of it. It's important for your mental health as well as your physical health to have your questions fully answered and your doubts resolved."

Denise Fuge, of NOW, recommends that you say something like, "Doctor, I came to you because I've been worried, and I need more time to talk to you. If you're too busy today, please tell me when you can spend more time with me and I'll come back." A women's medical-consumer group in New York, HealthRight, also suggests that you ask the nurse some of your unanswered questions; nurses are often sympathetic and less rushed than the doctor.

But if your doctor regularly allows less time than normal—15 minutes is the national average duration of routine office visits—and doesn't respond to your request for more time, he may be the wrong doctor for you.

7. *Don't let yourself be treated as an inferior.* This is one of the trickiest points, and perhaps one of the most important. Many doctors treat you in ways that puts you at a psychological disadvantage. Some gynecologists in particular address patients by their first names even when they scarcely know them; it makes the patient feel a little like a child. Many women resent this; a few fight back. When a gynecologist greeted one woman, whom he had seen only once before, with "What brings you here today, Lillian?" she said sweetly, "I've got galloping vaginitis again, Bernard." Bernard took the hint. Generally, though, a more formal way of setting the matter straight will work better. For instance: "Doctor, I would much prefer to be called Ms. So-and-so," or, "I really don't like being addressed by my first name."

Similarly, it may make you feel inferior to be undressed and in a gown when you first meet the doctor. If so, tell the nurse you want to speak to him before you undress. This is a delicate matter; the doctor may have set office rules. But Dr. Menninger points out that when you come to exhibit some disease to the doctor, you are apt to feel shame and humiliation, and since such feelings tend to make you a docile patient rather than an active one, it is important to resist anything that intensifies them.

Things will never be what they once were. But the new doctor-patient relationship need not be one of antagonism; it can be one of equality and cooperation. This is what most of the medical-consumer groups, and most active patients are really seeking.

And within the ranks of doctors there are signs of evolution toward a new image of the good doctor—no longer the wise patriarch whose word is law, but a dedicated expert who is ready to give you the help you need and the kind of help you choose. Increasingly, medical journals carry articles advocating democratic ways of dealing with patients and favoring patient participation in the making of medical decisions.

Professor Julia Frank, of the Yale University School of Medicine, writing in the New England Journal of Medicine, urges doctors everywhere to make the patient "an equal member of the team." An editorial in a recent issue of the Journal of the American Medical Association, noting the spread of "participatory democracy" in our society, says, "It is simply no longer possible for the physician to make moral and value decisions for his patients." And Professor Levin, writing in Public Health Reports, sounds a call for massive self-reform by the health professions: "The high value placed on the compliant patient must be transferred to the active, even resistant, patient." He predicts the creation of a "new social contract between professionals and lay persons"—a contract from which the doctor will benefit, by sharing responsibility with those he treats.

And it is a contract from which the patient will benefit by gaining self-respect and a sense of control over her own life—and by getting better quicker.

More Than One Womb

by Louise Marsden

For the first 31 years of my life, I thought I had a fairly good idea of what my body was like; it functioned 'normally', and since I had a paramedical education, having trained as a pharmacist, I thought that I was informed. Then for various reasons I decided to have a child. I am a women, I can bear children, so it should be straightforward, I thought. (It couldn't be quite straightforward, I am a lesbian.) I was trying for a year, towards the end of which I began to think I was infertile. I suspect that friends wondered at my continued attempts to become pregnant, as infertility seemed more and more of a possibility. Then one month just when my period was due, I became sick with what seemed incredibly like German measles. It *was* German measles, and my period did not come that month, and I was pregnant. There was no question of whether or not to have an abortion: the effects of German measles on a foetus are usually ghastly. It was not too difficult to get an NHS abortion, although there was some delay, of course! In my anaesthetic haze after the abortion (or termination as they say), the doctor came around and told me that there had been 'scanty products' from the abortion. He looked skeptical and told me to come back in ten days. By then the results of the histology tests—the examination of the embryonic tissue—would be ready. He did not stay to explain. The ward sister assured me that at least one woman every week has scanty products from an abortion.

During the next ten days I tried to find out why there would be 'scanty products'. Perhaps the embryo had already died. This sometimes happens and if it is in the first three months our bodies can reabsorb the 'products'. Perhaps with the German measles it had not grown much anyway. Perhaps the whole pregnancy had been hysterical. I had been trying hard to get pregnant, and maybe I'd forced my body to pretend that it was. Confidence in my own judgment seeped away a little. Were these symptoms psychological?

Anyway, I waited, searching for information as usual. On the appointed day I went, they did not have the histology results, of course. However, I was examined and my uterus was still swollen. It was a different doctor and he decided to have a look around, or rather a feel around. Finally he found something: 'a vaginal septum perhaps', yes, a vaginal septum. Did I mind a student doctor having a look? No, but what are you looking at? He explained that I had a piece of flesh dividing my vagina into two, nothing else. He asked for another sample of urine and I was asked to return to see the consultant in two days and dismissed.

I immediately did a pregnancy test at home, it was still positive. Great! The consultant was very apologetic, another abortion immediately. But it may not be simple; he may have to cut the septum; he may not be able to remove the foetus without doing a caesarean type abortion, which means cutting me open. He didn't quite know, but it seemed that I had a double uterus. Well, the abortion was quite straightforward fortunately (we have to be thankful for small mercies); my uterus is completely divided into two, it's a uterus didelphys. From

the outside I look like any woman does, there is one entrance to my vagina, but once inside a little, there is this tissue—septum—which divides the pathway into two, going up to two cervixes, then into the two uteruses. The pathway on the left is much narrower and until this abortion business, had never been discovered, although I had had countless internal examinations by doctors for one thing or another. What follows is what I've learned since. I want as many women as possible to know that these anomalies exist.

In the first 12 weeks when the egg is dividing into different cells (when it is called an embryo), two tubes form and they are called Mullerian ducts. There is one on either side, and they come together to form one tube or vessel, and eventually, the uterus, cervix and upper vagina. If they do not join together completely, and fuse, then these variations on the theme of the female reproductive system develop. The urinary tracts, the kidneys, urethras (tubes going down to the bladder) and bladder also form during this fusion of the Mullerian ducts. So if you get incomplete joining of those ducts, it is possible to have variations in that area too. I have a double lot of kidneys and urethras, but the urethras join together before getting to the bladder. Again they have never caused me any trouble, although some variations can.

It is not known why these things happen, they just do. These things are not passed on from mother to child, so they are not hereditary.

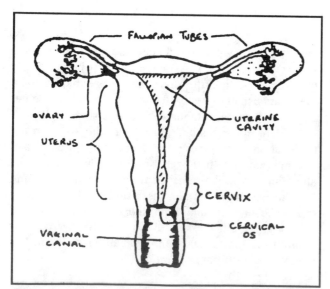

Figure 4 · Average female reproductive organs: here is a diagram of what are called 'the female reproductive organs', but we'll call them average female reproductive organs' *Teresa Savage* (*SR 88* October 1979).

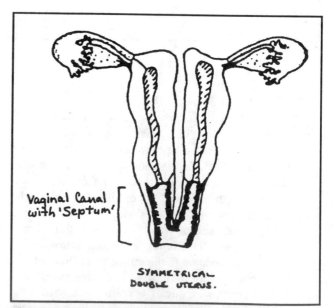

Figure 5 · Symmetrical double uterus: here you get two uteruses, two cervixes. There is a fallopian tube attached to each uterus, so the usual number of fallopian tubes and ovaries. The duplication can continue down to the vagina. This is called a Uterus Didelphys. *Teresa Savage* (*SR88* October 1979).

There are a number of possible variations in the uterus and vagina in the female reproductive system. You can have extra ovaries, but that seems to be extremely rare. You can be born without the top part of the vagina or with a very strong division across it.

The Problems Caused by the Different Variations

Infertility: there is complete infertility if the path to the cervix and vagina is blocked and there is relative infertility if the pathways are narrowed and there are divisions or septa in any of the paths. So with a Unicornuate uterus, one side is completely missing, including one ovary: this means fertility will be considerably reduced.

Miscarriage: miscarriage is more common because implantation of the fertilized egg can happen on a septum, and the septum is likely to have a weaker blood supply and will not be strong enough to support the growing egg (embryo). Also the space inside the uterus may be irregular, and this will prevent growth.

Premature Labour and Premature Rupture of the Membranes (Waters): both of these happen for the same reasons as miscarriage happens. The foetus may not be able to position itself properly for birth, because of the shape of the uterus. So 'malpresentation' is more common. The baby may lie across the uterus, or upside down (breech).

Dystocia (Abnormal Labour): the uterine contractions may not be co-ordinated, also the non-pregnant side of the uterus can block the way of the baby. Placenta can remain in the uterus, again because of the uncoordinated contractions, so it has to be removed by hand.

All of the above problems are to do with childbirth, but with a uterus which has a blind side, you can get a build up of menstrual blood because there is no way for it to come out. So periods can be very painful and eventually after some years, you can get a big lump which is made up of old menstrual blood and it falls down into the vagina. Its removal would have to be by surgery.

It is hard to find very much written on how often these variations occur; they are often not discovered at all because they are not always problematic. Ian Donald in *Practical Obstetric Problems* says that two out of every thousand women have a 'congenital deformity' that is bad enough to interfere with pregnancy. This is 0.2% and presumably he means that 0.2% of women have problems conceiving because of one of these variations. Belscher and Mackay in *Obstetrics and the New-born* say, however, that the incidence of variation is approximately 1%, but if minor forms of duplication like a septate uterus are included, it could be close to 5%. So five women in every 100 have some variation, and this knowledge is kept in weighty medical tomes, hidden from us.

The gynecology consultant whom I saw for the abortion said that he sees about one woman a year with some variation. I have spoken to midwives who have been practicing for years, and who have seen only two or three—not surprising, really, as midwives deal with women who have successfully conceived, and not with women who are having problems.

Until I decided to get pregnant, my double uterus caused me no difficulties at all; most of the problems do seem to happen in pregnancy. If a lot go unnoticed, it's possible that they are trouble free. Ian Donald quotes that from 42 pregnancies where there were uterine variations, 19 ended in miscarriage, five in premature labour, eight with unstable presentation, that is breech or sideways, and in five the placenta had to be removed by hand. Out of the 23 pregnancies reaching labour, four babies died. He also says that the more minor the variation, then the more treacherous; for example, in some variations the growing foetus could lie with its head in one side, and body in the other, and this would be very dangerous. Since mine is completely separate, the problems are minimized.

That is all the technical information I have been able to find; there is not a lot written, just two or three pages in gynecology books in chapters headed 'Congenital Anomalies/Abnormalities'. Are we not told much about the abnormalities of the female reproductive system because these women are not normal, possibly not reproductive, or is it a continuation of the mystification that prevents us from having control over our bodies and our lives?

In the past few months I have heard of other women with such variations, but as yet I have not met any others. It would be good to hear of other women's experience. I have not had a lot to do with doctors since the discovery. My GP was mildly amused and the consultant at the hospital objectively curious.

I am pregnant again now; it happened the first time I tried after the second abortion, clever body, so I have been to an antenatal clinic. I suspect that I am a curiosity there. I don't mind people learning from my parts; the more who know the better. But I think that I will have to undergo more examinations than usual for the sake of medical science and I also think that I will not be told what they are seeing or what they are thinking. I object to being seen as a medical specimen and not just as a variation. I am not sick. I do not feel any different from how I felt for the first 31 years of my life.

My present lover noticed ages ago that there were 'two ways that she could go' inside my vagina, and she often felt worried about it. Why don't we trust our own discoveries? The 'experts' have made us totally dependent. Now that I am pregnant, I feel less in control than I might overwise have felt. I keep thinking that perhaps I should be doing things that other pregnant women don't need to do, I don't know quite what. I suppose I am feeling that I do have some deformity for which I am responsible. The feeling is not strong and I resist it, but it's there. I feel angry that some of my confidence has been taken from me. We should know that these variations are possible, but of course there is so much that we should know and we don't.

Neither the woman I am involved with nor I were shocked or horrified by the knowledge, only curious and we sought out as much information as we could, as quickly as we could. Other women have been shocked and thought it peculiar, but I think that reflects a standard acceptance of what is 'normal'. We're fighting the 'norms' of this society.

They say that these variations often go undetected, that is until they present a problem. But if we knew about them, some we could easily discover ourselves like double vaginas. We would not be taken by surprise and the possibility of thinking it 'odd' would at least be reduced.

The Gynecologic Exam and the Training of Medical Students
An Opportunity for Health Education

by Judith Schmidt

This article is a personal account written by a senior health education major about her experience as a teaching associate (TA) in training medical students for the gynecological examination. This method of using teaching associates who "teach on their own bodies" has evolved in medical schools across the country in recent years. It is an attempt to counter inadequate medical school preparation in this important area of women's health and to improve the physician-patient relationship in gynecological medicine. Lack of sensitivity to female patients has taken the form of high rates of malpractice litigation in gynecology, a situation which might well be reversed given the improved communication between physician and patient. Medical school teaching staff across the country have now widely accepted the use of teaching associates as the most effective teaching method for this part of the complete physical examination.

One of the ideas emphasized in this approach is that of the "activated patient." An activated patient is one who is fully and equally involved as a participant in the examination process. One projected outcome of this approach is greater personal responsibility for one's health such as doing self-breast exams. But the potential of using this approach goes beyond mere "disease prevention" of traditional medical care. It gives female patients a sense of control over what happens to them—both inside and out of a gynecologist's office—and enters a psychological and social health dimension that makes the concept known as "high-level wellness" accessible. In the context of medical intervention by physicians during the gynecological exam, the potential exists to take steps toward the goal of optimal wellness. This article attempts to explore that potential.

From *Health Values*, Vol. 10, No. 2, March/April 1986, pp. 33–36. Copyright © 1986 by Judith Schmidt. Reprinted by permission of the author.

"What's it like doing that sort of thing?" curious and sometimes incredulous friends ask. I have just told them about my job. I am a teaching associate (TA) for the instruction of the gynecological examination to first and second-year medical students. As such, I am a "professional patient." I give feedback to these students about their technique and attitude, and most important, about the way they communicate with me as a patient during the gynecological exam.

I respond to my friends' questions by telling them my job is demanding. I experience the same feelings that any woman facing a breast and pelvic exam does, including anxiety and nervousness. But overall, I feel good about doing it. I feel that what I am doing is important.

The next question, "Does it pay well?" The implication is that the only reason for my engaging in such an occupation must be money. "Yes, it does," is my answer. "And well it should! My job takes a good deal of knowledge and ability." Not only does it require knowledge of female sexual and reproductive anatomy, but it means that I must be comfortable discussing my own anatomy with others. It requires good teaching and interpersonal skills, plus a lot of sensitivity about a topic that is emotionally loaded for students and patient alike.

"But money isn't the main reason I do it," I explain. My own experiences with gynecologists have for the most part not been satisfactory. The opportunity to improve this area of women's health through my input into the training of medical students appeals to me. Also, as a student majoring in health education at the same university, I see the potential for patient education and the role physicians might play in this process. As a TA, I feel I have some influence in this direction.

"Does your job take training?"

"Yes it does," I respond, as I visualize our initial training sessions. In these first sessions, we learn right along with the medical students. We all become part of a "learning team" which I can now see is beneficial for reducing anxiety and developing a comfortable working relationship with the students prior to the actual examination.

Just as the medical students do, we watch the Bates videotape, "Female Pelvic Examination." And just as they do, we practice inserting the speculum and examining internal anatomy manually on the plastic Gynny model. As I practice using the speculum on the Gynny model, the idea then seems less scary to me. I wonder, as a health educator, whether offering other women this experience on a Gynny model prior to a pelvic exam might lessen their anxiety, as it has mine.

In these initial training sessions my actual teaching role begins. I am called upon to recall my own feelings during the gynecological exam. The medical students are also encouraged to explore the kinds of feelings that they, as physicians, might experience. How should the physician, for example, handle a situation in the best interests of the patient and him or herself if sexually attracted to the patient prior to the examination? Issues such as these are dealt with in these sessions.

Emphasis in these training sessions is put on the importance of involving the patient during the process of the exam itself. An activated patient who is involved in such a way has some sense of control over what is happening to her during her exam. Again, as a teaching associate I am called upon to describe how being "activated" in this way as a patient allows me to feel less victimized during the gynecological exam.

Part of this initial discussion focuses on empathy. To learn to empathize with female patients, all the students are required to disrobe, drape, and get into the lithotomy position—or into the stirrups, as it is commonly called. Through this first-hand experience, medical students can vividly relate to the feelings of vulnerability shared by their female patients as they lie naked, legs suspended, waiting to be examined—covered only by a thin piece of paper that fails to intercept the cool flow of air over one's usually concealed private anatomy.

After these preliminary training sessions, my difficult work begins. I find that my anxiety soon disappears as I get actively involved in teaching. The students are much more nervous than I am so that relating to them in a calm and confident way has the effect of putting us both at ease.

The nature of the suggestions that I give during the actual examination stresses technique. I might suggest that a student flatten his or her hand while palpating my abdomen. I might help a student identify that fleeting moment when my ovaries roll past. But I do not emphasize the mechanics, as I know these will improve with practice.

The general feedback I give each student in turn afterward about how well he or she communicated with me and attended to my emotional needs is far more important. I begin by reinforcing those things which I like. This might include confirming that the student maintained eye contact with me and watched my face for non-verbal signals indicating discomfort. Or it might mean commending a student's effective use of firm and reassuring touch. Then, I follow with a suggestion for improvement. This might include suggesting to the student that he or she replace specialized medical jargon with common conversational language that the patient can more easily understand.

Occasionally, my job demands that I be assertive. For example, I had to tell a male student that I was uneasy having his groin against my knee, while having my breast examined—under ordinary circumstances a female patient might interpret this in a sexual way. We were both embarrassed, but he expressed appreciation for telling him this.

Only once did I find it necessary to tell a student about poor attitude. "I am uncomfortable with the way you treated me—as if I were a plastic model," I had to say. Fortunately, this is rare as most students are respectful and caring to the extreme.

I am proud of the student who is able to include me actively and equally as a participant. I keep a mental check-list during the exam of the various ways the student might accomplish this. Does the student remember to offer me a mirror? Does he or she offer it in such a way that is *not* just an off-hand question? ("Do you want a mirror?") But rather in a way so that *I,* as patient, understand that it is important and acceptable to know about my own female anatomy. "Would you like to hold a mirror while I examine your pelvic area? That way I can better explain to you what *I* see, and *you* can see everything for yourself?"

There are other check-offs on my mental list. Does the student offer me the option of having my head raised during the pelvic part of the examination to facilitate communication between us? Does the student actively solicit my verbal input; not just telling and explaining, but questioning and encouraging any questions *I,* as patient, might have regarding my anatomy or sexual functioning?

Finally, I consider certain non-verbal aspects of our communication exchange. I consider the student's attitude. Is it flippant or overbearing in any way? Does the student display appropriate respect and a willingness to share power in the interaction that goes on between us? What clues do I get from facial expression, body position and movement that support my assessment?

By assessing the answers to all these questions, I am able to evaluate how well I was activated as an involved and equal participant during the examination. When done effectively, this process allows me to feel in control—not as a passive bystander whose body is "being done to."

At this point, relating the notion of the activated patient to the idea of wellness begins. By actively engaging female patients in the gynecological exam itself, the physician can play an important role in aiding the female patient in knowing and being comfortable with her body. Not only might this have a spin-off effect of encouraging women to practice self-examination and prevention at home, (I am an example of one who only began doing regular self-breast exams since beginning this job even though I had long known the appalling statistics about breast cancer) but it might help overcome those cultur-

ally programmed negative feelings that many women still have about their bodies and lead to a greater degree of sexual satisfaction.

At the end of the teaching session, it is my time for reinforcement. The students all express their gratitude. They are relieved that doing a procedure that had worried them has turned into a positive learning experience; they give me credit. I accept their thanks and express my hope that they will use what they have learned here to make the experience of the gynecological exam a better one for their patients.

One of my fears when I took this job was how the students would react when we would meet in public after the training sessions. I knew this was inevitable as I am a student on the same campus in a small city. Contrary to my worries, I have not felt the slightest embarrassment. Rather I sense a mutual respect between us resulting from the difficult task we shared together.

This feeling of mutual respect might not be something peculiar to my own particular experience. Perhaps it is a reflection of this kind of interaction between a patient-oriented physician and an activated, involved patient. It is an interaction that is designed to allow the patient to feel more in control and, in so doing, to enhance her self-esteem.

The positive effect of this interaction for the patient and its contribution to her overall health status should not be minimized. Replacing negative feelings that many women still have regarding their sexual-reproductive anatomy with positive ones can enhance a woman's sense of well-being and personal fulfillment. Satisfying such a psychological health need represents a step on that continuum toward that elusive concept known as high level wellness. Entering this psychological and social health dimension goes beyond the purely physical realm of traditional medical care.

Medical intervention by a physician which attempts to accomplish such a task is a concrete way to lessen the gap between disease prevention and that lofty goal of optimal wellness. It is an intervention mutually rewarding to patient and physician alike.

BIBLIOGRAPHY

1. DiMatteo RM, Friedman HS: *Social Psychology and Medicine.* Oelgeschlager, West Germany, Gum and Hain, Publishers, Inc., 1982.
2. Miller GD: They gynecological examination as a learning experience. *Journal of the American College Health Association* 1974; 23(2).

Cadavers, Dolls, and Prostitutes:
Medical Pedagogy and the Pelvic Rehearsal

by Terri Kapsalis

My first question, as I suspect yours may be, was, "what *kind* of woman lets four or five novice medical students examine her?"—James G. Blythe, M.D.[1]

Fearing the Unknown

*I*n a paper entitled "The First Pelvic Examination: Helping Students Cope with Their Emotional Responses," printed in the *Journal of Medical Education* in 1979, Julius Buchwald, M.D., a psychiatrist, shares his findings after ten years of conducting seminars with medical students starting their training in OB/GYN.[2] He locates six primary fears associated with a first pelvic examination: (1) "hurting the patient"; (2) "being judged inept"; (3) the "inability to recognize pathology"; (4) "sexual arousal"; (5) "finding the examination unpleasant"; and (6) the "disturbance of the doctor-patient relationship" (when a patient reminded them of somebody they knew, e.g., mother or sister).

Because the pelvic exam produces fear and anxiety in medical students, numerous methods have been used to offer them a pelvic exam "rehearsal." This practice performance is meant to help soothe or disavow student fears while allowing them to practice manual skills. The types of practice performances adopted reveal and promote specific ideas about female bodies and sexuality held by the medical institution. The use of gynecology teaching associates (GTAS), trained lay women who teach students using their own bodies, is a relatively new addition to pelvic exam pedagogy that will be examined at length. Previous to and contemporaneous with this practice, medical schools have cast a variety of characters as subjects of this pelvic exam rehearsal, including actual patients, cadavers, anesthetized women, prostitutes, and plastic manikins such as "Gynny," "Betsi," and "Eva". The ways medical students have been taught to perform pelvic exams illustrate the predicament of the gynecological scenario, a situation in which a practitioner must, by definition, examine woman's genitals in a clinical and necessarily nonsexual manner. The array of pedagogical methods used to teach pelvic exams reveals how the medical institution views female bodies, female sexuality, and the treatment of women.

In pelvic exams, physicians-to-be are confronted with both female genital display and manipulation, two highly charged cultural acts. If students have previously engaged in gazing at or touching female genitals, most likely they have done so as a private sexual act (e.g., male students engaging in heterosexual activities and female students masturbating or engaging in lesbian activities). Occasionally there are male or female students who, for a variety of reasons, have had little or no exposure to naked female bodies, and their fears often revolve around a fear of the "unknown," which in the case of women's genitals takes the form of a particularly stigmatized mystery.

Students seem to find it very difficult to consider female genital display and manipulation in the medical context as entirely separate from sexual acts and their accompanying fears. Buchwald's list of fears makes explicit the perceived connection between a pelvic examination and a sexual act. "A fear of the inability to recognize pathology" also reflects a fear of contracting a sexually transmitted disease, an actual worry expressed by some of Buchwald's student doctors. Likewise, "a fear of sexual arousal" makes explicit the connection between the pelvic exam and various sexual acts. Buchwald notes that both men and women are subject to this fear of sexual arousal. "A fear of being judged inept" signals a kind of "performance anxiety," a feeling common in both inexperienced and experienced clinical and sexual performers. "A fear of the disturbance of the doctor-patient relationship" recognizes the existence of a type of "incest taboo" within the pelvic exam scenario. Buchwald shares anecdotes of students feeling sick or uncomfortable if the patient being examined reminded them of their mother or sister. Buchwald's work deviates from most publications dealing with the topic of medical students and pelvic exams. Largely, any acknowledgment of this precarious relationship between pelvic exams and sex acts is relatively private and informal, taking place in conversations between students, residents, and doctors, sometimes leaking into private patient interactions. For example, as a student in the 1960s, a male physician was told by the male OB/GYN resident in charge, "During your first 70 pelvic exams, the only anatomy you'll feel is your own." Cultural attitudes about women and their bodies are not checked at the hospital door. If women are largely marketed as sexualized objects of the gaze, why should a gynecological scenario necessarily produce different meanings?

Rehearsing Pelvics

Teaching medical practices is the act of constructing medical realities. In other words, the student is continuously learning by lecture and example what is right and acceptable and, conversely, what is wrong and unacceptable in medical practice. The intractability of medical teaching from medical practice is built into the very title of Foucault's *Birth of the Clinic*. The translator's note recognizes the importance of the choice of the word "clinic": "When Foucault speaks of *la clinique,* he is thinking of both clinical medicine and of the teaching hospital so if one wishes to retain the unity of the concept, one is obliged to use the rather odd-sounding clinic."[3] Medical pedagogy, including textbooks (the focus of the following chapter) and experiential learning, is symbiotic with medical practice; the two work together in the formation, transferal, and perpetuation of medical knowledge. With regard to pelvic exams, this medical knowledge has been acquired in a number of ways.

Many medical students have encountered their first performance of a pelvic exam on an actual patient. Oftentimes a group of students on rounds would repeat pelvic exams one after another on a chosen patient while the attending physician watched. If we consider that the pelvic exam is often sexualized by novice practitioners, this pedagogical situation resembles a "gang rape." Many times there is little communication with the woman being examined, nor is her explicit consent necessarily requested. Due to the intimidation of the medical institution, a woman may not resist repeated examination, even if she is adamantly against the use of her

body for pedagogical purposes. This actual patient situation is one that Buchwald locates as anxiety provoking for the medical student (he fails to mention the anxiety this may cause the woman being examined).[4] This situation adds to what Buchwald refers to as the student's "fear of being judged inept": "a frequent remark was, 'if the resident sees the way I'm going about it, he'll think I'm stupid.' In some respects what began to evolve was the image of the experienced, wise, worldly, and sexually competent adult (the resident or attending physician) sneering at the floundering explorations of an adolescent (the medical student) who is striving to become a 'man.'"[5] Buchwald's reading of this situation is gendered inasmuch as he compares the pelvic exam to an adolescent male rite of passage. This gendered reading is telling. The medical apparatus, particularly this 1970s version, incorporates specifically gendered male positions of physician and medical student. Even though there are increasing numbers of women medical students, physicians, and medical educators, the structures of this apparatus, specifically the structures of medical pedagogy, are in many instances unchanged or slow in changing and require a female medical student to fit into this masculinized subject position. Her relationship to this ascribed subject position, particularly as a medical student, may be uncomfortable, as she may be split between identifying with the woman pelvic patient (as she herself has most likely undergone such exams) and with her newly forming role as masculinized spectator. As a medical educator, I frequently witness such a split in female medical students. As Laura Mulvey describes, "trans-sex identification is a *habit* that very easily becomes *second nature*. However, this Nature does not sit easily and shifts restlessly in its borrowed transvestite clothes."[6] Although Mulvey is discussing female cinematic spectatorship, her words are applicable to female medical spectatorship as well. While the anxieties located and described by Buchwald as very "male" in nature may be the very same anxieties experienced by a female medical student, these anxieties take on different twists and meanings with female physicians-in-training.

Other than the attending physician, one person within the pelvic equation who might also judge the student as inept or whose presence might distract the student from performing a proper first exam and therefore cause the student anxiety, is the patient herself. Cadavers, anesthetized women, and anthropomorphic pelvic models like the plastic manikins "Gynny," "Betsi," and "Eva" are pelvic exam subjects who, for a variety of reasons, are rendered absent and therefore cannot talk back or have an opinion about the medical student's performance. These female models alleviate anxiety regarding inappropriate patient performance since they cannot possibly act out. The pedagogical use of these models may also have been developed in order to avert other student fears. If the woman's body is anesthetized, dead, or replaced altogether by a plastic model certainly there can be no fear of causing her pain. However, this logic is questionable in the case of the anesthetized patient: How might repeated pelvic exams under anesthetic affect how a woman "feels" both psychologically and physically when she wakens?

More importantly, the legality of this practice is extremely questionable. How many women would actually consent to this practice? Many women are anxious at the thought of a single pelvic exam, let alone multiple exams. Furthermore, the fear of a pelvic exam is often associated with feeling vulnerable and out of control; under anesthetic, a woman is particularly vulnerable and out of control. And yet teaching medical students how to do pelvic exams on anesthetized women appears to be widely practiced, although public discussion of this method outside (and inside) the medical community is relatively scarce.[7] At a 1979 conference sponsored by the Women's Medical Associations of New York City and State, New Jersey, and Connecticut held at Cornell University Medical College, this issue was discussed and found its way into the *New York Times,* where the conference recommendation was quoted: "If examined in the operating room, patients must be told prior to anesthesia that they will be examined by the members of the operating team, including the medical student."[8] Decades later this recommendation is often unheeded. For example, a surgical nurse I interviewed provided a common scenario: "While doing an exam on a woman who is sedated for a urological procedure, a physician may discover that she has a prolapsed uterus. The student or students observing the procedure will then be invited to perform a bi-manual exam on the woman [inserting two fingers in her vagina while pressing on her abdomen] in order to feel her uterus." I have overheard physicians at a prestigious Chicago medical school encouraging students to "get in surgery as much as possible to get pelvic exam practice." The assumption is that students will not be intimidated by an unconscious woman and that the patient will, in addition, have relaxed abdominal muscles, thus permitting easy palpation of her ovaries and uterus. Many physicians have not heard about such "practicing" and are outraged at the suggestion, maintaining that this is medically sanctioned sexual assault. Some physicians who are aware of the practice dodge the questionable issues, maintaining that for some students it is the only way they will learn.

But what *are* students learning in this scenario? By using anesthetized women, cadavers, or plastic models as pelvic exam subjects students are being taught that a model patient (or patient model) is one who is essentially unconscious or backstage to the performance of the pelvic exam; she should be numb to the exam, providing no feedback and offering no opinions. In the tradition of Sims's experiments, passive and powerless female patients are considered ideal "participants" in the learning process. In addition, students practicing on essentially silent and lifeless models are learning that the manual skills associated with completing a pelvic exam are more important than the fundamental skills needed to interact with the patient—skills that ideally would help the patient relax and participate in the exam.

Perhaps these rehearsal methods are used under the assumption that an anesthetized, dead, or plastic model is unerotic and will thus relieve students of Buchwald's fear #4, "a fear of sexual arousal." And yet the rendering of the object of manipulation or the gaze as passive simply heightens the power differential between examiner and examined that can in effect tap into an altogether different system of erotics. Necrophilia may be coded into a pelvic examination on a cadaver. Similarly, there have been noted cases of sexual abuse when patients are under anesthetic.[9] Likewise, the anthropomorphically named pelvic manikins "Gynny," "Betsi," and "Eva," with their custom orifices for medical penetration, could be recognized as the medical correlates to inflatable sex dolls.[10]

In the late 1970s, numerous medical pedagogues were reexamining what one physician referred to as "the time-honored methods" of pelvic exam pedagogy: students examining anesthetized women, conscious patients, cadavers, or plastic models.[11] The problems with these methods were discussed in a number of articles. The authors of the 1977 article "Professional Patients: An Improved Method of Teaching Breast and Pelvic Examination" in the *Journal of Reproductive Medicine* found that training medical students on actual patients "has many disadvantages, including infringement of patients' rights, inadequate feedback and moral and ethical concerns. Another approach that is widely used is the anesthetized preoperative patient. Again, problems include informed consent, increased cost and/or risk and lack of an interpersonal exchange. The introduction of the 'Gynny' and 'Betsi' models has been an attempt at improvement, but not without drawbacks, which include a lack of personal communication, unreal exposure and difficulty with 'live' correlation."[12] Where was the medical community to find these living models? Some went to what must have seemed a very natural source. In the early 1970s a number of schools, including the University of Washington Medical School and the University of Oklahoma Physician's Associate Program, hired prostitutes to serve as "patient simulators."[13] What other women would accept payment for spreading their legs? Logically, these educators felt that a prostitute would be the most fitting *kind* of woman for the job. In a sense, the patriarchal medical establishment took the position of a rich uncle, paying for his nephew, the medical student, to have his first sexual experience with a prostitute.

This gendered suggestion assumes that female medical students are structurally positioned as masculinized "nephew" subjects as well.

Although lip service has been paid to the supposed importance of desexualizing the pelvic patient, in choosing prostitute patient models, medical educators inadvertently situated the exam as a sexualized act. They must have thought that only a prostitute would voluntarily submit to exams repeatedly and for nondiagnostic purposes. Or perhaps the underlying assumption was that a lady *pays* to get examined whereas a whore *gets paid* for the same exam. It may have also been assumed that prostitutes are more accustomed to and have a higher tolerance for vaginal pain than other women and would thus be more fitting practice models for novice students. In choosing to hire prostitutes as patients the boundaries of pornographic and medical practice were collapsed. Within this scenario of a hired prostitute, the student physician was put in the position of a medicalized lover or "john." Certainly Buchwald's fear #3, "a fear of sexual arousal," was confirmed and even encouraged by hiring prostitutes. Buchwald notes that certain students "appeared to project their anxiety by asking, 'what should I do if the patient starts responding sexually?'"[14] By hiring prostitutes as pelvic patients, the medical establishment not only enforced the trope of the "seductive patient," but also paid for it.[15] "Playing doctor" in this pelvic rehearsal cast with patient prostitutes threatened to translate the pelvic exam into an act of sexualized penetration and bodily consumption.

In many cases when prostitutes were hired, the medical student was led to believe that the woman being examined was a clinical outpatient rather than a prostitute. Thus the prostitute still had a relatively passive position in the training of medical students. In order to properly perform her role as clinical outpatient, she could offer the student little feedback. In addition, the working logic of the medical educators remained relatively opaque inasmuch as the student was not directly learning about the medical establishment's opinion of model patients. And yet these attitudes undoubtedly found their way into medical practice. Years later, students are still told by certain unaware medical faculty that GTAS are prostitutes. Today certain faculty still conclude that no other *kind* of woman would submit her body to multiple exams in exchange for a fee. This points to the importance of understanding the recent history of pelvic pedagogy. Those physicians trained in the 1970s are the same physicians practicing and educating today.

Some physicians found fault with the use of prostitutes as pelvic models. According to the authors of "Utilization of Simulated Patients to Teach the Routine Pelvic Examination," "the employment of prostitute patient simulators is not satisfactory. The prostitutes employed by the PA (Physician's Associate) program were

not articulate enough to provide the quality of instructive feedback necessary for an optimal educational experience. Their employment was costly at $25 per hour, and that expense prohibited their extensive and long-term use. Also, and more importantly prostitutes had abnormal findings on examination prior to their utilization."[16] Pathology was not desirable in these model patients: in the pelvic rehearsal, students were not to be distracted by abnormal findings. Rather, the patient simulator needed to be standardized as normal like the plastic model. In addition, the prostitute was expensive. She received market value for her bodily consumption, unlike the income-free corpse, indebted actual patient, and the cut-rate graduate students that the authors of the article hired at $10 per hour. And although prostitutes did offer some student critique (comments such as "poor introduction," "too serious," "too rough," and "forgot to warm the speculum") their language skills were not medically acceptable.[17] What the medical establishment needed was a model who could engage in medicalese, was more cost efficient, and had normal, healthy anatomy. The GTA would be the answer.

The GTA Program

In 1968 at the University of Iowa Medical School's Department of Obstetrics and Gynecology, Dr. Robert Kretzschmar instituted a new method for teaching junior medical students how to perform the pelvic exam.[18] For the pelvic model he used a "simulated patient," first defined in the medical literature as a "person who has been trained to completely simulate a patient or any aspect of a patient's illness depending upon the educational need."[19] Many simulated patients were actresses and actors hired by the medical establishment to realistically portray a patient. Their critical feedback was not traditionally requested. They simply served as a warm body for the practicing student. This stage of Kretzschmar's program was not dissimilar to the other programs that hired prostitutes. Initially, Kretzschmar adhered to this simulated patient model. He hired a nurse for the role of patient. She agreed to repeated exams by medical students; "however, it was necessary to compromise open communication with her, as she was draped at her request in such a way as to remain anonymous."[20] The curtain rose but the nurse's knowledge, thoughts, feelings, and face remained backstage. All that was revealed was the object of the exam: the woman's pelvic region. The logic behind draping the simulated patient presumed that if "only a whore gets paid" for a nondiagnostic exam, perhaps the nurse could avoid whore status by becoming faceless and silent.

In many gynecology textbooks, as will be examined in the following chapter, a similar logic prevails. Photographs picturing women are cropped so that faces are not shown or bands are placed across eyes to maintain the model's anonymity. If the woman's face and eyes are pictured, the photo could enter the realm of pornography; the woman imaged cannot be soliciting or meeting the medical practitioner's gaze, a potentially sexualized act. If the nurse who served as simulated patient was draped to maintain her anonymity she was in effect attempting to desexualize her body for the medical gaze. But is this an effective strategy for the desexualization of the exam? Is a faceless, vulnerable female body less erotic? In addition, although this professional patient model rehearsal did save actual patients from the task of performing the role of pelvic model, it did little to encourage communication between student and patient. Maintaining such anonymity taught the students that it was acceptable and even preferable for them to ignore the woman backstage behind the drape. They were also shown that a modest woman, unlike a prostitute, would need to disassociate her face from her body. And therefore, a modest woman preferred to be treated as though she were anonymous and invisible.

In 1972, Kretzschmar instituted a different program. The new simulated patient, now named the gynecology teaching associate (GTA), would serve as both patient and instructor, stressing the importance of communication skills in addition to teaching the manual skills required to perform a proper pelvic exam. Unlike the nurse clinician who was first hired as a simulated patient in 1968, the GTA would actively teach and offer feedback to medical students, forsaking any anonymity through draping. The GTAS first hired by Kretzschmar were women who were working on or had received advanced degrees in the behavioral sciences but who had no formal medical training. The women had normal, healthy anatomy and were willing to undergo multiple exams. They then received elaborate instruction in female anatomy and physiology, pelvic and breast examination, self-breast-examination and abdominal examination, with an emphasis on normal anatomy. They worked in pairs, one GTA serving as "patient" TA, one as "instructor" TA. They were assigned a small group of medical students and conducted the educational session in an exam room. The "patient" TA received the exam, role-playing as patient and co-instructor, while the "instructor" TA remained alongside the students, helping and instructing them during the exam. After receiving two exams the "patient" TA changed from gown to street clothes and became "instructor" TA, and the "instructor" TA changed from street clothes to gown to become the "patient" TA. The teaching session was then repeated with a new group of medical students, thus assuring that one TA of each pair would not receive all the exams.

Kretzschmar's GTA model provided a radically new way of teaching medical students how to do pelvic and breast exams. No longer was the simulated patient a teaching tool; now she was both teacher and patient. The women's movement undoubtedly influenced this model. In the 1960s and '70s women were demanding better health care and some took matters into their own hands by establishing self-help groups and feminist clinics. In fact, many early GTAS were directly associated with these groups and clinics and believed their new position within the medical establishment as GTA could allow them to bring their alternative knowledge to the heart of the beast.

Kretzschmar received a variety of critical responses from the medical community for his new GTA program. Some were positive, applauding him for his innovative method and his success in avoiding a "men's club" attitude by hiring women as teachers.[21] Some, however, were skeptical at best. They were particularly cautious regarding the GTAS' motives for participating in such a perverse endeavor. The epigraph to this chapter—"What *kind* of woman lets four or five novice medical students examine her?"—was a question asked by many physicians, according to Kretzschmar. Some human subjects committee members who reviewed the GTA concept "felt that women who were willing to participate must be motivated by one or more of several questionable needs, such as desperate financial circumstances (in which case exploiting their need would be unethical). Others fear the women would be exhibitionists or that they would use the pelvic exam to serve some perverse internal sexual gratification (in which case portraying them as normal to medical students would be irresponsible)."[22] Once again, the pelvic exam was compared to a sexual act by the medical establishment. Cultural fears regarding female sexuality and its perversions surface in these objections to the GTA program. Only a nymphomaniac would seek out multiple exams, enjoying repeated penetration with speculums and fingers. Also, poor women might lower themselves to such embodied work out of desperation, thereby aligning the GTA with the prostitute in an explanatory narrative. Furthermore, the committee questioned the psychological stability of the GTA, with the assumption "that women who are emotionally unstable might be attracted to the program, or that undergoing repeated examination might be psychologically harmful."[23] These human subject committee members reveal their nineteenth-century ideas about (white) women: frail female psychological health and sexual health are seen as mutually dependent and delicate partners. If their equilibrium is tipped by the "pleasure" or pain incurred by the excessive sexualized act of multiple pelvic exams, then who knows what horrors will take place.

Unquestionably, teaching female genital display and manipulation has been the cause of a great deal of anxiety. These fears are much more reflective of the medical institution's constructions of the female psyche and female sexuality than of any actual threat to women posed by the role of GTA. One reason the role of GTA could seem threatening to these critics is that they were faced with a new and potentially powerful position for women in the predominantly male medical establishment. Their attempt at pathologizing the GTA could have been propelled by a desire to maintain the status quo: that *normal* women are passive, quiet, disembodied recipients of a hopelessly unpleasant but necessary pelvic exam. For them, perhaps this was the least threatening alternative.

Despite its early critics, Kretzschmar's model has become the pedagogical norm in the vast majority of institutions. Over 90 percent of North American medical schools employ this instructional method, recognized as "excellent" by the Association of Professors of Gynecology and Obstetrics Undergraduate Education Committee.[24] Many GTA programs throughout the country maintain the same basic form as Kretzschmar's 1972 incarnation, though there is some variation. For example, some schools have GTAS working alone, rather than in pairs; a few schools still hire the more passive live pelvic model or "professional patient" to be used in conjunction with an instructing physician. The use of pelvic manikins, anesthetized women, cadavers, and actual patients continues to supplement some student learning.

Beginning in 1988, I was employed as a GTA by the University of Illinois at Chicago (UIC) medical school. Periodically, I also taught at two other Chicago-area medical schools and in one physician's assistant program. Excepting one institution, all my teaching experiences have followed Kretzschmar's GTA model. For the institution that had not adopted Kretzschmar's model, I worked as a "professional patient." A physician or nurse-midwife served as instructor, and I was hired primarily to model the exam for three students and the instructor. Whenever a clinician-instructor was unable to attend, I volunteered to work as both instructor and model, adopting a variation of Kretzschmar's model.

In discussing the GTA, I will collapse the roles of instructor and patient GTA into a single role. While this is reductive of the complexity of the partner relationship assumed by the instructor and patient GTAS, it may help clarify their common mission. And indeed many schools have collapsed the roles of the two GTAS into a single GTA who is paired with three or four students. After years of teaching, I find this to be a better model. It is impossible for students to position the instructor as silent patient if she is the only educator in the room. When there is a single teacher who also serves as "patient" students are faced with the jarring experience of examining a woman who knows more about gynecological exam than they do.

The Teaching Session

The students enter the exam room, where the GTA wears a patient gown. She is both their teacher and the object of their examination. The GTA explains the purpose of the teaching session. She is a healthy woman with normal anatomy who is there to help the students learn how to perform a proper breast and pelvic exam. Medical students, however, have been indoctrinated into a system that privileges pathology. They have learned that what is normal and healthy is not as interesting as what is abnormal and unhealthy. Some students seem disappointed when they are told that the GTA session is one part of their medical education in which they will not be presented with pathology.

The GTA explains that the patient, performed by herself, is there for a yearly exam. She has no complaints. Rather, they are there to have the experience of examining a normal, healthy woman and thus should offer the "patient" feedback after each part of the exam, letting her know that "everything appears healthy and normal." The GTA emphasizes that no woman can hear the phrase "healthy and normal" too much. For many medical students "healthy" and "normal" are new additions to their medical script. Often, these second- and third-year medical students admit that the GTA session is the first time they have been encouraged to use these words. In a moment that struck me as simultaneously encouraging and tragicomic, one student, upon hearing me discuss the phrase "healthy and normal," pulled a 3 x 5 notecard and pen out of his pocket. He then said, "Tell me those words again. I want to write them down so I can remember them." In medical pedagogy, pathology is the norm, and normalcy is often viewed as mundane or unremarkable. For a woman in need of her yearly pap smear, the clinician's preoccupation with pathology can have sad consequences, both adding to the woman's anxiety about the possibility of the clinician finding that something is wrong and leaving her with the feeling that something is wrong regardless of actual clinical findings.

During the GTA session, other aspects of the students' scripts are rewritten and relearned. They are taught to use words that are less sexually connotative or awkward. For example, "I am going to *examine* your breasts now" as opposed to "I'm going to *feel* your breasts now." A number of script adjustments are made: "insert" or "place" the speculum as opposed to "stick in"; "healthy and normal" as opposed to "looks great." Changes are encouraged with regard to tool names: "footrests" as opposed to "stirrups"; "bills" rather than "blades" of the speculum.

When I was working as a "professional patient" with a young white woman physician as instructor, she kept referring to the "blades" of the speculum while teaching the students. I explained to her that many people within the medical community were replacing the term "blades" with "bills" because of the obvious violent connotations of the term, especially given that it refers to that part of the speculum placed inside the woman's body. The physician replied, agitated, "Well, we don't say it to the *patient*." Her assumption was that words that circulate within the medical community do not affect patient care or physician attitudes toward patients as long as those words do not reach the patient's ears. This is naive and faulty thinking, resistant to change, disabling the idea that language does indeed help structure attitudes and practice.

Furthermore, in that scenario *I* was the patient and the word "blade" was being used to refer to the part of an instrument that was to be placed inside *my* body. My thoughts were largely ignored even though I was hired to perform the role of patient. For the rest of the session, the physician begrudgingly used the word "bills," looking at me and punching the word each time she used it. Weeks later I worked at the same institution with a young white male physician whose language was considerate and carefully chosen and who continually encouraged my feedback and participation within the session. He consistently referred to the "bills" of the speculum of his own accord. By seeking out a patient's opinion and input within both a teaching situation and an actual exam, the clinician is relinquishing a portion of control and offering the patient more power within the exam scenario. As is evident in these two examples, gender does not necessarily determine a clinician's attitudes toward patients or the patient model.

The GTA offers many tips on how the clinician may help the patient feel more powerful and less frightened during an exam. "Talk before touch" is a technique used in the pelvic exam by which the clinician lets the patient know that she or he is about to examine the patient: with the phrase "You'll feel my hand now," the clinician applies the back of her or his hand to the more neutral space of the insides of a patient's thighs. Since the patient cannot *see* where the clinician's hands are, this technique offers her important information about where and when she will be touched.

Eye contact is another important and often ignored part of the pelvic exam. The GTA reminds the student to maintain eye contact with her throughout most parts of the exam. Many women complain that oftentimes clinicians have spoken at their genitals or breasts rather than to them. Eye contact not only offers the clinician another diagnostic tool, since discomfort and pain are often expressed in a patient's face, but it also makes the patient feel as though she is being treated as a person rather than as fragmented parts. In order to facilitate eye contact, the students are taught to raise the table to a 45-degree angle rather than leaving it flat. This has the added benefit of relaxing the woman's abdominal muscles. Specific draping techniques are taught so that the student-clinician cannot hide in front of the drape, ignoring the parts of the woman that reside backstage behind the curtain.

Given that the medical institution routinely segments and dissects bodies for examination, maintaining eye contact with the patient is often difficult for students. Considering the sexual overtones of this particular exam, many students (and practitioners) find it very difficult to meet their patient's gaze. Likewise, there are patients who will not look into their examiner's eyes due to shame or embarrassment or a desire to be "invisible." While this is always a possibility, the GTA asserts that the practitioner must initiate eye contact even if the patient declines the offer, so that the patient at least has a choice of whether to "look back" at the clinician.

Similarly, the GTA encourages students to continuously communicate with the patient, informing her as to what they are doing, how they are doing it, and why they are doing it. For example, the student must show the woman the speculum, holding it high enough so that she can see it (without aiming it at her like a gun), while explaining, "This is a speculum. I will insert this part, the bills, into your vagina, opening them so that I can see your cervix, the neck of your uterus. I do this so that I can take a pap smear, which is a screening test for cervical cancer." Many women have had dozens of pelvic exams without ever having had the opportunity to see a speculum. More often, they hear the clanking of metal as the speculum is snuck out of its drawer and into their vagina.

Clinicians should not use words that patients will not understand, nor should they patronize patients; rather, they should piggyback medical terms with simpler phrases. In addition, students are taught that women should be given verbal instruction when they need to move or undress. For example, the woman should not be handled like a limp doll as a clinician removes her gown for the breast exam; instead the woman should be asked to remove her own gown. This helps her feel a little more in control of her own body and space. Ideally, the pelvic exam can become an educational session and the patient a partner in her own exam.

Lilla Wallis, M.D., an OB/GYN professor at Cornell University Medical School and a strong advocate of the GTA program, promotes this idea of "the patient as partner in the pelvic exam,"[25] and in addition encourages the use of many techniques popular within the women's health movement. Wallis adopts what some institutions might consider radical techniques. For instance, she urges clinicians to offer patients a hand mirror so that they might see what is being done to them. The patient is encouraged to look at her own genitals and not feel as though this were a view limited to the practitioner. Wallis also questions the draping of the patient: "This separates the patient from her own body. It suggests that the genitals are a forbidden part of her body that she should modestly ignore. It also isolates the doctor."[26] Instead, she believes that patients should have the choice of whether to be draped or not. She refers to the use of GTAS as "a quiet revolution" in American medical schools, believing that GTA programs will lead to better, more thoughtful care by physicians.

Is the rehearsal with GTAS enough to change medical attitudes about women, female sexuality, and women's bodies? Can the use of GTAS actually affect these attitudes? While I was working as a "professional patient" or "model" at an esteemed Chicago-area medical school, an interesting sequence of events happened that pointed out to me the vast difference between teaching students as a GTA and serving as a "model." The physician I was to be working with was delayed at a meeting, so I started working with the four medical students. I stressed patient communication, helping the woman relax, "talk before touch," and educating the woman during the exam. The students were responsive, as the vast majority of students are, understanding my explanations for why these techniques were important and making an effort to adopt them as they made their way through the breast and pelvic exam.

I had finished teaching all four students how to do a breast exam and two students had completed pelvic exams, when the physician, a young white man, rushed in, apologizing for being late. He then proceeded to contradict much of what I had taught the students. I argued my points, but he insisted that many women were not interested in explanations or education but just "wanted it to be over with." He taught students a one-handed technique so that only one hand ever got "dirty," leaving the other hand free. He basically ignored my presence, so much so that at one point I had to dislodge his elbow, which was digging into my thigh as he leaned over, bracing himself on me, to see if my cervix was in view. The two remaining students were visibly more nervous than the students who had already had their turns. They were rushed and forgot "talk before touch" in an attempt to incorporate the shortcuts that the physician had taught them.

At the end of the session, he encouraged the students to get into surgery to examine as much pathology as possible: "I have an 18cm uterus I'll be working on. Come by." I pictured this enlarged uterus alone on a surgical table without it's woman-encasement. He assured the students, "The only way you're going to learn what is normal is to see a lot of pathology." I had emphasized the wide variety of what is normal, how vulvas were all different and that students would need to see a lot of normal anatomy to understand what was not normal. After this physician's intrusion, the lone female medical student in the group kept looking at me at each point the physician contradicted me. She smiled at me empathetically, understanding the severity of the emotional and political sabotage I must have been feeling as both an educator and a naked woman "patient." Before the students left, three of the four shook my hand, genuinely thanking me for helping them. The one student who had been resistant to some of the techniques I had taught them was more suspicious. He said to me sternly, "Can I ask you, what are your motivations for doing this?"

The View From the Table

Implicit in the role of the GTA is a fundamental contradiction. On the one hand, she is an educator, more knowledgeable than medical students about pelvic and breast exams although she holds no medical degree. In this sense she is in a position of power, disseminating various truths about the female body and it's examination. On the other hand, the GTA is bound to a traditionally vulnerable and powerless lithotomy position: lying on her back, heels in footrests. Oftentimes, her body is viewed as the true learning tool, with her words taking a back seat to this "hands-on" educational experience. In an interview, one GTA expressed her frustration: "Sometimes I feel like it's strange being nice, being like an airline hostess of the body. For example [she points two fingers as stewardesses do at cabin exits], 'Now we're coming to the *mons pubis.*' You have to be nice. I've seen some GTAS who were strong and businesslike about it, and I don't feel comfortable doing that but it's a strain having to be nice." This is a beautiful metaphor for describing the GTA'S predicament: She is there to make medical students comfortable as they journey across the female body. Comparing the GTA to an airline hostess highlights the pink-collar service role she performs: she is working for the medical school in a position that only women can fill and she is there to make the students feel less apprehensive and more knowledgeable. The fact that she needs to be "nice" while presenting her own body points to one of the performative aspects of the GTA'S role as educator. Like the stewardess, the GTA is costumed with a smile, a well-defined script, and a uniform.

In her book *The Managed Heart: Commercialization of Human Feeling,* Arlie Russell Hochschild connects Marx's factory worker to the flight attendant; both must "mentally detach themselves—the factory worker from his own body and physical labor, and the flight attendant from her own feelings and emotional labor."[27] The case of the GTA becomes an interesting blend of these two types of alienation. She is like the flight attendant in that she manages her own feelings, what the GTA above calls "being nice." She must learn how to deal with the occasional hostile or overtly sexual medical student customer. She is there to make the student's trip through the female body comfortable, safe, and enjoyable. But it is her own body, not the meal tray or the fuselage of the airplane, that she is presenting to the paying customer.[28] In this sense, the GTA is like Marx's factory laborer who uses his own body. She is getting paid for her body's use-value in the production of a trained medical student.

Structurally, with regard to physical labor and the management of feelings, the GTA resides in a position similar to that of a prostitute. Both GTAS and prostitutes sell the use of their body for what may be loosely termed "educational purposes." Both must manage their feelings, acting the part of willing recipient to probing instruments. Medical school history aside, GTAS and prostitutes have a good deal in common. This is perhaps why numerous GTAS have remarked on their husband's or partner's discomfort with their work. Certainly not all GTAS have partners who consider their teaching to be a sexual act and so object to or are threatened by it. But partner discontent is not uncommon. One GTA explains, "My boyfriend had problems with my teaching when I first moved in with him. It didn't bother him before I was living with him. I moved in only a couple of months before we got married and then he started voicing his complaints. . . I think they [significant others] are afraid it's sexual and I think the students are afraid it's sexual. They're afraid about how they're going to react, whether they're going to be aroused, but it's so clinical." Another GTA present at this interview said she had a similar problem in that her boyfriend was "concerned" and "uneasy": "I said to him if you're going to give me $150 to sit with you or have sex with you or whatever, fine, otherwise I'm going to make my money."

GTAS' partners are not the only ones who have been distressed by the GTA role. Some early women's health activists expressed a different kind of uneasiness as they quickly realized the pink-collar nature of the job. When the GTA program was first starting in the 1970S, these feminist health activists participating in the project sensed that they were still expected to mimic a patriarchal medical performance, employing language, techniques, and attitudes that reinforced the established power differential between pelvic exam clinician and female patient. These groups felt that working for a medical school did not allow them enough autonomy to teach what were, for them, important exam techniques. They believed that change within the medical establishment was virtually impossible and encouraged women not to participate in pelvic teaching within medical schools.[29] Of these GTAS, some simply discontinued their work with medical students. Others continued teaching self-motivated medical students who would voluntarily visit feminist self-help clinics for continuing education. These feminist teachers regarded this new experience as highly valuable. As one activist notes: "The rapport experienced by the program participants and the [feminist teaching] nurses had been astounding . . . The result was an exploration with students of such topics as sexuality, abortion, contraception and ambivalent feelings regarding their roles."[30] After refusing the medical institution's version of a proper pelvic exam rehearsal, these health activists composed their own.

In his article about medical students' six fears of pelvic exams, Buchwald accepted student fears without either questioning why young physicians-to-be would have such fears or searching for the cultural attitudes underlying them. Indeed, he might have been employing a Freudian psychoanalytic model that would entirely justify such fears: faced with the abject, castrated vulva, medical students *would* be terrified by the exam. These feminist teachers who rejected the GTA program, however, confronted and questioned student fears, realizing the importance of helping these future caregivers shed deep anxieties and ambivalences regarding female bodies. For years, medical pedagogues blatantly sidestepped these issues by employing teaching methods that would simply ignore or Band-aid student fears: hiring prostitutes would confirm student ideas regarding promiscuous female sexuality and its relationship to the pelvic exam; the use of plastic manikins would soothe student fears of touching real female genitals; while the use of anesthetized women and cadavers would present an unconscious "model" patient. Only with the use of GTAS have medical schools attempted to incorporate women patients' thoughts, feelings, and ideas into pelvic exam teaching. And yet, as these feminist teachers pointed out decades ago and as my experiences have occasionally confirmed, it may be impossible to educate students properly within the medical institution given unacknowledged cultural attitudes about female bodies and female sexuality.

• • •

The pelvic exam is in itself a pedagogical scenario. The woman receiving the exam, despite the political or philosophical orientation of the clinician, is taught attitudes about female bodies. In this respect, the physician is as much a pedagogue as a healer, if the two roles can be separated. In teaching medical students, one is therefore teaching teachers, transferring knowledge, methods, and attitudes to those practitioners who will in turn conduct private tutorials with individual women who seek their care. Thus the methods used to teach medical students how to do pelvic exams significantly structure how these physicians-to-be will educate their future patients. The various ways medical students have been taught to do pelvic exams are intimately related to the medical institution's attitudes toward women and in turn structure how future practitioners perceive and treat their women patients.

The use of GTAS alters the normal pelvic scenario to some degree. Here the "doctor" is being educated by the "patient," a potentially powerful role for the GTA. As an educator, she may critique the student from the patient's perspective (e.g., "Use less pressure," "you're not palpating the ovary there"). One would think that the medical student would not argue with the woman who is experiencing the exam. And yet, because the GTA is not a physician, the student is sometimes skeptical of her expertise, doubting her advice even if it is based on her bodily experience. The very fact that her experience is bodily may serve to deny the importance of her role. Her embodiment of the exam makes her a curious and suspect educator in the eyes of many since she is being *paid* for the use of her body in addition to her teaching skills. Her role continually elicits questions about what *kind* of woman she must be to undergo multiple exams.

In the GTA'S educational performance there is no hypothetical signified, no abstract female body; rather the GTA is a fleshy referent with her own shape, anatomical variation, and secretions. At the site of the GTA, medicine, pornography, and prostitution mingle, highlighting medical attitudes regarding female sexuality, vulvar display, and genital manipulation. The teaching session may be a "representation" of a "real" exam, but for the GTA, as well as the medical student, it is simultaneously representation *and* practice.

It is curious, but not surprising, that the medical institution has focused so much attention on the GTA'S role. Instead of focusing on what *kind* of woman would allow multiple exams to be performed on her, physicians might be more justified in asking how the medical establishment perceives the proper pelvic model or model patient. Or to turn the question back onto the medical institution itself, one might ask what *kind* of man or woman will *give* multiple exams. Unless there is a continued investigation of the medical structures that construct and reflect attitudes about female bodies and sexuality, the answer to this question might indeed something to really fear.

For references, see original source.

Health Care Rationing

— by Adriane Fugh-Berman, M.D.

Although health care rationing already exists in this country, it is more subtle, more convoluted, and more pathological rationing than that which exists in any other country. Poor people get less health care and the relatively rich get more health care. Ironically, neither group gets optimal health care. We tend to confuse high-tech diagnostics and therapeutics with good health care (as in the statement "The United States has the best health care in the world . . ."), but health itself is in short supply even in our well-insured populations.

We already have rationing—in the best light, it is random rationing; at worst, it is rationing only for the poor because it is based on the ability to pay. Emergency rooms (ERs) have become the primary care provider for many of the uninsured and underinsured. They are not very good places to get primary care: one rarely sees the same provider twice; ER personnel are so overworked that they are irritable with those they don't consider to be bonafide emergencies; preventive health care is not possible; and follow-up is rarely adequate. Emergency rooms have become a nightmare because once the wards fill up, there is no place to put new patients until an inpatient dies, is discharged, or is transferred. Meanwhile the patients stay in the emergency room, with more coming in all the time. At some point, the ER may close and is said to be "on diversion", meaning that ambulances are not to deliver patients there. There are occasions when every hospital in New York City is on diversion and ambulances must drive around until one of the ERs opens up. There is regular meal service in New York City ERs, a necessity because the average waiting period between the time a patient is officially admitted and the time he or she actually gets a bed is 24 hours. Some patients wait days, psychiatric patients may wait a week. Many of the doctors who work in the ER are excellent; care is compromised not because doctors aren't conscientious, but because they are overwhelmed.

Patients are sent home before they are ready to leave the hospital because DRGs (diagnostic-related groups) limit how long people can stay on the basis of their diagnosis, not their actual condition. Doctors learn tricks: I have kept a patient on intravenous medication when I could have switched him to oral medication because this would allow the patient to stay in the hospital longer. Patients are transferred from public to private hospitals if they can pay and, more commonly, from private to public hospitals if they cannot. It is not so very different from the days of segregated hospitals; these days we separate by ability to pay instead of by race.

Other public hospitals stagger and sway under the weight of the chronically ill, the acutely ill, the casualties of the drug wars, the boarder babies, the mental patients, the dysfunctional adults who cannot be discharged because they have no place to go. In New Jersey each hospital bill carries a 13% surcharge to help make up for uncollected bills (nationally, uncompensated care totaled more than $8 billion in 1988). Hospitals try to make up the money elsewhere, through such mechanisms as government subsidies. Private hospitals court well-off patients with carpeted floors, gourmet meals in private rooms, grooming services—or establish high-profit services such as open heart surgery.

Prince George's Hospital Center in Maryland was recently fined for its mini-version of an equitable health plan; they were charging patients who could pay more in order to subsidize patients who couldn't pay.

The Montefiore-associated Family Health Center is a model of excellent health care in the South Bronx. Because it is in an underserved area, it received Federal funds until some bureaucrat decided that because the clinic was now in the underserved area, the area was no longer underserved and therefore not entitled to more funds . . .

Public hospitals provide less than optimal care because they are overloaded. This results in a diffusion of attention to patients, a survivalist mentality among health care practitioners, and discouraging mortality statistics. Washington, D.C. General Hospital, for instance, has been disparaged unfairly. This hospital takes care of the poorest and the sickest patients, so the death rate is higher because patients arrive sick. Some of the patients who don't do well have been transferred from private hospitals, which are blatantly allergic to patients without insurance. One study found that 87% of patient transfers to Cook County Hospital in Chicago were the result of lack of medical insurance. Almost a quarter of the patients were medically unstable before being transferred and were transferred anyway (Schiff, et at., *New England Journal of Medicine* Vol. 314, no.9, Feb. 27, 1986, "Transfers to a public hospital").

Medicaid covers less than half of the nation's poor. It was not meant to do otherwise. One must be not only poor, but often far below the poverty level in order to qualify—in Alabama a family of three is ineligible for Medicaid if its annual income exceeds $1,416 (*Washington Post*, Jan. 6, 1991).

Many people who are not poor have no health insurance, including people working for small businesses, part-time workers, the self-employed, and those taking early retirement. Uninsured women are much less likely to undergo screening for breast cancer, cervical cancer, or glaucoma (diseases in which screening is worthwhile and where early intervention is crucial). Five million women of childbearing age (15–44 years) are covered by private health insurance—but it often doesn't even pay for prenatal care! (*Consumer Reports*, August 1990).

Employers are reluctant to hire older workers because their health insurance premiums are so high. Many insurance companies now require a negative HIV test result before granting coverage.

Insurance for Whitman-Walker Clinic health workers more than quadrupled in a year and a half, nearly driving the primary provider of service to HIV-positive patients in Washington D.C. bankrupt. Although HIV-positive patients are in the most dire need of insurance, they are the least likely to get it. We have accepted that the sickest patients should bear the greatest financial burden. Isn't that health care rationing?

In 1989 the American Medical Association took out a series of Canada-bashing ads which accused our northern neighbors of rationing health care. A picture shows a young girl with the caption: "In some countries she could wait months for her surgery." Another reads "Elective surgery: should it be up to you or up to a committee?" It is interesting that when the most powerful lobby for the medical profession in the U.S. takes aim at Canada, all it could come up with was diversionary whining. Yes, you may wait months for ELECTIVE surgery in Canada. It's called elective for a reason; it means it is not an emergency. If it's an emergency, you get faster service. There are far too many "elective" procedures done in the United States.

Canadians are very happy with their system; and a majority of Americans would prefer it too. So what if you have to wait for elective surgery—Canada has us beat on life expectancy (longer), infant mortality (lower), and spending percentage of GNP (lower).

Although England's National Health Service is having problems of its own because of intentional dismantling by Conservative governments, it's kind of fun to bring it up to those who oppose a National Health Plan. It always provokes the same response: "Did you know that you can't get kidney dialysis there if you're over 55?!" And in this single example it's true that it is relatively easy to obtain dialysis here (because of a rider attached to a Congressional bill). You're not entitled to preventive medicine, prenatal care, routine medical care, dental care, hospital care, prescriptions, home health care, or anything else—but if your kidneys fail, rest easy! It's the one medical condition that we actually take care of in this country.

While poor patients don't get enough health care, patients who can pay suffer excess procedures and tests. Good insurance, in fact, is a reliable risk factor for Caesarean-sections.

A study published in *JAMA* (Jan. 2, 1991) found that women with good insurance were much more likely to have repeat C-sections than were uninsured women. Despite recommendations that it is safer for women who have undergone a previous C-section to have vaginal births, 87% of women in this California study who had C-sections undergo repeat C-sections for later births. In private, for-profit hospitals, the rate was more than 95%

(*Washington Post* 1/2/91). It has been said that the only way to reduce C-section rates is to raise the physician compensation rate for vaginal deliveries above that for C-sections!

Some firms use telemarketers to contact patients and offer them free physicals. The offer is only made to well-insured patients whose insurance carriers are later billed for as much as $30,000. Patients may receive an 18-panel urinalysis, a 26-panel blood workup, an EKG, echocardiography, sonograms of vital organs and the vascular system, and pulmonary function tests. None of these tests are valuable for routine screening although telemarketers are instructed to tell the clients that these tests are good preventive medicine! (*Medical Economics,* July 23, 1990, "Is this the ultimate health care fraud?").

The answer to these problems is a national health plan. The answer is not to pour more money into Medicaid. It's not to pass a bill on long-term care. It's not to pass a catastrophic health bill. It's not to pass a women's health bill. The problems are all related to the fact that we have no minimum standard of care to which every person is entitled. As a society, we would rather complain about the inequity of rationing high-tech care while people are dying from lack of access to simple, boring, but essential, low-tech care. We have chosen to ration primary care and preventive medicine on the basis of ability to pay. We have chosen not to ration the resources to keep permanently comatose patients alive, to try to save babies who weigh less than a pound, to do organ transplants and other high-tech procedures. We can ration by choice or we can ration by chance. These are our only options. Isn't it time we made better choices?

Toward Universal Coverage

from Public Citizen Health Research Group's
Health Letter
September 1998 Vol. 14, No. 9

The following is a reprint of an op-ed by Robert Kuttner, co-editor of the *American Prospect,* that appeared in the 7/14/98 edition of *The Washington Post.*

President Clinton recently made headlines by ordering the Department of Health and Human Services to deny Medicare contracts to health insurance companies that discriminate against high-risk consumers. And the Democrats and Republicans are currently outdoing each other to crack down on the excesses of HMOs.

It is encouraging to see both parties addressing the public's distress over misdeeds by private health insurers. But this sort of piecemeal regulation is useful only to spotlight the abuses of the present system. As policy, it runs the risk of adding more layers of bureaucracy without addressing the deeper problem of a fragmented, profit-oriented health system.

In such a system, insurers pursue profits in two basic ways. They avoid covering people who are sick or likely to get sick. And they work to minimize the costs of treatment of sick people they can't avoid covering. This strategy, of course, is at odds with the whole point of health insurance.

HMOs put out a great deal of publicity about how they emphasize wellness, prevention and coordinated care. This certainly described the community-oriented, non-profit group health plans of a generation ago.

But today's for-profit HMO's lack that social mission. They are responsive mainly to Wall Street. They have much higher patient turnover than old-fashioned pre-paid group plans, so it doesn't make economic sense for them to invest in your lifetime wellness. And the cost savings that can be garnered by more comprehensive screenings and vaccinations pale next to the savings available from avoiding sick people and limiting care.

Current regulatory policy toward HMOs mirrors the patchwork nature of the health insurance system. Most states now prohibit health plans from denying a new mother two days in the hospital; they require HMOs to pay for reasonable emergency room care and inpatient mastectomies. But it is just not practical to regulate health care, one condition at a time.

The federal Kennedy-Kassebaum law requires insurance companies to offer coverage at reasonable prices to people who've lost their health insurance because they moved or changed jobs. However, Kennedy-Kassebaum offers no assistance to people seeking insurance for the first time, and it is maddeningly vague on what is meant by reasonable prices.

But the worst consumer abuses of the present HMO system are not touched by any of the proposed legislation or regulation. These include doctor-compensation formulas that make the doctor's income contingent on how much care is withheld; subtle marketing practices by managed care companies that make plans attractive to healthy subscribers and unattractive to sick ones; and elaborate protocols that get between doctor and patient, aimed mainly at saving money.

If government tries to remedy these abuses one at a time, the consequence will be ever more creative marketing and pricing by insurance plans, ever more astute legal maneuvers—and thicker books of regulations. Meanwhile, private insurers are turning away from seeking contracts to operate Medicare and Medicaid programs, because it turns out that the old and the poor are expensive to cover—imagine that. And with for-profit companies skimming the cream of the well population, government gets stuck with the costly cases, which then busts government's budgets, which then leads to reduced government payments and so the cycle continues.

The only way to cut through this mess is, of course, to have universal health insurance. All insurance is a kind of cross subsidy. The young, who on average need little care, subsidize the old. The well subsidize the sick.

With a universal system, there is no private insurance industry spending billions of dollars trying to target the well and avoid the sick, because everyone is in the same system. There is no worry about "portability" when you change jobs, because everyone is in the same system. And there are no problems choosing your preferred doctor or hospital, because everyone is in the same system. There's a common theme here.

All national health insurance systems are facing cost squeezes, because people are living longer and costly new medical technologies keep being invented. But no national health system rewards doctors for denying care. It took the U.S. private sector to come up with that one.

It is ironic, to say the least, that our desire to keep health insurance in the private sector led to less patient choice, more gaps in coverage, more clinical interference by private bureaucrats and a backlash of (mostly ineffectual) government regulation. At some point, one hopes soon, this system will collapse of it's own weight and universal health insurance will be back on the national agenda.

Scientific Terms Explained

by Adriane Fugh-Berman, M.D.

Some of the terms you'll come across repeatedly in this book may be unfamiliar to you. It's worth learning them, since they're universally used to explain the results of scientific experiments. and knowing them will not only help you read this book but will stand you in good stead when you read about scientific experiments elsewhere.

Fortunately, scientific terminology isn't hard to learn. That doesn't mean you're going to remember every single term after reading this chapter once. Just let whatever sticks in your mind stick, and ignore the rest. Then, when you encounter a term you're not sure about, refer back to this chapter, or look it up in the index. (I've boldfaced the terms where they're defined in this chapter, to make them easy to find.)

Study is a very broad term that covers almost everything that's looked at objectively. A human participant in a study—that is, one of the people whose responses, reactions or whatever are being studied—is called a **subject.**

A **case study** is a report on one unusual subject by a doctor. Both case studies and stories patients report themselves are called **anecdotal evidence.** Doctors joke that if we see two cases, we say we're seeing something "time after time," and if we see three cases, we call it a **case series.** Joking aside, a case series should consist of at least five cases. Case series are useful for indicating that something interesting is going on that may merit more formal study.

A **survey** is a kind of study that reports the results of interviewing people on whom no **intervention** is done. (Compare *trial,* below.) Since nothing new—no new drug, procedure, dietary restriction or whatever—is given to them or done to them, we say surveys are **observational.** Like the three studies cited in the *Introduction,* surveys simply try to discover how common a disease, treatment. condition or behavior is—or what **correlations,** or **associations,** there may be between various diseases, behaviors, etc. (There's a subtle distinction between a *correlation* and an *association* that isn't worth going into here.)

A **positive correlation** means that the more you have of A, the more you have of B. A **negative** (or **inverse) correlation** means that the more you have of A, the *less* you have of B. So, for example, there's a positive correlation between a high-fat diet and heart disease (the more fat you eat, the greater your chance of getting heart disease), and a negative correlation between eating broccoli and getting certain cancers (the more broccoli you eat, the smaller your chance of getting these cancers).

Correlations can't prove anything absolutely. For example, just because an increased number of storks in an area coincides with an increased number of births, that doesn't prove that storks bring babies.

How many people have a given condition at a given point in time is called its **prevalence** (for example, the number of color-blind people per 100,000 in the US today, or the number of people who were carrying tuberculosis bacteria on January 1, 1900). How many new cases of a condition occur over a given period of time is called its **incidence** (for example, the number of babies born in a given year who are color-blind, or the number of new TB cases in the last month). The study of prevalence and incidence falls into the field of **epidemiology,** which looks at patterns of disease and the factors that influence those patterns.

A **retrospective study** looks to the past for clues—you start with the disease and try to find out what caused it. For example, retrospective studies found that the prevalence of cigarette smoking among patients with lung cancer was higher than the prevalence of cigarette smoking among people without lung cancer. (Since you can't intervene in the past, all retrospective studies are observational.)

Retrospective studies can be large or small. To improve their quality, the **case-control** method is often used. This means that, when comparing a group with the disease to a group without it, the two groups are matched as closely as possible with regard to factors like age, sex, geographic location or any other variable that might affect the likelihood of getting the disease. The perfect case-control study would be of a group of identical twins where one twin in each pair developed a disease and the other twin in each pair didn't.

A **prospective study** is one in which subjects are followed forward in time instead of backward. Unlike retrospective studies, prospective studies can be either observational or interventional. Two famous prospective trials are the Nurses' Health Study, in which about 100,000 nurses have been answering annual questionnaires since 1976, and the Health Professionals Follow-up Study, in which about 50,000 physicians and other health professionals have been answering annual questionnaires since 1986.

By analyzing their responses, many associations have been discovered, including the positive correlation between hormone replacement therapy and breast cancer (that is, hormone replacement tends to increase one's risk of getting breast cancer) and the negative correlation between vitamin E intake and cardiovascular disease (that is, taking E tends to decrease heart disease risk).

Unlike a survey, a **trial** is a study in which the subjects receive an experimental intervention. Since you can only intervene in the present, not in the past, trials are always prospective. A **clinical trial** is one in which the subjects are human—as opposed to **preclinical trials** that use animals, bacteria, cells, etc.

In a **controlled trial,** at least two groups are compared. The **treated,** or **experimental** group receives the intervention, while the other—called the **control group** or simply the **control**—doesn't. Or different groups may receive different interventions. The groups studied in a trial are also called **arms.**

In a **placebo-controlled** trial, an inactive pill or procedure—the **placebo**—is given to the control group. *Placebo* is Latin for *I will please [you];* placebos got that name because any intervention, including simple attention, tends to make people feel better. Certain conditions, such as headaches, arthritis and hot flashes, are particularly responsive to placebos—as are some individuals.

Overall, the average **placebo effect** is an astonishing 33% (although it can range from much lower to much higher). In other words, an average of a third of the subjects in clinical trials will report significant improvement simply from being given a sugar pill (or some other placebo). So to demonstrate that a treatment works, you have to show that it does significantly better than the placebo that's given to the control group.

A **randomized** trial is one in which subjects are assigned to different groups as randomly as possible—by flipping a coin, or using a random number generator. If the researcher decides which subjects go into which group, or if the subjects assign themselves, intentional or unintentional **bias** can creep in and the groups may no longer be comparable (all the sicker patients might end up in one group, for example).

A **crossover** trial is one in which each patient is in each group at different times. For example, group A starts on drug X, and group B starts on the placebo; then, midway through the trial, the subjects are crossed over to the other arm (group A starts taking the placebo and group B starts taking the drug).

Blinding (sometimes, but less frequently, called **masking**) means that the researchers and/or the subjects don't know which group each subject is in. In a **single-blind** study, the subjects don't know but the researchers do (theoretically, it could also mean that the subjects know and the researchers don't, but there wouldn't be much point to that). Most nonsurgical studies are at least single-blind, since subjects' knowing whether they're getting an experimental treatment or a placebo is obviously likely to affect their responses.

In a **double-blind** study, neither the researchers nor the subjects know which group the subjects are in; all information is coded, and the code isn't broken until the end of the trial. (An exception is made when the difference between the two groups is so pronounced—everyone in the control group is dying, say, and everyone in the treated group is getting well—that it would be unethical to continue to deny the treatment to the controls.)

Double-blinding is important because researchers can give subtle, unconscious cues that can change subjects' responses quite independently of the treatment being tested. If the researchers don't know who's getting the treatment and who's getting the placebo, they can't put out those signals.

Saying that a treatment worked in 50% of the subjects tested obviously means a lot more if you're talking about 2000 subjects than if you're talking about two. So a good researcher involves statisticians before a trial begins in order to determine the **sample size** (the number of subjects) that will be necessary to show that the results are **statistically significant**—that is, unlikely to be due to chance.

Statistical significance isn't black and white; it's a matter of degree—what are the *odds* that this result was due to chance? It's measured by something called the **p value** (the *p* stands for *probability*). P values look like this: <.1, <.05, <.01, etc. (< means *less than*). To translate a p value into English, move the decimal point two spaces to the right and say "percent."

A p value of <.01 means that the probability that the results occurred by chance is less than 1%. That's a good study. A p value of <.1 means that the probability that the results occurred by chance is less than 10%. That isn't so great, since it means that there's almost one chance in ten that the results are meaningless. In general, a p value of <.05 is considered statistically significant.

A large sample size helps to control for **confounding variables** (also called **confounding factors** or simply **confounders**). For example, a small trial on cardiovascular disease might happen to have a larger number of smokers in one group than the other. In this case,

smoking would be a confounding variable, since it's known to cause cardiovascular disease.

If the sample size is large enough, however, one can assume that known—and unknown—confounders will be evenly distributed between the groups. To see why this is, imagine flipping a coin. If you flip it ten times, there's a reasonable chance it will come up heads 70% of the time (7 heads, 3 tails). If you flip it a thousand times, there's almost no chance it will come up heads 70% of the time (700 heads, 300 tails).

To put all this together—the gold standard for medical research is a prospective, randomized, double-blind, placebo-controlled trial with a sample size large enough to produce a p value of <.05 or lower. Many of the studies in this book don't achieve that standard—but then neither do most of the studies behind conventional medical therapies. If I limited the studies cited here to ones that meet that standard, this wouldn't be a book but an article . . . a short article.

Still, it's useful to know what the gold standard is, because everything—including trials of conventional medical therapies—should be held up to it. (Studies that don't meet the standard aren't necessarily wrong, but they're not proof. Future trials should adhere to the gold standard as much as possible.)

There are just a few more terms you should know. A **meta-analysis** is a relatively new kind of study in which you combine the results from a number of selected trials in order to come to some general conclusions. Meta-analyses are usually done when a number of small trials give ambiguous, conflicting or statistically insignificant results. When all of the decent trials are combined, there may be enough subjects in the combined treatment group to reach a statistically significant conclusion.

Let's say we're doing a survey of weights in a tiny village that has just eleven inhabitants. There are five children, who weigh 40, 50, 65, 65 and 65 lbs (the last three are triplets); three women, who weigh 105, 110 and 125 lbs; and three men, who weigh 150, 160 and 840 lbs (this last guy has a hormonal disorder).

If we add up all the weights, we get 1780 lbs; if we divide that by 11, we get 162 lbs. This is the **mean**—it's what we're talking about when we use the word *average* in everyday speech. But it would be very misleading to say that the average person in this village weighs 162 lbs, since all but one of the inhabitants weigh less than that. To deal with situations like this, statisticians have come up with two other kinds of averages—the median and the mode.

The **median** is the value in the middle of the distribution—the one halfway between the bottom and the top. In this particular example, the median—105 lbs—gives a much better idea of the average weight than the mean does.

The **mode** is the value that occurs most frequently; in this example, it would be 65 lbs (the triplets). In some distributions, the mode is a better indication of what's representative than either the mean or the median.

The **FDA** (the Food and Drug Administration, a regulatory agency of the federal government) requires specific kinds of trials on human subjects before it will approve new drugs. (Animal studies and the like have typically been done before these trials take place.) A **Phase I** trial simply tests for safety; it's usually done on healthy volunteers, without a control group.

In a **Phase II** trial, the drug is given to people with the condition or disease to be treated; it supplies some preliminary data on whether the treatment works, and supplements the safety data of the Phase I trial. Phase II trials may or may not use a control group.

A **Phase III** trial assesses efficacy, safety and dosage, compared with standard treatments or a placebo. Phase III trials are usually randomized and controlled.

Phase I, II, and III trials are usually performed as part of an **IND** (an *investigational new drug* application to the FDA). After the Phase III trial is completed, the manufacturer can submit an **NDA** (a *new drug application*) which requests permission to market the drug.

Not routinely required, **Phase IV** studies are done after drugs are approved by the FDA and can be sold to the public. They're randomized trials or surveys that attempt to evaluate longterm benefits and risks.

Finally, **in vitro** (literally, "in glass") refers to studies done in artificial environments like test tubes, and **in vivo** to studies done in living organisms.

The Safety of Silicone Breast Implants

by Diana Zuckerman, Ph.D.

Silicone breast implants have been sold in the United States since the early 1960's, although their long term safety in human beings was not studied until the 1990's. Because of the lack of medical scrutiny, it is not known how many women in the United States have silicone breast implants, although experts estimate one million. The major controversy that has emerged in recent years is whether silicone breast implants are safe, and whether they are responsible for the illnesses that have been reported by many of the more than 400,000 women who have filed law suits against the manufacturers. *This Briefing Paper focuses on the published epidemiological research on silicone breast implants, summarizing what is known and what is not known about the health risks.*

The use of silicone to increase breast size started shortly after the end of World War II, when liquid silicone was first injected directly into the breasts of Japanese prostitutes to make them more attractive to American G.I.'s (Anderson, 1990). In some cases, the silicone migrated to other parts of the body, such as the arms, lungs, and liver, causing horrible deformities or even death. Rather than stopping the procedures, how-ever, efforts were made to improve the results by mixing the liquid silicone with additives such as oil, to produce scarring that would keep the silicone in place. Within a few years, similar procedures spread to Las Vegas, Hollywood, and elsewhere in the United States, where equally disastrous results for an estimated 50,000 women led to controversy about whether the problems were caused by the silicone or the additives.

Because of the continuing safety and aesthetic problems, in the early 1960's two plastic surgeons suggested to Dow Corning Corporation that they develop silicone breast implants, which were composed of a silicone elastomer envelope containing silicone gel (Braley, 1972). Saline implants, which consist of silicone envelopes filled with saline, were developed in 1968. Like the injections, these implants were produced and sold without having been tested on human beings to determine whether they were safe or effective.

In 1976, the Medical Device Amendments to the Food, Drug, and Cosmetic Act gave the Food and Drug Administration (FDA) the responsibility to regulate all medical devices for the first time (see chronology in Table 1). Since breast implants had previously been sold in this country, they were "grandfathered in" and therefore allowed to stay on the market even though the manufacturers had not submitted proof of their safety and efficacy to the FDA (Kessler, Merkatz, & Schapiro, 1993). The FDA was responsible for eventually requiring that "grandfathered" medical devices be proven safe and effective, however, and FDA scientists considered implantable devices a high priority since their likelihood of harm seemed greater than for non-implanted devices such as surgical gloves, which the FDA also regulated.

By the 1980's, silicone breast implants had become a major segment of plastic surgery practices in the United States. Approximately 80 percent of the implants were used to increase the size of healthy breasts, while 20 percent were for reconstruction after mastectomy for cancer or other illnesses or trauma (Brown, Langone, & Brinton, 1998). In 1988, the FDA publicly announced that in 30 months, manufacturers would be required to submit research data proving that their silicone gel implants were safe and effective.

By 1990, approximately one million American women had breast implants, but there were still no published clinical trials, case/control studies, or epidemiological research studies indicating whether they were safe.[1] In December of 1990, a Congressional subcommittee responsible for monitoring the FDA, chaired by the late Rep. Ted Weiss (D-NY), held hearings aimed at encouraging the FDA to follow through on its 1988 announcement by requiring implant manufacturers to submit safety studies (Hearing of the Government Operations Subcommittee on Human Resources and Intergovernmental Relations, Dec. 18, 1990).[2] Dr. Diana Zuckerman of the Congressional committee staff reviewed copies of all the studies and other documents in the FDA's possession regarding the safety and efficacy of breast implants. In reading these boxes of documents, Congressional staff found that for many years, FDA scientists and advisors had expressed their concerns to FDA policy makers regarding the potential health risks of breast implants in internal memoranda (reproduced in Hearing, Dec.18, 1990). The staff concluded that there

was no evidence that independent, systematic research had been conducted on human beings to evaluate the long-term safety of the implants (Staff Report of the Committee on Government Operations, December 1992). Instead, most of the published reports were in plastic surgery or cosmetic surgery journals, where surgeons would describe the experiences of their patients, primarily in terms of cosmetic results. These case reports were not systematic studies and did not evaluate potentially serious short-term or long-term problems, such as silicone migration, implant rupture, infection, or systemic disease. There was also a survey distributed by plastic surgeons to their former patients, which indicated high customer satisfaction; although this was referred to as a study, it was a marketing survey rather than a scientific study, and could not provide accurate medical information.

In 1991, when the FDA finally reviewed the implant manufacturers' studies to determine the safety and efficacy of breast implants, it became clear that many of the studies of women with implants had just been started. After contentious FDA hearings and a great deal of public controversy, in 1992 the FDA removed silicone breast implants from the market because of the lack of safety data (Kessler, 1992). The greatest concern was the growing evidence that breast implants did not "last a lifetime" as had been claimed, and would eventually break, leaking silicone into the breast that could migrate to other parts of the body, including vital organs. There was also clear evidence that even implants that were intact could "bleed" liquid silicone into the breast area, and this silicone could also migrate. Several journal articles indicated that implant patients might be at risk for autoimmune disease or cancer as a result of this leaking silicone. In addition, breast cancer was considered a potentially serious risk, because the implants interfered with mammography.

Although there were serious safety concerns, the lack of adequate studies meant that there was no clear research evidence regarding whether or not breast implants increase the risk of disease. In response to the request of some breast cancer advocacy groups that silicone gel implants fulfilled a "public health need" after a mastectomy, they remained available in what were described as very large clinical trials for women with mastectomies or to replace implants that were broken (Kessler, 1992). In these "clinical trials," the FDA instructed the manufacturer to restrict the use of silicone gel implants to patients for whom the physician determined that saline breast implants were not appropriate.[3] FDA scientists believed that the saline implants were safer than the silicone gel implants, because although both types of implants were made with a silicone envelope, the saline and other chemicals inside the saline implants were believed to be safer than silicone gel.[4] However, the saline implants had also been grandfathered onto the market and their manufacturers had not yet been required to provide evidence of safety to the FDA.

Table 1. Chronology of Events Related to Breast Implants[1]

1962:	The first silicone breast implants, made by Dow Corning, are implanted.
1976:	The Medical Device Amendments to the Food, Drug, and Cosmetic Act gave the FDA the responsibility to regulate all medical devices, including breast implants, for the first time. An FDA expert panel recommended that breast implants be placed in class II[2] because their safety was considered well-established.
Jan. 1982:	Because of reported problems, the FDA announced a proposal to place breast implants in class III, which would require studies of safety and effectiveness.
June 1988:	The FDA classified all breast implants into class III. After 30 months, the FDA could require that manufacturers provide data showing the safety and effectiveness of these devices.
Dec. 1990:	The U.S. House of Representatives Subcommittee on Human Resources and Intergovernmental Relations held a hearing criticizing the FDA for not requiring manufacturers to submit safety data.
1991:	The manufacturer of polyurethane-coated silicone breast implants removed them from the market; research indicated that the foam would degrade and release TDA, a known animal carcinogen. About 10 percent of women with breast implants had the polyurethane-coated type.
Apr. 1991:	The FDA required manufacturers of silicone gel implants to submit data showing the safety and effectiveness of the implants by July 9, 1991.
Sept. 1991:	The FDA required manufacturers to disseminate information to patients on the risks associated with breast implants.
Nov. 1991:	The FDA convened an expert panel to consider whether the data were sufficient to establish that silicone gel implants are safe and effective. Despite the lack of data, the panel advised the FDA that breast implants filled a public health need and should continue to be available while the manufacturers collected additional data.
Dec. 1991:	A California jury awarded more than $7 million to an implant patient, primarily for punitive damages. Within a few weeks, internal Dow Corning documents from the trial came to the attention of the FDA and the media.
Jan. 1992:	The FDA called for a moratorium on the use of silicone gel implants until new safety information could be reviewed by the panel.
Feb. 1992:	The FDA's expert panel met again to review new information on silicone gel implants, including case reports of autoimmune diseases and evidence that some early models leaked excessively.
Mar. 1992:	Dow Corning stopped selling all types of silicone implants.
Apr. 1992:	The FDA announced that silicone gel implants could be sold only as part of controlled clinical studies for reconstruction after mastectomy, correction of congenital deformities, or replacement for ruptured silicone gel implants. The FDA approved Mentor Corporation's study in July.
Jan. 1993:	The U.S. House of Representatives Subcommittee on Human Resources and Intergovernmental Relations issued a report criticizing the FDA's poor monitoring of silicone breast implants. The FDA published a proposal in the Federal Register calling for safety and effectiveness data for saline breast implants.
Mar. 1994:	Four breast implant manufacturers put together a global settlement proposal with a cap of $4.25 billion over 30 years. This settlement collapsed when Dow Corning filed for bankruptcy protection in 1995.
Dec. 1994:	The FDA issued a Talk Paper describing the types of studies required to demonstrate the safety and effectiveness of saline breast implants. Pre-clinical data were submitted throughout 1995, and final clinical data are expected by early 1999.

[1] This chronology is based in part on the FDA's *Breast Implants* Information Update, July, 1997.
[2] The FDA has three regulatory categories for medical devices. Class I and class II are for devices whose safety and effectiveness are well-established. Class II devices require safeguards, such as performance standards or surveillance studies. Class III devices must be proven safe and effective before they can be sold.

Research Findings

In the last few years, several articles have been published in well-respected medical journals, supporting some of the concerns expressed in 1992, and contradicting others. There is now clear evidence that many silicone gel breast implants rupture in the body, leaking silicone, sometimes without the woman's knowledge, and that this is much more likely among the thinner "second generation" silicone gel implants that were sold between 1973–87 (Peters, Smith, Fornasier et al., 1997). There has been no epidemiological evidence of increased risk of breast cancer in the published studies, although more research is needed to rule out a long-term risk of cancer (Brinton & Brown, 1997). The research also seems to indicate that several specific connective tissue diseases are not frequent problems among women with breast implants. However, there are conflicting results in published research, and many of the studies have been criticized for not evaluating enough women to draw conclusions about rare diseases and for not studying many of the symptoms and illnesses that women with implants have reported to their doctors. The most recent review of the autoimmune research, published in the *Journal of the American Medical Women's Association* in 1998 by scientists at the FDA and the National Cancer Institute, concluded that "the samples were too small to rule out an increase" and the studies were not properly designed to evaluate an "atypical syndrome" that could be unique to silicone (Brown, Langone, & Brinton, 1998). The published studies with their findings and shortcomings are described in greater detail below.

Methodological Shortcomings of Existing Epidemiological Studies

In order to determine whether breast implants are safe, it is necessary to conduct systematic long-term studies that evaluate the association between breast implants and the illnesses and symptoms that women with breast implants report. Prospective studies, which evaluate patients during the years following their implantation, are expensive and take many years to complete, so most studies have instead looked back at the health problems of women who have had implants for periods of time ranging from a few months to a few years. This review by the Institute for Women's Policy Research of the major published studies and of the reviews of those studies (e.g. Brown, Langone, & Brinton, 1998; Rawls, 1995; Silverman, Brown, Bright et al., 1996) indicates several basic methodological weaknesses:

1. **Virtually all of the studies focus on auto-immune diseases or cancer rather than the other health problems that the women are reporting, such as muscle pain and memory loss.**

2. **Most studies evaluate whether an individual has a well-established diagnosis for specified diseases, such as lupus and scleroderma, rather than evaluating the prevalence of symptoms that could be associated with a new or "atypical" syndrome.** There is scientific evidence that chemical exposures can cause "scleroderma-like" symptoms and other rheumatic diseases (Miller, in press; Zschunke, Ziegler, & Haustein, 1990).

3. **The studies do not provide long-term data,** despite an expected latency period for many diseases. Systemic illnesses may be more likely after implants are ruptured, which typically occurs 8–14 years after implantation (Robinson, Bradley & Wilson, 1995).

4. **The comparison samples in some studies are women who sought medical care, rather than healthy women.** Since most women who choose implants for augmentation are young and healthy, implant patients should be compared to a "control group" of similarly young, healthy women.

5. **Even in the largest epidemiological studies, the sample sizes are not large enough to identify substantial increases in the rate of rare diseases.** Diseases such as scleroderma that are diagnosed in less than one in 10,000 women in the general population (Zschunke, Ziegler & Haustein, 1990) can only be meaningfully evaluated in large samples; it is therefore surprising that the studies that have been conducted included only a few hundred or, at most, a few thousand women with breast implants.

6. **Most of the studies used convenience samples, which collected information intended for a different purpose, or collected data on patients from a few medical practices.** The results are not necessarily generalizable to all women with implants, and the medical information is sometimes limited because the data that were collected did not necessarily include the most relevant information.

Two studies, conducted by researchers at the Mayo Clinic and Harvard, have been frequently cited by some manufacturers and physicians as "clear evidence" that silicone breast implants are safe. The authors of these studies are more cautious than the individuals who cite them, pointing out that the studies focused only on several well-defined diseases but not other diseases or symptoms, and that the study samples were too small to detect even a doubling of some rare diseases. These studies deserve careful scrutiny and several of their limitations are described below.

"Mayo Clinic" Study

The first published "Mayo Clinic" study compared patients in Olmstead County, Minnesota who had breast implants with patients without breast implants regarding the reporting of classic criteria of rheumatological diseases in their medical records (Gabriel, Fallon, Kurland et al., 1994). The study made good use of existing medical information, but it did not supplement medical records with questionnaire or interview data, and it focused on classic disease criteria, so the results do not include information about other symptoms or "atypical" diseases. In addition, the comparison sample consisted of patients receiving medical care in facilities in the county, whereas most breast implant patients are very healthy women. The 749 implant patients in this sample are too few to provide reliable information about an increase in rare diseases, such as lupus and scleroderma; the authors estimated that they would need to study 62,000 women with implants for an average of 10 years to determine whether there was a doubling of the risks of rare diseases such as scleroderma, since their estimated incidence is usually estimated to be less than two per 100,000 women.

"Harvard" Nurses Study

The nurses study, conducted by researchers at Harvard University, was somewhat larger, including 1,183 nurses with breast implants, but only 876 were classified as having silicone gel implants (Sanchez-Guerrero et al., 1993). Like the Mayo Clinic study, this study evaluated connective tissue diseases using standardized criteria and did not study other types of illnesses, and the number of implant patients was too small to study very rare diseases such as scleroderma and lupus. Although this study also evaluated 41 "signs or symptoms" of connective tissue disease, these symptoms were not evaluated individually; instead, they were used to create 'possible' diagnoses of classic connective tissue diseases for women with several symptoms of those diseases.

The Harvard study was designed to minimize "reporting bias" of health problems by implant patients, by excluding any health problems diagnosed after May 1990, which was six months before the major media coverage of implant problems. The study was not designed to minimize some other kinds of bias; for example, the authors did not remove from the analysis the women who reported having received breast implants between 1952–1961, an obviously inaccurate response since breast implants had not yet been invented during that time. The inclusion of these misreported years increased the average years of implantation, which was reported to be 10 years. Moreover, implants sold prior to 1973 were made of a more rubbery silicone envelope

and thicker gel and are less likely to break (Peters, Smith, Fornasier et al., 1997). Therefore, the experts who are most concerned about implants believe that these thicker implants are less likely to cause illness. If thicker implants are safer, including women with thicker implants in the same analysis with other implant patients decreases the likelihood of a significant association with health risks. The study also included women with implants for only one month; including women who have had implants for such a short time again decreases the likelihood of finding an association with systemic health problems.

Other Studies Often Cited as Finding No Significant Risk

There are more than one dozen other published abstracts and studies that found no statistically significant health risks associated with breast implants. Each of these studies has several of the shortcomings numbered above. The authors have noted that their studies are inconclusive, usually because of the sample sizes and sometimes for other reasons, such as the small number of years after implantation. Several abstracts are based on unpublished studies with extremely small samples, so this review will focus on the most substantial, published studies, which also have clear limitations. For example, one study of autoimmune diseases included only 250 patients who had implants for an average of approximately 2.5 years (Shusterman, Kroll, Reece et al., 1993), and another study evaluated connective tissue diseases among 125 implant patients (Weisman, Vecchione, Albert et al., 1998). Even with their larger comparison samples, both of these studies include too few implant patients to provide meaningful information about these rare diseases. A recent Scottish study contacted all patients in South East Scotland who had silicone breast implants inserted between 1982–1990, but this resulted in an analysis of only 110 augmentation patients and 207 mastectomy patients (Park, Black, Sarhadi et al., 1998); these two groups were analyzed separately, although they were much too small to provide useful data when analyzed either separately or together.[5]

A Swedish study was based on a much larger sample, of more than 7,400 women with implants, averaging 8 years of follow-up information (Nyren, McLaughlin, Yin et al. 1998; Nyren, Yin, Josefsson et al., 1998). The results indicated no statistically significant increase in hospitalization due to neurological or connective tissue disease among implant patients; however, the authors acknowledge that even this sample size is too small to draw conclusions about any link between breast implants and the rare diseases that were studied. This study had similar limitations to other implant studies: only 56 percent of the implant patients had silicone gel implants, many of the patients had implants for a short period of time and implant patients were compared to breast reduction patients. However, this study has a more important flaw that limits the usefulness of the results: patients were considered ill only if their illness resulted in hospitalization, which excludes many patients with these diseases.

Given the rarity of many of the diseases analyzed in these studies, focusing on women with connective tissue diseases rather than women with implants is a reasonable alternative strategy chosen by several researchers. However, because so few women have breast implants, these samples still need to exceed several thousand in order to have statistical power to determine whether the implants are associated with disease. They also need appropriate comparison samples of women in the general population with similar health habits and demographic backgrounds. Table 2 indicates the comparison samples and inadequate sample sizes of the studies that have been conducted. Two of these studies reported nonsignificant higher rates of illness among implant patients. A third study, which included rheumatological patients, as its comparison sample, found nonsignificantly lower prevalence of certain types of illness among implant patients, but neglected to mention that there were higher levels of many other types of rheumatological illnesses among implant patients. The samples were so small that none of the differences were statistically significant and therefore they could have occurred by chance.

STUDIES FINDING SIGNIFICANT HEALTH PROBLEMS AMONG IMPLANT PATIENTS

Two of the largest studies have found statistically significant health problems among breast implants patients. In a study of 10,800 American women with all types of breast implants, Hennekens, Lee, Cook et al. (1996) found a statistically significant 24 percent increase in self-reported connective tissue diseases among implant patients compared to other women. These women were part of a much larger study of more than 426,000 women health professionals, who completed questionnaires between 1992–95. Although self-reported illnesses are considered less accurate than medical diagnoses, the fact that the women reporting them are health professionals increases the findings' credibility. The results suggest that breast implant research might be more likely to indicate health risks when the samples are larger and a wider range of connective tissue diseases are evaluated.

A study of 2,570 Danish women with breast implants also found a statistically significant association between breast implants and "muscular rheumatism, fibrositis, and myalgia" but not with rarer connective tissue diseases such as scleroderma or lupus (Friis, Mellemkjaer, McLaughlin et al., 1997). These symptoms were more than twice as likely among breast implant patients. Breast reduction patients and breast cancer patients without implants also had higher than expected reports of these symptoms, although the increase was not as dramatic as for implant patients. Like the previous studies, this study sample was too small to study rare diseases. There were other shortcomings: a very small minority had their implants for ten years or more, not all the implants were silicone gel, and illness was measured by hospitalization.

A new area of research is examining possible effects on the children of women with silicone breast implants (e.g. Levine & Ilowite, 1994). Given the lack of epidemiological studies, children's health will not be included in this review.

What Kind of Research Is Needed?

Overall, most of the published epidemiological studies found no statistically significant health problems among implant patients, but they usually did not include information about many of the symptoms that breast

Table 2. Nonsignificant Findings in Studies of Connective Tissue Patients

Hochberg et al., 1996	837 scleroderma patients compared to random control group matched for race, sex, and age group	7% more implant patients among scleroderma patients
Burns et al., 1996	274 scleroderma patients compared to random control group matched for race, sex, and age	30% more implant patients among scleroderma patients
Goldman et al., 1995	721 patients with Rheumatoid Arthritis or connective tissue disease compared to other rheumatology patients	55% fewer implant patients with these illnesses, but higher rates of implant patients among other rheumatology patients

implant patients have reported to their physicians, and they had methodological shortcomings that minimized the likelihood of finding significant health risks. Well-designed epidemiological studies would be substantially different from most existing studies, and would include the following design and assessment strategies:

1. The first step would be to **analyze the effects of specific types of implants separately,** instead of combining them. For example, saline implants should be analyzed separately from silicone gel implants; if there are too few saline implant patients to analyze separately, they should be excluded from the analysis rather than be included with the silicone gel patients. This is important because many experts believe that saline implants are safer than silicone gel implants; by including saline implants in a study of silicone implants, the researchers have increased the likelihood of finding no health risks.

   There are also **different types of silicone implants that should be analyzed separately.** In an ideal study, each brand of implant would be studied separately, but since many women do not know what kind of implant they have, and since some implants were not used by large numbers of women, this is not possible. Nevertheless, it is essential to analyze the polyurethane-covered implants separately, since it is known that the polyurethane sometimes disintegrates and can break down into TDA, a known animal carcinogen (Brinton & Brown, 1997). Separate analyses should also be conducted on double lumen breast implants, which consist of a silicone envelope that contains saline, antibiotics, and other substances surrounding an inner silicone envelope filled with silicone gel.

   In addition, it is essential to **separately analyze different "generations" of silicone gel implants,** because the "second generation" implants sold between 1973–87 are thought to be the most likely to cause problems, and the newest implants are of great interest because they are still being sold today. The implants sold in the 1960's are thought to be relatively safe because they have a thicker gel and thicker envelope than those sold since then and are therefore unlikely to break and leak large amounts of silicone (Peters, Smith, Fornasier, et al., 1997). In contrast, the implants sold in the 1990's are reportedly thinner than those from the 1960's but possibly less likely to bleed silicone than those in the 1970's and 1980's; in addition, they have been implanted for fewer years so they probably are less likely to be associated with health problems at this point in time. Since virtually all the large studies have included implants from the 1960's, 1970's, 1980's, and several have included implants from the 1990's, one would expect that these studies would be less likely to find evidence of health risks than studies that focus on the thinner "second generation" implants.

2. Research should focus on **long-term implant use.** Most of the studies have included women who had implants for short periods of time, such as one month. Since experts believe that long-term implantation is more likely to cause problems, analyzing a group of women that includes women who had implants for less than one year, or even less than five years, probably decreases the likelihood of finding a statistically significant association with illness.

3. One cost-effective strategy would be to conduct research on women with **ruptured implants,** since experts believe that silicone gel or liquid that has escaped from the implant is more likely to cause problems than an intact implant. This is related to the first and second points noted above, since implants that have been in place longer are more likely to be ruptured than recently inserted implants, and second generation implants are probably more likely to rupture than those older or younger. There are many reports of implants that ruptured within the first five years of use, however, so the duration of the implant placement is not the only factor influencing likelihood of rupture. By focusing on the "worst case scenario" of women with ruptured implants, and comparing them to women with intact implants for similar periods of time and women of the same age and similar demographic traits but no implants, it would be possible to gather more meaningful information using smaller samples.

4. Another essential design issue is to **separately analyze breast cancer patients and augmentation patients.** They have been analyzed together in most studies. The "public health need" of breast cancer patients is a major reason why silicone breast implants have remained on the market despite limited safety information, and yet very few breast cancer patients have been studied. There is some evidence that they have more implant problems than augmentation patients. Most breast cancer patients do not choose silicone gel breast implants, but it is essential that research be conducted on an appropriate number of the women who do.

5. In terms of outcomes, research is needed to evaluate **many measures of illness and health, not just auto-immune disease and cancer.** Implanted women report many symptoms, and some of these symptoms are not necessarily related to auto-immune disease or cancer. The selection of those diseases as a focus may have more to do with litigation than with current knowledge about implant problems. It would be appropriate to look at a wider range of

illnesses and symptoms, and determine how women with implants differ from other women of similar age and health habits. After all, the important issue for women is whether implants increase their risk of serious illness, not limited to cancer and classically defined connective tissue diseases.

Of course, when rare diseases are being studied, the number of women with implants must be adequate to meaningfully evaluate an increased risk of that disease.

6. **More research is needed on "local" problems, such as pain, hardening, and rupture.** Previous studies have focused on systemic illnesses, but local complications can seriously threaten a woman's quality of life, and women need that information before they make a decision about whether to get implants or whether to remove them. Although there is general agreement that rupture and breast hardening are problems, there is considerable debate about the frequency and severity of these problems and whether they can evolve into diffuse soft tissue pain syndromes.

7. In all studies, every effort should be made to **statistically control for any differences between implant patients and other women that could influence health,** such as age, weight, diet, and health-related behaviors such as smoking. This is essential to any epidemiological study, but only the most basic factors, such as age and race, were taken into account in most of the published studies.

In summary, much remains unknown about the risks of silicone breast implants. Studies that are not well-designed cannot provide conclusive information, whether there are two studies, 20 studies, or 200 studies. Therefore, breast implants cannot be considered safe based on the available research to date, and well-designed studies are essential in order to inform women about the safety of the implants that are currently in their bodies, as well as the newest implants that are still being chosen by thousands of women every year. Thus far, the burden of proof of safety has fallen primarily on manufacturers of breast implants under the regulatory oversight of the FDA. Unfortunately, this strategy failed for more than three decades, resulting in no epidemiological studies until lawsuits created a strong financial incentive to conduct research that would prove that implants are safe. In recent years, the major studies have primarily been funded by those with a financial interest in the outcome, such as the manufacturers or the American Society of Plastic and Reconstructive Surgeons, and the studies have tended to address the questions raised by litigation. Because the financial stakes are so high, it is especially difficult to trust the objectivity of manufacturer-sponsored studies, even when conducted by well-respected researchers.

Meanwhile, the FDA has allowed silicone gel implants to stay on the market in poorly implemented "clinical trials," and still has not required a single study of saline breast implants to be submitted for review. The hope that new research will provide the answers must be tempered by the knowledge that there are strongly vested interests on both sides, because hundreds of thousands of women have silicone gel implants in their bodies and the number of women receiving saline breast implants is now more than 120,000 each year, an increase of more than 1,000 percent since 1990.

Among the many unanswered questions, one will determine whether the others are answered: will the scientific community, with the support of the U.S. Department of Health and Human Services and private foundations, have the will and the funding needed to conduct the well-designed, independent research necessary to determine the long-term and short-term safety of both silicone gel and saline breast implants?

ACKNOWLEDGEMENTS

IWPR wishes to thank the panel of experts that reviewed this briefing paper, which included faculty from the Yale University School of Public Health and Johns Hopkins School of Medicine, and a former epidemiologist at Dow Corning. IWPR also wishes to thank the authors of several of the cited studies for their clarifications regarding their research findings. This Briefing Paper was written by Diana Zuckerman and formatted by Anna Rockett in November 1998.

ABOUT THE INSTITUTE FOR WOMEN'S POLICY RESEARCH

The Institute for Women's Policy Research (IWPR) is a public policy research organization dedicated to informing and stimulating the debate on public policy issues of critical importance to women and their families. IWPR focuses on issues of poverty and welfare, affirmative action and pay equity, employment and earnings, work and family issues, and the economic and social aspects of health care and domestic violence. The Institute works with policymakers, scholars, and public interest groups around the country to design, execute, and disseminate research that illuminates economic and social policy issues affecting women and families, and to build a network of individuals and organizations that conduct and use women-oriented policy research. IWPR, an independent, nonprofit organization, also works in affiliation with the graduate programs in public policy and women's studies at the George Washington University.

INSTITUTE FOR WOMEN'S POLICY RESEARCH INFORMATION NETWORK

The IWPR Information Network is a service designed to make IWPR products available on a regular basis to the widest possible audience and to facilitate communication among it's members. Individual and organizational members may receive complimentary or discounted publications, discounted registration to IWPR's policy conferences, and Research News Reporter, a monthly service that disseminates research in the news relevant to women and families and includes citation and ordering information.

NOTES

1. In 1990, there were published estimates of 2 million implanted women, which were later determined to be approximately double the accurate number based on the approximately 2 million breast implants that had been sold. Since many implants have been replaced at least once, and many women have had their implants removed, the estimated number of implant patients has been one million since the early 1990's.
2. Hereinafter referred to as Hearing, Dec. 18, 1990.
3. These "clinical trials" do not have control groups or comparison samples, and patients have complained to the FDA that their efforts to report health problems have not been included in these "studies."
4. Plastic surgeons frequently mix antibiotics and other chemicals with the saline that they put in the implants.
5. The comparison samples in all these studies are larger, but the implant sample sizes remain a serious shortcoming.

REFERENCES

Anderson, N. Testimony before the Subcommittee on Human Resources and Intergovernmental Relations of the Committee on Government Operations, U.S. House of Representatives, December 18, 1990.

Braley, S.A. The use of silicones in plastic surgery. Plastic and Reconstructive Surgery 1973: 51: 280–88.

Brinton, L.A., and Brown, S.L. Breast implants and cancer. Journal of the National Cancer Institute 1997; 89: 1341–49.

Brown, S. L., Langone, J.J., and Brinton, L.A. Silicone breast implants. Journal of the American Medical Women's Association 1998; 53: 21–24.

Burns, CJ., Laing, TJ., Gillespie, B.W. et al. The epidemiology of scleroderma among women: Assessment of risk from exposures to silicone and silica. Journal of Rheumatology 1996: 23: 1904–11.

Friis, S., Mellemkjaer, L., McLaughlin, J.K. et al. Connective tissue disease and other rheumatic conditions following breast implants in Denmark. Annals of Plastic Surgery 1997; 39: 1–8.

Gabriel, S.E., O'Fallon, W.M., Kurland, L.T. et al. Risk of connective-tissue diseases and other disorders after breast implantation. New England Journal of Medicine 1994; 330:1697–702.

Goldman, J.A., Greenblatt, J., Joines, R. et al. Breast implants, rheumatoid arthritis, and connective tissue diseases in clinical practice. Journal of Clinical Epidemiology 1995; 48: 571–82.

Hearing on protecting patients from dangers of silicone breast implants. Human Resources and Intergovernmental Relations Subcommittee of the Committee on Government Operations, U.S. House of Representatives, December 18, 1990.

Hennekens, C H., Lee, I.M., Cook, N.R. et al. Self-reported breast implants and connective-tissue diseases in female health professionals: A retrospective cohort study. Journal of the American Medical Association 1996; 275: 616–625.

Hochberg, M. C., Perlmutter, D.L., Medsger, Jr., T.A. et al. Lack of association between augmentation mammoplasty and systemic sclerosis (Scleroderma). Arthritis and Rheumatism 1996; 39: 1125–1131.

Kessler, D.A., Merkatz, R.B. and Schapiro, R. A call for higher standards for breast implants. Journal of the American Medical Association 1993; 270: 2607–8.

Kessler, D.A. The basis of the FDA's decision on breast implants. New England Journal of Medicine 1992: 326: 1713–15.

Levine, JJ. and Ilowite, N.T. Sclerodermalike esophageal disease in children breast-fed by mothers with silicone breast implants. JAMA 1994; 271: 213–16.

Miller, F.W. Genetics of environmentally associated rheumatic disease. In Rheumatic Diseases and the Environment, New York: Thompson Science, in press. J. Varga (Ed.)

Nyren, O., McLaughlin, J.K., Yin, L. et al. Breast implants and risk of neurologic disease: A population-based cohort study in Sweden. Neurology 50 1998; 956–961.

Nyren, O., Yin, L., Josefsson, S. et al. Risk of connective tissue disease and related disorders among women with breast implants: a nation-wide retrospective cohort study in Sweden. British Medical Journal 1998; 316: 417–422.

Park, A. J., Black, R.J., Sarhadi, N.S. et al. Silicone gel-filled breast implants and connective tissue diseases. Plastic and Reconstructive Surgery 1998; 101: 261–268.

Peters, W., Smith, D., Fornasier, V. et al. An outcome analysis of 100 women after explanation of silicone gel breast implants. Annals of Plastic Surgery 1997; 39: 9–19.

Rawls, R.L. Epidemiological work clashes with case studies suggesting implant risk. Chemical and Engineering News, December 11, 1995; 15–17.

Robinson, Jr., O. G., Bradley, E. L., and Wilson, D.S. Analysis of explanted silicone implants: A report of 300 patients. Annals of Plastic Surgery 1995; 34: 1–7.

Sanchez-Guerrero, J., Colditz, G.A., Karlson, E.W. et al. Silicone breast implants and the risk of connective-tissue diseases and symptoms. New England Journal of Medicine 1995; 332: 1666–70.

Shusterman, M.A., Kroll, S.S., Reece, G.P. et al. Incidence of autoimmune disease in patients after breast reconstruction with silicone gel implants versus autogenous tissue: A preliminary report. Annals of Plastic Surgery 1993; 31: 1–6.

Silverman, B.G., Brown, S.L., Bright, R.A. Reported complications of silicone gel breast implants: An epidemiologic review. Annals of Internal Medicine 1996; 124: 744–56.

Staff Report, The FDA's Regulation of Silicone Breast Implants, Human Resources and Intergovernmental Relations Subcommittee of the Committee on Government Operations, U.S. House of Representatives, December 1992.

Weisman, M H., Vecchione, TR., Albert, D. et al. Connective tissue disease following breast augmentation: A preliminary test of the human adjuvant disease hypothesis. Plastic and Reconstructive Surgery 1988; 82: 626–30.

Zschunke, E, Ziegler, V., and Haustein, U. Occupationally induced connective tissue disorders. Pgs 172–82 in Occupational Skin Disease, R A. Adams (Ed.); Philadelphia W B. Saunders, 1990, 172–82.

WORKSHEET—CHAPTER 1

Women and the Health Care System

1. The list below mentions a few of the issues women's health activists have organized around:
   - more women doctors
   - women's health centers run *by* women *for* women
   - self-help groups
   - better information for personal information decision-making
   - excellent health services equally available for rich & poor
   - more research on women's health issues

   a. If you were to identify the priorities for the activities for a women's health organization, list the rank that you would give to each of the above. (Are there different issues you would add to your six priorities?)

issue	b	c
1.		
2.		
3.		
4.		
5.		
6.		

   b. In the column b, for each of the issues above, identify whether that issue can (yes) be taken care of within the present system or (no) whether such a "demand" calls for fundamental changes in the health care system.

   c. In column c, for each of the issues, identify whether you think the last 20+ years of activism have improved this issue.
   - \-   = there have been set-backs
   - 0   = little change
   - +   = situation improved
   - ++ = situation very much improved

2. Building on information in several of the articles, describe how the gynecological exam becomes symbolic of the consumer/health practitioner relationship and identify things every woman should be able to expect as a part of a good gynecological exam.

3. Describe your "best" and "worst" health care experiences. Briefly, identify the behaviors (or other characteristics) which were different for the health providers in the two situations. Referring to "How to Tell Your Doctor a Thing or Two," can you identify ways that you were or were not an "active patient" in the two situations?

4. Outline *both* sides of the debate on the question, "Will increasing the number of women doctors increase the quality of care which women receive as health care consumers?"

   yes

   no

5. Pretend that you have been asked to give a short presentation on the women's health movement(s) work on bringing attention to women's health issues. Using both the Ruzek and Becker article and the Chesney and Ozer article, identify several key points you would make and how you might organize such a talk.

6. Pretend you are editing this book, outline the decision-making process you would go through in thinking through where to put the article on silicone breast implants. (Be sure to read the introduction to this chapter and the article before you answer this question.)

CHAPTER 2

Diversity and Health Issues

A core part of developing an analysis of women's health issues is working towards an understanding of why "some women have a better chance of being healthy than other women." This involves learning how racism, anti-semitism, poverty, homophobia, ageism, attitudes towards disabilities, fatphobia, and other forms of oppression multiply the effects of sexism, impact on women's mental and physical health, affect access to the determinants of health (nutrition, environment, housing, education, and rewards for employment), and influence or determine one's access and/or relationship with the health care system. Articles in this chapter are chosen to stimulate dialogue on this and help us work towards a better understanding of how oppressions impact on health so that working against oppressions and our own ways of perpetuating oppressions can be an on-going part of our work towards a health care system more appropriate for *all* women (and men).

The reader is reminded that this book is planned to complement, rather than overlap with, *The Black Women's Health Book.* As African-American women, and the National Black Women's Health Project specifically, have played a leadership role in the documentation and expression of how racism is a major health issue, much of the most ground-breaking work on this topic is covered or reflected in *The Black Women's Health Book.*

The first three articles set the tone for how we have tried to work on diversity issues in this book. Audre Lorde's classics, "Age, Race, Class and Sex: Women Redefining Difference" and "There Is No Hierarchy of Oppressions" look at the interactions of *all* forms of oppression and how a basic understanding of power and control issues (who benefits from the inequalities in society and what weapons are used to keep the status quo/the inequalities in place) is fundamental to understanding any and all forms of oppression. (It is important to note that while Audre Lorde's life was devoted to educating us about the widest range of oppressions and begging us to look at their intersections rather than looking at a hierarchy of oppressions, Lorde also emphasized that in a racist society, racism plays a dominating role in maintaining power differentials.)

Ricky Sherover-Marcuse, a Jewish feminist, also devoted her life to anti-oppression work. Her "Unlearning Racism" article captures some of the essence of the powerful, life changing Unlearning Racism Workshops which she facilitated around the country, encouraging each of us to take responsibility for starting to unlearn oppressive misinformation which we have learned as a part of our socialization in a racist society. Perhaps her most inspiring work was to stimulate everyone committed to anti-oppression work to look at how we could consciously work at being *allies* for each other and for "each other's issues."

"Infant Mortality in the US" and "The Class Gap" provide rare discussions on the intersection of race and class as health determinants in the US and provide a feel for the complexity of these issues which too often are left out of our debates when we simply try to look at race or class issues. Internationally, infant mortality rate (IMR) is considered the key figure to use for comparing health determinants in different populations. When IMRs are used for looking internally at what is happening in the US, we see a drastic difference between the IMR for wealthy white populations and the IMR for poor Black communities. As Paul Wise says, "infant mortality represents a stark if not ultimate expression of social and economic injustice in our society." Sherrol Benton, in "Health of Baby Reflects Health of Community," which exposes the even more extreme problem of infant mortality among Native Americans, summarizes the key issue; "If a given population has a high infant mortality rate, it's generally thought of as a red flag that tells us there are health problems in that population group. And by health I mean not simply medical diagnosis, but a holistic view of health that takes into account mental health, spiritual health, and general well being."

"The Class Gap" provides an unusual glimpse at what we could learn about the influence of class on health *if* we had access to such information. Class analysis, building on officially published figures (always open to criticism, such as, why is a woman's class defined by her husband's occupation?), is core to women's health writing in many other countries, but "the U.S., unlike most industrialized nations, does not regularly collect and publish mortality statistics (or other health information) by class." Is that a reason for, or a reflection of, Americans' confusion about the role of class in our lives? "Strained Class Windows" is one of a series of articles in the special class issue of *Sojourner* (January 1994) looking at the role of class in women's lives. Class differs from other forms of oppression in a very fundamental way. For other issues, a goal is to celebrate and value our differences and to eliminate *the oppression* related to the issue. With class (poverty), the goal is to *eliminate that form of difference*. As Judith K. Witherow says at the end of her article, "I would like to see the problems caused by classism worked on continually until all women share equally in the benefits of society."

In order to recognize the ways that racism and other forms of oppression impact on every health issue, we have tried to include articles by a diverse group of women in many chapters of this book. The next articles in this chapter are intended to highlight, rather than isolate, a few of the many special issues which are related to racism, anti-semitism and disability issues. Vanessa Gamble's "Under the Shadow of Tuskegee: African Americans and Health Care" examines the long history of racism, including more recent examples of the ways racist medicine has hurt Black people, which results in the fact that many African Americans do not trust the health system. Excerpts from "Latino Women" similarly looks at particular barriers Latinas face in trying to access health care and "Expanding Health Options for Asian and Pacific Islander Women" looks at a project especially designed to gauge Asian and Pacific Island women's awareness of HIV and reproductive health issues and to develop peer leadership. Paula Gunn Allen's "Angry Women Are Building: Issues and Struggles Facing American Indian Women Today" summarizes many of the key issues Native American women live with daily when literal survival is the central issue in their lives. "Blazes of Truth" and "JAP: The New AntiSemitic Code Word" discuss the oppression and meanings of using the term "Jewish American Princess." "Disability and the Medical System," "On Being an Outreach Group: Women with Disabilities" and "Simply . . . Friend or Foe?" give us an overview of some of the health and medical abuse issues for women with disabilities, provide specific ideas for how women's organizations can make more meaningful connections with women with disabilities, and through illustrations, offers the able-bodied ideas for how to be allies to people with disabilities.

"Ideas for Anti-Racism and Pro-Diversity Work and Discussion in a Women's Health Class" brings together a number of ideas and exercises which have been used successfully in trying to make diversity and anti-oppression issues core to the teaching and learning about women's health.

White students are particularly encouraged to read and think about Peggy McIntosh's "White Privilege: Unpacking the Invisible Knapsack" and everyone may find it useful to examine ways in which they might have certain privileges in society, for example, because they are heterosexual or have no disabilities or are middle-class.

Age, Race, Class, and Sex
Women Redefining Difference*

by Audre Lorde

Much of western European history conditions us to see human differences in simplistic opposition to each other: dominant/subordinate, good/bad, up/down, superior/inferior. In a society where the good is defined in terms of profit rather than in terms of human need, there must always be some group of people who, through systematized oppression, can be made to feel surplus, to occupy the place of the dehumanized inferior. Within this society, that group is made up of Black and Third World people, working-class people, older people, and women.

As a forty-nine-year-old Black lesbian feminist socialist mother of two, including one boy, and a member of an interracial couple, I usually find myself a part of some group defined as other, deviant, inferior, or just plain wrong. Traditionally, in american society, it is the members of oppressed, objectified groups who are expected to stretch out and bridge the gap between the actualities of our lives and the consciousness of our oppressor. For in order to survive, those of us for whom oppression is as American as apple pie have always had to be watchers, to become familiar with the language and manners of the oppressor, even sometimes adopting them for some illusion of protection. Whenever the need for some pretense of communication arises, those who profit from our oppression call upon us to share our knowledge with them. In other words, it is the responsibility of the oppressed to teach the oppressors their mistakes. I am responsible for educating teachers who dismiss my children's culture in school. Black and Third World people are expected to educate white people as to our humanity. Women are expected to educate men. Lesbians and gay men are expected to educate the heterosexual world. The oppressors maintain their position and evade responsibility for their own actions. There is a constant drain of energy which might be better used in redefining ourselves and devising realistic scenarios for altering the present and constructing the future.

Institutionalized rejection of difference is an absolute necessity in a profit economy which needs outsiders as surplus people. As members of such an economy, we have *all* been programmed to respond to the human differences between us with fear and loathing and to handle that difference in one of three ways: ignore it, and if that is not possible, copy it if we think it is dominant, or destroy it if we think it is subordinate. But we have no patterns for relating across our human differences as equals. As a result, those differences have been misnamed and misused in the service of separation and confusion.

Certainly there are very real differences between us of race, age, and sex. But it is not those differences between us that are separating us. It is rather our refusal to recognize those differences, and to examine the distortions which result from our misnaming them and their effects upon human behavior and expectation.

Racism, the belief in the inherent superiority of one race over all others and thereby the right to dominance. Sexism, the belief in the inherent superiority of one sex over the other and thereby the right to dominance. Ageism. Heterosexism. Elitism, Classism.

It is a lifetime pursuit for each one of us to extract these distortions from our living at the same time as we recognize, reclaim, and define those differences upon which they are imposed. For we have all been raised in a society where those distortions were endemic within our living. Too often, we pour the energy needed for recognizing and exploring difference into pretending those differences are insurmountable barriers, or that they do not exist at all. This results in a voluntary isolation, or

*Paper delivered at the Copeland Colloquium, Amherst College, April 1980.

false and treacherous connections. Either way, we do not develop tools for using human difference as a springboard for creative change within our lives. We speak not of human difference, but of human deviance.

Somewhere, on the edge of consciousness, there is what I call a *mythical norm,* which each one of us within our hearts knows "that is not me." In america, this norm is usually defined as white, thin, male, young, heterosexual, christian, and financially secure. It is with this mythical norm that the trappings of power reside within this society. Those of us who stand outside that power often identify one way in which we are different, and we assume that to be the primary cause of all oppression, forgetting other distortions around difference, some of which we ourselves may be practicing. By and large within the women's movement today, white women focus upon their oppression as women and ignore differences of race, sexual preference, class, and age. There is a pretense to a homogeneity of experience covered by the word *sisterhood* that does not in fact exist.

Unacknowledged class differences rob women of each others' energy and creative insight. Recently a women's magazine collective made the decision for one issue to print only prose, saying poetry was a less "rigorous" or "serious" art form. Yet even the form our creativity takes is often a class issue. Of all the art forms, poetry is the most economical. It is the one which is the most secret, which requires the least physical labor, the least material, and the one which can be done between shifts, in the hospital pantry, on the subway, and on scraps of surplus paper. Over the last few years, writing a novel on tight finances, I came to appreciate the enormous differences in the material demands between poetry and prose. As we reclaim our literature, poetry has been the major voice of poor, working class, and Colored women. A room of one's own may be a necessity for writing prose, but so are reams of paper, a typewriter, and plenty of time. The actual requirements to produce the visual arts also help determine, along class lines, whose art is whose. In this day of inflated prices for material, who are our sculptors, our painters, our photographers? When we speak of a broadly based women's culture, we need to be aware of the effect of class and economic differences on the supplies available for producing art.

As we move toward creating a society within which we can each flourish, ageism is another distortion of relationship which interferes without vision. By ignoring the past, we are encouraged to repeat its mistakes. The "generation gap" is an important social tool for any repressive society. If the younger members of a community view the older members as contemptible or suspect or excess, they will never be able to join hands and examine the living memories of the community, nor ask the all important question, "Why?" This gives rise to a historical amnesia that keeps us working to invent the wheel every time we have to go to the store for bread.

We find ourselves having to repeat and relearn the same old lessons over and over that our mothers did because we do not pass on what we have learned, or because we are unable to listen. For instance, how many times has this all been said before? For another, who would have believed that once again our daughters are allowing their bodies to be hampered and purgatoried by girdles and high heels and hobble skirts?

Ignoring the differences of race between women and the implications of those differences presents the most serious threat to the mobilization of women's joint power.

As white women ignore their built-in privilege of whiteness and define *woman* in terms of their own experience alone, then women of Color become "other," the outsider whose experience and tradition is too "alien" to comprehend. An example of this is the signal absence of the experience of women of Color as a resource for women's studies courses. The literature of women of Color is seldom included in women's literature courses and almost never in other literature courses, nor in women's studies as a whole. All too often, the excuse given is that the literatures of women of Color can only be taught by Colored women, or that they are too difficult to understand, or that classes cannot "get into" them because they come out of experiences that are "too different." I have heard this argument presented by white women of otherwise quite clear intelligence, women who seem to have no trouble at all teaching and reviewing work that comes out of the vastly different experiences of Shakespeare, Molière, Dostoyefsky, and Aristophanes. Surely there must be some other explanation.

This is a very complex question, but I believe one of the reasons white women have such difficulty reading Black women's work is because of their reluctance to see Black women as women and different from themselves. To examine Black women's literature effectively requires that we be seen as whole people in our actual complexities—as individuals, as women, as human—rather than as one of those problematic but familiar stereotypes provided in this society in place of genuine images of Black women. And I believe this holds true for the literatures of other women of Color who are not Black.

The literatures of all women of Color recreate the textures of our lives, and many white women are heavily invested in ignoring the real differences. For as long as any difference between us means one of us must be inferior, then the recognition of any difference must be fraught with guilt. To allow women of Color to step out of stereotypes is too guilt provoking, for it threatens the complacency of those women who view oppression only in terms of sex.

Refusing to recognize difference makes it impossible to see the different problems and pitfalls facing us as women.

Thus, in a patriarchal power system where white-skin privilege is a major prop, the entrapments used to neutralize Black women and white women are not the same. For example, it is easy for Black women to be used by the power structure against Black men, not because they are men, but because they are Black. Therefore, for Black women, it is necessary at all times to separate the needs of the oppressor from our own legitimate conflicts within our communities. This same problem does not exist for white women. Black women and men have shared racist oppression and still share it, although in different ways. Out of that shared oppression we have developed joint defenses and joint vulnerabilities to each other that are not duplicated in the white community, with the exception of the relationship between Jewish women and Jewish men.

On the other hand, white women face the pitfall of being seduced into joining the oppressor under the pretense of sharing power. This possibility does not exist in the same way for women of Color. The tokenism that is sometimes extended to us is not an invitation to join power; our racial "otherness" is a visible reality that makes that quite clear. For white women there is a wider range of pretended choices and rewards for identifying with patriarchal power and its tools.

Today, with the defeat of ERA, the tightening economy, and increased conservatism, it is easier once again for white women to believe the dangerous fantasy that if you are good enough, pretty enough, sweet enough, quiet enough, teach the children to behave, hate the right people, and marry the right men, then you will be allowed to co-exist with patriarchy in relative peace, at least until a man needs your job or the neighborhood rapist happens along. And true, unless one lives and loves in the trenches it is difficult to remember that the war against dehumanization is ceaseless.

But Black women and our children know the fabric of our lives is stitched with violence and with hatred, that there is no rest. We do not deal with it only on the picket lines, or in dark midnight alleys, or in the places where we dare to verbalize our resistance. For us, increasingly, violence weaves through the daily tissues of our living—in the supermarket, in the classroom, in the elevator, in the clinic and the schoolyard, from the plumber, the baker, the saleswoman, the bus driver, the bank teller, the waitress who does not serve us.

Some problems we share as women, some we do not. You fear your children will grow up to join the patriarchy and testify against you, we fear our children will be dragged from a car and shot down in the street, and you will turn your backs upon the reasons they are dying.

The threat of difference has been no less blinding to people of Color. Those of us who are Black must see that the reality of our lives and our struggle does not make us immune to the errors of ignoring and misnaming difference. Within Black communities where racism is a living reality, differences among us often seem dangerous and suspect. The need for unity is often misnamed as a need for homogeneity, and a Black feminist vision mistaken for betrayal of our common interests as a people. Because of the continuous battle against racial erasure that Black women and Black men share, some Black women still refuse to recognize that we are also oppressed as women, and that sexual hostility against Black women is practiced not only by the white racist society, but implemented within our Black communities as well. It is a disease striking the heart of Black nationhood, and silence will not make it disappear. Exacerbated by racism and the pressures of powerlessness, violence against Black women and children often becomes a standard within our communities, one by which manliness can be measured. But these women-hating acts are rarely discussed as crimes against Black women.

As a group, women of Color are the lowest paid wage earners in america. We are the primary targets of abortion and sterilization abuse, here and abroad. In certain parts of Africa, small girls are still being sewed shut between their legs to keep them docile and for men's pleasure. This is known as female circumcision, and it is not a cultural affair as the late Jomo Kenyatta insisted, it is a crime against Black women.

Black women's literature is full of the pain of frequent assault, not only by a racist patriarchy, but also by Black men. Yet the necessity for and history of shared battle have made us, Black women, particularly vulnerable to the false accusation that anti-sexist is anti-Black. Meanwhile, womanhating as a recourse of the powerless is sapping strength from Black communities, and our very lives. Rape is on the increase, reported and unreported, and rape is not aggressive sexuality, it is sexualized aggression. As Kalamu ya Salaam, a Black male writer points out, "As long as male domination exists, rape will exist. Only women revolting and men made conscious of their responsibility to fight sexism can collectively stop rape."[1]

Differences between ourselves as Black women are also being misnamed and used to separate us from one another. As a Black lesbian feminist comfortable with the many different ingredients of my identity, and a woman committed to racial and sexual freedom from oppression, I find I am constantly being encouraged to pluck out some one aspect of myself and present this as the meaningful whole, eclipsing or denying the other parts of self. But this is a destructive and fragmenting way to live. My fullest concentration of energy is available to me only when I integrate all the parts of who I am, openly, allowing power from particular sources of my living to flow back and forth freely through all my different selves, without the restrictions of externally imposed definition. Only then can I bring myself and my energies as a whole to the service of those struggles which I embrace as part of my living.

A fear of lesbians, or of being accused of being a lesbian, has led many Black women into testifying against themselves. It has led some of us into destructive alliances, and others into despair and isolation. In the white women's communities, heterosexism is sometimes a result of identifying with the white patriarchy, a rejection of that interdependence between women-identified women which allows the self to be, rather than to be used in the service of men. Sometimes it reflects a die-hard belief in the protective coloration of heterosexual relationships, sometimes a self-hate which all women have to fight against, taught us from birth.

Although elements of these attitudes exist for all women, there are particular resonances of heterosexism and homophobia among Black women. Despite the fact that woman-bonding has a long and honorable history in the African and African-American communities, and despite the knowledge and accomplishments of many strong and creative women-identified Black women in the political, social and cultural fields, heterosexual Black women often tend to ignore or discount the existence and work of Black lesbians. Part of this attitude has come from an understandable terror of Black male attack within the close confines of Black society, where the punishment for any female self-assertion is still to be accused of being a lesbian and therefore unworthy of the attention or support of the scarce Black male. But part of this need to misname and ignore Black lesbians comes from a very real fear that openly women-identified Black women who are no longer dependent upon men for their self-definition may well reorder our whole concept of social relationships.

Black women who once insisted that lesbianism was a white woman's problem now insist that Black lesbians are a threat to Black nationhood, are consorting with the enemy, are basically un-Black. These accusations, coming from the very women to whom we look for deep and real understanding, have served to keep many Black lesbians in hiding, caught between the racism of white women and the homophobia of their sisters. Often, their work has been ignored, trivialized, or misnamed, as with the work of Angelina Grimke, Alice Dunbar-Nelson, Lorraine Hansberry. Yet women-bonded women have always been some part of the power of Black communities, from our unmarried aunts to the amazons of Dahomey.

And it is certainly not Black lesbians who are assaulting women and raping children and grandmothers on the streets of our communities.

Across this country, as in Boston during the spring of 1979 following the unsolved murders of twelve Black women, Black lesbians are spearheading movements against violence against Black women.

What are the particular details within each of our lives that can be scrutinized and altered to help bring about change? How do we redefine difference for all women? It is not our differences which separate women, but our reluctance to recognize those differences and to deal effectively with the distortions which have resulted from the ignoring and misnaming of those differences.

As a tool of social control, women have been encouraged to recognize only one area of human difference as legitimate, those differences which exist between women and men. And we have learned to deal across those differences with the urgency of all oppressed subordinates. All of us have had to learn to live or work or coexist with men, from our fathers on. We have recognized and negotiated these differences, even when this recognition only continued the old dominant/subordinate mode of human relationship, where the oppressed must recognize the masters' difference in order to survive.

But our future survival is predicated upon our ability to relate within equality. As women, we must root out internalized patterns of oppression within ourselves if we are to move beyond the most superficial aspects of social change. Now we must recognize differences among women who are our equals, neither inferior nor superior, and devise ways to use each others' difference to enrich our visions and our joint struggles.

The future of our earth may depend upon the ability of all women to identify and develop new definitions of power and new patterns of relating across difference. The old definitions have not served us, nor the earth that supports us. The old patterns, no matter how cleverly rearranged to imitate progress, still condemn us to cosmetically altered repetitions of the same old exchanges, the same old guilt, hatred, recrimination, lamentation, and suspicion.

For we have, built into all of us, old blueprints of expectation and response, old structures of oppression, and these must be altered at the same time as we alter the living conditions which are a result of those structures. For the master's tools will never dismantle the master's house.

As Paulo Freire shows so well in *The Pedagogy of the Oppressed,*[2] the true focus of revolutionary change is never merely the oppressive situations which we seek to escape, but that piece of the oppressor which is planted deep within each of us, and which knows only the oppressors' tactics, the oppressors' relationships.

Change means growth, and growth can be painful. But we sharpen self-definition by exposing the self in work and struggle together with those whom we define as different from ourselves, although sharing the same goals. For Black and white, old and young, lesbian and heterosexual women alike, this can mean new paths to our survival.

We have chosen each other
and the edge of each other battles
the war is the same
if we lose
someday women's blood will congeal
upon a dead planet
if we win
there is no telling
we seek beyond history
for a new and more possible meeting.[3]

NOTES

1. From "Rape: A Radical Analysis, An African-American Perspective" by Kalamu ya Salaam in *Black Books Bulletin,* vol. 6, no. 4 (1980).
2. Seabury Press, New York, 1970.
3. From "Outlines," unpublished poem.

There Is No Hierarchy of Oppression

— by Audre Lorde

I was born Black, and a woman. I am trying to become the strongest person I can become to live the life I have been given and to help effect change toward a liveable future for this earth and for my children. As a Black, lesbian, feminist, socialist, poet, mother of two including one boy and a member of an interracial couple, I usually find myself part of some group in which the majority defines me as deviant, difficult, inferior, or just plain "wrong."

From my membership in all of these groups I have learned that oppression and the intolerance of difference come in all shapes and sizes and colors and sexualities; and that among those of us who share the goals of liberation and a workable future for our children, there can be no hierarchies of oppression. I have learned that sexism (a belief in the inherent superiority of one sex over all others and thereby its right to dominance) and heterosexism (a belief in the inherent superiority of one pattern of loving over all others and thereby its right to dominance) both arise from the same source as racism—a belief in the inherent superiority of one race over all others and thereby its right to dominance.

"Oh," says a voice from the Black community, "but being Black is NORMAL!" Well, I and many Black people of my age can remember grimly the days when it didn't used to be!

I simply do not believe that one aspect of myself can possibly profit from the oppression of any other part of my identity. I know that my people cannot possibly profit from the oppression of any other group which seeks the right to peaceful existence. Rather, we diminish ourselves by denying to others what we have shed blood to obtain for our children. And those children need to learn that they do not have to become like each other in order to work together for a future they will all share.

The increasing attacks upon lesbians and gay men are only an introduction to the increasing attacks upon all Black people, for wherever oppression manifests itself in this country, Black people are potential victims. And it is a standard of right-wing cynicism to encourage members of oppressed groups to act against each other, and so long as we are divided because of our particular identities we cannot join together in effective political action.

Reprinted with permission from *Council on Interracial Books for Children Bulletin,* vol. 14, No. 3–4, 1983. (1841 Broadway, Rm. 500, New York, N.Y. 10023)

Within the lesbian community I am Black, and within the Black community I am a lesbian. Any attack against Black people is a lesbian and gay issue, because I and thousands of other Black women are part of the lesbian community. Any attack against lesbians and gays is a Black issue, because thousands of lesbians and gay men are Black. There is no hierarchy of oppression.

It is not accidental that the Family Protection Act, which is virulently anti-woman and anti-Black, is also anti-gay. As a Black person, I know who my enemies are, and when the Ku Klux Klan goes to court in Detroit to try and force the Board of Education to remove books the Klan believes "hint at homosexuality," then I know I cannot afford the luxury of fighting one form of oppression only. I cannot afford to believe that freedom from intolerance is the right of only one particular group. And I cannot afford to choose between the fronts upon which I must battle these forces of discrimination, wherever they appear to destroy me. And when they appear to destroy me, it will not be long before they appear to destroy you.

Unlearning Racism

by Ricky Sherover-Marcuse

Because racism is both institutional and attitudinal, effective strategies against it must recognize this dual character. The *undoing* of institutionalized racism must be accompanied by the *unlearning* of racist attitudes and beliefs, and the *unlearning* of racist patterns of thought and action must guide the practice of political and social change.

Institutionalized racism can be defined as the systematic mistreatment of people of color (Third World people). Defining racism in this way highlights the fact that racism is not a genetic disease which is inherent in white people, but that it is a form of social oppression which is the result of the institutionalized inequalities in the structure of a given society.

Attitudinal racism can be defined as the set of assumptions, feelings, beliefs, and attitudes about people of color and their cultures which are a mixture of *misinformation* and ignorance. By "misinformation" I mean any assumption or attitude which in any way implies that people of color are less than fully human. Defining attitudinal racism as misinformation about people of color which has been imposed upon white people means that racism is not a moral defect which some (bad) white individuals have, but a social poison which has been given to all of us, albeit in many different forms.

Attitudinal racism and institutional racism feed off each other. The systematic mistreatment of any group of people generates misinformation about them which in turn becomes "explanation" of or justification for their continued mistreatment. As a result, misinformation about the victims of social oppression becomes socially empowered or *socially sanctioned misinformation*. This is what differentiates this sort of misinformation from prejudice. Socially sanctioned misinformation gets recycled through the society as a form of conditioning which becomes part of our "ordinary" assumptions, and as a result social oppression is viewed either as "natural" or as the fault of the victims themselves.

For example, the misinformation that people of color are stupid or indifferent to the value of human life becomes the "explanation" as to why there is a higher rate of infant mortality among certain groups in the populations. This "explanation" then justifies the attitude that there is really nothing one can do about infant mortality since this problem is basically due to the character or personality structure of the ethnic group involved.

For the past five years I have been doing workshops with groups of white people on "Unlearning Racism". The purpose of these workshops is to help whites to become aware that we have a personal stake in overcoming and unlearning the racist conditioning that was imposed upon us. Having racist beliefs and attitudes is like having a clamp on one's mind. *Unlearning* racism is partly a process of *relearning* how to get accurate information from and about people of color. This involves *relearning* how to really listen to people of color without making judgments or assumptions about what we think they are going to tell us.

When white people become aware of the ways in which *our lives* have been limited and restricted by racism, we become aware of *our interest* in ending this oppression. The most effective action that white people can take against racism will be action which springs not from a sense of guilt or pity, but from our own *knowledge* that in working against racism we are moving towards our own human liberation.

Infant Mortality in the U.S.

by Paul Wise

*I*nfant mortality has a long history as a sensitive indicator of the general well being of a population in that it is closely related to the nutritional, sanitary, and medical conditions of a society. Early in 1983 a series of reports pointed to rising infant mortality rates in areas of high unemployment.[1] In response, the Senate committee charged with the oversight of childhood nutrition programs, the Committee on Agriculture, Nutrition and Forestry, chaired by Jesse Helms, held hearings on this issue.

The reaction of government officials and many academicians was to fault these reports on the unreliability of their statistics. They pointed to the "randomness" inherent in annual mortality data from a small geographic area (e.g., city or state) whereby increases in rates may occur by chance alone. Their advice was not to view these increases as real, and further that the declines in infant mortality over the past decade would indeed continue. The committee's dismissal of the short-term rise in mortality precluded, however, the very real possibility that the mortality reflected transitory but very real change in social conditions. A related issue underlying much of the debate was the notion that cities or states with large black populations should not be compared to others with primarily white populations or to a national average. Helms stated it best when he noted as part of a question:

> Some observers have noted that the comparative use of inner city statistics— where black populations are often higher —with the national average is inappropriate because black infant mortality is historically close to double the national rate.[2]

From *Science for the People,* March/April 1984, pp. 23–26. Copyright © 1984. Reprinted by permission of the author.

Paul Wise teaches pediatrics at Children's Hospital in Boston, and is in the Division of Health Policy Research and Education at Harvard University.

The implication is that rates for blacks and whites must be viewed separately, as black rates have been "historically" so much higher than those of whites. This discussion highlighted two fundamental observations. First, that racial differentials in infant mortality are enormous and persistent. Second, and far more subtle, was the unspoken attitude that high mortality was both tolerable and somehow related to inherent racial differences. The "history" of high black infant mortality implied some form of natural order, not particularly responsive to public policies, and a source of statistical error if not controlled for in comparative studies. The true implications of these differentials were rarely approached, and only in the written testimony of Dr. Peter Budetti, a respected public health researcher and child advocate, did their devastating presence receive the attention they deserved. The concentration of infant mortality in the black community has become so marked that the ranking of states by infant mortality generally corresponds to the percent of their population that is black. The precise causes of this high black infant mortality remain unclear. However, recent efforts to better understand the nature of infant mortality trends have shed light on some areas of special concern.

Neonatal Mortality: Disparity between Blacks and Whites

Infant mortality is defined as the number of deaths experienced in children from birth to one year of age, and is usually expressed per 1000 live births. In 1982, the infant mortality rate for the United States was 11.2. This implies that for every 1000 children born alive in the United States, an average of 11.2 of them will die before their first birthday. It has been known for some time that the majority of infant deaths occur shortly after birth from causes significantly different from those which kill infants later in the first year. In the United States approximately 70% of all infant deaths occur during the newborn, or "neonatal" period, defined as the first 28 days of life. Therefore, discussions of infant mortality must primarily address trends in neonatal mortality.

The neonatal mortality rate (NMR) in the U.S. has been falling for more than a century. However, despite the considerable variation in NMR over the years, there has been one constant observation: for any given year, the NMR for black newborns is substantially higher than that for whites. The long history of high black mortality rates has provided the basis for a widespread acceptance of unequal mortality and the accompanying view that it is in large part due to innate characteristics of black women and infants. A closer look at these data, how-

ever, suggests that black rates ultimately assume the level of white rates; it is just that it takes more than ten years to occur. The white rate was 17.2 in 1960, but it took until 1974 for the black rate to reach that level. The white rate reached 15 in 1967, while the black NMR did not fall below 15 until 1977.

Also intertwined with the issue of racial differentials is the larger question of class. In this society racial patterns of mortality are heavily influenced by social and economic forces. When one compares the neonatal mortality experience of wealthy whites with that of poor whites, poor whites reveal much higher rates of death. The same inverse relationship with income has been documented for black neonates. Therefore, poverty is associated with poor birth outcome for infants of both races. However, when neonatal mortality is analyzed for each race and income level, black mortality has been shown to be higher than that of whites even within the same income groups. This suggests that in the U.S., black neonatal mortality is associated not only with income effects but also residual social influences more closely related to race than to income.

Birth Weight as a Crucial Factor

An important insight into the nature of these patterns in neonatal mortality can be gained by partitioning neonatal mortality into its component parts. It has been well documented that the risk of death in a newborn is closely related to its weight at birth. In general the lower the birth weight the higher the risk of death. This is due to the fact the birth weight is a relatively good proxy measure of the maturity and intrauterine growth of the child. Neonates can then be categorized into various birth weight groupings each associated with its respective mortality risk. Commonly newborns under 1500 gm (3.3 lbs.) are termed very low birth weight (VLBW), below 2500 gm (5.6 lbs.) low birth weight (LBW) and above 2500 gm normal or high birth weight. The group with the highest mortality is the VLBW group. The smallest risk is in those newborns with birth weights above 2500 gm. This general framework of risk stratification allows neonatal mortality in a population to be broken down into two parts: 1) the distribution of birth weights in that population and 2) the relative survival of newborns in that population that are born at a given birth weight. The first component is usually labeled the "birthweight distribution," and the second the "birthweight-specific mortality." Therefore, to analyze differences in mortality one must establish whether one group had a higher proportion of births born with weights associated with high risk (VLBW and LBW groups) and subsequently any differences in survival once they are born at a given birth weight.

This partitioning has helped explain why newborns in the United States experience higher mortality than in 16 other industrialized countries. Comparisons between the U.S., Norway[3] and Sweden [4] reveal that the cause of relatively high NMR's in the U.S. are due to unfavorable birth weight distribution. The U.S. experiences much higher rates of VLBW and LBW births. Birth-weight-specific mortality rates were in fact significantly better for these newborns in the U.S. Once an infant is born in the U.S., its chances of survival are somewhat better than that of newborns of the same birth weight born in Norway and Sweden. The problem in the U.S. is that due in large part to poor nutrition particularly prevalent among black and low income mothers, a far higher percentage of infants are born at low birth weights.

When racial and income differentials are analyzed in this manner a similar pattern emerges. For the most part, black birthweight-specific mortality rates for LBW babies are better than those of white neonates. Once born at a given birth weight, black newborns' survival is even better than white survival. Then why are black NMR's so much higher than those of whites? The answer is that blacks have much higher rates of low birth weight births. In fact, blacks experience approximately twice the low birth weight rate of whites.

The Issue of Low Birth Weight

Unlike birth-weight-specific-mortality, declines in low birth-weight rates have not been similar for both races. Reports from diverse locations including North Carolina,[5] California,[6] and Boston,[7] have shown that white LBW rates fell more steeply than did those of blacks. National estimates have echoed these findings. This divergence has helped to widen the gap between white and black NMR's.

Attempts are often made to explain these observed racial and income differentials in NMR's based on differences in the demographic characteristics of the compared populations. Most notably has been the argument that the different rates are due to a higher portion of births to young women among blacks. It has been known for some time that newborns of women under 16 years are at significantly higher risk of death. It has also been well documented that the number of births for black and poor white teen-age women is almost double that for wealthy whites. This has led some to the conclusion that by preventing teen-age births much of this racial differential in NMR could be extinguished. This proves false, however, when one considers that less than 5% of black or low income white births occur to women under 16. If all births to women under 16 were prevented, less than 10% of the racial and income differential would be reduced. The mortality risk associated with births to

women 17 to 20 years is not appreciably higher than that of women 20 to 35 years. Therefore, teenage pregnancy cannot be held responsible for the mortality differentials. Programs dealing with pregnant teenagers and young parents are important because these births are associated with high medical and social risk and require special resources to help improve their outcome. However, they should not be viewed as a means of significantly reducing inequalities in overall neonatal mortality. Rather the focus must be on preventing the relatively high rates of low and very low birthweight births. Until this is accomplished the racial and income gaps in neonatal mortality rates will not be reduced, and indeed may widen.

The major recent declines in NMR's in the U.S. may have even exacerbated racial differences. Both national[8] and state-specific analyses [9, 10] have suggested that both blacks and whites have experienced remarkable reductions in birthweight-specific-mortality rates over the past decade. Once born at a given birthweight, newborns today are much more likely to survive than they were ten years ago. However, the birthweight distribution component has not fared as well. The percentages of all births which are of low birthweight has fallen much more slowly than birthweight-specific mortality rates. Continued efforts to improve the quality and access to intensive neonatal care when needed will remain an important aspect of neonatal care for all infants in the years to come. However, the concentration of mortality into the very low birthweight category of newborns makes it unlikely that differentials can be reduced through greater reliance on neonatal intensive care. What is needed is greater emphasis on preventive strategies.

Preventive Strategies

Nutrition supplementation programs have generally proved effective in increasing the birthweight of newborns. The most important of these has been the Women, Infant and Child (WIC) supplementation program. A federal program administered through state agencies, WIC provides coupons for nutritious foods for eligible pregnant and lactating women and children under five years of age. Eligibility is based on nutritional and income criteria. In conjunction with coupon distribution, nutritional and medical consultation is an ongoing requirement. While controversy over its impact persists, the WIC program has been shown to increase the birthweight of neonates born to enrolled women. The Reagan administration has made recent efforts to significantly reduce funding for WIC and lighten eligibility requirements despite the fact that less than half of all eligible women and children in the U.S. are presently served by WIC.[11]

Caring and conscientious monitoring of the woman, fetus, and family from the first trimester until delivery are directly associated with an improved rate of infant survival.[12] However, numerous studies have shown that poor black women are much less likely to receive prenatal care than are whites. In some cities as many as one half of all black women will receive no prenatal care or begin care just weeks before their scheduled due date.

Improvements in the quality of and access to comprehensive prenatal services, therefore, would seem to be more important than ever. The critical importance of LBW birth rates to overall racial differentials in NMR's has never been greater. However, all indications are that prenatal services for poor women in the U.S. are beginning to erode due to constriction of federal programs in this area. Cutbacks in the WIC program and funds supporting the delivery of general prenatal services have already occurred. Further efforts by the Reagan administration to curtail funding for these and related programs can only reduce the already inadequate resources dedicated to this area of preventive care.

While understanding the patterns of neonatal mortality is useful in assessing the need and nature of medical and social initiatives, it also helps focus attention on the presence and the scope of social disparity in the United States. That poor, black neonates experience almost four times the mortality of wealthy white neonates provides insight into the human toll of continued structural inequalities, and helps explain why the issue of infant mortality becomes so heavily contested in the political arena. It is in this sense that infant mortality represents a stark if not ultimate expression of social and economic injustice in our society, and at some level, reminds all of the brutal cost this disparity exacts from its youngest and most vulnerable citizens.

REFERENCES

1. For instance see Food Research and Action Center, "Infant Deaths Go Up, While WIC Program Funds Stay Low," presented in Hearings, Committee on Agriculture, Nutrition and Forestry, U.S. Senate, March 14, 1983

2. Hearings, Committee on Agriculture, Nutrition and Forestry, U.S. Senate, March 14, 1983

3. Erickson, J.D., F.B Bjerkedal, Fetal and infant mortality in Norway and the United States. JAMA 1982; 247:987–991.

4. Guyer, B., L.A. Waklack, S.L. Rosen. "Birth-weight standardized neonatal mortality rate and the prevention of low birth weight: how does Massachusetts compare with Sweden?" N. Engl. J. Med. 1982, 306:1230–1233.

5. David, R.J., E. Siegel. "Decline in neonatal mortality, 1968 to 1977: better babies or better care?" Pediatrics 1983; 17-531–540.

6. Williams, R., P.M. Chen. "Identifying the sources of the recent decline in perinatal mortality rates in California." N. Engl. J. Med. 1982; 306:207-214.

7. Wise, P.H., M. Wilson, M. Wills, M. Kotelchuck. *Childhood mortality in the City of Boston.* Part I: Neonatal Mortality. (In Press).

8. Lee, K, et al. "Neonatal mortality: an analysis of the recent improvements in the United States." Am. J. Public Health 1980; 70:15-21.

9. David, R.J., E. Siegel, 17–531–540.

10. Galdenberg, R.I., J.I. Humphrey, C.B. Hale. "Neonatal death in Alabama, 1970-1980: an analysis of birth weight and race specific neonatal mortality rates." Am. J. Obstet. Gynecol. 1983; 145:545–552.

11. Hearings, Committee on Agriculture, Nutrition and Forestry, U.S. Senate, March 14, 1983.

12. Ibid.

The Class Gap

by Vincente Navarro

*M*uch attention has recently been paid to the growing disparity in the mortality rates of blacks and whites. There is a moral imperative to mobilize social resources to reverse this trend. But there is another mortality gap, one that is not talked about: the social class gap. Because the United States, unlike most industrialized nations, does not regularly collect and publish mortality statistics by class, we do not know how many more years a corporate lawyer lives than an unskilled blue-collar or service worker.

On one of the few occasions that the government did gather such information, however, in 1986 (and measuring only deaths from heart and cerebrovascular diseases), the results were stunning. People of any race with less formal education, with lower incomes and belonging to the working class (those whom the Census classifies under the terms "operator" and "services") die at higher rates than people belonging to the upper classes (those designated "managers" and "professionals"). The death rate from heart disease, for example, was 2.3 times higher among unskilled blue-collar operators than among managers and professionals. By contrast, the mortality rate from heart disease in 1986 for blacks was 1.3 times higher than for whites.

Did these enormous gaps close or widen during the 1980s? We have no means of knowing. But we do know that class differentials in the rates at which people get sick have been growing. From 1983 to 1988 the percentage of individuals with an annual income over $60,000 who had limited activity due to a chronic condition declined, while for those with incomes less than $10,000, it increased. It is fair to assume that the class differentials in mortality have been increasing as well. And the rise in the black death rate offers further grounding for this assumption, since blacks, because of racism, are disproportionately concentrated in the low-income groups.

In the 1980s the U.S. population underwent severe class polarization, with a reduction of the middle class, a slow growth of the upper and upper-middle classes, and a rapid growth of the low-paid, unskilled working class. The low earners are a heterogeneous group—blacks, Latinos, whites, men and women—whose standard of living is fast deteriorating. They belong to the 40 percent of the population that received only 15.7 percent of the total income in 1984, the lowest amount since such figures were first kept, in 1947. On the other hand, the wealthiest 20 percent received 42.9 percent of the total income, the highest ever. This growing disparity of wealth and income is the main, if not exclusive, reason for the growing differentials in morbidity and mortality between whites and blacks. The deteriorating working and living conditions of the low-wage working class are reflected in the statistics on death and disease. Within each class, minorities are even worse off. This is why the life expectancy of blacks has been declining, and that of whites is improving at an unprecedentedly slow rate. It is also the reason that the publication of health statistics in racial terms is insufficient.

We as a nation need to do much more to eliminate racism, but we also need to eliminate the fatal consequences of classism. The growing mortality differentials between whites and blacks are part of larger mortality differentials—class differentials. The publication of health statistics in racial terms assumes that white unskilled workers have more in common with white lawyers, for example, than with black unskilled workers. They do not. White workers have far more in common, in the way they live, get sick and die, with black workers than with white lawyers. And the same may be said of black workers and black lawyers. Yet the way in which statistics are kept does not help to make white and black workers aware of the commonality of their predicament.

From *The Nation*, April 8, 1991, pp. 436–437. Copyright © 1991 by The Nation Company, Inc. Reprinted by permission.

Vincente Navarro is a professor of health policy and sociology at Johns Hopkins University.

The collection and publication of mortality statistics by race *and* class would help to unite rather than separate black and white laborers.

Class differentials in mortality rates are not unique to the United States. In other industrialized nations not only do they exist but they are on the rise, and great national and international debates on the reasons for this have begun. Meanwhile, in the United States the silence persists.

Health of Baby Reflects Health of Community

by Sherrol Benton, Ojibwe

Among the dead in 1990, there were more than a dozen newborn Native American children—victims of the sudden Infant Death Syndrome (SIDS). And, like other vital statistics, infant death rates are high among Indians.

Medical specialists believe that improving the health and lifestyle of Native Americans will have a direct affect upon the life of their infants.

Infant mortality is the death of a baby that is born alive and dies sometime within the first year of life. The mortality rate is the number of deaths per thousand of live births within a given population. Statisticians count the number of live births over a span of several years.

The national rate of infant deaths is approximately 9.1 in the United States. The infant death rates are 18.1 for Native Americans.

Dr. Marie Valdes-Dapena, University of Miami School of Medicine, completed a literature review of SIDS cases and found new concepts about the causes of SIDS.

"Many things may happen to different babies. But we are beginning to see SIDS as a two-staged event. In the first stage, something happens to the baby in utero. The mother may have a seemingly inconsequential viral infection like a cold that damages the baby slightly—probably in the brain stem. In the second stage, after birth, something may happen to challenge this baby like an upper respiratory infection. The baby isn't able to respond normally to that and dies," Dr. Valdes-Dapena said.

There are many different kinds of things that can trigger SIDS, but it is generally accepted that the baby has a slight handicap in the brain. The brain stem is the center of control for breathing, the heart beat, and for the coordination of not breathing while swallowing. When the baby has a slight handicap in the brain stem, the baby has a hard time sorting out difficult situations, according to Dr. Valdes-Dapena.

For example, a subtly handicapped baby won't lift its head and turn its nose away from poor air if it's lying on its stomach on a soft quilt. It will just keep breathing in carbon monoxide. A normal baby would try to lift its head and turn toward a better air supply.

"This concept may not apply in all cases. Other mechanisms apply in other cases. We're just beginning to understand it."

Susan Tillema, State Department of Health and Human Services, (DHHS) of Madison, Wisconsin, is a member of a task force investigating SIDS among tribal communities. The DHHS found that in the general population the infant death rate is approximately eight per thousand but for Indians the infant death rate is between 17 and 20 per thousand live births.

"The fact that the majority of Indian babies die after the first month of life leads us to believe that causes may be related to the environment in which they live. In particular, we're concerned about factors related to poverty such as nutrition, transportation, access to health care, and crowded living conditions. These kind of factors tend to cluster together when we're looking at high infant mortality rates," Tillema said.

Some causes that may be linked to SIDS can be traced to both the mother and father's health and lifestyle. It's well known that use of alcohol, illicit drugs, and cigarette smoking during pregnancy can affect an infant. New evidence shows that the father's health and lifestyle before conception also may contribute to the condition of a newborn.

David Savitz, Associate Professor of Epidemiology at the University of North Carolina, School of Public Health, said there is some evidence suggesting that there may be a link between the father's exposure to hazardous materials and some diseases in his children.

"There's a lot of interest and speculation and some evidence that suggests that the father's exposure to agents like lead, certain solvents and pesticides could alter the sperm and still leave it capable of producing conception that would result in the risk of miscarriage, or birth defects or those sorts of outcomes," Savitz said.

Lifestyle choices among men are more important than any biological effects upon the quality of his sperm. Savitz has found possible links from use of alcohol, drug abuse and cigarette smoking to some diseases in the newborn.

There's also some research that has looked at more lifestyle factors like cigarette smoking, alcohol use, and various other sorts of illicit drug use. And again it's not firm but there are suggestions. For example, we did a study that suggested that possibly the father's use of tobacco before conception might be related to childhood cancer or the risk of certain kinds of birth defects. Another study done shows how elements of cocaine can attach to sperm and enter the ovum. There's more evidence about what this does to the father, but nonetheless there is some suggestion that these exposures could effect his offspring as well," Savitz said.

Researchers have suggested that some causes may be related to different cultural practices, although evidence to prove that is very elusive. However, the IHS has found clear differences of infant death rates among several tribal groups.

The highest infant mortality rate is among the Plains Indians who have a rate of 20 to 23 infant deaths per thousand live births. The woodland tribes of Minnesota, Wisconsin and Michigan have an infant mortality rate of 13 per thousand live births. The infant mortality rate of the southwestern tribes like the Navajos and Pueblos is very low, even lower than the white population in that area.

"There are clear regional differences among tribes. They may have something to do with tribal differences or tribal practices or other factors that have nothing to do with race poverty or anything. It may just have to do with some lifestyle questions. For example, we do know that the southwestern tribes don't smoke as much as the northern tribes do. And passive smoke has been clearly implicated in the health of the fetus and the newborn. But, whether that is a factor in the tribal differences of infant deaths remains to be seen," according to Wegehaup.

Tillema applies worldwide standards to measure the health status of Indian populations. A high infant mortality rate is just one way to measure the vast health and wellness problems within a population.

"If a given population has a high infant mortality rate, it's generally thought of as a red flag that tells us that there are other health problems in that population group. And by health I mean not simply medical diagnosis, but a holistic view of health that takes into account mental health, spiritual health and general well being," Tillema said.

Some of Tillema's work involves launching a new program called Grandmothers, Aunties, Mothers and Sisters (GAMS), sponsored by the Great Lakes Inter-Tribal Council. GAMs has a novel approach to providing social support to mothers. It addresses the whole community using a multi-generational approach to supporting the pregnant mother, and a cultural base of values and knowledge about families, health and wellness.

"We are supporting the concept of "care coordination" as an important part in health care provision both for the mother's prenatal care and the baby's first year of life. Care coordination generally means helping someone understand the health and social service system, get what he or she needs from the system, and stay in the system."

Using the health and social service system includes regular visits to the doctor and dietician during pregnancy. Accessing the system also includes contacting a social worker for psycho-social support, or applying for housing and clothing assistance and other basic supplies when needed.

Tillema is a member of the American Indian Infant Mortality Work Group, (AIIMWG). This year, the goal of the AIIMWG is to find out what is causing the high rate of infant mortality. Their goal is to gather data about the circumstances of each infant's death and to develop prevention plans.

As part of its work AIIMWG is training grief counselors from each Wisconsin Reservation. The grief counselors will provide emotional support to grieving families of deceased infants.

The work group also plans to address to role of fathers, grandfathers, uncles and other men in the lives of pregnant mothers and newborns. Next year, the GAMS program plans to develop a father's program to involve them more in family, birthing and parenting.

"There are a lot of significant people surrounding that mother and baby. There is of course the grandmothers, aunts, and sisters. There's also the father, the partner of the mother, the grandfathers. All of these people need to understand the importance of the mother's care during pregnancy and then what provides a healthy environment for a new baby," Tillema said.

The most important role for a father is a social role in the emotional and psychological support of the pregnant mother. The father can be especially helpful in eliminating drugs and alcohol from the mother's environment to ensure the health of an infant. A well established

issue is the adverse effects of alcohol and illicit drug use during the mother's pregnancy.

"And it is also pretty clear that it is much more difficult for the woman to abstain if her partner is using drugs and alcohol. It's not a direct effect, but if the father is a heavy drinker or drug user, it's harder for the mother to abstain. The social role of the father is unarguable. It's quite clear that the father has an impact (upon the health of the fetus) in the way of abstaining from drugs and alcohol," Savitz said.

The IHS considers the Sudden Infant Death Syndrome as one its top 10 objectives to deal with within Native American communities. Also, the Wisconsin Division of Health has set "the reduction of infant mortality among Native Americans" as a top goal to reach in the year 2000.

Strained Class Windows

by Judith K. Witherow

You People. Every time I hear those ignoble words used, I know it isn't going to be good. They will always make me mentally and physically cringe.

When you hear those words from birth on, as part of your name, you know which rung of the ladder you're standing on.

"You People should have indoor plumbing. How can you stand that outhouse?" "You People need to have electricity and running water." "Your house looks so small. How many of You People sleep in one bed?" (I shared a bed with two sisters, and, in the winter, our body heat was probably the only thing that kept us from freezing to death.) "Why don't You People paint your house?"

Gee, poverty makes you so damned dumb that none of these things ever occur to you. Someone pointing them out is like a giant wake-up slap on the forehead.

We could have painted any bare wood shack we ever lived in seven different colors, and it wouldn't have changed a thing. Oh, people would have said, "You People are so gaudy," but that is how much tangible difference it would have made. There would have been less money for food and other survival necessities, but what the hell, it might have made us easier to look at. That's what it is all about, isn't it? Looks?

Not the kind of looks where someone is rolling their eyes while they are "trying" to talk to you. This habit is the twin of "You People," and you just want to haul out a piece of tape and hold their eyes still so they can clearly see what you are saying.

I'm 49 years old, and I still don't have this class thing figured out. For that matter, I don't know for sure whether classism or racism is worse. Most times I can't even figure out why I'm being treated the way I am.

I honestly thought I could be objective writing this article, but the deeper I dig into old buried familial grief graves, the more angry and sad I become. If this weren't so God awful important, I'd throw the dirt back on, but how are we ever going to change anything unless all sides are totally truthful?

As a poor, mixed blood Native American, raised in the northern Appalachians, I invite you into my life and reveal to you the sights, tastes, smells, and life-limiting experiences that you might not have been privy to.

I keep wanting to say I know all the big words I'm using. It's very important to me that you know I'm not being pretentious, that these are no one else's words but mine. If that is classism in reverse, I will readily say I am sorry. My partner, Sue, helps me proofread but that is the extent of the input. Sometimes people assume someone of my background could not be literate. I can't tell you how many times someone has asked me if I actually wrote a particular article.

I hear the same thing from many family members, but for a different reason. The first time I showed my mother a poem I had written, she asked if I really knew all those words, or did I find them in a dictionary? Often I get quizzed about an article I've written. Someone will say, "Did that really happen?" It's like, "Judith, you'll be in deep, deep trouble if you put a lie in print." Right. The nonfiction police will bust my butt.

The printed word has always been cause for heated discussion in my family. They don't believe anyone would print something that isn't true. This includes *The National Enquirer.* I've learned that the older generation can survive easier without the ugly truths at this late date, so I concentrate on working with the younger ones. The truth doesn't always set you free. It bruises and bleeds like no other injury ever could, but pain can open the gates to gain.

I graduated from high school and made my family very proud. Looking back, I can see I was purposely kept at lower class levels even though I had good grades. No one ever mentioned scholarships or college to me. (As a result, I earned a living as a textile factory worker, waitress, and housekeeper.) I believe you get weeded out of the further education track at an early age. It's not the grades that count. It's your family's potential that is measured by the class yardstick. (You People would just take up a space that could be used by someone really serious.) Some very fine minds get lost this way. Yes, you could go to college at a later date, but by then life has had so many whacks at you that it rarely leaves you with the time or confidence to try it. Survival often means feeding the belly before the brain. The deprivation of either causes lifelong pain. There is only so much humiliation you can cram into a child before you effectively crowd her out of the system.

My father quit school in third grade to help raise his brothers and sisters. He was self-educated and gave me an abiding love of the written word. My mother made it to the eighth grade. Her one clothing outfit for school was the top of a dress for a blouse and the bottom of a man's overcoat for a skirt. She never stopped grieving for her lost chance. She often spoke of her proudest moment as winning a poetry recital before she had to quit school.

When my father was in his seventies and dying of cancer, he asked me to cover for him because he had told the nurse a lie. I thought she must have asked him about smoking or drinking. He said, "She asked me how far I had went in school. I thought fifth grade sounded much better so I told her that. You back me up, kid." I asked him why he didn't just say he had graduated? He looked like someone had pulled a gun on him. "Jesus, girl, you can't say anything like that." I tried to explain to him it was a bullshit question, but he was having none of it.

You see, after many years of subjugation, you become your own overseer. To this day, I see my nieces and nephews trash each other before the rest of society gets a chance. I understand the dynamic perfectly. If you make fun of or hurt each other, then the second time around it doesn't hurt as much. You have already been prepared. When you depersonalize pain and suffering, you can ignore it. Only when a human face is superimposed on poverty will this barbaric practice end.

The first house I remember us living in contained three small rooms. (The next tenants used it as a chicken coop.) My father had to walk stooped over because the ceilings were about five feet high. He was six foot tall. There was no water or electricity, of course. The creek out back served as a washing machine, a refrigerator, and a bathtub.

We never lived in a place that had screen doors or screens in the windows. This allowed everything, including snakes, to come and go at will.

We learned at an early age to pound on the floor before getting out of bed. This was so you didn't accidentally step on a rat and get bitten. Why the hell do rats always overrun the poor? I can tell you it is not for the food. Maybe it's just easier access.

When it snowed in the mountains, it would drift in through all the cracks that weren't full of paper or rags. We had very few blankets, so coats, rugs, or clothes helped to keep us warm. The roof had so many holes that we didn't have enough pots or cans to catch all the rain that trickled through. Too bad we didn't have one of those glass ceilings I hear so much about. I'll bet those suckers could keep you dry, warm, and in your place.

This basically describes all the houses we grew up in. Each move was a little better than the last. When I was five, we moved to a house that had electricity. At age 14, we moved to a house that had both water and electricity. We never acquired a place with screens or one that wasn't overrun with rats. Yes, we set traps. Yes, we put out poison. Many times my brother and I would sit in the basement with a .22 rifle and pick them off when they popped their heads out.

People many times equate poverty with laziness. We always worked. Dad worked at a sawmill and as a lumberjack. Later on, he became a carpenter. He never missed work, and he never received any benefits.

My dad, a good-looking, proud man, came from a long line of alcoholics, as did my mother, but only he succumbed to it. It still follows the male lineage on both sides of the family. Twice while growing up, I heard people use my dad's name as a synonym for drunk. If the alcohol colored and clouded the ugliness and made it bearable, I can understand and forgive that. Yes, I'm sure the cheap wine he drank took material and mental tolls on all of us, but it was an illness he fought all of his life.

One time Dad committed himself to an alcohol rehabilitation institution. Mom had to apply for welfare and sign a non-support order that she was told would never be served. It was protocol. (It was the only time she applied for benefits.) On the day of Dad's release after two months of treatment, the police came and took him away in handcuffs because of the nonsupport warrant. On the way home from jail, he stopped and bought a bottle of wine. It caused a breach in my parents' relationship that never healed. None of us had ever been in any trouble with the law. The law was something you feared with all of your being. It still is for us older ones.

Mom worked as a housekeeper for several families. I was ashamed of her for doing that. When high school girls whose homes Mom cleaned would tell me in a loud voice at school what a wonderful job Mom did, I wanted to die. On the other hand, to Mom's dying day, she would brag about what a good job she had done and how pleased her employers were.

She also did waitress and factory work and thought it was a great honor that she had never been fired from any job. Me, I just wanted to shake her when she would start these raps and say, "Of course, they didn't fire you. You were every shit-working boss's dream. You never complained, and you left a piece of your heart and health everywhere you worked." Of course, I never said it out loud to her.

She looked at me in total amazement whenever I tried to say that perhaps things weren't as cut and dried as they appeared. She was the dearest, kindest woman I have ever known. I will never stop missing her truly honest compassion. May she rest in peace. I doubt I ever will.

Work. That's all we ever knew from childhood up. You name it, and we sold it or did it. We picked and sold strawberries, blackberries, elderberries, and blueberries.

We sold Rosebud salve by the gross. Remember those tacky cardboard mottos that said "HOME SWEET HOME?" Sold them. Countless packs of seeds also sold door to door. Lawnmowing, gardening, babysitting, etc.

One of the hardest jobs was picking princess pine. It's used to make funeral and Christmas wreaths, etc. You find it growing wild in the wintertime. It looks like wispy little pine trees. You get paid six cents a pound for it. Believe me, it takes more back-breaking work than you can ever imagine to fill a burlap sack with it. Digging through the snow in search of it without the benefit of gloves or boots is something you wouldn't wish on anyone. We would miss school to help with this. Whoever was the youngest at the time would be placed in a hurriedly fashioned lean-to for shelter from the elements. Another young one would stay nearby and keep the fire going while the rest of us picked.

Our favorite spot, one where you weren't walking forever to find the pine, was on a state game reserve. One time, after picking all day, we dragged our sacks up to the dirt road where Dad was to meet us. Instead of Dad, we were met by a game warden. He made us dump out all of our piney. He said he had been watching us work all day long, and he wanted to teach us a lesson. Granddad and the rest of us were scared, but Mom told us it would be all right.

Later that night we went back and picked it all up by the light of the moon. Mom said that it was too much work picking something growing wild—that should be yours for free—only to have it wasted by someone who didn't know the first thing about nature.

Because of background and lifestyle, our family is riddled with disease and disability. The water we drank wherever we lived came out of mountains that had been strip-mined for coal. This same water would flow down the river and kill all of the fish and other living organisms.

The little town of 400 where we were raised is now full of cancer, multiple sclerosis, and many other diseases. I had cancer and had a section of my right foot removed. I have multiple sclerosis as do other members of my family. It is uncommon to have so many cases in such a small region. It's not contagious, so what is the common denominator?

We moved from the mountains in 1964, but apparently not in time. All of us have arthritis. Most have several of the following: high blood pressure, diabetes, emphysema, vitiligo, learning disabilities, heart and lung disease, sarcoidosis, eczema, kidney or liver disease or alcoholism.

I wish there had been free lunch programs back then. I know our health problems due to malnutrition could have been avoided. When I hear anyone go into a diatribe about all You People wanting handouts, I go a bit crazy. My main memory of my childhood is always being hungry. Oh sure, we gardened, hunted, and fished, but it was never enough to feed eight or more people at one time.

Does society still not get it? An unhealthy child will be an even more unhealthy adult. A sick, uneducated adult will not be able to work and contribute like a healthy educated one can. This dynamic will cost from the cradle to the coffin if it is not interrupted. Unlimited resources that are now being spent to make war all over the globe could be redirected to save the same amount of people.

My hope is that after all of the articles on class are printed in this issue, they will not just be read and then forgotten. If more people aren't willing to work to help us change our destiny, the loss will soon be insurmountable. I would like to see the problems caused by classism worked on continually until all women share equally the benefits of society.

Under the Shadow of Tuskegee
African Americans and Health Care

by Vanessa Northington Gamble, MD, PhD

ABSTRACT The Tuskegee Syphilis Study continues to cast its long shadow on the contemporary relationship between African Americans and the biomedical community. Numerous reports have argued that the Tuskegee Syphilis Study is the most important reason why many African Americans distrust the institutions of medicine and public health. Such an interpretation neglects a critical historical point: the mistrust predated public revelations about the Tuskegee study. This paper places the syphilis study within a broader historical and social context to demonstrate that several factors have influenced—and continue to influence—African Americans' attitudes toward the biomedical community. (*Am J Public Health.* 1997;87:1773–1778)

Introduction

On May 16, 1997, in a White House ceremony, President Bill Clinton apologized for the Tuskegee Syphilis Study, the 40-year government study (1932 to 1972) in which 399 Black men from Macon County, Alabama, were deliberately denied effective treatment for syphilis in order to document the natural history of the disease.[1] "The legacy of the study at Tuskegee," the president remarked, "has reached far and deep, in ways that hurt our progress and divide our nation. We cannot be one America when a whole segment of our nation has no trust in America."[2] The president's comments underscore that in the 25 years since its public disclosure, the study has moved from being a singular historical event to a powerful metaphor. It has come to symbolize racism in medicine, misconduct in human research, the arrogance of physicians, and government abuse of Black people.

From *American Journal of Public Health*, Vol. 87, No. 11, November 1997, pp. 1173–78. Copyright © 1997 by the American Public Health Association. Reprinted by permission.

The author is with the History of Medicine and Family Medicine Departments and the Center for the Study of Race and Ethnicity in Medicine, University of Wisconsin School of Medicine, Madison.

Requests for reprints should be sent to Vanessa Northington Gamble, MD, PhD. University of Wisconsin School of Medicine, 1300 University Ave., Madison, WI 53706.

This paper was accepted July 24, 1997.

The continuing shadow cast by the Tuskegee Syphilis Study on efforts to improve the health status of Black Americans provided an impetus for the campaign for a presidential apology.[3] Numerous articles, in both the professional and popular press, have pointed out that the study predisposed many African Americans to distrust medical and public health authorities and has led to critically low Black participation in clinical trials and organ donation.[4]

The specter of Tuskegee has also been raised with respect to HIV/AIDS prevention and treatment programs. Health education researchers Dr Stephen B. Thomas and Dr Sandra Crouse Quinn have written extensively on the impact of the Tuskegee Syphilis Study on these programs.[5] They argue that "the legacy of this experiment, with its failure to educate the study participants and treat them adequately, laid the foundation for today's pervasive sense of black distrust of public health authorities."[6] The syphilis study has also been used to explain why many African Americans oppose needle exchange programs. Needle exchange programs provoke the image of the syphilis study and Black fears about genocide. These programs are not viewed as mechanisms to stop the spread of HIV/AIDS but rather as fodder for the drug epidemic that has devastated so many Black neighborhoods.[7] Fears that they will be used as guinea pigs like the men in the syphilis study have also led some African Americans with AIDS to refuse treatment with protease inhibitors.[8]

The Tuskegee Syphilis Study is frequently described as the singular reason behind African-American distrust of the institutions of medicine and public health. Such an interpretation neglects a critic historical point: the mistrust predated public revelations about the Tuskegee study. Furthermore, the narrowness of such a representation places emphasis on a single historical event to explain deeply entrenched and complex attitudes within the Black community. An examination of the syphilis study within a broader historical and social context makes plain that several factors have influenced, and continue to influence, African Americans' attitudes toward the biomedical community.

Black Americans' fears about exploitation by the medical profession date back to the antebellum period and the use of slaves and free Black people as subjects for dissection and medical experimentation.[9] Although physicians also used poor Whites as subjects, they used Black people far more often. During an 1835 trip to the United States, French visitor Harriet Martineau found that Black people lacked the power even to protect the graves of their dead. "In Baltimore the bodies of coloured people exclusively are taken for dissection," she remarked, "because the Whites do not like it, and the coloured people cannot resist."[10] Four years later, abolitionist Theodore Dwight Weld echoed Martineau's sentiment. "Public opinion," he wrote, "would tolerate surgical experiments, operations, processes, performed upon them [slaves], which it would execrate if performed upon their master or other whites."[11] Slaves found themselves as subjects of medical experiments because physicians needed bodies and because the state considered them property and denied them the legal right to refuse to participate.

Two antebellum experiments, one carried out in Georgia and the other in Alabama, illustrate the abuse that some slaves encountered at the hands of physicians. In the first, Georgia physician Thomas Hamilton conducted a series of brutal experiments on a slave to test remedies for heatstroke. The subject of these investigations, Fed, had been loaned to Hamilton as repayment for a debt owed by his owner. Hamilton forced Fed to sit naked on a stool placed on a platform in a pit that had been heated to a high temperature. Only the man's head was above ground. Over a period of 2 to 3 weeks, Hamilton placed Fed in the pit five or six times and gave him various medications to determine which enabled him best to withstand the heat. Each ordeal ended when Fed fainted and had to be revived. But note that Fed was not the only victim in this experiment; its whole purpose was to make it possible for masters to force slaves to work still longer hours on the hottest of days.[12]

In the second experiment, Dr J. Marion Sims, the so-called father of modern gynecology, used three Alabama slave women to develop an operation to repair vesicovaginal fistulas. Between 1845 and 1849, the three slave women on whom Sims operated each underwent up to 30 painful operations. The physician himself described the agony associated with some of the experiments[13]: "The first patient I operated on was Lucy. . . . That was before the days of anesthetics, and the poor girl, on her knees, bore the operation with great heroism and bravery." This operation was not successful, and Sims later attempted to repair the defect by placing a sponge in the bladder. This experiment, too, ended in failure. He noted:

> The whole urethra and the neck of the bladder were in a high state of inflammation, which came from the foreign substance. It had to come away, and there was nothing to do but to pull it away by main force. Lucy's agony was extreme. She was much prostrated, and I thought that she was going to die; but by irrigating the parts of the bladder she recovered with great rapidity.

Sims finally did perfect his technique and ultimately repaired the fistulas. Only after his experimentation with the slave women proved successful did the physician attempt the procedure, with anesthesia, on White women volunteers.

Exploitation after the Civil War

It is not known to what extent African Americans continued to be used as unwilling subjects for experimentation and dissection in the years after emancipation. However, an examination of African-American folklore at the turn of the century makes it clear that Black people believed that such practices persisted. Folktales are replete with references to night doctors, also called student doctors and Ku Klux doctors. In her book, *Night Riders in Black Folk History*, anthropologist Gladys-Marie Fry writes, "The term 'night doctor' (derived from the fact that victims were sought only at night) applies both to students of medicine, who supposedly stole cadavers from which to learn about body processes, and [to] professional thieves, who sold stolen bodies—living and dead—to physicians for medical research."[14] According to folk belief, these sinister characters would kidnap Black people, usually at night and in urban areas, and take them to hospitals to be killed and used in experiments. An 1889 *Boston Herald* article vividly captured the fears that African Americans in South Carolina had of night doctors. The report read, in part:

> The negroes of Clarendon, Williamsburg, and Sumter counties have for several weeks past been in a state of fear and trembling. They claim that there is a white man, a doctor, who at will can make himself invisible and who then approaches some unsuspecting darkey, and having rendered him or her insensible with chloroform, proceeds to fill up a bucket with the victim's blood, for the purpose of making medicine. After having drained the last drop of blood from the victim, the body is dumped into some secret place where it is impossible for any person to find it. The colored women are so worked up over this phantom that they will not venture out at night, or in the daytime in any sequestered place.[15]

Fry did not find any documented evidence of the existence of night riders. However, she demonstrated through extensive interviews that many African Americans expressed genuine fears that they would be kidnapped by night doctors and used for medical experimentation. Fry concludes that two factors explain this paradox. She argues that Whites, especially those in the rural South, deliberately spread rumors about night doctors in order to maintain psychological control over Blacks and to discourage their migration to the North so as to maintain a source of cheap labor. In addition, Fry asserts that the experiences of many African Americans as victims of medical experiments during slavery fostered their belief in the existence of night doctors.[16] It should also be added that, given the nation's racial and political climate, Black people recognized their inability to refuse to participate in medical experiments.

Reports about the medical exploitation of Black people in the name of medicine after the end of the Civil War were not restricted to the realm of folklore. Until it was exposed in 1882, a grave robbing ring operated in Philadelphia and provided bodies for the city's medical schools by plundering the graves at a Black cemetery. According to historian David C. Humphrey, southern grave robbers regularly sent bodies of southern Blacks to northern medical schools for use as anatomy cadavers.[17]

During the early 20th century, African-American medical leaders protested the abuse of Black people by the White-dominated medical profession and used their concerns about experimentation to press for the establishment of Black controlled hospitals.[18] Dr Daniel Hale Williams, the founder of Chicago's Provident Hospital (1891), the nation's first Black-controlled hospital, contended that White physicians, especially in the South, frequently used Black patients as guinea pigs.[19] Dr Nathan Francis Mossell, the founder of Philadelphia's Frederick Douglass Memorial Hospital (1895), described the "fears and prejudices" of Black people, especially those from the South, as "almost proverbial."[20] He attributed such attitudes to southern medicine practices in which Black people, "when forced to accept hospital attention, got only the poorest care, being placed in inferior wards set apart for them, suffering the brunt of all that is experimental in treatment, and all this is the sequence of their race variety and abject helplessness."[21] The founders of Black hospitals claimed that only Black physicians possessed the skills required to treat Black patients optimally and that Black hospitals provided these patients with the best possible care.[22]

Fears about the exploitation of African Americans by White physicians played a role in the establishment of a Black veterans hospital in Tuskegee, Ala. In 1923, 9 years before the initiation of the Tuskegee Syphilis Study, racial tensions had erupted in the town over control of the hospital. The federal government had pledged that the facility, an institution designed exclusively for Black patients, would be run by a Black professional staff But many Whites in the area, including members of the Ku Klux Klan, did not want a Black-operated federal facility in the heart of Dixie, even though it would serve only Black people.[23]

Black Americans sought control of the veterans hospital, in part because they believed that the ex-soldiers would receive the best possible care from Black physicians and nurses, who would be more caring and sympathetic to the veterans' needs. Some Black newspapers even warned that White southerners wanted command of the hospital as part of a racist plot to kill and sterilize

African-American men and to establish an "experiment station" for mediocre White physicians. Black physicians did eventually gain the right to operate the hospital, yet this did not stop the hospital from becoming an experiment station for Black men. The veterans hospital was one of the facilities used by the United States Public Health Service in the syphilis study.

During the 1920s and 1930s, Black physicians pushed for additional measures that would battle medical racism and advance their professional needs. Dr Charles Garvin, a prominent Cleveland physician and a member of the editorial board of the Black medical publication *The Journal of the National Medical Association,* urged his colleagues to engage in research in order to protect Black patients. He called for more research on diseases such as tuberculosis and pellagra that allegedly affected African Americans disproportionately or idiosyncratically. Garvin insisted that Black physicians investigate these racial diseases because "heretofore in literature, as in medicine, the Negro has been written about, exploited and experimented upon sometimes not to his physical betterment or to the advancement of science, but the advancement of the Nordic investigator." Moreover, he charged that "in the past, men of other races have for the large part interpreted our diseases, often tinctured with inborn prejudices."[25]

Fears of Genocide

These historical examples clearly demonstrate that African Americans' distrust of the medical profession has a longer history than the public revelations of the Tuskegee Syphilis Study. There is a collective memory among African Americans about their exploitation by the medical establishment. The Tuskegee Syphilis Study has emerged as the most prominent example of medical racism because it confirms, if not authenticates, long-held and deeply entrenched beliefs within the Black community. To be sure, the Tuskegee Syphilis Study does cast a long shadow. After the study had been exposed, charges surfaced that the experiment was part of a governmental plot to exterminate Black people.[26] Many Black people agreed with the charge that the study represented "nothing less than an official, premeditated policy of genocide."[27] Furthermore, this was not the first or last time that allegations of genocide have been launched against the government and the medical profession. The sickle cell anemia screening programs of the 1970s and birth control programs have also provoked such allegations.[28]

In recent years, links have been made between Tuskegee, AIDS, and genocide. In September 1990, the article "AIDS: Is It Genocide?" appeared in *Essence,* a Black woman's magazine. The author noted

"As an increasing number of African-Americans continue to sicken and die and as no cure for AIDS has been found some of us are beginning to think the unthinkable: Could AIDS be a virus that was manufactured to erase large numbers of us? Are they trying to kill us with this disease?"[29] In other words, some members of the Black community see AIDS as part of a conspiracy to exterminate African Americans.

Beliefs about the connection between AIDS and the purposeful destruction of African Americans should not be cavalierly dismissed as bizarre and paranoid. They are held by a significant number of Black people. For example, a 1990 survey conducted by the Southern Christian Leadership Conference found that 35% of the 1056 Black church members who responded believed that AIDS was a form of genocide.[30] A *New York Times*/WCBS TV News poll conducted the same year found that 10% of Black Americans thought that the AIDS virus had been created in a laboratory in order to infect Black people. Another 20% believed that it could be true.[31]

African Americans frequently point to the Tuskegee Syphilis Study as evidence to support their views about genocide, perhaps, in part, because many believe that the men in the study were actually injected with syphilis. Harlon Dalton, a Yale Law School professor and a former member of the National Commission on AIDS, wrote, in a 1989 article titled, "AIDS in Black Face," that "the government [had] purposefully exposed Black men to syphilis."[32] Six years later, Dr Eleanor Walker, a Detroit radiation oncologist, offered an explanation as to why few African Americans become bone marrow donors. "The biggest fear, she claimed, is that they will become victims of some misfeasance, like the Tuskegee incident where Black men were infected with syphilis and left untreated to die from the disease."[33] The January 25, 1996, episode of *New York Undercover,* a Fox Network police drama that is one of the top shows in Black households, also reinforced the rumor that the US Public Health Service physicians injected the men with syphilis.[34] The myth about deliberate infection is not limited to the Black community. On April 8, 1997, news anchor Tom Brokaw, on "NBC Nightly News," announced that the men had been infected by the government.[35]

Folklorist Patricia A. Turner, in her book *I Heard It through the Grapevine: Rumor and Resistance in African-American Culture,* underscores why it is important not to ridicule but to pay attention to these strongly held theories about genocide.[36] She argues that these rumors reveal much about what African Americans believe to be the state of their lives in this country. She contends that such views reflect Black beliefs that White Americans have historically been, and continue to be, ambivalent and perhaps hostile to the existence of Black people. Consequently, African-American attitudes toward biomedical research are not influenced solely by the Tuskegee Syphilis Study. African Americans' opinions about the value White society has attached to their lives should not be discounted. As Reverend Floyd Tompkins of Stanford University Memorial Church has said. "There is a sense in our community, and I think it shall be proved out, that if you are poor or you're a person of color, you were the guinea pig, and you continue to be the guinea pigs, and there is the fundamental belief that Black life is not valued like White life or like any other life in America."[37]

Not Just Paranoia

Lorene Cary, in a cogent essay in *Newsweek*, expands on Reverend Tompkins' point. In an essay titled "Why It's Not Just Paranoia," she writes:

We Americans continue to value the lives and humanity of some groups more than the lives and humanity of others. That is not paranoia. It is our historical legacy and a present fact; it influences domestic and foreign policy and the daily interaction of millions of Americans. It influences the way we spend our public money and explains how we can read the staggering statistics on Black Americans' infant mortality, youth mortality, mortality in middle and old age, and not be moved to action.[38]

African Americans' beliefs that their lives are devalued by White society also influence their relationships with the medical profession. They perceive, at times correctly, that they are treated differently in the health care system solely because of their race, and such perceptions fuel mistrust of the medical profession. For example, a national telephone survey conducted in 1986 revealed that African Americans were more likely than Whites to report that their physicians did not inquire sufficiently about their pain, did not tell them how long it would take for prescribed medicine to work, did not explain the seriousness of their illness or injury, and did not discuss test and examination findings.[39] A 1994 study published in the *American Journal of Public Health* found that physicians were less likely to give pregnant Black women information about the hazards of smoking and drinking during pregnancy.[40]

The powerful legacy of the Tuskegee Syphilis Study endures, in part, because the racism and disrespect for Black lives that it entailed mirror Black people's contemporary experiences with the medical profession. The anger and frustration that many African Americans feel when they encounter the health care system can be heard in the words of Alicia Georges, a professor of nursing at Lehman College and a former president of the National Black Nurses Association, as she recalled an emergency room experience. "Back a few years ago, I was having excruciating abdominal pain, and I wound up at a hospital in my area,' she recalled. "The first thing that they began to ask me was how many sexual partners I'd had. I was married and owned my own house. But immediately, in looking at me, they said, 'Oh, she just has pelvic inflammatory disease.'"[41] Perhaps because of her nursing background, Georges recognized the implications of the questioning. She had come face to face with the stereotype of Black women as sexually promiscuous. Similarly, the following story from the *Los Angeles Times* shows how racism can affect the practice of medicine:

When Althea Alexander broke her arm, the attending resident at Los Angeles County-USC Medical Center told her to "hold your arm like you usually hold your can of beer on Saturday night." Alexander who is Black, exploded. "What are you talking about? Do you think I'm a welfare mother?" The White resident shrugged: "Well aren't you?" Turned out she was an administrator at USC medical school.

This example graphically illustrates that health care providers are not immune to the beliefs and misconceptions of the wider community. They carry with them stereotypes about various groups of people.[42]

Beyond Tuskegee

There is also a growing body of medical research that vividly illustrates why discussions of the relationship of African Americans and the medical profession must go beyond the Tuskegee Syphilis Study. These studies demonstrate racial inequities in access to particular technologies and raise critical questions about the role of racism in medical decision making. For example, in 1989 *The Journal of the American Medical Association* published a report that demonstrated racial inequities in the treatment of heart disease. In this study, White and Black patients had similar rates of hospitalization for chest pain, but the White patients were one third more likely to undergo coronary angiography and more than twice as likely to be treated with bypass surgery or angioplasty. The racial disparities persisted even after adjustments were made for differences in income.[43] Three years later, another study appearing in that journal reinforced these findings. It revealed that older Black patients on Medicare received coronary artery bypass grafts only about a fourth as often as comparable

White patients. Disparities were greatest in the rural South, where White patients had the surgery seven times as often as Black patients. Medical factors did not fully explain the differences. This study suggests that an already-existing national health insurance program does not solve the access problems of African Americans.[44] Additional studies have confirmed the persistence of such inequities.[45]

Why the racial disparities? Possible explanations include health problems that precluded the use of procedures, patient unwillingness to accept medical advice or to undergo surgery, and differences in severity of illness. However, the role of racial bias cannot be discounted, as the American Medical Association's Council on Ethical and Judicial Affairs has recognized. In a 1990 report on Black-White disparities in health care, the council asserted:

> Because racial disparities may be occurring despite the lack of any intent or purposeful efforts to treat patients differently on the basis of race, physicians should examine their own practices to ensure that inappropriate considerations do not affect their clinical judgment. In addition, the profession should help increase the awareness of its members of racial disparities in medical treatment decisions by engaging in open and broad discussions about the issue. Such discussions should take place as part of the medical school curriculum, in medical journals, at professional conferences, and as part of professional peer review activities.[46]

The council's recommendation is a strong acknowledgment that racism can influence the practice of medicine.

After the public disclosures of the Tuskegee Syphilis Study, Congress passed the National Research Act of 1974. This act, established to protect subjects in human experimentation, mandates institutional review board approval of all federally funded research with human subjects. However, recent revelations about a measles vaccine study financed by the Centers for Disease Control and Prevention (CDC) demonstrate the inadequacies of these safeguards and illustrate why African Americans' historically based fears of medical research persist. In 1989, in the midst of a measles epidemic in Los Angeles, the CDC, in collaboration with Kaiser Permanente and the Los Angeles County Health Department, began a study to test whether the experimental Edmonston-Zagreb vaccine could be used to immunize children too young for the standard Moraten vaccine. By 1991, approximately 900 infants, mostly Black and Latino, had received the vaccine without difficulties. (Apparently, one infant died for reasons not related to the inoculations.) But the infants' parents had

not been informed that the vaccine was not licensed in the United States or that it had been associated with an increase in death rates in Africa. The 1996 disclosure of the study prompted charges of medical racism and of the continued exploitation of minority communities by medical professionals.[47]

The Tuskegee Syphilis Study continues to cast its shadow over the lives of African Americans. For many Black people, it has come to represent the racism that pervades American institutions and the disdain in which Black lives are often held. But despite its significance, it cannot be the only prism we use to examine the relationship of African Americans with the medical and public health communities. The problem we must face is not just the shadow of Tuskegee but the shadow of racism that so profoundly affects the lives and beliefs of all people in this country.

ENDNOTES

1. The most comprehensive history of the study is James H. Jones, *Bad Blood,* new and expanded edition (New York: Free Press, 1993).
2. "Remarks by the President in Apology for Study Done in Tuskegee," Press Release, the White House, Office of the Press Secretary, 16 May 1997.
3. "Final Report of the Tuskegee Syphilis Study Legacy Committee," Vanessa Northington Gamble, chair, and John C. Fletcher, co-chair, 20 May 1996.
4. Vanessa Northington Gamble, "A Legacy of Distrust: African Americans and Medical Research," *American Journal of Preventive Medicine 9* (1993): 35-38; Shari Roan, "A Medical Imbalance," *Los Angeles Times,* 1 November 1994; Carol Stevens, "Research: Distrust Runs Deep; Medical Community Seeks Solution," *The Detroit News,* 10 December 1995; Lini S. Radaba, "Minorities in Research," *Chicago Tribune,* 13 September 1993; Robert Steinbtook, "AIDS Ttials Short-change Minorities and Drug Users," *Los Angeles Times,* 25 September 1989; Mark D. Smith, "Zidovudine: Does It Work for Everyone?" *Journal of the American Medical Association* 266 (1991): 2750-2751; Charlise Lyles, "Blacks Hesitant to Donate; Cultural Beliefs, Misinformation, Mistrust Make It a Difficult Decision," *The Virginian-Pilot,* 15 August 1994; Jeanni Wong, "Mistrust Leaves Some Blacks Reluctant to Donate Organs," *Sacramento Bee,* 17 February 1993; "Nightline," ABC News, 6 April 1994; Patrice Gaines, "Armed with the Truth in a Fight for Lives," *Washington Post,* 10 April 1994; Fran Henry, "Encouraging Organ Donation from Blacks," *Cleveland Plain Dealer,* 23 April 1994, G. Marie Swanson and Amy J. Ward, "Recruiting Minorities into Clinical Trials: Toward a Participant-Friendly System," *Journal of the National Cancer Institute* 87 (1995): 1747–1759; Dewayne Wickham, "Why Blacks Are Wary of White MDs," *The Tennessean,* 21 May 1997, 13A.
5. For example, see Stephen B. Thomas and Sandra Crouse Quinn, "The Tuskegee Syphilis Study, 1932 to 1972: Im

plications for HIV Education and AIDS Risk Education Programs in the Black Community," *American Journal of Public Health* 81 (1991): 1498–1505; Stephen B. Thomas and Sandra Crouse Quinn, "Understanding the Attitudes of Black Americans," in *Dimensions of HIV Prevention. Needle Exchange,* ed. Jeff Stryker and Mark D. Smith (Menlo Park, Calif.: Henry J. Kaiser Family Foundation, 1993), 99–128; and Stephen B. Thomas and Sandra Crouse Quinn, "The AIDS Epidemic and the African-American Community: Toward an Ethical Framework for Service Delivery," in *"It Just Ain't Fair": The Ethics of Health Care for African Americans,* ed. Annette Dula and Sara Goering (Westport, Conn.: Praeger, 1994), 75–88.

6. Thomas and Quinn, "The AIDS Epidemic and the African-American Community," 83.

7. Thomas and Quinn, "Understanding the Attitudes of Black Americans," 108–109; David L. Kirp and Ronald Bayer, "Needles and Races," *Atlantic,* July 1993, 38–42.

8. Lynda Richardson, "An Old Experiment's Legacy: Distrust of AIDS Treatment," *New York Times,* 21 April 1997, Al, A7.

9. Todd L. Savitt, "The Use of Blacks for Medical Experimentation and Demonstration in the Old South" *Journal of Southern History* 48 (1982): 331–348; David C. Humphrey, "Dissection and Discrimination: The Social Origins of Cadavers in America, 1760–1915," *Bulletin of the New York Academy of Medicine* 49 (1973): 819–827.

10. Harriet Martineau, *Retrospect of Western Travel,* vol. I (London: Saunders & Ottley; New York: Harpers and Brothers; 1838), 140, quoted in Humphrey, "Dissection and Discrimination," 819.

11. Theodore Dwight Weld, *American Slavery As It Is: Testimony of a Thousand Witnesses* (New York: American Anti-Slavery Society, 1839), 170, quoted in Savitt, "The Use of Blacks," 341.

12. F. N. Boney, "Doctor Thomas Hamilton: Two Views of a Gentleman of the Old South, *Phylon* 28 (1967): 288–292.

13. J. Marion Sims, *The Story of My Life* (New York: Appleton, 1889), 236–237.

14. Gladys-Marie Fry, *Night Riders in Black Folk History* (Knoxville: University of Tennessee Press, 1984), 171.

15. "Concerning Negro Sorcery in the United States," *Journal of American Folk-Lore* 3 (1890): 285.

16. Ibid., 210.

17. Humphrey, "Dissection and Discrimination," 822–823.

18. A detailed examination of the campaign to establish Black hospitals can be found in Vanessa Northington Gamble, *Making a Place for Ourselves: The Black Hospital Movement, 1920–1945* (New York: Oxford University Press, 1995).

19. Eugene P. Link. "The Civil Rights Activities of Three Great Negro Physicians (1840–1940)," *Journal of Negro History* 52 (July 1969): 177.

20. Mossell graduated, with honors, from Penn in 1882 and founded the hospital in 1895.

21. "Seventh Annual Report of the Frederick Douglass Memorial Hospital and Training School" (Philadelphia, Pa.: 1902), 17.

22. H. M. Green, *A More or Less Critical Review of the Hospital Situation among Negroes in the United States* (n.d., circa 1930), 4–5.

23. For more in-depth discussions of the history of the Tuskegee Veterans Hospital, see Gamble, *Making a Place for Ourselves,* 70–104; Pete Daniel, "Black Power in the 1920's: The Case of Tuskegee Veterans Hospital," *Journal of Southern History* 36 (1970): 368–388; and Raymond Wolters, *The New Negro on Campus: Black College Rebellions of the 1920s* (Princeton, NJ: Princeton University Press, 1975), 137–191.

24. "Klan Halts March on Tuskegee," *Chicago Defender,* 4 August 1923.

25. Charles H. Garvin, "The 'New Negro' Physician," unpublished manuscript, n.d., box 1, Charles H. Garvin Papers, Western Reserve Historical Society Library, Cleveland, Ohio.

26. Ronald A. Taylor, "Conspiracy Theories Widely Accepted in U.S. Black Circles," *Washington Times,* 10 December 1991, Al; Frances Cress Welsing, *The Isis Papers: The Keys to the Colors* (Chicago: Third World Press, 1991), 298–299. Although she is not very well known outside of the African-American community, Welsing, a physician, is a popular figure within it. The *Isis Papers* headed for several weeks the best-seller list maintained by Black bookstores.

27. Jones, *Bad Blood,* 12.

28. For discussions of allegations of genocide in the implementation of these programs, see Robert G. Weisbord, "Birth Control and the Black American: A Matter of Genocide?" *Demography* 10 (1973): 571–590; Alex S. Jones, "Editorial Linking Blacks, Contraceptives Stirs Debate at Philadelphia Paper," *Arizona Daily Star,* 23 December 1990, F4; Doris Y. Wilkinson, "For Whose Benefit? Politics and Sickle Cell," *The Black Scholar* 5 (1974): 26–31.

29. Karen Grisby Bates, "Is It Genocide?" *Essence,* September 1990, 76.

30. Thomas and Quinn, "The Tuskegee Syphilis Study," 1499.

31. "The AIDS 'Plot' against Blacks," *New York Times,* 12 May 1992, A22.

32. Harlon L. Dalton, "AIDS in Blackface," *Daedalus* 118 (Summer 1989):220–221.

33. Rhonda Bates-Rudd, "State Campaign Encourages African Americans to Offer Others Gift of Bone Marrow." *Detroit News,* 7 December 1995.

34. From September 1995 to December 1995, *New York Undercover* was the top-ranked show in Black households. It ranked 122nd in White households. David Zurawik. "Poll: TV's Race Gap Growing," *Capital Times* (Madison. Wis), 14 May 1996, 5D.

35. Transcript, "NBC Nightly News." 8 April 1997.

36. Patricia A. Turner, *I Heard It through the Grapevine: Rumor in African-American Culture* (Berkeley: University of California Press, 1993).

37. "Fear Creates Lack of Donor Organs among Blacks," *Weekend Edition,* National Public Radio, 13 March 1994.

38. Lorene Cary, "Why It's Not Just Paranoia: An American History of 'Plans' for Blacks," *Newsweek,* 6 April 1992, 23.

39. Robert J. Blendon, "Access to Medical Care for Black and White Americans: A Matter of Continuing Concern. *Journal of the American Medical Association* 261 (1989): 278–281.

40. M. D. Rogan et al., "Racial Disparities in Reported Prenatal Care Advice from Health Care Providers." *American Journal of Public Health* 84 (1994): 82–88.

41. Julie Johnson et al., "Why Do Blacks Die Young? *Time,* 16 September 1991, 52.

42. Sonia Nazario, "Treating Doctors for Prejudice: Medical Schools Are Trying to Sensitize Students to 'Bedside Bias.'" *Los Angeles Times,* 20 December 1990.

43. Mark B. Wenneker and Arnold M. Epstein. "Racial Inequities in the Use of Procedures for Patients with Ischemic Heart Disease in Massachusetts," *Journal of the American Medical Association* 261 (1989): 253–257.

44. Kenneth C. Goldberg et al., "Racial and Community Factors Influencing Coronary Artery Bypass Graft Surgery Rates for All 1986 Medicare Patients," *Journal of the American Medical Association* 267 (1992):1473–1477.

45. John D. Ayanian, "Heart Disease in Black and White," *New England Journal of Medicine* 329 (1993): 656–658;

J. Whittle et al., "Racial Differences in the Use of Invasive Cardiovascular Procedures in the Department of Veterans Affairs Medical System," *New England Journal of Medicine* 329 (1993): 621–627; Eric D. Peterson et al., "Racial Variation in Cardiac Procedure Use and Survival following Acute Myocardial Infarction in the Department of Veterans Affairs," *Journal of the American Medical Association* 271 (1994): 1175–1180; Ronnie D. Homer et al., "Theories Explaining Racial Differences in the Utilization of Diagnostic and Therapeutic Procedures for Cerebrovascular Disease," *Milbank Quarterly* 73 (1995): 443–462; Richard D. Moore et al., "Racial Differences in the Use of Drug Therapy for HIV Disease in an Urban Community," *New England Journal of Medicine* 350 (1994): 763–768.

46. Council on Ethical and Judicial Affairs, "Black-White Disparities in Health Care," *Journal of the American Metical Association* 263 (1990): 2346.

47. Marlene Cimons, "CDC Says It Erred in Measles Study," *Los Angeles Times,* 17 June 1996, A 11; Beth Glenn, "Bad Blood Once Again," *St. Petersburg Times,* 21 July 1996, 5D.

Latino Women
Access to Health Care

by Aida L. Giachello

Lack of access to medical care is frequently cited as the single greatest problem that Latinos face in the health care system. Access is an indicator of the ability to obtain medical care for an immediate health need. It is also an indicator of the likelihood of receiving preventive and maintenance health care. Lack of access to the health care system results from financial, cultural, and institutional barriers. Latinos lack access to a broad array of health services, especially primary care. Poor and uninsured Latinos who turn to public facilities for routine care confront a lack of bilingual/bicultural services, long waiting times between calling for an appointment and the actual visit, and long waits once they get there.

These barriers contribute to their disproportionate use of more costly services, such as hospital emergency rooms, when symptoms of illness persist or when the illness has reached an advanced stage. Access to inpatient care is also a problem in many cities, such as Chicago, where during the past several years as many as 14 community hospitals serving low-income areas and providing charitable care to the poor have closed. There are several indicators of access: (a) whether or not a person has a regular source of care, (b) health insurance coverage/financial barriers, (c) inconveniences in obtaining care, and (d) the actual use of medical services. Research findings on these areas are briefly elaborated below.

The phrase *regular source of care* refers to an established and identifiable facility or medical source that an individual or a family uses on a routine basis. Having a regular source of care is a good indicator of health services use because it facilitates entry into the system and the continuity and quality of care. Studies consistently document that Latinos are less likely than any other group to be linked to a regular source of care. This is particularly true among those with low family income.

The situation appears to be worsening among Latinos. A 1986 national survey conducted by Lou Harris and Associates found that the percentage of Latinos without a regular source of care was almost double that for whites (30% vs. 16%). Furthermore, the percentage of Latinos without a regular source of care almost tripled in 4 years, from 11.8% in 1982 to 30% in 1986.

The 1982–1984 HHANES data show that, within Latino subgroups, the proportion of those having a regular source of care varies by gender and age-group. For instance, only 56% of Mexican American men aged 20 to 30 reported a regular source of care, compared with 69% for those aged 31 to 45 and 78% for those aged 46 to 74. Mexican American women consistently reported higher linkages with a regular source of care (78% for those aged 20 to 30).

LIMITED FLEXIBILITY OF THE HEALTH CARE SYSTEM

Other inconveniences in obtaining health care for Latinos are related to the fact that the health care system in the United States possesses limited flexibility to meet the needs of populations that are poor or that may have differing illnesses, cultural practices, diets, or languages (U.S. DHHS-HSRA,1990). Providers' inability to communicate is problematic because they not only do not know the language but also use technical jargon that further confuses the client.

Providers' lack of knowledge and sensitivity about Latino culture and health behavior may also result in a series of stereotypes negatively affecting the provider-consumer relationship. This effect may have implications not only in service delivery but also in patient compliance. For instance, some non-Latino providers may regard Latinos as superstitious, present oriented, uninterested in preventive exams, and noncompliant (Gregory, 1978).

In addition, prejudice and social discrimination against Latinos may maintain and reinforce the social distance between provider and consumer (Aponte & Giachello, 1989; Quesada & Heller, 1977). A mail survey done in Chicago documented providers' knowledge, attitudes, and practices toward Latino patients/clients (Aponte & Giachello, 1989). The study found that more than half of the health care providers who responded to a questionnaire reported not knowing about Latino health status and about the heterogeneity of the Latino population. They also reported not knowing the meaning of the terms *Latinos and Hispanics* and how they are used by many Latinos interchangeably. Also, 50% said that Latinos should learn English instead of expecting bilingual services to be provided. Clear differences emerged in this study in levels of knowledge and cultural sensitivity between health care providers serving high numbers of Latino clients as opposed to those serving relatively low numbers of Latinos. Those providers serving few Latino clients showed the least interest in learning about Latino health problems or about how to reach out and serve Latinos.

LANGUAGE AS A BARRIER

Much of the literature indicates that language is a major barrier to access and appropriate use of prenatal and obstetrical services. Language becomes a problem when the population to be served is primarily Spanish speaking. Edgerton and Karno (1971) found that language barriers may be linked to other barriers, depending on whether the individual is bilingual or mainly monolingual either in Spanish or English. For example, Latinos who were only Spanish speaking tended to have less education and lower income and tended to be older and more attached to their culture. The inability to speak English fluently has interfered with Latinos' ability to obtain important health information, to communicate with health professionals, and to locate health services available in their community.

Communication and the provider-consumer relationship may be negatively affected by the use of interpreters. Interpreters require a great deal of skill to describe and explain terms, ideas, and processes regarding patient care (Putsch, 1985). Usually, the responsibility for interpretation in a health or mental health facility falls, according to Putsch, to anyone who is bilingual, such as an employee, family members (e.g., child), or friend, usually with no formal interpretation training. This lack of training may lead to inaccuracies, failure to disclose information, violation of confidentiality, and failure of the provider to develop rapport with the patient (but with the interpreter).

The presence of bilingual staff does more than provide translation services. It also promotes a perception of caring about Latinos, opens the way for changes in service delivery that can contribute to better access for Latinos, and improves the quality of service delivery (Giachello, 1985). Understanding a patient's language is the beginning of understanding her or his health and illness beliefs and behavior and facilitates treating the patient as a whole person, and not just as a configuration of disease symptoms.

Even so, a citywide survey of health care providers' perceptions of Latino clients in Chicago found that only 28% of providers made any special efforts to recruit bilingual personnel (Aponte & Giachello, 1989). Nonprofit providers and those located in Latino areas were most likely to make such efforts (47% and 45%, respectively). Of those that did, providers located in Latino areas reported encountering the most difficulty in recruiting such personnel.

Limited provisions are being made in many health facilities that serve a large number of Latinos to establish procedures to handle the case of interpreters. For example, Aponte and Giachello (1989) found that only 40% of health care providers reported having a protocol for dealing with monolingual Spanish-speaking clients. Of those who reported a protocol, close to one third said that the protocol consisted of telling the client to bring her or his own interpreter, and two thirds indicated that an interpreter was available on site. Providers serving primarily Latino clients were least likely to report having any sorts of arrangements for serving their clients who spoke only Spanish.

HEALTH CARE COSTS

A 1990 study based on the 1982–1984 HHANES data examined specific barriers that Mexican Americans experience in using medical services. Cost of health care emerged as the number one factor, mentioned by 18% of the sample. Similarly, Andersen, Giachello, and Aday (1986) found in their national survey on access to health care that Latinos and African Americans in 1982 had more difficulty than whites in getting medical care because of financial reasons; similar findings were obtained by Garcia et al. (1985).

Analyses of the problem have indicated that lack of insurance among Latinos is related to employment status, type of industry, and income (GAO, 1992). A report issued by the General Accounting Office on Hispanic access to health care indicated that one third of Latinos (more than 6 million persons) were uninsured during all or part of 1989, compared with 19% of African Americans and 12% of whites (GAO, 1992). This report indicated that 78% of Latino family members under age 65 who were uninsured lived in families with an adult worker (p. 12). It also indicated that uninsured Latinos were more likely than whites and African Americans to work in industries that are less likely to provide health insurance coverage, such as construction and agriculture. Because health insurance coverage decreases with income, working Latinos with low incomes, particularly those below the poverty level, were much more likely to be uninsured than those with higher incomes. This finding is particularly true among

Latino males with lower incomes. They were twice as likely to be uninsured (64% vs. 30%), compared with Latino males with higher incomes.

Research on uninsured Latinos by gender also indicates differences in coverage among subpopulations. For instance, the 1982–1984 HHANES found that 34% of Mexican American males in the study reported no health insurance, compared with 28% for Cuban American males and 30% for Puerto Rican males. The percentages for Latino women were 34% for Mexican American, 25% for Cuban American, and 17% for Puerto Rican.

The problem of insurance coverage is even more severe among Latino children and adolescents. Two researchers in 1989 found that, in Chicago, 38% of Mexican American children and adolescents were uninsured. Mexican adolescents experienced the greatest disadvantage, with over half of 18- to 19-year-olds (56%) uninsured. Even in a more affluent Latino community, such as that of the Minneapolis-St. Paul metropolitan area, a 1990 telephone survey among Latinos found that only 27% of adolescents aged 16 to 21 had insurance (Giachello & Arrom, 1990).

Studies on type of health insurance coverage have found differences among racial and ethnic groups and among Latinos of various national origins. A group of researchers in 1991, using data from the 1989 Current Population Survey, found that Mexican Americans (43.7%) and Puerto Ricans (43.6%), followed closely by African Americans (45.4%), were least likely to have private health insurance. Furthermore, Puerto Ricans were most likely of all racial and ethnic groups to report Medicaid coverage (32.5%), followed by African Americans (23.3%), compared with Mexican Americans (13.7%), Cuban Americans (11.9%), and compared with the total U.S. population (8.3%).

One explanation for the high percentage of Puerto Ricans on Medicaid programs is that a high proportion of Puerto Rican poor families are female-headed households and thus are more likely to be eligible for Medicaid coverage. This eligibility is because many states exclude two-parent families from the Medicaid program regardless of whether they meet the income requirements. Another explanation is the difference in Medicaid eligibility criteria across states. Texas and Florida, where 3 of every 10 Latinos live in the United States, are the most restrictive states; New York and New Jersey, where Puerto Ricans are mostly concentrated, are not (GAO, 1992). Furthermore, Arizona and New Mexico do not have a medically needy program (GAO, 1992).

The National Coalition of Hispanic Health and Human Service Organizations explored in detail the Medicaid programs of seven states: Arizona, California, Florida, Illinois, New Jersey, New York, and Texas. The

Latino population in these states comprise 84.4% of the total Latino population in the United States. The survey found that the percentage of Latino Medicaid recipients varies by state, ranging from 0.4% in Florida to 33.7% in Texas. It also revealed that almost two of every three Latinos (65%) below age 65 and under the poverty level and not covered by private insurance coverage were not covered by Medicaid, compared with 36% of whites. For those covered, the per capita spending under the Medicaid program for a group of preventive care and acute illness services in all the states except New York and New Jersey was lower for Latinos than for whites.

Medicaid has not been a solution to the lack of insurance for all poor people, particularly Latinos and African Americans below the poverty level. Furthermore, studies show that health care providers are least likely to accept Latino patients with Medicaid than with Medicare. Providers located in Latino barrios and with at least 50% of Latino clients were the ones most likely to accept Latinos with Medicaid coverage (Aponte & Giachello, 1989).

Having insurance coverage, however, does not ensure equal access because of (a) inequities in benefits packages, (b) providers' discretion in deciding which health insurance company to accept, and (c) increased search costs due to private cost-containment efforts (e.g., deductibles, copayments). Latinos appear particularly vulnerable to these weaknesses in the current system of financing medical care.

The relationship between health insurance and use of services has been documented. Using data from the HHANES, a group of researchers in 1991 found that lack of health insurance reduces an individual's access to health care; a high proportion of the uninsured did not have a regular source of medical care, had not consulted a physician in the past year, and never had a routine medical examination, compared with the insured. Latinos with only Medicaid coverage were most likely to report a physician visit within the year, followed by those with Medicare and other public insurance programs. In 1989, Medicaid coverage was associated with an increase in the probability of hospital admission for Mexican Americans.

Finally, even the presence of insurance (public or private) may not provide adequate coverage for the needs of Latinos. More than half of private health insurance plans do not cover pre- or postnatal care, both critical time periods for ensuring a child's future health. Of employment-based insurance plans, only 9% cover preventive care, 15% cover eyeglasses, and 32% cover dental care. Similar inadequacies are also found in public programs.

Summary

It is clear that Latino women are experiencing serious health problems and that access to health care continues to be difficult for this population. They are experiencing a chronic lack of access to health care because of financial, cultural, and institutional barriers. Linkages with regular sources of medical care are limited, and differences exist in the sources, patterns, and quality of health care received by Latinos. There is also shortage of bilingual and bicultural health professionals, combined with drastic cuts in health and human services programs.

These problems are occurring at a time when Latino women's medical needs are becoming greater. Latinos with the worst health status and with poor access live in communities that are experiencing a series of health and social problems, such as family violence, crime and gang activities, and high school dropouts. A strong association appears to exist between poor health and poverty, both of which are the result of institutional racism, classism, and discrimination.

Recommendations

This chapter provided a review of the literature on Latino women's health. What follows are a series of recommendations for public policy formulation, for program planning and implementation, and for future research.

1. *It is critical that health care providers and policymakers give the proper attention to the special health needs of Latino women.* In doing so, it is necessary to take into consideration the tremendous diversity of the Latino women population in terms of national origin, age, socioeconomic status, levels of education, assimilation and acculturation into the mainstream society, and regional areas. Health care providers and policymakers must expand the network of Latino health professionals who are consulted on health and human services matters to include representatives from the different Latino women's health and social organizations and representatives of women of different Latino groups (e.g., Mexican Americans, Puerto Ricans, Cubans) and from different regions of the country.

2. *There is a need is for long-term institutional/ structural changes to deal effectively with the health problems of Latino women.* Social changes must

occur in society to minimize poverty and to improve levels of education and income among Latinos. For example, the health needs of Latino women cannot be adequately addressed unless the social and economic problems that women confront in society are addressed.

3. *More research and data are needed on Latino women.* Despite an increase of data on Latino women, tremendous gaps exist. For example, no recent data are available on health services use. Insufficient data are available on their health status regarding certain health problems and on health services use patterns. Practically no information is available on the health status of women from Central or South America; yet, this group is the fastest growing Hispanic population. Limited data are available on Latino life expectancy and on socioeconomics, life, and environmental factors that affect their health. More research is needed on the following:

- *Health and mental status of Latino women.* More data are needed on acute and chronic conditions (e.g., gestational diabetes, sexually transmitted diseases), pre- and postpartum depressions, attitudes toward pregnancy and birth, factors responsible for medical high-risk designations, and the long-term physical and mental health effects of bearing many children.

- *The lifestyle practices or personal health habits of Latino women, adolescents, and adults.* The limited data that exist are primarily in the areas of smoking, alcohol consumption, and selected nutritional habits.

- *Factors related to access to medical care.* Aspects that must be examined are financial barriers (e.g., cost of services, health insurance coverage, type of insurance—private as opposed to government sponsored), characteristics of the regular source of health care (e.g., private vs. public), and inconveniences of health care (e.g., clinic hours, appointment system, staff composition).

- *Sociocultural factors, including health beliefs and behaviors and their effects on health outcomes.* Elements of the culture have positive impacts on pregnancy outcome. These elements should be studied, and programs should be developed that can transfer these elements to other at-risk populations.

- *Programs that can educate Latino adolescents of both sexes about issues of sexuality; family planning methods, including abstinence; and the social and medical implications of teen pregnancy.* More important, Latino youths, particularly females, need assistance to increase their communication skills, decision-making skills, and negotiation skills regarding when, how, and under what circumstances they will become sexually active.

- *Programs at the community level that could provide the necessary support (e.g., mental health, training programs, day care service) and financial assistance to Latino women who are female heads of households to break the cycle of poverty for themselves and their children.*

4. *HIV/AIDS policies and funding must be more responsive to Latino women's needs.* A recent shift in policies occurred at the federal level from primary prevention and education to early intervention and treatment. Although proper attention should be given to these areas, drastic reductions are occurring, and more are expected, aimed at the area of primary prevention (e.g., general awareness campaign, HIV/AIDS education activities). Funds for prevention and education should not be taken away from communities of color. This shift may have negative consequences to the Latino communities that have just begun to be exposed to HIV/AIDS education and prevention activities. Many Latino women, particularly the poor and migrants or those living in small communities in the Midwest, have not been reached at all. For these populations already lacking access to medical care in general, HIV and AIDS are not a "chronic manageable disease," but a sentence to death.

Prevention and education remain the only effective tools in the fight against AIDS and are an inexpensive and extremely cost-effective way to fight the epidemic. A continuum of care policy is needed. In addition, prevention strategies that go beyond awareness levels have not been implemented. Prevention strategies require more intensive efforts at the community level to develop the infrastructure that will provide clear, unequivocal prevention messages and ensure that resources such as the distribution of condoms, which has proven effective, be expanded.

Congress needs to legislate and to recommend that federal agencies develop programmatic means that will minimize the competition for funding among groups at high risk for AIDS. The way the distribution of funds currently works, groups are forced to compete with one another for limited resources—for example, gay/bisexual groups competing for funds against racial/ethnic minorities.

5. *We need to increase Latino women's representation at the federal level.* This is particularly necessary in key administrative and policy-making positions addressing the needs of children and adolescents. A report from the Hispanic Health Policy Summit in 1992 indicates that Hispanics account for less than 3% of all employees in the federal government workforce. Among federal health professionals with doctoral degrees, Hispanics comprise less than 2% of employees. Of those federal health professionals in the U.S. DHHS who manage significant departmental budgets, Latinos constitute less than 1%. Evidence suggests that the Latino workforce in the federal government is declining.

6. *In the area of alcohol and substance abuse, there is a need for more drug treatment programs for Latino women addicted to drugs.* Practically no culturally appropriate and affordable programs are available for female adolescents and adult women dependent on alcohol and other drugs. The need is to strongly advocate for more treatment slots for women with alcohol and drug addiction who are pregnant. These women tend to be excluded from drug treatment programs. Arguments used are that these programs do not have birth centers and cannot handle complications that require neonatal care. The need is to make provision for the comprehensive care and services delivery for the growing number of drug-addicted Latino women and their babies.

Public health and social policies that promote the prosecution of women who use alcohol and drugs during pregnancy should be reexamined. A series of legal and ethical controversies has emerged regarding alcohol and drug use during pregnancy. Debate has been increasing on whether women who use drugs during pregnancy should be criminally prosecuted for their conduct. Criminalization of drug use during pregnancy may lead pregnant Latino women who are drug users to either delay their entry into the medical care system or not use the system at all for prenatal care because of fears of prosecution or of removal of the child after she or he is born. These actions would serve neither the baby's nor the mother's health.

It is imperative that the war against drugs, as well as any antidrug strategic plans, incorporate and bring for public discussion ways of minimizing and/or ultimately eliminating the abuse of legal (alcohol) and illegal drugs in the United States. The federal government should establish tough measures to keep the alcohol and tobacco industries away from Latino women, children, and youths.

It is important that state and local governments and the public recognize the direct relationship between HIV/AIDS and substance abuse. Funding should be made available for community-based organizations to develop the proper strategies for dealing effectively with this problem.

Expanding Health Options for Asian and Pacific Islander Women

by collective members of Massachusetts Asian AIDS Prevention Project
Edited by Ramani Sripada-Vaz and Sue Lowcock

Women of Asian and Pacific Islander (API) descent are often a forgotten group when it comes to access to health care and education. It is a difficult enough task to begin to dismantle the myth that APIs are a "model minority," that we are all academic and economic achievers with no health problems. API women are further marginalized when it comes to gaining culturally and linguistically appropriate reproductive health and HIV/AIDS information. Little research has been done to this date to determine the level of HIV awareness, risk factors for HIV transmission and accessibility of health services for women of API descent living in the United States.

According to the 1990 census, Asians made up 2.4 percent of the population in Massachusetts, with the Chinese community being the largest (37.5 percent), followed by Asian Indian (19 percent), Vietnamese (10.4 percent) and Cambodian (9 percent) populations. Though Boston had the largest Asian population in 1990, Lowell had the largest concentration of Asians, of which 56.3 percent were Cambodian. API women make up approximately half of the state's Asian population.

The Massachusetts Asian AIDS Prevention Project (MAAPP), a nonprofit organization established in 1995 to prevent the spread of HIV among APIs in Massachusetts, initiated the Women's Needs Assessment Project to focus on prevention of HIV. We targeted four separate groups of API women: Chinese, Vietnamese, Cambodian and Bangladeshi. This project was done in collaboration with South Asian Women for Action, South Cove Community Health Center, Refugee and Immigrant Health Program (Massachusetts Department of Public Health), and Vietnamese and Cambodian community-based individuals.

First, a knowledge questionnaire specific to women was developed and translated into four languages: Chinese, Vietnamese, Khmer and Bengali. Next, a list of focus group questions were designed to elicit ideas, behaviors and attitudes related to HIV, general reproductive health and access to health information. The participants and facilitators were also asked for suggestions about the best strategies for reaching API women.

All four focus groups were held from September to November 1996, with a total of 34 women attending. The majority of the women were from lower-income backgrounds and spoke some English. The following is a snapshot of what happened during one of the sessions:

A small group of women gathered together on a Sunday evening in October, and between cups of tea and occasional bursts of giggles, they chatted about how they feel HIV can affect their lives. Because of cultural and religious values, they had difficulty discussing premarital and extramarital sex. It was also difficult to talk about the critical subject of safer sex because their religions prohibit contraception. The women felt that they are not at risk for HIV because they do not engage in "sexual misconduct." In a social context, where the male partner is always perceived as dominant, many of the women felt the need for an outside third party to intervene in order for safer sex and condom-use to happen, since sex is not always negotiable within a marriage without the help of a medical, legal or familial authority figure.

Gaps in knowledge were common in all four ethnic groups, particularly regarding the transmission of HIV. Some misconceptions that were presented include:

- AIDS is a disease that only affects those who live in big cities and have multiple partners.
- Only anal sex transmits HIV.
- Nothing can be done to prevent a baby from getting infected during pregnancy/delivery.
- When people are married, there is no need to practice safer sex.
- Keeping in good physical shape is the best way to keep from getting AIDS.

From *Sojourner: The Women's Forum*, March 1998, Vol. 23, No. 7, p. 32. Copyright © 1998 by Sojourner. Reprinted by permission.

- A shower after sex reduces the risk of getting AIDS. Withdrawal by a man before orgasm prevents transmission of HIV.

These results have implications for the need to tailor HIV-prevention materials to be more woman-specific, taking into account basic transmission facts. In addition to these knowledge indicators, focus group discussions also identified key themes surrounding behaviors and attitudes. Some of these include:

- Poor knowledge of family planning methods and prevention of sexually transmitted disease, including condom use.
- Difficulty negotiating contraception with partners because of taboos around talking about sex and gender inequity.
- Reliance on personal physicians for health information. Emphasis on belief that HIV is transmitted only if there is "sexual misconduct."
- Homophobia and lack of familiarity with sexual diversity. Low self-perception of risk because the women were not "promiscuous." Fear of and stigmatization of people with HIV at workplaces. Fear of and stigmatization of children with HIV at their children's schools.

While discussion of these and other taboo topics was difficult for focus group participants, we did find that women were able to talk about sexuality, HIV/AIDS and gender issues. Such discussion was possible because the issues were raised in a safe, peer-supported environment, within the context of broader women's health issues. The ideas and recommendations that came from the focus group discussions, and which will be presented to other community members, form the basis for future advocacy efforts by MAAPP with providers and institutions serving API women.

MAAPP is currently organizing a Women's Advisory Group for our upcoming Women's Health Leadership Initiative, which aims to promote and expand API women's reproductive health options and knowledge through a process empowering women to learn about their reproductive health, discover their own bodies, and enhance their self esteem. We will encourage API women to educate their peers and become advocates for improved culturally competent and linguistically accessible reproductive health services.

The National Asian Women's Health Organization (NAWHO) advocates on a national level for such services, and has created an API women's health agenda. MAAPP is truly grateful for the opportunity to work with national organizations such as NAWHO because it is often difficult to work on the local and state level when policies are also being made on a national level. If you or anyone you know is interested in participating in MAAPP's women's program please call Ramani Sripada-Vaz at (617)262-2900.

Angry Women Are Building: Issues and Struggles Facing American Indian Women Today

by Paula Gunn Allen

The central issue that confronts American Indian women throughout the hemisphere is survival, *literal survival,* both on a cultural and biological level. According to the 1980 census, the population of American Indians is just over one million. This figure, which is disputed by some American Indians, is probably a fair estimate, and it carries certain implications.

Some researchers put our pre-contact population at more than 45 million, while others put it at around 20 million. The U.S. government long put it at 450,000—a comforting if imaginary figure, though at one point it was put at around 270,000. If our current population is around one million; if, as some researchers estimate, around 25 percent of Indian women and 10 percent of Indian men in the United States have been sterilized without informed consent; if our average life expectancy is, as the best-informed research presently says, 55 years; if our infant mortality rate continues at well above national standards; if our average unemployment for all segments of our population—male, female, young, adult, and middle-aged is between 60 and 90 percent; if the U.S. government continues its policy of termination, relocation, removal, and assimilation along with the destruction of wilderness, reservation land, and its resources, and severe curtailment of hunting, fishing, timber harvesting and water-use rights—then existing tribes are facing the threat of extinction which for several hundred tribal groups has already become fact in the past five hundred years.

In this nation of more than 200 million, the Indian people constitute less than one-half of one percent of the population. In a nation that offers refuge, sympathy, and billions of dollars in aid from federal and private sources in the form of food to the hungry, medicine to the sick, and comfort to the dying, the indigenous subject population goes hungry, homeless, impoverished, cut out of the American deal, new, old, and in between. Americans are daily made aware of the worldwide slaughter of native peoples such as the Cambodians, the Palestinians, the Armenians, the Jews—who constitute only a few groups faced with genocide in this century. We are horrified by South African apartheid and the removal of millions of indigenous African black natives to what is there called "homelands"—but this is simply a replay of nineteenth-century U.S. government removal of American Indians to reservations. Nor do many even notice the parallel or fight South African apartheid by demanding an end to its counterpart within the borders of the United States. The American Indian people are in a situation comparable to the imminent genocide in many parts of the world today. The plight of our people north and south of us is no better; to the south it is considerably worse. Consciously or unconsciously, deliberately, as a matter of national policy, or accidentally as a matter of "fate," *every single government,* right, left, or centrist in the western hemisphere is consciously or subconsciously dedicated to the extinction of those tribal people who live within its borders.

Within this geopolitical charnel house, American Indian women struggle on every front for the survival of our children, our people, our self-respect, our value systems, and our way of life. The past five hundred years testify to our skill at waging this struggle: for all the varied weapons of extinction pointed at our heads, we endure.

We survive war and conquest; we survive colonization, acculturation, assimilation; we survive beating, rape, starvation, mutilation, sterilization, abandonment, neglect, death of our children, our loved ones, destruction of our land, our homes, our past, and our future. We survive, and we do more than just survive. We bond, we care, we fight, we teach, we nurse, we bear, we feed, we earn, we laugh, we love, we hang in there, no matter what.

Of course, some, many of us, just give up. Many are alcoholics, many are addicts. Many abandon the children, the old ones. Many commit suicide. Many become violent, go insane. Many go "white" and are never seen or heard from again. But enough hold on to their traditions and their ways so that even after almost five hundred brutal years, we endure. And we even write songs and poems, make paintings and drawings that say "We walk in beauty. Let us continue."

Currently our struggles are on two fronts: physical survival and cultural survival. For women this means fighting alcoholism and drug abuse (our own and that of our husbands, lovers, parents, children);[1] poverty; affluence—a destroyer of people who are not traditionally socialized to deal with large sums of money; rape, incest, battering by Indian men; assaults on fertility and other health matters by the Indian Health Service and the Public Health Service; high infant mortality due to substandard medical care, nutrition, and health information; poor educational opportunities or education that takes us away from our traditions, language, and communities; suicide, homicide, or similar expressions of self-hatred; lack of economic opportunities; substandard housing; sometimes violent and always virulent racist attitudes and behaviors directed against us by an entertainment and educational system that wants only one thing from Indians: our silence, our invisibility, and our collective death.

A headline in the *Navajo Times* in the fall of 1979 reported that rape was the number one crime on the Navajo reservation. In a professional mental health journal of the Indian Health Services, Phyllis Old Dog Cross reported that incest and rape are common among Indian women seeking services and that their incidence is increasing. "It is believed that at least 80 percent of the Native Women seen at the regional psychiatric service center (5 state area) have experienced some sort of sexual assault."[2] Among the forms of abuse being suffered by Native American women, Old Dog Cross cites a recent phenomenon, something called "training." This form of gang rape is "a punitive act of a group of males who band together and get even or take revenge on a selected woman."[3]

These and other cases of violence against women are powerful evidence that the status of women within the tribes has suffered grievous decline since contact, and the decline has increased in intensity in recent years. The amount of violence against women, alcoholism, and violence, abuse, and neglect by women against their children and their aged relatives have all increased. These social ills were virtually unheard of among most tribes fifty years ago, popular American opinion to the contrary. As Old Dog Cross remarks:

Rapid, unstable and irrational change was required of the Indian people if they were to survive. Incredible loss of all that had meaning was the norm. Inhuman treatment, murder, death, and punishment was a typical experience for all the tribal groups and some didn't survive.

The dominant society devoted its efforts to the attempt to change the Indian into a white-Indian. No inhuman pressure to effect this change was overlooked. These pressures included starvation, incarceration and enforced education. Religious and healing customs were banished.

In spite of the years of oppression, the Indian and the Indian spirit survived. Not, however, without adverse effect. One of the major effects was the loss of cultured values and the concomitant loss of personal identity. . . . the Indian was taught to be ashamed of being Indian and to emulate the non-Indian. In short, "white was right." For the Indian male, the only route to be successful, to be good, to be right, and to have an identity was to be as much like the white man as he could.[4]

Often it is said that the increase of violence against women is a result of various sociological factors such as oppression, racism, poverty, hopelessness, emasculation of men, and loss of male self-esteem as their own place within traditional society has been systematically destroyed by increasing urbanization, industrialization, and institutionalization, but seldom do we notice that for the past forty to fifty years, American popular media have depicted American Indian men as bloodthirsty savages devoted to treating women cruelly. While traditional Indian men seldom did any such thing—and in fact among most tribes abuse of women was simply unthinkable, as was abuse of children or the aged—the lie about "usual" male Indian behavior seems to have taken root and now bears its brutal and bitter fruit.

Image casting and image control constitute the central process that American Indian women must come to terms with, for on that control rests our sense of self, our claim to a past and to a future that we define and that we build. Images of Indians in media and educational materials profoundly influence how we act, how we relate to the world and to each other, and how we value ourselves. They also determine to a large extent how our men act toward us, toward our children, and toward each other. The popular American media image of Indian people as savages with no conscience, no compassion, and no sense of the value of human life and human dignity was hardly true of the tribes—however true it was of the invaders. But as Adolf Hitler noted a little over fifty years ago, if you tell a lie big enough and often enough, it will be believed. Evidently, while Americans and people all over the world have been led into a deep and unquestioned belief that American Indians are cruel savages, a number of American Indian men have been equally deluded into internalizing that image and acting on it. Media images, literary images, and artistic images, particularly those embedded in popular culture, must be changed before Indian women will see much relief from the violence that destroys so many lives.

To survive culturally, American Indian women must often fight the United States government, the tribal governments, women and men of their tribe or their urban community who are virulently misogynist or who are threatened by attempts to change the images foisted on us over the centuries by whites. The colonizers' revisions of our lives, values, and histories have devastated us at the most critical level of all—that of our own minds, our own sense of who we are.

Many women express strong opposition to those who would alter our life supports, steal our tribal lands, colonize our cultures and cultural expressions, and revise our very identities. We must strive to maintain tribal status; we must make certain that the tribes continue to be legally recognized entities, sovereign nations within the larger United States, and we must wage this struggle in many ways—political, educational, literary, artistic, individual, and communal. We are doing all we can: as mothers and grandmothers; as family members and tribal members; as professionals, workers, artists, shamans, leaders, chiefs, speakers, writers, and organizers, we daily demonstrate that we have no intention of disappearing, of being silent, or of quietly acquiescing in our extinction.

NOTES

1. It is likely, say some researchers, that fetal alcohol syndrome, which is serious among many Indian groups, will be so serious among the White Mountain Apache and the Pine Ridge Sioux that if present trends continue, by the year 2000 some people estimate that almost one half of all children born on those reservations will in some way be affected by FAS. (Michael Dorris, Native American Studies, Dartmouth College, private conversation. Dorris has done extensive research into the syndrome as it affects native populations in the United states as well as in New Zealand.)

2. Phyllis Old Dog cross, "Sexual Abuse, a New Threat to the Native American woman: An Overview," *Listening Post: A Periodical of the Mental Health Programs of Indian Health Services.* vol. 6, no. 2 (April 1982), p. 18.

3. Old Dog cross, p. 18.

4. Old Dog cross, p. 20.

Blazes of Truth

by Susan Schnur

When I was 12 years old, my parents sent me off to Camp Ramah in the Poconos. That June, I was a dull kid in an undershirt from Trenton, New Jersey, outfitted in lime-green, mix-and-match irregulars from E.J. Korvette's. By the end of August, though—exposed as I was, for two months, to suburban Philadelphia's finest pre-adolescent fashion cognoscenti—I had contracted that dread disease: *"JAP* itis."*

Symptoms included not only the perfection of an elaborate, all-day, triple-sink procedure for dyeing white wool bobby socks to the requisite shade of dirty white (we called it oyster), but also my sudden, ignominious realization that the discount "Beatlemania" record my mother had bought for me the previous spring was not, after all, sung by the real group.

I'm not even sure that the term *JAP* existed yet back then (I don't think it did), but, in any case, by October I was—more or less—cured. I put the general themes of entitlement, of materialism, of canonized motifs (in those days, Lord and Taylor was the label of choice rather than Bloomingdale's) at the back of my mental medicine chest for the next two decades.

It wasn't until six months ago, actually—while teaching a course at Colgate University called "Contemporary Issues of Jewish Existence"—that I again gave the subject of *JAPs* a moment's pause.

A unit on *JAPs* was decidedly *not* on my course syllabus (I taught the standards: Holocaust—Faith—Immigration—Assimilation—Varieties of Religious Experience—Humor—Israel—Women). But my students, as it turned out, were obsessed with *JAPs.*

Week after week, in personal journals that they were keeping for me, they talked *JAPs:* the stereotypes, dating them, hating them, not *being* them, *JAP* graffiti, *JAP* com-petitiveness, *JAPs* who gave them the willies back home in Scarsdale over spring break.

I had been raised on moron jokes; *they* had been raised on JAP jokes. ("What does a *JAP* do with her asshole in the morning? Dresses him up and sends him to work.")

Little by little, I came to realize that the *JAP* theme was by no means a one-note samba. It was kaleidoscopic and self-revealing; the students plugged it into a whole range of Jewish issues. I began to encourage them to look at their throwaway *JAP* comments with a measure of scrutiny.

The first, and most striking, ostinato in the students' journals was the dissociative one. As one Jewish student framed it, "There are so many *JAPs* in this class, it makes me sick." (An astonishing number of students were desperate to let me know this.)

Since over one-third of the class was not Jewish (the enrollment was 30), and since there was no one in the class that I would have identified sartorially as a *JAP,* this was an interesting fillip.

"That's funny," I started commenting back in these students' journals. "The other students think *you're* a *JAP.*"

Eventually, one Jewish student wrote, "Maybe when I talk about *JAPs* and that whole negative thing, it's a way for me to get 'permission' to assimilate."

Another wondered why he feels "like every *JAP* on campus somehow implicates me. That's a very 'minority culture' reflex, isn't it? Why am I so hung up on how everyone else perceives Jews?"

Some students perceived the *JAP* phenomenon, interestingly, as a developmental phase in American Judaism—a phase in which one parades both one's success

This article was originally published in *Lilith,* the independent Jewish women's quarterly; subscriptions are $16.00 per year, from *Lilith,* 250 West 57th Street, New York, NY 10107. It is being reprinted here by permission.

Susan Schnur is a rabbi and a writer and has been a Visiting Professor in the Philosophy of Religion Department at Colgate University.

*The term JAP refers to Jewish American Princess.

and one's entitlement. "When my best girlfriend from childhood was bat mitzvahed," wrote one student after reading *A Bintel Brief* and *World of Our Fathers,* "her grandmother gave her a '*JAP*-in-training' diamond-chip necklace. It's like the grandmother was saying, "When I was your age, I had to sew plackets in a Lower East Side sweatshop. So you girls be *JAPs*. Take whatever you can and be proud of it."

A Black student mentioned—during a talk about the socialization of Jewish women—that Jewish women, like their Black counterparts, are encouraged to be extremely competent, but then are double-bound with the message that their competence must *only* be used for frivolous purposes. (Like Goldie Hawn, in *Private Benjamin,* scolding her upholsterer with impressive assertiveness: "I specifically said—the ottoman in mushroom!", or informing her superior officer that she refused to go to Guam because "my hair will frizz.") "Minority women are warned not to be a real threat to anyone," the student explained, "That's how *JAPs* evolve."

Another theme of the students touched on their perception that Jews are sometimes discriminated against not because they are *less* endowed than others, but because they are more endowed (smarter, richer, more "connected"). *JAPs,* then, become, in the words of an Irish Catholic student who was doing reading on theology and the theme of chosenness, "the 'chosen of the chosen'. Unlike Irish Catholics who have been discriminated against because we seem 'un-chosen'," she mused, "people hate *JAPs* because they seem to have everything: money, confidence, style."

Of course, it's probably unnecessary for me to point out that the most prolific *JAP* references had to do with the venerable old feud—the Jewish War-Between-The-Sexes.

One pre-law Jewish male in the class (who was under a lot of pressure and had developed colitis during that semester) stated point-blank that he did not date Jewish women. I was shocked by the number of 20-year-old, seemingly fully-assimilated Jewish males who were right up there with Alexander Portnoy on this subject.

Several students responded to his comment in their journals. "He's angry at *JAPs,*" one woman wrote, "because they get to be needy and dependent, whereas the expectations on him are really high."

Another student related the experience of two friends of hers at SUNY Binghamton: "Someone spray-painted the word *JAP* on their dormitory door," she recounted. "But now I wonder—which one of the girls was being called a *JAP?* The one with the dozen Benetton sweaters, or the one who'd gotten 750 on her L-SATs?" The question being, of course, which is ultimately more threatening . . . the demanding woman or the self-sufficient one?

An Hispanic woman in the class talked about what she called "the dialectic of prejudice"—that is, the contradictory nature of racist or sexist slurs as being, in itself, a diagnostic of irrational bias. "A JAP is portrayed as both frigid and nymphomaniacal," she wrote. "She's put down both because of her haughty strut that says, 'I'm independent', and because of her *kvetching* that says, 'I'm dependent'."

A twist on this theme was provided by a Jewish woman who commented, "Whatever Jewish men call us—cold, hot, leech, bitch—it's all the same thing: They're afraid they can't live up to our standards."

A psych major in the class took a different tack. "It's not that the Jewish male really believes Jewish women are terrible, rather that he simply wants majority culture males to believe it. It's like when territorial animals urinate on a tree," she explained. "It's a minority male's possessive instinct. Like a sign that says, 'Robert Redfords—stay away!'"

Finally, several Jewish students framed their relations with one another in the context of Jewish family systems. "Lashing out at Jewish women—calling them all *JAPs* or refusing to marry them—is a way to get back at the entire high-expectation, high-pressure Jewish family," stated one student in response to a film I showed in class called "Parenting and Ethnicity." "You can lash out by becoming an academic failure," he went on, "or you can become a doctor—which is less self-destructive—and then simply refuse to marry a Jewish woman."

Towards the end of the term, a feminist friend pointed out to me something I had not considered: that the characterizations of *JAPs* and Yuppies are often identical—the difference being, of course, that a Yuppie designation is still generally taken as neutral or even positive, whereas there is hardly one of us left—I don't think—who would compete for the label of *JAP.*

All in all, I trust that the larger lessons in all of these *JAP* ruminations have not been lost on my students. For example: Why has it become socially sanctioned to use a *Jewish* designation *(JAP)* for a description that fits as many Christians as Jews? Or why—along the same lines—is it okay to use a *female* designation (again, *JAP)* for a description that fits as many men as women? Or sensing what we now sense, shouldn't we refuse any truck altogether with the term *JAP?*

JAP: The New Antisemitic Code Word

by Francine Klagsbrun

Isn't it odd that the term *JAP*, referring to a spoiled, self-indulgent woman, should be so widely used at a time when women are working outside their homes in unprecedented numbers, struggling to balance their home lives and their work lives to give as much of themselves as they can to everybody—their husbands, their kids, their bosses?

Jewish women, like women throughout society, are trying to find their own paths, their own voices. And, along with other changes that have taken place, they have been finding themselves Jewishly. And yet we hear the term *JAP* being used, perhaps almost more now than ever before. Why?

The new found, or rather newly accepted, drive of women for achievement in many arenas threatens many men. What better put-down of the strong woman than to label her a "Princess"? She is not being attacked as a competitor—that would be too close to home. No—she's called a princess, and that label diminishes her, negating her ambition and her success.

One may note, and rightly so, that there are materialistic Jewish women—and men too. But are Jews the only people guilty of excesses in spending? Why should the word "Jewish" be used pejoratively to describe behavior we don't approve of?

I think the answer is that there is an underlying antisemitic message in that label. Loudness is somehow "Jewish." Vulgarity is somehow "Jewish." All the old stereotypes of Jews come into play in the use of the term *JAP*. In this day, polite Christian society would not *openly* make anti-Jewish slurs. But *JAP* is O.K. *JAP* is a kind of code word. It's a way of symbolically winking, poking with an elbow, and saying, "well you know how Jews are—so materialistic and pushy."

What is interesting is that this code word can be used in connection with *women*—the Jewish American *Princess*—and nobody protests its intrinsic antisemitism.

This article was originally published in LILITH, the independent Jewish women's quarterly; subscriptions are $16.00 per year, from LILITH, 250 West 57th Street, New York, NY 10107. It is being reprinted here by permission

Francine Klagsbrun is the author of *Married People: Staying Together in the Age of Divorce* (New York: Bantum, 1985) and of *Voices of Wisdom: Jewish Ideals and Ethics for Everyday* (New York: Pantheon Books, 1980). These excerpts are from a speech delivered by Klagsbrun recently at Temple Israel of Great Neck NY.

Disability and the Medical System

by the Boston Women's Health Book Collective

Women with disabilities constantly struggle to find health care workers who are sensitive to their needs. For nondisabled women, experiences such as childbirth tend to raise awareness of abuses in the medical system. But women with disabilities, particularly those raised with a disability or with very severe medical difficulties, constantly encounter patronizing attitudes and ignorance by health care practitioners, damaging their sense of independence and well-being, and seriously reducing the quality of care.

The overlap of sexism with discrimination against people with disabilities restricts employment, education, and participation in the community for the approximately 30 million U.S. women with disabilities, who are among the most frequent consumers of medical services. While not all disabled people need medical treatment, such non-medical services as Social Security benefits, wheelchair transportation, and personal care attendant benefits require "certification as disabled" by a doctor.

Yet physicians get little, if any, training about or exposure to people with disabilities. A woman with cerebral palsy reported going to the doctor for an ear infection; he told her he'd never met a person with CP and spent 20 minutes asking her probing questions unrelated to her ear. When another woman visited a dermatologist because of a blister from her brace, he became visibly alarmed to find a woman in a wheelchair in the examining room. On the other hand, some doctors only meet disabled people who are in medical crisis, and disability is viewed solely as a dysfunction; medical schools offer virtually no training in the social and political issues of disability, let alone the impact of sexism, racism, or homophobia on women with disabilities.

Preventing Doctor Abuse

1. Remember: you are in charge of your care; regard the doctor and other health workers as consultants who are employed by you.
2. Don't accept inappropriate or hurtful interaction. If confronting your doctor is hard, role playing first with friends may help you assert yourself.
3. Take a friend with you to take notes and provide support. Make sure the doctor knows that the friend or interpreter, if you use one, is not your guardian and that all communication should be directed to you.
4. To find a good doctor, ask women you trust; avoid the phone book or other listings. Call first to ask if the doctor has experience with your disability; ask about wheelchair or other accessibility.
5. Ask your general practitioner to find out about a specialist's experience with disabled people before referring you for an appointment.
6. Get a new doctor if you feel frightened, threatened, abused, or not respected as a capable adult; if your friend isn't allowed in the examination room without an acceptable reason; if the doctor isn't understandable and willing to learn from you about disabled people.
7. If you like your physician, tell her or him why. Refer others to that doctor.—M.S.

Marsha Saxton, a disability rights and women's health activist, herself disabled with spina bifida, is director of the Project on Women and Disability, a program sponsored by the Boston Women's Health Book Collective.

The recent passage of the Americans with Disabilities Act of 1990, which has sweeping provisions for accessibility of facilities and services, signals the growing political strength of disabled people. But the medical system lags behind in recognizing disabled women as adults, capable of independent, self-directed lives. For example, if a disabled woman questions a doctor's recommendation, the response is often brutal; a blind diabetic woman who questioned her doctor's prescription was told, "You are hardly in a position to decide. If you'd followed your doctor's advice, you probably wouldn't be blind."

Disabled women, often displayed with little or no clothing in front of groups of medical students, are beginning to communicate their feelings of violation and humiliation. Doctors justify this kind of objectification—bordering on abuse—as necessary to teach students; they are baffled that disabled women have begun to protest.

One of the most pervasive myths is that disabled women are not sexual beings capable of sexual relationships and motherhood. A woman with spina bifida asked her gynecologist for birth control and was asked, "What for? What would you do with it?" The medical system has lagged in addressing the reproductive health needs of women with various kinds of disabilities. By far, most of the medical research on the topic focuses on male reproduction and sexual function.

Medical benefits are another quagmire of inequity. Women with disabilities must fight harder than men to justify their need for benefits since women may not have "worked" in the Social Security system enough to qualify for Medicare. Often only the most sophisticated self-advocates who have access to legal advice can obtain their rights in the system. Others become discouraged by the vast bureaucratic requirements and give up.

With the increasing competition and privatization in the health care industry, hospitals are under pressure to be profitable. Screening technologies such as genetic testing, and extensive investigation into family medical histories, are being used increasingly to identify patients who may be poor financial risks. This strategy, called "skimming," often used by insurance companies to disqualify policyholders, hits women the hardest.

Another area of concern is personal care attendant services, which would allow severely disabled people to live in the community outside of institutions; obtaining such services is the new priority of the Denver-based activist organization Americans with Disabilities for Attendant Programs Today (ADAPT), which led the successful fight for wheelchair-accessible transportation.

Women with disabilities have few resources to challenge abuses; many are just now gaining the confidence to speak out, and their organizations have only begun to identify the nature of the mistreatment. As a group, disabled women tend to be poor, unemployed, and unlikely to pursue malpractice litigation; pro bono legal services are needed to support the legal rights of this emerging constituency.

We must assist disabled women in becoming more assertive, understanding their legal rights, and exploring medical alternatives, so that all of us can function as informed consumers of medical services.

For more information contact: ADAPT, (303) 733-9324; Disability Rights Education and Defense Fund, (202) 986-0375; Project on Women and Disability, (617) 277-5617. Also, the following books are available: *Past Due: A Story of Disability, Pregnancy and Birth,* by Anne Finger (Seal Press, $10.95); *Women with Disabilities: Essays in Psychology, Culture and Politics,* edited by Michelle Fine and Adrienne Asch (Temple University Press, $35); and *With Wings: An Anthology of Literature by and About Women with Disabilities,* edited by Marsha Saxton and Florence Howe (The Feminist Press, $12.95) —Marsha Saxton

On Being an Outreach Group: Women with Disabilities

by Marsha Saxton

A woman called me at my office recently, seeking a consultant on disability. She works for a women's organization which had gotten a grant that required her group to include people with disabilities. She asked me, "How do you get *them* to come to our events?" I guess she didn't realize that I am one of "them." Once again, I wondered, "Why is reaching out to people with disabilities so difficult?" After several years of doing consulting and training in disability awareness, I'm just starting to fathom how hard it is for people to think about access for people with disabilities. I've thought about disability all my life because of frequent hospitalizations and surgery at Shriner's Hospital to treat the weakness in my legs from my birth condition, spina bifida. I've been familiar with other disabled people, in wheelchairs, with speech differences, vision and hearing impairments, and with needs for various medical treatments. Disability doesn't seem like such a big deal for me. But it's clearly a big deal for people who are not familiar with it.

There have been many positive changes in the past few years, including the recent passage of the Americans with Disabilities Act, as well as a shift in women's organizations toward remembering to include disabled people in their "list" of outreach groups. Even so, it's not easy being an "outreach group." While everyone else is focusing on the topic of the event, "outreach groups" must field all the comments and behaviors that arise out of people's discomfort. We deal with feeling like one of "them," feeling objectified for being asked to join just because we're one of the target groups. We are the ones responsible for putting you at ease about our differences—differences which you may find distressing.

As disabled women, we must push through feeling like a bother if we need assistance, especially if the environment has not been made accessible so that we can function relatively independently. We are often expected to be a representative of our group in ways that are unreasonable: "Well Sarah, what do handicapped people feel about this issue?"

One of the most common assumptions that disabled women face is that efforts to include us are altruistic: we are being included through the generosity of others or we should be included so we won't have to feel so bad about ourselves. Other assumptions are made about us. Nearly everyone has had the flu or an injury, where daily activity and responsibilities are temporarily suspended and we need the help of others. But nondisabled people assume that a person with a chronic illness or disability must suspend their activities permanently. They express amazement at a disabled person's ability to adapt to physical limitations and proceed with life.

People are not relaxed around us. Some people are overly helpful: grabbing a blind person's arm to "assist" them or pushing a person's wheelchair without asking or introducing themselves. Some people show their fear by actually leaning backwards, as if to avoid physical contact. Some people attempt to ignore the disability entirely, assuming or pretending that the person's disability is not a factor in their life. I've had people tell me, "I've known someone for five years who uses a wheelchair, but I've never asked her why she doesn't walk."

What has made it so hard to include us? When I've asked people this question, the most common response initially is, "We don't know what to do about ramps or sign-language interpreters, or how to get materials done in Braille." While there are some key pieces of information that can help organizations with the logistics of accessibility, the real issue seems to be discomfort with the issue of disability.

Marsha Saxton is the director of the Project on Women and Disability, and a board member of the Boston Women's Health Book Collective. She coedited, with Florence Howe, *With Wings, An Anthology of Literature by and about Women with Disabilities* (The Feminist Press, 1987).

About one-sixth of the population, or 43 million people, has some sort of disability or illness that restricts daily life in some way and requires accommodation. Multiply that number by the family, friends, and coworkers of disabled people, and nearly everyone is currently directly or indirectly affected by disability. We rarely regard disability as the commonplace experience it actually is. Disability is a cultural taboo, like death or sex. When we were children, our natural and sometimes unabashed curiosity in encountering a disabled person was often met with our parents' embarrassed "Hush, don't ask and don't stare." Simple curiosity was replaced with embarrassment, fear, and mistrust.

Our culture's poor treatment of disabled people is evidence of our inability to think generally about all of our physical differences and physical needs. As a society, we tolerate poor quality air, water, and food, in exchange for convenience. We accept and wear uncomfortable fashions and even use harmful products to alter and disguise our bodies. Although we seem to value athletic prowess and reduced cholesterol, ironically, we place low value on the physical well-being of workers in the workplace. By choosing high-stress lifestyles, productivity and profit over our physical well-being, we are literally disabling ourselves.

Just as the fundamental behaviors and attitudes of racism and sexism are communicated to children from their earliest learning, disability oppression starts with child-rearing practices: we've all been babies and have had the experience of total dependence on others for feeding, dressing, bathing, mobility, communication, and so have, in a sense, experienced being "disabled" by cultural standards. The way our dependence and bodily needs were regarded by our caretakers, whether as a bothersome, disgusting burden or as a natural part of being human, affects our ability to think and function in a relaxed and thoughtful manner around someone else's physical needs.

We are entering a transition period where the taboo against acknowledging disability is lifting. The once common behaviors of shouting at a deaf person or of assuming that someone with another kind of disability can't hear, or even think, are declining. My friends who use wheelchairs report that waiters are somewhat less likely to ask the person accompanying them, "What would *she* like to eat?"

Because of this gradually increasing awareness, unasked questions are emerging. In disability awareness presentations I and friends of mine give to school children, we hear such honest and unabashed questions as, "What do blind people eat?" "How do you drive your wheelchair up onto the bed at night?" Adults never got a chance to ask all those questions, although they harbor the same kinds of confusions.

Americans with Disabilities Act

The Americans with Disabilities Act (ADA), signed into law on July 26, 1990, will significantly expand civil rights protection for people with physical and mental disabilities, in several key areas. They include:

- **Employment.** Private companies with more than 25 employees (and eventually those with more than 15 employees) cannot discriminate in hiring practices and must make their facilities accessible to disabled employees (unless the cost to do so is prohibitively expensive).
- **Public Access.** Public facilities, such as restaurants, stores and services, that are constructed after the bill was signed must be made accessible to persons with disabilities. Existing buildings, unless they are substantially rehabilitated, are not affected, except those for whom modifications are "readily achievable," i.e. not of excessive cost.
- **Transportation.** Newly purchased trains and buses with Amtrack, commuter rail systems, and local and intercity lines must be accessible to wheelchair users through lift devices or ramps. Station terminals must eventually be made accessible, though in some cases, with up to a 30-year time frame.
- **Communications.** Telephone companies are required to offer communication relay systems, to enable hearing- or speech-impaired people who have teletype devices to communicate with hearing people via phone lines.
- **State and Local Governments** must make their facilities and services accessible to people with disabilities.

Regulations for enforcement of the ADA will be developed by various federal agencies and phased in over the next few months or up to several years, depending on the scope of changes required.

For more information on the Americans with Disabilities Act, contact Disability Rights Education and Defense Fund, 1616 P Street, N.W., Suite 100, Washington, D.C. 20036, (202)328-5185, or the President's Committee on Employment of People with Disabilities, Suite 636, 1111 20th Street, N.W., Washington, DC, 20036-3470, (202)653-5044.

Go ahead and help us lift the taboo! Take the risk that you might make a mistake. In fact, if you are serious about moving through this oppression, you probably will. The worst that will happen is that you may feel embarrassed. The best will be that you will learn something about disability, and get to know us better. You might even learn something important about yourself.

Leaving out people with disabilities is a great loss to any movement for justice and equality. Despite the stereotypes, we have a full range of skills, and may have been forced, because of our disabilities, to sharpen our sense of setting priorities, organizing our time, asking for help and delegating, skills essential to any organization. Women with disabilities who have dealt with the oppression and have moved beyond the physical or emotional struggles of a disability are pretty tough characters and will be an asset to your organization.

When colleges in the '70s and '80s began reaching out to Black students, administrators couldn't comprehend the criticism that the traditional curricula, based on white culture, didn't address the educational needs of African-American students. By the same token, making an event logistically accessible to wheelchair users, for example, is just the beginning. In events such as lectures or concerts, accessibility is an adequate welcome to people with disabilities. But in events where the nature of the interaction requires thoughtfulness, attention, communication, and close physical proximity, there is need for sensitivity and openness to disability.

While the group "people with disabilities" do not share a common cultural background, the pervasive discrimination for disabled people means we do have common experiences. The way to make a program accessible and relevant to disabled people is to include us in the planning and leadership of your organization. In approaching disabled individuals or disability organizations that may be interested in your programs ask, "How can we include a broader group of people with disabilities? What would make our event welcoming and relevant?"

In the women's movement, we're slowly realizing that we can reach beyond our own groups to include other people with very different experiences, perspectives, and needs. Those of us from more mainstream groups are starting to realize that reaching out to people of various differences is for our own benefit, not just for the benefit of those typically left out.

But how easy it is to lose sight of the reasons for reaching out to underrepresented groups, and to proceed with the effort out of a sense of obligation. We sometimes forget that the goal of "diversity" is not improved percentages, or political correctness, but learning, pushing though fear, getting close to new friends and meeting and working with very different leaders in our many struggles for liberation. We benefit from the increased strength of a broad-based movement with diverse perspectives and sources of insight and power. Here are some guidelines in beginning to think about outreach:

1. If this group is not your priority to learn about and include, don't pretend it is. Just adding disability organizations to your mailing list doesn't mean you or your organization can really reach out in a manner that works.

2. If your organization is serious about reaching out to people with disabilities, get a group together for discussion about disability. Try reading, as a group, a good book on disability, such as one of the books listed below, and discuss what issues come up for members. Focus on such questions as: What have you been told about disabled people, by your family, your early schooling? What are common stereotypes? When was the first time you met, or saw, a disabled person? How did that encounter influence your feelings about disabled people? Do you know disabled people now? What do you imagine their lives to be like? Are you shy, awkward, or "not yourself" around disabled people? This kind of discussion and exploring of feelings helps defuse the discomfort and helps people be willing to risk making mistakes and move toward making friends with disabled people.

3. A good place to start with any effort to reach out to people with diverse backgrounds and experiences is to begin to explore and appreciate the diversity in your own group. Spend some time talking about ancestry, class backgrounds, lifestyle choices.

4. Encourage the members of your organization to talk about their own disabilities. When the taboo around disability is broken, often people will begin to reveal their previously unmentioned physical conditions: back problems, hearing losses, allergies, chronic illness and so forth. Discuss accommodations for the people already in your organization who have hidden disabilities.

5. Be honest. Don't advertise "wheelchair accessible" if your site doesn't comply with architectural standards, including the bathrooms. If your building has a level or ramped entrance, but no accessible bathrooms, state that on your flyers.

6. Publicize the accessibility you do have! Put "wheelchair accessible" or the universal access symbol if that's the case.

7. Plan ahead. If your organization doesn't have money for sign-language interpreters in your budget (which can cost up to $50 an hour depending on how long events are and how many interpreters are required) then reaching out to deaf people is not feasible for you now. Plan on including interpreters in next year's budget.

8. Set outreach goals that make logical sense for your organization's goals. You don't have to reach out to everybody all at once. (Unless your agency or business *is* covered by the Americans with Disabilities Act, in which case you must comply with the new law for public accommodation.) "Disabled people" is a diverse group of people. There may be subgroups of disabled people who find your services or activities relevant. For example, a literary group may decide to put materials on tape for blind people and publicize events within the blind community. A labor activist group may seek people disabled on the job.

9. Don't act on your guilt! Disabled people can sniff pity or guilt a mile away! If you are an activist organization, reach out to us because you want our input and involvement, not because you feel bad for having left us out. If you offer services, include us because you can competently serve this population.

10. Be flexible. Even if your building is not wheelchair accessible, you can consider holding events or services at other locations.

11. Be communicative and patient about accessibility with your membership. If you are reaching out to women with environmental illness (severe allergies) regularly mention to your members why wearing scented products make the environment inaccessible to some people. Keep remembering how hard it is for people to understand this issue, even after *you* catch on!

12. Remember to focus on what you're doing well. Change is slow, and less than instant results doesn't mean you're doing it wrong. If you or your group focus only on failures, frustration and self-blame will actually slow you down. It takes a long time for any new group to trust that you're earnest.

As social institutions recognize the legitimate needs of people with disabilities for access and accommodation, and as individuals become more familiar with disability issues, we can move beyond emotional reactions to disability and beyond the logistical issues of accessibility, and begin to ask questions that can move us all forward. For example: How does the economic system perpetuate the oppression of disabled people? How do racism, sexism, or other types of prejudice operate together with disability oppression? How does disability oppression hurt all people, disabled or not? How can women's peace, labor, or environmental groups take on the fight against disability oppression, and how can disabled people and disability organizations effectively participate and take leadership in these other movements? These are the exciting questions.

People with disabilities are a significant part of the population of every other constituency. Just as sexism hinders the effectiveness of any other movement—for economic justice, racial equality, or peace—the oppression of people with disabilities limits these movements. All other liberation movements must come to include people with disabilities. Your personal commitment to people with disabilities is a critical step in ending oppression of all people. Even more important, you can take the lead in your organizations, workplaces, families, and communities in joining us to end this oppression.

RESOURCES AND READINGS:

The Project on Women and Disability offers leadership training and resources for women interested in disability issues, and provides consultation and training on how to involve people with disabilities, and create programs and events which address the needs of women with disabilities. Call (617) 727-7440. Ask for our bibliography of readings on women and disability.

The Information Center for Individuals with Disabilities has extensive listings on disability organizations and resources in Massachusetts. They publish a monthly newsletter, *Together,* on local and national disability news. Call (617) 727-5540.

The Massachusetts Rehabilitation Commission Library is a good place to browse in the disability literature, at Fort Point Place, 27-43 Wormwood St., Boston.

With the Power of Each Breath: A Disabled Women's Anthology, edited by Susan Browne, Debra Connors, and Nanci Stern. Cleis Press, 1985.

Building Community: A Manual Exploring Issues of Women and Disability, by the Women and Disability Awareness Project. Educational Equity Concepts, Inc. 1985.

Past Due: A Story of Disability, Pregnancy and Birth, by Anne Finger. Seal Press, 1990.

With Wings: An Anthology of Literature by and about Women with Disabilities, edited by Marsha Saxton and Florence Howe. The Feminist Press, 1987.

Women with Disabilities: Essays in Psychology, Culture, and Politics, edited by Michelle Fine and Adrienne Asch. Temple University Press, 1988.

Disabled, Female, and Proud: Stories of Ten Women with Disabilities, by Harilyn Russo. Exceptional Parent Press, 1988.

Why Can't Sharon Kowalski Come Home? by Karen Thompson and Julie Andrzejewski. Spinsters/Aunt Lute, 1988.

Escape: A Handbook for Battered Women Who Have Disabilities. Finex House, 1988. Jamaica Plain, MA.

Dykes, Disability, and Stuff. Quarterly Journal, Catherine Lohr, Publisher, PO Box 6194, Boston, MA 02114.

Simply ... Friend or Foe?

from New Internationalist

The able-bodied can be allies of disabled people—or they can be patronizing oppressors. Here are a few ways in which non-disabled readers can be friends instead of foes.

ASK exactly what you can do if you want to help a disabled person — and listen to the reply. We know our needs best. Never help us without asking first whether your help is wanted. And don't expect us to be eternally grateful to you for the help you do offer...

RESPECT our privacy and our need for independence. Don't assume that because we are disabled you can ask us more personal questions than you would a non-disabled person.

ACKNOWLEDGE our differences. For many disabled people our difference is an important part of our identity. Don't assume that our one wish in life is to be 'normal' or imagine that it is 'progressive' or 'liberal' to ignore our differences.

THINK about the way society creates barriers for us. Take account of the social and economic context in which we experience our medical condition. But don't reduce us to our medical conditions. Why should it matter to you what our condition is called?

RECOGNIZE our existence. A gaze can express recognition and warmth. Talk to us directly. Neither stare at us — nor immediately look away either. And never talk about us as if we weren't there.

Challenge patronizing attitudes towards us. We want your empathy not your pity. Putting us on a pedestal or telling us how 'wonderful' and 'heroic' we are does not help. This attitude often conceals the judgment that having an impairment is intolerabale — which is very undermining for us.

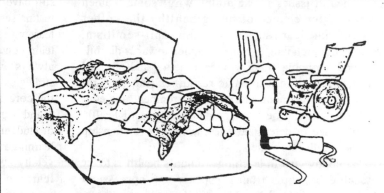

REALIZE that we are sexual beings, with the same wishes, needs and desire for fulfilling relationships as non-disabled people. Don't assume that we will never have children. And if a disabled person has a non-disabled lover don't jump to the conclusion that the latter is either a saint or has an ulterior motive.

APPRECIATE the contribution that we make to society in the fields of work, politics and culture. We engage in these activities for the same reasons as you do — but we may have some different insights to offer. Don't assume that we are passive — or that our activities are a form of 'therapy' to take our mind off our disability. Most disabled people are financially hard up and so we may have a greater need to earn a living than you.

This section is inspired by *Pride Against Prejudice* by Jenny Morris and produced in conjunction with Claire King and Beverly Ashton. The cartoons are by Tony Meredith.

Ideas for Anti-Racism and Pro-Diversity Work and Discussion in a Women's Health Class

by Nancy Worcester[1]

A core part of developing an analysis of women's health issues is examining why "some women have a better chance of being healthy than other women" and learning how racism, anti-semitism, poverty, homophobia, ageism, attitudes towards disabilities, and fatphobia affect women's mental and physical health, affect access to basic resources (housing, rewards for employment, nutrition, environment and education) which can be primary determinants of health, and influence or determine one's access or relationship with the health care system.

While my goal in teaching women's health is to try to teach every topic from an openly anti-oppression/pro-diversity viewpoint and to include readings and perspectives of many different women, I have found there are limitations to this approach. First, as a white woman struggling to unlearn my own racism (and other oppressive attitudes), I cannot always provide the leadership I strive for! Equally important, in a course where both the subject matter and the effort to build a pro-diversity classroom environment may be new to students[2], too often students (and teachers) find it challenging to deal with the already controversial topics and feel it is "too complicated" ("there isn't enough time" or "we don't have the tools/information to adequately deal with other issues") to look at the impact of racism and other oppressions on each topic. Even successfully managing to do exactly that can feel equally unsatisfactory if at the end of a class, there is the feeling that we have done a superficial "laundry list," mentioning a wide range of groups but never adequately reaching an understanding of the impact and perpetuation of institutional and attitudinal oppressions.

For these reasons, I try to plan at least one session, approximately a quarter of the way into the course (after we have started on the materials so it should be apparent why anti-oppression work is central to the course and we still have the rest of the semester to build on work done in this session) which concentrates on pro-diversity/unlearning racism exercises and discussions. The teaching team constantly experiments with different approaches, always evaluating (and debating) the most effective strategies. I believe that learning about racism must be the core of this work. However, at this stage, I have found it most effective (with groups where the majority of students are white and mostly new, but open, to unlearning racism) to do this as a part of workshops on diversity awareness rather than starting with specific unlearning racism workshops. The advantage of this approach is that people new to working against racism may be able to build on their experiences of working against other oppressions or their experiences of being a part of an oppressed group to see the similarities with racism. The disadvantages of this approach are that the facilitator and the group have to be careful that the racism component does not get "diluted", that attention is paid to ways that racism is unique and destructive in ways different from other oppressions, and that institutional as well as attitudinal oppression is addressed.

I. SETTING THE SCENE FOR UNLEARNING RACISM/ PRO-DIVERSITY WORK

A. It is useful to establish ground rules, such as the following:

- It will be hard work.
- We need to listen and think.
- We need to share and be honest when we do.

- We may not always feel comfortable.
- We may make mistakes. But it is a bigger mistake not to work on this.
- Guilt will only keep us stuck.
- Information shared in this session should not go out of this room.

Many people feel these two ground rules also help an introduction to racism:

- Our emphasis will not be on violent racism. We will concentrate on more subtle forms which are a part of everyday life for all people of color.
- We will not talk about reverse discrimination. In a society where one group has power over another, "reverse discrimination" is, in fact, a complex and inaccurate concept.

B. Working definitions of racism need to be clarified. Ricky Sherover-Marcuse's "Unlearning Racism" is a key article for this work (see p. 90). She uses these basic definitions:

> INSTITUTIONALIZED RACISM = Systematic mistreatment of people of color.
> ATTITUDINAL RACISM = set of assumptions, feelings, beliefs and attitudes about people of color and their culture which are a mixture of misinformation and ignorance.

C. It can also be useful at this stage to introduce the issues of internalized oppression and affirmative action. The paper by Thompson and Disch has excellent ideas for how to talk about affirmative action. These are issues which students often want to discuss, but they can side track the class from the more central topics unless they are planned to be a part of the other topics.

II. IDEAS/EXERCISES FOR PRO-DIVERSITY AWARENESS

Introduce Audre Lorde's concept of "mythical norm" (see p. 85) and Ricky Sherover-Marcuse's use of terms "target and non-target" (see IV. Target Group Exercise below.) Introduce the inter-relationships of power and control, attitudinal and institutional oppressions, and the perpetuation of "social order".

EXERCISES:

In setting up exercises, the challenge is to make sure that no one feels invisible, conspicuous, or is put in the position where they need to speak for everyone in a group.

Mythical Norm[1] (non-targets)[2]	Oppressions	Targets[2]
White People	Racism	People of Color
Men	Sexism	Women
Young (not too young)	Ageism	Old/Very Young
Heterosexual	Heterosexism/ Homophobia	Gays/Lesbians/ Bisexuals
Able-Bodied (mentally & physically)	Ableism	People with Disabilities
Christian	Anti-Semitism (Religious Narrowness)	Jews (Other Religious Groups)
Thin	Fatphobia	Fat People
Middle Class (access to resources)	Classism	Poor People

[1] The term "Mythical Norm" comes from Audre Lorde's writings, particularly in *Sister Outsider*.
[2] Ricky Sherover-Marcuse used the terms "non-target" and "target" groups in her Unlearning Racism Workshops.

A. Similarities and Differences

(This works well as a large group activity)

Have participants identify similarities between all forms of oppression and what is unique about different forms of oppression. (i.e. We want to work towards "celebrating" most differences but what is the one form of difference we want to eliminate? [class, poverty]. What is the one "difference" we all hope to grow into? [age] What is the role of invisibility with some oppressions? Are we better or worse at understanding the "differences" which could affect us [age, class, disability, body size, sexual identity] than those we know will never be personal issues [a change of sex or race]? In what ways is the impact of racism different than other forms of oppression?)

B. Target vs. Non-Target

(This works well as small group follow-up to the target exercise described below).

Have each person identify a *non-target* group they are in, list benefits and privileges they have simply because they are a part of this group, and at what age/in what situation they first remember recognizing this phenomena.

Have each person identify a *target* group they are in. How does the experience of being in a target group help them see ways that they can use their *non*-target group situation(s) to actively work against oppression?

Have each person identify a *target* group they are in and think of a time when *internalized oppression* has made them, as a member of the target group act in an oppressive way (jokes, comments, not hiring) towards someone of the same target group. Describe how effective internalized oppression is and why it is very confusing to people outside the target group who do not understand internalized oppression.

C. Sexism and Racism

For people who have actively worked against sexism, it is sometimes useful to look specifically at similarities between sexism and racism (In what ways is being a white woman in this society similar to being a Black man? As men have power, men must be involved in working against sexism, and as whites have power, white people must be involved in working against racism) before looking at ways in which racism and sexism are different.

QUESTIONS FOR DISCUSSION

Have people work in groups of 2 or 3 to discuss questions. If there is time, larger groups can discuss what came up in small groups.

a. (For women) Describe the first time you remember being at a disadvantage because you were female. How did you feel about that? Did you do anything to resist? Now, looking back on that stage, what do you wish you had done or what would you want a daughter or sister to do in that same situation today? (For men) Describe the first time you remember being at an advantage because you were male. How did you feel about that?

b. Think of some things you do now in your daily life to work towards equality for women.

c. Concerned men often want to know what they can do about sexism. What do you say to a man who asks "What can I do about sexism?"

d. Identify ways in which men working against sexism is similar to white women working against racism. List specific ways white people can do anti-racism work

D. Power and Control

The power & control wheel (p. 529) was put together by battered women to describe the many ways their abusers controlled them in their relationships. Using that wheel, identify similar ways institutional structures and different forms of oppression work to perpetuate inequalities.

E. Vision of a Diverse Society

Throughout the next week, every time you are in a group situation, observe the diversity or lack of diversity of the group. Identify who is making the decisions, who benefits from the present power dynamics, what are the visible and invisible barriers which keep others from participating in the group. Create a vision for yourself of a diverse group/community in which you *benefit* from working/playing with people different than you. Identify ways in which you can work toward making this diversity vision a reality for your life.

III. IDEAS FOR BEGINNING DISCUSSIONS ON RACISM

An introduction to racism needs to look at how all white people in a racist society are taught to be racist. (This helps to remove guilt and moves us on to more positive attitudes. It may help change the useless theme of "But I'm not racist" into "How can I work to not be racist?")

SOME QUESTIONS TO WORK ON IN SMALL GROUPS

Do you remember when you were first aware of there being people of color or that you were a person of color? What did you learn from this experience?

(For white people) How did you learn to be racist? How did your family or your home environment treat people of color? Did you learn that people of color (or a specific group) were "bad"? Do you remember early racist jokes/actions you witnessed? Did you learn to pretend that you didn't notice differences and to act like "we're all just alike"? Did you learn to be artificially nice to/to feel sorry for people of color? In what ways do white people benefit from being white? Why is racism a white person's issue?

(For people of color) Identify ways in which you observed racism affecting family members, friends, or people you didn't even know. Identify several different ways (overt, subtle, being ignored, or being treated as if someone didn't notice your race) racism has had an impact on your life as a child, as a teenager, and presently. Identify ways you have worked against racism. If you could say several things to white people about racism what would you say?

IV. Ricky Sherover-Marcuse's Target Group Exercise

This exercise is adapted from an exercise used by Ricky Sherover-Marcuse in Unlearning Racism Workshops I attended in Madison, WI and at the Iowa City Women Against Racism conferences. Ricky's workshops and this exercise in particular, were powerful and inspirational in helping me have the courage to play more of a leadership role in anti-racism work "even though I didn't feel ready." (The more I work on anti-racism, the more questions I have and the fewer answers, so I now realize I will never feel "ready"!) Writing up my version of this exercise (which I have now used successfully in various ways, in many settings) is one way I am keeping the promise I made to myself at the time of Ricky's death that I would do what I could to keep her work alive and inspiring to others.

Ricky Sherover-Marcuse suggested that by looking at groups as "targets" and "non-targets", rather than as "oppressed" and "oppressors", we can better:

- Avoid feeling guilty! None of us want to think of ourselves as oppressors.
- See that we benefit from being in a non-target group even if we do not actively engage in targeting the other group.

Purposes of this exercise:

- To help everyone see the wide range of target groups which are a part of our lives.
- To help individuals see for themselves that they probably belong to both target and non-target groups. We benefit whenever we are in a non-target group. We are at a disadvantage whenever we are a part of a target group.
- To help individuals have some sense of what it feels like to be in one group or another. (Does it feel worse to be in some target groups than others? Does it feel better to be a part of a target group if there are many people in that group? How does it feel to be the only person in a target group? What does it feel like to be separated from a friend or potential friends because of the group identified.)
- To help set the scene for looking at people of color as a target group and white people as a non-target group.

EXERCISE

A room with space for everyone to move around in is required for this exercise.

Everyone is in the middle of the room while the exercise is introduced.

The workshop leader will call out a target group/nontarget group combination. Each person in the target group moves to one side of the room. Each person in the non-target group moves to the other side of the room. Each person defines their own identity. People can stay in the middle of the room if they cannot decide which side they should be on or prefer not to identify with either group.

There should be a moment or two after everyone is in the appropriate place for everyone to quietly think about what it feels like to be a part of this particular target or non-target group. (There is no group discussion until the exercise is completed).

The workshop leader then calls out the next target group non-target group combination. The exercise is repeated with everyone moving to the side of the room which represents their identity on this particular issue. The exercise is repeated a number of times until 10–12 target/nontarget combinations have been called.

Target groups are always on the same side of the room. Nontarget groups are always on the opposite side of the room. If 10-12 combinations are used, many people will have had the experience of being on both the target and non-target sides of the room. (Warning! Often the non-target group is numerically small but they still have the power. This can be very confusing to someone new to the issues of power and control. A challenge of this exercise is to make sure that someone who is always on the nontarget side [i.e. a white, middle class man] or who is the only non-target [i.e. the only man in a women's studies class] sees the difference between the numerical size of a group and who has power in society)

TARGET GROUP EXERCISE
Non-target/Target Combinations

Non-target Groups	Target Groups
men	women
under 50	over 50
under 40	over 40
over 20	under 20
did not grow up poor	grew up poor
one parent went to college	neither parent went to college
parents' native language = English	parent's lang = not English
not Jewish	Jewish
non-rural	rural
never called or felt fat	called or felt fat
physically/mentally abled	disabled

Do *not* use examples where people have to choose between identifying themselves in a way which could put them at risk or denying a part of their identity. For example, in many situations it will not be safe to ask women to identify themselves on the basis of whether they are lesbians or battered women. In these situations, have the workshop leader explain why people are not being asked to identify on certain issues and have everyone stand in the middle of the room and think of the ramifications of not being able to identify with a particular group. (Contrast this situation to racism where most people of color do not have the choice not to identify themselves.)

V. Developing Diversity Exercises for Specific Organizations or Groups

This exercise can be specifically designed to fit the needs of any organization or group committed to becoming more diverse. Having a group of people work together to think up "situations" which fit their group can be as important as actually doing the exercise!

This exercise helps people see the difference between merely learning to cope with/interrupt oppression, educating against oppression, and pro-actively working for social change.

The right range of "situations" will cover a wide range of issues from the very subtle to the less subtle. Each "situation" is described on a card and all cards are put in a hat.

EXERCISE:

Groups of two draw a "situation" from the hat and discuss it. The "situation" is discussed from three perspectives:

1. How do you handle this situation when you merely want to cope with it in a sensitive way?

2. How do you use the situation as an "teachable moment?"

3. How do you work on this issue if you see yourself as a social change activist?

Small groups report to the larger group (many issues can be covered in a short time.) The larger group discusses those situations where the small group got stuck or where the topic generates discussion.

SAMPLE SITUATIONS

A. A person you are working with tells you that she is thinking of quitting because she feels overwhelmed by all the poverty/sadness she sees.

B. A new woman is working on your shift. She is about 60 years old. You realize that for the last few days all your conversations have been about periods and premenstrual syndrome.

C. You are designing a new poster to recruit volunteers/new workers. You realize that all the images on the poster are of young, white, able-bodied women.

D. You meet an old friend and tell her about the work you are doing. She says "How can you do that? Isn't that work that just takes care of poor Black people all the time?"

E. There is a new woman on your shift who you think is Jewish. (You don't know for sure!) Other people have been talking about recent anti-semitic incidents in your community in a way you feel may be hurtful to this woman.

F. You have been working for your organization for more than one year. You realize you have never been aware of disabled women participating in your events.

G. A group of you are sitting around talking about what you hope to be doing in a couple of years. All the plans discussed depend on people having had a good education or access to money. You realize that some women (without money/without a college degree) are being left out of this conversation.

H. A large woman walks into the room. You realize that all the chairs in the room are quite small with arms on them so there is nowhere the woman can sit.

I. An African-American woman is waiting for your coworker for help. You realize that your coworker is purposefully not paying any attention to this woman.

J. You meet an old friend and tell her about the women's organization you are working/volunteering for. She says, "I didn't know you are a lesbian."

K. Your organization has been trying to work against racism, but you have noticed that all the information you have (all situations you have discussed) deals with only African-American vs. white issues. You feel issues for other people of color need to be discussed.

Diversity Issues and Women's Health

It is important to make the connections between antiracism/pro-diversity exercises and the women's health course syllabus obvious to students. When articles from this book, readings from *The Black Women's Health Book,* newsletters from activist groups, etc. are assigned, it may be helpful if the discussions consciously refer back to and build on the issues covered in the exercises. For *every* women's health issue an effort can be made to work towards developing an over-all analysis of how the issues may be different, exaggerated, or multiply complex for women of color, Jewish women, lesbians, older women, poor women, fat women, or women with disabilities. The power and control exercise (IID) can be used as a basis for discussing many women's health topics. For example, with reproductive rights issues, how does institutional racism/oppression work (as the "using children" prong of the power and control wheel) to define who should and who should not have children? How does this affect access to infertility treatment, attitudes towards 'forced contraception or sterilization', and welfare and maternity leave policies?

Anti-oppression work can be very hard work: the issues can feel overwhelming. Without a clear vision of the long term goals of pro-diversity work, students can easily get "stuck" simply feeling that oppression is awful, only feeling sorry for their identified "victims" of oppression, and feeling that an individual can do little to change an oppressive system.

Just as easily, anti-oppression work can be the most rewarding work we do. My own commitment in teaching about oppressions is to thoroughly integrate identifying the problems and finding the solutions for each issue I teach. Positive images of women of color, Jews, lesbians, older women, fat women, and women with disabilities can be used as a central part of learning how oppression has affected these groups of women. Emphasizing the positive and influential work being done by activist groups can be a very empowering way to demonstrate that groups of women of all colors, sizes, ages, sexual identities, physical abilities, and classes, are already making huge changes in working for a society which values diversity and that a society which appreciates diversity will be a healthier society for all women.

The vision of a diverse society exercise (IIE) can be a powerful ending for a women's health course.

NOTES

1. This paper draws together some of the exercises and activities which I have designed or adapted from many workshops I have attended in England and the USA in the last fifteen years. I thank the many people who have inspired and supported my unlearning oppressions work. I would welcome feed-back on this article and am always anxious to learn new ideas and resources for diversity work. Write Nancy Worcester, Women's Studies Program, University of Wisconsin, 313 Lowell Center, 610 Langdon St., Madison, WI. 53703.

2. "Feminist, Anti-Racist, Anti-Oppression Teaching: Two White Women's Experience" by Becky Thompson and Estelle Disch in *Radical Teacher*, number 41, 1992, pp. 4–10.

White Privilege
Unpacking the Invisible Knapsack

by Peggy McIntosh

I was taught to see racism only in individual acts of meanness, not in invisible systems conferring dominance on my group.

Through work to bring materials from Women's Studies into the rest of the curriculum, I have often noticed men's unwillingness to grant that they are over-privileged, even though they may grant that women are disadvantaged. They may say they will work to improve women's status, in the society, the university, or the curriculum, but they can't or won't support the idea of lessening men's. Denials which amount to taboos surround the subject of advantages which men gain from women's disadvantages. These denials protect male privilege from being fully acknowledged, lessened or ended.

Thinking through unacknowledged male privilege as a phenomenon, I realized that since hierarchies in our society are interlocking, there was most likely a phenomenon of white privilege which was similarly denied and protected. As a white person, I realized I had been taught about racism as something which puts others at a disadvantage, but had been taught not to see one of its corollary aspects, white privilege, which puts me at an advantage.

I think whites are carefully taught not to recognize white privilege, as males are taught not to recognize male privilege. So I have begun in an untutored way to ask what it is like to have white privilege. I have come to see white privilege as an invisible package of un-earned assets which I can count on cashing in each day, but about which I was 'meant' to remain oblivious. White privilege is like an invisible weightless knapsack of special provisions, maps, passports, codebooks, visas, clothes, tools and blank checks.

Describing white privilege makes one newly accountable. As we in Women's Studies work to reveal male privilege and ask men to give up some of their power, so one who writes about having white privilege must ask, "Having described it, what will I do to lessen or end it?"

After I realized the extent to which men work from a base of unacknowledged privilege, I understood that much of their oppressiveness was unconscious. Then I remembered the frequent charges from women of color that white women whom they encounter are oppressive. I began to understand why we are justly seen as oppressive, even when we don't see ourselves that way. I began to count the ways in which I enjoy unearned skin privilege and have been conditioned into oblivion about its existence.

My schooling gave me no training in seeing myself as an oppressor, as an unfairly advantaged person, or as a participant in a damaged culture. I was taught to see myself as an individual whose moral state depended on her individual moral will. My schooling followed the pattern my colleague Elizabeth Minnich has pointed out: whites are taught to think of their lives as morally neutral, normative, and average, and also ideal, so that when we work to benefit others, this is seen as work which will allow "them" to be more like "us."

I decided to try to work on myself at least by identifying some of the daily effects of white privilege in my

Peggy McIntosh is Associate Director of the Wellesley College Center for Research on Women. This essay is excerpted from her working paper, "White Privilege and Male Privilege: A Personal Account of Coming to See Correspondences Through Work in Women's Studies," copyright © 1988 by Peggy McIntosh. Available for $6.00 from address below. The paper includes a longer list of privileges. Permission to excerpt or reprint must be obtained from Peggy McIntosh, Wellesley College Center for Research on Women, Wellesley, MA 02181; (781)283-2520.

life. I have chosen those conditions which I think in my case *attach somewhat more to skin-color privilege* than to class, religion, ethnic status, or geographical location, though of course all these other factors are intricately intertwined. As far as I can see, my African American co-workers, friends and acquaintances with whom I come into daily or frequent contact in this particular time, place, and line of work cannot count on most of these conditions.

1. I can if I wish arrange to be in the company of people of my race most of the time.
2. If I should need to move, I can be pretty sure of renting or purchasing housing in an area which I can afford and in which I would want to live.
3. I can be pretty sure that my neighbors in such a location will be neutral or pleasant to me.
4. I can go shopping alone most of the time, pretty well assured that I will not be followed or harassed.
5. I can turn on the television or open to the front page of the paper and see people of my race widely represented.
6. When I am told about our national heritage or about "civilization," I am shown that people of my color made it what it is.
7. I can be sure that my children will be given curricular materials that testify to the existence of their race.
8. If I want to, I can be pretty sure of finding a publisher for this piece on white privilege.
9. I can go into a music shop and count on finding the music of my race represented, into a supermarket and find the staple foods which fit with my cultural traditions, into a hairdresser's shop and find someone who can cut my hair.
10. Whether I use checks, credit cards, or cash, I can count on my skin color not to work against the appearance of financial reliability.
11. I can arrange to protect my children most of the time from people who might not like them.
12. I can swear, or dress in second hand clothes, or not answer letters, without having people attribute these choices to the bad morals, the poverty, or the illiteracy of my race.
13. I can speak in public to a powerful male group without putting my race on trial.
14. I can do well in a challenging situation without being called a credit to my race.
15. I am never asked to speak for all the people of my racial group.
16. I can remain oblivious of the language and customs of persons of color who constitute the world's majority without feeling in my culture any penalty for such oblivion.
17. I can criticize our government and talk about how much I fear its policies and behavior without being seen as a cultural outsider.
18. I can be pretty sure that if I ask to talk to "the person in charge," I will be facing a person of my race.
19. If a traffic cop pulls me over or if the IRS audits my tax return, I can be sure I haven't been singled out because of my race.
20. I can easily buy posters, postcards, picture books, greeting cards, dolls, toys, and children's magazines featuring people of my race.
21. I can go home from most meetings of organizations I belong to feeling somewhat tied in, rather than isolated, out-of-place, outnumbered, unheard, held at a distance, or feared.
22. I can take a job with an affirmative action employer without having coworkers on the job suspect that I got it because of race.
23. I can choose public accommodation without fearing that people of my race cannot get in or will be mistreated in the places I have chosen.
24. I can be sure that if I need legal or medical help, my race will not work against me.
25. If my day, week, or year is going badly, I need not ask of each negative episode or situation whether it has racial overtones.
26. I can choose blemish cover or bandages in "flesh" color and have them more or less match my skin.

I repeatedly forgot each of the realizations on this list until I wrote it down. For me white privilege has turned out to be an elusive and fugitive subject. The pressure to avoid it is great, for in facing it I must give up the myth of meritocracy. If these things are true, this is not such a free country; one's life is not what one makes it; many doors open for certain people through no virtues of their own.

In unpacking this invisible knapsack of white privilege, I have listed conditions of daily experience which I once took for granted. Nor did I think of any of these perquisites as bad for the holder. I now think that we need a more finely differentiated taxonomy of privilege, for some of these varieties are only what one would want for everyone in a just society, and others give license to be ignorant, oblivious, arrogant and destructive.

I see a pattern running through the matrix of white privilege, a pattern of assumptions which were passed on to me as a white person. There was one main piece of cultural turf; it was my own turf, and I was among those who could control the turf. *My skin color was an asset for any move I was educated to want to make.* I could think of myself as belonging in major ways, and of making social systems work for me. I could freely disparage, fear, neglect, or be oblivious to anything outside of the dominant cultural forms. Being of the main culture, I could also criticize it fairly freely.

In proportion as my racial group was being made confident, comfortable, and oblivious, other groups were likely being made inconfident, uncomfortable, and alienated. Whiteness protected me from many kinds of hostility, distress, and violence, which I was being subtly trained to visit in turn upon people of color.

For this reason, the word "privilege" now seems to me misleading. We usually think of privilege as being a favored state, whether earned or conferred by birth or luck. Yet some of the conditions I have described here work to systematically overempower certain groups. Such privilege simply *confers dominance* because of one's race or sex.

I want, then, to distinguish between earned strength and unearned power conferred systematically. Power from unearned privilege can look like strength when it is in fact permission to escape or to dominate. But not all of the privileges on my list are inevitably damaging. Some, like the expectation that neighbors will be decent to you, or that your race will not count against you in court, should be the norm in a just society. Others, like the privilege to ignore less powerful people, distort the humanity of the holders as well as the ignored groups.

We might at least start by distinguishing between positive advantages which we can work to spread, and negative types of advantages which unless rejected will always reinforce our present hierarchies. For example, the feeling that one belongs within the human circle, as Native Americans say, should not be seen as privilege for a few. Ideally it is an *unearned entitlement.* At present, since only a few have it, it is an *unearned advantage* for them. This paper results from a process of coming to see that some of the power which I originally saw as attendant on being a human being in the U.S. consisted in *unearned advantage* and *conferred dominance.*

I have met very few men who are truly distressed about systemic, unearned male advantage and conferred dominance. And so one question for me and others like me is whether we will be like them, or whether we will get truly distressed, even outraged, about unearned race advantage and conferred dominance and if so, what we will do to lessen them. In any case, we need to do more work in identifying how they actually affect our daily lives. Many, perhaps most, of our white students in the U.S. think that racism doesn't affect them because they are not people of color; they do not see "whiteness" as a racial identity. In addition, since race and sex are not the only advantaging systems at work, we need similarly to examine the daily experience of having age advantage, or ethnic advantage, or physical ability, or advantage related to nationality, religion, or sexual orientation.

Difficulties and dangers surrounding the task of finding parallels are many. Since racism, sexism, and heterosexism are not the same, the advantaging associated with them should not be seen as the same. In addition, it is hard to disentangle aspects of unearned advantage which rest more on social class, economic class, race, religion, sex and ethnic identity than on other factors. Still, all of the oppressions are interlocking, as the Combahee River Collective Statement of 1977 continues to remind us eloquently.

One factor seems clear about all of the interlocking oppressions. They take both active forms which we can see and embedded forms which as a member of the dominant group one is taught not to see. In my class and place, I did not see myself as a racist because I was taught to recognize racism only in individual acts of meanness by members of my group, never in invisible systems conferring unsought racial dominance on my group from birth.

Disapproving of the systems won't be enough to change them. I was taught to think that racism could end if white individuals changed their attitudes. [But] a "white" skin in the United States opens many doors for whites whether or not we approve of the way dominance has been conferred on us. Individual acts can palliate, but cannot end, these problems.

To redesign social systems we need first to acknowledge their colossal unseen dimensions. The silences and denials surrounding privilege are the key political tool here. They keep the thinking about equality or equity incomplete, protecting unearned advantage and conferred dominance by making these taboo subjects. Most talk by whites about equal opportunity seems to me now to be about equal opportunity to try to get into a position of dominance while denying that *systems* of dominance exist.

It seems to me that obliviousness about white advantage, like obliviousness about male advantage, is kept strongly inculturated in the United States so as to maintain the myth of meritocracy, the myth that democratic choice is equally available to all. Keeping most people unaware that freedom of confident action is there for just a small number of people props up those in power, and serves to keep power in the hands of the same groups that have most of it already.

Though systemic change takes many decades, there are pressing questions for me and I imagine for some others like me if we raise our daily consciousness on the perquisites of being light-skinned. What will we do with such knowledge? As we know from watching men, it is an open question whether we will choose to use unearned advantage to weaken hidden systems of advantage, and whether we will use any of our arbitrarily-awarded power to try to reconstruct power systems on a broader base.

WORKSHEET—CHAPTER 2

Diversity and Health Issues

1. Identify two ways that you think your sex, race, or family income have influenced your interactions with health care providers or your access to the health care system.

2. What is similar and what is different about the following?

    •   men working against sexism

    •   white people working against racism

    •   middle class people working against class oppression

3. For this question, refer to the "Ideas for Anti-Racism and Pro-Diversity Work" article and "White Privilege" articles.

    a.   Identify a *non*-target group you are in. Describe the age and situation in which you first became aware that you had certain privileges or power because of belonging to this group.

    b.   Identify a target group to which you belong. Identify ways in which you think this is similar and different from belonging to another target group. (Be specific about which two target groups your are comparing.)

c. Having identified a target group you are in, describe ways in which you feel you may have internalized society's negative messages about this group.

4. List ways that in your daily life you could or do interrupt sexist, racist, anti-semitic, ageist, or homophobic incidents or behaviors.

5. You are helping to plan a women's health course. Choose two different women's health topics. Suggest specific ideas of how you could plan to make sure that diversity issues were central to the material covered for these topics.

CHAPTER 3

Images and Gender Roles

*M*ost introductory women studies courses devote some class time to a discussion of gender roles. Many of the inequalities in our society are reinforced through the perpetuation of gender roles and through the arguments that these roles are somehow biologically determined and inevitable. (We use the term *gender* roles to emphasize that these roles are socially and culturally determined, not biologically determined *sex* roles). Sex role stereotyping plays a part in every issue discussed in this book and has an impact on women's roles as health care consumers and providers. The first article, "Hazards of Hearth and Home," gives an excellent overview of women's health issues in the context of women's roles in society, exploring, among other issues, both the physical and psychological hazards of housework, the stress of caretaking and "emotional housework," and the impact of economic inequalities on women's health.

"Male and Female Hormones Revisited" critiques the common use of the terms "male hormones" and "female hormones" and how this terminology reflects and perpetuates misunderstandings about the role of hormones vs. socialization in determining male and female similarities and differences. Many women and men find it liberating, or at least interesting, to learn that men and women are much more alike biologically than most of us have been led to believe and that many differences between boys and girls, men and women, are more socially constructed than biologically determined. Of course, in a society where both males and females were valued, it would not particularly matter what was biological or social/cultural in origin. However, in a society in which what is identified as "masculine" is valued/rewarded more than what is "feminine" (for example, see "If Men Could Menstruate," "Mental Health Issues," and many other articles in this book), demystifying biological vs. social roles of sex/gender differences is a very political issue and biological determinism (the attempt to explain complex human behaviors by simplistic biological explanations) has been used as a very powerful tool to maintain the status quo and inequalities.

Feminists and others working for social change have certainly questioned rigid sex role socialization. Similarly, transsexuals and transgendered people have questioned our narrow definitions of "male" and "female" as absolutes and moved (some of) us toward thinking about what more fluid definitions of sex and gender would mean. "Intersexuals: Exploding the Binary Sex System" looks quite specifically at how at least 1 of every 2000 people would benefit from living in a society in which the definitions of "male" vs. "female" would be less rigid and where the medical establishment was not given the power to mutilate the bodies of children who do not easily fit into the male/female sex system. The article introduces us to the Intersex Sex Society of North America (ISNA) and the issues they are raising about the routine practice of doctors' performing major surgery on young children. But more than that, it raises much more fundamental questions about whether we can even envision a society in which new parents could be told, "Your child is intersexual, in other words, neither a boy nor a girl. There are resources available to help you raise your child in a healthy way. Go home and love your child as you would any other." (For a discussion of the challenges for trans and intersexuals to live safely, read "Trans and Intersex Survivors of Domestic Violence" in Chapter 12).

Examining the ways that narrow definitions of male and female, masculinity and femininity, ethnic or cultural groups, or even "health," limit one's ability to maximize on mental and physical health, can be an important component of a women's health course. In "The Myth of the Latin Woman—I Just Met a Girl Named Maria," Judith Ortiz Cofer explores the way images of an ethnic group impact on and limit people. Although she describes her own and others' resistance to these racist stereotypes, she acknowledges that it is harder for some people (without the privilege of the education or the "entree into society" that she has) to struggle against misconceptions and stereotypes.

The film "Still Killing Us Softly," which focuses on images of women in advertising, is an excellent introduction to these issues which we use in our classes. In preparation for the film, to make discussions particularly focus on the health ramifications of images, students are asked to collect ads related to health issues which appear in advertising aimed at women as consumers or images of women as consumers which appear in medical journals. In their chapter, "Drug Marketing: Selling Women Out," Leslie Laurence and Beth Weinhouse summarize many of the key issues of how health related ads manipulate consumers just as much as do ads for laundry detergent. We see that drug advertisements have a powerful influence on physicians and that some pharmaceutical companies budget $5000 per physician per year to influence prescribing practices, but that many of the ads (92% of the ads examined) do not meet FDA standards. A major change in the last decade is that the FDA began to allow prescription drug advertising to be directly aimed at consumers. Laurence and Weinhouse outline the many ramifications of this trend for women's own health and for all the people for whom women make decisions.

How health is represented in photographs in health textbooks is explored in "The Picture of Health." In images very similar to those seen in advertising, those portrayed as "healthy" exclude large segments of the population, leaving a group of young, white, thin, and physically abled to represent health. Health is presented in these images as a commodity that many will not be able to attain, in other words, a privilege, not a right.

Hazards of Hearth and Home

by Lesley Doyal

Synopsis—Women's health cannot be understood simply in terms of their biological characteristics. Improved theoretical analysis and more effective political action both require an exploration of the causal links between women's daily lives and their experiences of health, illness and disability. Recent research relating to these issues is explored in two linked articles: "The Hazards of Hearth and Home" and "Waged Work and Women's Well Being" (Vol. 13 No. 6).

Domestic work varies around the world but it universally involves low status, lack of economic power, and extensive social and emotional responsibilities. The implications of this labour for women's health are explored in this first article through an examination of the physical and psychological hazards of housework, the impact of caring on women's well-being, the stresses of emotional housework, inequalities in the allocation of household resources, the social and economic context of the ageing process in women, and the effects of domestic violence. These issues are placed in the context of the feminisation of poverty and differences between women in the developed countries and the Third World are explored.

Introduction

Women's health has traditionally been understood in terms of their reproductive systems. Thus, doctors locate women's problems in the specialist areas of gynaecology and obstetrics and assume that this takes care of those health problems peculiar to the female sex. Even women's overrepresentation among those diagnosed as suffering from certain types of mental illness is frequently explained by reference to some ill-defined biological nature, related, however obscurely, to their reproductive characteristics.

The reductionist model of health and illness that lies behind these practices has come under increasing attack in recent years. Research has shown that social and economic factors such as class, race, and country of residence are crucially important in mediating the biological processes underlying disease, death, and disability in both sexes. People do not become sick or remain healthy simply because of their genetic inheritance and their accidental contact with disease causing agents. The causal processes involved are much broader, encompassing living and working conditions, access to basic necessities, power and autonomy, and the quality of human relationships.

Feminists have taken this analysis a step further, using these ideas to explore the particular health problems experienced by women. While most women have a longer life expectancy than men from the same social group as themselves, they report more ill health and distress than men, use primary care and hospital services more than men, and suffer more long-term disability. The nature and severity of women's health problems obviously vary according to race, class, and economic status, but this overall gender difference remains remarkably constant. Researchers are now beginning to explore the reasons for this, linking women's patterns of morbidity and mortality to the nature of gender divisions in society and particularly to the continuing inequalities between the sexes. Findings from this new research are used to explore the links between women's health and two main areas of activity in their lives—domestic labour and waged work.

Domestic Labour in a Global Context

Women have traditionally been responsible for most of the work done in the domestic sphere. However, very little is known officially about the nature of household work or the conditions under which it is performed. While there have been periodic panics about women's capacity to look after their families'—and therefore the nation's—health, the impact of their domestic work on women's own well-being has rarely been a cause for concern. Indeed the role(s) of housewife and mother have generally been seen as healthy, despite considerable evidence to the contrary. So what is the nature of this work that most women spend so much of their time performing?

Their domestic responsibilities involve women in a complex web of activities that are often difficult to disentangle. For most, the central threads consist of care of a husband (or male partner), care of children and other dependents, and housework. Although the balance of these responsibilities will vary during the life cycle, these basic jobs form the core of women's domestic work in most societies. Not surprisingly, the nature and volume of this labour and the circumstances under which it is carried out have profound effects on women's physical and mental health.

In the developed countries, the common stereotype of the housewife is of a consumer who does a relatively small amount of low status, unskilled work, much of which involves spending money earned by a man. The reality, however, is very different. In the first place, most domestic work is done not by full-time housewives, but by women who are also engaged in some combination of paid and unpaid work outside the home. This pattern now applies in the majority of countries around the world—rich and poor, socialist and capitalist. In the second place, domestic work involves many (often unrecognized) skills and much effort. Indeed, most women with children (with the exception of the very affluent) spend their lives in continuous activity, putting together what the Italian feminist Laura Balbo has called "survival strategies" for themselves and their families (Balbo, 1987, p. 45).

But despite its obvious social utility, women's domestic work is unpaid—a fact which demeans it, and sets it apart from most other work done by adults. This inevitably has psychological significance for women, lowering their self-esteem and minimizing their sense of their own worth. It also affects them in more material ways, by reinforcing their economic dependence on others. Although many mothers with young children are now in paid employment, few can earn enough to support themselves and their families while continuing to do unpaid domestic work. Hence, most are forced, along with full-time housewives, into economic dependence on a male wage earner. Others have to rely not on an individual man but on the state to provide for their basic needs. In either case, economic dependence seriously limits women's autonomy and inhibits their control over their own lives and their health.

At the same time, women also have to take responsibility for those who are dependent on them for emotional and physical sustenance. Most of their daily work involves women in the servicing of others (Kickbusch, 1981). Put in more romantic terms, women's work consists of care of their "loved ones." This care can range from washing a partner's clothes through cooking a child's dinner to comforting a teenager worried about spots or cleaning up after the dog has been sick. It is distinguished from the same work in a laundry, cafe, or health centre because it is done for love rather than money. That is to say, women are expected to care *about* other people as well as caring *for* them (Graham, 1984). Thus, many women bear the double burden of their own economic dependence on a man or the state along with the dependency of their families on them for physical and psychological survival.

So far we have been talking in general terms about the elements of domestic work as it is performed by women in most countries around the world. The recognition of these basic similarities is important in reminding us that whatever the circumstances, patriarchal societies give women ultimate responsibility for the well-being of their families, often at considerable cost to their own health. However, this responsibility will have different implications according to the socioeconomic circumstances in which it has to be fulfilled. This point is most clearly illustrated through contrasting the lot of the majority of women in the industrialized countries with those in the Third World.

Housework and childcare are not the same in Birmingham, England or Birmingham, Alabama, as they are in the slums of Sao Paolo or the rural wastes of the Sahel. The most obvious difference is the level of material resources to which a woman has access to meet her family's needs. As we shall see, poverty itself is a major factor influencing the impact that a woman's domestic work has on her health, and most Third World women are very poor by comparison with those in Britain or the United States. But taking the analysis one stage further, we also need to recognize that the nature of domestic work itself is very different in the Third World.

Women in the rich countries work out their survival strategies through their own and often a partner's negotiations with the labour market and/or the state. This will often be difficult, time-consuming and exhausting, and the impact on the health of poor women should not be underestimated as they cobble together wages, benefits, subsidies, or rebates to underwrite the purchase of their necessities. However, even these options are not available to millions of women in the Third World. They have little or no money to spend in the cash economy and welfare services are not available to fill the gap. As a result, they have to weave their patchwork of survival through the direct production of their own and their family's needs. Many are engaged in subsistence agriculture, growing and then processing the food they are not rich enough to buy. Fuel is collected in the form of firewood rather than purchased from a gas or electricity supply company and water is collected from a local source rather than flowing to the house through pipes. Thus, the physical burdens of their domestic labour are very much greater and this is clearly reflected in their experiences of morbidity and mortality. These international variations will be explored in more detail as we look at the different aspects of women's domestic work and its impact on their health.

The Hazards of Housework

Throughout the world, women perform many millions of hours of housework every day—most of it unacknowledged and barely visible. In the developed countries it is widely assumed that technological innovation has led to a reduction in the hours spent on housework. However, there is little evidence to support this belief. The introduction of basic services, such as running water and gas and electricity, along with the later development of vacuum cleaners, washing machines, and other domestic appliances certainly ameliorated the hard physical labour that characterized the lives of so many workingclass women in the 19th and early 20th centuries (Oren, 1974; Pember Reeves, 1980; Llewellyn Davies, 1978; Spring Rice, 1981). However, there was little reduction in the number of hours worked (Vanek, 1974; Meissner et al., 1988). Nor is there evidence that women's greater participation in waged work has led to a more equal division of domestic labour. Instead, women have retained the moral responsibility for ensuring that all domestic work is done, whether they are employed outside the home or not. They must organize it and worry about it, even if they do not do everything themselves, with inevitable effects on their health.

Despite (or sometimes because of) the development of modern technology, housework can still be physically and mentally exhausting, especially when conditions are difficult. Domestic accidents are a common hazard, especially for older women, and are more likely to happen when the fabric of the home is substandard. An old and dilapidated house will be more difficult to keep clean and will often threaten the safety of women and children. Since they have to spend more time than men indoors, women are more affected by defects, such as condensation and dampness which can aggravate respiratory

disorders, as well as increasing the physical burden of housework. Looking after a home and its inhabitants can also bring the worker into contact with a wide range of toxic chemicals that are largely unregulated and have often been inadequately tested (Dowie et al., 1982; Rosenberg, 1984). Most of these are domestic products of various kinds such as cleaning fluids, bleaches, detergents, insecticides, and pesticides that are commonly used in the home and garden. It has been estimated that the average household in the United States contains some 250 chemicals that could send a child to hospital (Rosenberg, 1984).

There is also growing evidence that in the course of their housework women may be put at risk by hazardous chemicals encountered by their partners at their place of work. Research has shown that they can be endangered by asbestos fibers and radiation brought home on their husband's clothes or on his person. It also seems likely that some cases of cervical cancer may be caused by substances to which the man is occupationally exposed, which are then passed on to the women during intercourse (Robinson, 1981). Thus, the domestic workplace is not necessarily free from the chemical hazards of the industrial setting. Toxic substances do not become safe simply because they cross the threshold of the home and more research is needed to identify these dangers, as well as more effective regulation to control them.

However, it is the psychological hazards of housework which have attracted most attention, at least in the developed countries. To understand the reasons for this we need to look more closely at the nature of the work itself, at its social and economic status, and at the conditions under which it is performed. We can then explore the effects these have on women's sense of themselves, their control over their lives, and their potential for growth.

In Ann Oakley's study of full-time British housewives, most saw the main advantage of their job as the negative one of freedom from the constraints of employment (Oakley 1974). Few were positively happy with their work, with 70% expressing themselves 'dissatisfied' overall (Oakley, 1974). The women described most of their household tasks as monotonous, boring, and repetitive. Interestingly, it is these very characteristics of unskilled labour that occupational psychologists have shown to be most stressful in the context of male waged work. Although they are not formally controlled by a boss, most women doing housework experience very powerful pressures, both from other people and from inside their own heads. Ann Oakley asked one of the women in her study whether she found housework monotonous. Sally Jordan replied:

> Well, I suppose I do really, because it's the same thing every day. You can't sort of say, "I'm not going to do it," because you've got to

do it. Take preparing a meal: it's got to be done, because if you didn't do it, the children wouldn't eat. I suppose you get so used to it, you do it automatically. When I'm doing housework, half the time I don't know what I'm thinking about. I'm sort of there, and I'm not there. Like when I'm doing the washing—I'm at the sink with my hands in water, and I drift off. I daydream when I'm doing anything really—I'm always going off in a trance, I don't hear people when they talk to me. (Oakley, 1976, p. 147)

Thus, women are able to get little job satisfaction from routine housework and this is exacerbated by their lack of social and economic status (Berk, 1980). Most adults are paid for their work, and lack of such rewards limits self-esteem and gives a sense of worthlessness. Moreover, housework tends to be noticed only when it has *not* been done, giving women little opportunity for positive reinforcement, even of a nonmaterial kind.

These negative feelings are reinforced by the circumstances under which domestic labour is carried out. Housework is paradoxical in that it is usually done at home in isolation from most other adults, but when combined with childcare it also offers little opportunity for solitude. Despite widespread social and economic change, women continue to do almost all their household tasks in individual nuclear family units, with modern architectural styles often reinforcing this separation. However, the housewife may also find that her time is not her own. She will have to respond to the needs of others, may find very little time or energy to do things for herself, and rarely has physical space of her own. Under these circumstances, the demands on women are often high, and the real possibilities for control are low—again a situation clearly identified as stressful in the context of waged work (Karasek, 1979).

An additional feature of domestic work which can pose a threat to women's health is its open-endedness. Just as there are no absolute goals or standards, so there is no obvious end to the working day. For men and older children, home is perceived as a place of rest and recovery from the stresses and strains of real work done in the world outside. However, for most women the home is also a workplace and remains so for most of their waking hours. Many find it difficult to separate work and leisure; indeed those with young children are never really off duty, and their working hours can even extend to periods of sleep.

Not surprisingly, surveys in the developed countries have shown that women indulge in fewer leisure activities than men. The hobbies and pastimes they do mention tend to be domestic or home-based (listening to records or tapes, watching TV, reading, needlework and knitting, crafts and cooking) and they are frequently combined with ironing or child care (Deem, 1986). Relatively few are able to have outside interests, and active participation in sport is rare indeed. The reasons for this are closely related to women's family situation: lack of material resources, reluctance of men to allow them out alone, and the difficulty of getting someone else to look after the children, as well as the male-domination of many leisure and sporting facilities. This lack of leisure in general, and sport in particular, has obvious implications for women's physical and mental health:

> . . . the notion of "wellbeing" is closely tied up with opportunities for leisure. The fewer opportunities women have for leisure, the less the chance that they will see themselves as enjoying such wellbeing, which includes more than feeling healthy and/or fit and implies a sense of confidence about and enjoyment of life in general, which is difficult if that life consists mainly of being stressed, overworked, tense and continually feeling tired as well as having a poor body image. (Deem, 1986, p. 425)

Ultimately, the most damaging aspect of housework for women's mental health may be the lack of opportunity it offers for personal development. Some women do get a great deal of satisfaction from tasks done in and for their households, and develop considerable skills in the process. However, the structure of the job offers no opportunity for growth or advancement and few chances of wider social recognition for achievement. Of course, women do learn to deal creatively with challenges and crises throughout their lives. Indeed many individuals and families would not have survived without their tenacity, problem-solving abilities, and sheer hard work. However, those tasks are rarely of their own choosing and may offer little in the way of increased personal autonomy.

Why then do so many women go on doing housework under these conditions with so little complaint? One reason is their early socialisation which means that many have extreme difficulty in expressing any dissatisfaction they may have with housework. To do so may be to threaten their identity as a good wife and loving mother.

The power of this repression is reflected in what Jessie Bernard has called the "paradox of the happy marriage." During her classic investigation of male and female perceptions of marriage, men expressed a considerable degree of dissatisfaction, but appeared to have relatively good mental health as measured by a questionnaire. Women, on the other hand, were more likely to say they were happily married but exhibited much poorer mental health (Bernard, 1972). This contradiction was especially acute among full time housewives, many of whom simultaneously expressed high levels of satisfaction with marriage, as well as serious psychiatric symptoms. Indeed Bernard describes what she calls the "housewife syndrome" consisting of nervousness, fainting, insomnia, trembling hands, nightmares, dizziness, heart palpitations, and other anxiety symptoms. She concluded that "the housewife syndrome is far from a figment of anyone's imagination" (p. 47) and that "being a housewife makes women sick" (p. 48).

But it is depression above all, that seems to be an occupational hazard among fulltime housewives, especially those with young children. Both clinical experience and community research have shown that many women staying at home experience intense frustration, which is usually expressed in feelings of emptiness, sadness and worthlessness (Brown & Harris, 1978; Nairne & Smith, 1984). Too often these feelings go unacknowledged; women are said to be "like that" and the front door closes on a great deal of misery and distress. George Brown and Tirril Harris working in South London found that one-third of a random sample of workingclass women with children under six who were fulltime caregivers were suffering from what could be classified as "clinical depression." However, few had sought medical help. When women do take emotional problems to their doctors they are usually offered a chemical solution. In reality, however, it is the nature of women's domestic labour, their relationships with other people and their dependent status that makes them more likely than any other group to experience depression and anxiety, but less likely to confront the real reasons for their frustrations and dissatisfactions.

Who Cares for the Caregivers?

As well as doing the housework the majority of women also care for dependents. The intensity of this work varies over the lifecycle and some women never do it at all. However the vast majority become mothers at least once in their lives—in Britain the figure is now about 80%. This can be immensely rewarding and for many women motherhood is the most important and creative aspect of their lives. However, the reality of day to day childcare can also be both physically and emotionally demanding, especially under difficult circumstances (Graham & McKee, 1980; Richman, 1976; Boulton, 1983). For first-time mothers in particular, the responsibility of a tiny baby can be very onerous and nights without sleep exhausting and demoralizing.

Despite the lip service paid to motherhood as a social duty and a valued activity, few researchers have explored the reality of childcare from a woman's perspective. In an attempt to fill this gap, the British sociologist Mary Boulton recently carried out a series of in-depth interviews with young mothers (Boulton, 1983). Her intention was to disentangle women's feelings about the daily labour of childcare from their love for their children or their response to the status of motherhood itself. Almost two-thirds of women in the study experienced a strong sense of meaning, value, and significance in looking after their children. This is clearly important because a purpose in life is central to a feeling of well-being. However over one third did not feel this way (Boulton, 1983). Moreover, some 60% of her middle-class respondents and 44% of those who were working class found looking after children to be predominantly an irritating experience. Thus, the majority did not find childcare "naturally rewarding." Yet this was their fulltime work.

Many of the women referred to stress in their lives and identified a number of factors contributing to it. The lack of boundaries to their role meant that they were always trying to create structures and find themselves physical and mental space. They complained that childcare interfered with other activities, especially housework, and that children often undid what had just been achieved. For some women, childcare was isolating and limited them to relationships with other women in a similar position. Many also pointed out that children greatly curtailed their freedom of action because there was so much effort and anxiety involved in taking them out.

Overall, about 50% of Mary Boulton's sample said they were wholly content with their lives as mothers, about one-fifth were wholly discontented, while about one-quarter were in between. That is to say they accepted the situation, but wished it could be different. Significantly however, many of those who reported themselves satisfied also stated that their experiences of childcare were negative. This suggests that, as we saw in the context of housework, many women may simply accept situations over which they have no control, living much of their lives vicariously through others, with inevitable effects on their own well-being.

As well as caring for healthy children, women also look after dependent adults and chronically sick children. Again, precise information is difficult to obtain because this domesticated nursing is one of the most invisible of all forms of labour. In the British context, estimates suggest that at least 1.4 million people (out of a total population of just over 60 million) act as principal caregivers to adults and children with disabilities severe enough to warrant support in daily living tasks (Green, 1988). The vast majority of these are women. Some 15% of all British women of working age care for dependents over and above their normal family duties and many of them are also in paid employment (Martin & Roberts, 1984). Moreover, the need for such care is rising as the number of elderly and disabled people in the population increases. Indeed, the community care policies now fashionable in much of the industrialized world are based on the implicit assumption that women will continue with these unpaid labours (Osterbusch et al., 1987; Finch, 1984; Finch & Groves, 1983). Yet there is evidence that they may not be conducive to the promotion of women's own well-being.

The daily grind of caring has been well documented in a number of research studies (Equal Opportunities Commission, 1982; Finch & Groves, 1983; Briggs & Oliver, 1985). Caring for adults can be especially demanding both physically and psychologically. Much of the strain comes from the nature of the job itself—long hours, nightly disturbances and sometimes the trying behaviour of the person being cared for or the inability to hold a serious conversation. Stress is also caused by the conditions of caring, particularly the isolation that often results when the person cannot be taken out and no substitute care is available. Above all, caring for adults can cause emotional problems that do not arise in caring for normal children. The daughter who cares for a parent and the wife who cares for a husband may have to negotiate new relationships under difficult circumstances, often with very little support. One British woman looking after her husband has described her experiences in the following terms:

> The tiredness associated with looking after someone disabled was the hardest thing for me to adjust to . . . the tiredness is, of course, due to different causes for each caregiver, but the exhaustive effect is the same—for me, the tiredness comes from the physical exertion of caring for someone with severe multiple sclerosis, and from the mental stress of seeing the person you love best in the world suffering from such a disease. (Briggs & Oliver, 1985, p. 39)

Under these circumstances, women's own health will often suffer. This is especially true for women on what has been called the caring tricycle—the lifetime of responsibility which begins with care of children, continues into middle age with care of an aging parent, and ends with responsibility for a frail partner.

Doing Emotional Housework

Some of the more subtle aspects of women's domestic labour can be summarized as emotional housework. This is the least visible part of their work and consists of activities designed to ensure the happiness and emotional wellbeing of other family members—managing social relationships within the home to keep the old man happy and the kids quiet. While this labour is rarely perceived as such by women or their families, it is often a major burden. Arlie Hochschild has vividly described the processes involved:

> The emotion work of enhancing the status and wellbeing of others is a form of what Ivan Illich has called "shadow labour": an unseen effort which, like housework, does not quite count as labour but is nevertheless crucial in getting things done. As with doing housework the trick is to erase any evidence of effort, to offer only the clean house and the welcoming smile. (Hochschild, 1983)

But who is looking after women's needs while they smile for others? Sadly, the answer for many is no one. The traditional division of labour in the family means that women frequently do not receive the emotional sustenance they might have expected from their nearest and dearest. While adult daughters may provide support, this is rarely true of grown-up sons and male partners.

Luise Eichenbaum and Susie Orbach have written extensively on this problem from their experiences as feminist psychotherapists (Orbach & Eichenbaum, 1984; Eichenbaum & Orbach, 1985). They make the important point that the social stereotype of the clinging, passive female leaning on a strong and independent man is usually the reverse of the truth. Most men, they say, are looked after by women all their lives, from their mothers and other female relatives through female teachers to their wives or female partners in adulthood. A girl, on the other hand, is brought up to assume that she will marry a man and provide nurturance, care, and emotional support for him and his children. While she is expected to *appear* "dependent, incompetent and somewhat fragile," the internal reality is rather different:

> . . . behind this outward facade is someone who, whatever the inner state, will have to deal with the emotional problems met in family relationships, a person who knows that others will expect to rely and lean on her, a person who fears that she will never really be able to depend on others or never feels content about her dependency. (Eichenbaum & Orbach, 1985, p. 21)

Thus, many adult women cannot fulfill their own basic need for nurturance and emotional fulfillment, despite—or because of—their position at the hub of what is widely regarded as the most caring institution in modern society.

These insights derived from the psychoanalytic tradition are consonant with women's own accounts of their situation, as reported in a number of recent studies. Agnes Miles, a British sociologist, recently carried out in-depth interviews with some 65 women and men diagnosed as suffering from depression. About half of the women blamed their depression on an unhappy marriage, whereas most men referred to work and health problems (Miles, 1988). When asked about the support they had received, only 24 out of 65 women named their male partner as their main confidante and not all of these were satisfied with the quality of the relationship:

> (Iris, 24, no children). "There is only my husband. I wish there was someone else. Mostly I keep my thoughts to myself. I hoard my thoughts, then I get upset and tell my husband because there is nobody else. I usually regret it afterwards. He is part of the trouble, but who else can I talk to?"

> (Bridget, 29, two children 4 and 7). "I wish I had more people, I wish I had a woman friend. My husband is there but he doesn't want to talk, not like women talk to each other. He doesn't understand. He just says, don't bother me with nonsense." (Miles, 1988, pp. 94–95)

Many of the women in Miles' sample also expressed their fear of putting too much of a burden on other people. They were afraid that what little help was available would be withdrawn and, even more fundamentally, saw themselves as unworthy of support. Interestingly, the men in Miles' sample did not report the same problems in getting support from their wives. As Miles expressed it, "both took for granted that this was the natural order of things" (p. 113).

Susannah Ginsberg and George Brown uncovered a similar pattern in their study of women in the North London suburb of Islington. Again they were interviewing women who would be clinically diagnosed as a case of depression, in an attempt to see how relatives, friends, and doctors responded to their problems. This research repeated the now-common finding that signs of depression in women (such as inexplicable crying) are often given little attention since they are regarded as normal for women, especially when they are young mothers or menopausal (Ginsberg & Brown, 1982). Three quarters of those interviewed (27/37) who were living with their husbands felt that he had given little or no support. Mrs. Thomas, for instance, commented as follows:

> "I told my husband how depressed I've been feeling. He just sits in silence. If he could just talk things out and suggest something—but he doesn't."

> "Has he suggested you should go to the doctor?"

> "No, he doesn't realize anything is wrong. He doesn't notice that I haven't been getting on with things." (Ginsberg & Brown, 1982, p. 93)

Three quarters of the women (34/45) also felt they received little or no support from their mother or other relatives such as sister, or friends. The majority (32/37) who were living with their husbands said they did try to talk about their depression but most were unsuccessful. The majority of husbands apparently responded with such comments as "You're imagining it all," "Stop being silly," or "You mustn't talk like that, there's the baby" (Ginsberg & Brown, 1982, p. 95).

It seems, then, that women's domestic labour, especially their role in caring for others, is not always conducive to their own good health. Their mental well-being in particular will often be put at risk, and adequate support is not available when they are in need. As we shall see, this is especially true in the context of material poverty.

The Feminisation of Poverty

Women have always been overrepresented among the world's poor and recent years have seen a worsening of their situation (Scott, 1984). Although impoverished women are to be found in all countries, the majority live in underdeveloped parts of the world and it is here that the rigours of domestic work are at their most severe (Buvinic, Lycette, & McGreavey, 1983). Of course, men in the Third World are also poor, but it is women who must manage the consequences of poverty for the whole family. This often means performing physically heavier work and working longer hours than men (Dankelman & Davidson, 1988; Momsen & Townsend, 1987; Sen & Grown, 1988). In Tanzania, for instance, a recent study showed that women work an average of 3069 hours a year compared with 1829 hours for men (Taylor, 1985). Similarly, women in the Gambia spend 159 days a year on farmwork compared to men's 103 days (Mair, 1984). Moving to Asia, a study conducted in several rural villages in Kaunataka showed that the labour of women and children together contributed almost 70% of the total human energy expended on village work, even when strictly domestic tasks such as sweeping, washing clothes and childcare were excluded (Kishwar & Vanita, 1984).

Thus, women in the Third World bear a heavy weight of domestic responsibilities. Moreover, their material poverty and, for many, the exhaustion of frequent childbearing, add to their burdens. While climate, culture, and conditions vary between countries, these women are united by their poverty and the harshness of the social, economic, and physical environment in which they carry out their labours. As we shall see, this daily struggle is reflected in their general state of health and well-being.

In the richer parts of the world, most housewives can take for granted the existence of a constant supply of clean water. However, there are millions of women from rural areas of Bangladesh to the crowded barrios of Latin America who must face the daily task of acquiring enough water to meet the needs of their families. This is a physically demanding job which in rural areas will often mean a lengthy journey, but it is very rarely done by men.

Water is needed not just for drinking, but for sanitation and waste disposal, washing, childcare, vegetable growing, and food processing and also for economic uses such as keeping animals, irrigating crops, and brewing beer (Dankelman & Davidson, 1988). All this has to be fetched by women—usually on their heads because few have access to a vehicle of any kind or even a donkey (Wijk-Sijbesma, 1983). Many walk miles every day to a stream, well, or pond for a few pots of water. In urban areas, women depend on public taps which will usually mean long waits and no privacy for bathing. In many slums even public taps are not available, so that women face a long journey or the payment of a high price to a street vendor for water of dubious quality (Dankelman & Davidson, 1988).

Under these circumstances, water will have to be consumed sparingly, making other domestic tasks more difficult. Moreover, insufficient or polluted water will often result in illness, adding to the woman's burden. It is generally assumed that some 80% of all diseases in Third World countries are water-related. Diarrhoea, for instance, is a major cause of death among young children and is closely correlated with the absence of a clean water supply. Women themselves suffer additional problems caused by lack of adequate sanitation because religious and moral prohibitions mean they often have to wait until dark to avoid being seen in the act of defecation. This can lead to constipation and strain on the bladder and also exposes them to the risk of assault (Dietrich, 1986).

As well as supplying water, many Third World women are also responsible for ensuring an adequate amount of fuel for cooking, boiling water, and heating and lighting the house. Again, this very arduous task is rarely done by men and is a significant factor in the endemic exhaustion of many rural women. Throughout the world women are carrying loads of up to 35 kilograms, distances as much as 10 kilometers from home. This weight exceeds the legal allowance for women carrying

heavy loads in an industrial setting in many countries. The distance women have to travel varies depending on where they live, and the time taken can be as much as three or four hours per day. In some areas including the Sahel, Gambia, and parts of India, the journeys can be even longer and deforestation means that they are increasing (Agarwal, 1986). As supplies of firewood diminish, women and children are having to spend even more time on collection. In parts of Bihar, for instance, where seven to eight years ago poor women could get enough wood at 1.5 to 2 kilometers, they now have to trek 8 to 10 kilometers every day (Agarwal, 1986).

This growing shortage of fuel has meant that cooking has now become more labour-intensive and traditional methods have to be adapted to conserve energy. In some places the traditional wood fuel has been replaced by substances, such as cattle dung and crop residues. These biomass fuels are less convenient for cooking; the fire has to be stoked continuously and the smoke is even more dangerous than woodsmoke (WHO, 1984). Emissions from biomass fuels are major sources of air pollution in the home, and studies have shown that cooks inhale more smoke and pollutants than the inhabitants of the dirtiest cities. In one study quoted by WHO, a female cook was said to inhale an amount of benzopyrene (a known carcinogen) equivalent to 20 packs of cigarettes a day. Chronic carbon monoxide poisoning has also been reported (Dankelman & Davidson, 1988). Pollution of this kind has been identified as a causal factor in the high level of respiratory and eye disease found among Third World women. It can also cause acute bronchitis and pneumonia, as well as nasopharyngeal cancer among those exposed from early infancy (WHO, 1984).

As well as ensuring supplies of water and fuel, many Third World women are also directly involved in the production of food for their families (Dixon-Mueller, 1985). They grow a variety of crops either for immediate consumption or to be sold or bartered in the village or local market, and raise poultry or small animals. When food is scarce or there is a drought, they may have to scour the countryside for edible matter such as the roots and leaves of plants. This raw food then has to be processed, often by laborious and lengthy methods. These processes will vary between cultures and climates, but Madhu Kishwar's account of Indian peasant women gives some indication of the quantity of work involved:

> Grain or pulses to be consumed have to be hard-cleaned, little pebbles or pieces of dirt hand-sifted or painstakingly removed, one by one before the cooking of every meal. Many women have to hand-pound the paddy or grind the wheat two or three days a week in order to make it consumable. The paddy first has to be boiled and dried in the sun before it is husked.

To husk 20 pounds of paddy, two women can easily spend two to three hours, and it takes much longer if a woman has to do it alone . . . Thus, cooking even the most simple and basic foods commonly used in the diet of ordinary families is very exhausting. (Kishwar & Vanita, 1984, p. 4)

These accounts make it clear that the domestic labour of most Third World women is extremely hard. The work is physically strenuous and the hours are long, leaving many millions exhausted, undernourished, and vulnerable to premature death. Moreover, most are involved in frequent childbearing, resulting in levels of debility which can only be guessed at, since morbidity data for rural women are rare, and mortality data crude and uninformative.

While some of the worst living and working conditions are suffered by women in the Third World, this should not blind us to the fact that there are also many women in the developed countries who suffer the ill effects of both absolute and relative poverty on their health (Gelpi, Hartsock, Novack, & Strober, 1983; Glendinning & Millar, 1987; Scott, 1984). In the United States, the richest country in the world, almost two-thirds of impoverished adults are women. This overrepresentation of women among the poor must be explained by reference to the sexual division of labour in the wider society. Women are confined to a secondary status in the labour market, yet their work in the home is not financially rewarded. State welfare benefits mirror this low earning capacity, thus perpetuating a lifetime of economic dependence and poverty for many working-class women. In Britain, for instance, working women make up over two-thirds of the 8 million people whose wages are below the poverty line. Similarly, some two-thirds of all elderly people live in poverty and six million of this nine million are women. Female-headed families, too, represent a significant group in poverty. Thus, many women in rich as well as poor countries suffer the ill-effects of poverty.

The ill health women experience as a result of deprivation is often compounded by the allocation of resources within the family. Research has shown that even in households where the aggregate income is above the poverty line, women may not have enough to meet their own needs. This is because the division of income and wealth between individuals is often unequal (Glendinning & Millar, 1987; Land, 1983; Pahl, 1980). Women tend to get (or take) less both because of their economic dependence and lack of power, but also because of their concern for other family members. Thus, women are more likely than men to be poor when living alone, they may be poor members in nonpoor households, or they may be the poorest in a poor household. In all cases, their health will be at risk.

Bread for the Breadwinner?

We can illustrate these inequalities in the allocation of household resources by looking at gender differences in nutrition. Although women are usually responsible for the purchase and preparation of food and often its production too, many do not have the power to determine distribution between family members, and their own health may suffer as a consequence. Adequate nutrition is a basic human need which cannot always be met for the entire household in conditions of poverty. Research in many countries around the world has shown that when the family income is too low, it is women who are especially prone to nutritional deficiency. Under these circumstances, food is often the only item of expenditure that can be manipulated to make ends meet and it is usually women who go short to ensure that the needs of the children and the breadwinner are met (Oren, 1974).

Yet women themselves have particular nutritional needs, which often go unrecognized or ignored. Menstruation, pregnancy, and lactation all increase women's need for protein and iron. This is difficult to measure precisely, but it has been estimated that pregnant women need 350 extra Calories per day, while those feeding their babies need another 550 Calories, as well as three times the normal intake of calcium and double the amount of vitamin A (Protein-Calorie Advisory Group, 1977). Research in both the developed countries and the Third World has shown that many women do not get enough of the right food to meet these needs.

A study carried out by the London-based Maternity Alliance in 1984 showed that despite the existence of the British welfare state some women are still not able to feed themselves adequately during pregnancy. The average cost of the diet recommended for pregnant women by the Department of Health in 1988 was £15.88. This represented nearly half the weekly benefit payable to a single person and a third of that for a couple (Durward, 1988). As a result, the many pregnant women on supplementary benefit could not afford to eat what was officially defined as necessary to sustain their own health and that of their unborn children.

In the Third World, the nutritional problems of poor women are, of course, much greater. The combination of lack of food and, in some countries, severe discrimination against women, results in serious undernutrition for many mothers and daughters (World Health Organization, 1986). According to the Protein-Calorie Advisory

Group of the United Nations (PAG), there are definite indications of maldistribution of food at the family level in many parts of Africa with women getting the least even in pregnancy (Protein-Calorie Advisory Group, 1977). In some cultures, it is common for boys to be breastfed considerably longer than girls and for girl children to be fed less well than boys, thus reducing their chances of surviving infancy. Adult men often sit down to eat before their women and children, who get what remains (Leghorn & Roodkowsky, 1977; Carloni, 1981; Maher, 1981). Thus, food which is itself in scarce supply is distributed according to the prestige of family members rather than their nutritional needs. As a result, many women become anemic, especially during pregnancy, due to a lack of basic nutrients. Estimates suggest that in the Third World as many as half of nonpregnant women and two-thirds of pregnant women are anemic due to iron deficiency and folate and vitamin B12 deficiency combined with parasitic infections (WHO, 1979).

The authors of a recent study in Bangladesh set out to determine whether or not the very poor health record of women in that country could be explained by inequalities in the allocation of food and medical care (Chen, Huq, & d'Souza, 1981). The results were startling. Fourteen and four-tenths percent of female children in the sample were found to be severely malnourished, compared with 5.1% of males. This appeared to be directly related to food intake because dietary surveys showed that per capita male food intake considerably exceeded that of females at all ages. Overall, males averaged 1,927 calories per capita compared with 1,599 calories for females. The male excess was as high as 29% during the childbearing years of 15 to 44. These differences remained even when the data were adjusted for body weight, pregnancy, lactation, and activity levels, indicating that they must be seen as a relevant factor in explaining women's excess mortality.

In concluding, the authors of the study make the important point that these gender inequalities in life and death should not be seen as merely the response to scarcity. Indeed, they were found in rich as well as poor families, reflecting the fundamental inferiority of women's position in a profoundly patriarchal society. Of course, the reasons for male preference are a complicated mixture of the material as well as the ideological—girls cannot earn as much to help the family budget, have to be given a dowry, and are not able to support their parents during old age. But all too often the end result is serious damage to the health of girls, with many of those who survive to adulthood passing on their debility to future generations.

Older Women: The Invisible Majority

So far we have talked mainly about the impact of domestic tasks on the health of women in their childbearing years. However, in the developed countries, at least, it is older women who are most often confined to the home and who form the largest single group living in poverty. Even those who are not materially deprived frequently face serious health problems, yet these go largely unnoticed in societies that prioritize youth, vitality, and innovation. A combination of ageism and sexism means that older women are all too often marginalised sexually, socially, and economically in ways that threaten their well-being.

Older women are now the fastest growing group in poverty in the United States and Britain. In the United States, one-fifth of women aged 65 and over are below the poverty line, and women are twice as likely as men to experience poverty in old age. The single elderly are poorest of all and are predominantly female—three-fifths of women over 65 are alone compared with only a quarter of men. This reflects both the age difference of most couples at marriage and women's longer life expectancy. Older women from ethnic minorities suffer disproportionately from the effects of poverty. Forty-two percent of aged black women are in absolute poverty and a staggering 82% in near poverty, according to the 1980 U.S. Census. A similar situation prevails in Britain, with two-fifths of elderly women (38%) living on or below the poverty line, compared with 25% of men; two-thirds of all older British women are on the margins of poverty (Walker, 1987).

The poverty of older women stems directly from their lifelong economic dependency on men, the nature of their domestic responsibilities, and the existence of a dual labour market. Those women who do not engage in waged work are never able to earn state benefit in their own right. Hence, dependency in their early and middle years is carried over into old age. Even those who do work outside the home are often unable to build up a reasonable income for themselves in retirement. Many worked in low paid jobs without pension provision. Moreover, their working lives are usually disrupted by childrearing and sometimes caring for elderly parents, giving them little opportunity to build up a reasonable contributions record. Most, therefore, remain dependent on men, who usually die first, leaving them with only a minimal state pension to rely on. As a result, many experience health problems either caused or exacerbated by inadequate living conditions, insufficient heating, and lack of a nutritionally balanced diet.

Of course, not all the health problems older women face can be related directly to poverty. Many also suffer the psychological problems associated with retirement from work. Almost no research has been carried out on this topic because it has generally been assumed either that women do not work outside the home or that they are not deeply attached to their jobs (Fennell, Phillipson, & Evers, 1988). Thus, women appear only as shadowy wives in studies of men's retirement problems. Yet the few accounts we have from older women themselves suggest that the tensions are very similar for both sexes, and are likely to result in similar health problems (Ford & Sinclair, 1987). Most older women also have to cope with the denial of their sexuality at the same time as the physical and psychological distancing of their children.

Very few studies have investigated the health problems of older women, and routine medical statistics tell us little about their well-being. However, we know that in both the United Kingdom and the United States, elderly women are much more likely than men to be disabled. Twice as many British women in the over-65 age group are severely or very severely disabled compared with men of the same age, while the figure is five times greater in the 75-plus age group (Harris, Cox, & Smith, 1971). Women suffer three times as much arthritis as men and osteoporosis is also a significant cause of reduced female mobility. Mental health problems are even more difficult to identify and measure, but older women appear to continue the excess identified in younger age groups, with higher rates of depression and dementia than their male counterparts. Alan Walker comments on the basis of British data that older women are "more likely than men to suffer from psychological problems such as loneliness or anxiety and to have lower levels of morale and life satisfaction" (Walker, 1987).

Overall, women seem to suffer longer periods of chronic ill health than men, but their deaths are rarely caused by the same disease(s) that disabled them in life. Men, on the other hand, tend to have shorter periods of disability and to die from the problems that have bothered them while they are alive (Verbrugge, 1985). Interestingly many older women seem to play down their ill health, either because of low expectations—"You can't expect much at my age"—or shame at being unable to manage any more (Fennell et al., 1988, p. 109). However, others seem to welcome illness as liberating them from a lifetime of caring for others, especially when their dependents are no longer alive (Herzlich, 1973). In any case, too many remain behind closed doors, struggling to look after themselves with little material or emotional support.

The situation of older women in underdeveloped countries is obviously different in several ways. In the first place, relatively few survive to old age at all, and those who do are often severely debilitated by frequent childbearing and hard physical labour. Second, they are more likely than women in the developed countries to be supported and looked after within the extended family.

Indeed in many societies older women occupy important social roles—grandmother, mother, or mother in law, performer of religious or magical rites, senior wife—which offer more status than those of younger men. Those societies where women are required to be attached to a male adult usually have mechanisms to ensure that widows are not left alone. In India, for instance, remarriage is not encouraged among high-caste Hindu women and a son will be expected to support his mother while in some African societies, a widow is inherited by her husband's brother. Thus, older women in many parts of the Third World are less likely to suffer the isolation and invisibility of those in the developed countries, and in some cultures their status is even enhanced.

However, this is by no means always the case. Childless widows in particular often find themselves without social or financial security. Moreover, there is growing evidence that in many countries the breakdown of the traditional family-support system with industrialization and urbanization is increasing the vulnerability of divorced and widowed women (Youssef & Hetler, 1983). In parts of India, the expectation that a widowed daughter-in-law will be absorbed into her husband's family is no longer always adhered to. Instead, widows often return to their own families or set up (often very poor) households. Similar findings of lack of support for widows have been reported from Africa, from Upper Volta, Morocco, Zambia, and Swaziland (Youssef & Hetler, 1983). Thus, the problems of older women in the industrialized countries are increasingly being felt by those in the Third World as modernization removes their traditional sources of emotional and material sustenance, and therefore their access to reasonable health.

The Home as Haven?

Despite the dangers discussed above, it is a common myth that the home is a haven, offering protection from the dangers of the world outside. Indeed, many women are afraid to go out at night, staying behind closed doors to ensure their safety. The reality, however, is very different, as I explore in this final section.

It is clear that both the fear and the reality of domestic violence constitute a major threat to women's health. The use of physical force in the home is relatively common and most of it is inflicted on women by men (Dobash & Dobash, 1980). Precise estimates are difficult to achieve because so many victims are reluctant to reveal their private suffering. Indeed, the authors of a major British study suggest that only 2% of such assaults are reported to the police (Dobash & Dobash 1980). However, a number of studies designed to reveal the extent of this hidden violence have given broadly similar findings for the United States and Britain. A large-scale national study carried out by Murray Straus and his colleagues in the United States reported that over 12% of the married women interviewed had suffered severe violence at some point in their marriage, while a total of 28% had experienced physical violence of some kind (Straus et al., 1980). A British study involved interviews with all the women living in seven neighbouring streets in inner Leeds. About one-fifth of those interviewed had been the victims of violent attacks in their homes during the previous year (Hanmer & Saunders, 1984).

There is evidence of domestic violence in most countries around the world. In India, in particular, the uncovering of this abuse and its elimination has been a major focus of the new feminist movement (Mies, 1986). Urban and rural women, working class and middle class are all potential victims of domestic violence and Mies argues that their suffering has increased as the process of modernization gets under way. The most dramatic and widely publicized cases include the so-called dowry murders, in which women have been abused and eventually murdered because their husband and often his family are not satisfied with the money and goods she brought to the marriage. Many are deliberately burnt to death, but a cooking accident is blamed. Others commit suicide because the pressures on them are too great (Mies, 1986; Kishwar & Vanita, 1984).

Thus, the evidence demonstrates that a significant proportion of the women who live with men have the quality of their lives diminished by domestic violence. Moreover, this experience is shared by those in different social groups and societies, uniting women across class and racial divides. All women are potentially at risk from male violence, but paradoxically it is wives or cohabitees who get the worst treatment. Moreover, it is often their domestic work that provides the immediate excuse for a battering—a meal not ready on the table, a shirt not ironed, the house not clean enough, too much money spent on food, or a bout of "nagging." The physical damage caused is often severe, necessitating medical treatment or hospitalization. In the Dobashes' study of the survivors of violence, nearly 80% reported visiting the doctor at least once during their marriage for injuries inflicted by their husbands. Nearly 40% said they had sought medical care on five or more occasions and many felt their husbands had prevented them from getting medical help when they needed it. Another study of women in British refuges found that 73% had put up with violence for three or more years. Thirty percent had suffered life threatening attacks or had been hospitalized for serious injuries such as fractured bones (Binney, Harkell, & Nixon, 1981).

As well as the physical damage, it is clear that domestic violence is a major cause of psychological stress and trauma. Sixty-eight percent of the British women

in refuges said that mental cruelty was one of the reasons they left home (Binney et al., 1981). Many victims are emotionally debilitated by anxiety about the next attack and feel shocked, upset, angry, and bitter at what is happening to them. Sadly, many feel guilty and blame themselves:

> I actually thought if I only learned to cook better or keep a cleaner house everything would be OK. . . It took me five years to get over the shame and embarrassment of being beaten. I figured there had to be something wrong with me. (Dobash & Dobash, 1980, p. 119)

The authors of a recent study in North London found that women who had been battered were twice as likely to be depressed and had lower self-esteem than those who had not received such treatment (Andrews & Brown, 1988). Years of violence often leave women in a situation where alternatives are difficult to visualize. The socially constructed dependencies that they already experience are exacerbated by physical intimidation and violence. Moreover, attempts to get help from social workers, police, and other authorities too often lead to further humiliation and rejection (Stark, Flitcraft, & Frazier, 1979).

Thus, women become double victims of the batterer and the social agencies who too often assign the blame to women and resist any intervention in the private lives of man and wife. Indeed, one American writer has used the term *learned helplessness* to describe the condition in which so many battered women find themselves (Walker, 1979). Constrained by lack of confidence, isolation, fear, and lack of money, too many are forced to remain for lengthy periods in relationships that threaten their health and sometimes even their lives.

Conclusion

Thus, research findings accord with some women's own subjective experience in associating many of their health problems with their domestic responsibilities. Women's traditional duties are not always good for their health, given the circumstances of inequality and sometimes deprivation under which they often have to be carried out. Not surprisingly perhaps, there is growing evidence that despite their subordination in the labour market, women sometimes improve their health by working outside the home. I explore the implications of this in Part Two.

REFERENCES

Agarwal, Bina (1986). *Cold hearths and barren slopes: the woodfuel crisis in the Third World*. London: Zed Press.

Andrews, Bernice, & Brown, George. (1988). Violence in the community: A biographical approach. *British Journal of Psychiatry*, 153, 305–321.

Balbo, Laura (1987). Crazy quilts: Rethinking the welfare state debate from a woman's point of view. In Anne Showstack Sassoon (Ed.), *Woman and the state*. London: Hutchinson.

Berk, Sarah. (1980). *Women and household labor*. Beverly Hills: Sage.

Bernard, Jessie. (1972). *The future of marriage*. New York: World Publishing.

Binney, Val, Harkell, Gina, & Nixon, Judy. (1981). *Leaving violent men*. Leeds: National Womens Aid Federation.

Boulton, Mary. (1983). *On being a mother*. London: Tavistock.

Briggs, Anna, & Oliver, Judith. (1985). Caring: *Experiences of looking after disabled relatives*. London: Routledge and Kegan Paul.

Brown, George, & Harris, Tirril. (1978). *Social origins of depression*. London: Tavistock.

Buvinic, Mayra, Lycette, Margaret, & McGreavey, William. (Eds.). (1983). *Women and poverty in the Third World*. Baltimore: Johns Hopkins Press.

Carloni, Alice. (1981). Sex disparities in the distribution of food in rural households. *Food and Nutrition*, 7, 3 12.

Chen, Lincoln, Huq, Emdadul, & d'Souza, Stan. (1981). Sex bias in the allocation of food and health care in rural Bangladesh. *Population and Development Review*, 7, 55–70.

Dankelman, Irene, & Davidson, Joan. (1988). *Women and environment in the Third World*. London: Earthscan.

Deem, Rosemary. (1986). *All work and no play*. Milton Keynes: Open University Press.

Dietrich, Gabriele. (1986). Our bodies, ourselves; organizing women on health issues. *Socialist Health Review*, March, 79–184.

Dixon-Mueller, Ruth. (1985). *Women's work in Third World agriculture*. Geneva: ILO.

Dobash, R. Emerson, & Dobash, Russell. (1980). *Violence against wives: A case against the patriarchy*. London: Open Books.

Dowie, Mark, et al. (1982). The illusion of safety. *Mother Jones*, June, 38–48.

Durward, Lyn. (1988). *Poverty in pregnancy* (with 1988 update). London: Maternity Alliance.

Eichenbaum, Luise, & Orbach, Susie. (1985). *Understanding women*. Harmondsworth: Penguin.

Equal Opportunities Commission. (1982). *Caring for the elderly and handicapped: Community care policies and women's lives*. Manchester: Author.

Fennell, Graham, Phillipson, Chris, & Evers, Helen. (1988). *The sociology of old age*. Milton Keynes: Open University Press.

Finch, Janet. (1984). Community care: Developing nonsexist alternatives. *Critical Social Policy* 9, 6–18.

Finch, Janet, & Groves, Dulcie. (1983). *A labour of love: Women work and caring*. London: Routledge and Kegan Paul.

Ford, Janet, & Sinclair, Ruth. (1987). *Sixty years on: Women talk about old age*. London: Women's Press.

Gelpi, Barbara, Hartsock, Nancy, Novack, Clare, & Strober, Myra. (1983). *Women and poverty*. Chicago: University of Chicago Press.

Ginsberg, Susannah, & Brown, George. (1982). No time for depression: A study of help seeking among mothers of preschool children. In David Mechanic (Ed.), *Symptoms, illness behaviour and help seeking*. New York: Prodist.

Glendinning, Caroline, & Millar, Jane. (1987). *Women and poverty in Britain*. Brighton: Harvester.

Graham, Hilary. (1984). *Women, health and the family*. Brighton: Harvester.

Graham, Hilary, & McKee, Lorna. (1980). *The first months of motherhood*. Research Monograph No. 3. London: Health Education Council.

Green, Hazel. (1988). *Informal careers (General Household Survey 1985—GHS no. 15 supplement* A). London: HMSO.

Hanmer, Jalna, & Saunders, Sheila. (1984). Well founded fear. London: Hutchinson.

Harris, Amelia, Cox, Elizabeth. & Smith, Christopher. (1971). *Handicapped and impaired in Great Britain*, pt. 1. London: HMSO.

Herzlich, Claudine. (1973). *Health and illness: A social psychological analysis*. London: Academic Press.

Hochschild, Arlie. (1983). *The managed heart: Commercialization of human feeling*. San Francisco: University of California Press.

Karasek, Robert. (1979). Job demands, job decision latitude and mental strain: implications for job redesign. *Administrative Science Quarterly* 24, 285–308.

Kickbusch, Ilona. (1981). A hard day's night—on women, reproduction and service society. In Margarita Rendel (Ed.), *Women, power and political systems*. London: Croom Helm.

Kishwar, Madhu, & Vanita, Ruth. (1984). *In search of answers: Indian women's voices from Manushi*. London: Zed Press.

Land, Hilary. (1983). Poverty and gender, the distribution of resources within families. In Muriel Brown (Ed.), *The structure of disadvantage*. London: Heinemann.

Leghorn, Lisa, & Roodkowsky, Mary. (1977). *Who really starves? Women and world hunger*. New York: Friendship Press.

Llewellyn Davies, Margaret. (1978). *Maternity: Letters from working women*. London: Virago.

Maher, Vanessa. (1981). Work, consumption and authority within the household: A Moroccan case. In Kate Young, Carol Wolkowitz, and Roslyn McCullagh (Eds.), *Of marriage and the market*. CSE books.

Mair, Lucy. (1984). *Anthropology and development*. London: Macmillan.

Martin, Jean, & Roberts, Ceridwen. (1984). *Women and employment: A lifetime perspective*. London: Department of Employment.

Meissner, Martin et al. (1988). No exit for wives: Sexual division of labour and the cumulation of household demands in Canada. In Ray Pahl (Ed.), *On work*. Polity Press.

Mies, Maria. (1986). *Patriarchy and accumulation on a world scale.* London: Zed Press.

Miles, Agnes. (1988). *Women and mental illness: The social context of female neurosis.* Brighton: Harvester Press.

Momsen, Janet, & Townsend, Janet. (1987). *Geography of gender in the Third World.* London: Hutchinson.

Nairne, Kathy, & Smith, Gerrilyn. (1984). *Dealing with depression.* London: Women's Press.

Oakley, Ann . (1974) . *The sociology of housework.* London: Martin Robertson.

Oakley, Ann. (1976). *Housewife.* Harmondsworth: Penguin.

Orbach, Susie, & Eichenbaum, Luise. (1984). *What do women want?* London: Fontana.

Oren, Laura. (1974). The welfare of women in labouring families in England 1860-1950. In Mary Hartman & Lois Banner (Eds.), *Clio's consciousness raised: new perspectives on the history of women.* London: Harper & Row.

Osterbusch, Suzanne, Keigher, Sharon, Miller, Baila, & Linsk, Nathan. (1987). Community care policies and gender justice. *International Journal of Health Services,* 17, 217–232.

Pahl, Jan. (1980). Patterns of money management within marriage. *Journal of Social Policy* 9, 313–335.

Pember Reeves, Maude. (1980). *Round about a pound a week.* London: Virago.

Protein-Calorie Advisory Group (PAC). (1977). *Women in food production, food handling and nutrition: With special emphasis on Africa.* Final report. New York: Author.

Richman, Naomi. (1976). Depression in mothers of preschool children. *Journal of Child Psychology and Psychiatry,* 17, 75–78.

Robinson, Jean. (1981). Cancer of the cervix: Occupational risks of husbands and wives and possible preventive strategies. In Joe Jordan, Frank Sharp, & Albert Singer (Eds.), *Preclinical neoplasia of the cervix.* London: Royal College of Obstetricians and Gynaecologists.

Rosenberg, Harriet. (1984). The home is the workplace: Hazards, stress and pollutants in the household. In Wendy Chavkin (Ed.), *Double exposure: women's health hazards on the job and at home.* New York: Monthly Review Press.

Scott, Hilda. (1984). *Working your way to the bottom: The feminisation of poverty.* London: Pandora Press.

Sen, Gita, & Grown, Caren. (1988). *Development, crises and alternative visions.* London: Earthscan.

Spring Rice, Margery. (1981). *Working class wives.* London: Virago. (Originally published in 1939.)

Stark, Evan, Flitcraft, Anne, & Frazier, William. (1979). Medicine and patriarchal violence. *International Journal of Health Services,* 9, 461–493.

Straus, Murray, Gelles, Richard, & Steinmetz, Suzanne. (1980). *Behind closed doors.* New York: Anchor Books.

Taylor, Debbie. (1985). Women: an analysis. *In Women: A world report.* London: Methuen and New Internationalist.

Vanek, Joann. (1974). Time spent on housework. Scientific American, 231, 116-120. (Reprinted in Amsden, Ann. [Ed.] *The economics of women and work.* Harmondsworth: Penguin.)

Verbrugge, Lois. (1985). An epidemiological profile of older women. In Marie Haug, Amasa Ford, & Marian Sheator (Eds.), *The physical and mental health of aged women.* New York: Springer.

Walker, Lenore. (1979). The battered woman. New York: Harper & Row.

Walker, Alan. (1987). The poor relation: Poverty among older women. In Caroline Glendinning, & Jane Millar (Eds.), *Women and poverty in Britain.* Brighton: Harvester.

Wijk-Sijbesma, Christine van. (1983). *Participation of women in water supply and sanitation: Roles and realities.* Technical Paper 22. The Hague: International Reference Center for Water Supply and Sanitation.

World Health Organization. (1979). *The prevalence of nutritional anaemia in women in developing countries:* Country project. WHO Document FHE/79.3. Geneva: Author.

World Health Organization. (1984). *Biomass fuel combustion and health.* Geneva: Author.

World Health Organization. (1986). *Health implications of sex discrimination in childhood: Review and bibliography.* Geneva: WHO/UNICEF.

Youssef, Nadia, & Hetler, Carol. (1983). Establishing the economic condition of women headed households in the Third World: A new approach. In Mayra Buvinic, Margaret Lycette, & William McGreavey (Eds.), *Women and poverty in the Third World.* Baltimore: Johns Hopkins University Press.

Male and Female Hormones Revisited

by Mariamne H. Whatley

In 1985 a chapter I wrote, "Male and Female Hormones: Misinterpretations of Biology in School Health and Sex Education," in which I examined in detail problems with both content and language in health and sexuality texts, was published in *Women, Biology, and Public Policy* (edited by Virginia Sapiro, Sage Yearbooks in Public Policy Studies, vol 10). Since then there have been a lot of changes in health education, sexuality education, and general knowledge about women's health and biology. However, when I reread the chapter to see how out-of-date it was, I was interested to find that the main points I made then are still very relevant.

One of central examples I presented was of the common use of the terms "male hormones" and "female hormones" to refer to androgens and estrogens respectively. By using this terminology, educators imply that men and women have two very different sets of hormones, which naturally could be seen as affecting development, behavior, and abilities, and could serve as the basis for believing incorrectly that there are biologically-determined sex roles, rather than culturally and socially influenced gender roles. In fact, men and women share the same hormones, but they appear in varying amounts. The average man will have higher levels of androgens than the average woman and the average woman will have higher levels of estrogen than the average man. However, just by looking at hormone levels a scientist could not determine with certainty whether an individual were male or female, because there is so much variation across individuals, across the lifespan, at different parts of the menstrual cycle for women, and even at different times of the day (Men's levels of androgens may vary more in a day than a woman's estrogen levels do over a month). There are a number of reasons, therefore, why it is scientifically inaccurate to refer to male hormones and female hormones:

1. Both males and females produce both androgens and estrogens.
2. The adrenal glands and the gonads (ovaries, testes) produce both hormones in both sexes.
3. Both males and females need both androgens and estrogens for normal development.
4. Both hormones increase in both males and females at puberty.
5. Androgens and estrogens are steroids which are very similar in structure and can be interconverted (changed from one to the other) in our bodies.
6. Knowing hormone levels alone is not enough to determine whether an individual is biologically male or female.

In spite of these facts, much sexuality and puberty education material still refers to estrogens and androgens as very distinctly female or male. For example, in discussing female puberty, only estrogen will be discussed as a factor in changes in development, leaving out the fact that androgens do play a role in the development of girls, as well as of boys, in such changes as muscle growth, hair distribution, acne, and libido (sex drive). If androgen is presented as only a *male* hormone, then muscle development in girls is seen as abnormal. Boys on the other hand also normally produce estrogen, which sometimes reaches high levels at puberty, causing changes that may be seen as "female," such as temporary breast enlargement (gynecomastia) or more fat distribution on the hips. A boy with gynecomastia will undoubtedly feel uncomfortable no matter how sensitively the topic is handled, but it certainly won't help if he and his peers have all learned that breast enlargement is caused by estrogen, the *female* hormone. On the other hand, if the message is that all boys and men produce estrogens but that the levels can fluctuate, especially during

Printed by permission of the author, 1999.

puberty, and cause temporary breast enlargement, that boy might at least have some assurance that he is "normal."

At the other end of the reproductive cycle, there are often discussions of hormones in relationship to aging. Information on menopause may present postmenopausal women as becoming more "male" as their estrogen decreases and androgen becomes proportionately higher. Such changes may have to do with loss of breast size and density, growth of facial hair, and redistribution of body fat, so there is less on hips and thighs and more in the abdomen. Because her whole life, a woman has been told that she has "female hormones," the menopause literature which presents menopause as a total lack of estrogen or an "estrogen deficiency disease" is giving the message that the factor that makes her female is gone. She is, therefore, not really female any longer. When Robert Wilson wrote the book *Feminine Forever,* which extolled the virtues of exogenous estrogen to counter the effects of menopause, much of his focus was on the loss of estrogen as causing a loss in femininity and sexuality. While there has been much criticism of his work and, in recent years, there has been a decrease in the negative descriptions of menopause, these views do still persist. Discussing the fact that estrogen does not disappear after menopause and that androgens are actually converted to estrogens in fat and muscle cells can help give women a clearer view of what the real hormonal changes are. Also recognizing that their whole lives, they have gone through changing balances of hormones places menopause more in the context of ongoing biological processes rather than a new, completely different stage. Before puberty, girls and boys have very similar levels of hormones and the low estrogen in girls is certainly not considered an "estrogen deficiency disease" that needs to be treated with "estrogen replacement."

There are other implications of viewing estrogens and androgens as distinct hormones not shared by the sexes. If hormones are believed to have certain effects on behavior or abilities, then the association of a hormone with only one sex will imply biological limitations. For example, some scientists believe that androgen levels cause changes in aggression. There has been a long debate about this which includes such key opposing arguments as: the fact that behavior and environment can themselves alter hormone levels, so a high level of androgen may be a *result* of being in an aggressive position rather than a *cause* of it; the definition of aggression as very loose, ranging from rough and tumble play in primates to success in business and politics. If it were accepted that androgen levels cause aggression and aggression were loosely defined as meaning being able to compete in a highly competitive field, such as business or politics, then women would be seen as unable to compete in these areas. And, of course, women who are as aggressive (or assertive) as men may be seen as not really normal women. While we hope most people have discarded these outdated views, the basic misunderstanding of biology seeps into many discussions of women's abilities in general and in discussions of specific women. When someone refers to a woman as "ballsy," it may be seen as a compliment for her being a gutsy woman ready to take on challenges, but is also a backhanded compliment because it also implies she is not fully a woman, figuratively possessing testes—the major producer of androgens.

A discussion of changing the language which is used to describe hormones may seem trivial, as did attention to changing the generic male (e.g., mankind). However, a view of the world underlies choices we make in language and a change in language—however small—can cause a shift in perception. Just as we now refer to firefighters and police officers rather than firemen and policemen, to represent more accurately the status of women in the workforce, so must we also clean up our scientific language to reflect scientific reality, which is so often distorted and misrepresented.

Intersexuals: Exploding the Binary Sex System

by Kim Klausner

I sat in a restaurant in the Castro section of San Francisco waiting to meet Cheryl Chase, founder of the Intersex Sex Society of North America (ISNA). A lone woman entered the eatery and it soon became clear that this was the person I was waiting for. After settling ourselves at a table I did my best with innocuous small talk, hoping to find a connection with this person I would soon be interviewing. "So, you were born in New York City?" I ventured. Cheryl looked at me oddly and replied, "No, why?" I scratched my head and mentioned that I had seen a reference to her being operated on as an infant at a prestigious New York City hospital. She matter-of-factly said, "I wasn't born in New York; I was mutilated there."

Cheryl's response took my breath away, and well it should have. I gazed at this courageous woman and saw someone who was determined to transform an intensely personal experience into far reaching political action. As we ate, she willingly revealed intimate details about her life and body to me, a stranger, with the hope that I would join her effort to change oppressive medical practices and the assumptions behind them. Her particular experience is important to know only insofar as it can be used to illustrate larger social relations. During our lunch I was alternately struck by two processes that seemed to underlie all that Cheryl talked about: 1) that the personal is the political and 2) that the medical profession embodies the prevailing cultural assumptions about sex, biology, and gender and uses its authority to enforce particular power relations.

Before I get too far along with *my* thoughts, however, let me share a little about what ISNA is, mostly in the words of the organization itself. ISNA is "a peer support, education, and advocacy group founded and operated by and for intersexuals, individuals born with anatomy or physiology which differs from cultural ideals of male and female." Intersexuals, sometimes called hermaphrodites, are a physically diverse group of people, with bodies that are not easily categorized in our either/or male/female sex system. According to doctors, intersexuals are females born with clitorises that the doctors consider too long and males born with penises that are deemed too short. In a certain sense, the medical establishment hardly recognizes the integrity of the category "intersexual," preferring to dismiss intersexuals as deficient males or females. One of ISNA's first goals is to redefine the terms of their very existence.

The concept of intersexuality confronts the dominant cultural conception of "sex anatomy as a dichotomy: humans come in two sexes, conceived of as so different as to be nearly different species." ISNA challenges this view with the assertion that "anatomic sex differentiation occurs on a male/female continuum with several dimensions."

(If your eyes glaze over at the mention of chromosomes and you can't quite remember, or never knew, what gonads are, feel free to skip the next two paragraphs.) ISNA continues its explanation of intersexuality with, "Genetic sex, or the organization of the 'sex chromosomes,' is commonly thought to be isomorphic to some idea of 'true sex.' However, something like 1/500 of the population have a karyotype [that is, chromosomal arrangement] other than XX (most females) or XY (most males)." As an example, ISNA points to women athletes subject to genetic testing. In recent years, women Olympic athletes have had to undergo genetic tests, and as a result a number of them have been disqualified as 'not women,' after winning. These women, of course are

From *Sojourner*, January 1997, Vol. 22, No. 5, pp. 7–8. Copyright © by Kim Klausner. Reprinted by permission.

Author's note: If you want to know more about inersexuality or ISNA, contact the organization by e-mail (info@isna.org or cchase@isna.org), at their web site (http://www.isna.org), or by snailmail at P.O. Box 31791, San Francisco, CA 94131.

Kim Klausner is an archivist at the Western Jewish History Center and the treasurer of the Buena Vista PTA.

not men—they, like many other intersexuals, have atypical karotypes (though one gave birth to a healthy child after having been barred from competition).

The genitals of intersexual people vary along the male-female continuum. As is pointed out in ISNA literature:

> Intersexual genitals may look nearly female, with a large clitoris, or with some degree of posterior labial fusion. They may look nearly male, with a small penis, or with hypospadias [a condition where the urethra opens on the under surface of the penis]. They may be truly "right in the middle," with a phallus that can be considered either a large clitoris or a small penis, with a structure that might be a split, empty scrotum, or outer labia, and with a small vagina that opens into the urethra rather than into the perineum.

> Internal reproductive organs may be partially developed or discordant with external genitals. For instance, there are people whose genitals have the same appearance as most females, but inside have testes and no uterus or ovaries. Some people have combined gonads, that is, ovo-testes. Some people who have male-appearing genitals have a uterus, ovaries, and tubes.

To summarize, ISNA asserts that medical science has effectively promoted the "objective fact" that there are but two sexes, male and female, and that people are either one or the other. If truth be told, and it is, thanks to ISNA, people can be virtually all male, all female, or some of both (though, the popular concept of two sets of genitals—male and female—is not possible). It should be noted that we're just talking biology here; this doesn't even attempt to address questions about the social construction of gender or how children are raised to be boys or girls.

ISNA wants the immediate end to practices that arise from the medical model established in the 1950s that asserts that "children with visibly intersexual anatomy cannot develop into healthy adults." They want to stop emergency sex assignment and reinforcement of sex assignment with early genital surgery, which often causes serious sexual dysfunction. They also want an end to the dishonesty of health care providers who, in their discussions with parents and intersexuals, cover up the true status of the intersex child. ISNA does not, however, oppose using medical technology when it is necessary. "For instance," Chase explains, "some children are born with ambiguous genitals because of adrenal hyperplasia, which can be life threatening. Doctors should treat those aspects of this condition that affect the health and comfort of the child, such as preventing him or her from going into salt shock."

When an infant is born with genitals that don't conform to our idea of either male or female, ISNA wants doctors to be honest and not say, as they currently do, "Well, we can't determine what sex your child is by looking at it, but we can perform tests that will tell us, and then we can alter its genitals so it looks more like the sex it is." Rather, they'd prefer that new parents be told, "Your child is intersexual, in other words, neither a boy nor a girl. There are resources available to help you raise your child in a healthy way. Go home and love this child as you would any other." Chase succinctly sums it up with "we want an end to harmful and medically unnecessary cosmetic surgery, secrecy, and lying."

Obviously, this approach requires a radical rearrangement of our society. At the least, we need some new pronouns since "it" hardly describes a new baby. What ISNA is advocating is so profoundly disorienting that I've even had feminist friends roll their eyes at me and say, "So what, these people want to dismantle our society's concept of the male-female dichotomy? Good luck!" Or "How many people does this affect anyway? I mean, shouldn't we be dealing with issues like racism or poverty, things that affect much larger groups of people?" The number of people born intersexual is not huge, although it is probably greater than you imagine (1 out of every 2,000 births).

Accepting ISNA's claims means recovering the authority we have given to the medical establishment to assign and enforce sex roles. Most people hardly give the concept that sexes are assigned by society a thought. It is something that is determined by biology; if an infant has a penis, then it is a boy. It sounds simple enough. But transgendered people, who don't fit neatly into male or female categories, know that the medical establishment closely guards its prerogative to enforce sex roles. In most parts of the United States, transpeople have to feign a mental disorder to obtain an operation that is forced on intersexual children. In both cases the medical profession assumes the role of sex judge. Doctors tell the parents of the intersexual infant, "Based on the evidence, this is a girl, even though part of her anatomy looks almost male," while telling the person who wants to take hormones in the hopes of uncovering a body that more closely resembles their identity, "I will not prescribe these drugs unless you prove to me that you think you're really a (wo)man (and straight, too)."

If we are to honor the experience of many transsexuals, we must admit it is possible to be a female born with a penis or a male born with a vagina. We feel compelled to identify newborns as male or female, but maybe we should wait and let the kid decide whether s/he is male, female, or both. Chase points out that it's only been in the past 50 years or so that the medical profession has arbitrated these questions. For centuries, intersexuals navigated without the "help" of the sex judges. In some cultures, intersexuals were ignored, in some they were accorded high status, and in others they were reviled.

Feminists have long advocated that gender is culturally constructed. Well, why not sex? Somehow, the material nature of genitals, internal organs, and even hormones coursing through our bloodstreams lends credence to the medically or biologically based construction of sex. You cannot be fooled by something you can actually see or touch. Intersexuals and transpeople are starting to tell us otherwise. Sex cannot always be easily articulated in morphological terms and the diversity of anatomical differences among humans arrays us along a sex spectrum, not into two mutually exclusive categories.

The argument that sex is not biologically determined challenges decades of feminist theory and practice. If it is no longer clear that there are two distinct sexes, a theory resting on these two categories of existence becomes unstable. How can men oppress women if the boundaries between each group are permeable? Or if we no longer know who fits in each category? For these reasons, some feminists have found transpeople and intersexuals threatening. But do intersexuals alter the paradigm?

Unfortunately, oppressive relations can flourish without immutable, biologically based categories. The existence of mixed-race people has not brought an end to racism. While some Black civil rights organizations may fear that the institutionalization of mixed-race categories on the census will dilute their political power, I doubt that any of them think that the disappearance of mixed-race people from their statistical ranks will cause racism to crumble. And a person with parents of different races still faces racist prejudice and discrimination as s/he walks through life. In the case of men and women, perhaps imagining a sex continuum makes gender more important than sex. And this raises the question of the connection between gender and sex. The more I think about it, the more unsure I am that things are as they seem. But of course, many queer people have known this with their bodies and minds since they were young children.

Having the medical establishment (aided and abetted by the legal system) in charge of defining what the sexes are and how individual people fit into this schema provides reassurance—at least to those who have faith in the medical-judicial system—that sex assignment is not done on an arbitrary or capricious basis. It is, after all, scientifically proven. But what happens when people's experiences deviate from the accepted medical facts? Intersexual bodies are mutilated to maintain the current paradigm, just as gay people are institutionalized,

women are called hysterical, and transpeople are thwarted in their efforts to realize themselves.

Here you might ask, "Why wouldn't a parent want to take advantage of the amazing medical techniques we have available to help her newborn child adjust to the world as it is? Wouldn't it be cruel to the child to force it to lead a life of being different?" The intersexuals connected with ISNA are saying simply and clearly they would rather be "different" than mutilated. Further, they want to help change our conception of normal so they won't have to feel out of place. Since an intersexual person knows, at some level, that s/he is different, the only thing surgical alteration seems to accomplish is the mental well-being of doctors, parents, and others who are more concerned with the intersexual's body than their mental well-being. In fact, the doctor's or parents' peace of mind is sometimes obtained at a monumental price: intersexuals report both sexual dysfunction and profound feelings of being unacceptable.

(It is certainly possible that some intersexuals are happy that they were altered. But they are the only ones who know. There have been no long-term studies on the effects of surgery on intersexual infants. The medical profession seems remarkably uninterested in knowing about the lives of intersexual adults. Perhaps if you are in this situation you will share your feelings with other *Sojourner* readers.)

This professionally sanctioned violation of a human body not only causes physical trauma but is also accompanied by a tremendous sense of shame about one's body. When an intersexual is born, a life of secrecy begins. It starts in the labor and delivery room. One can feel the palpable discomfort of the medical staff when they are unable to quickly answer the question, "is it a girl or a boy?" The intersexual teen is generally not told the truth about what has been done to his/her body, which magnifies an already difficult period of transition. And many intersexual people eventually carry the secret themselves as they hide their status from lovers.

When Cheryl Chase was born, the doctors told her parents that their child was a boy. When their son was a year old, a medical expert informed them, "This child is not really a boy. We will fix the problem by removing what looks like a penis but we suggest that you move to another city and start over again, telling people you have a daughter." Her parents renamed her Cheryl and did exactly that. Does the shame and secrecy sound similar to that experienced by the child of alcoholics or one who is sexually abused?

At 40, Cheryl still feels the painful reverberations of how the medical profession and her family treated her as someone born intersexual. Of this experience, she says simply, "It destroyed my whole family; we are scattered to the winds." From her mother who was given tranquilizers in response to her concerns about her infant's body, to her father who lay on his deathbed telling Cheryl that she was "bad from the day you were born," to her sisters who do not want biological children of their own, to her aunt who was unable to support Cheryl in her quest for the truth out of "loyalty" to her sister, there have been no winners here.

ISNA provides ample material from which to analyze power relations, particularly the way that science, as it is embedded in our particular culture, helps maintain a sexist hierarchy. For me, as someone who fits quite easily into a binary sex system, intersexual liberation is somewhat of an intellectual issue, removed from my day-to-day identity experience. At the same time, I recognize that this movement is led by people whose very core identities and bodies are at stake. As a political activist, I am incredibly rejuvenated by being a witness to this movement. There is something very powerful about a group of people who fuse the intensely personal with the theoretical to create change. I can take this concentrated sense of mission to other political work I do.

The process by which ISNA formed echoes the women's movement of the late '60s. A severe emotional breakdown provoked Chase to start asking questions about how her body came to be. In the course of her investigation, she found other people who had had similar experiences. Last summer, a group of ten intersexual people met for a weekend in Northern California. I happened to meet two of these people shortly after their gathering. They shared a small pile of photographs taken during the weekend. The photos show a bunch of people hanging out in a nice place, nothing remarkable at all. The photos, though, stimulated these two women to recount parts of the weekend, and it soon became clear how potent it had been. The simple act of coming together to share experiences was what they needed to name an oppressive force. Speaking the unspoken is at once both personal and political. In this case, collective action arises from the recognition that one's individual life is not an isolated experience. Cheryl says of her work with ISNA, "If I wasn't doing this, I'd be dead now." Cheryl and other ISNA members are providing an opportunity for other intersexuals, who may be confused or despairing, to continue their healing among those who know the pain from first hand experience. And in doing so, they will change the world.

I am a lesbian parent of two sons. (Or at least I'm assuming they're male, until they tell me otherwise.) When my oldest child was born eight years ago, a lot of people thought that it was unfair to bring a child into the world to face the anticipated harassment he would receive as the son of lesbians. As a parent, it is painful to think that my children will face prejudice (and they will never face discrimination based on their skin color, language learned at home, or income level). I didn't send my son to be raised by a straight couple; instead, I've tried to do what I can to reduce negative attitudes about lesbians. I am lucky that I live in a community that supports me in doing this. It certainly would have been harder and more isolating to take this approach in other parts of the country (even 50 miles from here). But not impossible. Some people are willing to take risks in the hopes that oppressive attitudes or power structures will change. As feminists, what can we do to help parents of intersexual children accept their children as they are and fight to change a world that says they should be changed?

The Myth of the Latin Woman
I Just Met a Girl Named María

by Judith Ortiz Cofer

On a bus trip to London from Oxford University where I was earning some graduate credits one summer, a young man, obviously fresh from a pub, spotted me and as if struck by inspiration went down on his knees in the aisle. With both hands over his heart he broke into an Irish tenor's rendition of "María" from *West Side Story*. My politely amused fellow passengers gave his lovely voice the round of gentle applause it deserved. Though I was not quite as amused, I managed my version of an English smile: no show of teeth, no extreme contortions of the facial muscles—I was at this time of my life practicing reserve and cool. Oh, that British control, how I coveted it. But María had followed me to London, reminding me of a prime fact of my life: you can leave the Island, master the English language, and travel as far as you can, but if you are a Latina, especially one like me who so obviously belongs to Rita Moreno's gene pool, the Island travels with you.

This is sometimes a very good thing—it may win you that extra minute of someone's attention. But with some people, the same things can make *you* an island—not so much a tropical paradise as an Alcatraz, a place nobody wants to visit. As a Puerto Rican girl growing up in the United States and wanting like most children to "belong," I resented the stereotype that my Hispanic appearance called forth from many people I met.

Our family lived in a large urban center in New Jersey during the sixties, where life was designed as a microcosm of my parents' casas on the island. We spoke in Spanish, we ate Puerto Rican food bought at the bodega, and we practiced strict Catholicism complete with Saturday confession and Sunday mass at a church where our parents were accommodated into a one-hour Spanish mass slot, performed by a Chinese priest trained as a missionary for Latin America.

As a girl I was kept under strict surveillance, since virtue and modesty were, by cultural equation, the same as family honor. As a teenager I was instructed on how to behave as a proper señorita. But it was a conflicting message girls got, since the Puerto Rican mothers also encouraged their daughters to look and act like women and to dress in clothes our Anglo friends and their mothers found too "mature" for our age. It was, and is, cultural, yet I often felt humiliated when I appeared at an American friend's party wearing a dress more suitable to a semiformal than to a playroom birthday celebration. At Puerto Rican festivities, neither the music nor the colors we wore could be too loud. I still experience a vague sense of letdown when I'm invited to a "party" and it turns out to be a marathon conversation in hushed tones rather than a fiesta with salsa, laughter and dancing—the kind of celebration I remember from my childhood.

I remember Career Day in our high school, when teachers told us to come dressed as if for a job interview. It quickly became obvious that to the barrio girls, "dressing up" sometimes meant wearing ornate jewelry and clothing that would be more appropriate (by mainstream standards) for the company Christmas party than as daily office attire. That morning I had agonized in front of my closet, trying to figure out what a "career girl" would wear because, essentially, except for Marlo Thomas on TV, I had no models on which to base my decision. I knew how to dress for school: at the Catholic school I attended we all wore uniforms; I knew how to dress for Sunday mass, and I knew what dresses to wear for parties at my relatives' homes. Though I do not recall the precise details of my Career Day outfit, it must have been a composite of the above choices. But I remember a comment my friend (an Italian-American) made in later years that coalesced my impressions of that day. She said that at the business school she was attending the Puerto Rican girls always stood out for wearing "everything at once." She meant, of course, too much jewelry, too many accessories. On that day at school, we were simply made the negative models by the nuns who were themselves not credible fashion experts to any of us. But it was painfully obvious to me that to the others, in their tailored skirts and silk blouses, we must have seemed "hopeless" and "vulgar." Though I now know that most adolescents feel out of step much of the time, I also know that for the Puerto Rican girls of my generation that sense was intensified. The way our teachers and classmates looked at us that day in school was just a taste of the culture clash that awaited us in the real world, where prospective employers and men on the street would often misinterpret our tight skirts and jingling bracelets as a come-on.

Mixed cultural signals have perpetuated certain stereotypes—for example, that of the Hispanic woman as the "Hot Tamale" or sexual firebrand. It is a one-dimensional view that the media have found easy to promote. In their special vocabulary, advertisers have designated "sizzling" and "smoldering" as the adjectives of choice for describing not only the foods but also the women of Latin America. From conversations in my house I recall hearing about the harassment that Puerto Rican women endured in factories where the "boss men" talked to them as if sexual innuendo was all they understood and, worse, often gave them the choice of submitting to advances or being fired.

It is custom, however, not chromosomes, that leads us to choose scarlet over pale pink. As young girls, we were influenced in our decisions about clothes and colors by the women—older sisters and mothers who had grown up on a tropical island where the natural environment was a riot of primary colors, where showing your skin was one way to keep cool as well as to look sexy. Most important of all, on the island, women perhaps felt freer to dress and move more provocatively, since, in most cases, they were protected by the traditions, mores, and laws of a Spanish/Catholic system of morality and machismo whose main rule was: *You may look at my sister, but if you touch her I will kill you.* The extended family and church structure could provide a young woman with a circle of safety in her small pueblo on the island; if a man "wronged" a girl, everyone would close in to save her family honor.

This is what I have gleaned from my discussions as an adult with older Puerto Rican women. They have told me about dressing in their best party clothes on Saturday nights and going to the town's plaza to promenade with their girlfriends in front of the boys they liked. The males were thus given an opportunity to admire the women and to express their admiration in the form of *piropos:* erotically charged street poems they composed on the spot. I have been subjected to a few piropos while visiting the Island, and they can be outrageous, although custom dictates that they must never cross into obscenity. This ritual, as I understand it, also entails a show of

studied indifference on the woman's part; if she is "decent," she must not acknowledge the man's impassioned words. So I do understand how things can be lost in translation. When a Puerto Rican girl dressed in her idea of what is attractive meets a man from the mainstream culture who has been trained to react to certain types of clothing as a sexual signal, a clash is likely to take place. The line I first heard based on this aspect of the myth happened when the boy who took me to my first formal dance leaned over to plant a sloppy overeager kiss painfully on my mouth, and when I didn't respond with sufficient passion said in a resentful tone: "I thought you Latin girls were supposed to mature early"—my first instance of being thought of as a fruit or vegetable—I was supposed to *ripen,* not just grow into womanhood like other girls.

It is surprising to some of my professional friends that some people, including those who should know better, still put others "in their place." Though rarer, these incidents are still commonplace in my life. It happened to me most recently during a stay at a very classy metropolitan hotel favored by young professional couples for their weddings. Late one evening after the theater, as I walked toward my room with my new colleague (a woman with whom I was coordinating an arts program), a middle-aged man in a tuxedo, a young girl in satin and lace on his arm, stepped directly into our path. With his champagne glass extended toward me, he exclaimed, "Evita!"

Our way blocked, my companion and I listened as the man half-recited, half-bellowed "Don't Cry for Me, Argentina." When he finished, the young girl said: "How about a round of applause for my daddy?" We complied, hoping this would bring the silly spectacle to a close. I was becoming aware that our little group was attracting the attention of the other guests. "Daddy" must have perceived this too, and he once more barred the way as we tried to walk past him. He began to shout-sing a ditty to the tune of "La Bamba"—except the lyrics were about a girl named María whose exploits all rhymed with her name and gonorrhea. The girl kept saying "Oh, Daddy" and looking at me with pleading eyes. She wanted me to laugh along with the others. My companion and I stood silently waiting for the man to end his offensive song. When he finished, I looked not at him but at his daughter. I advised her calmly never to ask her father what he had done in the army. Then I walked between them and to my room. My friend complimented me on my cool handling of the situation. I confessed to her that I really had wanted to push the jerk into the swimming pool. I knew that this same man—probably a corporate executive, well educated, even worldly by most standards—would not have been likely to regale a white woman with a dirty song in public. He would perhaps have checked his impulse by assuming that she could be somebody's wife or mother, or at least *somebody* who might take offense. But to him, I was just an Evita or a Maria: merely a character in his cartoon-populated universe.

Because of my education and my proficiency with the English language, I have acquired many mechanisms for dealing with the anger I experience. This was not true for my parents, nor is it true for the many Latin women working at menial jobs who must put up with stereotypes about our ethnic group such as: "They make good domestics." This is another facet of the myth of the Latin women in the United States. Its origin is simple to deduce. Work as domestics, waitressing, and factory jobs are all that's available to women with little English and few skills. The myth of the Hispanic menial has been sustained by the same media phenomenon that made "Mammy" from *Gone with the Wind* America's idea of the black woman for generations; María, the housemaid or counter girl, is now indelibly etched into the national psyche. The big and the little screens have presented us with the picture of the funny Hispanic maid, mispronouncing words and cooking up a spicy storm in a shiny California kitchen.

This media-engendered image of the Latina in the United States has been documented by feminist Hispanic scholars, who claim that such portrayals are partially responsible for the denial of opportunities for upward mobility among Latinas in the professions. I have a Chicana friend working on a Ph.D. in philosophy at a major university. She says her doctor still shakes his head in puzzled amazement at all the "big words" she uses. Since I do not wear my diplomas around my neck for all to see, I too have on occasion been sent to that "kitchen," where some think I obviously belong.

One such incident that has stayed with me, though I recognize it as a minor offense, happened on the day of my first public poetry reading. It took place in Miami in a boat-restaurant where we were having lunch before the event. I was nervous and excited as I walked in with my notebook in hand. An older woman motioned me to her table. Thinking (foolish me) that she wanted me to autograph a copy of my brand new slender volume of verse, I went over. She ordered a cup of coffee from me, assuming that I was the waitress. Easy enough to mistake my poems for menus, I suppose. I know that it wasn't an intentional act of cruelty, yet of all the good things that happened that day, I remember that scene most clearly, because it reminded me of what I had to overcome before

anyone would take me seriously. In retrospect I understand that my anger gave my reading fire, that I have almost always taken doubts in my abilities as a challenge—and that the result is, most times, a feeling of satisfaction at having won a convert when I see the cold, appraising eyes warm to my words, the body language change, the smile that indicates that I have opened some avenue for communication. That day I read to that woman and her lowered eyes told me that she was embarrassed at her little faux pas, and when I willed her to look up to me, it was my victory, and she graciously allowed me to punish her with my full attention. We shook hands at the end of the reading, and I never saw her again. She has probably forgotten the whole thing but maybe not.

Yet I am one of the lucky ones. My parents made it possible for me to acquire a stronger footing in the mainstream culture by giving me the chance at an education. And books and art have saved me from the harsher forms of ethnic and racial prejudice that many of my Hispanic *compañeras* have had to endure. I travel a lot around the United States, reading from my books of poetry and my novel, and the reception I most often receive is one of positive interest by people who want to know more about my culture. There are, however, thousands of Latinas without the privilege of an education or the entrée into society that I have. For them life is a struggle against the misconceptions perpetuated by the myth of the Latina as whore, domestic, or criminal. We cannot change this by legislating the way people look at us. The transformation, as I see it, has to occur at a much more individual level. My personal goal in my public life is to try to replace the old pervasive stereotypes and myths about Latinas with a much more interesting set of realities. Every time I give a reading, I hope the stories I tell, the dreams and fears I examine in my work, can achieve some universal truth which will get my audience past the particulars of my skin color, my accent, or my clothes.

I once wrote a poem in which I called us Latinas "God's brown daughters." This poem is really a prayer of sorts, offered upward, but also, through the human-to-human channel of art, outward. It is a prayer for communication, and for respect. In it, Latin women pray "in Spanish to an Anglo God/with a Jewish heritage," and they are "fervently hoping/that if not omnipotent/at least He be bilingual."

Drug Marketing Selling Women Out

by Leslie Laurence and Beth Weinhouse

In most businesses, products are tested on the segment of the population that will be using the product. Not so with the pharmaceutical industry. Although most of the prescription and over-the-counter drugs now on the market were tested primarily on men, women are the biggest customers. Women take more prescription drugs than men and buy more over-the-counter medications for themselves and their families.

The lack of knowledge about how drugs affect women's bodies and women's health has not stopped pharmaceutical manufacturers from encouraging physicians to prescribe their products to women. They also pitch advertising directly to women, who see doctors more than men and make up 70 percent of drugstore shoppers.

The magazine ads and television commercials that pharmaceutical firms produce, whether aimed at doctors or consumers, are just as manipulative in their imagery as ads for a new laundry detergent or brand of ketchup. The difference is the consequence: In the long run it matters little what brand of soap a woman buys. But how much and what kind of drugs she buys for herself and/or her family may matter a great deal and have a profound impact on health and well-being.

Studies show that physicians receive most of their information about new prescription medications from advertising and from the "detail men," representatives of the drug companies who visit medical offices to tout new products and offer incentives for physicians to prescribe their companies' drugs. Detail men give away free samples of the drugs, plus T-shirts, coffee mugs, pens, and notepads imprinted with the products' names. Pharmaceutical companies spend much of their budgets on lavish promotional schemes: gifts, dinners, and travel for doctors who prescribe the most drugs. For example, the maker of the estrogen skin patch flew gynecologists who had prescribed large numbers of patches to the Caribbean for a "conference" touting the benefits of supplemental estrogen. Pharmaceutical drug-promotion budgets can be as high as five thousand dollars per physician per year. One study found that three-quarters of physicians had received money from pharmaceutical companies within the preceding two years.

"Clearly because of the number of drugs on the market, no practitioner can keep up today," says Joellen W. Hawkins, RNC, Ph.D., a professor at Boston College's School of Nursing who has examined gender bias and sex stereotyping in pharmaceutical advertising. "So physicians rely very heavily on medication advertisements. And if the detail person has been in with something that week, they're very likely to use it, or if they have a pen or pad on their desk with the product's name." Studies show that even when doctors *think* they get their information on drugs from the medical literature, much of their information actually comes from advertisements. "Drug advertisements are simply more visually arresting and conceptually accessible than are papers in the medical literature, and physicians appear to respond to this difference," concluded one study. Three-quarters of physicians read the drug advertisements in medical journals, and about 80 percent of those physicians find the ads helpful.

Unfortunately the ads may be horribly inaccurate. An article in the professional journal *Annals of Internal Medicine* found that 92 percent of the ads examined did not meet the standards for fairness, accuracy, and balance set by the Food and Drug Administration. The study also found that nearly half—44 percent—of the ads could lead doctors to prescribe the drugs inappropriately if they relied solely on the advertisements for information.

The pharmaceutical industry's hard-sell advertising tactics, coupled with the lack of good data on how drugs affect women, make it highly unlikely that every prescription a physician writes for a woman is absolutely necessary and is the best drug for that individual's specific condition. Targeting drugs toward women is not altruism but capitalism, with serious consequences for women's health.

Advertising Images: Cranky Old Women and Sexy Young Girls

The medical information in pharmaceutical ads isn't all that is inaccurate. The images used to sell the product may also mislead. Pharmaceutical advertising tends to reinforce the beliefs that physicians have about female patients, for instance that women's symptoms are "all in their head" and that women patients are more demanding, more complaining, and more anxious about their health than men. Drug company advertising exploits these myths to encourage doctors to prescribe their product as a way of placating supposedly demanding women with supposedly psychosomatic symptoms. The drug ads in the professional journals read by physicians also tend to show older, depressed, anxious women, or very sexy and voluptuous young women.

Joellen Hawkins and colleague Cynthia Aber did several studies looking at gender images in medical ads. What they found were ads filled with white male doctors and white female nurses (generally wearing short white uniforms), and women patients looking up at godlike father-image physicians. "Interestingly, we did not find one ad with a woman physician and a male consumer," says Hawkins. In fact, there were hardly any women physicians in the ads at all, and when there were, "they were usually only in ads having something to do with women, such as contraceptive drugs or yeast medications. Heaven forbid they show a woman surgeon or pathologist."

Ronda Macchello, M.D., an internist at the Palo Alto Medical Clinic, has also examined medical advertising. She does a presentation at medical conferences, complete with dozens of slides of offensive drug ads, hoping to show other physicians the bias inherent in the messages that bombard them. She found that the advertisers "seem to feel that the only doctor who is going to have any credibility for other doctors is someone who looks like Marcus Welby. When there are women physicians in the ad, they are quite strikingly young and pretty—they look like models with white coats and stethoscopes on."

Women in drug ads are more likely than men to be naked, with full body exposed. When men are naked, it is generally from the waist up only. "Not one ad portrays a man as a sex object, nor do many portray men with negative characteristics," says Hawkins. When men in these ads are stressed, it's from work, but women are stressed from family, housework, and menial tasks. Men are active, women passive. The women are often posed provocatively. Write Hawkins and Aber, "Some of the women have obviously dyed or bleached hair. Many have exaggerated makeup, long painted nails, long flowing hair, low-cut, sheer, or nude-tone outfits."

Hawkins is particularly appalled by ads in orthopedic journals for equipment such as hip-pinning machines. Pandering to the libidos of predominantly male orthopedic surgeons, these ads use sex to sell expensive medical equipment. "These ads show very young models in skintight outfits, even though young women are not the patients getting their hips replaced. In one ad there's a young woman on a hip-pinning machine with the post jammed into her crotch. If there are men in the ads, they're always in loose-fitting running shorts, but the women in the same ads are wearing skintight exercise clothes."

Macchello found an ad for a bowel prep (a liquid patients drink before having diagnostic images of the gastrointestinal tract) that used a subliminal sex image to sell the product. "Bowel preps are about the least sexy thing you can imagine," she says. "They really taste foul. The ad shows a woman with her mouth open, ready to drink the stuff. And in the glass, in a bubble, is an image of a penis. She's drinking a penis."

Sex may sell, whether the product is medicine or blue jeans, but the predominant image of the woman patient in pharmaceutical ads is the cranky old woman.

One popular ad for an antianxiety drug shows three different photographs of the same late-middle-aged woman. She is wearing a different outfit in each picture, but with similar pained, unpleasant expressions. The headline reads: "Varied complaints . . . Repeat visits . . . Negative workups . . . Suspect persistent anxiety." The implication is that this woman has visited her doctor at least three different times, complaining of a medical problem. The doctor has not been able to figure out what is wrong. Therefore the problem must be all in her head. The copy reads, "You probably see patients like this every day." Says Dr. Macchello, "The implication is that the patient is a horrible, whiny woman who keeps coming back to you with no problem, and if you give her this medicine, she'll be out of your face."

Women make up 80 percent of the "patients" in ads for psychotropic drugs, and the advertisers' message is obviously getting through to physicians, who write women more prescriptions than men for antidepressant drugs and tranquilizers (see chapter 11). "There's a real abuse of women patients. The idea is, 'Give her something to shut her up,'" says Ann R. Turkel, M.D., assistant clinical professor of psychiatry, Columbia University College of Physicians and Surgeons.

The ads for these drugs seem to confirm something physicians already believe, or plant a mental seed that perhaps women really do complain for no reason. The result for women may be too many prescriptions for psychoactive drugs, but men's health care may also be affected.

"If a woman comes in and you can't find anything wrong, they think it must be something in her mind. But if a man comes in, it must be something physical," says Hawkins. "So men get disserviced too. They get overtested, and nobody ever thinks it may be something psychological. Their psychological needs sometimes get ignored, although they certainly don't get mistreated in the way that women do."

Macchello found that women were overrepresented in ads for psychotropic drugs but underrepresented in ads for drugs to treat physical conditions such as high blood pressure, heart disease, arthritis, ulcers, and diabetes. Eva Lynn Thompson, who published another study of sex bias in drug ads warns, "By showing patients of a particular age or sex group, a drug advertisement is implying that the age or sex group is likely to have the condition which the advertised drug ameliorates." Biased ads can mislead by omission, too. For instance, because of the male bias in advertisements for cardiovascular drugs, "some physicians might be less likely to note early signs of these conditions in women," says Thompson. As chapter 4 showed, underdiagnosis of women's heart problems is rampant. Drug ads may be partly to blame.

Hawkins describes another ad, for Tenormin, a hypertension medication. The photograph shows a group of six people. The sex ratio is equal—three men and three women—but that's about all that's equal. Two of the men look like businessmen; one is a construction worker. The women include an old lady in hair curlers and a bathrobe with a sour expression, an overweight woman sitting down to a large meal, and a masculine-looking woman clutching a cat.

And these ads are not isolated examples. "There was a series of ads that told physicians the drug would allow patients to 'get on with their lives,'" says Hawkins. "The man would be portrayed as being able to get back to his job, but the woman would be sitting on a bench knitting. In another ad one side showed a man as a truck driver. The caption said the drug allowed him to 'follow normal daily routines.' But the caption near the woman in the ad, who doesn't seem to have a job, reads, 'enhance patient compliance.'"

The theme of compliance—how well patients follow doctors' orders—runs through many ads for prescription drugs. Convenience is stressed for the man, compliance for the woman. That's because drug ads suggest that most women are too stupid to follow directions. "It's very typical to portray women as dumb," says Hawkins. "There are drug ads that call women pillskippers, suggesting that they're not bright enough to remember to take their medicine."

Hawkins and Macchello's findings are particularly discouraging when compared with similar studies done in the 1970s, all of which came to conclusions nearly identical to those of the more recent work.

In one of the earliest studies of how pharmaceutical advertising affects physicians' perceptions of their patients, in 1971, Robert Seidenberg, M.D., found that advertisements for mood-altering drugs seemed to exploit the boredom that many women felt as housewives. He wrote, "The burden of giving a child a bath at night, or a distaste for washing dishes might be converted into medically treatable syndromes . . . one often sees women portrayed in their humdrum environment with the recommendation that they be drugged to become adjusted to their lot. The drug industry openly acknowledges the enslavement of women, as shown in an ad with a woman behind bars made up of brooms and mops. The caption reads, 'You can't set her free but you can help make her feel less anxious.'"

By making everyday boredom into a psychological illness, drug manufacturers have created an enormous market for tranquilizers and antidepressants. Many of these ads still show women as unable to handle daily life without their bottle of pills. If washing dishes were really causing major depression, it might make more sense for women to avoid the expensive medication and spend their money on a dishwasher instead.

Jane Prather and Linda S. Fidell found in 1975 that ads for mood-altering drugs tended to show women while those for other drugs showed men, and the women tended to be shown as suffering from primarily emotional illness while men are shown as having primarily organic illness. "That is, women may display (or be interpreted as displaying) emotional symptoms when the problem is organic, while men show (or are thought to show) organic symptoms when the 'cause' is emotional. The possibility for misdiagnosis of both sexes would appear therefore to be increased."

In another study from the 1970s, psychiatrists were asked about the images in psychotropic drug ads. They admitted that physicians' thinking might be affected by seeing women portrayed as the majority of patients. Some of the comments were: "Tends to perpetrate general trend of thinking of women as weaker, more sick," "subliminally might indicate women are crazier," "might imprint male M.D.'s with the impression that mental illness and femaleness go together."

Some of the same characters that inhabited drug advertisements in the 1970s still grace the pages of medical journals. One early study listed such female stereotypes as the irritable old lady, the overwrought mother, the depressed housewife, the complaining matron, and the attractive seductress—a cast familiar to any casual reader flipping through the medical literature. More than other types of advertising, the pharmaceutical ads that appear in professional journals still seem to rely on these outdated depictions of women.

The Drug Ads That Patients See

Both prescription and over-the-counter drugs are advertised directly to patients. But the drug ads shown in women's magazines are very different from those in the medical journals. All of a sudden the young sexpots and old sourpusses have metamorphosed into efficient, capable working women and mothers who intelligently weigh all the information before purchasing medicine for themselves and their families. Ironically, while professional ads exploit negative images of women patients to encourage physicians to prescribe more drugs, consumer ads exploit the idea of women's greater health knowledge and concerns to get women to buy more drugs for themselves and their families.

Since 1986 the FDA has allowed makers of prescription drugs to advertise their products directly to consumers, mainly women. "It takes a certain amount of confidence to have a dialogue with the doctor rather than accept everything he says, to talk to him rather than go for the over-the-counter drug," says Joan Lemler, an account supervisor at Medicus Consumer-DMB&B, who has worked on advertising campaigns for Seldane (an antihistamine), Nicorette (a nicotine chewing gum to help smokers quit), Cardizem (a drug to treat angina), and Peridex (an oral rinse to treat gum disease). "I think there's been a lot of respect for that audience because it's been a progressive audience."

Market research indicates that even when a drug is for a medical condition that affects men and women equally, the ads will be most effective when aimed at women. "Women are an easier group to target if the drug is appropriate," says Lemler. "They tend to accept treatment more than men, and they're more proactive, more into preventive medicine." So even though the incidence of allergies is pretty much equal, most of the advertising for Seldane was aimed at women and advertised in women's magazines. These ads were "nonbranded," meaning that the manufacturer, Merrell Dow, did not mention the drug by name but advised women to ask their doctors about prescription medicine for hayfever.

So great is women's appeal for advertisers that even drugs taken exclusively by men are often advertised to women. A woman who has worked in the art department of a pharmaceutical agency says, "When we were deciding what to do with Proscar [a drug used to treat enlarged prostate glands], there was a campaign geared toward women, even though it's a drug for men. Women tend to be the ones who make lots of decisions in the household and who get their husbands to go to the doctor."

This woman, who asked not to be named, says that advertising, whether for medical products or any other kind of product, is still a male-dominated business. While male copywriters and art directors work on campaigns for female products such as tampons and birth control pills, "I was only allowed to work on the Proscar campaign aimed at women. I was told I wouldn't understand the campaign for men."

Ads for over-the-counter (OTC) medications also play on women's greater health knowledge. These ads—for cold and cough medicines, analgesics, and so on—often feature capable homemakers happily medicating their families. "Advertisers of over-the-counter drugs have no problem exploiting the homemaker mythology, the idea of the woman as being the person in the home who is responsible for medical care, and who is knowledgeable about it," says R. Stephen Craig, Ph.D., a communications professor at the University of Maine.

Craig's study of over-the-counter drug commercials found that women were significantly more likely than men to appear in drug ads than in ads for other products. He writes, "This supports the hypothesis that drug advertisers take advantage of stereotypical images of women as home medical caregivers. It also raises the question of whether female consumers are being encouraged by these ads to overuse OTC medications as a way of gaining the family's love and respect."

Some of the commercials, says Craig, are quite explicit in their imagery. "There is one commercial for a cough syrup [Robitussin] that has a woman's family lined up outside a door, waiting for her to give them medicine, just like in a doctor's office. In this glorification [of women's knowledge of health care] women are being encouraged to use more over the-counter medications. What I'm suggesting is that women who feel alienated in the home and relish being experts in the few things they're allowed to be experts in, use medications as a way of confirming their value and their personal worth."

Unlike the men in prescription drug ads, the men in OTC drug commercials "were either absent altogether or appeared to be unrealistic exaggerations, relying on the wife/mother to make even the simplest decisions on home medical care."

Another TV commercial Craig describes starts with an announcer asking, "Home alone?" while the screen shows a father and son. The father is in a quandary because his child is sick and he doesn't know how to medicate the problem . . . until the mother comes home. "She's explicitly portrayed as the expert in the family," says Craig.

In yet another, a man and woman are in bed. She's sleeping, but he's coughing, and nudges her awake for some medicine.

Milk of Magnesia even uses the initials M.O.M.

In these ads, women give medication to others—husbands, children—more often than to themselves. "There's an analogy with food commercials. Instead of being shown eating their own food, women are shown preparing food which is then eaten by a husband or child," says Craig. "It's reaffirming the mother's value both to herself and to her family. [The commercials imply that] it's more important to the woman that her family enjoys her cooking than that she does. And more important that she care for her family than care for herself"

Again there's a medical danger to such lopsided messages. While most physicians would agree that less medicine is better, these ads encourage women to medicate their partners and children as a way of showing love. There may even be a more subtle message. According to Craig's study, "Such commercials may encourage women to use OTC medications as a way of establishing a limited power over husband/children, and therefore as a path of self-actualization. Should this be the case, such advertising may . . . reinforce the model of drug-taking as a solution to problems."

There's even been a suggestion in drug abuse circles that the promotion of OTC medications in commercials tends to glorify the use of all drugs and may increase the use of all drugs—legal and illegal, safe and dangerous. Some over-the-counter drug ads practically turn women into drug pushers for their families, creating a future generation of potential drug abusers.

As with prescription drugs, the advertising for over-the-counter health products is aimed at women even when the product is used by men. When condoms' main purpose was to prevent pregnancy and sexually transmitted diseases, there was little advertising. But in this age of AIDS, condoms are suddenly the best protection men and women have against HIV transmission. Most condoms (with the exception of the new, so-called female condom) are worn by men, but much of the advertising is designed to get women to purchase them and to bear the responsibility for having their partners wear them.

"I never understood the concept of targeting condoms at women," says Janet L. Mitchell, M.D., MPH, chief of perinatology at Harlem Hospital in New York. "It's a male device. It also puts women in a precarious position in the bedroom. It blames women, telling them it's their fault if they can't get their man to wear a condom. Historically in this country, in bedrooms, men are in control. But condom messages are directed at women. Why not target *men*? It's their responsibility."

Women's greater concern about health care means they are more susceptible to appeals that tout the *preventive* benefits of some medications. This may be the case with ads for female hormones—both estrogen replacement therapy and oral contraceptives. One way that companies have tried to widen the market for these products is to advertise that they prevent disease as well as treat menopausal symptoms and prevent pregnancy.

Women are currently getting a hard sell on both postmenopausal replacement therapy and oral contraceptives. Manufacturers are trying to convince women and their physicians that all, or most, women should be taking

hormones for the health benefits. For instance, oral contraceptives have been shown to help prevent ovarian and endometrial cancer. Postmenopausal hormone replacement therapy can help prevent osteoporosis. Advertisements for these drugs stress their preventive effects, while putting the side effects and health risks—stroke and breast cancer for the birth control pill, endometrial cancer for hormone replacement therapy—in small print. The idea is that you don't need to have any menopausal symptoms to take estrogen, and you don't even have to be sexually active to benefit from oral contraceptives.

One brochure for a birth control pill claims "Added Noncontraceptive Benefits," including cycle regularity, reduced blood loss and anemia, and more comfortable periods. And, boasts the ad, there's no generic equivalent (meaning that women do not have a lower-cost alternative).

Another ad has a woman saying, "I always knew the Pill was effective birth control. . . . Now I know it can give me more." The copy promises "extra noncontraceptive health benefits for the days ahead" (including reduction of irregular menses, dysmenorrhea, pelvic inflammatory disease, ectopic pregnancy, benign breast disease, ovarian cysts, endometrial and ovarian cancer).

In an ad for estrogen replacement therapy, which runs in many women's magazines, the copy reads, "Menopause is the reason most women start on Premarin. Ask your doctor if osteoporosis is a reason to stay on it." It continues, "Symptoms of menopause will pass. The risk of osteoporosis won't." But the ad doesn't mention that neither will the risk of cancer from taking the drug.

In an attempt to create a bigger market for their products, the manufacturers may be going too far. It is now possible for teenage girls to start taking birth control pills, continue on them without a break until menopause (since the FDA recently ruled that oral contraceptives are safe after age thirty-five), and then switch to hormone replacement therapy at menopause. Encouraged by physicians and pharmaceutical manufacturers, women may wind up taking hormones for nearly their entire lives, although there are no studies to show that this kind of long-term use is safe. At some point health has to win out over hype.

The Woman Consumer

Advertisements aren't the only way pharmaceutical firms are biased against women. Just as dry cleaners often take advantage of women by charging more to clean a woman's shirt than a man's, drug companies may also overcharge women. A casual look around the neighborhood drugstore shows some obvious instances. Many "women's" deodorant formulas cost more than men's. Cortisone creams (for treating minor skin itches and irritations) cost more when they have the prefix *gyne,* meaning they can be used on the female genitals. Yet the less expensive, regular cortisone cream is perfectly safe for use in the vaginal area.

In general, drugs are more expensive in America than in most other countries. A General Accounting Office study found that drugs cost an average of 60 percent less in the United Kingdom. Since women receive more prescriptions, live longer, and are sicker and poorer, the price-gouging affects them most. In addition, women buy medicines for their families as well as for themselves. So the burdens of drug and contraceptive costs fall squarely on women.

While many drugs are overpriced, medicines taken by women seem to be especially costly. Premarin (estrogen), for example, costs twenty-eight cents a pill in the United States, but only nine cents in Great Britain.

Norplant, the recently approved contraceptive implant, was selling in Sweden and some developing countries for as little as $23. When the drug became available in the United States in 1991, Wyeth-Ayerst started charging $365. The cost to make and market the drug is estimated to be just $16 per implant. Additionally, $17 million of taxpayers' money was used to help develop the device, along with another $25 million from foundations. Under pressure from family-planning groups, the pharmaceutical company agreed to cut the price to public clinics as of December 1995—but did not specify by how much.

When Upjohn began marketing Depo-Provera—a drug that has been sold for two decades to treat cancer—as a contraceptive in 1992, the price went from $12 to $29 per dose. Upjohn claimed it was recouping development costs, but critics argued that research had ended years ago and that the drug was already available as a contraceptive in many countries.

There is a sense among health care reformers and physicians that drug company prices are out of control. At one recent conference of the American College of Obstetricians and Gynecologists, a doctor who had just attended an elegant breakfast and received a leather briefcase and tape recorder from a company that manufactured birth control pills muttered, "I wish they'd keep the briefcases and lower the cost of the pills." (Of course the price of drugs doesn't just affect women. For instance, when Levamisole, a veterinary medication used to cure worm infestations in sheep, was approved to treat colon cancer in humans, the price of a dose went from six cents to six dollars.)

Drugs with cosmetic rather than medical uses are especially lucrative for manufacturers. Just as with cosmetic surgery, these drugs may be heavily advertised and steeply priced. One example is Rogaine Topical Solution for growing hair. Although few studies have been done on the effectiveness of Rogaine in women, when sales to men were disappointing, the manufacturer went after the women's market.

The Food and Drug Administration approved Rogaine in August 1988 as a treatment for androgenic alopecia, also called male-pattern baldness. Analysts predicted first-year sales of $500 million, but they overestimated men's desperation. First-year sales were only $70 million, and men seemed to find the drug expensive, messy, inconvenient, and ultimately ineffective. But Upjohn figured out a way to double the potential market for the drug. They got it approved for women in August 1991.

"That nod of approval increased the product's target market from 30 million men to 50 million people and made Rogaine available to an entire universe of customers who are already comfortable with hair treatment products and who feel enormous social pressure to do something, anything, to stop hair loss," said an article in *American Druggist.* An advertising campaign appeared in women's magazines. The pictures show just the back of a woman's head. Her medium-length blond hair is tied in a ponytail, and a floppy hat with flowers covers her head. The copy says she is twenty-five years old—hardly the product's typical user.

Upjohn admits the drug doesn't work for everyone, that it must be used for six months to a year before the results are known. If the product *does* work, it must be applied twice daily for life, or the effects reverse. But when Rogaine *does* work and *is* used for life, the profits to the company are enormous. The average cost of treatment is seven hundred dollars a year. U.S. sales of the drug are now $84 million per year, with 25–30 percent of sales—about $21–25 million—to women.

The *American Druggist* article cites pharmacists as saying Rogaine doesn't work at growing hair for many people, although it does seem to halt hair loss or thinning. Instead of purchasing thousands of dollars' worth of Rogaine, perhaps the young woman in the ad should just keep her hat.

Targeting Aging Baby Boomers

Another way drug companies increase profits is by focusing on small market niches to sell products. The idea is that wherever a problem can be identified, a drug solution can be manufactured.

The best example of this trend is the growing market for vaginal "moisturizers" for postmenopausal women. There used to be vaginal lubricants designed primarily for sexual purposes, and prescription estrogen creams for postmenopausal women. Now there's a new category of "personal" moisturizers that can be purchased over-the-counter. While K-Y jelly, the old standard, still commands over 50 percent of the market, new products are aimed directly at postmenopausal women: Parke Davis's Replens, and Schering Plough's Gyne-Moistrin are two examples. As the first wave of baby boomers, who came of age in the sexual revolution reach menopause, pharmaceutical manufacturers see an ever-expanding population of customers with uncomfortably dry vaginas, willing to buy expensive products to remedy the problem. An estimated forty million women baby boomers will reach menopause in the next twenty years.

Another article in *American Druggist,* titled "The New VD," equates vaginal dryness with sexually transmitted diseases. Of course, sexually transmitted diseases are caused by pathogenic organisms and require medical treatment; vaginal dryness is a normal part of aging. But the manufacturers of the new moisturizers stress that vaginal dryness is a medical problem with an easily purchased solution—much as the manufacturers of expensive facial moisturizers try to convince women that the normal aging of human skin is a pathological condition, too.

According to the article, "The $40 million personal lubricant market has grown 30% in the last year and is one of the 10 fastest-growing health and beauty aid categories." Says Georgia Witkin, Ph.D., clinical instructor of obstetrics and gynecology at Mount Sinai School of Medicine in New York, "Vaginal dryness is the new VD. The symptoms make women feel like their bodies have betrayed them."

Manufacturers stress that the new moisturizers are superior to the old lubricants, which simply eased friction during intercourse. New products supposedly suffuse vaginal tissues with moisture. Women will have to decide for themselves whether a simple, inexpensive product like K-Y jelly is as effective as the high-tech, much-hyped newcomers.

Because the FDA classifies these products as cosmetics, not drugs, the manufacturers can't make specific medical claims on the label. But they can expand their market by emphasizing that not only postmenopausal women need extra vaginal moisture. Those who may suffer from vaginal dryness include: women who are postpartum, breast-feeding, undergoing certain cancer treatments, exercising, under stress, or taking antibiotics, fertility drugs, endometriosis drugs, or oral contraceptives. The market is estimated at between twenty-five and fifty million women. In one study 90 percent of women with vaginal dryness who wanted to have more comfortable sex said the moisturizers helped. The researchers even got grateful phone calls from the women's husbands.

Because the products have the potential for big sales, manufacturers are urging *pharmacists* to counsel women. "Traditionally, vaginal dryness has not been covered well in pharmacy schools, and pharmacists are poorly prepared to counsel about it," said an expert

quoted in the article. "But it just takes a little initiative." By selling moisturizers as medical rather than recreational relief, "lubricants will never be a neglected category again."

Over-The-Counter Drugs: Better for Women or Not?

Pharmaceutical profits can be greatly increased by getting rid of the middle man, that is, the physician. When a drug switches from prescription to over-the-counter sales, profits rise dramatically. For instance, in early 1991 when Monistat 7 and Gyne-Lotrimin, two treatments for vaginal yeast infections, went over the counter, yearly sales soared. One pharmacy industry newspaper referred to the feminine hygiene category as one of the OTC department's "shining stars. Strong sales in recent years, largely attributable to the Rx-to-OTC switch of the antifungal preparations, are expected to continue."

To pharmaceutical companies and many consumers, prescriptions are like censorship, blocking people's access to the medications they desire. Shouldn't people have the right to take an antibiotic when they feel like it, the same way they can buy aspirin and antihistamines? When vaginal yeast medications were sold by prescription only, was it denying women control over their own health, or protecting them from potential harm? The answer depends on whom you ask.

"There are advantages to women in having access, but the problem I am concerned about is misdiagnosis or mistreatment of what they think is vaginitis," says Joellen Hawkins. "We get a lot of women who have tried a fungicide, but they didn't have a fungus infection. Or they had some concomitant infection that the medicine didn't touch. We're also seeing overtreatment. At the first little glimmer of something, if they think they're a little itchy, they'll use the medication. And then you kill off a lot of organisms in the vagina, change the pH, and something else can move in or overgrow." Physicians are also concerned that women will treat recurrent vaginal yeast infections by simply buying more tubes of medicine, not finding out until later that the recurrent infections are due to underlying diabetes or HIV infection.

In fact, when yeast medications went over-the-counter, the decision was prompted less by concerns about women's health and more by worry that the patent on the medication was running out. The pharmaceutical companies had a limited amount of time to make as much money as possible before lower-priced generic versions reached the market. Commercials for the drugs Monistat, Gyne-Lotrimin, and others stress what a breakthrough the over-the-counter availability is for women. But the companies are still charging high prices for the medications, and insurance companies will no longer reimburse women, since they pay only for prescription drugs. The sole party to benefit may be the manufacturers.

One pharmacy journal ran an article by the man responsible for the marketing campaign for Gyne-Lotrimin, who wrote, "We knew that approximately 22 million women are diagnosed with vaginal yeast infections every year; that 14 percent of the female population suffer from the ailment; but we couldn't target any particular group. We decided, therefore, to address *all* adult women [emphasis added]." Although, as mentioned earlier, female physicians rarely appear in the ads that run in medical journals, the company decided to use female gynecologists as spokespeople for Gyne-Lotrimin, because of their greater credibility with women.

Now the biggest controversy in the prescription versus over-the-counter debate is birth control pills, which some women's health advocates believe should be sold in drugstores nationwide as a remedy for the epidemic of teen pregnancies. But encouraging millions of teenage girls to skip seeing the doctor and begin taking hormones daily may not be the best way to promote women's health.

In 1993 the FDA's Fertility and Maternal Health Drugs Advisory Committee voted to change the labeling on oral contraceptive pills. The old labels read that a physician should take a medical history and perform a physical exam, including pelvic exam and Pap smear, before prescribing birth control pills, and then at least yearly while the pills are being taken. The new label would be revised to reflect the lower doses of hormones now in oral contraceptives. It would say that the physical exam could be deferred if the patient requested it and the physician agreed. In other words, anyone who wanted birth control pills could just request a prescription. This labeling change would open the door for OTC status.

Advocates for making the Pill available without a prescription say that unintended pregnancies will decline, while health risks will be negligible. The new low-dose pills, they say, are safe enough to sell without a doctor's permission. Some of these health advocates argue that from a public health standpoint it would make more sense to sell birth control pills in vending machines and cigarettes by prescription only.

Those who oppose selling oral contraceptives over-the-counter believe that unintended pregnancies may actually *rise* if women don't receive a health professional's instructions on pill taking, and that women's general health may suffer if they no longer have to check in with the doctor to get their prescription refilled. Women might have gone to their gynecologist for a Pill prescription, but while they were there they also received a Pap smear, breast exam, and so on.

"European countries have had birth control pills over-the-counter for a long time," says Hawkins. "The problem is, how are we going to monitor women who are at risk for taking birth control pills because they have a bad family history or bad personal history or are heavy smokers? How are we going to make sure they don't have high blood pressure or a high risk for thrombophlebitis? And how are we going to get them in for Pap smears? We're seeing so many abnormal Pap smears now in young women."

How do women feel about it? The National Women's Health Network, a feminist advocacy group, opposes the sale of birth control pills without a prescription. And the American College of Obstetricians and Gynecologists commissioned a Gallup survey in 1993 to discover the public's views on this controversial issue. The poll, of 997 women ages eighteen and over, found that 86 percent do *not* believe that oral contraceptives are safe enough to buy without first seeing a doctor.

In January 1993 the FDA canceled a meeting to discuss the proposal to allow over-the-counter sales of birth control pills, citing the need to consult with a wider range of interest groups. Right now the issue is on hold, but selling the Pill over-the-counter would mean enormous profits for pharmaceutical manufacturers, so it's a safe bet that the discussion is far from over.

Making Drug Marketing Women-Friendly

While the Pill's status is still being debated, there are signs that other aspects of the pharmaceutical industry may become more women-friendly. For one thing, health care reformers have already put pharmaceutical firms on notice that they must curb their exorbitant prices.

Pharmaceutical manufacturers are also showing interest in developing and testing drugs specifically for women. In 1993, jumping on the new women's health bandwagon, the Pharmaceutical Manufacturers Association placed stories in several medical and pharmaceutical journals boasting that 301 new drugs were in development for use by women. They defined women's drugs as those for treating diseases that affect only women, that disproportionately affect women, or that are among the top ten causes of death in women.

While the association's announcement is welcome, it is not as altruistic as it seems. The top ten causes of death are nearly identical for men and women, with heart disease, cancer, and stroke at the top of the list. And the majority of these drugs heralded for women were simply new drugs for women *and* men that were finally being tested on women.

One drug that would make a real difference in women's lives, RU-486, is not on this list. So far no pharmaceutical manufacturer has shown any interest in manufacturing and marketing the drug for sale in the United States. The drug is not only an abortifacient, but may also be a treatment for breast and brain cancer, uterine fibroids, endometriosis and Epstein-Barr virus. In addition, RU-486 may be useful for inducing labor, or as an oral contraceptive. But fear of the vocal anti-abortion minority prevents pharmaceutical manufacturers from testing and marketing the drug.

Now that pharmaceutical manufacturers are generally embracing the women's market, their advertising campaigns are finally showing some signs of change. Rather than show photographs of "patients," ads now use fewer people and more abstract images: diagrams, drawings of molecules, photographs of the product, and so on. "This may be the way the companies are skirting the whole issue of gender bias," says Dr. Macchello.

Ads that do use models are starting to use fewer stereotyped images and less degrading copy. For instance, a new ad for Tums antacid, which can be used as a calcium supplement to prevent bone loss in postmenopausal women, shows a healthy-looking older woman under the slogan "This woman is going through a major loss." The old slogan read, "This woman is a loser." "I have a feeling there must have been a lot of complaints," says Dr. Macchello.

An ad for Procardia, a heart medication, also underwent a transformation. The old ad showed three men and a woman. The men were a construction worker in a hardhat, a man in overalls who obviously engaged in some kind of outdoor labor, and a business executive. The only woman in the picture was a waitress with bleached hair and carmine lips.

The first page of the new ad is a composite photograph of eight faces—five men and three women. The two-page spread that follows shows a group portrait of all eight, shown only from the shoulders up. Their occupations are impossible to discern, but all are smiling.

Even ads for psychotropic drugs are improving. An ad for Zoloft, a popular antidepressant, shows a woman patient, but instead of looking depressed she's pictured dancing, playing with her grandchildren, giving a business presentation, having a dinner date, and jogging.

The men in drug ads aren't all hardhats and business executives anymore. Campaigns for Proscar (to treat enlarged prostate glands) and Cognex (an anti-Alzheimer's drug) show men hugging their grandchildren. Lodine, an arthritis drug, features a man returning to his gardening. There seems to have been a conscious decision to change outdated stereotypes and make new ads reflect today's reality rather than the 1950s' rigid gender roles. After one of Dr. Macchello's presentations a woman representative from one of the pharmaceutical companies came up to her and said, "I wish we could videotape this and send it to my marketing people. I've been telling this to them for years."

Gender bias has been a part of pharmaceutical advertising for so long that it's impossible to sort out which came first, physicians' biased attitudes toward women patients or the pharmaceutical ads that reflect them. But the recent change in advertising may finally portend a shift away from biased treatment and prescribing.

At least when drugs are advertised directly to the public, women can disregard them or regard them with healthy skepticism. But in the case of ads directed toward physicians, the images and text may alter a doctor's prescribing habits without patients having any knowledge of their influence.

Although the pharmaceutical industry is becoming more sensitive to women's health needs, it still has a long way to go. In spite of some recent changes, much of the medical information in drug ads is inaccurate, and many of the images are still biased. And, of course, most of the drugs being advertised were never adequately tested in women. Continued change is essential to ensure that the medications women receive from their doctors or buy for themselves are safe, effective, and appropriate.

The Picture of Health
How Textbook Photographs Construct Health

by Mariamne H. Whatley

Photographs in textbooks may serve the roles of breaking up a long text, emphasizing or clarifying information in the text, attracting the buyer (the professor, teacher, or administrator who selects texts), and engaging the reader. But photographs cannot be dismissed merely as either decorative additions or straightforward illustrations of the text. Photographs are often far more memorable than the passages they illustrate and, because they are seen as objective representations of reality, rather than artists' constructions (Barthes, 1977), may have more impact than drawings or other forms of artwork. In textbooks, photographs can carry connotations, intentional or not, never stated in the text. The selection of photographs for a text is not a neutral process that simply involves being "realistic" or "objective"; selection must take into account issues such as audience expectations and dominant meanings in a given cultural/historical context (Whatley, 1988). In order to understand the ideological work of a textbook, a critique of the photographs is as crucial as a critique of the text itself.

Using ideological analysis to identify patterns of inclusion and exclusion, I examined photographs in the seven best-selling, college-level personal health textbooks. This chapter presents the results of that research. In the first part of the analysis, I examined the photographs that represent "health," describing who and what is "healthy," according to these representations. In the second part of the analysis, I determined where those excluded from the definition of health are represented in the approximately 1,100 remaining photographs in the texts.

Selling Health in Textbooks

Generally, textbook authors do not select specific photographs but may give publishers general descriptions of the type of photographs they wish to have included (for example, a scene showing urban crowding, a woman in a nontraditional job). Due to the great expense involved, new photographs are not usually taken specifically for texts. Instead publishers hire photo researchers to find appropriate photographs, drawing on already existing photographic collections. The result is that the choice of photographs depends on what is already available, and what is available depends to some extent on what has been requested in the past. In fact, because the same sources of photographs may be used by a number of different publishers, identical photographs may appear in competing books. Although authors may have visions of their books' "artwork," the reality may be limited by the selection already on the market. In addition, editors and publishers make decisions about what "artwork" will sell or is considered appropriate, sometimes overruling the authors' choices.

Photographs, especially cover-photos and special color sections, are considered features that sell textbooks, but they also can work as part of another selling process. Textbooks, in many cases, sell the reader a system of belief. An economics text, for example, may "sell" capitalism, and a science text may "sell" the scientific method, both of which help support dominant ideologies. Health textbooks may be even more invested in this selling process because, in addition to convincing readers to "believe" in health, their "success" depends on the readers' adoption of very specific personal behavioral programs to attain health. Health textbooks hold up the ideals of "total wellness" or "holistic fitness" as goals we can attain by exercising, eating right, reducing stress, and avoiding drugs. The readers' belief in health and their ability to attain it by specific behaviors is seen by many health educators as necessary to relevant educational goals; the belief in a clearly marked pathway to health is also part of a process of the commodification of health.

In North America and Western Europe, health is currently a very marketable commodity. This can be seen in its most exaggerated form in the United States in the proliferation of "health" clubs, in the trend among hospitals and clinics to attract a healthy clientele by advertising their abilities to make healthy people healthier (Worcester & Whatley, 1988), and in the advertisements that link a wide range of products, such as high fiber cereals and calcium rich antacids, to health. In a recent article in a medical journal, a physician examined this commercialization of health:

> Health is industrialized and commercialized in a fashion that enhances many people's dissatisfaction with their health. Advertisers, manufacturers, advocacy groups, and proprietary health care corporations promote the myth that good health can be purchased; they market products and services that purport to deliver the consumer into the promised land of wellness. (Barsky, 1988, p. 415)

Photographs in health textbooks can play a role in this selling of health similar to that played by visual images in advertising a product in the popular media. According to Berger (1972), the role of advertising or publicity is to

> make the spectator marginally dissatisfied with his present way of life. Not with the way of life of society, but with his own place within it. It suggests that if he buys what it is offering, his life will become better. It offers him an improved alternative to what he is. (p. 142)

The ideal of the healthy person and the healthy lifestyle can be seen as the "improved alternative" to what we are. It can be assumed that most of us will be dissatisfied with ourselves when measured against that ideal, just as most women are dissatisfied with their body shapes and sizes when compared with ideal media representations.

In effective advertising campaigns the visual image is designed to provoke powerful audience responses. In

health textbooks the visual representation of "health" is calculated to sell, and it is likely to have a greater impact on the reader than discussions about lengthened life expectancy, reduction in chronic illness, or enhanced cardiovascular fitness. The image of health, not health itself, may be what most people strive for. In the attempt to look healthy, many sacrifice health. For example, people go through very unhealthy practices to lose "extra" weight that is in itself not unhealthy; being slim, however, is a basic component of the *appearance* of health. A recent survey found that people who eat healthy foods do so for their appearance and *not* for their health. "Tanning parlors" have become common features of health and fitness centers, though tanning in itself is unhealthy. As with being slim, having a good tan contributes to the appearance of what is currently defined as health.

The use of color photographs is particularly effective in selling the healthy image, for, as Berger (1972) points out, both oil painting and color photography "use similar highly tactile means to play upon the spectator's sense of acquiring the *real* thing which the image shows" (p. 141). The recent improvement in quality and the increase in number of color photographs in textbooks provide an opportunity to sell the image of health even more effectively than black and white photographs could.

Selection of Textbooks

Rather than trying to examine all college-level personal health (as opposed to community health) textbooks, I selected the best-selling ones, since those would have the widest impact. Based on the sales figures provided by the publisher of one popular text, I selected seven texts published from 1985 to 1988. Sales of these textbooks ranged from approximately 15,000 to 50,000 for each edition. (Complete bibliographic information on these textbooks is provided in the Appendix. Author-date information to these textbooks refer to the Appendix, rather than the chapter references.) Obviously, the sales figures depend on the number of years a specific edition has been in print. For one text (Insel & Roth, 1988), I examined the newest edition (for which there could be no sales figures), based on the fact that its previous editions had high sales. A paper on the readability of personal health textbooks (Overman, Mimms, & Harris, 1987), using a similar selection process, examined the seven top-selling textbooks for the 1984–85 school year, plus three other random titles. Their list has an overlap with mine of only four texts, which may be due to a number of factors, including differences in editions and changing sales figures.

Analysis I: Healthy-Image Photographs

The first step in my analysis was a close examination of the photographs that I saw as representing "health," the images intended to show who is healthy and illustrate the healthy lifestyle. These included photographs used on covers, opposite title pages, and as openers to units or chapters on wellness or health (as opposed to specific topics such as nutrition, drugs, and mental health). While other pictures throughout the texts may represent healthy individuals, the ones selected, by their placement in conjunction with the book title or chapter title, can be seen as clearly connoting "health." I will refer to these as healthy-image photographs. I included in this analysis only photographs in which there were people. While an apple on a cover conveys a message about health, I was interested only in the question of who is healthy.

A total of 18 different photographs fit my criteria for representing health. I have eliminated three of these from discussion: the cover from Insel and Roth (1988) showing flowers and, from Dinitiman and Greenberg (1986), both the cover photograph of apples and the health unit opener of a movie still from the *Wizard of Oz.* (This textbook uses movie stills as openers for all chapters; this moves the photograph away from its perceived "objective" status toward that of an obvious construction.)

There are a number of points of similarity in the 15 remaining photographs. In several photographs (windsurfing, hang gliding), it is hard to determine race, but all individuals whose faces can clearly be seen are white. Except for those who cannot be seen clearly and for several of the eight skydivers in a health unit opener, all are young. No one in these photographs is fat or has any identifiable physical disability. Sports dominate the activities, which, with the exception of rhythmic gymnastics and volleyball played in a gym, are outdoor activities in nonurban settings. Five of these involve beaches or open water. All the activities are leisure activities, with no evidence of work. While it is impossible to say anything definitive about class from these photographs, several of the activities are expensive (hang gliding, skydiving, windsurfing), and others may take money and/or sufficient time off from work to get to places where they can be done (beaches, biking in countryside); these suggest middle-class activities, whether the actual individuals are middle class or not. In several photographs (windsurfing, hang gliding, swimming) it is hard to determine gender. However, excluding these and the large group of male runners in a cross-country race, the overall balance is 23 males to 18 females, so it does seem that there is an attempt to show women both as healthy individuals and in active roles.

HOW HEALTH IS PORTRAYED

A detailed analysis of three photographs can provide insight into how these text photographs construct health. The first is a color photograph of a volleyball game on a beach from the back cover of *Understanding Your Health* (Payne & Hahn, 1986). As with most of these images of health, the setting is outdoors, clearly at a distance from urban life. The steep rock walls that serve as a backdrop to the volleyball game additionally isolate the natural beach setting from the invasion of cars[1] and other symbols of "man-made" environmental destruction and ill health. The volleyball players appear to have escaped into a protected idyllic setting of sun, sand, and, we assume, water. They also have clearly escaped from work, since they are engaged in a common leisure activity associated with picnics and holidays. None of them appears to be contemplating the beauty of the natural setting, but merely using it as a location for a game that could go on anywhere in which there is room to set up a net.

The photograph is framed in such a way that the whole net and area of the "court" are not included, so that some players may also not be visible. On one side of the net are three women and a man, on the other two women and a man. While this is not necessarily a representation of heterosexual interactions, it can be read that way. Two players are the focus of the picture, with the other five essentially out of the action. The woman who has just hit the ball, with her back toward the camera, has her arms outstretched, her legs slightly spread, and one foot partly off the ground. The man who is waiting for the ball is crouched slightly, looking expectantly upward. Her body is partially superimposed on his, her leg crossed over his. This is essentially an interaction between one man and one woman. It would not work the same way if the key players were both female or both male, since part of the "healthiness" of this image appears to be the heterosexual interaction. For heterosexual men, this scene might be viewed as ideal—a great male-female ratio on an isolated beach; perhaps this is their reward for having arrived at the end of this book—this photograph is on the *back* cover—attaining their goal of health.

All the volleyball players are white, young, and slim. The woman farthest left in the frame appears slightly heavier than the others; she is the only woman wearing a shirt, rather than a bikini top, and is also wearing shorts. Besides being an outsider in terms of weight, dress, and location in the frame, she is the only woman who clearly has short hair (three have long hair tied back in ponytails, one cannot be seen completely). Perhaps she can move "inside" by losing weight and changing her image. As viewers, we are just a few steps beyond the end of the court and are also outsiders. As with pickup games, there is room for observers to enter the game—if they are deemed acceptable by the other players. By achieving health, perhaps the observer can step into the game, among the young, white, slim, heterosexual, and physically active. But if the definition of health includes young, white, slim, heterosexual, and physically active, many observers are relegated permanently to the outside.

If this photograph serves as an invitation to join in the lifestyle of the young and healthy, the second photograph, facing the title page of another book, serves the same function, with the additional written message provided by the title of the book—*An Invitation to Health* (Hales & Williams, 1986). The photograph is of six bicycle riders, three women and three men, resting astride their bicycles. This photograph is in black and white, so it is perhaps not as seductive as the sunny color of the first cover. However, the people in this photograph are all smiling directly at the viewer (rather than just leaving a space in back where the viewer could join in). Two of the women, in the middle and the right, have poses and smiles that could be described as flirtatious. They are taking a break from their riding, so it is an opportune moment to join the fun of being healthy.

As with the volleyball players, all the bicycle riders are young, slim, white, and apparently fit. Another similarity is the amount of skin that is exposed. Playing volleyball on the beach and riding bikes in warm weather are activities for which shorts and short-sleeved shirts are preferable to sweatpants and sweatshirts. The choice of these types of activities to represent health results in photographs in which legs and arms are not covered. Appearing healthy apparently involves no need to cover up unsightly flab, "cellulite," or stretch marks. A healthy body is a body that can be revealed.

The bikers are in a fairly isolated, rural setting. While they are clearly on the road, it appears to be a rural, relatively untraveled road. Two cars can be seen far in the distance, and there may also be a house in the distance on the right side of the frame. Otherwise, the landscape is dominated by hills, trees, and grass, the setting and the activity clearly distance the bike riders both from urban life and from work.

In a third photograph, a health unit chapter opener (Levy, Dignan, & Shirreffs, 1987), we can see a possible beginning to alternative images of health. The players in this volleyball game are still slim, young, and apparently white. However, the setting is a gym, which could be urban, suburban, or rural. While four players are wearing shorts, one woman is wearing sweatpants; there are T-shirts rather than bikini tops, and gym socks rather than bare legs. The impression is that they are there to play a hard game of volleyball rather than to bask in the sun and each other's gaze. Two men are going for the ball from opposite sides, while a woman facing the net is clearly ready to move. Compared with the other volleyball scene, this photograph gives more of a sense of action, of actual physical exertion, as well as a sense of real people, rather than models.

It is interesting to imagine how healthy the volleyball players and bike riders actually are, underneath the appearance of health. The outdoor groups, especially the beach group, are susceptible to skin cancer from overexposure to the sun. Cycling is a healthy aerobic sport, though it can be hard on the knees and back. It is particularly surprising, however, to find that the bikers represented in a health text are not wearing helmets, thus modeling behavior that is considered very risky. Compared with biking, volleyball is the kind of weekend activity that sends the enthusiastic untrained player home with pulled muscles, jammed fingers, and not much of a useful workout. The question also arises as to how the particularly thin women on the beach achieved their weight—by unhealthy weight-loss diets, by anorexia, by purging? The glowing image of health may have little to do with the reality.

SIMILARITIES TO ADVERTISING

Shortly after I began the research for this chapter, I was startled, while waiting for a movie to begin, to see a soft drink advertisement from which almost any still could have been substituted for a healthy-image photograph I had examined. There were the same thin, young, white men and women frolicking on the beach, playing volleyball, and windsurfing. They were clearly occupying the same territory: a never-never land of eternal sunshine, eternal youth, and eternal leisure. Given my argument that these textbook photographs are selling health, the similarities between soft drink advertising images and textbook healthy images are not surprising. They are appealing to the same groups of people, and they are both attempting to create an association between a desirable lifestyle and their product. You can enjoy this fun in the sun if you are part of the "Pepsi generation" or think "Coke is it" or follow the textbook's path to health. These can be considered one variant of the lifestyle format in advertising, as described by Leiss, Kline, and Jhally (1986).

> Here the activity invoked in text or image becomes the central cue for relating the person, product, and setting codes. Lifestyle ads commonly depict a variety of leisure activities (entertaining, going out, holidaying, relaxing). Implicit in each of these activities, however, is the placing of the product within a consumption style by its link to an activity. (p. 210)

Even a naive critic of advertising could point out that drinking a carbonated beverage could not possibly help anyone attain this lifestyle; on the other hand, it might be easier to accept that the same lifestyle is a result of achieving health. However, the association between health and this leisure lifestyle is as much a construction as that created in the soft drink ads. Following all the advice in these textbooks as to diet, exercise, coping with stress, and attaining a healthy sexuality will not help anyone achieve this sun-and-fun fantasy lifestyle any more than drinking Coke or Pepsi would.

These healthy-image photographs borrow directly from popular images of ideal lifestyles already very familiar to viewers through advertising[2] and clearly reflect the current marketing of health. The result is that health is being sold with as much connection to real life and real people's needs as liquor ads that suggest major lifestyle changes associated with changing one's brand of scotch.

Analysis II: Where Are the Excluded?

For each textbook, the next step was to write brief descriptions of all other photographs in the books, totaling approximately 1,100. The results of the analysis of the healthy image photographs suggested a focus on specific aspects of the description of the individuals and activities in examining the remaining 1,100 photographs. The areas I selected for discussion are those in which "health" is linked to specific lifestyles or factors that determine social position/power in our society. I described the setting, the activity, and a number of observable points about the people, including gender, race, age, physical ability/disability, and weight. These photographs were all listed by chapter and when appropriate, by particular topic in that chapter. For example, a chapter on mental health might have images of positive mental health and also images representing problems such as severe depression or stress. These descriptions of photographs were used to establish whether there were images with characteristics not found in the healthy images and, if so, the context in which these characteristics were present. For example, finding no urban representations among the healthy images, I identified topic headings under which I did find photographs of urban settings.

White, young, thin, physically abled, middle-class people in the healthy images represent the mythical norm with whom the audience is supposed to identify. This not only creates difficulties in identification for whose who do not meet these criteria, but also creates a limiting and limited definition of health. I examined the photographs that did not fit the healthy-image definition to find the invisible—those absent from the healthy images:

people of color, people with physical disabilities, fat people, and old people. I also attempted to identify two other absences—the urban setting and work environment. Because there were no obvious gender discrepancies in the healthy images, I did not examine gender as a separate category.

PEOPLE OF COLOR

After going through the remaining photographs, it was clear that there had been an attempt to include photographs of people of color in a variety of settings, but no obvious patterns emerged. In a previous paper, I examined representations of African-Americans in sexuality texts, finding that positive attempts at being nonracist could be undermined by the patterns of photographs in textbooks that, for example, draw on stereotypes and myths of "dangerous" black sexuality (Whatley, 1988). Rather than reviewing all the representations of people of color in these health textbooks, I will simply repeat what I pointed out earlier—that there is a strong and clear *absence* of photographs of people of color in the healthy-images category. People of color may appear as healthy people elsewhere in the text, but not on covers, title pages, and chapter openers. If publishers wanted to correct this situation, they could simply substitute group photographs that show some diversity for the current all-white covers and title pages.

PEOPLE WITH DISABILITIES

From the healthy-image photographs, it is apparent that people with visible physical disabilities are excluded from the definition of healthy. Therefore, I examined the contexts in which people with disabilities appear in the other photographs. Out of the approximately 1,100 photos, only 9 show people with physical disabilities, with 2 of these showing isolated body parts only (arthritic hands and knees). One shows an old woman being pushed in a wheelchair, while the six remaining photographs all are "positive" images: a number of men playing wheelchair basketball, a man in a wheelchair doing carpentry, a woman walking with her arm around a man in a wheelchair, a man with an amputated leg walking across Canada, children with cancer (which can be seen both as a disease and a disability) at a camp (these last two both in a cancer chapter), and a wheelchair racer. However, three of these six are from one textbook (Payne & Hahn, 1986), and two are from another (Levy, Dignan, & Shirreffs, 1987), so the inclusion of these few positive images is over-shadowed by the fact that three books show absolutely none. In addition, none of these positive images are of women, and the only disabilities represented are those in which an individual uses a wheelchair or has cancer.

This absence of representation of disabled people, particularly women, clearly reflects the invisibility of the physically disabled in our society.

> It would be easy to blame the media for creating and maintaining many of the stereotypes with which the disabled still have to live. But the media only reflect attitudes that already exist in a body-beautiful society that tends to either ignore or ostracize people who don't measure up to the norm. This state of "invisibility" is particularly true for disabled women. (Israel & McPherson, 1983, pp. 4–15)

In a society that values the constructed image of health over health itself, a person with a disability does not fit the definition of healthy. In addition, since the person with a disability may be seen as representing a "failure" of modern medicine and health care (Matthews, 1983), there is no place for her or him in a book that promises people that they can attain health. The common attitude that disability and health are incompatible was expressed in its extreme by a faculty member who questioned the affirmative action statement in a position description for a health education faculty member; he wanted to know if encouraging "handicapped" people to apply was appropriate for a *health* education position.

Looking at the issue of health education and disabilities, it should be clear that it is easier for able-bodied people to be healthy, so more energy should be put into helping people with disabilities maximize their health. Able-bodied people often have more access to exercise, to rewarding work (economically[3] as well as emotionally), to leisure activities, and to health care facilities. Health care practitioners receive very little training about health issues relating to disability (self-care, sexual health), though they may receive information about specific pathologies, such as multiple sclerosis or muscular dystrophy. The inability to see, hear, or walk need not be the impairments to health they often are considered in our society. Health education is an obvious place to begin to change the societal attitudes toward disability that can help lead to poor physical and emotional health for disabled people. Health textbooks could present possibilities for change by showing ways that both disabled and able-bodied people can maximize health, and this could be done in both the text and the photographs. For example, one of those color chapter openers could include people with disabilities as healthy people. This might mean changing some of the representative "healthy" activities, such as windsurfing. While there are people with disabilities who participate in challenging and risky physical activities, there is no need for pressure to achieve *beyond* what would be expected of the able-bodied.[4] Showing a range of healthy activities that might be more accessible to both the physically disabled and the less physically active able-bodied would be appropriate.

FAT PEOPLE

There are no fat people in the healthy-image photographs. Some people who agree with the rest of my analysis may here respond, "Of course not!" because there is a common assumption in our society that being thin is healthy and that any weight gain reduces health. In fact, evidence shows that being overweight (but not obese) is *not unhealthy*. In many cases, being very fat is a lot healthier than the ways people are encouraged to attempt to reduce weight—from extreme low-calorie diets, some of which are fatal, to stomach stapling and other surgeries (Norsigian, 1986). In addition, dieting does not work for 99 percent of dieters, with 95 percent ending up heavier than before they started. Repeated dieting stresses the heart, as well as other organs (Norsigian, 1986). Our national obsession with thinness is certainly one factor leading to an unhealthy range of eating behaviors, including, but not limited to, bulimia and anorexia. While health textbooks warn against dangerous diets and "eating disorders," and encourage safe, sensible weight-loss diets, they do nothing to counter the image of thin as healthy.

Defining which people are "fat" in photographs is obviously problematic. In doing so, I am giving my subjective interpretation of what I see as society's definition of ideal weight. The photographs I have identified as "fat" are of people who by common societal definitions would be seen as "needing to lose weight." In the United States most women are dissatisfied with their own body weight, so are more likely to place themselves in the "need to lose weight" category than to give that label to someone else of the same size.

Not counting people who were part of a crowd scene, I found 14 photographs that clearly showed people who were fat. One appeared in a chapter on the health care system with a caption referring to "lack of preventive maintenance leading to medical problems" (Carroll & Miller, 1986, p. 471), one in a chapter on drinking, and one under cardiovascular problems. The remaining 11 appeared in chapters on weight control or diet and nutrition. Of the 11, one was the "before" of "before and after" weight-loss photographs. One showed a woman walking briskly as part of a "fat-management program" (Mullen, Gold, Belcastro, & McDermott, 1986, p. 125); that was the most positive of the images. Most of the photographs were of people doing nothing but being fat or adding to that fat (eating or cooking). Three of the photographs showed women with children, referring by caption or topic heading to causes of obesity, either genetic or environmental. Only 3 of the 11 photographs were of men. In these photographs, it seems we are not being shown a person or an activity, but a disease—a disease called obesity that we all might "catch" if we don't carefully follow the prescriptions for health. Fat people's excess weight is seen as their fault for not following these prescriptions. This failure results from a lack of either willpower or restraint, as implied by the photographs that show fat people eating and thus both draw on and lend support to the myth that fat people eat too much. The only health problem of fat people is seen as their weight; if that were changed, all other problems would presumably disappear. As pointed out earlier, the health problems of losing excess weight, particularly in the yo-yo pattern of weight loss/gain, may be greater than those created by the extra weight. In addition, the emotional and mental health problems caused by our society's fatphobia may be more serious than the physical problems (Worcester, 1988). These texts strongly reinforce fatphobia by validating it with health "science."

Health educators who consciously work against racism and sexism should carefully reevaluate how our attitudes help perpetuate discrimination against all groups. As Nancy Worcester (1988) points out,

> The animosity towards fat people is such a fundamental part of our society, that people who have consciously worked on their other prejudices have not questioned their attitude towards body weight. People who would not think of laughing at a sexist or racist joke ridicule and make comments about fat people without recognizing that they are simply perpetuating another set of attitudes which negatively affect a whole group of people. (p. 234)

An alternative approach would be to recognize that people would be healthier if less pressure were put on them to lose weight. Fat people can benefit from exercise, if it is accessible and appropriate (low impact aerobics, for example), without the goal needing to be weight loss (Sternhell, 1985). Photographs of "not thin" people, involved in a variety of activities, could be scattered throughout the text, and the pictures of those labeled obese could be eliminated completely. We all know what an obese person looks like; we do not need to have that person held up as a symbol of both unhealthiness and lack of moral character.

OLD PEOPLE

The healthy-image photographs show people who appeared to be predominantly in their teens and twenties, which is the age group toward which these college texts would be geared. Rather subjectively, as with the issue of weight, I will describe as old[5] those who appear to be about 65 or older. Obviously I probably judged incorrectly on some photographs, but since the representations seem to be skewed toward the young or the old, with the middle-aged not so prominent, my task was relatively easy. I identified 84 photographs that contained people I classified as old. Of these, 52 appeared in chapters specifically on aging or growing older, 10 appeared in chapters on death and dying, and the remaining 22 were distributed in a wide range of topics. Of these 22, several still focused on the issue of age. For example, a photograph of an old heterosexual couple in a chapter entitled "Courtship and Marriage" is captioned, "While some people change partners repeatedly, many others spend their lifetime with a single spouse" (Carroll & Miller, 1986, p. 271). One text showed a similar photo and caption of a heterosexual couple, but also included an old gay male couple on the next page (Levy, Dignan, & Shirreffs, 1987). This represents an important step in terms of deghettoization of gay and lesbian images, and a broadening of views about sexuality and aging. Two photos showed old people as "non-traditional students"; another depicted a man running after recovering from a stroke; and yet another featured George Burns as a representative of someone who has lived a long life. In others of the 22, the age is incidental, as in a man painting (mental health), people shopping in an open market (nutrition), people walking (fitness), a man smoking.

As the societally stereotyped *appearance* of health diminishes, as occurs with aging, it is assumed that health unavoidably diminishes. In fact, while there is some inevitable biological decline with age, many health problems can be averted by good nutrition, exercise, and preventive health care. Many of the health problems of aging have economic, rather than biological, causes, such as lack of appropriate health insurance coverage (Sidel, 1986). In a society that is afraid to face aging, people may not be able to accept that they will experience the effects of aging that they so carefully avoid (if they are lucky enough to live that long). In addition, as with disability, the people who may need to do more to maintain health are those being most ignored.

It is significant that these texts have sections on aging, which contain many positive images, but it is also crucial that health be seen as something that can be attained and maintained by people of all ages. The attempt to include representations of aging in these books must be expanded so that people of all ages are seen to be able to be healthy—a state now seemingly, in those images of health, to be enjoyed only by the young.

URBAN SETTING

The healthy-image photographs showing outdoor scenes are situated at the beach or in other nonurban settings; it is possible some were set in city parks, but there are no urban markers in the photographs. Bike riding, running, kicking a soccer ball, playing volleyball can all be done in urban settings, though the hang gliding and sky diving would obviously be difficult. Considering the high percentage of the U.S. population that lives in cities (and the numbers of those that cannot easily get out), it seems that urban settings should be represented in the texts. Of the 28 other photographs I identified as clearly having urban settings, I could see only 4 as positive. Two of these showed outdoor vegetable/fruit markets, one showed bike riding as a way of both reducing pollution and getting exercise in the city, and one showed a family playing ball together. Of the rest, 9 appeared in chapters on the environment, with negative images of urban decay, smog, and crowded streets; 10 were in chapters on mental health or stress, showing scenes representing loneliness, stress, or anger, such as a crowded subway or a potential fight on a street corner. Drinking and drug chapters had two urban scenes: "skid row" alcoholics and an apparently drunk man unconscious on the street. There were also three urban scenes in sexuality chapters—two of streets with marquees for sex shows and one showing a "man 'flashing' Central Park" (Payne & Hahn, 1986, p. 348).

There is a clear message that it is unhealthy to live in the city. While this is partly true—that is, the city may have increased pollution of various kinds, specific stresses, less access to certain forms of exercise, and other problems—there are healthy ways to live in a city. One of the roles of health education should be to help us recognize healthier options within the limits imposed on us by economic or other factors. Rather than conveying the message that urban dwelling inevitably condemns people to ill health (unless they can afford to get away periodically to the beach or the mountains), scenes showing health within the city could be presented.

Options for positive images include scenes of outdoor activities in what are clearly city parks, people enjoying cultural events found more easily in cities, gardening in a vacant lot, or a neighborhood block party. Urban settings are excellent for representing walking as a healthy activity. City dwellers are more likely to walk to work, to shopping, and to social activities than are suburbanites, many of whom habitually drive. Urban walking can be presented as free, accessible, and healthy in terms of exercise, stress reduction, and reducing pollution. More indoor activities could be shown so that the external environment is not seen as a determinant of "healthy" activity. These might give a sense of the possibilities for health within what otherwise might appear to be a very dirty, dangerous, stressful place to be.

WORK AND LEISURE

The healthy-image photographs I analyzed were all associated with leisure activities, so I tried to establish how these texts represent work in relationship to health. For this analysis, all photographs of health care workers were excluded, since these are used predominantly to illustrate health or medical issues. Of the 16 other photographs showing people at work, 4 were related to discussions of sex roles and women doing nontraditional work (phone "lineman," lawyer). This seems part of a positive trend in textbooks to reduce sexism. An obvious next step would be to show women in nontraditional work roles without commenting on them, as is done with a number of photographs of women as doctors. Six of the photographs of work accompany discussions of stress. Besides stress, there are no illustrations of health hazards at work except for one photograph of a farm worker being sprayed with pesticides. Three positive references to work show someone working at a computer (illustrating self-development), a man in a wheelchair doing carpentry, and an old man continuing to work.

Overall, the number of photographs representing work seems low, considering the amount of time we put into work during our lifetime. Blue-collar work is represented by trash collectors in an environmental health section, police officers in a weight control chapter, firefighters under stress, a construction worker in the opener for a stress chapter, the farm worker mentioned above, and women in nontraditional work. Blue-collar work is seen in terms of neither potential health hazards beyond stress nor the positive health aspects of working. The strongest connection between health and work presented involves the stress of white-collar jobs (symbolized by a man at a desk talking on the phone). The message seems to be that health is not affected by work, unless it is emotionally stressful.

The photographs in this book seem to be aimed at middle-class students who assume they will become white-collar workers or professionals who can afford leisure activities, both in terms of time and money. Those who work in obviously physically dangerous jobs, such as construction work, or in jobs that have stress as only one of many health hazards, are rarely portrayed. These people are also likely not to be able to afford recreation such as hang gliding (and also might not need the stimulus of physical risk taking if their job is physically risky in itself). These photographs serve to compartmentalize work as if it were not part of life and not relevant to health.

Rather than selecting photographs that reinforce the work-leisure split and the alienation of the worker from work, editors could include photographs that show the health rewards of work and the real health risks of a wide variety of work. For example, a photograph of a group of workers talking on a lunch break could be captioned, "Many people find strong support networks among their co-workers." Another photograph could be of a union meeting, illustrating that work-related stress is reduced when we have more control over the conditions of our work. In addition the mental health benefits of a rewarding job might be emphasized, perhaps in contrast with the stress of unemployment. Health risks, and ways to minimize them, could be illustrated with photographs ranging from typists using video display terminals to mine workers. A very important addition would be inclusion in the healthy-image photographs of some representation of work.

Conclusion

The definition of health that emerges from an examination of the healthy-image photographs is very narrow. The healthy person is young, slim, white, physically abled, physically active, and, apparently, comfortable financially. Since these books are trying to "sell" their image of health to college students, the photographs presumably can be seen as representing people whom the students would wish to become. Some students, however, cannot or may not wish to become part of this vision of the healthy person. For example, students of color may feel alienated by this all-white vision. What may be most problematic is that in defining the healthy person, these photographs also define *who can become healthy*. By this definition many are excluded from the potential for health: people who are physically disabled, no longer young, not slim (unless they can lose weight, even if in unhealthy ways), urban dwellers, poor people, and people of color. For various social, economic, and political reasons, these may be among the least healthy groups in the United States, but the potential for health is there if the health care and health education systems do not disenfranchise them.

The healthy-image photographs represent the healthy lifestyle, not in the sense of the lifestyle that will help someone attain health, but the white, middle-class, heterosexual, leisure, active lifestyle that is the reward of attaining health. These glowing images imitate common advertising representations. An ice chest of beer would not be out of place next to the volleyball players on the beach, and a soft drink slogan would fit well with the windsurfers or sky divers. It must be remembered, however, that while college students may be the market for beer, soft drinks, and "health," they are not the market

for textbooks. Obviously, the biggest single factor affecting a student's purchase of a text is whether it is required. The decision may also be based on how much reading in the book is assigned, whether exam questions will be drawn from the text, its potential future usefulness, or its resale value.

The market for textbooks is the faculty who make text selections for courses (Coser, Kadushin, & Powell, 1982). While the photographs may be designed to create in students a desire for health, they are also there to sell health educators the book. Therefore, health educators should take some time examining the representations in these texts, while questioning their own definitions of who is healthy and who can become healthy. Do they actually wish to imply that access to health is limited to young, white, slim, middle-class, physically abled, and physically active people? If health educators are committed to increasing the potential for health for *all* people, then the focus should not be directed primarily at those for whom health is most easily attained and maintained. Rethinking the images that represent health may help restructure health educators' goals.

It is an interesting exercise to try to envision alternative healthy-image photographs. Here is one of my choices for a cover photograph. An old woman of color, sitting on a chair with a book in her lap, is looking out at a small garden that has been reclaimed from an urban backlot.

Acknowledgments I would like to thank Nancy Worcester, Julie D'Acci, Sally Lesher, and Elizabeth Ellsworth for their critical readings of this chapter and their valuable suggestions.

Notes

1. Cars appear in health textbook photographs primarily in the context of either environmental concerns or the stresses of modern life.

2. Occasionally, photographs used were actually taken for advertising purposes. For example, in a chapter on exercise there is a full-page color photograph of a runner with the credit "Photo by Jerry LaRocca for Nike" (Insel & Roth, 1988, p. 316).

3. Examining the wages of disabled women can give a sense of the potential economic problems: "The 1981 Census revealed that disabled women earn less than 24 cents for each dollar earned by nondisabled men; black disabled women earn 12 cents for each dollar. Disabled women earn approximately 52 percent of what nondisabled women earn" (Saxton & Howe, 1987, p xii).

4. "Supercrip" is a term sometimes used among people with disabilities to describe people with disabilities who go beyond what would be expected of those with no disabilities. It should not be necessary to be a one-legged ski champion or a blind physician to prove that people with disabilities deserve the opportunities available to the

able-bodied. By emphasizing the individual "heroes," the focus shifts away from societal barriers and obstacles to individual responsibility to excel.

5. I am using "old" rather than "older" for two reasons that have been identified by many writing about ageism. "Older" seems a euphemism that attempts to lessen the impact of discussing someone's age, along with such terms as senior citizen or golden ager. The second point is the simple question: "Older than whom?"

References

Barsky, A.J. (1988). The paradox of health. *The New England Journal of Medicine, 318* (7), 414–418.

Barthes, R. (1977). *Image-music-text.* (S. Heath, Trans.). New York: Hill and Wang.

Berger, J. (1972). *Ways of seeing.* London: British Broadcasting Corporation and Penguin Books.

Coser, L.A., Kadushin, C., & Powell, W. (1982). *Books: The culture and commerce of publishing.* New York: Basic Books.

Israel, P., & McPherson, C. (1982). Introduction. In G.F. Matthews, *Voices from the shadows: women with disabilities speak out* (pp. 13–21). Toronto: Women's Educational Press.

Leiss, W., Kline, S., & Jhally, S. (1986). *Social communication in advertising: Persons, products and images of well-being.* Toronto: Methuen.

Matthews, G.F. (1983). *Voices from the shadows: Women with disabilities speak out.* Toronto: Women's Educational Press.

Norsigian, J. (1986, May/June). Dieting is dangerous to your health. *The Network News.* National Women's Health Network, 4, 6.

Overman, S.J., Mimms, S.E., & Harris, J.B. (1987). Readability of selected college personal health textbooks. *Health Education, 18* (4), 28–30.

Saxton, M., & Howe, F. (EDs). (1987). *With wings: An anthology of literature by and about women with disabilities.* New York: Feminist Press at the City University of New York.

Sidel, R. (1986). *Women and children last.* New York: Viking Penguin.

Sternhell, C. (1985, May). We'll always be fat but fat can be fit. *Ms.,* pp. 66–68, 141, 154.

Whatley, M.H. (1988). Photographic images of blacks in sexuality texts. *Curriculum Inquiry, 18*(2), 137–155.

Worcester, N. (1988). Fatophobia. In N. Worcester & M.H. Whatley (Eds.), *Women's health: Readings on social, economic, and political issues.* Dubuque, IA: Kendall/Hunt.

Worcester, N., & Whatley, M.H. (1988). The response of the health care system to the women's health movement. In S. Rosser (Ed.), *Feminism within the science and health care professions: Overcoming resistance* (pp. 117–130). New York: Pergamon.

Appendix: Textbooks Examined for this Chapter

Carroll, C., & Miller, D. (1986). *Health: The science of human adaptation* (4th ed.). Dubuque, IA: Wm. C. Brown.

Dintiman, G.B., & Greenberg, J. (1986). *Health through discovery* (3rd ed.). New York: Random House.

Hales, D.R., & Williams, B.K. (1986). *An invitation to health: Your personal responsibility* (3rd ed.). Menlo Park, CA: Benjamin/Cummings Publishing Company.

Insel, P.M., & Roth, W.T. (1988). *Core concepts in health* (5th ed.). Mountain View, CA: Mayfield Publishing.

Levy, M.R., Dignan, M., & Shirreffs, J.H. (1987). *Life and health.* (5th ed.). New York: Random House.

Mullen, K.D., Gold, R.S., Belcastro, P.A., & McDermott, R.J. (1986). *Connections for health.* Dubuque, IA: Wm. C. Brown.

Payne, W.A., & Hahn, D.B. (1986). *Understanding your health,* St. Louis: Times Mirror/Mosby.

Images and Gender Roles

1. Make a list of characteristics which get identified as "masculine" and "feminine." By each characteristic write "yes" or "no" as to whether this is a characteristic which is valued and rewarded by our society.

female characteristics	valued?	male characteristics	valued?

2. In what ways is it just as dangerous or more dangerous for women to say, "Women are more nurturing than men" as it is for people to say that "Men are better at certain things?"

3. A longtime peace activist has said, "A prerequisite for being president of the USA should be that a person has to be a mother before they can be president." Describe your reaction to this statement and problems with such statements.

4. Check below which strategies you think are likely to help improve the role of women in society?

_____ Trying to eliminate differences between sexes/genders
_____ Trying to make men more like women
_____ Trying to make women more like men
_____ Making it possible for both men and women to explore both masculine and feminine sides of themselves
_____ Trying to make society value a much wider range of characteristics and behaviors

Briefly comment on why you made the choices you did:

5. Compare the messages girls and boys in your family got about "appropriate" vs. "inappropriate" behavior for their sex. When were girls praised for feminine behavior? for masculine behavior? Were boys ever praised for feminine behavior?

6. Collect several ads related to health issues which are in advertising aimed at women as consumers and/or images of women as consumers which appear in medical journals. Compare what you find with the issues raised in "Drug Marketing—Selling Women Out."

7. After reading "The Picutre of Health," describe a more appropriate image of health which you would like to include if you were designing a health textbook.

8. If average untrained college-age men and women are tested for physical fitness, the men are likely to appear to be more fit, particularly in the area of strength. These results fit with the assumption that many make that women naturally have less physical potential than men. However, exercise physiologists find very different results. For example, men tend to have greater strength in both upper (back, arms, shoulders) and lower body, but when the measurement is adjusted relative to body weight, the differences in lower body strength disappear. When untrained men and women begin to do weight-training, the women often progress much faster because they are farther below their potential. Androgens are needed for muscle proliferation, so the fact that the average woman has lower levels of androgens than the average man means there is some limit on her muscle bulk. However, this does not mean much in terms of strength limitation since women can increase greatly in strength without "bulking" (muscles increasing in size). Right now we have no idea what the strength capability of women is since women are so undertrained in terms of strength.

Women have a great capacity for developing endurance. Leading women marathoners can beat all but the best male runners and would, in fact, have won many past Olympic men's marathons with their current times. Women do even better in relation to men in ultra marathons (50 or 100 miles). Women hold many long-distance swimming records and compete directly with men.

When boys and girls are tested for physical performance, they are matched up to ages 10 to 12. In fact, girls are often faster than their male classmates in elementary school. After age 12, boys tend to increase in strength and cardiovascular fitness more than girls. Exercise physiologists believe these differences may be more social than biological in origin. It is not hormones that make women weaker but social and cultural processes.

DISCUSSION QUESTIONS

a. Untrained males and females show little difference in lower body strength but larger differences in upper body strength. Show how this situation might arise by examining the activities from early childhood through adulthood that males and females might engage in that are likely to develop upper or lower body strength.

b. Differences in physical performance between males and females generally first appear around puberty. What are the changes in physical activity around puberty that might affect this? What are the social and cultural messages that may limit girls' activities at puberty? Compare your own forms of exercise before and after puberty.

c. How does the definition of women as "weaker" limit women's lives? Examine such issues as work, recreation, safety. Who benefits from the definition of women as weaker?

CHAPTER 4

Mental Health

*M*any formerly battered women who have been close to death with life threatening physical injuries have said the physical violence had less impact on them than the day to day psychological/emotional abuse they survived. Many women with chronic fatigue syndrome so severe that taking a shower became a major goal have said that the worst part of their condition was that people (including doctors) would not believe they were ill and had said the condition was "all in their head." Mental and physical health issues have so much impact on each other that in many cases it may be misleading to try to make a distinction and in other cases it can be very dangerous to confuse mental and physical health ramifications of a situation. Readers will notice that mental health components are central to every topic in this book.

"Women and Mental Health," by Marian Murphy, provides an overview of definitions of mental health, gender differences in patterns of mental ill health, women and depression, women and mental health services, and positive suggestions for change. This article very clearly identifies that women's ill health (particularly depression) is very obviously related to the fact that women find themselves in depressing situations. Being active agents to change those situations goes against how women/girls are socialized and the types of activities which are accepted as "suitably feminine" in a world where healthy females are defined as being submissive, dependent, easily influenced and not competitive.

Going into more depth on the same themes, Fiona Rummery provides specific examples of how femininity is socially constructed. She explains that what "is generally regarded as the woman's role happens to coincide with what is regarded as mentally unhealthy" so that "whether women comply with or rebel against traditional precepts of femininity, we risk being labelled 'dysfunctional.'" Of course, the dilemma then, as described by both Murphy and Rummery, is that mental health services also reflect the values of society. Therefore, a woman's mental health issues get her labelled and treated (often medicalized) as having an individual problem unrelated to the social context of the oppression of trying to "adjust/accept" an inferior role in life. (The article on postpartum depression, "You Never Saw June Cleaver Weeping, Did You?" in Chapter 10, describes another women's mental health issue which is often ignored or individualized, but needs serious research on how it relates to wider social issues.)

The good news is that the availability of feminist therapy, women's self-help groups, and other resources very specifically supports women to explore and confront the social and cultural contexts of what is making them unhealthy. Now that women who choose to be in therapy have identified that they want counseling which relates to their socialization in a sexist society, consumers need to be alerted to the trend for some therapists to market themselves as "feminist therapists" even if their therapy techniques are fairly traditional. Both the Murphy and Rummery articles describe guiding philosophies a woman seeking feminist therapy should be able to expect.

Although the Rummery article is titled "Mad Woman or Mad Society: Towards a Feminist Practice with Women Survivors of Child Sexual Assault," it is included in this chapter because it so well describes wider mental health issues and feminist theory and practice in addressing the core social context of women's mental ill health. Readers are encouraged to contrast this feminist response to incest with the medical model critiqued in Louise Armstrong's "Surviving the Incest Industry" (p. 560).

"Co-dependency: A Feminist Critique" looks at how the co-dependency label gets put on many of the same behaviors which our society encourages as positive for women and then, "because codependency so accurately describes what many of us experience in our lives, we blame ourselves for the behaviors." Bette Tallen's thought provoking article looks at how the concept of co-dependency depoliticizes feminism (or any other movement by people who fight against sexism and racism) but also appeals to many women.

In a book which is trying to look at both recurring global issues and specific issues for particular groups of women, "Mental Health Issues for Asian/Pacific Island Women" is included for both reasons. The reader is encouraged to use the article both to learn about specific mental health issues for Japanese, Chinese, Vietnamese, Laotian, Cambodian, Korean, Filipino, or other Asian/Pacific Island women, and also to think about how to pay attention to the very different factors which may have an impact on mental health issues for other specific groups of women.

The article introduces us to some of the many factors which prove to be important in influencing mental health: where someone is born, whether or how well they speak the dominant language and how important that is in their day to day life, exposure to trauma both before or after immigration, familiarity with urban life, personal or ethnic group history of acceptance in the U.S., gender issues within their own culture, social support networks in their local community, educational and employment expectations and opportunities, and intergenerational harmony or conflict. Similarly, we are introduced to some of the barriers to utilizing mental health services and recommendations for making mental health services more appropriate for Asian/Pacific Island women. We hope that as we read that only 32% of Japanese Americans were born in Japan but nearly 80% of Vietnamese, Laotians, and Cambodians were born in their home countries, or that 80% of Filipino-American women abstain from alcohol compared to 33% of Japanese-American women, and that the number of Japanese-American women who drink alcohol increased from 13% in 1954 to 53% in 1964, we will learn to be careful not to generalize about groups which have much diversity within the group or to think that health issues remain static. As we read about the stigma and barriers to using mental health services, we hope we will learn to recognize that just because something has not been identified or "counted" by studies, it does not mean that it is not an issue.

True describes the experience of some Cambodian women refugees who were diagnosed as functionally blind even though there was no organic basis for their blindness. Because they had lost relatives and witnessed the massacre of family members, their blindness is described as "almost as if their traumas were so great that they did not wish to see anything." Comparing this article to the co-dependency article, one might wonder how much women's attraction to explanations of "co-dependency" is related to not wanting to see the "trauma" of sexism, racism, and other forms of oppression.

Women and Mental Health

by Marian Murphy

What We Mean by Mental Health

Mental health, as opposed to mere absence of mental illness is a complex and often controversial subject. What defines mental health? Who defines it? In terms of women, notions of mental health carry an added burden of value judgments and traditional beliefs. It is my view that mental health is a concept that needs constant redefinition in the light of new knowledge and, within the framework of this discussion, mental health refers not simply to the absence of symptoms or problems but to the presence in a woman of *well-being* and *growth* and the ability of a woman to solve problems in a reality-based way.

A healthy and growing person can be described as moving towards increased acceptance of and openness to herself and others; increased self-support and self-esteem; growing capacity to give and receive love; increased intellectual competence and creativity; greater freshness of perception and richness of feelings (both joy and pain); a more aware, autonomous, and caring value system; a growing sense of closeness to the natural world; a greater frequency of moments of transcendence; a growing enjoyment of living in her present experience. Using this kind of standard, most people live in a state of permanent mental ill health.[1] At the very least, it is estimated that on average we each fulfil less than 10 per cent of our potential for this kind of growth. The extreme forms of this general ill health are reflected in the increasing numbers of people using psychiatric and counselling services and increasing rates of suicide, alcohol/drug abuse and crime.

In the case of women, this situation is compounded by the very standards used to define mental health/illness. There are differing standards of mental health for women than for men among mental health professionals. An often-cited study carried out by Broverman and colleagues (1970)[2] showed that a double standard is employed when assessing the mental health of women and men. Behaviour that was regarded as healthy for an adult, sex unspecified, and thus viewed from an ideal absolute standpoint, was identical to behaviour considered healthy for men, but not for women. This finding that psychiatrists, psychologists and social workers ascribe male-valued stereotypic traits more often to healthy men than to healthy women conceals a powerful, negative assessment of women in general. For instance, these professionals were more likely to suggest that healthy women differ from healthy men by being more submissive; less independent; more easily influenced; more excitable in minor crises; less competitive. Such a combination of traits is a most unusual way of describing any mature, healthy individual.

Another important factor here is the notion of health itself that is used by many professionals working in health services, i.e., an adjustment notion of health. This would suggest that one of the most important factors involved in mental health is adjustment to one's environment. This, together with the existence of different norms of female and male behaviour, also leads to different standards of mental health for women and men. Thus for women to be healthy from an adjustment viewpoint, we must adjust to and accept the behavioural norms for our sex, even though these behaviours are generally less valued socially and are considered less healthy for the generalised competent, mature adult. Acceptance of this adjustment notion of health places women in the difficult position of having to decide whether to exhibit those positive characteristics considered desirable for men and adults such as assertiveness and ambition, thus calling our 'femininity' into question; or to behave in the prescribed 'feminine' manner, accept second-class adult status and possibly live a lie to boot. This strongly suggests that mental health professionals should be concerned that the influence of sex-role stereotypes on their professional activities actually reinforces social and psychological conflict.

Reprinted with permission from *Personally Speaking* ed. Liz Steiner Scott, Attic Press Dublin, Ireland 1985.

Thus, before we even get to the point of looking at the different mental health statistics of women and men, we can begin to consider the possible effects of this double standard of health. A possible implication is that (a) behaviours and feelings exhibited by women and considered 'normal' for us, (e.g., low self-esteem, feelings of depression) and thus not requiring treatment, would be seen as 'symptoms' in men and would be treated; (b) women exhibiting behaviour which did not conform to these female stereotypes (non-nurturing, lack of interest in childbearing) would be considered 'abnormal' and in need of psychiatric treatment. There is much evidence that this is in fact the case. There are, therefore, numerous implications for both sexes, in the way in which they view themselves and how they should deal with life problems and also in the kinds of treatment they receive from the mental health and medical professions.

Differences in Patterns of Mental Ill Health

The worldwide picture is that the majority of clients for mental health services are women. In North America, for example, women comprise 60-75 percent of clients. In Canada, it has consistently been demonstrated that women receive more prescriptions for all drugs than men and this difference is even more noticeable in the case of psychotropic (mood-changing) drugs, with between 67–72 per cent of these drugs going to women. In Britain, 12 per cent of women take tranquillisers daily for a month or more each year. Although there are no statistics for Ireland, doctors' reports would suggest an equally high level of usage of tranquillisers by women. Women have consistently higher levels of medical consultations than men, both with general practitioners and specialist consultants. What is even more striking than these overall rates of usage of mental health services, which, after all can sometimes be dismissed as differences in help-seeking patterns and willingness to talk about distress etc., is the different patterns of illness displayed by women and men.

In community studies in Britain and the USA where people who have not sought help at all are studied, women consistently report more distress, anxiety and depression. In diagnostic terms, doctors are treating large numbers of women with such clinical conditions as hysteria, eating disorders such as anorexia nervosa (under eating) and bulimia (binge eating) and, most particularly, depression. The incidence of depression in women (matched only by rates of alcoholism in men in Ireland) illustrates the internalised way in which women deal with problems, whereas it appears that men cope by ex-

ternalising their frustrations. As depression is the most prevalent mental illness among women and has been extensively studied, it may be useful to spend some time on it here.

Women and Depression

Is there something inherent in being a woman that predisposes us to developing an emotional illness? There are a number of possible answers to this question. Firstly, it is suggested that the incidence of depression is actually more equally divided between women and men but that each sex expresses it differently. It is suggested that men often develop mechanisms such as excessive drinking, or have outbursts of violence. Many treated alcoholics do have symptoms of depression so it would not be unreasonable to infer that men may use alcohol to hide their symptoms of depression. For others, chronic alcohol abuse and the cause and effect factors have not yet been sorted out and, although it is possible to speculate that there are large numbers of depressed men in the community who are simply not visible because of the masking effects of alcoholism, there is no evidence that this is the case.

The differing ratios of depressive ill health in women and men is often accounted for by the fact that women perceive, acknowledge, report and seek help for stress and its related symptoms more readily than men. However, recent studies have shown that women do not experience or report more stressful events than do men nor do we evaluate the standard lists of life events (death of a spouse, separation, change in jobs, etc.) as having greater impact than do men. We must, therefore, conclude that women do actually experience more frequent and more severe symptoms of depression than men.

Could women's depression be accounted for by biological factors? While there is now some evidence to suggest that there is a genetic factor operating in depression, the samples that have been studied are few and there is insufficient evidence to draw conclusions about the way depression is transmitted or to explain the sex differences. Similarly, while there is good evidence that premenstrual tension (PMT) increases rates of depression, it is not a major cause. Also, the amount of female depression that is attributable to the possible effects of oral contraceptives is extremely small indeed.[3] There is excellent evidence that the period following childbirth does induce an increase in depression. However, contrary to widely held views, there is now evidence to show that the menopause has virtually no effect in increasing depression rates.[4] While, therefore, some portion of the sex differences in depression, probably during the child-bearing years, may be explained by reference to biological and hormonal factors, it is not sufficient to account for the consistently large differences.

Sociologists, psychologists, feminists and others concerned with women have become increasingly occupied with explaining why more of us become depressed. The conventional belief is that our long-standing disadvantaged social status causes women to become depressed. The persistence of social status discrimination for women therefore is proposed to explain the greater numbers of us suffering from depression. One extensive study on depression in women[5] suggests that there are two main reasons why we become depressed. This study holds that many women find their situations depressing because of the real social discrimination we experience in our everyday lives; this makes it difficult for us to achieve control by direct action and self-assertion, further contributing to our psychological distress. Such discrimination leads to legal and economic helplessness, dependency on others, chronically low self-esteem, low aspirations and ultimately clinical depression. The second reason why women become depressed is that our socialisation discourages assertiveness. Young women learn to be helpless while we are growing up and thus develop a limited ability to respond when under stress. Instead of learning to act out in frustration or anger as young men do, young women internalise these feelings and become depressed.

Attempts to test these hypotheses have focused on the different rates of mental illness among married and unmarried women.

If these hypotheses are correct, marriage should be of greater disadvantage to women than to men, and since married women are more likely to embody or find themselves in the traditional stereotyped role, they should, therefore, have higher rates of depression. In one study it was found that the higher overall rates of many mental illnesses for women are largely accounted for by higher rates for married women.[6] In every other marital status category, single, divorced and widowed women have lower rates of mental illness. It concludes that being married has a protective effect for males but a detrimental effect for women. Similar conclusions have been reached by researchers in several different countries.

This study and others attribute the disadvantage of the married women to several factors: role restrictions (most men occupy two roles and therefore have two sources of gratification whereas many women have only one); the low prestige of housekeeping and its frustrating effect for many women; the unstructured role of 'housewife', allowing time for brooding and the fact that even if a married woman works, her position is usually less favourable than a working man's.

There are, of course, other important intervening factors such as family size and financial resources. Other researchers have examined the relationship between psychological stress and subsequent affective disorders.[7] They found that working-class married women with young children living at home had the highest rates of depression. Subject to equivalent levels of stress, working-class women were five times more likely than middle-class women to become depressed. Four factors were found to contribute to this class difference: loss of a mother in childhood; three or more children under the age of fourteen living at home; absence of an intimate and confiding relationship with partner; lack of full- or part-time employment outside the home. The first three factors were more frequent among working-class women. Employment outside the home, it was suggested, provided some protection by alleviating boredom, increasing self-esteem, improving economic circumstances and increasing social contact.

From these studies, it can be concluded that the excess of depressive symptoms in women is not entirely due to biological factors inherent in being female, but is contributed to by the conflicts generated by the traditional female role, and the isolation that this role may bring.

The Mental Health Services: How Women Use Them and How Women Are Treated by Them

Given that more women than men experience symptoms of depression and other mental ill health, how is this maniifested when we look at the mental health services? To begin with, as already noted, rates of consultation are higher. The usual avenue to the health services is through contact with general practitioners. In this country general practitioners say that at least 25 per cent of the consultations are due to psychological factors and that they have neither the training, the time nor the resources to provide appropriate treatment. Moreover, many problems which result from a way of life or a particular difficulty or habit have come to be regarded as diseases rather than problems. Some women's problems which may actually be social, economic, ethical or legal, may be misidentified or wrongly regarded as psychiatric disturbances.

However, there have been few attempts by any western governments to introduce professionals with other than medical training into the first line of contact with people suffering from these kinds of problems and similarly, no attempts have been made to implement programmes of primary prevention and mental health education. The most likely form of treatment, therefore, that a woman will receive for a variety of these problems, is medical, in the form of mood-changing drugs. In fact doctors are more likely to offer tranquillisers to us than to men who present the same complaints, specifically complaints which involve the client being: unhappy, crying, depressed, nervous, worried, restless and tense. For these kinds of complaints men are more likely to receive more physical therapies, laboratory tests and referrals to specialists. Here again the double standard is apparent.

A major contributing factor to this scenario is women ourselves who, in fact, frequently request our doctors to prescribe drug treatment for such symptoms. It has been suggested that this comes about as a result of women's view of our situation, a view which society teaches us. Women have learned to see our resentment and despair about our place in the social structure, as an individual problem, an emotional disorder. Women are trained to invalidate our own experiences, understanding and feelings and to look to men to tell us how to view ourselves. Ideas, concepts, images and vocabularies available to women to think about our experiences have been formulated from the male viewpoint by universities, professionals, industries and other organisations. These are reinforced by images of women in the media: women's magazines, women's novels, women as depicted in advertisements, children's stories and much more. These views are supported by the findings of a Vancouver study that questioned groups of women about their understanding of the uses of minor tranquillisers. Women felt that tranquillisers were sometimes needed to help them cope; coping, for them, meant the management of their roles as housewife and mother. In retrospect, some women expressed doubts about the role of illness that they had accepted and wondered about other options. One woman said: 'I feel that, essentially, when a doctor prescribes a pill for me, it's to put him out of my misery'. Another commented that a prescription for babysitters would have been more useful than a prescription for tranquillisers.[8]

When we look at the training attitudes and practices of doctors and psychiatrists, we see even more blatant examples of sex-bias in treatment. In 1974 a study highlighted the process by which medical schools teach demeaning and derogatory attitudes to women, both as patients and as students.[9] Physicians are taught that women's illnesses are not worth understanding, are unimportant and are of emotional origin. The woman 'patient' is objectified and made fun of. These assumptions about women are part of the very fabric of our society—this appears to be borne out by several studies in the USA on the amount of sex-bias and sex-role stereotyping involved in psychotherapeutic practice. In July 1974, responding to requests by the American Psychological Association Committee on Women in Psychology, a task force was established to look at this whole area. The task force identified four general areas

affecting women as clients. The first of these was in the area of support for traditional sex roles. Here the therapists assumed that resolving of problems and self-fulfillment for women come from marriage or perfecting the role of wife without any recognition of women's other potential roles in society. The second general area was the above-mentioned bias in the medical profession's expectations and devaluation of women. This was exemplified in practice by the use of theoretical terms and concepts (e.g., masochism), to ignore or condone violence towards and victimisation of women; and by the use of demeaning labels such as manipulative, hysterical etc. when describing female patients. The third general area was the sexist use of psychoanalytic concepts, e.g. labelling assertiveness and ambition with the Freudian concept of penis envy. The fourth area of discrimination identified was the therapist's response to women as sex objects, e.g., heavily weighing physical appearance in the selection of patients or having a double standard for male and female sexual activities and even going as far as seducing female clients.

In view of these findings the American Psychological Association subsequently advocated a whole range of educational efforts to overcome these appalling practices and injustices. There is little evidence to show that these findings have had any effect on the practice of many psychiatrists. In fact, the realisation that 'feminine' characteristics can, in fact, be seen as those of any oppressed group of people tends to be astounding to the psychiatrist.

It is obvious then that the three interacting sets of factors briefly discussed here (a) the medical and mental health systems and the process of medicalisation; (b) the mental health professionals and their attitudes and theoretical backgrounds and (c) the woman and her socialisation; perpetuate a situation which predisposes women to mental, and particularly depressive, illness. Women's problems are treated only as psychological problems, without any prospect of addressing and dealing with the root causes.

Where Do Women Go from Here?

Internationally, the future for our mental health is bleak. In Ireland, as everywhere, additional stress factors such as high unemployment rates and the consequent lack of access to work outside the home for many women, interact with a traditionally male medical and psychiatric culture emanating from a society that clings stubbornly to a view of woman as homemaker and mother. Realisation of the need for a new medical model is appearing, however, and the supposed scientific basis of psychiatry has been greatly criticised. Psychiatrists are beginning to see sexism as a barrier to our understanding of the family and to acknowledge the 'much patriarchal rhetoric has masqueraded as theory.'[10]

Theoretical and practical alternatives are emerging that approach women's problems in ways that are more closely connected with our life experiences. Worldwide, feminist therapy is developing to such a degree that it has been suggested that it has some of the characteristics of a school of psychotherapy. The increased equality of client and therapist, the main focus on environmental interpretations, the movement away from sex-role prescriptions and the role of the features of this new therapy. In Ireland some alternatives to traditional psychotherapy are available but only in urban centres. Women's self-help groups and consciousness-raising groups can be particularly useful here. Women in groups can come to realise that cultural values we have accepted unquestioningly such as maternal success, complete devotion of self to motherhood, and consumerism, as a major source of our tensions and dissatisfactions. Researchers have found that consciousness-raising groups provide a forum in which mildly depressed women with low self-esteem can explore our feelings about ourselves and our life situations. Obviously, participation in such groups is not a substitute for psychotherapy for those women whose problems are long-standing and severe. However, they can provide a useful starting point for women who are beginning to take more personal responsibility for the quality of our lives.

A range of other resources has also begun to emerge which provide support and reduce the isolation of women in extended families. These include family and community resource centres which often provide mother and child clubs, pre-school and day-care facilities, discussion and personal development groups, employment counselling, assertiveness training and legal clinics. 'Return to work' courses, creches in a variety of educational facilities and opportunities for women to come together to work at co-operative ventures are playing a vital role in preventing the development of further mental illness among women. In Ireland, there are few counselling centres which provide education and treatment that is not sex biased, but beginnings are being made.

For women undergoing particular crises, facilities such as rape crisis centres supply practical help, enabling us to confront our anger and avoid chronic and disabling shame and embarrassment. Advice is also available on possible legal action and its implications. Transition houses provide shelter for battered women and their children and have served to alert the community to the enormity of this problem.

Notwithstanding these developments, a great deal still needs to be done. Generally, we need to be more aware of the factors leading to stress and mental ill health. Preventive programmes should be established to help people discover and use their own coping mecha-

nisms and recognise the value of yoga, relaxation techniques, akido, a balanced lifestyle, and other alternatives to the traditional medical response to mental illness.

Caution must be exercised by women anxious to develop alternatives outside the traditional framework of 'the home'. They should not swing to the opposite extreme and create new kinds of 'career' and other pressures that can equally cause an imbalance—to behave like men under stress is not a solution. The ideal would be to redistribute nurturing and work roles between women and men allowing for more balanced lifestyles for all. It is also vital that the new kinds of services already discussed at some length be encouraged and recognised as viable sources of help for women who have hitherto all too often been seen as in need of psychiatric treatment.

Finally, it is imperative that those working in the mental health professions be encouraged, both at pre- and post-qualifying levels, to employ the following guidelines in their dealings with women and that we in turn begin to seek and insist upon a service that embodies the following principles: (1) an equal relationship with shared responsibility between counsellor and client; (2) provision of help in differentiating between the politics of the sexist social structure and those problems over which, realistically, we have personal control; (3) provision of help in exploring our personal strength and how we can use it constructively in personal, work and political relationships; (4) provision of help in confronting unexpressed anger in order to combat depression and to make choices about how to use our anger constructively; (5) provision for helping women to redefine ourselves apart from our relationships to men, children and home including exploration of fears about parental role changes; (6) encouragement to women to nurture ourselves as well as caring for others, thereby raising self-confidence and self-esteem; (7) encouragement of the development of a range of skills to increase women's competence and productivity. This may include assertiveness training, economic and career skills and advice on how to reeducate family and friends who resist change. Although not every counselling situation with women will necessarily incorporate all of these principles they provide a basis for mental health professionals as well as a standard which can be used by women to evaluate the treatment we receive. Women clients, no less than men, have a right to mental health services that are sex-fair, competent and ethical.

Conclusion

Moving from an 'ideal-type' definition of mental health, through some of the examples of ill health in women, and how these are currently treated, I have

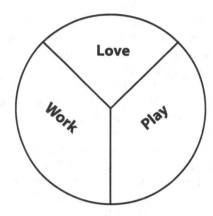

arrived at suggestions which I believe would help to promote better levels of mental health in women. These suggestions are underlined by a view of people and their psychological needs which I, together with others, working in the mental health services, hold. This view presupposes that mental health involves a balance between three basic areas of life (see diagram): love, based on self-acceptance and self-esteem; work, providing opportunities for a sense of achievement, recognition and status; play, allowing for relaxation and forgetting of self and other preoccupations.

Traditionally, women have loved and worked, men have worked and played. This imbalance has impoverished the lives of both sexes. Ironically, now that some men are beginning to learn to feel and show emotions, affection in relationships is being awarded a status it did not enjoy when found predominantly among women. Women, however, must not only achieve recognition status for the work we do, we must also learn to look after our own needs for relaxation, play and satisfying work and above all for a sense of self that is not defined for us either by society or by our relationships with others. For each individual woman this means maximising existing opportunities for looking at and, if necessary, reordering her lifestyle. For members of the health profession, it means reorganising and eliminating sex-biased practices.

For the community as a whole, it not only means making a commitment to programmes of prevention in the mental health field, but also rejecting the rigid adherence to the stereotypical division of roles, responsibilities and acceptable behaviours between women and men.

It has been because of the growth of feminist thinking and 'psychotherapy' that changes and reanalysis of women and mental health have begun to take place. This development must be guided and supported. It is important for women to recognise our own strengths and contributions in this field and to look to each other for the shared experience and discussion which will allow greater control and responsibilities in our lives.

QUESTIONS FOR DISCUSSION

1. Do you think that the family as we know it is to blame for a considerable amount of mental ill health in women? Discuss.
2. Some women become depressed after childbirth. Why? What other events in women's lives might be the cause of their depression?
3. From your own experience, how does the medical profession treat women as clients? How might you change that attitude?
4. Is it in women's 'nature' to be more prone to mental ill health, especially depression, than men? Discuss.
5. If you have ever taken tranquillisers for any length of time, can you assess how they affected you? Did they help? How? Was it difficult to stop taking them?
6. In what ways can women's groups be a positive force for mental health?
7. If you were in need of professional help, where would you go? Can you think of any alternatives to professional help that might be of use?

References available in original source.

Mad Women or Mad Society: Towards a Feminist Practice with Women Survivors of Child Sexual Assault

by Fiona Rummery

This chapter examines an aspect of structural violence as embodied in traditional psychiatric labels of mental ill health. Although this discussion revolves around the issues of child sexual assault (which is constituted by physical violation) it does not focus on the interpersonal aspects of such abuse. Rather, it explores the subtler abuse which often informs the framework of societal institutions, such as medicine. When considering violence against women, it is usually overt and direct experiences of violence which are highlighted. It is arguable that women's experiences of systemic violence when seeking assistance are as worthy of detailed assessment. As Irwin and Thorpe argue in the opening chapter in this collection, systemic violence plays a crucial role in allowing interpersonal violence to continue, partly through the processes of silencing and discrediting, as this chapter details.

This chapter considers the question of what it is about a feminist counselling practice that differentiates it from other, more traditional modes of working. It will thus utilise an illustrative discussion of an issue which arose for me whilst working as a sexual assault counsellor. This involved working with an incest survivor who had an extensive history with the psychiatric profession, and my subsequent investigation into this area. As such, this chapter encompasses discussions of the issues involved in child sexual assault generally; women and notions of madness and the way these intersect with constructions of femininity; as well as ideas about working as a feminist practitioner. This is not an exhaustive discussion but rather exists as an exploration of some of the more subtle ways in which we, as workers, must always consider and reconsider the theoretical underpinnings of any practice, as well as constantly analyzing the practical implications of any theoretical formulation.

Child Sexual Assault

Misconceptions, fear and denial surround the issue of child sexual assault, as its existence problematises popular ideas about the fundamental institution of the family. In most cases of child sexual assault the perpetrator is known to the child, and the abuse continues over some time (Waldby 1985). The dominant cultural discourses which attempt to deal with child sexual assault form a powerful and ubiquitous part of the social fabric. More importantly (and confusingly) they are bizarrely contradictory in their nature:

> It doesn't happen; it only happens to poor families; it doesn't happen to THIS family; men do it when their wives are frigid or otherwise unavailable; children are naturally seductive; it doesn't do any harm; it damages for life. (Linnell & Cora 1993, 24)

The sexual assault of children usually involves progressive intrusion over a long period of time, with gradual coercion or co-option of the child, and with disclosure not occurring until some time after the abuse has ended (Cashmore & Bussey 1988). Child sexual assault is a particularly silenced experience; still commonly eliciting responses of disbelief and stigmatisation. It is also a particularly silencing experience in that the intensity and intimacy of violation often leads women to such a state of depression, self-hatred and/or distrust that they are unable or reluctant to talk about it (Stanko 1985; Ward 1984). Much of the early literature on child sexual assault documented the ravages of abuse, focussing on the tragedy of supposedly ruined lives. More recently the focus has shifted towards the process of recovery, with the aid of appropriate intervention. Incest survivors need to be provided with appropriate supportive services that allow them to actively and consciously confront the legacy of their abusive history.

One of the issues that I experienced when I began working with incest survivors, was that a high number had some psychiatric history or diagnosis. Approximately seventy per cent of the clients I had seen had been categorised with Borderline Personality Disorder, or as Manic Depressive or as having psychotic episodes and as a result had been hospitalised or prescribed medication. When I questioned these women as to the details of the exact nature of the causes of their depression—or psychotic episodes—I was again surprised by the manner in which the symptoms manifested by these women seemed to me to be normal reactions to abusive situations. This led me to do some reading into women and psychiatry so that I could better understand theoretically the unease I felt intuitively to such psychiatric labelling of women's distress. Moreover, I wanted to incorporate this unease more effectively into my practice.

Women and Madness

The history of the connections between women and madness has been examined by a number of feminist writers in the last twenty years. These have ranged from historians (such as Matthews 1984) through to psychiatrists and social workers (such as Penfold & Walker 1983) and to philosophers (Russell, 1986, 1995). They have examined the manner in which what is defined as 'madness' has changed over time according to context. In addition, they have exposed the manner in which the mental health profession has been used as a mechanism of social control, inextricably intertwined with notions of what constitutes 'femininity'.

The 'science' of mental health will be treated in this discussion as an elastic and value-driven social science. Whilst I acknowledge that some women may be genuinely suffering from psychiatric illnesses, there are also many whose emotions, responses and 'symptoms' are unnecessarily deemed 'sick' within a psychiatric framework. It is this process of pathologising women's behaviour with which this paper is most concerned.

Phyllis Chesler says of her interviews with sixty women aged 17–70 with regard to their experiences in both private therapy and mental asylums: 'Most were simply unhappy and self-destructive in typically (and approved) female ways. Their experiences made it very clear to me that help-seeking or help-needing behaviour is not particularly valued or understood in our culture' (Chesler 1973, XXII).

Central to the definition of what constitutes madness then, is the manner in which femininity is socially constructed. Caplan like Chesler, asserts that: 'A misogynist society has created a myriad of situations that make women unhappy. And then that same society uses the myth of women's masochism to blame the women themselves for their misery' (Caplan 1985, 9).

The traditional 'psychology of women' correlates closely with the 'characteristics of oppression' (Penfold & Walker 1983). Women's sane, average, even self-preserving responses to situations of abuse or oppression are often used as evidence of their own lack of mental health.

Debra

I want at this point to introduce a case example in order to highlight some of the issues referred to throughout. Whilst I am loathe to do this in some senses—as it easily becomes voyeuristic and simplistically condenses a woman's struggle and life—it elucidates my point at different stages of this discussion more effectively than any abstract discussion of 'women' can.

Debra was a woman whom I saw for counselling after she referred herself to the sexual assault service. It was largely through my contact with her that I undertook this research into women and psychiatry. She was thirty-four at the time and had a nine-year-old daughter. She was chronically and sadistically sexually abused by a male family member from the age of approximately eight until sixteen. She has had extensive contact with the psychiatric profession, has had a variety of diagnoses and been prescribed nearly every type of medication. Her first contact with psychiatrists was at age eight when she attempted suicide. After hospitalisation she was labelled 'depressed' and given Valium and sleeping tablets for a number of years.

Her first psychotic episode occurred after the birth of her daughter, at which time she was placed in a psychiatric institution for some months. Since then, intrusive flashbacks of the sexual abuse she had experienced as a child have increased and intensified. She regularly had bouts of depression, suicidal feelings and tendencies as well as repeated psychotic episodes during which time she was hospitalised. She had been prescribed a plethora of drugs, none of which alleviate either the psychotic episodes or her flashbacks. Debra sought counselling at the sexual assault service as her flashbacks had further intensified since the time her daughter turned eight, and she felt strongly that there were things about the sexual assault which she needed to resolve.

Although Debra had a history of extensive contact with health professionals, at no time was she asked about her childhood. Even at age eight, and during her adolescence when Debra was medicated and hospitalised a number of times, the safety and stability of her family life was not questioned. The psychiatrists she saw did not ask her whether she had any ideas about what might be causing her distress. Rather, the manifestations of her emotional distress in response to abuse were treated as symptoms of an illness which could be cured by psychiatric intervention, such as medication.

It became clear to me quite early on that the messages which I was giving Debra directly contradicted those of her psychiatrist, whom she was still seeing. The things that he said to her are best encapsulated in the following examples:

You have no control over this.

You don't know what you need, I know what's *best for you.*

Just do as I say and take the medication.

The sexual assault is not *particularly relevant.* You must not indulge in self-pity and dwell on it. Put it out of your mind, it is in the past now

You are psychotic and manic depressive. There is nothing you can do about it. You must learn to live with your mental illness.

The work that I undertook with Debra, some of which will be described here, focussed upon validating both her feelings and memories, believing her, and giving her control over the counselling relationship. This approach stems from the belief that the core experiences of child sexual assault are disempowerment and disconnection from self and others. Recovery, therefore, is based primarily upon the empowerment of the incest survivor and the creation of new relationships which are non-abusive. 'No intervention that takes power away from the Survivor can possibly foster her recovery, regardless of how much it appears to be in her best interest' (Herman 1992, 133).

The way in which Debra's psychotic episodes were dealt with by psychiatrists provides an illuminating illustration of the manner in which women's distress is pathologised rather than validated. When I questioned Debra as to the exact nature of her psychotic episodes, these were revealed (over some time) to be a series of extremely distressing memory flashbacks. To label these 'psychotic' effectively removes them from her reality, thereby denying her the opportunity of integration. Whilst these memories were extremely distressing and often bizarre in nature, it was only through exploring

them fully that Debra was able to become less afraid of them. As one survivor of childhood sexual abuse wrote: 'I've looked memories in the face and smelled their breath. They can't hurt me any more' (Bass & Davis 1988, 70).

The validation that her terror of flashbacks was an expression of the terror she had felt at the time of the abuse enabled Debra to remove these from the realm of paranoia. By extension, she was then able to turn fear into (justifiable) rage toward a perpetrator who could do such cruel things to a child. This change was in direct contrast to her previous self-blame and confusion about feeling crazy due to her mood hallucinations. The process of remembering and mourning has been well-documented by feminist practitioners as a crucial stage in recovery from childhood trauma of any kind, as it is only through knowing what happened that women can begin to heal and recover from the damage done to them (Herman 1992, 155).

THE PROBLEMS WITH CATEGORISATION

A major part of the construction of femininity is the emphasis which is placed upon serving others. This is exemplified in the importance which is accorded to motherhood and women's roles in providing for children. This role, however, has gradually become devalued in western society, so women are ensnared within the paradox of being both glorified and trapped within an oppressive definition of what they should be. At its extreme, some feminist commentators have argued that concepts of femininity and madness are actually interchangeable.

Numerous psychological studies have pointed out that what in the west is generally regarded as the woman's role happens to coincide with what is regarded as mentally unhealthy (Russell 1986, 86; Russell 1995). *The Diagnostic and Statistical Manual of Mental Disorders* (DSM-IIIR), created by the American Psychiatric Association, lists symptoms of all psychiatric disorders and is considered to be the essential reference for those working in Mental Health in the western world. Whilst the length of this chapter prevents greater exposition, it is useful to compare the set of criteria for certain diagnoses, particularly those which are most often assigned to women.

Kaplan (cited in Russell 1986, 82–90) undertook a comparison of the DSM-III description of Histrionic Personality Disorder (which is far more frequently diagnosed in women than in men) with the findings of Broverman's (1972, in Russell) research into what constitutes a mentally healthy woman. The criteria for a diagnosis of Histrionic Personality Disorder are 'self-dramatization, for example exaggerated expression of emotions, overreaction to minor events' (Spitzer & Williams 1987). Remarkably similar is the woman deemed mentally healthy in Broverman's research 'being more emotional and more excitable in minor crises' (as cited in Russell 1986, 82–90).

This comparison illustrates the paradox in which women are placed, in that what are described as healthy feminine attributes can equally be seen as symptoms of psychiatric disorders. Thus, through assumptions about appropriate sex roles on the part of practitioners, a woman who is 'successfully' fulfilling the feminine role by 'revealing emotional responsibility, naivete, dependency and childishness' (Lerner & Wolowitz as cited in Russell 1986, 88) can be very easily diagnosed and labelled. The example used here is by no means the only one. A woman conforming to the female role can also be deemed to have a 'dependent personality disorder', or 'avoidant personality disorder'. These definitions also include a high level of ambiguity, allowing for much interpretation on the part of the practitioner.

Whether women comply with or rebel against traditional precepts of femininity, we risk being labelled 'dysfunctional'. As the above examples reveal, compliance with femininity is not necessarily the safer option, as it can imply any variety of mental disorders; but rebellion against it can be seen as signifying aggressiveness, lack of gender identity, and social maladjustment. The 'catch-22' inherent in this paradox is treacherous for women.

Constructing Reality

The dominant group in any society controls the meaning of what is valid information. For women and other subordinate groups, the version of the world which has been sanctioned as reality does not address their lived experience . . . (Penfold & Walker 1983, 56)

When there is a disjunction between the world as women experience it and the terms given them to understand the experience, women often have little alternative but to feel 'crazy'. Labels of mental ill-health thus create and authorise ways in which women can conceptualise their unhappiness and despair, in a societally acceptable manner. In struggling against this, rather than treating Debra's symptoms as hers alone, a feminist approach seeks to normalise these by placing them within a context. Whilst this does not necessarily alter the feelings she experiences, it does alleviate accompanying feelings of isolation and fault. For example, when I pointed out to Debra that many women experience an increase in in-

tensity and number of memory flashbacks after the birth of a child, or when a daughter reaches the age that they were when the abuse began, she was relieved, and we were able to explore what a daughter's vulnerability might mean to her. I would stress again that this does not necessarily relieve the distress experienced during these flashback episodes, but rather that the panic of feeling 'crazy' and out of control during and afterwards is alleviated. Thus, Debra was able to view her symptoms as having a cause, rather than being something intrinsic to her as an individual which she needed to 'learn to live with'. It is important to remember that women's symptoms are real. Although this chapter criticises the fact that these symptoms are seen to constitute an identifiable (or classifiable) mental illness, this does not negate the fact that the symptoms as experienced by individual women can be intense and overpowering. Thus, the theoretical underpinnings of one's practice are revealed in the manner in which one defines women's distress. The psychiatrists who saw Debra acknowledged her distress, as did I. It is the framework in which we interpreted this that differed dramatically.

Mental Illness as Social Control

The institution of psychiatry presents itself as healing, benign and compassionate while obscuring its function as part of the apparatus through which society is ordered. (Penfold & Walker 1983, 244)

Depressed or subservient women serve a social function in that they are unlikely to question their subordinate gender roles nor challenge broader social structures. This is exemplified by Miles (1988) in her discussion of the role of housewife:

The stresses inherent in domestic work and the role of the housewife can lead to neurosis which in its turn is likely to make her even more home-centered and thus vulnerable to further stress . . . [T]he home can become . . . a setting which, by its peculiar strains, 'drives her mad' yet which provides asylum from the impossible demands of the world outside with which she feels that she can no longer cope. (Miles 1988, 7)

If one accepts the premise that the construction of mental health reflects a social ordering of gender, one must then ask what purpose the pathologising of women's behaviour serves. To medicate Debra meant that she remained socially compliant. To label her as crazy enabled both professionals and her family to dismiss those disclosures she did make about the child sexual assault as imagined or exaggerated. This silenced her more effectively than any terror she may have felt.

Jordanova (1981, 106) expands upon this idea, by examining depression within the paradigm of an 'illness'. She compares those illnesses from which men most commonly suffer, with those of women, highlighting how rarely women are allowed to take on the 'sick role': a role which provides relief from day-to-day burdens of work. This is not to negate the underlying framework which operates to posit the female condition as continuously or innately 'sick'. Rather, my point is that men are given societal access to a 'legitimate' sick role. Jordanova effectively contrasts a woman who is depressed and on medication but still expected to perform familial duties, with the more 'serious' illnesses which lead to time spent in bed, relaxation, holidays, and time off work for men. Again, Debra had been medicated and encouraged to 'cope'. For ten years her ability to care for her child and elderly relatives (including her and her partner's grandparents) domestically was actively rewarded, and the time that she spent in hospital frowned upon as indulgent. At no point was she offered the space, time or care to understand and deal with the cause of her distress.

Strategies for a Feminist Practice

Practicing from a feminist perspective will involve a variety of methodological approaches depending upon the context in which one is working. Thus, I do not intend to discuss method, but rather the underlying ideals informing a feminist approach. The ideal is to empower clients to challenge both external power structures and their own internalised oppression. This is necessary because both external and internal oppression can be equally debilitating and disempowering in the manner in which they are personally experienced (Fook 1990, 30).

A feminist approach cannot be a set of 'how-to's' which can be easily adopted. A feminist framework is flexible and evolving, and involves as much an analysis of one's self, as that of the women with whom one is working. This is not to simplify feminism, nor to unify all feminist counsellors into the one category. I acknowledge the diversities within the existing definitions of feminism (and women) and the way in which these manifest in work practices. In order to establish and maintain a feminist practice, the worker must firstly be a feminist. This is in some senses stating the obvious, but I would reiterate that undertaking counselling in a feminist manner is not simply a job or framework which can be utilised and then discarded. Feminist practice is also not merely client-focused. Rather, it extends into all areas of work, examining and analysing the structures in which one is working and in the dynamics between staff members. An example which is pertinent is that of working within a psychiatric institution. In such an environment, one's feminist perspective would be of crucial motivation when interacting with other staff members in the organisation, particularly doctors, and others in positions of power in the hierarchy—in challenging the established frameworks in which they think and label people and which influence their practice.

A feminist approach values collective rather than hierarchical structures and seeks to deconstruct the 'expert worker'—'client in need of help' dynamic, favoring instead empowerment of clients. This is particularly pertinent to a discussion on working with incest survivors. Working from a feminist perspective in essence allows women to be the expert of their own lives. This structuring of one's practices, so that the client is more than merely a recipient, allows the space for them to control the relationship. This is crucial as Herman points out, 'The first principle of recovery is the empowerment of the Survivor. Others may offer advice, support, assistance, affection and care, but not cure' (Herman 1992, 133).

A feminist focus upon validating women's experiences is paramount—indicating to them that they have been listened to, heard, and believed, as this so rarely occurs elsewhere. This again is particularly pertinent to working with victims of sexual assault whose experiences of abuse may have been denied, trivialised or ignored—as in Debra's situation. The silence surrounding sexual assault makes it incredibly difficult for women to speak of their experiences; thus it is not possible to underestimate the impact on a personal level of a worker hearing and believing a woman's disclosure. Working with Debra involved providing constant reassurance that I did believe her memories and that I did not think that she was lying. At times, her fear of having spoken the abuse was palpable. This again reinforces the transformative power of merely disclosing the abusive experiences. It has been stressed that as workers we should never lose sight of the terror of disclosure, adding that on many occasions it is actually as if the perpetrator were in the room: 'The terror is as though the patient and therapist convene in the presence of yet another person. The third image is of the victimiser, who . . . demanded silence and whose command is now being broken' (Herman 1992, 137).

This also highlights the importance of the manner in which the counsellor perceives of change. The worker should not view change simply as a change in behaviour, but rather expand this to create an environment in which it is recognised that change does not have to be structural or large to be of importance. The emphasis is therefore shifted so that an apparently slight change in awareness is valued and its ability to facilitate considerable difference in a woman's life is acknowledged. For Debra this type of change in awareness allowed her to begin to redefine her self and formulate a differing self-image from that previously provided to her. The creation of a new manner in which to perceive her self and her life allowed her to reinterpret her own life experience (Linnell & Cora 1993, 36). This newfound ability to resist the dominant discourse of her experience facilitates the potential for both social and personal empowerment. Goldstein comments that the personal narrative has been the way in which women have attempted (often privately and without recognition) to link up their lived experiences and feelings in the face of social definitions: 'The use of this method is most instructive for social work because it reveals how personal and social change may be spurred by the kind of consciousness raising that occurs when people explore their own stories' (Goldstein 1990, 40).

Another essential feature of a feminist practice is that the worker's values are stated, and there is no pretence at objectivity or impartiality: 'The consciousness of oppression has implications for alternative approaches such as those developed in self-help groups, women's studies, political action and consciousness raising' (Penfold & Walker 1983, XI).

In my practice, in order to challenge dominant constructions of power and knowledge, I take an overtly non-neutral position. This is achieved through providing the woman with the space, opportunity and information which is necessary for her to begin to consider her own experiences in the light of the broader cultural and social context. An example of this involves providing women with knowledge of the incidence of child sexual assault (as well as common reactions and experiences as detailed previously). This broader context allows the woman's perspective to encompass her own experience as well as the knowledge of a complex social dynamic. It is then possible to provide questions and possibilities which facilitate the reframing of personal experience within the context of this new knowledge (Linnell & Cora 1993, 34). Whilst this mode of working could be accused of not being 'impartial' enough by traditional practitioners, it is important to differentiate here between making one's political and social ideologies clear without rupturing the boundaries of the counselling relationship, and importing the worker's own emotional personal agenda into the working relationship. Herman provides a poignant explanation of the difference between the technical neutrality of the practitioner as opposed to what she calls moral neutrality: 'Working with victimised people requires a committed moral stand. The therapist is called upon to bear witness to a crime. She must affirm a position of solidarity with the victim' (Herman 1992, 135).

She further extends this notion to explain that it does not necessitate a simplicity which assumes that the victim can do no wrong and asserts that rather it involves an understanding of the fundamental injustice of the child sexual assault and the victim's subsequent need for 'a resolution that restores some sense of social justice' (Herman 1992, 135).

If we see that the depression of women speaks their lived experiences and represents a feminised manner of calling for some kind of understanding, then 'a detailed examination is called for which concerns itself not just with which women in the population get depressed, but how and why' (Jordanova 1981, 106–07)

Social analysis does not necessarily help those women who feel unable to cope with their day-to-day existence. Knowledge that their 'illness' is part of broader structural problems, and attributable to their social situation does not automatically endow them with feelings of joy and liberation. Whilst this is an important long-term aim, it does little to alleviate the suffering women individually experience. It 'highlights the immediacy of the problem for women, and the need to think in terms of immediate action, not just the distant solutions implied in abstract analysis' (Jordanova 1981, 105).

If counselling is about negotiating an adjustment between client and environment (Fook 1990), then the treatment undertaken for women deemed 'mentally unhealthy' has largely sought to adapt them to their environment. A feminist approach, however, would necessitate an examination of the societal factors which have led to the level of emotional distress present. Essentially then, public and private struggles are as inextricably linked as are theory and practice. Most importantly, neither partner in either equation should be treated as superior as each is crucial to the other.

Conclusion

It is necessary for a feminist practice to examine the oppression of women in both private and public, individual and institutional, structural contexts. Although this chapter has utilised the example of parts of one woman's story, as stated earlier this is representative of the experiences of many of the women with whom I have worked. The process of labelling these women when they exhibit intense emotional distress as 'disordered' or 'sick', effectively silences their disclosures of abuse. To accept that there are extremely cruel and sadistic acts perpetrated against children within our society is confronting and difficult. The manner in which social institutions and scientific discourse interact with the ideologies of patriarchy, needs to be exposed, and such interactions condemned for the manner in which they subjugate women.

Labels of mental illness do not exist in a social vacuum. To deny the importance of an individual's abusive childhood is to abdicate the responsibility that we all have for the impact of our actions on others. Such denial contributes to the continuation of such abuse. Links between madness as a social construction, and madness as a subjective experience (or as a 'sane' response to abusive or oppressive experiences) need to be explored. Further, the label of 'madness' when applied to women needs to be viewed with utter skepticism before being accepted as an appropriate diagnosis.

References available in original source.

Co-dependency
A Feminist Critique

by Bette S. Tallen
Graduate Studies in Education and Human Development
Rollins College

Thanks to Elliott, Donna Langston, Mara, Rosemary Curb for comments and suggestions although only I am responsible for the opinions expressed here.

I live in a community where co-dependency is big business, where women have had in-hospital treatment for it, where many belong to Co-dependents Anonymous, where therapists advertise in the women's community as specialists in co-dependent treatment. Many women have described themselves to me as co-dependent. This behavior is neither new nor unique. In 1989 when I worked in a Women's Studies Department in a state university in southern Minnesota, we offered a one-credit workshop on co-dependency, we were so flooded by student demand for the course that we had to schedule a second section. This was in a community of less than 40,000 people. Moreover, the more I talk to other women around the country the more I realize none of this behavior is all that unusual. Books on co-dependency are best sellers, not only in feminist bookstores but on national best-seller lists. Women-only and lesbian-only co-dependent groups abound. Treatment centers for women advertise in newspapers as well as on TV.

In short, co-dependency is an idea whose time has come. Sharon Wegscheider-Cruise defines co-dependents as "all persons who (1) are in a love or marriage relationship with an alcoholic, (2) have one or more alcoholic parents or grandparents, or (3) grew up in an emotionally repressive family." (Wegscheider-Cruise, as quoted in Anne Wilson Schaef, *Co-Dependence: Misunderstood—Mistreated*, p.14.) Feminists and non-feminists alike embrace the concept of co-dependency to describe a phenomena that, according to Wegscheider-Cruise affects 96% of the population. *(Ibid.)*

Startlingly few critiques of the concept of co-dependency have emerged from our lesbian and feminist communities. We have no sustained analysis of the history of the term and have had little or no discussion of the political implications of using it as a method of understanding women's lives. Recently, I heard a woman describe another woman who is dying of cancer as only sick because she was co-dependent (cancer being one of several fatal diseases that co-dependency "causes," at least according to Anne Wilson Schaef. (*Co-Dependence*, p.8.) I was enraged, both as a cancer survivor and as a teacher of courses on women and health, I know only too well about the environmental and political issues that are critical to any discussion of cancer. African-American women and men suffer from and die from cancer in far greater numbers than do white people. Women continue to die from such drugs as DES. Are we all co-dependent? Or are we all suffering from a

From Sojourner: The Women's Forum, (January, 1990). Illustration © 1990 by Linda Bourke.

system that systematically targets certain groups as expendable? In short, what do we as women gain from explaining aspects of our lives as stemming from co-dependency?

Who is a co-dependent person? Who gets to say? Who has the appropriate credentials and skill to label someone as co-dependent? The list of symptoms of co-dependency sounds like a catalogue of our lives. Anne Wilson Schaef, for example, lists the following as characteristics of co-dependency: dishonesty, not dealing with feelings in a healthy way, control, confusion, thinking disorders, perfectionism, external referencing, dependency issues, fear, rigidity, judgmentalism, depression, inferiority/grandiosity, self-centeredness, loss of personal morality, stasis and negativism. (*Co-Dependence*, pp. 42–43.) Who hasn't experienced these feelings? John and Linda Friel argue,

> Is it not true that almost everyone had some form of dysfunction in their childhood that could lead to co-dependent symptoms? And if everyone has "it," does it not lose its conceptual and diagnostic meaning. . . . The [DSM-III-R] always describes symptoms, but asks us to look at length and severity of symptoms . . . before we make a definite diagnosis. (*Adult Children: The Secrets of Dysfunctional Families*, p.161)

Since apparently only the "experts" can label co-dependents and since all of us potentially suffer from "it," we are all forced to seek their "expert" advice, treatment, and workshops in order to "get well," or opinion to determine if we are sick in the first place.

Co-dependency as a concept emerged during the late 70's from the therapy community. Melody Beattie suggests that the term emerged simultaneously from several treatment centers in Minnesota. (*Co-dependent No More*, p. 29.) With the concept of co-dependency the therapeutic community attempts to co-opt both the feminist movement and the Twelve Step movement represented by Alcoholics Anonymous.

Alcoholics Anonymous, one of the most successful grassroots movements of our time, was founded in 1935 by two upper-middle-class white males, Bill Wilson and Dr. Robert Smith. It has literally saved the lives of thousands of men and women who would have otherwise died because of their drinking. Much is quite admirable about Alcoholics Anonymous, its offshoot organizations, and the Twelve Steps themselves. However, feminists and lesbians need to examine the roots of AA, et. al. We must also make distinctions between those groups that are under the AA umbrella (such as Al-Anon and Alateen) and are therefore governed by AA's Traditions and those that are not (such as Co-dependents Anonymous). Alcoholics Anonymous attempts to combine the medical knowledge of alcoholism with the pragmatism of William James ("Keep on coming back! It works!") and a form of Christian fundamentalism which is peculiarly American ("Let Go. Let God.")* The founders of AA believed in scaring the alcoholic by hitting "him" (in its early days AA did not admit women) with the medical facts about *his* "disease." Only when the alcoholic had sunk as low as possible, would *he* be amenable to treatment. Underlying the Twelve Step approach to the treatment of alcoholism is a conversion experience, being "born again," after one hit rock bottom. This can involve either a religious experience, as traditionally understood (belief in a patriarchal God) or can also mean an immersion in a community (the community of those recovering) or any number of possibilities in-between. AA historian, Ernest Kurtz, describes it as a, *"salvation* attained through a *conversion,* the precondition of which was the act of *surrender."* (Ernest Kurtz, *Not-God: A History of Alcoholics Anonymous,* p.182.) Critical to this conversion is not only an understanding of the Twelve Steps but also its grounding in the Twelve Traditions of Alcoholics Anonymous.

The Twelve Traditions are the governing principles of AA, they express many of the principles of first century Christian anarchism on which AA was based. They were designed to keep AA a grassroots, member-focused organization. Not only do the Traditions distance the organization from experts and from treatment approaches, but they also address the forms of self-aggrandizement and endorsement that are seen at the core of alcoholic behavior. They fully explain the Anonymous part of the

AA name. Twelve Step groups not under the AA umbrella are not bound by the Traditions. And it is precisely these traditions, to my mind the most positive features of AA, that are getting lost in the Recovery Industry.

It does not take a particularly astute observer of American life to realize how big the Recovery Industry is, judging from its numerous publications, workshops, treatment centers, best-selling books, etc. Its big names are major media stars: their words and ideas come at us from all directions. We are literally bombarded with their messages. And what they have done to the Twelve Step movement is most interesting indeed.

Recently a friend and I visited one of the largest treatment centers for women in southern Minnesota, we were both suitably impressed by the presentation. It was slick, the brochures impeccable, the grounds immaculate, and of course, the facility spacious and inviting (providing the patient was not on medicaid or public assistance, they treat only those with adequate insurance or cash). Critical to the center's treatment program is its inpatient Twelve Step groups. In fact, one of the therapists mentioned that because the center was not given enough time and money from insurance companies to provide truly adequate de-tox (e.g., for some addicted to prescription medications it could take months to bring them safely off the drug but most insurance plans pay only for no more than thirty days in-hospital treatment), groups (along with individual counseling) were the primary treatment. When I questioned the head psychiatrist about requiring patients to attend Twelve Step meetings, since required attendance is antithetical to AA practice, she replied, "Yes, that is a problem," and changed the subject. Questions about how the therapists (many of whom were neither recovering substance abusers nor self-identified co-dependents) could participate in recovery groups were met with the same gracious stonewall of polite avoidance. The presence of therapists as experts, qualified only by training and not by experience, in such meetings, and the compulsory attendance contradict the Traditions and practices of AA (e.g., therapists cannot remain anonymous in group meetings when they see the same clients in individual counseling). Further, this takes place, not in a grassroots setting accessible to all who need help, but in an expensive facility which is enormously profitable. One of the therapists frankly admitted that she had never even heard of the Twelve Traditions. She stated that the only reason the hospital had started the women's unit was because they knew it would make money. And lots of money it makes.

Co-dependency and its treatment lie at the heart of how the Recovery Industry seeks to manipulate and control women. Ostensibly the concept arises out of the Al-Anon movement, the group started by Lois Wilson and Anne Smith that was initially composed of wives of men in AA. Al-Anon was founded on the concept that those who lived with alcoholics were affected by alcohol in some of the same ways as the alcoholic. However, at no time during its founding or since, was it held that alcohol affected the spouse physically, as it affected the alcoholic. The behaviors of the alcoholic were the primary issues. Enabling behaviors of the significant other were not seen as a disease or an addiction, but as a stumbling block to the alcoholic's recovery. The current concept of co-dependency varies from this quite significantly.

First, and perhaps most important, co-dependency is seen as a disease, a progressive, definable disease, with an inevitable outcome, and which, if not treated will result in death. Schaef even argues that, left untreated, the co-dependent will likely die before the addict. (*Co-Dependence*, p. 6.) There is the implication that co-dependency may actually be a more serious condition than addiction to a substance. Co-dependency is characterized as an addiction that produces significant physical symptoms, which some experts believe occur before the co-dependent becomes involved with the substance abuser. As the Friels argue, "[W]e are stating clearly that we do not believe that people become co-dependent because they have been living with an addict. Rather we are stating that they are in a relationship with an addict *because* they are co-dependent." (*Adult Children*, p.157.) The difference between the stance taken by the Recovery Industry and that of Al-Anon is huge. People in Al-Anon, are encouraged to create a healthy distance between themselves and the behaviors of the alcoholic, but they are not viewed as being ill prior to the relationship. Feminists and others who have critiqued Al-Anon say it too often focuses only on the alcoholic and not enough on the significant other.

Second, almost all the behaviors ascribed to co-dependents are traditionally seen as feminine behaviors in this society. How the experts on co-dependency handle this, I believe, underlies much of how the co-dependent movement itself seeks to de-politicize feminism. Melody Beattie, for example, describes the characteristics of co-dependent behavior as low self-worth, repression, obsession, controlling, denial, dependency, poor communication, weak boundaries, lack of trust, anger, and sex problems. (*Co-dependent No More*, pp. 35–47.) These behaviors form feminine identity in American culture. Growing up female means identifying ourselves as weaker, less-worthy, dependent on men, etc., in order to survive. If we resist these messages, we are penalized for our anger and lack of trust.

Because co-dependency so accurately describes what many of us experience in our lives, we blame ourselves for the behavior. In an introductory women's studies class I taught, a student talked about how much she learned from the book *Women Who Love Too Much* and how it helped her understand her feelings about her ex-husband, who battered her. I made an off-handed comment that perhaps the best book would not be on women who love too much but one on men who hit too much. In her journal, she wrote about how my comment "blew her away;" she never thought she could hold him responsible for his own behavior. Co-dependency, thus teaches us that femininity is a pathology, and we blame ourselves for self-destructive feminine behavior, letting men evade any real responsibility for their violent and abusive behavior. The Friels state, "If some one tried to make love to me when I said I didn't want to, this would be an individual boundary invasion." (*Adult Children*, p. 58.) I would call that rape. (They consider incest the result of "weak intergenerational boundaries," p. 60.) Redefining rape as weak boundaries on the part of both victim and perpetrator blames the victim.

Critical to co-dependency analysis is the view that you cannot control the behavior of the addicted person. Although obviously it is true that no one can control anyone else's behavior, the extension of the argument is that a co-dependent cannot even criticize the behavior of the addicted person rather they are taught to focus exclusively on their own health. Anne Wilson Schaef states that responsibility should no longer imply any kind of obligation, but rather should only be seen as the ability to respond, to explain one's own behavior. She writes, "responsibility is the *ability to respond.* In the Addictive System responsibility involves *accountability and blame.*" (*When Society Becomes an Addict,* p. 42.) In this view, women's responsibility is to look at their own behavior: they can neither blame nor hold men accountable for violent and abusive behavior. Sexism, and by extension, any system of oppression, becomes only the problem of the victim; the perpetrator can no longer be held responsible.

Third, the therapy community de-politicizes feminism by insisting that the root cause of co-dependent behavior is being raised in a dysfunctional family. The concept of dysfunctional family is based on the idea that it is possible to have a warm, loving, close nuclear family within the context of racist, capitalist, heteropatriarchy. It betrays the fundamental feminist insight that the patriarchal family itself is the primary institution in the oppression of women. As Simone de Beauvoir states, "Since the oppression of women has its cause in the will to perpetuate the family and to keep the patrimony intact, woman escapes complete dependency to the degree in which she escapes from the family." (*The Second Sex,* p. 82.) Not only does the concept of dysfunctional family ignore the sexism and heterosexism involved in the reality of family life, but it also renders invisible the racism and classism inevitably underlying the "warm, loving, family" conceived of by family therapists and psychologists. It creates, in Audre Lorde's term, a "mythical norm:" a standard by which we all judge ourselves to be wanting. ("Age, Race, Class and Sex: Women Redefining Difference," in *Sister Outsider,* p. 116.) The fantasy of the "functional" family imagines a well-employed father, and perhaps now, an equally well-employed mother, and children, able-bodied and well-adapted to society's definition of their race, class and gender. Families, such as the single-parent African-American family or gay and lesbian families, are seen as dysfunctional by definition and are therefore dismissed without any understanding of how those families may function far better for their members than the white, middle-class, "ideal" family. As Donna Langston has pointed out to me, many of the characteristics of co-dependent behavior, when seen in a working-class context, are actually critical aspects of survival skills. To learn to depend on others is what enables poor and working-class people to survive. To work only on healing the pain from having been raised in an "dysfunctional" family, holds out the hope that it is possible to achieve a fundamentally healthy family in this society without challenging the basic institutions of capitalism, heterosexism, sexism, racism, and classism that produced the patriarchal family in the first place. When we, as feminists, work on our issues of childhood abuse and neglect, part of the purpose is healing our own pain, but we also must seek to understand the political context that makes such abuse widespread, accepted, and an everyday occurrence, and fight collectively to stop it. The lack of any racial or class analysis in any of the literature on co-dependency underlines the white, middle-class nature of its roots in the therapy community and reinforces my belief that it represents an attempt to de-politicize feminism. Co-dependency adherents argue that we can get "well" without fundamentally altering the very institutions that created the situation in the first place. Beattie goes so far as to argue, that a preoccupation with injustice is a further proof of addiction. (*Co-dependent No More,* p.33.)

Why then is the concept of co-dependency so attractive to so many feminists and lesbians? A primary reason, in my view, is that co-dependency theory so accurately describes the reality of many of our lives. We feel powerless and unhappy. We live in a woman-hating culture where we pay a high price for resisting internalizing messages of feminine weakness and unworthiness. We are taught to depend on men for our survival. Co-dependency treatment offers hope that we can achieve our own private health. It allows those privileged by race, class, or sexual identity, among others to avoid looking at our privileged statuses. Co-dependency theory feeds on our complacency: we are no more responsible for behavior oppressive to others than any man is for his behavior to women. It teaches us that only we are responsible for our fate, that social activism and discontent are merely further symptoms of our "disease." When white women are confronted by women of color about their racism, they can now claim that racism is another symptom of their addiction, and their major task is to "get well." White people are not racist because they are sick, they are racist because they benefit from a system of racial superiority, they are privileged.

Co-dependency offers a relatively safe haven for those who can afford treatment. Its theory addresses many of the same concerns that we as feminists address, but without asking us to pay the high personal price of challenge and criticism. How many times have we felt judged wrongly or trashed in feminist groups without being given adequate space to explain? Co-dependency treatment offers a context of personal support that is all too often missing in our communities.

Co-dependency provides another way to resist the messages of femininity without fundamentally questioning the values of the racist, capitalist, heteropatriarchy we live with. We can get well, are encouraged to resist on a personal level, without ever really having to examine what made us "ill" in the first place. Therefore as we get "better," millions of other women will continue to be born into a culture that is misogynist to the core. Co-dependency theory offers a way to achieve a personal peace without examining the cost of that peace to others.

NOTES

*For a more detailed discussion of the history and roots of AA see my paper, "Twelve-Step Programs: A Lesbian-Feminist Analysis," in *NWSA Journal*, Summer 1990.

BIBLIOGRAPHY

Melody Beattie, *Co-dependent No More*. New York: Harper/Hazelden, 1987.

Simone de Beauvoir, *The Second Sex*. New York: Bantam, 1961.

John Friel and Linda Friel, *Adult Children: The Secrets of Dysfunctional Families*. Pompano Beach, Florida: Heath Communications, 1988.

Ernest Kurtz, *Not-God: A History of Alcoholics Anonymous*. Center City, Minn.: Hazelden, 1979.

Audre Lorde, *Sister Outsider*. Trumansburg, N.Y.: Crossing, 1984.

Anne Wilson Schaef, *Co-Dependence: Misunderstood—Mistreated*. Minneapolis: Winston,1986.

Anne Wilson Schaef, *When Society Becomes an Addict*. San Francisco: Harper & Row, 1987.

Mental Health Issues of Asian/Pacific Island Women

by Reiko Homma True

Although women's health and mental health issues are now beginning to attract national concerns in the United States, little support has been given so far to identify minority women's mental health needs, including those of Asian/Pacific Island (A/PI) women, or to provide funding for services that are culturally appropriate for their needs.

American society treats mental health issues with a general lack of understanding and reluctance. In the case of A/PI women, this is exacerbated by other factors:

- The relatively small number of people, and the perception that their needs are of lesser significance or nonexistent
- The wide geographic distribution and diverse nature of the A/PI population, which creates methodological problems for epidemiological needs assessment and other research investigations
- Perceptions of Asian Americans as a model minority with few problems, particularly related to mental illness or psychological distress

Diane L. Adams (ed.), *Health Issues for Women of Color (A Cultural Diversity Perspective)*, pp. 89–111. Copyright © 1995 by Sage Publications, Inc. Reprinted by permission of Sage Publications, Inc.

Until recently, A/PI leaders themselves were reluctant to focus on the possible existence of mental health issues in their communities. Their reluctance was partly due to the cultural stigma of mental illness, but they were also strongly influenced by their fear of attracting more negative publicity about their communities when they have already suffered persistent racism and hostility from the dominant groups for many years. However, as a result of a growing awareness about women's issues, an emerging group of A/PI women, from both professional and community groups, is beginning to speak out and identify the unique mental health needs and problems faced by their compatriots. The goal of this chapter is to review the information available to date and to help readers develop greater cultural understanding about the needs of A/PI women.

Demographic Profile

Although they are viewed by the U.S. public as a fairly homogenous group, the umbrella term *Asian and Pacific Islander women* covers a diverse group, representing as many as 27 Asian American and over 30 Pacific Islander groups, including Chinese, Filipinos, Japanese, Koreans, East Indians, and Southeast Asians, as well as Hawaiians, Samoans, and Guamanians. The 1990 U. S. census counted over 7.27 million Asians and Pacific Islanders, of whom 3.715 million (51% of the population) were women.

A/PI women are on average older than men, with a median age of 31.8 years, compared to 29.0 years for males, reflecting the generally longer life expectancy of females in the United States. Although data are not available by sex, it is important to note that 65.6% of all Asians are foreign born and 75.4% speak a language other than English at home. Although Pacific Islanders have a lower percentage of foreign born (12%), subgroup variations include 60.9% foreign-born Tongans and 77.9% foreign-born Melanesians (U.S. Bureau of the Census, 1992).

Although most A/PI women are married, Census Bureau (1992) data indicate that as of March 1991, 26% had never married, 8% were widowed, and 6% were divorced, compared to 28%, 2.5%, and 7% of white women, respectively. Whereas the percentage of all U.S. households headed by females was 16.5% in 1990, the figure for Asians was 12%. However, 26.2% of Cambodian households had female heads (U.S. Bureau of the Census, 1993). Overall educational achievement by A/PI women was high (74% high school graduates or higher, 31.8% with bachelor's degree or more), compared to the general U.S. population (74.8% and 17.6%), but there was great subgroup variability. Those from rural areas had the least education—the percentages of Hmong, Cambodians, and Laotians with a high school diploma or more were 19%, 25.3%, and 29.8% respectively (U.S. Bureau of the Census, 1993).

Most adult Asian (60%) and Pacific Islander (62.5%) women were in the labor force, compared to 56.8% of all total U.S. women, but the rates for some refugee groups were very low (19.9% for Hmong, 37.3% for Cambodians, and 49.5% for Laotians). The median earnings of A/PI women in 1990 was $21,320, higher than for white women ($20,050). However, the figure masks a great variability, with some women working as highly trained managers and professionals, and others earning marginal wages as sweatshop seamstresses or hotel maids. Of those below poverty level, 36% were in female-headed households (U.S. Bureau of the Census, 1993).

Historical Background

Because of laws restricting entry by women in the early years of Asian immigration, the number of women was small to start. However, as the immigration laws were revised to permit families to immigrate together and wives to rejoin their husbands, the number of Asian women immigrants increased rapidly, and they now outnumber men by 158,000.

Historically, the first group of Asian women to immigrate were the Chinese, who arrived nearly 150 years ago in the mid-1800s. Because of the prohibitive cost of the long journey from China and the traditional reluctance to send women overseas, only a small number of women were able to accompany their husbands at the early stage of Chinese immigration. Before more Chinese women had the chance to enter the United States, strong anti-Chinese sentiment erupted after Chinese male laborers began to achieve some level of economic success in various enterprises. The Chinese were quickly perceived as potential threats to the socioeconomic security of the white Americans, and exclusionary immigration laws were created, beginning in 1882, to severely limit further entry of Chinese, including women. In their place, a large number of Japanese males were brought in as cheap laborers to fill the back-breaking jobs no one else wanted. The Japanese government actively encouraged the immigration of women as wives of male laborers, a strategy for preventing problems endemic to bachelor societies, such as prostitution, violence, and gambling. Although the Japanese immigrants were subsequently perceived as a new threat, a significant number of Japanese women settled in the United States with their husbands before the restrictions were extended to them through the National Origins Act in 1924 (Nakano, 1990).

The groups that followed the Chinese and Japanese were Korean and Filipino laborers. However, in the early 1900s, their number was relatively small, and the number of women who came with their husbands was small until recently (Takaki, 1989).

In 1965, the immigration laws were significantly liberalized to permit increased numbers of immigrants from Asian countries and to allow the reunion of family members, including wives who had been separated from their husbands for many years. This made it possible for a large number of Chinese, Filipino, and Korean women to bring their families and rejoin husbands (Lee, 1985; Navarro, 1976; Yung 1986).

After the end of the Vietnam War in 1975, a large wave of Southeast Asian refugee women were forced to flee their countries, and many of them resettled in the United States with their families (Tien, 1994). More recently, immigration from the Indian subcontinent is also increasing (Jayakar, 1994).

Because of these historical differences, there are important diversities among the A/PI women. For example, although there are significant numbers of fourth- or fifth-generation, U.S.-born Japanese- and Chinese-American women, at least 63% of Asian Americans are foreign born. The differences among subgroups are dramatic: Nearly 80% of Vietnamese, Laotians, and Cambodians are foreign born, compared to only 32% of Japanese Americans (U.S. Bureau of the Census, 1993).

Extent and Nature of Mental Health Problems

Prevalence Data. In the absence of comprehensive epidemiological data on the mental health status of Asians and Pacific Islanders in the United States, regardless of gender, information specific to A/PI women is virtually nonexistent. Most policymakers did not support the effort to make this information a priority for investigation, tending to assume that A/PI people had few mental health problems, and that families and community would prefer to take care of those who did.

It may be helpful to review some findings from epidemiological studies conducted in Asia, mainly in Japan, China, and Taiwan. Some studies were modeled after the epidemiological studies attempted in the United States in the 1950s and 1960s, designed to be quite extensive for certain defined geographic regions. The findings from these studies were cross-tabulated by gender and provide information concerning the extent or prevalence of mental health problems among women in the area. To some extent, these data may be applicable to A/PI women in the United States. For example, Lin, Rin, Yeh, Hsu, and Chu (1969) investigated the prevalence of various cate-

gories of mental illness in three communities in Taiwan in 1963 and found an overall rate for all mental disorders for men and women to be 16.1 and 18.3 per 1,000, respectively. Although the difference in overall rates for the sexes was not statistically significant, there were significant differences within subcategories: high rates of mental deficiency and psychopathic personality for males; high rates of psychoneuroses for women, particularly in middle to older age. Also of note was a significantly higher incidence of schizophrenia among the 51 to 60 (7.1) and 61 to 70-year-old women (7.8) than among men in the same age groups (2.5 and 2.0 respectively). The overall findings seem to correspond to those of the epidemiological studies in the United States, in which women had higher rates of affective disorders, panic/obsessive-compulsive disorders, somatization, and phobias, apparently subsumed under the diagnosis of psychoneuroses in Lin et al.'s investigation. The higher rate of antisocial personality disorder for men in U.S. studies also corresponds with the Taiwan study's psychopathic personality (Robbins, Locke, & Regier, 1991).

In the absence of national data on A/PI women, it is helpful to consider the implications of some of the regional data about their mental health. For example, Ying (1988) attempted to explore the level of depressive symptomatology among San Francisco-based Chinese Americans through a telephone survey using the Center for Epidemiological Studies-Depression Scale (CES-D). Among the 360 subjects who agreed to be interviewed, 182 were women. Their mean depression score was 12.83, somewhat higher than the mean score of 10.25 for men. The score was also considerably higher than the mean score (ranging from 7.94 to 9.25) for a predominantly white sample in a study by Radloff (1977). Among the general population, a CES-D mean of 16 and above was used to indicate clinical depression. In the sample reported by Radloff for the white population, 19% scored 16 or above, whereas 24% of the Ying's (1988) combined male and female sample scored 16 or above. Ying also found that those who belonged to a lower socioeconomic level (as measured by education and occupation) scored as significantly more depressed than those who were at higher socioeconomic levels.

In a study in Chicago, Hurh and Kim (1990) conducted diagnostic interviews with 622 Korean immigrants (20 years and older) to explore the extent of mental health problems among more recent immigrants, using the CES-D scale, the Health Opinion Survey (HOS), and the Memorial University of Newfoundland Scale of Happiness (MUNSH). Their findings indicated that those who were married, highly educated, and currently employed in a high-status occupation indicated better subjective mental health than others. They also found significant gender differences in that the correlates for mental health for males were a set of work-related variables, whereas family life satisfaction and several ethnic attachment variables were moderately related for females.

Among Asian immigrant groups, it is generally agreed that Southeast Asian refugees face the greatest stress in adjusting to a new life in the United States. Many women suffered traumatic experiences and major losses of close family members before their immigration and frequently experience recurring symptoms of post-traumatic stress disorder (PTSD) (Rumbaut, 1985). In a statewide needs assessment study in California, Gong-Guy (1987) found that refugees from rural areas such as Cambodia and Laos, who had little previous exposure to modern urban living, were particularly ill-prepared for large, complex urban communities and were often experiencing significant psychiatric symptoms, such as high levels of depression, anxiety, and various psychosocial dysfunctions (difficulty performing tasks of daily living, school, or work). Among the refugee groups, Cambodians were exposed to the most atrocities and had to remain in camps much longer than others. Using the data from Gong-Guy's study (1987), Chung (1991) examined the gender and subgroup differences among the refugees—Cambodians, Laotians, and Vietnamese—and found that women in all three groups were more distressed than men. Among the three groups, she found that the Cambodians were the most distressed, followed by Laotians and Vietnamese.

The experience of Cambodian women refugees in Long Beach, California, reported by Rozee and Van Boemel (1989), provided a glimpse into the harrowing experience of war trauma and abuse suffered by older Cambodian women. The researchers conducted a series of supportive group services for refugee women who were diagnosed as functionally blind without organic basis, and therefore could not qualify for disability assistance. Among them, 90% reported losing 1 to 10 relatives and witnessing the massacre of family members. It was almost as if their traumas were so great that they did not wish to see anything; they suffered from severe depression, nightmares, sleep disturbances, and other symptoms associated with PTSD.

Another group of Asian Pacific Americans who were subjected to significant trauma were Japanese Americans, who were labeled enemy aliens in the United States during World War II and confined in concentration camps, euphemistically called "internment camps." The experience of being uprooted from their own homes, labeled enemy aliens even when they were born in the United States, deprived of their civil rights, and subjected to subhuman conditions was devastating to most Japanese Americans. Although most tried to rebuild their lives after the war, many carried lasting psychic scars, such as a pervasive sense of insecurity, de-

pression, and low self-esteem. In her interview of third-generation Japanese Americans, many of whom were women, Nagata (1991) identified how the psychological trauma, humiliation, and fears about future persecution were passed on to subsequent generations of Japanese Americans, even though they were not personally subjected to the trauma.

Utilization Data. Although mental health service utilization data are often accepted as a measure of the level of mental health problems present in communities, they provide little help in understanding the problems in the A/PI community; their record of service use has traditionally been very low (Snowden & Cheung, 1990; Sue & McKinney, 1975). For example, while the A/PI population constitutes 9.5% of the total in California (1990 Census), their statewide use of community mental health services during fiscal year 1989-1990 was 4.29% (2.32% for women; 1.97% for men) (California Department of Mental Health, 1992).

The San Francisco Community Mental Health Services showed 10.8% A/PI clients during the same period. Although this use figure represents a significant improvement over the past 15 years, made possible through the concerted effort of service providers to develop culturally sensitive, bilingual programs, it still represents underuse of mental health services by Asian Pacific citizens, who constitute 25% of the city's total population.

Some factors affecting low service use are thought to include

fear of establishment authorities;
absence of bilingual, culturally sensitive service
   providers;
cultural stigma among Asians about mental illness, creating family shame to acknowledge having psychiatric problems;
traditional reluctance to seek outside help;
cost of seeking help; and
institutional barriers such as geographic location or
   hours of operation.

Recognizing that the mental health problems in A/PI communities were much more extensive, community leaders and mental health professionals in key communities began to advocate for and develop programs that were more culturally responsive (President's Commission on Mental Health, 1978). For this reason, in some communities that made the effort to be more responsive, service use by A/PI clients has increased significantly (Sue, 1988). Although research about the gender differences among Asian American mental health clients is still limited, the usage data from Los Angeles and San Francisco counties in California provide some information.

As part of the extensive Los Angeles County Mental Health Service data analysis at the National Research Center on Asian American Mental Health, Fujino and Chung (1991) analyzed the gender differences in rates of psychiatric disorders among four ethnic groups of mental health clients. Besides confirming previous studies showing that Asian Americans tended to under use available services, the authors also found significant gender differences in rates of psychiatric disorders among the Asian American users of mental health services: Males (19.8%) significantly outnumbered females (10.4%) in the schizophrenic diagnosis, whereas females (21.2%) were more likely to suffer depressive disorder than males (15.1%). The rate for anxiety disorder among Asian males was higher than among females, 8.3% versus 7.4%. Although adjustment disorder was greater among female patients, the difference was not statistically significant.

Medical Service Utilization. In their review of U.S. women's mental health service use data, Mowbray and Benedek (1988) noted that a significantly greater number of women went to primary care physicians for help with their emotional problems. When Yu, Liu, & Wong (1987) reviewed the use data of a Chinatown health clinic in Boston, they also found that a significant number of Chinese women seen at the clinic were being treated for symptoms related to depression.

Additional support for this trend was also identified by Ying (1990), when she conducted a survey in San Francisco on the help-seeking attitude of Chinese women when dealing with potential psychiatric problems. Using a vignette depicting a major depression in a Chinese married woman, she interviewed a group of Chinese immigrant women at a San Francisco health center to explore the relationship between problem conceptualization and help-seeking behavior. When presented with the vignette, most women who conceptualized the problem as psychological did not suggest seeking professional psychological help; rather, they urged turning to family and friends or trying to resolve the problems themselves. On the other hand, those who conceptualized the problem as physical recommended seeking medical services.

Although data from other primary care providers serving Asian patients are not available, the impression of the community-based Asian health care providers is that many immigrant women, as well as men, are experiencing the strains of adapting to and surviving in a culturally divergent society and are expressing these strains as somatic complaints.

An explanation for this pattern is the significant cultural stigma attached to mental illness in most Asian countries; asking for help for somatic symptoms, however, is culturally acceptable. Compounding this cultural stigma, mental health services in Asian countries are designed to help the most seriously mentally ill. For this reason, those with moderate or less severe symptoms find it inconceivable to go to professionals for fear they might be considered "crazy." Under these circumstances, it will be important for mental health professionals to collaborate with primary care providers and provide consultation and training to improve their ability to deal with psychosomatic problems and to know when to make appropriate referrals to mental health providers.

Substance Abuse Problems. Although data on drug and alcohol abuse for the A/PI group are extremely limited, preliminary information includes data on gender differences. Several studies on the alcohol consumption patterns among Chinese, Japanese, Korean, Filipino, and Vietnamese Americans (Chi, Lubben, & Kitano, 1989; Padilla, Sung, & Nam, 1993) found that Asian American women were generally moderate or nondrinkers. Their low rate of drinking behavior is thought to be based on the strong cultural sanction in most Asian cultures against drinking by women. However, the pattern may be changing. For example, research conducted in Japan (Kono, Saito, Shimada, & Nakagawa, 1977) indicated a dramatic increase in the rate of women who drink, from 13% in 1954 to 53% in 1964.

Chi et al.'s (1989) survey of Asian Americans in the Los Angeles area revealed that Japanese women had the highest rate of heavy drinkers, 11.7%, and the lowest rate of abstainers, 33.4%; comparable rates for Chinese were 0% and 68.8%, for Koreans, .8% and 81.6%, and for Filipinos, 3.5% and 80.0%. Some contributing factors for these changes may be the impact of social changes, including blurring of sex roles, greater freedom for women, greater prosperity, and increased psychosocial stresses. The impact of acculturation is another factor to be considered for those living in the United States, as it was identified as the key factor for the changes in drinking patterns among Mexican American women (Markides, Ray, Stroup-Bebham, & Trevino, 1990).

The information on the use or abuse of drugs among A/PI women is even more limited, with conflicting findings. For example, Nakagawa and Watanabe (1973) interviewed Asian junior and senior high school students in Seattle and found that the use of hard drugs, excluding marijuana and alcohol, was considerable: 17% of female and 12% of male students were identified as users. Although gender differences were not cited, the differences between ethnic groups were significant in that 45% of the Filipino, 29% of the Japanese, and 22% of the Chinese students had some experience with hard drugs, including amphetamines, barbiturates, psychedelics, cocaine, and heroin (in descending order of frequency of use). However, more recent data from national surveys of high school seniors between 1976 and 1989 (Backman et al., 1991) indicate that the rates for Asian American females were significantly lower than those for white or Native American females for use of cigarettes, alcohol, and illicit drugs. Because information about country of origin or length of stay in the United States was not available, the question remains if acculturation is a factor in the increased rates of substance use for Asian American females.

Domestic Violence

Although data available on the extent of domestic violence against A/PI women are limited, many social service and women's shelter providers are concerned about the increasing incidence of abuse in A/PI communities in various parts of the country (Ho, 1990; Rimonte, 1989). They are particularly concerned about a possibly greater risk among more recently arrived A/PI immigrant and refugee women. A major contributing factor appears to be the significant level of frustration experienced by their male counterparts as they try unsuccessfully to establish themselves in the new country and find ways of supporting their families. In spite of their desire and effort, many of them have difficulty with English and do not have job skills that are transferrable and marketable in the United States.

On the other hand, women can find many jobs, although they are poorly paid, in domestic or other unskilled work; U.S.-born women are not willing to accept such work. When A/PI husbands are unable to find work or unable to support their families with marginal income, many women who did not work before immigration choose to get jobs to help support the family. In such situations, their husbands often feel humiliated, as if their masculinity or their authority as the patriarchal family head were damaged by having to rely on wives to support their families. At the same time, some wives become more assertive, feeling that with their greater role in supporting the family, they can expect to share decision-making authority on family matters. These changes in marital roles and relationship dynamics could often lead to considerable marital strife. Unaccustomed to such changes, some husbands take out their sense of powerlessness, rage, and frustration by abusing their wives, or they find escape in use of alcohol or drugs, which often leads to aggression against wives or children (Masaki, 1992; Rimonte, 1989).

Many abused A/PI women are reluctant to seek outside help, partly because of feelings of shame, fear of greater reprisals from abusers, and a sense of powerlessness. When they finally seek outside help, their plights are often ignored by service providers who do not understand the severity of the situation and are not sympathetic. Most appalling is when those with authority to intervene fail to do so and justify their nonaction by citing the need to respect Asian cultural tradition, which they believe condones oppression and violence against women. The case of a New York probation officer who recommended probation for a Chinese immigrant husband who murdered his wife, and the judge who accepted his recommendation, is the most galling instance of a failing system that ignores the plight of A/PI women (Hurtado, 1989). The argument used to justify such a light sentence for a heinous crime was based on their judgment that such an act was culturally acceptable in the family's native country (China) and that the husband was unlikely to commit other violent acts in the future (Hurtado, 1989). However, China has already made significant changes in recent years to protect the rights of women, establishing appropriate standards for punishment. Although acts of physical violence against women and wives still occur with some frequency and are overlooked in a few Asian countries, women advocates are increasingly challenging the oppressive conditions in their countries (Sunda, 1994). Regardless of the conditions in Asia, A/PI women in the United States should be accorded the same protections as other American women and not be subjected to the abusive treatment that may still exist in other countries.

Suicides

Although suicide rates for combined age categories for A/PI Americans is low, some of the age and ethnicity subgroups are at higher risk than others, data indicate. For example, Yu and Liu (1986) analyzed the existing suicide data on Chinese and Japanese Americans and found that the rate for Chinese women increased dramatically beginning at ages 45 to 54; that rate was 15.52 per 100,000, increasing to 44.32 at ages 75 to 84 and 49.93 at ages 85 and over. In contrast, the rates for white women successively declined across the same age categories, beginning with a high of 11.18 at ages 45 to 54 (see Table 1).

Some of the stress factors that may be increasing suicide among elderly A/PI women include death of spouses whom they depended on for dealing with the English-speaking world, economic hardships, deteriorating health, decreasing support from their adult children, and the breakdown of extended family support networks.

Table 1 Whites, Chinese, and Japanese: Average Annual Death Rates for Suicide, United States, 1980

| | Deaths per 100,000 Population | | | | | |
| Age Group | White | | Chinese | | Hispanics | |
	Male	Female	Male	Female	Male	Female
All ages, crude	20.57	6.43	8.26	8.28	12.57	6.14
Age-adjusted	19.41	6.20	7.93	8.08	11.08	5.00
5–14 years	0.75	0.28		0.61	1.69	
15–24 years	21.91	5.00	8.07	4.65	14.09	4.52
25–34 years	26.99	7.98	8.59	5.72	16.72	7.82
35–44 years	24.27	9.93	8.94	9.09	12.68	6.39
45–54 years	24.55	11.18	10.77	13.89	9.81	8.22
55–64 years	26.52	9.59	9.37	15.52	12.38	7.78
65–74 years	32.41	7.45	25.85	22.61	11.17	2.17
75–84 years	46.18	6.03	21.82	44.32	39.56	15.75
85 years +	53.28	4.92	64.10	49.93	139.76	19.50

SOURCE: U.S. Department of Health and Human Services (1986, p. 26).
NOTE: In calculating age-specific death rates, the numerator consisted of 1979-1981 cumulative number of deaths and the denominator was based on the total enumerated in the 1981 U.S. census.

Although traditional A/PI cultures place a strong value on treating elders with respect and care, immigrant families are separated from the extended family network and have limited resources to care for aging parents. Some families have to live and work in areas far away from their parents so that it is not possible for them to provide day-to-day support.

The number of A/PI people over 65 years of age is projected to increase dramatically, from 450,000 to 2.1 million by 2020, representing a 355% increase (Ong & Hee, 1992), and A/PI women, like women in general, tend to live longer than men. Thus, they will likely continue to experience significant stresses from poverty, isolation, lack of support, and declining health and be at risk for suicide.

Psychosocial Stressors

Many sources of stress contribute to the development of mental health problems for A/PI women. Foremost among these are those related to immigration and acculturation. When they arrive in the United States, many immigrant women are confronted by an unfamiliar language, lifestyle changes, and day-to-day survival issues. Although many had to deal with survival issues in their old country, they were able to rely on a supportive extended family and community network for help; now

they can no longer rely on this help. Although some are able to replace the lost support with new neighbors, many are unable to create another network, perhaps due to work or their traditional reluctance to seek help beyond the family kinship network (Bradshaw, 1994; True, 1991).

Immigrant women also experience significant conflict with their children, who become more rapidly acculturated and demand greater independence and freedom in making their own choices about friends, dating, sexuality, field of study, and occupation. Meanwhile, parents often become much more restrictive in an effort to shield children from what they perceive as negative influences in the outside community. Because of the old-world attitude toward women, parents are often more restrictive toward daughters, believing they need to work hard to protect them against "loose morals" so that they will not fall prey to such social ills as promiscuity, teenage pregnancy, and substance abuse. However, this, in turn, makes daughters resentful and rebellious: They know American girls are given much greater freedom than they have. The conflict is often most keenly felt between mothers and daughters, because mothers are expected to socialize their daughters to be compliant with the proper expectations for Asian women, that is, to be faithful to their parents, to be submissive to their men, and so on. Such struggles are poignantly portrayed in Amy Tan's (1989) book, *The Joy Luck Club*, and have been described by mental health professionals working with adolescent girls who struggle not only with their parents at home but with a variety of adjustment problems at schools (Kope & Sack, 1987; Williams & Westermeyer, 1983).

Native-born Asian American women and others who are freer of the basic survival needs faced by immigrant women face different types of stresses. Frequently, they are subjected to the double jeopardy of discrimination in various social and work settings because of their status as members of racial and sexual minority groups. Whatever their own individual strengths and abilities, A/PI women are often treated according to stereotypes that have a negative impact on them. For example, because the media often portray them as sexually promiscuous and easily accommodating, in such roles as Suzy Wong and Miss Saigon, they may be perceived as sex objects to be exploited. They are also often considered to be subservient, passive handmaidens or weak, helpless, dependent women who will be good office helpers, but who do not possess much leadership quality in work settings and are not deserving of promotional opportunities. If an A/PI woman is somewhat aggressive, she is quickly typecast as a power-hungry, ruthless "dragon lady."

A/PI women also experience difficulties within their own families and communities, where they are often treated as inferior to men in status and are expected to sacrifice their own personal needs to the needs of their men. This is a legacy of traditional, patriarchal Asian cultures, where women were oppressed for centuries and were expected to be subservient to males in all stages of their lives. It is generally assumed that older Asian women, particularly those who were born abroad and have had limited exposure to the more liberal Western perception of women's status and roles, are more accepting or resigned to this cultural expectation (True, 1991).

However, many younger women are dissatisfied with the traditional expectations imposed on them as second-class citizens in their community. Increasing numbers of these women now have the opportunity to seek higher education and are exposed to the radically different treatment of women in the larger American community. During the period when university campuses throughout the United States were activated by the civil rights movement, many A/PI women students became involved in campus activities and had their consciousness raised by the feminist movement (Chow, 1989; Fujitomi & Wong, 1973). Although initially apprehensive about the potential conflict of feminist ideologies and minority concerns related to the experience of racism, many younger A/PI women are now convinced that they need to challenge the pervasive stereotypes and discriminatory treatment of their counterparts, and they are struggling to define their new identity so that they can take pride in their individuality and be accepted by others on equal terms.

Another recent trend emerging as potential source of strain for A/PI women is the increasing number of interethnic and interracial marriages. Although interracial marriages were strongly discouraged in the United States by both Asian and mainstream communities, as well as antimiscegenation legislation in the early years of Asian immigration, it is begrudgingly recognized now as a trend that will grow in the future (Kikumura & Kitano, 1973; Shinagawa & Pang, 1988). When young people are first swept away by romantic love, many do not realize the potential conflicts associated with the fact they grew up with divergent cultural backgrounds, values, beliefs, and so on, and are ill-prepared to deal with these differences (Ho, 1990). This is particularly true for partners with widely divergent backgrounds, such as those involving the so-called war brides from Asian countries where U.S. servicemen were stationed (Kim, 1977) or more recent "mail-order brides," who are being brought in through advertisements from Asian countries. Although U.S.-born A/PI women who outmarry do not suffer from language problems and share more cultural experiences with their partners than their foreign-born counterparts, they also find themselves confronted with relationship problems they did not anticipate, often rooted in cultural differences. In addition to the strains due to cultural differences, both Asian-born and U.S.-born women are often subjected to racist hostilities from others because of long-standing social prejudices against intermarriage.

The challenges faced by biracial or multiracial Asian women, the offspring of these marriages, are also complex. Those who are more vulnerable will face additional strains, but the multicultural environment can also provide rich opportunities for personal growth for those who are willing or able to embrace the challenges (Root, 1992).

Service Strategies

Most service providers working with A/PI women received their training in U.S. educational institutions and use a variety of psychotherapeutic approaches based on Western conceptual and theoretical orientations. These include a variety of psychodynamic approaches, cognitive therapy, behavioral therapy, and various family therapy approaches. Although more Westernized A/PI women can benefit from application of these treatment approaches, many service providers have learned that considerable adjustment is needed for services to many A/PI women (Bradshaw, 1994; Shon & Ja, 1982; Sue & Morishima, 1982; Tien, 1994; True, 1990).

Some key elements of effective service strategies for A/PI individuals in general also apply to A/PI women. They include the following:

Availability of bilingual, bicultural therapists for non-English speaking clients. It is critical that every effort be made to make bilingual and bicultural mental health providers available to non-English speaking clients. In their guidelines for working with ethnic, linguistic, and culturally diverse populations, the American Psychological Association (1991) acknowledges the need for competent interpreters or translators in the absence of bilingual, bicultural professionals, but it also cautions about the limitations and risk of reliance on interpreters.

Location of services within geographically accessible locations and flexible hours. Many immigrant women are not only fearful of approaching a mental health program because of the cultural stigma, but they have a great deal of difficulty traveling outside of their communities to an impersonal institution.

Collaboration with primary care clinics and providers to deal with the tendency to somatize psychological distress. As demonstrated by Yu et al. (1987) and Ying (1990), many A/PI women are more receptive to receiving help in the early stages of difficulties at primary care health service sites, and efforts should be made to collaborate with these service providers.

Multiservice approach. Discussing mental health services for work with minority women, Olmedo and Parron (1981) advocated linking psychotherapy with education, health, and social services on the basis that this approach can address not only the immediate mental health problems, but also the environmental, economic, and social factors that affect the mental health of minority women. Such an approach is particularly helpful with Asian American women, whose mental health problems are often directly related to adverse financial and social problems.

Involvement of families. Because A/PI groups are strongly family oriented, it is important, when working with individual clients, to consider the interrelationship between them and family members. Often, it is important to involve parents, spouses, and other family members in working with individual clients. When talking about the need for a family-focused approach, many of the Asian therapists also stress the need to respect the traditional patriarchal family structure (Shon & Ja, 1982). Particular attention is paid to the role of the husband and father as the key decision maker in the family. This is followed by the need to respect the parents as part of filial obligations. However, others are beginning to raise concerns about the need to balance family integrity and the degree to which a woman's own personal needs should be sacrificed. For Asian women, the personal cost of accepting the stressful family status quo could eventually lead to serious psychiatric difficulties. When domestic violence is involved, failure to intervene could lead to tragic consequences.

Sensitivity to women's unique needs and problems. Much has been written about sex role stereotyping and treatment bias of practicing U.S. therapists toward female patients. Many concerned female mental health professionals have pioneered the development of treatment approaches and advocated for the efficacy of gender matches for certain types of female patients (Mowbray & Benedek, 1988). Because of the pervasive sexism toward A/PI women, they are also often given inappropriate treatment that does not resolve the destructive status quo. In this respect, A/PI women therapists, who are more sensitized about the plight of their counterparts, can be helpful in advocating for their needs (True, 1990). A review of Los Angeles County data at the National Research Center for Asian American Mental Health (Sue, Fujino, Hu, Takeuchi, & Zane, 1991) also seems to suggest that gender match was helpful for Asian American clients in lowering dropout rates and achieving better treatment outcomes.

Conclusion and Recommendations

Despite a lack of specific data about the mental health status or service use of A/PI women, indications are that they experience considerable stress. Some factors affecting their mental health status were identified as stresses related to their pre- and postimmigration strains, acculturation conflict, marital and family conflict, and various experiences of racism and sexism. In spite of the problems they are experiencing, however, A/PI women are reluctant to seek professional mental health services. The factors influencing their service underuse were identified as partly due to the cultural stigma within their communities. Other factors include unavailability of bilingual, bicultural service providers, fears about institutional agencies, and the problem of accessibility due to geographic location and available hours. Creative approaches could reverse this situation.

As the number of A/PI women is growing rapidly, their problems are also expected to increase. It is critical that greater attention and support be provided to identify and address their mental health issues The following are some of the actions needed to improve this situation:

- Funding and technical support is needed for research focused on the mental health needs of Asian Pacific American women, for example epidemiology, psychosocial stressors, and risk factors, with provisions for identifying subgroup and regional differences.

- Aggressive recruitment and support should be provided for training of A/PI mental health professionals to develop expertise on A/PI women's issues, as well as linguistic, bicultural capacity.

- Both non-A/PI professionals and A/PI male professionals need training to increase their cultural sensitivity toward A/PI women's needs.

- There should be increased funding to develop linguistically and culturally appropriate services for A/PI women, including outreach and education.

- Provision of ancillary services, such as social services, child care, vocational training, housing, and homemaker services to high-risk populations is needed to reduce the level of psychosocial stresses that often lead to the development of psychiatric and psychological difficulties.

REFERENCES

American Psychological Association. (1991). *Guidelines for providers of psychological services to ethnic, linguistic, and culturally diverse population.* Washington, DC:Author

Backman, J. G., Wallace, J. M., O'Malley, P. M., Johnston, L. D., Kurth, C. L., & Neighbors, H. W. (1991). Racial/ethnic differences in smoking, drinking, and illicit drug use among American high school seniors, 1976-1989. *American Journal of Public Health, 81*(3), 372–377.

Bradshaw, C. K. (1994). Asian and Asian American women: Historical and political considerations in psychotherapy. In L. Comas-Diaz & B. Greene (Eds.), *Women of color: Integrating ethnic and gender identities in psychotherapy* (pp. 72–113). New York: Guilford.

California Department of Mental Health. (1992). *Local mental health programs: Unduplicated clients served fiscal year 1989–90.* Sacramento, CA: Author.

Chi, I., Lubben, J. D., & Kitano, H. H. L. (1989). Differences in drinking behavior among three Asian American groups. *Journal of Studies on Alcohol, 50*(1), 15–23

Chow, E. N.-L. (1989). The feminist movement: Where are all the Asian American women. In Asian Women United of California (Ed.), *Making waves: An anthology of writings by and about Asian-American women* (pp. 362–377). Boston: Beacon Press.

Chung, R. C. (1991, August). *Predictors of distress among Southeast Asian refugees: Group and gender differences.* Paper presented at Asian American Psychological Association Conference, San Francisco.

Fujino, D. C., & Chung, R. C. (1991, August). *Asian American mental health: An examination of gender issues.* Paper presented at the annual convention of Asian American Psychological Association, San Francisco.

Fujitomi I., & Wong, D. (1973). The new Asian American women. in S. Sue & N. Wagner (Eds.), *Asian Americans: Psychological perspectives.* (pp. 252–263). Palo Alto, CA: Science and Behavior Books.

Gong-Guy, E. (1987). *The California Southeast Asian mental health needs assessment.* Oakland, CA: Asian Community Mental Health Services.

Ho, C. (1990). An analysis of domestic violence in Asian American communities. *Women and Therapy, 9*(1–2), 129–150.

Hurh, W. M., & Kim, K. C. (1990). Correlates of Korean immigrants' mental health. *Journal of Nervous and Mental Disorder, 178*(11), 703–711.

Hurtado, P. (1989, April 4). Killer's sentence defended: "He's not a loose cannon." *Newsday,* pp. 3, 25.

Jayakar, K. (1994). Women of the Indian subcontinent. In L Comas-Diaz & B. Greene (Eds.), *Women of color: Integrating ethnic and gender identities in psychotherapy* (pp. 161–184). New York: Guilford.

Kikumura, A., & Kitano, H. (1973). Interracial marriage: A picture of the Japanese Americans. *Journal of Social Issues, 29*(2), 67–81.

Kim, B.-L C. (1977). Asian wives of US. servicemen: Women in shadows. *Amerasia, 4,* 91–115.

Kono, II., Saito, S., Shimada, K., & Nakagawa, J. (1977). *Drinking habits of the Japanese,* Tokyo. Leisure Development Center.

Kope, T. M., & Sack, W. H. (1987). Anorexia nervosa in Southeast Asian refugees: A report on three cases. *Journal of American Academy of Child and Adolescent Psychiatry, 26*(5), 794–797.

Lee, I. S. (Ed.). (1985). *Korean American Women: Toward self-realization.* Mansfield, OH: Association of Korean Christian Scholars in Northern America.

Lin, T. Y., Rin, H., Yeh, E., Hsu, C., & Chu, H. (1969). Mental disorder in Taiwan, fifteen years later: A preliminary report. In W. Caudill & T. Y. Liu (Eds.), *Mental health research in Asia and the Pacific* (pp. 66–91). Honolulu: East-West Press.

Markides K., Ray, L., Stroup-Bebham, C., & Trevino, F. (1990). Acculturation and alcohol consumption in the Mexican American population of the Southwestern United States: Findings from HHANES, 1982–84. *American Journal of Public Health, 80,* 42–46.

Masaki, B. (1992). Shattered myths: Battered women in the A/PI community. *Focus, 3,* 1, 3.

Mowbray, C. T., & Benedek, E. P. (1988). *Women's mental health research agenda. Services and treatment of mental disorders in women* (Women's Mental Health Occasional Paper Series). Rockville, MD: National Institute of Mental Health.

Nagata, D. (1991). Transgenerational impact of the Japanese-American internment: Clinical issues in working with children of former internees. *Psychotherapy, 28(1),* 121–128.

Nakagawa, B., & Watanabe, R. (1973). *A study of the use of drugs among Asian American youths of Seattle.* Seattle: Demonstration Project for Asian Americans.

Nakano, M. (1990). *Japanese American women: Three generations 1890–1990.* Berkeley: MINA Press.

Navarro, J. (1976). Immigration of Filipino women to America. In *Asian American women* (pp. 18–22). Stanford, CA: Asian American Studies, Stanford University.

Olmedo, E. L., & Parron, D. L. (1981). Mental health of minority women: Some special issues. *Professional Psychology, 12*(1), 103–111.

Ong, P., & Hee, S. J. (1992). The growth of the Asian Pacific American population: Twenty million in 2020. In LEAP Asian Pacific American Public Policy Institute and UCLA Asian American Studies Center (Eds.), *The state of Asian Pacific America: Policy Issues to the year 2020* (pp. 11–24). Los Angeles: LEAP Asian Pacific American Public Policy Institute and UCLA Asian American Studies Center.

Padilla, A., Sung, H., & Nam, T. V. (1993, Winter). Attitudes toward alcohol and drinking practices in two Vietnamese samples in Santa Clara County. *Horizons of Vietnamese Thought and Experience, 2*(1), 53–71.

President's Commission on Mental Health. (1978). *Report to the president: Volume 4.* Washington, DC: Government Printing Office.

Radloff, L. S. (1977). The CES-D scale: A self-report depression scale for research in the general population. *Applied Psychological Measurement, 1,* 385–401.

Rimonte, N. (1989). Domestic violence among Pacific Asians. In Asian Women United of California (Ed.), *Making waves: An anthology of writings by and about Asian American women* (pp. 327–336). Boston: Beacon Press.

Robbins, L. N., Locke, B., & Regier, D. A. (1991). An overview of psychiatric disorders in America. In L. N. Robbins & D. A. Regier (Eds.), *Psychiatric disorders in America: The Epidemiologic Catchment Area study* (p. 350). New York Free Press.

Rozee, P. D., & Van Boemel, G. (1989). The psychological effects of war trauma and abuse on older Cambodian refugee women. *Women and Therapy, 8*(4), 23–49.

Rumbaut, R. G. (1985). Mental health and the refugee experience: A comparative study of Southeast Asian refugees. In T. C. Owan (Ed.), *Southeast Asian mental health: Treatment, prevention, services, training, and research* (pp. 433–486). Washington, DC: National Institute of Mental Health.

Shinagawa, L. H., & Pang, G. Y. (1988). Intraethnic, interethnic, and interracial marriages among Asian Americans in California. *Berkeley Journal of Sociology, 33,* 95–114.

Shon, S. P., & Ja, D. Y. (1982). Asian families. In M. McGodrick, J. K. Pearce, & J. Giordano (Eds.), *Ethnicity and family therapy* (pp. 208–228). New York: Guilford.

Snowden, L. R., & Cheung, F. K. (1990). Use of inpatient mental health services by members of ethnic minority groups. *American Psychologist, 45,* 347–355.

Sue, S. (1988). Psychotherapeutic services for ethnic minorities: Two decades of research findings. *American Psychologist, 43,* 301–308.

Sue, S., Fujino, D. C., Hu, L., Takeuchi, D. T., & Zane, N. W. S. (1991). Community mental health services for ethnic minority groups: A test of the cultural responsiveness hypothesis. *Journal of Clinical and Consulting Psychology, 59*(4), 533–540.

Sue, S., & McKinney, H. (1975). Asian Americans in the community mental health care system. *American Journal of Orthopsychiatry, 45,* 11–18.

Sue, S., & Morishima, J. K. (1982). *The mental health of Asian Americans.* San Francisco: Jossey-Bass.

Sunda, M. (1994). India: Rethinking sex crimes. *Ms., 4,* 5, 20.

Takaki; R. (1989). *Strangers from a different shore: History of Asian Americans.* Boston: Little, Brown.

Tan, A. (1989). *The joy luck club.* New York Ballantine.

Tien, L. (1994). Southeast Asian American refugee women. In L. Comas-Diaz & B. Greene (Eds.), *Women of color: Integrating ethnic and gender identities in psychotherapy* (pp. 479–504). New York: Guilford.

True, R. H. (1990). Psychotherapeutic issues with Asian American women. *Sex Roles, 22*(7/8), 477–486.

True, R. H. (1991, August). *Psychosocial impact of immigration on Asian women.* Paper presented at the annual convention of American Psychological Association, San Francisco.

U.S. Bureau of the Census. (1992, August). The Asian and Pacific Islander population in the United States: March 1991 and 1990. In *Current population reports* (pp.20–459). Washington, DC: Government Printing Office.

US. Bureau of the Census. (1993). *We, the American . . . Asians.* Washington, DC: Government Printing Office.

U.S. Department of Health and Human Services (1986). *Report of the Secretary's Task Force on Black and Minority Health Vol. 5. Homicide, suicide, and unintentional injuries.* Washington, DC: Author.

Williams, C. L., & Westermeyer, J. (1983). Psychiatric problems among adolescent Southeast Asian refugees. *Journal of Nervous and Mental Disease, 171*(2), 79–85.

Ying, Y. W. (1988). Depressive symptomatology among Chinese-American as measured by the CES-D. *Journal of Clinical Psychology,44*(5), 739–746.

Ying, Y. W. (1990). Explanatory models of major depression and implications for help-seeking among immigrant Chinese-American women. *Culture, Medicine, and Psychiatry, 14,* 393–408.

Yu, E. S. H., & Liu, W. T. (1986). Whites, Chinese, and Japanese: Average annual death rates for suicide, United States, 1980. In *Report of the Secretary's Task Force on Black and Minority Health Vol. 5. Homicide, suicide, and unintentional injuries* (p. 26). Washington, DC: U.S. Department of Health and Human Services.

Yu, E. S. H., Liu, W. T., & Wong S. C. (1987). Measurement of depression in a Chinatown health clinic. In W. T. Liu (Ed.), *A decade review of mental health research, training, and services* (pp. 95–100). Chicago: Pacific/Asian American Mental Health Research Center, University of Illinois at Chicago.

Yung, J. (1986). *Chinese women of America: A pictorial history.* Seattle: University of Washington Press.

WORKSHEET—CHAPTER 4

Mental Health

1. Stress is defined as the non-specific response of the body to demands made on it. These demands can be physical or emotional. The response is non-specific in the sense that, no matter whether the stressor (cause of stress) is seemingly negative or positive, the body responds the same way physiologically. On scales that measure stress of life-events, marriage, graduation, and promotion get high stress ratings, along with break-up of a relationship, death in the family, and a jail sentence. If we cannot find ways to manage stress, there can be many possible long term health consequences, such as high blood pressure, high cholesterol (both of which increase the risk of heart disease), at least in men lowered resistance to infectious diseases, more migraines if prone to them, various disturbances of the digestive system (including ulcers and colitis), and sleep problems.

    a. List five stressors in your life.
        1.
        2.
        3.
        4.
        5.

    b. List five ways you cope with or manage stress.
        1.

        2.

        3.

        4.

        5.

    c. If any of the answers in b. have potential negative consequences, identify an alternative positive approach. For example, some people deal with stress by shopping, but a shopping spree can create more stress when the bills have to be paid. Others may turn to alcohol or binge eating. What are "healthy" alternatives to these strategies?

    d. Are there differences in the stressors women and men in this society may experience? Are there differences in the way women and men may choose to or be able to deal with stress? Compare your answer to Marian Murphy's statement, "it appears that men cope by externalising their frustrations."

2. Mental health is said to be related to maintaining a balance of work, play and love in our lives.

   a. How do these elements balance out in your life?

   b. Thinking through the roles that women and men play in this society, and by reading Lesley Doyal's "Hazards of Hearth and Home" article in chapter 3, think of whether there may be differences for women and men in trying to maintain a balance in their lives. If so, describe some specific differences:

3. What does it mean that mental health professionals give similar definitions for healthy adults and healthy men but describe healthy women as more submissive, less independent, more easily influenced, less competitive?

   a. Does this mean "the only mentally healthy women are the ones who adjust to a world where women are considered inferior?"

   b. Does questioning sexism mean that someone is mentally unhealthy?!

4. The article "Mental Health Issues of Asian/Pacific Islander Women" was supposed to stimulate you to think about specific issues for Asian/Pacific Islanders and to think more broadly about what factors affect mental health issues for different groups.

    a.   Identify three specific things you learned about mental health issues for particular groups of Asian/Pacific Islanders?

    h   Identify what you have leaned from this article which may help you think about mental health issues for a different group of women.

CHAPTER 5

Drugs, Alcohol, and Smoking

*T*he "war on drugs" in the United States has targeted illegal drugs, especially cocaine. However, if we examine which drugs are responsible for the majority of drug-related health problems, the focus changes to legal drugs. Use and abuse of alcohol, tobacco, and psychoactive prescription drugs are responsible for more deaths and disease than the well-publicized "crack epidemic." The first article in this section, "Addictive Behaviors" from *The Women's Health Data Book*, presents an excellent overview of the use of these common drugs by women and what is known about the ways in which women's physiology (hormones, menstrual cycle, total water content) must be considered to understand the effects of these drugs. Unfortunately, women are often under pressure to use legal drugs (medical prescriptions for psychoactive drugs; alcohol and tobacco advertising targeted at women) and then receive information on the dangers only when pregnant. The protection of the fetus is often presented as more important than the health of the woman herself.

In fact, Lorraine Greaves' thought-provoking work on theories of women's smoking and how societies benefit from it says that pregnancy is really the only time when society worries very much about women's smoking: "Indeed, as long as it [smoking] does not interfere with childbearing, childrearing and the maintenance of heterosexuality, women's smoking can be regarded as useful by advocates of the status quo to both the woman and her society." Greaves is careful not to paint women as victims, describing ways women use cigarettes as "shock absorbers" to "suck back anger" so that they can cope with their realities. Greaves thus identifies the role smoking plays in maintaining inequalities and silencing the need for social change: "When smoking reduces or erases women's demands, emotions or challenges, women can be seen as compliant and less troublesome. The true scope of women's feelings, particularly anger, remains invisible." It certainly is no accident that the tobacco industry has increasingly aimed its products and its advertising at women. "How Women are Targeted by the Tobacco Industry" examines this drug that has helped women reach parity with men in the areas of lung cancer and other respiratory diseases. The article examines the ways women, especially younger women, have been targeted by the tobacco industry as an important market, both in the United States and internationally. Advertising approaches and themes are described, and the article concludes with some specific suggested ground rules for women's magazines around tobacco advertising.

Greaves argues that women's alcohol use is much less acceptable than smoking because it interferes with women's role as mothers. However, it is tragic to read how little alcohol treatment programs have catered to the unique needs of women as mothers and people socialized to take care of others' needs before their own. "Alcoholics Invisible: The Ordeal of the Female Alcoholic" is Marian Sandmeier's classic 1980 article which identified the *many* ways the health care system had failed to deal appropriately with women's problems with alcohol. It is depressing to compare Sandmeier's 1980 article with Sue Creamer's and Claire McMurtrie's excellent 1998 article, "Special Needs of Pregnant and Parenting

Women in Recovery: A Move Toward a More Woman-Centered Approach." Although this new article showcases model programs designed to empower women and recognize their unique needs, it is obvious that nearly 20 years after Sandmeier's article, such programs remain the exception to the male model of alcohol treatment: "Changing the mindset from one that colludes with the larger culture's sometimes subtle critique of women's relational orientation to one that recognizes these tendencies as strengths to be built upon in treatment was (and is) not an easy task."

In the article "The Twelve-Step Controversy," Charlotte Davis Kasl, a psychologist and former member of 12-step programs, continues this discussion by examining programs modeled after Alcoholics Anonymous, which was originally designed for and by men. In contrast, she suggests a 12-step model built on the reality of women's lives, which may be more useful to women trying to heal and move from "*recovery* to *dis*covery."

The devastation of fetal alcohol syndrome (FAS) in Native American communities is analyzed by Charon Asetoyer, a Native American health activist and educator. She emphasizes the need to end victim blaming approaches and repressive measures (such as forced sterilization) and calls for leadership to examine and correct the underlying societal and economic factors that lead to alcohol abuse among Native Americans. A follow-up letter to Asetoyer's article by Ruth Hubbard adds research data to support the importance of the role of economic and social factors in FAS.

Although the newspaper article, "College Life a Blur of Booze, Bar Crawls," does not analyze gender differences in the impact of college drinking, it surely demonstrates the seriousness of the issue. The author worries that the college pattern of drinking makes it difficult for students to feel whole and complete unless drunk. However, after reading that alcohol was involved in 90% of college rapes and that it was related to much unplanned sexual activity and not using protection when sexually active, it should be obvious that the long term consequences of college drinking may be particularly serious for women. Besides the other issues of alcohol consumption for women outlined in this chapter, women are particularly hurt by the double standard related to the combination of alcohol and violence. If a man hurts someone while he is drunk, he is less likely to be held accountable "because the alcohol made him do it." In contrast, a woman who is assaulted when she is intoxicated is doubly blamed both for drinking and for "letting it happen." The United Council of UW Students Factsheet warning students about drugs used to rape summarizes the crucial issue, "If a sexual assault does occur when someone is intoxicated or drugged, it is *NEVER* the victim's fault."

Mood altering drugs are prescribed for women twice as often as for men. There are certainly many times when mood altering drugs are beneficial to women, particularly for short periods of time in conjunction with therapy. However, the overall pattern of high prescription rates for women is of concern and is symbolic of how often women are told directly or indirectly that their problems are "all in their heads." Just as Greaves identified that many women use cigarettes as a way to cope with their lives, mood altering drugs have often been a physician's way of calming a woman down without addressing the real life issues which are upsetting her. The problems of such a pattern are particularly well documented for battered women when mood altering drugs do nothing to stop her abuser's violence but may actually increase her danger by making her miss warning signs of escalating violence, reinforcing what her batterer told her about "it all being in her head," and also giving her the tools to commit suicide.

Sidney Wolfe's chapter, "Tranquilizers and Sleeping Pills—Two Groups of Dangerously Overprescribed Drugs" in his *Women's Health Alert,* strongly encourages women to minimize their use of tranquilizers and sleeping pills: "No studies have proven a therapeutic benefit to long term use (more than four months for tranquilizers, four weeks for sleeping pills). It therefore makes no sense at all to keep taking these drugs in the face of their proven addictive risk." The "Finding a Supportive Doctor" part of his chapter reprinted here presents contrasting scenarios of a doctor who supports a woman trying to go off medication and a doctor who becomes part of the addiction problem.

Although the "Prozac Use Up at UW" article says little about gender issues (except the ratio of females to males seen at the Counseling and Consultation Services is 60:40), it is easy to assume that college women are particularly affected by the reported high rates of depression and use of antidepressants. It seems as if it would be important to understand why more young people are on antidepressants even in high school.

Addictive Behaviors

from The Women's Health Data Book

Alcohol Use

The use of alcohol by women is prevalent in American society. The limited data that are available indicate that alcohol affects women differently than men. Regarding alcohol use by women, the Report of the Public Health Task Force on Women's Health Issues notes that "there are few areas in which conclusions can be stated categorically, and fewer still in which our knowledge . . . is more than fragmentary."

Survey results cited in this section are often based on small numbers of subjects, which may produce unstable estimates. Self-reports of alcohol consumption are often used in surveys. These estimates are more often underestimates than overestimates of consumption.

Discussion of the complex issues surrounding alcohol use by women is hampered by the fact that scientific research has often ignored differences in alcohol use by women and men. In studies that have examined these differences, the research findings have often been inconclusive because of small sample size. Furthermore, the interrelationships between physiology, social factors, and alcohol use are not well understood. Although it is convenient to discuss prevalence, causal factors, and correlates of alcohol use separately from issues related to mental and emotional problems, these problems are often interrelated and frequently occur together.

Two national surveys have filled some of the gaps in our knowledge. One is a periodic survey called the National Household Survey on Drug Abuse and is conducted by the National Institute of Drug Abuse. It measures the prevalence of drug use among the household population aged 12 years and over, using a random sample of the population to provide the latest data. This survey includes persons living in some group quarters, such as college dormitories and homeless shelters. The 1991 survey also included Alaska and Hawaii for the first time. Another survey is the National Survey of Drinking, which is conducted by the National Institute of Alcohol Abuse and Alcoholism. This survey, based on self-reported information, was designed to represent adults over 18 years of age.

USE OF ALCOHOL BY WOMEN

Women who consume alcohol have been stigmatized since ancient times, particularly if their drinking was excessive according to the prevailing standards of their society. This stigmatization has led to an unwillingness on the part of women, as well as clinicians and researchers, to acknowledge the problem of alcoholism in women, making it difficult to estimate the magnitude of the problem.

It is agreed that women drink less than men. At all ages, women are less likely than men to have consumed alcohol in their lifetime, in the past year, or in the past month. On the other hand, women are more likely than men to be lifetime abstainers. In one study, 45% of women reported that they had never used alcohol, compared with 18% of men. While there is agreement that women on average drink less alcohol than men, there is mounting evidence that when they drink comparable amounts they are likely to be more impaired than men, both immediately and over longer periods of time.

It has been reported that one reason alcohol has a greater intoxicating effect on women than on men is that total body water content differs between the sexes. In general, women have smaller body water quantities than men of similar size because they have a higher proportion of fatty tissue. The result is higher blood alcohol concentrations in women. It has also been reported that women respond differently to alcohol throughout their menstrual cycle, but the mechanisms involved are not fully understood. Further study is needed on the basic processes involved in alcohol metabolism during the menstrual cycle and the role that estrogen levels play, since lower peak blood alcohol levels and alcohol clearance rates have been found in women taking oral contraceptives.

ALCOHOL-RELATED MORBIDITY AND MORTALITY

Alcohol abuse is the principal cause of cirrhosis of the liver, which is the ninth leading cause of death in the United States. There is some evidence that women are more likely than men to develop advanced liver disease, even with similar drinking histories. One of the few longitudinal studies of alcoholic women estimated that their average life span is reduced by 15 years because of both alcohol-related disorders such as liver disease and a higher incidence of alcohol-related accidents and suicides. In that study, more than 30% of the alcoholic women had died after 12 years of follow-up, a rate 4.5 times higher than the controls selected from other hospital patients.

Although the liver is the organ most seriously affected by alcohol consumption, women experience many other alcohol-related disorders, including hypertension, obesity, anemia, malnutrition, and gastrointestinal hemorrhage. Rates of obstetric and gynecologic conditions, including amenorrhea, miscarriage, early menopause, gynecologic surgery, and infertility, are higher than expected in alcoholic women than in other women. The reasons for these increased rates are unclear, although both biologic and psychosocial factors are thought to be involved.

ALCOHOL USE DURING PREGNANCY

Alcohol use during pregnancy has been identified as the leading preventable cause of birth defects. Although alcohol crosses the placental barrier, its effects on the developing fetus are variable because of differences in the degree and timing of exposure, genetic differences in maternal metabolism of alcohol, maternal nutritional status, and possible interaction with other drugs.

Fetal alcohol syndrome is a set of birth defects characterized by abnormal features of the face and head, growth retardation, and central nervous system abnormalities often reflected in mental retardation. It has been noted in some of the babies born to mothers who drank heavily during their pregnancy. Babies with milder symptoms are said to have fetal alcohol effects, which may not be apparent until the child is older. The most common fetal alcohol effects are learning disabilities, retarded growth, and mental retardation.

It is disturbing to find in one study that, although the prevalence of alcohol consumption reported by preg-

nant women in the United States showed a relative decline of 38% from 1985 to 1988, women who drank during pregnancy did not decrease the number of drinks consumed. This study also found that the prevalence of alcohol use remained highest among women who may be at higher risk for poor pregnancy outcome: pregnant smokers, single mothers, and the youngest and the least-educated women in the study showed no reduction in their use of alcohol.

MINORITY WOMEN

Seventy-five percent of black women, 70% of Hispanic women, and 83% of white women have reported that they have used alcohol at some point in their lives. In general, regardless of age, white women are more likely than black women to report alcohol use. Black and white women are equally likely, however, to drink heavily. In one study, binge drinking reported by mothers was higher among whites (11%) than among blacks (9%). At the same time, the rate of fetal alcohol syndrome among blacks in another study was seven times that among whites. The reason for this apparent contradiction is not understood, and further research is needed. Despite the overall lower reports of use, black alcoholic women who were followed for 12 years after treatment were found to have higher mortality than the white alcoholic women in the same study (6.7% versus 3.9%). Black women also report more alcohol-related health problems than white women.

High rates of fetal alcohol syndrome have also been found in some American Indian tribes in the Southwest. Several factors, including cultural influences, patterns of alcohol consumption, and nutrition, are thought to be associated with the prevalence of fetal alcohol syndrome in this population.

ADOLESCENTS AND YOUNG ADULTS

Self-reports of alcohol use by young females aged 12–25 years indicate that drinking is widespread in this age group. In 1990, 53% of women aged 18–25 years and 24% of girls aged 12–17 years reported that they had used alcohol in the past month. Although the proportion of young females reporting that they currently use alcohol has declined from a peak (76%) in 1979, these levels of alcohol use remain high. Furthermore, about 35% of female college students report patterns of recent heavy drinking, defined as five or more drinks in a row in the past 2 weeks. Among high school seniors, 29% of females and 46% of males report similar heavy drinking patterns.

The leading cause of death among young people in the United States is accidents and injuries. Alcohol has been implicated in nearly half of all deaths caused by motor vehicle accidents, suicides, and homicides and in one-third of all drownings and boating accident deaths.

The complex interaction of biologic differences and psychosocial factors seem to influence women's patterns of alcohol use. It is readily apparent, however, that additional research efforts are required to increase the limited knowledge that is currently available.

Drug Use

Females use virtually all types of illicit drugs, but they use them less frequently than males. Data from the 1991 National Household Survey of Drug Abuse indicate that among persons 12 years of age and older, females are less likely than males to have ever used, or to have used in the past year or the past month, any illicit drug. Illicit drug use by women in all three of these categories (lifetime use, use in the past year, and current use) is highest among women during their peak childbearing years. Perhaps the most striking statistic is that 53–57% of women aged 18–34 years reported using an illicit drug at least once in their lifetime.

MEDICAL AND NONMEDICAL USE OF PSYCHOTHERAPEUTIC DRUGS

Incidence of Use. The major exception to the generalization that drug use by men exceeds that by women is in regard to the use of medically prescribed psychotherapeutic drugs (sedatives, tranquilizers, stimulants, and analgesics). Prescribed medications may be used medically to serve a legitimate therapeutic function, or they may be used nonmedically, that is, in a manner inconsistent with prescribed instructions. It is not possible from the data available to determine how much of the reported use of prescribed drugs in men and women is appropriate and medically justified.

Almost without exception, regardless of age, women who reported that they had used psychotherapeutic drugs at some time in their lives were more likely than men to have had the drug prescribed for them. Seventy-one percent of adolescent females who reported that they had used a tranquilizer during their lifetime indicated that they had received it as a prescribed medication. Women over 18 years of age reported higher use of stimulants than men. Among youths aged 12–17 years, females had higher rates than males of nonmedical use of sedatives (54% versus 48%), stimulants (79% versus 55%), and analgesics (13% versus 8%).

Consequences of Use. Women are more likely than men to become addicted to prescription drugs and

to use them, often with alcohol, to medicate themselves to cope with anxiety, depression, and painful reactions to life stresses. Adverse consequences associated with the medical use of psychotherapeutic drugs are infrequently reported. However, persons who misuse psychotherapeutic drugs are more likely to report problems such as depression and argumentativeness.

DRUG-RELATED MORBIDITY

Drug-related morbidity is difficult to estimate. The Drug Abuse Warning Network (DAWN) is a surveillance system designed to monitor drug-related visits to hospital emergency rooms in 21 metropolitan areas of the United States. In 1990, there were more than 370,000 emergency-room episodes related to drug abuse. Provisional data indicate that the total number of drug-related visits to emergency rooms increased from more than 89,000 in the fourth quarter of 1990 to more than 100,000 in the second quarter of 1991. During the same period, cocaine-related visits increased by 31%, from nearly 20,000 to more than 25,000. In addition, there was a 26% increase in the number of emergency-room visits related to heroin use.

It is not clear whether these changes represent an increase in cocaine and heroin abuse or whether they reflect the severe medical complications that may result from prolonged drug use. Changes in the rate of drug overdoses could also contribute to greater use of emergency-room services. In contrast, data available for 1988-1989 show that there was a decrease in visits to emergency rooms for cocaine-related problems among young women of all races and ethnic groups. In the same year, however, there was an increase among older women, particularly among older white women. More recent data on these trends are not available at this time.

DRUG ABUSE DURING PREGNANCY

Thirty percent of women of childbearing age report that they have used marijuana at least once in their lifetime, and at least 3% have reported that they are current users. No studies have demonstrated abnormal pregnancy outcome attributable to the effects of marijuana use during pregnancy.

Opiate (heroin) addiction is less common than marijuana use among women, but the health risks to the mother and baby are serious. Women who are addicted to opiates are often in poor general health. They have a higher incidence of chronic infections, gynecologic problems, anemia, and sexually transmitted diseases, including human immunodeficiency virus (HIV) infection.

Because these women often use other drugs, have poor nutrition, and lack adequate prenatal care, serious obstetric complications can occur. Women using opiates during pregnancy are at higher risk for preterm labor, intrauterine growth retardation, and preeclampsia. Use of opiates close to the end of pregnancy can result in babies who suffer from drug withdrawal after birth. Unfortunately, opiate-dependent women are less likely to seek treatment than opiate-dependent men, and those who do seek treatment often find that services to meet their needs are almost nonexistent.

In 1991, 9% of women reported that they had used cocaine (including crack cocaine) at some point in their lives. Cocaine is highly addictive and produces an immediate but brief period of intense euphoria followed by a period of severe depression and agitation. Cocaine users frequently use various combinations of drugs and alcohol to prolong the period of euphoria. Cocaine has severe behavioral and biologic effects, including impulsivity, hypertension, seizures, cardiac arrhythmia, tachycardia, myocardial infarction, and sometimes death. Decreased interest in food over a long period can lead to malnutrition.

During pregnancy, cocaine can affect the fetus, resulting in an increased incidence of spontaneous abortion and fetal death. A higher risk of preterm labor, precipitous delivery, placental abruption, and fetal distress with meconium staining has been observed among women using cocaine. Higher rates of congenital malformations have also been noted in babies born to mothers who used cocaine. An increased rate of sudden infant death syndrome among infants born to mothers who used cocaine during pregnancy has also been observed.

SPECIAL POPULATIONS

Minority Women. The National Household Survey on Drug Abuse found that white women were more likely (35%) than black (33%) or Hispanic (25%) women to have used an illicit drug at some point in their lives. Current use of any illicit drug was also found to be slightly higher among black females (7%) than among white or Hispanic females (5%).

Elderly Women. Although the elderly are generally not users of illicit drugs, they are recognized as having high levels of legal drug use. Elderly women constitute 11% of the population, yet 25% of all prescriptions are written for this group. It has been reported that older patients may have as many as 30 drugs prescribed for them each year. Prescriptions for elderly women often include estrogen replacement therapy, sedatives, hypnotics, antianxiety drugs, antihypertensive drugs, vitamins, analgesics, diuretics, laxatives, and tranquilizers, which are prescribed for elderly women at a rate 2.5 times that of elderly men.

It is clear that the potential for harmful drug interactions is a serious threat to older women. Research has shown that women experience more adverse drug reactions than men, possibly due to the large number of drugs they take. Other health consequences associated with drug use in the elderly are suicide, insomnia, affective disturbance, and impairment of cognitive and motor function, which can be severe enough to lead to institutionalization.

Currently, it appears that drug misuse, rather than abuse, is more common in the elderly. However, some experts believe that as more people who were drug abusers in their early years reach older ages, they may be more likely to abuse psychoactive drugs that may be prescribed for them.

Although the available evidence suggests that women's experience with drug use and abuse is different from men's, the data are limited. More research is essential to provide an understanding of the physiologic, psychosocial, and behavioral dimensions of drug use throughout women's lives.

Smoking

The fact that the year Eleanor Roosevelt smoked a cigarette in public is recorded (1934) is an indication that such an event was rare. At that time there were little national data available on the prevalence of smoking, but it was estimated that 17% of adult women in the United States were smokers. By 1965, 34% of American women smoked, an all-time high.

Although the rate of cigarette smoking has never been as high among women as among men, the rate for both men and women has declined. The decline has been less dramatic for women, and the latest data show that 27% of women in the United States currently smoke. About one in every four women under 25 years of age is a current smoker. After age 25, approximately one in every three women smokes. Of great health significance is the fact that between 1965 and 1985, the percentage of women who are heavy smokers, defined as those who smoke 25 or more cigarettes a day, increased from 13% to 23%.

The good news is that there has been a 21% decline in the prevalence of smoking among women since 1965. Current female smokers are more likely to be separated or divorced women, women who have less than 12 years of education, and women with annual family incomes of less than $20,000. The highest proportion of former smokers are found among college-educated women, women who are married, and those with high incomes.

SMOKING INITIATION

Fifty-six percent of all adult women have never smoked. Fewer females than males start smoking before age 20, but regardless of the age at which they begin to smoke, women are more likely to continue to smoke. Furthermore, the younger a woman is when she starts to smoke, the more likely she is to be a current smoker.

Between 1965 and 1985, the percentage of former smokers has increased among adult women. The percentage of lifetime smokers (both current and former smokers), however, has remained constant since 1970, suggesting that the proportion of women who start to smoke has not declined.

SMOKING CESSATION

Seventeen percent of all adult females are former smokers. Smoking cessation may be accompanied by a wide range of withdrawal symptoms that vary considerably among individuals. Data about withdrawal and smoking cessation strategies in women versus men, however, are scarce. National data indicate that both former and current smokers cite present and future health concerns as reasons for quitting. Women smokers report more concern than men about gaining weight as a result of quitting.

SMOKING-RELATED MORBIDITY AND MORTALITY

Because cigarette smoking by women did not become widespread until during World War II, women are just now facing the increased morbidity and mortality associated with cigarette smoking. Cigarette smoking contributes to one of every five newly diagnosed cases of cancer and up to one-fourth of all cancer deaths among women.

As a result of the increase in cigarette smoking among women, the rate of deaths from lung cancer has increased dramatically in women. In 1988, lung cancer exceeded breast cancer as the leading cause of cancer death in white women. It has been estimated that it takes about 15 years after a smoker quits for her risk of lung cancer to return to that of a nonsmoker. A marked increase in deaths from chronic obstructive pulmonary disease (COPD) among women is expected in the next few decades, because an estimated 82% of all COPD deaths are attributable to cigarette smoking.

Heart disease is the leading cause of death for both men and women in the United States. Women with smoking patterns similar to those of men experience similar rates of cardiovascular morbidity and mortality, although studies have shown that women have a protective factor for heart disease prior to the age of menopause. Other cardiovascular conditions associated with smoking in women include lower levels of high-density lipoproteins, peripheral vascular disease, subarachnoid hemorrhage, and severe or malignant hypertension. Like their male counterparts, current female smokers have an increased incidence of sudden death. Women smokers over the age of 35 years are advised not to use oral contraceptives because their risk of heart attack and stroke is increased.

SMOKING AND PREGNANCY

Cigarette smoking has been implicated as a risk factor in about one-quarter of all births of babies weighing less than 2,500 g at birth. Babies born to women who smoke are, on average, 200 g lighter than babies born to comparable non-smoking mothers. Increasing levels of maternal smoking result in an increased risk of obstetric complications such as abruptio placentae, placenta previa, premature or prolonged rupture of membranes, and preterm delivery. The risk of miscarriage, stillbirth, and neonatal death increases directly with increasing levels of smoking during pregnancy. Further study of the role of smoking and other factors that may confound the relationship with perinatal outcome is warranted.

A recent study used cross-sectional data obtained by telephone interview from the Behavioral Risk Factor Surveillance System (BRFSS), a system of participating state health departments collaborating with the Centers for Disease Control. It was found that 21% of pregnant women and 30% of nonpregnant women were current smokers at the time of the study. Because the prevalence of having ever smoked was similar in the two groups, the difference in the current smoking rates was due to the fact that the pregnant women had quit smoking rather than to differences in when smoking had commenced.

These findings were supported by another study in which it was found that one-third of white women aged 20–44 years smoked prior to pregnancy and 39% of the smokers indicated that they quit while pregnant. Among current smokers in the BRFSS study, 38% of pregnant women and 53% of nonpregnant women reported that they were heavy smokers (smoking 20 or more cigarettes per day). Pregnant women over 30 years of age were less likely to smoke than women in their 20s. Unmarried pregnant women were more likely than married women to be smokers both before and during pregnancy. The prevalence of smoking decreased sharply with increasing education. Seventy percent of the women who quit smoking while pregnant resumed within 1 year, with the majority relapsing in the first 3 months after delivery.

SPECIAL POPULATIONS

Minority Women. Although the prevalence of smoking is high among all women, black and Hispanic women have lower overall current and lifetime rates of cigarette use than white women. The 1988 National Household Survey on Drug Abuse found lifetime use of cigarettes to be higher among white females (73%) than either Hispanic females (52%) or black females (63%). In this survey, similar patterns of current smoking were found. Only 20% of Hispanic and 24% of black women reported that they were smokers at the present time, compared with 26% of white women. This represents a decline among white and black women from the 1987 National Health Interview Survey findings. In that survey, an equally high percentage of current smokers was found among black and white females (27%). It is not clear whether this difference between the two surveys is due to methodologic factors or whether it represents a real decline.

Black women have consistently been shown to have a lower prevalence of smoking during pregnancy than whites. It has also been found that black women are less likely to quit after they become pregnant. This suggests that the difference in the prevalence of smoking among black pregnant women is due to the lower prevalence of ever having smoked in that population. Because other data suggest that there is no racial difference in prevalence of ever having smoked, however, these findings await further clarification.

Adolescent Women. Despite all of the publicity given to the health risks associated with cigarette smoking, adolescent females are more likely to smoke than their male counterparts in high school and in young adulthood, whether or not they are in college. Studies have shown that students who smoke are also more likely to use alcohol and illicit drugs, particularly marijuana.

A 1987 follow-up study of adolescents in the southeastern United States showed that among teenagers who did not smoke in 1985, more whites than blacks started smoking. White females in the study were more likely than blacks to start smoking at 12 years. Peer pressure was correlated with the likelihood that a white teenager would smoke, but this factor was not important for black teenagers in this study.

Tobacco use has been identified as the single most preventable cause of death and disease. Although progress has been made in social interventions to decrease smoking, the adverse health effects of smoking become apparent over a long interval, and the effects of the increased use of tobacco by women are just beginning to be felt. There is an immediate need for vigorous action to decrease smoking among women in order to improve health outcomes in the years ahead.

What Is a Theory of Women's Smoking? and How Do Societies Benefit?

by Lorraine Greaves

The analysis expressed in the first part of this chapter forms a useful starting point from which to develop a more thorough explanation of women's smoking:

> Smoking may be an important means through which women control and adapt to both internal and external realities. It mediates between the world of emotions and outside circumstances. It is both a means of reacting to and/or acting upon social reality, and a significant route to self-definition.

This view reflects the words of the women in this book. A consciousness and self-analysis is revealed by the women smokers, showing awareness of the discrepancies between emotional states and cultural and social expectations. Smoking mediates between these two fields. Women smokers use cigarettes to assist with their taking responsibility for social relationships and the maintenance of emotional equilibrium in their social groups.

Each cigarette serves as a temporary answer to these women's search for meaning. But as each one is stubbed out, the limitations of the answer it provided likely becomes clear. Not only do unpleasant aspects of life reenter consciousness, but the guilt. contradiction and tension associated with smoking also re-emerge.

Smoking a pack of cigarettes per day may offer repeated "meditations." It protects against full engagement with reality, allowing those realities to continue unabated. This is how smoking benefits the social order surrounding women. Not simply a lucrative and desirable aspect of commerce, fashion or femininity, smoking is also a way of perpetuating unsatisfying and unequal social relations.

The question remains whether women's smoking is a passive or active response to the world. Women can be either "passive victims" of or "active resisters" to patriarchal domination or possibly both, depending on their cultural or subcultural milieu. In some instances, women are victims and are limited to reacting. Other times, we have the energy and opportunity to be proactive in defining the self and negotiating social life. Depending on time, place and personal circumstance, women can use smoking to absorb inequality or resist it.

It is facile to assume that all women are victims. Seen this way, women smokers would be understood to be either completely duped by the culture or driven to smoke as a direct result of their treatment in the world. Neither of these is true. But it is equally facile to assume that a clear sense of self can be forged in a world that largely excludes the female experience in defining female identity. Smoking seems to assist in the assertion of the self in such circumstances.

Women across the social spectrum experience the failure of the ideal, but specific experiences such as abuse help expose the range of ways in which smoking can serve women. These interviews suggest that cigarettes are shock absorbers for abused women; smoking mediates between reality and ideal and eases the rawness of women's pain and life. Not surprisingly, suppressing negative emotions and using cigarettes as comfort were both more common in the testimony of abused women smokers. Many abused women know that directly expressing emotions could be perceived as aggressive and, as such, could potentially further endanger them.

The feminist smokers interviewed consciously analyze their reality. Their conflict centres on the discrepancy between their experience (as feminists and smokers) and their own and others' definitions of feminists and smokers. Is smoking liberating or did they just buy the advertising line? Is their continuing to smoke evidence of disempowerment? Is there a way to analyze this that fits with a feminist critique of the world? Tensions surround the personal and the political and are the source of self-punishment and guilt. The politics of empowerment clash with the fact that these women are being controlled to varying degrees by their need to smoke. But throughout, smoking is useful in negotiating life circumstances.

How *Do* Societies Benefit?

In industrial countries when women use smoking to mediate existence, whether taking the edge off their emotional reactions, giving themselves space and time away from pressures or even staying thin and looking sophisticated, there is often a tangible benefit to others in their society.

Culturally and economically, women's smoking is approved of (in some cultures) in advertising, movies and fashion and as a weight control method. Women's image, size and superficial beauty is treated as a commodity. Generally, when a fashion magazine shows a thin model with a cigarette or a film shows an independent woman defiantly smoking, smoking is seen as positive in the industrial world. Several industries, including the tobacco industry, will benefit directly. Naomi Wolf describes the Western patriarchal definitions of women's beauty and the lucrative industries and practices that support these definitions. She argues that women who smoke to control their weight are actually reflecting the logic of the (North American) culture where women's external body image is valued far more than their internal health. She says women should not be blamed for making the decision to smoke as there is no real social or economic reward for choosing otherwise, nor is there any particular reward for women who live longer (1990, 229–30).

When smoking reduces or erases women's demands, emotions or challenges, women can be seen as compliant and less troublesome. The true scope of women's feelings, particularly anger, remains invisible. Women smokers describe "sucking back anger" with each drag on a cigarette. If women smokers continue to internalize the tensions of interpersonal and social relations, the responsibility of others in their lives to deal with legitimate emotions is lifted.

Some women describe quit attempts that appear to be sabotaged by partners or family members. Sometimes cigarettes will be presented to a woman struggling to quit simply because she is being too irritable or difficult. In fact, this pattern indicates the strength and impact of emotions concealed by smoking.

When women depend on cigarettes instead of a partner or friend in cultures which approve of women's smoking, the pressure and collective responsibility to offer comfort and care is often relieved. The intensity of feelings toward cigarettes as friends and the grief con-

nected to giving them up is a key indicator of some women's security needs that go unfulfilled by others. Both individual and collective responsibility for providing comfort and consistency to women may be abrogated. Recognizing and countering this situation is critical to effective and ethical cessation programming for women. If women are being asked to give up smoking, what can be offered to replace it?

Women smokers are using a socially acceptable (among some cultures) form of self-medication. Unlike alcohol and most other drugs, tobacco does not render a woman incapable of carrying out her more traditional nurturing and caretaking social roles. In fact, as we have seen, it often helps women carry out numerous social roles that are unequal and unsatisfying.

The women in this study generally have few legitimate avenues for expression of negative emotion and angst. While smoking is profoundly self-destructive for a woman, it does not undermine the patriarchal family. Indeed, as long as it does not interfere with child bearing, childrearing and the maintenance of heterosexuality, women's smoking can be regarded as useful by advocates of the status quo to both the woman and her society.

On the other hand, women who get drunk or stoned are unable to care for children or continue working. This is one explanation why women's use of alcohol and drugs is much less acceptable from a Western societal point of view, despite the fact that alcohol consumption and drug use cause much less death and disease than does smoking. Several of the women interviewed, especially the First Nations women, were particularly clear about this. Smoking is most similar to the use of legal drugs—the traditionally overprescribed tranquilizers and sedatives—which have also been used in the service of pacifying women. In this sense, tobacco is a preferred drug, a socially acceptable form of medication.

There are rare exceptions to this. Pregnant women who smoke are the subject of a great deal of attention regarding women and smoking. Indeed, for many years in industrial countries the only form of attention paid to women smokers focused on smoking in pregnancy. Even now, there is an overemphasis on pregnant smokers. Not discounting the serious health problems created by smoking during pregnancy, the best intervention would be respectfully focused on women, not the fetus, long before and long after pregnancy.

A related, more recent concern among anti-smoking activists is the effect of women's smoking on children they are looking after. The issue of children being exposed to smoke, while very important, arouses passions in anti-smoking activists far in excess of the concern invested in women's health. In many instances involving children, societal reaction and attention from the international tobacco control movement has been, and continues to be, swift, sexist and woman-blaming (see Jacobson 1986, 124–26). There is a widespread and strong motivation to intervene in these circumstances.

How can we specify the benefits of women's smoking to a society? As we have seen in Chapter 1, the cultural meaning of women's smoking changes rapidly over time and from place to place. These shifts often affect the development of women's identity and pressure it to fit with new prevailing values and political realities. Over time, this has led to many social meanings being applied to women's smoking. Cultural meanings have demarcated occupations and class groups and evoked images, qualities and aspirations. In contemporary industrialized societies, smoking serves as a socially useful and legal method of self-medication for some women. In Third World countries, or countries where women's smoking rates are low it may still be a mark of resistance, the emblem of the "bad girl." In either case, smoking is a form of social control.

What would industrial societies do if women did not suppress emotions through smoking? What would happen if women refused to overwork instead of coping through smoking? What would happen if women took control and stopped adapting? Even anti-tobacco activists in the West fail to consider these questions! Could it be that women's health is so undervalued that the benefits to industrial societies of women's smoking will likely be perpetuated and the negative effects of smoking on women will not arouse a great deal of effective concern?

For references, see original.

How Women Are Targeted by the Tobacco Industry

by Amanda Amos

If women in many parts of the world are smoking in greater numbers than ever before, it is probably no coincidence. Women represent a fresh and lucrative target group for the tobacco industry, which has learned to tailor its products and promotion to women's presumed tastes. The promotion images, themes and devices used are analysed in the following article, which also suggests some healthy ground rules for women's magazines to consider adopting.

*I*n the last few years the tobacco industry has aimed both its products and its advertising increasingly at women. Tobacco companies have always been keen to develop the female market. Given the decline in smoking in many developed countries (especially among men) and the fact that tobacco kills off a quarter of its consumers, however, these companies are resorting more than ever before to the creation and expansion of new markets. Women are key target groups in both developed and Third World countries.

Items in the tobacco and advertising press are explicit about the importance attached to targeting women. Articles entitled "Suggesting that retailers should 'look to the ladies',"[1] "Women—a separate market,"[2] and "Creating a female taste,"[3] have appeared in the British journal *Tobacco*, as have similar articles in the United States press.[4,5] The international journal *Tobacco Reporter*, which has featured such articles as "Targeting the female smoker,"[6] concludes that "women are a prime target as far as any alert European marketing man is concerned."[7]

From *World Health Forum,* Vol.. 11, 1990, pp. 416–422. Copyright © 1990 by World Health Organization. Reprinted by permission.

Dr. Amos is Lecturer in Health Education, Department of Community Medicine, Usher Institute, University of Edinburgh Medical School, Teviot Place, Edinburgh EH8 9AG, Scotland.

How Are Women Targeted?

The overall objective of any campaign is to make smoking cigarettes in general, and one brand in particular, more appealing. This is achieved by tailoring the marketing mix to specific groups, which may involve altering the product, its price, its availability and its image through packaging and promotion. The particular marketing strategy used to target women will vary with factors such as: the tobacco company; the country—its culture, smoking patterns and trends, and its restrictions on advertising and promotion; and whether the campaign is aimed at a particular subgroup of women, defined by characteristics such as age, ethnicity and affluence.

In the USA and Europe several complementary strategies have been adopted, the most important being:

- promoting images designed to appeal specifically to women;
- producing new brands for women only;
- using women's magazines to direct advertising at women.

Creating the Right Image

"The image is luxury and sophistication, confidence and style, as manufacturers pursue half of America's smokers: the women." *Tobacco Reporter*[6]

Since the 1920s, when women first began to be targeted, various attractive images and themes have been used to encourage smoking, promote its social acceptability, and highlight the supposed desirable attributes of particular brands of cigarettes. A number of times smoking has been advertised as being glamorous, sophisticated, fun, romantic, sexually attractive, healthy, sporty, sociable, relaxing, calming, emancipated or liberated, rebellious and—last but definitely not least—an aid to slimming.[8-10] These images and themes have been conveyed by a variety of means ranging from straightforward verbal and visual messages, for example, advertisements featuring young attractive women and slogans such as "You've come a long way, baby", to the more subtle visual imagery of luxury represented by silk or satin and by symbols of success or high style such as expensive and exotic locations.

The message that smoking helps you stay slim appeared very early in the USA with the infamous ad of the 1930s encouraging women to reach for a cigarette "instead of a sweet". This message continues to be promoted today, although more subtly, through the association of slender female models with slender cigarettes. For example, in a recent German advertisement that depicted three people smoking different versions of the same brand of cigarette, it was the woman who was smoking the "slim line" cigarette.

Even in the United Kingdom and other countries that have more stringent restrictions on the content of tobacco advertisements, words such as long, slim and slender frequently appear in advertising copy. While they supposedly describe the merits of the cigarettes, clearly they also serve to associate the product with the aspirations of a large section of the target audience: women.

Cigarette manufacturers and advertisers argue that these messages and imagery merely encourage brand-switching or sustain brand loyalty among those who already smoke. However, there is increasing research evidence that such advertisements serve to encourage and reinforce smoking among the young.[11-13] A recent report by the New Zealand Toxic Substances Board[13] has concluded that brand-switching accounts for only 7% of the economic return from maintaining tobacco advertising and sponsorship. In the developing world, enormous amounts of money are spent on tobacco ads directed at women—even in places such as Hong Kong, where only some 3% of women are smokers.

> Given the decline in smoking (especially among men) and the fact that tobacco kills off a quarter of its consumers, tobacco companies are resorting more than ever before to the creation and expansion of new markets. Women are a key target group.

Women are targeted through a variety of other promotional activities as well. These have included special offers such as free silk stockings, contests, free cosmetics, and clothing carrying the brand logo. Another popular method is the sponsorship of women's sports (e.g., tennis) which receive widespread media coverage, and of women's events such as fashion shows. Again, the aim is to enhance the brand's image by associating it with socially valued activities.

> At various times smoking has been advertised as being glamorous, sophisticated, fun, romantic, sexually attractive, healthy, sporty, sociable, relaxing, calming, emancipated or liberated, rebellious and—last but definitely not least—an aid to slimming.

For Women Only—Women's Brands

"Question—what have Kim, Benson and Hedges Longer Length, and More got in common? . . . All three brands are calculated to appeal to the growing women's sector of the cigarette market.

Tobacco[1]

The targeting of women entered a new phase in the late 1960s with the launch in the USA of Kim, the first of a new wave of brands aimed solely at women. These "women only" brands use advertising and packaging which emphasize feminine characteristics and positive female images. For example, Eve—with its archetypal female name—has a filter tip decorated with a flower motif; Satin has a special luxury satin-like paper tip. Then there are the "designer" brands such as Ritz, which carries the logo of Yves St. Laurent, and Cartier. As mentioned above, there has also been an explosion in the number of extra-long (over 100 mm) cigarettes, which are particularly popular among women. A recent arrival in Europe is Vogue, a new brand described by *Tobacco* as a "stylish type of cigarette with obvious feminine appeal, being slim and therefore highly distinctive."[14] This has been followed by Capri, the world's first "ultraslim" cigarette, and Dakota, launched in the USA for "virile females."[15]

Women's Magazines—Readers' Health or Magazines' Wealth?

"For a number of years women's magazines have been a favourite advertising medium for all the best selling uni-sex brands."

Tobacco[16]

In many countries, particularly where tobacco advertising is banned from television, the most popular medium for targeting women is women's magazines. Cigarette advertising in these magazines has grown substantially. In the USA eight of the twenty magazines receiving the most cigarette advertising are women's magazines.[9] In the United Kingdom revenue from tobacco ads in women's magazines increased by 50% in real terms between 1977 and 1982[17] and by 10% between 1984 and 1988[18]. In 1988 nearly £9.7 million was spent on cigarette advertisements compared with some £7.2 million in 1984. A recent survey of the top women's magazines in 14 European countries found that 72% of them accepted cigarette advertisements.[19]

There are several reasons why women's magazines are so popular with tobacco advertisers.

Magazines in the European survey which did not accept cigarette advertisements, 1988.

		Reason for non-acceptance		
		Total media ban	Partial media ban	Magazine's policy
Finland	Gloria	x		
	Me Naiset	x		
France	Vogue			x
Greece	Domino			x
	Seventeen			x
Ireland/ United Kingdom	Company		x	
	Cosmopolitan		x	
	Elle		x	
	Just Seventeen		x	
	Marie Claire		x	
	Smash Hits		x	
	Vogue		x	
Italy	Vogue	x		
Netherlands	Yes			x
Portugal	Elle	x		
	Guia	x		
	Maria	x		
	Marie Claire	x		
	Maxima	x		
	Muhler Moderna	x		
Spain	Greca			x
Sweden	Frida		x	

Source: reference 19 and unpublished data.

- They have an enormous number of readers. In the United Kingdom around half of all women are regular readers of women's magazines.[17,18]
- They are read by women of all ages and backgrounds. Hence, through the careful selection of magazines, specific groups such as young women or black women can be reached. A recent survey in the USA found more tobacco ads in women's and youth magazines than in magazines targeted at other population segments.[20]
- Magazines can lend a spurious social acceptability or stylish image to smoking. In a British study the health editor of high-fashion magazine said that publication of an ad in that magazine was "as good as a stamp of acceptability."[17]
- The presence of tobacco ads in a magazine may dilute the impact of articles on tobacco and health. Alternatively, they may induce magazine editors to downplay this issue or avoid covering it altogether. There are numerous examples of magazines in the USA which have allegedly lost tobacco advertising because they reported on the adverse health

effects of smoking, or which have reportedly refused to cover this health issue or altered articles to de-emphasize its importance because they were worried about losing lucrative sources of advertising revenue.[21] New evidence from the USA shows that women's magazines as a group are more sensitive to the presence of cigarette advertising than are other magazines.[22]

Thus women's magazines represent a battleground between the competing interests of, on the one hand, the tobacco companies and advertisers wishing to target their massive female audience and the magazines wishing to maximize their own revenues, and, on the other, editors and journalists wishing to report the facts without bias and to protect the health of their readers. At present, the tobacco interests seem to be winning the battle.

> In the developing world, enormous amounts of money are spent on tobacco ads directed at women—even in places such as Hong Kong, where only some 3% of women are smokers.

Recent studies of women's magazines in the USA[23], the United Kingdom[18], and in Europe[19] have found that smoking, a major cause of ill-health and premature death among their readers, is receiving scant coverage in the medium most trusted by women—women's magazines. Only 29% of British women's magazines had published a major article on smoking and health in the year preceding the survey.[18] The preliminary findings of a survey of the top women's magazines in 14 countries in Europe showed that only half had recently covered this issue.[19] Indeed, some of the editors said that they would never cover it or had stopped covering it. The coverage that was given was often brief and considerably less than that given to tobacco advertisements. In the top French magazines, for example, only 24 articles appeared in 1988, as compared with 123 pages of tobacco advertisements.

> The targeting of women entered a new phase in the late 1960s with the launch of the first of a new wave of brands aimed solely at women.

Magazines' attitudes to coverage of the health hazards of smoking varied considerably, both in the United Kingdom and in other European countries. One key factor was the personal interest and commitment of the editor with regard to smoking and health. Another factor,

though many editors denied its importance, was the desire not to offend tobacco advertisers. The following candid comments came from the advertising department of one of the top-selling British women's magazines. "The difficulty is that we take money from these people. It does not matter how much we take from them, it's difficult for us to endorse anything that goes against the companies. Even editorially, they have to go carefully. The tobacco companies are very sensitive about their image."[17]

In the British and United States studies, the magazines that were most dependent on tobacco advertising gave least coverage to the health hazards of smoking. As remarked by a well-known editor who has come herself from the advertising world, "I think 'who needs somebody you're paying millions of dollars a year to come back and bite you on the ankle'?"[23]

Not only do many magazines avoid reporting on smoking and health while giving considerable space to tobacco ads. They also feature pictures of glamorous models smoking in their fashion pages. The European survey found that a third of the magazines had no policy on the editorial portrayal of positive images of smoking.[19] Fewer than half said that they would not publish such pictures. Magazines in Denmark, France and Spain had the worst records. For example, in 1988 one major French fashion magazine published 20 fashion photos depicting models smoking, and another published 25. The double standards of many magazines was illustrated in one issue of a Spanish magazine, where an article on the health of Spanish women—which included a section on smoking—was sandwiched between cigarette advertisements and photos of fashion models smoking.

The Way Forward

Numerous expert national and international bodies that have looked at the issue of tobacco and health, including the WHO Expert Committee on Smoking Control[24] and the Royal College of Physicians in London[25], have all reached the same conclusion. Smoking and smoking-related disease will decline only if a comprehensive approach is taken to tackling the problem. This includes a ban on all tobacco advertising and promotion.

Many countries have already adopted such a ban and many more are considering it. In the meantime, action should be taken to reduce the tobacco industry's ability to target key groups such as young people and women. Just as many women's magazines now play a negative role by allowing companies to promote their lethal product, they can also play an important positive role by encouraging their younger readers not to start smoking and helping their older readers to kick the habit. Women's magazines throughout the world could take the lead in protecting and improving the health of their readers by adopting these ground rules.

- Follow the example of several magazines in Europe and refuse to accept cigarette advertisements (see table). Although most of the magazines listed in the table were not allowed to accept advertisements because of national laws or regulations, five had voluntarily decided to refuse tobacco advertisements. These were French *Vogue*, Greek *Domino* and *Seventeen*, Spanish *Greca*, and Netherlands *Yes*.
- Give regular coverage to aspects of smoking including health hazards, how to give up smoking, and non-smokers' rights.
- In the case of a teenage or youth magazine, make a special effort to increase awareness of the special risks that smoking poses to young women, such as smoking while being on the pill, and smoking and pregnancy.
- Avoid the use of glamorous pictures of people, including fashion models, smoking.

REFERENCES

1. Reisman, E. Suggesting that retailers should "look to the ladies". *Tobacco* March 1983, pp. 17–19.
2. Cole, J. Women—a separate market. *Tobacco*, March 1988, pp. 7–9.
3. Gill, B. & Garrett, S. Creating a female taste. *Tobacco*, March 1989, pp. 6–7.
4. Sobczynski, A. Marketers clamor to offer lady a cigaret. *Advertising age*, 31 January 1983. pp. 14–16.
5. O'Connor, J.J. Women top cig target. *Advertising age*, 28 September 1981, pp. 9, 93.
6. Anon. Targeting the female smoker. *Tobacco reporter*, April 1983, pp. 44–45.
7. Rogers, D. Editorial. *Tobacco reporter*, February 1987, p. 8
8. Ernster, V.L. Mixed messages for women: a social history of cigarette smoking and advertising. *New York State journal of medicine*, 85: 335–340 (1985).
9. Davis, R.M. Current trends in cigarette advertising and marketing. *New England journal of medicine*, 316: 725–732 (1987).
10. Jacobson, B. *Beating the ladykillers*. London, Gollancz, 1988.
11. Aitken, P.P. et al. Cigarette brand preferences of teenagers and adults. *Health promotion*, 2: 219–226 (1988).
12. Chapman, S. & Fitzgerald, B. Brand preferences and advertising recall in adolescent smokers: some implications for health promotion. *American journal of public health*, 72: 491–494 (1982).
13. Toxic Substances Board. *Health or tobacco*. Wellington, New Zealand Department of Health, 1989.
14. Cole, J. For a special occasion. *Tobacco*. December 1988, pp. 15–16.
15. Specter, M. Uneducated white women are target of new cigarette. *Washington Post*, 17 March 1990, pp. D1, D10.
16. Anon. Are there now more women smokers than men? *Tobacco*, November 1985, pp. 29–32.
17. Jacobson, B. & Amos, A. *When smoke gets in your eyes: cigarette advertising policy and coverage of smoking and health in women's magazines*. London, British Medical Association/Health Education Council, 1985.
18. ASH Women and Smoking Working Group. *Smoke still gets in her eyes—a report on cigarette advertising in British women's magazines*. London, British Medical Association/ASH, 1990.
19. Amos, A. Women's magazines and tobacco—preliminary findings of a survey of the tobacco policies of the top women's magazines in Europe. In: *Proceedings of the 7th World Conference on Tobacco and Health*, Perth, Health Department of Western Australia (in press).
20. Allright, C.C. et al. Cigarette advertisements in magazines: evidence for a differential focus on women's and youth magazines. *Health education quarterly*, 15: 225–233 (1988).
21. Warner, K.E. Cigarette advertising and media coverage of smoking and health. *New England journal of medicine*, 312: 384–388 (1985).
22. Warner, K. et al. The economics of cigarette advertising: impacts on magazines' revenues and editorial practice regarding coverage of smoking and health. In: *Proceedings of the 7th World Conference on Tobacco and Health*. Perth, Health Department of Western Australia (in press).
23. White, L. & Whelan, E.M. How well do American magazines cover the health hazards of smoking? *ACSH news and views*, 7(3): 1, 8–11 (1986).
24. *Controlling the smoking epidemic. Report of the WHO Expert Committee on Smoking Control*. Geneva, World Health Organization, 1979 (Technical Report Series, No. 636).
25. Royal College of Physicians. *Health or smoking?* London, Pitman 1983.

If you know of any women's magazines that carry tobacco advertising you might like to bring this article to the attention of their Editors.

Alcoholics Invisible: The Ordeal of the Female Alcoholic

by Marian Sandmaier

*E*ven under the best of circumstances, the ability to turn away from a drug to which one is physically and psychologically addicted requires uncommon courage and determination. But most of the women whom I interviewed recovered from alcoholism in the face of an appalling lack of support from the doctors, therapists, alcoholism personnel, and others charged with diagnosing and treating their illness. With a few notable exceptions, these women were discouraged by the health system from embarking on alcoholism treatment to begin with, and once involved in treatment, were denied supports and services important to their recovery. They discovered what most alcoholic women who seek help are forced to recognize: that contemptuous attitudes and sheer ignorance about women with alcohol problems pervade the health system as thoroughly and destructively as any other segment of society. There, as anywhere, the real needs and the very humanity of alcoholic women remain invisible.

Within the health system, the first person an alcoholic woman is likely to encounter is her own doctor. And at first glance, he* would seem to be in an excellent position to identify her alcohol problem and steer her toward appropriate treatment.

Diagnosis

Yet physicians appear highly unlikely to diagnose alcoholism in their female patients. In a 1975 survey of 89 women in Alcoholics Anonymous, fully half of the women surveyed said they had tried to discuss their drinking problem with someone who told them they couldn't possibly be alcoholic; twelve received such advice from physicians, five of these psychiatrists.[1] Of the 50 women I interviewed, 45 had been seen by doctors while they were drinking alcoholically, but only seven were ever confronted by their physicians about their alcohol abuse. A 54 year-old Boston woman recalled: "In all of the times I landed in the hospital during my drinking years, no doctor ever said anything to me about alcoholism. I always either had colitis or a kidney problem or pneumonia, and when they couldn't think of anything else, I would have nerves. Twice I attempted suicide and once wound up in a hospital afterward for three months. And in those three months, I saw a psychiatrist every day and not once did he say a word to me about being alcoholic. And at that point I had been drinking almost around the clock."

Some physicians fail to respond to even clear-cut evidence of alcohol problems in their women patients. "I used to carry a big purse full of beer into my psychiatrist's office and drink right through the sessions," recalled a young social scientist from Virginia. "He never said a word to me about it. As I look back, I think I was probably challenging him to say something, to do something, to help me. But he never dealt with it." A Detroit homemaker who had a drinking problem while still in college encountered the same kind of reaction from her therapist at a university health service. "There were times when my husband called my psychiatrist in the middle of the night because I'd be so out of control and drunk and hysterical. . . . But when I would come in for my next session . . . the drinking would never get mentioned as a problem in itself."

Probably the primary reason for many doctors' failure to confront alcohol problems in their patients is, perhaps surprisingly, sheer ignorance of alcoholism itself. Although alcohol abuse affects at least 10 million persons in the United States and is considered the third

From *Social Policy.* Jan/Feb 1980, pp. 25–30. Reprinted with permission of the author from *The Invisible Alcoholics,* McGraw Hill, New York.

*I use the pronoun "he" deliberately because the medical profession is still overwhelmingly masculine; at present only 12 percent of physicians are women.

largest health problem in the country, it is one of the most neglected areas of study in medical schools. Although this situation is slowly being corrected, few medical schools even today offer more than one course on the subject, and many limit their coverage to a single lecture. This gap in education is largely due to alcoholism's heritage as a moral problem rather than a medical one, despite its obvious physical and emotional consequences. In a 1972 nationwide survey of 13,000 physicians who treat alcoholism, 70 percent declared alcoholics to be difficult and uncooperative patients, while a sizable minority believed alcoholism indicated a "lack of will or morality."[2]

Further, as the research of Phyllis Chester and others has demonstrated, doctors as a group hold notably stereotypical attitudes about appropriate behavior for women.[3] Consequently, many physicians who believe that alcoholism is a sign of moral laxity may well also subscribe to the double standard rendering alcoholism—i.c., immorality—more shameful in a woman than a man, and thus more discomfiting to discuss with a female patient. Indeed, a study of the attitudes of 161 physicians toward their alcoholic clients revealed that a substantial number of doctors believed that, compared to the alcoholic man, the alcoholic woman "had loose sexual morals, had more psychosexual conflict such as homosexuality, and was more likely to get into social difficulties."[4]

But if a doctor is unable or unwilling to diagnose a woman as alcoholic, he may give her condition another label instead. All too often, a physician notes the distraught state of his alcoholic female client, makes a primary diagnosis of "depression" or "anxiety," and proceeds to prescribe a pill to alter her mood, most commonly a tranquilizer, sedative, or antidepressant. Consequently, many alcoholic women walk out of their doctors' offices not only with their alcoholism undiagnosed but with a second powerful potentially addictive psychoactive drug in hand. A 50-year-old Maryland woman who abused both alcohol and a variety of pills described her introduction to mood-altering drugs: "I was incredibly jumpy from all the booze I was drinking, so my doctor put me on both Librium and Nembutal—one to calm me during the day and the other to get me to sleep at night. Then about a year later, he put me on Dexedrine to get me going in the morning, to counteract the effects of the pills—and the alcohol. He actually knew I was drinking, but he never seemed to see it as a major problem." A young Black woman from Washington, D.C. recalled her first visit with a psychiatrist during one of her worst periods of drinking. "I told this man I was depressed and exhausted all the time, but I also told him I thought my drinking might be getting a little out of hand. He told me to be cool about it and handed me a prescription for an antidepressant. In three months, I was going through a month's worth of that prescription every ten days."

Both their professional training and prevailing societal attitudes influence doctors and therapists to view women as inherently less stable emotionally than men by virtue of their female biology, and therefore more prone to psychological disturbances. Consequently, many doctors may be likely to misread a number of serious medical problems in women—including alcoholism—as merely "nerves," depression, or another emotional ailment. This image of women as "naturally" given to mental disorders is the content of much of the advertising by which the powerful American drug industry, at a cost of 1 billion dollars per year—approximately $5,000 per physician—tries to persuade doctors to prescribe mood-altering drugs to their patients.

Psychoactive drug use is not risk free for anyone, but it is especially dangerous for problem drinkers for several reasons. Perhaps the most obvious danger is that of mixing a mood-altering drug with alcohol. The combination of alcohol and certain psychoactive drugs produces a supra-addictive effect substantially more powerful than the effects of any of the drugs taken alone, and consequently increases the possibility of accidental death by an overdose. Access to both alcohol and psychoactive drugs also makes suicide attempts a relatively easy matter, a serious concern in view of the high rate of such attempts—many of them successful—among alcoholic women.

The other major danger of prescribing mood-altering drugs to an alcoholic is the possibility of cross-addiction, that is, dependence on both alcohol and one or more other drugs. Anyone who habitually uses psychoactive drugs may become addicted to them, but the alcoholic is a particularly high risk as she has already established an addictive drug use pattern with alcohol. Cross addiction sometimes keeps a woman drinking for a longer period of time, because she may be able to switch to Valium or another pill temporarily when the effects of alcohol become too staggering for her body to bear. And a woman addicted to both alcohol and pills is likely to face more difficulties in treatment, because she must withdraw and recover from the effects of two or more powerful drugs instead of alcohol alone.

Yet despite these multiple dangers, many physicians distribute these drugs to alcoholic women with an alarmingly free hand. According to Dr. LeClair Bissell, chief of the Smithers Alcoholism Center of New York City's Roosevelt Hospital, it is so easy for alcoholic women to get prescriptions for these drugs that, once addicted, many obtain their maintenance supply from several physicians simultaneously. "If a doctor is giving an alcoholic woman pills, don't imagine he is her only source. He is probably part of a long succession of people who are prescribing for her. For instance, the gynecologist is quite capable of writing prescriptions for Librium and Valium. The general practitioner, if there is one, will hear some of her problems and prescribe pills too. If there's been an emergency room afterward, that may result in yet another prescription for tranquilizers. Even the ophthalmologist taking care of the glasses can prescribe pills. The possibilities are endless."

Since physicians prescribe psychoactive drugs for women in the general population at almost twice the rate they prescribe them for men,[5] it is perhaps not surprising that alcoholic women are far more likely to be cross-addicted than alcoholic men. A 1977 nationwide survey of more than 15,000 Alcoholics Anonymous members showed that 29 percent of the women but only 15 percent of the men were addicted to other drugs besides alcohol. Of new AA members 30 years old or younger, a startling 55 percent of women were cross-addicted, compared to 36 percent of men.[6] Smaller surveys report similar findings: a study of residents in 36 alcoholism halfway houses in Minnesota, for example, found that nearly twice as many women as men were addicted to both alcohol and drugs.[7] Studies of individual treatment programs report similar female-male ratios for cross-addiction.[8]

Treatment

Not every physician, of course, acts as an obstacle to treatment. Some doctors are not only impressively knowledgeable about alcoholism, but will forthrightly confront any patient, regardless of sex, who shows symptoms of the illness. But even if an alcoholic woman is fortunate enough to come into contact with such a physician—and the odds are not good—he can provide no guarantee that she will ultimately receive caring and effective treatment. For once a woman acknowledges her alcohol problem and is ready to seek help, she is then faced with an alcoholism treatment system that, by and large, neither welcomes nor understands her.

The first challenge a woman may confront is simply finding an alcoholism program that has room for her. A 1976 study conducted by the Association of Halfway House Alcoholism Programs of North America reported that of a representative nationwide sample of 161 alcoholism halfway houses, 56 percent served men only, 35 percent were coed, and only nine percent were open only to women. Further, and perhaps more important, women occupied only 19 percent of all available beds in the 161 houses, because the "coed" units reserved only ten to 30 percent of their beds for women.[9] Another survey, conducted by the New York State Commission on Women and Alcoholism, found that in 45 inpatient alcoholism facilities in the state, only 17 percent of all beds were allocated for women. Some surveyed centers refused to treat women at all, citing inadequate budgets and, in one case, the lack of space for a second bathroom.[10]

The scarcity of treatment space for women stems largely from the long-standing assumption by the health system that alcoholism is essentially a male illness. Prior to 1970, the year Congress passed legislation requiring alcoholism programs to offer services to women as a criterion for receiving federal funding, relatively few alcoholism programs admitted women on any basis. And even after the legislation was enacted, many programs added only a few token beds for women rather than providing space on a par with the actual numbers of alcoholic women in the population. It is not uncommon, even today, for a 30-bed treatment center to reserve only four or five beds for women clients.

Consequently, some women seeking help for alcoholism become names on waiting lists, or are forced to travel far out of their communities to find programs with room for them. Others, like the many women in our society who are considered troublesome and who lack other options, end up in mental institutions. Although they are resorted to less often now than in the past, psychiatric hospitals are still used as dumping grounds for some women with drinking problems. Dr. LeClair Bissell described the typical experience of an alcoholic woman consigned to a psychiatric ward: "First of all, it's usually not hard to get her in there because women have always been willing to self-define as mentally ill more readily than men, especially if the alternative is to be called an alcoholic. And as for her drinking, it plays right into the psychiatric approach that says, 'Find the underlying cause, get a lot of insight, pull up your socks, honey, and guess what? You won't be drinking like that anymore and you'll be having two drinks before dinner just like everybody else.' Never mind that she is physically addicted to alcohol."

The "treatment" of alcoholic women in mental wards is sometimes marked not only by ignorance but outright brutality. A Washington, D.C. businesswoman remembered: "My husband told me he was taking me to a hospital and I went willingly, no questions asked. I was diagnosed as alcoholic. My husband left and I was told to follow the man who was carrying my bags. And as we walked along I noticed that he was locking doors behind him and I said: 'What are you doing that for?' And he said, 'Don't you know where you are?' And I said, 'No' and he said, 'You're at a federal facility for the insane.'

"It turned out that the hospital had an alcoholism program for men but none for women, so if you were unfortunate enough to be taken there as an alcoholic woman, you got thrown in with the violently insane. I will never forget it. I was put in a ward where people were defecating in the corner and ladies were walking around nude. And the people working there were just brutal. Really brutal. Full of contempt. I was treated like an animal just like everyone else there. There were no doors on the johns. You had to take a shower with somebody watching you. The blanket on my bed smelled like urine. For the first three days I just shook—I was having junior grade DTs. I was withdrawing from alcohol for the first time in my life and they didn't give me any drugs or any other kind of help. I just lay on my cot and shook."

But even if a woman is able to avoid the route of the psychiatric ward and finds an alcoholism program that has room for her, adequate treatment is by no means guaranteed. For by and large, the alcoholism treatment system is still very much a man's world, with most recovery programs primarily used, staffed, and directed by men and designed to meet male needs. As Rita Zimmer, director of a New York Bowery area alcoholism program, summarized the situation: "Just because most facilities now admit some women doesn't mean that most of them make any attempt to develop programs that relate to women. It doesn't mean they really try to reach out to find alcoholic women in the community. It doesn't even mean they hire staff who have an interest in working with women or who have any knowledge of how to work with women." Consequently, many women find themselves in treatment programs which are neither prepared nor committed to meeting many of their fundamental psychological and practical needs.

Perhaps more than anything else, a woman beginning treatment for alcoholism needs to feel cared about and believed in. In most cases, she has weathered years—sometimes decades—of a brutalizing addiction that has left her overwhelmed with feelings of failure and hopelessness about the possibility of acceptance by others. Dr. Edith Gomberg, professor of psychology at the University of Michigan and a pioneering researcher on women and alcoholism, noted from her experience: ". . . in a deviance disorder like alcoholism, the attitude (conscious and unconscious) of the therapist toward women and toward alcoholism and the enthusiasm and interest of the therapist seem far more related to outcome than the technique used."[11] Given the importance of these factors, the attitudes of many treatment professionals toward alcoholic women are deeply disturbing. A survey of 161 physicians involved in alcoholism treatment revealed that they generally believed that "women have more basic personality disorders: they are more hostile, angry, unhappy, self-centered, withdrawn, depressed and more subject to mood swings; they are more emotional, lonely, nervous; they have less insight, and are not as likable as men alcoholics."[12] Other surveys note similar negative views of women among treatment personnel, in particular the notions that alcoholic women are more emotionally unbalanced than alcoholic men, and by implication, more difficult to treat. Such attitudes

are deeply destructive to recovering women because they are likely to become self-fulfilling prophecies.

As the theory that women are more psychologically maladjusted than men appears to be widespread among alcoholism-treatment personnel and can seriously undermine a woman's successful recovery, its origins need to be examined more closely. It is possible that on the average, an alcoholic woman may actually enter rehabilitation more emotionally impaired than an alcoholic man, due to the psychic strain of the particularly harsh stigma attached to female alcoholism. But it is also likely that the "sicker" label springs from deeply sexist notions about the psychology of women held by mental health professionals. In the study most clearly illustrating these attitudes, conducted in 1970 by Dr. Inge Broverman and Dr. Donald Broverman, a group of psychotherapists was asked to define, respectively, a mature healthy man, a mature healthy woman, and a mature healthy adult. The clinicians, who displayed a high level of consensus in their conclusions, described a healthy male and a healthy female in very different terms. Specifically, they characterized a healthy, mature woman as more submissive, less independent, less adventurous, less competitive, more excitable in minor crises, more easily hurt and more emotional than a mature, healthy man. Equally significant, their description of a healthy adult closely paralleled their characterization of a healthy man, and thereby differed radically from their assessment of a healthy woman.[13] This landmark study, along with others which have replicated its findings, indicates that the standard of mental health in our culture is a clearly masculine one, and conversely, that feminine behavior is basically inconsistent with society's concept of adult mental health.

Stereotypical views of women among alcoholism professionals not only earn many women the damaging labels of "sick" and "hard to treat" but almost inevitably shape the criteria used for women's recovery. If a "healthy" woman is considered relatively submissive, dependent, and noncompetitive, such behaviors are likely to be urged on alcoholic women as evidence of emotional maturity, while behaviors that fail to conform to conventional feminine norms are apt to be punished. When Ardelle Schultz first joined the staff of a drug-alcohol program near Philadelphia in the early 1970s, she found that the staff—until her arrival entirely male—was bent on such a "reeducation" program for women clients:

Women were being taught a new set of behaviors to please males. They were told to give up their sleazy bitch ways. . . . If a woman happened to be naturally sexy and sensuous, she was accused of seducing the men and chastised. If she was unfemininely aggressive and angry, she was told she was treacherous and that she was losing her sensitivity and humanity. If she was lesbian, she was accused of being a man-hater and "sick." In other words, she was learning, again, to repress a part of herself that belonged to her and to become an "honest paper doll" cut out in man's image.[14]

Pressure to conform to such narrowly sexist standards of behavior is seriously damaging to any woman, but it is apt to be particularly destructive to a woman who is alcoholic. The heavy load of guilt, self-hatred, and worthlessness that an alcoholic woman drags with her into treatment is inextricably linked to her failure to live up to a self-denying and impossible ideal of womanhood—the sexual innocent, the nurturing mother, the dutiful wife, the consummate "lady." To be assaulted in treatment with further accusations of her sins against femininity—whether blatantly or subtly conveyed—can only reinforce her already profound conviction of failure as a woman.

Indeed, therapy that imposes a stereotyped vision of femininity on recovering women may also intensify the very kinds of conflicts that triggered their abusive drinking in the first place. Recent research by Dr. Sharon Wilsnack and others indicates that many women who become alcoholic suffer painful sex-role conflicts, usually between a consciously desired "feminine" self-image and unconscious "masculine" strivings which they experience as unacceptable and acutely threatening to their identities. This research shows that drinking may stifle this conflict, allowing a woman to temporarily integrate the masculine and feminine sides of her personality, and that uncontrolled drinking may be activated by a crisis that forces her forbidden "unfeminine" feelings to the fore.

The Social Context

Insensitivity to the psychological needs of alcoholic women is often coupled with apparent indifference to some of their most urgent practical concerns. For example, the typical woman entering an alcoholism treatment program is in serious financial difficulty and badly needs job training. More often than not, she is divorced, has custody of her children, and is receiving little or no support money from her ex-husband. Her job skills are likely to be minimal and she probably has been unable to work steadily for some time. A 1977 survey by the National Institute on Alcohol Abuse and Alcoholism revealed that of the some 60,000 women in federally funded treatment programs, approximately 30 percent were unemployed at the time of entering treatment, and only about seven percent held professional-level jobs.

The mean household income of all the women surveyed was about $7,000.[15]

Yet, regardless of these stark financial realities, few alcoholism programs offer serious job training to recovering alcoholic women, either within the facilities themselves or through arrangements with outside agencies. The myth appears to linger among program staff that women don't really need jobs, that their own and their children's survival are never wholly or even primarily dependent on their own wage-earning abilities. This obliviousness to the economic realities of women's lives was underscored in a recent study of staff attitudes toward clients at a Newark, New Jersey, drug-alcohol program, in which researchers asked the 25 male and nine female staff members their perceptions of the major problems faced by their clients. Less than a quarter of the staff believed that lack of job training was a significant problem for women, although it was seen as a major need for male clients. But when the clients themselves were asked what they perceived as their most serious problems, an overwhelming 96 percent of the women named lack of job training. No other single problem was named by as many women.[16]

When job training is offered to women at all, it is usually for low-paying "women's work" such as typing and other clerical functions, while men in the same program are often trained for more lucrative, highly skilled occupations. Many alcoholism programs provide no job training opportunities whatever for women, instead assigning them the "occupational therapy" of household chores within the program residence, or brush-up courses on cooking, sewing, and home management. Although these skills may be useful and even necessary to some women, to offer them in lieu of hard-nosed job training almost ensures continuing financial hardship for many women once they leave a treatment program. Unable to find a job that pays enough to support themselves and possibly children as well, many find themselves on welfare shortly after completing treatment, or are forced to work two jobs simply in order to pay the bills. Clearly, it is not a way of life conducive to staying sober.

Child care is another service crucially needed by recovering women and almost never provided by alcoholism programs. As most recovery facilities are designed for and by men, this gap is not altogether surprising, since men who enter rehabilitation programs ordinarily leave their children in the care of their wives. But women who begin alcoholism treatment have no such convenient caretakers. Even if a woman's husband is still living with her, which is unlikely, he is rarely able or willing to undertake primary care of the children while she gets help for her alcoholism. Foster care is generally a risky choice, since poor women in particular may be declared "unfit mothers" on the basis of their alcoholism and lose custody of their children, sometimes permanently. As for private day care and other kinds of child care services, New York City family alcoholism counselor Sheila Salcedo observed: "Day care centers are prohibitively expensive and have incredible waiting lists, and the homemaker services charge so much money that your average woman could never afford it. So if you have a lady in need of immediate detoxification and other treatment and she happens to have children, you're really in trouble."

Despite this clear and pressing need for child care services, to date only two alcoholism programs in the entire country offer in-house child care, and few others offer even minimal outside arrangements. Consequently, many women are literally prevented from getting any kind of alcoholism treatment because they can't find anyone to take care of their children. And if a woman tries to begin treatment without having made workable child care arrangements, her recovery is undermined from the start. Salcedo noted: "It is very difficult for most women to get the rest they need in treatment if the kids aren't in good hands. It's easy enough to say, 'OK, let's send the woman into rehab', but if she's got five kids at home, one of whom is on drugs and another who is failing school, and a husband who never really wanted her to go into treatment in the first place, nothing that happens in that treatment program is going to make any kind of impression on her. She gets phone calls from home, she worries, she feels guilty. What kind of treatment does that amount to?"

The realities of women's lives are such that they also may need more intensive follow-up than men after completing a formal program of treatment. In general, women are likely to both face greater pressures than men and receive less support from others once they return from a rehabilitation program to the "real world." Dr. LeClair Bissell observed: "There is much less support from the family of the alcoholic woman than the man. As soon as she returns from treatment she is expected to begin taking care of the children and cooking dinner for the husband and whatnot. And AA (Alcoholics Anonymous) sometimes rather blandly advocates '90 meetings in 90 days' at the beginning, which is fine in theory, but what about the woman who has a job and whose babysitter leaves every day at five o'clock? Or whose husband refuses to take care of the kids every night? How is she going to work the mechanics of that?"

The acute stress and isolation faced by many women following treatment can seriously threaten their sobriety. "You can't just treat a woman, show her how to stop drinking and then tell her to go out and do her own thing," said Clara Synical, founder and director of Interim House, a halfway house for alcoholic women in Philadelphia. "You have to go step by step, follow through, and keep in touch with her so she knows she has a home where she can get support at all times." Yet few alcoholism facilities provide any sustained follow-up services to clients once they complete treatment, in terms of either counseling or practical help in rebuilding their lives. Without such support, many women become quickly overwhelmed by the multiple pressures of their new situations and, sometimes within a few months or even weeks of completing treatment, turn back to the bottle for relief.

The disregard for women's concerns which marks many rehabilitation programs has sparked a small but vigorous movement within the alcoholism field to develop treatment programs specifically designed for women. These programs, which are often staffed and used entirely by women, are committed to providing alcoholic women with a strongly supportive, caring environment and to approaching their recovery needs in the context of women's total experience in society.

Yet, within the alcoholism field, support for women's programs has been grudging at best. Organizers of such programs have found funding hard to come by in a field that has yet to fully recognize the extent of female alcoholism, much less the inability of many traditional programs to meet women's needs. The National Institute on Alcohol Abuse and Alcoholism has funded only 29 women's programs in a total of some 500 treatment facilities, and although some of these federally supported programs are excellent, they clearly do not begin to meet the extent of women's needs. At present, many major metropolitan areas and even entire states are without a single women's program or even a coed program that has instituted special services for female clients.

Since alcoholism programs sensitive to women's concerns still comprise only a tiny percentage of existing programs, the vast majority of women continue to be treated in facilities that fail to meet many of their most pressing needs. Many women drop out of these programs before completing treatment. The reasons they cite are varied: lack of emotional support from staff, an inability to make suitable child care arrangements, diffuse feelings of alienation and isolation, sometimes simply an overwhelming sense that "it's not helping." Occasionally, women leave because of sexual harassment or abuse from male staff or residents. Of those who complete treatment, most studies show a significantly lower rate of recovery by alcoholic women than men, in some cases less than half the rate for men.[17] A good number of women who resume abusive drinking after leaving treatment become part of the "revolving door" syndrome, making their way in and out of treatment programs over and over again for years, endlessly searching for a way out of their addiction, and endlessly failing to find it.

NOTES

1. Jane E. James, "Symptoms of Alcoholism in Women: A Preliminary Survey of A. A. Members," *Journal of Studies on Alcohol,* 36 (1975), p. 1567.

2. Robert W. Jones and Alice R Heinch, "Treatment of Alcoholism by Physicians in Private Practice: A National Survey," *Quarterly Journal of Studies on Alcoholism,* 33 (1972), pp. 117–131.

3. Phyllis Chesler, *Women and Madness* (New York: Avon Books, 1972).

4. Marilyn W. Johnson, "Physicians' Views on Alcoholism with Special Reference to Alcoholism in Women." *Nebraska State Medical Journal,* 50 (1965), p. 380.

5. Herbert I. Abelson et al., *National Survey on Drug Abuse: 1977,* vol.. 1 (Rockville, Md.: National Institute on Drug Abuse. U.S. Department of Health, Education and Welfare, 1977). p. 102.

6. John L. Norris, "Analysis of the 1977 Survey of the Membership of Alcoholics Anonymous" (Paper presented at the Thirty-second International Congress on Alcoholism and Drug Dependence. Warsaw, Poland Sept. 3–8, 1978), p. 20.

7. Luise K Forseth, "A Survey of Minnesota's Halfway Houses for the Chemically Dependent" (Unpublished paper, 1976), p. 9.

8. Ingrid Waldron, "Increased Prescribing of Valium, Librium and Other Drugs: An Example of the Influence of Economic and Social Factors on the Practice of Medicine," *International Journal of Health Sciences,* 7 (1977), p. 55.

9. Association of Halfway House Alcoholism Programs of North America, "Statistical Survey of Full Member Halfway House Alcoholism Programs" (St. Paul, Minn.: 1976), pp 6–7.

10. Cheryl Gillen *et al.,* "Report on Survey of Eighty-Eight New York State Outpatient Detoxification Halfway House and Rehabilitation Facilities" (New York: Committee on Women and Alcoholism in New York State, 1977), p. 1.

11. Edith S. Gomberg, "Women and Alcoholism," in V. Franks and V. Burtle (ed.), *Women in Therapy* (New York: Brunner/Mazel, 1974), p. 183.

12. Johnson, "Physicians' Views on Alcoholism," p. 380.

13. Inge Broverman et al., "Sex Role Stereotypes and Clinical Judgments of Mental Health," *Journal of Consulting and Clinical Psychology,* 34 (1970), pp. 1–7.

14. Ardelle M. Schulz, "Women and Addiction" (Paper presented to Ohio Bureau of Drug Abuse, Cleveland, Oh., June 17, 1974), pp. 23–24.

15. National Institute on Alcohol Abuse and Alcoholism, U.S. Dept.. of Health, Education and Welfare, *Women in Treatment for Alcoholism in NIAAA Funded Facilities,* 1977 (Rockville, Md.: 1978), p. 8.

16. Stephen J. Levy and Kathleen M. Doyle, "Attitudes Toward Women in a Drug Treatment Program," p. 431.

17. David A. Pemberton, "A Comparison of the Outcome of Treatment in Female and Male Alcoholics," *British Journal of Psychiatry,* 133 (1967), pp. 367–373.

Special Needs of Pregnant and Parenting Women in Recovery: A Move Toward a More Woman-Centered Approach

by Sue Creamer, MSW
MIC-TIP
New York, New York
and
Claire McMurtrie, MPH
Harbor-UCLA Research and Education Institute
Torrance, California

In 1989, the Center for Substance Abuse Prevention (CSAP) launched a national effort to systematically explore prevention and treatment intervention options for pregnant women who used alcohol, tobacco, and other drugs (ATOD), representing a major step toward understanding the prevention and treatment needs of women. Although endorsement of a "women's health perspective" was not required from projects receiving CSAP funds, there was a growing, sometimes separate, awareness among many of CSAP's Pregnant and Post-partum Women and Infant (PPWI) projects that something needed to be done to address the fact that a male-as-norm bias in addiction models affects the theoretical questions in research and also ultimately affects assessment techniques, treatment interventions, and follow-up care.[1] As the literature about treatment models for PPWI grew, CSAP developed a National Resource Center for the Prevention of Perinatal Abuse of Alcohol and Other Drugs (which provides tools, training assistance, findings, and ideas relevant to treatment for this population) and an active learning community that convenes at national conferences. The result is an ever-growing knowledge base about how to create environments that foster women's recovery from ATOD use.

Genesis of Woman-Sensitive Treatment

As providers sought ways to engage pregnant women in treatment, it was becoming apparent that treatment programs accustomed to serving predominantly male individuals were not equipped to meet the needs of pregnant women.[2] Based on early methadone models that treated male convicts, programs did little over the years to accommodate women. An awareness that pregnant ATOD users might constitute a "special population" with a different set of treatment needs than those of men (and the nonpregnant ATOD user) gradually evolved. This awareness may have been compelled by the unprecedented increase in the number of single-parent families entering the child welfare system as a result of maternal ATOD use, as well as the acknowledgment by treatment providers that women are often the primary family caregivers.[3] An almost universal finding among nine New York City (NYC) projects was that women tended to be very involved with their children and were often unable or unwilling to separate themselves from their caregiver role to attend exclusively to their own needs. Additionally, most women (whether

Reprinted with permission from the *Jacobs Institute of Women's Health* (Women's Health Issues, Vol. 8, No. 4, 1998, pp. 239–245).

they were involved with child protective services or not) were reluctant to enter treatment if it meant relinquishing their children to relatives or foster parents. Pregnant women posed additional problems for traditional programs because of medical liability issues and the lack of staff trained in prenatal care and child welfare. One of the most basic ways, therefore, in which the NYC CSAP programs felt that they had to accommodate women was to acknowledge their child-rearing roles and responsibilities. Adaptations to this single fact require a theoretical reorientation concerned with the way we frame the problem of maternal ATOD use—that we understand women's roles, and socialization and women's relative status within the larger culture and the developmental and psychological theories that inform our clinical interventions. In addition, logistical planning, having to do with the way systems are structured and concrete services are developed, needs to be reconceptualized.

Relational Theory

One of the most important contributions to the development of a more woman-sensitive treatment is Finkelstein's application of Jean Baker Miller and the Stone Center's "self-in-relation theory" to treatment modalities for women.[4] Miller was one of the first clinicians to challenge the assumption that principles of male development are universal principles of human development.[5] She argued that women in Western society have been "carriers" of certain aspects of the human experience, and a full understanding of human development can be derived only from a thorough elucidation of both female and male experience.

According to Miller and her colleagues, traditional notions of ego strength have overemphasized separateness, autonomy, and objectivity. Boys in this culture are encouraged to disidentify with their mothers and suppress certain "relational sensitivities" in order to gain acceptance, value, and prestige in the eyes of men. They are taught to accept peer standards of toughness and invulnerability. Self-in-relation theory maintains that the direction of growth for girls is not toward greater degrees of autonomy or individuation and the breaking of early emotional ties, but toward a process of growth within relationship, where both or all people involved are encouraged and challenged to maintain connection and to foster, adapt to, and change with the growth of the other. The qualities of relatedness, intimacy, mutuality, and empathy are highly valued and remain central throughout.[6]

Since the dominant culture stresses separation as an ideal, however, women's relational qualities have often been framed as pathologic or have been phrased in regressive terms such as *merged, symbiotic, or undifferen-*tiated by traditional psychology.[6] The larger culture has often viewed relational qualities in terms of emotional fragility, dependency, passivity, and weakness. So-called "women's work" that concerns itself with fostering growth and connection has often taken a back seat to work that emphasizes individual profitability and success.[7] More positive aspects of so-called women's differences, such as receptivity, concern for others, emotional expressiveness, and capacity for empathy, have been largely ignored. Gilligan argued that these qualities are in fact the strengths that allow women to arrive at well-informed conclusions by looking at a situation from many angles and understanding its complexity.[8]

Implications for Treatment

When Finkelstein applied relational theory to drug treatment for women, she shed some much-needed light on a phenomenon that had been occurring with great frequency.[4] Despite clinicians' well-intentioned efforts to convince women that they needed to "work on themselves, first" before they could devote time and energy to their roles within families, women were leaving traditional treatment programs in great numbers. It used to be that, when a woman left a traditional residential treatment program or intensive outpatient program prematurely in order to be with a romantic partner or with children, treatment providers would throw up their hands, shake their heads, and complain that her "codependence" sabotaged her treatment. The implication was that there was something pathologic—or at least, headstrong and unwise—about her choice to be in relationship.[9] Typically men or women entering residential treatment go through an initial phase in which contacts with the outside world are extremely limited. The rationale is that distractions should be kept to a minimum (drug-world related as well social and familial), so that the client can focus on his or her individual issues. Men and women in residential treatment are further discouraged (and often prohibited) from carrying on intimate relationships while in treatment, as these relationships are seen as threats to the development or reconstruction of a stable, separate sense of self. While some NYC CSAP women with prior treatment episodes in more traditional programs reported that they benefited from this approach, self-in-relationship theory asserts that women can build self-esteem and a locus of control within the context of relationships. Since the reality was that most of the NYC CSAP clientele were in relationships already, it made sense to try approaches more consistent with clients' preferences. This was true even in cases where women's partners were abusive. Generally, NYC CSAP programs found that it made more sense to accept a client's choices (rather than make the often unrealistic demand that she leave the abusive relationship) and try to work with her to establish mutual goals. This approach is compatible with the basic social work practice tenet of "starting where the client is" and is by no means a new practice; however, it does mark a departure from the more directive approaches of traditional programs.

Finkelstein believes that self-in-relation theory offers us a rich framework for viewing the socioeconomic, clinical, and systemic treatment issues of ATOD-using women.[10] She suggests that traditional programs that do not acknowledge the importance of relationships and relational sensitivities in a woman's life and help her foster healthy connections cut her off from an important source of self-esteem. Since many women in treatment lack satisfying jobs and other outlets for building self-esteem, the mothering and partnering roles assume central importance. When ATOD-using women face failure on these fronts (in the form of abusive and neglectful relationships, for example), the effects on their self-esteem are often devastating. A frequently cited reason for abusing substances among NYC CSAP clients is to relieve the anxiety associated with such failure. Finkelstein argues that a key focus of any intervention with pregnant ATOD-using women, therefore, should be to enhance (or repair) her connections and help her to embrace her relational self.[10] For these reasons, several NYC programs agreed with Covington that terms like "codependent" must be used cautiously, as they may be contrary to efforts aimed at empowering women and supporting her relational qualities.[11]

TREATMENT APPLICATIONS

Changing the mindset from one that colludes with the larger culture's sometimes subtle critique of women's relational orientation to one that recognizes these tendencies as strengths to be built upon in treatment was (and is) not an easy task. Perhaps now that we are hearing more about a women's health perspective, empowerment models, and strength-based interventions, the relational model makes more sense. However, when the NYC CSAP projects were starting out in 1989, the system was laden with barriers, not the least of which were attitudes and unexamined biases on the part of staff who did not easily entertain such new practices. PACE (Parent and Child Enrichment) underestimated the difficulty of developing a model of treatment that was flexible and more tailored to women within Reality House, a program whose clients were mostly male and whose style of drug treatment was traditional. For example, some Reality House staff believed that pregnant women, even given their additional concrete needs, should not receive special attention. PACE clients occasionally felt judged by other Reality House clients and staff for using drugs while pregnant, reflecting the stigma of the larger culture. Furthermore, some PACE staff corroborated Reed's finding that traditional techniques of confrontation that were used to break down denial (often employing harsh and condescending words) sometimes only served to exacerbate feelings of learned helplessness and hopelessness that are characteristic of women who have been abused.[2] At PACE, there continued to be tension over differing treatment styles and approaches, despite extensive staff training.

Even in NYC CSAP programs where there were fewer older traditions to be overcome and where staff were more open to the notion of women-sensitive treatment, some staff members' predictable, knee-jerk negative reactions to ATOD-using pregnant women needed to be checked, contained, and managed skillfully. Some NYC programs felt that more staff supervision around this and other countertransference issues would have been helpful.

Adopting global and consistent policies and procedures of honoring and supporting women's roles as caregivers and partners was critical in all projects. Recognizing that children can be a support system to women, motivators for remaining in treatment, and a source of self-esteem, SISTERS Intervention Services (a paraprofessional case management program) had an on-site parent child resource room staffed by an early childhood educator, pediatric nurse practitioner, and family specialist. Children received breakfast and light snacks, and both children and their mothers received hot meals every day. Women at SISTERS could leave their children for brief periods of time while they received acupuncture treatment, attended Narcotics Anonymous meetings, or saw a nurse practitioner. However, they were also required to spend time with their children in an interactive educational or play activity with guidance and feedback from staff. SISTERS also made attempts to incorporate a more family-oriented approach by offering services to willing ATOD-using male partners in a parallel clinic. INCEPT, a foster care nursery that was conceived exclusively for families involved with child protective services, offered family therapy in addition to child care. Their staff received twice monthly family systems training and employed an empowerment perspective. Family members were defined as the experts in knowing what was best for them.

Empowering versus Blaming and Pathologizing Approach

For some NYC CSAP programs, assessing strengths required a paradigm shift—a shift away from stigma, blame, confrontation, and shame to one that recognized that "defenses and dysfunction are adaptive and necessary responses to particular experiences."[12] Reed points out that traditional confrontational strategies may be very inappropriate and even harmful for women who enter treatment with an intense feeling of powerlessness that may have contributed to the addictive behavior.[2] This suggests that one of the first tasks of counselors who deal with pregnant addicted women is to take an inventory of their strengths. To name just a few, that inventory might include incredible adaptive skills, resourcefulness, and street smarts; the ability to be financially solvent despite a limited income; the desire to be a good parent and partner; the ability to parent children without the help of fathers; humor; spirituality; adaptability; and an enormous capacity for survival. Moreover, this empowerment approach to treatment is critical given that many women as young girls experience a gender-bound socialization process that encourages them to focus on others' needs at the expense of their own and that is censorial of expressing their own needs and feelings, often leading to depression, low self-esteem, and dysfunctional relationships.[5,8]

A key finding of many of the NYC CSAP programs was that, when treatment goals were a process of negotiation between client and therapist, outcomes were more successful. The theoretical orientation of the prevention and education program of the Multicultural Prenatal Drug and Alcohol Prevention Project (MPDAPP) and Choices recognized this from the start and was reflected in the projects' ability to accommodate input from clients as they went along. PACE was also able to adapt to clients' needs and added a childcare component.

FLEXIBILITY

NYC CSAP programs concurred that flexibility is essential when dealing with pregnant drug users. In addition to being able to respond to clients' needs as they arose and adjust program policies accordingly, many programs found that they had to offer women flexible hours in order to retain them in treatment. In focus groups, several Maternity, Infant Care-Treatment Intervention Program (MIC-TIP) clients cited this as one of the most appealing aspects of the program. Other programs found that the strategy of establishing abstinence before treating issues that may have led to ATOD use (eg, sexual abuse) was too rigid and merely set women up for treatment failure. MIC-TIP tried to accommodate this by encouraging abstinence but allowing women to come and go for counseling regardless of their ATOD-use status (providing they were sober for sessions). This strategy was useful for some women who were not "treatment ready" when they entered MIC-TIP, but rather used it as a stepping stone to more intensive treatment in the future.

Comprehensive Care, Spirituality, and Other Supportive Services

One final aspect of a more woman-sensitive treatment approach that experts promote and NYC CSAP grantees' experiences confirm is the necessity for comprehensive care.[13] The provision of multiple services—preferably in one location—simply make logistics easier, which is an important consideration for pregnant women with a disease characterized by resistance and with children in tow. It decreases the amount of time and money spent and increases the chances of use of services.

Services that NYC CSAP programs feel are essential are prenatal and postpartum care, pediatric care, individual and group ATOD counseling, education (eg, parenting, nutrition, GED, vocational, family planning, ATOD use, stress management, relapse), child care, and social services. Additional services that were found to be very helpful were acupuncture, peer counseling, outreach workers, meals and snacks, spirituality groups, services to address violence and sexual abuse, assistance with finding suitable housing, twelve-step programs, and after care services. Twelve-step groups and other groups or methods that addressed women's spirituality were also found to be extremely helpful. The MPDAPP's project CHOICE used spirituality in its support groups by incorporating culturally relevant poetry, music, stories, and media to acknowledge the strong spiritual component in African tradition. Participants reported that this approach validated their cultural and spiritual beliefs, building strength and confidence in their abilities to have control over their lives. MIC-TIP counselors often worked within the framework of clients' personal spiritual beliefs to enhance treatment.

Programs that could not provide a wide array of services in one location benefitted from strong linkages and case management services that included features such as transportation (eg, vans to transport clients) and extensive outreach and follow-up on appointments. Programs that could not offer some of the components that are considered important (such as child care, vocational training, housing) were able to compensate to some degree by providing aggressive case management and outreach.

Recommendations

The relational model offers an approach that takes into account the reality of women's lives and may account for why so many women who used NYC CSAP services cited caring staff as the key to the success of their treatment. Their message was clear: positive relationships go a long way toward helping women recover from ATOD use. Accordingly, a woman-sensitive treatment program should aim for the following: empowerment and strength-based approaches; regular clinical training and supervision of staff; greater flexibility in treatment planning and program structure; group work, peer counseling, and therapeutic relationships that model healthy relationships; and comprehensive services in a one-stop-shopping model.

REFERENCES

1. Wilke D. Women and alcoholism: how a male-as-norm bias affects research, assessment and treatment. Health Social Work 1994;19:29–35.
2. Reed BG. Developing women-sensitive drug dependence treatment programs: why so difficult? J Psychoactive Drugs 1987;19:151–64.
3. Azzi-Lessing L, Olsen LJ. Substance abuse-affected families in the child welfare system: new challenges, new alliances. Social Work J National Association Social Workers 1996;41:15–23.
4. Finkelstein N. In: Kronstadt D, Green PF, Marcus C, editors. Pregnancy and exposure to alcohol and other drug use: the relational model. Center for Substance Abuse Prevention Report. Washington (DC): US Department of Health and Human Services, 1993:126–63.
5. Miller JB. Towards a new psychology of women. Boston: Beacon Press, 1976.
6. Jordan JV, Kaplan AG, Surrey JL. Women and empathy: implications for psychological development and psychotherapy. In: Women's growth in connection: writings from the Stone Center. New York: Guilford Press, 1991:27–50.
7. Surrey JL. The self-in-relation: a theory of woman's development. In: Women's growth in connection: writings from the Stone Center. New York: Guilford Press, 1991:51–66.
8. Gilligan C. In a different voice. Cambridge (MA): Harvard University Press, 1982.
9. Frank PB, Golden GK. Blaming by naming: battered women and the epidemic of codependence. Social Work 1992;37:5–6.
10. Finkelstein N. Treatment issues for alcohol and drug-dependent pregnant and parenting women. Health Social Work 1994;19:7–15.
11. Covington S. Presentation at Center for Substance Abuse Prevention National Perinatal Conference. Washington, DC, July, 1993.
12. Bean K, Egan P. Women-specific. AOD prevention and treatment. Handout at Center for Substance Abuse Prevention National Perinatal Conference. Washington, DC, 1992.
13. Chavkin W. Treatment for crack-using mothers: a study and guidelines for program design: executive summary. Handout at March of Dimes Perinatal Addiction Conference, New York, 1989.

The Twelve-Step Controversy

by Charlotte Davis Kasl

Drug addiction, codependency, incest, compulsive eating, sex, gambling, and shopping—multitudes of people are using 12-step programs modeled after Alcoholics Anonymous (AA) to recover from these problems. But beneath the surface of this massive movement, women are asking, is this really good for women? While female dissatisfaction with AA is not new (Jean Kirkpatrick founded Women for Sobriety in 1976), widespread questioning of these programs has only begun recently.

In workshops and group interviews, women repeatedly expressed fear about opening up the sacrosanct 12-step institution to scrutiny: "I'm afraid if we talk about this I'll lose something that helped me," or "I questioned the steps in my training program and they said I'd have to leave if I kept that up."

Women who question "the program," as it's often called, have been shamed, called resistant, and threatened with abandonment. They have been trained to believe that male models of nearly anything are better than whatever they might create for themselves.

Some women are grateful for what 12-step programs have given them: a generally available peer model providing support and understanding at no cost. Yet no one way works for everyone. The steps were formulated by a white, middle-class male in the 1930s; not surprisingly, they work to break down an overinflated ego, and put reliance on an all-powerful male God. But most women suffer from the *lack* of a healthy, aware ego, and need to strengthen their sense of self by affirming their own inner wisdom.

Research strongly indicates that alcohol addiction has links to genetic predisposition. A vital point that seems overlooked in AA is that in the case of nearly all substance abuse, the brain chemistry and the body ecology need extensive healing in order to prevent the protracted withdrawal syndrome of depression, anxiety, volatile emotions, and obsessive thinking that can last for years. Too often women endlessly attend groups, have psychotherapy, or take antidepressants when their emotions are actually being influenced by a chemical imbalance that could be helped by proper nutrition and exercise.

Other addictions, and codependency (as well as the will to recover), are influenced by cultural *oppression,* which includes poverty, battering, racism, sexism, and homophobia. Treatment programs need to incorporate understanding—and advocacy—regarding these concerns.

As a psychologist and a former member of 12-step programs, I have encouraged women to write steps that resonate with their own inner selves, putting the focus on self-empowerment.

Here are the 12 steps (as published by AA World Services) followed by a critique and by some possible empowerment steps:

1. "We admitted we were powerless over [our addiction]—that our lives had become unmanageable." The purpose of this step is to crack through denial or an inflated ego and acknowledge a destructive problem. It can be helpful to say "I am powerless to change my partner," but many women abuse chemicals or stay in harmful relationships *because* they feel powerless in their lives. Thus, many women prefer to affirm that they have the power to *choose* not to use chemicals or have dependent relationships. So, alternatively: *We acknowledge we were out of control with _____ but have the power to take charge of our lives and stop being dependent on others for our self esteem and security.*

From *Ms. Magazine,* Nov./Dec. 1990, pp. 30–31. Copyright © 1990 by Ms. Magazine. Reprinted by permission.

Charlotte Davis Kasl is the author of "Women, Sex, and Addiction: A Search for Love and Power" (Harper & Row 1990) and is currently writing "Many Roads, One Journey: Moving Beyond the Twelve Steps" (Harper & Row, to be published in 1992). Her monograph, "Paths of Recovery," is $7.00, from Box 7073, Minneapolis, Minn. 55407.

2. "Came to believe that a Power greater than ourselves could restore us to sanity." I believe that spiritual power is neither higher nor lower but all pervasive. I would replace the passivity implied in this step—that something external will magically restore us to sanity—with "affirmative action": *I came to believe that the Universe/Goddess/Great Spirit would awaken the healing wisdom within me if I opened myself to that power.*

3 "Made a decision to turn our will and our lives over to the care of God *as we understood Him.*" This conjures up images of women passively submitting their lives to male doctors, teachers, ministers, often with devastating consequences. Instead: *I declared myself willing to tune into my inner wisdom, to listen and act based upon these truths.*

The following steps are grouped together here because they all ask women to focus on negative aspects themselves:

4. "Made a searching and fearless *moral inventory* of ourselves."
5. "Admitted to God, to ourselves, and to another human being the exact nature of our *wrongs.*"
6. "Were entirely ready to have God remove all these *defects of character.*"
7. "*Humbly* asked Him to remove our *shortcomings.*"
8. "Made a list of all *persons we had harmed,* and became willing to *make amends* to them all."
9. "*Made direct amends* to such people wherever possible, except when to do so would injure them or others." (All emphases mine.)

We women need to make a searching and fearless inventory of how the culture has mired *us* down with guilt and shame, recognizing how hierarchy has harmed *us* and how *we* have been complicit in harming ourselves and only then look at how we have harmed others. So, instead:

We examined our behavior and beliefs in the context of living in a hierarchal, male-dominated culture.

We shared with others the ways we have been harmed, harmed ourselves and others, striving to forgive ourselves and to change our behavior.

We admitted to our talents, strengths, and accomplishments, agreeing not to hide these qualities to protect others' egos.

We became willing to let go of our shame, guilt, and other behavior that prevents us from taking control of our lives and loving ourselves.

We took steps to clear out all negative feelings between us and other people by sharing grievances in a respectful way and making amends when appropriate.

10. "Continued to take personal inventory and when we were wrong promptly admitted it." As one woman said in a group, "Admit that I'm wrong? I say I'm wrong for breathing air. I need to say I'm *right* for a change." *Continued to trust my reality, and when I was right promptly admitted it and refused to back down. We do not take responsibility for, analyze, or cover up the shortcomings of others.*

11. "Sought through prayer and meditation to improve our conscious contact with God *as we understood Him,* praying only for knowledge of His will for us and the power to carry that out." Instead of looking to an external power, women need to reach inside and ask, What do I believe, what feels right to me? For example:

Sought through meditation and inner awareness the ability to listen to our inward calling and gain the will and wisdom to follow it.

12. "Having had a spiritual awakening as the result of these steps, we tried to carry this message to [others], and to practice these principles in all our affairs." The desire to reach out to others is a natural step that comes with healing, but women need to remember to first care for and love themselves and then to give from choice, not from guilt, emptiness, or to prevent abandonment.

Most important is that we not identify ourselves with such labels as codependent or addict, or get stuck in chronic recovery as if we were constantly in need of fixing.

The goal is to heal and move on, embrace life's ups and downs, and move from *recovery* to *discovery.* Then we can break through the limitations imposed by hierarchy, work together for a just society, and free our capacity for courage, joy, power, and love.

Fetal Alcohol Syndrome: A Nation in Distress

by Charon Asetoyer

And indeed, if it be the design of Providence to extirpate these Savages in order to make room for cultivators of the earth, it seems not improbable that Rum may be the appointed means. It has already annihilated all the tribes who formerly inhabited the sea coast.

—from the diary of Ben Franklin (1700s)

Let us put our minds together and see what kind of life we can make for our children.

—Sitting Bull (1800s)

It becomes clear who was the savage and who was the civilized man.

Historical Overview

In 1973, two doctors from Seattle, Washington, David Smith and Kenneth Jones, identified an irreversible birth defect that occurs when alcohol is consumed during pregnancy. They called it fetal alcohol syndrome (FAS) and noted its effects: mental retardation, deformed facial features, and stiff joints in the hands, arms, hips, and legs.

This naming of FAS by "modern man," however, was not our first knowledge of the connection between alcohol and the birth of unhealthy children. As early as 428–347 B.C., in the Laws of Plato, we find warnings about alcohol consumption during pregnancy: "Any man or woman who is intending to create children should be barred from drinking alcohol." Plato believed that all citizens of the state should be prohibited from drinking alcohol during the daytime and that children should not be made in bodies saturated with drunkenness. He went on to say: "What is growing in the mother should be compact, well attached, and calm."

In 322 B.C., Aristotle was quoted as saying: "Foolish, drunken, hair-brained women most often bring forth children like themselves, morose and languid." In ancient Sparta and Carthage, the laws prohibited bridal couples from drinking on their wedding night for fear of producing defective children. Even in the Bible (Book of Judges 13:7), an angel warns the wife of Manoah: "Behold, thou shalt conceive and bear a son, and now drink no wine or strong drink."

If the great philosophers were aware of the relationship between alcohol and birth defects, why has it taken so long for modern medicine to reach the same conclusion?

Ben Franklin's diary serves as a reminder that the colonial governments of what are now referred to as the United States, Africa, and Australia all used alcohol, in one form or another, to manipulate and control the local inhabitants of the continents they invaded. Alcohol was often used as a form of money with which to barter with local inhabitants for land, food, and animal hides. Colonial governments knew that indigenous people had no experience with alcohol and, therefore, were vulnerable to its effects. As Franklin makes clear, annihilation of indigenous people through alcohol became the unofficial policy of the colonial (U.S.) government.

Charon Asetoyer is the founder and director of the Native American Women's Health Education Resource Center in Lake Andes, South Dakota.

Throughout U.S. history, the government has continued to use alcohol to control, manipulate, and murder Native Americans. Alcohol has been legal, illegal, and legal again at the whim of various presidents. The most recent change in the law pertaining to alcohol use among Native Americans was in 1953, when the Eisenhower administration once again legalized the sale of alcohol to Native Americans. Knowing this history, we should not be surprised that alcoholism remains a major health problem among Native Americans, nor that alcoholism results in the birth of significant numbers of children with FAS.

The Women and Children in Alcohol Program

Of all women who drink alcohol during pregnancy, 40 percent will give birth to children suffering from either FAS or a lesser condition known as fetal alcohol effects (FAE). FAE occurs four to six times more often than FAS, and though a less serious birth defect, we must not underestimate it. The effects are: below average intelligence; learning disabilities; visual, speech, and hearing problems; hyperactive behavior; and a short attention span. FAE may also be accompanied by some of the same physical disabilities as FAS. FAE children usually are not detected until they enter school, where they are often seen as children with discipline problems. On Native American reservations, it is estimated that anywhere from one in nine to one in four children are born with FAS or FAE.

To address the problems of alcohol consumption among Native American women and its impact on their children, the Native American Community Board (NACB), a nonprofit project based on the Yankton Sioux Reservation in Lake Andes, South Dakota, developed the Women and Children in Alcohol program. NACB was founded in 1985 to improve the quality of life for indigenous people and to ensure the survival of our culture through increasing awareness of health issues pertinent to our communities and encouraging community involvement in economic development efforts.

Women and Children in Alcohol was the first program of the NACB, and this focus resulted in NACB opening the first Native American Women's Health Education Resource Center in 1988. Located on the Yankton Sioux Reservation, the center addresses many of the unmet needs of women and children identified during the initial program, including child development; nutrition; adult learning; women's health issues, especially reproduction, AIDS and other sexually transmitted diseases, and cancer prevention; and environmental issues. It is not enough to go out into the community and spread the word about FAS/FAE. Information is important; however, there is more to it than that.

Blaming the Women

Early on, we discovered that when people learned of FAS/FAE, they were quick to blame mothers and their children. No one wanted to examine the larger picture, to ask questions about why women drink when pregnant. What about men's involvement in this, the peer pressure to drink in a community where alcohol use has become the accepted norm? What about the idle time in communities where the unemployment rate is often as high as 85 percent and the high school drop-out rate is over 60 percent? What about the high rates of domestic violence and sexual assault in our communities and the lack of community agencies to address these issues? It is easy to say that a mother's drinking causes an FAS/FAE child to be born, but it is far from the whole truth.

Women who are chemically dependent don't plan to get pregnant and give birth to unhealthy children. They are often the products of abusive childhoods or of homes where their parents drank. They were introduced to alcohol at an early age—I've known children on reservations addicted by the time they were ten or eleven years old. As adults, these women have many health problems of their own—liver damage, diabetes, and other conditions related to alcohol abuse. But these are not uncaring mothers. Chemically dependent mothers love their children as much as other mothers—no matter how unlikely this may seem to outsiders. They must also live with the guilt that society imposes upon them for having given birth to imperfect children. Every day they are reminded that had they not consumed alcohol during pregnancy, their children would probably have been normal and healthy. Chemically dependent women who seek treatment find one barrier after another blocking their paths. Only a small number of alcohol and drug treatment centers take pregnant women. In our four-state area, there is only one such center designed for Native American women. The Kateri program, in St. Paul, Minnesota, will take women through their sixth month of pregnancy (due to complications with Title 19, women cannot receive medical coverage if they stay beyond this point). This program, however, is in the process of being closed down because of problems with state and county funding.

Even if a woman is able to find a treatment center, in most cases, she will be unable to have her children there with her. If she is lucky enough to have supportive and available family members, she can leave her children with them; otherwise, she must turn them over to foster care, where she may fear that they will be abused and neglected. Most Native American women will not turn their children over to foster care unless ordered to do so by the courts.

Of course, someone must pay for women to enter treatment centers. Often, for poor women, the only means of gaining access to treatment is through a court order. But more often than not, when a woman is prosecuted for crimes related to chemical dependency, the courts find it easier and cheaper to terminate parental rights or to sentence a woman to jail than to provide treatment.

In recent years, it has become more and more common for prosecutors to charge women with child abuse or with giving a controlled substance to a minor in cases where a woman has continued to drink or take drugs during pregnancy. Judges want to punish women for engaging in what they consider self-indulgent behavior. They see these mothers as abusive rather than ill. The court may not even consider the fact that the woman being prosecuted may have tried to gain access to unavailable services.

Women of color are reported to authorities eight times more often than white women for giving birth to babies who are drunk or who have controlled substances in their blood. These women are often brought to the attention of authorities by social workers or doctors who deliver their children. But what have these service providers done to help these women deal with their addictions? In our communities, it is a sad fact that social-service and child-protection workers are often aware of alcohol problems among children and adults but are unwilling to intervene because those in need of assistance are part of their own extended family or the family of a tribal council member. Because of the politics involved, a social worker may lose his or her job for trying to assist a child in need of services.

Several years ago, a doctor at the Indian Health Services Hospital on our reservation diagnosed a child with FAS. It turned out to be the tribal chairman's child. The doctor was transferred out of our hospital. It is easier for the problems of families and children to be ignored, for the entire system to become dysfunctional, and for all of the blame to fall on alcoholic mothers, who are given little or no support in the first place.

Sterilization Abuse

Since the courts are rarely interested in helping women to overcome their additions, they have instead focused on how to prevent alcoholic and drug-addicted women from having children. Although judges have shied away from permanent surgical sterilization of women because of fear of violating women's civil rights, new contraceptive technologies have allowed judges to order women to be temporarily sterilized. This, too, is a violation of civil rights.

Norplant, a surgically implanted contraceptive that prevents pregnancy for up to five years, has become the sterilization method of choice among judges. Norplant must be implanted, and removed, by a physician; thus, the woman who is subjected to Norplant has no control over her fertility. She is sterilized. The same is true with the contraceptive Depo-Provera (an injected contraceptive that lasts for approximately three months), which was used to sterilize mentally ill Native American women in the 1980s. Not only were these Indian women injected with Depo-Provera without their approval, but they were given the contraceptive before the FDA had even approved it for use in this country.

The first case in which a judge, as part of a plea bargain, ordered a woman to use Norplant, was in California in 1991. The woman, Darlene Johnson, was African American. The judge had little, if any, understanding of the potential harm that Norplant might do to this woman. He did not know that Johnson had health conditions that could become life-threatening if she were to be given Norplant. Should court officials who have no medical background be prescribing powerful medications? Will the courts assume legal responsibility if they endanger a woman's life in prescribing a potentially harmful drug?

Poor women, many of them women of color, have been targeted for sterilization not only through the courts but through bills in a number of states that require the use of Norplant as a condition for receiving welfare. Clearly, society takes the attitude that you reduce the risk of FAS/FAE babies by sterilizing women at high risk for giving birth to these babies. Reducing the risk of alcoholism and drug addiction among women of color and providing treatment for those in need is not a priority. This means that FAS/FAE and chemically dependent children often end up as orphans, dependent on the state for medical treatment as well as other social services.

Addicted mothers end up absent from home because they are still "using" and are out in the streets, in jail, or are dead after many years of substance abuse. Others must care for the children who may end up in foster homes or state facilities for the remainder of their lives. I have a close family member who has FAE. He lost his mother when he was seven years old due to an alcohol-related car accident. By the time he was fourteen, he had been in ten foster homes. Some were so bad that he experienced sexual abuse, drug abuse, and neglect. He is now 25 and has many problems with chemical dependency as well as with the law.

Society must take some responsibility for allowing a system to continue to function in this manner. It seems that it is easier to allow a system to be ill than to assist it in trying to get healthy. Both tribal and state courts have overstepped their authority in recommending or sentencing women to use Norplant or Depo-Provera. The bottom line is that this is sterilization, whether short-term or permanent, and such a policy carries with it strong connotations of racism and genocide when women of color are the intended targets. We cannot forget that in the mid '70s, the surgical sterilization of Native American women was common practice, with estimates running as high as 25 percent of all child-bearing age women having been permanently sterilized against their will.

CONCLUSION

It is easier to blame women for being alcohol- or drug-addicted than to admit that society has failed to provide services that will help these women to work toward a healthy lifestyle. Though not entirely surprised by the response of the courts, I have been shocked by hearing health care professionals support sterilization policies. In a recent interview with an Indian Health Service doctor concerning Norplant and Native American women, he said that he "would support court ordering of Norplant for the prevention of FAS/FAE." Never during the entire interview did he mention or suggest that the system had failed in trying to assist women who are alcohol or drug addicted.

Fetal alcohol births are an indicator of a Nation in distress. What does this mean for the future of a Nation? For the existence of a culture? The quality of a Nation's leadership is derived from its people and the vulnerability of a Nation lies in its leadership. Health care professionals, social service workers, tribal leaders, lawyers, and judges—people in a position to create a positive response to this issue—have chosen not to do so. Thus, they must share the burden of guilt each time an FAS/FAE or chemically dependent baby is born.

Fetal Alcohol Syndrome Class Related

by Ruth Hubbard

Readers of Charon Asetoyer's article about fetal alcohol syndrome in the March health supplement might like to know about a paper published in the journal *Advances in Alcohol and Substance Abuse* in summer 1987. The article, written by Nesrin Bingol and six others and entitled "The Influence of Socioeconomic Factors on the Occurrence of Fetal Alcohol Syndrome," reports the results from a study comparing the children of 36 upper-middle or upper-class chronic alcoholic women and the children of 48 chronic alcoholic women receiving public assistance in New York City. The authors found that whereas 4.6 percent of the children of the affluent mothers exhibited Fetal Alcohol Syndrome and other alcohol-related effects, 71 percent (or 15 times as many) of the children of the poor mothers did. Both groups of women were heavy drinkers, but their lives differed in many ways. For example, the poor women were more likely to have had alcoholic parents and grandparents and less likely to eat regular and balanced meals than the affluent women. The results of this study show clearly that Fetal Alcohol Syndrome is not just the result of pregnant women drinking too much alcohol, but of the economic, social, and physical neglect entire segments of our population experience all their lives.

College Life a Blur of Booze, Bar Crawls
UW 1st in Binge-Drinking; Students Explain Behavior

by Debbie Stone
Wisconsin State Journal

Shawn Fisher couldn't possibly have realized how vulnerable she looked earlier this month, wobbling in the doorway of a jammed State Street bar, her blond hair messy and her eyelids at half-mast.

She eventually managed a few staggering steps, dazed but ready to charge onward.

"I want to go to another bar," the 21-year-old UW-Madison student said, as if it was plainly the next logical step after downing 10 rum "Captain Cokes" in the last several hours. "It is a fun way to meet people."

For many students, getting drunk is a weekly rite that is as much a part of their college experience as lectures and final exams. On any night of the weekend, particularly during fall football season, they pack into noisy bars that reek of smoke and cheap tap beer.

Researchers say college students are the heaviest drinkers in America. And UW-Madison students have the distinction of topping that list.

According to a 1994 Harvard University study of drinking on college campuses, more than half of UW-Madison students reported that they drink alcohol with the sole intent of getting drunk. That's significantly higher than the national average for large public colleges.

The study also showed that more than one-third of UW-Madison students binge-drink three or more times every two weeks—again, significantly higher than the national average. Binge-drinking is defined in the study as downing five or more drinks in a row.

Ask students why they drink and repeatedly they will give you the same answer that Kevin Pote, 23, does:

"Drinking is a serious part of college life."

"It's expected of you. It's a bonding thing," said senior Joe Binder, 22.

And they're right.

Football games begin and end with beer fests. Campus bars lure students' business with all-you-can-drink specials. One of the favorites is the $5 "Bar Card" available for sale at Pizza Hut on State Street that allows students to get two-for-one drinks at nine bars around Downtown. The bars also offer hangover brunch specials on Sunday morning.

"We glamorize drinking as part of the college ritual," said Felix Savino, the university's coordinator of education for alcohol, tobacco and other drug use.

The Onion, a weekly newspaper in Madison, runs a feature titled "Drunk of the Week," a photo of a particularly crazy wasted person. It's a feature that is beloved by many students.

Some adults encourage the drinking as well. They come onto campus for football weekends and get hammered alongside the young people, several students said.

At UW-Madison, many students, even those who are underage, start drinking on Thursday and sometimes do not come up for air until Monday morning.

Getting drunk is how they reward themselves for making it through a tough week.

"I'm not planning on passing out, blacking out or puking on myself," said the freshly showered and coiffed Jason Norine, 21, before he began a night of drinking two weeks ago. "But I definitely will be intoxicated."

For many adults, it may be difficult to understand the harm in such partying, especially when they used to do it when they were young and today are leading healthy, productive lives.

But there are consequences to the consistent heavy drinking of college students, researchers say.

More than 40 percent of the UW-Madison students surveyed in the Harvard study reported that they did something they regretted when they were drunk. Either they had sex when they didn't want to, got into a fight or may have simply been unable to study when they should have because they were hung over.

A 1994 Columbia University study concluded that alcohol was involved in two-thirds of student suicides, in 90 percent of campus rapes, and in 95 percent of violent crime on campuses.

On rare occasions, students drink so much they end up in the hospital or dead. Earlier this month a Janesville 16-year-old nearly died when he drank rum, vodka and beer in his older brother's college dormitory.

"The students are playing roulette," said drug and alcohol abuse counselor Marlin Kriss.

What is clear, however, is students are willing to risk harming themselves to get drunk week after week.

"These are the four years where you essentially can be an idiot," said Bob Kula, 21.

Stroll down Langdon Street near campus at about 8:30 p.m. most Thursday nights as students gear up for hours of partying. Some have been sipping keg beer since early afternoon.

They sit on their front stoops and discuss their route—a pre-bar party at someone's apartment, a stint at the bars and then an after-bar party at someone's house or fraternity. A pizza truck that sells slices parks and waits for drunk students seeking munchies.

On the Thursday before the Wisconsin-Ohio State football game, students were particularly eager to begin a night of revelry, planning on drinking well into the wee hours Friday.

Not only was there a big game on the horizon, but most students had just finished a grueling week of midterm exams.

"It's probably the most hectic week I have ever had and now I want to let loose," said senior Norine.

Norine and his roommates spend about $300 to stock their bar with whiskey and vodka and to buy a quarter-barrel of beer for a pre-bar cocktail party at their apartment on East Johnson Street.

The young men were excited about their spread, the variety of liquor and the hors d'oeuvres of chips and salsa. "I'm going to have a drink in my hands for the next three to four hours," said Gus Zinn, 21, with a huge smile.

The young men's friends were sufficiently impressed. "Parties usually aren't like this," said one young woman. "There's food and everything here."

What soon became apparent was that the students could handle considerable amounts of liquor. From 9:30 to 10:30 p.m. most of the 30 students at the party had downed at least three hard drinks, mainly rum and Cokes, and didn't appear affected. Everyone was drinking.

There seemed to be an understanding among them that the heavy drinking would begin later when they went to the bars.

"People start out sober and then by midnight or 1 a.m., they've lost their inhibitions," said Amy Potts, 21.

By 12:30 a.m., most of the students had left to go to the bars, except for three young men who were jumping up and down to some loud rock music.

Some students walked to the bars with drinks in their hands. By this time, their conversations were bordering on the ridiculous. One student talked on and on about how he wanted Tom Brokaw's job and would accept nothing less.

Many of the bars looked like dark caves, with students crammed next to each other, shoulder to shoulder, gripping plastic cups. The concrete floors were sticky from spilled beer.

It was hard to follow any conversations because of the number of voices that blended together into a loud buzz.

Many of the students didn't seem to be talking at all and just looked around at each other with glassy eyes.

"All right, I'm bombed right now," said one student, caustically. "What's wrong with that?" he asked. "I've had 10 beers. What's the big deal?"

One of the bars known for its $5 all-you-can-drink beer bargain had a line in front of it a couple of blocks long.

Brian Metelak, who was celebrating his 21st birthday, was so drunk he could hardly stand up or keep his eyes open while waiting in line. "Give me a shot of anything and I will drink it." he said, teetering back and forth. "You only live once."

Looking into the glass windows in some of the bars, it was easy to spot the wasted ones. They had trouble keeping their eyes open, were constantly running their hands through their hair, or talking with wild hand gestures and using lots of profanity.

A patch of vomit carpeted the sidewalk in front of one bar.

Students said they know they drink too much, but they are convinced they will not be harmed by the indulgence.

"We are not alcoholics," Zinn said. "But we definitely abuse alcohol."

Once they graduate and begin full-time jobs, students said they will stop getting sloshed.

Binge drinking is "just a stage people go through in college. Eventually, most people grow out of it." said Kelly Conway, 20.

"I binge-drink and do bad stuff now because this is my time to do it," senior Kula said.

Students Norine and Zinn, for instance, said they both have grade-point averages above 3.0 and look forward to successful careers in business. They are confident they would not let alcohol disrupt their goals once they graduate. "We come from good families. We've seen the way career people live." Zinn said. "Our dads have careers."

The students' point of view is a rational one, said Bob Trumpy, a consultant with National Health Awareness Services in Madison. Since they have been in school they have been taught that the people most susceptible to alcohol problems are people with low self-esteem who are shy and need to drink to make friends, Trumpy said.

"Most of these kids have high self-esteem and are gregarious." Trumpy said. "What has happened is that on some level, these kids have been told it's not going to happen to you."

While researchers say most students will curb their drinking once they graduate, they said college is the training ground for how they will use alcohol throughout their lives.

"The reality is they have an inability to party without alcohol." Trumpy said. "They don't feel whole and complete unless they're drunk. That's not real life."

How UW-Madison drinkers stack up against others

17,592 students at 140 colleges nationwide were surveyed by mail about their alcohol consumption by researchers with the Harvard School of Public Health. The researchers conducted the survey in 1993 and released it in December, 1994

	UW-MADISON	LARGE PUBLIC COLLEGES	ALL COLLEGES SURVEYED
Level of Drinking and Binging			
Past year abstainers/lifetime abstainers	5.7%	12.5%	15.7%
Drank, but did not binge	28.9%	37.2%	40.7%
Binged 1–2 times in the past two weeks	34.6%	26.7%	24.1%
Binged 3 or more times in the past two weeks	30.8%	23.7%	19.5%
Drinking styles of students who had a drink in the past month			
Drank on 10 or more occasions in the past 30 days	16.6%	19.5%	17.7%
Usually binged when drank	51.5%	44.4%	39.9%
Was drunk 3 or more times in the past month	32.4%	26.1%	22.7%
Drinking has caused you to:			
Have a hangover	79.1%	62.3%	58.5%
Miss class	34.5%	30.9%	28.0%
Get behind in school work	28.4%	22.7%	19.6%
Do something you regret	42.6%	35.0%	31.7%
Forget where you were or what you did	37.8%	27.4%	23.8%
Argue with friends	22.3%	20.6%	19.3%
Engaged in unplanned sexual activity	24.3%	20.4%	18.9%
Not use protection when having sex	12.8%	10.4%	9.7%
Damage property	10.8%	9.3%	8.6%
Get into trouble with campus or local police	4.1%	4.5%	4.3%
Get hurt or injured	12.8%	10.0%	9.0%
Require medical treatment for alcohol overdose	0%	0.2%	0.4%
Have five or more of the above problems, excluding hangover but including driving and drinking	23.0%	18.5%	16.1%
Reason for drinking			
Drink to get drunk	54.4%	42.9%	39.0%

The Dangers of Rohypnol

United Council of UW Students

The Scenario: You are at a bar with friends. The cute guy across from you hands you a drink. You drink it and start to feel drunk and confused after a few minutes, as if you are going to pass out. The man offers to walk you outside to get some air. This is the last of what you remember. You wake up the next morning at home with your clothes disheveled and absolutely no memory of the events from the night before.

What It Is

Rohypnol (flunitrazapam) is a benzodiazepine prescribed by physicians for debilitating sleep disorders in 64 countries, but is illegal in the U.S.

How to Recognize It

Small white tablet commonly found in its 1 mg tablet form with an encircled "1" and the word "roche" on one side and a single cross score on the other.

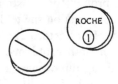

How It Is Abused

Rohypnol is a colorless, odorless, tasteless drug that is slipped into victims' drinks as a prelude to rape. It is used as a "date rape drug" because its sedative effects are felt within 20–30 minutes and possess an amnesia effect, causing a victim to pass out and not remember being sexually assaulted.

The Effects of Rohypnol

Effects are similar to other sedatives: a drunk appearance (drowsiness, light-headed, dizziness) muscle weakness, fatigue, slurred speech, motor incoordination, loss of judgment, and amnesia that lasts up to 24 hours.

Death can result when Rohypnol is mixed with alcohol, narcotics, or other depressant drugs. Strongest effects occur within 1 to 2 hours.

Street Names

- Roofies
- Roachies
- R-2
- Rope
- Lemons
- Mexican Valium
- Circles

How to Reduce the Risk of Substance-Related Rape:

1. Do not leave beverages unattended.
2. Do not take any beverages, including alcohol, from someone you do not know well.
3. At a bar, accept drinks only from the bartender or waitstaff.
4. At parties, do not accept open-container drinks from anyone.
5. Be alert to the behavior of friends appearing disproportionately drunk.
6. Anyone who believes they have consumed a sedative-like substance should be driven to a hospital emergency room immediately.

If You Suspect That You Have Been Drugged and/or Raped:

- Contact your local Rape Crisis Center
- Call the Police (911) for Assistance
- Seek Immediate Medical Help

If a sexual assault does occur when someone is intoxicated or drugged, it is NEVER the victim's fault.

For more general information on Rohypnol, contact the **Hoffmann-La Roche Drug Company** at 800/720-1076 For additional information, contact **United Council,** 122 State Street, Suite 500, Madison, WI 53703; 608/263-3422; Fax: 608/265-4070; ucwomen@macc.wisc.edu.

Find a Helpful, Supportive Doctor

by Sidney M. Wolfe, M.D.
with Rhoda Donkin Jones

If you think you may be addicted to tranquilizers or sleeping pills and would like to do something about it, the first thing to do is to have a talk with your doctor. Depending on what kind of doctor you have, you will get a receptive or not so receptive response. What follows are scenarios, each representing a type of doctor or situation you may encounter.

Scenario A: Doctor Knows Best?

Edith has had a rocky year. Her divorce became final after years of bitter wrangling with her now ex-husband. Required to work for the first time in her life, she started out as a salesperson in a boutique. Soon her natural fashion sense landed her the job of buyer and assistant manager.

The divorce, her job, her relationship with two lively children now entering adolescence, and her reentry into the "singles" scene have all been sources of anxiety as Edith attempted to cope with the many changes in her life.

About two years ago, when it was clear that her marriage was breaking up, Edith went to see her doctor about a backache brought on by strenuous household work. During the conversation she told her doctor about the tension at home. Her doctor gave her a prescription for tranquilizers for both problems. At first her prescription was for 5 mg three times a day, and it made her feel more in control of her life; but mounting tension at home, protracted legal proceedings, and entry into the job scene all increased her anxiety until her doctor suggested that more tranquilizers might be in order. Now she is taking one 10 mg pill four times a day, as her doctor has prescribed.

On a recent buying trip for the boutique, Edith picked up a book at the airport: *I'm Dancing as Fast as I Can,* an autobiography of a professional woman who had become addicted to tranquilizers. She noticed the parallels between her life and the author's, and when she returned from the trip she made an appointment with her doctor.

Edith: Doctor, I am worried about the tranquilizers I'm taking. I have been taking tranquilizers for over two years now, and I wonder if I could be getting addicted.

Doctor: Well now Edith, I guess you've been reading some of those scare stories in the popular press.

Edith: Yes, I have, Doctor. I read a book about a woman a lot like me who began taking tranquilizers because of the stress in her life, and wound up in terrible shape when she tried to quit. Ann Landers wrote a warning about tranquilizers, too, and now I'm worried.

Doctor: Well, I can assure you, that I keep right up to date with professional literature, not the headline-making stuff you've been reading, and there really isn't any danger.

Edith: But, Doctor, I asked the druggist about this, and he showed me the *Physicians' Desk Reference,* and it said that I was taking the maximum dosage permitted, and that even the manufacturer doesn't know very much about the long-term effects of the drug. The book also said I shouldn't be taking it with alcohol. I had two glasses of wine with dinner just a few days ago.

Doctor: And did anything bad happen?

Edith: Well, no, not really, but . . .

Doctor: So you see, it's perfectly safe!

Edith: The book the druggist showed me also said I should be careful driving. I do a lot of driving as part of my job.

Doctor: And have you had an accident?

Edith: Well, no, but maybe I've been lucky.

Doctor: I don't see why you are complaining. These pills are doing you good and I don't see why you are taking up my time with these questions.

Edith: I'm worried about taking these pills. I think they are bad for me to be taking for such a long time. My life is on a pretty even keel now and I don't think I need a crutch; in fact, I wonder if I ever really did. I know now I could have used a counsellor during the time of my divorce, but no one ever suggested it and I didn't think of it myself. I really

don't like the idea of using chemicals like this, and I think it would be best if I stopped using tranquilizers.

Doctor: You do, eh? Now where did you get your medical degree? Don't you think I know what's best for you? Of course I do.

Edith: Oh, Doctor, I don't want to have a fight over this, but I would like your help; I know I still have some personal problems, but my back feels fine now, and perhaps with counseling . . .

Doctor: I can see you are not interested in my advice. Well then, do whatever you want to do. If you don't want to take the pills, just don't take them. I don't care. It's your problem. Now, I think the appointment is over.

Edith: But Doctor, is it safe to just stop all of a sudden like that? Couldn't I get withdrawal symptoms?

Doctor: If you really wanted my advice you would have taken it, and taken your pills just as I prescribed. I'm really very busy now; good day.

Edith left the doctor's office. She still had one refill of her tranquilizer prescription, so she continued using it as directed.

However, she went directly to a drug information hotline for a referral to a physician who would help her get off tranquilizers safely. She was lucky, for if she had followed her doctor's advice and quit cold turkey she might have experienced severe withdrawal symptoms.

Scenario B: Working with the Doctor

Ann is a housewife and mother of three. Two years ago, her doctor prescribed tranquilizers for her after one of her children was seriously injured in an accident. The child is now fine, but keeping a home and raising three children has brought many new stresses, and Ann is always expected to be friendly and responsible. Tranquilizers seemed to help, so her doctor has kept giving her prescriptions for tranquilizers and she has kept taking them. She takes tranquilizers only as directed: a 10 mg pill two to three times a day. Ann also has had several attacks of lower back pain since she hurt her back a few years ago. Her doctor has told her that tranquilizers will help her back pain, too.

Recently, Ann has read articles warning that tranquilizers can be addicting. Although she is taking it only as prescribed, she is worried. After some thought, Ann writes down a list of questions and decides to talk to her doctor about tranquilizers.

Ann: Doctor, I recently read that taking tranquilizers can be addicting. I've been taking the tranquilizers you prescribed for me for two years, now, and I'm a little worried. Could I be getting addicted to tranquilizers?

Doctor: You certainly shouldn't take more tranquilizers than you need, Ann, but tranquilizers are actually quite safe. Very few people get addicted to tranquilizers. And people who do get addicted are usually those who take very high doses of tranquilizers.

Ann: I understand that. But I've read that even doses of tranquilizers prescribed by doctors can be dangerous if I take them for a long time. Isn't two years getting to be a long time?

Doctor: Well, yes, it's a pretty long time. You certainly don't want to take it if you don't need it. But if you do need a drug for tension, it's really a pretty safe drug.

Ann: Is it really safe? I've read that tranquilizers can affect my mind—that it could make my memory worse, or make it harder for me to think clearly. I do seem to forget things more than I did. Could that be the tranquilizers?

Doctor: Well, many things can make you forgetful, and I wouldn't just blame the drug. Tranquilizers do seem to have some effects on a few people's mental functions. But so does anxiety! It's very hard to think well when you're upset.

Ann: That's true, but I do worry about muddling up my mind even more. And I'm also worried about drowsiness. I do feel a little slow sometimes after taking tranquilizers. Is it safe for me to drive?

Doctor: It is pretty common for tranquilizers to slow you down. Some studies even suggest that it slows your reactions down and may affect your coordination. You certainly don't want to drive when you're at all drowsy, or to take anything else that could make you drowsy when you're taking tranquilizers.

Ann: You mean things like sleeping pills?

Doctor: Yes, sleeping pills. And also alcohol, and other tranquilizers. And antihistamines, too.

Ann: I'm glad you told me that. But it does worry me; I often have my children in the car with me, and I'd hate to drive if I'm not quite alert. I'm still a little worried about addiction, too. Wouldn't taking a tranquilizer for this long change my system somehow? Ten milligrams of tranquilizers used to knock me out, and now I take it and hardly notice the difference.

Doctor: It's true, you do seem to get used to a drug when you take it a long time.

Ann: Then is it really worth the risk? If it can slow me down, and if there's even a small chance I could get addicted, should I be taking a drug like this?

Doctor: That depends on whether you need it.

Ann: Does it even work when you take it for this long? It really knocked me out at first. but is it doing anything now?

Doctor: It's hard to say. The label does say that it hasn't been studied well for periods over four months.

Ann: Do you have a copy of the label that I can see? My bottle just says, "Take one pill two or three times a day as needed."

Doctor: You can get the label from your pharmacist. But it's written for doctors, and you may find it hard to read.

Ann: Can I call you if I have any questions?

Doctor: Of course.

Ann: But if you're not sure the tranquilizers are doing anything, and if they can be dangerous, wouldn't I be better off trying to do without them?

Doctor: Well, if you'd like to try, it might be a good idea to try to cut down.

Ann: How about trying to do without them entirely?

Doctor: You could try that too, if you want.

Ann: Can I just quit "cold turkey"?

Doctor: Well, it might not be a good idea. If you stop taking tranquilizers suddenly after two years, you can have bad reactions. You get nervous or shaky, or you may have trouble sleeping.

Ann: It sounds like I could be a little addicted, then.

Doctor: Well, you're used to the drug. Or it could just be your old anxiety coming back.

Ann: But I wasn't that anxious before my son was hurt. And since then, I've been taking tranquilizers all the time.

Doctor: You are used to taking tranquilizers, too. So it is better if you cut back gradually.

Ann: How should I take them when I'm cutting back? I'm taking two to three pills a day.

Doctor: You want to lower your dose over about four weeks. So take two pills a day for a week. Then take 1 1/2 pills a day for the next week. Then take one pill a day or half a pill twice a day for a week. Then cut down to half a pill a day for a week, and then stop.

Ann: Will I have problems right away if I quit suddenly?

Doctor: No. If you stop taking tranquilizers after taking them a long time, they stay in your body in some form for over a week. So it takes a few days before you develop symptoms.

Ann: But I've heard that you can still get withdrawal symptoms.

Doctor: Well, if you were addicted, you could get severe symptoms. They start a few days after you stop.

Ann: What about my back pain? Will that get worse if I don't use tranquilizers?

Doctor: Tranquilizers are only one of the treatments for back pain, and they shouldn't be used alone. Aspirin, rest, and heating pads are very helpful, and they probably will be all you need. You should also be doing back exercises to keep your back from acting up. I can give you a sheet describing some back exercises, if you'd like.

Ann: That would be nice. What about tension? What can I do for tension besides take pills?

Doctor: It depends on what causes it. If you have serious problems, you may want to get counselling. If someone upsets you, try talking to that person. When you can do it, changing situations that upset you is the best thing to do to help tension.

Ann: That makes sense to me. I think I could really use a week's vacation. I haven't had a vacation in years!

Doctor: It sounds like a good idea.

Ann: It sounds much better to me than taking pills. I really like the idea of getting off these tranquilizers. I've felt sort of guilty about them, like they're a crutch. I'd feel a lot more free if I could do without them. I do want to quit, even though it's a little scary.

Doctor: You seem to have thought about it a lot. And I'll be happy to try to help you through the rough spots, if you find you have trouble quitting.

Ann: Good. I need your help.

Doctor: Let me write down a schedule for cutting down, and I'll see you in a month. Give me a call if you have any problems while you're cutting down your dose.

Ann: Thanks. I will.

Doctor: You may find that you need to cut down your dose more slowly. Don't feel that you need to keep to this schedule. Some people take months to stop entirely.

Ann: I'll see how I do.

Doctor: I'll see you in a month, but call me sooner if you have any problems.

Ann: See you then. Hey! I'm leaving here without any prescriptions at all! I feel better already.

Prozac Use Up at UW

by Amy Zarlenga
The Capital Times

UW-Madison health providers are seeing a steady rise in use of anti-depressants on campus with 30 percent of students who go to counseling clinics now on some form of mood-altering medication.

Dr. Eric Heiligenstein, a psychiatrist at Counseling and Consultation Services and a clinical assistant professor in the UW Medical School, estimated about 12 percent of all UW students have mood disorders, and depression is the most common. National surveys of college-age students show the same figure.

About 30 percent of students seen by health counselors take psychotropic medication, and anti-depressants comprise the bulk of them, Heiligenstein said. The most often prescribed anti-depressants are Prozac and its chemically similar cousins, Paxil and Zoloft.

The number of students using counseling services has dramatically increased by almost 50 percent since 1993 and has forced the number of full-time employees to double, from nine to 20 today. About 12,000 visits were made to campus counselors last year, Heiligenstein said, and much of this is caused by increases in the number of depression cases.

• • •

Julie's story: Julie started taking Prozac, an anti-depressant hailed since its creation as a miracle drug for depression, when she was a UW-Madison freshman and had been feeling different than her usual self.

"I was always tired, and I would just cry forever," said Julie, who went to the University of Wisconsin-Madison's Counseling and Consultation Services to get help. There, she was prescribed the drug and worked with a psychotherapist by talking out many of the problems she didn't even know she had.

And cases like Julie's are on the upswing, Heiligenstein said.

Julie soon found out some of her closest friends were taking anti-depressants for the same reason. And today—three years later—she's still taking the drug and claims that without it she'd have flunked out of school and would be living with her parents again.

Anti-depressants stimulate the brain to increase it's production of serotonin, a chemical that is at low levels in people with depression.

Although anti-depressants are most often used to treat the illness for which they were created, they can be used to treat a variety of mental and physical illnesses or ailments, Heiligenstein said, including anxiety, migraine headaches, compulsive behaviors, smoking addiction, and attention deficit hyperactivity disorder.

Prozac was introduced 10 years ago by Eli Lilly & Co. Since then, more than 27 million people, 17 million of whom are Americans, have used the drug.

• • •

Counseling: Most college students respond best to anti-depressants when combined with psychotherapy, Heiligenstein said. Only in rare cases do campus psychiatrists prescribe the drugs without requiring counseling.

"Students come in asking for anti-depressants, and we don't explicitly say this, but we're not waiters or waitresses in a restaurant where people order what they want," he said. "If they want prescriptions alone, we will point them in the right direction, because there are lots of doctors in Madison who will do it that way. But we won't."

Students who go to counseling services have a brief meeting with a therapist or psychiatrist within 24 hours of their request. Staff assess the patients' greatest needs and set up a one-hour appointment for them to meet again.

After the one-hour visit, decisions are made on what route of therapy to take with a patient. Some require medications and therapy, but therapy alone could work for others.

The ratio of females to males seen at the clinic is about 60 percent to 40 percent, respectively. Heiligenstein attributes this to females historically being higher consumers of health care.

Some students are coming to UW already on anti-depressants from doctors in their hometowns, Heiligenstein said.

"I'm getting a lot more calls than I've ever had from parents who have a son or daughter with depression coming to the university and want to make sure we will see them," he said. "We even get calls from the students' doctors. It's a big trend I'm seeing."

The danger involved, however, is some students come to campus unprepared. They run out of pills or only keep contact with their doctor at home for refills. Discontinuing anti-depressants too quickly can result in a depression relapse, Heiligenstein said, and students who simply take the drugs forget the importance of therapy.

• • •

Adolescents' Use Up: The number of adolescents taking antidepressants is also on the rise, leading to more UW students coming into the university with depression, said Sharon Foster, associate professor and assistant clinical professor of pediatrics.

"More adolescents are facing harder situations now than like those 20 years ago," she said. "There's a lot more risk out there now with drugs and alcohol."

Depression is becoming more acceptable as an illness and not a weakness in society, Foster said. The debate continues in current research about how well anti-depressants work on young people, but children as young as 5 are taking them, she said.

The UW drinking culture is distracting for students taking anti-depressants, Heiligenstein said. Because alcohol is a depressant, it can wear down the anti-depressant's effect.

"I've often been asked if it's safe to drink with these drugs by students, and we're really careful about this," he said. "I don't feel comfortable giving the blanket statement of 'nothing will happen' because you never know. But I do tell them they won't get better if they keep drinking."

People who take tricyclic anti-depressants—some of the older drugs that include Imipramine, Nortriptyline and Doxepin—can have "horrendous" depressive effects if they drink alcohol, Heiligenstein said. He said the clinic uses the newer anti-depressants partly because employees know many UW students drink.

Julie said that despite an occasional headache and being a little more tired than before taking Prozac, she believes the drug has helped divert her from drinking and keeps her on a schedule.

"I don't really credit the drug itself," she said. "My roommate is the one who woke me up and told me to get help—but it has definitely helped me."

Heiligenstein said the best way to stop taking anti-depressants is to very gradually lower the dosage. The process can take months or even years for people who relapse into depression. But long-term effects of anti-depressants are not dangerous because the drugs are not addictive, he said.

WORKSHEET—CHAPTER 5

Drugs, Alcohol, and Smoking

1. The articles by Lorraine Greaves describe how cigarette smoking helps women cope with rather than change their lives and that this helps maintain the status quo. Interview two women who smoke now or have smoked to see if their experiences support or contradict Greaves's ideas.

2. "How Women Are Targeted by the Tobacco Industry" examines the marketing of cigarettes to women. Collect cigarette advertisements from magazines and other sources. Find ads in magazines aimed at white audiences and ads aimed at people of color.

   a. Compare the strategies in the ads that seem to be directed at women with those aimed at men. Are there recurring themes?

   b. Compare the messages to white people with the messages to people of color.

   c. Most adult smokers began smoking before they were 20. Are there any educational strategies you can think of to counter the ads aimed at young women?

3. You have been asked to consult on a new alcohol treatment center for your community. All the other "experts" on the committee have years of experience in setting up treatment centers for men. Drawing on at least three articles in this chapter and other information and experience, identify a number of issues which you may need to address to insure that this new facility will be appropriate for women.

4. "College Life a Blur of Booze, Bar Crawls" describes many problems associated with college drinking. Give two specific examples of what could be done to create a healthier approach to alcohol on college campuses.

5. "Prozac Use Up at UW" reports that many young people are on antidepressants in high school and that this problem is increasing. Identify factors which you think may be related to this.

CHAPTER 6

Menstruation

We begin this chapter with the classic "If Men Could Menstruate" by Gloria Steinem. Besides demonstrating that feminists *do* have a sense of humor, this enjoyable, popular article really sets the framework for this chapter. Indeed, it is often the first article discussed in "Women and Their Bodies in Health and Disease" because it sets a theme to be addressed throughout the course: when there are inequalities in a society, everything associated with the valued group will be valued and anything connected with the devalued group will not be valued.

The normal physiological process of menstruation has been defined and redefined by male "experts." It has been labeled a disability or illness, as a barrier to higher education for women, as a weakness that justified keeping middle-class women from working outside the home (working class women were expected to continue their work). Later, menstrual cramps were identified as psychogenic in origin, brought on by the fear of femininity or sexuality. Now hormonal fluctuations are blamed for a wide range of symptoms premenstrually, from acne and water retention to homicidal behavior and self-mutilation. The next article in this section, "Women, Menstruation, and Nineteenth Century Medicine," puts the changing definitions and meanings of menstruation within their historical contexts, while at the same time addressing a recurring theme in medical history—"the reluctance of physicians to accept new scientific findings." In "The Meaning of Menstruation," Louise Lander examines what the social sciences say about the meaning of menstruation, concluding that the meanings will always change because menstruation will always be one aspect of what it means to be a woman in a given cultural and historical context.

With all the changes in labels and definitions, one view of menstruation has remained relatively constant in recent years: menstruation is a big money-maker, with a huge market of healthy women for various industries to target. For example, when it was discovered that cramps were not in our heads, but in our uteruses and the causal agent, prostaglandins, was found, pharmaceutical firms began putting a lot of advertising dollars into selling over-the-counter anti-prostaglandin drugs. While this has largely been a benefit for women who experience dysmenorrhea, we should be alert to potential problems whenever any new groups of drugs are mass-marketed to healthy people. PMS provides an even more dramatic example relating to menstruation, as "The Selling of Premenstrual Syndrome" clearly explains. This classic uses PMS as a teaching tool to remind the reader that there is now a history of healthy women being used as guinea pigs for products (oral contraceptives, DES, estrogen replacement therapy) for which the promises were too good to be true. Progesterone has been widely prescribed without any solid data on effectiveness or risks. While a small percentage of women may suffer from severe PMS and benefit from this treatment, there is a clear attempt to convince a lot more women that they have this "disease" and need treatment. PMS is symbolic of the "double-edged sword" women face when asking that our health issues be taken more seriously. We need good scientific research and health system response to the issues which affect us, but we do not want these issues to be medicalized or used against women.

Since women went "off the rag" and began using disposable menstrual products, there has been a large profitable business in tampons, napkins, and pads. While these are products most women want to keep on the market, the competition and profit motive sometimes mean that consumer health and safety receive minimal attention. The most obvious example was the Rely superabsorbent tampon, marketed by Proctor and Gamble, which was associated with toxic shock syndrome deaths. In *The Price of a Life,* Tom Riley, the lawyer for Pat Kelm, a young woman from Cedar Rapids, Iowa, who died from toxic shock syndrome four days after using her first Rely tampon, describes how Proctor and Gamble intentionally ignored reports of problems and instead chose to spend more than all other tampon manufacturers combined marketing their wonder product as the tampon which "even absorbs the worry." Now that toxic shock syndrome (TSS) is no longer the women's health issue in the headlines and in women's magazines, we are concerned that young women (TSS mainly strikes menstruating women under age 30 using tampons) are not learning what they need to know to protect themselves from products (high absorbency products) or circumstances (leaving a tampon in for many hours) which increase risk of TSS.

The worksheet on menstrual products provides a tool for calculating the personal financial costs of menstruation related products for one woman in her lifetime. Any reader who multiplies that figure by the number of menstruating women will see dollar signs which tempt companies to get a piece of the menstruation product market.

In spite of all the negative views, women have been redefining menstruation for ourselves—as a normal, healthy physiological process. Some women have even developed celebratory menstrual rituals. (It is important to note, however, that many women cannot menstruate and for women who are trying to become pregnant, menstruation can be viewed with great disappointment and sadness).

This chapter concludes with the voices of many women describing their experiences and messages they received connected with menarche as their introduction to menstruation and womanhood. In "Menarche and the (Hetero)Sexualization of the Female Body," Janet Lee summarizes 40 narratives about menarche from women ages 18–80 and concludes, "While women internalize negative scripts associated with the bleeding female body, they also respond with consciousness and resistance."

If Men Could Menstruate—
A Political Fantasy

by Gloria Steinem

A white minority of the world has spent centuries conning us into thinking that a white skin makes people superior—even though the only thing it really does is make them more subject to ultraviolet rays and to wrinkles. Male human beings have built whole cultures around the idea that penis-envy is "natural" to women—though having such an unprotected organ might be said to make men vulnerable, and the power to give birth makes womb-envy at least as logical.

In short, the characteristics of the powerful, whatever they may be, are thought to be better than the characteristics of the powerless—and logic has nothing to do with it.

What would happen, for instance, if suddenly, magically, men could menstruate and women could not?

The answer is clear—menstruation would become an enviable, boast-worthy, masculine event:

Men would brag about how long and how much.

Boys would mark the onset of menses, that longed for proof of manhood, with religious ritual and stag parties.

Congress would fund a National Institute of Dysmenorrhea to help stamp out monthly discomforts.

Sanitary supplies would be federally funded and free. (Of course, some men would still pay for the prestige of commercial brands such as John Wayne Tampons, Muhammad Ali's Rope-a-dope Pads, Joe Namath Jock Shields—"For Those Light Bachelor Days," and Robert "Baretta" Blake Maxi-Pads.)

Military men, right-wing politicians, and religious fundamentalists would cite menstruation ("*men*struation") as proof that only men could serve in the Army ("you have to give blood to take blood"), occupy political office ("can women be aggressive without that steadfast cycle governed by the planet Mars?"), be priests and ministers ("how could a woman give her blood for our sins?"), or rabbis ("without the monthly loss of impurities, women remain unclean").

Male radicals, left wing politicians, mystics, however, would insist that women are equal, just different, and that any woman could enter their ranks if only she were willing to self-inflict a major wound every month ("you *must* give blood for the revolution"), recognize the pre-eminence of menstrual issues, or subordinate her selfness to all men in their Cycle of Enlightenment.

Street guys would brag ("I'm a three-pad man") or answer praise from a buddy ("Man, you lookin good!") by giving fives and saying, "Yeah, man, I'm on the rag!"

TV shows would treat the subject at length. ("Happy Days": Richie and Potsie try to convince Fonzie that he is still "The Fonz," though he has missed two periods in a row.) So would newspapers. (SHARKS SCARE THREATENS MENSTRUATING MEN. JUDGE CITES MONTHLY STRESS IN PARDONING RAPIST.) And movies. (Newman and Redford in "Blood Brothers"!)

Men would convince women that intercourse was *more* pleasurable at "that time of the month." Lesbians would be said to fear blood and therefore life itself—though probably only because they needed a good menstruating man.

Of course, male intellectuals would offer the most moral and logical arguments. How could a woman master any discipline that demanded a sense of time, space, mathematics, or measurement, for instance, without that in-built gift for measuring the cycles of the moon and planets—and thus for measuring anything at all? In the rarefied fields of philosophy and religion, could women compensate for missing the rhythm of the universe? Or for their lack of symbolic death-and-resurrection every month?

Liberal males in every field would try to be kind: the fact that "these people" have no gift for measuring life or connecting to the universe, the liberals would explain, should be punishment enough.

And how would women be trained to react? One can imagine traditional women agreeing to all these arguments with a staunch and smiling masochism. ("The ERA would force housewives to wound themselves every month": Phyllis Schlafly. "Your husband's blood is as sacred as that of Jesus—and so sexy, too!": Marabel Morgan.) Reformers and Queen Bees would try to imitate men, and *pretend* to have a monthly cycle. All feminists would explain endlessly that men, too, needed to be liberated from the false idea of Martian aggressiveness, just as women needed to escape the bonds of menses-envy. Radical feminists would add that the oppression of the nonmenstrual was the pattern for all other oppressions ("Vampires were our first freedom fighters!") Cultural feminists would develop a bloodless imagery in art and literature. Socialist feminists would insist that only under capitalism would men be able to monopolize menstrual blood. . . .

In fact, if men could menstruate, the power justifications could probably go on forever.

If we let them.

Women, Menstruation, and Nineteenth-Century Medicine

by Vern Bullough • Martha Voght

One of the recurrent themes in medical history is the reluctance of physicians to accept new scientific findings. This may well be due to the innate conservatism of medical practitioners and their unwillingness to use patients as guinea pigs for treatment about which they are unsure. Sometimes, too, the reluctance comes because new findings demonstrate that previous practices might have been harmful to the patient; this turn of events is difficult to accept. Often, however, the reluctance is not attributable to any medical reason but results when new findings upset the emotional attachments, some would say political prejudices, that most physicians hold and which have little to do with medicine itself. This paper is concerned with this kind of of position.

When the belief structure of the physician is threatened, even in fields outside of medicine, he often uses his medical expertise to justify his prejudices and in the process strikes back with value-laden responses which have nothing to do with scientific medicine. Unfortunately, since he is assumed to speak with authority, his response, perhaps as he intended, has influence far beyond that of ordinary men. One of the best examples of this is the controversy over the physical disabilities of women which took place in the last part of the nineteenth century as women began to demand more education and greater political equality and to challenge many of the male stereotypes about woman's place. Since medical practitioners were almost all men, and many of them were hostile to any change in the status quo in male-female relationships, they inevitably entered the struggle with arguments which not only appear today as ludicrous, but even in the period they were writing were not based upon any scientific findings and in fact went contrary to those findings. This is particularly true in their understanding of the consequences of menstruation.

From *Bulletin of the History of Medicine* 47 (1973): 66–82. Copyright © 1973 by Johns Hopkins University Press. Reprinted by permission.

This article is also reprinted in the excellent collection *Women's Health in America*, edited by Judy Walzer Leavitt, University of Wisconsin Press, 1984.

VERN L. BULLOUGH is Dean of the Faculty of Natural and Social Sciences, State University of New York College, Buffalo, New York.

MARTHA L. VOGHT is a free-lance writer of educational materials in Bishop, California. Reprinted with permission from Bulletin of the History of Medicine 47 (1973) 66 82.

During the last part of the nineteenth century American physicians toyed with several theories of menstruation. In general they were aware of the theories of John Power of London who postulated that ovulation and menstruation were connected. American medical journals also made an attempt to keep their readers current on the English research which tended to support his theories.[1] At the same time, however, many physicians seriously discussed various folk theories about menstruation, retaining with little change in content ideas which appear in the Hippocratic corpus or in Aristotle. Many still held that it was the effect of the moon upon women that caused them to menstruate; others held that the fetus was formed from the menstrual flow. The popular underground pseudonymous marriage manual *Aristotle's Masterpiece* held that menstruation was due to the casting out of the excess blood which would have nourished the embryo if pregnancy had occurred.[2] Even as late as the 1890s when the first experimental work leading to the understanding of human hormones was taking place, American physicians were still discussing the question of whether the ovaries triggered menstruation, whether the uterus was an independent organ and performed the menstrual function without external aid, or whether the fallopian tubes were responsible for the monthly flow.[3] A few, however, perhaps influenced by the Victorian disgust at the sexual and reproductive processes, considered menstruation a pathological condition. These physicians believed that in Paradise humans had reproduced asexually and it was only when man had fallen that perfection had been replaced by the evil of sex. An article in the *American Journal of Obstetrics* in 1875, for example, argued that menstruation was pathological, proof of the inactivity and threatened atrophy of the uterus. As evidence of its unnaturalness the author claimed that conception was most likely when intercourse occurred during the monthly flow, but intercourse at such times was dangerous and forbidden because the menstrual blood was the source of male gonorrhea. Since menstruation therefore stood in the way of fruitful coitus it obviously had not been ordained by nature.[4]

In 1861 E.F. Pflüger demonstrated that menstruation did not take place in women whose ovaries had been removed, a finding which reinforced the ovarian theory but did not end the debate since Pflüger himself in 1863 hypothesized that there was a mechanical stimulus of nerves by the growing follicle which was responsible for congestion and menstrual bleeding. This led him to believe that menstruation and ovulation occurred simultaneously.[5] It was not until the twentieth century and a better understanding of the hormonal process that the timing of ovulation was fully understood. In the meantime, many American physicians accepted Pflüger's theory that nervous stimulation triggered menstruation, and it was this belief which led large numbers of physicians to express opposition to any emancipation of women.

This paper is not the place to discuss the movement for female emancipation, but even a brief synopsis must point out that women were much more assertive of their rights in the last part of the nineteenth century than earlier. Though traditionally women in the United States had received some sort of primary education, if only to learn to read the Bible, they had been denied entrance to any of the grammar schools or colleges. In 1783, for example, twelve-year-old Lucinda Foote was examined for admission to Yale and found capable of giving the "true meaning of passages in the *Aeneid* of Virgil, the *Select Orations* of Cicero and the Greek *Testament."* She was, however, declared unqualified to enter the college because of her sex.[6] Physicians of the time were generally more inclined to favor female education than oppose it. Perhaps the best example is Benjamin Rush. He urged female education on the grounds that it would allow women to better fulfill their familial responsibilities, be less prone to superstition, have talent in managing their family's affairs, and be better teachers for their sons. Rush also pointed out to his fellow males who might be somewhat hesitant to accept his ideas that the ignorant were the most difficult to govern and an educated wife could, by virtue of her education, be more easily shown the wisdom of her husband's orders and decisions.[7] It was only later that a significant portion of the medical community appear in opposition to female education.

During the first part of the nineteenth century the female academies and seminaries began to multiply, and in the 1830s full-fledged colleges were proposed for women and Oberlin College opened its doors to both sexes.[8] Soon medical schools also found themselves under attack for failure to admit women, and a few women such as Elizabeth Blackwell managed to receive medical training. Most women, however, turned to nursing as an alternative to challenging the male bastion of medicine,[9] but it is perhaps no accident that medical opposition to feminine emancipation began to increase as the physician himself felt threatened by the few women attempting to enter medical school. About 1870 several medical writers began proclaiming that education for women was a disastrous error since girls between twelve and twenty could not stand the strain of higher education, in large part because of the physiological strains which puberty and ovulation put upon them.

Among the first theorists of menstrual disability, by far the most influential was Edward H. Clarke, a professor of materia medica at Harvard and a fellow of the American Academy of Arts and Sciences. In 1873 he wrote that though women undoubtedly have the right to do anything of which they are physically capable, one of the things they could not do and still retain their good health was to be educated on the pattern and model of men. He held that while the male developed steadily and gradually from birth to manhood, the female, at puberty, had a sudden and unique period of growth when the development of the reproductive system took place.[10] If this did not take place at puberty, it would never occur, and since the system can never do "two things well at the same time," the female between twelve and twenty must concentrate on developing her reproductive system. To digest one's dinner, he held it was necessary to temper exercise and brain work; likewise, during the growth of the female reproductive system, brain work must be avoided. The overuse of the central nervous system would overload the switchboard, so to speak, and signals from the developing organs of reproduction would be ignored in favor of those coming from the overactive brain. Even after puberty females were not to exercise their minds without restriction because of their monthly cycle. The menstrual period was vital, Clarke held, and any mental activity during the "catamenial week"[11] would interfere with ovulation and menstruation,[11] the necessary physiological processes of being female.

He then proceeded to demonstrate, at least to his own satisfaction, that higher education left a great number of its female adherents in poor health for life. He was alarmed that the increase in the number of young women being educated would so deplete the population that within fifty years "the wives who are to be mothers in our republic must be drawn from trans-Atlantic homes."[12] For proof of his assertion he offered as evidence the cases of young women he had as patients whose ill health he ascribed to hard study. One had entered a female seminary at fifteen in good health but after a year of application to her studies and following the routine of the school, which included standing to recite, she was pale and tired "every fourth week." A summer's rest restored her but by the end of the second year she was not only pale but suffering from an "uncontrollable twitching of a rhythmical sort" in the muscles of her face. On the advice of the family physician she was taken for a year of travel in Europe and returned cured. Unfortunately she then returned to school where she studied without regard to her menstrual periods and, though she graduated at nineteen as valedictorian, she was an invalid and it took two years in Europe for her to recover. Her illness, according to Dr. Clarke's diagnosis, resulted from making her body do two things at once. He reported the case of another young woman, a student at Vassar, who began to have fainting spells and suffer painful and sparse menses. Inevitably she graduated at nineteen as an invalid, suffering from constant headaches. Dr. Clarke believed this was because she suffered from the arrested development of her reproductive system due to her education. As evidence he claimed she

not only had menstrual troubles but was rather flat chested. Another young college woman came to him with a history of diminishing menstrual flow, constant headaches, mental depression, acne, and rough skin. Eventually Dr. Clarke committed her to an asylum.[13] It was also of some concern to Dr. Clarke that young women of the lower classes were expected, during puberty, to take jobs in domestic service or in factories. In his practice he had seen evidences of ill health among such women which he blamed upon their work. Yet, he concluded that labor in factory at a loom was far less damaging than study to a woman, because it worked the body, not the brain. It was primarily brain work which destroyed feminine capabilities.[14]

Women who concentrated upon education rather than the development of their reproductive system also underwent mental changes, according to Clarke. Not possessing the physical attributes of a man, they also tended to lose the "maternal instincts" of a woman to become coarse and forceful. By educating women, said Dr. Clarke, we were creating a class of sexless humans analogous to eunuchs. To solve this alarming problem, he recommended strict separation of the sexes during education, particularly after elementary school. He urged that female schools provide periodic rest periods for students during their menstrual periods. The young women would also have shorter study periods since they were by nature weak and less able to cope with long hours.

> A girl cannot spend more than four, or, in occasional instances, five hours of force daily upon her studies, and leave sufficient margin for the general physical growth that she must make. . . . If she puts as much force into her brain education as a boy, the brain or the special apparatus (i.e., the reproductive system) will suffer.[15]

He held up as models some reports on German education, showing that menstrual rest for female students was practiced.[16]

Though there was immediate unfavorable reaction to Clarke's thesis, it still became widely accepted. His critics pointed out, for example, that Clarke had done no scientific study on the matter, that he generalized from a few clinical cases in his own practice, and that his description of periodic rests in European education were totally untrue. One critic commented that "Dr. Clarke has thrown out to a popular audience a hypothesis of his own, which has no place in physiological or medical science. His whole reasoning is singularly unsound."[17] There was some suspicion that Clarke's argument was designed to end speculation at Harvard about admitting female students.[18] Nevertheless, the popularity of his message is indicated by the fact that within thirteen years, *Sex in Education* went through seventeen editions.

Those physicians who followed Clarke tended to exaggerate his position and to ascribe far more harm to the education of women than even he had dared. T.S. Clouston, a physician of Edinburgh, Scotland, wrote a lengthy series for the *Popular Science Monthly* to demonstrate to the public the dangers of the education of females. He pointed out that it was medically accepted that the "female organism is far more delicate than that of men; . . . it is not fitted for the regular grind that the man can keep up." Over-stimulation of the female brain causes stunted growth, nervousness, headaches and neuralgias, difficult childbirth, hysteria, inflammation of the brain, and insanity. The female character is likewise altered by education; the educated woman becomes cultured, but "is unsympathetic; learned, but not self denying." Clouston admitted the weak point of his argument, "that it is not founded on any basis of collated statistical facts," based only upon observations of physicians of their own patients. Nonetheless, he expressed the hope that research to gather the facts would be carried on in the future.[19]

This, in fact, began to happen but the results were not what Clouston anticipated. The Massachusetts Labor Bureau made the first report on the health of American college women based upon statistical evidence and not the "haphazard estimate of physicians and college instructors."[20] The results indicated that of 705 college women, 78 percent were in good or excellent health, 5 percent were classed as in fair health, and 17 percent were in poor health. When these women had started college, 20 percent were in poor health. The report concluded that there were no marked differences in health between college women and the national average.[21] John Dewey, in his analysis of the report, decided that worry over personal matters was more harmful to health than overstudy.[22]

In spite of the publicity given the study, there was little change in attitudes among those who believed women and education made a dangerous mixture. In the same year that it appeared, Henry Maudsley wrote in *Sex in Mind and in Education* that the concurrence of puberty and higher education meant that mental development was accomplished at the expense of physical. While acknowledging that there were no facts to provide an answer to the question—what are the effects of coeducation?—he nonetheless answered the question by citing Clarke and declaring that girls educated in the traditional ways were losing "their strength and health." The imperfect development of the reproductive system interfered with the development of the feminine character leaving the educated woman without a sufficiently feminine frame of mind. The education of women must be designed to prepare them for their proper sphere.

It will have to be considered whether women can scorn delights and live laborious days of intellectual exercise and production, without injury to their functions as the conceivers, mothers, and nurses of children. For, it would be an ill thing, if it should so happen that we got the advantage of a quantity of female intellectual work at the price of a puny, enfeebled, and sickly race.[23]

Clarke and most of his imitators subscribed to the Pflüger theory of menstruation, but it was not a necessary preliminary to the belief in the physical disability of women. John Goodman, a Louisville physician, believed that the ovular theory of menstruation was untenable. Instead menstruation was "presided over by a law of monthly periodicity," a "menstrual wave" which affected the entire female being and from whose dictates women could not escape.[24] This theory, although in conflict with that of Pflüger, was appropriated to the cause of those who opposed female education. A good example is George J. Englemann who, in his presidential address before the American Gynecological Society in 1900, expressed the opinion that female schools should heed the "instability and susceptibility of the girl during the functional waves which permeate her entire being," and provide rest during the menstrual periods. At the same time he said that menstruation was controlled by "physical conditions and nerve influences," and that the first menses were accelerated by mental stimulation. His observations contradicted those of Clarke, since while Clarke found educated women ceasing menstruation, Englemann found that mental work increased the frequency of menstrual flow.[25] Nevertheless he would agree with Clarke that women could not endure the rigors of higher education.

J.H. Kellogg, whose *Plain Facts for Old and Young* was responsible for inculcating vast numbers of Americans with the idea that masturbation led to insanity, added also to the public misinformation about menstruation. Part of Kellogg's success was due to the fact that he appeared to be so scientific:

There has been a great amount of speculation concerning the cause and nature of the menstrual process. No entirely satisfactory conclusions have been reached, however, except that it is usually accompanied by the maturation and expulsion from the ovary of an ovum, which is termed ovulation. But menstruation may occur without ovulation, and vice versa.[26]

He then stated that the first occurrence of menstruation is a very critical period in the life of a female, that each recurrence renders her specially susceptible to morbid influences and liable to serious derangements, and that she must carefully watch out during these periods.

> There is no doubt that many young women have permanently injured their constitutions while at school by excessive mental taxation during the catamenial period, to which they were prompted by ambition to excel, or were compelled by the "cramming" system too generally pursued in our schools, and particularly in young ladies' seminaries.

He added, however, that a moderate amount of study would not be injurious, and he had no doubt that a large share of the injury which has been attributed to over-study during the catamenia was caused by improper dress, exposure to cold, keeping late hours, and improper diet. Kellogg also wondered about women workers and felt that female workers should be protected during their periods. He felt it was wrong that women in order to keep their situations were required to be on hand daily and allowed no opportunity for rest at the menstrual period.

> In many cases, too, they are compelled to remain upon their feet all day behind a counter, or at a work table, even at periods when a recumbent position is actually demanded by nature. There should be less delicacy in relation to this subject on the part of young women, and more consideration on the part of employers.[27]

As the movement for female emancipation grew, the physicians who discussed the frailties of the female did so with increasing emotional fervor. The president of the Oregon State Medical Society, F.W. Van Dyke, in 1905, claimed that hard study killed sexual desire in women, took away their beauty, and brought on hysteria, neurasthenia, dyspepsia, astigmatism, and dysmenorrhea. Educated women, he added, could not bear children with ease because study arrested the development of the pelvis at the same time it increased the size of the child's brain, and therefore its head. The result was extensive suffering in childbirth by educated women. Van Dyke concluded by declaring that the women who were remembered in history were faithful wives and good mothers such as Penelope, Cornelia, St. Elizabeth; and these would still be remembered when "the name of the last graduate of the woman's college shall have faded from the recollection of men forever."[28]

Dr. Ralph W. Parsons in the *New York Medical Journal* in 1907 cited many of the above authorities to show that the results of higher education for women could lead only to ill health. He claimed college women

suffered from digestive disorders as well as nervous and mental diseases.

> The nervous system has been developed at the expense of other bodily organs and structures. The delicate organism and sensitive and highly developed nervous system of our girls was never intended by the Creator to undergo the stress and strain of the modern system of higher education, and the baneful results are becoming more and more apparent as the years go by.[29]

He offered as proof the fact that in 1902, 42 percent of the women admitted to New York insane asylums were well educated, while only 16 percent of the men admitted had gone beyond grade school He concluded that women "who have undergone the strain of the modern system of education, are much more liable to become victims of insanity than men of the same class."

One of the mental diseases to which college women were prone was the modification of feminine traits of mind. These women developed distaste for the duties of home life, were egotistical, assumed independence of speech and manner, and were not attentive to the advice of their parents. Educated women neglected to cultivate refined speech, had loud voices, laughed with gusto, and sometimes even used slang and profanity. "They do not exhibit," said Dr. Parsons, "the modesty of demeanor which we have been taught to believe is one of the most admirable traits of the feminine character." Colleges encouraged unwomanly behavior. At one school girls publicly appeared on stage in knee breeches, and in the performance used such words as "devilish" and "damned." Such women as these would never be able to fulfill their female functions, for not only was their reproductive apparatus stunted by education, but no man would ever love them. This was because men had deep sentiment for women with "feminine traits of character with which God intended they should be endowed."

Parson's solution went far beyond anything proposed in the nineteenth century by medical men. Girls, he decided, should not learn Latin, Greek, civics, political economy, or higher math, for these subjects could be of no use to them in their proper sphere. They should have shorter school hours than boys, and spend most of their time in home economics classes.[30]

All of these twentieth-century physicians had available to them a careful study on the health of college and noncollege women, printed in the *Publications* of the American Statistical Association, 1900–1901. This study, carried out during the 1890's, compared college women, not to the "average" woman of the census, as past projects had done, but to a control group of noncollege women composed of their own relatives and friends of their own social class. The study found that though college women married two years later than noncollege women there was a growing tendency to marry later among both groups. Noncollege women had "a slightly larger number of children," but college women had more children per years of married life. There were no differences in problems of pregnancy and mortality of children. The health of the children was roughly equal; although among college-educated mothers the researchers felt they detected slightly fewer delicate children and slightly more robust children. The study found no significant difference between the health of the two groups of women before or after college age. Seventy-five percent of the college women had been employed before marriage, while only 34 percent of the noncollege women had had outside employment. The college women chose different kinds of husbands than the control group. Seventy-five percent of them married college men, while their noneducated cousins married a college-educated husband in only half the cases. Sixty-five percent of college women married professional men, while only 37 percent of the noncollege women had husbands in the professions.[31]

The physicians who persisted in accepting the theories of Clarke et al. simply ignored such studies. G. Stanley Hall who, though one of the outstanding psychologists of the early twentieth century, strongly believed that woman's place was in the home, simply dismissed the statistical studies as inaccurate. Instead, he felt, physicians who treated overeducated women were more likely to see the true circumstances. Inevitably Hall's classic *Adolescence* repeated all the fears and superstitions concerning female education. For example, he connected menstruation to mental exercise. As proof he offered the fact that American girls had their first menses at an average of 14 years of age, while European girls were, on the average, 15.5 years of age before menstruation started. This precocity of American girls was "due chiefly to mentality and nerve stimulation," in other words, education. "Education," theorized Hall, "in a temperate or subartic zone is more productive of precocity than in the south, and if general nervous stimulus is the cause, the same schooling is more dangerous in the city than in the country."[32] Hall was heavily influenced by Clarke's concept of rest during the menstrual periods, and suggested that the female, rather than observing the weekly Sabbath, should have rest periods of four successive days per month. These days would be devoted to leisure and religion, since during menstruation the female was inclined "to a natural piety and sense of dependence" which accounted for the fact that women were more religious than men.[33] Women were by nature intuitive, Hall claimed, not mental. By being "bookish"

woman lapsed into male manners and fashions, declined from "her orbit," and obscured her "original divinity."[34]

He believed with Goodman that the ruling factor of female life was periodicity. For most of her life a woman had no alternative but to give way to its dictates, and for this reason special schools should be established for girls. Under no circumstances should coeducation exist, for putting adolescents in the intimacy of the classroom destroyed "the bloom and delicacy" of the girls. Female schools should be in the country, with plenty of places for exercise and privacy. All students should observe the "monthly Sabbath" during their menstrual periods, during which time

the paradise of stated rest should be revisited, idleness be actively cultivated; reverie, in which the soul, which needs these seasons of withdrawal for its own development, expatiates over the whole life of the race, should be provided for and encouraged in every legitimate way, for in rest the whole momentum of heredity is felt in ways most favorable to full and complete development. Then woman should realize that *to be* is greater than *to do;* should step reverently aside from her daily routine and let Lord Nature work.[35]

Such opinions as this were unlikely, in 1905, to go unchallenged by the feminists. Martha Carey Thomas, president of Bryn Mawr College, attacked this lyrical report on periodicity as "sickening sentimentality" and "pseudo-scientific." She held that the seventh and seventeenth chapters of Hall's work were more degrading to womanhood than anything written since Michelet's *La Femme.* She recalled her student days, when she was "terror-struck lest I, and every other woman with me, were doomed to live as pathological invalids in a universe merciless to woman as a sex." Now "we know" that it is not "we," but the "man who believes such things about us, who is himself pathological, blinded by neurotic mists of sex, unable to see that women form one-half of the kindly race of normal, healthy human creatures in the world."[36]

Serious research also questioned the point of view Hall represented. One such study hypothesized that if the menstrual cycle had such influence on women, it ought to show up on tests comparing motor and mental abilities of both men and women. When the results were analyzed it was found that none of the efficiency curves correlated with the menstrual cycles and that the males in the tests had varying efficiencies similar to the females rather than being stable and unvarying as had been thought. In fact, the curves produced by the two sexes were indistinguishable when the notations of the menstrual periods were removed. How, asked the researcher Leta Stetter Hollingworth, was such a striking disparity from what had been the accepted scientific position to be accounted for. Two possible explanations were offered. First the scientific and medically accepted facts were not facts at all but traditions carried on by mystic and romantic writers that "woman is a mysterious being, half hysteric, half angel," and this attitude had somehow found its way into the scientific writing. Scientists seeking to justify this had "seized" upon the menstrual cycle as the probable source of the alleged "mystery" and "caprice of womankind." Once formulated, then, the dogma became cited as authority from author to author until the present day. A second possible explanation of the error was that physicians had not based their conclusions upon accurate evidence. She postulated that normal women did not come under the care and observations of physicians but rather only those with mental and physical diseases. Physicians generalized from these patients, and determined that women were chronically ill. Moreover, once these observations were accepted, experiments to disprove them were difficult since, until the end of the nineteenth century, all investigators were men and the taboo upon mention of the menstrual function made such research next to impossible.[37]

In actuality the explanation is probably far more complex than this. It is quite possible that physicians were simply blind to what was going on and were so prejudiced than they refused to see reality. There is also the possibility that during the nineteenth century young women did have more than their share of menstrual difficulties. One source of such problems was undoubtedly diet. It was generally believed a century ago that certain foods, especially highly flavored dishes and meats, aroused the sexual appetites. It was, accordingly, desirable to regulate the diets of young girls so as to protect them from unhealthy desires, and physicians found that protein deprivation was a successful cure for female masturbation.[38] Female boarding schools, to minimize sexual interest among their charges, were likely to follow such a prescribed vegetable diet. A study of female higher education in the 1890s deplored the low state of boarding school health, due, it was believed, to diet and lack of exercise, as well as the pressures of the curriculum.[39]

Clelia Mosher, whose research into menstruation among college women spanned several generations between 1890 and 1920, found that girls in the earlier period probably did have greater menstrual difficulties than those in the 1920s. She at first concluded that the reason for this was that during the nineteenth century girls were taught that they were going to be sick during menstruation and the result was a self-fulfilling prophecy. She also found, however, that there was a correlation between dress and menstrual difficulties. During the 1890s and the early years of the twentieth century most young women were put into tight corsets, banded clothing, and unsupported heavy skirts. This clothing interfered with the respiration, made the abdominal muscles flabby, restricted physical activity, and deformed the body on the same principle that the binding of feet in China did. The result was, Mosher held, chronic disturbances of the organs and prolonged menstrual flow.[40] She prepared tables correlating menstrual pain among college women with the width and weight of their skirts and the measurements of their waists. Her figures showed that as the skirt grew shorter and skimpier, and the waist larger, the functional health of women improved. In 1894, 19 percent of the college women were free from menstrual difficulties; in 1915–16, 68 percent considered their periods no problem. In the earlier period the average skirt was 13.5 feet around the hem, the average waist measurement was twenty inches, and the woman also wore several petticoats, some fifteen pounds of clothing hanging from a constricted waist. By the beginning of World War I women wore their skirts above the ankle, skirts were narrowed, petticoats fewer, and waist measurements had increased by 40 percent.[41]

Such studies did much to ease the traumas inflicted by some of the male medical writers of the last part of the nineteenth century. Increasing reassurance came from the growing numbers of college-educated and career women who seemed none the worse for their years of hard study or work. While the generation of Martha Thomas had been haunted by the "clanging chains of that gloomy little specter," Dr. Edward H. Clarke's *Sex in Education,* several generations of educated women tended to prove that "college women were not only not invalids, but that they [were] better physically than other women in their own class of life."[42] In part too, the development of the sanitary pad in the aftermath of World War I also freed women from some of the more confining aspects of menstruation. Not all physicians, however, adjusted their thinking to correspond with the latest scientific findings. At the beginning of the twentieth century most sex manuals warned against exciting lives and mental stimulation for pubertal girls.[43] Perhaps this was to be expected but, when the same sort of material was still being published thirty years later, it is possible to wonder what motivated the physicians who wrote it. William J. Robinson's book, for example, in 1931 in its twenty-second edition, still warned that only a minority of women were free from illness during their menstrual periods, and that most should rest at least two days, avoid dancing, cycling, riding, rowing, or any other athletic exercises, and probably postpone travel by auto, train, or carriage.[44]

That some of the medical hesitation to change seems political, a hesitation to accept women as equals, is evident even in the 1970s. After all it was in 1970 that Edgar Berman, previously best known as the friend and physician of Hubert Humphrey, remarked that women could not fill leadership roles because of the influences of their periodicity, that is their menstrual cycles and menopause.[45] This statement cost him his position in the Democratic Party and made not only him but Humphrey an object of attack by the militant members of women's lib. That the belief still has currency is also indicated by the fact that the first issue of the new woman's magazine *Ms.* found it relevant enough to counter with an article on male cycles and gave hints to women on how to discover whether the men in their lives were ebbing or flowing.[46]

This is not the place to argue the existence of male cycles, however, but only to indicate that it is very possible for medical concepts to get mixed up with political and social beliefs. Perhaps this is inevitable since we are human, but it ought to make the physician a little more cautious in distinguishing his biases from his objective findings. In retrospect it does seem that the nineteenth-century physician grew somewhat more shrill in his emphasis on the instability of the female at the very time that women and their male allies were challenging the old stereotypes. A few physicians jumped into the controversy citing their own clinical observations as evidence in ways that today we can regard only as ludicrous. This in fact happened with a whole series of physiological functions and human activities but was particularly harmful when such sexual topics as menstruation, masturbation, or birth control were dealt with. Obviously women are anatomically different from men, and they do have monthly periods, but to generalize from this and a few isolated patients to a whole theory of female inferiority seems to be an example of poor medical theorizing. The difficulty with past medical theory, whether good or bad, however, is that it often remains a part of the popular ideology of a later generation. One of the things that women of today have to overcome is some of the mistaken concepts about menstruation and its effect.[47]

Notes

This paper was presented at the 45th annual meeting of the American Association for the History of Medicine, Montreal, Canada, May 4, 1972. Research sponsored by the Erickson Educational Foundation, Baton Rouge, La.

1. John Power, *Essays on the Female Economy* (London: Burgess and Hill, 1831); G.F. Girdwood, "Theory of menstruation," *Lancet*, 1842-43 , i: 825–30; J.Bennet, "On healthy and morbid menstruation," *Lancet, 1852, i:* 35, 65, 215, 328, 353.
2. Aristotle [pseud.], *The Works of Aristotle in Four Parts,* containing I. *His complete Master-piece; . . . II. His Experienced Midwife; . . . III. His Book of Problems; . . . IV.*

His Last Legacy . . . (London: published for the bookseller, 1808), 126.
3. See M.M. Smith, "Menstruation and some of its effects upon the normal mentalization of woman," *Memphis Medical Monthly,* 1896, *16:* 393–99; C. Frederick Fluhmann, *Menstrual Disorders, Diagnosis and Treatment* (Philadelphia: W.B. Saunders, 1939), 17-26.
4. A.F.A. King, "A new basis for uterine pathology," *American Journal of Obstetrics,* 1875–76, 8: 242–43.
5. E.F.W.Pflüger, *Ueber die Eierstöke der Sügethiere und des Menschen* (Leipzig: Englemann, 1863).
6. Thomas Woody, *A History of Women's Education in the United States,* 2 vols. (New York: The Science Press, 1929), 2: 137.
7. Benjamin Rush, *Essays, Literary, Moral and Philosophical* (Philadelphia: Thomas & Samuel Bradford, 1798), 75–92.
8. Woody, *History of Women's Education,* 2: 231.
9. See Vern Bullough and Bonnie Bullough, *Emergence of Modern Nursing* (New York: Macmillan, 1969), passim.
10. Edward H. Clarke, *Sex in Education; or, A Fair Chance for Girls* (Boston: James R. Osgood & Co., 1873), 37–38.
11. Ibid., 40–41.
12. Ibid., 63.
13. Ibid., 65–72.
14. Ibid., 133.
15. Ibid., 156–57
16. Ibid., 162–81.
17. George F. Comfort and Anna Manning Comfort, *Woman's Education and Woman's Health* (Syracuse: Thomas W. Durston & Co., 1874), 154.
18. G. Stanley Hall, *Adolescence, Its Psychology and Its Relations to Physiology, Anthropology, Sociology, Sex, Crime, Religions and Education,* 2 vols. (New York: D. Appleton and Co., 1904), 2: 569.
19. T.S. Clouston, "Female education from a medical point of view," *Popular Science* Monthly 24 (Dec. 1883–Jan. 1884): 322–33.
20. John Dewey, "Health and sex in higher education," *Popular Science Monthly* 28 (March 1886): 606.
21. Annie G. Howes et al. *Health Studies of Women College Graduates: Report of a Special Committee of the Association of Collegiate Alumnae* (Boston: Wright & Potter, 1885),9.
22. Dewey, "Health and sex in higher education," 611.
23. Henry Maudsley, *Sex in Mind and in Education* (Syracuse: C.W.Bardeen, 1884), 14.
24. John Goodman, "The menstrual cycle," *Transactions,* American Gynecological Society, 1877, 2: 650–62; "The cyclical theory of menstruation," *American Journal of Obstetrics,* 1878. 11: 673–94.
25. George J. Englemann, "The American girl of today: the influence of modern education on functional development," *Transactions,* American Gynecological Society, 1900, 25: 8–45.
26. J.H. Kellogg, *Plain Facts for Old and Young* (Burlington, Iowa: I.F. Segner, 1882), 83.
27. Ibid., 86.

28. F.W. Van Dyke, "Higher education a cause of physical decay in women," *Medical Records,* 1905, 67: 296–98.
29. Ralph Wait Parsons, "The American girl *versus* higher education, considered from a medical point of view," *New York Medical Journal,* 1907, 85: 116.
30. Ibid., 119.
31. Mary Roberts Smith, "Statistics of college and noncollege women," *Publications,* American Statistical Association, 1900-1901, 7, *nos. 49–56:* 1–26.
32. Hall, *Adolescence,* 1: 478.
33. Ibid., 1: 511.
34. Ibid., 2: 646.
35. Ibid., 2: 639.
36. M. Carey Thomas, "Present tendencies in women's college and university education," Feb., 1908, in *The Woman Movement: Feminism in the United States and England,* ed., William O'Neill (Chicago: Quadrangle Books, 1969), 168.
37. Leta Stetter Hollingworth, *Functional Periodicity: An Experimental Study of the Mental and Motor Abilities of Women during Menstruation,* Teachers College, Columbia University Contributions to Education, No. 69 (New York: Columbia University Press, 1914), 44, 66, 93, 95.
38. John Tompkins Walton, "Case of nymphomania successfully treated," *American Journal of the Medical Sciences,* 1857, *33:* 47–50.
39. Anna C. Brackett, ed., *Women and the Higher Education* (New York: Harper, 1893), 90.
40. Clelia Duel Mosher, "Normal menstruation and some of the factors modifying it," *Johns Hopkins Hospital Bulletin,* 1901, *12:* 178–79.
41. Clelia Duel Mosher, *Women's Physical Freedom* (New York: The Woman's Press, 1923), 1, 29.
42. Thomas, "Present tendencies in women's college and university education," 169.
43. See, for example, William H. Walling, *Sexology* (Philadelphia: Puritan Publishing Co., 1904), 207.
44. William J. Robinson, *Woman: Her Sex and Love Life,* 22d ed. (New York: Eugenics Publishing Col., 1931), 80–81.
45. *New York Times,* July 26, 1970; *Los Angeles Times,* Feb. 21, 1972.
46. Estelle Ramey, "Men's cycles," *Ms.* Spring 1972, 8–15.
47. For a survey of some recent research on the topic see Mary E. Luschen and David M. Pierce, "Menstrual cycle, mood and arousability," *Sex Research* 8 (February 1972): 41–47.

The Meaning of Menstruation

by Louise Lander

In our search for the hidden treasure that is the meaning of menstruation for modern women, we have so far found some clues in the realm of biology: that cyclicity is a function of life, not of femaleness; that hormonal influences affect both sexes and operate in extremely complex ways, with the causal arrows between hormones and behavior pointing in both directions; and that from an evolutionary perspective the way modern human females experience menstruation is anomalous. If biological science has this to offer, what help can social science provide?

Social Science as Spinning Wheels

The short answer is, not a lot. Social scientists concerning themselves with menstruation have had to expend large amounts of energy discrediting a body of masculinist research that was on its way to entrenching menstrual stereotypes as scientific fact. Having accomplished that task, they have been expending their energies trying to design methodologically sound research that fits the human experience of the menstrual cycle into neat social scientific categories—dependent and independent variables, correlations and tests of statistical significance. Contradictory findings abound, perhaps because the subjects and their lives are more complex than the methodology by which they are being examined. A mass of material yields only a little of interest, that concerning the different ways human beings explain how they feel, depending on the social context of their being asked. But in fairness to the social scientists, we should note that the interesting material from biology has come less from studies of the menstrual cycle itself than from work that incidentally casts light on that phenomenon; when it has looked at menstruation directly, biomedical science has given us the morass we examined in Chapter 5.

Social scientists used to be fascinated with the subject of mood changes as a function of the menstrual cycle, using elaborate questionnaires to ask batteries of women how they felt during the various stages of past menstrual cycles and coming up with findings that served to buttress the concept of a premenstrual syndrome. By now that body of research has been pretty thoroughly discredited: It has been well established that a study that asks women to record their moods day by day produces different results from one asking them to record their moods from memory of the past; that women taking part in a study they know concerns the menstrual cycle will give different answers from those in a study whose purpose is disguised; that looking at data in terms of group averages frequently presents a different picture from that produced by individual responses; and that negative moods found in the premenstrual stage of the cycle may reflect stresses that are themselves changing the length of the cycle and determining when the premenstrual stage occurs.[1]

Attempts to construct new bodies of social scientific research concerning menstruation have been less successful than attempts to discredit the research of the past. Studies looking for correlations between personality types or socialization categories and the experience of menstruation have given us a wealth of contradictions: High femininity scores on a personality test, for example, have been found to correlate positively, negatively, or not at all with severity of menstrual symptoms, depending on the study. Some studies, in other words, suggest that women identifying with those characteristics traditionally defined as feminine (being nurturant, supportive, and deferential) experience greater menstrual distress than less conventional women, other studies suggest the reverse, and still others find no association between such personality measures and the degree of menstrual discomfort.[2]

Research attempting to correlate cultural attitudes surrounding menstruation with the extent of menstrual distress has been similarly inconclusive.[3] One study, which hoped to correlate stress and traditional socialization with menstrual symptoms and attitudes, found that its strongest correlation reflected what might be called the reality effect: Women with the most severe menstrual symptoms had the most negative attitude toward menstruation. "Thus," concludes the researcher, "it appears that menstrual attitudes are not merely a product of socialization but also a function of women's experiences with symptoms that disrupt their lives."[4] Apparently it surprises social scientists to find that women are in touch with reality, that menstrual experience is more than a web of outdated taboo.

Menstruation as Label

But just as menstrual pain is real, so other—perhaps more subtle but no less real—feelings may or may not be labeled menstrual by the women experiencing them. A study comparing women taking oral contraceptives with women not taking them, for example, inquired about conditions such as headache, backache, irritability, abdominal and breast swelling, cramps, depression, and happiness, and asked the subjects to what they attributed these various conditions—tension, illness, the menstrual cycle, a good or bad day, something else, or unknown. It turned out that during the premenstrual phase of the cycle, women on the pill were more likely to connect their state of being to their menstrual cycle than women not on the pill. This finding logically reflects the fact that the contraceptive pill creates an artificial menstrual cycle in which menstruation is totally predictable, unlike the usual situation for women whose cyclicity is not under artificial control; thus the explanation of being premenstrual is more readily available to women on the pill as a way to make sense of how they feel.[5]

This analysis, called attribution or cognitive labeling theory, harks back to the research described in the chapter on hormones in which subjects were injected with adrenaline thinking it was a vitamin supplement, sometimes told and sometimes not told that they might experience certain physical effects, and then put in a room with a stooge who acted either euphoric or angry. The subjects who had access to a physiological explanation for the way they felt experienced less anger or euphoria than those who were uninformed.[6] Other research has found that negative behavior described as occurring during a woman's premenstrual period is likely to be attributed to the menstrual cycle but that positive behavior is more likely to be attributed to factors in the woman's personality or situation.[7]

There are a number of states and actions, in other words, that are sufficiently ambiguous that they might or might not be a function of menstrual cyclicity; whether or not they are put in that category has something to do with the availability of cyclicity as an explanation and something to do with the positive or negative nature of what needs to be explained—biology, especially menstrual biology, being seen as a negative element in a woman's life, and the concept of premenstrual syndrome being a conveniently available label to attach to any negativity that occurs during the premenstrual phase.[8]

To say that attribution theory is about all the social sciences have to offer us is to say as much about the complexity of human beings as about the deficiencies of researchers. Human beings stubbornly refuse to keep their variables well separated—the premenstrual phase, for example, which social scientists would like to assume "causes" certain states, may itself be determined by certain states, as when the stress of, say, final exams accelerates the start of one's period. In that case, a state is causing the premenstrual phase, rather than the reverse.[9] Or negative premenstrual feelings may be a realistic reflection of painful experiences of menstruation in the past rather than a psychological expression of a hormonal state in the present.[10]

Menstruation as Synchrony

One of the most fascinating findings of menstrual cycle research—some of it conducted by psychologists, some by biologists—is located precisely on the border between biology and culture. This is the phenomenon known as menstrual synchrony, an old wives' tale become scientifically established fact. Three studies of college women have found that close association between women over a number of months leads to a significant coming closer together of the dates their periods start. Two studies found this convergence operating among roommates and among pairs of women who identified each other as closest friends; the third study used a population of women living in single rooms and thus dealt only with closest friends.

The first menstrual synchrony study, conducted in the early seventies at a women's college, also looked at the correlation between contact with men and the length of the menstrual cycle. Comparing women who spent time with men at least three times a week with those whose association with men was less frequent, the women who interacted infrequently with the opposite sex had significantly longer menstrual cycles. The other two studies were unable to duplicate this finding, but they were carried out at coeducational institutions and thus could not replicate the extent of the separation of the sexes; they distinguished their subjects in terms of frequency of social contact with men, but all of the subjects were seeing men as fellow students every day.[11]

The phenomenon of menstrual synchrony is a perfect example of the convergence of the biological and the social, a social situation shaping a biological process.

As we saw was often the case with hormones, this phenomenon is the opposite of the conventional assumption that female biology affects conduct; here conduct—being in close association with another woman—is affecting biology—the endocrine events that determine the timing of the menstrual cycle.

What causes menstrual synchrony? No one knows, but some speculate about the possibility of substances known as pheromones. These are a class of chemicals used by many species to effect communication between members of the species, one individual releasing the substance into the environment and another receiving it and reacting to it. It is not clear whether human pheromones exist, but one intriguing study took underarm perspiration from one woman and applied it to the upper lip of several other women; a control group received plain alcohol instead of sweat. After four months, the women in the experimental group but not in the control group showed a significant shift in the timing of their menstrual cycle toward that of the donor of the perspiration.[12]

Menstrual synchrony is not the only example of social situations affecting menstruation, although it is the most elegantly established. Wartime has provided an unwanted laboratory for studying the effects of extreme situations, and wartime catastrophes including air raids, internment, and the threat of extermination have been seen to bring about the cessation of menstruation in women with previously normal cycles. Among women in concentration camps, the frequency of amenorrhea has seemed to vary with the harshness of conditions and the danger of death, although there is some evidence that malnutrition also played a part. Peacetime studies have found a connection between food intake and menstruation, with the menses stopping among women who are malnourished and among obese women who lose substantial amounts of weight.[13]

Less drastic life changes, such as going away to a new environment—a convent, the armed forces, or a residential school—have also been found to trigger amenorrhea in a substantial percentage of women.[14] Anxiety about exams can have the same effect.[15] In social-scientific terms, menstruation turns out not to be an independent variable; in real-life terms, menstruation is an integral part of what it means to live as a human being, a creature of culture as much as biology, the two merging and mutually interacting so that the distinction becomes meaningless.

Menstruation as Pain

But then there is the problem of pain—and it exists across cultures, an apparently irreducible biological core of menstrual negativity. A study conducted by the World

Health Organization in the early eighties surveyed women in ten countries in various stages of development (Egypt, England, India, Indonesia, Jamaica, Korea, Mexico, Pakistan, the Philippines, and Yugoslavia) and found that women all over the world, rural and urban, of low and high social status, experienced physical discomfort in connection with menstruation, with frequencies ranging from 50 to 70 percent. Younger women tended to experience discomfort during their periods; older women, before bleeding began. Women using an IUD were more likely to complain of discomfort that women using no contraception or using some other method—suggesting that a total escape from the cultural into the biological is impossible after all. The most commonly reported symptoms were back pain and abdominal pain.

The reported experience of mood changes in connection with menstruation was much more varied than was the case with physical discomfort—ranging from 23 percent among the Sudanese in Indonesia (surveyed separately from the Javanese) to 71 percent in England (home of the doyenne of PMS, Katharina Dalton) and 73 percent among the Moslems in Yugoslavia (surveyed separately from non-Moslems). The Indonesian Sudanese reported both the lowest incidence of mood changes (23 percent) and the highest incidence of physical discomfort (71 percent); this intriguing pattern provides another suggestion that total escape from the cultural is impossible, for it might mean that this is a culture in which somatic symptoms are more socially acceptable than changes in mood.[16]

The general response to menstrual discomfort, it might be noted, is apparently stoicism—most women reported doing nothing by way of treatment (the minority who took analgesic drugs tended to be urban, better-educated women), and, outside of India, menstruating women made little change in their daily routine, inside or outside the home. (In India the concept of menstrual pollution leads most women to avoid many household tasks during menstruation.)[17]

Pain as Culture

But even to the extent that there is an irreducible, crosscultural core of menstrual pain, looking like a purely biological phenomenon—ignoring for the moment the cultural elements that crept into the WHO data—pain itself turns out to be a cultural phenomenon, its extent and meaning shaped by the surrounding circumstances. Perhaps the most clear-cut demonstration of pain as culture is a classic study, conducted in the forties and fifties, comparing the experience of pain of soldiers wounded in battle and male patients coming out of surgery. Both groups were asked whether they were in pain and, if so, were asked to rate their pain as slight, moderate, or severe; those experiencing pain were also asked if they would like something to relieve it. Both groups had suffered wounds, battle wounds or surgical wounds, in the areas of the chest and abdomen or in the bones.

Although the damage to tissue inflicted on the soldiers by high explosive shell fragments was far greater than the damage inflicted on the surgical patients by their surgery, the experience of pain was far greater for the patients than for the soldiers: 83 percent of the patients, but only 32 percent of the soldiers asked for something to relieve their pain; 14 percent of the soldiers, but only 4 percent of the patients claimed not to be in pain at all.[18]

What was clearly more important than traumatized nerve endings to the experience of pain was the meaning of what was happening at the source of the pain. For the soldiers, being wounded was a blessing; having been in constant danger of imminent death, to be wounded and still alive was an immense relief, heightened by the awarness that their wounds had taken them away from the battlefield for good. For the surgical patients, having surgery was a disaster, upsetting the order of their lives, instilling a fear of death or disability— in general, a source of enormous anxiety. Thus the positivity or negativity of what was underlying the tissue trauma shaped the extent to which that physiological condition was experienced as pain.

For menstruating women, the experience of menstruation is negative or at best ambivalent—just as the experience of being female has reason to be negative or at best ambivalent. An irregularly contracting uterus—or whatever physiological process may be generating a pain stimulus—has no favorable context, no positive meaning to alleviate its effect. Far from being a route off the battlefield, menstruation is another sector of the battlefield—a symbol, in a masculinist culture, of a woman's inferior position.

The Negativity of Female Physicality

Menstruation also reminds a woman of her body, and women generally live in their bodies in a state of uneasy alliance at best. There is some evidence that athletes suffer less menstrual discomfort than sedentary women,[19] which may have something to do with lower levels of prostaglandins or higher tolerances for pain, but may also have something to do with athletes being on better terms with their physicality. To a person who is physically fit, her body is both more important and less important than to the sedentary— more important in the sense that its being in peak condition is something she values, less important in that her attitude toward her body is more detached, more that of an outside observer.

She simultaneously lives in her body more comfortably and can step outside her body and analyze its condition, good or bad, more matter-of-factly.

The estrangement that most women feel from their bodies was nicely demonstrated by a study in which women and men were shown nine line drawings of women and men ranging from extremely thin to extremely heavy and asked to note which represented themselves, which the body they would like to have, which the body they thought was most attractive to the opposite sex, and which drawing of the opposite sex was most attractive to them. Women consistently rated their own bodies as heavier than what they would like to be and what they thought was attractive to men, whereas for men the three ratings were almost identical. (What women rated as the ideal male body was lighter than the male ratings, but what men rated as the most attractive female body was heavier than what women rated as ideal and what they thought was attractive to men.) Another statistical tidbit suggesting women's estrangement from their bodies is the fact that about 90 percent of cases of anorexia and bulimia are women.[20]

Studies comparing high school and college women athletes with nonathletes, on the other hand, have found that the athletes have a much more positive image of their bodies than the nonathletes; one such study also found the athletes expressing much more satisfaction with life in general than the nonathletes.[21]

None of this is to promote jogging or yoga as a sure-fire cure for menstrual cramps or premenstrual bloating, only to suggest that the experience of menstrual discomfort may frequently be part of a package that includes estrangement from our physicality and that learning to inhabit our bodies more comfortably, a lesson that athletics can teach, might make the experience of menstruation less problematic. Attaining a state of physical fitness can demonstrate that there is more to the female body than the capacity to grow babies, can impart a sense of strength and self-assurance that, among other benefits, can make coping with physical inconveniences a more matter-of-fact proposition.

Biomedicine versus Holism

Still, we are faced with the lesson—and the problem—of the previous chapter that regular menstrual cyclicity, month in and month out for years at a time, is a condition that the human female body has not had time to adapt to on an evolutionary time scale, and that menstrual discomforts of various kinds may be the price we pay for that disjunction between human evolution and human culture. Just as high blood pressure,

for example, is a disease of civilization, reflecting the damage wrought by the fight-or-flight response as evolutionary anomaly, so menstrual distress might be called a discomfort of civilization. But just as one can take a high-tech route or a holistic route to coping with one's hypertension, taking medication or doing meditation, so one can make similar choices about coping with menstrual distress.

A few studies by psychologists, for example, starting from the premise that menstrual cramps have something to do with painful contractions of the uterine muscle, have explored the possibility that learning to relax one's musculature can alleviate menstrual pain. In one study, subjects were trained to achieve a state of deep muscle relaxation and at the same time to imagine scenes relating to menstruation, in all of which they remained calm and comfortable while thinking of all that they had to do during their period, just as it was beginning. The participants were instructed to carry out this procedure on their own at least twice a day. Two months after the training, symptoms that subjects had reported feeling often on a before-and-after questionnaire were being experienced only rarely.[22]

Another study used a different relaxation technique combined with biofeedback measuring the temperature of the vagina; this because muscle relaxation is accompanied by dilation of blood vessels and a rise in temperature (and there is a common artery supplying the uterus and the vaginal wall) and the researcher hypothesized that temperature biofeedback would reinforce the relaxation training. After eight weekly training sessions, with instructions to do the relaxation exercises daily on their own, subjects' scores on an index designed to measure dysmenorrhea went down by more than two-thirds.[23]

As we saw in Chapter 5, one can also take antiprostaglandin pills for cramps. The difference, of course, is that pills merely reinforce our typical alienation from our physicality—our body becomes something to chemically zap when it misbehaves—whereas an approach like visualization or deep muscle relaxation promotes the integration of psyche and soma, the mind coaxing the muscles to relax, the pleasurable feeling of relaxed muscles then alleviating the anxiety in the mind that was caused by the pain and was also intensifying the pain, the lessened anxiety then making it easier for the muscles to relax further, which further alleviates the anxiety, and so on. All of which is not to provide a primer on the holistic treatment of menstrual distress, only to note that anomalous human states, whether hypertension or dysmenorrhea, can be coped with in ways that reflect humankind's technological alienation from itself or in ways that reflect humankind's complex integration of soma and psyche, biology and culture.

Menstruation as Culture

The problem of culture outpacing evolution and the physiological quirks that accompany that phenomenon is a problem of the human species, not a problem unique to women. What is uniquely a problem of women is being put down for our biology—or, more precisely, being put down for other reasons and our biology then being called upon as a convenient justification of the putdown. Men's problems with their prostate glands or their greater susceptibility to heart attacks have never been thought reason to disbar them from full participation in social and political life. President Jefferson suffered from migraines; President Kennedy had Addison's disease, which is a serious hormonal disorder, and a bad back.[24] When people are valued, their physiological problems are taken in stride. If women were valued, their menstrual aches and pains would be inconsequential—and the fact of being valued would itself have the effect of reducing those aches and pains.

Modern women's constant menstrual cyclicity is a result of, is symbolic of, our escape from compulsory motherhood. When that escape becomes threatening—when the alternative to compulsory motherhood is female encroachment on formerly male domains—it becomes useful to call menstrual cyclicity a disability.

Then women are disabled from full participation in social and political life either because they are having babies or because they are not having babies.

But if regular menstruation is a concomitant of our escape from compulsory motherhood, it does not define modern women any more than a high rate of heart disease defines modern men. It does illustrate that modern human societies, like earlier ones, are places where biology and culture are inseparable—where menstruation is both a biological event whose nature is profoundly shaped by cultural forces and a biological event that is frequently used as a political weapon by cultural forces.

Thus menstruation per se has no meaning, for menstruation per se does not exist. The physical flow that comes monthly—the evolutionary anomaly—only exists as one aspect of what it means to be a woman at the turn of the twenty-first century. As that meaning changes, the meaning of menstruation will change—will become more negative, more positive, more ambivalent, or perhaps free of emotional baggage altogether. Ultimately, the question of menstruation is not a problem to be solved, it is an issue that needs to become a nonissue, like the question of how many angels can dance on the head of a pin; for it would and will become a nonissue if and when women are fully accepted as full-fledged human beings.

For references, see original.

The Selling of Premenstrual Syndrome
Who Profits from Making PMS "The Disease of the 80s"?

by Andrea Eagan

In the summer of 1961, I was working as a laboratory assistant at a major pharmaceutical firm. Seminars were regularly given on recent scientific developments, and that summer, one of them, on the oral contraceptive, was given by an associate of Dr. Gregory Pincus, who was instrumental in the development of the Pill. As a rule, only the scientists went to the seminars. But for this one, every woman in the place—receptionists and bottle washers, technicians and cleaners—showed up. Oral contraception sounded like a miracle, a dream come true.

During the discussion, someone asked whether the drug was safe. Yes, we were assured, it was perfectly safe. It had been thoroughly tested in Puerto Rico, and besides, you were only adjusting the proportions of naturally occurring substances in the body, putting in a little estrogen and progesterone to fool the body into thinking that it was "just a little bit pregnant." The Food and Drug Administration had approved the sale of the birth-control pill in the United States the year before. News of it was everywhere. Women flocked to their doctors to get it. The dream, we now know, was much too good to be true. But we learned that only after years of using the Pill, after we had already become a generation of guinea pigs.

Since then, and because of similar experiences with DES and with estrogen replacement therapy (ERT), because of the work of the women's health movement and of health activists like Barbara Seaman, we have presumably learned something: we have become cautious about medical miracles and scientific breakthroughs. To suddenly discover, then, that thousands of women are rushing to get an untested drug to cure a suspected but entirely unproved hormone deficiency which manifests itself as a condition with a startling variety of symptoms—known by the catchall name premenstrual syndrome (PMS)—is a little shocking.

Often when a drug suddenly makes the news, or when a new "disease" for which there is a patented cure is discovered, it is fairly easy to find the public relations work of the drug manufacturers behind the story. As just one example, estrogen replacement therapy for the symptoms of menopause had been around since the 1940s. But in 1966, a Brooklyn physician by the name of Robert Wilson wrote a book called *Feminine Forever,* which extolled the benefits of ERT in preventing what the author called "living decay." Wilson went on TV and radio, was interviewed for scores of articles. He claimed that *lifelong* ERT, starting well before menopause, would prevent or cure more than 20 different conditions, ranging from backaches to insomnia and irritability. Wilson ran an operation called the Wilson Research Foundation that put out information to the media and received grants from drug companies. Among those contributing to the Wilson Foundation was Ayerst Laboratories, the largest manufacturer of the estrogen used in the treatment of menopause symptoms. Ayerst also funded a group called the Information Center on the Mature Woman, from which regular information bulletins were sent to the media.

Many doctors had misgivings about ERT (the link between estrogen and cancer had been reported since the 1930s), but the information that the public received about ERT was almost entirely positive. One of the few warnings against ERT appeared in *Ms.* in December, 1972. Three years later, in 1975, a study was published in the *New England Journal of Medicine* reporting that estrogen users had a five to 14 times greater incidence of uterine cancer than did nonusers. This *was* news, and it made the papers. (The *New England Journal,* like several other prestigious medical journals, sends out advance issues to some news services, which is why the networks all have the same story on the same day.)

Women, needless to say, were concerned about ERT. Many simply stopped taking the drug, and sales of Premarin (the brand name of Ayerst's ERT preparation, which accounted for 80 percent of the market) dropped.

Soon after this, Ayerst received a memo on media strategy from Hill & Knowlton, its public relations firm. This memo, the sort that is supposed to be absolutely confidential, became public when someone sent a copy to the New York women's newspaper, *Majority Report. MR* published the entire memo under the headline, "New Discovery: Public Relations Cures Cancer." The first part of the plan was to take the spotlight off estrogen and refocus it on menopause. The "estrogen message," said the memo, "can be effectively conveyed by discreet references to `products that your doctor may prescribe.'" Articles on menopause were to be placed in major women's magazines. Information was also to be fed to syndicated women's page columnists, general magazines and prominent science writers and editors.

The second part of Hill & Knowlton's plan was to counter anticipated negative publicity. A list of potentially damaging events—research reports (one was expected from the Mayo Clinic), FDA announcements, lawsuits—was given. News releases were to be prepared in *advance* of the "damaging commentary . . . in as much detail as possible." When this memo became public (Jack Anderson picked it up after *MR's* publication), Ayerst denied any intention of following its recommendations, but the memo actually outlines the kinds of steps some drug manufacturers take to bring their products to the attention of the public and to counteract criticism.

The same story, with only minor changes, can be told for a number of other drugs, so when I began seeing articles about PMS and progesterone treatment, I immediately had some questions. Why was PMS suddenly "news"? What do we really know about progesterone? And who are the advocates of this treatment?

PMS stories began appearing rather suddenly about two years ago, after two Englishwomen claimed PMS as a mitigating factor in their defense against murder charges. When the stories about these cases appeared, many American women who suffer from cyclical problems naturally became interested in finding out all they could about the condition.

PMS itself is not news. It was first mentioned in the medical literature in the 1930s, and women presumably had it before then. Estimates on the numbers of women affected by PMS vary wildly. Some claim that as many as 80 percent are affected while others place estimates at only 20 percent. Similarly, doctors' opinions vary on the number and type of symptoms that may indicate PMS. They cite from 20 up to 150 physical and psychological symptoms, ranging from bloating to rage. The key to recognizing PMS and differentiating it from anything else that might cause some or all of a woman's symptoms is timing. The symptoms appear at some point after ovulation (around mid-cycle) and disappear at the beginning of the menstrual period. (It should not be confused with dysmenorrhea or menstrual discomfort, about which much is known, and for which several effective, safe treatments have been developed.)

While PMS is now generally acknowledged to be a physical, as well as a psychological disorder, there is little agreement on what causes it or how it should be treated. There are at least half a dozen theories as to its cause—ranging from an alteration in the way that the body uses glucose to excessive estrogen levels—none of which have been convincingly demonstrated.

One of the most vocal proponents of PMS treatment is Katharina Dalton, a British physician who has been treating the condition for more than 30 years. Dalton believes that PMS results from a deficiency of progesterone, a hormone that is normally present at high levels during the second half of the menstrual cycle and during pregnancy. Her treatment, and that of her followers, relies on the administration of progesterone during the premenstrual phase of the cycle.

Progesterone is not absorbed effectively when taken by mouth. Powdered progesterone, derived from yams or soybeans, can be dissolved in oil and given in a deep, painful muscular injection. Or the powder can be absorbed from vaginal or rectal suppositories, a more popular form. (In this country the Upjohn Company is the major manufacturer of progesterone, which they sell only in bulk to pharmacies where pharmacists then package it for sale. Upjohn makes no recommendation for the use of progesterone and is conducting no tests on the product.)

Although she promotes the progesterone treatment, Dalton has no direct evidence of a hormone deficiency in PMS sufferers. Because progesterone is secreted cyclically in irregular bursts, and testing of blood levels of progesterone is complicated and expensive, studies have been unable to show conclusively that women with PMS symptoms have lower levels of progesterone than other women. Dalton's evidence is indirect: the symptoms of PMS are relieved by the administration of progesterone.

Upon learning about Dalton's diagnosis-and-cure, many women concluded that they had the symptoms she was talking about. But when they asked their doctors for progesterone treatment, they generally got nowhere. Progesterone is not approved by the FDA for treatment of PMS (the only approved uses are for treating cessation of menstrual flow and abnormal uterine bleeding due to hormone imbalance); there is *nothing* in the medical literature showing clearly what causes PMS; and there has never been a well-designed, controlled study here or in England of the effect of progesterone on PMS.

Despite some doctors' reluctance to prescribe progesterone, self-help groups began springing up, and special clinics were established to treat PMS. Women who had any of the reported symptoms (cyclical or not) headed en masse for the clinics or flew thousands of miles to doctors whose willingness to prescribe progesterone had become known through the PMS network. And a few pharmacists began putting up progesterone powder in suppository form and doing a thriving business.

How did PMS suddenly become the rage, or what one New York gynecologist called "the hypoglycemia of the 1980s"? At least part of the publicity can be traced to an enterprising young man named James Hovey. He is reported to have claimed he had a B.A. in public health from UCLA despite the fact that, aside from extension courses, he had been there less than a year. (UCLA does not even have a B.A. program in public health.) He met Katharina Dalton in Holland several years ago at a conference on the biological basis of violent behavior. Returning to the United States, he worked with a Boston physician who opened the first PMS clinic in Lynnfield. A few months later, Hovey left the clinic. He then started The National Center for Premenstrual Syndrome and Menstrual Distress in New York City, Boston, Memphis, and Los Angeles—each with a local doctor as medical director.

For $265 (paid in advance), you got three visits. The initial visit consisted of a physical exam and interview, and a lengthy questionnaire on symptoms. During the second visit, the clinic dispensed advice on diet and vitamins, and reviewed a monthly record the patient was asked to keep. On the third visit, if symptoms still persisted, most patients received a prescription for progesterone.

Last year, James Hovey's wife Donna, a nurse who was working in his New York clinic, told me that they were participating in an FDA-approved study of progesterone, in conjunction with a doctor from the University of Tennessee. In fact, to date the FDA has approved only one study on progesterone treatment of PMS, which is conducted at the National Institute of Child Health and Human Development, an organization unrelated to James Hovey.

Similar contradictions and misrepresentations, as well as Hovey's lack of qualifications to be conducting research or running a medical facility, were exposed by two journalists last year. Marilyn Webb in the *Village Voice* and Jennifer Allen in *New York* magazine both dug into the operation of the clinic and Hovey's past to reveal him as a former Army medical corpsman turned entrepreneur. Hovey left New York and gave up his interest in the New York and Boston clinics. He is cur-

rently running a nationwide PMS referral service out of New Hampshire.

In a recent interview, Hovey said that the clinic business is too time-consuming, and that he is getting out. His "only interest is research" he says. He was associated with two scientists who applied to the FDA for permission to do progesterone studies but who were rejected because the FDA considered the doses of progesterone to be too high. At last report, Hovey still headed H and K Pharmaceuticals, a company founded in 1981 for the manufacture of progesterone suppositories, and it is as a supplier that his name has appeared on FDA applications.

Hovey's involvement in PMS treatment seems to have centered on the commercial opportunities. Others, such as Virginia Cassara, became interested in PMS for more personal reasons.

Cassara, a social worker from Wisconsin, went to England in 1979 to be treated by Dalton for severe PMS. The treatment was successful and Cassara returned to spread the good news. She invited Katharina Dalton to Wisconsin to speak and notified the press. Though only one article appeared, it brought women "out of the closet," Cassara says. Cassara began counseling and speaking, selling Dalton's books and other literature. Her national group, PMS Action, now has an annual budget of $650,000, 17 paid staff members, and 40 volunteers. Cassara spends most of her time traveling and speaking.

Cassara's argument is compelling, at least initially. She describes the misery of PMS sufferers, and the variety of ineffective medical treatments they have been subjected to in their search for relief. For anyone who is sensitive to women's health issues, it is a familiar tale: a condition that afflicts perhaps millions of women has never been studied; a treatment that gives relief is ignored. Women, says Cassara, are pushed into diet and exercise regimens that are difficult to maintain and don't always work. One valid solution, she feels, lies in progesterone.

According to FDA spokesperson Roger Eastep, Phase I studies—those that determine how much a particular substance is absorbed by the body and how it works—have yet to be done for progesterone. But in the meantime, more and more doctors are prescribing the hormone for PMS.

Dr. Michelle Harrison, a gynecologist practicing in Cambridge, Massachusetts, and a spokesperson for the National Women's Health Network, is one physician who does prescribe progesterone to some women, with mixed feelings. "I've seen it dramatically temper women's reactions," she says. "For those women whose lives are shattered by PMS, who've made repeated suicide attempts or who are unable to keep a job, you have to do something. But I have a very frightening consent form that they have to sign before I'll give progesterone to them." Harrison also stresses that a lot of PMS is iatrogenic; that is, it is caused by medical treatment. It often appears for the first time after a woman has stopped taking birth-control pills, after tubal ligation or even after a hysterectomy, in which the ovaries have been removed.

When doctors do prescribe progesterone, their ideas of the appropriate dosage can vary from 50 to 2,400 mg. per day. For some women, dosages at the lower end of the scale do not bring relief from their symptoms. It has also been reported by women taking progesterone and in medical literature that the effect of a particular dose diminishes after a few months. Some women are symptom-free as long as they are taking the drug, but the symptoms reappear as soon as they stop, regardless of where they are in the menstrual cycle.

For all these reasons, some women are taking much higher doses than their doctors prescribe. Michelle Harrison had heard of women taking 2,400 mg. per day; Dalton had heard about 3,000; Cassara knows women who take 4,000. Because PMS symptoms tend to occur when progesterone is not being taken, some women take it every day, instead of only during the premenstrual phase. Some bleed all the time; others don't menstruate at all. Vaginal and rectal swelling are common. Animal studies have shown increased rates of breast tumors and cervical cancer. Marilyn Webb, a reporter who began taking progesterone while working on a story about PMS, developed chest pains after several months. She asked all the doctors she interviewed whether any of their patients had experienced chest pains. Every one said that she or he had at least one patient who had.

Reminding her of the history of the Pill, of DES, and of ERT, I asked Virginia Cassara whether she was concerned about the long-term effects of progesterone on women. "I guess I don't think there could be anything worse than serious PMS," she responded. "Even cancer?" I asked. "Absolutely. Even cancer." Later, she said, "I think it's paternalistic of the FDA to make those choices for us, to tell us what we can and cannot put in our bodies. Women with PMS are competent beings, capable of making their own choices."

I don't have severe PMS, and I don't think I fully understand the desperation of women who do and who see help at last within reach. But given our limited understanding of how progesterone works, I do not understand why women like Cassara are echoing drug company complaints of overregulation by the FDA. I'm alarmed to see women flocking to use an untested substance about which there is substantial suspicion, whose mode of action is not known, to treat a condition whose very cause is a mystery. And I fear that, somewhere down the line, we will finally learn all about progesterone treatment and it won't be what we wanted to know.

One doctor, who refused to be quoted by name, cheerfully assured me that progesterone was safe. "Even if a woman is taking 1,600 milligrams per day, the amount of circulating progesterone is still only a quarter of what is normally circulating during pregnancy." And I couldn't help but think of the doctor at the seminar more than 20 years ago: "Of course it's safe. It's just like being a little bit pregnant."

The Vitamin Cure

Diet and vitamin therapies are, according to many doctors, effective in the large majority of PMS cases. Michelle Harrison has found that most of her patients will respond to a hypoglycemia diet: whole grains, no caffeine, lots of water, no sugar, frequent small meals. To this, she adds up to 800 mg. per day of vitamin B6 during the premenstrual phase. Harrison has written a clear and useful 50-page booklet, *Self-Help for Premenstrual Syndrome* ($4.50, plus $1.50 postage and handling, from Matrix Press, Box 740M, Cambridge, Massachusetts 02238), which includes charts for keeping track of symptoms and lots of good advice about diagnosis and treatment, as well as a look at the social and political questions raised by PMS.

Dr. Marcia Storch (author of *How To Relieve Cramps and Other Menstrual Problems*, Workman Publishing, $3.95) and her associate, Dr. Shelley Kolton, believe that reducing salt intake helps to curb water retention and headaches that result from it. They also prescribe 300 to 500 mg. daily of vitamin B_6. Kolton says that this therapy is effective in about 80 percent of all cases, though it may take several months for the treatment to work. (Storch and Kolton do not recommend progesterone because of safety concerns.)—A.E.

Menarche and the (Hetero) Sexualization of the Female Body

by Janet Lee
Oregon State University

Menarche—or a woman's first menstrual period—is a central aspect of body politics. Through explorations of oral and written narratives, I suggest that girls' subjective sense of themselves as maturing women at menarche develops simultaneously with a process of sexualization whereby young women experience themselves as sexualized, and their bodies are produced as sexual objects. While women internalize negative scripts associated with the bleeding female body, they also respond with consciousness and resistance.

In high school I wanted to be a beatnik. I too wanted to go on the road, but I could never figure out what would happen if, travelling in Mexico in 1958, I got my period. Were you supposed to carry a supply of Kotex with you? How many could you carry? If you took all you needed, there wouldn't be any room for all those nice jugs of wine in Jack Kerouac's car. The only beatnik I know who even considered this question was Diana diPrima in Memoirs of a Beatnik. She describes her first big orgy, the one with the works, including Allen Ginsburg. As she takes a deep breath and decided to plunge in, so to speak, she pulls out her Tampax and flings it across the room where somehow it gets irretrievably lost. A grand moment, that. Do I hear you thinking, How gross? Or, How irrelevant? Gross, yes: irrelevant, no. And that's the point. Having to worry about the gross mess becomes a part of life from puberty on (Dimen 1986, 32–3).

Menstruation is a biological act fraught with cultural implications, helping to produce the body and women as cultural entities. The body is a "text" of culture; it is a symbolic form upon which the norms and practices of society are inscribed (Bartky 1992; Bordo 1989; Haug et al. 1987). Male desire and policy have been scripted onto the female body at the same time that "woman" has been overdetermined and overrepresented in contemporary art, social science and politics, as well as scientific and medical discourses. In this article I share stories of the body in an analysis of the menarche (or first period) experiences of ordinary women who participated in an ongoing oral and written history project. It is primarily through the body that women are inserted, and insert themselves, into the hierarchical ordering of the sexual.

I explore menarche as a central aspect of body politics since it is loaded with the ambivalence associated with being a woman in Western society today. Menarche represents the entrance into womanhood in a society that devalues women through cultural scripts associated with the body. Overwhelmingly, messages associated with menarche in a wide range of cultural and historical contexts are ambivalent (Buckley and Gottlieb 1988;

Janet Lee, *Gender and Society*, Vol. 8, No. 3. Copyright © 1994. Reprinted by permission of Sage Publications, Inc.

Janet Lee is Associate Professor and Director of Women's Studies at Oregon State University in Corvallis, Oregon. One of her general research interests concerns the social construction of women's bodies and its consequences for women's sense of self and identity. Most recently, she has begun to investigate the meaning of menarche as a significant adolescent life experience in the context of a society that devalues and degrades women and their bodies.

AUTHOR'S NOTE: *This article and ongoing project have been funded by the Oregon Council for the Humanities, a fellowship at the Center for the Humanities at Oregon State University, and by grants from the Research Office and the College of Liberal Arts at Oregon State University. I would especially like to thank my research assistants, Alida Benthin, Jennifer Sasser-Coen, Sindy Mau, and Tamara Schaub, for their help with interviewing, as well as all the women who so graciously shared their memories of menarche.*

Delaney, Lupton, and Toth 1988; Golub 1983, 1992; Lander 1988). Even those women who have reflected on this experience with positive thoughts and memories have been found to articulate its negative and shameful aspects (Hays, 1987; Jackson 1992; Koff, Rierdan, and Jacobson 1981; Martin 1987; Weideger 1976; Whisnant and Zegans 1975). To talk of menstruation in contemporary Western culture is to articulate its secretive, emotionally laden, and shame filled aspects (Thorne 1993).

Within patriarchal and heterosexist societies menarche simultaneously signifies both emerging sexual availability and reproductive potential. While I do not suggest that sexuality and reproduction must be, or have always been, conflated (D'Emilio and Freedman 1988), to focus on menarche is unavoidably to deal with both. In terms of sexuality, the process of sexualization whereby women experience themselves as sexualized in current Western society is a thoroughly heterosexual one; the use of sexuality as a generic term implying heterosexuality illustrates the normalizing powers of language. Sexualization implies heterosexualization, meaning that women are taught to live and discipline their bodies in accordance with the prescriptions of heterosexuality, experiencing themselves as sexual objects for heterosexual male viewing, pleasure, and also as mothers of men's children (Haug et al. 1987; Young 1990). As Thorne (1993, 170) suggests: "it is during the transition from 'child' to 'teen' that girls start negotiating the forces of adult femininity, a set of structures and meanings that more fully inscribe their subordination on the basis of gender." I emphasize that menarche symbolizes this process, and must therefore be framed within the discourses of the heterosexual, emphasizing its importance in the relationship between reproduction and sexuality generally.

While women's bodies are produced discursively within misogynist societies (Bartky 1992; Foucault 1978; Scott 1992), women's everyday experiences negotiating adolescence are concretely lived in ways that not only internalize and maintain such discourses, but also actively resist them through appropriation and/or the integration of more positive discourses of the body (Martin 1987). While, as Smith (1992, 91) suggests, women are always located in a particular configuration of the everyday, "the standpoint of women never leaves the actual," this "actual" involves the negotiation of subject positions through discourse and from which women as subjects emerge. Women's thoughts and behavior are grounded in these particular discursive spaces at the same time that their agency to comply with and resist such discourses is recognized. Attention to the discursive formation of the body does not remove agency from the human subject; instead, it problematizes human behavior and emphasizes how individuals negotiate identities

and subject positions. Narratives of women's memories of menarche highlight this interactive nature of discourse and agency; when women remember their first menses, their memories are framed by many competing discourses, having become subjects through the sifting and making meaning out of their experiences.

My methodological focus is phenomenological. I explore the meanings women attribute to menarche, what they think and feel, and the significance of this event as represented in what they say and write. I analyzed forty narratives (twenty-eight oral and twelve written narratives), listening and reading for interpretations of menarche embedded within the everyday, lived experience of women. Written narratives were collected when women could not be interviewed in person, but agreed to share written accounts of their menarche. The oral history interviews were conducted either in women's homes or in an office or seminar room, and sometimes in a public space, although the latter occurred rarely. With participants' consent, a tape recorder was used and interviews were then transcribed. Participants were also asked if they wanted to use a pseudonym; most chose to do this, though some preferred to use their real names. Participants were volunteers who had agreed to participate as word of the project spread through presentations made in classes, flyers in a local physician's office, and through contact with colleagues, students, and friends and the Extended Education Office at Oregon State University.

This local sample was Eurocentric, including thirty white women, three Jews, two African Americans, one biracial woman, three Asian Americans, two Mexican Americans, and three women each from Nepal, Malaysia, and Iran. Since three-quarters of the participants were white, reflecting the general lack of racial and ethnic diversity in Oregon, where this study was done, I must emphasize its limitations and the dangers of overgeneralization. The age range spanned from 18 to 80 years. Five women identified themselves as lesbians and three as bisexuals, although none said they identified as such during early adolescence. Nineteen of the participants are working class and twenty-one are middle class, all residing in the Willammette Valley and south and central Oregon.

I suggest here that menarche is an important time when young women become inserted and insert themselves into the dominant patterns of sexuality. As a crucial signifier of reproductive potential and thus embodied womanhood, menarche becomes intertwined with sexuality. Certain orifices and their secretions take on sexual significance and menarche marks a simultaneous entry into adult womanhood and adult female sexualization. I will share excerpts from the narratives to illustrate themes associated with female sexualization at menarche, exploring the ways these women relate to the female body and menstrual blood. I focus on issues of contamination and alienation, and the relationship between menarche, boys, and developing bodies. Finally, I will discuss issues of consciousness and resistance, exploring ways women have coped with menarche in their everyday lives.

Contaminating Bodies

Historically and cross-culturally, menstrual blood has been considered both magical and poisonous, and menstrual taboos have structured and restricted women's lives (Buckley and Gottlieb 1988; Golub 1992). Since women are associated with the body, earth, and nature, and men with the abstract powers of reason, women's bodies connote words like *earthy, fleshy,* and *smelly,* reminding humans of their mortality and vulnerability. Dorothy Dinnerstein (1976) captures this in her discussion of the deep-seated cultural perceptions of the female body as corrupting, contaminating, unclean, and sinful. On the one hand, woman is associated with life, while on the other, her bleeding and oozing body is met with disgust, reminiscent of earthly vulnerabilities. Male bodies are not so symbolically marked with such connotations; men are more easily able to imagine their bodies free of such constraints, and they are allowed to project their fears and hatred onto women's flesh. Cultural contexts provide mythologies and images of disgust for women's bleeding that are deeply internalized into the psyche, encouraging women to hate their bodies and men to hate things they recognize as feminine in themselves (Ussher 1989).

Repeatedly, women in this study stated that their monthly bleeding made them feel ambivalent about their bodies, menarche being clouded by negativity. Almost half of the sample specifically mentioned "the curse" as a term they and others had used to describe menstruation. Edith, a 66-year-old mother and grandmother emphasized the gloom associated with menarche:

> It's so long ago . . . I guess it was mid-winter, and waking after dozing to sleep, briefly, having had a "funny" tummy ache—to a sticky, nasty uncomfortable feeling between my legs; slightly smelly too, if I really think deeply, ugh. . . . There was this dark, clammy, gloominess and sort of "dread" accompanying it.

Others also stated that their first menstrual blood made them feel dirty and unclean, ashamed and fearful. Bertha, a Jewish woman in her forties, remembered her menarche as similar to "a feeling I used to feel when I was young and wet my pants. . . . It was a feeling of hav-

ing soiled myself." Such feelings affect women's sense of self and worth, establishing female bodies and sexuality as bad and corrupting. These memories of shame and embarrassment were shared by Northstar, a Chinese American woman in her late twenties who grew up in Taiwan:

> I feel I have a big diaper. I feel everyone can see me . . . Very embarrassed. . . . I know sometimes when I went to my uncle's house that sometimes my aunt would forbid my uncle to take garbage out because she said that we have "women's mess" inside so men cannot carry the garbage out because there are women's pads inside.

With similar sentiment, a white working-class woman in her thirties named Anna wrote that she was "mortified," and felt she needed to hide her shame and embarrassment:

> When I first started menstruating (the very first time) I had experienced incredible stomach pains the night before. I stayed in bed all night and was the first one up in the morning. I went to the bathroom and lo and behold there was blood. I felt mortified because I knew what had happened. I felt incredibly ashamed and didn't tell anyone for a year (I used tissue paper). Now I was like my mother, a woman who had a bad smelly part of her. This, for the most part, is also how men see menstruation, as something filthy belonging to a woman that makes them mentally unstable

The disdain associated with menstrual blood encouraged many women to go to great lengths to hide such evidence of their contamination from the potentially disapproving gaze of others. There was overwhelming evidence of women's fears of showing evidence of wearing pads or staining garments or sheets. Three-quarters of all women in the sample specifically shared a story of the embarrassment associated with staining, or a fear that it might happen to them. This illustrates how the bulge or stain becomes a visible emblem of their contamination and shame. Announcing their "condition" for all to see. It also symbolizes a lapse in women's task of maintaining the taboo, concealing the evidence and preventing the embarrassment of others (Laws 1990). Seventy-four-year-old Laverne shared the following;

> A problem with menstruating at that time was the napkin pads. They were made out of absorbent cotton with a cotton mesh cover (no

shields). They soaked through easily and you often stained your underwear. I always worried that my skirt might be stained and would sometimes wear my coat in school all day long. At Girls High, it was the custom for the Seniors to wear all white every Friday. When I was a Junior, I happened to notice that one of the Seniors was wearing a thin white skirt which showed the outline of her sanitary pad so when I had my Senior skirt made I bought rather heavy material and had a double panel put in the back.

Women tended to see themselves as becoming more visible at the same time that they felt the pressure to conceal evidence of menstruation. Many women talked about wearing baggy clothes or coats to hide evidence of menstruation. Other research has also reported such findings, with women sharing feelings of being afraid of being found out with a strong desire to hide any traces of their period (Patterson and Hale 1985). One study found that it was only after several menstrual periods that girls would share their experiences with anyone other than their mothers (Brooks-Gunn and Ruble 1983). Similar results were found here, with several women using tissue and toilet paper for months, or hiding soiled underwear at the back of drawers and closets.

The most intense and poignant stories of contamination came from childhood survivors of violence. Of the 10 women who shared experiences of incest or child sexual abuse, all connected the violation of their bodies to menarche as a contaminating experience and said that they felt their bodies were dirty and shameful. Hannah, a young, white lesbian spoke poignantly of the way her feelings about her contaminated body as a survivor coincided with her feelings about her menstrual flow:

> The abuse made me feel awful. It colored everything, so much of what I did, how I felt about my body and my self-esteem. . . . I felt really dirty and you know because I was on my period, and I would cramp more and I just felt dirty, I felt icky, I felt horrible, like people could smell me and I just felt subhuman. . . . I felt kind of shameful to be around men and I don't want to be around people and I don't want people to know at all. . . . I hated the feeling of flowing, I hated just that warm feeling whenever. . . . I felt as if it was something dirty, something horrible coming out and I wanted to not flow as much as possible and if I got really active I would flow more and I didn't want to flow. I just wanted it to stop.

Child sexual abuse survivors' words illustrate the way the vulnerabilities associated with women's emerging sexuality (and in these cases, the exploitation of what these little girls' bodies signified in the context of a society that exploits female sexuality) become integrated so that the body becomes and is experienced by girls as something acted upon, used, and soiled.

Alienated Bodies

Many of the women interviewed experienced menarche as something that was happening *to* them, as something outside of themselves and frequently referred to as "it," giving an illusion of a self that was fragmented. Overwhelmingly, women used the passive voice to describe menarche. Examples include: "I couldn't believe it was happening to me," "we called it 'the visitor,'" "I got it when I was fourteen," "I remember exactly when it started," "this monthly event," and (my favorite) "when it came I was at home."

Karin, a 22-year-old white woman, shared the following:

> I mean she [her sister] had no problem with it. I don't know if she was happy about it because she was on good terms with it. . . . I guess I'm not really in control of it because I just felt like it happened to me, I didn't ask for it, it just suddenly happened.

Similarly, Barbara, a 19-year-old lesbian, also clearly illustrates this sense of bodily alienation: "It was unknown and I really didn't understand it and it was something I couldn't control so it seemed kind of abstract and not within me."

With their passive construction and imagery, these quotes suggest a fragmentation between self and body, a sense of menarche as something a woman has to cope with, adjust to, and manage. Menarche is something that seems to appear from outside, invading the self. Such findings were also reported by Martin (1987), who wrote of the women she interviewed as seeing menstruation as something that happened *to* them, rather than seeing the process as being a part *of* them. While she explained this in terms of the medicalization of the female body and the way a scientifically based society produces images of human bodies as machines, I suggest that there is more at work here, since many women framed menarche as happening "to them" in the context of their emerging understandings of sexuality. Charlotte, a white bisexual mother in her late thirties, shared her feelings about this fragmentation and lack of control, illustrating how menarche is intimately connected to feelings about sexual alienation and objectification (the "it" is her first period):

> When it came, I was a high school exchange student in Europe, staying with the family of a friend. I felt like I was out of control, that something was happening to me that I couldn't stop. I bled terribly all over the sheets and was horribly embarrassed telling my friend's aunt (especially since I didn't know the right words, menstruation is hardly one of the common vocabulary words you have to learn). I remember distinctly being embarrassed because this blood seemed like an emblem of my sexuality, like somehow it indicated that I might run out and have sex, yet really I felt like it was all happening to someone else, not me, like I was watching myself in a movie and now was this sexual being.

The passive, indirect, fragmented language of menarche and menstruation is about sexual objectification and alienation. This sense of bodily alienation is entwined with women's object status in patriarchal societies that allow men subjectivity but construct femininity as a mirror through which men see themselves as human (Irigaray 1985). Adolescence and the journey from girlhood to womanhood involve forms of self-silencing whereby girls become preoccupied with how they are perceived and by others (Brown and Gilligan 1992; Gilligan, Lyons, and Hanmer 1990). Femininity means moving from assertive actor to developing woman, learning to respond to the word indirectly through the filter of relationships. Women are encouraged to accommodate male needs, understand themselves as others see them, and feel pleasure through their own bodily objectification, especially being looked at and identified as objects of male desire (Connell 1987). Again, the voice of a survivor, this time Susan, is especially poignant in illustrating this objectification:

> Becoming a woman kind of opened the avenues which I think I unconsciously kind of knew that men would start looking at me more which was, I think, a little bit scary in a sense. I mean I was confused, I think I wanted to be accepted by the male gender, but yet with this experience [incest] it was a frightening thing because, it wasn't even me, it was like my body, and it was happening to my body. . . . It was no longer my mind or who I was, I mean it was like I was nothing. But yet my body was something, a sex object or something and I couldn't have said it. I didn't think that my body was

like a sex object. I mean I couldn't clarify what was a norm, but, to look back now, that is what it was, my body was a sex object and the menstruation process was, just defined it that much more that I was a woman. . . . You know what I am saying? Because I related to the menstrual cycle, I connected it directly with all this. . . . So there is a connection there, one part of me, I wanted to be that woman for the opposite sex, because it was kind of like expected of me, you know, that I be pleasing to look at and starting that menstrual cycle was my direct link with that, wow, I am a woman. But then there is bad incident that I don't think had a lot of negative influence on that, but yet it must have somehow, you know, been buried there.

Anxious Bodies

Adolescence is a difficult and vulnerable time when girls focus attention on their bodies (Koff 1983; Rierdan and Koff 1980; Koff, Rierdan, and Silverstone 1978; Ussher 1989) in the context of a culture that demands perfect female bodies (Brownmiller 1984; Coward 1985). In a study that asked pre- and postmenarcheal girls to draw pictures of women, Koff found that girls who had experienced menarche drew considerably more sexually differentiated bodies. She writes about how girls come to experience themselves as more sexually mature at menarche: "It appears that regardless of the actual physical changes that are taking place, the girl at menarche anticipates and experiences a reorganization of her body image in the direction of greater sexual maturity and feminine differentiation" (1983, 83).

For many women, the increasing focus on their bodies was associated with painful cramps or even severe dysmenorrhea or painful periods. For example, Mehra, a young Iranian woman, spoke of how she noticed her body more at this time: "Yes, I felt like I paid more attention to my body, how it looked, felt, but also about where the pain comes from. . . . I would focus on that because of the pain." Some, like Laurence, a 20-year-old Malaysian student, started tuning into their body at menarche, becoming more self-conscious generally: "Yes, I guess mentally I became more aware of my body and what you would say 'the journey to womanhood,' yeah, and I became more self-conscious when I had my period. . . . I did become more self-conscious."

Others, like Robin, a young, lesbian biracial woman, were aware that other people treated their bodies differently, and felt that this contributed to their interpretations of menarche:

Then they [her brothers] started becoming critical of the way I dressed, and my hair and the way I spoke . . . And criticizing and saying you need to go over that way and you need to start wearing skirts and you need to start doing your hair, and you need to care about what you look like and not talk like this or that. So, I think there was a definite change in how they saw me. . . . I think it did set inside their heads "she is woman, I mean she is not a boy. Yeah, she is different, other."

For most women, anxieties about their developing bodies at menarche concerned the way these bodies looked and might be interpreted by others, rather than how they looked or felt to themselves. Breast development seemed especially fraught with such anxiety. When recounting their first period stories, many women described their feelings toward their breasts, emphasizing how menarche is so often framed within the discourse of the sexual. Although enlarging breasts and hips are visual representations of femaleness, they are also highly constituted in our culture as objects of male desire (to be gazed at) and contribute to the experience of menarche as connected to the process of sexualization. As Haug et al. (1987, 139) suggest, "female breasts are never innocent." The excerpt below from Madeleine, a white woman in her thirties, illustrates the anxiety and self-consciousness associated with the developing body at menarche; a body that is being increasingly viewed as sexual, and, given the patriarchal context, a body that is becoming increasingly objectified.

I remember when I was in 6th grade and this boy called me "stuffy," in other words he was accusing me of stuffing my bra, because I wore a sweater that was, you know, more fitted than the day before and I was developing very early as a 6th grader and I didn't like my body at all, in fact I had a breast reduction when I was in 10th grade. . . . But so, I had a lot of hang-ups about that and they were very painful to me and so it just, my boobs were just to big that, I mean, I am still busty and I mean, they are huge and I was a small person and they got in my way (long laugh) and I really hated them. . . . I just remember feeling that I was going to grow up and the only thing that I would be good for was something like a Playboy bunny or something really you know . . . disgusting or just to be a housewife which was like a fate worse than death. . . . So, I guess that maybe that's why I felt so angry about my period because I associated it with these feelings about my boobs, you know.

At menarche, women say that their physical bodies are becoming problematic; women report that their breasts are too small or too big, hips tend to become enemy sites and there is the overwhelming fear of fat. These reports spanned generations as Florence, an 80-year-old Jewish woman remembered feeling "ugly and fat," just as did 18-year-old Marie, who, when asked how she felt about her body, responded: "I had a really low self-esteem about my physical appear;ance and stuff . . . It was pretty heavy dislike." Ambivalence is a good word to describe the feeling that many women report since, while many felt okay about their developing bodies, (especially in the context of competition with female friends and the relief from the embarrassment that goes along with being undeveloped—of not "measuring up," so to speak), these were accompanied by strong negative experiences of self-consciousness and embarrassment, and the internalization of ambivalence about women's flesh and sexuality. The relationship here between menarche and sexuality is illustrated by several women who commented that friends of theirs whose bodies had developed early were somehow seen as promiscuous, even though they were just young girls with no active sexual relationships. The use of the term "precocious puberty" in the literature to describe girls with early puberty and onset of menarche is also an example of this issue. Robin shares the following:

Oh, there was one person I knew who had it before any of us you know . . . this is really terrible, but I think that I thought that she was just a little more ahead of us sexually. I am positive the woman wasn't sexual, but I knew that was a part of getting older, and I knew that getting older meant having sex, and I think seeing someone else with their period made me feel that they were a lot further ahead than I was. . . . I am sure they probably weren't having sex, I don't know, but I saw them as more promiscuous.

Bodies and Boys

Women also make a clear association between menarche and changing relationships with boys through the language of the body. Many were distressed that their camaraderie with boys dissipated. They felt they could no longer be "one of the boys" or their friendships became infused with the sexual tensions of early adolescence and its budding compulsory heterosexuality. Barbara, a strong athlete during adolescence, illustrates this:

Yeah, I think it was in the sense that it [her menarche] separated me from the boys, and so I felt like I was going to have to dress up and just drop sports by the wayside because now it was like some way of being notified that well, you have had your fun as a tomboy but it is time to really do what you are "supposed" to do.

Women worried about what boys might think, if boys noticed them, if they didn't. Sixty-two-year-old Rowena remembered distinctly how her behavior changed. She wrote, "I began to 'be careful' at school, to not act 'too smart' although I continued to get straight A's. That was stupid."

Women remembered being embarrassed around boys, and especially remembered the teasing and crude comments about menstruation. Urmila, in her twenties and raised in Nepal, shared her memories of such teasing:

> Maybe the [boys] don't understand it, so the only way of doing it is by laughing, making fun . . . they just laugh, making it feel for the girls that they do know, so it sort of makes them dominant and makes the girls feel like "oh, my goodness, I have done something wrong."

Women reported that they learned early that they must hide all evidence of menstruation from boys and men, brothers and fathers. This set up a self-consciousness for girls who were used to playing with boys. Crystal, a young, white, bisexual woman, summed this best: "When I didn't have my period I didn't mind playing with the guys, but when I did, I was afraid someone would see me, like something might leak through or things like that."

In terms of potential sexual relationships with boys, the risk of pregnancy that sets in at menarche influences family dynamics. Research suggests that parents tend to see their daughter's emerging sexuality as more problematic than their son's, with early sexual maturation being associated with greater independence and achievement from parents for boys, and to a lesser extent for girls (Fine 1988; Hill and Lynch 1983; Ussher 1989). Hill and Holmbeck (1987) found that menarche was accompanied by intense family turmoil for a large number of the girls in their sample, with daughters reporting more parental control in the first six months after menarche than at any other time. The comments of Elizabeth, a white woman in her forties who grew up in a Catholic home with thirteen brothers and sister, is illustrative of this:

> When I hit my adolescent years our relationship [with her mother] really split because my mother all of a sudden was very suspicious of everything I did. . . . I still remember her just all of a sudden, a suspicion about me, maybe I was becoming sexual.

In predictable ways the double standard of sexual conduct plays itself out as boys are encouraged to sow their wild oats and girls are chastised for similar behavior, resulting in closer monitoring. "I was told by my mother that I was a lady now, so that I had to act like one, and not play with the boys anymore," recalled Darlene, a white working-class woman in her forties. She followed this statement with:

> I started to cry, I said "I'm not ready to be a lady and I like playing with the boys." I guessed the reason I couldn't play with them anymore is that they would smell me too and know my horrible secret. I felt dirty, humiliated and angry.

Finally, the remarks of 77-year-old Greta, a widow and retired teacher, illustrate the responsibilities of potential sexual relations that girls have to assume at menarche:

> During the "curse" as we termed it, I was concerned about odor and spotting. My mother made it clear that now necking and petting could have serious results if we went "all the way"—which could happen if emotions got out of hand.

Consciousness and Resistance

To study menarche is to study the female body as it is contextualized through the sociopolitical constructs of specific societies. In this study, the words that women used to describe menarche are those that symbolize the relationship of women to their bodies in a misogynist society: fear, shame, embarrassment, humiliation, preoccupation, mess, hassle, and so on; however, running through these stories are also tales of consciousness, agency, and resistance. Women are not merely acted upon, nor are they merely powerless pawns embedded in the discursive struggles that determine existence. While these discourses do frame the body, the woman in the body does resist, as Martin (1987) has suggested. Women show their resistance to the destructive and alienating discourses associated with menarche through insight and analysis, through telling their stories, and through the many ways that women have learned to cope. Some spoke of increasing solidarity with girls, of using menstruation as a way to manipulate and get their way; many spoke of having done or having a desire to do things differently when their own daughters start to menstruate. It is to these forms of consciousness and resistance that I now turn.

TELLING THE STORY

Since this project involved participants who were volunteers, the women's voices I share here are all those who wanted to have the opportunity to tell their stories. Usually, when the tape had been switched off and women were leaving, they would comment on the benefits of speaking about something that they had never really spoken of in any public way before, something that was an important experience in their lives, but which the society in which they lived, as well as academia, has tended to ignore. "I don't know if it's making any real sense, but it is starting to make more sense to me when I talk about it" was a comment often heard.

For many, the telling of their stories took the form of ongoing analysis and commentary on those experiences, speaking or writing with insight into body politics and the effects of those politics on women's everyday lives. Kay, a white mother and student in her thirties wrote the following, nicely illustrating this consciousness and insightful analysis:

First, in fifth or sixth grade, at my elementary school, we were separated from the boys and shown a film about menstruation. Next we were given a packet which contained some kind of feminine hygiene products and propaganda. We considered this whole affair hilarious, embarrassing and yet it took the place of what could be considered a puberty ritual for us girls. We never knew what the boys talked about or what they were told about us, reproductively, etc. But I always somehow felt that they had been given some important secret that day, that we, as girls, were not privy to, and that this was just some kind of weird, divisive act on the part of the administration to distract and codify us. I suppose that sounds like a true paranoid at work, or perhaps hindsight talking, eh? But it's true I did feel that way. . . . I also believe that most of what I experienced, or did not experience, were [sic] consistent with much of the cultural conditioning that women receive from the media and the medical establishment.

Many women revealed a form of resistance in the contradictory voices used to tell their stories. Women moved between the anxious, hesitant and fearful disclosure complete with multiple "umms" and "you knows" to the staging of their stories as a series of adventures, gaining control over the experience and framing it in hindsight as ridiculous. In so doing, they claimed control over events, appropriating them and defusing the pain and anguish. This emphasizes the sometimes contradictory ways gender is negotiated, discourses of resistance

being crucial components of this negotiation. Virginia, a 38-year-old white student, illustrates this as she jokes about the story of her first period, laughing and describing the event as a funny experience:

So I was 10 years old and didn't understand any of it. In fact I misunderstood most of it. What I remember about it from the book was that somehow the menstrual blood came out on the outside of your lower abdomen somehow like it seeped through your skin! (Laugh) . . . and so here's the book telling me that these napkins don't show and I'm holding them up to my stomach and saying year, right (laugh), that is going to show, you can't tell me that is not going to show. . . . So I told my mother and it was like "oh," she did seem rather pleased but it wasn't like the kind of pleased where if I got a really good grade or you know, gotten the solo in the school play (laugh). . . . She pulls out the Kotex kit and that is when I begin to connect, this is what it is, it doesn't come out of your stomach!

Hannah, an incest survivor, spoke very poignantly about her first menses. Despite her sadness she tells funny stories of menarche, her humor helping her gain control over he pain:

I saw blood in my underwear and it was like I just sat on the toilet (laugh) and I am like "mom." She comes in and she was like, "What? Well honey, congratulations, you are a little lady now." I am like, "Say what?!!" I was cramping really bad and I was given medication. It was to get me regulated. . . . I remember lying on the floor and my mom, she used to have bad cramps because she had a tipped uterus, so my grandfather used to buy her a pint of alcohol because they didn't have medication then, and she would drink it and she would pass out and she would be out for a day, so my mom gave me some brandy because she thought it would solve it! (Laugh) Well, after I had the brandy I just started to york it, I was throwing up left and right, so it seems like after that time every period I ever had I would throw up!

ACCEPTANCE, COPING, AND APPROPRIATION

For some women, especially those at midlife and beyond, there was a general sense of acceptance or resignation to the politics of menarche that was apparent in the narratives. I had never thought of this as a form of resistance until I read Emily Martin's discussion of acceptance, lament, and nonaction as a way of responding to women's reproductive restrictions (Martin 1987, 184-6); yet these ways of coping and surviving are important, and they also subvert the masculinist idea of resistance as oppositional action and behavior. When asked about the specifics of their menarche, many women responded with such comments as "people didn't talk about such things back then," "it was just something I had to endure," "that's the way it was back then." The comments of Alex, an 80-year-old white woman, were typical:

> And in those days we didn't have the sanitary napkins we have today, or even now the Tampax and so on, but you always had that laundry to do. That was just not very pleasant, but it was a thing you did. I mean, that was the way it went.

This acceptance did not always take the form of resignation. Many women, such as Yvonne, an African American woman in her thirties, were angry that they had had to endure certain experiences. "I was pissed" was among Yvonne's comments. Some tempered their frustrations with observations such as "Well, that's just the way it was then you see." The important point is that these were survival and coping mechanisms.

Louis, age 73, talked about the hardships associated with menstruation before the onset of disposable sanitary supplies. She remembers being in a tight spot with no menstrual cloths: "I had a jack knife and I cut up one of my blankets for pads and used those." Women of all ages reported using toiled paper, tissue, and underwear to help them hide their bleeding and cope with their first menses. Some hid evidence, some threw it away, some washed it out when no one was around. Many worked out ways to avoid going to a grocery store where they might be recognized, and others modified their clothes and activities to avoid embarrassment.

Many women told stories of using menstruation as a way to manipulate and have some control over situations. A Mexican American woman in her thirties was not alone in sharing how she avoided showers in school by telling the teacher she had her period, and also telling her boyfriend the same to avoid sexual contact. Greta spoke for many as she wrote:

> As far as school was concerned—during Physical Education, we were benched for three days. CLUB members [those girls who had already started their periods] often considered this a plus as we were not required to wear gym attire.

BONDING AND SOLIDARITY

Some women found that the experience of menarche helped girls identify and bond with each other, providing support and solidarity. Amy, an African American student and mother, told how she had pretended to have her period for several months before she actually experienced it in order to feel accepted by her friends. She said: "I was happy because I didn't have to lie anymore, now I was one of the girls. . . . It was important for me to be accepted as one of the group, it was a significant event for that reason." Greta, almost 40 years Amy's senior, talked bout how friends who had "joined the Club" were closer and held in a higher regard by other girls. For many women, then, first menses was an ambivalent time; it was framed by negativity, but at the same time, symbolic of maturation, it brought status. This was usually acted out in the context of sisters and peers, where girls wanted very much to be included in the group. As Thorne (1993) suggests, the "popular" girls set the stage; if they were perceived as having started their period, then this development was seen as desirable. Since this status is intertwined with their sexual status, it is complex: girls do not want to start too soon and be seen as too advanced or promiscuous, but they do not want to start last and be branded a less mature child. Timing is definitely of the essence.

The importance such a personal event held within girls' groups was illustrated by Robin, who reported that she was obsessed with the idea of starting her period and looked forward to the drama of it all: "Blood would run down your leg and you would have to run out of class!" She was not daunted by this thought and said, "I wanted very much for it to begin at school. . . . Just for the attention I guess. . . . It was a social thing. All my friends were going to get their period and I wanted to be social."

While most girls suffered the embarrassment of menarche alone, some reported how friends had supported and helped them. Laurence, a young Malaysian woman, spoke of the support and solidarity received from friends when she started her period while away at boarding school:

> It was during choir practice, we were just singing and I felt something weird and so a girl said "you have a little stain on your skirt." The girls' side of the choir was really restless and the guys had no idea what was happening. A bunch of girls, about three of them my close friends, escorted me to the bathroom and everything happened, they got me the pads, told me what to do, everything.

Others also talked and wrote about friends and older sisters who helped them figure out what was happening to their bodies, as well as helped them access and use menstrual products. Karin emphasized how she felt closer to her friends after she started her period:

> I think it kind of brought me closer to girls in a certain way because when you talk about things that are personal it really kind of strengthens your friendships I think, and I think it makes it a very intimate friendship. So I realize that [with] some of my girlfriends I was really closer, I felt very close to them.

CHANGING THE SCRIPTS

For many women, the framing of womanhood at menarche occurred within the context of the complex dynamic of their relationship with their mothers. Scholars have suggested (and the data here certainly support this) that since girls rely on their mothers at menarche, they report either increased conflict or closeness, depending on the relationship and communication patterns before puberty (Brooks-Gunn and Petersen 1983; Danza 1983; Orbach 1986). Mothers often socialize their daughters into the same restrictions associated with femininity that they have endured, ensuring that their daughters will fit into society and maintaining a shared compliance in the development of a submissive femininity and gendered sexual identity. Girls may grow to resent their mothers for their role in this at the same time that they may fear becoming what they perceive their mothers have become; however, there is much evidence here to suggest that these patterns are being disrupted. Many of the women who had negative experiences with their mothers at menarche also said that they would never want that to happen to their own daughter, and several went on to tell stories of positive experiences of menarche with adolescent children. Nonetheless, several women also emphasized that even though they had prepared their children and made it a positive experience, their daughters still felt some shame and embarrassment. The values of the culture are strong; children are not raised in a vacuum and quickly internalize the negative messages associated with menstruation.

Judy, a Japanese American in her twenties, shared her desire for a better experience for any future daughters:

> If I have daughters of my own in the future, I will tell them more positive things about periods, such as that it's not something you should be ashamed of or something dirty. I would make sure that they'll have some knowledge about menstruation before it starts because, when my period started, I didn't have any knowledge why women have [a] period or how it starts or anything.

Ann, a white mother of two daughters and a grandmother, spoke with regret that she acted very much like her own mother and was not able to give information and help her daughters feel good about their first menses. She is, however, committed to undoing this piece of family history with her granddaughter:

> My mother neglected telling me and I neglected telling my girls and I wouldn't want that to happen to my granddaughter . . . Because I wouldn't want it to come from an outside source like from girls at school. I feel that my daughter really should do this, but like I said, if she doesn't I am prepared to do it for her.

Conclusion

Although women's bodies have been the object of derogation and admiration, women themselves have not had the power to control how their bodies might look, act, and feel. Menarche is an event that symbolizes both reproductive and sexual potential and centers attention on the body. Since "woman" is overrepresented through the practices and values of sexuality, menarche takes on loaded meanings that have consequences for women and their everyday lives, scripting relations of power into the discourses and practices that surround women's bodies. The women who participated in the study remembered menarche as an important experience and, for most, this experience provoked anxiety, reminding them of their contaminating natures and encouraging them to hide evidence of their bleeding, while focusing attention on the sexualized body and changing relationships with others. Bodies are contextualized in a society that devalues and trivializes women; however, while adult women have internalized the stigma and shame associated with having bodies that bleed and all that this entails in terms of restrictions on body, mind, and soul, they have responded as active agents, and have resisted these discourses through a variety of means. They continue to resist them as they reminisce about their first menses, viewing their experiences retrospectively, framing and reframing them, hoping to neutralize the pain, perhaps taking back their power.

Menarche is a physiological happening, framed by the biomedical metaphors of current scientific knowledge, yet also a gendered sexualized happening, a transition to womanhood as objectified other. What is crucial here is that this juncture, menarche, is a site where girls become women and gender relations are reproduced. Such relations are about power and its absence; power to define the body and live in it with dignity and safety; power to move through the world with credibility and respect. May this be in our futures.

REFERENCES

Bartky, S. 1992. Foucault, femininity, and the modernization of patriarchal power. In *Feminist philosophies: Problems, theories and applications,* edited by J.A. Kourany, J.P. Sterba, and R. Tong. Englewood Cliffs, NJ: Prentice Hall.

Bordo, S.R. 1989. The body and the reproduction of femininity: A feminist appropriation of Foucault. In *Gender/body/knowledge: A feminist reconstruction of being and knowing,* edited by A.M. Jaggar and S.R. Bordo. New Brunswick, NJ: Rutgers University Press.

Brooks-Gunn, J., and A. C. Peterson, 1983. The experience of menarche from a developmental perspective. In *Girls at puberty,* edited by J. Brooks-Gunn and A. C. Petersen. New York: Plenum.

Brooks-Gunn, J., and D. N. Ruble. 1983. Dysmenorrhea in adolescence. In *Menarche: The transition from girl to woman,* edited by S. Golub. Lexington, MA: D.C. Health.

Brown, L.M., and C. Gilligan. 1992. *Meeting at the crossroads: Women's psychology and girls' development.* Cambridge, MA: Harvard University Press.

Brownmiller, S. 1984. *Femininity.* New York: Ballantine.

Buckley, T., and A. Gottlieb. 1988. *Blood magic: The anthropology of menstruation.* Berkeley: University of California Press.

Connell, R. W. 1987. *Gender and power.* Stanford, CA: Stanford University Press.

Coward, R. 1985. *Female desires: How they are sought, bought and packaged.* New York: Grove Press.

Danza, R. 1983. Menarche: Its effects on mother-daughter and father-daughter interactions. In *Menarche: The transition from girl to woman,* edited by S. Golub. Lexington, MA: D.C. Heath.

Delaney, J., M. J. Lupton, and E. Toth. 1988. *The curse: The cultural history of menstruation.* Urbana: University of Illinois Press.

D'Emilio, J., and E. B. Freedman. 1988. *Intimate matters: A history of sexuality in America.* New York: Harper & Row.

Dimen, M. 1986. *Surviving sexual contradictions: A startling and different look at a day in the life of a contemporary professional woman.* New York: Macmillan.

Dinnerstein, D. 1976. *The mermaid and the minotaur: Sexual arrangements and human malaise.* New York: Harper & Row.

Fine, M. 1988. Sexuality, schooling and adolescent females: The missing discourse of desire. *Harvard Educational Review* 58:29–53.

Foucault, M. 1978. *The history of sexuality, volume 1: An introduction.* Translated by R. Hurley. New York: Pantheon.

Gilligan, C., N. P. Lyons, and T. J. Hanmer, eds. 1990. *Making connections: The relational worlds of adolescent girls at Emma Willard School.* Cambridge, MA: Harvard University Press.

Golub, S., ed. 1983. Menarche: *The transformation from girl to woman.* Lexington, MA: D.C. Heath.

———. 1992. *Periods: From menarche to menopause.* Newbury Park, CA: Sage.

Haug, V. et al. 1987. *Female sexualization.* London: Verso.

Hays, T. E. 1987. Menstrual expressions and menstrual attitudes. *Sex Roles* 16:605–14.

Hill, J. P. And G. N. Holmbeck. 1987. Familial adaptation to biological change during adolescence. In *Biological-psychological interactions of early adolescence,* edited by R. M. Lerner and T. T. Foch. Hillsdale, NJ: Lawrence Erlbaum.

Hill, J. P., and M. E. Lynch. 1983. The intensification of gender-related role expectations during early adolescence. In *Girls at puberty,* edited by J. Brooks-Gunn and A. C. Petersen, New York: Plenum.

Irigaray, L. 1985. *Speculum of the other woman.* Translated by G. C. Gill, Ithaca, NY: Cornell University Press.

Jackson, B. B. 1992. Black women's responses to menarche and menopause. In *Menstrual health in women's lives,* edited by A. J. Dan and L. L Lewis. Urbana: University of Illinois Press.

Koff, E. 1983. Through the looking glass of menarche: What the adolescent girl sees. In *Menarche: The transition from girl to woman,* edited by S. Golub. Lexington, MA: D.C. Heath.

Koff, E., J. Rierdan, and S. Jacobson. 1981. The personal and interpersonal significance of menarche. *Journal of the American Academy of Child Psychiatry* 20:148-58.

Koff, E., J. Rierdan, and E. Silverstone. 1978. Changes in representation of body image as a function of menarcheal status. *Developmental Psychology* 14:635-42.

Lander, L. 1988. *Images of bleeding: Menstruation as ideology.* New York: Orlando Press.

Laws, S. 1990. *Issues of blood.* London: Macmillan.

Martin, E. 1987. *The woman in the body: A cultural analysis of reproduction.* Boston: Beacon Press.

Orbach, S. 1986. *Hunger strike.* London: Faber and Faber.

Patterson, E. T., and E. S. Hale. 1985. Making sure: Integrating menstrual care practices into activities of everyday living. *Advances in Nursing Science* 7:18–31.

Rierdan, J., and E. Koff. 1980. Representation of the female body by early and late adolescent girls. *Journal of Youth and Adolescence* 9:339–96.

Scott, J. W. 1992. Experience. In *Feminists theorize the political,* edited by J. Butler and J. W. Scott. New York: Routledge.

Smith, D. E. 1992. Sociology from women's experience. *Sociological Theory* 10:88–98.

Thorne, B. 1993. *Gender play: Girls and boys in school.* New Brunswick, NJ: Rutgers University Press.

Ussher, Jane. 1989. *The psychology of the female body.* New York: Routledge.

Weideger, P.; 1976. *Menstruation and menopause; The physiology and psychology: The myth and reality.* New York: Knopf.

Whisnant, L., and L. Zegans. 1975. A study of attitudes towards menarche in white, middle-class American adolescent girls. *American Journal of Psychiatry* 132.809–14.

Young, I. 1990. *Throwing like a girl and other essays in feminist philosophy.* Bloomington: Indiana University Press.

WORKSHEET—CHAPTER 6

Menstruation

This worksheet must be optional. Some parts of this worksheet are designed for women who go through reproductive cycles. Women who do not have reproductive cycles and men may or may not want to interview women about the personal questions asked in I and III.

1. **Your menstrual cycle**

   Observe changes your body goes through during a monthly cycle. Here are a few things you may want to note. You may think of others you would find interesting to record (cravings, water retention, etc.). See if you can identify when you are ovulating/have ovulated. If you are on oral contraceptives, how will your observations differ from those of women not on synthetic hormones?

   Temperature Record body temperature (by mouth is fine) first thing in the morning before you get up, have anything to drink or smoke. You are more likely to note changes if you have a fairly regular schedule and if you use a very accurate thermometer.

   Mucus (secreted by the cervical glands) Observe changes in mucus. Choose your own words to describe what you feel. Words like much, some, scant, clear and watery like egg-whites, and sticky are sometimes useful. Remember that contraceptive gels, creams, foams, and semen in the vagina will mask much of what you might notice about mucus.

   Breasts—Fuller, less full, lumpier, tender, "What I think of as 'normal'", and sore may be words useful to describe breast changes.

Date	Temperature	Mucus	Breasts	Other Observations
1				
2				
3				
4				
5				
6				
7				
8				
9				
10				
11				
12				
13				
14				
15				
16				
17				
18				
19				
20				
21				
22				
23				
24				
25				
26				
27				
28				
29				
30				
31				
32				
33				
34				
35				

II. Menstruation Products

Calculate how much you or an "average" woman spends on menstruation products in a lifetime. (These calculations can be based on today's prices.) Check current prices for one or two brands of tampons, napkins, or other "menstrual hygiene products". Estimate how much of this product is used each menstrual period. (A woman with a heavy flow will use many more than a woman with a light flow.) For your calculations you will need to figure how many years a woman will menstruate (age of menopause—age of menarche), and how many times a year a woman menstruates. Show your work. (For a very accurate estimation, you would want to think about how pregnancies, lactation, choice of contraception and menstrual changes at different ages would influence your calculations, but you do not need to do this for this question.)

III. Premenstrual syndrome

The publicity about premenstrual syndrome (PMS) and advertising for drugs promising a medical-fix for PMS have worked to make women and men regard the days pre-menstrually as "the bad time of the month" for women.

A. If a few days are regarded as the relatively "bad" days, then other parts of the month must be viewed as relatively "good". Identify "good" things you associate with different parts of your cycle. (These might include such things as times of high energy, times when you require less sleep, times when you most enjoy how your body feels, times when you especially enjoy exercising, times when you find it easy to resist sweet foods.)

B. Some women identify very positive things about their premenstrual days. For many women this is a time when they are most creative, their dreaming is most vivid, they are the most sexually aroused, they find it easiest to "justify" taking time for themselves, they feel most in touch with things in their life which need changing. Identify positive things you, your friends, or your mother notice about premenstrual days.

IV. Compare your own or (other) women's stories about menarche with the experiences described in "Menarche and the (Hetero) Sexualization of the Female Body." Describe how you learned about menarche/menstruation and compare this to how you wish you had learned about it.

V. Think of ways in which menarche/menstruation could be introduced to young people as a positive part of women's and men's lives.

    A. Suggest one or more ways to introduce menarche/menstruation as positive to young women.

    B. Suggest one or more ways to introduce menarche/menstruation as positive to young men.

CHAPTER 7

Aging, Ageism, Mid-life and Older Women's Health Issues

A core theme of this book is to remember that different women have different chances of being healthy and/or having access to health services appropriate to their needs. This chapter specifically looks at a few issues for mid-life and older women.

Aging is certainly a woman's health issue because almost all people have more health concerns and call upon the health system more as they grow older. As women outnumber men 2:1 in the over 75 group, health issues of aging are disproportionately women's health issues. Both because of women's roles and status in society and because of their longer life expectancy, women have very different experiences of aging and being old as compared to men. Older women's incomes are on average 58% of the incomes of older men; women over 65 are almost twice as likely to have incomes below the poverty line as men over 65 (Ruth Sidel, "The Special Plight of Older Women" in *Women and Children Last*). Men are much more likely to be cared for by a loved one in their dying days; women are much more likely than men to spend their last days or years in nursing homes.

When younger students suggest that the issues of aging are not relevant to their lives, it is very appropriate to point out that we are all, constantly, in the process of aging! Patsy Murphy's "Ageing" article bring this point home by looking at the issues of aging from the vantage point of a 43-year old. Questions on the worksheet try to guide students of all ages to an awareness that aging is a lifelong process and that taking care of our bodies in our younger years may be the best investment we can make in order to maximize on our old age. In the case of osteoporosis, young people who do weight-bearing exercise and eat a diet which promotes healthy bones literally build for their future; reaching age 35 with the strongest bones possible does more to prevent osteoporosis than most decisions made after 35. There is increasing evidence that the time between a woman's first period and her first pregnancy is the time when her body is most vulnerable to carcinogens. The decisions a woman makes in her teens and early twenties about exercise, fat consumption, alcohol use, and exposure to radiation, pesticides or other environmental hazards (often not a choice at all) may influence her chances of developing breast cancer later in life more than decisions she makes later. Harvard's Rose Frisch published studies showing that women involved in athletics in high school and college have a decreased risk of breast cancer, and Susan Love, breast cancer specialist (see p. 473), concludes, "A theory has been very seriously put forth that I find delightful: put public health funding into high school athletics for girls -not a bad use of our resources. This wold likely decrease breast cancer; also it strengthens bones and helps prevent heart disease" (*Dr. Susan Love's Breast Book,* 1995, p. 239).

Ageism is, of course, a mental and physical health issue for older women. In "Women and Ageing: The Dreaded Old Woman Fights Back," Madge Sceriha identifies how sexism and society's lack of respect for older people come together in anophobia, the irrational fear of old women. Although she describes this powerful social, economic, and political issue, as the title of her article suggests, she also emphasizes how older women are actively organizing and fighting against their oppression. Similarly, building on the theme that even women's movements have too often ignored the issues of older women, in "An Open Letter to the Women's Movement," Barbara Macdonald identifies ways we can all work against our own ageism. In "The Need for Intimacy," Jane Porcino movingly emphasizes a need we all have which is too often ignored for older women.

The last three articles in this chapter explore topics related to the mass marketing of products to menopausal age women and women's resistance or lack of resistance to this marketing hype. So much attention has been focused on the range of products available to menopausal women that many perimenopausal women come to our menopause classes feeling an urgent need to decide *which* pill to swallow for the rest of their lives! In "More Selling of Hormones: Still Playing on the Fear Factor," we try to demystify many of the complex issues students in menopause classes ask about, give a summary of what is and is not known scientifically, and identify many of the debates which *should* be taking place on the use of hormonal products for mid-life and older women. This article and "The Bitter Pill" provide more examples of the consequences when drug advertising is a major source of information for consumers (and their physicians), as introduced and analyzed in "Drug Marketing—Selling Women Out" (see page 166). "The Bitter Pill" looks at the lack of debate over whether a less expensive, generic version of Premarin, the most popular estrogen "replacement" product, should be available. Looking at the power of pharmaceutical companies, Leora Tanenbaum shows how many players, including women as consumers, the FDA. and politicians were manipulated into protecting the profits of Wyeth-Ayerst.

Although both "More Selling of Hormones" and "The Bitter Pill" express the need for women to be *more* active in countering the influence of powerful pharmaceutical industries, there certainly is an increasing movement of people trying to explore healthy alternatives to drugs. There is particular interest in these other approaches as related to menopause and ageing. In "Phytoestrogens: A New Alternative for Women?" Dr. Adriane Fugh-Berman, author of *Alternative Medicine: What Works,* answers many questions women ask about taking plant products with estrogenic effects for menopausal concerns and disease prevention.

Ageing

by Patsy J. Murphy

I cried bitterly when I reached my twenty-third birthday because everyone else in my year in college was nineteen or thereabouts and I felt life passing me by. I dreaded thirty with a passion which in retrospect was idiotic—I had the happiest time of my life between thirty and thirty-five. I walked the beach at Dunquin on my fortieth birthday on a lovely June day and felt terrific, and when asked at forty-three to write on ageing I felt resentful—it's hip to be over forty in New York and ageing is something I wasn't thinking about anyway. Now I've been thinking about it for the last month and what I feel about ageing is GUILT. Lots of Guilt and mostly about the things that I haven't done that I thought I would have—I haven't written a book, made a movie, seen Vienna—I haven't, in short sorted out my life and it's time I did. . . . On the other hand, I've enjoyed myself, reared a daughter (almost), supported us both and today I am starting to sort out my life.

I believe that most of the time ageing isn't so dreadful. A friend of mine told me crisply that ageing is what other people notice about you—you don't monitor its progress. My daughter used to carefully count the lines on my forehead when I was thirty-three and I know they've increased and multiplied, but I remain unaware of it until I pass a shop window and see this Winnie-the-Pooh-shaped middle-aged woman and then I reel in horror at the vision that is me.

But the vision isn't as dreadful as the guilt, which has to do with things I've left undone. At my back I always hear time's winged chariot. I've run a questionnaire amongst some of my contemporaries, who are, as a French woman I know puts it, `happy in their skin'—that is doing what they want to do and liking themselves. They don't mind ageing. I asked the cleverest woman I know how she felt about it and she said that 99 percent of the time she was totally unconscious of ageing—ageing was no bother But the one per cent was the awful, awful nostalgia about the past. I'll come back to the past later, but 99 percent is OK. The message for me is to do things that make me like myself and avoid the many, many things that make me hate myself—drinking too much, not making dental appointments. The message is the same for us all, sisters.

I asked a psychologist about guilt—it's normal he says, but it's useless: 'Take it out into the back garden and get rid of it,' he says. So, guilt apart, what does ageing mean? It means the body ain't what it used to be, but what the hell—the mind has more information and the body more experience. Ageing means that situations don't scare you as much as they did when you were young. I no longer feel terror when I walk into a room full of people. I no longer dread having to speak in public. I no longer think that someone else is going to sort out my life for me though I often wish that someone would.

For many women ageing brings freedom—a time to do things for themselves, by themselves, things that family responsibilities excluded for years. You don't have to be twenty to be knocked out by Venice, and the southern sun beams as benignly on your back at forty as at eighteen. A good book is still a good book. A glass of wine is still a glass of wine.

I've convinced myself that ageing has its compensations, but I'm still frightened of old age. I'm frightened of all the things that I presume everyone fears, being on my own, having no one to love, no one loving me, not being able to manage, the fear that the whole structure that one calls one's life, which I often feel I have small control over, will collapse around me and that I won't have the health or the energy to put it together again. Old age is not a subject one hears discussed. People on the radio and in books talk to the old, not about being old, but about their past, their part in the revolution, their girlhood, their village long ago. My fear of old age is the fear of death, which I have only experienced as the loss of other people, particularly the dreadful loss of

Reprinted with permission from *Personally Speaking,* ed. Liz Steiner-Scott, Attic Press, Dublin, Ireland 1985.

my father. I couldn't bear his death—I hated to think of him in the cold ground. I still cannot face the idea of my own death.

I can face the more immediate horrors, though. I don't believe that the menopause is such a big deal or that it's going to make me feel useless. I imagine it must be quite a relief—no more periods—and it can hardly make me more evil-tempered than I can be now. So what is it that worries me? I'm back where I started. I'm back with my friend talking about the awful nostalgia. I'm there in my past looking at a photograph of us all sitting on a wall in Paris in 1958, skinny, happy, hopeful. . . . Or I'm back in a place of which I can say, like Edna O'Brien's green-eyed girl, 'I was happy here' and I feel my ghost, I see my former self, before motherhood, before mortgages, before security mattered. This is agony, the skewer in the heart and it has to be borne. Yeats felt it, Dylan Thomas, Simone de Beauvoir . . . we all feel it, bear it, hate it. Sometimes I want it back, my lovely lost past. Well, it's gone.

When I was young, I read a lot. I've continued to do so, and I will always do so, and if I'm blind I'll ask someone to read to me because books at any age are a passport to freedom. Once, in a very gloomy period of my existence, I kept sane by reading Simone de Beauvoir's series of autobiographies. I would mechanically get through my horrid day and then, clutching twenty cigarettes, get under the blanket and live a different life, a life that became more real than my own. Unhealthy, you may say, but it got me through a bad time in my life and I imagine that books will have to and will get me through more bad times. I don't have enough life left to read all that remains to be read. Apart from such old pleasures I've found new ones in middle age—gardening, listening to opera. The pleasures of the flesh? To be candid I haven't experienced them for some time but I don't think they have disimproved and I suppose everyone's life has lulls in sensuality.

Last week I saw David Shaw Smith's TV film on the life of Pauline Bewick, an artist whose work is a total celebration of womankind. In a very beautiful film, the thing that touched me most was her triumphant feeling about her future and her work now she's fifty. She looked to her future with such a shout of confidence. I would like to be like that, although I'm not.

Our friends are the most important source of pleasure. I still have the same friends that I had in my twenties, and the friendship of women is something that improves with time, because women share their sorrows, drink over them, laugh over them, grow close over them. I hope when we're old we'll be laughing more than crying.

My friends and I laughed a lot in our twenties, we got up late, looked out the window with a cup of coffee and a fag in hand and surveyed the long carefree day ahead. Then, as it was the sixties, we all got jobs we loved, and had love-lives and money and lots of crack. Then we got pregnant, and the hassles and stratagem and patchwork that are the lot of women who bring up children—especially on their own—followed. But we survived and we still enjoyed ourselves, frazzled, broke and unperceptibly ageing. We survived. What we lost with youth was freedom, the freedom, as one friend says wistfully, just to fling stuff into a rucksack and go. I was never one for rucksacks, but I know how she feels.

So I sit here at the typewriter aged forty-three and how I do feel? I think that I have not done all that I should with my life. There are moments when I feel panic-stricken and desolate: 'What if this or that happens?' 'What if it doesn't?' There are times when I trail home from work clutching the shopping and sink in front of the telly, immersed in *Hill Street Blues,* and scream silently to myself 'Is there a life out there in the world?' And yes, I know there is and I'm going out to tackle it one of these days. Perhaps I'll tackle it today. I'll put the photograph of our hopeful selves sitting on a wall in Paris in 1958 back in the album and I'll go out and confront this grey city and my life ahead.

Questions for Discussion

1. How do you feel about getting old?
2. What are the things that bother you the most about getting old? What are the things that make you feel good about ageing?
3. How does society treat older women? With respect? With indifference? With contempt? Why?
4. What relationship, if any, do younger women have with older women outside their families? Do you think that this is a source of worry for young and old?
5. Imagine yourself when you are old. What will you look like? What will you be doing? Where will you be living? With whom? How do you think you will feel?
6. Why do we try to stay 'looking young' for as long as possible? Why are we so concerned with the signs of ageing: getting grey hair, wrinkles, loose skin, etc.?
7. What effect does the menopause have on women? Do you think it is a cause of depression in women?
8. Do you think that your attitude towards sexuality will change when you're old? How?
9. What place do older women have in the women's movement? What role should they have?
10. If you are taking care of an elderly woman, how do you feel about her? How does she feel about you? Why is there so much guilt and resentment built into these relationships? What can be done about it?

SUGGESTED READING

Jane Barker and Rosie Graham, 'Change of Life?' *Spare Rib*, No. 51 (London: October 1976) pp. 41–3.

Colette, *Earthly Paradise: An Autobiography drawn from her lifetime writings,* Edited by Robert Phelps, (Harmondsworth: Penguin 1974).

Simone de Beauvoir, *All Said and Done* (Harmondsworth: Penguin 1977). *Old Age* (Harmondsworth: Penguin).

Barbara Macdonald with Cynthia Rich, *Look Me in the Eye: Old Women. Aging and Ageism* (London: The Women's Press 1984).

Adrienne Rich, *Of Woman Born. Motherhood as Experience and Institution* (London: Virago 1977).

Virginia Woolf, *A Room of One's Own* (Harmondsworth: Penguin 1963).

Women and Ageing: The Dreaded Old Woman Fights Back

by Madge Sceriha

Introduction

Ageism is one sociopolitical issue which has been conspicuously absent from the agenda of mainstream feminism over the years since its second wave surged some thirty years ago. For those feminists like myself who are presently facing the challenge of growing old, there is an immediacy to our concern that this omission be addressed. One compelling reason is that, while older women are increasingly evident in demographic data describing our ageing population, they are virtually *invisible* elsewhere in literature about women except as depressed, despairing, demented burdens.

Over the last decade, however, there has been a vocal and determined resistance movement gathering momentum among older women. To a large extent this represents a grassroots rebellion against the socially invalidating experience of older women's virtual invisibility within white, male-dominated western societies. Many within this movement have brought a feminist consciousness to the analysis of their experience and this has contributed to a more encompassing awareness of the effects of all forms of oppression on women throughout their lives. (Anike & Ariel 1987; Ford & Sinclair 1987; Job 1984; Rosenthal 1990; Scutt 1993; Walker 1985). Pioneers of second-wave feminism and public figures such as Germaine Greer (1991), Betty Friedan (1993) and Robin Morgan, the woman who coined the slogan 'the personal is political' and who is now editor-in-chief of *Ms Magazine*, have joined the ranks too and added strength to the movement.

It is still early days though, and inspiring women who are ageing to challenge the stereotype of the 'old woman' is no easy task. This chapter will highlight the insidiousness of ageism as it affects women: the 'links between the social devaluation of women and their own self deprecating beliefs' (Fook 1993, 15).

Anophobia

When I am an old woman I shall wear purple . . .' (Jenny Joseph, cited in Martz 1991, 1)

These opening words from Jenny Joseph, in the now familiar poem `Warning', sound as if they were written especially for feminists growing old. It certainly is a poem of protest against conventional role expectations for women and paints a picture of the old woman as defiant and outrageous. Yet such is the power of ageism that it is more than likely that the woman who emulates this poem's urgings would be ridiculed and her purpose in rebelling ignored or trivialised.

Most older women are not overtly rebellious. Instead they have learned to step out carefully amid the minefields of patriarchal capitalism and ever more so as they negotiate the added dangers of ageism. Were they to look more closely at ageism though, they would see that their experience of it is neither gender neutral nor new. In a different form, which Germaine Greer (1991, 2) has called 'anophobia', it has stalked them throughout their lives as women.

'Anophobia' means 'the irrational fear of old women'. This is the fear that has made being called an 'old woman' one of the most insulting things that can be said by one man about another man. This is the fear which, because it is internalized by women from an early age, complicates their own inevitable ageing experience. This is the fear that is in effect yet another way in which women are systematically oppressed in our white, male supremacist society. Anophobia is the fuel which feeds sexist ageism.

Anophobia is a most effective social control mechanism every time it silences the rage and pain of old women's existence as they struggle to survive against the constraints of economic, social and political marginalisation. It is effective too when it perpetuates divisiveness among women of different ages. Perhaps the worst outcome of all is its effectiveness in reinforcing fear and a sense of helplessness in women as ageing progresses and their capacity to serve others diminishes. For many, all that seems to be left for them is to passively serve out their time till death comes as a welcome release.

Serving and servicing others still characterises the work women do in the home and in the paid workforce and, although this 'women's work' has traditionally been devalued as low status in a male-defined model of work, it has provided many older women with a role identity over their lifetime. Where there is unquestioned commitment to this role, it can drain women physically and emotionally. An example of this is the work older women do in caring for a partner who is dying or who has some lingering illness requiring constant care. This work is all too easily taken for granted because most women in traditional marriages:

> . . . honour their commitment to selfless caregiving in line with religious beliefs as well as sex role expectations . . . [at the cost of] social isolation and problematic return to life outside family relations [when the caring role ends]. (Rosenthal 1990, 4)

The exploitation of women this represents is seldom if ever recognised on a societal basis nor is the work

costed and thereby included as contributing to the economy. To have the courage to reject the caring role is not without its costs either, for the woman who fails to fulfil her role in selfless serving is all too often labelled selfish. This negative label is particularly effective as a means of social control when applied to women, especially those who are conditioned to put others' needs before their own.

The women's movement certainly has challenged structural inequalities with respect to work because such inequalities discount the value of what women do and consequently deny women as a social group access to economic power and independence. These structural inequalities have, however, not yet yielded to change fast enough or far enough for this to be reflected in major changes to women's identification with traditional roles. Ageing women therefore face an identity crisis when they contemplate a future in which they are increasingly likely to need the services of others rather than being the ones providing the services.

This identity crisis is exacerbated by the stereotypes which have been perpetuated under anophobic influence; stereotypes which infiltrate our awareness from an early age in fairy tales, legends, books, movies and television. Think about these all too familiar examples:

- the wicked witch with superhuman powers, sharp featured, hunched over her evil brew, cackling to herself or shrieking curses;
- this is not far removed from the feared and reviled matriarch who, with her razor-sharp tongue and control of the purse strings emasculates the males of the household and enslaves the females;
- in contrast there's the pathetic, useless, dried up, shabby shadow of a woman who is the ultimate form of female passivity and powerlessness, huddled in a lonely room waiting to die;
- then there's the old maid who, unfulfilled without a man and children in her life, is portrayed as an object of scorn or pity;
- for a good opportunity to ridicule think of Dame Edna Everage, an image created and exploited by a man which gives it just that extra impact;
- and of course there's Maggie in 'Mother and Son' whose image reminds us of our fears of becoming a burden, of losing our memories and doing outrageous things which shame our families and we're meant to laugh *at* her not *with* her;
- the best that is offered is the idealised grandmother image, but it is an image of a paragon of smiling, ever-available sacrifice whose own needs are always secondary to those of family and community.

Words too which are typically associated with old women are loaded with derision: 'dithering', 'dotty', 'doddering', 'little old lady', 'shrivelled shrew' and 'old bag' are telling examples. Woe betide her too if she's sexual because then she's grotesque or disgusting, especially if her partner is a younger man or, even more unspeakable, a woman.

Then there are the doom and gloom projections about the future sensationalised by the media which tell us that 'by the year 2021, 17% of our population will be over the age of 65' (Cross 1992, 13). We are warned that this will burden the young and strain the health services to say nothing of all the other services which will be clogged with these dependent, decrepit drains on the public purse. Let's face it though, the bulk of the older persons likely to be affected by such messages are women. It is women who are likely to spend most of our years supposedly 'past our prime' for it is suggested that 'women get pushed into the category of non-persons our society calls older people twenty years or so before men do.' (Cross 1992, 14). Because women also live longer on average than men, we are likely to experience the loss of status associated with ageing as a double burden—it starts earlier and lasts longer. Anophobia ensures also that we are likely to experience it more intensely.

This gender dimension has until recently been largely ignored in the literature on ageing as indeed has race and ethnicity. 'Very few Aboriginal people or Torres Strait Islanders survive to old age' we are reminded in a recent report. This report reminds us also of the 'growing numbers of migrants in the older population who are increasingly . . . from non-English speaking backgrounds,' (Davison, Kendig, Stephens & Merrill 1993, 16-17). These two facts can very easily be ignored when neither of the groups concerned has yet a voice (least of all a female voice) that commands attention in male-dominated, white, English-speaking Australian society.

The dominant societal voice is rather one that sounds out loudly and clearly that to be an old woman is the pits in the destiny stakes. Searching for an identity as an old woman is therefore fraught with anxiety when selfless sacrifice appears to be the only alternative to her more blatantly negative stereotypes. All too often we defend ourselves against this anxiety with denial, and fall back on the belief that age is a state of mind not a matter of chronological years. This belief is reflected in the observation that 'most people perceive themselves as essentially younger than they are' (Greer 1991, 272) and is exploited by advertisers every time they target older people and promote their products with images that evoke fantasies of passing for or emulating youth.

Every time we succumb to such propaganda we reinforce our own internalised anophobia. This is evident with regard to health and self-care products and procedures which are promoted through association with youthful attractiveness and youthful desirability. The

success of sales of pills and potions from the health food stores, pins and tucks from cosmetic surgeons, the creams and dyes from the cosmetic houses, to say nothing of weight control regimes, is founded on unrealistic expectations for miracles of repair, restoration, reconstruction and, in terms of weight, reduction. What publicity there has been about the costs in economic terms, emotional anguish and often enough, the traumatising physical consequences of these examples of the pursuit of beauty has not had a marked impact on the thriving beauty industries which benefit from women's fear of growing old.

The Beginning of the End or the End of the Beginning

It hasn't been so easy though to deny the menopause which marks the end of women's reproductive years and, it is suggested, the end of her 'prime time' as well (Cross 1992, 14). Not so easy that is until the advent of the menopause industry. Working on the premise that menopause is an endocrine deficiency disease, the medical profession with quite a little help from the media has effectively promoted the idea that what women need to carry them through the 'dreaded change of life' is a steady dose of medicalisation in the form of hormone replacement therapy (HRT). It'll calm them down, keep them cool, and even allow them to have a bleed once a month if they want.

It's certainly a lot easier for the medical profession to prescribe pills than it is for them to deal with the social reality that this is likely to be a particularly stressful time in many women's lives. One such stressful social reality is the powerful influence of anophobia. Small wonder then that the 'quick fix' promise of HRT is so widely taken up when it is presented as providing the possibility 'of eliminating menopause and keeping all women both appetising and responsive to male demand from puberty to the grave [thereby] driving the dreaded old woman off the face of the earth forever' (Greer 1992, 2).

Women are certainly not expected to think about the fact that HRT is a very lucrative product for the drug companies if they can be assured of a population of consumers with some thirty years of consuming to do from menopause to death. We're not expected to think either about the costs to women (economic, emotional and physical) of a regime of HRT. Nor perhaps are we expected to remember that, before HRT, a woman at menopause who experienced symptoms which led her to seek out help was likely to be dismissed or trivialised, whereas now, as a potential consumer of HRT, the midlife woman is much sought after.

Nowhere is this more obvious than in the marketing of osteoporosis. In *The Menopause Industry* Sandra Coney cautions us to question the motives of that industry, in particular the pharmaceutical companies, that would have us believe that osteoporosis is a 'silent epidemic' with the potential to leave us all deformed past midlife. 'Osteoporosis sells things' she reminds us, like calcium supplements and HRT and its sales success is based on our fear of the little old lady who may turn out to be even 'littler' than our worst fears could imagine (Coney 1991, 105ff). Fear is the enemy as much as any potentially debilitating condition though, especially if we allow ourselves to be 'persuaded to feel anxious, fragile and prey to a host of unpleasant diseases [thereby] . . . worrying ourselves half to death,' (Coney 1991, 277).

We might otherwise recognise that osteoporosis could have as much to do with chronic dieting and overexercising and the tendency some women have to wear themselves out or starve themselves half to death because of an obsession with slenderness. It appears that there is advantage in the presence of a little padding as we grow older provided we also keep fit. Not only does carrying this weight benefit bone structure, it cushions any falls that could lead to fractures as well. It appears also that this padding is involved in the process of oestrogen production in our bodies after menopause. This process involves the conversion of androgens, which are produced by the ovaries and the adrenal glands, into a form of oestrogen called oestrone and this process takes place primarily in the fat of women's breasts and stomach (Coney 1991, 85, 149).

It is significant too that anophobic obsession with the idea that the young female is the yardstick of what is worthwhile and desirable in a woman is divisive and keeps women in competition with each other between and within age groupings. We must remember though that it is a particular image of the young female which is idealized. An image which, furthermore, is elusive because it is created by the media in collusion with advertisers who have no scruples about using the airbrush and computer technology to shape their models to their whim. Magazines, we are told,

> ignore older women or pretend they don't exist
> . . . [and] consciously or half consciously, must
> project the attitude that looking one's age is bad
> because $650 million of their ad revenue comes
> from people who would go out of business if
> visible age looked good. (Wolf 1990, 82–4)

That age is airbrushed off the faces of any older women who do happen to be featured 'has the same political echo that would resound if all positive images of blacks were routinely lightened, . . . that less is more' (Wolf 1990, 82–4).

Even within the covers of those magazines which target an older female population, the emphasis is on the message that 'it's all right to get older as long as you look as young as possible' (Gerike 1990, 42). Thus, although there are many articles featured in these magazines which take up social issues of concern to older women, they appear alongside a proliferation of advertisements in which the models are young, trim and trendy. For good measure there are the occasional accounts of celebrities like Elizabeth Taylor who at sixty still appear ever young and ravishing. It isn't surprising therefore that so many women find comfort and reassurance from being told that they've 'worn well' or they 'don't look their age' and who dread being judged as having 'let themselves go.'

There are limits to what is tolerated in the effort to pass as or emulate the young though, and this has been very clearly demonstrated in the widespread controversy attendant on the news that two post-menopausal women have given birth after undergoing fertility treatment in an Italian clinic. Reports about the international uproar these events have caused focus on concerns for the future welfare of children of an elderly mother who might die or, for some other reason, not be able to care for her children (*Townsville Bulletin*, 31 December 1993). The double standard this represents is ignored, for males past 'their prime' who father a child are more than likely to get a pat on the back because what they've done shows that there's 'life in the old dog yet'.

Within the politics of reproduction, reproductive technology has emerged as a new frontier for the women's movement in its protracted struggle against patriarchal-capitalist power and control. 'Science and commercial enterprises (forms of institutional power) join forces with ideological forms of power (the control myth of woman as mother) in their attempt to control woman's procreative power' (Rowland 1988, 163–64). Reproductive technology stands alongside the medicalisation of childbirth and menopause, the radical invasive surgery of hysterectomy and the castration of women through oophorectomy as sociopolitical issues about which we need to develop a rigorous woman-honouring 'reproductive consciousness' (Rowland 1988, 165).

We certainly need such a consciousness to counteract complacency about the effects of the removal of a woman's uterus, cervix and ovaries when she is close to menopause. The removal of these organs is often justified on the basis of the argument that they are 'useless organs, sources of potential disease and decay' (Schumacher 1990, 58). Yet evidence is accumulating that, far from being useless, these organs have lifelong structural and functional significance for women's health and well-being other than that associated with reproduction.

Not least of the functional aspects is the part these organs play in woman's sexual pleasure from arousal to orgasm. Women have been too easily persuaded to accept the 'take it all out' technique and then later, when they experience the very real sexual losses this entails, to accept that '[s]ex is all psychological' anyway (Schumacher 1990, 55).

Seldom though have we heard it suggested that we name the indiscriminate use of medical practices and procedures that experiment on, invade, mutilate and manipulate women's bodies for what they are—another form of sexual abuse (Schumacher 1990, 64). Seldom too do we reflect on the marked contrast there is in our attitudes to the prospect of hysterectomy as opposed to mastectomy. "Hysterectomy is trivialised where mastectomy is dramatised; the visible mutilation . . . is dreaded in the same irrational proportion as the internal mutilation is courted' (Greer 1992, 52). Prescriptive body image beliefs and the sexual objectification of women once again triumph when we fail to make such connections.

Women still trust the male-dominated medical profession to give them authoritative advice. Perhaps though we should remind ourselves of the absurdity of such authority about women's reproductive processes as it fuelled nineteenth-century arguments that women should not be admitted to universities. Then it was said that women's monthly bleeding would rob their brains 'of the constant and substantial flow of blood . . . required for intellectual activity' (Scutt 1993, 3). Keeping them out once menopause removed this impediment to participation was then left to other mechanisms of social control, not least of which was anophobic-driven sexist-ageism. Even today when menopause could be perceived as the beginning of another developmental stage in women's lives, prevailing medical authority favours a deficiency-disease diagnosis.

Medical authority is a form of institutionalised power which can influence our beliefs about ourselves. Where that authority influences us to believe the ageing woman's body is deficient and her once valued organs of reproduction are useless, it becomes another source of tacit legitimation for the continued medicalisation of women's lives and the social practices which devalue older women on the basis of their perceived biological inferiority. It is as if '[o]ur society has the idea that the value of women over 40 starts dropping rapidly and makes it a reality by turning the assumptions into facts' (Anike 1987, 26).

The Dreaded Old Women Unmasked

Devaluing is a form of social abuse which is 'so systematic that it . . . is considered normal by the society at large' (Dworkin 1988, 133). Its purpose is to marginalise and disempower and it is most successful when it generates feelings of revulsion and fear of the devalued group. Anophobia is such an abuse. Its obvious expression is in the pathological representation and negative stereotyping of women's ageing. It is much less obvious and therefore more difficult to confront when it takes the form of patronising tolerance. Worst of all though is when women start to feel that they are invisible, as this tends to silence them as well. It is not uncommon for women to remark that they really became aware of feeling old when they were ignored in shops and bumped into in the street as if they weren't there. Experiences of that sort soon erode self-esteem and self-confidence, especially if there were little of either at the outset.

The life expectancy of women in white Australian society has increased by some thirty years over this century and women outnumber men in all age groups after the age of 65 (Parliamentary Report 1992, 18–19). Women are the majority of the aged population and will be into the future and that population is projected to increase dramatically.

Alarmist reports in the media about the consequences of this demographic phenomenon refer to a '. . . "time-bomb" that threatens to blow the economy to pieces' (Parliamentary Report 1992, 52). It isn't difficult to see how the fear this has generated already in our society will attach to women in particular because they live longer. The double standard which persists in granting males as they age greater status and privilege than women accentuates this possibility. It is not that males are immune to ageist oppression but there is no male equivalent of anophobia nor is the image of unattractiveness, asexuality, passivity, dependency and incompetence associated with being old thrust upon them so early nor so destructively.

A 1992 Parliamentary Report observes,

Demographic change may expose inadequacies in economic and social institutions and practices, but the former is not in itself the problem . . . The debate over how best to run an economic system is not primarily an ageing discussion . . . the ageing of populations may have little to do with the outcome. (Parliamentary Report 1992, 68, 70)

We must therefore maintain a critical consciousness of how easily the aged (and most particularly women) could be scapegoated when politicians blame welfare spending for the country's economic crises. Our society would have more to fear if older women were to withdraw the unpaid caring work they do within family networks and as volunteers in the community which is a contribution they are likely to make as long as they are able. Research indicates that older people are more likely to be providers than recipients of any kinds of support . . . [In addition it seems that more than 60% of the over 65 population have no limit on their functional ability and about 30% report only some minor restrictions to their activity. (Edgar 1991, 17)

There is a danger in focusing on 'use value' as a justification for older women's right to more visibility and respect though, especially where it is so closely linked to privatisation of service provision within the family structure. Such a view constrains women who want to 'retire' from such role expectations and venture into other pursuits which interest them and negates those women who are frail or disabled. These issues are among the many which increasing numbers of older women are coming together to confront as part of an older women's movement which has the potential to become as politically significant as any of the radical movements which developed in the 1960s.

Accounts of this movement worldwide are proliferating. The Older Women's League (OWL) in America, The Older Feminist's Network and the Growing Older Disgracefully Collective in the United Kingdom, the Older Women's Network (OWN) in Australia and the Raging Grannies in Canada are examples of action groups that are inspiring older women to be who they are with courage, openness and a commitment to living more fully than they have ever before been allowed to think possible. These groups offer support and encouragement for women to explore their potential without imposing expectations for dramatic change. In such an environment it is more possible to become aware of internalised anophobia and all other forms of oppression

which ageist prejudice exacerbates. They are not about establishing new stereotypes for old women for not all women have secret burning desires to abseil or bungee jump or even to join in direct social action. Not all women could, even if they wanted to, because of frailty, disability and/or economic constraints.

Many of these groups are encouraging women to write their own stories, to join in theatre workshops, to learn public speaking, to lead discussions, to learn self-defence, to be involved in environmental and peace issues and to link in with younger women's groups for events like International Women's Day and Reclaim the Night marches and rallies. Through involvement in such activities and action women can break down the barriers isolating them from each other within and between age groups, break the silence about their concerns and discover that the world of the young woman is no utopia nor is the world of the old woman necessarily a hell on earth.

That it is a hell on earth for too many is a fact that all women, both young and old, have a stake in addressing. We know that old women are likely to be victims of socio-economic violence (or what has been more euphemistically labelled the 'feminisation of poverty') because structural inequalities in our society continue to disproportionately disadvantage women throughout their lives. We know from the burgeoning literature on elder abuse that old women are often victims of emotional, physical and sexual violence just as their younger sisters are. We know that many feel isolated, lonely, hopeless and helpless because poverty, prejudice and powerlessness confine them to the margins of societal concerns. There is good reason, therefore, for all women to be actively anti-ageist and, in particular, anti-anophobic for it is an investment in their own future.

For references, see the original.

An Open Letter to the Women's Movement

by Barbara Macdonald

The following suggestions conclude a longer article entitled "An Open Letter to the Women's Movement" which deals with the widespread ageism in the women's community. The book from which this article is taken, *Look Me in the Eye,* is about women and ageing.

The following are a few suggestions to all of us for working on our ageism:

1. Don't expect that older women are there to serve you because you are younger—and *don't think the only alternative is for you to serve us.*
2. Don't continue to say "the women's movement," . . . until all the invisible women are present—all races and cultures, and *all ages* of all races and cultures.
3. Don't believe you are complimenting an old woman by letting her know that you think she is "different from" (more fun, more gutsy, more interesting than) other older women. To accept the compliment, she has to join in your rejection of old women.
4. Don't point out to an old woman how strong she is, how she is more capable in certain situations than you are. Not only is this patronizing, but the implication is that you admire the way she does not show her age, and it follows that you do not admire the ways in which she does, or soon will, show her age.
5. If an old woman talks about arthritis or cataracts, don't think old women are constantly complaining. We are just trying to get a word in edgewise while you talk and write about abortions, contraception, premenstrual syndromes, toxic shock, or turkey basters.
6. Don't feel guilty. You will then avoid us because you are afraid we might become dependent and you know you can't meet our needs. Don't burden us with *your* idea of dependency and *your* idea of obligation.
7. By the year 2000, approximately one out of every four adults will be over 50. The marketplace is ready now to present a new public image of the aging American, just as it developed an image of American youth and the "youth movement" at a time when a larger section of the population was young. Don't trust the glossy images that are about to bombard you in the media. In order to sell products to a burgeoning population of older women, they will tell you that we are all white, comfortably middle class, and able to "pass" if we just use enough creams and hair dyes. Old women are the single poorest minority group in this country. Only ageism makes us feel a need to pass.
8. Don't think that an old woman has always been old. She is in the process of discovering what 70, 80, and 90 mean. As more and more old women talk and write about the reality of this process, in a world that negates us, we will all discover how revolutionary that is.
9. Don't assume that every old woman is not ageist. Don't assume that I'm not.
10. If you have insights you can bring to bear from your racial background or ethnic culture—bring them. We need to pool all of our resources to deal with this issue. But don't talk about your grandmother as the bearer of your culture—don't objectify her. Don't make her a museum piece or a woman whose value is that she has sacrificed and continues to sacrifice on your behalf. Tell us who she is now, a woman in process. Better yet, encourage *her* to tell us. I wish you luck in your beginning. We are all beginning.

Reprinted with permission from *Look Me in the Eye* by Barbara Macdonald and Cynthia Rich, Spinsters/Aunt Lute Book Co., 1983. (Available from P.O. Box 410687, San Francisco, CA 94141).

The Need for Intimacy

by Jane Porcino

How long has it been since someone touched me? Twenty years? Twenty years I've been a widow, respected, smiled at, but never touched. Never held so close that loneliness was blotted out. . . .Oh, God, I'm so lonely.

These poignant words from the poem "Minnie Remembers," by Donna Swanson, reflect one of our deepest fears about aging. No matter what our age, we each need intimacy in our lives—at least one other person with whom we can share both pleasure and pain. We hunger for someone who will accept us as delightfully different. This other person can be female or male, young or old.

Research demonstrates that babies who never are held or touched suffer psychologically and may actually wither and die. This also is true as we grow older. And yet, an increasing number of women over 65 live alone, without partners, many of them deprived of any expression of intimacy.

One reality we will face as we grow older female is that there are more women than men; we are likely to find ourselves without a male partner. In the beginning decades of this century, there were equal numbers of women and men over the age of 65. Today, there are almost 150 older women for every 100 men. Divorce after 25 to 30 years of marriage is becoming commonplace, and the average age for a widow is only 56. Complicating all of this is the fact that men who are widowed or divorced in mid- or late-life quickly remarry, most often to younger women. There are nine bridegrooms to every bride over the age 65. Not only is remarriage rare for older women, but there are few social opportunities for close relationships with men. As a result, almost half of all older women live alone—many of them lonely. One women stated the problem well when she wrote to me:

One thing unites us all—babies, adults, and grandmothers—our need for response from some living creature. Of course, tender loving care would be better, but we can survive without that luxury. What we cannot do without is some kind of reciprocal sharing of life experiences.

Are millions of us doomed to loneliness in old age? Not if we are willing to plan now for our later years, and not just let them happen to us. First, it is important to strengthen and nurture our friendships with women—indeed, glory in them. Fortunately, we were encouraged to develop close female friendships, to share trust and confidences, and to express our feelings to one another. Many of us, even many married women whose relationships with their husbands lack intimacy, presently share much of our social life with women. We seek out environments in which we can express our innermost thoughts. The coffeeklatch, PTA-days have evolved to rap groups, consciousness-raising meetings, and professional networking (the "old girls' club").

Collective living is one way to counter loneliness in our later years. Small groups of us can join together to share living space, incomes, companionship, thoughts, and tasks in a supportive environment. Women are successfully doing this throughout the country. There is a great deal that we can do together that we cannot do alone.

The seeking of intimacy could be encouraged even within nursing homes. My own mother lived out her last years in such a facility, where she developed a close friendship with another woman. They shared all the details of their daily lives, and yet to the end, these two proper women called each other "Mrs.," and rarely touched. The friendship was so deep that when one died, the other followed in a few months.

Reprinted with permission of the author, from *Ms.* Magazine, January, 1982, p. 104.

A prevailing fear of homosexuality among many heterosexual older women may prevent them from acknowledging their human need for intimacy. Some women have shared sexual intimacy with other women most of their adult years. Even women who prefer heterosexuality are moving toward intimacy with women in their later years because of the limited choices available to them. Only a few women may find sexual gratification in their female relationships. But they will find many other kinds of intimacy. Women I know say that they enjoy the companionship of other women; many say they have no desire at all to make the accommodations that would be necessary to form new heterosexual relationships. Two wrote the following to me:

> I am blessed with a few special women friendships. They are nonsexual, greatly sharing, mutually supportive "conversational love affairs."

> I've a whole circle of supportive, nutritive, loving women friends. I talk over life circumstances, problems and interests with them very openly, receive a great deal of support from them, and give the same. We often have just fun together. I love them and they love me. These friendships have been the most stable thing in my life.

The upcoming generation of elderly women (those now in their late 30s and 40s—the baby-boom generation) are more open to exploring different ways to be intimate. Those of us presently in our middle or late years can learn from them. Although we have been socialized to seek only one significant other, perhaps our search should be for a few such people in our lives—people to have fun with, to share our pleasure and pain, and to give us the physical touching we need.

Love has the potential for deepening as we age. We have years of experience behind us, and now we have the time. Sensuous grandmothers abound—women like Lena Horne, Mary Calderone, and Ingrid Bergman, whose vibrant way of being in the world draws people to them. Our only limit may be a weak imagination.

More Selling of HRT: Still Playing on the Fear Factor

by Nancy Worcester • Mariamne H. Whatley
University of Wisconsin—Madison

Introduction

For decades, women's health activists were critical of the medical system's lack of interest in older women's issues. Osteoporosis and heart disease were excellent examples of the problematic relationship between the medical system and women who use it. These prevalent, serious, life threatening conditions were characterized by an almost total lack of information and research. Until the early 1980s, most women had never heard of osteoporosis, and cardiovascular disease was so consistently labelled as a 'men's' disease that the major studies included tens of thousands of men and *no* women.

The situation has changed dramatically in the last decade. Osteoporosis and heart disease can no longer serve as examples of neglect of older women's issues. Osteoporosis has become a household word (clearly indicated by the fact that we no longer have to teach our students how to spell it), there must not be a woman in the industrialized world who has not seen a headline announcing 'heart disease is the number one killer of women', and the prevention of both osteoporosis and heart disease in women has become 'hot' research.

This is an updated version (1999) of "The Selling of HRT: Playing on the Fear Factor" by Nancy Worcester and Mariamne H. Whatley which was published in *Feminist Review* (London, England) no. 41, summer, 1992, pp. 1–26.

It might seem that feminist activists should be applauding this response of the medical establishment. Any woman approaching menopause is likely to receive information from her health care practitioners on the dangers of osteoporosis and heart disease. So why are we complaining? Aren't feminists ever satisfied?

PREVENTION CONSCIOUSNESS

The interest in older women's issues is directly related to the fact that the medical establishment and the drug industry have 'discovered' that healthy menopausal and post-menopausal women represent a huge market. The selling of hormones and services which promote or follow up on them fits neatly into the needs of the drug industry, as well as health service providers and consumers. Restrictions by the government and insurance companies in the US have meant the health system cannot make enough money on sick people and women are not having 'enough' babies; the health system has had to search for previously untapped markets of healthy people. Consumers may feel the health system is finally responding to their needs if services and products are marketed to play on their new found prevention consciousness.

Contemporary US and British societies, especially the middle classes, have become highly health conscious. Advertisements in which bran cereals are pushed to prevent cancer, low cholesterol foods to reduce heart attack risk, and exercise machines to promote 'wellness' reveal the dominance of the prevention ideology in health awareness. Sometimes the meaning is sufficiently clouded that it seems that the appearance of health may be an end in itself rather than a means towards a higher quality life.

The focus on prevention and self-help is a part of an overall trend among consumers away from the sick-care model of the medical industry which devotes few resources to environmental and occupational issues, disease detection and control, or medical education, and instead prioritizes drugs, surgery, hospitals and high-technology equipment. This sick-care model may do an impressive job of patching up accident victims or putting a new heart into someone who has eaten the typical high fat, low fiber, western diet, but it does practically nothing to keep us well. The initial resistance to the medical model was often political, based, for example, on the analysis generated by the women's health movement; prevention was a way of wrestling control away from doctors and returning it to consumer.

However, it took the medical establishment and others little time to coopt the emphasis on prevention. This consciousness has been intentionally constructed to be very individualistic—'take care of *yourself*' (i.e. don't expect society, the government or the health system to take care of you)—and victim-blaming—'it's their fault if they choose to live unhealthy lifestyles'. As major consumers in the health care system, responsible for their own health and that of other family members, women quickly were targeted as the major customers of prevention services. In her seminars on how to market women's health, Sally Rynne, consultant to for-profit women's health centers throughout the USA, noted that 18 per cent of women's medical visits are preventative, that women are the major subscribers to the prevention/wellness type magazines and that the audiences at health promotion programs are predominantly women (Whatley and Worcester, 1988). Ironically, though the emphasis on prevention originated as a way to become less dependent on the medical establishment, it is now being used as a marketing technique to attract people back into the system: you cannot prevent osteoporosis or heart disease with HRT without having a doctor's prescription and surrounding services to monitor your 'progress' toward prevention!

SELLING THE FEAR FACTOR

In order to maximize the market value of 'prevention', the condition to be avoided must be sufficiently serious or highly undesirable. Individuals must view the condition in question as highly prevalent or believe themselves to have a high level of personal susceptibility. Fear can become an important selling point for either true prevention or early detection tests.

As diseases become 'popular', there is a time of intense interest, during which we are inundated with media coverage of the newest plague, whether it is genital herpes, toxic shock syndrome, premenstrual tension, or chlamydia. Accurate and complete information is needed about these issues; increased awareness is essential for all individuals who want to have some control over their health. However, sensational media coverage often does little besides create fear, as the early media coverage of AIDS clearly demonstrated. Those who benefit from this fear-based media coverage are those who offer prevention, tests for diagnosis, or treatment, whether they are effective or not.

The marketing of hormone products to menopausal and postmenopausal women is particularly sadistic in the way that it plays not only on the fears of specific disabling or life-threatening conditions but also on women's fear of ageing. Disabling or life-threatening conditions are frightening enough in themselves, but once totally associated with the ageing process, growing older or *being old,* take on an increased meaning for women in an ageist society which particularly devalues older women. It is no coincidence that *Feminine*

Forever was the name of the 1966 book which first popularized the notion that a wonder drug (estrogen) could prevent the ageing process in women.

SWALLOWING HRT AND FORGETTING ITS HISTORY

Feminine Forever, whose author was funded by Wyeth-Ayerst, the manufacturer of the menopausal estrogen product Premarin, promised that estrogen could keep women young forever and prevent the natural 'decaying' process of ageing. It is not surprising that by 1970 Premarin had become one of the top four prescription drugs in the USA (Eagan, 1989.) By the mid-1970s, there were cities in the US where more than half of the menopausal women were taking estrogen (Sloane,1985). But, by the mid-1970s, studies were starting to show a marked increase in endometrial (lining of the uterus) cancer in women who had taken menopausal estrogens. While Wyeth-Ayerst denied the estrogen-endometrial cancer link and even resorted to sending 'Dear Doctor' letters to all gynecologists in the US (Waterhouse, 1990), women became afraid of menopausal estrogen, doctors feared lawsuits if they prescribed it, and at least another fifteen studies proved that estrogen use was associated with a marked increase in endometrial cancer (Sloane, 1985). By 1979, a consensus conference of the National Institutes of Health had rejected almost all claims which had been made for the physical or psychological benefits of estrogen replacement therapy. The conference committee concluded that of all the presumed symptoms of menopause, there were only two which could be established as uniquely characteristic of menopause and that are uniformly relieved by estrogen therapy. Estrogen is only effective for controlling hot flashes (vasomotor instability) and changes in the genitals (which text books refer to as genital atrophy—no wonder women will resort to anything to avoid this condition!)

One might think that would be the end of a product which lived up to few of its claims, in which consumers and physicians had lost confidence and which was known as a cancer-causing agent. But, drug companies had tasted the potential of marketing products to menopausal women: in the US more than 28 million prescriptions for estrogen had been filled in 1975. (National Prescriptions Audit).

The 1980s saw two changes in the marketing of estrogens. 1) Public relations firms were hired to promote estrogen products in the same way that candy, breakfast cereals or soaps are advertised, and 2) estrogens were reintroduced onto the market in combination with progestins.

Feminist health activists have found the mass marketing of estrogen products to be irresponsible. Starting in 1985, Premarin's manufacturer, Wyeth-Ayerst, hired a public relations firm to conduct a public education campaign aimed at encouraging *all* women over thirty-five years to consider estrogens to prevent osteoporosis instead of targeting the twenty-five percent of women at high risk of suffering consequence of osteoporosis. Later, Ciba Geigy, manufacturer of an estrogen patch, began mass direct mail solicitations promoting their patch to women throughout the US. Testifying before the Food and Drug Administration against the mass promotion of estrogens, Cindy Pearson stated, 'The National Women's Health Network is outraged that a potentially risky drug is being promoted with the same techniques used by Publishers Clearinghouse Sweepstakes' (Pearson, 1991).

By the drug companies' criteria, such promotion of estrogen products must seem phenomenally successful. In 1985, when Wyeth-Ayerst first started its 'education' campaign on osteoporosis, a survey found that 77 per cent of women had not heard of this condition (Dejanikus, 1985). Now, women have not only heard of osteoporosis, they are also frightened by the seeming inevitability of postmenopausal hip fractures or of becoming like the elderly woman with the severely bent spine they have seen in advertisements. Having dropped to approximately 15 million prescriptions per year in the US in 1979/80, estrogen prescriptions were back up to nearly 32 million by 1989 (National Prescription Audit). According to federal health statistics, as many as half of all postmenopausal American women take some form of hormone 'replacement' at sometime and at least 15 percent are taking the drugs at any one time (Michael Specter, 1989). A recent telephone survey of 500 women ages 50–74 in the US found that 38% currently used estrogen (Keating et al, 1999).

PACKAGING AS HRT OR ERT

Consumers are now faced with a 'choice' of hormonal products. By the early 1980s estrogen was often prescribed in combination with a progestin. It was believed that the progestin component would protect against the risk of endometrial cancer which was associated with estrogen on its own.

For the rest of this paper two different terms will be used to identify the two different forms in which estrogen is most commonly prescribed. **HRT (hormone replacement therapy)** will be used in reference to products or regimes where a woman is given *both* an estrogen and a progestin hormone. **ERT (estrogen replacement therapy)** will be used when a woman is given estrogen on its own. At this stage of the debate about postmenopausal hormones, it is absolutely essential that we keep track of whether we are talking about HRT or ERT.

It is accepted that ERT is related to an increase in endometrial cancer, whereas HRT is not associated with that cancer and may even have a protective effect against endometrial cancer. Any woman with a uterus (i.e. women who have not had a hysterectomy) should be informed of this and offered HRT instead of ERT if HRT is believed to fulfill the purpose for which she is considering hormones. If a woman with a uterus chooses to take ERT instead of HRT (for example, some women find they feel depressed and/or less sexually responsive on progestins), it will be essential that she have regular endometrial biopsies to check for endometrial cancer. As this paper will discuss, it is a confusing moment in history for women to be making choices about postmenopausal hormones. Many of the studies have been done with ERT, but not on HRT. As the studies have not been done, it is simply too early to know whether the progestin component of HRT diminishes or reverses effects expected of estrogen. The Women's Health Initiative, the largest randomized, controlled study ever done on women, is monitoring many thousands of women from diverse populations for the effect of ERT, HRT, or placebo (no hormone) on heart disease, cancers, osteoporosis and cognitive function (including dementia.) But, the results from this important study will not be available until 2007. As Kathleen MacPherson (1987) points out in her important article "Osteoporosis: The New Flaw in Women or Science?", some physicians will not prescribe the HRT combination because: 1) research on its long term effects is scant, 2) progestins in the contraceptive pills increased the risk of hypertension and strokes, and 3) postmenopausal women may not want to have break through bleeding which occurs monthly if they take the estrogen-progestin combination.

Women who are considering taking ERT, estrogen on its own, should be informed that in addition to the approximately five to fourteen fold increase in endometrial cancer (National Women's Health Network, 1989), women on this regimen also increase the risk of abnormal bleeding 7.8 times, need dilation and curettage 4.9 times as often, and have hysterectomy rates 6.6 times higher, than non-users (Ettinger, 1987). Women who take estrogens after menopause also have a two to three fold increase in their risk of gallbladder disease (National Women's Health Network, 1989).

Clearly the goal of estrogen manufacturers is to find a way to package estrogens so that women are willing to stay on them for their *entire postmenopausal life:*

> We are still learning ways to administer estrogen and progestogen to obtain maximum effectiveness with minimum side effects. New formulations of estrogens and progestogens, new routes of administration, and improved dosage schedules should provide more conve-

nient and acceptable long term hormone replacement, one that women can use for their entire postmenopausal life time without the inconvenience of menstrual bleeding and concern about possible side effects. (Ettinger, 1987: 36)

In contrast to the drug manufacturers' goal to have women stay on hormones from perimenopause until end of life, there is much evidence that many menopausal women who "try" hormones do not stay on them long term. Short term use of low dose hormones are safer than long term use of higher doses of hormones, so it will often be appropriate for women to use hormones to ease the transition through menopause. However, women using hormones to reduce osteoporosis or heart disease will lose any protective effect soon after they stop taking hormones. The "yo-yo" effect of going on and off hormones can *cause* hot flashes and other menopausal symptoms by artificially creating the hormone fluctuations which cause these symptoms. Additionally, there is some question whether "on and off" use of hormones might actually increase bone loss. This paper will emphasize the importance of deciding *when* to take hormones as well as deciding *whether* to take them.

HORMONES DOMINATE THE SYSTEM BOTH PHYSIOLOGICALLY AND POLITICALLY

Hormones hold potential for improving quality and quantity of life for some menopausal and postmenopausal women. It will be important to come back to this point and question how feminists can better look at the potential for these hormones. Unfortunately, we seldom have the luxury of being able to do this because major forces are so persistently pushing hormones and because most information is so pro-hormones. In an effort to "balance" the discussion, feminist health activists have often ended up as lone voices critiquing the premature, routine prescribing of these drugs of unknown safety. It is interesting to note that anyone asking for this more "balanced" view of hormones (trying to shift the emphasis to asking which particular women will most benefit from which hormones and when) gets labelled as being "anti-hormones." Ironically, although postmenopausal hormones are increasingly pushed as something *all* women need, in reality, it is predominately white middle and upper class women who even get to make choices about hormones. Few low or no income women have access to hormones and with the important exception of the new Women's Health Initiative, women of color have been noticeably missing from other hormonal studies.

Even if women have *all the* available information on postmenopausal hormones, with the present state of knowledge it is extremely difficult to weigh the potential benefits and the unknown risks. But, in fact, very few women 'choosing' to embark upon hormone treatment even know that the drugs they are taking are controversial and possibly hazardous. The information women get in the lay press is very much biased towards the use of hormones. A survey of thirty-six menopause articles in the most popular women's magazine found that three-quarters of the articles were clearly pro-hormone and half the articles did not even mention any risks of hormone use. (Pearson, 1991). The information women get from their doctors may be nearly as biased: over 75 per cent of US gynecologists routinely prescribe hormones to all menopausal women.

Even the smallest doses of ERT or HRT have very powerful effects on a woman's body and totally dominate her body's own regulation and production of hormones. How desirable or safe this is physiologically is a question which remains to be answered. What is known at this time is that the way hormones are being promoted is very dangerous for women politically and must be seen as the part of the purposeful medicalization of women's lives.

Feminists have long been critical of the ways in which normal, healthy processes such as contraception, pregnancy and childbirth have been medicalized. We used to criticize the fact that real health issues such as premenstrual tension, infertility, and osteoporosis were ignored by the health system. Now that women's health issues have been 'discovered' and there are money-making drugs or technologies to offer, we see an expansion into medicalizing whole new areas of women's lives. We are already witnessing what this means. The medical profession is taking control over more aspects of women's lives, more conditions are being labelled as illness and used against the equality of women, drugs or high technology procedures have been identified as the solution to newly targeted 'problems' and, in the name of prevention, more women are being hooked into a medical system which does not meet their needs.

The medicalization of menopause means that menopause and postmenopause are defined as 'deficiency illnesses'. Even the terms 'hormone replacement therapy' and 'estrogen replacement therapy' wrongly imply that something is missing which must be replaced. The fact that this misinformation can so easily be used as a selling point for products is a sad reflection on how little information most women have about their own bodies. As the National Women's Health Network's position paper on hormone therapy puts it, **'We object to the view of normal menopause as a deficiency disease.**

Menopause does not automatically require "treatment".' (National Women's Health Network, 1999)

Menopause is a normal, healthy transition phase of a woman's life when her body has within it all the mechanisms necessary to gradually change from dealing with demanding reproductive cycles to meeting the different, post-reproduction, physiological needs of post-menopause. The postmenopausal women is still capable of making the estrogens she needs: the older woman's body needs less estrogen and makes it in a different way. During the reproductive years, a woman's ovaries will be the main producers of estrogens and relatively high quantities of estrogens will be produced. Menopause is the time when the ovaries gradually decrease their production of estrogens, with the dominant form of estrogen changing from estradiol to estrone, and the estrogens produced by the adrenal glands and converted from androgens by fat and muscle tissue become the major estrogens in a woman's body. Menopause should be viewed as the healthy transition from premenopause to postmenopause in the same way that puberty is recognized as the time when young women make the transition from pre-reproduction to being capable of reproduction.

Viewing menopause as a normal, healthy transition does not imply that transition is easy for all women. Although many of the problems faced by menopausal women are social rather than physiological, woman may experience symptoms such as hot flashes when or if their estrogen levels drop rapidly (which is what happens if a woman's ovaries are surgically removed). Taking ERT or HRT works to *delay* the transition by keeping hormone levels artificially high. If a woman suddenly stops taking hormones she can experience the same or worse symptoms than the ones for which she was taking hormones. If a woman chooses to take ERT or HRT to relieve hot flashes or genital changes, to *ease* the transition she would want to take gradually reduced amounts of hormones for as short a period of time as possible for specific complaints (National Women's Health Network, 1999).

The medicalization of menopause is particularly dangerous in that *all* attention has become focused on hormones as the 'answer' to whatever is identified as the menopausal/postmenopausal 'problem'. While some women may benefit from hormones, many or most women will be able to go through the transition phase and minimize osteoporosis and heart disease risks with less hazardous measures such as a healthy diet, appropriate physical exercise, and using alternatives to hormones. Whether in determining research priorities or influencing the information the mass media should give to empower women through informed decision making, much more attention needs to be focused on healthy alternatives to hormones. As Kathleen MacPherson (1987: 60) puts it,

> To recommend widespread use of HRT as a public health measure to prevent osteoporosis without assessing the needs of individual women would be the same as recommending that everyone take antihypertensive drugs because so many people have high blood pressure. For no other condition is anything as potentially dangerous as hormones being recommended as a preventative measure.

Osteoporosis

CREATING THE FEAR OF OSTEOPOROSIS

In order to create markets for their products, both drug companies and calcium manufactures effectively used the media to introduce people to osteoporosis, a previously ignored condition, and to scare them into buying products which promised to prevent this. Both prevention consciousness and fear of aging contributed to the success of osteoporosis-related advertising. Many advertisements played on both of these, such as the spot for a calcium supplement which showed a healthy thirty year old transformed to a stooped sixty-five year old within thirty seconds (Giges, 1986). Such an image not only capitalizes on the fear of losing youthful beauty, it also draws on even deeper fears of disability leading to loss of independence. In another very recent advertisement, Merck used a similar scare tactic before their drug (Fosamax) to treat osteoporosis was even available. The advertisement did not name a specific product but helped build on women's fears of disability and aging; the image was of a young woman riding a bicycle and the large shadow cast—that of a wheelchair. The information on hip fractures has been presented in an even more frightening way. For example, a popular guide to preventing osteoporosis states: 'The consequences of hip fractures can be devastating. Fewer than one-half of all women who suffer a hip fracture regain normal function. Fifteen percent die shortly after their injury, and nearly 30 percent die within a year' (Notelovitz and Ware 1982: 37). The deaths are not inevitable and are related to complications such as pneumonia but they certainly serve as a useful scare tactic.

Because the lethality of hip fractures has been used so effectively as a scare tactic in the marketing of a whole new range of products to prevent, treat, or identify osteoporosis, it may be useful to know a little more about hip fractures. What happens to a healthy vigorous 80 year old who breaks her hip and what happens to a frail, unhealthy 80 year old who breaks her hip are as different as the women's health conditions were before the hip fractures. In her *Dr. Susan Love's Hormone Book,* Susan Love contrasts ramifications of hip fracture on her step mother and mother-in-law. The healthy woman broke her hip while traveling in Cambodia, flew home to have the hip fracture nailed, recovered promptly, and a year later returned to Cambodia to "finish" her trip. In contrast, the frail woman became less and less independent after a broken hip and a year later broke her other hip; as she was becoming less and less healthy her hip fracture(s) were the last straw (Love, 1997). Instead of simply seeing that adults often have major life threatening problems after suffering a hip fracture, it is important to question whether hip fractures initiate or reflect the process of health deterioration (Wolinsky, 1997). Osteoporosis researcher Steven R. Cummings, University of California Medical Center, San Francisco, has summarized the situation as, 'Hip fractures may often be a marker and not the cause of declining health and impending death. Most patients who suffer a hip fracture have severe concomitant illness that accounts for much of the increased mortality after hip fractures' (Cummings, 1990: 4). Ironically, even though the fear of hip fractures has been used primarily to market products to white women, this population is the least likely to die after hip fracture. In a study of 712,027 persons covered by Medicare, white women experienced the lowest mortality rate following a fracture of the hip, 17.2 per 1000 person months, in contrast to 22.9 for Black women, 33.5 for Black men, and 33.7 for white men (Jacobsen, 1992).

The information about complications of osteoporosis as a major 'killer' of women in their 80s and the linking of osteoporosis with menopause in such a way that osteoporosis practically becomes identified as a symptom of menopause, can be further connected to imply that menopause itself is a killer unless hormones are taken to stop this process.

In fact, osteoporosis and how it affects people are much more complicated and unpredictable than the hormone and calcium promoting information suggest. Osteoporosis is not an 'all or nothing' condition, it is 'not a disease like tuberculosis that a person either has or does not have' (Parfitt, 1988). Indeed, there is much controversy over how osteoporosis should even be defined. The World Health Organization (WHO) defines osteoporosis as a value for bone mineral density (BMD) which is 2.5 standard deviations or more below the mean peak bone density in young adults (aged 25–40.) A definition this broad means that a very high proportion of older women eventually get defined as having a disease. The National Women's Health Network says, "This is a case where a definition has created a disease!" (NWHN, 1999). The National Women's Health Network believes that "low" bone density levels should be determined for older women by comparing older women to healthy older women rather than to the standard of a 25–40 year old reaching their optimum lifetime bone mass.

A statement like, 'It would appear inevitable that if a person lives long enough, he or she will suffer from osteoporosis' (Kirkpatrick, 1987) may help British or American women put their newly created fear of osteoporosis into perspective. However, taking a more cross-cultural approach such as, 'osteoporosis is not a natural part of aging and does not occur all over the world, even among the elderly'(Brown, 1988) will be more useful for understanding that osteoporosis is not inevitable, is very much related to industrialized/western diets and lifestyles, and that *real* prevention has nothing to do with hormones.

> Looking at cross-cultural data, we see that blaming osteoporosis on an estrogen deficiency is just a little less absurd than blaming heart attacks on a deficiency of by-pass surgery. Surgery might solve the problem for a while, but it is not a deficiency of the operation that caused the problem. (Brown, 1988.6)

Osteoporosis often is billed as a major health issue for all older women, when, in fact, some women are much more at risk than others. The fact that lighter complexioned women with ancestors from northern Europe or Asia are much more likely to develop osteoporosis than darker complexioned women with African, Hispanic, Mediterranean or Native American ancestry probably accounts for this condition finally receiving the attention it has. Real pressing health needs of 'minority' older women as defined by the women themselves still tend to get ignored.

However, while critiquing the misinformation that osteoporosis is equally an issue for all older women, it is also important to emphasize that just because certain groups have lower rates of osteoporosis that does not mean that no one in those groups is at risk. Osteoporosis may have different impacts on white women and women of color, as is the case with other diseases. For example, it has long been noted that Black women have a lower incidence of breast cancer than white women but a disproportionally high percentage of Black women compared to white women die of breast cancer and five year breast cancer survival rates are considerably lower in Black women than white women. An unpublished study by Lian Partlow (1991) traces how Black women gradually got left out from the osteoporosis literature. She cites earlier studies which concluded that 'hip fractures are three times greater in white women than Negro women' or 'Black women in the US have age-specific incidence rates for hip fractures of about half of those of

white women.' However, by the 1980s and 90s when osteoporosis became a major research topic, those important though not equal rates of osteoporosis in Black women disappeared and almost all scientific articles included a statement such as, 'Black women were excluded from this study because of their low risk for hip fracture' (Cauley, 1995). Osteoporosis, like breast cancer, seems to be less common in Black women than white women, but potentially more lethal for Black women than white women. (See hip fracture mortality rates above.)

FRACTURES ARE NOT SYNONYMOUS WITH OSTEOPOROSIS

Disabling or life-threatening fractures must not be seen as synonymous with osteoporosis. Not all women with osteoporosis have fractures, not all women with fractures have osteoporosis, studies have shown that women with and without hip fractures had similar bone densities, and women in other cultures have low rates of bone fractures even with low bone density (National Women's Health Network, 1999).

The *real* health issue for women is the prevention of fracture and the best was to prevent fractures is to prevent falls. Falls are the immediate precipitating factor for approximately 90% of hip fractures and 80% of other fractures in women (Cummings, 1993). Factors such as impaired vision (including poor depth perception), muscle strength, balance, flexibility, obstacles in the home, having to walk on icy sidewalks, and advancing age have been demonstrated to influence the chance of fracture more than the density of bone mass (Whatley, 1988a, Atkins, 1996). Dr. Carol Frey (1998), Director of the Foot and Ankle Center at the Los Angeles Orthopedic Hospital, says that avoiding falls can often be as simple as choosing appropriate shoes for different situations. Her research has found that 28% of falls in older people were blamed on the "wrong" shoes: 60% wearing sneakers fell because their shoes caught or dragged on the floor and 40% had fallen in situations where their athletic shoes became too slippery. Falls among elderly people are known to be significantly greater for those using antidepressants, sedative/hypnotics and vasodilators (drugs that dilate blood vessels) (Myers, 1991; Tromp, 1998) and modification of medications has been shown to be an effective method of reducing falls and fractures in both community and nursing home settings (Wolfe, 1991a; Close, 1999). Even a simple home-based exercise program for elderly women also significantly reduced the risk for falls and resulting fractures (Campbell et al, 1997). So, in many cases reducing, rather than increasing, drugs, and taking fairly simple measures will be the key preventative issues for minimizing complications of osteoporosis in elderly women.

A more creative and caring, less profit-motivated approach might come up with some very interesting ideas about what to do about osteoporosis (Whatley, 1988). For example, Kathleen MacPherson emphasizes that health policies must reflect the need for bold structural changes in our society instead of the usual incremental or "bandaid" policies suggested as osteoporosis prevention (MacPherson, 1987: 61). Her recommendations are for policies to "alleviate the feminization of poverty, a living wage, pension plans, social security, benefits for homemakers, and a national health care plan to provide ongoing health promotion and maintenance for all citizens." Ending violence against women so that more women felt safe walking and running and getting a wide range of exercise in various settings would certainly improve more than just bone mass!

It is now accepted that standard doses of ERT and HRT slow loss of bone mass in most women and can reduce the risk of hip fractures while it is taken (Writing Group for PEPI, 1996; Cauley, 1995; Assessment of Fracture Risk, WHO, 1994). Articles also refer to estrogen increasing bone density up to 5% (Genant, 1997, Libanati, 1999) but *Dr. Susan Love's Hormone Book* (1997, p. 94) emphasizes that, 'estrogen appears to halt or slow bone resorption rather than actually building bones: thus the 5% represents a filling in of resorption pits rather than the development of new bones.'

Now that osteoporosis is a 'hot' topic, the market is being flooded with a range of new products promising to be miracle drugs for preventing or treating osteoporosis. Because of recent changes in Food and Drug Administration (FDA) regulations, it is easier to get new products onto the market than it used to be and drug companies are allowed to advertise their products directly to consumers rather than just to physicians and other health practitioners with prescribing privileges. Consumers need to be aware that most new products have been tested for only short term effects and safety.

Two osteoporosis treatment products deserve mention because of the aggressive marketing and attention they are getting. Calcitonin, a version of the hormone produced by the parathyroid gland, is now available as the nasal spray, Miacalcin. Fosamax (alendronate) is a bisphosphonate that works to inhibit resorption and increase bone density. Comparing the two products, *The Medical Letter* (January 5, 1996) concluded, 'Miacalcin offers the least concern about safety, but its effectiveness is limited. Fosamax is probably more effective, but its long term safety remains to be established.'

Fosamax is being marketed very aggressively by its manufacturer, Merck, but in its first years on the market there have been a very high number of adverse drug reactions reported against it (Annual Adverse Drug Experience Report, 1996) and the FDA Regulatory Review Office had to contact Merck more than once about mis-leading claims in violation of the Federal Food, Drug and Cosmetic Act (Reb, 1997). It should be emphasized that Fosamax is for *treating* not preventing osteoporosis and anyone taking Fosamax has to follow a very strict regimen (i.e. take the drug with sufficient water but absolutely no other food or drugs and do not lie down for at least one half hour) (Cummings, 1998b).

Women wanting to make decisions about osteoporosis prevention and treatment will want to keep in mind a number of issues. Some methods (Miacalcin and Fosamax) work only on the bone and do not provide other health benefits. ERT and HRT work to reduce bone loss and may have additional benefits but benefits need to be weighed against risks, particularly breast cancer. In contrast, appropriate dietary and physical activity changes may reduce osteoporosis and provide other health promotion benefits (particularly in relation to heart disease and fracture reduction) without risks. For many women, a major issue will be whether they can afford the method(s) they would like to use. The following information is given as the name of the drug or product, the suggested dose per day, and the average wholesale cost per month (Freeman, 1998):

1) Vitamin D = 400 units = $0.30–0.75
2) Calcium Carbonate = 1000mg = $2.25
3) Estrogen pills = 1.0mg - 0.625mg = $10.00
4) Estrogen patches = 0.05mg/week = $20.00
5) Estrogen/progestin combined = 0.625/2.5 = $17.60–19.20
6) Alendronate (Fosamax) = 10mg = $52.00
7) Calcitonin injection = 100 units = $96.00
8) Calcitonin spray (Miacalcin) = 100 units = $100.00

OSTEOPOROSIS SCREENING

Detecting osteoporosis also gets deliberately confused with preventing the condition. In the US and Canada, osteoporosis screening has been widely promoted. Finding a noninvasive way to predict a woman's risk for fractures may seem a benefit of medical science with which few could find fault. Certainly the prevalence and potential consequences of osteoporosis are serious enough to justify screening.

An editorial in the *Journal of the American Medical Association* observed, 'The field of osteoporosis has been overwhelmingly focused on bone mass, both because imagers can measure it and because clinicians can affect it' (Heaney, 1998: 2119). However, just because you can measure and change something doesn't mean that that's the most important or even appropriate procedure to follow! It is not a coincidence that much of the information on the dangers of osteoporosis and the value of bone screening and much bone screening equipment are paid for by pharmaceutical companies with osteoporosis products. How many people know that the work of the National Osteoporosis Foundation (including their toll free hotline and research) is largely funded by Merck? An evaluation of bone mass measurements as a screening procedure reveals serious limitations in what can be learned from bone density readings (Napoli, 1988; Whatley and Worcester, 1989). In the most comprehensive review and evaluation of the literature on bone density issues, the British Columbia Office of Health and Technology (1997) concluded, "Research evidence does not support whole populations or selective bone mineral density (BMD) testing of well women at or near menopause as a means to predict future fractures. On some issues, evidence is insufficient because the research has not been done. Existing research evidence, though imperfect, indicates substantial limitations of BMD testing."

Several techniques are currently being used to detect osteoporosis and these techniques vary in availability, cost, accuracy, reproducibility, and what they actually measure. But, there are certain problems with all of them and the most available techniques are the least reliable. Speakers at a recent osteoporosis conference noted that the pace of technological change in the bone density field is such that women are being screened today with technology which will be out of date by the time she has a second screening. ("Emerging Approach" 1997)

While screening can show that bone mass has been lost, screening cannot predict how rapidly someone will be losing bone and cannot predict whether or not someone is at risk for osteoporosis. Bone loss is neither constant nor predictable. Knowing someone's bone mass at one age does not help predict how fast that women will lose bone mass; a woman with a low bone mass may end up losing at a very slow rate and a woman with a much higher bone mass might end up losing rapidly (Whatley, 1988). Screening is even limited in its ability to identify full-blown cases of the disease. While bone density screening would be expected to differentiate between those who do and do not have osteoporosis related hip fractures, these measurements are of little use in the most at-risk elderly population because, 'if the highest bone mass seen in patients with fractures is designated as the 'fracture threshold', then nearly all women over 70 will by definition have osteoporosis' (Ott, 1986, p. 875). Bone density of one bone does not necessarily predict bone density elsewhere. For example, many right handed women have higher bone mass in their right wrist than their left wrist. Measurements of the wrist do not necessarily reflect bone density at the hip (Ott, 1986; Riggs and Melton, 1986). One study found a 150% increase in the number of women who would be defined as having osteoporosis if they took BMD measurements at two sites per woman rather than

just one site because bone densities are so different from one part of the body than another (Abrahamson, 1997).

It must be emphasized that techniques for measuring bone mass are extremely useful for research purposes. However, at this stage, unreliable but sophisticated, expensive screening has little to offer the consumer. Requiring regular monitoring of bone mass, osteoporosis screening offers enormous potential for clinics as a profitable procedure and enormous risk to women that it will hook them into a system which has little to offer them except hormone prescriptions (Worcester and Whatley, 1988). There is now considerable evidence that BMD measurement is useful, and used, to convince women to use hormones. Because women do not necessarily have the information they need to make informed decisions about what BMD results mean, studies show 'screening for low bone density significantly increases the use of HRT . . . but without any immediate adverse or positive effects on the quality of life' (Torgerson, 1997: 2121–2125; Silverman, 1997). The sentiment, 'Women who refuse HRT for osteoporosis prevention should be offered a BMD measurement' ("Emerging Approach, 1998, p. 590), which shows up in the medical literature, may be common in clinical practice. Another study which demonstrated that bone density screening can be influential in pushing women to use hormones also showed that women who were told they had low BMD became fearful of falling and began to limit their activities to avoid falling (Rubin, 1992). Bone screening could be counterproductive if it results in less physical activity by exactly the women who might most benefit from physical activity to strengthen bone mass!

ROLE OF DIET

There is plenty of evidence that western/industrialized lifestyles and diets are responsible for the prevalence of osteoporosis and the fact that it affects women much more than men. Britain and the US report much higher rates of osteoporosis than less industrialized/westernized countries. For example, the US rate is 24 times higher than that of some other countries. People in Singapore, Hong Kong, certain parts of Yugoslavia and the Maori of New Zealand have very low rates of osteoporosis caused fractures and Africans and people living traditional indigenous lifestyles have been described as 'almost immune' to osteoporosis (Brown, 1988).

Osteoporosis as a male disease in Britain and the US gets very little attention (because no one has figured out how to convince men that their problems are all due to 'estrogen deficiency'?) despite the fact that (US) men suffer one-sixth the spinal fractures and approximately one-half the hip fractures as women. In other parts of the world, i.e. Hong Kong, some parts of Yugoslavia, and in the South African Bantu, it has been documented that men experience osteoporosis and fractures at the same or higher rates than women. Medical anthropologist Susan Brown (1988) gives the following explanations for the excessive development of osteoporosis in western women: 1) as a group, women have less exposure to sunlight which helps the body make vitamin D which is essential for calcium absorption, 2) women are not encouraged to be as physically active, 3) women use more prescription drugs, 4) women are more subject to removal of the sex hormone producing gonads, the ovaries (i.e. if the testes are removed, men also develop osteoporosis), and 5) men generally consume a higher quality/more nutritional diet than women.

Western diets contribute to the development of osteoporosis both by not providing enough calcium in the first place, and more importantly, by "wasting" the calcium which is ingested. The typical western diet encourages a heavy imbalance in the ratio of phosphorus (high levels in carbonated beverages and high protein foods, including meats) to calcium which can cause a loss of bone calcium, low levels of vitamin D and high levels of fiber, oxalates, and phytates interfere with calcium absorption and high intakes of caffeine and alcohol also significantly contribute to excessive bone loss (Abelow, 1992, Campbell, 1997, Finn, 1987 and Brown, 1988, and Hu, 1993). Instead of dealing with anything as complex as the calcium-wasting effects of our diet, or questioning high consumption of foods like meat which are central to our diet and economy, calcium has been promoted as something one can simply add to what one already consumes. Retail sales of calcium supplements grew from $18 million in 1980 to $166 million in 1986, a calcium-fortified sugar-free drink mix was marketed, and the sales of the diet cola, Tab, tripled when calcium was added. Jumping on the calcium bandwagon and hoping it would make people forget their cholesterol concern, the dairy industry launched a campaign with the theme 'dairy foods: calcium the way nature intended' (Giges, 1986). In the 1990s, calcium-fortified orange juice has become readily available.

It is well established that because bone mass peaks at age 35 years, the greatest benefit from calcium occurs in the years from birth to age 35 (Finn, 1987). However, it is discouraging to see how, in the push towards hormones, the role of calcium for menopausal and post-menopausal women has been ignored or discounted. In explaining why recommended intakes of calcium for older women had not been increased in the Food and Nutrition Board's latest (10th edition) *Recommendation for Daily Nutrient Allowances,* the director stated, 'because estrogen is more effective in preventing osteoporosis than calcium.'

That answer is much too simplistic and totally ignores the risks of estrogens and the fact that many women cannot or will not take hormones. Most importantly, such attitudes influence research and policy agendas so that the potential of calcium alone or in sufficient quantities to reduce the amount of estrogens needed, are not being explored despite work showing the merit of this approach. In a study believed to be the first one looking at both lifelong and current calcium intake in normal postmenopausal women not taking estrogens, researchers found a protective effect of calcium on bone density in women who reported high calcium intakes *both* throughout their lifetime and presently (Cauley, 1988). The excellent review article, 'Calcium for Prevention of Osteoporotic Fractures in Postmenopausal Women' by Robert G. Cumming and Michael C. Nevitt (1997) summarizes results from 37 calcium studies published between 1966 and early 1997. Using meta-analysis techniques (combining information from many studies) these authors found that 1000 mg/day of dietary calcium was associated with a 24% reduction in hip fracture risk, and stated, 'Our conclusion is that calcium supplements and dietary calcium probably reduce the risk of osteoporotic fractures in older women. The consistency in effect size between small randomized trials and pooled observational studies (after adjustments for measurement error) is particularly impressive. Our systematic review of the evidence supports the current clinical and public health policy of advising older women to increase their calcium intake' (Cumming and Nevitt, 1997, p. 1329).

Even Bruce Ettinger (1987: 33–34), previously quoted as supporting the goal of keeping women on estrogens for their entire postmenopausal lives, gives us reason to remind pro-hormone scientists that calcium deserves more attention. He states, 'Although calcium given alone is incapable of maintaining skeletal mass, high intakes of calcium allow estrogen to be more effective; by simply augmenting calcium intake to 1,500 mg. per day, women may be adequately protected while taking half the usual dosage of estrogen . . . It has also been suggested but not proven that very low intake of calcium—perhaps less than 300 mg. per day—can also diminish or abolish estrogen's protection.'

Thinking of *real* osteoporosis prevention is a useful case study of how life long interactions of social, economic, and political issues affect women's health and how factors in a young woman's life affect her chances of being able to maximize on her full potential. With 'femininity' so closely associated with an obsession with thinness and the conflicting, never appropriate messages given to young women about physical activity, sex role socialization and gender identity have to be seen as causal agents of osteoporosis. The obsession with thinness and fear of fat promote osteoporosis in several different ways. First, avoiding high calcium foods because of caloric content, dieting that results in nutritional deficiencies or nutritional imbalances, fasting, and purging can be identified as behaviors which interfere with calcium absorption and contribute to low peak bone mass (Kirkpatrick, 1987). The benefits of increased calcium intake for young women was demonstrated in a study on the effect of increased milk intake in adolescent girls (median age 12.2), which found that, compared to the control, the increased milk group gained a significant amount of bone mineral with no other significant changes, such as in weight or fat mass (Cadogan et al, 1997). Secondly, low body weight reduces the mechanical forces applied to the skeleton by gravity and muscle contraction so there is less 'built-in' stimulation for bone formation. As a generalization, heavier people tend towards more bone mass (Goodman, 1987). Additionally, it is well established that fat tissue in a woman's body produces estrogen and the more fat a woman has, the more estrogen she will produce. But how many women know this or can listen to the message if they hear it? Society so consistently pushes thinness and hormones, that contradictory healthy advice such as that in Mary Kirkpatrick's 'A Self Care Model for Osteoporosis' is seldom mentioned:

> Ironically, midlife may be a good time to have a little extra weight to act as a protective mechanism against osteoporosis. If fat tissue provides more estrogen, the bone loss at menopause may be slowed. Also, body weight can act as a loading factor and can produce necessary stress on the bony structure to form bone mass. (Kirkpatrick, 1987, pp.48–49).

PHYSICAL ACTIVITY

Numerous studies have shown that exercise, particularly of the weight-bearing type, can promote bone strength in women under 35 and help maintain bone mass in women over 35. But, how often do women, particularly young women, get useful, sensible advice about the health benefits of moderate exercise? Too often women get only one of two equally inappropriate messages: don't exercise or do too much of it!

When tested for physical performance, girls and boys are matched up to ages 10 to 12. Thereafter, they receive very different messages about what is 'lady like' or 'masculine' and after age 12, boys tend to increase in strength and cardiovascular fitness more than girls who are discouraged from being physically active (Whatley, 1988b). The young women who resist the pressure to be sedentary, are often encouraged to go to the other extreme. Both the "cosmetic athletes" who obsessively exercise to achieve "beauty" and the serious athletes who exercise too strenuously, can delay menarche or cause amenorrhea which can be detrimental to building bone density (Goodman, 1987).

Interestingly, the relationship of 'athletic amenorrhea' to osteoporosis started attracting quite a bit of media attention as more young women have begun to explore their athletic capabilities. Physiologically, the explanation and consequences of amenorrhea may be the same whether caused by athletic training, ballet dancing or extreme dieting. However, as western cultures find ballet and dieting to be ideal 'feminine' activities, the media attention has focused almost exclusively on the potential osteoporotic risks of athletic amenorrhea. Regular, moderate, weight-bearing exercise is undoubtedly a healthier approach to osteoporosis prevention. Further research is needed to determine the type, intensity, duration, and frequency of physical activity which best builds and maintains bone mass (Goodman, 1987).

WHEN TO START HORMONES?

The emphasis on taking hormones at perimenopause or menopause to prevent bone loss has been based on the thinking that the most rapid bone loss takes place during the first six years after menstruation ceases so that hormonal 'treatment' would have the greatest impact on reducing bone loss if begun within three years after natural menopause. However, recent studies show that when and how women lose bone mass is far less predictable. The importance of preventing bone loss at menopause seems to have been overemphasized. One longitudinal study of bone loss in postmenopausal women described two quite distinct groups: although one third of women lose significant bone mineral (the 'fast losers'), two-thirds lose only a minor amount of bone mineral (Riis, 1995). Other longitudinal studies have shown that bone loss continues or even accelerates with increasing age (Ensrud, 1994). 'It is becoming clear that, at least at sites other than the spine, bone loss continues unabated into the oldest age ranges and probably accelerates at the hip, the most important region for predicting hip fractures' (Black, 1995: 2A–69S).

Even people who promote hormones for osteoporosis prevention debate whether hormones should be started before or after menopause. Since bone loss similar to normal loss during menopause years sets in as soon as the hormones are stopped, estrogen started at menopause, even if taken for as long as ten years, does not protect women into their late seventies. Serious fractures are most common in the elderly: the average age of hip fracture is 80 (Cauley, 1995). As a result, treatment started at menopause would need to continue lifelong, possibly for 30 or more years with all the associated risks.

Starting estrogen before menopause may increase breast cancer risks without increasing osteoporosis benefits. A meta-analysis of studies on ERT found that studies in which estrogen therapy was started before menopause showed a much greater increase in breast cancer than studies of women who started estrogen after menopause (Steinberg, 1991).

A woman's decisions regarding hormones for osteoporosis prevention can be made many years after menopause. The emphasis on menopause as a time for intervention has more to do with it being an easily identifiable marker in a woman's life than that it is the optimal time for intervention. It may also have to do with the fact that women at the age of menopause are more likely to be covered by health insurance that covers prescription drugs than are elderly women. The Rancho Bernardo Study of 740 women over 60 found that there was no significant difference in bone mineral density between women who started estrogen at menopause and those who started after 60 (Schneider, 1997).

Although the Osteoporotic Fractures Research Study (a study of 9704 women) emphasized that estrogen is most effective if initiated soon after menopause and continued indefinitely, the conclusion of the study was that current use of estrogen in women 65 years of age and older, whether started 'early' (up to 5 years after menopause) or 'late' (more than 5 years after menopause) reduces the risk for fractures (Cauley, 1995). Dr. Dennis Black, UC-San Francisco, has argued that 'stopping bone loss at age 65–70 can still prevent most instances of very low bone mass in women over 80, that screening at age 65 can more precisely identify risk of hip fracture at age 80, and that treatment beginning at age 65 may be more cost-effective than earlier screening and treatment' (Black, 1995).

In terms of osteoporosis prevention, it is more effective for a woman to delay her decision about starting hormones rather than going on and off hormones. Theoretically, going on and off hormones post-menopausally could mean the body goes through accelerated 'transitional bone loss' more than once.

Heart Disease

Women may have become saturated with information about ERT and osteoporosis; a new angle has been necessary to raise anxiety to the point at which a new group of women will actively seek ERT prescriptions. The long overdue attention to *prevention* of heart disease in women has provided exactly the right focus for an expanded ERT market, giving physicians an additional rationale to prescribe it. The new media coverage of women and heart disease has helped generate fears and then ERT has been offered as the solution.

This contrasts with approaches in the past when very little attention had been paid to either prevention or treatment of heart disease in women, for it has traditionally been viewed as a man's disease. While men experience heart disease at younger ages and have more heart attacks than women, women account for 47 per cent of the heart attack deaths in the United States, making it the leading cause of death for women (Winslow, 1991). In addition, women who suffer a heart attack are more likely to die than men (39 per cent vs. 31 per cent) and more likely to suffer a second heart attack within four years (20 per cent vs. 15 per cent) (Winslow, 1991). However, these high risks for women have not been reflected in treatment. For example, in one study of patients hospitalized for coronary heart disease, men were 28 per cent more likely to have angiography, a procedure to determine the extent of arterial blockage, and 48 per cent more likely to have bypass surgery or balloon angioplasty. In another study of men and women hospitalized for major heart attacks, men were nearly twice as likely to have angiography and bypass surgery (Winslow, 1991). This study also found that, before the heart attack, chest pains and other symptoms were more disabling for women than men. One of the authors of the latter report emphasized her concern that women who continued to have chest pains after their heart attacks still do not receive angiography (Kolata, 1991a).

These studies and others document the lack of attention by the medical profession to heart disease as a major women's health issue, but the fact that these studies exist at all is a sign that there is finally some concern. If heart disease is the leading killer of women in the United States, why has there been so little emphasis on it before? Why do so many women fear breast cancer but are apparently unaware of their risks of heart disease? Without going into reasons for past neglect, it is possible to offer some explanations for the new-found hype of heart disease as '#1 killer of women.' One view is that the market is fickle and there needs to be a 'disease of the month' to capture the interest of the media, consumers, practitioners, and the people (politicians included) who control research funding. However, with an old disease, only a new angle, preferably with something to sell, will generate the necessary interest. For example, there was considerable media attention when a study suggested that aspirin reduced the risk of heart attacks in men (Steering Committee of the Physician's Health Study Group, 1989). Aspirin manufacturers must have been delighted by the press aspirin received, especially after the earlier negative publicity about Reye syndrome, a potentially fatal condition in children caused by aspirin being given during a viral infection such as flu or chickenpox. However, the media reports rarely mentioned that the study was done on men only and could not be extrapolated to women. In response to the gap in the research, a study reported that women who took one to six aspirin a week experienced a 25 per cent reduction in risk of heart attack compared to women who took no aspirin (Manson, Stampfer, and Colditz, 1991). The results are hardly conclusive, however. The study, which included only nurses, was an observational study (the women made their own choices about aspirin and reported it, while the researchers just looked for the effects), not an experimental one. This leads to the strong possibility of confounding variables, for the groups may vary in much more than the factor of aspirin use (Appel and Bush, 1991).

In spite of the flaws, this study received a lot of publicity and generated more interest in women and heart disease, providing a good opening for calling attention to the role of ERT in preventing heart disease. In an apparent attempt to expand their market, Wyeth-Ayerst, the manufacturers of Premarin, the most commonly prescribed oral estrogen, requested that the U.S. Food and Drug Administration (FDA) allow promotion of Premarin for the prevention of heart disease, at least for women who have had hysterectomies (Rovner, 1990). The FDA Advisory Committee concluded, after listening to much conflicting testimony, that 'the cardiovascular benefits of estrogen replacement therapy with Premarin in women without a uterus may outweigh the risks, considering the individual patient's risk for various estrogen-related diseases and conditions' (Rovner, 1990: 9). Dangerously, this statement, as it has been reported and repeated has been reduced to a simple 'benefits outweigh the risks;' in addition, the distinctions between ERT and HRT are rarely clarified.

In terms of the research itself, the results are not clear-cut. Generalizability is limited because almost all the subjects have been white and middle-class. As with the aspirin study, these studies have been observational; the researchers did not control the choice of treatments but merely observed the results based on the women's choices. A major confounding factor is that the women who *choose* Premarin may be at reduced risk for heart attack anyway. For example, a co-author of the major lipid study cited in the FDA hearings, Elizabeth Barrett-Connor said that women who used Premarin were also less likely to smoke, were thinner, and were better educated than non-users, all of which might have been factors in reducing risk (Rovner, 1990). One of the clearest ways to emphasize that users and non-users may represent different populations is the result of one study which found users of estrogen had lower mortality rates, not only from heart disease, but also from accidents, suicide, and homicide. As Cindy Pearson, of the National Women's Health Network, asked, when she was testifying *against* FDA approval for Premarin being promoted for the prevention of heart disease,

'Does this mean we can conclude that estrogen use protects one from being murdered?' (Rovner, 1990, p. 9).

Until recently, no study has been without the major flaw of lack of comparability between users and non-users of ERT. This is well illustrated in a study published after the FDA hearings, which was heralded as more good news about ERT. The study of 49,000 post-menopausal women showed 44 per cent fewer heart attacks and 39 per cent reduced risk of heart attack death in those who took ERT (Kolata, 1991b). However, the study was on nurses, 98 per cent of whom were white, who had made their own choices about use of ERT. As an example of this problem, a very heavy woman, who might be more at risk for heart attack, might also be less likely to select ERT because she would also be *less* likely to experience menopausal changes for which ERT is recommended. A nurse who considered herself at risk for heart disease might not have taken ERT because physicians in the 1970s were discouraging women at risk of heart disease from taking estrogen at all (Sojourner, 1991). Up until recently, all the evidence for the role of estrogen in preventing heart disease was based on non-randomized observational studies. In 1998, an important randomized study on HRT compared to placebo in postmenopausal women with preexisting coronary disease was published (Hulley et al, 1998). While the lipid profile was better in the HRT group, there was no difference in cardiovascular outcomes at the end of the study and, in the first year, there were more heart attacks and deaths from heart disease in the HRT group. The results do not preclude possible benefits to women with no known coronary disease, but they do raise questions about the benefits of estrogen, which it was assumed would be especially beneficial to the group of women in the study.

Besides the studies directed at heart attack risks, much of the support for the role of ERT in preventing heart disease comes from data on HDL (high density lipoprotein) and LDL (low density lipoprotein). *Higher* HDL and *lower* LDL are favorable to reduced risk of heart disease. A review article by Bush and colleagues (Bush et al, 1988) provides a good summary of the factors affecting these lipoproteins in women. These include genetics, diet, obesity, exercise, alcohol, cigarette smoking, oral contraceptives.

The data on oral contraceptives is particularly interesting. All formulations increase LDL, the 'bad lipoprotein.' The largest increases in LDL occur with the lowest estrogen dose and the strongest anti-estrogenic progestin. As the potency of progestin increases, HDL, the 'good' lipoprotein decreases. The implications from the oral contraceptive data for the use of ERT as compared to HRT are borne out by the studies on estrogens as menopausal therapy. According to Bush and colleagues

(Bush et al, 1988), use of unopposed and synthetic estrogens leads to the more favorable HDL/LDL profile. However, cyclic estrogen-progestin therapy (HRT) has either a minimal or adverse effect on lipoproteins, depending on the progestin used. In other words, while estrogen therapy by itself may have very positive effects, the addition of progestins at least partially negates those effects. HRT, therefore, in the best case, provides little benefit in terms of HDL/LDL profile, the main route by which ERT is believed to have a protective effect against heart disease. However, many women take HRT to avoid the increased risks from ERT in terms of endometrial cancer. If the progestin component protects against endometrial cancer but at least partially undoes the protective effects against heart disease, women may have to make difficult decisions about which disease they fear most.

The lipoprotein data also provides some interesting results about alcohol. Bush et (1988) state that moderate alcohol consumption is strongly related to increased HDL levels in men and women. A recent report suggested that moderate alcohol consumption has a protective effect against heart disease in men, which supports previous work finding benefits for men and women. If estrogen manufacturers are allowed to say their products reduce heart disease, why shouldn't beer and wine companies request that the FDA allow them to promote their products as reducing risk of heart disease? Such a claim would surely be countered with the argument that the risks of alcohol consumption outweigh the benefits. But do we really know that benefits of ERT outweigh the risks?

While much of the discussion has focused on the effects of HDL and LDL, recently more attention is being paid to high levels of triglycerides as a possible risk factor for heart disease. It is now theorized that in women high triglycerides are more predictive of risk than high total cholesterol and that high HDL cannot counter the negative effects of high triglycerides. In discussions of the effects of estrogen on the lipid profile, it is often not emphasized that ERT *increases* triglycerides, thereby potentially *increasing* risk of heart disease.

Some of the answers about ERT and HRT should come from the Women's Health Initiative, mentioned previously. When the data from this study is analyzed completely, it may be appropriate to make some recommendations about HRT and ERT. In the meantime, while we wait for the data to come in, perhaps it would be more appropriate to focus on what we do know about preventing heart disease in women and provide education about diet, exercise, smoking, and treating high blood pressure (Wolfe, 1991b).

Breast Cancer

In the attempt to reduce the risk of heart disease or osteoporosis by taking ERT or HRT, women may be replacing one disease with another. There is strong evidence that estrogens increase the risk of breast cancer, but the issue seems to be how big a risk that really is. A Swedish study, published in 1989, showed a 10 per cent increased relative risk of breast cancer in women on estrogens, with the risk increasing with length of treatment. After nine years of use, there was an excess risk of 70 per cent. The addition of progestins did not reduce the risk and may even have increased it slightly (Bergkvist et al, 1989). The differences in the estrogen of choice in the U.S. and Sweden was apparently one reason why this study did not receive more press, as well as the fact that the risk was seen as only slightly increased.

A later study from the United States received more attention but also was presented as showing a slight risk. In a study that followed over 12,000 nurses for 10 years, Colditz and colleagues found that women taking estrogen were 30 to 40 per cent more likely to develop breast cancer than those who did not (Colditz et al, 1990). This might be seen by many as a serious risk in a disease that is said to strike one out of eight women in the United States. However, the media coverage played down the effects as slight. For example, referring to the increased risk of 30 to 40 per cent, one article claimed, 'But this risk is considered small; it is only about half the risk a woman faces if her mother had breast cancer' (Kolata, 1990: A11). This is hardly reassuring for women considering ERT who have other risk factors, particularly the woman whose mother had breast cancer. The one note that women may actually find reassuring is that the additional risk seems to disappear a year after stopping estrogens. However, that does not help much for women who are on the long-term plan for estrogen to maintain the reduced risk of osteoporosis and heart disease until death.

A large number of studies on ERT and breast cancer were evaluated using meta-analysis, a statistical method to evaluate data from a number of studies, which can give a more accurate picture than a single study (Steinberg et al, 1991). The data suggest an increased risk of breast cancer for women who used estrogen for more than five years. Women with a family history of breast cancer had a markedly increased risk. A particularly interesting finding was that the studies in which estrogen therapy was started before menopause showed a much greater increase in risk than those which included only women who started estrogen after menopause. The duration of estrogen therapy is clearly related to risk and going off it seems the only way to reduce the risk. While progestins may protect these women against endometrial cancer, it will apparently do nothing to reduce breast cancer risks. The most recent studies conclude that there is an increased risk of breast cancer with ERT/HRT. In 1997 a detailed analysis of data from 51 studies involving large numbers of post-menopausal women concluded that breast cancer risks were increased a small but significant amount, with increased duration of use increasing risk (Collaborative Group, 1997). It is important to note that with one out of eight women in the U.S. developing breast cancer, even a small percentage increased risk leads to many more women with cancer.

In weighing up the risks of breast cancer versus the possibility that ERT or HRT can prevent osteoporosis or heart disease, women essentially need to decide which disease they fear the most. Dr. Lynn Rosenberg, a Boston epidemiologist, says that most women decide whether to take estrogen by a sort of fear meter, asking themselves which diseases or discomforts they most dread (Kolata, 1991c). Even more to the point, Dr. Adriaane Fugh-Berman (1991, p. 3), speaking on behalf of the National Women's Health Network puts it,

> We are concerned that the concept of disease prevention may be expanded to include the concept of disease substitution.

Dr. Fugh-Berman's statement was made in reference to tamoxifen, a totally different topic, but one which we mention here for the purpose of emphasizing the complications and unknowns of menopausal/post-menopausal hormones. Tamoxifen is a drug which has been recognized for its effectiveness in prolonging the disease-free interval in postmenopausal women with estrogen receptor-positive breast cancer. However, now, tamoxifen is being experimented with in both England and the US as a way to *prevent* breast cancer in normal healthy women. In the US, the National Women's Health Network was the only organization to present testimony to the Food and Drug Administration Committee on Oncology Drugs opposing the trial. This is not the place to detail why the trial was 'premature in its assumptions, weak in its hypotheses, questionable in its ethics, and misguided in its public health ramifications' (Fugh-Berman, 1991:3). Relevant to this paper is the fact that tamoxifen is known to be effective as breast cancer treatment because it works as an *anti*-estrogen: it blocks the effect of estrogen on the breast. Researchers justified studying the effects of tamoxifen on healthy

women because they felt there was sufficient evidence to suggest that blocking the effects of estrogen on the breasts may be a way of preventing (delaying?) breast cancer.

The irony of the situation must be obvious to anyone reading this paper. How can it be that at this particular moment in history, in the name of 'prevention', huge numbers of women are being given estrogen products and another group is being studied with anti-estrogens? *All* the women taking either estrogens or anti-estrogens are part of massive experiments which should help us learn more about hormones but do *nothing* to support health-promoting methods of disease prevention.

The tamoxifen as 'prevention' trial received a great deal of attention recently because of the apparent success in reducing the risk of breast cancer. However, in the flurry of announcements about tamoxifen as preventing breast cancer, it was not well-publicized that there was an increase in endometrial cancer, pulmonary embolism, and stroke in the tamoxifen group (Fisher et al, 1998). In fact, Fugh-Berman's prediction of 'disease substitution' was correct.

'DESIGNER ESTROGENS'

Tamoxifen is now being marketed by its manufacturer, Zeneca, in a direct to consumer advertising campaign that implies that it can be taken by healthy women to prevent cancer (*Network News,* 1999a), but tamoxifen is only the beginning of a new approach to estrogens. It is one of a group of drugs called selective estrogen receptor modulators or SERMs, also known as 'designer estrogens.' These are being developed with the goal of having all the beneficial (proven or alleged) effects of estrogens, with none of the negative effects, that is, having both estrogenic and anti-estrogenic effects. Tamoxifen, for example, may reduce the risk of breast cancer but it still has the estrogenic effect of increasing the risk of endometrial cancer. Another SERM, raloxifene, manufactured by Eli Lilly under the name Evista, has been widely promoted in direct to consumer advertising, in magazines such as *Parade.* Raloxifene has been approved by the FDA for prevention of osteoporosis in postmenopausal women. Though the research is still in a relatively early stage, the popular media coverage of this drug suggests that it has the estrogenic effects of reducing osteoporosis and promoting a good lipid profile, while having anti-estrogenic effects of reducing risk of breast cancer and not stimulating the endometrium. At this point there is simply insufficient data and the studies have not been conducted for a long enough period to draw conclusions about the benefits, risks, or safety of raloxifene. As of 1999, there are plans for a large study comparing tamoxifen and raloxifene in reducing risk of breast cancer. In the mean time, both Lilly and Zeneca have direct to consumer campaigns, some of which have been identified as misleading. In fact, in response to complaints by the National Women's Health Network to the FDA, both companies have had to pull some of their ads (*Network News,* 1999b). As more of these drugs are developed and tested, consumers will be bombarded with advertising that tries to convince them that one form or another of estrogen or 'designer estrogens' is the real 'answer' to their fears about osteoporosis, bone density, heart disease, etc.

Conclusion

HRT raises large questions for individual women trying to decide whether to take it and for women's health movements which must analyze why it is that once again huge numbers of women are swallowing a product of unknown safety. There are no simple answers for either individual women or for feminist health activists.

The marketing of ERT/HRT has escalated in the 1990s as new research suggests—but has not proven—new benefits from these hormones. For example, women are now being told that ERT will prevent memory loss and dementia, including Alzheimer's disease. Certainly, the threat of losing our mental capabilities and memory is a powerful scare tactic. The fear of Alzheimer's disease may easily outweigh fear of other risks, since there are no other 'answers' for preventing this serious condition. The media has hyped the benefits of estrogen in this area and the manufacturers of Premarin have, without going beyond what they legally can, suggested in advertisements that estrogen may help. However, even though the media may accept estrogen as a proven prevention or treatment for loss of cognitive function, especially Alzheimer's disease, right now there is no proof for these benefits. Two detailed thorough reviews of the literature conclude that the evidence does *not* support recommending estrogen for prevention or treatment of dementia or loss of cognitive function (Haskell et al, 1997; Yaffe et al, 1998).

This paper has covered many of the issues which individual women will want to weigh as they make their own decisions. At some level, it is a very personal decision to balance known and unknown risks with the narrow range of choices available. Each woman will want to make today's and tomorrow's decisions based on her own personal hormone history. Most of the studies which have been done have been on women for whom oral contraceptives were not available. It remains to be seen how much different formulations of oral contraceptives taken for different lengths of time influence issues related to ERT or HRT. Much research will be done on many aspects of hormone use in the next few years. Any woman taking, or considering, hormones should find a source of information which she trusts such as the National Women's Health Network. Excellent health check ups, including pelvic exams, mammography and physical breast exams, pap smears, monitoring of blood lipids and blood pressure, and endometrial biopsies, must be available to all women who are or have been on hormones for any length of time.

HRT raises enormous challenges for women's health movements. Many of us have lived through the tragedies of DES, the Dalkon Shield, thalidomide, and toxic shock syndrome. One of the biggest questions must be, why aren't the lessons from the immediate past more central to our present debates? Why do large numbers of women not know about, or choose to ignore, the tremendous risks involved in taking drugs whose long term safety is not known? An even trickier question is why are so few people questioning the long term safety of hormonal products for menopausal and post-menopausal women? A number of people who have been allies in the struggle for safer contraceptives are not involved in evaluating and critiquing the mass marketing of ERT and HRT. Is ageism a factor? Are we willing to accept a few more side effects in a product designed specifically for older women? Are we willing to lower our standards just a little bit for products which promise to interfere with the ageing process?

The HRT debate—or more accurately, the *lack* of debate—serves as a reminder of the urgency of empowering *all* women to understand their own bodies and having access to appropriate (language, reading level, relevant to own issues) information for the 'choices' they face. One of the biggest lessons in the marketing of HRT has been that many women still do not know enough about the normal healthy workings of their bodies to resist a mass manipulation of the fear factor.

ERT and HRT are very valuable products to have available. They will definitely make a difference in the quality and length of life for *some* women. However, they will probably never be products which should be given to *most* women for a long length of time. If these products are as valuable as the manufacturers say, these products should be available to the women who would most benefit from them rather than the present situation where it tends to be the healthiest groups of women with easy access to the medical system which are given hormones.

To answer any of the questions raised in this paper, long term, controlled studies which look at multiple parameters and the interactions of many factors must be done with diverse groups of women. Without a clearer understanding of the actual value and risks of ERT and HRT, the mass marketing of these products is certainly premature. A renewed focus on *real* prevention and self help as a way of wrestling control *for* the consumer, *away* from the medical system and makers of highly profitable products, continues to be a most urgent priority for women's health movements.

References

Abelow, B. J., et al., study reported in *Calcified Tissue International,* January, 1992, referred to in Health Facts (Center for Medical Consumers) vol. 22, no. 10, October, 1997, pp. 4–5.

Abrahamsen, B, T.B. Hansen, L. Bjorn Jensen, A.P. Hermann, and P. Eiken (1997) "Site of Osteodensitometry in Perimenopausal Women: Correlation and Limits of Agreement Between Anatomic Regions," *Journal of Bone and Mineral Research,* vol. 12, no. 9, pp. 1471–1479.

Appel, Lawrence J. and Bush, Trudy (1991) 'Preventing Heart Disease in Women. Another Role for Aspirin' *Journal of the American Medical Association,* vol. 266, (pp. 565–566).

Annual Adverse Drug Experience Report, 1996, http://www.fda.gov/cder/dpe/annrep96/index.htm

Assessment of fracture risk and its application to screening for postmenopausal osteoporosis, WHO Technical Report Series 843. Geneva: WHO, 1994 cited by John A. Kanis, "Treatment of Osteoporosis in Elderly Women" in *The American Journal of Medicine,* vol. 98 (supple 2A), February 27, 1995a, p. 2A–60S.

Atkins, D., telephone interview with Atkins, reported in *HealthFacts* [Center for Medical Consumers] July 1996, vol. XXI, no. 206, pp. 1 & 4)

Bergvist, L. et al (1989) 'The Risk of Breast Cancer after Estrogen and Estrogen-progestin Replacement' *The New England Journal of Medicine,* vol. 321. no. 5, (pp. 293–297).

Black, Dennis M., "Why Elderly Women Should be Screened and Treated to Prevent Osteoporosis" in *The American Journal of Medicine,* vol. 98, suppl 2A, February 27, 1995, pp. 2A–67S–2A–75S.

Brown, Susan (1988) 'Osteoporosis: An Anthropologist Sorts Fact from Fallacy', unpublished longer version of article which was edited and appeared as 'Osteoporosis: Sorting Fact from Fallacy' in (National Women's Health Network) *Network News,* July/August, (pp. 1, 5–6).

Bush, Trudy, Fried, Linda P., and Barrett-Connor, Elizabeth (1988) 'Cholesterol Lipoproteins and Coronary Heart Disease in Women' Clinical Chemistry, vol. 34. no. 8(B), (pp. B60–B70).

Cadogan, J. et al (1997) 'Milk intake and bone mineral acquisition in adolescent girls: Randomised, controlled intervention trial' *British Medical Journal,* vol. 315 (Nov 15) (pp. 1255–1260).

Campbell, J. et al (1997) 'Randomised controlled trial of a general practice programme of home based exercise to prevent falls in elderly women' *British Medical Journal,* vol. 315 (Oct 25) (pp. 1065–1069).

Campbell, T. Colin, interview in *Health Facts* (Center for Medical Consumers) vol 22, no. 10, October, 1997, pp 4–5.

Cauley, Jane A. (1988) and Gutai, James P., Kuller, Lewis H., Ledonna Dorothea, Sandler, Rivka B., Sashin, Donald, and Powell, John G. (1988) 'Endogenous Estrogen Levels and Calcium Intakes in Postmenopausal Women' *Journal of the American Medical Association,* vol. 260, no. 21, (pp. 3150-3155).

Cauley, Jane A., Dana G. Seeley, Kristine Ensrud, Bruce Ettinger, Dennis Black, and Steven Cummings, for the Study of Osteoporotic Fractures Research Group, "Estrogen Replacement Therapy and Fractures in Older Women" *Annals of Internal Medicine,* vol. 122, no. 1, January 1, 1995, pp. 9-16

Cedar Rapids Gazette (1991) 'Estrogen Cuts Heart Disease Risk: Study' *Cedar Rapids (Iowa) Gazette,* September 12.

Close, Jacqueline, Margaret Ellis, Richard Hooper, Edward Glucksman, Stephan Jackson, and Cameron Swift, "Prevention of Falls in the Elderly Trial (PROFET); A Randomised Controlled Trail, *Lancet,* vol. 353, January 9, 1999, pp. 93-97.

Colditz, G.A. Stampfer, M.J., Willett, W.C. *et al* (1990) 'Prospective Study of Estrogen Replacement Therapy and Risk of Breast Cancer in Postmenopausal Women' *Journal of the American Medical Association,* vol. 264, (pp. 2648–2653).

Collaborative Group on Hormonal Factors in Breast Cancer (1997) 'Breast cancer and hormone replacement therapy: Collaborative reanalysis of data from 51 epidemiologic studies of 52,705 women with breast cancer and 108,411 women without breast cancer' *Lancet,* vol. 350 (Oct 11) (pp. 1047–1059).

Cumming, Robert G. and Michael C. Nevitt (1997) "Calcium for the Prevention of Osteoporotic Fractures in Postmenopausal Women," *Journal of Bone and Mineral Research,* vol. 12, no. 9, pp. 1321–1329.

Cummings, S. R., "Bone Mass and Bone Loss in the Elderly: A Special Case?" *Int. J. Fertil Menopausal Stud,* 38 Supple 2, 1993, pp 92–97.

Cummings, Steven R., in *Annals of Internal Medicine,* 15 October, 1990 article, quoted in *HealthFacts,* vol. XXI, no. 206, July 1996, p. 4.

Cummings, Steven R., Dennis M. Black, Desmond E. Thompson, William B. Applegate, Elizabeth Barrett-Connor, Thomas A. Musliner, Lisa Palermo, Ronald Prineas, Susan M. Rubin, Jean C. Scott, Thomas Vogt, Robert Wallace, A. John Yates, Andrea Z. Lacroix, for the Fracture Intervention Trial Research Group, "Effect of Alendronate on Risk of Fracture in Women with Low Bone Density but Without Vertebral Fractures," *Journal of the American Medical Association,* vol. 280, no. 24, December 23/30, 1998, pp. 2077–2082.

Dejanikus, Tacie (1985) 'Major Drug Manufacturer Funds Osteoporosis Education Campaign' (National Women's Health Network) *Network News,* May/June, (pp. 1,3).

Eagan, Andrea Boroff (1989) 'Hormone Replacement Therapy Overview' (National Women's Health Network) *Network News,* May/June, (pp. 1,3)

"An Emerging Approach to Osteoporosis Prevention" discussion at Clinical and Economic Considerations in the Prevention of Osteoporosis Among Postmenopausal Women Conference, September 19, 1997, reported in *The American Journal of Managed Care,* February, 1998, vol. 4, No. 2, Sup., pp. S85–S93.

Ensrud KE, Palermo L, Black DM, et al. Hip bone loss increases with advancing age: longitudinal results from the study of osteoporotic fractures. In: LG Raisz, ed. *Sixteenth Annual Meeting of the American Society for Bone and Mineral Research.* Kansas City, Missouri: Mary Ann Liebert, 1994; S153, cited in Dennis M. Black, "Why Elderly Women Should be Screened and Treated to Prevent Osteoporosis" in *The American Journal of Medicine,* vol. 98, suppl 2A, February 27, 1995, pp. 2A–67S–2A–75S.

Ettinger, Bruce (1987) 'Update: Estrogen and Postmenopausal Osteoporosis 1976–1986' Health Values, Vol. 11, no. 4, (pp. 31–36).

Finn, Susan (1987) 'Osteoporosis: A Nutritionist's Approach' *Health Values,* vol. 11, no. 4, (pp. 20–23).

Fisher, B. et al (1998) 'Tamoxifen for prevention of breast cancer: Report of the National Surgical Adjuvant Breast and Bowel Project P-1 Study,' *Journal of the National Cancer Institute,* Vol. 90, no. 18, (pp. 1371–1389).

Freeman, Ruth, "The Management of the Patient with Osteoporosis—A Modern Epidemic," *American Journal of Managed Care,* February 1998, vol. 4, no. 2, sup, pp S94–S107.

Frey, Carol—article to be published in *Biomechanics* in 1998, cited in Jane E. Brody's "When the Elderly Fall, Shoes May Be to Blame," *New York Times,* February 24, 1998, p. C7.

Fugh-Berman, Adriane (1991) 'Tamoxifen in Healthy Women: Preventative Health or Preventing Health?' (National Women's Health Network) *Network News,* September/October (pp. 3–4).

Genant, Harry K., Johna Lucas, Stuart Weiss, Mark Akin, Ronald Emkey, Heidi McNaney-Flint, Robert Downs, Joseph Mortola, Nelson Watts, Hwa Ming Yang, Niranyan Banav, John J. Brennan, and Joseph C. Nolan, for the Estratab/Osteoporosis Study Group, "Low Dose Estrified Estrogen Therapy," *Archives of Internal Medicine,* vol. 157, December 8/22, 1997, pp. 2609–2615.

Giges, Nancy (1986) 'Calcium Market Shrugs Off Study' *Advertising Age,* vol. 59, (pp. 49,56).

Goodman, Carol E. (1987) 'Osteoporosis and Physical Activity' *Health Values,* vol. 11. no. 4 (pp. 24–30).

Haskell, S.G., Richardson, E.D., and Horvitz, R.I. (1997) 'The effect of estrogen replacement therapy on cognitive function in women: A critical review of the literature' *Journal of Clinical Epidemiology,* vol. 50, no. 11, (pp. 1249–1264).

Heaney, Robert D., "Bone Mass, Bone Fragility, and the Decision to Treat," *Journal of the American Medical Association,* vol. 28, no. 24, December 23/30, 1998, pp. 2119–2120.

Hu, J-F., Zhao, X-H., Jia, J-B., Parpia, B., Campbell, T.C. "Dietary Calcium and Bone density Among Middle-aged and Elderly Women in China," *Am. J. Clin. Nutr.* 58: 219–227, 1993.

Hulley, S. et al (1998) 'Randomised trial of estrogen plus progestin for secondary prevention of coronary heart disease in postmenopausal women' *Journal of the American Medical Association,* vol. 280 (Aug 19) (pp. 605–613).

Jacobsen, Steven J., Jack Goldberg, Toni P. Miles, Jacob A. Brody, William Stiers, and Alfred A. Rimm, "Race and Sex Differences in Mortality following Fracture of the Hip," *American Journal of Public Health,* August 1992, vol. 82, no. 8, pp. 1147–1150.

Keating, N.L. et al (1999) 'Use of hormone replacement therapy by postmenopausal women in the United States' *Annals of Internal Medicine,* vol. 130, (pp. 545–553).

Kirkpatrick, Mary (1987) 'A Self Care Model for Osteoporosis' *Health Values,* vol. 11, no. 4, (pp. 44-50).

Kolata, Gina (1990) 'Cancer Risk in Estrogen is Slight, Study Asserts' *New York Times,* 28 November, (p. A11).

————(1991a) 'Women Don't Get Equal Heart Care' *New York Times,* 25 July, (pp. A1, A9).

————(1991b) 'Estrogen After Menopause Cuts Heart Attack Risk, Study Finds' *New York Times,* 12 September, (pp. A1, A13).

————(1991c) 'Women Face Dilemma Over Estrogen Therapy' *New York Times,* 17 September.

Libanati, Cesar, "Prevention and Treatment of Osteoporosis," *Primary Care Reports,* vol. 5, no. 5, February 22, 1999, pp. 27-4.

Love Susan, with Karen Lindsey, *Dr. Susan Love's Hormone Book,* Random House, New York, 1997.

Macpherson, Kathleen I. (1987) 'Osteoporosis: The New Flaw in Woman or in Science?' *Health Values,* vol. 11, no. 4, (pp. 57–61).

Manson, J.E., Stampfer, M.J., Colditz, G.A. *et al* (1991) 'A Prospective Study of Aspirin Use and Primary Prevention of Cardiovascular Disease in Women' *Journal of the American Medical Association,* vol. 266, (pp. 521–527).

The Medical Letter, January 5, 1996 report on osteoporosis products, reported in *HealthFacts,* Center for Medical Consumers, February 1996, vol. XXI, no. 201, pp. 3–4.

Myers, Ann H., Baker, Susan P., Vannatta, Mark L., Abbey, Helen, and Robinson, Elizabeth G. (1991) 'Risk Factors Associated with Falls and Injuries among Elderly Institutionalized Persons' *American Journal of Epidemiology,* vol. 133, no. 11, (pp. 1179–1190).

Napoli, Maryann (1988) 'Screening for Osteoporosis: An Idea Whose Time Has Not Yet Come' (pp.115–119) in Worcester, Nancy and Whatley, Mariamne H. (1988) *Women's Health: Readings on Social, Economic, and Political Issues,* Dubuque, Iowa: Kendall/Hunt Publishing Company.

National Prescriptions Audit, IMS America Ltd., prepared for the National Women's Health Network (hormones and breast cancer files) by the USA Food and Drug Administration Staff, February, 1990.

National Women's Health Network (1999) *Taking Hormones and Women's Health* (available from the NWHN, 514 10th St., N.W., Suite 400, Washington D.C. 20004)

Network News (National Women's Health Network) (1999a) 'Tamoxifen approved for risk reduction: Network criticizes first ad' January/February (p. 4).

Network News (National Women's Health Network)(1999b) 'Zeneca vs. Lilly vs. Zeneca: Will lawsuits lead to better information?' March/April (p. 6).

Ott, Susan (1986) 'Should Women Get Screening Bone Mass Measurements?' *Annals of Internal Medicine,* vol. 104, no. 6 (pp. 874–876).

Parfitt, M. (1984) 'Definition of Osteoporosis: Age-related Loss of Bone and its Relationship to Increased Fracture Risk', presented at the National Institutes of Health Consensus Development Conference on Osteoporosis, Bethesda, Maryland, April 1-2, quoted in MacPherson (1987).

Partlow, Lian (1991) Personal communication.

Pearson, Cindy (1991) Testimony before the USA Food and Drug Administration Select Committee on Aging, Subcommittee on Housing and Consumer Interests, 30 May.

Reb, Anne M., (Regulatory Review Officer, Division of Drug Marketing, Advertising, and Communications, Food and Drug Administration) letters dated (approximately) April 14, 1997 and July 2, 1997, to Ellen R. Westrick, Senior Director, Office of Medical/Legal Issues, Merck.

Riis, Bente Juel, "The Role of Bone Loss" in *The American Journal of Medicine,* vol. 98, suppl 2A, February 27, 1995, pp. 2A–29S–2A–32S.

Riggs, B, Lawrence and L. Joseph Melton (1986) "Involutional osteoporosis," *New England Journal of Medicine* 314, no. 26 1, 676–684

Rubin, S.M. and S.R. Cummings, "Results of Bone Densitometry Affect Women's Decisions About Taking Measures to Prevent Fractures," *Annals of Internal Medicine,* vol. 116, no. 12 pt 1, June 15, 1992, pp. 990–995.

Rovner, Sandy (1990) 'Estrogen Therapy: More Data, Less Certainty' *Washington Post Health,* 4 September, (p. 9).

Schneider, Diane L., Elizabeth L. Barrett-Connor, Deborah J. Morton, "Timing of Postmenopausal Estrogen for Optimal Bone Mineral Density" *JAMA,* February 19, 1997, pp. 543–547.

Silverman SL, Greenwald M, Klein R, Drinkwater BL. "Effect of Bone Density Information on Decisions about Hormone Replacement Therapy: A Randomized Trial," *Obstet Gynecol* 1997; 89: 321–325., referred to in Robert Lindsay, Nelson B. Watts, and Donna Shoupe, symposium presentation "Current Approaches to Osteoporosis Prevention" in *The American Journal of Managed Care,* vol. 4, no. 2, sup, pp. S64–S69.

Sloane, Ethel (1985) *Biology of Women,* New York: John Wiley.

Sojourner (1991) 'Debating Estrogen Replacement Therapy' *Sojourner—The Women's Forum,* November, (pp. 13–14).

Specter, Michael (1989) 'Hormone Use in Menopause Tied to Cancer' *Washington Post,* 3 August, (p. 1).

Steering Committee of the Physician's Health Study Group (1989) 'Final Report on the Aspirin Component of the Ongoing Physician's Health Study' *New England Journal of Medicine,* vol. 321, (pp. 129–135).

Steinberg, Karen, Thacker, Stephen, Smith, Jay *et al* (1991) 'A Meta-analysis of the Effect of Estrogen Replacement Therapy on the Risk of Breast Cancer' *Journal of the American Medical Association,* vol. 265, (pp. 1985–1990).

Torgerson, David J., Ruth E. Thomas, Marion K. Campbell, David M. Reid, "Randomized Trial of Osteoporosis Screening: Use of Hormone Replacement therapy and Quality of Life Results," *Arch Intern Med,* vol. 157, Oct. 13, 1997, pp. 2121–2125.

Tromp, A.M., J.H. Smit, D.J.H. Deeg, L.M. Bouter, and P. Lips, "Predictors for Falls and Fractures in Longitudinal Aging Study Amsterdam," *Journal of Bone and Mineral Research,* vol. 13, no. 12, 1998, pp. 1932–1939.

Whatley, Marianne H. (1988a) 'Screening is Calculated Exploitation', (National Women's Health Network) *Network News,* January/February, (pp. 1, 3).

——(1988b) 'Women, Exercise and Physical Potential' in Worcester, Nancy and Whatley, Mariamne H. editors, *Women's Health: Readings on Social, Economic, and Political Issues,* Dubuque, Iowa: Kendall/Hunt.

Whatley, Mariamne H. and Worcester, Nancy (1989) 'The Role of Technology in the Co-optation of the Women's Health Movement: The Case Study of Osteoporosis and Breast Cancer Screening' (pp. 199-220) in RATCLIFF, Kathryn Strother, et. al., *Healing Technology—Feminist Perspectives,* Ann Arbor, Michigan: University of Michigan Press.

Winslow, Ron (1991) 'Women Face Treatment Gap in Heart Disease' *Wall Street Journal,* July 25, (pp. B1, B4).

Writing Group for the PEPI Trial, "Effects of Hormone Therapy on Bone Mineral Density—Results from the Postmenopausal Estrogen/Progestin Interventions (PEPI) Trial", *JAMA,* November 6, 1996, vol. 276, no. 17, pp. 1389–1396.

Wolfe, Sidney M., editor, (1991a) 'Risk Factors for Falls in the Elderly' (Public Citizens Health Research Group) *Health Letter,* nol. 7, no. 8, (p. 10).

——(1991b) 'New Evidence that Menopausal Estrogens Cause Breast Cancer; Further Doubts About Prevention of Heart Disease' (Public Citizens Health Research Group) *Health Letter,* June (pp. 4–6).

Wolinsky, Fredric D., John F. Fitzgerald, & Timothy E. Stump, "The Effect of Hip Fracture on Mortality, hospitalization, and Functional Status: A Prospective Study," *American Journal of Public Health,* March 1997, vol. 87, no. 3, pp. 398–403.

Worcester, Nancy and Whatley, Mariamne H. (1988) 'The Response of the Health Care System to the Women's Health Movement: The Selling of Women's Health Centers' (pp. 117–130) in Rosser, Sue V. (1988) *Feminism Within the Science and Health Care Professions: Overcoming Resistance,* Oxford: Pergamon Press.

Yaffe, K. et al (1998) 'Estrogen therapy in postmenopausal women—Effects on cognitive function and dementia' *Journal of the American Medical Association,* vol. 279, no. 9 (pp. 688–695).

ACKNOWLEDGEMENT

The authors want to acknowledge the work of the National Women's Health Network's Hormone Education Campaign in providing the key leadership for US women in the evaluation and critique of menopausal hormones. The excellent publications and testimonies before Food and Drug Administration Committees have been extremely valuable in preparing this paper. *Taking Hormones and Women's Health* is available from The National Women's Health Network, 514 10th Street, N.W., Suite 400, Washington D.C., 20004 (USA).

The Bitter Pill
Bombarded by Propaganda on Premarin,
We Can't Trust our Doctors and
We Can't Trust Ourselves

by Leora Tanenbaum

Barbara Dworkin, 61, is one of eight million American women taking Premarin, an estrogen replacement that eases menopausal symptoms such as hot flashes and dry skin. Dworkin started on Premarin 15 years ago and plans to take the drug for the rest of her life. Although studies have shown that Premarin may increase the risk of breast cancer by 30 percent, as well as cause fatal blood clots, the drug also offers protection against osteoporosis and decreases the risk of fatal heart disease by 53 percent. Besides, as a 911 operator living on Long Island, NY, she leads stressful days fielding emergency calls and feels thankful for Premarin because it "makes my life much more pleasant and secure."

But Premarin costs between $15 and $25 a month. If there were a generic version, Suffolk County, New York (which covers Dworkin's drug plan) could cut its costs by 30 percent—over $3,000 for her lifetime. If you consider that millions of other women lack health insurance or prescription drug coverage, a generic could save them more than $300 million a year.

But economizing isn't the only reason to push for a generic. Premarin is derived from the urine of pregnant horses, a fact that concerns animal rights supporters—and repulses many users. People for the Ethical Treatment of Animals (PETA) claims that the collection methods on "urine farms" are barbaric: some 80,000 pregnant mares are confined to stalls for six months out of the year so that their urine can be collected; the 65,000 foals born to them are slaughtered as unusable byproducts of these pregnancies. PETA advises women to switch to an alternative hormone treatment that doesn't harm animals.

An alternative, however, will not be forthcoming. The FDA announced in May that it will not approve a recently manufactured, affordable, plant-based generic form of Premarin, even though FDA research has shown the generic to be just as effective as the brand-name drug. Rather than heed the recommendation of its own Office of Pharmaceutical Science, the FDA appears to have bowed to political pressure—at the expense of women. While there are several plant-derived, FDA-approved estrogen regimens such as Estrace and Estraderm, they have not been proven to offer long-term health benefits. Only those who can afford Premarin—or whose insurance will pay—will be able to relieve their menopausal symptoms, ward off heart attacks and avoid bone fractures.

Leora Tanenbaum has written a book *(Slut)* about teen girls labeled "sluts" by their peers. She has written for *Ms., The Nation, Seventeen, Newsday,* and *The Women's Review of Books.*

It's no surprise that the common interests of Premarin's manufacturer, Wyeth-Ayerst, have superseded health considerations, but the tactics involved are particularly outrageous. Wyeth-Ayerst cultivated influential supporters through financial contributions. Then, when the company needed them, it prodded its beneficiaries to take a stand against their competition. The result? Several highly visible politicians and advocacy groups—who knew nothing about the issues involved—testified before the FDA against the generic form of Premarin. In the end, the consumer's ability to get the best drugs for the lowest price was sacrificed The saddest part of this whole incident? Feminist politicians and women's groups were key players.

"Doctor, I Want My Premarin"

You don't have to be menopausal to recognize the brand-name Premarin. No doubt you've seen the drug's fear-inducing magazine ads, which suggest that midlife women who don't take estrogen will be crippled by osteoporosis—if they don't die from a heart attack first. The ads also intimate that midlife women who don't take estrogen can never hope to achieve the care-free, wrinkle-free look of the models depicted.

Premarin, of course, is merely one of dozens of prescription drugs aggressively advertised in magazines such as *Newsweek, Redbook, Mirabella,* and *The New Yorker.* In recent years, drug companies have bypassed physicians and marketed their products directly to consumers. Eli Lilly's multimillion dollar campaign for Prozac, for instance, includes ads in more than 20 magazines. Some magazines, like *Good Housekeeping* and the *Ladies' Home Journal,* contain so many drug ads you might be tempted to double-check the cover to make sure you're not reading a professional medical journal Which is precisely the point: drug manufacturers want consumers to play doctor by asking their physicians to prescribe particular drugs. And 99 percent of physicians do comply with patients' requests, market research confirms. In this era of "managed care," when physicians are pressed to see as many patients as possible in the shortest amount of time, educated patients who know how they want to be treated are a dream come true.

A dream come true, that is, for physicians and drug companies—but not necessarily for the patients. We may believe that by asking our physicians for Premarin or Prozac we are empowering ourselves by being more assertive in our relationships with our physicians, because only we really know our bodies and what's best for our health But in reality, the drug companies are taking advantage of our adherence to this *Our Bodies, Ourselves* credo. We are intermediaries in a loop of influence that originates in magazine ads and culminates in a prescription.

Last year alone, pharmaceutical companies spent nearly $600 million advertising prescription drugs directly to consumers—twice as much as they spent in 1995 and almost 10 times more than they spent in 1991, according to Competitive Media Reporting, a company that tracks ad spending. None of that money, however, seems to be spent on factual research: more than half of the drug ads scrutinized last year by the Consumers' Union advocacy group contained misleading information on risks and benefits and false claims about efficacy.

Politics vs. Science

But as the case of the massively popular Premarin shows, the influence of drug companies goes far beyond false advertising. Wyeth-Ayerst Laboratories is a pharmaceutical Goliath that garners $1 billion a year in revenue from Premarin, the most commonly prescribed drug in America. Owned by American Home Products, Wyeth-Ayerst has maintained a monopoly on Premarin ever since it began manufacturing the estrogen replacement in 1942. Even though the patent expired over 25 years ago, Wyeth has gotten the FDA to change its guidelines in determining bioequivalence in generics, making it difficult for competitors to match Premarin. A lot is at stake: sales could reach $3 billion within five years, with more than one-third of all women in the United States currently over the age of 50, and another 20 million entering the menopausal years within the next decade.

Because of the size of that market, two small generic drug companies have decided to compete with Wyeth. After the FDA concluded in 1991 that an effective generic requires only two active ingredients (estrone and equilin), Duramed Pharmaceuticals Corp. and Barr Laboratories Inc. teamed up to develop a urine-free generic according to FDA guidelines. In response, Wyeth filed a citizens petition requesting that one of Premarin's ingredients (an obscure estrogen called delta 8,9 dehydroestrone sulfate or DHES) be reclassified as a necessary component. Duramed has not been able to replicate an equivalent of DHES and Wyeth holds the patent on the estrogen. Furthermore, in 1995 the FDA found that based on clinical trials, there was no evidence that DHES was anything other than an impurity.

And so Wyeth shrewdly lined up the support of several influential women's and health groups by making donations to Business and Professional Women/USA, the American Medical Women's Association, the National Consumers League, and the National Osteoporosis Foundation, among others. Representatives of these groups testified before the FDA on the drug company's behalf, saying that they opposed the approval of a generic that lacks DHES, despite the FDA's own contention that the estrogen wasn't essential The president of the Women's Legal Defense Fund also testified although this group did not accept money from Wyeth. None of these groups had taken a position on DHES prior to being contacted by Wyeth.

The company also developed close ties to the White House and the Senate. John Stafford, chairman and CEO of Wyeth-Ayerst's parent company, American Home Products, attended an intimate 17-person White House "coffee klatsch" with President Clinton in November 1995. And in June 1996, according to the Federal Elections Commission, American Home Products made a $50,000 contribution to the Democratic National Committee. Several months later, Democratic senators Barbara Mikulski (Md.) and Patty Murray (Wash.) wrote the FDA for assurance that "it has no intention of approving a generic version of Premarin that lacks the 'same' active ingredient as the innovator." According to her press secretary, Murray became involved in this issue after she "was contacted by women's groups. As a result, our office spoke with the manufacturer, who was in contact with the same women's groups."

Lo and behold, the FDA reversed its stance. Janet Woodcock, M.D., director of the FDA's Center for Drug Evaluation and Research, announced on May 5 that "based on currently available data, there is at this time no way to assure that synthetic generic forms of Premarin have the same active ingredients as the [urine-based] drug." Or, put another way "Perhaps everything in this pool of animal waste could have benefits for human females," in the words of Duramed CEO and president E. Thomas Arington.

No matter how you look at it, the FDA flip-flop appears to be the result of Wyeth-Ayerst's considerable lobbying muscle. Of course, just because a decision is politically influenced doesn't mean it's wrong. But an internal FDA memo dated May 3 (two days before the decision was announced) supports the generic, saying that DHES is not a necessary component. Even the vice president of Wyeth-Ayerst's regulatory affairs department admitted to *The Wall Street Journal* that there's "probably nothing" special about DHES, and that "it's but one of many components in Premarin."

Consumer health is clearly the last thing on the minds of everyone involved in the Premarin debacle. "This decision is pure politics," fumes Cynthia Pearson, executive director of the National Women's Health Network, the only women's organization that publicly supports the generic. Coincidentally, the network does not accept donations from drug companies. The decision "was not backed up by science," says Pearson. "This

never would have happened without political pressure orchestrated by Wyeth-Ayerst."

Duramed has challenged the FDA decision in an administrative appeal; the company intends to file a court appeal if it is turned down. But Wyeth is already a step ahead: it is busily working to ensure that no matter what happens, it will continue to dominate the estrogen replacement market. After all, Wyeth is the sole sponsor of an important "memory study" on Premarin's effectiveness in warding off Alzheimer's disease, a study conducted under the aegis of the government-sponsored Women's Health Initiative. If a correlation is found, physicians and consumers alike will naturally turn to Premarin as a preventative for Alzheimer's.

Commercially Sponsored Medicine

Wyeth is hardly the only drug company to use political leverage to protect its turf. The *Journal of the American Medical Association (JAMA)* recently published results of a 1990 study on thyroid medications and reported that the maker of Synthroid, one of the drugs under study, had suppressed for years the fact that three other medications were equally effective. Like Premarin, Synthroid has long enjoyed domination in a lucrative market because its manufacturer falsely claims that its product is superior to the competition.

Ten years ago, in order to establish Synthroid as the most effective drug in its class, Flint Laboratories (then the drugs manufacturer) approached researcher Betty Dong of the University of California, San Francisco. Dong signed a contract with Flint to conduct comparative studies of the bioequivalence of Synthroid and three other preparations. When her research was completed in 1990, Dong submitted the results to Boots Pharmaceuticals (which had since taken over Flint). It turned out that all four drugs were bioequivalent, and that consumers who chose the other drugs over Synthroid could save $356 million annually. Boots became alarmed: after all, it is the leader in a $600 million-a-year market.

With so much revenue at stake, Boots did everything it could to publicly discredit Dong's research. It dishonestly claimed that the research was flawed in design and execution, and that Dong had breached research ethics. It then published Dong's results in a "reanalysis" that reached the opposite conclusion. Conveniently, Boots was able to prevent publication of Dong's own account of her research, since the contract she originally signed stipulated that nothing could be published without written consent from the drug company.

Finally, under pressure from the FDA, Boots (now part of Knoll Pharmaceutical) agreed to allow Dong's results to be published—seven years after the study was completed. And in August, Boots/Knoll agreed to pay $98 million in a settlement to consumers who purchased Synthroid between 1990 and 1997. But despite the settlement, Boots/Knoll has had the last laugh. A highly-placed physician who refuses to be identified points out that Boots/Knoll earned over $2 billion during the time that it suppressed the research, and that the settlement represents less than one-twentieth of the extra profits.

A Matter of Trust

The growing power of pharmaceutical companies is troubling on a number of levels. It is frightening how poorly we are informed about the appalling treatment of animals in drug manufacturing. It is wasteful to pay for needlessly expensive medications. Forget about President Clinton's 1992 plea to the drug companies to control their prices. In the last few years, big-name drug companies such as Merck and Hoechst have withdrawn from the generics field because they realized they could make far more money selling brand-name drugs. But the real bottom line is that the drug companies have robbed consumers of the ability to trust anyone in the area of drug research: commercialism has infected everyone involved. We can't trust those companies to which we entrust our health to accurately represent their products. We can't assume that the FDA has weighed all of the scientific research fairly. We can't even take for granted that the scientists who perform drug research are working independently.

Savvy consumers, of course, realize that drug companies are motivated by profit. But what about advocacy groups, including women's and health organizations? Aren't they supposed to be looking out for the public good? It's in this arena that consumers are really misled. "I can't understand how any woman in a position of influence would deliberately deny a high-quality, low-cost alternative [the Premarin generic] to postmenopausal women who need this important drug," says Duramed's Arington. It seems that advocates, in the public or private sphere, will do anything for the right price. Even the American Medical Association, whose own internationally respected journal previously disclosed the Synthroid saga, agreed in August to endorse Sunbeam health products in exchange for royalties until, stung by charges of conflict of interest and commercialism, it decided to abandon the plan.

"All medical organizations receive money from the pharmaceutical companies," rationalizes Debra R. Judelson, MD., president of the American Medical Women's Association, one of the organizations that accepted money from Wyeth and testified before the FDA on the same issue. "There are no virgins. We've all been lobbied by the pharmaceuticals on all the issues." The National Women's Health Network, the lone women's advocacy group to support the Premarin generic, must be the only virgin at the orgy.

But perhaps the ever-increasing power and determination of certain drug companies to quash their competition isn't so terrible. Look, if we all just took Prozac, it wouldn't seem so bad.

Phytoestrogens: A New Alternative for Women?

by Adriane Fugh-Berman, M.D.

Phytoestrogens, or plant estrogens, are much weaker estrogens than our own bodies make. Phytoestrogens are only about 1/200th the strength of endogenous estrogens. There are two main kinds of phytoestrogens: lignans and isoflavones. Foods that contain lignans include oily seeds, especially flaxseed (also called linseed) and also cereal grains, beans, vegetables and fruits. Premenopausal women fed 10 grams a day of flaxseed powder multiplied their lignan excretion 3 to 285 fold. Isoflavones are less common, occurring mainly in soybeans, chickpeas, and other legumes (Knight). Some phytoestrogens are also found in black cohosh, clover and other medicinal herbs, but these are different than phytoestrogens found in food plants and should not be treated the same in terms of safety.

Hot Flashes and Vaginal Dryness

Whole grains and beans (especially soybeans) are the most commonly eaten source of phytoestrogens. Asian women complain less of hot flashes than Western women do, and it may be that eating soy products serves as a type of hormone replacement therapy (Adlercreutz). There is evidence that supplementing with phytoestrogens can help hot flashes and vaginal dryness. A study of 145 Israeli women with menopausal symptoms found that the 78 women assigned to a phytoestrogen-rich diet had fewer hot flashes and less vaginal dryness than the 36 women in the control group who did not change their diet (Adlercreutz 1997). The study lasted twelve weeks and women in the treatment group substituted phytoestrogen-rich foods (including tofu, soy drink, miso, and flax seed) for approximately one fourth of their daily caloric intake (Brzezinski). Two studies have looked at whether supplementing the diet with phytoestrogens resulted in estrogenic changes in vaginal cells. One study found a positive result (Wilcox) and the other a negative result (Baird), but the study that did not find an effect used an unusual method of collecting vaginal cells that may have underestimated estrogenized cells (Knight).

Breast Cancer Prevention

What is the effect of phytoestrogens on breast cancer risk? Although there has not been a prospective study on this, studies of different populations show that groups that consume a lot of phytoestrogens have a lower rate of breast cancer. A recent case control study found that women with breast cancer excreted much lower amounts of phytoestrogens in their urine than women without breast cancer (Ingram).

However, this protective effect may be strongest in premenopausal women. Soybeans are quite high in phytoestrogens, and there is a high intake of soy products in some Asian countries, especially China, Japan, and Korea. A study of Chinese women in Singapore found that soy product intake seemed to protect premenopausal women, but not postmenopausal women, from breast cancer (Lee).

From *The Network News*, May–June 1998, pp. 1, 4, 7. Copyright © 1998 by the National Women's Health Network. Reprinted by permission

Adriane Fugh-Berman writes on a variety of women's health topics. Her book, *Alterative Medicine: What Works*, was reviewed in the July/August 1996 *Network News*.

This article was taken from a new edition of the Network's *Taking Hormones and Women's Health: Choices, Risks, and Benefits*.

Different Effects in Premenopausal and Postmenopausal Women

The above result is not all that surprising because phytoestrogens may have opposite effects in pre-menopausal and postmenopausal women. Pre-menopausal women have nominally higher estrogen levels than postmenopausal women. In premenopausal women who eat a lot of plant estrogens, the weak plant estrogens perform some of the same functions as our own, stronger estrogens. Chemical messengers regulate estrogen in our bodies by determining when more or less estrogen is needed; when weak plant estrogens are meeting our estrogen needs, our own hormone factories take a break. So premenopausal women with normally high estrogen levels who eat plant estrogens everyday have a constantly lower rate of production of homegrown estrogens, and the total estrogen effect on their bodies (lower internal estrogen production plus weak plant estrogens) is lower. So in premenopausal women, the effect of a diet high in phytoestrogens is actually anti-estrogenic.

"Background" estrogen levels are already low in postmenopausal women, so eating phytoestrogens boosts the estrogen levels. So for postmenopausal women, phytoestrogens may have an estrogenic effect. This estrogenic effect may affect different organs differently. A high soy intake appears to protect against endometrial cancer in both premenopausal and postmenopausal women (Goodman).

Different Menopausal Experiences in Asian and Western Women

Some people theorize that hot flashes and other menopausal symptoms may be due less to low estrogen levels than to a sudden drop in estrogen levels. According to this theory, Asian women complain less of hot flashes and other menopause-related complaints because decades of eating soy products may have lowered estrogen levels sufficiently that the menopausal drop, especially cushioned by continued high intake of phytoestrogens, may be an easy hormonal descent. Westerners start at a higher estrogen level and fall to a lower level; we plummet over a hormonal cliff.

Other factors may be equally important, of course; it is difficult to determine the importance of the fact that Asians respect age while Westerners worship youth. The transition to menopause in the West might be very different if we looked forward to an honored place in society rather than discrimination and poverty.

If You Have Breast Cancer

Phytoestrogens in food have been consumed for thousands of years by Asian women, who have a lower risk of breast cancer than Western women at all ages, and the idea that these foods are dangerous is clearly absurd. For premenopausal women with breast cancer, phytoestrogen would be expected to lower circulating estrogen levels and thus be beneficial.

For postmenopausal women with breast cancer the situation is more complicated. Soybeans contain substances that are estrogenic and substances that are anti-cancer. It is not clear whether the estrogenic properties of soybeans could cause breast cancer to grow. In cultured breast cancer cells, both estradiol and a phytoestrogen stimulated cell growth, but when added together, little to no growth stimulation occurred. But in an immunocompromised mouse model, phytoestrogen implants caused estrogen receptor positive (but not estrogen receptor negative) breast cancer implants to grow (Helferich).

On the other hand, phytoestrogen supplementation in postmenopausal women markedly increased sex hormone binding globulin (SHBG) (Brzezinski). High levels of SHBG are associated with lower breast cancer risk.

The Network believes that supplementing one's diet with phytoestrogens makes sense for premenopausal women. Whether postmenopausal women with breast cancer should avoid supplementing with phytoestrogens is an open question. The Network believes that there is no need for postmenopausal women with breast cancer to actively avoid phytoestrogens, which are consumed in quantity in many countries with low breast cancer rates, and are found in many foods with high nutritive value. Whether or not to actively supplement a diet with phytoestrogens is a different story.

Some people argue that Asian women have lower breast cancer rates at all ages than Westerners, so phytoestrogen intake can't be harmful. But Asians consume high levels of phytoestrogens throughout their lifetime, and this may create a very different hormonal situation than a Western woman who has a low phytoestrogen intake premenopausally and then suddenly increases her phytoestrogen intake postmenopausally. It is theoretically possible that that scenario increases her lifetime exposure to estrogens. Also, other factors may contribute to a lower rate of breast cancer in Asian women, who generally consume a low-fat, high-fiber diet, and have different exposures to environmental factors. A case can be made for postmenopausal women with breast cancer to maximize or minimize phytoestrogen intake, but there is not adequate evidence to justify a strong recommendation either for supplementing or avoiding phytoestrogens.

Should breast cancer patients who are being treated with the hormonal drug tamoxifen supplement with phytoestrogens? These two substances have similar effects in terms of having some estrogenic and some antiestrogenic properties. There are no studies on what the effects are of combining the use of phytoestrogens and tamoxifen. The Network believes that once again, a case can be made either for supplementing or avoiding phytoestrogens, and that the most prudent decision may be to do neither.

Cardiovascular Disease

Soybeans also may have a beneficial effect on cardiovascular disease. A meta-analysis of 38 controlled clinical trials found that eating a lot of soy protein was associated with reduced cholesterol (9.3% less than controls), reduced LDL cholesterol (12.9%), reduced triglycerides (10.5%). HDL cholesterol was unaffected (Anderson).

Osteoporosis

The effect of phytoestrogens on bone has not been well studied, but there is reason to believe that there may be some effect on bone. Asians have a lower rate of osteoporotic bone fracture than Western women do, despite the fact that the bones of Asian women are thinner and their calcium intake is far lower than Western women. And genistein, the predominant isoflavone in soybeans, helps to maintain bone in rats that have had their ovaries removed (Knight).

If You Want to Supplement with Phytoestrogens

Soybean products are the most widely consumed source of isoflavones and also contain some lignan precursors. Chick peas (garbanzo beans), lima beans, other beans, and peas are also good sources of isoflavones.

In Asia, consumption of legumes (soybeans, lentils, other beans, and peas) provides 25–45 mg of total isoflavones a day, compared with Western countries, where less than 5 mg/day is eaten. In Japan, where soy consumption is very high, up to 200 mg/day of isoflavones are consumed (Knight).

Not all soy products are equal in terms of phytoestrogen content. Soy oil and soy sauce don't have measurable amounts of phytoestrogens in them.

Tofu (soy bean curd) comes in many different textures and is almost tasteless on its own; it easily takes on other flavors. "Silken" tofu is the softest and is best for blending; try making shakes with fruit juice or substituting it for oil in your favorite salad dressing recipe. Very firm tofu can be cut up and put into soups and curries or marinated and stir-fried with vegetables.

An added bonus for eating tofu is that many brands are made with calcium sulfate and can supply a significant amount of this important nutrient. According to the USDA, 1/4 block (116 mg) of tofu made with calcium supplies 406 mg. of calcium, and 1/4 block of firm tofu (81 gm) supplies 553 mg of calcium. Read the label to see if your brand of tofu is made with calcium.

You can increase your intake of lignans by eating more whole grains (especially rye) and eating flaxseed. Several breakfast cereals are made with flaxseed. It tastes nutty when toasted and can be sprinkled on hot or cold cereal, yogurt, etc.

Summary

The Network believes that phytoestrogens are safe and beneficial to the health of premenopausal women, and may alleviate menopausal symptoms in postmenopausal women, but that the safety of supplemental phytoestrogens in postmenopausal women with breast cancer has not been clearly established.

References are available from the office of the National Women's Health Network.

WORKSHEET—CHAPTER 7

Aging, Ageism, Mid-life and Older Women's Health Issues

1. It is often hard to think about aging when we are young. However, there are many lifestyle factors throughout our lives that can have an impact on the health we experience when we get old. (Be sure to read the introduction to this chapter and the articles before completing these questions.)

   a. Examine your own health-related behaviors (nutrition, exercise, use of drugs, etc.) to see how these might affect risks for both osteoporosis and heart disease.

   b. What changes could you make now to decrease these risks? *Be specific!*

   c. Do you think the answers for question b will be different for a 20 year old, a 40 year old, or a 60 year old?

   d. How could health policies and health education for young people be most appropriate for maximizing the possibility of a healthy old age?

2. Interview two older women. What are the key health issues, if any, in their lives? How secure do they feel about being able to meet their health needs in the next five years? Identify social, economic, and heredity factors which you think influences these women's lives today.

3. *ERT/HRT Summary Sheet.* On the basis of information in "More Selling of HRT" and other information, try to summarize what is and is not known which would help women evaluate and balance "choices" about the following situations:

For the "taking ERT/HRT/SERMS" column, try to answer:
- would it be better to take a specific product? (Would the answer be different for different women?)
- when would one start taking the product?
- when would one stop taking the product?
- what other specific issues would influence this "choice"?

PURPOSE	TAKING ERT/HRT/SERMS	OTHER ALTERNATIVES
Easing the transition through menopause		
Reducing or coping with specific symptoms of menopause		
Reducing risks of osteoporosis		
Reducing risks of heart disease		
Reducing risks of breast cancer		
Other		

CHAPTER 8

Sexuality

$\mathcal{T}$his chapter emphasizes how social and cultural definitions of sexuality can be detrimental to our emotional and physical health. The male emphasis on vaginal intercourse as the "real thing" limits or invalidates the experiences and preferences of many women. The question of who defines sexuality, and whether those definitions encourage or limit women's enjoyment of sexuality and maximizing on sexual health, will be central to this chapter.

"Exposed at Last: The Truth About Your Clitoris" is an appropriate way to begin this sexuality chapter. Although textbooks have often defined the clitoris as the "key" to female sexuality (the term clitoris is derived from the Greek word for key), they have also hidden it and presented it as very small, described as pea-sized. Jennifer Johnson's article notes that "the clitoris was more accurately described in some 19th century anatomy texts, but then it was mysteriously shrunk into a mere speck on the anatomical map." When the clitoris is more fully and accurately described as homologous (arising from the same structure) to the penis (see Sloane's *Biology of Women* for details of the sex differentiation of the embryo), many things about female anatomy and sexual response make more sense. As we read this article, we should once again ask ourselves whether different things would be considered "scientifically interesting" and studied if more scientific decision-makers were women.

"How Being a Good Girl Can Be Bad for Girls," by Deborah Tolman and Tracy Higgins, gives both a societal overview and three specific adolescent girls' experiences of how "women's sexuality is frequently suspect in our culture, particularly when it is expressed outside the bounds of monogamous heterosexual marriage." In the same way that we have seen healthy women defined as passive and dependent (see "Mental Health Issues," chapter 4), "good" women are sexually defined as "passive and threatened sexual objects" with no sexual desire. Tolman and Higgins point out that "When women act as sexual agents, expressing their own sexual desire rather than serving as objects of men's desire, they are portrayed as threatening, deviant, and bad." This chapter looks at all the no-win situations this puts girls and women in as they are held responsible for sexual gate-keeping. Within this framework, girls/women do not have permission to discover, express or enjoy their own sexual desire, but are too often held culturally or legally responsible for not stopping rape. This chapter starts the discussion of how such good girl/bad girl dynamics can be resisted and feminists are encouraged "to analyze the complexity of living in women's bodies within a culture that divides girls and women within themselves and against each other."

The question of who defines women's sexuality is next explored in terms of issues of disability. Social attitudes about women's sexuality are exaggerated and even more problematic in their impact on women with disabilities. In "Forbidden Fruit," Anne Finger examines the strong prejudice against people with disabilities in our society—the belief that they should neither be sexual nor have children.

"Invisible Women: Lesbians and Health Care" shows how a woman's sexuality often becomes a factor in the health care she receives. The article dearly demonstrates how damaging heterosexism can be to the mental and physical health of lesbians. June Jordan's essay "The New Politics of Sexuality" asserts the important points that freedom is indivisible, that the politics of sexuality are not the province of "special interest" groups, and that bisexuality gives an important perspective on the complexity of sexuality.

Because feminism often focuses on the problems of heterosexuality, it is sometimes difficult for heterosexuals to be comfortable with both their sexuality and their politics. Naomi Wolf's article, "Radical Heterosexuality," explores feminist models for healthy heterosexual relationships. In response to our decision to include this article in this book, Professor Laura McEnaney, a former teaching assistant in women's health who often spoke as a heterosexual on the sexuality panel for the class, offers her critique both of this particular article and of other work by Naomi Wolf.

Whether identifying as heterosexual, lesbian, bisexual, or celibate, rather than just accepting male definitions of women's sexuality (and the negative consequences associated with those definitions), women have been redefining sexuality in our own terms. These redefinitions can be empowering and validating for all women.

Exposed at Last
The Truth About Your Clitoris

by Jennifer Johnson

"At a witch trial in 1593, the investigating lawyer (a married man) apparently discovered a clitoris for the first time; he identified it as a devil's teat, sure proof of the witch's guilt. It was 'a little lump of flesh, in a manner sticking out as if it had been a teat, to the length of half an inch,' which the gaoler, 'perceiving at the first sight there of, meant not to disclose, because it was adjoining to so secret a place which was not decent to be seen. Yet in the end, not willing to conceal so strange a matter,' he showed it to various bystanders. The witch was convicted."

from The Vagina Monologues *by Eve Ensler* [Villard].

Pick up almost any medical, anatomy or biology text and you'll find something missing: the greater part of the clitoris.

The clitoris is like an iceberg; only the tip is visible on the outside, its larger mass is under the surface. The visible tip is the glans, or head of the organ. While modern medical science books stop there, the clitoris actually continues under the pelvic bone, then turns down to surround the vagina from above and on either side. The structure forms a dense pyramid of tissue, well-supplied with nerve and vascular network, and is comparable in size to the penis. Like the male organ, the clitoris is flaccid when unaroused and erect when aroused.

And yet, even in the most ponderous, detailed texts, the clitoris is described as a "vestigial organ," or "pea-sized." The diagrams typically show a diagram of a spread-legged female, with a little bulb arrowed "clitoris." The internal diagrams show her reproductive organs, but the bulk of the clitoris—the shaft (body), legs (crura), and bulbs—are missing. Next to the illustration showing the female sex organ as a bump usually appears a drawing of the male sex organ on an extremely well-hung man. Even *Gray's Anatomy*—the authoritative text of biologists—doesn't accurately depict the clitoris.

As a biologist, I first discovered this while doing an anatomical study (dissection) on a human subject. I was shocked to discover that the clitoris was far larger than I had been taught. I could not understand how such a basic—not to mention crucial—piece of biological infor-

mation had been neglected. I searched textbooks, consulted doctors and professors and found all of them unaware of the actual size of the clitoris.

Of course, I was not the only student of science to discover this. When Helen O'Connell became curious about why the female sex organ was "glossed over" in

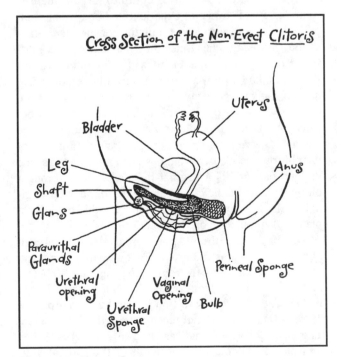

Illustration: Noreen Stevens

the texts, she made it her business to take a closer look when she became a doctor. Now a surgeon at the Royal Melbourne Hospital in Australia, she and her colleagues have been dissecting and measuring the clitoris; her findings were reported in a recent article in *New Scientist.* "Sometimes the whole structure is drawn as a dot," says Dr. O'Connell. In fact, the legs of the clitoris, called the crura, are five to nine centimeters long, extending from the body (shaft) of the clitoris and filling the space between its legs are two bulbs, one on either side of the vaginal cavity. Contrary to the belief that the urethra and clitoris are entirely separate, the clitoris actually encompasses the urethra. Dr. O'Connell believes the clitoris squeezes the urethra shut during sex, reducing the entry of bacteria.

Drawing a more accurate picture of the female sexual anatomy explains a few things. It helps explain why some women are not having orgasms, since women must first be erect before they can reach orgasm. It may also explain why Viagra appears to work for women even though it's not supposed to—suggesting that women may be impotent for the same physiological reasons as men. It also explains why women frequently report that their sex lives were damaged following some types of pelvic surgery—the nerves to the clitoris, and sometimes the organ itself, can be damaged or severed during surgery. It also sheds light on the controversy of the clitoral vs. vaginal orgasm that was debated a few years ago.

When seen as an entire complex organ, there is room for a wide range of experiences. Some women experience orgasm through stimulation of the outer glans of the clitoris; at other times they may experience a different orgasm when combined with penetration. An orgasm reached through external stimulation may feel quite different. For many women, orgasm is intense and relatively easy to reach with digital or oral contact because this is the most direct way to stimulate the large pudendal nerve which runs straight down into the tip of the clitoris (the glans.) What has been referred to as "the vaginal orgasm" is a vaginal-induced orgasm, brought on by stimulating the clitoris indirectly through the vaginal walls. (Of course, it's common to add some direct pudendal stimulation on the outside.)

Then there is the G-spot. Part of the vaginal wall clinically known as the urethral sponge, the G-spot can be found by exploring the roof of the vagina. It's about a knuckle-length in—from one and a half to three inches inside. The easiest way to find it is to have your partner crook a finger or two and reach toward the belly button. The size varies from half an inch to 1.5 inches. When unaroused, it feels like the back of the roof of your mouth. If your partner presses up on this spot and you feel like you have to urinate, they've found it. When it is stroked, it will puff out and feel like a marshmallow.

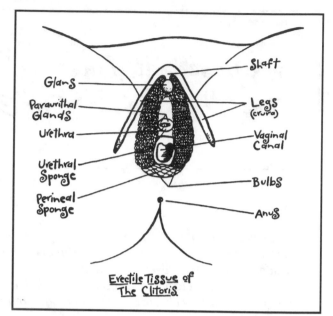

Erectile Tissue of The Clitoris

Illustration: Noreen Stevens

While there are many differences between male and female sexual responses, there are unmistakably many similarities. When the clitoris is engorged and erect, endorphins are released and induce a 'high.' The long bands of the crura become hard and flare out along the pubic bones. Vaginal blood vessels widen and fill with blood and the perineal sponge thickens. The uterus balloons forward, the tubes and ovaries swell. The broad ligament tightens, pulling up the uterus and causing the vagina to enlarge. The neck of the cervix is flexible, like an accordion and during orgasm, the cervix moves forward and down, dipping its head in the seminal pool if a male partner has ejaculated. As well, ejaculation fluid squirts from the woman's paraurithal glands, located on either side of the urethra. This may come as news to women who haven't had a female sexual partner and therefore may not have experienced a female ejaculation first hand. The ejaculate may be a small amount and not noticeable, or it may be a copious amount that 'soaks the sheets.'

The size of the clitoris is actually not a new 'discovery' but the revealing of a secret. The clitoris was more accurately described in some 19th century anatomy texts, but then it was mysteriously shrunk into a mere speck on the anatomical map. The French, however, have been more accurately depicting the clitoris since before the turn of the century.

While doing research for this article, I contacted many sex-related organizations, including the famous Kinsey Institute, the British Association for Sexual and Marital Therapy, even the German Society for Sex Research. None had accurate information on the clitoris, and most did not believe that the clitoris is larger and more complex than medical texts indicate. In bookstores, found current sexology books that didn't have more than a paragraph on the clitoris, some only a few lines, many did not have "clitoris" indexed at all! Even the famous British 'feminist' scientist Desmond Morris's new book, *The Human Sexes,* contains no indexed references for clitoris. Without exception, every sex book gave 'penis' all kinds of room—entire sections, chapters and references.

What does it all mean? Dr. Jennifer Berman, director of the Women's Sexual Health Clinic at Boston University, predicts that knowing the proper female anatomy will lead to research in this area of female function and dysfunction, which she says has been "grossly neglected."

In an article published with her colleagues in *The Journal of Urology* in June 1998, Dr. O'Connell and her colleagues wrote, "Since the studies of Masters and Johnson, there has been surprisingly little investigation of basic female sexual anatomy or physiology." The arti-cle describes the intricate connection between the urethra and the clitoris and says that surgeons should be made aware of the damage that can be done to the organ during urethral surgery. O'Connell says anatomy texts should be changed to accurately depict the clitoris and perineal anatomy. She is now mapping the nerves to the pelvic region innervating the female sex organ.

"They were mapped in men a decade ago," says O'Connell, "but they've never been mapped in women."

It does beg the question doesn't it? Why not? One anthropologist I spoke to explained that the size of the clitoris may have been overlooked because "the size of the male phallus" is a symbol of power; admitting women have the same size organ would be like admitting they are equally powerful. Indeed.

Sex psychologist Dr. Micheal Bailey doesn't buy into the patriarchal conspiracy theory. "There's been very little scientific interest in female sexuality," he insists. Then adds, "It's possible *we* didn't look."

How Being a Good Girl Can Be Bad for Girls

by Deborah L. Tolman • Tracy E. Higgins

Women's sexuality is frequently suspect in our culture, particularly when it is expressed outside the bounds of monogamous heterosexual marriage. This suspicion is reflected in the dominant cultural accounts of women's sexuality, which posit good, decent, and normal women as passive and threatened sexual objects. When women act as sexual agents, expressing their own sexual desire rather than serving as the objects of men's desire, they are often portrayed as threatening, deviant, and bad. Missing is any affirmative account of women's sexual desire. Yet, even while women's sexuality is denied or problematized, the culture and the law tend to assign to women the responsibility for regulating heterosexual sex by resisting male aggression. Defined as natural, urgent, and aggressive, male sexuality is bounded, both in law and in culture, by the limits of women's consent. Women who wish to avoid the consequences of being labeled "bad" are expected to define the boundaries of sexual behavior, outlined by men's desire, and to ignore or deny their own sexual desire as a guide to their choices.

The cultural anxiety precipitated by unbounded female sexuality is perhaps most apparent with regard to adolescent girls. Coming under scrutiny from across the political spectrum, girls' sexuality has been deemed threatening either to girls themselves (potentially resulting in rape, sexually transmitted diseases, unwanted pregnancy), or to society (as evidenced by the single mother, school dropout, welfare dependent). Although none of these issues is limited to teenage girls, all frequently arise in that context because of society's sense of entitlement, or, indeed, obligation, to regulate teen sexuality. Accordingly, the cultural and legal sanctions on teenage girls' sexuality convey a simple message: good girls are not sexual; girls who are sexual are either (1) bad girls, if they have been active, desiring sexual agents or (2) good girls, who have been passively victimized by boys' raging hormones. Buttressed by the real concerns that girls themselves have about pregnancy, AIDS, and parental as well as peer disapproval, the good-girl/bad-girl dichotomy organizes sexuality for young women. This cultural story may increase girls' vulnerability to sexual coercion and psychological distress and disable them from effectively seeking legal protection.

The Cultural Story of Girls' Sexuality in the Media and in Law

Sexually assertive girls are making the news. A disturbed mother of a teenage boy wrote to Ann Landers, complaining of the behavior of teenage girls who had telephoned him, leaving sexually suggestive messages. After publishing the letter, Landers received twenty thousand responses and noted, "If I'm hearing about it from so many places, then I worry about what's going on out there. . . . What this says to me is that a good many young girls really are out of control. Their hormones are raging and they have not had adequate supervision" (qtd. In Yoffe 1991). What were these girls doing? Calling boys, asking them out, threatening to buy them gifts, and to "make love to [them] all night." In the *Newsweek* story, "Girls Who Go Too Far," in which the writer described this Ann Landers column, such girls were referred to as "obsessed," "confused," "emotionally disturbed," "bizarre," "abused," "troubled." Parents described the girls' behavior as "bewilder[ing]" or even "frighten[ing]" to boys. A similar, more recent story in the *Orlando Sentinel* noted that "girls today have few qualms about asking a boy out—and they have no qualms about calling a boy on the telephone" (Shrieves 1993). Describing late-night telephone calls from girls to their teenage sons, the adults interviewed characterized the situation as "frustrating" and "shocking" and suggested that "parents should be paying more attention to what their daughters are going." Girls' behavior, including "suggestive notes stuck to a boy's locker or even outright propositions," was deemed "obsessive."

In contrast, media accounts of boys' sexuality tend to reflect what Wendy Hollway has called the "discourse of male sexual drive," wherein male sexuality is portrayed as natural, relentless, and demanding attention, an urge that boys and men cannot help or control (Hollway 1984). Media coverage of the so-called Spur Posse in

Lakewood, California, reflects this discourse. Members of the Spur Posse, a group of popular white high school boys in a middle-class California suburb, competed with one another using a point system for their sexual "conquests" (Smolowe 1993). When girls eventually complained, several boys were charged with crimes ranging from sexual molestation to rape. Although many criticized the incident as an example of unchecked adolescent sexuality, others excused or even defended the boys' behavior. One father explained, "Nothing my boy did was anything any red-blooded American boy wouldn't do at his age." Their mother commented, "What can you do? It's a testosterone thing."

A comparison of the different boundaries of acceptable sexual behavior for girls and boys illustrates the force of the cultural assumption of female passivity and male aggression. Although the Spur Posse incident was covered as a troubling example of male sexuality out of control, the point at which adolescent sexual aggression becomes suspect is strikingly different for girls and boys. For girls, it's phone calls; for boys, it's rape. The girls' suggestive phone calling is described as shocking to the parents and even threatening to the sons, not because the desire expressed was unusual in the realm of teen sexuality, but because the agents were girls and the objects were boys. In the Spur Posse incident, the possibility of girls' sexual agency or desire shifted responsibility from the boys' aggression to the girls' failure to resist. For some observers, whether or not the boys in the Spur Posse were considered to have acted inappropriately depended upon an assessment of the sexual conduct of the girls involved. If the girls were shown to have expressed any sexual agency, their desire was treated by some as excusing and justifying the boys' treatment of them as objects or points to be collected. As one mother, invoking cultural shorthand put it, "Those girls are trash." The boys' behavior was excused as natural, "a testosterone thing," and the girls were deemed culpable for their failure to control the boys' behavior.

Through these cultural stories, girls are simultaneously taught that they are valued in terms of their sexual desirability and that their own desire makes them vulnerable. If they are economically privileged and white, they become vulnerable because desiring (read "bad") girls lose credibility and protection from male aggression. If they are poor and/or of color, or bisexual or lesbian, they are assumed to be bad, as refracted through the lenses of racism, classism, and homophobia that anchor the cultural story (Tolman forthcoming). While in some communities girls' and women's sexuality is acknowledged and more accepted (Omolade 1983), the force of cultural stories permeating the dominant cultural presses upon all girls. This constant pressure often inflames the desire of marginalized girls to be thought of as good, moral, and normal, status denied them by mainstream standards.[1]

Moreover, all girls' vulnerability is compounded by the extraordinary license given to adolescent boys regarding the urgency of their sexuality. Perhaps more than any other group of men, teenage boys are assumed to be least in control of their sexuality. The responsibility for making sexual choices, therefore, falls to their partners, usually teenage girls, yet these "choices" are to be enacted through passivity rather than agency. Girls who attain good girlhood are at constant risk of becoming bad girls if they fail in their obligation to regulate their own sexual behavior and that of their partners. It is during adolescence, then, that girls are both most responsible for sexual decision making and most penalized for acting on their own sexual desires. It is also during adolescence that girls are socialized into cultural stories about being sexual and being women (Brown and Gilligan 1992; Tolman 1994a and 1994b).

The power of these cultural norms to mediate the interpretation of teen sexuality is perhaps most vividly revealed in the comments of those who would defend "aggressive" girls. Teenage girls interviewed in the *Sentinel* story explained their peers' behavior in terms of girls giving boys what the boys wanted. One suggested that "sometimes girls, in order to get certain guys, will do anything the guy wants. And that includes sex." That would include propositioning a boy "[I]f that's what she thinks *he wants.*" The girl's actions are reinterpreted in terms of satisfying the boy's desire rather than her own. Explaining away the possibility of the girls' sexual desire, one counselor suggested that the girls may not really be "sex-crazed." Rather, they are probably simply "desperate for a relationship" (Shrieves 1993). Describing the girls as trading sex for relationships, the counselor reinterprets their actions in a manner that is consistent with the cultural story of male aggression and female responsibility, which is devoid of female desire. The girl gives the boy what he (inevitably or naturally) wants, negotiating her need only for a relationship by managing his drive for sexual pleasure.

The contrasting media coverage of teenage girls' and teenage boys' sexuality stands as one manifestation of a broader cultural message about gendered norms of sexual behavior. Feminists have documented and discussed this message as a theme present throughout literature, law, film, advertising, and general sources of cultural wisdom on sexuality such as self-help books, advice columns, and medical treatises. The story of male aggression and female responsibility suffuses the culture and operates to regulate human sexuality on conscious and subconscious levels in a gender-specific way. By discouraging women's sexual agency and men's sexual responsibility, these cultural norms undermine communication and encourage coercion and violence. This effect is perhaps nowhere more clear than in the legal regulation of sexuality through rape statutes and the media coverage of rape trials.

Premised on the notion of male sexual aggression and irresponsibility, the law of rape incorporates cultural norms that place upon the woman the burden of regulating sexual activity and, at the same time, penalize her for acting as a sexual subject (Henderson 1992). In so doing, the law of rape incorporates both sides of the good girl/bad girl dynamic. The good girl's attempt to exercise her responsibility to regulate male sexuality is encoded in the requirement of nonconsent to sexual intercourse. Proof of nonconsent, however, frequently depends upon establishing an absence of desire. To be a victimized good girl and therefore entitled to protection, a girl or woman must both resist *and* lack desire. A desiring bad girl, on the other hand, is often deemed deserving of the consequences of her desire.

In cases of nonstranger (acquaintance) rape, rape trials frequently hinge upon whether nonconsent is established, a standard which, as feminists have noted, takes little account of women's sexuality. As Carol Smart has argued, the consent/nonconsent dyad fails to capture the complexity of a woman's experience (Smart 1989). A woman may seek and initiate physical intimacy, which may be an expression of her own sexual desire, while not consenting to intercourse. Nevertheless, by imposing the consent/nonconsent interpretive framework, rape law renders a woman's expression of any desire immediately suspect. Expression of desire that leads to intimacy and ultimately submission to unwanted sex falls on the side of consent. As the "trashy" girls who were the victims of the Spur Posse illustrate, to want anything is to consent to everything. The woman has, in effect, sacrificed her right to refuse intercourse by the expression of her own sexual desire. Or, more precisely, the expression of her desire undermines the credibility of her refusal. Evidence that the rape victim initiated sexual interaction at any level operates to undermine her story at every stage of the process—police disbelieve her account, prosecutors refuse to press the case, and juries refuse to convict. At trial, the issue of consent may be indistinguishable from the quation of whether the woman experienced pleasure. Thus, within rape law, a woman's behavior as a sexual subject shifts power to the aggressor, thereby maintaining the power hierarchy of the traditional story of male aggression and female submission. As in pulp romance, to desire is to surrender.

The centrality of the absence of female desire to the definition of rape cuts across racial lines, albeit in complicated ways. As African American feminists have pointed out, rape and race are historically interwoven in a way that divides the experiences of women of color from white women (i.e., Collins 1990 and Harris 1990; see also Caraway 1991). Nevertheless, whatever the woman's race, the absence of female desire stands as a prerequisite to the identification of a sexual act as rape. The difference emerges as a product of the interlocking elements of the cultural story about women's sexuality which segregate white women and women of color. For example, a key element in the cultural story about women's sexuality is that African American women are sexually voracious, thereby making them unrapable—as distinguished from white women, who are asexual and thus in a constant state of rapability. The absence-of-desire standard is still applied to women of color but presumed impossible to meet. Conversely, when white women accuse African American men of raping them, the required absence of female desire is simply presumed.

If, under ordinary rape law, expression of female sexual desire takes women and girls outside the protection of the law, rendering them unrapable, statutory rape law defines female sexuality as outside the law in a different way. By criminalizing all intercourse with minors, statutory rape laws literally outlaw girls' expression of their own sexuality.[2] In terms of female sexual desire, statutory rape laws represent a complete mirroring of rape law regulating men's access to adult women—with statutory rape, absence of desire is presumed. Instead of rendering a woman unrapable or fully accessible to men, the law simply makes young women's expression of sexual desire illegal.

Both rape law and statutory rape law reinforce cultural norms of female sexuality be penalizing female sexual desire. The coverage of rape in the media, in turn, frequently heightens the focus on the sexuality of the victim, casting her as either good (innocent) or bad (desiring). For example, in the coverage of the Mike Tyson rape trial, the media referred repeatedly to the fact that Desiree Washington taught Sunday school, as though that fact were necessary to rebut the possibility that she invited the attack by acting on her own sexual desire. In an even more extreme case, the mentally disabled adolescent girl who was raped by a group of teenage boys in her Glen Ridge, New Jersey, neighborhood was portrayed both by her lawyers and by the media as largely asexual. To establish nonconsent, the prosecution argued explicitly that she was incapable of knowing or expressing her sexuality.[3] Although she was not sexually inexperienced, this strategy rendered her sexually innocent. Coverage of these two trials stands in sharp contrast to another highly publicized rape trial at the time, that of William Kennedy Smith, in which the media revealed not only the victim's name but her sexual history and her driving record. Much was made in the media of the victim's sexual history and her apparent willingness to accompany Smith home that night. Her desire to engage in flirtation and foreplay meant that her alleged refusal of intercourse could never be sufficiently credible to convict. Smith was acquitted.

As illustrated by the coverage of rape trials, the media and the law interact to reinforce the cultural story of male aggression and female passivity, reinforcing the good girl/bad girl distinction. With the suffusion of this story throughout our culture, girls and women come to understand the norms of acceptable sexual behavior—that good girls are those who are sexually innocent, meaning without sexual desire, although not necessarily without sexual experience. These girls are sexual objects, not subjects, charged with defending the boundaries of their own sexual activity by resisting male aggression. In contrast, bad girls are girls who express their desire, acting as sexual subjects on their own behalf. They are assertive girls, "girls who go too far." Vilified by the media and the culture more broadly as deviant and threatening, these girls are rendered far less likely than good girls to be able to invoke the protection of rape laws and are thus made doubly vulnerable.

Problem of Desire for Adolescent Girls

In this section, we turn to the voices of adolescent young women speaking about their experiences. We rely on a feminist method of analyzing interviews to understand how cultural stories about girls' sexuality may create vulnerability for girls rather than protect them from it.[4] This method takes women as authorities on their own experiences. We listen to what they say and how they say it so that our role as interpreters of their words is clear; that is, we do not claim the authority to say what they are saying but convey how we understand the stories they tell, given our perspective on these issues. We have drawn two case studies from a psychological study of adolescent girls' experience of desire (Tolman 1994a and 1994b),[5] and one from the legal literature. We selected the cases from the study because each of these girls chose to speak about a sexual experience with a boy who was not her boyfriend. Although each associated her experience with sexual violence, the two girls differ profoundly in their understanding of these experiences and also in their critical perspective on gender relations, the cultural story about male and female sexuality, and the good girl/bad girl dynamic. In Jenny's case, a lack of a critical perspective on these issues disables her from feeling outraged or empowered to act on her own behalf. For Pauline, such a perspective appears to enhance her sense of entitlement and ability to act. Through this contrast, we demonstrate how being a good girl can be bad for girls and, conversely, how challenging the terms of the good girl/bad girl dichotomy can be enabling. Finally, we selected the case of Sharon from the legal literature to underscore our point that denying desire in the name of good girlhood can diminish girls' ability to garner protection under the law.

Jenny: When Bad Things Happen to Good Girls

Sixteen-year-old Jenny, who lives in a suburb of a large city, looks like the quintessential good girl. She is white, has long, straight, blond hair framing a lightly freckled, fair face. She is slim, dressed fashionably yet unassumingly. She sits with her legs tensely crossed; she is polite and cooperative and smiles often. Like many girls in this study, throughout the interview Jenny describes how she lives her life by trying to stay carefully within the boundaries of good girl. She and her mother are "very close," and it is very important to her to be "nice" and a "good friend"—even if it means silencing her own displeasure or dissent in relationships.[6] Complying with conventional norms of femininity, Jenny explains that she has never experienced feelings she calls sexual desire: "I actually really don't think I've ever like, wanted anything, like sexually that bad. I mean I don't think I've ever been like sexually deprived or like saying, oh I need sex now or anything, I've never really felt that way before, so, I don't know. I don't really think that there's anything that I would, I mean want," Given Jenny's concern about and success at being a good girl in other domains of her life, it is not surprising that she does not report feeling desire. Having a "silent body" is a psychological response to the belief that good girls are not sexual (Tolman 1994a).

The vulnerability of this silence in her life is tangible in the narrative she tells about the first time she had sexual intercourse, which occurred just prior to our interview. This experience was not what she had hoped it would be:

> We got alone together, and we started just basically fooling around and not doing many things. And then he asked me if I would have sex with him, and I said, well I didn't think I, I mean I said I wanted to wait, 'cause I didn't want to. I mean I like him, but I don't like him so, and I mean he sorta pushed it on me, but it wasn't like I absolutely said no, don't, I—it was sort of a weird experience. I just, I sort of let it happen to me and never like really said no, I don't want to do this. I mean I said no, but I never, I mean I never stopped him from doing anything. . . . I guess maybe I wanted to get it over with, I guess . . . I don't know. I, I just, I mean I could've said no, I guess and I could've pushed him off or whatever 'cause he, I mean, he wasn't, he's not the type of person who would like rape me or whatever, I mean, well I don't think he's that way at all. . . . I was always like, well I want to wait, and I want to be in a relationship with someone who I really

like, and I want it to be a special moment and everything, and then it just sort of like happened so quickly, and it happened with someone who I didn't like and who I didn't want a relationship with and who didn't want a relationship with me, and it was just sort of, I don't, I don't know, I regret it. . . . I wish I had just said no. I mean I could've, and I did for once but then I just let it go. And I wish that I had stood up for myself and really just like stood up and said no, I don't want to do this. I'm not ready or I want it to be a different experience. I mean I could've told him exactly how I felt. . . .I don't know why I didn't.

In this story, Jenny is unsure about how to understand her first experience with sexual intercourse. In listening to her, we, too, are unsure. When she begins this story, Jenny knows that she did not want to have sexual intercourse with this boy, although she did want to "fool around." She, in fact, said "no" when the boy asked her if she would have sex with him. There is a clarity to her no that she substantiates with a set of compelling reasons for not wanting to have sex with this boy: she "wanted to wait," she didn't "like him" or "want a relationship with him." After the fact, she is again clear that she did not want to have sex with this boy. She "regrets it." But we notice that this clarity gives way to a sense of confusion that colors Jenny's voice and gains momentum as her narrative, itself an interplay of description and assessment, unfolds. Cleaving to the convention that girls are ultimately responsible for boys' sexual behavior, she attempts to make sense of the fact that this boy behaved as though she had not said no. Assuming responsibility, Jenny suggests that she had "never stopped him from doing anything," implying, perhaps, that she had not meant the no that she had said.

Jenny's suggestion that she might have said *no* and meant *yes* raises a troubling issue for feminists who have rallied around the claim that "no means no." Although "no means no" is effective as an educational or political slogan or perhaps even as a legal norm, such norms protect girls only at the margin. Within the broader context of adolescent sexuality, girls' no must be credible both to girls and to their partners. Yet the cultural story that good girls do not have sexual desire undermines the credibility of their no, not only to others but also to themselves. When girls cannot say yes, no (or silence) is their only alternative and must express the range of their choices. Some have suggested that girls can ameliorate the problem by simply taking responsibility for communicating their desire (e.g., Roiphe 1993). This answer falls short and, in fact, leaves girls in the lurch by failing to account for the cultural sanctions on girls' expression of their sexuality. Leaving those sanctions unaddressed, so-called power feminists reinforce the assignment of responsibility to girls for sexual decision making without criticizing the constraints under which such decisions are made.

Jenny struggles within those constraints as she attempts to take seriously the possibility that she may have wanted to have sex with the boy despite having said no; the possibility that her no meant yes. Yet her reflection, "I guess maybe I wanted to get it over with, I guess" is literally buttressed by doubt. While this statement stands as a potential explanation of why she had sex even though she said no, Jenny herself does not sound convinced. The explanation sounds even less plausible when compared to the clarity of her elaborated and unambiguous statements about why she did not want to have sex. She explains, "I want to be in a relationship with someone who I really like, and I want it to be a special moment and everything."

As her story progresses, we hear Jenny's confusion about what she wanted intensify. This confusion seems to undermine Jenny's knowledge that she had actually said no to this boy. Eventually, Jenny seems to forget that she ever said no at all. Despite having just explained that she had not wanted to have sex with this boy and had told him so, Jenny starts to speak as if she had not said no. "I said no" becomes "I sort of let it happen to me and never like, really said no, I don't want to do this." She progressively undoes her knowledge that she articulated her wish not to have sex. "I mean I could've said no, I guess, and I could've pushed him off or whatever," finally becomes "I wish I had just said no." Thus, when this boy behaved as though Jenny had not said no, Jenny loses track of her knowledge and her voice, becoming confused not only about what she wanted but also about what she said.

The conditions Jenny gives for an appropriate sexual encounter—"a special relationship," someone she "really like[s]"—resonate with the cultural story that girls' sexuality is about relationships and not desire. Because the encounter she describes did not meet these conditions, she decided that she did not want to have sex and told the boy no. Yet these conditions did not supply an adequate framework for Jenny either to make a clear decision and insist that it be respected, or, if it was not respected, to identify the incident as one of violation. In this context, it is significant that Jenny makes no reference to her own sexual desire. It is only later in the interview, in response to a direct question, that Jenny reports that she "hadn't felt desire for the person I was with." She notes, however, that this absence of desire does not distinguish this encounter from any other: "I've never like had sexual feelings to want to do something or anything." We wonder whether, in the moment, Jenny was not able to hold onto her knowledge that she did not want to have sex because her own desire has never been

available as a guide to her choices. We suggest that not feeling desire is one way to cope with the good girl/bad girl dichotomy. Were Jenny not subject to the good girl standard that prevents her from attending to her own sexual feelings, perhaps she would feel desire in some situations, and her lack of sexual desire could operate as a clear signal to her, perhaps leaving her less vulnerable to such confusion.

The consequences of Jenny's confusion include physical and psychological vulnerability. Her difficulty in holding on to her no and insisting that her no be respected leaves her physically vulnerable to sexual encounters that she does not in any clear way want. Jenny's confusion makes her vulnerable psychologically as well. By discounting her own thoughts and feelings, she risks becoming dissociated from her own experience and from reality. Such dissociation makes it difficult for Jenny to be able to know and name sexual exploitation. Accustomed to being the object of someone else's sexual desire, not considering that her own sexual desire might be relevant or significant, Jenny pastes over the complexity of what did, in fact, happen with the phrase "it just sort of like happened." This "cover story" symbolizes and sustains Jenny's vulnerability in a culture that leaves out her sexual desire.

At the same time, Jenny's suggestion that "it just sort of like happened" keeps another story at bay, a story of a girl whose spoken wish was not heeded, who was coerced. Was Jenny raped? Jenny herself brings the word "rape" into her story: "I mean I could've said no, I guess and I could've pushed him off or whatever 'cause he, I mean, he wasn't, he's not the type of person who would like rape me, or whatever. I mean, well I don't think he's that way at all." She seems to wonder whether this experience might somehow be connected to rape. She may associate this experience with rape because the word signifies something about what it felt like for her, a violation. Although she stopped saying no and apparently assented nonverbally to the act, this sexual experience was not related to any feeling of yes on Jenny's part. Jenny's experience of having passively consented and of having been violated suggests the disjuncture between consent and desire in women's experience, a disjuncture that likely heightens Jenny's confusion over how to interpret what happened to her. Such confusion prevents Jenny from speaking clearly in the first instance about her desire and from later interpreting what happened in a way that acknowledges her own resistance.

Nonetheless Jenny is an astute observer of the social landscape of adolescent heterosexual relationships. She identifies some imbalances in how girls and boys behave and in how they are treated by others in response to their behavior. Later in the interview, she notes that "whenever like a girl and a guy do something and people find out, it's always the girl that messed up or, I mean, maybe the guy messed up, but the guys like get praise for it [laughing] and the girl's sort of like called, either a slut or something, or just like has a bad reputation. Which is sort of [laughing] awful." Jenny believes that "it is just as much the guy's fault as it is the girl's fault. . . . It's just like the guys and the girls make fun of the girls but no one makes fun of the guys [laughing]." What Jenny needs is an analytic framework that links the inequities she observes to cultural stories about sexuality. She suspects, but does not know, that these stories operate in a way that creates gendered power differences. Identifying the good girl/bad girl divide, Jenny tries without success to make sense of the contradiction she observes, that both girls and buys may be at "fault" in sexual situations like hers, but only girls are chastised. We notice that she does not say what she thinks about this contradiction. When she is asked directly, her constant confusion about gender relations is audible: "I really don't know."

Sharon: The Slippery Slope off Good Girlhood

The legal vulnerability created when girls become confused about their own desire is illustrated by the testimony of Sharon, the victim in the U.S. Supreme Court's statutory rape case *Michael M.* v. *Sonoma County*. In her portion of the trial transcript reproduced in the Supreme Court's opinion, Sharon, who, like Jenny, is sixteen and white, is being questioned by the defendant's lawyer about whether she wanted to have sex with the defendant, a boy who was not her boyfriend. Ordinary rape law requires that she make a clear claim that she did not want to have sex with the defendant in order to gain legal recourse. The confusion that emerges as she testifies not only renders the case problematic under ordinary rape law but also calls into question the legitimacy of the statutory rape prosecution. The lawyer's questions about Sharon's desire subtly garner the good girl/bad girl dynamic as part of a strategy to undermine the credibility of her claim that she did not want to have sexual intercourse. In the face of these questions, Sharon appears to lose her clarity about the exact parameters of her desire:

Q: Now, after you met the defendant, what happened?

A: We walked down to the railroad tracks.

Q: What happened at the railroad tracks?

A: We were drinking at the railroad tracks and we walked over to this bus and he started kissing me and stuff, and I was kissing him back, too, at first. Then I was telling him to stop—

Q: Yes.

A: —and I was telling him to slow down and stop. He said, "Ok, Ok." But then he just kept doing it. He just kept doing it and then my sister and two other guys came over to where we were and my sister told me to get up and come home. And then I didn't. . . . We were laying there and we were kissing each other, and then he asked me if I wanted to walk with him over to the park. We walked over to the park, and then we sat down on a bench, and then he started kissing me again, and we were laying on the bench. And he told me to take my pants off. I said "No," and I was trying to get up and he hit me back down on the bench, and then I just said to myself, "Forget it," and I let him do what he wanted to do and he took my pants off and he was telling me to put my legs around him and stuff.

Q: Did you have sexual intercourse with the defendant?

A: Yeah.

Q Did you go off with [the defendant] away from the others?

A: Yeah.

Q: Why did you do that?

A: I don't know. I guess I wanted to. (Michael M. *v.* Sonoma County 450 U.S. 464 [1980]: 483–488)

Sharon begins by speaking clearly about what she did and did not want to do with the boy. She wanted to kiss him back, she wanted him to slow down and stop, and she also wanted to walk over to the park with him. However, when the sexual interaction turned from kissing or "fooling around" to "tak[ing] off [her] pants," she said "no," unequivocally and clearly and "tri[ed] to get up." We hear that her desire had specific contours: while she had wanted to "fool around," she did not want to have sexual intercourse. Nevertheless, like Jenny, she stopped saying no and "let him do what he wanted to do." In so doing, she may have given her consent legally although not emotionally or psychologically.

Initially Sharon maintains clarity about the limits of her desire. Confusion creeps into her previously straightforward account, however, as she is asked about her motives for having gone to the park with the defendant. Implicit in the lawyer's question "[why] did you go off with [the defendant] away from the others?" is the unspoken condemnation of the actions of a bad girl, the conditional phrase *"unless you wanted to have sexual intercourse with him?"* So understood, the question is really about her desire. Having been asked to speak about her own desire, Sharon loses the clarity of her earlier explanation. She seems to suspect (along with the lawyer) that there is an inconsistency between having wanted to go to the park and having not wanted to have sex with the boy.

Confronted with the threat of bad girl status, Sharon retreats from the earlier articulation of her desire. Following on the heels of an unequivocal account that portrays the parameters of her desire, Sharon's statement of ambivalence makes her seem confused and uncertain. By responding that she does not know what she wanted, that she "guess[es]" that she "wanted to," Sharon undermines the credibility of her previous testimony. As a witness, Sharon becomes trapped within the good girl/bad girl dichotomy. Her admission of her desire to go to the park with the boy undermines the credibility of her claim that she was coerced. At this point, her reiteration of her direct statement that she wanted to go to the park coupled with her retreat from that statement render her testimony unreliable. Her mistake, as she seems to realize, was to relinquish good girl status by confessing her desire.

Paulina: Empowerment through Rejecting the Good Girl/Bad Girl Dichotomy

Paulina, a white girl who lives in a urban environment, tells stories that offer a counterpoint to Jenny's. Seventeen-year-old Paulina looks like the other adolescent girls in this study: long, dark hair frames her pretty, open face; stylish jeans and sweater clothe a slim figure. Despite her appearance, Paulina does not sound like the other girls: having immigrated from Eastern Europe several years prior to the interview, Paulina speaks with a strong accent. It is the content of her narrative, however, that distinguishes her from most other study participants. Like Jenny, Paulina is also a competent consumer of cultural stories about girls and sexuality, and can recite them without a moment's hesitation:

They expect the woman to be pure, I mean, she has to be holy and everything, and it's okay for a guy to have any feelings or anything, and the girl has to be this little virgin who is obedient to the men. . . . usually a guy makes the first move, not the girl, or the girl's not supposed to do it, the girl's supposed to sit there going, no,

no you can't. I can't do that. . . . I mean the guy expects the girl to be a sweet little virgin when he marries her, and then he can be running around with ten other women, but when he's getting married to her, she's not supposed to have any relationship with anybody else.[7]

Paulina echoes Jenny's observation about how the label "slut" is—and is not— used: "Guys, they just like to brag about girls. Oh she does this, and she's a slut because she slept with this guy, and with this guy, but they don't say that about guys. It's okay for them to do it, but when a girl sleeps with two guys it's wrong, she shouldn't do that, she automatically becomes a slut."

In contrast to Jenny's ambivalence and uncertainty, Paulina has strong opinions about the sexual double standard: "I just don't agree with it. . . . I just don't think so." A sense of entitlement, accompanied by outrage, suffuses her well-articulated view of female sexual agency: "Woman can do whatever they want to, why shouldn't they?. . . . I think that women have the same feelings as men do, I mean, I think it's okay to express them too. . . . I mean, they have the same feelings, they're human, why should they like keep away from them?" While Jenny seems unable to make sense of this inequity, Paulina grounds her dissension in an analysis linking gender and power: "I think males are kind of dominant, and they feel that they have the power to do whatever they want, that the woman should give in to them." Paulina also parts from Jenny in her detailed knowledge about her own sexual desire.

Perhaps not coincidentally, Paulina speaks of this embodied experience with an ease that reflects and underscores her belief that girls' sexual desire is normal or, in her words, "natural": "I feel really hot, like, my temperature is really hot. . . . I felt like a rush of blood like pumping to my heart, my heart would really beat fast, and it's just, everything are combined, you're extremely aware of every touch, and everything, everything together. . . . you have all those feelings of want." Paulina is clear that this desire can guide her choices and that it should be respected: "To me if you have like a partner that you're close to, then it's okay. And if you feel comfortable with it, 'cause if you don't, then you shouldn't do it. You just don't want to." Thus, Paulina grounds her sexual decisions in her own feelings and beliefs—she can identify and is able to account for the presence and absence of her own desire. As a result, Paulina appears to be less vulnerable to becoming confused about what she feels and what she has said.

Like Jenny, Paulina has had a "bad" sexual experience with a boy whom she thought of as a friend. In the interview, she describes a time when this male friend tried to force her to have sex with him:

There was one experience, the guy wanted to have sexual intercourse and I didn't. I didn't have sex with him. He, he like pulled me over to the couch, and I just kept on fighting. . . . I was just like begging him to like not to do anything, and like, I really did not have like much choice. Because I had my hands behind me. And he just like kept on touching me, and I was just like, just get off me. He goes, you know that you want to, and I said no I don't. Get off me, I hate you. . . . So he's like, well, I'll let you go if you're gonna kiss me. So I kissed him, and I'm like well I can go now. And he was like no. But um, the phone rang later on, I said I have to answer this, it's my mother. . . . So he let me answer the phone. So. And it was my friend and I just said, oh can you come over? And, since I'm Polish I spoke Polish, so I'm like oh just come over, come over as soon as you can.

Ultimately, when her friend arrived, she was able to convince the boy to leave.

Paulina's assailant attacked her both physically and psychologically, telling her, "You know that you want to." However, because Paulina had a clear understanding of her sexual feelings, she is able to speak clearly about not feeling sexual desire. In response to his coaxing, Paulina's retort is direct and unequivocal: "No, I don't. Get off me. I hate you." Unlike Jenny and Sharon, Paulina does not become confused: she has no doubt in her mind about the parameters of her own sexual feelings; she did not want any sexual interaction with this young man. Her sense of entitlement to her feelings and choices empowers her to resist the attack.

It must be emphasized that Paulina was very lucky in this situation. She was able to think clearly and take advantage of an opportunity—her friend's phone call—to protect herself from being raped. The critical point is not that she was able to avoid assault in this case, but that she was clear about the threat of violence. Had Paulina not escaped attack, it seems likely that she would have maintained her clarity about her own actions and desires, a clarity that would enable her to claim the protection the law offers.

Conclusion

In listening to three adolescent girls voice experiences with their own sexuality, we hear both how the good girl/bad girl dynamic becomes embodied and embedded in girls' psyches and relationships and how it can be resisted. We suggest that Paulina's ability to know her desire and know its absence, in contrast to Jenny's "silent body" and Sharon's confusion, is linked to her critical consciousness about how male power and dominance underpin the good girl/bad girl dichotomy. Because she rejects a cultural story about her sexuality that makes her own desire dangerous, we think she is less vulnerable to the confusion that Sharon and Jenny voice and more empowered to know and to speak with clarity about her sexual interactions and the social landscape of gendered relationships.

The voices of these three girls living (with) the good girl/bad girl dynamic suggest the necessity of what Michelle Fine terms an affirmative discourse of desire (Fine 1988) for adolescent girls. Such a discourse must recognize, reveal, and then reject the good girl/bad girl categories as patriarchal strategies that keep girls and women from the power of their own bodies and their bonds with one another. It should center on all girls' entitlement to their sexuality, rather than focus solely on the threat of lost status and respect or diminished safety. With the words and analysis to interrupt the good girl/bad girl dynamic, girls and women can identify and critique cultural stories that impair them psychologically and under the law.

The task for feminists, then, is to help adolescent girls and women to analyze the complexity of living in women's bodies within a culture that divides girls and women within themselves and against each other. It is true that the threat of sexual violence against girls and women, as well as social isolation, is real and constant, effectively keeping girls' and women's bodies and psyches filled with fear, rendering sexual desire difficult and dangerous. Yet it is also true that girls and women at this moment in history can feel profound pleasure and desire and should be entitled to rely on their own feelings as an important aspect of sexual choices. By holding the contradiction of pleasure and danger, girls and women can expose and loosen the tight weave seamlessly worked by the good girl/bad girl dynamic in society and in their individual lives.

NOTES

1. Some young women are able to resist such norms by anchoring their sexual self-concept in their culture of origin (Robinson and Ward 1991).

2. Although the modern reinterpretation of the purpose of statutory rape laws is that such legislation is designed to prevent teen pregnancy, the historical justification was the protection of female virtue. For example, in 1895, the California Supreme Court explained:

The obvious purpose of [the statutory rape law] is the protection of society by protecting from violation the virtue of young unsophisticated girls. . . . It is the insidious approach and vile tampering with their persons that primarily undermines the virtue of young girls, and eventually destroys it; and the prevention of this, as much as the principal act, must undoubtedly have been the intent of the legislature. (People v. Verdegreen, 106 Cal. 211, 214–215, 39 P. 607, 607–609 [1895]

In 1964, the same court explained that "an unwise disposition of her sexual favor is deemed to do harm both to herself and the social mores by which the community's conduct patterns are established. Hence the law of statutory rape intervenes in an effort to avoid such a disposition" (People v. Hernandez, 61 Cal. 2d 531, 393 P. 2d 674 [1964]).

As Professor Fran Olsen has argued, although the boy's conduct is punished by criminal sanction, it is the girl who is denied the capacity to consent. Under gender-specific statutory rape laws, the boy may legally have intercourse with women who are over the age of consent (Olsen, 1984).

3. The prosecution's strategy to portray the victim as asexual was controversial among advocates for people with mental disabilities. (See Houppert 1993, citing Leslie Walker-Hirsch, president of the American Association on Mental Retardation's special interest group on sexual and social concerns). Nevertheless, in this, as in many other rape trials, the surest means of establishing lack of consent was to establish the sexual innocence of the victim.

4. This method adopts the psychodynamic concept of the layered psyche in interpreting girls' and women's narratives in individual interviews conducted by women (Brown et al. 1991). Importing this clinical construct into empirical research is not by fiat a feminist act. But requiring the interpreter to focus actively on her own subjectivity and theoretical framework in the act of interpretation subverts the tendency in psychology of an authoritative, expert "voice over" of a girl or woman's words. This psychological method, called the Listening Guide, enables an exploration of ways in which internalized oppression may operate to constrain what a girl or woman says, thinks, or knows, and how she may resist such oppressions. This method asks us to consider what is not said as well as what is said and how power differences embedded in the brief research relationship may circulate through the narrative. The method obligates the interpreter to ask herself persistently how a woman's structural position in society or individual relational history may contribute to layered ways of understanding her voice—what she says, where she falters, when she is silent. The use of this method yields multiple interpretations of women's narratives by highlighting different voices or perspectives audible in a single story. Using this method means creating a dialectic between the way one girl or woman speaks and how another woman, from a distinctly feminist point of view, hears her story.

5. The study was designed to fill in a gap in the psychological literature on adolescent girls' sexuality: how girls experience their own sexual feelings, particularly their bodies. This feminist question challenged the belief that girls' sexuality is essentially a response to boys' sexual feelings and began to flesh out how sexual desire is a part of ado-

lescent girls' lives. For her dissertation, Tolman interviewed a random sample of thirty girls from two different social contexts: they were juniors, aged fifteen to eighteen, at a suburban and an urban public high school. These girls were black, Hispanic, and white and represented a range of religious backgrounds, sexual experiences, and ethnicities. The interviews often had a conversational tone because the feminist approach used emphasizes listening to girls, in contrast to the traditional procedure of strict adherence to a preset questionnaire. Overall these girls reported that their own desire was a dilemma for them because they were not supposed to experience sexual feelings but, in fact, did. For more on this study see Tolman 1994a, 1994b, and forthcoming. The analyses of this data have focused on class rather than race differences, due to the demographics of the sample. Both qualitative and quantitative analyses revealed similarities across class, such as in the proportion of girls who reported an absence of or confusion about desire and those who reported an awareness of their own desire, and significant class differences in the association of desire with vulnerability and pleasure. Urban girls' narratives were more likely to be about vulnerability and not about pleasure, while suburban girls' narratives were more likely to be about pleasure rather than vulnerability.

6. Brown and Gilligan 1992 and Jack 1991 describe these qualities of the "tyranny of nice and kind" and the tendency to silence or sacrifice the self's disruptive feelings as characteristic of girls' and women's descriptions of their relationships.

7. Paulina's responses have been reported previously in Tolman 1994b.

REFERENCES

Brown, Lynn, and Carol Gilligan. 1992. *Meeting at the Crossroads.* Cambridge, MA: Harvard University Press.

Brown, Lynn, Elizabeth Debold, Mark Tappan, and Carol Gilligan. 1991. "Reading Narratives of Conflict for Self and Moral Voice: A Relational Method." In *Handbook of Moral Behavior and Development: Theory, Research and Application,* ed. William Kurtines and Jacob Gewirtz. Hillsdale, NJ: Lawrence Erlbaum.

Caraway, Nancie. 1991. *Segregated Sisterhood.* Knoxville: University of Tennessee Press.

Collins, Patricia Hill. 1990. *Black Feminist Thought.* New York: Routledge

Fine, Michelle. 1988. "Sexuality, Schooling, and Adolescent Females: The Missing Discourse of Desire." *Harvard Educational Review* 58 (10: 29–53.

Harris, Angela. 1990. "Race and Essentialism in Feminist Legal Theory." *Stanford Law Review* 42: 581–592.

Henderson, Lynne. 1992. "Rape and Responsibility." *Law and Philosophy* 11 (1–2): 127–128.

Hollway, Wendy. 1984. "Women's Power in Heterosexual Sex." *Women's Studies International Forum* 7 (1): 63 68.

Houppert, Karen. 1993. "The Glen Ridge Rape Draws to a Close." *Village Voice* (March 16): 29–33.

Jack, Dana. 1991. *Silencing the Self.* Cambridge, MA: Harvard University Press.

Michael M. v. Sonoma County, 450 U.S. 464 (1980).

Olsen, Frances. 1984. "Statutory Rape: A Feminist Critique of Rights Analysis." *Texas Law Review* 63: 387.

Omadale, Barbara, 1983. "Hearts of Darkness." In *Powers of Desire: The Politics of Sexuality,* ed. Ann Snitow, Christine Stansell, and Sharon Thompson. New York: Monthly Review Press.

Robinson, Tracy and Janie Ward. 1991. "A Belief in Self Far Greater than Anyone's Disbelief: Cultivating Resistance Among African American Female Adolescents." In *Women, Girls, and Psychotherapy: Reframing Resistance,* ed. Carol Gilligan, Annie Rogers, and Deborah Tolman. New York: Haworth Press.

Roiphe, Katie: 1993. *The Morning After: Sex, Fear, and Feminism on Campus.* Boston: Little, Brown.

Shrieves, Linda. 1993. "The Bold New World of Boy Chasing." *Orlando Sentinel* (22 December): E1.

Smart, Carole. 1989. *Feminism and the Power of the Law.* New York: Routledge

Smolowe, Jill. 1993. "Sex with a Scorecard." *Time* (5 April):41.

Tolman, Deborah. Forthcoming. "Adolescent Girls' Sexuality: Debunking the Myth of the Urban Girl." In *Urban Adolescent Girls: Resisting Stereotypes,* ed. Bonnie Leadbetter and Niobe Way. New York: New York University Press.

———. 1994a. "Daring to Desire; Culture and the Bodies of Adolescent Girls." In *Sexual Cultures: Adolescents, Communities and the Construction of Identity,* ed. Janice Irvine. Philadelphia: Temple University Press.

———.1994b. "Doing Desire: Adolescent Girls' Struggle for/with Sexuality." *Gender and Society* 8(3); 324–342.

Yoffe, Emily. 1991. "Girls Who Go Too Far." *Newsweek* (22 July): 58.

Forbidden Fruit

by Anne Finger

Before she became a paraplegic, Los Angeles resident DeVonna Cervantes liked to dye her pubic hair 'fun colours'—turquoise, purple, jet black. After DeVonna became disabled, a beautician friend of hers came to the rehabilitation unit and, as a Christmas present, dyed DeVonna's pubic hair a hot pink.

But there's no such thing as 'private parts' in a rehab hospital. Soon the staff, who'd seen her dye job when they were catheterizing her, sent the staff psychiatrist around to see her. Cervantes says that he told her: 'I know it is very hard to accept that you have lost your sexuality but you don't need to draw attention to it this way.' Cervantes spent the remainder of the 50-minute session arguing with him, and, in perhaps the only true medical miracle I've ever heard of, convinced him that he was wrong—that this was normal behaviour for her.

Cervantes' story not only illustrates woeful ignorance on the part of a 'medical expert'; equating genital sensation with sexuality. But it shows clearly a disabled woman's determination to define her own sexuality.

Sadly, it's not just medical experts who are guilty of ignoring the reproductive and sexual rights and needs of people with disabilities. The movements for sexual and reproductive freedom have paid little attention to disability issues. And the abortion rights movement has sometimes crudely exploited fears about 'defective fetuses' as a reason to keep abortion legal.

From *New Internationalist,* July 1992, pp. 8–10. copyright © 1992 by New Internationalist. Reprinted by permission.

Anne Finger teaches English literature at Wayne State University, Detroit, US. In her book *Past Due* (Women's Press, 1990) she describes her experience of childbirth as a disabled woman.

Because the initial focus of the women's movement was set by women who were overwhelmingly non-disabled (as well as young, white, and middle-class), the agenda of reproductive rights has tended to focus on the right to abortion as the central issue. Yet for disabled women, the right to bear and rear children is more at risk. Zoe Washburn, in her poem, 'Hannah', grieves the child she wanted to have and the abortion she was coerced into: '. . . so she went to the doctor, and let him suck Hannah out with a vacuum cleaner. . . . The family stroked her hair when she cried and cried because her belly was empty and Hannah was not only dead, but never born. They looked at her strange crippled-up body and thought to themselves, thank God that's over.'

Yet the disability rights movement has certainly not put sexual rights at the forefront of its agenda. Sexuality is often the source of our deepest oppression; it is also often the source of our deepest pain. It's easier for us to talk about—and formulate strategies for changing—discrimination in employment, education, and housing than to talk about our exclusion from sexuality and reproduction. Also, although it is changing, the disability rights movement in the US has tended to focus its energies on lobbying legislators and creating an image of 'the able disabled'.

Barbara Waxman and I once published an article in *Disability Rag* about the US Supreme Court's decision that states could outlaw 'unnatural' sex acts, pointing out the effect it could have on disabled people—especially those who were unable to have 'standard' intercourse. The *Rag* then received a letter asking how 'the handicapped' could ever be expected to be accepted as 'normal' when we espoused such disgusting ideas.

Because reproduction is seen as a 'women's issue', it is often relegated to the back burner. Yet it is crucial that the disability-rights movement starts to deal with it. Perhaps the most chilling situation exists in China where a number of provinces ban marriages between people with developmental and other disabilities unless the parties have been sterilized. In Gansu Province more than 5,000 people have been sterilized since 1988. Officials in Szechuan province stated: 'Couples who have serious hereditary diseases including psychosis, mental deficiency and deformity must not be allowed to bear children'. When disabled women are found to be pregnant, they are sometimes subjected to forced abortions. But despite widespread criticism of China's population policies, there was almost no public outcry following these revelations.

Even in the absence of outright bans on reproduction, the attitude that disabled people should not have children is common. Disabled women and men are still sometimes subject to forced and coerced sterilizations—including hysterectomies performed without medical justification but to prevent the 'bother' of menstruation.

Los Angeles newscaster Bree Walker has a genetically transmitted disability, ectrodactyly, which results in fused bones in her hands and feet. Pregnant with her second child, last year, she found her pregnancy the subject of a call-in radio show. Broadcaster Jane Norris informed listeners in a shocked and mournful tone of voice that Bree's child had a 50-percent chance of being born with the same disability. 'Is it fair to bring a child into the world knowing there's two strikes against it at birth? . . . Is it socially responsible?' When a caller objected that it was no one else's business, Norris argued, 'It's everybody's business.' And many callers agreed with Norris's viewpoint. One horrified caller said, 'It's not just her hands—it's her feet, too. She has to [dramatic pause] wear orthopaedic shoes.'

The attitude that disabled people should not have children is certainly linked with the notion that we should not even be sexual. Yet, as with society's silence about the sexuality of children, this attitude exists alongside widespread sexual abuse. Some authorities estimate that people with disabilities are twice as likely to be victims of rape and other forms of sexual abuse as the general population. While the story of rape and sexual abuse of disabled people must be told and while we must find ways to end it, the current focus on sexual exploitation of disabled people can itself become oppressive.

As Barbara Faye Waxman, the former Disability Project Director for Los Angeles Planned Parenthood states, 'The message for disabled kids is that their sexuality will be realized through their sexual victimization. . . . I don't see an idea that good things can happen, like pleasure, intimacy, like a greater understanding of ourselves, a love of our bodies.' Waxman sees a 'double whammy' effect for disabled people, for whom there are few, if any, positive models of sexuality, and virtually no social expectation that they will become sexual beings.

The attitude that we are and should be asexual seems to exist across a broad range of cultures. Ralf Hotchkiss, famous for developing wheelchairs in Third World countries, has travelled widely in Latin America and Asia. He says that while attitudes vary 'from culture to culture, from subculture to subculture,' he sees nearly everywhere he travels, 'extreme irritation [on the part of disabled people] at the stereotypical assumptions that people . . . make about their sexuality, their lack of it.' He also noted: 'In Latin American countries once they hear I'm married, the next question is always, "How old are your kids?"'

Some of these prejudices are enshrined in law. In the US, 'marital disincentives' remain a significant barrier. To explain this Byzantine system briefly: benefits (including government-funded health care) are greatly reduced and sometimes even eliminated when a disabled person marries. Tom Fambro writes of his own difficulties with the system: 'I am a 46-year-old black man with cerebral palsy. A number of years ago I met a young lady who was sexually attracted to me (a real miracle).' Fambro learned, however, that he would lose his income support and, most crucially, his medical benefits, if he married. 'People told us that we should just live together . . . but because both of us were born-again Christians that was unthinkable. . . . The Social Security Administration has the idea that disabled people are not to fall in love, get married, have sex or have a life of our own. Instead, we are to be sexual eunuchs. They are full of shit.'

Institutions—whether traditional hospitals or euphemistically named 'homes', 'schools', or newer community care facilities—often out-and-out forbid sexual contact for their residents. Or they may outlaw gay and lesbian relationships, while allowing heterosexual ones. Disabled lesbians and gays may also find that their sexual orientation is presumed to occur by default. Restriction of access to sexual information occurs on both a legal and a social plane. The US Library of Congress, a primary source of material for blind and other print-handicapped people, was instructed by Congress in 1985 to no longer make *Playboy* available in braille or on tape. And relay services, which provide telecommunication between deaf and hearing people have sometimes refused to translate sexually explicit speech. In her poem, 'Seeing', blind poet Mary McGinnis writes of a woman being watched by sighted men while bathing nude:

. . . the guys sitting at the edge of the pond
looked at her, but she couldn't see them . . .
and whose skin, hair, shirts and belts
would remain unknown to her
because she couldn't go up to them
and say, now fair is fair, let me touch the places
on your bodies you try to hide,
it's my turn—don't draw back or sit on
your hands, let me count your rings, your scars,
the hairs coming from your nose. . . .

I have quoted poets several times in this piece; many disability-rights activists now see that while we need changes in laws and policies, the formation of culture is a key part of winning our freedom. Disabled writers and artists are shaping work that is often powerful in both its rage and its affirmation.

In Cheryl Marie Wade's 'side and belly', she writes:

He is wilty muscle sack and sharp bones fitting my gnarlypaws. I am soft cellulite and green eyes of middle-age memory. We are side and belly trading dreams and fantasies of able-bodied former and not real selves: high-heel booted dancers making love from black rooftops and naked dim doorways. . . .
. . . Contradictions in the starry night of wars within and being not quite whole together and whole. Together in sighs we say yes broken and fire and yes singing.

Invisible Women
Lesbians and Health Care

by Risa Denenberg

In the 1960s, when women were disclosing the intimate details of their private lives to one another in consciousness-raising groups, a body of knowledge began to emerge about women's health care experiences. The early women's health movement, which fought primarily for women's autonomy in reproduction and in opposition to medical authority, was resisted with all the force that the medical profession could muster. Despite that resistance, the women's health movement flourished and helped to usher in an era in which women have more knowledge of their bodies and a greater sense of ownership than they did in any previous generation.

As a participant in both the women's movement and the women's health movement, I know that many of the leaders were lesbians. During the years of struggling to create an autonomous movement, fighting for abortion rights, looking at our own and each other's bodies with plastic vaginal speculums, and creating feminist clinics, a mere handful of projects and programs for lesbians were developed. Our issues were subsumed within the more visible agenda for heterosexual women's rights. The women's movement both faltered and flourished. It undertook the complex task of broadening to include issues of race and class, and the single-issue battle for abortion rights became a call for prenatal and child care and against sterilization abuse. And in the 1980s, the reality of how women were being affected by AIDS became a consuming item on the women's agenda. Finally, after years of working on such crucial issues, it is still difficult for lesbians to articulate our own health care needs.

It is an even greater task to get our needs recognized by others, given the widespread view of homosexuality and lesbianism. Heterosexuality is still seen as the universal norm, and the notion persists that homosexuality, and particularly lesbianism, doesn't matter. In the right-wing, conservative view, homosexuality is sinful, and therefore matters more, but a great many liberals, and even progressives, remain doggedly blind to sexuality. This blindness comes in many forms: keeping gay concerns a low priority in progressive movements, closeting of gay leaders in such groups, and widespread discomfort with public sexuality: "That's their business, but I just wish they didn't feel such a need to flaunt it in our faces." Although the AIDS crisis and the gay response to it has opened the door to overcoming this invisibility and legitimizing the health needs of gay men, the attention it demands has set lesbians even further back from having our health care needs recognized—even when we have AIDS, are dying in astounding numbers from breast cancer and other cancers, and neglect our health care needs in order to care for others. And while AIDS has disproportionately affected gay men, the increase in anti-gay violence that has accompanied the epidemic affects gay men and lesbians equally.

Invisibility and Discrimination

Lesbians are like other women in their vulnerability to illness and to the damaging effect of sexism in the health care system. Lesbians also have unique concerns and experiences that must inform their health care services if individual needs are to be met. A few examples give some hint of the specific problems of discrimination that lesbians face within the health care system:

- Doris entered a therapeutic community to recover from drug and alcohol use, but she found it necessary to hide her gay life-style from the other clients and the staff.

Risa Denenberg is a family nurse practitioner at Bronx Lebanon Hospital in New York City and a health writer.

- Evelyn was in therapy for depression for about six months when her female therapist made an overtly homophobic remark. She decided against revealing her growing sexual feelings toward a woman at her job.
- Lori was unable to find a specialist to treat her infertility and assist her with artificial insemination because she is a lesbian.
- Fran came out as a lesbian to her doctor when he was asking her about birth control. During the exam, when he was placing the speculum in her vagina, he was extremely rough, and he used a size that was uncomfortable for her. When Fran complained, he said, "I'm just trying to change your mind."
- Vivian was committed at age 15 to a psychiatric hospital by her parents when they discovered her having sex with another girl.

Although such invisibility and discrimination are not always life and death matters, they bear upon clinical practice, access to health care services, medical decision making, and the level of discomfort we all feel with wholly depersonalized, even antagonistic health care. Lesbians live in all communities and are diverse in race, ethnicity, class, and political outlook, and are not easily distinguished within health care settings. As seen in the following examples, this invisibility can thwart the receipt of decent health care:

- Sharon had a bad experience with an insensitive gynecologist when she was in her twenties. Now, at 43, she hasn't had a Pap smear in 16 years.
- Marcia was unemployed and had no health insurance when she discovered that she had a breast lump. Her lover of eight years had a job with heath insurance, but couldn't place Marcia on her policy.
- Joan was given a hysterectomy at age 27 for a small fibroid tumor on her uterus. At one point her doctor mentioned doing a myomectomy—removing the tumor and saving the uterus—but after he found out that she was lesbian, he never brought it up again. He never asked her if she wanted children.
- After Sonja's surgery for breast cancer, her lover Michelle was not allowed into the recovery room. As she sat in the waiting room for three hours, Michelle noticed the nurses escorting other people in to see family members. She was afraid to complain, lest they treat Sonja badly.

Huge gaps exist in the public's and the medical establishment's understanding of lesbian culture and lifestyle that make it difficult to confront our invisibility. There is no standard definition of who is a lesbian. Many female couples exist in satisfying, long-term relationships without ever uttering the words lesbian or gay. Other women boldly proclaim a lesbian identity, yet at times have sexual relations with men. Lesbians live in the same unhealthy environments and engage in the same kinds of risky health behaviors as other women—drug and alcohol abuse, eating disorders, smoking, unsafe sex. Yet, lesbians are virtually unstudied as a population by any discipline.

Lesbians exhibit a wide and fluid range of attitudes, behaviors, and self-identities. One common denominator in their relationships, expression of sexuality, life-style, and experiences, however, is that they are all outsiders when it comes to getting their health needs met. When lesbians' health care needs are the same as those of other women for screening, prevention, treatment of illness, education and crisis intervention, lesbians' needs are less well met than those of heterosexuals. And when lesbians present unique problems and concerns, the medical system generally can't or won't meet them. Health care services must be evaluated to determine whether or not they are discriminatory and offensive to lesbians.

Most lesbians have heard of or personally experienced abuses within the health care system because of their sexual preference. These experiences include sexual assault, patronizing treatment, neglect, intimidation, ignorance, and discrimination. Homophobia, in the form of heterosexual presumption, is a common experience shared by all lesbians entering the health system. This is layered on top of the sexism that all women continue to meet in this arena. For lesbians of color, racism within the system adds another layer of discrimination. Poor lesbians, lesbian intravenous drug users, and lesbian mothers all face additional bias.

The collective experience of lesbians rings an alarm bell of terror for any lesbian entering the system. It is not surprising, then, that lesbians often avoid receiving health care in traditional settings as long as it is possible for them to do so. A variety of other elements and experiences help to determine lesbians' health status and relationship to the health care system, including their financial standing, work life, sexuality, reproductive life, and support systems.

Money and Work

As women, lesbians earn less money, since, according to the Census Bureau, women's earnings are only two thirds that of men. In addition, lesbians generally have less access than other women to men's resources. Thus, a lesbian household is likely to earn less than a heterosexual household—whether single, coupled, or collective—and is likely to have fewer dollars to spend on health care services. This is compounded by discrimination against lesbians in the work world, which leads to a lack of job mobility. Lesbians may also tend to choose jobs that will not put extra stress on them if their lesbian identity is known. In addition, along with gay men and others in nontraditional families, lesbians usually cannot place a lover or a partner's children on their health insurance policy. Furthermore, lesbians may be less able to recruit support and resources from their family of origin, who often reserve such favors for their married children.

The workplace itself places enormous stress upon lesbians. In the work world one often must make the choice between being out, with the accompanying torture of gay baiting and harassment, or remaining in the closet, with the constant fear of being exposed.

Although not everyone finds pleasure in tapping into the social network in the workplace, to some extent everyone attempts to ease stress on the job by fitting in and getting along with their co-workers. It is difficult to negotiate the pressures to fit into the social networks that develop among co-workers, and camaraderie creates yet another pressure with negative effects on lesbians who must be closeted in a heterosexual world. Women often invent a "boyfriend," invert pronouns, appear falsely naive about relationships, and stay away from office parties or picnics where a male escort would be expected. For lesbians, work, however satisfying in theory, can be a stress that adversely affects self-image, mental health, household finances, and physical well-being.

Sexuality and Lesbian Relationships

Lesbians often feel isolated, especially when single, and have difficulty finding positive images of lesbian relationships and sexuality. Gay women have similar inhibitions as heterosexual women about approaching, pursuing and expressing desire to other people. The sexual or romantic isolation that a single lesbian feels may be exacerbated if her friends are competing for lovers within their small circle.

Lesbians are often singled out in medical discussion for the dubious achievement of engaging in low-risk sex. One inaccurate portrayal of lesbian sexuality is that sex is generally chaste, dry, and monogamous. This leads to the idea that lesbians are not at risk of sexually transmitted infections or HIV. It is dangerous to suggest that any category of sex is completely safe from HIV transmission. Furthermore, this stereotype contributes to the myth that lesbians don't have much sex and that this is a frequent cause of failure for lesbian relationships. Lesbian sexuality, like all sexuality, is polymorphous and diverse, and it has never been adequately described in research or literature. But clearly, sexuality is neither the only inspiration, nor the usual cause of failure for female bonding. Gay relationships are generally unsupported by families and communities, are bound by fewer legal ties, and have fewer common children to draw parties together when the relationship feels threatened from within.

Reproductive Health

Lesbians' health needs clearly differ from those of heterosexual women in the area of reproductive health. Lesbians generally have fewer pregnancies in the course of their lifetimes than other women and, hence, longer years of unrelieved menstruation. Anecdotal reports from clinicians providing care to lesbians suggest that lesbians have more complaints about menstruation and fewer about menopause. Women who have sex exclusively with women may have a lower overall incidence of sexually transmitted infections, which translates into a lower incidence of pelvic infections, ectopic pregnancies, and cervical cancer. Women who have never been pregnant have a higher incidence of breast cancer. Thus, there are a few differences that may be based on sexual preference; however, this is not the case in the incidence of most gynecological complaints: fibroid tumors, ovarian cancer, ovarian cysts, endometriosis, cystic breast disease, vaginitis, and urinary tract infections. Yet lesbians receive fewer gynecological services than other women who must seek medical care for birth control, treatment of sexually transmitted infections, and pregnancies.

While a lesbian identity does not preclude sexual activity for money or with men, lesbians often simply deny and ignore needs rather than submit to gynecologists. Often problems such as bad cramps, heavy periods, pain from endometriosis or fibroid tumors, or severe hot flashes during menopause go untreated. Lesbians skip Pap smears, breast exams, and mammograms, and, in omitting these key health care events, often receive no preventive health care services. Thus, they enter the health care system only during crisis.

Lesbians are as likely to want children as other women, but are less likely to act on these desires. External and internalized homophobic messages cast doubt on the appropriateness of raising children for all lesbians and gay men. Both public and private adoption agencies usually bar adoption for gay couples and singles. However, many lesbians are mothers, having born children during prior relationships with men. But many of these lesbians, once out of the marriage and out of the closet, have lost custody of their children.

Mental Health and Emotional Support

In terms of emotional well-being, many gays have experienced early rejection from family, peers, and co-workers because of their sexual orientation. Many young lesbians have been confined in mental hospitals or ordered to therapy by parents for the crime of engaging in same-sex relationships. Lesbians experience the same sexist violence as other women in the form of early sexual abuse, sexual harassment on the job, and rape, and they suffer from the added abuse of homophobic assaults in all forms—comments, threats, beatings, and sexual assault—as well. Lesbians are not exempt from violence within relationships either, but they are less able to seek and receive sensitive support, refuge, and crisis intervention when battering occurs. Several studies show a higher rate of alcoholism and drug abuse among gays.

The gay community offers support to lesbians but may not be a haven. Gay and lesbian community centers—when they exist at all—often have much male and little female leadership and programming. And most towns and cities have no lesbian projects at all—no twelve-step groups, social activities, or educational programs geared for lesbians. Bars are often the only place to connect with lesbians. Rural communities often have informal social networks, but, because they are small, tend to enforce conformity. Such networks also set unrealistic expectations to provide support to group members when illness or crises occur.

Lesbians and AIDS

Lesbians have worked as activists and service workers throughout the AIDS epidemic, yet there is still controversy over whether or not AIDS is a lesbian issue. Lesbians constitute a growing segment of those who are HIV-positive. Lesbians engage in risky behaviors, including sex with those at risk (both men and women) and unsafe use of needles. Lesbian AIDS Project researchers conducted a small study of lesbian intravenous drug users in San Francisco in 1987 and found that many of these women also engaged in other high-risk behaviors such as unprotected sex with men, sex in exchange for money or drugs, and unprotected sex with other women during their periods. Similarly, a study of lesbian sexual behavior conducted by the Kinsey Institute also in 1987 revealed that 45 percent of the 262 self-identified lesbians sampled had been sexually active with men since 1980. Despite this reality, lesbians' risk of disease is overlooked because of dangerous myths about their sexual behavior.

Among groups and organizations doing work on AIDS, research, education, and outreach for lesbians is all but nonexistent. A few projects exist, created by lesbians, that deal with issues relevant to lesbians with HIV/AIDS, and there are a few support groups for HIV-positive lesbians in some communities. The Lesbians' Educational AIDS Resource Network in Tampa, Florida, has the goal of providing a forum for HIV prevention in the lesbian and female bisexual communities. Groups of lesbians working in AIDS have formed to provide support and activities for lesbians involved in advocacy and service for people with AIDS and also to specifically address lesbian HIV issues.

An important link needs to be made between HIV/AIDS issues and drug use in the lesbian communities. At present, as noted, recovery programs and twelve-step meetings specifically for lesbians are few, but such groups are an important place for lesbians to get help with drinking and drug problems.

Lesbians and Cancer

The health focus for lesbians in the 1990s appears to be cancer. The leadership and involvement of lesbians in the women's cancer movement and its projects has been significant. Composed of networks of local cancer projects, these groups reflect the community's cumulative grief and anger at too many women dying with too little being done in areas of research and meaningful prevention. In 1990, 45,000 women died of breast cancer. At least 10 percent of these were lesbian, probably more, both because the number of lesbians in the general population is usually underestimated, and because of the increased risk of breast cancer in women who have never been pregnant.

Most other cancers and chronic and life-threatening illnesses affect gay and straight women with similar frequency, but they often affect lesbians in a different way than other women. The problems lesbians often confront in dealing with the health care system—lack of health insurance, resources for health care services, and community support, the invisibility of lesbians and hostility towards the ill person's partner—all surface with particular harshness at times of immense crisis—at diagnosis, during treatment, at death. Heartbreaking stories, such as that of Sharon Kowalski (see "The Fragile Rights of Sharon Kowalski," Spring 1989 issue) are commonplace in the lesbian community.

Cancer activism is an integral part of lesbian communities throughout the country. Several projects have formed to deal exclusively with lesbian cancer issues: the Chicago Lesbian Cancer Project, the Women's Cancer Resource Center in Oakland, California, and the Mary Helen Mautner Project for Lesbians with Cancer in Washington, DC. Lesbian cancer projects organize support groups and provide services such as transportation, child care, and housekeeping for sick lesbians in addition to outreach, education, and activism. But just as gay men cannot cope with the AIDS epidemic without external supports, lesbians cannot tend to each other adequately without leadership and initiative from the medical community, the government, and the community-based organizations.

Resources

Some resources have already been created to help lesbians deal with their health problems, although these are far too few and limited to meet the existing need. Among the published pamphlets, books, and other literature on lesbian health, the original prototype is the still-in-print *Lesbian Health Matters!* published and distributed by the Santa Cruz Women's Health Collective. *Our Bodies, Ourselves* has a chapter about lesbians, and several other books have been published by women's and gay presses (see end of article).

Some lesbian health projects have been developed over the years by various women's and gay groups. In the 1970s, feminist-run clinics such as the Santa Cruz Women's Health Center, the several Feminist Women's Health Centers, and the Cambridge Women's Health Center commonly set aside certain nights for lesbians. Although these "lesbians nights" smacked of segregation, they allowed an unprecedented level of individual attention to the health and sexuality concerns of gay women. Most of these clinics had a majority of lesbians in leadership roles, who frequently found themselves working on heterosexual issues while complaining about "not getting to our own issues," just as lesbians now debate the virtues of fighting AIDS along with gay men while perpetually relegating lesbian issues to the back burner. Many feminist clinics have foundered altogether in the recent climate of cutbacks and anti-abortion activism, and those that continue to function have fewer resources for special programs.

Other projects were developed in the 1980s, including the Lesbian Insemination Project, the Lesbian AIDS Project, the Lesbian Health Information Project in San Francisco and Lesbian Illness Support Group in New York.

Less than a handful of lesbian health clinics currently exist. At some, including the Lyon-Martin Clinic in San Francisco and the St. Marks Women's Clinic in New York City, many straight and bisexual women also receive health care. Others are gay/lesbian clinics, such as the Community Health Project in New York, Fenway Community Health Center in Boston, and Whitman Walker in Washington, DC. Lesbians working in these projects voice concern that gay men have always been better served, and that now AIDS programming has left scant resources to serve gay women, even gay women with AIDS.

New York City has an office on lesbian and gay health concerns that functions as a liaison between the lesbian and gay communities and the health service sector. The emphasis is on providing training and education to health professionals so that they can better serve the gay community. The office also provides technical assistance and support to community organizations and co-sponsored a conference on Lesbians and Life-Altering Illness in Fall 1991.

Research

There is little research on the health of lesbians and even less that would provide evidence of the kinds of changes needed in the health care system to appropriately address lesbians' needs within the health care system. One of the few surveys of health care experiences, attitudes, and needs of lesbians was undertaken by Judith Bradford and Caitlin Ryan in 1984 through the National Lesbian and Gay Health Foundation. This ambitious 104 question survey was answered by nearly 2,000 lesbians throughout the United States. Most of the respondents were white, college-educated professionals. Some principal findings from this study include the following:

- Fifty percent of the lesbians surveyed had not had a Pap smear in the previous 12 months, and many of the respondents were not receiving any care for existing gynecological problems.
- The most common health problem reported was depression.
- Most women felt unable to disclose their sexual preference to their usual health care provider—yet 80 percent reported experiencing discrimination based on their sexual identity.
- The most frequently reported concern regarding access to health care services was insufficient money; this was the primary reason cited for not seeking health care.
- Of the women who reported the experience of rape, only one-third ever sought help.
- Stress-related illnesses, including ulcers, allergies, and hypertension, were common among the lesbians responding.

The authors conclude that the data confirm that lesbians face many obstacles in negotiating the health care system, often do not receive important health care, and have health concerns in a variety of areas. They cite the need for further research and documentation in the areas of "discrimination, physical and sexual abuse, . . . the need for mental health services and the training of providers; the impact of outness/closetness on mental health, and access to non-discriminatory and informed services."

Other research into lesbian health needs has also been conducted by the gay and lesbian community. Small-scale, unpublished, and uncompleted research exists and is passed along within small circles of lesbians involved in health politics and clinical practice. Studies of breast cancer, HIV seroprevalence, psychological needs of lesbian couples, attitudes about sexuality, sexual transmission of vaginitis between women, and incidence of environmental illnesses in lesbians all exist in various stages of completion. This type of research is severely underfunded and underreported. Nevertheless, an informal network among lesbian activists, researchers, and clinicians passes along important findings and ideas. Funding and support for this type of work would bring important information into a more public forum.

Lesbian Health Agenda

Lesbians clearly experience health and illness differently from both gay men and heterosexual women, and their differing needs constitute a lesbian health agenda that must be articulated and made visible. The involvement and action of the health community would hasten the development and enactment of such an agenda. Identifying key issues and appropriate approaches by talking to lesbian leaders is imperative. Health planning agencies need to consult lesbian health experts to determine whether or not services are targeted to, reaching, and acceptable to lesbian clients. Slotting a seat for a lesbian on community advisory boards, medical committees, and planning boards would also be useful.

To begin work on lesbians' concerns in clinical settings, lesbians might be identified and rendered visible by asking relevant questions and using appropriate language on health forms. For example, terms such as sexual partner or significant other are non-threatening. Heterosexual presumption can be eliminated from history-taking, and lesbian-positive images and literature can be placed along with other educational materials in waiting rooms. Funding is needed immediately for lesbian programming, technical assistance, relevant educational materials, and advocacy. Among the issues on a lesbian health agenda that health professionals need to support are the following items that have already been identified.

Cancer is a serious concern of lesbians, claiming many lives and causing much disability and loss of productivity. Lesbian-informed research will continue to look for earlier detection methods and investigate both environmental and personal risk. Partners and children of lesbians who face serious illness or death need legal protection within the framework of lesbian families and relationships.

Childbearing and parenting is another primary concern for lesbians, whether single or coupled. Few sperm banks are receptive to lesbians, and discrimination hampers many lesbians' efforts to get pregnant. This often leads to informal insemination with semen from donors who are not screened for HIV and other sexually transmitted diseases. The pervasive discrimination against lesbians in custody proceedings also requires more supportive services and advocacy for lesbian families.

Drug and alcohol abuse is a high-priority issue within the lesbian community that requires research as well as community support. Lesbians and gay men cannot recover from addiction while in the closet and being bombarded with homophobic messages. Lesbians benefit tremendously from participating in lesbian recovery groups, but most communities have none.

Mental health services are a significant need in the gay community. Lesbians seek mental health services most often for depression. There is a growing body of writing and research on battering in lesbian relationships and on the effects of sexual assault and homophobic violence on lesbians. Rejection for early expression of lesbian sexuality and life-style may mark the beginning of a lifetime of alienation from family, teachers, old friends, and co-workers. The closet is a breeding ground for depression, anxiety, and physical complaints as well. Lesbians should be able to choose lesbian therapists, attend lesbian support groups, and be able to identify with a lesbian political action group.

Gynecology represents an area of dissatisfaction for almost all women. Gynecologists are still schooled in sexism. Women report being patronized, misinformed, lied to, and talked over and about in the third person. They suffer the abuses of unnecessary surgeries, sterilizations, and drug experimentation. Lesbians need lesbian-informed and sensitive obstetric and gynecological services in order to ever consider participating in the basic women's health care services.

Lesbians, like other women, are vulnerable to HIV infection and need to be rendered visible in the AIDS epidemic. A network of services, research, and support needs to be built that includes the lesbian experience of HIV/AIDS.

The time is long overdue for this agenda to be recognized and addressed by the medical community. Lesbians have contributed richly to progressive movements that have brought about changes in the health care system for heterosexual women, for gay men, and for other minority communities. We will continue to do that work, but lesbians' health needs must no longer be left off of the agenda as we fight for the changes that are so sorely needed in the health care system.

BOOKS ON LESBIAN HEALTH

The Advocate's Guide To Gay Health, Alyson Publishers 1982.

Alive and Well: A Lesbian Health Guide, by Hepburn and Gutirrez, Crossing Press, 1988.

Artificial Insemination: An Alternative Conception for the Lesbian and Gay Community, by the Lesbian Health Information Project. Order from San Francisco Women's Centers, 3548 18th Street, San Francisco, CA 94110.

Cancer as a Women's Issue, Edited by Midge Stocker, Third Side Press, 1991.

Cancer Journals, by Audre Lorde, Spinsters Ink.

Cancer in Two Voices, by Sandra Butler and Barbara Rosenblum, Spinsters Books, 1991.

Considering Parenthood: A Workbook for Lesbians, by Cheri Pies, Spinsters Books, 1985.

Lesbian Health Matters! by Santa Cruz Women's Health Collective, 1979. Write Santa Cruz Women's Health Center, 250 Locust Street, Santa Cruz, CA 95060.

Lesbian Psychologies, by Boston Lesbian Psychologies Collective, University of Illinois Press, 1987.

Lesbian Sex, by JoAnn Loulan, Spinsters Ink, 1984.

The Lesbian S/M Safety Manual, by Pat Califia, Lace Publications, 1988.

Naming the Violence: Speaking Out About Lesbian Battering, edited by Kerry Lobel, Seal Press, 1986.

The New Our Bodies, Ourselves, by the Boston Women's Book Collective, Simon and Schuster, 1992.

One in Three: Women with Cancer Confront an Epidemic, by Judith Brady, Cleis Press, 1991.

Out From Under: Sober Dykes and Their Friends, edited by Jean Swallow, Spinsters Ink, 1983.

Suzie Sexpert's Lesbian Sex World, by Suzie Bright, Cleis Press, 1990.

A New Politics of Sexuality

by June Jordan

As a young worried mother, I remember turning to Dr. Benjamin Spock's *Common Sense Book of Baby and Child Care* just about as often as I'd pick up the telephone. He was God. I was ignorant but striving to be good: a good Mother. And so it was there, in that bestseller pocketbook of do's and don't's, that I came upon this doozie of a guideline: Do not wear miniskirts or other provocative clothing because that will upset your child, especially if your child happens to be a boy. If you give your offspring "cause" to think of you as a sexual being, he will, at the least, become disturbed; you will derail the equilibrium of his notions about your possible identity and meaning in the world.

It had never occurred to me that anyone, especially my son, might look upon me as an asexual being. I had never supposed that "asexual" was some kind of positive designation I should, so to speak, lust after. I was pretty surprised by Dr. Spock. However, I was also, by habit, a creature of obedience. For a couple of weeks I actually experimented with lusterless colors and dowdy tops and bottoms, self-consciously hoping thereby to prove myself as a lusterless and dowdy and, therefore, excellent female parent.

Years would have to pass before I could recognize the familiar, by then, absurdity of a man setting himself up as the expert on a subject that presupposed women as the primary objects for his patriarchal discourse—on motherhood, no less! Years passed before I came to perceive the perversity of dominant power assumed by men, and the perversity of self-determining power ceded to men by women.

June Jordan writes for *The Progressive* every other month. This column was adapted from her keynote address to the Bisexual, Gay, and Lesbian Student Association at Stanford University on April 29, 1991.

A lot of years went by before I understood the dynamics of what anyone could summarize as the Politics of Sexuality.

I believe the Politics of Sexuality is the most ancient and probably the most profound arena for human conflict. Increasingly, it seems clear to me that deeper and more pervasive than any other oppression, than any other bitterly contested human domain, is the oppression of sexuality, the exploitation of the human domain of sexuality for power.

When I say sexuality, I mean gender: I mean male subjugation of human beings because they are female. When I say sexuality, I mean heterosexual institutionalization of rights and privileges denied to homosexual men and women. When I say sexuality I mean gay or lesbian contempt for bisexual modes of human relationship.

The Politics of Sexuality therefore subsumes all of the different ways in which some of us seek to dictate to others of us what we should do, what we should desire, what we should dream about, and how we should behave ourselves, generally, on the planet. From China to Iran, from Nigeria to Czechoslovakia, from Chile to California, the politics of sexuality—enforced by traditions of state-sanctioned violence plus religion and the law—reduces to male domination of women, heterosexist tyranny, and, among those of us who are in any case deemed despicable or deviant by the powerful, we find intolerance for those who choose a different, a more complicated—for example, an interracial or bisexual—mode of rebellion and freedom.

We must move out from the shadows of our collective subjugation—as people of color/as women/as gay/as lesbian/as bisexual human beings.

. . .

I can voice my ideas without hesitation or fear because I am speaking, finally, about myself. I am black and I am female and I am a mother and I am bisexual and I am a nationalist and I am an anti-nationalist. And I mean to be fully and freely all that I am!

Conversely, I do not accept that any white or black or Chinese man—I do not accept that, for instance, Dr. Spock—should presume to tell me, or any other woman, how to mother a child. He has no right. He is not a mother. My child is not his child. And, likewise, I do not accept that anyone—any woman or any man who is not inextricably part of the subject he or she dares to address—should attempt to tell any of us, the objects of her or his presumptuous discourse, what we should do or what we should not do.

Recently, I have come upon gratuitous and appalling pseudoliberal pronouncements on sexuality. Too often, these utterances fall out of the mouths of men and women who first disclaim any sentiment remotely related to homophobia, but who then proceed to issue outrageous opinions like the following.

That it is blasphemous to compare the oppression of gay, lesbian, or bisexual people to the oppression, say, of black people, or of the Palestinians.

That the bottom line about gay or lesbian or bisexual identity is that you can conceal it whenever necessary and, so, therefore, why don't you do just that? Why don't you keep your deviant sexuality in the closet and let the rest of us—we who suffer oppression for reasons of our ineradicable and always visible components of our personhood such as race or gender—get on with our more necessary, our more beleaguered struggle to survive?

Well, number one: I believe I have worked as hard as I could, and then harder than that, on behalf of equality and justice for African-Americans, for the Palestinian people, and for people of color everywhere.

And no, I do not believe it is blasphemous to compare oppressions of sexuality to oppressions of race and ethnicity: Freedom is indivisible or it is nothing at all besides sloganeering and temporary, short-sighted, and short-lived advancement for a few. Freedom is indivisible, and either we are working for freedom or you are working for the sake of your self-interests and I am working for mine.

If you can finally go to the bathroom, wherever you find one, if you can finally order a cup of coffee and drink it wherever coffee is available, but you cannot follow your heart—you cannot respect the response of your own honest body in the world—then how much of what kind of freedom does any one of us possess?

Or, conversely, if your heart and your honest body can be controlled by the state, or controlled by community taboo, are you not then, and in that case, no more than a slave ruled by outside force?

What tyranny could exceed a tyranny that dictates to the human heart, and that attempts to dictate the public career of an honest human body?

Freedom is indivisible; the Politics of Sexuality is not some optional "special-interest" concern for serious, progressive folk.

And, on another level, let me assure you: If every single gay or lesbian or bisexual man or woman active on the Left of American politics decided to stay home, there would be *no* Left left.

. . .

One of the things I want to propose is that we act on that reality: that we insistently demand reciprocal respect and concern from those who cheerfully depend upon our brains and our energies for their, and our, effective impact on the political landscape.

Last spring, at Berkeley, some students asked me to speak at a rally against racism. And I did. There were 400 or 500 people massed on Sproul Plaza, standing together against that evil. And, on the next day, on that same Plaza, there was a rally for bisexual and gay and lesbian rights, and students asked me to speak at that rally. And I did. There were fewer than seventy-five people stranded, pitiful, on that public space. And I said then what I say today: That was disgraceful! There should have been just one rally. One rally: Freedom is indivisible.

As for the second, nefarious pronouncement on sexuality that now enjoys mass-media currency: the idiot notion of keeping yourself in the closet—that is very much the same thing as the suggestion that black folks and Asian-Americans and Mexican-Americans should assimilate and become as "white" as possible—in our walk/talk/music/food/values—or else. Or else? Or else we should, deservedly, perish.

Sure enough, we have plenty of exposure to white everything so why would we opt to remain our African/Asian/Mexican selves? The answer is that suicide is absolute, and if you think you will survive by hiding who you really are, you are sadly misled: There is no such thing as partial or intermittent suicide. You can only survive if you—who you really are—do survive.

Likewise, we who are not men and we who are not heterosexual—we, sure enough, have plenty of exposure to male-dominated/heterosexist this and that.

But a struggle to survive cannot lead to suicide: Suicide is the opposite of survival. And so we must not conceal/assimilate/ integrate into the would-be dominant culture and political system that despises us. Our survival requires that we alter our environment so that we can live and so that we can hold each other's hands and so that we can kiss each other on the streets, and in the daylight of our existence, without terror and without violent and sometimes fatal reactions from the busybodies of America.

Finally, I need to speak on bisexuality. I do believe that the analogy is interracial or multiracial identity. I do believe that the analogy for bisexuality is a multicultural, multi-ethnic, multiracial world view. Bisexuality follows from such a perspective and leads to it, as well.

Just as there are many men and women in the United States whose parents have given them more than one racial, more than one ethnic identity and cultural heritage to honor; and just as these men and women must deny no given part of themselves except at the risk of self-deception and the insanities that must issue from that; and just as these men and women embody the principle of equality among races and ethnic communities; and just as these men and women falter and anguish and choose and then falter again and then anguish and then choose yet again how they will honor the irreducible complexity of their God-given human being—even so, there are many men and women, especially young men and women, who seek to embrace the complexity of their total, always-changing social and political circumstance.

They seek to embrace our increasing global complexity on the basis of the heart and on the basis of an honest human body. Not according to ideology. Not according to group pressure. Not according to anybody's concept of "correct."

This is a New Politics of Sexuality. And even as I despair of identity politics—because identity is given and principles of justice/equality/freedom cut across given gender and given racial definitions of being, and because I will call you my brother, I will call you my sister, on the basis of what you *do* for justice, what you *do* for equality, what you *do* for freedom and *not* on the basis of who you are, even so I look with admiration and respect upon the new, bisexual politics of sexuality.

This emerging movement politicizes the so-called middle ground: Bisexuality invalidates either/or formulation, either/or analysis. Bisexuality means I am free and I am as likely to want and to love a woman as I am likely to want and to love a man, and what about that? Isn't that what freedom implies?

If you are free you are not predictable and you are not controllable. To my mind, that is the keenly positive, politicizing significance of bisexual affirmation:

To insist upon complexity, to insist upon the validity of all of the components of social/sexual complexity, to insist upon the equal validity of all of the components of social/sexual complexity.

This seems to me a unifying, 1990s mandate for revolutionary Americans planning to make it into the Twenty-first Century on the basis of the heart, on the basis of an honest human body, consecrated to every struggle for justice, every struggle for equality, every struggle for freedom.

Radical Heterosexuality

by Naomi Wolf

All over the country, millions of feminists have a secret indulgence. By day they fight gender injustice; by night they sleep with men. Is this a dual life? A core contradiction? Is sleeping with a man "sleeping with the enemy"? And is razor burn from kissing inherently oppressive?

It's time to say you *can* hate sexism and love men. As the feminist movement grows more mature and our understanding of our enemies more nuanced, three terms assumed to be in contradiction—radical feminist heterosexuality—can and must be brought together.

Rules of the Relationship

But how? Andrea Dworkin and Catharine MacKinnon have pointed out that sexism limits women to such a degree that it's questionable whether the decision to live with a man can ever truly be free. If you want to use their sound, if depressing, reasoning to a brighter end, turn the thesis around: radical heterosexuality demands substituting choice for dependency.

Radical heterosexuality requires that the woman be able to support herself. This is not to belittle women who must depend financially on men; it is to recognize that when our daughters are raised with the skills that would let them leave abusers, they need not call financial dependence love.

Radical heterosexuality needs alternative institutions. As the child of a good lifetime union, I believe in them. But when I think of pledging my heart and body to a man—even the best and kindest man—within the existing institution of marriage, I feel faint. The more you learn about its legal structure, the less likely you are to call the caterers.

In the nineteenth century, when a judge ruled that a husband could not imprison and rape his wife, the London *Times* bemoaned, "One fine morning last month, marriage in England was suddenly abolished." The phrase "rule of thumb" descends from English common law that said a man could legally beat his wife with a switch "no thicker than his thumb."

If these nightmarish echoes were confined to history, I might feel more nuptial; but look at our own time. Do I want the blessing of an institution that doesn't provide adequate protection from marital rape? That gives a woman less protection from assault by her husband than by a stranger? That assigns men 70 percent of contested child custodies?

Of course I do not fear any such brutality from the man I want to marry (no bride does). But marriage means that his respectful treatment of me and our children becomes, despite our intentions, a kindness rather than a legally grounded right.

We need a heterosexual version of the marriages that gay and lesbian activists are seeking: a commitment untainted by centuries of inequality; a ritual that invites the community to rejoice in the making of a new freely chosen family.

The radical heterosexual man must yield the automatic benefits conferred by gender. I had a lover once who did not want to give up playing sports in a club that had a separate door for women. It must be tempting to imagine you can have both—great squash courts *and* the bed of a liberated woman—but in the mess hall of gender relations, there is *no such thing as a free lunch.*

Radical heterosexual women too must give up gender benefits (such as they are). I know scores of women—independent, autonomous—who avoid assuming any of the risk for a romantic or sexual approach.

From *Ms. Magazine,* July, August 1992, pp. 29–31. Copyright © 1992 by Ms. Magazine. Reprinted by permission.

Naomi Wolf's book "The Beauty Myth" is available in Anchor Books paperback. She has written on feminist issues for "Esquire," "The New Republic," and "The Wall Street Journal," and speaks to college audiences on feminism.

I have watched myself stand complacently by while my partner wrestles with a stuck window, an intractable computer printer, maps, or locks. Sisters, I am not proud of this, and I'm working on it. But people are lazy—or at least I am—and it's easy to rationalize that the person with the penis is the one who should get out of a warm bed to fix the snow on the TV screen. After all, it's the very least owed to me *personally* in compensation for centuries of virtual enslavement.

Radical heterosexuals must try to stay conscious— at all times, I'm afraid—of their gender imprinting, and how it plays out in their erotic melodramas. My own psyche is a flagrant *son et lumière* of political incorrectness. Three of my boyfriends had motorcycles; I am easy pickings for the silent and dysfunctional. My roving eye is so taken by the oil-stained persona of the labor organizer that myopic intellectuals have gained access to my favors merely by sporting a Trotsky button.

We feminists are hard on each other for admitting to weakness. Gloria Steinem caught flak from her left-wing sisters for acknowledging in *Revolution from Within* that she was drawn to a man because he could do the things with money and power that we are taught men must do. And some were appalled when Simone de Beauvoir's letter revealed how she coddled Sartre.

But the antifeminist erotic template is *in* us. We would not be citizens of this culture if swooning damsels and abandoned vixens had not been beamed at us from our first solid food to our first vote. We can't fight it until we admit to it. And we can't identify it until we drag it, its taffeta billowing and its bosom heaving, into the light of day.

I have done embarrassing, reactionary, abject deeds out of love and sexual passion. So, no doubt, has Norman Schwarzkopf. Only when we reveal our conditioning can we tell how much of our self-abasement is neurotic femininity, and how much is the flawed but impressive human apparatus of love.

In the Bedroom

Those are the conditions for the radical heterosexual couple. What might this new creation look like in bed? It will look like something we have no words or images for—the eroticization of consent, the equal primacy of female and male desire.

We will need to tell some secrets—to map our desire for the male body and admit to our fascination with the rhythms and forces of male arousal, its uncanny counterintuitive spell.

We will also need to face our creature qualities. Animality has for so long been used against us—bitch, fox, *Penthouse* pet—that we struggle for the merit badges of higher rationality, ambivalent about our animal nature.

The truth is that heterosexual women believe that men, on some level, are animals; as they believe that we are animals. But what does "animal" mean?

Racism and sexism have long used animal metaphors to distance and degrade the Other. Let us redefine "animal" to make room for that otherness between the genders, an otherness fierce and worthy of respect. Let us define animal as an inchoate kinship, a comradeship, that finds a language beyond our species.

I want the love of two unlikes: the look of astonishment a woman has at the sight of a male back bending. These manifestations of difference confirm in heterosexuals the beauty that similarity confirms in the lesbian or gay imagination. Difference and animality do not have to mean hierarchy.

Men We Love

What must the men be like? Obviously, they're not going to be just anyone. *Esquire* runs infantile disquisitions on "Women We Love" (suggesting, Lucky Girls!). Well, I think that the men who are loved by feminists are lucky. Here's how they qualify to join this fortunate club.

Men We Love understand that, no matter how similar our backgrounds, we are engaged in a cross-cultural (if not practically biracial) relationship. They know that we know much about their world and they but little of ours. They accept what white people must accept in relationships with people of other ethnicities: to know that they do not know.

Men We Love don't hold a baby as if it is a still-squirming, unidentifiable catch from the sea.

Men We Love don't tell women what to feel about sexism. (There's a postcard that shows a dashing young fellow, drawn Love-comix-style, saying to a woman, "Let me explicate to you the nature of your oppression.") They do not presume that there is a line in the sand called "enlightened male," and that all they need is a paperback copy of Djuna Barnes and good digital technique. They understand that unlearning gender oppressiveness means untying the very core of how we become female and male. They know this pursuit takes a lifetime at the minimum.

Sadly, men in our lives sometime come through on personal feminism but balk at it intellectually. A year ago, I had a bruising debate with my father and brother about the patriarchal nature of traditional religious and literary canons. I almost seized them by their collars, howling "Read Mary Daly! Read Toni Morrison! Take Feminism 101. *No, I can't* explain it to you between the entrée and dessert!"

By spring, my dad, bless his heart, had asked for a bibliography, and last week my brother sent me *Standing*

Again at Sinai, a Jewish-feminist classic. Men We Love are willing, sooner or later, to read the Books We Love.

Men We Love accept that successful training in manhood makes them blind to phenomena that are fact to women. Recently, I walked down a New York City avenue with a woman friend, X, and a man friend, Y. I pointed out to Y the leers, hisses, and invitations to sit on faces. Each woman saw clearly what the other woman saw, but Y was baffled. Sexual harassers have superb timing. A passerby makes kissy-noises with his tongue while Y is scrutinizing the menu of the nearest bistro. "There, there! Look! Listen!" we cried. "What? Where? Who?" wailed poor Y, valiantly, uselessly spinning.

What if, hard as they try to see, they cannot hear? Once I was at lunch with a renowned male crusader for the First Amendment. Another Alpha male was present, and the venue was the Supreme Court lunchroom—two power factors that automatically press the "mute" button on the male ability to detect a female voice on the audioscope. The two men began to rev their motors; soon they were off and racing in a policy-wonk grand prix. I tried, once or twice, to ask questions. But the free-speech champions couldn't hear me over the testosterone roar.

Men We Love undertake half the care and cost of contraception. They realize that it's not fair to wallow in the fun without sharing the responsibility. When stocking up for long weekends, they brave the amused glances when they ask, "Do you have this in unscented?"

Men We Love know that just because we can be irrational doesn't mean we're insane. When we burst into premenstrual tears—having just realized the cosmic fragility of creation—they comfort us. Not until we feel better do they dare remind us gently that we had this same revelation exactly 28 days ago.

Men We Love must make a leap of imagination to believe in the female experience. They do not call women nags or paranoid when we embark on the arduous, often boring, nonnegotiable daily chore of drawing attention to sexism. They treat it like adults taking driving lessons: if irked in the short term at being treated like babies, they're grateful in the long term that someone is willing to teach them patiently how to move through the world without harming the pedestrians. Men We Love don't drive without their gender glasses on.

A Place for Them

It's not simple gender that pits Us against Them. In the fight against sexism, it's those who are for us versus those who are against us—of either gender.

When I was 16, my boyfriend came with me to hear Andrea Dworkin speak. While hearing great feminist oratory in a sea of furious women changed my life, it nearly ended my boyfriend's: he barely escaped being drawn and quartered.

It is time to direct our anger more acutely at the Men We Hate—like George Bush—and give the Men We Love something useful to do. Not to take over meetings, or to set agendas; not to whine, "Why can't feminists teach us how to be free?" but to add their bodies, their hearts, and their numbers, to support us.

I meet many young men who are brought to feminism by love for a woman who has been raped, or by watching their single mothers struggle against great odds, or by simple common sense. Their most frequent question is, "What can I do to help?"

Imagine a rear battalion of committed "Men Against Violence Against Women" (or Men for Choice, or what have you)—of all races, ages, and classes. Wouldn't that be a fine sight to fix in the eyes of a five-year-old boy?

Finally, the place to make room for radical feminist heterosexuality is within our heads. If the movement that I dearly love has a flaw, it is a tendency toward orthodoxies about other women's pleasures and needs. This impulse is historically understandable: in the past, we needed to define ourselves against men if we were to define ourselves at all. But today, the most revolutionary choice we can make is to affirm other women's choices, whether lesbian or straight, bisexual or celibate.

NOW President Patricia Ireland speaks for me even though our sexual lives are not identical. Simone de Beauvoir speaks for me even though our sexual lives are not identical. Audre Lorde speaks for me even though our sexual lives are not identical. Is it the chromosomes of your lovers that establish you as a feminist? Or is it the life you make out of the love you make?

Response to Naomi Wolf's "Radical Heterosexuality"

— by Laura McEnaney

I never thought about heterosexuality as anything but sexual behavior until I got to college. I took a women's studies course my freshman year, and my teacher introduced the term "sexual politics" to me. I resisted thinking about sexuality as political—I couldn't connect what I understood as "political," (elections, the presidency, etc.) with heterosexuality. And I was disturbed that my teacher had stirred up self-doubt and curiosity about something I thought was completely "natural." Now, ten years later, I cannot see sexuality as anything but political. As a graduate student, I have had the privilege of reading about heterosexuality from a historical perspective. As a teacher, I have listened to the viewpoints of many undergraduates—male and female—as they have grappled with their experiences of heterosexuality in the 1980s and 1990s. As a feminist, I have spent many hours trying to understand how feminist insights have challenged and changed this sexual identity. And as someone who identifies as heterosexual and has been in a number of relationships with men—who have ranged from feminist to sexist to anti-feminist—I have long grappled with the question posed by Naomi Wolf: "how to love a man and save your feminist soul." So, I am happy to see that Wolf has created another forum to define and debate heterosexuality as a political concept. Still, I find myself quite disturbed by her article. I have no real answers about the dilemma Wolf describes, but I am troubled by some of her depictions of feminism and by her vision of what is radical and possible for contemporary heterosexual relations.

First, I want to agree with some of Wolf's observations. I am pleased that she demands we take a more critical, less romantic look at marriage. I like the idea of celebrating freely chosen families. I agree with her argument that gender struggles do not follow neat biological categories—that women's problems cannot be explained exclusively as a battle of women versus men. The political struggles of the last twenty years have

shown us that women can be anti-feminists and men can be feminists—and many other confusing variations on the political continuum. And I like her assertion that men must make a concerted effort to see sexism in all of its guises, and that they should "add their bodies, their hearts, and their numbers" to support women's causes. These are all important components of any feminist program that attempts to remap heterosexual relations.

Yet, I am uncomfortable with many of Wolf's assertions, as well as with the overall tone of her article. First, I depart from Wolf in my understanding of what feminism has offered to women as they have struggled to find sexual identities that feel comfortable for them. Like so many other contemporary journalists, Wolf implies that the feminist movement has taken the pleasure out of heterosexual romance and ritual. She suggests that feminism has diminished women's erotic agency, and that pure "animal" sex has been replaced by political correctness. Feminism's flaw, she says, "is a tendency toward orthodoxies about other women's pleasures and needs." She uses Andrea Dworkin, in particular, as the icon of an angry, man-hating, anti-heterosexual feminism that can chew up sympathetic boyfriends at public lectures. Now that feminism has become "more mature," she says, "it's time" to challenge the ideological purity of a movement that dictated, instead of liberated, women's sexual choices.

I am confused by this. One of the chief contributions of feminist movements has been the insistence that women have a right to sexual pleasure on their own terms. Sexual liberation has always been a central tenet of second-wave women's movements. An enormous body of feminist literature has documented the diversity and variety of female sexualities. *Our Bodies, Ourselves* is the culmination of over two decades of feminist thinking and debate about sex. It is a classic feminist text that affirms women as sexual beings and offers them a very expansive, non-judgmental definition of female sexuality. Feminist movements have made women's claims to an enjoyable sex life a sign of health, not deviance, and the scores of self-help books and talk shows that encourage female pleasure attest to feminism's mainstream success in reclaiming the bedroom (and other space!) for women.

Strangely, Wolf does not acknowledge the rich history of spirited debate about sexuality within feminisms. Nor does she mention the enormous diversity of opinion about sexual politics among contemporary feminists. Instead, she suggests that feminists are a sexual monolith, disciples of a sexual-political correctness. Gloria Steinem "caught flak" from some feminists not, as Wolf says, for her sexual fantasies, but for her recent emphasis on creating "revolution from within," a frightening departure for some second-wave feminists who are still invested in fighting for equality at structural levels. I don't agree with much of what Andrea Dworkin says about sexuality, but Wolf's depiction of her (and her followers) as a force that could "draw and quarter" men is a classic stereotyping of women who speak angrily about sexism. And why does she choose Dworkin and Catharine MacKinnon as "the feminists" to argue with? Is it because they—especially Dworkin—represent the most extreme example of female anger about the violence and powerlessness so many women have experienced in their heterosexual relationships? I wish that Wolf would have at least acknowledged some of the terrific radical thinking about heterosexuality by other feminists, such as Ellen Willis, who share Dworkin's anger about inequality, but offer different possibilities for heterosexual relations. When Wolf says, "It's time to say you *can* hate sexism and love men," she implies that she is one of the first to think through this dilemma—that as a representative of younger women who didn't fight the battles of the sixties, she can bring a fresh, more ideologically fluid perspective to this issue. She makes invisible all of the radical heterosexual women who have played key roles in women's movement activism around sexuality. And she doesn't give enough credit to feminist movements for creating the space for debate about heterosexuality. In fact, she and I wouldn't be having this printed conversation if it weren't for feminism.

I am growing weary of women like Wolf (Katie Roiphe and Karen Lehrman included) who blame feminism for ruining the romance of heterosexuality. And it worries me that this notion carries so much weight in the mainstream media. Recent episodes of "Beverly Hills 90210" and "Picket Fences," for example, have suggested that feminists have gone too far in politicizing the bedroom. I think if there are any feminist orthodoxies about sex (which I don't believe there are), they might be that women must have the right to define their own sexual identities, and that inequality between men and

women makes it imperative that women understand sex as a political category. What's constricting or orthodox about this? These feminist tenets seem to *open,* not foreclose, sexual possibilities for women. Men and women do not enter a relationship as equals in society, so why shouldn't heterosexuals interested in forging equality in their relationship examine the ways in which sex, itself, is part of the larger struggle for gender equity? In fact, I think exposing how sexism shapes heterosexual relationships has the potential to make sexual relations *more,* not less, satisfying; it frees *both* men and women to challenge repressive gender expectations so that they can experience fully their relational and erotic desires. I think Wolf sometimes confuses feminist critiques of heterosexuality, which have always focused on liberation, with the mainstream media's anxious and inaccurate translation of those critiques.

I am also frustrated by the political program Wolf offers women who identify as heterosexual: out of bed, men's reeducation and making good choices; in bed, a reclaiming of the "animal." First, out of bed. Wolf is very optimistic about the possibility of raising men's consciousness about sex discrimination. Her stories of fighting with male family members, men's blindness to street harassment, and male domination of conversation are all painfully familiar to women. The story of her father and brother eventually acknowledging her feminist viewpoints tells us that men can "get it." Women and men, she argues, should be partners in the task of men's reeducation. Men shouldn't expect women to do all of the work for them, but women should direct their anger at the men they hate (nasty politicians), and "give the Men (They) Love something useful to do."

So, what's wrong with this? I'm not sure I see Wolf asking men in any concrete way to concede power. It seems like she is asking men to tolerate women more than she is demanding that they share power with them. Sharing contraception, lovingly accepting women's "irrational" premenstrual emotions, and listening to women's "often boring" chore of complaining about sexism seems to be about as radical as Wolf's vision gets. Why do women have to settle for men's understanding? Why can't women demand changes in behavior, concessions about the household division of labor, and power-sharing in and out of the bedroom? Conventional sex roles within heterosexual relationships have amazing resilience, and I think Wolf underestimates the staying power—and comfort—of those conventions. It is much easier to be angry at George Bush (what have you got to lose?) than it is to confront power differentials with the person you sleep with. Wolf suggests that men unlearn sexism, but she is unwilling to spell out exactly what that means for heterosexual relations. Who will be the tutors for these men? When a man has not yet unlearned his sexism and refuses to wear a condom, what then does his partner do? Where are the institutional and psychological supports for a man to unlearn sexism? What if "the men we love" don't change? I am all for consciousness-raising, but it can function as only one part of a much larger political movement that attacks the economic and cultural roots of men's dominance over women.

In bed, Wolf offers heterosexual women "the equal primacy of female and male desire" and a redefinition of "the animal." Well, feminism has already claimed for women the right to desire and fantasize, and I, again, state it's important for Wolf to credit feminism for this. As for her call for women to face their "creature qualities" and to "define animal as an inchoate kinship, a comradeship, that finds a language beyond our species," I am not sure I understand her meaning. What are women's "creature qualities"? Something "natural" or biologically ordained? A person's desire is shaped by the culture; there is nothing biological abut the fact that our culture finds thin blonde white women the most desirous. And how can reclaiming "our animal nature" help women? Why does Wolf accept the term "animal" for men and women at all? As she points out, this term is a by-product of racism and sexism. I think it is naive to reclaim the "animal" in a society where the term is still used so derisively against women—especially women of color. Redefining "the animal" as a program of heterosexual liberation is a political fantasy and a slippery slope. It assumes women have enough political power in society to mediate how "animal" will be redefined, and it embraces dangerous pre-feminist notions that ascribed male domination and women's supposed passionlessness to hormones. Wolf could have simply called for the continuation of feminist criticism of conventional heterosexuality, emphasizing the importance of women reclaiming the erotic, however they want to define it.

I envision a different kind of radical heterosexuality than Wolf. A radical heterosexuality challenges the notion of a fixed, biologically-determined sexual identity. In other words, radical heterosexuality challenges itself. Radical heterosexuals think about heterosexuality as part of a sexual continuum that includes bisexual and homosexual fantasizing and activity. Politically, it is not enough to define radical heterosexuality as a way to reeducate a boyfriend and make sex more enjoyable for women. We need to complicate the very idea of "heterosexuality" in a way that exposes how it can reinforce conventional gender roles and foreclose opportunities for us to explore sexual aspects of ourselves that don't follow neat and supposedly biologically-determined categories of "gay" and "straight." This is controversial, I know. Some believe that sexuality is genetically determined. But radical heterosexuality should offer women a way of honestly questioning how one's sexual desires

and relationships are constructed by a larger culture that is extremely uncomfortable with bi- or homosexuality.

I also think radical heterosexuality should involve an investment in building and maintaining friendships. Most of us have had the experience of either being "dropped" by a woman friend who begins a relationship, or ourselves have neglected friends as we have entered new relationships. It is a challenge to maintain friendships while we are in relationships because there is very little encouragement to do so. The contemporary notion of romantic love suggests that women (and men) can find all of their emotional fulfillment in one person— their partner/spouse. Friends are important, but are sidelined somewhat, because "the relationship" takes precedence. I think a radical heterosexuality should challenge this cultural script and blur the lines between friendship and relationship. This is not to say that relationships and friendships are or should be exactly the same; sex complicates things tremendously. But I think a radical heterosexuality should offer a better awareness about the privileging of sexual relationships at the cost of building and sustaining other friendships.

Finally, radical heterosexuality should be about, at the very least, the exposure and active challenging of heterosexual privilege. Heterosexuality is rewarded in so many invisible ways in this society—marriage and its attendant economic benefits being one of the most obvious illustrations of this. Radical heterosexuals should make themselves aware of the privileges they enjoy just for identifying as heterosexual: public displays of affection, a basic level of family approval for partner choice, and health benefits, to name only a few. This is not an exercise in liberal guilt, but an act of consciousness raising to alert people to the power they have—whether they want it or not—because of their sexual identity. Radical heterosexuality offers heterosexuals a way to openly criticize that power and a way to act against it or simply retreat from using it. It also provides an understanding of the kind of oppression that "non-heterosexuals" are bound to experience because of their sexual identities. Radical heterosexuality must always be a sexual identity engaged in fighting homophobia and heterosexual privilege, otherwise it becomes only a utopian celebration of itself.

I have previously offered some of these views as a speaker on the Women's Studies 103 sexuality panel, and some students have responded by saying I am not a "real heterosexual." I can imagine some people reading my response and thinking I am overly pessimistic, bitter, and too much of a "PC-feminist." I offer these views as an optimistic contribution to the spirited debate about sexuality that has always characterized feminism. I think pushing ourselves to question every fixed category with presumed "natural" origins is liberating, not politically stifling. It frees us from gender conventions, from being suspect for knowing our desires don't follow clear, predetermined categories, and from regulating ourselves—or being forced to live with the sexual regulation of others. No, I am not as optimistic as Wolf about the future of heterosexual relations, and I find her agenda lacking in anger, radical imagination, and concrete political meaning. But I am not pessimistic either. I think forging an equal relationship with a man is hard work, but possible. Instead of criticizing feminism for making heterosexuality less enjoyable, I credit it for creating more options for men and women in relationships. Without a feminist critique of heterosexuality, the hard work of building equality on the micro and macro level would be impossible between women and men.

WORKSHEET—CHAPTER 8

Sexuality

This worksheet should be optional. It asks personal questions which no one should be required to answer.

I. Sexual Preference

Society, parents, and friends give very clear messages about who one should relate to sexually, how and when! We are all aware that we are "breaking the rules" if we are sexually involved with someone of the "wrong" age, the "wrong" color, the "wrong" social status, or the "wrong" sex.

Heterosexism is so prevalent that most heterosexuals never think about why they relate sexually to the opposite sex. Imagine a mother asking her 18 year old daughter to explain why she is going out with men instead of women. But most lesbians and bisexuals have had to think through, question, and explain their choices.

Answer the following questions for yourself. Ask friends who would identify their sexual preference (or situation) as different from yours (lesbian—bisexual—celibate—heterosexual—virgin) to answer the same set of questions.

A. Briefly describe your present lifestyle and your sexual identity.

B. Describe how you made this choice about your sexuality. (Was it a gradual evolution or a sudden awareness? Has your sexuality changed or stayed the same since your first sexual identity? What factors have influenced this?)

C. Do you have a sexual partner or partners now? Would your sexual identity be the same if you did not have a partner/partners?

D. In what specific ways do you consciously work towards a balance of power in your relationship? How equal is your relationship sexually?

E. How does your sexual relationship/identity affect your relationships with friends, both men and women, with whom you are not having a sexual relationship?

F. How does your sexuality affect your choices regarding children?

G. The women's movement has emphasized that "the personal is political": the decisions we make in our personal lives and the way we live our lives are political issues. How do you see "the personal being political" relating to your sexuality and your sexual choices?

H. Do you feel there is such a thing as "heterosexual privilege"? If so, how does this affect your life?

II. Kegel Exercises

The pubococcygeus (P.C.) muscle supports the walls of the vagina, the urethra and rectum. Good, strong P.C. muscles can be important for childbirth, preventing stress incontinence (loss of urine when coughing or sneezing), and can enhance sexual enjoyment.

Kegel exercises (developed by Dr. Arnold Kegel) are designed to strengthen the P.C. muscle. Unlike most exercises, no special clothes, gyms, etc., are required. These exercises can be done anywhere and no one else will even know you are doing them.

A. Find your P.C. muscle. When you are urinating, stop the flow of urine in midstream. The muscle you do this with is your pubococcygeus muscle and is the muscle you want to strengthen.

B. Examples of Kegel Exercises:

Flicks—Do a series of contractions as rapidly as possible. It has been suggested that one does this in time to the car's turn signals.

Squeeze and hold for as long as possible, trying to work up to holding for 8–10 seconds.

Take a slow, deep breath, squeezing the P.C. muscle as you are breathing in. Pretend you are slowly drawing something into your vagina.

CHAPTER 9

Fertility, Infertility and Reproductive Rights/Freedom*

*R*eal reproductive rights would mean that a woman is able to choose when, whether, and under what conditions to have children, how many children to have, and to assume that she and her children would survive (and thrive) during pregnancy, childbirth, and the post-partum periods. What kind of health system would truly allow *all* women to have healthy babies, healthy children, and healthy families? What other societal changes need to happen for women to be able to make their own "choices" not to have children or to have the number of children they want?

Too often the media, and maybe even the movements themselves, have promoted the image that the struggle for reproductive rights is about abortion and contraceptive issues. Certainly access to affordable, safe contraception, with affordable, safe abortion as a back-up, is an essential part of women being able to control their bodies and their lives, but many other issues are also part of the bigger picture of what reproductive rights and reproductive freedom* really mean.

Building on the work of the Black Women's Health Project and African-American Women for Reproductive Rights (see *The Black Women's Health Book*), other women of color groups have been actively organizing around and clearly articulating that an agenda for reproductive rights must be much more broadly defined to include many other issues central to their lives. The articles, "Empowerment Through Dialogue: Native American Women Hold Historic Meeting, "For Native Women Reproductive Rights Mean:" and "Latinas for Reproductive Choice" summarize more inclusive, more culturally relevant definitions of reproductive freedom and provide examples of ways Native American women and Latinas are organizing around these issues.

"Women in Prison, Women in Danger: Reproductive Health Care Denied" talks about the literal barriers to health care, especially reproductive health care, for women in prison, which are almost always forgotten in debates about access to the health system and the privilege of being able to take care of one's own body. Having taught women's health courses in prison, we have become aware of the physical and mental health hazards which many women face in prison. We have been impressed

---

*Loretta Ross, a long-term women's health activist, uses the term reproductive rights in connection with the more white-dominated movements which have focused very much on abortion and contraceptive issues, and the term reproductive freedom for the organizations, with women of color leadership, which have worked on a much wider range of issues related to women's reproductive lives.

with how many women in prison, against all odds, were still trying to take care of health needs for themselves and their families—teaching each other yoga so they could find a healthy way to relieve stress in the confines of their cells, asking specific questions about contraceptives and STDs so they could share this information with their teenagers in the next phone call, trying to organize for an additional source of vitamin C so that, if they missed orange juice at breakfast, they had not missed the day's only vitamin C source. Seeing the physical bars which kept women in prison from taking care of their health issues was a thought-provoking reminder to us to be more aware of the less visible bars which keep millions of women from being able to maximize on their health, including reproductive health.

In working for a broader definition of reproductive rights which includes women being able to have as many children as they choose, we need to have an analysis of how the issue of infertility has been medicalized. High tech medicine certainly promises exciting possibilities for offering some women with infertility the possibility of producing a baby. In many cities, it is already routine to offer in vitro fertilization, bypassing blocked fallopian tubes, to many heterosexual women who happen to have an extra $5000 to try it. But, health activists have questioned who benefits, who makes money, and who is determining the priorities in the rapidly growing field of infertility technology? Why is all the research emphasis on finding expensive high technological solutions instead of looking at ways to prevent infertility (safer contraceptive methods, safer work and living environments) which could benefit far more people? Which women do and do not have access to infertility investigations and infertility treatments and should it be a goal to make these resources equally available to all women? Anne Woollett's moving personal diary (from a book by Pfeffer and Woollett) serves to remind us that there is much more to infertility than sophisticated medical technology: how does the health care system respond to many of the key issues of the experience of infertility (including the tests and treatments) which are related to self-image, sexuality, relationships and dreams for the future? Anne Woollett and Naomi Pfeffer have written an update to their 1983 book, especially for this book, to answer all the students who read Anne's diary and ask how the field of infertility has changed since the early 1980's and want to know what happened to the authors themselves after they wrote *The Experience of Infertility*. Both Dr. Anne Woollett and Dr. Naomi Pfeffer are very visible, much published women's health lecturers, working in London universities. In their update, they describe how infertility technology may have changed since 1983 but how many of the personal and social issues remain the same. Anne moves us on to having us share in her thinking of herself as "childless" rather than "infertile" and trying to disentangle what it means to be a "mother" and to be a "woman."

The article "Donor Egg Conception for Lesbian and Heterosexual Women" takes one very specific medical process for infertility to show how the science of medicine intersects with economic and social issues for different women.

We live in a reactionary climate where our access to safe, legal abortion is threatened or eroded by state decisions to restrict the availability of abortions. The "Shortage of Abortion Providers Fact Sheet" summarizes the ways the political climate has had an impact on the availability of medical personnel able to provide abortion services.

Working against the backlash to the few reproductive rights which we have won often takes so much of our energy that we do not take the time to discuss controversial and contradictory issues about abortion with other reproductive rights activists. The next three articles should be thought provoking enough to stimulate some healthy debates among friends or students who usually simply pride themselves on being "pro-choice." Both "Born and Unborn: The Implications of 'Choice' for People with Disabilities" and "The Bad Baby Blues—Reproductive Technology and the Threat to Diversity" ask us to remember that real choice must include the choice to have a child with disabilities and to look at how oppressive societal attitudes about disability impact on pregnant women facing prenatal screening. We might ask ourselves what the role of prenatal screening would be in a society where many of the societal "handicaps" of disability had been eliminated or minimized.

Connie S. Chan's "Reproductive Issues Are Essential Survival Issues for Asian American Communities" describes how she, as a middle-class, educated, bi-lingual Asian American, was unaware of the reproductive health issues of poor, non-English speaking immigrant women and what she learned as a translator. This article is a reminder of how easy it is not to understand what reproductive rights mean to another woman or groups of women; it begs us to think through the ramifications for poor women when health care benefits are not available to them because of their immigrant status or because Medicaid benefits will not cover abortion. At its most provocative level, this article asks us to think about the many ways the health system and society have failed a woman and her children when abortion becomes the only "choice" for basic survival for the members of a family unit.

The issues of who even gets to make decisions about contraception and sterilization and whether women have the information they need for informed decision-making are addressed in the next four articles. "Sterilization Abuse: The Policies Behind the Practice" presents a brief review of some of the history of sterilization abuse and the activism of Dr. Helen Rodriguez-Trias, the Committee to End Sterilization Abuse, and many others to gain more reproductive freedom for women. Because of the "success" of organizing and educating against sterilization abuse, such abuse is now more subtle and much harder to document or count. In many ways, the sterilization abuse issues of the 1960's and 1970's have been updated into 1990's controversies related to the abuse of long-term contraception, particularly Norplant. In their "Norplant Information Sheet" questioning the safety and use of Norplant for women on welfare, immigrant women, and women of color, the National Latina Health Organization states, "We are not being paranoid when we question the ethics of Norplant. We have been victims of selective reproductive control before. The forced sterilization of Latinas and other women of color was blatant and widespread until the class action suit against U.S.C.-Los Angeles County Medical Center in 1975. "The Misuses of Norplant: Who Gets Stuck?H acknowledges that many women are very satisfied with Norplant. However, this article further looks at how many low income women and women of color have had Norplant "pushed" on them without adequate information or choice and at the physical, financial, and political problems of women's being able to have the five-year implants removed if they want to.

The seemingly apolitical article from the *FDA Consumer,* "'The Pill' May Not Mix Well with Other Drugs," raises very worrying questions about the politics of information when the reader realizes that very basic information with life-changing ramifications, "certain drugs many decrease the effectiveness of your contraceptive or your contraceptive may alter the way your body responds to other medications," is not available to many women choosing to use the contraceptive pill.

Another major political question is why are "reproductive rights" so much seen as issues for women? If we lived in a more egalitarian society or if men shared equally in the responsibility for childcare, how would that affect *all* reproductive rights and health issues? Why has almost all of reproductive research focused on finding ways to interfere with a woman's body to prevent pregnancy or understanding how a pregnant woman's environment affects fetal health? Do you think we would see more articles and research like "Eight New Nonhormonal Contraceptives Methods for Men" if more women had the power to help determine reproductive health research priorities?

Empowerment Through Dialogue:
Native American Women Hold Historic Meeting

by Donna Haukaas

Ten years ago, a young Indian woman on the Pine Ridge Indian Reservation went to the local Indian Health Service hospital and sought advice on birth control. The doctors prescribed Provera, the pill form of Depo-Provera, a drug known for its cancer-causing properties. Last year, the woman was diagnosed as having cervical cancer. She said she was never told of the drug's possible side effects by hospital staff. Ever since, this woman has blamed herself, until she went to a very important conference where she met other Indian women with similar stories and realized she was not alone.

The conference, "Empowerment Through Dialogue: Native American Women & Reproductive Rights" held in Pierre, South Dakota, was the first time ever Indian women have participated in a reproductive rights conference planned by and for Native American women. More than 30 women representing 11 tribes from South Dakota and North Dakota attended this three-day conference which was co-sponsored by the Women of Color Partnership Program of the Religious Coalition for Abortion Rights of Washington, D.C. and the Native American Women's Health Education Resource Center of Lake Andes, South Dakota.

"The purpose of the conference (is) to bring together women from across South Dakota in a collective decision-making process to recommend an agenda for Native American women's reproductive rights," said Charon Asetoyer, Executive Director of the Native American Women's Health Education Resource Center (NAWHERC). "Our reproductive rights are much broader than abortion."

Sabrae Jenkins, Director of RCAR's Women of Color Partnership Program, gave a national overview of reproductive rights and women of color. "We, as women of color, cannot afford to look at the issue of abortion in a vacuum like middle-class white women; we have too many other things to deal with," said Jenkins. "The issue of choosing when, if, where and how to have a child is tied to access to education, housing, employment, health care and child care.

"Then you bring in the issues of racism, women of color's disproportionate low-income status and sexism—we are at the bottom of the rung." she said.

Mary Louise Defender, a member of the Standing Rock Tribe of North Dakota, addressed "The Reproductive History and Tradition Within the Native American Community" from the perspective that for Indian women the past and present are tied to the future. She talked about how elders would teach the young girls about menstruation and the meaning behind it as well as child spacing. "There were ladies who would tell you how not to have a child, but this was not to be used to sleep around" she said.

"The coming generation depends on no one but we women. Our role models should be those grandmas from generations ago who took no guff. Somewhere along the way our women became a little bit shy. But we need to remember those grandmas, and think of how they were and how they would take control and do it," said Defender.

Karen Artichoker of the South Dakota Coalition for Sexual Assault and Domestic Violence spoke on "The Status of Native American Women in South Dakota." From her many travels around the state, Artichoker relayed a dismal picture to the women regarding high unemployment, the horrendous health conditions of Indian families and alcoholism.

During the second day, Charon Asetoyer discussed "Reproductive Technologies and Concerns for Native American Women" where the participants were made

From *Common Ground—Different Planes,* July 1990, pp. 1 and 5. Copyright © 1990 by The Women of Color Partnership Program of the Religious Coalition for Reproductive Choice. Reprinted by permission.

Donna Haukaas is a Lakota Indian and a writer for the Rosebud Reservation Newsservice. A domestic violence activist, Ms. Haukaas was a conference participant.

aware of the new technologies like RU-486 and Norplant as well as Depo Provera and forced sterilization. She also addressed "Choices After Conception" which included abortion, fetal alcohol syndrome, and prenatal care.

"In South Dakota only 37% of pregnant Indian women receive regular prenatal care compared to 64% of white women. Consequently, the South Dakota non-white population which is 90% Native American has one of the highest infant mortality rates in the country at 27.5 deaths per 1,000 live births" stated Asetoyer.

Brenda Hill closed out the second day of speakers with a frank presentation on "The Impact of Domestic Violence & Sexual Abuse on Reproductive Rights." She told the audience that the violation of reproductive rights is directly linked to sexual assault and domestic violence.

Brenda made the conference participants clearly aware of the high rates of violence which currently exist within the Indian community and why it occurs. While Native Americans only make up 6.25% of the total population of South Dakota, 50% of all domestic abuse cases occur within the Native American Community.

"We have the right to comprehensive, culturally-relevant health care that recognizes and prioritizes the safety issues of battered women and children, and that each woman has the courage to take personal responsibility to say 'violence against women is not right,'" said

Tillie Black Bear of St. Francis, South Dakota and Chair of the National Coalition Against Domestic Violence.

"We have a right to come together as sisters. This includes a recognition that we are all doing the best we can at the present time, given our own oppression and internalized oppression," said Black Bear.

During the third and final day of the conference, the participants reflected on all the discussion of the previous days within small groups. Utilizing the African American Women for Reproductive Rights manifesto as a model, the women came back to the conference body with items which should be included in a reproductive rights agenda for Native American women and formed a committee to write a narrative explaining their support for reproductive rights as well as to integrate the agenda items from the small groups into one.

The participants said they were encouraged by the conference and felt inspired to pursue a broad agenda in the next year that would aid women in taking greater control over their lives. As the conference came to a close, these women discussed a specific desire to organize a coalition where the information sharing started at the conference could continue and where they could collectively fight for reproductive health care changes within their own communities.

For Native Women Reproductive Rights Mean . . .

by Native Women for Reproductive Rights Coalition

1. The right to knowledge and education for all family members concerning sexuality and reproduction that is age, culture and gender appropriate.

2. The right to all reproductive alternatives and the right to choose the size of our families.

3. The right to affordable health care, including safe deliveries within our communities.

4. The right to access safe, free, and/or affordable abortions, regardless of age, with confidentiality and free pre and post counseling.

5. The right to active involvement in the development and implementation of policies concerning reproductive issues, to include, but not limited to, pharmaceuticals and technology.

6. The right to include domestic violence, sexual assault and AIDS as reproductive rights issues.

7. The right to programs which meet the nutritional needs of women and families.

8. The right to programs to reduce the rate of infant mortality and high risk pregnancies.

9. The right to culturally specific comprehensive chemical dependency prenatal programs, including, but not limited to, prevention of Fetal Alcohol Syndrome and Effects.

10. The right to stop coerced sterilization.

11. The right to a forum for cultural/spiritual development, culturally-oriented health care, and the right to live as Native women.

12. The right to be fully informed about, and to consent to any forms of medical treatment

13. The right to determine who are members of our Nations.

14. The right to continuous, consistent and quality health care for Native People.

15. The right to reproductive rights and support for women with disabilities.

16. The right to parent our children in a non-sexist, non-racist environment.

In order to accomplish the foregoing stated rights, the Native Women for Reproductive Rights will create coalitions and alliances to network with other groups.

Latinas for Reproductive Choice

by Latinas for Reproductive Choice

*T*he National Latina Health Organization was co-founded by four Latinas on March 8, 1986, International Women's Day. The NLHO was formed to raise Latina consciousness about our health and health problems, so that we can begin to take control of our health and our lives. We are committed to work towards the goal of bilingual access to quality health care and the self-empowerment of Latinas through educational programs, outreach and research.

The National Latina Health Organization has been redefining reproductive issues from our very beginning. We have been actively advocating the expansion of abortion rights to include all the reproductive issues . . . family planning, prenatal care, education and information on sexuality that is culturally relevant and in our language, birth control, freedom from sterilization abuses; and above all, access to all health services. This is being done with our constituents locally and nationally.

At the beginning of 1990, the NLHO, along with other community activists, created "Latinas for Reproductive Choice", a project of the NLHO. We feel strongly that Latinas need to take a public stand on reproductive issues in the way that they affect us. We launched our project with a press conference in San Francisco on October 3, 1990, the thirteenth anniversary of the death of Rosie Jimenez. Our legislators and the general public need to become aware that we are now ready to become a very visible, public, vocal and very strong force in this historic debate that will decide the future of all women. Another very important effect of our becoming public is that other Latinas who have never openly dealt with these issues, even though they themselves may have had an abortion, will finally have the support that they need to make a personal difference. It is very historic, that Latinas are coming together in coalition to publicly take a stand on reproductive issues.

As Latinas for Reproductive Choice we propose to:

1. Break the silence on reproductive rights issues within the Latina community and provide a platform for open discussion.
2. Debunk the myths that surround Latinas through public education.
3. Include Latinas in the national reproductive rights debate by promoting Latinas on the boards of the traditional reproductive rights groups.
4. Monitor elected officials who represent Latino communities.
5. Advocate and pressure elected officials, organizations, and individuals to support reproductive choice issues for Latinas.

We are using the following letter to bring our community together on these vital issues.

. . .

Dear Amiga,

Did you know . . .

. . . Latinas make up 8.4% of women 15-44 years of age in the United States, yet 13% of all abortions are performed on Latinas in that age group?

. . . the abortion rate for Latinas is 42.6 per 1,000 compared to 26.6 per 1,000 for non-Latinas aged 15-44?

. . . it is easier today for a poor Latina to be sterilized than it is for her to receive quality family planning services and obstetrical care?

. . . In some areas of the U.S., 65% of all Latina women have been sterilized?

Do you care . . .

. . . that because Latinas have been left out of the abortion debate a myth has been promulgated by others that Latinas don't have abortions (after all, we're all Roman Catholic aren't we?)

. . . that if abortion rights are restricted, Latinas will be among the first victims of illegal abortions?

. . . that a group of Latinas has banded together to address these issues and do something about them?

We are Latinas for Reproductive Choice and we will no longer stand on the sidelines and let others decide our fate. We have come together to make sure Latina voices are part of the debate and to mobilize Latinas who are as alarmed as we are at what has been happening to our hermanas across the nation.

On October 3, 1977 a poor, young Latina died because of an illegal Texas abortion. That was the year Medicaid funding for abortions was cut. The young Latina was Rosie Jimenez, the first women to die from such an operation following the cutoff of Medicaid funds for abortions. Lack of reproductive choice killed Rosie Jimenez. And we can't afford to lose any more Rosies to this kind of murder! Yet, there continue to be millions of young women just like Rosie Jimenez today. Right now, in 1990, most Latinas still do not have reproductive choice. If we do not fight to maintain access to safe and legal abortions thousands more young women like Rosie Jimenez will die needlessly.

Access to abortion is only half the issue for Latinas. Reproductive choice for us is much more than abortion—it is the ability to have healthy babies when, and if, we want. It means the freedom to choose to have one child or 10. Or even none. Reproductive choice means access to culturally-relevant, quality health care and information, education about sexuality and contraception for our daughters, and access to alternative forms of birth control, regardless of cost. Sterilization should not be our only choice simply because it is federally funded. Reproductive choice means the freedom to make informed choices about our bodies.

Reproductive health and abortion issues will dominate the 1990's. Candidates in the upcoming November election will be elected on the basis of their positions on reproductive issues. In recent months the United States Supreme Court has upheld more and more state restrictions on the right to an abortion and with the resignation of Justice William Brennan, the future is not encouraging. For the first time since the historic Roe v. Wade decision the Supreme Court appears willing to overturn a woman's right to a safe and legal abortion.

It is clear that if we do not speak for ourselves, no one else will. We need to ensure that Latina voices are heard in this historic debate because we have a unique perspective that has been ignored for too long.

This is why we have come together as Latinas for Reproductive Choice. Won't you join with us to make sure Rosie Jimenez did not die in vain? Help us provide a voice for all other Latinas who find themselves without choice. Help us speak out as Latinas on the most momentous issue of this decade. We can no longer afford to be silent. Add your name to the list of Latinas who are willing to take a stand.

Sinceramente,

LATINAS FOR REPRODUCTIVE CHOICE
PO BOX 7567
OAKLAND, CA 94601
(415) 534-1362

Women in Prison, Women in Danger: Reproductive Health Care Denied

by Brenda V. Smith

While much has been written over the past months about the increasing prison population in this country, little attention has been paid to the fastest growing group among the incarcerated population, women, and in particular women of color. With the number of women prisoners growing and prison health care, particularly reproductive health care, existing at a substandard level, we are on the verge of a crisis—depriving prisoners of their rights and endangering their very lives. The examples illustrated below suggest the potential of this crisis.

In the last decade, female prison population growth has significantly outstripped that of the male prison population. In 1980, there were approximately 13,000 women serving sentences in state and federal prisons. By the end of 1989, that number had risen to over 41,000. In 1989 alone, the female prison population grew by 24% compared to a 13% growth in the male prison population.

Preliminary figures from 1990 suggest that this trend has abated somewhat and that for the first time since 1981, the male growth rate in the prison population exceeded the growth rate in the female population (8.3% and 7.8% respectively).

The primary reason for the increase in both the male and female prison population has been this country's war on drugs. By primarily focussing the war on interdiction, not on treatment and prevention, the prison population has witnessed an astronomical increase. While the male prison population has increased by 112% since 1980, the female prison population increased by over 200%.

A larger percentage of women than men are serving sentences for drug offenses. The most current information from the Bureau of Justice Statistics, collected in 1986, reveal that 22% of all women prisoners compared to 16% of men prisoners were serving sentences for drug offenses.

Recent figures suggest that figure has only increased. For example, the Federal Bureau of Prisons reports that while 55.1% of all federal prisoners are serving sentences for drug offenses, 62% of women prisoners are serving sentences for drug offenses. Though disturbing, this statistic is not surprising since women are overwhelmingly convicted of non-violent crimes with an economic motive such as drug sales, theft, forgery and prostitution.

Women prisoners are disproportionately women of color. African-American women comprise over 50% of the total female prison population. In the District of Columbia, 99% of women prisoners are African-American.

The majority of these women are between 21 and 35, in their prime childbearing years. About 80% of women prisoners have children. Almost 90% of those who reported having children indicated that at least one of their children was under the age of eighteen. About 25% of women prisoners are pregnant or postpartum (8-10% are pregnant). The District of Columbia Department of Corrections estimates that 20% of women prisoners are pregnant at intake.

Typically, women enter prisons and jails with a host of medical problems including HIV infection and other sexually transmitted diseases, diseases associated with poor nutrition such as obesity, diabetes, hypertension, and alcohol and other drug addictions. A conservative estimate suggests that 70% of women prisoners have alcohol and other drug problems. These women are clearly in need of comprehensive health care services.

While the system of medical care for all prisoners is poor, the situation is far worse for women prisoners. Prison medical care systems were created for men. Essentially, women must "fit in" to the existing inadequate framework. Though the situations of individual women outlined below may appear extreme, they are unfortunately all too common.

Routine gynecological care, such as pap smears, breast exams and mammograms, is very rare in state or federal prison systems. The care that exists is generally administered only when the medical situation becomes an emergency. As demonstrated, the emergency often becomes a disaster, with women dying or becoming severely injured.

Quality prenatal care has become another pressing need, given the increasing numbers of pregnant women entering prison. Many pregnant prisoners suffer from alcohol and drug problems. Most prisons, however, offer these women little or no assistance in detoxing, despite clear medical data which shows the serious harm both women and their fetuses can suffer when allowed to detoxify without appropriate medical supervision. Prenatal care for these women is even more vital given the increased chances of complications with the pregnancy or the newborn due to prior drug and alcohol use.

Pregnant women also have increased nutritional needs which are not met in jails and prisons. Though Congress passed legislation last year allowing states, at their option, to provide the Women, Infant and Children ("WIC") food program to pregnant prisoners, only Alabama and Arizona have chosen to do so. The WIC program provides additional food such as cheese, milk, cereal, infant formula, eggs, peanut butter and juice for pregnant women, new mothers, infants and children under age five with family incomes below 185% of the poverty level.

In addition to food supplements, WIC provides health and nutritional counseling—including smoking cessation, and alcohol and drug abuse prevention—to foster comprehensive long-term improvement in the health status of WIC program participants and their families.

These WIC programs are core services pregnant prisoners need in order to ensure the healthiest pregnancies and outcomes for them and their children. Practically speaking, the WIC program could be used to expand services to pregnant prison population and provide services which prisons and jails cannot fund through their own budgets.

Women prisoners also desperately need access to reproductive counseling. There is little health care counseling within prisons and even less related to women's reproductive health. Male and female prisoners engage in sexual practices both before and after their incarceration that put them at high risk for unplanned pregnancies and for sexually transmitted diseases, including HIV infection.

Though abortion is technically available for prisoners, depending on the laws of the particular state, it is difficult and practically impossible for most women to obtain. In the District of Columbia a pregnant prisoner who wishes to obtain an abortion has a number of seemingly insurmountable obstacles.

A District of Columbia prisoner must be able to pay for the abortion. While government funds can be used for almost any type approved medical procedure for prisoners, District of Columbia funds cannot be used to pay for elective abortions for women prisoners (or any other low-income woman for that matter). Because most women prisoners were unemployed prior to their incarceration, they have little personal or family resources to pay for the procedure.

Even if a D.C. prisoner can pay for an abortion, she must make her own arrangements to have the abortion performed at a private clinic. D.C. General which provides routine medical care for prisoners no longer performs abortions. Generally, women prisoners get ten minutes per day to make phone calls. If she is able to make the arrangements, she must then secure approval to have a guard transport her to the facility to have the abortion performed.

Approval could take weeks because of the shortage of guards or because of prison overcrowding. If all these obstacles are surmounted, she will be transported by a guard, often male, who is required by prison regulations to be present at all times during the procedure.

Comprehensive counseling on reproductive health is essential to the health of prisoners. Additionally, they must have meaningful access to abortion and contraception. As noted, sex continues even during incarceration. Though prison administrators have in the past turned a blind eye to sexual practices within prisons, they can no longer afford to ignore the consequences of such activity. Contraception, both barrier and oral methods, must be made available to women prisoners.

Women prisoners are a forgotten and underserved population. Both prison officials and the public justify their neglect of women prisoners because they are law violators, drug addicts, "bad" mothers or all of the above. These women reflect the end product of what happens when we ignore the needs of low-income women, in particular the need for economic and family support and good health care including reproductive services and counseling.

The need for these services does not halt when women are incarcerated. These women have needs which are just as critical, if not more critical, than the needs of women in the free world. We must press prison officials, public health officials, and the public to respond to the concerns of these women in a comprehensive and caring manner. Services to these women will benefit not just them but their children and the communities to which they will ultimately return.

Discovering That You Are Infertile:
One Woman's Experience

by Naomi Pfeffer and Anne Woollett

'Well,' they said, 'If you're going to have a baby you should start soon. You're not getting any younger you know.'

It took me a long time to decide that I wanted a child. I started thinking about it perhaps four years ago. I thought about it. I talked to other women. I listened to other women, to mothers and women without children. I found out about childcare arrangements. I thought about my job and how having a child would influence my work. I talked to the man I live with about a child and the effects one might have on our lives and on our relationship. We thought about when would be a good time to have a child. A baby born in the spring or summer would fit in well with my work.

April 1978. I put my cap away.

August 1978. We go away on holiday.

September 1978. Period two days late and breasts feel very tender. Are they normally tender just before my period? I become much more sensitive to my body. I live inside myself, my centre of gravity seems to be somewhere inside my uterus. I feel full, preoccupied, pleased that I might be pregnant. Then blood. No pregnancy. No baby. Perhaps next month.

1 October 1978. Perhaps next month.

30 October 1978. Blood, period, perhaps next month. Why am I not getting pregnant? I begin to ask questions about my body. I've been taking my temperature for several months and I know that I am ovulating. How long does it normally take to get pregnant? I had assumed it could take up to six months and we have been trying for that time.

People reassure me. Sometimes it takes a long time. I'm given advice, information, details about how other people did it. I'm consoled, never mind, you'll make it. I'm trying to grapple with the idea that perhaps I won't make it. That idea creeps into my mind and I want to discuss it. But it's not something people are willing to discuss. A friend gets pregnant. It didn't take her long. She gets bigger. We discuss home confinements, epidurals, baby clothes, names. The world seems to be full of pregnant women, in the streets, holding babies, pushing prams. I'm surrounded by pregnant women. I read up on conception and find that infertility tests begin with an examination of the man's sperm.

4 December 1978. A friend, a nurse, arranges for us to have a sperm test. She provides us with the plastic container in its brown box, complete with instructions. `The sperm must be produced by masturbation and reach the laboratory within four hours.' So today, the alarm goes off, I get up and make a cup of tea while Paul produces the specimen (how quickly we get into the jargon) and we rush it up the road to my friend who takes it to the lab at work.

The same friend arranges for us to attend the fertility clinic attached to the birth control clinic where she works. This is the same clinic I have been attending for years. The appointment is for after Christmas. We hope that I get pregnant over Christmas so that we won't need to keep the appointment. In the meantime I read up on infertility investigations.

5 January 1979. Our first appointment. Our medical histories are taken and we are both examined physically. We are seen by the consultant separately and then he talks to us together. `Yes, everything seems quite normal.' But we are told that the sperm count is not terribly high, about thirty million, but high enough. Conception is possible with lowish sperm counts. Paul is told to give up his Y-fronts and to wear boxer shorts. This may increase the sperm count. I'm told that from my charts it

Reprinted with permission from *The Experience of Infertility* by Naomi Pfeffer and Anne Woollett, Virago Press, London, England, 1983.

looks as though I'm ovulating. I'm to continue taking my temperature but I must use the official forms rather than bits of graph paper. We are told that the next step is the post-coital test for which I am to make an appointment after my next period has started.

In some ways I feel quite elated after this first appointment. Our problem has been recognized and something is being done for us. We go straight to Marks and Spencers to buy the shorts, feeling that things had started, that we had acquired some kind of control.

7 January 1979. Period begins. I start my new temperature chart on the official form and ring the hospital to make an appointment for a post-coital test. At this particular clinic post-coital tests are done only on Tuesday mornings.

16 January 1979. First post-coital test. Attending the clinic is a depressing experience. A feeling of heaviness comes over me as I get closer to the clinic. I walk past the Family Planning clinic which I've attended for many years, down the corridor, past the row of women waiting their turn, to the door marked `Subfertility Clinic'. I am redefined. I am now infertile, a woman with a problem. I announce my arrival, show my card with my new number on it. When I was fertile I was E34976. Now that I'm infertile, I'm 4032.

I wait my turn, sitting by myself, getting lower and lower, trying to fight the tears, and the feelings of self-pity. It is my turn. I go in and undress, and lie on the couch as instructed. A doctor, a woman, not the one we'd seen previously, inserts a speculum and then using a long rubber tube takes a sample of my cervical mucus. While I get dressed, she goes over to the other side of the room to examine my mucus under a microscope. `I don't like this at all,' she says. I panic. What have I done? Hadn't we followed the instructions? I feel like a naughty child and I start to cry. The tears stream down my face and they continue unabated for the rest of my appointment. It transpires that what she doesn't like is the way the sperm and the mucus are getting along. There aren't enough sperm and they don't seem to be surviving well in my mucus. The doctor suggests that Paul sprays his testicles twice a day with cold water using one of those small indoor plant sprays. I don't know how he will take to that. If this spraying is such a good idea, then why hadn't the doctor suggested it on our first visit when Paul was there. That way at least he'd have been told directly. Now it was up to me to tell him. I'd brought his sperm to them and now I was taking bad news back home. My mucus didn't meet with her approval either. It was described on my form as `tacky.' I am given a prescription for some oestrogen tablets and told to come back next month for another post-coital test.

There are lots of questions I want to ask. But the tears are still streaming down my face and I feel far too distraught to ask them. So I fumble around for my coat and bag and leave, while the doctor talks into her tape recorder about my case.

The force of my feelings and my inability to cope with them surprises me. During the next month I think a great deal about what happened and how I might cope in the future.

8 February 1979. Period starts. I feel depressed. I've got to go back to the clinic again. I ring up to make an appointment. Tuesdays arrive this cycle either on day eight or day fifteen of my cycle. The nurse thinks that I should go for the earlier date. I take the oestrogen tablets in preparation for the appointment.

16 February 1979. Second post-coital test. This time I feel much stronger. When the doctor appears and calls my name my stomach turns over. I force it back into place and I follow her into the room. I try to attend very carefully to what she does. Both the procedure and the doctor are the same as before. `Well, the mucus is better, but the sperm are much the same as before.' She writes this down. I confess that Paul has refused to spray his testicles. The doctor points out that this is quite important as the present emphasis is to get the balance right between my mucus and his sperm. She suggests that I douche myself with a solution of bicarbonate of soda just before intercourse during the fertile days. This may make my vagina more conducive to the survival of Paul's sperm. I tell her that I am puzzled. Should I take the oestrogen tablets for my mucus to coincide with my clinic appointments or around ovulation as the two days are a week apart? Am I undergoing tests or treatment? The doctor says that, as she has an empty slot the following Tuesday, I can return for another post-coital so she can check the sperm and the mucus nearer to ovulation and after I have been using the douche. When she'd got the mucus right, she'd move on to other things, in particular, on to checking whether my tubes were unblocked. I'm even more puzzled. Why bother spending months checking my mucus if we then discover that my tubes are blocked? Why is only one test done at a time? I suppose I'd expected the investigation to be more like an MOT, where your car is given a whole range of tests at one go, and so you know what's wrong fairly rapidly. I tell the doctor how depressed I feel and that I'm worried that the investigations might destroy the relationship into which the child would be born. But any talk of emotions is brushed aside with the comment that some people feel quite heartened to think that treatment is being offered and that some couples are willing to go to the most elaborate extremes to have a child. I take the hint and shut up.

The clinic nurse shows me how to use the douche. She is much more cheery and tries to boost me by telling me how successful the doctor is at getting women pregnant.

The visit is over. The tension gradually subsides. At least this time I didn't collapse and I did manage to ask most of my questions. Now I have to go home with my collection of bits and pieces, instructions and information and prepare us for the next appointment.

I tell Paul what the doctor said about spraying his testicles, that he must do it to improve motility. He refuses. She made it clear that this is the next step in the proceedings. If he's not prepared to do it then we've reached a stalemate. Will they be prepared to continue the investigations if he's uncooperative? I feel cross with him. I've had to go to the clinic, go through the humiliating examinations and face the doctor and now he won't do his share. Later he agrees to try. Our sex life has taken on new elements: Paul sprays his balls twice a day; just before intercourse I pop into the bathroom and spend five minutes with the douche.

20 February 1979. Third post-coital test. My mucus has remained good and the number of sperm has improved but their motility is still low. The doctor suggests I continue with the current regime of tablets, douche and spray. We now move on to other things: an X-ray of my Fallopian tubes. A form is filled in and I am told to ring the hospital's X-ray department when my next period arrives to make an appointment for day ten of my cycle. Via me, Paul is advised to see the semenologist, in six weeks' time.

26 February 1979. My fertile period is over and so the rites can cease for a while till next month. I can stop gently bullying Paul for a while, and relax. My friend has had her baby and I go to see it. I feel very thrilled for her. But after the excitement wears off I feel very sad. If I'd got pregnant quickly my baby would be almost due. I realize how much I'd stopped thinking about children and babies. My goal now is conception.

13 March 1979. Period starts. It is about three days late and I'd just begun to feel really hopeful. Yesterday I'd had moments of discomfort; and stomach ache but I'd ignored them till I saw the blood today. I feel weak and tearful. All the strength I thought I'd acquired just seems to have drained away. The discomfort serves as a reminder of my failure. So much for menstruation as a sign of femininity and the potential for motherhood. All it signifies to me is my failure.

21 March 1979. To the hospital for an HSG (X-ray of my Fallopian tubes). I had rung them beforehand to find out how long it would take and whether I would feel well enough to go back to work afterwards. I'm nervous so I've asked my friend to come with me. In the X-ray department, I undress completely and put all my clothes into a brown paper bag and cover myself with one of the hospital's green overalls. I'm shown into the X-ray room and told to sit on a long table with the equipment all around and above it. The doctor and radiographer, both men, arrive. My friend who is a nurse and works at the hospital is allowed to stay. The doctor tells me what will happen. I can watch the proceedings on a TV screen. The insertion of the dye may feel like a period pain. He inserts the dye. It is very painful and the pain gets worse. I pass out. When I come round the doctor shows me the X-ray. I try to concentrate but I can't take in what he's saying. The left tube appears to be clear but my right tube has gone into spasm. I fear there may never be a baby. I am put on to a trolley and wheeled into the corridor where I lie in pain for some time. Gradually the pain begins to ease and I am able to get dressed. My friend finds a taxi, takes me home and puts me to bed with a hot water bottle. By the evening I feel better.

The investigations seem to be taking so long. A day does not pass by without my thinking about them and my infertility. I feel I must go on with the tests, and all the pain they cause, because I need to know if I will ever be able to have a child, and because there is no other source of help for my infertility to which I can turn.

19 April 1979. Appointment with the semenologist. The appointment is at 3:40 and so at 2:30 Paul produced his sperm sample into the little plastic container provided by the hospital. We then rush to the hospital, clutching the sample. The doctor looks at some of the sperm under the microscope and sends the rest to the lab for a sperm count. He thinks that the count and motility are increased, but this will be confirmed by the laboratory test. That's it basically. It's heartening to think there's an improvement. The spraying must be working so Paul will continue with that. We fix another appointment with the semenologist to see whether the improvement has continued.

26 April 1979. I'm in contact with children who have German measles so I have a blood test to see whether I am immune to German measles.

1 May 1979. Appointment at the Infertility Clinic to hear the results of the HSG. The doctor tells me the same tale as I was told in the X-ray room. One tube is definitely clear but the result is uncertain for the other. This tube may be blocked or it might be a technical problem which made it difficult for the dye to get through. My agony is reduced to a technical hitch. If I have not conceived in three months time, I am to have a laparoscopy. This will involve a short stay in hospital. The waiting list is long so she will put my name down on it the next time I see her, in three months' time. Why do I have to wait till then? Why can't my name be put on the list now? Meanwhile, the doctor suggests I try an insemination cap. I am to return to the clinic in two days to be shown how to use it. I am to use it in the middle of the cycle and then come back to her with it in place to see if I am using it properly and to check whether it's improving the sperms' chances of survival. This calls for another new element in our sex life: I take the oestrogen tablets around the time of ovulation; then before `intercourse' I am to spend five minutes in the bathroom with the douche after which I am to insert the insemination cap. Meanwhile Paul is masturbating into the hospital's plastic pot, with his balls nicely chilled twice daily. I am then to syringe his sperm into the tube which dangles from the insemination cap. What erotic excitement!

3 May 1979. To the hospital to learn how to use the insemination cap. It's a bit fiddly and difficult to get into place.

19 May 1979. Fourth post-coital but with insemination cap in place. The results seem exactly the same as for the test we had in February. Mucus is okay, sperm count is fine, but the motility is low. The insemination cap has not made any difference so the doctor doesn't think it's worth continuing with it. I indicate my relief at that news. We are sent back to the semenologist for a sperm-mucus compatibility test to see if my mucus is killing off Paul's sperm.

12 June 1979. Second appointment with semenologist. We go together with a sperm sample in a little container. The semenologist examines it and pronounces his approval of both the count and motility. We then persuade him to do the sperm-mucus compatibility test which is the reason we came to see him. He seems happy with the result. I feel totally confused. One doctor says the motility is low. Another says it's fine. One tells me to douche. The other says that it's unnecessary. How am I to deal with this lack of consensus? The only response seems to be to feel cheerful. At least someone has said we're okay. I may not be pregnant but any ray of hope is to be appreciated.

1 August 1979. Appointment to see the consultant. He puts me on the list for a laparoscopy. I should have an appointment within six months. It's just a question of waiting. And because my cycle is somewhat irregular, he decides to put me on an ovulation-inducing drug. I am given one month's supply. Am I to go back each month for another prescription?

10 August 1979. We go on holiday. It is the second holiday we've taken since trying to get pregnant. Events like this remind me of time passing.

On our return from holiday, we decide to buy a house. We had been thinking for some time about where we were going to live. The flat was a bit small for a child. We had no garden and getting up and down the stairs would not have been easy with a small baby. When we first started trying to conceive, our plan had been to move out soon after the baby's birth. But as the months passed with no signs of a baby, we put this plan to one side. It just did not seem possible to make any decisions about where we were to live until we knew more about whether we were likely to have a baby. How much longer could we go on delaying plans and decisions because one day there might be a baby? So many aspects of our lives were becoming controlled by our frustrated attempts to become parents. We went ahead and bought a house. It is a large house—one that gives us plenty of space for us and for children.

15 October 1979. Receive a card from the hospital telling me to fix the date for a laparoscopy in the second half of my next cycle.

7 November 1979. I enter hospital for a laparoscopy the next afternoon. I have never been in hospital before and I am nervous. It is much jollier than I expected. There are thirteen women in the ward and we quickly discover who we all are. Six of us are to be operated on tomorrow. As we have all come in for different operations, we each have different anxieties, but we are great company for one another, laughing and joking together. I realize how much more pleasant it is to have other women around you while going through tests, someone to share the worries and the news. There are two other women on the ward who are having problems in conceiving. It is good to talk to them, to compare notes about the tests and their reactions to infertility. I realize that I did not know anyone who had been through the investigations or who is infertile. While a lot of women have been very kind and listened to my tales of tests and anguish, none of them have been through similar experiences or had similar feelings. This is the first time I've spoken to women who've said, 'Yes, they did that to me,' or 'Yes, I felt like that too'. I see that I've become very careful about the people I get close to. I am only relating to close friends and relatives who know about my problem. I feel very vulnerable about stepping outside of that group into the great beyond of those who don't know.

9 November 1979. The doctor comes round to tell us all about the results of our operations. He confirms that I am ovulating and that my tubes, ovaries and uterus are okay. So I am proclaimed fit and told to report back to the consultant in six weeks' time.

I feel now as though I have done the rounds. A series of tests have revealed little that was seriously wrong with either Paul or myself. I imagined that at the next appointment I would be told that medical science had its way with us and that now it was up to us to go away, to forget the hassles we had been through, to relax and conceive.

24 November 1979. Period starts.

22 December 1979. It comes again. Another Christmas passes and I'm not pregnant.

4 January 1980. Appointment to see the consultant. This is the anniversary of my first appointment at the Infertility Clinic. The consultant looks at the report of my laparoscopy, reads all the notes and thinks. He suggests a blood test to check my progesterone level. This is fixed for 13 January as it has to be done late in my cycle. I'm also told to make an appointment for a fifth post-coital test to check that everything is still all right there.

13 January 1980. I have a blood sample taken for the progesterone test. I delay making the appointment for a fifth post-coital.

2 February 1980. We move into our new house. It requires a lot of work which the builders have started. At first I organize the rooms around a child. One room is to be a nursery. Later that same room becomes my study.

8 May 1980. I make an appointment for a post-coital test.

20 May 1980. Fifth post-coital test. I have taken the oestrogen tablets for the first time in months. I had a hard job finding them. When I arrive at the clinic, I feel that I need to explain to the nurse why I hadn't come sooner. The doctor, however, either doesn't notice or doesn't ask about the long delay. So I say nothing. I take off my knickers. I get on the couch. It's all so familiar, I feel positively light-headed. A seasoned traveller. The result seems the same as ever. The sperm are there but not very motile. So one year and a half later, we are back where we started. The results of the progesterone test are not too encouraging. I am ovulating, but not very well. To improve my ovulation, I am given Clomid as well as

oestrogen tablets. I am also sent off to have a blood test to see if I have antibodies to sperm.

I go away feeling fed-up. It seems as if a whole lot of new problems are coming up—low progesterone, sperm antibodies. If they are significant factors, why were they not looked for months ago. I've had a number of blood tests. Why hadn't these been included then? And I don't understand why the motility of Paul's sperm is a matter of differing opinions. If it is a significant factor in our infertility then why put me on Clomid? We seem to be going round in circles, backtracking over ground that I thought we'd explored. I feel like a detective story, with the doctors sniffing round for clues, going over old suspects as well as checking on esoteric possibilities. Nevertheless, I take the Clomid in my next cycle as well as the oestrogen tablets.

20 June 1980. I feel very ill.

4 July 1980. Period starts. It's fourteen days since I felt so ill so I feel sure that it was due to the Clomid. Why hadn't I been warned of the side-effects? Also, how am I to know if the Clomid is working? No tests are being done to check on my defective progesterone levels. I am depressed.

31 July 1980. Period starts. I've run out of oestrogen tablets. The hospital no longer dispenses them so I have to go to my GP. Since I moved, I haven't found a new GP. By the time I work all this out, it's too late to take Clomid this cycle.

This summer is the third since we tried to conceive. We work on the house. I find out through my friend at the hospital that the test showed that I do not have antibodies to Paul's sperm. It dawns on me that I have decided by default not to continue with the Clomid or with the tests. I feel uneasy about giving up the investigations. Having gone so far it seems silly not to continue. The next test might be the one which gives me the answer. They might just find something that works for me. But then I remember what the tests were like and I feel loathe to go back to the hospital and try again.

I feel the key question is changing slowly. I am asking less why am I infertile. Instead, I am thinking about how to reconcile myself with my infertility, and how I can move forward into a life in which children may not have a central role. I feel that this is where I prefer to put my energies, and that continuing with the tests will interfere with this. So I do not go back to the clinic.

Update to "Discovering that You Are Infertile: One Woman's Experience"

by Anne Woollett and Naomi Pfeffer

"Discovering that You Are Infertile" was written some years ago. In a number of respects infertility, its impact for women and their reproductive decisions have changed considerably. Treatment options have increased, so that while many of the investigations mentioned in the diary continue to be part of their experiences, the decisions infertile men and women now commonly make include those which relate to the new techniques of assisted conception, such as IVF and surrogacy (Franklin, 1997).

These techniques are complex and expensive and so are available only to those who can afford the costs of treatment and associated drugs, travel and accommodation. In the US, they are rarely covered by health insurance (King and Meyer, 1997). These techniques of assisted conception are seen as producing new treatment opportunities (and career and financial opportunities for medical and scientific staff). The first child conceived by IVF was born in 1978 and we have, as yet, little evidence about the effects and long term psychological development of children conceived in these ways (McMahon and Ungerer, 1998). There is now more recognition of the emotional and psychological costs of treatment for women and partners (Sandelowski, 1993), but there is still little discussion about and research into the effects on the long term health of women of IVF and especially drugs employed to stimulate ovulation (Klein and Rowland, 1989).

The techniques of assisted conception have opened up treatment options and fertility choices for some women and their partners. However, these treatments still have a low success rate, and hence result in the birth of a live baby for only a minority of infertile couples (Pfeffer, 1993). For many women, therefore, coming to terms with infertility and finding ways of relating to others as infertile/childless women remains as much of an issue as when this diary was written (Franklin, 1997).

The new techniques of assisted conception have changed considerably the ways in which infertility is represented and written about. There is now more discussion of infertility in professional accounts (medical, bioethical, psychological, sociological) and in popular culture. These suggest that while women may find it easier to recognize infertility as a 'problem', many women still experience a strong desire to become mothers and motherhood is viewed as a central, 'normal', and expected role for women (Phoenix, Woollett and Lloyd, 1991; Morrell, 1994). As Mardy Ireland (1993) argues within this framework infertility continues to be construed as a shock, a loss, and as a lack of reproductive choice. A different representation of infertile women (but not infertile men) has emerged in the debates about the ethics of the new techniques. Women prepared to become mothers by means of these unconventional routes are said to threaten the stability of the nuclear family. Yet, ironically, it is the nuclear family which many of these women are seeking to create.

However, in spite of greater public recognition, there are still many unasked and unanswered questions about infertility. One concerns the diversity of women's lives, their social and economic situations, and ideas about motherhood and mothering (Collins, 1994) hence how they view infertility and being childless (Woollett, 1996). Another concerns the ways in which women's ideas about infertility change over time. The diary points to some ways in which one woman's thinking about infertility changed over time: from concerns about being a mother and how motherhood would fit into her life and relationships, to concerns about her body, why she was not getting pregnant, what 'the problem' was, and about the swings in her mood during her menstrual cycle. Since writing that diary, Anne's thinking about infertility has changed considerably. She decided to step off what felt

This update was written specifically for *Women's Health: Readings on Social, Economic and Political Issues.*

like an emotionally draining and isolating roundabout of infertility investigations. This meant thinking of herself not so much as 'infertile' as 'childless' (Woollett, 1996). Professionally she became more interested in how women resist representations of themselves as 'mad', 'sad' or 'desperate'. Drawing on research such as that of Morell (1994) and Ireland (1993) she began to think about the identities, activities and ways in which childless women relate to others, and to disentangle what it means to be a 'mother' and to be a 'woman'.

REFERENCES

Collins, P.H. (1994) Shifting The Centre: Race, Class and Feminist Theorizing about Motherhood. In E.N. Glenn, G. Chang, and L.R. Forcey (eds) Mothering: Ideology, Experience and Agency. New York. Routledge.

Franklin, S. (1997) Embodied Progress: A Cultural Account of Assisted Conception. London. Routledge.

Ireland, M.S. (1993) Reconceiving Women: Separating Motherhood from Female Identity. New York. The Guilford Press.

King, L. and Meyer, M.M. (1997) The politics of reproductive benefits: US insurance cover of contraceptive and infertility treatments. Gender and Society, 11, 3–30.

McMahon, C.A. and Ungerer, J.A. (1998) Parenting and infant development following conception by reproductive technology. In C.A. Niven and A. Walker (eds) Current Issues in Infancy and Parenthood. Oxford. Butterworth Heinemann.

Morell, C. (1994) Unwomanly Conduct: The Challenge of Intentional Childlessness. London. Routledge.

Pfeffer, N. (1993) The Stork and The Syringe: A Political History of Reproductive Medicine. Cambridge. Polity.

Phoenix, A., Woollett, A. and Lloyd, E. (eds) (1991) Motherhood: Meanings, Practices and Ideologies. London. Sage.

Sandelowski, M. (1993). With Child In Mind: Studies of the Personal Encounter with Infertility. Philadelphia. University of Pennsylvania Press.

Woollett, A. (1996) Infertility: From 'Inside/Out' to 'Outside/In'. Feminism Psychology, 6, 74–78.

Donor Egg Conception for Lesbian and Heterosexual Women

by Loret Waldal and Gretchen Sewall, RN, MSW

Abstract. The medical process of donor egg conception is identical for both lesbian and heterosexual women; however, the legal and psychological issues which confront lesbians are different. There are few laws which deal with egg donation, so lesbians must be careful to use consent forms and contracts which clearly state their intentions and the intentions of the gamete donors. Social attitudes are slowly changing and numbers of lesbian mothers are increasing. However, lesbians may still face animosity and rejection from friends and family when they decide to conceive. Lesbian women must be selective when choosing health care providers who are sensitive to these issues. This article outlines the medical procedure of egg donation and addresses its legal and psychological aspects as they apply to lesbian women.

From *Journal of Naturopathic Medicine,* Vol. 7, No. 1, Winter 1997, pp. 42–46. Copyright © 1997 by the Journal of Naturopathic Medicine. Reprinted by permission.

Introduction

*L*esbian women confront obstacles not encountered by heterosexual women when seeking to conceive children. They may fear ostracism from their families, friends, and co-workers when deciding to conceive a child. Lesbian women need to seek out health care providers who are sensitive to their needs and desires. They must also go through the process of procuring a sperm donor and insemination, either in a medical setting or at home. To add infertility to this formidable list of concerns and hurdles may be overwhelming for some lesbians. There are also various legal issues to contend with for both heterosexual and lesbian women.

Various Assisted Reproductive Technologies (ART) such as In Vitro Fertilization (IVF), and Gamete Intra-Fallopian Transfer (GIFT) are now widely used to treat female infertility. For the purposes of this article we will focus on one treatment option: donor egg IVF and its medical, legal and psychological aspects. This article provides a medical description of IVF egg donation and is intended to serve as a guide to health care providers and their patients.

Donor Egg IVF

Egg donation is the process by which women who are unable to use their own eggs to achieve pregnancy receive eggs (oocytes) from a donor. The donor's ovaries are stimulated with hormonal medication to produce multiple eggs which are then retrieved from the ovaries and fertilized with sperm. The resulting embryos are placed in the uterus of the recipient woman which has been prepared by hormonal therapy. Anonymous egg donors are screened for medical and genetic anomalies as well as psychosocial risk factors and then matched with recipients. Women may also have a friend or a relative who is willing to serve as their known donor. In the case of a lesbian couple in which one partner is infertile or of advanced maternal age, it is possible for a woman to donate eggs to her infertile partner. Both genetic and gestational contribution would then be accomplished by the two intended parents.

INDICATIONS FOR DONOR EGG IVF

There are several situations in which a physician may recommend a donor egg cycle. Indications for IVF with donor eggs are:[1]

1. premature ovarian failure
2. oophorectomy
3. genetic indications
4. poor response to ovarian stimulation
5. natural menopause
6. persistently abnormal oocytes obtained at IVF
7. ART candidates ≥ 40 years of age who wish to optimize their pregnancy rate and decrease their rate of spontaneous abortion.

Women aged ≥ 40 years have a lower chance of pregnancy than younger women due to the effects of aging on the quality of their eggs and embryos. These older women may benefit from significantly improved fecundity rates and reduced spontaneous abortion rates with the use of donor gametes.[1] Even women who have experienced natural menopause are able to conceive with donor oocytes.[2]

It is not uncommon for lesbian women to decide late in their reproductive years to conceive a child. For many lesbians, the process of coming out, finding a partner, establishing a supportive social network and achieving financial security may delay the decision to bear a child. Although lesbian couples are seeking donor insemination in increasing numbers[3], they are still subject to widespread prejudice and animosity. For most lesbians, the decision to conceive is one that is made after considerable deliberation.[4] Several studies have revealed that when deciding to bear a child, lesbian women feared loss of support from the gay community, opposition from friends and rejection from family.[5,6,7,8] Lesbians have also reported difficulty in finding health care providers who are sympathetic to their needs and who support their wish to conceive.[9]

The first successful human donor egg cycle was performed in 1984.[10] Since then, the success rate for oocyte donation has exceeded that of IVF and GIFT, approaching as much as 50% in established programs. Using a woman's own eggs for in vitro fertilization yields a much lower pregnancy rate (10%–15%) if she is over age 40 or shows signs of premature ovarian failure. The higher pregnancy rate with donor eggs is due to the younger age of the donor and possibly the hormonal preparation and support of the recipient's endometrium.

MEDICAL SCREENING REQUIREMENTS

Women requesting donor egg must first go through a screening process which includes:

1. medical history and physical examination
2. uterine sounding to measure the depth of the endometrial cavity

3. hysterosalpingogram is recommended to evaluate for uterine integrity and ectopic pregnancy risk in the following cases:
   a. patient is nulliparous
   b. history of infertility in the presence of ovarian function
   c. patient is at risk for spontaneous abortion (e.g., fibroids, recurrent abortion, abnormal bleeding, diethylstilbestrol exposure or previous uterine instrumentation)
4. serology testing for sexually transmitted diseases

Most programs establish an upper age limit of 50 years of age for recipients. The increase in maternal obstetric mortality in women ≥ 35 years of age is well established and pregnancy outcome data for women over the age of 50 is scarce. Although the use of young donor gametes may counteract the age-related decline in fertility, the incidence of chronic medical illness (i.e., hypertension and diabetes) increases with age and may contribute to an increase in maternal morbidity.[1] Women over 40 conceiving naturally are at risk for low birth weight babies, pregnancy induced hypertension, increased miscarriage, and increased Cesarean section rate.[1] Therefore, recipient women 45 years of age or older should have a complete medical evaluation beyond the initial screening process, including[1]:

1. mammogram
2. fasting and 2-hour postprandial glucose
3. fasting lipoprotein profile
4. complete blood count
5. serum chemistries, including electrolytes, blood urea nitrogen, creatinine and hepatic enzymes
6. electrocardiogram

If risk factors are identified, the woman should be advised regarding the risks of pregnancy and then referred for preconceptual counseling.

A donor egg cycle consists of five basic components:1) ovarian stimulation in the donor; 2) hormonal preparation of the recipient's uterus: 3) transvaginal, ultrasound guided removal of the oocytes from the donor: 4) fertilization and development of the embryo(s); 5) transfer of the embryo(s) into the recipient woman's uterus.

OVARIAN FOLLICLE DEVELOPMENT (DONOR)

In donor egg cycles, the donor's ovaries are hyperstimulated with gonadotropins (e.g., Metrodin™ and/or Humegon™) so that multiple follicles and oocytes will develop. The development of the follicles is monitored via serum estradiols and transvaginal ultrasounds. On approximately cycle day 10 or 11, human chorionic gonadotropin (Profasi®) is administered to induce final maturation of the oocytes.

EGG RECOVERY (DONOR)

Thirty-four to 36 hours after Profasi® administration, a transvaginal ultrasound is performed with an aspiration needle to remove the mature oocytes from the ovaries. The physician places the ultrasound probe into the vagina and guides the needle through the vaginal wall into follicles on each ovary. The procedure is usually performed under conscious sedation using benzadiazepines and intravenous narcotics. Promethazine is also administered as prophylaxis for nausea. If the ovaries are difficult to access, or if the patient is particularly sensitive to pain, the donor or the physician may elect to use general anesthesia. The oocytes are obtained by aspirating fluid from the follicles. The embryologist immediately inspects the follicular fluid under a microscope for the presence of an egg.

CULTURE AND FERTILIZATION OF THE OOCYTE(S)

Immediately following egg retrieval, eggs are cultured and fertilized with donor sperm in the embryology laboratory. Not all follicles aspirated can be expected to yield an oocyte. Immature, post-mature or degenerate oocytes may be recovered as well as mature ones. The eggs are examined to see if they have fertilized and developed normally, and the resulting embryo(s) are then transferred into the recipient woman's uterus approximately 48 hours after egg recovery.

UTERINE PREPARATION AND EMBRYO TRANSFER (RECIPIENT)

Recipients follow a standard hormonal replacement protocol to prepare the uterine lining for implantation and pregnancy. If the recipient woman menstruates, she is first suppressed with a GnRH agonist. For approximately two weeks, she is given increasing doses of estradiol (transdermal, oral or intramuscular). Two or three days before embryo transfer, progesterone support (50 to 100 mgs intramuscularly daily) is administered. Hormone therapy is continued until the pregnancy test and then daily until about 10 weeks gestation (after which placental steroidogenesis is adequate to support the pregnancy).

Ideally, two to three embryo(s) are transferred into the uterus via a very fine catheter placed inside the uterus through the cervix. No anesthesia is required. The recipient woman is asked to limit physical activities for the first 48 hours following embryo transfer. A serum pregnancy test is done 13 days after embryo transfer.

If more than four eggs develop into embryos, there is the option of cryopreserving (freezing) the remaining embryos for thawing and replacement in a later cycle. Cryopreservation is used to minimize the risk of multiple gestations.

COST INFORMATION

The cost of IVF with donor eggs may be prohibitive. The total cost of one donor egg cycle ranges from $9,000 to $14,000. Recipients are responsible for all costs associated with the cycle, which include donor compensation, donor screening, medications, monitoring costs, egg recovery, embryo transfer, and laboratory charges. For lesbians, and some heterosexual women there is also the additional cost of donor sperm, which ranges from $375–$450 per cycle, depending on the sperm bank and number of vials used. If a woman wishes to use a known sperm donor, that donor must undergo the same screening as anonymous donors. This will add more cost to the total charges.

Infertility treatment is rarely covered by health insurance. Even with insurance coverage, the policy will not include donor compensation.[11] Some insurers have an age criteria of 40–42 for limiting coverage[11]. As a result, the high cost of donor egg may make it implausible for some women to utilize this technology.

Legal Aspects of Donor Egg

The involvement of third parties in reproduction raises legal issues and alters the traditional concept of family. The conventional notion of family as defined by genetic relations is changing as advances in medical technology allow for new family configurations. It is possible for single women to be inseminated with donor sperm; for single men to hire a surrogate; and for lesbian couples to conceive with donor sperm or donor egg. Laws have been slow to keep up with the progress of medical science and there is now a need for legislation which addresses assisted reproductive technology.

There are many ethical concerns which surround the legality of gamete donation and compensation. Different states have various laws regarding parental rights and genetic or biological links. Many states' laws apply only to married women, and some states have no laws regarding artificial insemination.[12] For the purposes of this article, we will cover the legal aspects of egg and sperm donation in general and the use of anonymous vs. known donors.

SPERM DONORS

Anonymous sperm donation has been practiced for many more years and is more commonplace than egg donation, and for this reason there is more legislation surrounding it. The sperm recipient and her consenting husband are declared the legal parents of the child in all of the 35 states which regulate anonymous sperm donation.[11] In the case of single women or lesbians, 12 states affirm that the sperm recipient is the sole parent of the child.[11] In general, the use of anonymous sperm eliminates the possibility that the donor will be able to establish parental rights. Once a sperm donor has voluntarily relinquished parental rights, courts have asserted that he has no further link to the child, even if he changes his mind after the child is born.[11]

It is difficult to generalize about known sperm donation and the legal rights of the donor. States vary in their treatment of this matter, and courts within states may disagree. In New York, a known sperm donor for a lesbian couple claimed parental rights to the child. One court denied his claims, but an intermediate appellate court ruled in his favor. The case is now on further appeal.[11] Known donor insemination can bring up additional complications such as the possibility of an ongoing relationship between the sperm donor and the child. In cases of known donation, it is advisable to have a legal contract (which may or may not be binding) between the recipient and the donor in which the donor relinquishes all parental rights to the child. However, there is always the risk with known sperm donation that the donor will attempt to assert his parental rights.

EGG DONORS

There is very little legislation which addresses donation of oocytes. Only five states, Florida, North Dakota, Oklahoma, Texas and Virginia, have laws concerning egg donation. The statutes which these states have adopted relieve the egg donor of all parental rights and responsibilities, as with donor sperm.[11] Because of the paucity of legislation on egg donation, it is undoubtedly in the recipient's best interest to execute consent forms for both the donor and recipient which clearly state their intentions. As with sperm donation, anonymous egg donation carries less risk in terms of the donor vying for parental rights.

The cryopreservation of embryos may bring up further legal complications. It is possible to imagine a situation in which an egg donor may try to assert her claim to preserved embryos. Health care providers also need to be prepared for situations in which the recipient woman dies or is disabled, or cannot continue to pay storage fees.[13] A lesbian partner may wish to bear a child from the cryopreserved embryos so that the children born into their partnership are biological siblings. In any case, it is in the best interest of the recipient woman and her partner to create legal documents with the assistance of an attorney who specializes in reproductive law and sign consent forms which clarify their intentions.

PARENTAGE

Advanced reproductive technology has begun to change the concept of what constitutes a parent, and whether or not genetic, biological, or psychological ties grant parental privileges. It would seem that in different cases, different measures of parental bonds exist. A couple may use their own gametes and then hire a gestational carrier to carry and give birth to their child. They may be awarded custody based on their genetic relationship and any contract made before the birth of the child. In a traditional surrogate arrangement, the intended mother or recipient may be awarded custody over the genetically related woman who gives birth to the child. In these cases, the best interests of the child and any agreements made before the birth are both considered.

For lesbians who wish to conceive via egg donation, there are two donors involved in the process: both sperm and egg. This could also be the case for some heterosexual couples. It is therefore imperative for the future parents in this situation to sign consent forms and contracts which protect their parental rights to the child and relinquish those of the donors. A women who conceives via egg donation is legally the parent of the resulting child.[12] It may be difficult, however, for a lesbian to secure the parental rights of her female partner, to whom she is not legally married. Her partner also has no genetic or gestational links to the child. Some states have granted second parent adoptions to partners of lesbian mothers, but lesbian couples should be legally prepared for the event of the gestational mother's death or the dissolution of the partnership and resulting custody complications. Since laws are scarce and situations remain unclear, it is necessary to take all possible steps to ensure that parental rights are not challenged.

Psychological Aspects of Donor Egg

Women enduring infertility report the experience to be a major life stress.[13,14,15] A study of lesbians undergoing infertility treatment suggests that they are much more likely to report stress due to their treatment than married couples.[3] Some typical psychological responses to infertility are: guilt for being infertile and for being upset over it; anger at the unfairness of it; and depression from the loss. The grief associated with infertility has even been compared to the loss of a child.[16] A failed ART cycle may be perceived as proof of the unlikeliness of ever experiencing pregnancy and childbirth.[15]

Most lesbians, when they decide to conceive a child, have already accepted the idea of a sperm donor. The use of donor eggs, however, means the loss of their genetic link to the child. For many, this loss is significant and requires additional time and counseling prior to attempting donor egg conception. After the birth, comments from others about the child's talents, traits and physical characteristics will remind the parents of this loss.[16] This could impact bonding with the child. For some parents, continued counseling is necessary.

Parents must also decide whether or not to tell the child about their genetic heritage. Lesbians are generally more open and accepting of different interpretations of family, since the families they create are by definition "alternative" families. Interviews with lesbian couples who had conceived with donor sperm revealed that all of them planned to tell their children how they were conceived.[17] In a separate study, 100% of lesbian couples surveyed said they planned to tell the child about the donor insemination and that they felt the child had a right to know.[3] In the case of egg donation, there is no obvious need for an explanation of where the egg came from. The lesbian parent may feel that disclosure of this information will lead the child to believe that she is not the "real" mother. However, "a commitment to tell the child and the expression of positive feelings regarding the donor, will provide the child with a sound emotional climate from the beginning."[18] The important thing to emphasize when telling such children about their conception is that they were wanted and planned for and that their conception is just one of the ways in which children are born into families.

Summary

This article has presented the medical process of donor egg IVF as a treatment option for infertile women. Inherent in the medical procedure are legal and psychosocial issues. Infertility and treatment are stressful for women and perhaps more difficult for lesbian women as they have additional psychosocial and legal obstacles to contend with. As more lesbian women seek infertility treatments such as donor egg IVF, health care providers need to develop sensitivity and awareness of the complexities that face this patient population. The health care provider may be called upon to identify additional community resources and offer assistance reaching beyond the medical management of infertility.

Acknowledgments: The authors wish to thank Nancy A. Klein, MD of the University of Washington, Seattle, Washington for providing valuable comments on the manuscript.

REFERENCES

1. Klein N, Sewall G, Soules M. University of Washington Medical Center Donor Oocyte Program. In Cohen C. (Ed.), New Ways of Making Babies: The Case of Egg Donation. Bloomington & Indianapolis, IN, Indiana University Press, 1996; 5.

2. Sauer M, Paulson R, Lobo R. Reversing the natural decline in human fertility. JAMA 1992; 268:1275

3. Wendland C, Byrn F, Hill C. Donor Insemination: a comparison of lesbian couples, heterosexual couples and single women. Fertility and Sterility 1996; 65:764.

4. Kennedy J, Tash D. Lesbian childbearing couples' dilemmas and decisions. Health Care for Women International 1992; 13:209.

5. Hill K. Mothers by insemination: Interviews. In Pollack S & Vaughn J. (Eds.), Politics of the Heart: A Lesbian Parenting Anthology. Ithaca, NY, Firebrand Books, 1987: 111.

6. Pollack S. A lesbian-feminist perspective on research. In Pollack S & Vaughn J. (Eds.), Politics of the Heart: A Lesbian Parenting Anthology. Ithaca, NY, Firebrand Books, 1987: 316.

7. Wismont J, Reame N. The lesbian childbearing experience: assessing developmental tasks. Image: Journal of nursing scholarship 1989;21:137.

8. Murphy M. And baby makes two, In Pollack S & Vaughn J (Eds.), Politics of the Heart: A Lesbian Parenting Anthology. Ithaca, NY, Firebrand Books, 1987: 125.

9. Zook N, Hallenback R. Lesbian coparenting: creating connections. In Pollack S & Vaughn J (Eds.), Politics of the Heart: A Lesbian Parenting Anthology. Ithaca, NY, Firebrand Books, 1987: 89.

10. Lutjen P, Trounson A, Leeton J. Findlay J, Wood C, Renov P. The establishment and maintenance of pregnancy using in vitro fertilization and embryo donation in a patient with primary ovarian failure. Nature 1984; 3 07:174.

11. Seibel M, Crockin S. Family building through egg and sperm donation. Sudbury, MA, Jones and Bartlett Publishers 1996.

12. Curry H, Clifford D, Leonard R. A Legal Guide for Lesbian and Gay Couples. Berkeley, CA. Nolo Press, 1993.

13. Greenfeld D, Olive D. Psychospecific treatments in ART. Assisted Reproduction Reviews 1993; 3:190.

14. Reading A, Kerin J. Psychologic aspects of providing infertility services. The Journal of Reproductive Medicine 1989; 34:861.

15. Mazure C, Greenfeld D. Psychological studies of in vitro fertilization/embryo transfer participants. Journal of in Vitro Fertilization and Embryo Transfer 1989; 6:24:242.

16. Mahlstedt P, Greenfeld D. Assisted reproductive technology with donor gametes: the need for patient preparation. Fertility and Sterility 1989; 52:908.

17. Brewaeys, A. Ponjaert-Kristofferson I, Van Steirteghem AC, Devroey P. Children from anonymous donors: an inquiry into homosexual and heterosexual parents' attitudes. Journal of Psychosomatic Obstetrics and Gynecology. 1993; 14:23.

18. Probasco K. Discussion with children about their donor conception. Unpublished client information, Overland Park, KS, 1992.

Fact Sheet
The Shortage of Abortion Providers

by The Abortion Access Project

- 84% of all U.S. counties and 94% of all rural U.S. counties have no abortion provider.[1]
- Half of all OB-GYNs who provide abortion are 50 years of age or older.[2]
- In 1983 42% of all OB-GYN doctors offered abortion services; in 1995 only 33% did.[3]
- 2% of OB-GYNs perform the majority of abortions in the U.S.[3]
- Only 12% of OB-GYN residency programs require training in first trimester abortion.[4]
- Only 7% of OB-GYN residency programs require training in second trimester abortion.[4]
- Only 15% of chief residents in family medicine residency programs had clinical experience providing first trimester abortions.[5]
- 44 states have "physician only" provisions in their abortion laws which prevent qualified practitioners such as nurse-midwives, nurse practitioners, and physician assistants from performing abortions.[6]
- 7% of abortions are performed in hospitals, 4% are performed in private doctor's offices, 89% are performed in clinics.[1]
- Between 1988 and 1992 the number of U.S. hospitals providing abortions decreased by 18%.[1]
- There have been approximately 2,100 reported instances of violence against abortion providers since 1977, including 6 murders and 15 attempted murders (actual instances are most likely higher).[7]
- Abortion is the only medical procedure with a "conscience clause" that allows medical providers to refuse to participate in the care of a patient.

Sources: [1]S.K. Henshaw and J. Van Vort, "Abortion Services in the United States, 1991 and 1992," *Family Planning Perspectives,* 26:100-112, 1994. [2]Kaiser Family Foundation Media Briefing, 1995. [3]J. Hitt, "Who Will Do Abortions Here?", *New York Times Magazine,* January 18, 1998. [4]H.T. MacKay and A.P. MacKay, "Abortion Training in Obstetrics and Gynecology Residency Programs in the United States, 1991-1992," *Family Planning Perspectives,* 27:112-115, 1995. [5]J.E. Steinauer et al., "Training Family Practice Residents in Abortion and Other Reproductive Health Care: A Nationwide Survey," *Family Planning Perspectives* 29:222-227, 1997. [6]National Abortion Federation, "The Role of Physician Assistants, Nurse Practitioners, and Nurse-Midwives in Providing Abortions," 1997. [7]National Abortion Federation, "NAF Violence & Disruption Statistics," 1997.

Born and Unborn:
The Implications of "Choice" for People with Disabilities

by Marsha Saxton

Some time in the first month after my conception, a disruption occurred in the growth of my lower spine, and the nerves coursing through my bladder and down to my lower legs and feet, the "perineal" tract, did not develop normally. About two out of a thousand babies are affected by this "neural tube defect" or "NTD," the second most common birth difference after cerebral palsy. The range of disability varies considerably from "spina bifida occulta" (or a slight niche in the spine which the individual my be unaware of, or experience back pain) to Myelomenigacele like mine, but sometimes characterized by paraplegia and including Hydrocephally (fluid on the brain). Some babies are born with such severe NTD they have no brain and die soon after birth.

I have been told many times how 'lucky' I am to be only moderately disabled. 'It could have been much worse,' they say, an attitude which perplexes me. I have never been told how unlucky I am to be disabled at all. At thirty-two, I have a slight limp, and somewhat skinny legs lined with pale incisions.

I have always planned and looked forward to becoming a mother. The varying statistics from doctors or books over the years about the possibility of my having a baby with my disability have not caused me to reconsider this.

As a feminist I have supported the pro-choice position on the question of abortion. I feel a woman must be able to choose motherhood or not and exert control over her own body. I view abortion as a stop-gap measure which women must maintain to counteract the oppressive forces that limit women's control over our lives, which include poor access to, and harmful birth control methods. Because of the emotional and social costs of abortion to the individual mother, fetus, and society, I cannot view abortion as another form of birth control. The debate "at what age does the fetus constitute a human life," in my estimation, can never be satisfactorily resolved. Indeed, such an argument misses the point of the true issues at hand, namely, the real resources, financial, social, and emotional of the parents and the community to welcome the child.

It is on this basis that I question the practice of systematically ending the life of a fetus *because it is disabled.* Real "choice" involves an understanding of all the options and the opportunity for flexible decision-making for the individual woman in her own situation based on an accurate assessment of her available resources. It also necessitates closely scrutinizing society's view of "ablebodiedness." We need to better understand disability and our relationship to it. In particular,

1. How does society define and treat disability?
2. What are the implications of prenatal technology in relation to societal oppression of disabled persons?
3. How are disabled women affected by the new technologies and the attitudes surrounding them?
4. How can both consumers and health-care professionals more rationally consider these issues and act in humanly responsible ways?

Disability triggers much fear in our culture. Some of the recent media coverage on the topic has begun to challenge the widespread ignorance in this area, but the old attitudes persist. Perhaps from prehistoric times, disability must have appeared to humans as some mysterious force leaving many human beings with physical limitation, loss of body functions, constant pain, disfigurement, and sometimes early death. It is no wonder that we have feelings of powerlessness about disability. It forces us to confront our own vulnerability.

We, especially in the U.S., live in a culture obsessed with health and well-being. We value rugged self-reliance, athletic prowess, and rigid standards of beauty.

We incessantly pursue eternal youth, and our treatment of our elders attests to an ingrained denial, fear, and even hate of our own aging and accompanying physical limitation. The disabled person in our society is the target of attitudes and behaviors from the able-bodied world ranging from gawking to avoidance, pity to resentment, or from vastly lower expectations to awe. Along with these attitudes disabled persons confront a variety of tangible barriers: architectural inaccessibility, lack of sign-language interpreters for deaf people, insufficient taped or brailled materials for blind persons. In addition, disabled persons confront less tangible barriers: discrimination in employment, second-class education, and restricted opportunities for full participation in the life of the community.

As in any kind of oppression, the attitudes are self-perpetuating, the stereotypes in the literature are reinforced in the popular media. The isolation of disabled persons limits the larger culture's exposure to their life experiences, needs, and common humanness. The child's natural curiosity and inquisitiveness in encountering the disabled person for the first time is so often met with a parent's embarrassed, "Hush, don't ask and don't stare." This child's simple wonder is thus replaced with mistrust and fear, and so handed down the generations. It is surprising to learn that as recently as the 1950's, laws remained on the books in some states prohibiting the public presence of persons "diseased, maimed, mutilated or in any way deformed so as to be an unsightly or disgusting object." The fear of vulnerability, the flight from physical limitation (perhaps from death) is at the root of such phenomena as the Eugenics Movement in the early 1900's. By 1937, 28 states had adopted Eugenics Sterilization laws aimed at persons with epilepsy, mental retardation, mental illness, and other kinds of differences where "procreation was deemed unadvisable." Such attitudes are still with us.

From the youth and beauty oriented culture we are beset with messages to buy products which hide or disguise our differences and body functions, and strive to achieve rigid standards of appearance. Such standards are particularly harsh on disabled women whose appearance or body function may be further from "acceptable."

Do we want a world of "perfect people?" I really wonder what have been the human costs of our attempts to control our differences, our vulnerability. There is tremendous pressure upon us to have "perfect babies." Where disabled persons are stigmatized, so are their parents. In some societies, including the U.S., parents have concealed the birth of disabled infants and in some cases killed or allowed the infant to die of hunger or exposure. (A contradiction to this comes from other cultures including some Native American cultures, where disabled persons are regarded as "spiritually special" and are revered and assigned specific religious or healing roles.)

I have heard of cases as recently as the 1950's in Britain where Spina Bifida newborns were denied sustenance until death.

It is important to point out that physicians are to a certain extent under pressure to encourage prenatal screening and even abortion. Physicians, out of fear of malpractice suits, may lobby for enforced screening. A further concern is that women undergoing screening yet not choosing abortion would be the target of further oppression. This possibility to those of us acquainted with the mothers of disabled, particularly retarded children, does not seem so remote. They are already the target of considerable social stigma. If we are to maintain our "choice" we must include the *choice to have a disabled child.*

How do the oppressive attitudes about disability affect the woman facing prenatal screening? Very often prospective parents have never considered the issue of disability until it is raised in relation to testing. What comes to mind to most prospective parents at the mention of the term "birth defects?" Our exposure to disabled children has been so limited by their isolation that most people have only stereotyped views which include telethons, displays in drugstore counters depicting attractive "crippled" youngsters soliciting our pity and loose change. The image of a child with Down's Syndrome elicits an even more intense assumption of eternal parental burden.

The issue of the burden of a handicapped child seems to be a prominent one in the decision to abort. How much reality is there to the "burden of the disabled?"

Our assessment of the "costs" of raising a disabled child are vastly distorted by the oppressive assumptions. A common theory applied in parent counseling is that parents who gave birth to a disabled child must "grieve for the normal child they didn't have." While it is certainly helpful for parents to release feelings of sadness, shock, and so forth, this theory fails to recognize a prominent feature of this experience; parents bring a lifetime of loss, disappointment, feelings of failure, guilt, etc. to every parent-child relationship (for the most part repressed). This "grieving" point of view blames the child, but often the disabled infant is not the cause of the parents' grief but a reminder of a backlog of old pain. Very often in successful parent counseling, when parents "come to grips" with the issues in their relationship with their child, they identify previously unresolved issues from their past that were being played out in the current relationship.

Of course we cannot chastise or applaud any parent for feeling whatever one might feel about their child. Not "good" or "bad," our feelings are an expression of our history of experiences, our learning over time, and our resource to deal with past distress. But what has been confirmed for me is that one's attitude toward a disabled baby is a *point of view, a relative position.*

Related to this issue is the fact that the oppression of women as the sole and often isolated caretakers of children affect the resources of many mothers in caring for their disabled children, an issue which deserves considerably more attention. The oppression of disabled persons falls upon the parents who may be limited in obtaining needed compensatory aids, medical assistance, and respite care. Many factors in the culture, such as the weakening of the extended family, contribute to the isolation and feelings of overwhelm by the mother. Such issues are typically ignored, again placing the blame of "burden" on the disabled child.

Another of the myths affecting prospective mothers is about the "suffering" of the disabled.

There is no doubt that there are disabled people who "suffer" from their physical conditions. There are even those who may choose to end their lives rather than continue in pain or with severe limitations, but is this not obviously as true for nondisabled people who suffer from emotional pain and limitation of resource? As a group, people with disabilities do not "suffer" any more than any other group or category of humans. Our limitations may be more outwardly visible, our need for help more apparent, but like anybody else, the "suffering" we may experience is a result of not enough human caring, acceptance, and respect. The discriminatory attitudes and thoughtless behaviors, that's what makes life difficult. This is the source of the real limits: the oppression, the architectural barriers, the pitying stares or frightened avoidance, the unaware assumptions that you couldn't do the job, couldn't order for yourself in a restaurant, couldn't find a mate or direct your own life.

How Women Typically Learn about Their Options about Pre-natal Testing

"Choice" requires that information be presented in an unbiased way. Most physicians will indicate their intention to adhere to a "nondirective" philosophy where decisions are left up to the patient. However, not just in my childhood, but recently when I have mentioned to medical professionals my intention to get pregnant, I have encountered a wide array of emotional responses. An orthopedic surgeon to whom I indicated a desire to minimize the use of X-ray while I was trying to conceive blurted out, "You're going to get pregnant? I hope you'll get an amniocentesis."

The standard philosophy in relation to amniocentesis for women particularly over thirty-five years of age is that given the low risk to the fetus, why not go ahead and do it? Very often women are encouraged to have an amniocentesis without reconsideration to what action the parents might take if an abnormality is discovered. This attitude is not derived from careful individualized consideration of the parent's values and decision options, including an appraisal of the risks and consequences of miscarriage for *these particular individuals* is irresponsible, needlessly expensive, and ultimately hurtful to the parent, child, and society.

Medical services consumers tend to put considerable faith in their physicians and assume that physicians are acting in their best interest. Few consumers are made aware that while some medical procedures may be necessary and life sustaining, many are also in the financial interest of the health care industry. Ninety-five percent of all amniocenteses performed indicate no anomaly, and thus function only to reassure parents that their baby is fine. The real value of such an invasive, risky, and expensive procedure must be questioned. As my genetics counselor stated, screening is "sometimes used as a substitute for thinking." On this basis the American College of Obstetrics and Gynecology, and the American Academy of Pediatrics oppose routine Alpha-feto protein screening.

The biggest challenge to health care workers who are counseling both disabled and nondisabled prospective parents about options and the use of reproductive technologies is in presenting the information in understandable and nonbiased ways.

Almost every health care professional is motivated by a deep sense of human caring, and yet is as subject to confusion and prejudice as anyone. While health care professionals have a responsibility to present information in as unbiased a way as possible, blaming them for not doing so does not advance the cause of the consumer. Regarding ourselves as hapless victims of an oppressive profit-motivated health care system does nothing to enhance our power or to challenge the institutionalized patterns of the health care industry. We as women consumers have to regard ourselves as powerful and assert this power in the face of others' possible confusion and prejudice.

We must regard ourselves as the directors of our own needs. Health care professionals are available to us as educators and consultants, but we must be the ones to make the decisions. To do this we must take responsibility for obtaining the necessary information and we must trust our own thinking. We, more than any other, know of our own life circumstances, goals, and capabilities. Disabled women, in our more frequent encounters with the medical system, are particularly vulnerable to feelings of powerlessness to challenge stereotyped and hurtful interactions with unaware professionals. An important goal for us as women and mothers is to make our decisions based on clarity about our values, adequate knowledge of the issues, and an accurate appraisal of our own resources. One avenue toward obtaining that needed confidence is through meeting and sharing with other women where we can gain safety, clarity, and strength. Peer groups are an excellent place to begin discussion about the issues raised here. (Saxton, 1981)

What would I ask or tell another woman considering an amniocentesis with intent to abort a disabled fetus? Was she satisfied that she had sufficient knowledge about disability, an awareness of her own feelings, that she could make a rational choice? Did she personally know any disabled adults or children? What was she taught about disability by adults when she was young? Was she aware of the distorted picture of the lives of disabled people presented by the posters, telethons, and stereotyped characters in the literature and media? I would also ask her to consider the personal and emotional cost that abortion could take. Was the elimination of a disabled fetus worth that cost?

Do I think all disabled fetuses should be born to this world as it is now? Do I think parents should be forced to accept and care for a baby born disabled? No, I don't. I feel our priority should be to assess our current capabilities, determine the realities of the situation, and make decisions that are workable for all concerned.

The questioning by disabled activists of abortion of disabled fetuses has been criticized by some feminists as "too much like Right to Life." I can understand this fear, for the control over our lives as women that access to abortion has provided is currently so tentative that any challenge to abortion may feel threatening. But I feel that it's important to point out that the basis for choosing to abort a disabled fetus is the same basis for choosing to abort a fetus *because it is female,* a practice clearly denounced by the Women's Movement. But regardless of the logic of our current views as activists, we have a responsibility to persistently re-evaluate the implications of our position and examine how they apply to individuals and specific populations.

At this point, if I became aware that the fetus I was carrying would be disabled, I would not choose to abort it. These are my reasons: I hope for and look forward to a time when all children can be welcomed to a world without oppression. I would like to exercise this view if only in my own personal world.

Marsha Saxton's article is an edited excerpt from a paper which appears in Test-Tube Women, *1984, Pandora Press (Routledge & Kegan Paul) and is reprinted with their permission.*

The Bad Baby Blues
Reproductive Technology and the Threat to Diversity

— by Lisa Blumberg

The public discourse we need has been stalled—even in the disability community—because when people discuss the implication of the new reproductive technology at all, they tend to do so within the framework of their views on abortion. Yet these issues transcend the abortion controversy.

It was my feminist leanings superimposed on my disability orientation that fueled my interest in the implications of reproductive technology. In 1980, a woman I worked with who was pregnant told me she was having amniocentesis. "I really don't want the test," she said. "I don't know what I'm supposed to do if there is a problem. I don't want to make a decision about having the child." When I asked why she was having it, she said, "I'm 37, and my doctor told me every expectant mother over 35 needs to have it. He wouldn't feel comfortable if I refused."

From *Ragged Edge (The Disability Experience in America),* July/August 1998, Vol. 19, No. 4, pp. 12–14, 16, by Lisa Blumberg. Copyright © 1998 by Lisa Blumberg. Reprinted by permission.

I just said "good luck" (as is usually the case, the test, revealed nothing) without telling her that her doctor's stance made me uncomfortable. Until then, I thought that whether to have prenatal tests was a decision that prospective parents made for themselves, based on their own attitudes on pregnancy, disability, family life and a host of other things. Without being able to articulate why, I thought it was dangerous for a doctor to impose an obligation on a woman to learn beforehand whether her child might be disabled.

A few years later, I was a watching a news story on the merits of a predictive test for spine bifida. A woman explaining why she had gotten an abortion after test results had been positive said, "I defy any woman, no matter how much she wants a child, to continue a pregnancy after they show her a picture of a deformed baby and tell her that 'this is going to be yours.'"

I thought about that woman a lot. What concerned me was not so much the choice she made as the approach of her medical advisors. What a baby with an untreated medical problem looks like does not indicate what a person with a disability can become. Was it fair to urge people to make such a profound decision as to whether to bring a particular type of child into world on the basis of such a firsthand visceral response?

I started seeing articles in news magazines suggesting that if prenatal testing were used widely and women were then "willing" to abort fetuses found to be "defective," the incidence of children with certain types of disabilities could be significantly reduced.

The word "willing" always jumped out at me. Amniocentesis had originally been touted as a way to expand pregnant women's options, but now it seemed that women were expected to use the knowledge that could be gained by prenatal testing in a way that satisfied others.

In the past decade, prenatal testing has become a multi-billion dollar industry, with hundred of conditions now capable of pre-birth detection. Screening methods, some invasive and some not, are constantly evolving. Ultrasound, which used to just measure fetal growth and position, is giving way to targeted ultrasound which can zero in on a specific body part of the fetus such as the face. In most cases (but by no means in all) when a fetus is diagnosed as having a permanent disability, the pregnancy is terminated.

It is amazing that there has been scant public debate about this revolutionary new technology that allows us for the first time in all of human history to ascertain certain medical facts before one is even a person. Nothing that earlier generations dealt with during pregnancy was in any way comparable. In what varying ways can we react as individuals? How should we react as a society? What are legitimate public health goals? Can we view all people as equals and still feel that it is important to identify some traits prenatally? These are some of the questions that we must start addressing or else we could find ourselves drifting toward a society where there is little tolerance for either physical diversity or diversity in decision-making.

Disability activists need to be aggressive in initiating and framing the debate because our interests, along with those of women, are the most directly involved.

There are differences between ordinary abortion and selective abortion. Most abortion occurs because the pregnancy is unexpected and the prospect of parenthood itself is creating a crisis for the woman. Selective abortion, which constitutes a tiny fraction of all abortions, occurs when the pregnancy is planned but the fetus is perceived as having undesirable characteristics. In other words, selective abortion involves judgments about people. Indeed, women who abort due to fetal "defect" are often urged to get pregnant again quickly.

Almost everyone, regardless of how pro-choice they are, has views on where a moral line should be drawn in selective abortion. Where the difference in opinion arises is the positioning of that line. Many feminists express misgivings over abortion based on sex. Most medical ethnicists would oppose abortion based on eye color. The idea that a couple who share an inherited trait such as some types of deafness might want to end a pregnancy involving a fetus that did not have the same gene and "try again" out of the belief that their family will work better if all members have the same characteristics is controversial even in the disability community.

Without suggesting there should be restrictions on abortion, it is legitimate for disability activists to question the general public consensus that fetal disability is one of the "best" reasons for abortion—right up there with rape or incest and what right-to-lifers call "hard cases." It is not inevitable that prenatal diagnosis must change a wanted future baby into a "defective" fetus about which a decision must be made. As Adrienne Asch, a professor at Wellesley College has written, "suppose Down syndrome, cystic fibrosis or spina bifida were depicted not as an incalculable, irreparable tragedy but as a fact of being human? Would we abort because of those conditions or seek to limit their adverse impact on life?"

The disability rights movement in the quarter century it has been in existence has been successful on some nuts-and-bolts access issues. Important civil rights laws have been passed. However, basic attitudes towards disability really have not changed. It is a premise of the movement that a person with a disability is limited more by society's prejudices than by the practical difficulties that may be created by the disability. Unfortunately, by and large, nondisabled people don't believe it. Most people, to the extent they must think about disability at all adhere to the medical model of disability. Under the medical model, a person's disability is seen to be the cause and sum of that person's problems, with the paramount question therefore being whether the impairment can be alleviated.

Nowhere is the medical model more entrenched than with medical professionals. And it is medical professionals, and in particular genetic counselors, who help prospective parents evaluate their options after prenatal diagnosis.

The role of genetic counselors is to give prospective parents advice about how their child's expected condition can affect people—so the parents can make an informed decision regarding whether to continue the pregnancy. Genetic counseling is intended to be "nondirective," and most counselors do refrain from telling their clients what their decision should actually be. However, when counselors provide prospective parents with merely a list of deficits their future child may have (or may not have, since the same diagnostic label can reflect itself in different individuals in widely disparate ways), they are only telling half of the story. The other half is how people cope with these limitations and what other factors may influence their lives.

Perhaps the most serious limitation of genetic counseling is that counselors rarely offer clients the opportunity to meet persons with disabilities similar to those their child might have or to talk with parents of disabled children. Indeed, some genetic counselors resist the idea out of the belief that this would increase the discomfort of their clients. Yet clients who did not want to accept the offer could just say so. We can and must urge that the sources of information people have access to within the genetic counseling process be broadened.

Persons affected by disability are the most qualified to provide insight on the lifestyle concerns that prospective parents will have after prenatal diagnosis. We cannot tell others what they can personally cope with, but we can tell them how it is for us—and we can share with them our individuality and the range of our views. We can suggest that it is alright to embark on an endeavor which sometimes may be hard, which may make one an outsider and where there are few signposts. We can point out that it is O.K to do the unusual thing.

On a more general social level, consideration also needs to be given to how the emphasis on prenatal testing and the perceived need to make decisions after diagnosis affect people's relations with one another. A prominent newspaper columnist once described the reactions she got to her veto of her doctor's age-based recommendation that she have amniocentesis. She chose to forego the option of termination in the unlikely evens the fetus was disabled, she said, because of the children she already had. She did not know how she could find the words to explain to them a decision not to have a child who might use a wheelchair or always need special guidance, she said, and still affirm for them her view that differences in people should be accepted.

She pointed out that this was not a snap judgment but something she had reflected upon at length. However, she said, people she thought knew her well dismissed her desire to contemplate older motherhood without prenatal tests with an "Oh, it must be because you're Catholic." She is, in fact, pro-choice.

The woman had hit upon something important. In an open letter to genetic counselors published in a professional journal, one woman described the aftermath for her family of a decision to end a pregnancy involving a fetus with Down syndrome. Her school-aged children disturbed by their parents' grief, asked what was so bad about this type of disability.

Their father, said the letter writer, then had to instruct the children on the realities of life with a "handicapped child"—or at least what he thought the realities were. He asked them to imagine what it would be like to be trying to cross a street and always get confused about whether red meant "go" or green meant "go."

Later, when the children were asked to write down their feelings about what had happened, the older one told how sad it had been, and said "the only good thing is not having a child like that in our family." One wonders how children specifically encouraged to see disability as an all-encompassing burden both for the person who has it and for others will interact with the people with noticeable disabilities that they will most certainly meet in life.

Genetic counselors should be urged to help parents who do decide to abort after prenatal diagnosis to find "disability neutral" ways to talk about their decision with children—discussions which focus on the limitations or competing priorities of the family, rather than on assumptions about the potential of people with disabilities.

Reproductive technology can be divisive. It can reinforce prejudices.

There is another side of prenatal testing though. At a conference designed to start a dialogue between disability rights activists and the medical community, I listened as a parent recounted how, after her first child died from Tay-Sachs, she chose to have Tay-Sachs screening in her subsequent pregnancies. All she wanted was children who would live, she said; and eventually she had them. She told us, "I was given an option which I would not otherwise have had—the option to have a family."Another woman with a family history of cystic fibrosis had a predictive test when she was pregnant because, if her child were effected, she wanted to get on a particular doctor's roster right away. There are people who do want the tests, and people who have benefitted from them.

However, it is one thing to acknowledge a couple's right to make a personal and private decision to use prenatal testing based on their own unique circumstances, it is quite another thing for there to be a general expectation that every pregnant woman over 35 will go on defect alert.

What scares me is not the individual decisions people make—although I may disagree with some of these decisions—but the fact that society has latched onto the new reproductive technology as a lead weapon in a simplistic war against "birth defects." It is chilling to read decisions in wrongful birth and wrongful life suits where judges opine that avoiding the births of disabled children is a social good. It is equally chilling to hear public health analysts debate whether the abortion rate of "defective fetuses" will be high enough to make state-sponsored prenatal programs cost effective and efficacious. The legislature of at least one state (Alabama, in a law first passed in the late 1970s) has declared it to be state policy "to encourage the prevention of birth defects and mental retardation through education, genetic counseling and amniocentesis . . ."(Section 22-lOA-l of the Alabama statutes).

How easily ignored is the ethical imperative placed on genetic counselors to be nondirective! And how easily blurred is the critical distinction between preventing persons from *having* disabilities and preventing persons *with* disabilities! Most frightening in my view, though, are the articles in legal and medical journals suggesting that carrying a disabled fetus to term constitutes "fetal abuse" on the part of the woman.

Ruth Hubbard, professor emeritus of Biology at Harvard, has written, "my problems with amniocentesis stem mostly from my concern about how it creates eugenic thinking. We act as if we can look at a gene and say 'Ah-ha, this gene causes this . . . disability' when in fact the interactions between the gene and environment are enormously complex. It moves our focus from the environmental causes of disabilities—which are terrifying and increasing daily—to individual genetic ones." This misplaced focus will not only result in individuals acquiring disabilities unnecessarily: it will undermine the status of people with disabilities, regardless of the origins of their disabilities, and of women.

The new reproductive technology represents a boon for some and terror for others.

It is startlingly new but it invokes feelings that are age-old. I believe that the public discourse that we need has been stalled—even in the disability community—because when people discuss the implication of the new reproductive technology at all, they tend to do so within the framework of their views on abortion. Yet these issues transcend the abortion controversy, even as they cut across both sides of that debate. Somehow, we must begin to think more creatively and learn to meld together different world views. It is only then that we will have the hope of solving the conundrums created by the new reproductive technology in ways that will respect the individuality of us all.

Reproductive Issues Are Essential Survival Issues for Asian American Communities

by Connie S. Chan

When the Asian-American communities in the U.S. list their priorities for political action and organizing, several issues concerning basic survival are usually included: access to bi-lingual education, housing, health, and child care, among others. Yet the essential survival issue of access to reproductive counseling, education, and abortion is frequently missing. Why are reproductive issues perceived as unimportant to the Asian-American communities? I think there are several reasons—ignorance, classism, sexism, and language barriers. Of course, these issues are interrelated, and I'll try to make the connections between them.

First, let me state that I am not an "expert" on the topic of reproductive issues in Asian-American communities, but that I have some firsthand experiences which have given me some insight into the problems. Several years ago, I was a staff psychologist at a local community health center serving the greater Boston Asian population. Most of our patients were recent immigrants from China, Vietnam, Cambodia, Laos, and Hong Kong. Almost all of these new immigrants understood little or no English. With few resources (financial or otherwise) many newcomers struggled to make sense of life in America and to survive in whatever fashion they could.

At the health center, the staff tried to help by providing information and advocacy in getting through our confusing system. I thought we did a pretty good job until I found out that neither our health education department nor our ob/gyn department provided *any* counseling or information about birth control or abortion services. The medical department had interpreted our federal funding regulations as prohibiting not only the performance of abortions on-site, but prohibiting the dissemination of information which might lead to, or help patients to obtain an abortion.

Needless to say, as a feminist and as an activist, I was horrified. When I found out that pregnant women who inquired about abortions were given only a name of a white, English speaking ob/gyn doctor and sent out alone, this practice seemed morally and ethically neglectful. One of the nurse-midwives agreed with me and suggested that I could serve as an interpreter/advocate for pregnant women who needed to have abortions or at least wanted to discuss the option with the English-speaking ob/gyn doctor. The only catch was that I would have to do it on my own time, that I could not claim any affiliation with the health center, and that I could not suggest follow-up care at the health center.

Not fully knowing the nature of what I was volunteering for, I agreed to interpret and advocate for Cantonese-speaking pregnant women at their appointments with the obstetrician. It turned out that over the course of three years I interpreted during at least a hundred abortions for Asian immigrant women who spoke no English. After the first few abortions, the obstetrician realized how essential it was to have an interpreter present, and began to require that all non-English speaking women have an interpreter during the abortion procedure.

As a middle-class, educated, bi-lingual Asian-American woman, I was aware of the importance of having the choice to have an abortion, and the necessity to fight for the right to choose for myself, but I had been unaware of how the right to have an abortion is also a right to survival in this country if you are a poor, uneducated, non-English speaking immigrant.

From *Common Ground—Different Planes,* July 1990, pp. 6, 12. Copyright © 1990 by The Women of Color Partnership Program of the Religious Coalition for Reproductive Choice.

Connie Chan is a native Hawaiian. An activist and feminist, Ms. Chan is an Associate Professor of Human Service at the University of Massachusetts in Boston.

The women I interpreted for were for the most part not young. Nor were they single. They ranged in age from 25–45, with a majority in their late twenties and early thirties. Almost all of the women were married and had two or more children. Some had as many as five or six children. They needed to have an abortion because they had been unlucky enough to have gotten pregnant after arriving in this country. Their families were barely surviving on the low wages that many new immigrant workers earned as restaurant workers, garment factory workers, or as domestic help.

Almost all of the women worked full-time: the ones who had young children left them with older retired family members or did piecework at home; those with older children worked in the factories or hotels. Without fail, each woman would tell me that each needed to have an abortion because her family could not afford another mouth to feed, that they could not afford to lose her salary contribution, not even for a few months, to care for an infant. In some ways, one could not even say that these women were *choosing* to have abortions. The choice had already been made for them and it was a choice of basic survival for the members of their family unit.

Kai was one of the women for whom I interpreted. A 35-year old mother of four children, ages 2 to 7, she and her husband emigrated to the U.S. from Vietnam. They had no choice in their immigration, either, they were refugees whose village had been destroyed, and felt fortunate to escape with their lives and all four of their children. Life in the U.S. was difficult, but they were scraping by, living with another family in a small apartment where their entire family slept in one room. Their hope was that their children would receive an education and make it in American society: They lived with the day-to-day hope of that deferred dream for the next generation.

When Kai found out that she was pregnant she felt desperate. Because she and her husband love children and live for their children, they wanted desperately to keep the child, this one that would be born in America and be an American citizen from birth. Yet they sadly realized that they could not afford another child, they could not survive on just one salary, they could not feed another one. Their commitment was to the children they already had, and keeping their family together.

When I accompanied Kai to her abortion, she was saddened, but resigned to what she had to do. The $300 that she brought to the clinic represented almost a month of wages for her, she had borrowed the money from family and friends. She would pay it back, she said, by working weekends for the next ten weeks. Her major re-

gret was that she would not be able to buy any new clothes for her children this year because of this unexpected expense.

Kai spoke very little English. She did not understand why she had to go to a white American doctor for her abortion, instead of receiving services from her Asian doctor at the health center. She had no understanding, really, of reproductive rights issues, of *Roe v. Wade,* or why there were demonstrators waving pictures of fetuses and yelling at her as we entered the clinic. Mercifully, she did not understand the questions they shouted at her in English, and she did not ask me what they said, remarking only that they (the protestors) seemed very angry at someone. She felt sure, I think, that they were not angry at *her.* She had done nothing to provoke anyone's anger. She was merely trying to survive in this country under this country's rules.

It is a moral crime and an injustice that Kai could not receive counseling in her language by her doctors at the Asian neighborhood health center. It is an injustice that she had to borrow $300 to pay for her own abortion, because her Medicaid benefits did not pay for it. It is a grave injustice that she had to have me, a stranger, interpreting for her during her abortion because her own doctor could not perform the procedure at her clinic . Again, it was not a matter of choice for her to abort her pregnancy, but a matter of basic survival.

Kai will probably never attend a march or rally for choice. She will not sign any petitions. She might not even vote. But it is for her and the countless thousands of immigrant women like her that we need to continue the struggle for reproductive rights. Within the Asian American community, the immigrant women who are most affected by the lack of access to abortions have the least power. They do not speak English, they do not demand equal access to health care; their needs are easily overlooked.

Thus it is up to us who are bi-lingual, those of us who can speak English and who can speak to these issues, to do so. We need to insure that the issue of reproductive rights is an essential one in the Asian American political agenda. It is not a woman's issue; it is a community issue.

We must speak for the Kais, for their children, for their right to survive as a family. We must, as activists, make the connection between the issues of oppression based upon gender, race, national origin, sexual orientation, class or language. We can, and must lead the Asian American community to recognize the importance of the essential issue of reproductive rights for the community's survival.

Sterilization Abuse: The Policies Behind the Practice

by Kathryn Krase

This is the eighth in a series of articles commemorating the history of the women's health movement and featuring the founders of the National Women's Health Network.

In 1968, a Puerto Rican demographer reported that women of childbearing age in Puerto Rico were more than ten times more likely to be sterilized than were women from the United States. The Puerto Rican sterilization rate of over 35% led to questions about systematic biases that influenced the practice of sterilization.

Since the United States assumed governance of Puerto Rico in 1898, population control has been a major effort. The US., worried that overpopulation of the island would lead to disastrous social and economic conditions, instituted public policies aimed at controlling the rapid growth of the population. The passage of Law 116 in 1937 signified the institutionalization of the population control program. This program, designed by the Eugenics Board, was intended to "catalyze economic growth," and respond to "depression-era unemployment." Both U.S. government funds and contributions from private individuals supported the initiative.

Instead of providing women with access to alternative forms of safe, legal, and reversible contraception, U.S. policy promoted the use of permanent sterilization. Institutionalized encouragement of sterilization through the use of "door-to-door" visits by health workers, financial subsidy of the operation, and industrial employer favoritism toward sterilized women pushed women towards having "la operacion." These coercive strategies denied women access to informed consent. More than one third of the women in the 1968 study didn't know that sterilization through tubal ligation was a permanent form of contraception. The euphemism "tying the tubes" made women think that the procedure was easily reversible.

The practice of sterilization abuse was challenged by local coalitions. Puerto Rican women's groups, along with the movement for Puerto Rican independence, took up the fight against the injustices of the campaign to sterilize women. The economically disadvantaged women of Puerto Rico lacked access to information that would make contraceptive alternatives available to them. By denying access to reproductive health services for the women who were most in need of them, US. policy exerted its control over the growth of the Puerto Rican population, as well as over the lives of many Puerto Rican women. Dr. Helen Rodriguez-Trias, M.D. summarized the situation in Puerto Rico: "Women make choices based on alternatives, and there haven't been many alternatives in Puerto Rico."

The U.S., like Puerto Rico, was not a stranger to forced sterilizations. As early as 1907, the United States had instituted public policy that gave the state the right "to sterilize unwilling and unwitting people." Laws, similar to Law 116, were passed in 30 states. These policies listed the insane, the "feeble-minded," the "dependent," and the "diseased" as incapable of regulating their own reproductive abilities, therefore justifying government-forced sterilizations. Legitimizing sterilization for certain groups led to further exploitation, as group divisions were made along race and class lines.

In the early 1970's, Dr. Rodriguez-Trias was invited by a New York University Law School student organization to give a short talk about Puerto Rican sterilization abuse after viewing a related film. After her talk, Dr. Rodriguez-Trias was approached by a

From *The Network News,* January–February 1996, pp. 1, 4–5. Copyright © 1996 by the National Woman's Health Network. Reprinted by permission.

Kathryn Krase was a Network intern.

handful of audience members. Some were hospital workers who recalled stories of minority and disadvantaged women who were coerced into signing sterilization consent forms. Full information on the procedure and its alternatives was not provided. The case of a young woman, incarcerated by the New York City Police, was brought up in discussion. While being detained, the woman discovered she was pregnant and wished to have an abortion. She was taken to a public city hospital for the procedure. During counseling for the abortion, sterilization was offered as the best prevention of future unwanted pregnancies. Uninformed and misled, the young woman signed the papers and later regretted the procedure. In response to the treatment of this young woman, and the many other disadvantaged women who had been coerced into giving up their reproductive rights, Dr. Rodriguez-Trias and a handful of other New Yorkers formed CESA, the Committee to End Sterilization Abuse.

As awareness of abuses increased, the call for action became stronger. In 1974, the Department of Health, Education and Welfare (now Health and Human Services) published guidelines for sterilization procedures. These guidelines established a moratorium on sterilization of women under the age of 21 and on others without the legal ability to provide consent. A 72-hour waiting period between the signing of a consent form and the procedure was mandated. A written statement that women would not lose their welfare benefits if they refused the sterilization procedure, and that reserved a woman's right to change her mind and refuse the procedure anytime up until the surgery, even after granting original consent, served as informed consent. However, studies conducted by the ACLU and the Center for Disease Control in 1975 showed that noncompliance with the guidelines was widespread.

At this time, New York City public hospitals were bearing the brunt of regional complaints. These hospitals were the major source of health care for the city's economically disadvantaged, and consequently provided reproductive services for many of the city's poor women. The Health and Hospitals Corporation (HHC), the group that oversees the city's hospitals, became an important tool in the study, identification, and monitoring of sterilization abuse practices.

In early 1975, the HHC called on members of CESA, including Dr. Rodriguez-Trias, and members of other reproductive rights organizations, to serve on an ad hoc Advisory Committee on Sterilization Guidelines. The goal of the advisory committee was to set guidelines, like the HEW guidelines, for the public hospitals of New York City. These local guidelines hoped to promote the successful monitoring of sterilization practices.

By identifying the weaknesses of the HEW guidelines, the advisory committee drafted a more effective set of regulations that were aimed at protecting the rights of the women who were mistreated in the past. The committee's guidelines required a 30-day waiting period from the signing of the consent to the procedure. During this time, hospitals were required to offer counseling services. These services were to be provided in the language that the woman spoke, and would not be given by the doctors themselves, but by a counselor removed from the clinical experience. As part of the consent, women described their understanding of the procedure and the alternatives available, so that there was no doubt that she understood the permanence of the procedure. The guidelines suggested by the advisory committee became effective HHC rules on November 1, 1975.

The guidelines set forth by the HHC could only be applied to the city's public hospitals. In response, Public Law #37 was passed by the New York City Council in April of 1977, making the HHC guidelines the law of the city, applicable to both public and private facilities. Failure to comply with these regulations would result in a penalty. Public Law #37 was unique in that past guidelines were expanded to include the regulation of the practice of sterilization on men as well as women.

With success in New York City, groups in other regions looked toward pursuing similar goals. In Los Angeles, a group of ten Mexican-American women successfully sued the County Hospital for denying them informed consent. These women, who only spoke Spanish, were coerced into signing consent forms in English, while some were in labor and others were under anesthesia. Since the successful settlement of this case, the L.A. County Hospital has become squeaky clean when it comes to following sterilization guidelines.

In response to regional action, the HEW redesigned their national guidelines for sterilization practices to embody the provisions of New York's Public Law #37 in 1978. The national guidelines received widespread support from CESA as well as over one hundred other regional and national organizations, but also faced opposition from organizations that saw the guidelines as limiting women's access to sterilization as a choice for contraception.

Even with these many successes, less fortunate and poorly educated women are still being denied the reproductive freedoms available to other women, and entitled to all. Dr. Rodriguez-Trias believes that although the organization of local groups has been effective in the sharing of information as well as in applying pressure to policy makers, only with raised consciousness, informed consent, and the existence and accessibility to real alternatives, can freedom of choice become a reality for all women.

REFERENCES

Bauza, Vanessa. "Puerto Rico: The Covert Campaign to Sterilize Women. *Ms. Magazine.* Sept./Oct. 1994.

Corea, Gena. *The Hidden Malpractice: How American Medicine Treats Women as Patients and Professionals.* New York: William Morrow. 1977, p. 128.

Dreifus, Claudia. "Sterilizing the Poor. *The Progressive.* Dec. 1975, p. 13.

Rodriguez-Trias, Helen. Telephone Interview. Oct. 13, 1995.

Rodriguez-Trias, Helen. "Puerto Rico, Where Sterilization of Women Became 'La Operacion.'"

Rodriguez-Trias, Helen. "Sterilization Abuse" Lecture. 1976. Published by The Women's Center, Bamard College, 1978.

Tyler, Jr., Carl W. "An Assessment of Policy Compliance with the Federal Control of Sterilization" Atlanta, GA. Centers for Disease Control. June 1975.

Norplant Information Sheet

by National Latina Health Organization

The National Latina Health Organization (NLHO) is committed to work toward the goal of bilingual access to quality health care and the empowerment of Latinas through culturally sensitive educational programs, health advocacy, outreach, research and the development of public policy.

The NLHO would like to break some myths and set the record straight. . . Latinas do believe in reproductive rights, do use birth control, do get abortions, and do believe passionately that women should be able to make their own reproductive decisions without any political, social or religious interference. An eighty-four year-old Mexican Catholic woman sums it up very neatly: "If women don't have that (right), what do they have?"

Norplant. . . is it the answer to a woman's prayers? Or is it a form of social control that will be used to control the reproduction of particular groups of women? Is it a safe form of birth control?

The National Latina Health Organization (NLHO) is very concerned with its safety. The NLHO does not feel that there has been sufficient research done. We are not convinced that twenty years of research is enough to give us information on long-term effects and generational effects. No research or testing has been conducted on women under eighteen years of age so we don't know the short or long-term effects on them. Federal Drug Administration (FDA) requirements and criteria and the FDA seal of approval do not guarantee the complete safety of Norplant. We are still living with the results of the Dalkon Shield, Depo-Provera and silicone breast implants.

We are concerned that actual and possible side-effects and the degree of their seriousness have been down-played by many health practitioners. Irregular bleeding occurs in 80% of all women. This can mean bleeding two weeks out of the month or not having periods at all. We are concerned that irregular bleeding, an early symptom of uterine cancer is not being dealt with. Once women are implanted, how will they know whether the irregular bleeding is due to Norplant or an actual symptom of cancer? There is no set protocol on how soon a woman should be examined after Norplant insertion. Will those women who do not have access to regular health care but have been implanted with Norplant, have the regular exams that they need?

Side effects also include headaches, mood changes and acne. The so-called 'experts' are saying that women with high-blood pressure and smokers don't have any special concerns. But the Office of Family Planning Policy Statement Guidelines of California and the Wyeth "Norplant System Patient Labeling" make a point of this. To quote, "Women who use the oral contraceptives should not smoke as it greatly increases the risk of serious adverse effects on the heart and blood vessels; therefore, it is likely that it may be a problem with Norplant use." There is no consensus in the medical field that side effects and conditions that are specific to estrogen-based oral contraceptives need not be considered with Norplant.

We are concerned with how quickly Norplant and funding was made available in all fifty states and the District of Columbia. So quickly that there wasn't adequate or language appropriate information available so women could truly be able to make an informed decision. In February of 1992, the state of California made $5 million dollars available to provide Norplant to women eligible for the Office of Family Planning and Medi-Cal services. How much of this money is being used to target and inform specific or particular groups of women, i.e. women on welfare, Immigrant women or women of color? This has never been done before for any other type of birth control. Hundreds of health personnel have been trained to implant Norplant, but they have not all been trained to remove it.

We are not being paranoid when we question the ethics of Norplant. We have been victims of selective reproductive control before. The forced sterilization of Latinas and other women of color was blatant and widespread until the class action suit against U.S.C.-Los Angeles County Medical Center in 1975. Approximately twelve Chicanas had undergone forced sterilization, in some instances, without their knowledge. One of the results of this case is that sterilization consent forms are now multilingual. Yet these abuses continue to happen, sometimes in very subtle ways. . . doctors will not give all information necessary so women can make their own decisions; or they will give their 'medical opinion' for what they think is 'best'.

The overt and covert coercion of the 'Norping' of women is our biggest concern. When women go to their clinics for birth control, is Norplant the only birth control method available at their clinic? Is it low-cost or free? Are other forms of birth control equally available, equally recommended, and equally funded? Are appointments for other forms of birth control difficult to schedule? Once Norplant is implanted, will there be trained personnel available to remove it at the end of five years? If a woman wants it removed before the fifth year, will it be difficult to schedule an appointment for its removal? Will her request be granted? Will she be encouraged to keep it in another few months? Will it be removed regardless of whether she can afford the removal fee that can be as high as $300?

Obviously this is the real issue. Norplant is NOT WOMAN CONTROLLED. So whose control is it under?

What is most alarming about Norplant is the immediate potential for, and actual abuse. Norplant was approved by the FDA in late December, 1990. By January 5th, 1991, Judge Broadman in Visalia, California ordered a woman to have Norplant implanted as a condition of her probation. Seven states have introduced legislative bills involving Norplant since then. One type links the use of Norplant and public assistance benefits, either by providing financial incentives to encourage women who receive financial assistance to use Norplant; or by requiring Norplant use as a condition for receiving public assistance. The second mandates that women convicted of particular crimes, usually child abuse, child neglect or drug use, be required to have Norplant implanted. Assemblyman Murry in the 56th District of California attempted to pass a bill that linked AFDC benefits to Norplant. Fortunately this bill no longer exists in any recognizable form because of the NLHO involvement at the state level.

We are hearing from Latinas that they are being pressured into using Norplant rather than other contraceptives. We know that some clinics have Spanish language Norplant pamphlets in their waiting rooms, but none in English. We know that Native American women on reservations are being `Norped'. On a reservation in Montana, a large majority of the young teens, have been 'Norped', yet nowhere on the reservation are there condoms available. A woman from another state came to an Oakland clinic during the summer of 1992 to have Norplant removed after a judge in her home state had ordered her implanted. The clinic did not remove the Norplant until they had called a meeting of their medical board. Why wasn't it removed on demand?

We know that there are very unethical practices being used when training health providers to implant Norplant. A woman in Southern California complained that after being recruited to have Norplant implanted free of charge, her calls were not returned when she requested that Norplant be removed because of the side effects. When her call was finally returned, she was told that it would cost her $300 to have it removed. We alerted "Street Stories", a television program in New York that was preparing a story on Norplant. With the permission of the young woman, a "Street Stories" reporter contacted the clinic. The Clinic providers were very upset, and couldn't understand why the young woman thought she could not have it removed. Why must we go through these extraordinary efforts?

The Baltimore School is now making Norplant available through their school clinic. It is extremely important to note that the Norplant 'consent forms' state that the removal of Norplant may not be available through their clinic and that one may have to go to another clinic for removal at the individual's own expense. In addition, when the Health Department Director and the clinic director were questioned about the sex education that was provided for their students, they admitted that students only get a few hours of sex education during their entire junior high and high school career.

A clinic provider (who wishes to remain anonymous) in Savannah, Georgia, claims that young adolescent women are being encouraged to accept Norplant. The Norplant 'consent form' states that if the individual wants it removed, she will have to go to a local hospital for the procedure; and that it is up to the hospital to decide whether it will be removed or not.

Clinics in South Dakota are adopting the policy of not removing Norplant unless it is 'medically indicated'. A woman cannot have it removed simply because she requests it for whatever reason. If side-effects are intolerable to her, it is still up to the provider to decide whether it should be removed.

A social worker in New Jersey has counseled a young mother that cut the Norplant out of her own arm because her clinic providers refused to remove it.

After having Norplant implanted, a young black adolescent in Atlanta complained about irregular bleeding to her provider. The provider prescribed oral contraceptives to regulate her menstrual cycle. Now this young women has two systemic hormonal contraceptives coursing through her body.

A clinic in San Francisco at first refused to accept young Asian women in their clinic because they were prostitutes. They were told that they did not accept "their kind of people", that they served middle-class white women. Once an advocate intervened so that the women could be taken care of, the clinic provider kept encouraging the use of Norplant and would not offer another method.

These are the stories we are hearing; there are hundreds more untold stories that have not reached us yet. The women of Color Coalition for Reproductive Health Rights, along with other organizations, has been meeting with David Kessler, Commissioner of the FDA and his staff; and Patsy Fleming and Dennis Hayashi of Donna Shalala's office to discuss our deep concerns regarding the abuse of Norplant. We must keep telling these stories and advocating for and intervening for women that have no other recourse.

The National Latina Health Organization believes that women should have all reproductive options available . . . culturally relevant quality health care and information; education about sexuality; alternative forms of woman-controlled birth control that are safe and affordable; prenatal care so that we can have healthy babies; fertility services; safe and legal abortions; and freedom from reproductive abuses. The NLHO also believes that all forms of birth control be developed with the purpose of giving safe, affordable choices to women of all ages so that they can control their own reproductive lives. This is not an unreasonable expectation. It is a very sane and logical expectation.

The Misuses of Norplant: Who Gets Stuck?

by Jennifer Washburn

Su Juan Fields was 21 years old when she gave birth to her daughter, Mikyah. Shortly thereafter, in November 1991, she decided to look into getting Norplant. Approved by the Food and Drug Administration (FDA) in 1990, Norplant consists of six matchstick-size capsules made of silastic (the same material that encases breast implants) inserted into a woman's arm, which secrete a synthetic progestin and provide up to five years of highly effective contraception.

At Detroit's Metro Medical Clinic, Fields learned that Norplant was fully covered by Medicaid, but she would have to wait three months for insertion because so many women were getting it. "I thought that meant it was a good thing. Even the receptionist said she had it and liked it. So I told them I was interested." Fields says she was never counseled about any other contraceptive methods, and that Ellen Morin, her nurse practitioner, never discussed Norplant's contraindications or side effects except to say that Fields might experience three to six months of irregular bleeding.

Immediately after the capsules were inserted, Fields suffered continual bleeding, severe cramping, migraine headaches, fatigue, and dizziness. She had trouble going to work. "I never had a migraine before Norplant. I was feeling weak, I lost so much blood. I told [Morin], 'I don't want it in me anymore.' I explained the product was not working, but she wouldn't take it out."

Fields says she regularly returned to the clinic to describe her illnesses and request removal but, each time, Morin expressed reluctance to remove it and instead prescribed new things to alleviate the symptoms: estrogen, birth control pills, Motrin, even vitamin C. For two and a half years, the Metro Medical Clinic refused Fields's request to have the Norplant removed. When Fields finally switched to another clinic and found a doctor willing to perform the removal, she was told that the Norplant capsules had been inserted too deeply. After an

hour of painful surgery, which tore ligaments in her arm, the doctor was unable to find the sixth capsule and opted to leave it in.

Two years have passed and Su Juan Fields has still not fully recovered from her ordeal. Though the bleeding stopped, the migraines recur, and she is concerned about the effect of the remaining capsule, should she decide to have another child. (A startling 18 percent of the accidental pregnancies that occur on Norplant, which she is technically still on, are reported to be ectopic [outside the uterus], posing a danger to the woman's life.)

Feeling angry and violated by her experience, Fields has joined 4,700 other women in a class action lawsuit against Wyeth-Ayerst Laboratories, the manufacturer of Norplant. Jewel Klein, a Chicago-based lawyer who handles this class of suit, has filed claims against the company for its misrepresentation of Norplant's side effects and removal problems. In 1994 and 1995, Wyeth-Ayerst, responding to the suits and negative publicity, substantially revised its product warnings to include the severity of certain side effects, and new medical complications previously not reported. The first hearings will begin in February.

Though no one knows how many of the estimated one million Norplant users in this country have experienced problems, some 400 lawsuits have been filed, including class actions representing 50,000 women. Klein estimates that at least a quarter of her plaintiffs had to undergo surgery more than once in order to remove all the Norplant capsules. Problems arise for a variety of reasons: doctors are often nor properly trained in insertion, thick scar tissue can build up around even the most carefully inserted capsules, and capsules can migrate inside the arm. Norplant is particularly inappropriate for women predisposed to keloid scarring, an overproduction of external scar tissue that affects black women at a much higher rate than other women. Many Norplant

From *Ms. Magazine,* Nov/Dec, 1996, pp. 32–36. Reprinted by permission of *Ms. Magazine,* © 1996.

Jennifer Washburn is a New York City-based freelance journalist.

recipients request removal before the full five years. A University of California study, financed by Wyeth-Ayerst and the Population Council—the developer of Norplant—found that 54 percent of 205 Norplant recipients discontinued use within a little more than three years. Reasons cited for early removal included chronic bleeding, sexual problems, headaches, weight fluctuation, and acne.

But besides the well-documented medical complications associated with Norplant, there is a more obscured, yet no less important, dimension of economics and class at play. Norplant costs $365, not including the medical fees for insertion and removal, which can raise the cost to more than $700 for private-sector patients. In 1993, Congressman Ron Wyden (D.-Oreg.) attacked Wyeth-Ayerst for refusing to lower its price, pointing out that more than 17 million taxpayer dollars went into the research and development of the device, and that Medicaid—one of Norplant's largest buyers—was paying more than 22 times its actual cost. So, while politicians scream about taxes paying for women and children on welfare, we hear nothing about those same taxes underwriting Wyeth-Ayerst.

In addition, as Lisa Kaeser of the Alan Guttmacher Institute explains, because Wyeth-Ayerst refused to market Norplant to family planning clinics at a discount (standard practice with contraceptives) "only women on Medicaid and wealthy women have access to Norplant—women who fall in between do not."

Though class issues are seldom discussed, it is clear that the vast majority of women affected by the litigation and controversies surrounding Norplant are poor, and a disproportionate number are women of color. Both Jewel Klein and Sybil Shainwald, a New York City lawyer, confirm that most of their clients in Norplant cases are low-income women; many of Klein's clients are on public assistance. Still, Medicaid coverage of Norplant is only one factor explaining its prevalence among low-income women. Another lies in our society's misguided attempts to embrace birth control as the sole cure for poverty.

Norplant was the first major contraceptive method to hit the U.S. market since the Pill's arrival in 1965. Understandably, the device garnered considerable enthusiasm given how dissatisfied many women still feel about birth control options. Less than a week after FDA approval, however, the Philadelphia *Inquirer* featured an editorial entitled "Poverty and Norplant: Can Contraception Reduce the Underclass?" Though the paper's editorial board was promptly forced to apologize, its suggestion that "welfare mothers" be "offered an increased benefit for agreeing to use this new, safe, long-term contraceptive" began popping up all over. A flurry of legislation in more than 13 states proposed offering financial incentives for women on welfare to "choose" Norplant. In 1994, legislators in Connecticut proposed paying recipients of Aid to Families with Dependent children

(AFDC) $700 to use Norplant, and $200 more for each year of continued use. In Oklahoma, lawmakers proposed giving a $500 income tax credit to any health care provider who gave Norplant to a woman on AFDC. During 1992 and 1993, Mississippi, South Carolina, North Carolina, and Ohio even considered *mandating* sterilization or the use of a long-term hormonal contraceptive for any AFDC recipient.

Thanks to a concerted campaign by women's rights advocates, as well as the negative publicity generated from Norplant lawsuits, none of these laws passed, and new coercive proposals did not reappear in 1996. But Norplant continues to be misused in other ways. State Medicaid agencies, for example, often generously cover the cost of Norplant insertion but don't cover removal if a woman wants the device out before the full five years. With any contraceptive that requires a medical provider to start and terminate the method, it's imperative that the patient have access to removal at any time.

Shortly after the Indian Health Service began to offer Norplant on reservations in South Dakota, Charon Asetoyer, a Native American women's health advocate, started receiving phone calls from women being denied removal. Asetoyer discovered, to her dismay, that South Dakota's Medicaid policy covers early removal "only due to infection or rejection or when determined medically necessary. If removal . . . is to reverse the intent of the implant, the recipient is responsible for the cost."

Of course, medical "necessity" is defined by the provider and the Medicaid agency, not the patient. "We have women who've gained 40 and 50 pounds on Norplant, who are denied removal," says Asetoyer. When the life of the woman is at risk, doctors "are supposed to remove it, regardless. Instead, doctors are trying to talk women into waiting; they say weight gain is not a serious issue."

Although Medicaid is federally funded, states are given remarkable autonomy in determining what they will and will not cover The provider manual in South Carolina is particularly blunt: removal is "reimbursable only if medically necessary due to medical complications directly related to Norplant. . . . Normal side effects related to Norplant are not considered medical complications and the removal will be denied payment." Utah Medicaid spokesperson Raydell Ashley justified the state's removal restrictions in terms of an investment: "We have [patients who] want reversal early. But we won't pay $500 for putting it in, another $100 for reversal, and then start paying for birth control pills." In Oklahoma, as in these other states, the chronic side effects Su Juan Fields suffered from Norplant would not be adequate cause for removal. As Oklahoma Medicaid spokesperson Nan Hastings explained dismissively: "A lot of women will say, 'I'm having headaches.' But we don't cover removals for that because we told women [when they chose Norplant] about the side effects."

Thousands of low-income women receive Norplant through Medicaid during a brief period that lasts from childbirth to 60 days postpartum (the so-called pregnancy loophole), after which time they are no longer eligible for aid—and removal is not covered. Another catch-22 is related to our tricky welfare laws; Medicaid coverage is lost when women leave welfare to take jobs—jobs that frequently do not provide health insurance.

While several national organizations regularly track reproductive rights in state legislatures, few monitor these issues at the state Medicaid level. Natalie Gomez-Vélez, a staff attorney at the American Civil Liberties Union, was deeply troubled to learn that such coercive Norplant policies exist: "This is part of a trend, long-practiced in this country, of denying certain populations their reproductive rights. This underhanded method of inserting language in the state books shows that regulators have no qualms about interfering with a woman's most basic human rights."

So, where is Wyeth-Ayerst in all this mess? Early on, the company saw the potential for a public relations disaster if thousands of low-income women were unable to afford removal. In March 1995, already on the defensive because Norplant's high price had cut middle-income women out of the market (leaving the company with a disproportionate number of low-income users), Wyeth-Ayerst created the Norplant Foundation Removal Assistance Network to provide free removal services to low-income women who lack health coverage. In a recent interview, Liz Walton, manager of client services for the foundation, said that "at least half of our Medicaid patients can't get removal before the five years." The network has stepped in and provided more than 11,000 women with free removals thus far. Sounds nice, but the company's intentions were far from altruistic. In April 1995, attorney Klein discovered that women who qualified for free removals were also required to sign a paper releasing the foundation and any of its "agents"—which include Wyeth-Ayerst itself—from all legal actions related to Norplant removal. By exposing this sleight of hand, Klein won a court guarantee that any woman who signed papers would not jeopardize her future legal rights against Wyeth-Ayerst, should she suffer deleterious effects from Norplant.

While Norplant use has by all accounts been dropping steadily—largely because of the medical complications that have come to light—the class issues surrounding it and other contraceptives remain very much alive. As the welfare legislation passed last summer demonstrates, politicians have declared open season on poor women with children. They impugn teen mothers, without improving their educational opportunities or job prospects; and impose rigid work requirements and benefit limits, without providing day care services or job training. In such an environment, it's hardly surprising that states, newly liberated from federal oversight, promote birth control in increasingly coercive ways.

With Norplant's popularity waning, women's groups are shifting their attention to Depo-Provera, another provider dependent contraceptive that is very popular among women of color, especially teenagers. Women's health activists worry that once this three-month synthetic progestin shot enters a patient's bloodstream, it cannot be reversed or neutralized if she suffers adverse effects.

It should be acknowledged that many women are thoroughly satisfied with both Depo-Provera and Norplant. In low-income communities, however, problems are exacerbated by the substandard levels of medical treatment that many poor women receive. As Julia Scott of the National Black Women's Health Project told the New York Times: "The opposition that you will hear from some of the progressive women's groups and most of the women-of-color groups is not against technology or against new methods . . . but against how we know it will eventually be used with poor women."

Efforts to control the fertility of low income women, without concern for their bodily integrity or reproductive rights, extend to today's welfare debate. vowing to "end welfare as we know it," Republicans and Democrats alike have embraced faulty assumptions about poor women on welfare. Even before the welfare bill was signed, the federal government had approved "family caps" in 16 states, which deny additional benefits to children born to a mother on welfare. The autonomy that states have gained under the welfare bill will only make these laws more popular.

Like coercive Medicaid and Norplant policies, child exclusion laws are based on the erroneous assumption that poor women are unable to control their fertility, so society must do it for them. The truth? The average AFDC family has two children—slightly less than the average non-AFDC family. Overwhelming evidence has shown that assistance levels do not affect family size. States that have the lowest percentage of welfare families with four or more children have the highest grant levels. And Mississippi, the state with the lowest AFDC grant level ($1.33 a day, per person, for a family of three), has the highest percentage of families with four or more kids.

Preventing poor women from having children, without addressing the root causes of poverty, creates the climate for the kinds of abuses already seen with Norplant and Depo-Provera. The more that politicians demonize poor women, peppering their speeches with code words like "dependency," "illegitimacy," and "teen pregnancy," the more likely such abuses become. A society so focused on controlling poor women's reproductive choices swerves close to reviving a long and ugly history of eugenics.

And, as Asetoyer notes, society's current message to low-income women is clear: "Stay poor, but not pregnant."

'The Pill' May Not Mix Well with Other Drugs

by Judith Willis

A young newlywed had been taking birth control pills several months in the early 1970s when she developed a bladder infection. She consulted her doctor, who prescribed an antibiotic. The infection cleared up quickly. But nine months later she gave birth to her first child.

Today, with proper communication between physician and patient, the inadvertent pregnancy in this mythical example would be far less likely to occur. Many interactions between oral contraceptives (OC's) containing both estrogen and progestogen and other drugs are now well-known and included in both the physician and patient labeling of the pill.

Such interactions can not only diminish the contraceptive's effectiveness, but also increase or decrease the potency of the other drug. Both those who take oral contraceptives and those who don't may find it interesting to look at what is known about the how and why of such OC-drug interactions.

Some drugs decrease contraceptive effectiveness apparently because they increase the metabolism of the contraceptives. This means that the liver breaks down the hormones in the contraceptive faster, and they are eliminated from the body more quickly. Thus, the levels of estrogen and progestogen are reduced, sometimes so much that they no longer suppress ovulation. Breakthrough bleeding is often a symptom of this reduced effectiveness. This type of interaction is of even more concern with the very-low-dose contraceptives, since the level of hormones they contain is already low.

The first drug with which that type of OC interaction was reported was rifampicin, used to treat tuberculosis. In the early 1970s, medical journals reported breakthrough bleeding and contraceptive failure in OC users taking rifampicin. Alerted to this effect with one drug, physicians over the next few years noted the possibility of this type of decreased effectiveness with many different drugs. They include:

- antibiotics such as isoniazid, ampicillin, neomycin, penicillin V, tetracycline, chloramphenicol, sulfonamides, nitrofurantoin, and griseofulvin,
- barbiturates,
- anticonvulsants such as phenytoin and primidone, and
- the anti-inflammatory phenylbutazone.

Also, some analgesics, tranquilizers and anti-migraine preparations may have this type of interaction. OC users taking such drugs are advised *to use an additional form of contraception until they discontinue therapy with the second drug.*

When it comes to the other side of the coin—OC's affecting the potency of other drugs—knowledge about such interactions is more limited. But again, the how and why seem to be tied to the way the drug is metabolized; that is, changed into a form that can be eliminated from the body.

Some drugs are metabolized in the liver primarily by oxidation, and thus are excreted through the kidneys rather than the bowels. These drugs appear to be metabolized more slowly in OC users, according to research by a group of scientists headed by Darrell Abernathy, M.D., Ph.D., and reported in the April 1, 1982, *New England Journal of Medicine.* The researchers reported that long-term use of low-dose estrogen-containing OC's may cause diazepam (Valium), a benzodiazepine anti-anxiety drug, to stay in the body longer. This means that OC users may require lower dosages of diazepam and other drugs that are metabolized in the same way. However, since not all people metabolize drugs in the same way, the patient should be monitored by her physician to

From *FDA Consumer,* March 1987, Government Printing Office, by the U.S. Department of Health and Human Services.

Judith Willis is editor of the *FDA Drug Bulletin,* a publication for health professionals.

see if the dose should be adjusted. Other drugs that may stay in the body longer because of OC's include: other benzodiazepines such as chlordiazepoxide (Librium); hydrocortisone; antipyrine; phenothiazines; and some tricyclic antidepressants.

In contrast, some drugs that are excreted mainly through the bowels (and at times partly through the kidneys) may be eliminated more quickly in OC users. Even though the metabolism of some benzodiazepines may be slowed by OC's, there are other benzodiazepines (such as lorazepam, oxazepam and tamazepam) whose metabolism may be enhanced, so they may be excreted more quickly in women taking birth control pills. However, information on exactly how such drugs interact with OC's is scarce. In an article in the September 1982 issue of *Obstetrics & Gynecology,* Abernathy reported that, in women using low-dose OC's containing estrogen for more than three months, acetaminophen (Tylenol) was eliminated more quickly than in non-OC users. The authors theorized that this increase in the speed at which the drug is eliminated from the body might offer some protection against liver toxicity in cases of acetaminophen overdose.

But OC users taking only the recommended dosages of acetaminophen might need a higher dosage than non-OC users. Again, because response to medication is so individual and because different combinations and dosages of estrogen and progestogen may have different effects, OC users should consult their physicians about any deviation from recommended dosages.

OC users taking other drugs may need to have the dosage monitored and possibly adjusted for a variety of reasons. Some epileptics may need a change in the dosage of an anticonvulsant drug they are taking, depending on the type of OC they're using. But other women taking the same combination may not need the dosage changed. The exact reason for this "iffiness" is not known, but it may be because OC-related changes in fluid retention could influence the frequency of seizures. Because of these difficulties, many doctors recommend that women taking anticonvulsants rely on another contraceptive than birth control pills.

A similar recommendation is often made for diabetics, because OC's may cause blood sugar levels to rise. If a diabetic does take birth control pills, she should be closely monitored to see if there needs to be a change in her diabetes medication.

Hypertension can be a problem in women on birth control pills, and elevated blood pressure has been known to occur in women not hypertensive before taking OC's. To complicate matters further, some of the medications used to control high blood pressure do not work the same way in those on The Pill as in non-OC users. In particular, the blood pressure drug guanethidine often does not adequately control hypertension in OC users. OC users taking blood pressure drugs need to be more carefully monitored.

In addition to interactions with drugs, OC's may also interact with certain vitamins. Labeling for birth control pills notes that OC users may have disturbances in the metabolism of tryptophan, an amino acid. Although such a disturbance is not considered cause for undue concern, it may result in a deficiency of pyridoxine (vitamin B6). Whether that is a cause for concern is not known. Also, in rare cases, megaloblastic anemia, a certain type of anemia due to insufficient pyridoxine, has been reported in OC users. In addition, levels of folic acid—one of the B vitamins—may be lower in women on The Pill.

Preliminary studies have shown that vitamin C may increase the bio-availability of estrogens. This means that women using birth control pills who take large doses of vitamin C may be risking increased side effects from the pill's estrogen. For this reason, some experts suggest that OC users take no more than 1,000 milligrams of vitamin C daily.

Some laboratory test results can be altered by OC use. The pathologist or other lab personnel should be informed when a woman undergoing lab tests is taking birth control pills so that this can be taken into consideration when evaluating the tests. Tests that are altered by OC use include those measuring: liver function, coagulation (clotting), thyroid function, blood triglycerides and phospholipid (fats) concentrations, serum folate, glucose tolerance, and plasma levels of some trace minerals.

In most young, healthy women, the effects of taking other drugs while using oral contraceptives are no cause for alarm and should not keep women who can benefit from the contraceptive effectiveness of OC's from taking them. The effects of OC-drug interactions may vary greatly from woman to woman. Yet women should be aware of the possibility of such interactions and tell their doctor if they are taking birth control pills so that other therapy can be properly coordinated.

Eight New Nonhormonal Contraceptive Methods for Men

by Elaine Lissner

Can you think of a male contraceptive other than the condom and vasectomy? Probably not, and for good reason: though more than eight new methods exist, some of them ready to use, none have been publicized. The methods range from simpler, safer, less surgical vasectomy to ancient "folk" methods which have performed well under scientific scrutiny. They are:

#1 No-scalpel vasectomy. According to Dr. Douglas Huber, recent medical director of the Association for Voluntary Surgical Contraception, "The no-scalpel vasectomy technique is the way all vasectomies should be done. If a vasectomy can be accomplished with this minimal surgery, then any surgeon doing more surgery should justify why more is necessary."

No-scalpel vasectomy, which has been performed for 4-8 million men in China and more than 1500 men in the rest of the world, involves gently poking and stretching a small opening in the scrotal skin rather than cutting the skin. Each vas deferens (sperm duct) is then blocked just as in a standard vasectomy. No-scalpel vasectomies bleed less and heal faster than standard vasectomies; they also eliminate the need for stitches. A list of U.S. physicians who perform no-scalpel vasectomy can be obtained from the Association for Voluntary Surgical Contraception at (212) 561-8000.

#2 Permanent contraception by injection. In this experimental method, an injection of chemicals is used to close off the vas deferens, rather than cutting it surgically.

#3 Potentially reversible contraception by injectible vas deferens plug. Tests in China in over 512,000 men have shown a 98% effectiveness rate, and all the men who have had their plugs removed for at least a year have regained fertility. Encouraged by these results, the World Health Organization recently started tests in ten men. Continued success will reportedly lead to a trial in 3500 men around the world (and availability in some parts of the world within two years).

#4 Potentially reversible contraception by surgically implanted vas deferens plug. Here, a soft silicone plug, or "Shug," is implanted in the vas deferens in an operation similar to vasectomy. The Shug's main advantage over injectible plugs is its two-plugs-in-one design, which gives it the potential to be more leak-free. Any sperm which leak past the first plug are likely to stay in the space between the plugs rather than continuing on their course. Currently being studied on men in the Chicago area, the Shug is proceeding slowly but steadily.

#5 Temporary injectible contraception. The interior of the vas deferens is coated with a sperm-killing solution that keeps its effects for up to five years and can be reversed before then with a simple injection. Fertility can be restored at any time. This method has been completely safe and effective in ten years of animal trials.

From *Changing Men*, issue 24, Summer/Fall 1992, pp. 24–25. Copyright © 1992 by Elaine Lissner. Reprinted by permission of the author.

Elaine Lissner has been studying nonhormonal male contraception for the past several years. She recently established the Male Contraception Information Project, a national effort to publicize the methods. This article is based on her work, "Frontiers in Nonhormonal Male Contraceptive Research," which can be obtained (along with more information) by writing to Elaine Lissner, P.O. Box 3674, Stanford, CA 94309. Please include 75 cents in postage stamps.

Human trials are beginning in India, but testing in the United States is stalled partly because the necessary polymer has not been sent to the National Institutes of Health.

#6 Wet Heat method. The deleterious effect of heat on male fertility has been known since the time of Hippocrates. Much as aspirin was "discovered" in the 1800s from a bark that Native Americans had long been accustomed to chewing to relieve pain, heat methods are now being "discovered" as a new form of male contraception. In this method, the testes are bathed in hot water every night for three weeks. Effectiveness goes up with increased temperature (hot tub temperature is not enough). At the recommended temperature, 116 degrees Fahrenheit, forty-five minutes per day provides contraceptive effect for six months. Although 116 degrees may sound very hot, one man has reported that this temperature is actually more comfortable on the testes than on any other part of the body.

Heat methods should be used in conjunction with sperm count checks (unless, for example, the heat method is just being used to enhance another method such as condoms or diaphragms). Sperm count can be checked easily at a doctor's or urologist's office.

#7 Artificial Cryptorchidism ("Jockey Method"). Special jockey shorts are worn during the day to hold the testes inside the inguinal canal (the same tube to which the testes retract naturally during cold or dangerous conditions.) This raises the testes to body temperature, thereby achieving the heat effect. Men appear to be about equally divided between those who find it a strange feeling and those who wouldn't mind it. Some men have expressed concern that this method would cause "jock itch," but this problem has not arisen for volunteers.

#8 Ultrasound method. Ultra-short sound waves (the same type used by physical therapists to heal injuries) are applied to the testes for ten minutes once every six months, efficiently achieving the heat effect. Ultrasound should be used only after knowing all the details, as it may also be a permanent method in much greater doses.

All of these methods are nonhormonal (and thus not as prone to complicated side effects). Two of the methods (artificial cryptorchidism and wet heat) require little or no doctor intervention and could be put to use almost immediately. In addition to providing self-determination to men, any of these methods would improve the health, economic status and survival rates of women in countries (including the United States) where inadequate medical care makes many female methods unsafe or unavailable.

Do you wonder why you've never heard of these? In addition to the hurdles which face all contraceptive development, research bias has played a large part. In the past, funding agencies have found reasons not to fund research on male contraceptives, such as claiming that men are not committed to contraception (even though vasectomy makes up 12% of the world's contraceptive use) and that new male methods shouldn't be developed because they don't prevent the spread of HIV (even though new female methods such as Norplant don't either). Simple methods with low profit-margins have received even less support. With funding levels so low, even supportive researchers couldn't accomplish much.

According to a 1990 committee convened by the Institute of Medicine/National Research Council, "Unless immediate steps are taken to change public policy, the choice of contraceptives in the United States in the next century will not differ appreciably from what it is today." However, many researchers and policymakers believe men don't care about contraception.

How can this be changed? Read up on the subject and make it one of your priorities, since research will increase only when public pressure is strong enough to provide incentive. Think about these methods, talk about them, and share this article with a friend. Bias is already fading, and with eight new methods in the wings, men and women don't need to wait any longer.

If You Want to Use These Methods

The only methods which are "ready to go" are wet heat, artificial cryptorchidism and no-scalpel vasectomy.

No-scalpel vasectomy is a small improvement on vasectomy. However, if you or someone you know is considering a vasectomy, this is the way to do it. To get a list of physicians who perform no-scalpel vasectomies, call the Association for Voluntary Surgical Contraception's general number at (212)561-8000. No-scalpel vasectomy is even safer and less invasive than the already safe vasectomy procedure.

Wet-Heat method and artificial cryptorchidism ("jockey method") are in some sense ready to use—if you are willing to be your own researcher, method user, doctor and critical thinker all rolled into one. Neither of these methods is in widespread use or well-known to doctors. Hopefully, in the near future men will be able to go to their doctors for an ultrasound treatment or for a "do's and don'ts" manual for using the other heat methods. However, until that time men and women who use these methods must take full responsibility for reading up, knowing what they're doing and making a fully informed choice.

If you are interested, start by reading the original paper, **"Frontiers in Nonhormonal Male Contraceptive Research."** Then go to a medical library and photocopy all the references in that citation on heat methods in general and the specific method you're interested in. Be certain to read the Kandeel and Swerdloff paper, even though it is very technical. **Contact the Male Contraception Information Project if you need more information.**

If you decide to use the wet heat method you'll have to experiment a bit to find a way to keep the water hot. Be creative. For example, modified old-style baby bottle warmers might work. If you come up with a good idea, let us know so we can pass it on. Regarding the use of hot tubs, you should know that it would take hours of hot-tubbing every day to produce contraceptive effect. That is why the wet heat method involves testes only bathing at higher temperatures.

—Elaine Lissner
Male Contraception Information Project

WORKSHEET—CHAPTER 9

Fertility, Infertility, and Reproductive Rights/Freedom

1. Three situations are described below. Make a list of all possible contraceptives which are options in the situations and briefly comment on the pros and cons for each.

Linda and Larry

Linda and Larry are 22. They have been married for one year and want a family someday. Linda feels it is very important that she does not get pregnant now while she is supporting both of them because Larry (a scientist) is unemployed. Because of their shared religious beliefs, Larry is not happy about Linda using birth control and both feel very strongly against abortion. Linda does not feel comfortable with her own body and does not have much understanding of the menstrual cycle or the process of fertilization.

Betsy and Bob

Betsy and Bob are 22. They have been married for one year and want a family someday, but want to wait until they are older. Betsy and Bob are working towards equality in their relationship so both are working half time and going to school half time. Although Betsy and Bob hope to prevent an unplanned pregnancy, they have the money and "attitude" which would permit abortion as back-up to failed contraception. Both Betsy and Bob feel pretty comfortable with their bodies and both recently got A's in a women's health course.

Susie and Sam

Susie and Sam are 22. Susie identifies as bisexual. She is mostly sexually active with women, but once in awhile she is still sexually active with her old boyfriend, Sam. Both Susie and Sam are responsible and well informed about sexual relationships. Both Susie and Sam feel strongly that their infrequent sexual encounters should not result in a pregnancy.

2. We get very used to thinking about ways a woman can control her fertility to limit the number of children she has. As reflected in the articles in this chapter, true reproductive freedom means being able to have as many or as few children as desired. List a wide range of factors which would enable women to have as *many* children as they wish:

3. After reading "Born and Unborn: The Implications of 'Choice' for People with Disabilities," and "The Bad Baby Blues" identify some of the ramifications of routine prenatal genetic testing.

   a. Give a reason why a woman might choose to have prenatal genetic testing even if she knew she would not choose to have an abortion.

   b. What could our society do to make it easier for women to choose to have a child with a disability?

4. Identify ways in which reproductive freedom and being valued by society are closely related issues. List specific examples of how reproductive issues are related to racism, homophobia, ageism, poverty, and other issues.

CHAPTER 10

Childbearing

*M*any of the problems in the relationship between women and the health care system are clearly visible in the area of childbearing. The paternalism, the reliance on technology, and the performance of unnecessary surgery characterizing the medical profession in the United States are all evident. On a positive note, this is also an area in which organized movements by women have had an impact in improving care for women and their babies and increasing the options available. It is an area of continuing struggle, in which apparent victories may sometimes actually weaken the movement for more fundamental changes. For example, in some cases, "birthing centers" are merely hospital rooms decorated to look like home, with families allowed to be present for the birth, sometimes with a nurse midwife attending, but with the same medical interventions and little change in who is making the decisions. However, such birthing centers may "pacify" some women who would otherwise work for more major changes.

As with organizing around any women's health issue, activism for increasing choices for women during pregnancy and childbirth have had to take into account the ways different women benefit from different choices. For example, many women have worked to increase the availability of home births, but this is certainly not an option for homeless women or women in many other living situations. Similarly, many women have worked to have husbands, boyfriends, and female partners present during childbirth but the now routine practice of having a partner present may not be appropriate for a battered woman because battering very often begins or escalates during pregnancy. A theme of this book is the importance of activism to make information and choices available so women can empower themselves and have more control over their decisions affecting their health. However, as we read critiques of the medicalization of childbirth, we must remember that at a time when many women died of childbirth, women wanted more, not less, intervention, and medicalization plus improved hygiene and a better understanding of disease processes played important roles in making childbirth safer for women and babies. Also, consumer lawsuits are a driving force in pushing health care providers to "over" medicalize childbirth, and women are not all equally excited about being involved in medical decision-making.

Doris Haire's classic paper "The Cultural Warping of Childbirth," was first published in the *International Childbirth Education Association News* in 1972. It was a very influential article, comparing the experience and outcomes of childbirth in the U.S. with that of other countries. It identified common pathologically orientated obstetrical practices throughout the entire pregnancy and post-partum period which "served to warp and distort the childbearing experience in the United States." The specific issues defined in this paper became many of the key issues around which childbirth activists organized for the next twenty years.

Written more than twenty years after Doris Haire's classic, the more recent "Childbearing Policy within a National Health Program: An Evolving Consensus for New Directions" is remarkably similar. The need for redefining childbirth as a natural healthy process with midwives as the appropriate caretaker for many childbearing women, instead of viewing childbirth as a medical event requiring maximum technological intervention, seems as urgent as ever. The childbearing policy paper serves as an excellent representation of a collaborative effort of a number of women's health organizations, trying to make sure that women's voices and women's issues are core to national debates on health reform.

Although childbirth remains one of the most medicalized areas of women's lives, the two 1998 articles from the *Boston Globe,* "Midwives' Time Has Come Again" and "Some Nations Cite Lower Mortality Rates," demonstrate that by 1996, 6.5% of U.S. women were able to choose to have midwife assisted deliveries compared to only 1% in 1975.

Although many factors influence birth outcomes and infant mortality rates (and people with vested interests in different agendas will always disagree about the relative importance of different factors or how to measure cause and effect), it is important to note that both U.S. studies and cross cultural data reported in this chapter demonstrate consistently good birth outcomes with midwife assisted childbirth.

Students new to childbirth issues often talk about the *new* trend towards woman-assisted and midwifery deliveries, but the reader is reminded that childbirth has historically been "women's business." Judith Walzer Leavitt's excellent book *Brought to Bed: Childbearing in America 1750–1950* tells us that, "Before 1760 birth was a woman's affair . . . When a woman went into labor, she 'called her women together' and left her husband and other male family members outside . . . Only in cases where women were not available did men participate in labor and delivery, and only in cases where labor did not progress normally did physicians intervene and perhaps extricate a dead fetus. The midwife orchestrated the events of labor and delivery, and the women neighbors and relatives comforted and shared advice with the parturient" (pp. 36–37). An article by Linda Janet Holmes, "Thank You Jesus to Myself: The Life of a Traditional Black Midwife" (in *The Black Women's Health Book*), reminds us that while some white middle class women are gaining the option of a midwife assisted delivery, many Black women are losing their tradition of granny midwives assisting in their births.

Building on themes introduced in this chapter, the "Breast Milk" article traces some of the history of how and why U.S. women stopped breastfeeding their babies. While the article outlines many of the factors responsible for the overall low rates of breastfeeding, we are left to think about why the barriers to breastfeeding affect different groups in different ways and why the babies who might most benefit from breastfeeding are very likely not to be breastfed.

Similarly, the article summarizing much of what is known about postpartum depression ("You Never Saw June Cleaver Weeping, Did You?") leaves us with as many questions as answers. However, the information that Westerners seem to have the highest rates and prevalence of postpartum depression and that "women who feel let down by the medical system, their doctor, or by their own body, report a greater sense of depressive symptoms than women who gave birth the way they imagined and planned," certainly seems to indicate that postpartum depression could be related to other issues explored in this chapter. Postpartum depression emerges as a topic which deserves much more serious attention.

The Cultural Warping of Childbirth

by Doris Haire

While Sweden and the Netherlands compete for the honor of having the lowest incidence of infant deaths per one thousand live births, the United States continues to find itself outranked by fourteen other developed countries.[1] A spokesman for the National Foundation March of Dimes recently stated that according to the most recent data, the United States leads all developed countries in the rate of infant deaths due to birth injury and respiratory distress such as postnatal asphyxia and atelectasis. According to the National Association for Retarded Children there are now six million retarded children and adults in the United States with a predicted annual increase of over 100,000 a year. The number of children and adults with behavioral difficulties or perceptual dysfunction resulting from minimal brain damage is an ever growing challenge to society and to the economy.

While it may be easier on the conscience to blame such numbing facts solely on socioeconomic factors and birth defects, recent research makes it evident that obstetrical medication can play a role in our staggering incidence of neurological impairment. It may be convenient to blame our relatively poor infant outcome on a lack of facilities or inadequate government funding, but it is obvious from the research being carried out that we could effect an immediate improvement in infant outcome by changing the pattern of obstetrical care in the United States. It is time that we take a good look at the overall experience of childbirth in this country and begin to recognize how our culture has warped this experience for the majority of American mothers and their newborn infants.

As an officer of the International Childbirth Education Association, I have visited hundreds of maternity hospitals throughout the world—in Great Britain, Western Europe, Russia, Asia, Australia, New Zealand, the South Pacific, the Americas, and Africa. During my visits I was privileged to observe obstetric techniques and procedures and to interview physicians, professional midwives, and parents in the various countries. My companion on many of my visits was Dorothea Lang, C.N.M. (Certified Nurse-Midwife), Director of Nurse-Midwifery for New York City. Miss Lang's experience as both a nurse-midwife and a former head nurse of the labor and delivery unit of the New York-Cornell Medical Center made her a particularly well-qualified observer and companion. As we traveled from country to country certain patterns of care soon became evident. For one, in those countries that enjoy an incidence of infant mortality and birth trauma significantly lower than that of the United States, highly trained professional midwives are an important source of obstetrical care and family planning services for normal women, whether the births take place in the hospital or in the home. In these countries the expertise of the physician is called upon only when the expectant mother is ill during pregnancy, or when labor or birth is anticipated to be, or is found to be, abnormal. Under this system, the high-risk mother—the one who is most likely to bear an impaired or stillborn child—has a better opportunity to obtain in-depth medical attention than is possible under our existing American system of obstetrical care where the obstetrician is also called upon to play the role of midwife.

Deprivation, birth defects, prematurity, and low birth weight are not unique to the United States. While it is tempting to blame our comparatively high incidence of infant mortality solely on a lack of available prenatal care and on socioeconomic factors, our observations indicate that, comparatively, the prenatal care we offer most clinic patients in the United States is not grossly inferior to that available in other developed countries. Furthermore, the diet and standard of living in many countries which have a lower incidence of infant mortality than ours would be considered inadequate by American standards.

As an example, when one compares the availability of prenatal care, the incidence of premature births, the average diet of various economic groups, and the equipment available to aid in newborn-infant survival in two such diverse countries as the United States and Japan, there are no major differences between the two countries. The differences lie in (a) our frequent use of prenatal and obstetrical medication, (b) our pathologically oriented management of pregnancy, labor, birth, and postpartum, and (c) the predominance of artificial feeding in the United States, in contrast to Japan.

If present statistics follow the trend of recent years, an infant born in the United States is more than four times more likely to die in the first day of life than an infant born in Japan. But a survival of the birth process should not be our singular goal. For every American newborn infant who dies there are likely to be several who are neurologically damaged.

Unfortunately, the American tendency to warp the birth experience, distorting it into a pathological event rather than a physiological one for the normal childbearing woman, is no longer peculiar to just the United States. In my visits to hospitals in various countries I was distressed to find that some physicians, anxious to impress their colleagues with their "Americanized" techniques, have unfortunately adopted many of our obstetrical practices without stopping to question their scientific or social merit.

Few American babies are born today as nature intended them to be.

It is not unlikely that unnecessary alterations in the normal fetal environment may play a role in the incidence of neurological impairment and infant mortality in the United States. Infant resuscitation, other than routine suctioning, is rarely needed in countries such as Sweden, the Netherlands, and Japan, where the skillful psychological management of labor usually precludes the need for obstetrical medication. In contrast, in those European countries, such as Belgium, where the overall pattern of obstetrical care is similar to our own, the incidence of infant mortality also approaches our own.

Obviously there will always be medical indications which dictate the use of various obstetrical procedures, but to apply the following American practices and procedures routinely to the vast majority of mothers who are capable of giving birth without complication is to create added stress which is not in the best interests of either the mother or her newborn infant.

Let us take a close look at some of our common obstetrical practices from early pregnancy to postpartum which have served to warp and distort the childbearing

experience in the United States. While not all of the practices below affect infant mortality, it is equally apparent that they do not contribute to the reduction of infant morbidity or mortality and therefore should be reevaluated.

Withholding information on the disadvantages of obstetrical medication. Ignorance of the possible hazards of obstetrical medication appears to encourage the misuse and abuse of obstetrical medication, for in those countries where mothers are not told routinely of the possible disadvantages of obstetrical medication to themselves or to their babies the use of such medication is on the increase.

There is no research or evidence which indicates that mothers will be emotionally damaged if they are advised, prior to birth, that obstetrical medication may be to the disadvantage of their newborn infants.

Requiring all normal women to give birth in the hospital. While ICEA does not encourage home births, there is ample evidence in the Netherlands and in Chicago (Chicago Maternity Center) to demonstrate that normal women who have received adequate prenatal care can safely give birth at home if a proper system is developed for home deliveries. Over half of the mothers in the Netherlands give birth at home with the assistance of a professional midwife and a maternity aide. The comparatively low incidence of infant deaths and birth trauma in the Netherlands, a country of diverse ethnic composition and intermarriage, is evidence of the comparative safety of a properly developed home delivery service.

Dutch obstetricians point out that when the labor of a normal woman is unhurried and allowed to progress normally, unexpected emergencies rarely occur. They also point out that the small risk involved in a Dutch home delivery is more than offset by the increased hazards resulting from the use of obstetrical medication and obstetrical tampering which are more likely to occur in a hospital environment, especially in countries where professionals have had little or no exposure to normal labor and birth in a home environment during their training.

Elective induction of labor. The elective induction of labor (where there is no clear medical indication) appears to be an American idiosyncrasy which is frowned upon in other developed countries.

The elective induction of labor has been found almost to double the incidence of fetomaternal transfusion and its attendant hazards.[1] But perhaps the least appreciated problem of elective induction is the fact that the abrupt onset of artificially induced labor tends to make it extremely difficult for even the well-prepared mother to tolerate the discomfort of the intensified contractions without the aid of obstetrical medication. When the onset of labor occurs spontaneously, the normal, gradual increase in contraction length and intensity appears to provoke in the mother an accompanying tolerance for discomfort or pain.

Since the British Perinatal Hazards Study found no increase in perinatal mortality or impairment of learning ability at age seven among full-term infants unless gestation had extended beyond forty-one weeks,[3] there would appear to be no medical justification for subjecting a mother or her baby to the possible hazards of elective induction in order to terminate the pregnancy prior to forty-one weeks' gestation.

Separating the mother from familial support during labor and birth. Research indicates that fear adversely affects uterine motility and blood flow,[4] and yet many American mothers are routinely separated from a family member or close friend at this time of emotional crisis.

In most developed countries, other than the United States and the Eastern European countries, mothers are encouraged to walk about or to sit and chat with a family member or supportive person in what is called an "early labor lounge." This lounge is usually located near but outside the labor-delivery area in order to provide a more relaxed atmosphere during much of labor. The mother is taken to the labor-delivery area to be checked periodically, then allowed to return to the labor lounge for as long as she likes or until her membranes have ruptured.

Confining the normal laboring woman to bed. In virtually all countries except the United States, a woman in labor is routinely encouraged to walk about during labor for as long as she wishes or until her membranes have ruptured. Such activity is considered to facilitate labor by distracting the mother's attention from the discomfort or pain of her contractions and to encourage a more rapid engagement of the fetal head. In America, where drugs are frequently administered either orally or parenterally to laboring mothers, such ambulation is discouraged—not only for the patient's safety but also to avoid possible legal complications in the event of an accident.

Shaving the birth area. Research involving 7,600 mothers has demonstrated that the practice of shaving the perineum and pubis does not reduce the incidence of infection. In fact, the incidence of infection was slightly higher among those mothers who were shaved.[5] Yet this procedure, which tends to create apprehension in laboring women, is still carried out routinely in most American hospitals. Clipping the perineal or pudendal hair closely with surgical scissors is far less disturbing to the mother and is less likely to result in infection caused by razor abrasions.

Professional dependence on technology and pharmacological methods of pain relief. Most of the world's mothers receive little or no drugs during pregnancy, labor, or birth. The constant emotional support provided the laboring woman in other countries by the nurse-midwife, and often by her husband, appears greatly to improve the mother's tolerance for discomfort. In contrast, the American labor room nurse is frequently assigned to look after several women in labor, all or most of whom have had no preparation to cope with the discomfort or pain of childbearing. Under the circumstances, drugs, rather than skillful emotional support, are employed to relieve the mother's apprehension and discomfort (and perhaps to assuage the harried labor attendant's feeling of inadequacy).

Routine Electronic Fetal Monitoring. The wisdom of depending on an experienced nurse using a stethoscope to monitor accurately the effects of obstetrical medication on the well-being of the fetus has been demonstrated by Haverkamp.[6] No one knows the long-term or delayed consequences of ultrasonic fetal monitoring on subsequent human development. The fact that some electronic fetal monitoring devices require that a mother's membranes be ruptured and the electrode be screwed into the skin of the fetal scalp creates hazards of its own. Current research indicates that obstetrical management which reduces the need for such monitoring is advisable.

Chemical stimulation of labor. Oxytocic agents are frequently administered to American mothers in order to intensify artificially the frequency or the strength of the mother's contractions, as a means of shortening the mother's labor. While chemical stimulation is sometimes medically indicated, often it is undertaken to satisfy the American propensity for efficiency and speed. Hon suggests that the overenthusiastic use of oxytocic stimulants sometimes results in alterations in the normal fetal heart rate.[7] Fields points out that the possible hazards inherent in elective induction are also possible in artificially stimulated labor unless the mother and fetus are carefully monitored.[8]

Shortening the phases of normal labor when there is no sign of fetal distress has not been shown to improve infant outcome. Little is known of the long-term effects of artificially stimulating labor contractions. During a contraction the unborn child normally receives less oxygen. The gradual buildup of intensity, which occurs when the onset of labor is allowed to occur spontaneously and to proceed without chemical stimulation, appears likely to be a protective mechanism that is best left unaltered unless there is a clear medical indication for the artificial stimulation of labor.

Delaying birth until the physician arrives. Because of the increased likelihood of resultant brain damage to the infant the practice of delaying birth by anesthesia or physical restraint until the physician arrives to deliver the infant is frowned upon in most countries. Yet the practice still occurs occasionally in the United States and in countries where hospital-assigned midwives do not routinely manage the labor and delivery of normal mothers.

Requiring the mother to assume the lithotomy position for birth. There is gathering scientific evidence that the unphysiological lithotomy position (back flat, with knees drawn up and spread wide apart by "stirrups"), which is preferred by most American physicians because it is more convenient for the *accoucheur,* tends to alter the normal fetal environment and obstruct the normal process of childbearing, making spontaneous birth more difficult or impossible.

The lithotomy and dorsal positions tend to:

1. Adversely affect the mother's blood pressure, cardiac return, and pulmonary ventilation.[9]
2. Decrease the normal intensity of the contractions.[10]
3. Inhibit the mother's voluntary efforts to push her baby out spontaneously[11] which, in turn, increases the need for fundal pressure or forceps and increases the traction necessary for a forceps extraction.
4. Inhibit the spontaneous expulsion of the placenta[12] which, in turn, increases the need for cord traction, forced expression, or manual removal of the placenta[13]—procedures which significantly increase the incidence of fetomaternal hemorrhage.[14]
5. Increase the need for episiotomy because of the increased tension on the pelvic floor and the stretching of the perineal tissue.[15]

Australian, Russian, and American research bears out the clinical experience of European physicians and midwives—that when mothers are supported to a semisitting position for birth, with their feet supported by the lower section of the labor-delivery bed, mothers tend to push more effectively, appear to need less pain relief, are more likely to want to be conscious for birth, and are less likely to need an episiotomy.[16]

The increased efficiency of the semisitting position, combined with a minimum use of medication for birth, is evidenced by the fact that the combined use of both forceps and the vacuum extractor rarely exceeds 4 percent to 5 percent of all births in the Netherlands, as compared to an incidence of 65 percent in many American hospitals. (Cesarean section occurs in approximately 1.5 percent of all Dutch births.)

The routine use of regional or general anesthesia for delivery. In light of the current shortage of qualified anesthetists and anesthesiologists and the frequent scientific papers now being published on the possible hazards resulting from the use of regional and general anesthesia, it would seem prudent to make every effort to prepare the mother physically and mentally to cope with the sensations and discomfort of birth in order to avoid the use of such medicaments. Regional and general anesthesia not only tend adversely to affect fetal environment pharmacologically, which has been discussed previously herein, but their use also increases the need for obstetrical intervention in the normal process of birth, since both types of anesthesia tend to prolong labor.[17] Johnson points out that epidural and spinal anesthesia significantly increase the incidence of midforceps delivery and its attendant hazards.[18] Pudendal block anesthesia not only tends to interfere with the mother's ability effectively to push her baby down the birth canal due to the blocking of the afferent path of the pushing reflex, but also appears to interfere with the mother's normal protective reflexes, thus making "an explosive" birth and perineal damage more likely to occur.

The routine use of forceps for delivery. There is no scientific justification for the routine application of forceps for delivery.[19] The incidence of delivery by forceps and vacuum extractor, combined, rarely rises above 5 percent in countries where mothers actively participate in the births of their babies. In contrast, as mentioned previously, the incidence of forceps extraction frequently rises to as high as 65 percent in some American hospitals.

Routine episiotomy. There is no research or evidence to indicate that routine episiotomy (a surgical incision to enlarge the vaginal orifice) reduces the incidence of pelvic relaxation (structural damage to the pelvic floor musculature) in the mother. Nor is there any research or evidence that routine episiotomy reduces neurological impairment in the child who has shown no signs of fetal distress or that the procedure helps to maintain subsequent male or female sexual response.

The incidence of pelvic floor relaxation appears to be on the decline throughout the world, even in those countries where episiotomy is still comparatively rare. The contention that the modern washing machine has been more effective in reducing pelvic relaxation among American mothers than has routine episiotomy is given some credence by the fact that in areas of the United States where life is still hard for the woman pelvic relaxation appears in white women who have never borne children.

In developed countries where episiotomy is comparatively rare the physiotherapist is considered an important member of the obstetrical team—before as well as after birth. The physiotherapist is responsible for seeing that each mother begins exercises the day following birth which will help to restore the normal elasticity and tone of the mother's perineal and abdominal muscles. In countries where every effort is made to avoid the need for an episiotomy, interviews with both parents and professionals indicate that an intact perineum which is strengthened by postpartum exercises is more apt to result in both male and female sexual satisfaction than is a perineum that has been incised and reconstructed.

Why then, is there such an emotional attachment among professionals to routine episiotomy? A prominent European professor of obstetrics and gynecology recently made the following comment on the American penchant for routine episiotomy, "Since all the physician can really do to affect the course of childbirth for the 95 percent of mothers who are capable of giving birth without complication is to offer the mother pharmacological relief from discomfort or pain and to perform an episiotomy, there is probably an unconscious tendency for many professionals to see these practices as indispensable."

Interviews with obstetrician-gynecologists in many countries indicate that they tend to agree that a superficial, first degree tear is less traumatic to the perineal tissue than an incision which requires several sutures for reconstruction. There is no research which would indicate otherwise.

Early clamping or "milking" of the umbilical cord. Several years ago De Marsh stated that the placental blood normally belongs to the infant and his or her failure to get this blood is equivalent to submitting him or her to a rather severe hemorrhage. Despite the fact that placental transfusion normally occurs in every corner of the world without adverse consequences, there is still a great effort in the United States and Canada to deprecate the practice. One must read the literature carefully to find that placental transfusion has not been demonstrated to increase the incidence of morbidity or mortality in the placentally transfused infant.[20]

Delaying the first breast-feeding. The common American practice of routinely delaying the time of the first breast-feeding has not been shown to be in the best interest of either the conscious mother or her newborn infant. Clinical experience with the early feeding of newborn infants has shown this practice to be safe.[21] If the mother feels well enough and the infant is capable of suckling while they are still in the delivery room then it would seem more cautious, in the event of tracheoesophageal abnormality, to permit the infant to suckle for the first time under the watchful eye of the physician or nurse-midwife rather than delay the feeding for several

hours when the expertise of the professional may not be immediately available.

In light of the many protective antibodies contained in colostrum it would seem likely that the earlier the infant's intake of species specific colostrum, the sooner the antibodies can be accrued by the infant.

Offering water and formula to the breast-fed newborn infant. The common American practice of giving water or formula to a newborn infant prior to the first breast-feeding or as a supplement during the first days of life has not been shown to be in the best interests of the infant. There are now indications that these practices may, in fact, be harmful. Glucose water, once the standby in every American hospital, has now been designated a potential hazard if aspirated by the newborn infant, yet it is still used in many American hospitals.

Restricting newborn infants to a four-hour feeding schedule and withholding nightime feedings. Although widely spaced infant feedings may be more convenient for hospital personnel, the practice of feeding a newborn infant only every four hours and not permitting the infant to breast-feed at all during the night cannot be justified on any scientific grounds. Such a regimen restricts the suckling stimulation necessary to bring about the normally rapid onset and adequate production of the mother's milk. In countries where custom permits the infant to suckle immediately after birth and on demand from that time, first-time mothers frequently begin to produce breast milk for their babies within twenty-four hours after birth. In contrast, in countries where hospital routines prevent normal demand feeding from birth, mothers frequently do not produce breast milk for their babies until the third day following birth.

Overdistention of the breast or engorgement is a hospital acquired condition which does not occur to any comparable degree in cultures where mothers are permitted to breast-feed their babies on demand from birth.[22]

Preventing early father-child contact. Permitting fathers to hold their newborn infants immediately following birth and during the postpartum hospital stay has not been shown by research or clinical experience to increase the incidence of infection among newborns, even when those infants are returned to a regular or central nursery. Yet only in the Eastern European countries is the father permitted less involvement in the immediate postpartum period than in the United States.

Research has consistently confirmed the fact that the greatest sources of infection to the newborn infant are the nursery and nursery personnel.[23] One has only to observe a mother holding her newborn infant against her bathrobe, which has probably been exposed to abundant hospital-borne bacteria, to realize the fallacy of preventing a father from holding his baby during the hospital stay.

Restricting intermittent rooming-in to specific room requirements. Throughout the world great effort is made to keep mothers and babies together in the hospital, no matter how inconvenient the accommodations. There is no research or evidence which indicates that intermittent rooming-in should be restricted to private rooms or to rooms which have a sink, or which provide at least eighty square feet for mother and baby. Such requirements are based on conjecture and not on controlled evaluation.

Restricting sibling visitation. The common American practice of prohibiting toddlers and children from visiting their mothers during the hospital stay is an emotional hardship on both the mothers and their children and is unsupported by scientific research or evidence. Experience in other countries and in several hospitals here in the United States suggests that where sibling visitation is permitted, a short explanation as to the importance of not bringing suspect illnesses into the hospital seems to be effective in controlling infection.

Summary

As mentioned previously, most of the practices discussed above have developed not from a lack of concern for the well-being of the mother and baby but from a lack of awareness as to the problems which can arise from each progressive digression from the normal childbearing experience. Like a snowball rolling down hill, as one unphysiological practice is employed, for one reason or another, another frequently becomes necessary to counteract some of the disadvantages, large or small, inherent in the previous procedure.

The higher incidence of fetal, neonatal, and maternal deaths occurring in our large urban hospitals, as opposed to our smaller community hospitals,[24] is undoubtedly due, in part, to the greater proportion of high-risk mothers in the urban areas. But we in the United States must stop looking for scapegoats and face up to the fact that by individualizing the care offered to maternity patients, much can be done immediately to improve infant outcome without the slightest outlay of capital.

There is currently an increasing emphasis on consolidating maternity facilities. However, we in ICEA do not see the consolidation of community obstetrical facilities as being always in the best interest of the vast majority of mothers who are capable of giving birth without complications. There should, of course, be centers where those mothers who have had no prenatal care or who are

anticipated to be obstetrical risks can be properly cared for. But to insist that every healthy mother must go to a major maternity facility which is unnecessary for her needs and inconvenient for her family, and where she is very apt to be "lost in the crowd," will only spur the growing trend in the United States toward professionally unattended home births.

Throughout the United States the current inclination of many expectant parents is to seek out, to "shop around" for the type of physician and hospital they feel they need in order to have the type of childbearing experience they want. They not only want a doctor who will support them in their efforts to have a prepared, natural birth, with a minimum of or no medication; they also want a hospital which offers education for childbearing and a supportive family-centered atmosphere. These expectant mothers appreciate the availability of such facilities as an early labor lounge, a dual purpose labor-delivery room, a mother-baby recovery room, and a children's visiting room if they have older children. But most of all they want a supportive atmosphere in which they can share the childbearing experience to the extent that they desire, and one which makes an effort to meet the individual needs of the mother, the father, and their newborn baby as they form their family bonds during the hospital stay.

Notes

1. H. Chase, "Ranking Countries by Infant Mortality Rates," Public Health Reports 84 (1969): 19–27; M. Wegman, "Annual Summary of Vital Statistics—1969," Pediatrics 47 (1971): 461-64.
2. A. Beer, "Fetal Erythrocytes in Maternal Circulation of 155 Rh-Negative Women," *Obstet. & Gynec.* 34 (1969): 143–50.
3. N. Butler, "A National Long-Term Study of Perinatal Hazards," Sixth World Congress of the Federation of International Gynecology & Obstetrics, 1970.
4. J. Kelly, "Effect of Fear Upon Uterine Motility," *Am. J. Obstet. & Gynec.* 83 (1962): 576–81.
5. R. Burchell, "Predelivery Removal of Pubic Hair," *Obstet. & Gynec.* 24 (1964): 272–73; H. Kantor et al., "Value of Shaving the Pudendal-Perineal Area in Delivery Preparation," *Obstet. & Gynec.* 25 (1965) 509–12.
6. Haverkamp, A. D., Thompson, H. E., McFee, J. G. et al., "The Evaluation of Continuous Fetal-Heart Monitoring for High Risk Pregnancies." *Am. J. Obstet. & Gynec.* 125, no. 3 (June 1, 1926): 310–20.
7. E. Hon, "Direct Monitoring of the Fetal Heart," *Hospital Practice* (September 1970): 91–97.
8. H. Fields, "Complications of Elective Induction" *Obstet. & Gynec.* 15 (1960): 476–80; H. Fields, "Induction of Labor: Methods, Hazards, Complications, and Contraindications," *Hospital Topics* (December 1968): 63–68.
9. C. Flowers, *Obstetric Analgesia and Anesthesia* (New York: Hoeber, Harper & Row, 1967); L. S. James, "The

Effects of Pain Relief for Labor and Delivery on the Fetus and Newborn," *Anesthesiology* 21 (1960): 405–30; A. Blankfield, "The Optimum Position for Childbirth," *Med. J. Australia* 2 (1965): 666–68.

10. Blankfield, "The Optimum Position for Childbirth"; F. H. Howard, "Delivery in the Physiologic Position," *Obstet. & Gynec.* 11 (1958): 318–22; I. Gritsiuk, "Position in Labor," *Ob-Gyn Observer* (September 1968).

11. Blankfield, "The Optimum Position for Childbirth"; Howard, "Delivery in the Physiologic Position"; N. Newton and M. Newton "The Propped Position for the Second Stage of Labor," *Obstet. & Gynec.* 15 (1960): 28–34.

12. Newton and Newton, "The Propped Position for the Second Stage of Labor."

13. M. Botha, "The Management of the Umbilical Cord in Labour," *S. Afr. J. Obstet.* 6, no. 2 (1968): 30–33.

14. Beer, "Fetal Erythrocytes in Maternal Circulation of 155 Rh-Negative Women."

15. Blankfield, "The Optimum Position for Childbirth."

16. Ibid.; Newton and Newton, "The Propped Position for the Second Stage of Labor."

17. L. Hellman and J. Pritchard, *Williams Obstetrics,* 14th ed. (New York: Appleton-Century-Crofts, 1971).

18. W. Johnson, "Regionals Can Prolong Labor," *Medical World News,* October 15, 1971.

19. Butler, "A National Long-Term Study of Perinatal Hazards."

20. S. Saigal et al., "Placental Transfusion and Hyperbilirubinemia in the Premature," *Pediatrics* 49 (1972): 406–19.

21. H. Eppink, "Time of Initial Breast Feeding Surveyed in Michigan Hospitals," *Hospital Topics* (June 1968): 116–17.

22. M. Newton and N. Newton, "Postpartum Engorgement of the Breast," *Am. J. Obstet. & Gynec.* 61 (1951): 664–67.

23. H. Gezon et al., "Some Controversial Aspects in the Epidemiology of Hospital Nursery Staphylococcal Infections," *Amer. J. of Public Health* 50 (1960): 473–84; R. Ravenholt and G. LaVeck, "Staphylococcal Disease—An Obstetric, Pediatric & Community Problem," *Amer. J. of Public Health* 46 (1956): 1287–96.

24. E. Bishop, "The National Study of Maternity Care." *Obstet. & Gynec.* (1971): 745–50.

*Excerpts from
Childbearing Policy within
a National Health Program:
An Evolving Consensus for New Directions*

A collaborative paper by:
Boston Women's Health Book Collective
National Black Woman's Health Project
National Women's Health Network
Women's Institute for Childbearing Policy

Note from the collaborating organizations: The following selection is excerpted from a large booklet. In addition to the material that appears here, the booklet contains acknowledgments, a summary, an opening section on "The Failure of the Present System to Meet Needs of Childbearing Women and Families" with extensive supporting documentation, eight appendices presenting a broad range of information and additional support for the positions taken in the paper, and information about the four collaborating organizations. The complete document may be obtained for $10 postpaid (checks made out to Women's Institute for Childbearing Policy) from: Jane Pincus, WICP, PO Box 72, Roxbury, VT 05669. The collaborative paper is a project of the Women's Institute for Childbearing Policy. We are grateful to the Midwifery Communication and Accountability Project for support that enabled the creation of the revised and expanded 1994 edition.

The Value of Women's Health and Public Health Perspectives

The solution to current problems lies in a shift from the present emphasis on a medical approach to an approach that combines women's health and public health perspectives. *From a women's health perspective, the needs of women and children are central.[18] In the best public health tradition, in this country as well as Europe, clinical services are only one component of a broader approach; moreover, these clinical services give priority to primary care.* Many advocates of reform speak of a National *Health* Program, when what they really mean is a National *Medical Care* Program. Our challenge is to develop and implement a genuine National Health Program that includes the conditions of daily life that influence health, provides universal access to prevention-oriented health care services, and insures medical services when necessary.

Childbearing policies that reflect women's health and public health perspectives would promote healthful living conditions. As the National Association for Public Health Policy asserts, the campaign for a national program of clinical services "must be part of an overall movement for full employment, higher wages, improved working conditions, decent housing, better education, and affirmative action to end discrimination in all areas of our national life" (1989). Public policies must assure: access to adequate family leave and social supports; availability of adequate housing and nourishing food; control of environmental hazards; and freedom from the havoc of violence and of alcohol, tobacco, cocaine and other drugs. *Social and economic conditions, and the presence or lack of social supports, are directly linked to the quality of birth outcomes* (Barrera et al.1992; Terris 1990a, 1990b; Elbourne et al. 1989; Ottawa Charter for Health Promotion 1986).

Maternity care services based upon women's and public health perspectives would be provided routinely by primary caregivers who are trained to understand, promote and sustain health. These caregivers would recognize the importance of nutritional, educational, social, psychological, and cultural factors. They would pay vigilant attention to mothers and babies, consult and refer when appropriate, and provide continuous, individualized care and a range of basic services. They would develop a trusting relationship with the woman and her support network. Care would be given in small-scale, community-based settings that give priority to community participation, employ community residents, and provide convenient and coherent services. All women would be able to give birth in the location of their choice, including freestanding birth centers and homes. Consultative and specialist back-up services would always be readily available.[19]

On a small scale within this country, and on a large scale in Europe and other nations, midwives most consistently offer this optimal care for women and newborns. We call for a national health program that recognizes that midwives' philosophy, education and standards of practice make them the most effective and optimal front-line caregivers for the great majority of childbearing women.[20] The Core Values segment of the "Statement of Values and Ethics" of the Midwives Alliance of North America reflects many of the distinctive elements of midwifery care and underscores the sharp contrast between prevailing medical approaches and midwifery approaches to maternity care.[21]

It is important to note that obstetricians and family practitioners can, and occasionally do, provide midwifery care as we describe it below. Unfortunately, however, the limitations of medical education and practice and the potential for restrictive and punitive behavior by colleagues severely limit the ability of physicians to deviate from medical standards.[22]

Similarly, we call for a national health program that recognizes that freestanding birth centers and homes are the most appropriate and enabling settings for Primary Maternity Care. These community-based sites enhance the likelihood that care will be non-bureaucratic; individualized; woman- and family-oriented; protected from unnecessary medicalization and interventions; and physically, culturally and psychologically accessible.

In advocating such care, we do not mean the mere substitution of one type of practitioner and site of practice for another, but the *substitution of one system and philosophy of care for another.* It is critical that the reconfiguration of maternity care addresses appropriate

type of front-line caregiver, settings for care, and content and philosophy of care. Addressing only one or two of these dimensions will not assure necessary change in the maternity care system.

Benefits of a Primary Maternity Care System

1. Primary Maternity Care involves education, health promotion, social support, clinical assessment, and continuity of care. Midwifery care is primary care at its best. Midwives have regularly demonstrated a commitment to understanding and maintaining normal birth and the health of women and infants. Basic preventive practices, such as offering information and advice on diet and breastfeeding, and enhancing the integrity of the childbearing family, are the foundation of midwifery practice. Midwives address social, cultural, psychological, ethical, and political aspects of pregnancy, birth, and parenthood. They recognize and affirm the meaning and importance of childbearing in the lives of women and their families. They work to build a trusting, close relationship with women, which tends to be the cornerstone of their practice. Many midwives choose to work in community-based settings. Within this framework, they offer prenatal care that is rich, contextual, multifaceted, accessible and acceptable to women and that promotes the health of mothers and babies.[23]

2. Primary Maternity Care is safe. Numerous studies, some of which have been controlled, have shown that the maternity care provided by nurse-midwives and other midwives in hospitals, birth centers and homes result in birthweights, mortality rates, and other health indicators that are similar to, or better than, those obtained by specialists in acute medical settings (Durand 1992; Mayes et al.1987; Feldman and Hurst 1987; Scupholme et al.1986; Piechnik and Corbett 1985; Baruffi et al.1984a; Beal 1984; Mehl et al. 1980; Slome et al. 1976). In the United States, most of the published studies describe the practice of certified nurse-midwives. However, extensive data from European studies demonstrate the excellent record of non-nurse-midwives working in many settings.[24]

Investigators of the large multi-site National Birth Center Study similarly conclude that freestanding "birth centers offer a safe and acceptable alternative to hospital confinement" (Rooks et al.1989). The absence of maternal mortality and low intrapartum and neonatal mortality experiences in this study compare favorably with mortality rates of low-risk women using hospitals (Rooks et al. 1992c).[25] Despite the widespread belief in the U.S. that home birth involves greater risk than hospital birth, the hospital has never been shown to be safer than home or birth center births (Hughes 1992; Campbell and MacFarlane 1986; Institute of Medicine 1982). On a large scale in the Netherlands and on a smaller scale in the United States, the United Kingdom and other nations, birth at home has involved very low mortality rates (Hughes 1992; Treffers et al. 1990; Campbell and MacFarlane 1986; Treffers and Laan 1986; van Alten 1989). In a meta-analysis pooling data from U.S. studies and considering international data, Hughes concludes, "Currently available research suggests that home birth, in the presence of qualified and appropriately equipped attendants, is . . . at least as safe as hospital birth" (1992). This finding is echoed both by the Oxford Database of Perinatal Trials project, whose organizers conclude that policies for "universal institutional confinement" should be abandoned in light of available data (Chalmers et al. 1989b), and by a recent House of Commons report that supports the choice of home birth (Great Britain 1992).

Several studies suggest that healthy women using more technology-intensive birth settings experience greater morbidity than those in less intensive sites (Campbell and MacFarlane 1986; Baruffi et al. 1984a, 1984b; Mehl and Peterson 1981). These diverse and consistent studies, and the vital statistics of several European nations (Miller 1987; Wagner 1988), thus contradict the prevalent belief that healthy women inevitably experience excess morbidity and mortality when *not* attended by specialists in acute care settings.

3. Primary Maternity Care enhances access.
Midwives have been honored to serve women of all social groups and to work in diverse community-based settings. They have provided effective, sensitive, respectful, empowering, community-oriented services to women who have often been rejected by physicians by virtue of their insurance status, economic class, race, ethnicity, foreign birth or geographical location. They have worked disproportionately in underserved areas, with underserved populations, and with women lacking private insurance (Scupholme et al. 1992; Declercq 1992; U.S. Department of Health and Human Services 1984; Langwell et al. 1980).[26] In addition to their willingness to care for the underserved, the sensitive *way* midwives have regularly been found to care for all types of women, and the cost effectiveness of their care, enhance access. The increased access has been associated with significant, and dramatic, improvements in health status indicators of more vulnerable women and infants (e.g., Levy et al. 1971; Montgomery 1969).

Attributes of freestanding birth centers similarly enhance access to maternity care. They can be situated in communities and oriented toward the needs of communities, creating a sense of ownership, belonging and familiarity. They avoid the barriers of large-scale, bureaucratic institutions, which can be alienating and difficult and time-consuming to negotiate (see Institute of Medicine 1988). These centers may thus have a major role to play in improving the care of more vulnerable childbearing families who now rely extensively upon services in tertiary hospitals. Because freestanding birth centers can operate in rural areas that do not have hospital obstetrics departments (Rooks et al. 1989), they also can play a major role in bringing access to the many rural areas that now lack adequate maternity services (see Lewis-Idema 1989).

4. Primary Maternity Care offers special benefits for virtually all childbearing women.
With their commitment to education, prevention, providing social support and individualized care, and developing a close relationship with the childbearing woman and her family, midwives provide excellent and particularly appropriate care to women who are often considered "high-risk" (Reedy 1979). Their approach is well-suited, for example, to providing support for pregnant adolescents, helping women with gestational diabetes maintain a healthy diet, and working with women who are HIV-positive or are addicted to drugs. (When indicated by medical conditions, midwives and physicians collaborate in the care of childbearing women.) So-called high-risk women who receive midwifery care consistently attain excellent outcomes, which are typically more favorable than those of the general population. Midwifery care is also ideally suited for the special needs and interests of many other women, including single mothers, lesbian mothers, childbearing women who are older, childbearing women with disabilities, and those who wish to incorporate personal or cultural rituals into their unique childbearing experiences. Women in the United States from every kind of social and economic background have sought out and benefited from this care.

In a similar fashion, freestanding birth centers and homes offer possibilities for personal and individualized care and the fulfillment of diverse wishes and expectations of childbearing families that are difficult or impossible to provide in clinic and hospital settings. They also offer these families greater amounts of privacy and greater opportunities for control of the care environment.[27]

5. Primary Maternity Care involves judicious use of technology.
In a system of Primary Maternity Care, technological interventions are used only when needed to promote the health and well-being of mother and baby, and not as routine interventions or substitutes for social support, education, attentiveness, patience or preventive measures. Controlled studies repeatedly show that, relative to standard medical care, midwifery care involves significantly less use of such interventions as anesthesia, intravenous hydration, electronic fetal monitoring, artificial augmentation of labor, episiotomy, forceps and

cesarean birth (Feldman and Hurst 1987; Scupholme et al. 1986; Baruffi et al. 1984b; Beal 1984).

Primary Maternity Care sites have also been associated with relatively low rates of interventions. For example, relatively few women participating in the National Birth Center Study experienced continuous electronic fetal monitoring (8%), artificial augmentation of labor (2%), and cesarean section (4%) (Rooks et al. 1992b). Many obstetrical technologies are simply unavailable in home settings. Those who provide care in home settings tend to work to avoid interventions or to use lower technology interventions.[28]

The differences in rates of procedures between Primary Maternity Care and conventional maternity care can be quite substantial. For example, a comparison of a group of women who began their labors at home with independent midwives and a similar group using conventional care found that the former had 91% fewer cesarean births (1.5% vs.16.5% cesarean rates) (Durand 1992). These studies find that the reduced use of technology does not compromise outcome; in fact, women receiving such care benefit by avoiding the risks, discomfort and disruption that these procedures impose.[29]

6. Primary Maternity Care is associated with a highly favorable liability record.

In 1987 surveys, 10% of nurse-midwives had been named in one or more liability claims, as opposed to 71% of obstetrician-gynecologists (Adams 1989; Opinion Research Corporation 1988). This comparison is not adjusted for years of practice, severity of caseload and other factors that could influence experience with claims. However, the size of the difference strongly suggests that it is real. Aspects of midwifery care and freestanding birth center and home care settings that have been associated with favorable liability experiences include avoiding unnecessary procedures, developing a personal and trusting relationship, and carefully observing principles of informed consent (Relman 1989; O'Reilly et al. 1986; Gilfix 1984; Shearer et al. 1976). In accord with their philosophy and values, midwives usually provide more satisfactory communication and greater continuity of care than obstetricians; spend more time with women prenatally, during labor and following birth; and show greater care and respect to women. These practices are likely to contribute to their more favorable liability experience. Physicians in hospital settings may be sued more often because of their tendency to have brief prenatal visits, to have relatively limited contact during labor and birth, to use as birth attendants on-call physicians whom women do not know, to work in settings that emphasize efficiency and focus excessively on progress in labor, and to prefer hierarchical relationships that inhibit satisfactory communication. LoCicero identifies a variety of ways

that medical maternity care thwarts common expectations of childbearing women (1993). Such a mismatch may help to explain why obstetricians' liability experiences are disproportionately unfavorable relative to nearly all other medical specialties.[30]

7. Primary Maternity Care is well-received by women.

As women, we value patient, personalized, respectful, non-hierarchical care that addresses many dimensions of our lives and helps us to take responsibility for our health. We have regularly welcomed midwives' commitment to principles of informed choice and the opportunity for genuine participation in decisions about our care. We often feel especially comfortable with caregivers who are women and who are often themselves experienced mothers (Kelly-McCormick 1989; Lazarus 1988b; Wellish and Root 1987).[31]

Women participating in the National Birth Center Study also reported high rates of satisfaction with their care. Ninety-nine percent of those giving birth in the centers said that they would recommend the center to friends and 94% said they would use the center in a subsequent pregnancy. Of those who were transferred to hospitals for their birth, 97% said they would recommend the center and 83% would use it again (Rooks et al. 1989, 1992c).

Interestingly, it is difficult to find informative studies on women's satisfaction with home birth. Since home birth is actively sought out and women continue to choose home birth in spite of cultural, economic and institutional obstacles to this choice, it seems clear that they are highly satisfied with their experiences. Women choosing home birth have been very articulate about their experiences, describing them, as well as the reasons for their choices in great detail in magazines, journals and books (e.g., *Birth Gazette; C/SEC Newsletter, The Clarion;* Gaskin 1990; Kitzinger 1988; Wellish and Root 1987; Ashford 1984).

8. Primary Maternity Care is highly cost-effective.

Studies of midwifery care, both in and out of hospitals, show major cost savings relative to dominant medicalized maternity care (e.g., Krumlauf et al. 1988; Seiner and Lairson 1985; Cherry and Foster 1982; Reid and Morris 1979). Midwifery fees tend to be lower than physician fees despite the fact that midwives spend considerably more time with women and offer services that may otherwise be provided by an entire team. Other aspects of midwifery care that involve significant cost savings relative to the present reliance upon front-line physician care include the considerably lower costs to educate midwives, their much more favorable experience with legal claims and suits, the lower rates of intervention associated with their care, the shorter length of hospital or birth center stay of midwifery clients (e.g., Baruffi et al.1984a; Cherry and Foster 1982), and midwives' greater willingness to work in non-hospital settings.[32]

Primary Maternity Care sites have similar cost advantages. Charges of freestanding birth centers have consistently been found to be well below those of hospitals. In 1989, for example, the average cost of birth center care, including prenatal and postpartum visits, was about one-half of the average cost of a vaginal birth in the hospital and about two-thirds of a one-day hospital maternity stay (Health Insurance Association of America 1989).[33] Birth at home eliminates facility expenses entirely and involves modest expenses for supplies and equipment.

. . .

The system we are proposing has important precedents. At the present time and on a national scale, the Netherlands has the most exemplary system of Primary Maternity Care in the world and there is much we can learn and adapt from it. We must be aware, however, that the Dutch system is experiencing various types of pressure to become more medicalized and technology intensive. Presently, to give citizens the benefits of primary care, facilitate use of appropriate levels of care, and contain costs, Dutch government policies strongly support home births, midwives and the avoidance of unnecessary obstetrical procedures (World Health Organization 1986). Structural incentives contribute to the maintenance of this system of Primary Maternity Care. For example, maternity care costs for healthy women are only covered in full if such women use midwifery services (where available) and give birth at home or in short-stay "polyclinic" settings. At present, midwives attend about 43% of births and about 35% occur at home (Treffers et al. 1990). A large proportion of the institutional births are polyclinic births of less than 36 hours (Hingstman and Boon 1988). Other administrative and organizational features help sustain this primary care system. Midwives are educated to function as independent practitioners with the authority to screen and refer.

Although the Netherlands has a socio-demographic profile similar to the U.S., with a diverse immigrant and indigenous population, the Dutch infant mortality rate has consistently been among the lowest in the world. In 1989, it ranked 4th compared to 19th for the U.S. (Rosenbaum et al. 1991). Another distinctive feature of this system is the social support available through its postpartum home care program. Women are entitled to eight days of assistance by trained maternity home aides who care for them and their babies, assist with breastfeeding, care for older children, and perform housekeeping tasks. The health promoting primary care system in the Netherlands is associated with low rates of obstetrical intervention, and the standards of midwifery home

care have a restraining influence on interventive patterns of obstetrical care. In 1985, for example, when the U.S. cesarean rate was 22.7%, the Dutch rate was 6.6%.[34]

Policy Proposals: Improved Standards of Living and Systematic Transition to a Primary Maternity Care System

We intend to work with other groups to develop the following proposals about childbearing policy in a national health program.[35]

1. As a society, we should work to enhance the conditions of everyday life that influence the health of women and their infants. Favorable conditions include: economic security, high-quality education, the availability of adequate family leave provisions and other social supports, the elimination of occupational and environmental hazards, the availability of safe housing and nourishing food, and the eradication of harmful drugs and violence. Shortterm policies should specifically address the effect of these areas on childbearing women and their infants, while longterm policies should be developed to improve the conditions of everyday life for all citizens. We must implement a true National Health Program that addresses these primary determinants of health. While neither national health care policy nor a National Health Care Program in themselves can create the kind of social change we describe, policy makers can build coalitions with groups working on these issues and stress the critical nature of such efforts to their own work.

2. We who are taking the leadership for a national health program should establish a task force to investigate and propose guidelines for systematic transition to a system of Primary Maternity Care. This task force should reflect appropriate racial and economic diversity and be composed of leaders who represent the following perspectives: women's health, childbirth reform, midwifery, and public health, as well as other health and medical professionals and community representatives who are engaged in health planning and decision making, committed to a primary care model and knowledgeable about the distinctive record of midwifery care, freestanding birth centers and home birth.

This task force should carefully consider past and present exemplary models of Primary Maternity Care. In the U.S., these include the Frontier Nursing Service in rural Kentucky; Boston's Traditional Childbearing Group; the Maternity Center Association's Childbearing

Center in New York; the Childbearing Center of Morris Heights; other members of the National Association of Childbearing Centers; and midwives who have traditionally served women in our African American, Latino, Native American and Asian American communities (Rooks et al. 1992a, 1992b, 1992c; Sakala 1989; Holmes 1986; Branca et al. 1984; Lubic and Ernst 1978; and Breckinridge 1952).

The task force should take into account the growing data affirming the relative safety of home birth in the U.S., data which are supported by the home birth experience in the Netherlands and research conducted on out-of-hospital births in the United Kingdom (Hughes 1992; Campbell and MacFarlane 1986; Great Britain 1992; Tew and Damstra-Wigmenga 1991; Mehl 1981). On an international level, the task force should study the Dutch maternity care model and strengthen and adapt it to conditions in the U.S.

In addition, the task force should critically appraise medical education, the training of midwives and nurses, the scope and standards of practice of various practitioners, approaches to regulation, mechanisms for integrating current midwives, and projected need for primary and specialist maternity caregivers and primary and acute maternity care settings. Utilizing all this information, the task force should develop related policy recommendations leading to a strong system of Primary Maternity Care that gives priority to the interests of childbearing families and resists cooptation involving acute and other medical settings and specialist and other medical caregivers.[36]

3. We should greatly expand opportunities to educate midwives, the most appropriate providers of Primary Maternity Care. Midwifery can and should be an autonomous profession. This position is supported by the boards of the Midwives Alliance of North America and the American College of Nurse-Midwives. Both nurses and those with other backgrounds should be welcomed into midwifery education programs and, on demonstrating proficiency in midwifery knowledge and skills, be recognized as fully competent midwives. The International Confederation of Midwives and the International Federation of Gynecologists and Obstetricians recognize multiple routes of entry into the practice of midwifery. Many states legally recognize well-educated and well-trained community midwives (also known as direct-entry, independent, empirical, traditional, or lay midwives), who have a strong record throughout the country and have begun to receive Medicaid reimbursement in various state programs. Similarly, European nations have had outstanding experiences with midwives from many backgrounds.[37]

U.S. training programs should make special efforts to recruit and educate women of color, low-income women and women from rural areas, many of whom will choose and be most qualified to provide services within their own communities. Although the Clinton proposal includes midwives, it fails to address the systemic issues related to site and content of care addressed in this paper, fails to recognize multiple routes to midwifery practice, and fails, to acknowledge the barriers faced by currently practicing midwives.

4. We should greatly expand opportunities for women to give birth in freestanding birth centers and at home, if they choose. Community-based freestanding birth centers, are, in our judgment, highly appropriate maternity care sites. They are the most feasible sites for Primary Maternity Care from social, psychological, organizational, political, and economic perspectives.[38] These centers should provide a broad range of formal and informal health and support services for childbearing women and their infants and should also help involve fathers in the childbearing process and in parenting. Women who wish to give birth at home must be supported in this choice as a covered service and by hospitals and medical caregivers providing full cooperative back-up. Of all sites, home tends to be the most demedicalized, to involve the least high-tech interventions, and to offer women and their families the greatest freedom of choice.[39]

5. We should emphasize and develop small-scale community-based and -oriented services. This goal should be a priority when recruiting caregivers, establishing the location of maternity services, and determining the type of care provided. Women who use the services should have substantial input into the development of policies and programs through participatory processes for resource allocation and other decisions.[40] We should give special attention to the development of supportive client-oriented services for women who have limited social supports and negative, stressful life circumstances.[41]

6. We should develop effective policies that commit our national health program to a system of Primary Maternity Care. These policies should ensure that midwives are autonomous practitioners and that specialist and tertiary care back-up are readily available for any medical problems. Women should have ready access to midwifery, home birth and freestanding birth center services in their communities and should be free to choose their caregiver and the place where they receive maternity care and give birth; policies should ensure that all women receive accurate and detailed information about these choices. Adequate funds should be available for widespread public education about the benefits of Primary Maternity Care, for Primary Maternity

Caregiver education and training programs, and for all Primary Maternity Care services. Present difficulties in securing reimbursement for these services should be eliminated. Primary Maternity Care services, as well as any necessary medical care, should be covered in full, with no co-payments or other out-of-pocket expenses. Finally, ongoing mechanisms of accountability must be established to apply research findings and ensure that maternity practices are safe, effective, and conducive to a positive quality of life.

7. We should regulate Primary Maternity Care through independent boards. In order to assure public accountability, these boards should be composed predominantly of public members; they should also include midwives and other health professionals who are knowledgeable about and respect the primary care model. Board composition should reflect the diversity of community women, including women of color and women of various economic backgrounds.

8. We should establish a major research program to support Primary Maternity Care. Research on normal childbearing and prevention of complications should be given priority. Childbearing technology assessment should address many dimensions, including positive and negative impact on physical, psychological and social well-being (both short- and long-term); political and ethical issues; and economic implications. Sensitive morbidity measures should be developed to address the period from pregnancy through the child's first year, and data on these measures should be regularly collected. All aspects of the Primary Maternity Care system should be thoroughly evaluated, with systematic mechanisms for incorporation of relevant findings into future programs.

• • •

As women's health advocates, we support childbearing policies and programs that are in the best interests of women and infants. We must ensure that a national health program addresses healthy living conditions as the major determinants of health. Clinical services can never compensate for inadequate social supports, and high-cost, high-tech medical approaches do not solve economic and social problems. With respect to maternity care services, the optimal form of care is a system that gives priority to Primary Maternity Care and utilizes midwives and free-standing birth centers as recommended forms of care for most childbearing women. It is our conviction that this best form of care for mothers and babies will also be of great interest to policy makers: it is safe, of high quality, cost-effective, and greatly appreciated by women. The solution to many of our pressing childbearing problems is within our reach.

NOTES

18. A women's health perspective addresses not just the health status of women but how women relate to the system, are treated by it and are workers within it. This approach looks at the needs of women beyond medical needs and addresses the way gender differences, ways of knowing, psychosocial development and power differentials within the culture affect maternity care (Jordan 1987). In an article addressing the non-medical factors that contribute to high rates of intervention, LoCicero (1993) considers contemporary theories of gender and psychosocial development. Her analysis concerns gender difference (in cognition, moral development, sense of self, empathy and helpfulness, and power), gender role expectations, and gender identity. She concludes that in each of these dimensions prevailing medical approaches are compatible with conventional masculine standards and fundamentally incompatible with the needs and expectations of most women, and are likely to have a negative effect on women's ability to labor effectively. Midwifery care, she proposes, is far more compatible with women's needs in these respects.

19. In their summary of the longitudinal Oxford Database of Perinatal Trials project, which identifies and synthesizes thousands of perinatal trials, Enkin and colleagues endorse the primary care concept:

> . . . . it is inherently unwise, and perhaps unsafe, for women with normal pregnancies to be cared for by obstetric specialists . . .
>
> Midwives and general practitioners, on the other hand, are primarily oriented to the care of women with normal pregnancies, and are likely to have more detailed knowledge of the particular circumstances of individual women. The care that they can give to the majority of women whose pregnancies are not affected by any major illness or serious complication will often be more responsive to their needs than that given by specialist obstetricians.
>
> Optimal care can only occur when both primary and secondary caregivers recognize their complementary roles. There is no place for rivalry or competition between those whose expertise is in the supervision of health and the detection of disease, and those whose specialty is in the management of disease and the restoration of health. [1989]

The authors also state that policies supporting "universal institutional confinement" should be abandoned in light of existing evidence (1989).

20. Obstetrician-gynecologists serve as the first contact with the medical care system for many women. The usual care that these surgeon-specialists provide, however, *cannot be considered to be primary care* (see Burkons and Willson [1975] and accompanying discussion). The most appropriate role for the obstetrical specialist is (1) as direct caregiver for women who are at high medical risk or have developed serious medical complications and (2) as consultant and back-up to midwives who serve as Primary Maternity Caregivers to all other women.

We are not optimistic about the use of family physicians for Primary Maternity Care. Although we respect and applaud their primary care philosophy, we regret that in their provision of maternity services, the great majority of family practitioners have been obliged to emulate and practice the specialist model (Brody and Thompson 1981). Additional constraints are provided by the challenge of incorporating maternity services and of supporting maternity liability premiums within a general practice. We also respect the primary care philosophy of nurse-practitioners and their work with childbearing women. We cannot, however, recommend that they have a major role in a Primary Maternity Care system because they cannot provide continuity of care during the critical period of labor, birth and early postpartum.

21. The ethics statement was the result of a two-year consensus-building process that involved hundreds of practicing midwives.

A focus on life and health pervades this statement. Sakala (1993d) summarizes the values articulated in this statement:

> The midwives emphasize that pregnancy and birth are intrinsically normal life processes, and that it is desirable to enhance this normalcy . . . and to help women with complications move toward greater well-being. . . The statement places childbearing within the context of the totality of women's lives. . . . It asserts that physical, emotional, mental, psychological, and spiritual dimensions of life experiences are interrelated and cannot be viewed in isolation. . . . Pregnancy and birth are simultaneously personal, intimate, sexual, and social events; these experiences in turn influence women's self-esteem, health, ability to nurture, and personal growth.
>
> The midwives also give priority to respect for the mother. . . and the baby and the integrity of their relationship. . . . They enhance childbearing by respecting women's capabilities, . . . empowering women to be confident and strong . . . and identifying other sources of support. . . . They value honesty and communication. . . and honor women's right to self determination. They value the diversity of women's experiences and needs, and individualized care. . . .

22. For examples of physicians who have adopted a frame of reference and attitudes compatible with midwifery see Odent (1984) and Sagov et al. (1984). For examples of impediments that physicians place before reformist colleagues, see Savage (1986) and Harrison (1983). On the effectiveness of medical education in socializing physicians into medical approaches to care, see Davis-Floyd (1992).

23. Descriptions of midwifery care include Rothman (1989), Sullivan and Weitz (1988) and Annandale (1988). Kitzinger (1988) provides a comparison, in their own words, of the position of midwives in the medical systems of different nations. She sees midwives as the greatest challenge world-wide to high-technology, conveyer-belt obstetrics. On how midwives see themselves, their practice and education, see Gaskin (1990), Steiger (1987), Varney (1987) and Davis (1987).

Roger A. Rosenblatt points to an important policy benefit of such a broad and continuous view of maternal and child health. This view involves "longitudinal responsibility for a series of intertwined clinical interventions," and provides incentives to emphasize prevention and minimize use of costly, disruptive and ethically complex salvage technologies. He argues that we should encourage this perspective by capitating caregivers for the entire period from conception through the neonatal period, in contrast to our present policies of economic and service fragmentation (1989). The recent Public Health Service report on prenatal care strongly recommends that the prevailing emphasis on medical concerns be balanced by greatly increased attention to social, psychological and educational concerns (United States Department of Health and Human Services 1989).

Rates of breastfeeding might be considered to be a measure of midwives' commitment to and effectiveness with health-promoting care. Reported rates of early postpartum breastfeeding by women who have received midwifery care are consistently higher than rates in the general population, ranging from 78% to 99% (Nichols 1985; Baruffi et al.1984a; Bennetts and Lubic 1982; Mann 1981; Hewitt and Hangsleben 1981; and Gaskin and Gaskin 1979). These reports describe women of many social and economic backgrounds, including women using clinic services. By contrast, the Public Health Service reports that in 1988 54% of women in the U.S. were breastfeeding in the early postpartum period. This figure drops to 32% for low-income mothers and 25% for Black mothers (United States Department of Health and Human Services 1991).

24. While there is a growing body of research suggesting that care provided by independent (non-nurse) midwives is as safe, effective and desirable as that provided by nurse-midwives (e.g., Durand 1992; Hinds et al. 1985; Sullivan and Beeman 1983; Burnett et al.1980; McCallum 1979), most research in the United States has been conducted on nurse-midwives and has focused on assessing the care they provide. Institutional support and funding as well as the presence of nurse-midwifery training programs in academic settings have fostered this research. Independent midwives place high value on knowledge, experience, and the refinement of skills (Davis 1981; Steiger 1987). These are acquired in a variety of ways, including study groups, apprenticeships, classes, and highly structured programs such as the Seattle Midwifery School. The Pilot Data Collection Project of the Midwives Alliance of North America (MANA), which includes both independent midwives and nurse-midwives, has been designed to gather information needed for further research, both quantitative and qualitative, on independent midwifery practice and home birth. This information will complement the data from the Netherlands and throughout Europe (Miller 1987) that reveal the excellent record of non-nurse midwives practicing in many settings. See also note 34.

25. The National Birth Center Study involved nearly 12,000 women who received care during labor and birth at 84 centers throughout the nation (Rooks et al. 1992a, 1992b, 1992c, 1989). For a summary of birth center outcome research and a report of consistent and favorable outcome data from a similar study of over 3,400 women receiving this same care at 25 California birth centers, see Eakins (1989).

26. A 1991 national survey found that 34% of clients of active certified nurse-midwives reside in low-income inner-city areas and 22% in rural areas. Eighty percent of respondents described their practices as including women from at least five of the following eight vulnerable groups: adolescents, African Americans, Native Americans, Asian Americans, Latinas, low income individuals, migrant workers, and people without insurance (Scupholme et al. 1992). A small areas analysis indicates that U.S. counties with the highest ratios of nurse-midwives per 100,000 15- to 44-year-old women are low-income areas with small populations, few hospital beds and high birth rates (Langwell et al.1980). Nationally, about 40% of reimbursement for services of certified nurse-midwives is from Medicaid (Scupholme et al.1992), whereas the average obstetrician receives not more than 8% from that program (Schappert 1993).

On studies assessing the effectiveness of midwives working with low-income or otherwise disadvantaged women and their infants, see note 27.

27. Midwifery programs for historically vulnerable women have regularly been associated with physical outcomes superior to those in the local area, state and/or nation. These programs have served many rural and urban areas in the country and have provided care in hospitals, freestanding birth centers and homes. See Cavero et al. (1991), Haire and Elsberry (1991), Brucker and Muellner (1985), Mann (1981), Haire (1981), Burnett et al. (1980), Reid and Morris (1979), Browne and Isaacs (1976), Murdaugh (1976), Meglen (1972), Levy et al. (1971), Montgomery (1969), Metropolitan Life Insurance Company (1960) and Laird (1955). One study found similar or better physical outcomes among higher-risk women receiving midwifery care in a maternity center when compared to matched women receiving usual care, that is, dominant medical care, in a tertiary teaching hospital (Baruffi et al. 1984a). Whether analyzed by education, age, parity, race, or place of birth, national birthweight data from 1978 are consistent with the favorable evaluations of individual midwifery programs: in every group the percentage of low birthweight babies is lower for midwives than for all hospital births, physician-attended out-of-hospital births, and other categories (Declercq 1984).

The repeated finding that women who historically have experienced high rates of adverse physical outcomes experience rates more favorable than the mean for the general population when using midwifery care suggests that lack of access to appropriate services is a major and common risk factor for vulnerable women and their infants. Unfortunately, this risk factor has not been considered in the many studies examining risk factors for mothers and infants (e.g., Nersesian 1988).

Lisbeth Schorr has written an important book on the distinguishing characteristics of successful intervention programs for vulnerable children. *Within Out Reach* identifies general qualities that precisely describe midwifery care and the kind of care that is regularly and readily provided in freestanding birth centers and homes. She argues that successful programs: offer a broad spectrum of services that transcend conventional professional and bureaucratic boundaries, maintain flexibility and continuity, offer coherent services that are easy to use, consider people in the context of their broader life circumstances, and convey a sense of respect and trustworthiness. These programs, Schorr argues, fundamentally "take their shape from the needs of those they serve rather than from the precepts, demands, and boundaries set by professionalism and bureaucracies" (1988). Similarly, these forms of Primary Maternity Care have much in common with the recommendations that came out of the World Health Organization conferences on appropriate technology and childbearing.

28. Research reports comparing midwifery and medical approaches to common indications for cesarean birth and to pain suggest that midwives tend to understand these situations in different ways and to address them with a wide range of techniques that tend to be relatively simple, inexpensive and noninvasive. Their knowledge and practice are to a great extent derived from and oriented toward women's childbearing experience (Sakala 1993c, 1988).

Nurse-midwives in acute settings are more interventive than those who practice in childbearing centers (Fullerton and Severino 1992). Similarly, California childbearing centers with obstetricians as sole provider use a range of interventions and technology not used in centers with nurse-midwives as sole providers. Nationally, centers where physicians attend any or all births tend to be more technologically intensive than those with only midwives (Eakins 1989).

It is important to note that midwives are inevitably vulnerable to medicalization when they are educated in and/or practice in medical environments. These environments (including clinics, hospitals or nursing schools) influence how midwives practice, how they think and the language they use. For example, women receiving care in hospitals tend to become "patients," regardless of their health status, with all the associations of illness, passivity and impaired ability. When midwives adopt the language of obstetrics, they tend to adopt the values and limitations of obstetrics, in ways of which they may not be aware.

29. Two carefully matched studies comparing midwifery care to usual care found significant excess morbidity among low-risk women in the usual care group. Authors of these reports hypothesize that this finding is attributable to risks associated with more extensive use of procedures in the usual care groups. See Baruffi et al. (1984a) and Mehl et al. (1980).

30. The Department of Professional Liability of the American College of Obstetricians and Gynecologists publishes a series of risk management circulars for the association's membership. These guidelines emphasize such routine attributes of midwifery care as commitment to good communication and rapport, provision of fully informed consent, and acknowledgment of the possibility of undesirable outcomes, all of which are in conflict with the time constraints and professional training of medical specialists (1983).

31. A greater-than-sixfold increase in the number of births attended by midwives from 1975, when this figure first became available, to 1991 (National Center for Health Statistics 1993; U.S. Department of Health and Human Services 1984) strongly suggests the degree to which women appreciate midwifery care.

In a randomized controlled trial, Flint (1988) found that women working with midwives perceived their experience of mothering to be easier than those working with obstetricians. This suggests that the care received, and the birth experience facilitated by the midwives, increase women's self-esteem and sense of competence as parents. Similarly, a randomized controlled trial considering the impact of a supportive companion throughout labor found differences favoring the supported group in many "psychosocial" areas in the day, weeks, and/or months after birth. These include the mothers': anxiety level, impression of how well their labors and births had gone, experience of discomfort, sense that the transition to motherhood had been easy, sense they were doing a good job of mothering, report of exclusive breastfeeding, report of their babies' appetites, report that breastfeeding had primarily been discontinued due to insufficiency of milk, report of how long it had taken them to establish a relationship with the baby, report of number of hours per week spent apart from the baby, and depression scores (Trotter et al.1992; Klaus et al. 1992; Hofmeyr et al. 1991). This line of inquiry warrants a major systematic research program to identify the range and duration of differences in psychosocial effects of different forms of care. A series of randomized controlled trials throughout the world have similarly documented consistently favorable experiences with the course of labor, interventions during labor and birth, and physical outcomes through use of supportive labor companions (Klaus et al 1992).

32. The Health Insurance Association of America reports that the average physician's fee for vaginal birth in 1989 was $1,492, in contrast to $994 for the average fee of midwives (1989). The Office of Technology Assessment compares the estimated cost of training a physician in 1985—$86,100—to the estimated cost of obtaining a nurse-midwifery certificate and master's degree—$16,800 (United States Congress 1986). Saving associated with differences in interventions may be considerable. As noted above, for example, midwifery care has been associated with up to 91% fewer caesareans than medical care of similar women, with no apparent compromise in safety. Nearly one million caesareans are performed annually in the U.S., and on the average a cesarean birth cost $2,852 more than a vaginal birth in 1989 (Health Insurance Association of America 1989).

33. In 1989, the average hospital stay for a vaginal birth cost $4,334, and a one-day hospital stay averaged $3,233; by contrast, a one-day birth center stay averaged $2,111. The latter charge includes laboratory tests, childbirth education, home visits, prenatal visits and postpartum visits (Health Insurance Association of America 1989).

34. On general health policies of the Netherlands, see World Health Organization (1986) and Tiddens et al. (1984). On the Dutch maternity care system, see Treffers et al. (1990), Smulders (1989), Smulders and Limburg (1988), Miller (1987), Hingstman and Boon (1988), Phaff (1986), Ris (1986), and Verbrugge (1968). Tew and Damstra-Wijimenga (1991), Treffers et al. (1990), van Alten et al. (1989), van Alten (1986), and Ris (1986) offer data on the relative safety of that system. On international cesarean trends, see Notzon (1990) and Notzon et al. (1987).

35. We are aware that these proposals often conflict with the interests of many groups, including physicians and other medical personnel, hospitals and medical and insurance industries. These groups have had the power to shape both knowledge and practice, including what ideas are respected and what is done to women in childbirth. They have been able to maintain their positions in a society that has little faith in women's ability to give birth and great faith in technology and the authority of powerful professions and institutions. In addition, marketing strategies have led much of the public to believe that significant change has already taken place. These strategies have also led many women to believe they are receiving the highest quality of care.

   While most women and infants emerge from this system in a physically healthy state, we believe the changes we advocate will improve the pregnancy and birth experiences for large numbers of women and make important contributions to disadvantaged and minority women. They will also reduce the rate of cesarean sections and of many other procedures and tests and, combined with increased social supports and improved economic and social conditions, reduce the infant mortality and low birthweight rates for disadvantaged women. There is also the possibility, increasingly suggested in the research literature, that the kind of care we describe will contribute to the self-esteem of many childbearing women and their sense of competence as individuals, caregivers and parents, and will decrease postpartum depression, improve family relationships, increase participation of fathers in caretaking, and so forth (e.g., Mutryn 1993; Trotter et al. 1992; Hofmeyr et al. 1991). Extensive research needs to be done in this direction.

36. The recent report and other activities of the Task Force on the Implementation of Midwifery in Ontario can serve as an important model for this work (Task Force on the Implementation of Midwifery in Ontario, 1987), as can the British Health Committee Report on Maternity Services from the House of Commons (Great Britain 1992).

37. On a small scale in the United States and on a larger scale in other nations, independent midwives have a strong record with respect to access, quality and cost (Durand 1992; Tew and Damstra-Wijimenga 1991; van Alten et al. 1989; Ris 1986; Hinds et al. 1985; Sullivan and Beeman 1883; Burnett et al. 1980; Mehl et al. 1980; McCallum 1979).

38. Approximately one hundred and thirty freestanding childbearing centers are operating presently in the United States, and the National Association for Childbearing Centers has about 55 Developing Birth Center members (Ernst 1992). Important mechanisms to support birth center development are in place and the Commission for the Accreditation of Freestanding Birth Centers has been active since 1985. Reports of the National Birth Center Study (Rooks et al. 1989; Rooks et al. 1992a,1992b,1992c), and additional studies using that data-base (Fullerton and Severino 1992) demonstrate advantages of this form of care. The National Birth Center Study provides data from 84 childbearing centers and summarizes the experience of 18,000 women using these centers. A study of 25 California birth centers produced similar findings (Eakins 1989). Branca et al. (1984) project that freestanding birth centers have the potential to offer high quality care with major cost savings to a large proportion of childbearing women and infants in the United States.

   A study done by Scupholme and Kamons (1987) sheds an interesting light on consumer preference. This study involved a group of women who were assigned involuntarily to a birth center due to hospital overcrowding. It found that these women had positive experiences and that their outcomes were comparable to women who had chosen to use that site. Significantly, these women tended to choose the birth center for subsequent births and to refer family members and friends to the center.

   Most people do not know that facilities and procedures for birth in U.S. hospitals were modeled on arrangements for industrial production, including operations research techniques designed for efficient production of weapons during World War II (Lindheim 1981; see also Martin 1987). Emphasis on standardization and rapid processing of childbearing women disregards physiologic patterns of labor, involves unnecessarily high rates of interventions, and dehumanizes participants. Simply put, hospitals are not healthy places for childbearing women or practitioners who want to function as primary care providers, and support and facilitate normal birth. Medical clinics similarly involve inappropriate medical values, beliefs, and practices and impose these on women and infants who have no medical problems.

   Social science research has consistency identified the great degree to which hospital and clinic routines and provider interests take precedence over the pregnant and birthing woman's own situation and preferences in determining the type of care she receives. See Sakala (1993a, 1993d), Davis-Floyd (1992), Lichtman (1988), Danziger (1986, 1980), Rothman (1983), Scully (1980), Shaw (1974), Kovit (1972), and Rosengram and Devault (1963).

39. Hughes (1992) used meta-analytic techniques to pool data from U.S. studies and looked at studies of home birth from other nations. She concludes that available research finds planned home birth to be as safe as hospital birth. Anderson and Greener (1991) did a descriptive analysis of home births attended by CNMs in two nurse-midwifery services. The British House of Commons Report (Great Britain 1992) gives strong support for the availability of home birth services for women who choose them and underscores the value and appropriateness of the style of care that occurs at home. Even on a small scale, birth at home clarifies that childbirth is not inherently a medical matter, but is fundamentally related to the life and well-being of women, infants and families. Demedicalized birth is also the best way for practitioners and researchers to understand normal birth and the most effective ways to support it (Rothman 1983).

40. The distribution of knowledge and power is influenced by the social environment in which care takes place. Low technology birth settings—i.e., freestanding birth centers and homes—that rely primarily on everyday materials and language involve a far more equal balance of knowledge and power than acute and other medical settings. In low-technology settings, caretakers tend to show greater respect for the individual woman's self-knowledge and capabilities and encourage and allow for greater involvement in decision-making. Care marked by this kind of respect and mutuality empowers women and families in their early parenting and postpartum adaptation (Hofmeyr et al. 1991), and in ways that may have long-term effects. In hierarchical hospital settings, where information is tied to sophisticated technology, only highly trained professionals are considered competent to interpret and apply it to the situation (Jordan 1987). This applies equally to midwives, family physicians and obstetricians. The degree of knowledge and power sharing appears to be linked to the kind and amount of intervention in the birth process that takes place. Refer back to notes 28 and 29.

41. The director of one center, located in the South Bronx, reports that activities such as these have helped a community of women who live under difficult circumstances to come together and support one another. Individual women in these groups have made significant changes in their lives such as returning to school and finding employment. Community women have also been empowered by serving on the birth center's advisory committee and by learning new skills through their employment at the center (Sanders 1992; Dohrn, interview with Gaskin 1991).

Midwives' Time Has Come—Again

by Judy Foreman

Carol Rose, a Harvard-trained lawyer from Melrose, was pregnant with her first child two years ago when her health plan pulled a switch.

She was in the exam room, waiting for her female doctor when a male doctor walked in. She's not anti-men, or anti-doctor, but this guy was a bad match. "I had a bunch of questions," she says. "He said, 'I have limited time.' I felt so dehumanized and medicalized that I left."

When she turned to Leslie Ludka, a nurse-midwife who heads the midwifery program at Brigham and Women's Hospital, she discovered "the best of both world"—someone with time to answer questions, yet backed by doctors at a major hospital.

When the big day came, says Rose, Ludka was great. "When the pain was at it's peak, I said, 'I'm not sure I can do this.' She said, 'The pain will not get worse than it is right now.'" It didn't. Rose had a drug-free delivery just as she had hoped.

Midwifery—the art of helping a woman through childbirth—is as low-tech as mother's milk, as ancient as womankind. But until recently, it had been squeezed out of the birthing room by doctors and their gadgets, much as death has been hustled out of homes and into hospitals.

That is changing—6.5 percent of American babies are now delivered by midwives, usually in hospitals, compared to 1 percent in 1975. And this could be good news for babies.

A study published in May by the National Center for Health Statistics found babies delivered by certified nurse-midwives were less likely to die than those delivered by doctors.

The study, by researchers Marian MacDorman and Gopal Singh, looked at all singleton babies delivered vaginally in the United States in 1991 at 35 to 43 weeks of gestation—roughly full term. (The study did not look at multiple births or Caesareans, which account for about one quarter of all births.)

Of the 2.8 million births studied, the team focused on about 1 million: a sampling of doctor-attended births (850,000) and all 153,194 births attended by certified nurse-midwives.

The results were striking:

- After controlling for socioeconomic and medical risk factors, the infant mortality rate—death during the first year—was 19 percent lower for certified nurse-midwives than for physicians.
- The death rate in the first 28 days—was 33 percent lower.
- And the risk of low birthweight infants was 31 percent lower.

Some doctors, among them Dr. Michael Greene, director of maternal-fetal medicine at Massachusetts General Hospital, suspect that the midwives' better track record may be due to their having patients who were "healthier to begin with."

Dr. Fredric Frigoletto, chief of obstetrics at MGH and a past president of the American College of Obstetricians and Gynecologists, agrees. This study has "significant limitations," he says, because it's not clear "how patients found themselves in the midwife or doctor cohort."

Statistician MacDorman agrees that any study like hers based on data from birth certificates can't control for all factors, but she notes that since her study deliberately left out multiple births, preterm births and Caesarean deliveries, the women *were* comparable in that they all had normal deliveries.

From *The Boston Globe,* November 2, 1998.

HEALTH SENSE reprinted by permission of United Feature Syndicate, Inc.

Judy Foreman is a member of the Globe staff. Her e-mail address is: foreman@globe.com

Previous "Health Sense" columns are available through the Globe Online searchable archives at **http://www.boston.com.** Use the keyword **columnists** and then click on Judy Foreman's name.

Furthermore, her study showed that midwives were more likely than doctors to care for women at higher socioeconomic risk—black women, American Indians, teenagers, women with three or more previous births, unmarried women, those with less than a high school education and those with late or no prenatal care.

The doctors were somewhat more likely to have medically difficult cases, she says, but "the differences were small."

So if there's magic in midwifery, what is it? Midwives say it's time and support—during prenatal visits and labor.

One study cited by MacDorman found certified nurse-midwives spent an average of 49.3 minutes on the first visit—versus 29.8 minutes for doctors. Subsequent visits averaged 29.3 minutes for midwives, against 14.6 minutes for doctors.

Frigoletto counters that if you add up the time the doctor, the nurse and the nurse's assistant spend with each patient, "the total visit might be just as long."

Unlike doctors, most midwives stay with the woman—not just nearby—for the duration. This allows quick action if the baby's heart rate soars or plummets. If low-tech remedies such as having the woman change position or drink fluids don't help, the midwife can then call in the doctor.

Often, the combination of massage, position changes, breathing exercises and moral support do the trick, though Frigoletto warns there's little data linking these interventions with birth outcomes.

Midwives believe they have economics on their side, too. A 1996 study of 1,000 patients showed that hospital charges for midwife births were 21 percent lower than those for doctors, perhaps because they're less likely to use interventions such as electronic fetal monitors and to do procedures such as episiotomies (surgical cuts to enlarge the vaginal opening).

Though midwives, like doctors, can use painkilling medications and drugs such as oxytocin (Pitocin) to induce or speed up labor, they do so sparingly lest they trigger a vicious circle: Painkillers may slow labor, which means a woman may need oxytocin, which causes more pain, which may necessitate more painkillers.

"There's some truth to that" scenario, says Frigoletto. But usually, the need for drugs depends on the individual and how many previous births she's had. He adds that doctors, like midwives, are cautious about using drugs too early in labor.

And midwives have some time-honored tricks up their sleeves. Instead of using forceps, midwives often ask a woman to stand and rock her hips or squat to free a stuck baby. They also may use nipple stimulation, which can help a woman's body release it's own natural oxytocin.

"What was nice," Rose says of her son's birth two years ago, was having "all the advantages of a midwife, yet if something went wrong, there was a doctor on call and a neonatal intensive care unit 30 seconds away."

So nice, in fact, that Rose and her husband asked Ludka to deliver their second child, who arrived last month—with the help of another midwife at the Brigham. Ludka was fast asleep—she'd been delivering a baby the whole night before.

Some Nations Cite Lower Mortality Rates

by Judy Foreman

*L*ong a staple of medical care in other countries, midwifery is growing steadily in the United States.

In 1975, only 1 percent of American babies were delivered by midwives, according to government statistics. By 1991, it was up to 4.4 percent; by 1996, 6.5 percent.

Worldwide, the use of midwives is often associated with lower infant mortality, says Lisa Paine, head of maternal and child health at the Boston University School of Public Health.

In most countries that are "ahead of us in infant mortality rates, there is greater reliance on care provided by midwives," she says.

But interpreting such data can be tricky, warns Dr. Fredric Frigoletto, chief of obstetrics at Massachusetts General Hospital. Neonatal mortality (deaths in the first month of life) are a big contributor toward infant mortality (deaths in the first year). The United States counts deaths of premature and low birthweight infants as neonatal deaths, but some countries might not count them at all, which skews the statistics, he says.

Still, the apparent link between reliance on midwives and low infant mortality is intriguing. In Britain, about 70 percent of births are attended by midwives and the infant mortality rate is 6.1 per 1,000—versus 7.8 per 1,000 in this country, says Paine. In the Netherlands, where nearly half of all births are attended by midwives, the rate is 5.2.

In Canada, midwifery is less common than in the United States, but the infant mortality rate is lower (6.0), for unclear reasons.

Japan, whose infant mortality rate is the world's lowest (3.8 per 1,000), is facing a potential midwife shortage. Many of Japan's midwives are over 65, and it's not clear there will be enough younger midwives to take their place.

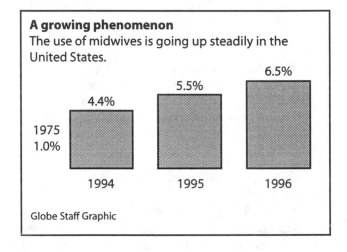

A growing phenomenon
The use of midwives is going up steadily in the United States.

Globe Staff Graphic

In the United States, there are now an estimated 5,500 certified nurse-midwives, according to the American College of Nurse-Midwives, an advocacy and lobbying group in Washington, D.C.

Certified nurse-midwives—nurses who have taken accredited midwifery training and have passed a national certification exam—are licensed in all 50 states. In addition, there are several thousand lay midwives. They are not licensed in Massachusetts and many other states. But in some cases, they have passed a different exam and may be certified by the National Association for the Registry of Midwives, in which case they're called CPMs: certified professional midwives.

In a few states, they may deliver babies in hospitals; they deliver babies at home and in birth centers.

Despite the growth in midwifery, there are "not enough midwives to meet the demand," says Judy Norsigian, program director of the Boston Women's Health Book Collective, the women's health group that wrote the self-help book "Our Bodies, Ourselves."

From *The Boston Globe,* November 2, 1998.

HEALTH SENSE reprinted by permission of United Feature Syndicate, Inc.

Judy Foreman is a member of the Globe staff. Her e-mail address is: foreman@globe.com

Previous "Health Sense" columns are available through the Globe Online searchable archives at **http://www.boston.com.** Use the keyword **columnists** and then click on Judy Foreman's name.

Breast Milk:
It Does a Body Good

by Barbara Quick

If a medicine were to be developed that could prevent the deaths of a million or more children per year, greatly reduce childhood illness and disease, produce healthier and perhaps even smarter adults, and, in its administration, contribute to preventing ovarian and premenopausal breast cancer and osteoporosis in women, it would certainly be hailed as the greatest miracle in the history of medical science. If, furthermore, this medicine had no ill side effects, and its production had absolutely no adverse environmental impact, we would scarcely be able to believe our good fortune as a species. Now, what if the fantasy were to be extended a bit, so that we imagine this miracle substance to be not only all of the above, but also free of charge? In other words, no one stands to profit economically from its production, promotion, or distribution. In fact, the only adverse impact at all would be an economic one on a billion-dollar multinational industry built upon a competing but clearly inferior product. Would the makers of that lesser product raise their hands in thanks for the blessing to humankind and close up shop? Would the medical establishment rise in a collective cheer at the prospect of fewer sick people needing its services?

It is unnecessary to venture into the realm of fantasy to find the answers to these questions, as the miracle substance—breast milk—already exists, although it is only in the last 25 years or so that the full range of its medicinal properties has begun to be understood and recognized by the worldwide scientific community.

Until the 1930s, practically all American babies were breast-fed by either their mother or a wet nurse. As more women gave birth in hospitals, and doctors exerted increasing control over childbirth and baby care, the notion of artificial feeding began to catch on. Formula companies, capitalizing on the "better living through chemistry" ethos of the 1950s, marketed their products as an improvement on Mother Nature. For baby boomers' parents, formula feeding became the norm; only 18 percent of babies born in U.S. hospitals in 1956, for example, were breast-fed for their first week.

Between 1970 and 1980, the percentage of mothers choosing to breast-feed in hospital increased from 27 percent to 55 percent, with the highest rates among higher-income and college-educated women. The percentage peaked in 1984 at 60 percent, only to decline for the following six years.

The U.S. now has one of the lowest breast-feeding rates of all industrialized nations—and one of the highest rates of infant mortality. Since 1991, there has been a resurgence in breast-feeding, but as of 1995 only 48 percent of all babies in the U.S. were exclusively breast-fed during their first day or two in the hospital. In Finland, by way of contrast, 95 percent of babies are breast-fed from birth. In Germany, almost 70 percent of babies are being breast-fed at two months of age. By the time they are five months old, just 20 percent of American infants receive any breast milk at all. Among African American women, only 12 percent are breast-feeding when their babies are five to six months old; the figures for white and Latina women are 26 and 21 percent, respectively. Yet World Health Organization (WHO) guidelines for optimal mother and child health recommend breast-feeding for the first two years.

The disenfranchised of this nation—women who have the least income and least education—have the lowest rates of breast-feeding and the highest rates of infant mortality, and—even though they can least afford it—they are the greatest consumers of infant formula. The estimated cost of the artificial baby milk needed to bottle-feed a child in the first year is between $900 and $1,200.

Infant formula is nothing more than powdered cow's milk with chemical additives designed (so far, in vain) to "humanize" it. Breast milk is a live substance, replete with at least 11 anti-infectious factors and antibodies,

Reprinted by permission of *Ms. Magazine,* © 1997. January/February, pp. 32–35.

Barbara Quick is the author of "Northern Edge: A Novel of Survival in Alaska's Arctic" (HarperCollins West).

protecting the newborn not only from germs, but also from the absorption of proteins that can cause the development of allergies: breast-fed infants are seven times less likely to develop allergies than infants fed on cow's milk preparations. Unlike artificial baby milk, breast milk is easily digested and assimilated by human babies, and contains all the vitamins, minerals, and nutrients they require in their first five to six months of life. Any one mother's breast milk is constantly changing and adapting to her individual baby's needs from day to day and month to month. If uninterrupted by the introduction of formula supplements or bottles, the breast-feeding dyad is an elegant illustration of the law of supply and demand: as the infant suckles, the woman's breasts respond by producing more milk. (This is why—given sufficient food, liquid, and moral support—women with more than one baby can breast-feed successfully.)

The health benefits to babies are overwhelming. A 1995 study in the *Journal of Pediatrics* states: "Breast-feeding during the first year of life is protective against diarrheal illness and otitis media [ear infections], even in a relatively affluent, highly educated population." Furthermore, "The reduction in morbidity associated with breast-feeding is of sufficient magnitude to be of public health significance." Among the results of other studies, breast-fed children were found to be half as likely to have any illness during the first year of life as those fed artificially; had half the risk of becoming diabetic; were ten times less likely to be admitted to the hospital during their first year of life; were one third less likely to die of sudden infant death syndrome; and, if breast-fed exclusively for at least six months, were half as likely to develop cancer before age 15 than children who were fed formula.

Nonetheless, artificial baby milk, initially developed as a way to feed infants whose mothers had abandoned them or died, has gained widespread acceptance as a perfectly good alternative to breast milk for all babies.

How can this possibly have happened? The answer involves attitudes as much as economics. Women who have grown up with no exposure to breast-feeding may face prejudice and criticism instead of instruction and support. The breast has been so sexualized in our culture that women are often shamed into nursing their babies in bathroom stalls. It can be difficult to continue to breast-feeding while facing the disapproval of employers, acquaintances, and scandalized passers-by at the mall.

Taking advantage of this discomfort, the formula industry is coming up with ever more brilliant and insidious marketing practices to promote its products and maintain its profit. In *Milk, Money, and Madness: The Culture and Politics of Breast-feeding*, Naomi Baumslag, M.D., lays out the issues clearly and eloquently: "The lack of accurate information about breast-feeding makes it hard for women to understand how their right to breast-feed is manipulated by those who profit when they choose not to."

The medical establishment today is mired in a complex economic relationship with the formula companies, which donate tremendous amounts of money for medical training, research, and professional meetings, and provide formula free of charge to many U.S. hospitals. The big three U.S. formula manufacturers—Abbott Laboratories (Ross Laboratories), American Home Products (Wyeth-Ayerst Laboratories), and Bristol Myers (Mead Johnson)—contribute millions of dollars per year to the American Academy of Pediatrics, the American College of Obstetricians and Gynecologists, and the American Medical Association, even though these groups are on record as strongly supporting breast-feeding.

There is ardent competition between the big three to win the privilege of "donating" their brand of formula and supplies to hospitals in exchange for exclusive representation in the hospitals' "discharge packs" for new mothers—often a diaper bag filled with cute little rattles, baby hats, and samples of infant formula. Market research has shown that 93 percent of mothers will continue to buy the brand of formula given to them at the hospital. Many studies, including a 1996 article in *Pediatrics,* show that infants of mothers who receive formula or coupons upon their discharge are significantly more likely to be fed artificially at one month of age, while the infants of mothers given the names of lactation support groups or individuals instead are more likely to be fully breast-feeding at four months.

Other hospital routines that are largely taken for granted in this country—such as placing infants in nurseries rather than "rooming in" with the mother, or separating newborns and mothers for four hours after delivery—contribute to our woefully low rates of breast-feeding. The authors of the article in *Pediatrics* note that "other structural problems, particularly the fact that the labor and delivery department is on a different floor from both the newborn nursery and the maternity ward, made it difficult for mothers and infants to transition together."

In 1991 UNICEF and WHO launched the Baby-Friendly Hospital Initiative, a program designed to promote breast-feeding by recognizing health care providers who encourage and support the practice. Although there are more than 8,000 certified Baby-Friendly Hospitals world-wide, only one hospital in the United States has received certification.

Not all physicians have been willing to jump on the formula band-wagon. Some doctors have allied themselves in practice as well as in theory with lay organizations, such as La Leche League International, dedicated to breast-feeding promotion and education. A study in the September 1995 issue of *Pediatrics* found that "residency training does not adequately prepare pediatricians for their role in breast-feeding promotion," and recommended that lactation training—including direct patient interaction and the practice of counseling and problem-solving skills—become part of the medical school curriculum. Even the federal WIC program (Special Supplemental Nutrition Program for Women, Infants, and Children)—which serves one in three infants and accounts for 40 percent of all infant formula sales in the U.S.—has begun energetically promoting breast-feeding among its clients.

Fortunately for the continuation of our species, breast-feeding makes economic (as well as ecological) sense. A study conducted by a California company found that breast-feeding among its female employees resulted in a 36 percent reduction in infant illnesses and 27 percent reduction in mothers' absenteeism from work. An in-house publication for Kaiser Permanente estimates a savings of $1,000,000 to the HMO merely from the reduced incidence of ear infections that would result from an increase in breast-feeding among its members. Statistics compiled by La Leche League International in 1993 estimate that the WIC program would garner savings of at least $29 million per year if mothers in the program would breast-feed their infants for just one month. One expert has estimated that universal breast-feeding for the first three months could decrease hospitalization costs for infants in the U.S. by $2 billion to $4 billion per year.

The "Healthy People 2000" report issued in 1990 by the U.S. Department of Health and Human Services proposed ambitious national goals for breast-feeding initiation (75 percent of all mothers and infants by the year 2000) and duration (50 percent still breast-feeding at five to six months postpartum). The only way we could possibly achieve these goals in the next three years would be through a massive educational campaign that might convince individual women as well as the medical establishment to spurn artificial baby milk in favor of "the right stuff."

RESOURCES

BOOKS

Beyond the Breast-Bottle Controversy, by Penny Van Estereik (Rutgers University Press, New Brunswick, N.J.)

Milk, Money, and Madness, by Naomi Baumslag and Dia L. Michels (Bergin and Garvey, Westport, Conn.)

The Nursing Mother's Companion: Third Revision Edition, by Kathleen Higgins, R.N., M.S. (The Harvard Common Press, Boston)

A Practical Guide to Breastfeeding, by Janice Riordan (C.V. Mosby, St. Louis)

So That's What They're For! Breast-feeding Basics, by Janet Tamaro (Adams Media Corporation, Holbrook, Mass.)

The Womanly Art of Breastfeeding, published by La Leche League.

The Working Woman's Guide to Breastfeeding, by Nancy Dana and Anne Price (Meadowbrook, Deephaven, Minn.)

GROUPS

La Leche League International, 1400 North Meacham Road, Box 4079, Schaumburg, Ill. 60168-4079; (847)519-7730, (800)LA-LECHE; Web site http://www.lalechleague.org./ Nursing mothers' support group. Call for breast-feeding help and information on your local chapter.

Nursing Mothers Counsel, P.O. Box 50063, Palo Alto, Calif. 94303; (415)599-3669. Nursing mothers' support group. Call for information or referral to a local chapter.

You Never Saw June Cleaver Weeping, Did You?

by Danielle Kuhlmann, RNC, BSN

For many women, the birth of a child is an extraordinary event filled with intense emotions. It is the culmination of hopes and dreams, futures and pasts, all rolled into one small wonderful package. The birth also initiates a permanent role change that can leave a woman feeling helpless, hopeless, and depressed. Her role as a woman is altered: she is now the mother of a totally dependent being. A dual responsibility is now present. Women who were once working or socially connected to the community may feel the isolation associated with having a new baby at home. Relationships with childless friends can be altered to a point where women find themselves unable to relate to the difference in lifestyles. If the woman has a career, then her time is now divided

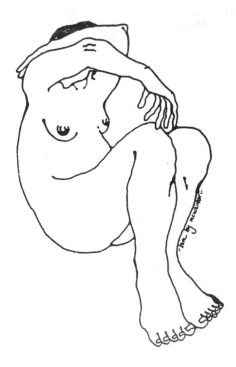

between the responsibility of her job and her family. Social outings are decreased because the focus is on getting to know the new person in the family and the new routine for care.

Her role as a sexual being is changed. Sexual intimacy is often temporarily decreased and may feel different than before the birth. Physiologically, her body has made an incredible change. Her breasts are more full, they are now the object of food, not of sexuality. If she is breast feeding, her vagina is drier due to the lack of estrogen, and she may feel uncomfortable from the vaginal delivery. A cesarean section will have left a permanent scar that makes her feel "altered" in some way. In our culture, men often believe, consciously or unconsciously, in a "madonna/whore" complex: women who are mothers are not supposed to be sexualized. Loss of spontaneity and the need to schedule intimate moments can have an effect on relationships. Resentment may occur between partners because now one is the primary bread-winner of the family, while the other is the primary care giver of the new baby.

Depressive symptoms may occur because the woman may not be emotionally ready for the change which has happened. Her expectations of what motherhood was supposed to be like may be completely different than reality. Women who thought that a troubled marriage would be solved by the addition of a baby, or that somehow low self-esteem would be cured by having a little baby who loves and needs them are often jolted by the reality that motherhood brings.

Most all women feel a range of emotions immediately after giving birth, some very high and frantic, and some very, very low. These common feelings are called the "baby blues". The baby blues are characterized by bouts of crying for no apparent reason, fatigue over the

From *WomenWise,* Winter 1998, pp. 6–8. Copyright © 1998 by Concord Feminist Health Center. Reprinted by permission.

Danielle Kuhlmann is a perinatal nurse at Concord Hospital in Concord, New Hampshire, and an aspiring midwife. All she really wants to be is a princess, complete with elbow length gloves and a tiara.

new strange hours that new mothers find themselves keeping, irritability, anxiety at the sudden reality of a new helpless baby, sleeplessness and restlessness. These symptoms are often thought to be present because of the letdown period after the profound emotional experience of childbirth. Some women who haven't experienced these feelings before report that they feel overwhelmed by it all.

These feelings are temporary, and usually resolve themselves. As one woman I spoke with said, "It was my fourth baby, and I knew what was happening. I would just stand in my hospital room and bawl for no apparent reason. I was so worried that this time it was going to be so much harder after I left the hospital. I was terrified! Then, just a few days later, when I got back into the routine of my daily life, it all just disappeared."

Because of the wide range of emotions that are felt by women after childbirth, postpartum depression is often overlooked, and undertreated. Postpartum depression (PPD) may start early, like the "baby blues", and is characterized by the same uncontrollable crying, irritability, anxiety, loneliness, and isolation as the "baby blues". Its distinction is that it lasts longer and has a more debilitating effect.

During pregnancy, and particularly in the last trimester, the hormones estrogen and progesterone are at an all time high. Within twenty-four to forty-eight hours after the delivery of the placenta, serum levels of these hormones drop to the lowest level recorded in non-pregnant states. Estrogen, in particular, is a hormone that is responsible for the development of the secondary sexual characteristics, and for the changes in the tissue of the vagina and the uterus. Fluctuating levels during women's menstrual cycles are thought to play a role in mood changes, especially mood instability. Oddly enough, the word "estrogen" comes from the Greek oistros, meaning "mad desire"! Apparently, there was a connection to moods long before "modern medicine" deemed it so.

Twenty-four hours after delivery, estrogen is at a concentration that reaches only two percent of levels that were present before conception. Also during pregnancy, a woman's blood volume nearly doubles, and within forty-eight hours after delivery, returns to the pre-pregnant volume. Such a dramatic decrease in volume and hormone levels affect a woman's emotional state. The social adjustment that women must make to a new baby is further enhanced by hormonal forces occurring in the body.

Progesterone, a hormone that works in concert with estrogen, is responsible for the development of the endometrial lining of the uterus before the implantation of the fertilized egg, development of the placenta after implantation, and development of the mammary glands to support breast feeding. Decreased estrogen levels in the postpartum period have been associated with increased sleep disturbances, and decreased progesterone levels with depressive feelings. A less pronounced elevation of progesterone in the menstrual cycle is associated with Premenstrual Syndrome (PMS).

Prolactin, a pituitary hormone that supports milk production, soars after delivery. Even in non-breast feeding mothers, the presence of prolactin further suppresses estrogen and progesterone, perhaps enhancing the "hormone effects" of the post-partum period. There is conflicting research on whether or not breast feeding is a factor in postpartum depression. Another hormone present in pregnancy and postpartum, especially those women who are depressed, is the stress hormone cortisol. High levels of cortisol in women have been and are currently being studied as to their role in postpartum depression.

Thyroid hormones and their shift may play a part in the lavish scene of postpartum depression. These levels are naturally low in the postpartum period, and the drop in levels may account for the depressive feelings many women report. Although a true clinical hypothyroid state may not be present, just the abrupt decrease in the levels can begin the cascade of symptoms of postpartum depression.

Postpartum depression is an altogether larger, and more complex state than the "baby blues". It, too, is characterized by extreme emotional lability, exhaustion, uncontrollable and unpredictable crying, and anxiety. The depression itself can start gradually or abruptly, and last from a few months to well up to a year after delivery. It can be extremely debilitating, causing a disturbance in the mother-infant bonding relationship, as well as the relationship between the mother and her partner. Symptoms such as fatigue, headaches, loss of appetite, memory loss, poor concentration, confusion, and thoughts of harming or over-protecting the baby can accompany postpartum depression. PPD differs from the "baby blues" by increased intensity and duration of symptoms. "Baby blues" is a temporary adjustment, both physically and emotionally, but depression is a clinical state that usually requires some sort of treatment, be it medical, psychological, or homeopathic.

Susan, a 34 year old woman with her second child, described her feelings like this: "With my first baby, I knew something was amiss, but I didn't have any frame of reference, so I just smiled through the tears and tried the best way I knew how to eke out a semi-normal life for myself. After my son was born, I was scared that it was going to happen again. Sure enough, about six days after he was born, I could feel this sense of unrest rolling in. I couldn't find any reason to be happy. I mean, I loved my son and I had a beautiful three year old daughter, my husband and I were at good points in our careers, but everything seemed so sad to me. I would be lying in my bed in the morning, I could hear my son crying for me but I just couldn't find it in myself to get out of bed and go to him. I knew I was crumbling on the inside, I just wasn't able to muster up enough strength to do anything about it. I think I was crying out for help when I went to see my doctor six weeks after the baby was born. I had this monster list of complaints that were so small and insignificant, she knew I was depressed. She looked up at me and asked how I really felt inside. I sobbed so uncontrollably, I think I was partially relieved that someone knew that I wasn't getting it together."

Just as there are a myriad of symptoms associated with this unique depression, there are also a number of theories regarding its causes.

It has been said that what the mind forgets, the body remembers, and traumatic birth experiences certainly have an effect on a woman's emotional well being. Women who feel let down by the medical system, their doctor, or by their own body, report a greater sense of depressive symptoms than women who gave birth in the way that they had imagined and planned. Most medical researchers who have delved into the possibility of depression after major surgery will agree that there exists a real potential for depression following cesarean delivery of a baby. The conflict arises when people assume that because the woman got a healthy baby out of the procedure, her depression should then be lessened. Feeling "ruined" by a surgical scar on the abdomen or the perineum contributes to the poor body image, and possibly the depressive state often following delivery.

Several "red flags" can alert us to the potential for the problem. Physicians and medical researchers currently estimate that ten to twenty percent of birthing women will develop postpartum depression of some sort, although the estimation is thought to be conservatively low by other physicians and medical researchers, nurses and those who actually work directly with the depressed women themselves. Not surprisingly, lack of emotional, family, or financial support is thought to be major risk factors.

Katie, a 19 year old first time mother, stated, "The whole thing started out bad. First, me and my boyfriend broke up, then he found out I was pregnant so we got back together. His family and my mother were against it from the beginning. They kicked both of us out. We had nowhere to go, so we stayed with friends and moved every couple of months. He got sick of me and went back home, but I couldn't go anywhere. Anyway, I had the baby and I felt good and all, but I guess something wasn't right because all of a sudden I freaked out. All I wanted to do was sleep, I couldn't eat, I just hated myself. I thought that I would have this baby and everything would be all right. My mom let me and my daughter move back in, and she had to take care of the baby because I couldn't. Sure, I thought of killing

myself because that is the only way that I knew would solve all of my problems. I felt guilty enough getting pregnant, I didn't want to hurt any more."

Unrealistic expectations of parenthood, with drastic changes in role responsibility, can also influence feelings in the postpartum period. In our culture, we are taught to value the highly productive and efficient. Motherhood is a nurturing job, one that takes place in an intimate setting and isn't regulated by the job market. Creating a family requires a slower paced, more evolutionary style of productivity. A woman's parenting skills (or lack thereof) aren't seen in the "finished product" until later in her child's life.

Women in high-powered careers often report depression with the sudden role change and categorically different responsibilities of motherhood. No longer is she running an efficient, money-making company, one with clearly defined goals of profit and production, striving for a bigger piece of the economic pie, and one that is more goal-oriented than people-oriented. A job where workers and the inefficient are replaceable, constantly turning out new, younger and better. Now she is challenged by a small infant who needs her for security, food, love and affections, stimulation, and nurturing. What happens with motherhood is an altogether micromanagement of the formation of a person. This is a job where there are no rigorous schedules, there is no "technical manual" from which to consult. Here is a twenty-four hour, seven day a week job that will last a lifetime. Coffee breaks may not come around for several years.

Women have been duped in the last decade or two by the notion that the "Super Mom" actually exists. It's no wonder that postpartum depression rates are rising; we've come to think that the strong '90s woman can run a high-powered job with expert precision, while tending to the needs of her well taken care of and well behaved children. This notion is promoted by television shows (notice how The Cosby Show's Mrs. Huxtable had a successful law practice, and her children were smartly dressed and well adjusted, and she still managed to make a nice home). Magazines have their part in all of this, too. *Working Mother,* and other magazines that cater to the mainstream, are routinely filled with articles on how to get "quality time in just ten minutes" or "how to make delicious meals in thirty minutes that your family will think you slaved over for hours".

The fact that we had to wage a political fight for maternity leave with a guarantee of job security, and that we still don't have a system set up for both partners to take an extended leave to start their families, says volumes about the current socio-political state of motherhood. Women ourselves don't do a fabulous job at creating a supportive network for new mothers. It starts with the dreadful pregnancy horror stories that so many of us like to relate: "Oh, the stretch marks I had were all over my body, and the hemorrhoids the size of pillows, it's no wonder my husband didn't want to touch me, I was a whale" And it continues with the birth nightmare situations: "I was in labor for six days before I finally begged the doctor to rip the kid out of me." Finally, it culminates with "I had 45 minutes of sleep per week, the kid was constantly nursing, I couldn't hear the doorbell through the din of the shrieking, colicky baby." Of course, these quotes are a bit of an embellishment, but certainly one can get the idea of the setup new mothers face.

When postpartum depression recognition and treatment is ignored or delayed, the more severe types can surface and become demonstrably more grim. This is the point where the risk of suicide and infanticide rises.

Postpartum psychosis, the most severe form of postpartum depression in terms of its side effects and consequences, is also the most rare. Postpartum psychosis may begin immediately after the birth, or its onset may be delayed by a few weeks. Usually this kind of psychosis can be identified when the woman involved experiences some profound psychotic break: she may try to hurt or kill her child, or she may become self-destructive. This unique level of PPD affects about one in one thousand postpartum women.

Although its exact time of onset varies from woman to woman, experts can all agree that the danger and severity of postpartum psychosis are equal regardless of the time at which it occurs. Symptoms include hallucinations (all-sensory), delirium, severe mania and/or depression, an overwhelming urge to harm or kill the infant, and a desire to kill oneself. These symptoms manifest themselves in unique ways. One mother reported that before her admission to the psychiatric ward of a hospital, she was sleeping a maximum of three hours a night. She would write all of her Thank-you notes, iron all the baby clothes, wash all the floors and begin to prepare the storage of homemade baby food she would need for the next several months, all in one night.

Tragically, there are numerous reports of women killing their infants when the psychotic episodes begin. One woman thought she heard the voice of God tell her that her baby was evil, and the fate of humanity rested upon this baby's death. Reports exist of women driving over their infants, shooting, stabbing, drowning, and suffocating them all because "a voice" told them to do it, or that the babies were fussing or crying to a point that the women felt that death was the only outlet.

Postpartum psychosis results in the news events all too familiar to every reader of a daily paper: the baby shaken into a coma, the baby found abandoned in a trash bag, the young mother who surprises everyone by hurling herself off a bridge. The infant appears to these women to present an insurmountable state of need, and these mothers just don't feel as though they can ever accommodate these needs. Mothers report "hating" their babies, feeling completely at odds with this small creature that is seeming to take over their lives.

Accompanying Obsessive-Compulsive Disorder with postpartum illness is less common than severe postpartum depression. Symptoms include obsessive, intrusive thoughts about harming the baby, anxiety and panic attacks, and avoidance behaviors. These are the women who check their child's carseat hundreds of times during each brief car trip. Some women begin to compulsively hide all the kitchen knives, fearful that the new baby will "hurt itself" with them. They may spend all of their available time cleaning, cleaning, recleaning their homes. These women also find themselves obsessing on ways to harm their babies, much to their own secret horror.

Fortunately, postpartum psychosis is easily treated and the prognosis for most women is good. Treatment is the same for non-postpartum psychotic episodes: medications, hospitalization, and longer-term psychotherapy and follow up.

Treatment is based on the severity of the depression. For years, women who complained of not feeling "quite right" were told that they should be happy with their new baby, and to "get over it". Usually a prescription of Valium was written, and they would be sent along their merry way. However, three million women "not getting over it" seemed to indicate that something a little more serious was involved than mere coping skills. Nowadays, with the endless number of antidepressants that are available, a depressed new mother is sure to receive a prescription for at least one of these medications. In addition to medication for the depression, a sleeping medication may be given, as well as an anti-anxiety medication. In more severe cases, in-hospital treatment is usually the safest situation for the mother (and her baby).

Medications include Prozac, the 1990s panacea for ill feelings, Paxil, Wellbutrin, Elavil, Pamelor, Desipramine, Zoloft, and Tofranil. Prozac is somewhat in a class of its own, but works much like the other antidepressants. Other antidepressants and Prozac work by making the neurotransmitters serotonin and norepinephrine more available to receptors in the central nervous system, essentially by inhibiting their degradation. Low levels of these neurotransmitters are thought to contribute to depressive disorders. Antidepressants' most common and harshest side effect is its inhibitory function of the sexual drive (a particularly unfortunate effect regarding postpartum depression). Other side effects include dry mouth, dizziness, diarrhea, and fatigue. Effectiveness is seen in about two to four weeks, so patience and close monitoring by a professional is necessary in cases where the symptoms of PPD have reached the point of suicidal ideation. These medications are not recommended for breast-feeding mothers, except that Zoloft has some promise in that its levels in human milk are found to be negligible. It is considered safe to use with lactation, so the bonding process between mother and infant can be unhindered. Luvox is another antidepressant that is used primarily for the treatment of the obsessive-compulsive disorders associated with postpartum depression, and it, too, works by inhibiting the reuptake of serotonin. Side effects of Luvox include headaches, nausea, insomnia or drowsiness. Sometimes an anti-anxiety medication like Xanax, Buspar, Valium or Librium will be prescribed in conjunction with an antidepressant to combat some of the anxiety, restlessness and sleeplessness associated with PPD.

Another class of antidepressants are Monoamine Oxidase Inhibitors (MAOIs). These drugs are usually used for severe forms of PPD. MAOIs work by interfering with the enzymes responsible for the breakdown of neurotransmitters, thus providing the same type of improved symptoms that the other antidepressant medications offer. Women on an MAOI antidepressant need to be extremely careful with their diets. Foods containing tyramine and tryptophan should be avoided, due to the potentially harmful and even life threatening effects that may result, such as heart arrhythmia. Foods like aged cheeses, red wines, large amounts of caffeine, beer, chocolate, bananas, avocados, chicken livers, cured meats and soy sauce all contain tyramine and/or tryptophan. Side effects of MAOI antidepressants include dizziness, insomnia, dry mouth and anorexia.

Western medical management is only one of the therapies available. If traditional Western medicine does not satisfy or appeal to a woman experiencing postpartum depression, she will be happy to know that PPD has been treated safely and effectively for many years by naturopathic doctors, homeopathic practitioners, herbalists, acupuncturists, and doctors of Chinese Medicine. Anyone can drop into a natural food store or drug store and find a multitude of homeopathic remedies, but the safest and real benefit comes from seeking out the services of a Naturopathic Doctor, one who has specific training in homeopathic remedies. This person is likely to treat the whole person physically, emotionally, and spiritually.

St. John's Wort, a name that is frequently appearing in medical literature around the world, is an herbal (and therefore natural) antidepressant. St. John's Wort works in the same way that synthetic antidepressants do, by inhibiting reuptake of serotonin. It also is a powerful antiviral that works by boosting the body's own immune system. Unlike the chemical antidepressants, St. John's Wort can be taken while breast feeding, and has no known side effects. It is useful for mild to moderate depression; more severe forms will require exploration of complementary therapies.

Women can help themselves in the postpartum state whether or not they are "depressed" by treating some of

Post Partum Depression Sources

- Hale, Thomas, PhD. *Medications and Mothers' Milk* (sixth ed.) Amarillo: Pharmasoft Medical Publishing, 1997.
- Hamilton, J.A. & P.N. Harberger. *Postpartum Psychiatril Illnesses: A Picture Puzzle,* Philadelphia: University of Pennsylvania Press, 1992.
- Kendall-Tackett, K.A. & G. Kaufman-Kantor. *Postpartum Depression: A Comprehensive Approach for Nurses.* New York: Sage Publications, 1993.
- Skodol-Wilson, H. & C. Ren-Kneisl. *Psychiatric Nursing* (fourth ed.) New York: Addison-Wesley, 1992.
- Spratto, A. & A. Woods, *Delmar's Nurse's Drug Reference.* Albany: Delmar Publishing, 1996.

the symptoms associated with PPD. As everyone who has had a child knows, sleep is a highly scarce and valuable commodity, and too little will eventually wreak havoc on the emotional and physical body. So, plenty of rest is important. Proper nutrition is a given, but an often difficult task to undertake, especially when the needs of a newborn are the priority. Vitamin supplementation cannot be overemphasized; if a woman is given a prescription for prenatal vitamins during pregnancy, it will do her good to continue taking them. Vitamin B complexes are important for energy, alertness, good digestion, healthy skin and eyes. Vitamin C is important for healing of wounds, iron absorption and absorption of Vitamin E and several of the Vitamin Bs. Of course, most women can benefit from calcium and magnesium supplementation, the latter more important in mood stabilization, muscle tone and with depressive symptoms.

Chinese herbs that treat the kidneys, their adrenal glands, and the liver may be prescribed to the depressed woman by a naturopath to retone those organs primarily affected by the depletion state of postpartum.

Natural progesterone is useful in the treatment of mild PPD. It comes in either pill or cream form and, unlike the synthetic progesterone pills, women can breast feed their babies while taking natural progesterone. This natural form also does not cause the bloating, irritability, breast tenderness, and mood swings so commonly reported with the synthetic progesterone.

Any form of nurturing and self-healing therapy can only make a woman feel better. Such complementary therapies may include: Massage (there are numerous forms such as deep, Swedish, Rolfing, etc. that will suit just about everyone's needs); Reikki (an Eastern-based form of energy releasing therapeutic touch); Shiatsu (accupressure); and Laying on of Hands (the Christian form of Therapeutic Touch). The women should be encouraged to let someone dote on her for a change. It never hurts, and often helps.

Outside of the realm of medications, support groups are very therapeutic; just casually taking to other women who have been through this is extremely helpful for someone in the midst of her struggle with postpartum depression. Exercise is also a key, getting out of the house with or without the baby. Exercise helps a woman feel mentally and physically better, gets her pregnancy weight off and will help give her more energy in the long run.

Seeking treatment within a traditional hospital setting, particularly a traditional psyche ward, is not really therapeutic, since a woman is not allowed to have her baby with her at all. Twenty-four hour nursing observation and medical attention is great for the person who is feeling compelled to hurt herself or her baby, however. Therapy that is tailored especially to the postpartum mother is essential in getting her needs recognized and adequately treated. Some responsive clinics in both Europe and America have special postpartum units where mothers and babies can both stay; the facility will offer rooming-in service for the mother and baby during the acute phase of the illness, so that she can still have the opportunity to bond with her baby. Psychotherapy is often offered in conjunction with the medical management of depression, and can improve outcomes for both mother and family. Parenting skills, along with stress reduction techniques and coping skills, are taught to the woman during her stay.

As one can clearly ascertain, the impact of postpartum depression and its related symptoms can have far reaching effects. The maternal infant bond can be temporarily or permanently altered. How? Well, it's possible to view the child as responsible for the feelings accompanying childbirth. As a result, mothers can feel somewhat detached from the traditional mother/infant bond. Does this lead to a greater incidence of child abuse? Who knows. I do know that the baby itself must sense something is up and may not feel very loved. The older siblings may not treat this child well if they see it as the cause for the change in behavior of their once "normal" mother. The relationships of spouses and partners are profoundly affected. If this is the first baby, then both may wonder about the possibility of having subsequent children. Are they doomed as parents? The mother's partner may not trust her to be alone with the child. Both may wonder what their family and friends will think about their situation. Larger scope family and community relationships don't escape unscathed. For the woman herself, self-esteem, coping mechanisms, role attainment, familial attachment and development are all hindered. It becomes understandable why the potential for violence all around is increased.

With the seemingly varied population that is affected by postpartum mood disorders (the more severe manifestations of postpartum depression, like psychosis and obsessive compulsive disorder, are currently referred to as "mood disorders"), how do we tell who is most likely to experience postpartum depression? Experts and researchers cannot conclusively agree on the type of person or situation that will trigger the onset of postpartum depression and/or postpartum mood disorder. The list of potential causative factors reads long, and the true challenge for the researcher is to find a woman who isn't in one or another of these "risk groups".

They include: One who has a history of "pure" depression (depression without the proximity of childbirth); previous history of postpartum mood disorder; depression during pregnancy; anxiety disorder during pregnancy; family history of depression or postpartum depression; single mothers; marital discord; low socioeconomic status; high powered job status; poor relationship with the woman's own mother; very young mother; childbirth after the age of thirty-five; short interval in years between children; long interval in years between children; unrealistic expectations of motherhood; stressful recent or remote life events; lack of family and friends' support; and difficult infant behavior. All are said to predict postpartum depression.

Support of the woman and validation of her feelings is essential for her recovery, allowing her to voice her frustrations and work through some of the emotional difficulty that can accompany parenthood. It's odd that Westerners have the highest rates and prevalence of postpartum depression. Is it that Asian women's depression is somehow masked through cultural patterns, or is it that many Asian cultures provide some sort of effective rituals for the transition period of postpartum? Many of these cultures also lavish attention on mothers, and less so on the infant. Perhaps attending to all these needs, physical, emotional and spiritual, is in some way a comprehensive postpartum depression treatment that nips it in the bud.

As I was doing research for this article, I came upon volumes of writings and studies, but no real definitive answers. I searched and searched for the one article that wrapped postpartum depression up in a neat little package, but to no avail. I think that this, in and of itself, says something altogether more important about the state of knowledge and remedy that the subject of postpartum depression is in today.

I was talking to a friend of mine who recently had a baby, and as I was explaining the woes of my research and details of my finding, I looked up at her and saw tears welling in her eyes. I then realized that this was the face of postpartum depression: no rhyme or reason to it. It just was.

WORKSHEET—CHAPTER 10

Childbearing

1. Doris Haire's "The Cultural Warping of Childbirth" identified many common obstetrical practices from early pregnancy to post partum which "served to warp and distort the childbearing experience in the U.S." List ten of the practices Haire identified. For each practice, identify how you think the situation has or has not changed since 1972: If you do not know much about present childbirth practices, prepare to include this information in the interviews you do for question 2.

+ = totally improved, issue no longer an issue for activists
= = remains a problem
x = situation is even more exaggerated today than it was in 1972
? = not known
new = new technology/changed situation impacts on this issue

Practices	Changed?
1	
2	
3	
4	
5	
6	
7	
8	
9	
10	

2. Interview two women who have given birth or interview a woman who has given birth at least twice. (If you have given birth, you are encouraged to ask yourself these questions.) Ask the following questions about each pregnancy and birth.

a. How was she treated in pregnancy by health providers and others? Was she healthy during the pregnancy? Did she have access to regular pre-natal care? During her pregnancy, did she have strong ideas of what she wanted the childbirth experience to be?

birth 1 | birth 2

b. For the birth event, where was the birth, who assisted in the delivery, and what kind of birth was it (natural childbirth, some intervention, cesarean section)?

birth 1 | birth 2

c. Did the woman feel she had control in the process and did she have the childbirth experience she had hoped for?

birth 1 | birth 2

3. For the two pregnancy and birth experiences described above, identify social and economic factors which you think influenced similarities and differences in the two childbirths.

4. Many students think of childbirth experiences as being one extreme (doctor assisted—much medical intervention—birth in a hospital) or the other (non-doctor woman assisted—no medical intervention—birth at home); whereas all three factors 1) who assists, 2) type of delivery, including different interventions, and 3) where the birth takes place should be able to be negotiated. Ideally, of course, a woman should be able to have good medical backup if she chooses to try a non-medical type delivery or plans not to deliver in a medical setting.

   a. Read about Carol Rose's birth in "Midwives' Time Has Come Again." Describe the particular combination of 1) who, 2) type and 3) where choices she made and the advantages or disadvantages of her choices.

   b. Make up your own scenario of a birth plan for a woman where she does not want either of the "extremes."

5. The introduction to this chapter emphasizes that increasing choices for women during childbirth must take into account that different women will benefit from different choices. Identify two examples of a "choice" in childbirth which some women might want but which might not be desirable or appropriate for other women. (Give if a brief explanation if the explanation is not obvious.)

CHAPTER 11

Politics of Disease

*T*he politics of disease can be seen in the decisions made by government agencies, pharmaceutical companies, and the health care industry regarding priorities in funding, research, and education. Another aspect of the politics of disease is how women interact as both consumers and practitioners with these systems to fight for the priorities we identify. The first section focuses on breast cancer, which it is estimated one out of eight women in the United States will develop. Currently, there is a network of breast cancer activists around the country pushing for changes in research and the health care system. The chapter begins with an excerpt, "Breast Cancer: Power vs. Prosthesis," from *The Cancer Journals* by Audre Lorde, an extraordinary writer who died of breast cancer (also see her essays in this book: "There Is No Hierarchy of Oppressions" and "Age, Race, and Sex: Women Redefining Difference"). The excerpt examines from a very personal and political perspective the complexities around her decision not to use a prosthesis after mastectomy. Following this is an article on Dr. Susan Love, a surgeon who specializes in breast cancer, who can serve as a model of what women should be able to expect from a physician when dealing with breast cancer diagnosis and treatment. The article also touches on some of the controversies around breast cancer—such as the value of mammography for women under age 50. While breast cancer affects all groups of women, incidence, mortality rates, and survival rates may vary considerably. Some of these differences may reflect access to health care, though there certainly may be other factors such as diet and exposure to environmental carcinogens. The four fact sheets produced by the National Women's Health Network on breast cancer issues for Asian American, Native American, Latina, and African American women highlight these differences and remind us that, in analyzing any health issue, we need to keep in mind a diverse population of women.

The next three articles focus on the difficult area of prevention of breast cancer. In recent years, there has been a great deal of attention to "breast cancer genes." When these genes were first discovered, many thought the key to understanding the cause and prevention of breast cancer had been found. However, as the fact sheet on "Breast Cancer Genes" produced by the Boston Women's Health Book Collective (authors of *Our Bodies, Ourselves*) clarifies, only about 5% of breast and ovarian cancer can be attributed to inherited mutations and knowing there is an increased genetic risk does not aid in prevention. This sheet and its companion fact sheet on "Genetics, Health and Human Rights" present some of the complexities and ethical issues involved in genetic testing, whether for "breast cancer genes" or other genetic diseases. Another approach to prevention has been through the use of a drug called tamoxifen, which has been successfully used as a *treatment* for breast cancer. Rita Arditti's article on tamoxifen critiques the use of this drug, which has powerful side-effects (including endometrial cancer), for preventing breast cancer in healthy women, pointing out that, if there is not a better definition of prevention, "exchanging breast cancer for other life-threatening problems will be considered a success."

The last article on breast cancer, co-authored by Rita Arditti and Tatiana Schreiber, "Breast Cancer: The Environmental Connection," continues with the issue of defining true prevention, that is, keeping women from developing cancer, not merely detecting it early. After examining the roles of radiation, pesticides, and other forms of pollution in causing cancer, the authors call for a grass-roots movement that will push for changes in governmental priorities towards the elimination of environmental causes of cancer. (See also the Ruzek and Becker article in Chapter 1 on the history of the women's health movement for a description of breast cancer activism.)

Following up on the importance of consumer activism, "Ten Years of Self Help Achievement" is an interview with a co-founder of the Endometriosis Association. This group has been able to influence the health care system by providing information about endometriosis, as learned from the women who experience this disease, as well as providing support and information for those women. A companion 1998 article shows how much work remains to be done in this area, as its title, "Endometriosis Still Underdiagnosed," indicates.

The next three articles focus on AIDS, a disease that was once incorrectly considered a man's disease. However, it is now recognized that HIV infection is rapidly increasing in women and AIDS is a leading cause of death in women in certain age groups and geographic locations. Because most of the early cases of AIDS in the U.S. were men, the definitions of the disease were originally based on the opportunistic infections that men experienced. A person who was HIV+ (had antibodies to HIV, the virus that causes AIDS) and had specific symptoms was given the diagnosis of AIDS. Because women do not get the same opportunistic infections as men (women may have pelvic inflammatory disease, invasive cervical cancer, persistent and severe vaginal yeast infection, for example), HIV+ women were not being diagnosed with AIDS. It wasn't until 1993 that the Centers for Disease Control (CDC) changed the definitions to be more inclusive, especially of women. However, even with the changing definitions and a greater recognition of the need to focus on HIV/AIDS in women, as Lise Alschuler's article on "Women and HIV" points out, "there is still a relative lack of research on women with HIV disease. More research is needed to improve the early diagnosis and treatment of women with HIV disease."

The next two articles examine issues around preventing transmission of HIV and other sexually transmitted diseases (STDs). First, Jane Juffer, in "Spermicides, Virucides, and HIV," examines what is known about options in addition to condoms for preventing HIV transmission, emphasizing the need for women-controlled methods. (The careful reader will note that Alschuler and Jaffer offer somewhat contradictory information on the effectiveness of nonoxynol-9 in preventing HIV transmission. We see this as a reminder that we need more information on the effectiveness nonoxynol-9 in many different situations.) Next, Carol Camlin presents the debates about safer sex for lesbians. Although focusing on lesbian issues, the article is a presentation of explicit and concrete information that may be useful to anyone who is sexually active with one or more partners. She gives practical advice about reducing risk while putting that risk in clear perspective.

The last three articles in this section examine three different health issues that disproportionately affect women and that are often trivialized or assumed to be "all in her head." Donna Kiefer describes how she learned to live with Chronic Fatigue Immune Dysfunction Syndrome (CFIDS), "struggling just to make breakfast or take a shower," when she had previously led an extremely active life, working as an EPA attorney. Patricia Hanvey, a former Women's Studies 103 student, tells a parallel story in "Overcoming Obstacles," as she describes the way Lupus (Systemic Lupus Erythematosus or SLE) completely changed her life. Her article explores a number of key themes in this book and the course about the relationship of women to the health care system, including an examination of disability rights issues and the effects of homophobia. The last article examines a topic rarely discussed as a women's health issue as its title, "Recurrent Headache—A Neglected Women's Health Issue," indicates. The authors point out that not only do women report more frequent and more severe headaches than men, but also that, according to recent research, "the only disease found to affect patient quality of life and functioning more adversely than headache was AIDS."

Together the articles in this chapter illustrate the need for input by women—both as consumers and practitioners—into the decisions that are made about research priorities, policies, and the information/education about diseases that can affect our lives.

Breast Cancer
Power vs. Prosthesis

by Audre Lorde

On Labor Day, 1978, during my regular monthly self-examination, I discovered a lump in my right breast which later proved to be malignant. During my following hospitalization, my mastectomy and its aftermath, I passed through many stages of pain, despair, fury, sadness and growth. I moved through these stages, sometimes feeling as if I had no choice, other times recognizing that I could choose oblivion—or a passivity that is very close to oblivion—but did not want to. As I slowly began to feel more equal to processing and examining the different parts of this experience, I also began to feel that in the process of losing a breast I had become a more whole person.

After a mastectomy, for many women including myself, there is a feeling of wanting to go back, of not wanting to persevere through this experience to whatever enlightenment might be at the core of it. And it is this feeling, this nostalgia, which is encouraged by most of the post-surgical counselling for women with breast cancer. This regressive tie to the past is emphasized by the concentration upon breast cancer as a cosmetic problem, one which can be solved by a prosthetic pretence. The American Cancer Society's Reach for Recovery Program, while doing a valuable service in contacting women immediately after surgery and letting them know they are not alone, nonetheless encourages this false and dangerous nostalgia in the mistaken belief that women are too weak to deal directly and courageously with the realities of our lives.

The woman from Reach for Recovery who came to see me in the hospital, while quite admirable and even impressive in her own right, certainly did not speak to my experience nor my concerns. As a 44-year-old Black lesbian feminist, I knew there were very few role models around for me in this situation, but my primary concerns two days after mastectomy were hardly about what man I could capture in the future, whether or not my old boyfriend would still find me attractive enough, and even less about whether my two children would be embarrassed by me around their friends

My concerns were about my chances for survival, the effects of a possibly shortened life upon my work and my priorities. Could this cancer have been prevented, and what could I do in the future to prevent its recurrence? Would I be able to maintain the control over my life that I had always taken for granted? A lifetime of loving women had taught me that when women love each other, physical change does not alter that love. It did not occur to me that anyone who really loved me would love me any less because I had one breast instead of two, although it did occur to me to wonder if they would be able to love and deal with the new me.

In the critical and vulnerable period following surgery, self-examination and self-evaluation are positive steps. To imply to a woman that yes, she can be the 'same' as before surgery, with the skillful application of a little puff of lambswool, and/or silicone gel, is to place an emphasis upon prosthesis which encourages her not to deal with herself as physically and emotionally real, even though altered and traumatized. This emphasis upon the cosmetic after surgery reinforces this society's stereotype of women, that we are only what we look or appear, so this is the only aspect of our existence we need to address. Any woman who has had a breast removed because of cancer knows she does not feel the same. But we are allowed no psychic time or space to examine what our true feelings are, to make them our own.

Ten days after having my breast removed, I went to my doctor's office to have the stitches taken out. This was my first journey out since coming home from the hospital, and I was truly looking forward to it. A friend had washed my hair for me and it was black and shining, with my new grey hairs glistening in the sun. Colour was starting to come back into my face and around my eyes, I wore the most opalescent of my moonstones, and a single floating bird dangling from my right ear in the name of grand asymmetry. With an African kentecloth tunic and new leather boots, I knew I looked fine, with that brave new-born security of a beautiful woman having come through a very hard time and being very glad to be alive.

The doctor's nurse, a charmingly bright and steady woman of about my own age who had always given me a feeling of quiet no-nonsense support on my other visits, called me into the examining room. On the way, she asked me how I was feeling.

'Pretty good,' I said, half-expecting her to make some comment about how good I looked.

'You're not wearing a prosthesis,' she said, a little anxiously, and not at all like a question.

'No,' I said, thrown off my guard for a minute. 'It really doesn't feel right,' referring to the lambswool puff given to me by the Reach For Recovery volunteer in the hospital.

Usually supportive and understanding, the nurse now looked at me urgently and disapprovingly as she told me that even if it didn't look exactly right, it was 'better than nothing,' and that as soon as my stitches were out I could be fitted for a 'real form'.

'You will feel so much better with it on,' she said. 'And besides, we really like you to wear something, at least when you come in. Otherwise it's bad for the morale of the office.'

I could hardly believe my ears! I was too outraged to speak then, but this was to be only the first such assault on my right to define and to claim my own body.

A woman who is attempting to come to terms with her changed landscape and changed timetable of life and with her own body and pain and beauty and strength, that woman is seen as a threat to the 'morale' of a breast surgeon's office!

Yet when Moishe Dayan, the Prime Minister of Israel, stands up in front of parliament or on TV with an eye patch over his empty eye socket, nobody tells him to go get a glass eye, or that he is bad for the morale of the office. The world sees him as a warrior with an honourable wound, and a loss of a piece of himself which he has marked, and mourned, and moved beyond. And if you have trouble dealing with Moishe Dayan's empty eye-socket, everyone recognises that it is your problem to solve, not his.

Well, women with breast cancer are warriors, also. I have been to war, and still am. So has every women who had had one or both breasts amputated because of the cancer that is becoming the primary physical scourge of our time. For me, my scars are an honorable reminder that I may be a casualty in the cosmic war against radiation, animal fat, air pollution, McDonald's hamburgers and Red Dye no. 2, but the fight is still going on, and I am still a part of it. I refuse to have my scars hidden or trivialised behind lambswool or silicone gel. I refuse to be reduced in my own eyes or in the eyes of others from

warrior to mere victim, simply because it might render me a fraction more acceptable or less dangerous to the still complacent, those who believe if you cover up a problem it ceases to exist. I refuse to hide my body simply because it might make a woman-phobic world more comfortable.

Prosthesis offers the empty comfort of 'nobody will know the difference'. But it is that very difference which I wish to affirm, because I had lived it, and survived it, and wish to share that strength with other women. If we are to translate the silence surrounding breast cancer into language and action against this scourge, then the first step is that women with mastectomies must become visible to each other. For silence and invisibility go hand in hand with powerlessness. By accepting the mask or prosthesis, one-breasted women proclaim ourselves as insufficients dependent upon pretence.

In addition, we withhold that visibility and support from one another which is such an aid to perspective and self-acceptance.

As women, we cannot afford to look the other way, nor to consider the incidence of breast cancer as a private or secret personal problem. It is no secret that breast cancer is on the increase among women in America. According to the American Cancer Society's own statistics on breast cancer survival, of women stricken, only 50% are still alive after three years. This figure drops to 30% if you are poor, or Black, or in any other way part of the underside of this society. We cannot ignore these facts, nor their implications, nor their effect upon our lives, individually and collectively. Early detection and early treatment is crucial in the management of breast cancer if those sorry statistics of survival are to improve. But for the incidence of early detection and early treatment to increase, American women must become free enough from social stereotypes concerning their appearance to realize that losing a breast is infinitely preferable to losing one's life (or one's eyes, or one's hands . . .).

Although breast self-examination does not reduce the incidence of breast cancer, it does markedly reduce the rate of mortality, since most early tumours are found by women themselves. I discovered my own tumour upon a monthly breast exam, and so report most of the other women I know with a good prognosis for survival. With our alert awareness making such a difference in the survival rate for breast cancer, women need to face the possibility and the actuality of breast cancer as a reality rather than a myth, or retribution, or terror in the night, or a bad dream that will disappear if ignored. After surgery, there is a need for women to be aware of the possibility of bilateral recurrence, with vigilance rather than terror. This is not a spread of cancer, but a new occurrence in the other breast. Each woman must be aware that an honest acquaintanceship with and evaluation of her own body is the best tool of detection.

The greatest incidence of breast cancer in American women appears between the ages of 40 to 55. These are the very years when women are portrayed in the popular media as fading and desexualised figures. Contrary to the media picture, I find myself as a woman of insight ascending into my highest powers, my greatest psychic strengths, and my fullest satisfactions. I am freer of the constraints and fears and indecisions of my younger years, and survival throughout these years has taught me how to value my own beauty, and how to look closely into the beauty of others.

There is nothing wrong, *per se,* with the use of prostheses, if they can be chosen freely, for whatever reason, after a woman has had a chance to accept her new body. But usually prostheses serve a real function, to approximate the performance of a missing physical part. In other amputations and with other prosthetic devices, function is the main point of their existence. Artificial limbs perform specific tasks, allowing us to manipulate or to walk. Dentures allow us to chew our food. Only false breasts are designed for appearance only, as if the only real function of women's breasts were to appear in a certain shape and size and symmetry to onlookers, or to yield to external pressure. For no woman wearing a prosthesis can even for one moment believe it is her own breast, any more than a woman wearing falsies can.

Attitudes towards the necessity for prostheses after breast surgery are merely a reflection of those attitudes within our society towards women in general as objectified and depersonalised sexual conveniences. Women have been programmed to view our bodies only in terms of how they look and feel to others, rather than how they feel to ourselves, and how we wish to use them. As women, we fight this depersonalisation every day, this pressure towards the conversion of one's own self-image into a media expectation of what might satisfy male demand. The insistence upon breast prosthesis as 'decent' rather than functional is an additional example of that wipe-out of self in which women are constantly encouraged to take part. I am personally affronted by the message that I am only acceptable if I look 'right' or 'normal', where those norms have nothing to do with my own perceptions of who I am. Where 'normal' means the 'right' colour, shape, size, or number of breasts, a woman's perception of her own body and the strengths that come from that perception are discouraged, trivialised, and ignored.

Every woman has a right to define her own desires, make her own choices. But prostheses are often chosen, not from desire, but in default. Some women complain it is too much effort to fight the concerted pressure exerted by the fashion industry. Being one-breasted does not mean being unfashionable; it means giving some time and energy to choosing or constructing the proper clothes. In some cases, it means making or remaking clothing or jewelry. The fact that the fashion needs of one-breasted women are not currently being met doesn't mean that the concerted pressure of our demands cannot change that.

Some women believe that a breast prosthesis is necessary to preserve correct posture and physical balance. But the weight of each breast is never the same to begin with, nor is the human body ever exactly the same on both sides. With a minimum of exercises to develop the habit of straight posture, the body can accommodate to one-breastedness quite easily, even when the breasts were quite heavy.

Women in public and private employment have reported the loss of jobs and promotions upon their return to work after a mastectomy, without regard to whether or not they wore prostheses. The social and economic discrimination practised against women who have breast cancer is not diminished by pretending that mastectomies do not exist. Where a woman's job is at risk because of her health history, employment discrimination cannot be fought with a sack of silicone gel, nor with the constant fear and anxiety to which such subterfuge gives rise. Suggesting prosthesis as a solution to employment discrimination is like saying that the way to fight prejudice is for Black people to pretend to be white. Employment discrimination against post-mastectomy women can only be fought in the open, with head-on attacks by strong and self-accepting women who refuse to be relegated to an inferior position, or to cower in a corner because they have one breast.

Within the framework of superficiality and pretence, the next logical step of a depersonalising and woman-devaluating culture is the advent of the atrocity euphemistically called 'breast reconstruction'. It should be noted that research being done on this potentially life-threatening practice represents time and research money spent—not on how to prevent the cancers that cost us our breasts and our lives—but rather upon how to pretend that our breasts are not gone, nor we as women at risk with our lives.

Any information about the prevention or treatment of breast cancer which might possibly threaten the vested interests of the American medical establishment is difficult to acquire in the country. Only through continuing scrutiny of various non-mainstream sources of information, such as alternative and women's presses, can a picture of new possibilities for prevention and treatment of breast cancer emerge.

The mortality for breast cancer treated by conventional therapies has not decreased in over 40 years (Rose Kushner, *Breast Cancer,* Harcourt, Brace & Jovanovitch, 1975, p. 161). Since the American medical establishment and the ACS are determined to suppress any cancer information not dependent upon western medical bias, whether this information is ultimately useful or not, we must pierce this silence ourselves and aggressively seek answers to these questions about new therapies. We must also heed the unavoidable evidence pointing towards the nutritional and environmental aspects of cancer prevention.

Cancer is not just another degenerative and unavoidable disease of the ageing process. It has distinct and identifiable causes, and these are mainly exposures to chemical or physical agents in the environment. In the medical literature, there is mounting evidence that breast cancer is a chronic systemic disease. Post-mastectomy women must be vigilantly aware that, contrary to the 'lightning strikes' theory, we are the most likely of all women to develop cancer somewhere else in the body.

Every woman has a militant responsibility to involve herself actively with her own health. We owe ourselves the protection of all the information we can acquire about the treatment of cancer and its causes, as well as about the recent findings concerning immunology, nutrition, environment and stress. And we owe ourselves this information *before* we may have a reason to use it.

It was very important for me, after my mastectomy, to develop and encourage my own internal sense of power. At all times, it felt crucial to me that I make a conscious commitment to survival. It is physically important for me to be loving my life rather than to be mourning my breast. I believe it is this love of my life and myself, and the careful tending of that love which was done by women who love and support me, which has been largely responsible for my strong and healthy recovery from the effects of my mastectomy. But a clear distinction must be made between this affirmation of self and the superficial farce of 'looking on the bright side of things'.

Last week I read a letter from a doctor in a medical magazine which said that no truly happy person ever gets cancer. Despite my knowing better, and despite my having dealt with this blame-the-victim thinking for years, for a moment this letter hit my guilt button. Had I really been guilty of the crime of not being happy in this best of all possible infernos?

The idea that the cancer patient should be made to feel guilty about having had cancer, as if in some way it were all her fault for not having been in the right psychological frame of mind at all times to prevent cancer, is a monstrous distortion of the idea that we can use our psychic strengths to help heal ourselves. This guilt trip which many cancer patients have been led into (you see, it is a shameful thing because you could have prevented it if only you had been more . . .) is an extension of the blame-the-victim syndrome. It does nothing to encourage the mobilisation of our psychic defenses against the

very real forms of death which surround us. It is easier to demand happiness than to clean up the environment. The acceptance of illusion and appearance as reality is another symptom of this same refusal to examine the realities of our lives. Let us seek 'joy' rather than real food and clean air and a saner future on a liveable earth! As if happiness alone can protect us from the results of profit-madness.

Was I wrong to be working so hard against the oppressions afflicting women and Black people? Was I in error to be speaking out against our silent passivity and the cynicism of a mechanized and inhuman civilisation that is destroying our earth and those who live upon it? Was I really fighting the spread of radiation, racism, woman-slaughter, chemical invasion of our food, pollution of our environment, the abuse and psychic destruction of our young, merely to avoid dealing with my first and greatest responsibility—to be happy?

The only really happy people I have ever met are those of us who work against these deaths with all the energy of our living, recognising the deep and fundamental unhappiness with which we are surrounded, at the same time as we fight to keep from being submerged by it. The idea that happiness can insulate us against the results of our environmental madness is a rumour circulated by our enemies to destroy us. And what Woman of Colour in America over the age of 15 does not live with the knowledge that our daily lives are stitched with violence and with hatred, and to naively ignore that reality can mean destruction? We are equally destroyed by false happiness and false breasts, and the passive acceptance of false values which corrupt our lives and distort our experience.

The idea of having a breast removed was much more traumatic for me before my mastectomy than after the fact, but it certainly took time and the loving support of other women before I could once again look at and love my altered body with the warmth I had done before. But I did.

Right after surgery I had a sense that I would never be able to bear missing that great well of sexual pleasure that I connected with my right breast. That sense has completely passed away, as I have come to realise that that well of feeling was within me. I alone own my feelings. I can never lose that feeling because I own it, because it comes out of myself. I can attach it anywhere I want to, because my feelings are a part of me, my sorrow and my joy.

I would never have chosen this path, but I am very glad to be who I am, here.

30 March 1979

Dr. Susan Love:
Making Patients Medical Partners

by Sue Frederick

On a warm March day in Boston, surgical oncologist Dr. Susan Love, wearing a pin that reads "Keep ABreast: Get A Second Opinion," is seven hours into her 12-hour day at the Faulkner Breast Centre, examining yet another patient after a morning spent performing a lumpectomy.

Love sits patiently with the frightened woman, explaining cancer, how it spreads, and the pros and cons of treatment options. Love adds gently, "It's not going to hurt anything if you wait a few weeks to consider your options."

Then the room is quiet, almost like a confessional, as the woman whispers her fears and questions to the doctor. After answering all of them, Love sits calmly, willing to talk some more. And suddenly, to hear her patients tell it, breast cancer just isn't such a big deal.

Indeed, that's Love's intention: To help women face the trauma of a disease that the American Cancer Society estimates will strike one of every 10 women in their lifetime. She goes about it in a uniquely feminine—some say feminist—way by arming her patients with knowledge, which she considers the antidote to fear.

She isn't afraid to speak her mind. According to Love:

- Breast self-exams, invented by men, are taught wrongly, and that may be why nobody does them.
- Fibrocystic disease is a "garbage" term.
- Most women aren't given enough time and information to make a wise treatment decision when it comes to breast cancer.

But to hear her patients tell it, this outspoken woman is the doctor to see after a breast cancer diagnosis. As one woman says of Love, "She makes me feel at ease. She treats me like an intelligent human being."

Elaine Ullian, president of Boston's Faulkner Hospital where Love is director of the Breast Centre, is another admirer.

"I made up my mind to recruit her here before I'd even met her," she recalls. "Her reputation is incredible, not only in the medical community. Every woman I'd ever heard of who had breast disease was beating a path to Dr. Love's office."

Indeed, Love, who's also an assistant surgery professor at the Harvard Medical School and a surgical oncologist in the breast-evaluation center at Boston's Dana-Farber Institute, has impressive credentials and a growing reputation as a top-notch breast-cancer specialist. Yet, not all medical experts are enamored with her, a fact Love is quite aware of.

"My reputation is that I'm outspoken, that I speak my mind. And that's good and bad," she admits. "It's blocked off some avenues for my career."

Dr. Robert Goldwyn, head of the plastic surgery division at Beth Israel Hospital and another surgery professor at the Harvard Medical School, is quite familiar with Love's reputation.

"I think she's done a lot for medicine and for patients. She's done a lot for us here at Beth Israel," he says. "It's certainly not a dull experience working with her.

"But there are people, and I'm not one of them, who think she's rather extreme and champions a philosophy that might be detrimental to patients in the long run. But they don't want to speak out against her because she's a feminist and it would look like they were speaking out against feminism. People don't want to attack feminism."

Yet Love's honesty and directness, which may cause her problems in the medical world, are traits that pay off well in the examining room. That's where she kicks into gear, often seeming more a teacher than a surgeon, what with her charts and X-rays and detailed explanations of cancer.

"This isn't so bad," she says softly to a patient who has tears in her eyes. "Breast cancer is scary business. But we still cure 80 percent of all early breast cancers. Most people don't hear about those survivors. You hear about the ones who go downhill fast. You don't hear about those who go on quietly with their lives."

As Ullian puts it: "She has the wonderful combination of being an excellent surgeon and also having an incredible ability to talk to her patients. These women get a difficult diagnosis from one doctor that leaves them feeling utterly destroyed, and they go see Dr. Love, who gives them the same diagnosis. But the women walk out of her office feeling hopeful and not powerless anymore."

"I feel like I'm a teacher with these women," Love says. "My job is to educate the woman so she understands what's going on, so together we can come up with the best plan for her care. Teaching is very important."

Indeed, those who appear in her office face a challenge. This year, the American Cancer Society estimates some 135,000 women will be diagnosed with breast cancer in the United States, and 42,000 will die from it. But Love is used to tackling challenges, a necessary skill for a woman fighting her way up the ranks of a male-dominated system. When she entered medical school in 1971, only 8% of the physicians in this country were women; the figure now stands at around 15%.

Along the way, Love has collected quite a few stories about being a woman in medicine.

When she applied for a residency at Columbia University in 1974, they asked her what type of birth control she used, and if she planned to have children—"standard questions back then," remembers Love, who ended up doing her residency at Beth Israel Hospital in Boston, where she spent seven years as breast-clinic director.

She has since become somewhat infamous in her medical circles for her professional, as well as personal, style.

She is 40 years old, unmarried, and plans to raise her three-month-old girl, Katy, with her female companion. In her examining room, there are buttons with feminist observations that not all men find amusing, slogans like, "On the seventh day, when God created man, she made a mistake."

However, Love's opinion of men is not as extreme as it would initially seem. For one, her mentor is Dr. William Silen, the chief of surgery at Beth Israel.

"I truly respect Dr. Silen," Love says. "He's been a real role model for me in terms of taking patients seriously. And he's somebody who knows how you can still be caring and compassionate and still be a very good surgeon."

But her opinions about breast cancer do raise eyebrows—opinions that would be controversial even if they weren't coming from a woman. For example, she calls fibrocystic disease a "garbage term."

"It doesn't mean anything," she says flatly. "It means lumpy, painful breasts that don't have anything to do with cancer. To pathologists, it covers 15 different pathological entities common in all breasts, yet none causes lumps or pain. And on a mammogram, it's a term used for dense breasts.

"So they're all talking about a different thing, which would be okay except that some doctors say it increases your chance of getting breast cancer, which it doesn't. We need to get rid of the term and call them lumpy breasts or painful breasts."

Dr. Norman Sadowsky, chief of radiology at Faulkner Hospital and director of the diagnostic branch of the Faulkner Breast Centre, agrees.

"Most people know fibrocystic disease is a waste-basket term, but people still tell their patients they have it, and the patient thinks something is wrong with them.

"It's normal to have nodular breasts and painful breasts at certain times of the month, and there's nothing wrong with you if you have that. Love is mainly responsible for populating the idea that that's not a disease. She's had a big effect on doctors' thinking. They won't use the term now without thinking about it a little more."

But Dr. Ezra Greenspan, a clinical professor of medicine and the associate chief of the oncology division at New York's Mount Sinai School of Medicine, sees it differently.

"What she [Love] says about fibrocystic disease is a gross overstatement," he declares. "True, it is a 'dump' term covering several different conditions, but some of those conditions are not normal. And studies have shown that 30 percent of women with breast cancer have fibrocystic disease.

"And there are dozens of papers showing these women with fibrocystic disease do have a slightly higher incidence of cancer. So she's not quite accurate there."

Love says it can be argued both ways: "[Greenspan] is right in a way. In its broadest sense, fibrocystic disease covers a precancerous condition called atypia hyperplasia, which is not common and doesn't cause lumps or pain, but is under the broad pathological umbrella of the term fibrocystic disease."

The controversies continue.

Love was one of the few doctors to criticize Nancy Reagan's decision to go immediately from biopsy to surgery after the first lady was diagnosed with breast cancer last year.

"That really put us back," says Love. "Not that she chose to have a mastectomy, but that she didn't explore the options. She said she did before the biopsy, but you can't know the options before the biopsy.

"I think her choice is fine, but doing it in one stick is what I don't agree with. She should've taken the time to get a second opinion."

Indeed, Love encourages her own patients to take the time to make good treatment decisions: "Basically, the old theory was that breast cancer would go up the lymph nodes and get out into the body fast. So women went straight to surgery from the biopsy. But now, we know it takes 90 days for one cancer cell to become two cells.

"And most cancers are present 8 to 10 years before we feel the lump or see it on the mammogram. So if it wanted to get out, it's gotten out already, and it's a question then of how well your immune system has taken care of it. But the idea of it getting out tomorrow is baloney."

Love believes that when a woman is diagnosed with breast cancer, she goes into a temporary state of shock, which isn't a good state of mind in which to make decisions that will affect the rest of her life. As she says, "It is much safer to take a deep breath and wait a day or two, or a week or two, and get a second opinion and figure out the best treatment for you. If you rush in, you can't change things later."

Perhaps because of this outspokenness, or perhaps because she is a successful female surgical oncologist with a six month backlog of patients waiting to see her, Love has suddenly, quite to her own surprise, become a public figure. Recently, she was featured on the Public Broadcasting System's *Nova* series, as well as on ABC's *20/20*. And *The New York Times Magazine* shot her photo for a story on women surgeons.

"My success has surprised me, but it shows there's an enormous demand for physicians who will spend time talking to patients," she explains. "My success is not based on my skills in the O.R., which are okay, but it's based on the time I take to talk to women.

"If you can take a very scary crisis situation and explain it to someone clearly, and explain the unknown, you can empower them."

Love does know how to put women at ease. Her earthy honesty, her confident voice and her clear explanations are a salve to the women who seek her out. In fact, Love often puts women at ease with a subject few doctors are willing to sway from the party-line about: breast self-exams.

At least once a day, Love finds herself talking to a woman who feels terribly guilty and scared because she doesn't perform BSE's the way they're described in the American Cancer Society pamphlets. To that, Love says, "Stop feeling guilty. Nobody's doing them."

To her, these elaborate exams where a woman carefully searches her breasts for hidden lumps were born out of a male perspective on a female problem.

"These were invented by a man and nobody does them, but everybody feels guilty about it," she says. "Doing it like the ads say, in front of the mirror, is too much of a deal. You don't do it. You feel little things everywhere and don't know what they are. You don't

know what you're looking for, so you get anxious and stop doing it. Then you feel guilty for not doing it. It's another example of blame the patient."

But Dr. Arthur Holleb, the former senior vice president of medical affairs for the American Cancer Society, has long believed in the value of thorough BSE's in early cancer detection.

"If a woman is terrified of doing the self-exam and has nodular breasts, I'd say come to me every three months, and I'll do the exam for you and won't charge you. I did this in my practice," he explains.

Silen at Beth Israel sides with Love.

"I don't disagree with her about self-exams," he explains. "They've never really taken hold. Studies suggest they aren't making a huge difference. Women don't follow the routine taught by the ACS anyhow."

Indeed, a recent Oregon Medical Association survey of 618 Oregon women with breast cancer showed that many women never perform the technique. In fact, only 63% of that group detected their lumps either by self-exam or accidental discovery. The reason they cited for avoiding the technique: Their breasts were lumpy anyway.

Even the New York-based National Alliance of Breast Cancer Organizations acknowledges that the elaborate procedure intimidates some women. NABCO estimates that only 30% of women who know about BSE's regularly practice the procedure. Says a NABCO spokesperson: "We encourage women to examine their breasts in any way they can, however they're comfortable doing it. It's better than not doing it at all."

Holleb says doctors should be teaching the procedure to women: "We recommend the doctor teach the technique to the woman when he examines her. The advantage of the BSE is that the woman can do it every month, and the more frequently you do the BSE, the better your chance of finding an early cancer."

Holleb's main contention with Love's approach is that a large number of women in this country can't afford to visit a doctor for regular check-ups; often, they can't afford mammograms, either.

"If we discard BSE's, we're doing a great disservice to these women especially . . . and, really, to all women," Holleb says. "In the past, there were few rewards for doing the BSE and finding an early cancer. The reward then was a radical mastectomy. But nowadays, if you find it early, you can often save the breast and have a much better chance of survival."

But Love contends that, "There are no studies that show breast self-exams increase the survival rate of breast-cancer patients.

"Cancer can't be felt when it's a little bee-bee, so the little lumps she finds aren't usually cancer. And by the time a woman finds a cancerous lump, it's pretty advanced.

"These exams were invented at a time when women never touched themselves 'down there.' Now, women do run their hands over their bodies and are acquainted with their breasts."

Her recommendation: "Once a month in the shower when you're soaped up, run your hands over your body and get acquainted with your breasts, not looking for anything. Don't focus on anything. And you'll notice a change if there is one."

Love agrees with the ACS, however, that mammograms are the best way to detect cancer since they can find a malignancy in an early stage when it's far too small to be detected by hand.

But Love isn't crazy about their use in women under 40: "When they first came out, the doctors thought, 'Hey this is great. We'll do mammograms every year.' And they discovered they'd cause as many cancers as they cured if they did that."

"So, the answer is somewhere in between. The radiation risk is greater in younger women than older women. So if you're over 50, there's no question that mammograms improve the cure rate of breast cancer. From 40 to 50, it doesn't seem to have as much impact. The breasts are denser. Things are harder to see."

Nevertheless, Love says women over 40 should probably have them done every year, but she doesn't recommend them for women 35 to 40: "We need to get rid of the idea of a baseline mammogram. That idea comes from tuberculosis. The chest doesn't change every year, but breasts do change every year. So it's not a good comparison point. To compare one mammogram to another from one year to the next is false information."

Dr. Paul Stomper, a radiologist at the Dana-Farber Cancer Center and an assistant professor of radiology at the Harvard Medical School, disagrees.

"There's no data to back up her comments," he says. "As someone who takes mammograms everyday, I know that a woman's breast doesn't change that much on a mammogram from age 35 to 40. And studies have shown that the cut-off for radiation risks at low doses is at age 30. It stops being dangerous to have a mammogram at age 30. The risk then is negligible if at all . . .

"Mammograms are the only way to beat breast cancer, and physicians must be responsible and explain both sides of the issue to their patients. It's a very complex area."

Love's next patient of the day is 31-year-old Luz Landrau, who has just had a lumpectomy after six months of chemotherapy. Love examines the woman's breasts, asks about her energy since the surgery, and then makes her raise her left arm. Landrau raises the limb halfway and winces. Love says "good, great," and they laugh together.

Landrau is grateful to Love for getting her through what she calls the "toughest year of my life." After

being diagnosed and starting her chemotherapy regimen, Landrau decided that treatment wasn't for her and she stopped it. She told Love she wanted to cure herself "the natural way" with diet and vitamins.

Love was patient, continuing to see Landrau for check-ups. "She made me reason with her logically," Landrau recalls. "The tumor grew when I stopped chemo and she showed it to me on the mammogram. So after two months, I went back to chemo."

But that wasn't the end of Landrau's struggles. After completing the rigorous chemotherapy regimen, Love scheduled her for a lumpectomy. The night before the operation, Landrau called and said she was too afraid to go through with the surgery.

"Dr. Love said okay and gave me two weeks to get ready. She calmly helped me through my fears. She's a very special doctor," says Landrau.

Love says she's not angered by patients who want to try alternative therapies: "There's no question there's a real mind-body connection. The danger is using any one therapy to the exclusion of all others.

"With surgery, radiation therapy and chemo, we're trying to get rid of the large number of cancer cells, so the immune system can take care of itself. Many alternative therapies boost the immune system, so it makes sense to combine the two methods. And the macrobiotic diet is not well-tested, but it makes sense that a diet low in animal fat could improve the treatment of cancer. But it should be combined with conventional treatment.

"I tell patients the important thing is to make a package deal that combines the methods they like, and to be sure to include everything: prayer is probably as viable as diet or anything else."

Landrau's choice of a lumpectomy over a mastectomy is a common one in Love's office.

"Ninety percent of my patients have lumpectomy and radiation, and if they choose mastectomy, they often have immediate reconstruction," Love explains.

However, NABCO cites a 1985 study conducted by Dr. Bernard Fisher of the University of Pittsburgh School of Medicine who determined that, nationwide, only 30% of the women eligible for lumpectomies choose that procedure over mastectomies.

Says a NABCO spokesperson: "Dr. Sue Love's experience is very unusual. It shows she's in a very sophisticated medical community."

Love points to an Italian study that showed no difference in survival rates between patients with lumpectomies and those with mastectomies.

"But the American doctors didn't believe it," she says. "Now there's been an American study that shows the same thing—no difference in survival between lumpectomies with radiation versus radical mastectomies. Now the question is, 'Do you always have to use radiation?'"

Love is currently conducting a study with Boston's Joint Center for Radiation Therapy on the use of lumpectomy without radiation in negative-lymph-node women. It's an ongoing study with 50 patients so far, but many more are needed. They plan to follow these patients for some 15 to 20 years and won't have preliminary results for five years.

Silen at Beth Israel agrees with Love about the benefits of lumpectomies:

"The doctors can twist it anyway they want with body English and the way they explain the options. There are still physicians who believe the gold-standard treatment is a radical mastectomy, yet no studies have confirmed that."

But then again, Love is always pushing the boundaries of "standard treatments"—asking why and why not at every turn. It was these types of questions that first drew her into science as a child, when she took biology and physiology courses.

Her strong character may have been molded by her unusual childhood that began in New Jersey, where she was the oldest of five children. Her father, who worked for a large corporation, was transferred to Puerto Rico when Love was in the seventh grade. And due to another family move, Love spent her high school years in Mexico.

"I think there's a real advantage to growing up in other parts of the world. You realize that there's not only one way to live, and you realize what it's like to be in the minority," she says. "It makes you strong in a way, especially to do that during your high school years. My parents never really pushed us or anything, but all of us have turned out to be independent."

Indeed, it was Love's natural sense of adventure and her love of science and teaching that led her to study medicine. When she spent time in college working for the Red Cross in Latin America, it became clear to her that she would become a doctor.

However, Love didn't intend to specialize in breast surgery. She began her career as a general surgeon until she realized that women with breast cancer wanted to be treated by women doctors: "I found I made the most difference in breast surgery. Women liked women doctors—felt they had more sensitivity. So I saw lots of women. At Dana-Farber, I was seeing 90% breast cases and got more interested in it.

"It seems to me that women think differently from men. It's hard for a man to understand breast lumps and what it's like to face a mastectomy. I think that's where I can make a difference.

Later, walking down the hall to see her next patient, Love says: "If you can explain things, it takes away fear. Women are better at explaining these things than men are, because I think women spend more time empathizing and are socialized to talk more openly. And lots of men don't want to take the time."

Love says she has a male physician friend who's always able to take new patients immediately, rather than have them wait months, and who sees several more patients a day than Love can ever fit in.

"I asked him how he does it, how he could be seeing so many patients. And he said, 'Susan, you talk to the patients too much.'"

Leona Mendelbaum and her husband are sitting in the waiting room. "I've come to Dr. Love to get a second opinion," she says quietly. "I'm not happy with what my physician in New York told me, and I did some checking and Dr. Love has an excellent reputation."

Her doctor in New York told her she had a precancerous condition and recommended a mastectomy as a preventive measure; another doctor told her to do nothing. Mendelbaum says there must be an alternative.

In the examining room, Mendelbaum tells Love she was having strange discomfort in her breasts before she went for an exam. Her doctor found a cyst, aspirated it, found atypical cells, and called it lobular carcinoma *in situ*.

Love says, "We don't consider that cancer. And later I'll explain everything you ever wanted to know about lobular carcinoma *in situ*."

She gets a history from Mendelbaum, about the births of her four children. Then, she asks the patient to put her hands on her hips, her arms up, her arms together, and to lean forward. "You have a nice matched set of ribs," she says, making Mendelbaum laugh. "Look, you know what you have here. Feel that line, that dimple. It's an irritated vein. That's not bad at all. Just interesting."

She stands facing Mendelbaum, puts her hands on the woman's shoulders, looks her in the eyes, and says, "It's nothing to worry about."

Mendelbaum smiles gratefully and the exam is over. Back in the office, Mendelbaum confesses that she's very worried about having cancer. Love begins her lecture, the one she gives to all new patients. She holds up Mendelbaum's mammogram film and explains, "The breast is a milk gland with two parts to it: lobules and ducts that carry the milk. Everything that happens in the breast happens in the ducts or the lobules . . .

"Lobular carcinoma *in situ* is too many cells in these lobules. It doesn't cause lumps, and it's not detected on mammograms, either. What this is is just a marker that says this woman has a 1% higher chance of getting cancer each year, or 30% in 30 years. It's the same as if your mom had it, and now we should watch you carefully."

At these moments, Love is a teacher, clear and succinct in her explanations: "And there's two school of thoughts about how to treat it. At Sloan-Kettering, they see this and say, 'Take both breasts off to prevent it from turning into cancer.' But if only 30% of women will get cancer, this means you'll take the breasts off of 70% of the women for no reason.

"But over at Columbia, the doctors say, 'Just watch these women. They don't need a mastectomy.' A researcher there says that of the patients he's followed with this condition, no one ever died of breast cancer.

"So the choices are either take off both the breasts to be 100% sure you never get breast cancer, or wait and watch it. And if it appears, find it early, and do a lumpectomy. And there is a 1 percent chance you'll get a cancer so aggressive we wouldn't find it in time. But that's the same chance any woman has of getting cancer."

Love says gently, "I think you'll be fine. I can follow you here, or you can go back to your first doctor, whatever you're comfortable doing."

Mendelbaum pauses, takes a long deep breath and smiles at the doctor.

"I feel very comfortable with you. You're a woman and can offer me a woman's perspective. I'd rather come to you."

Four Fact Sheets on Breast Cancer and Women of Color

by the National Women's Health Network

These four fact sheets on breast cancer and women of color are produced by The NWHN. The fact sheets are intended to provide both statistics and analysis of the current situation. Production and distribution of these fact sheets has been supported by a grant from The Breast Cancer Fund.

Breast Cancer and Asian American Women

INCIDENCE

Statistics documenting the breast cancer incidence. in Asian American women living in the United States have only recently been published. For Chinese women the reported incidence was 55 per 100,000 women, for Japanese women 82 per 100,000 women, for Filipino women 73 per 100,000 women, Korean women 29 per 100,000, Vietnamese women 38 per 100,000, and Native Hawaiian women 106 per 100,000. In comparison, White women had a reported incidence of 112 per 100,000 women.[1]

MORTALITY

The mortality rate in Asian-American women is the lowest of the main ethnic populations in the United States. Asian-American women have a combined mortality rate of 13 deaths for every 100,000 women.[2] This. compares to a rate of 27 out of every 100,000 White women, and 15 out of 100,000 Latina women who die from the disease. Among Asian-Americans, the mortality ranged from 7 per 100,000 for Korean and Southeast Asian women, to 12 for Filipino and 13 for Japanese women. For Chinese women the deaths were 11 per 100,000.[1] The lower number of Asian-American women who die of breast cancer reflects the lower incidence of the disease, as cited above.

SURVIVAL

The population of Hawaii is comprised of five major ethnic groups: Japanese, White, ethnic Hawaiians, Filipinos, and Chinese. According to a study of breast cancer in Hawaii, the Japanese and Chinese women in this population were more likely to have their breast cancers diagnosed at an earlier stage, therefore resulting maybe in a better survival rate for these women. In contrast, a later stage of breast cancer at the time of diagnosis was more common for Filipino and Hawaiian women.[3]

FURTHER CONSIDERATIONS

According to a national study on reproductive health, Asian women are the least likely to have an annual gynecological exam, or to ever have had a mammogram.[4] Numerous barriers exist which affect access to medical screening and treatment for Asian women, including cultural beliefs and practices, mistrust of Western medicine, and socioeconomic factors.[5]

It is important to note that when Asian women migrate to the United States their risk of breast cancer rises considerably, a six fold increase compared to the women in their native countries[6] and the rates approach those of White women. Exposure to Western lifestyles,[6] particularly diet and nutrition, has most recently been cited as an explanation for the dramatic differences in incidence rates for Asian women living in the United States and in Asia.[7] A recent study found that changes in reproductive patterns do not explain the increased risk of Asian-American women compared to Asian women. Thus, the overall lower incidence of breast cancer among this population can mask the sub-groups who may have risks similar to White American women.[8]

For more recent immigrants, a further problem of language barriers and residency status often influences the willingness to seek care, which may lead to late diagnosis. Continued outreach education and intervention efforts are needed that are culturally sensitive to the special considerations of Asian-American women.

ADVOCACY GROUPS

National Asian Women's Health Organization (NAWHO)
250 Montgomery Street, Suite 410
San Francisco, CA 94104
(415) 989-9747

Community-based health advocacy organization focused on the health status of Asian women and girls. Conducting a comprehensive review of breast cancer materials addressing for Asian-American women.

NOTES

1. National Cancer Institute. *Racial Patterns of Cancer in the United States 1988–1992.* NIH Publication 96 4104. April 1996.
2. Perkins CI, Morris CR, Wright WE, and Young JL. *Cancer Incidence and Mortality in California by Detailed Race/Ethnicity, 1988–1992.* Sacramento, CA: California Department of Health Services, Cancer Surveillance Section, April 1995.
3. Goodman MJ. Breast Cancer in multi-ethnic Population: The Hawaii Perspective. *Breast Cancer Research and Treatment.* The Netherlands: Kluwer Academic Publishers. Vol. 18, 1991, pp. S5–S9.
4. Communications Consortium Media Center and the National Council of Negro Women. (1992) The 1991–1992 Women of Color Reproductive Health Poll.
5. Varricchio CG. Issues to Consider When Planning Cancer Control Interventions for Women. *Women's Health Issues.* Vol. 5, No. 2, Summer 1995, pp. 64–72.
6. Ziegler, RG, Hoover, RN, et al., Relative Weight, Weight Change, height, and Breast Cancer Risk in Asian American Women. *Journal of the National Cancer Institute.* Vol. 88, No. 10, May 1996, pp. 650–660.
7. Ziegler RG, Hoover RN, Pike MC, et al. Migration Patterns and Breast Cancer Risk in Asian-American Women. *Journal of the National Cancer Institute.* Vol. 85, No. 22, November 1993, pp. 1819–1827.
8. Wu, AH, Ziegler, RG, Pike, MD, et al. Menstrual and Reproductive Factors and Risk of Breast Cancer in Asian-Americans. *British Journal of Cancer.* Vol. 73, No. 5, March 1996, pp. 680–686.

Breast Cancer and Native American Women

INCIDENCE

The breast cancer incidence for Native American women varies depending on region. Incidence rates are lower among American Indian women living in Arizona and New Mexico, as well as Alaska Native women, than among White and African American women. In any one year, 32 out of every 100,000 American Indian women, and 79 out of every 100,000 Alaska Native women are diagnosed with breast cancer. In comparison, 112 out of every 100,000 White women, 95 out of every 100,000 African American women, and 70 out of every 100,000

Latina women are diagnosed with breast cancer.[1] Native Hawaiian women have a breast cancer incidence comparable to White women at 106 per 100,000 women, and higher than other Native American women, African American women and Latinas.[1] American Indian women living in the northern states have higher rates in comparison to other Native American women.[2]

MORTALITY

The breast cancer mortality rate for most Native American women is lower than for White and African American women, and Latinas. In any one year, 9 out of every 100,000 American Indian women, and 13 out of every 100,000 Alaska Native women die of breast cancer. In comparison, 27 out of every 100,000 White women, 31 out of every 100,000 African American women, and. 15 out of every 100,000 Latinas die of breast cancer. Similar to incidence rates, regional variability exists in mortality rates for Native American women. The mortality rate for Native Hawaiian women, at 38 per 100,000 women, is higher than for other Native American women, White and African American women, and Latinas. The Billings IHS Area mortality rate is comparable to White women at 25 per 100,000 women.[3] Many Native Americans believe the incidence and deaths caused by certain diseases are underestimated due to the misclassification of ethnicity in health statistics.[4]

In a study of Native Americans in selected states, the breast cancer morality rates for most of the areas showed a clear increase in the late 70s and after. The overall U.S. rate during this time was comparatively unchanged.[4]

SURVIVAL

The five-year breast cancer survival rate for American Indian women is lower than all other ethnic and racial groups living in the United States. For Native Hawaiian women the survival rate is higher than for American Indian and African American woman, but lower than for White women. The five-year survival is 49% for American Indians, 69% for Native Hawaiian women, 84% for White women, 69% for African American women, and 70% for Latinas.[1,3]

INSURANCE AND ACCESS TO SERVICES

Although Native Americans are eligible for free comprehensive health care through the Indian Health Service (IHS), only half choose or are able to use it. Some Native Americans do not use the IHS because they have other medical insurance. However, many Native Americans find that no IHS facility is accessible to them. For example, no IHS facilities exist in California which is the state with the second largest population of Native Americans[2], and IHS usually does not cover the cost of care provided outside its system. The establishment and maintenance of breast cancer/mammography outreach efforts and clinical services for Native American women is important.

FURTHER CONSIDERATIONS

In 1989, 30.9% of American Indians and Alaska Natives lived at or below the poverty level. In the same year only 9.8% of whites and 13.1% of the total U.S. population were living in poverty.[2]

Racial information is no longer standard on many forms used in hospitals. When it is requested, the health care provider often assumes and records race by visual observation. This can result in a misclassification of Native Americans as white or Hispanic. The extent of this varies from state to state and, from area to area.[2]

ADVOCACY GROUPS

Native American Women's Health Education Resource Center
P.O. Box 572
Lake Andes, SD 57356-0572
(605) 487-7072

Reservation-based, provides comprehensive women's health services and education, and technical assistance to other groups.

NOTES

1. National Cancer Institute, *Racial/Ethnic Patterns of Cancer in the United States 1988-1992*. NIH Publication 96–4104. April, 1996.
2. *Native American Monograph No. 1. Documentation of the Cancer Research Needs of American Indians and Alaska Natives.* National Cancer Institute, National Institutes of Health, reprinted June 1994, pp. 1–11.
3. Native American Women: Breast Cancer and Mammography facts. *Cancer Facts.* National Cancer Institute, National Institute of Health. Printed August 1995.
4. Valway, S. *Cancer Mortality Among Native Americans in the United States: Regional Differences in Indian Health, 1984–1988 & Trends Over Time, 1968–1987.* Indian Health Services Cancer Prevention and Control Programs, U.S. Department of Health and Human Services, chart 31, p. 38.

Breast Cancer and Latinas

INCIDENCE

The breast cancer incidence for Latinas is lower than for White or African American women. In any one year, 70 out of every 100,000 Latinas are diagnosed with breast cancer. In comparison, 112 out of every 100,000 White women, and 95 out of every 100,000 African American women are diagnosed with breast cancer. However, the incidence is increasing faster for Latinas than for other women.[1]

MORTALITY

The breast cancer mortality rate for Latinas is lower than for White or African American women. In any one year, 15 out of every 100,000 Latinas die of breast cancer. In comparison, 27 out of every 100,000 White women, and 31 out of every 100,000 African American women die of breast cancer. The lower number of Latinas who die of breast cancer reflects the lower number of Latinas who get it.[1]

SURVIVAL

However, those Latinas who do get breast cancer are less likely to survive for five years after diagnosis than are White women. The five-year survival is 70% for Latinas, 84% for White women, and 69% for African American women.[1] Little research has been done on the poor survival of Latinas diagnosed with breast cancer, but it may be because Latinas are more likely to be diagnosed after the disease has spread.

MAMMOGRAPHY SCREENING

Latinas are as likely as White women to have had at least one mammogram. According to a National Health Interview Survey in 1992, the percentage of Latinas who had ever been screened was 70%, for White women 69%, and, for African American women 64%.[1] Being screened just once does not reduce the likelihood of dying from breast cancer, though, and research has not been done to identify how many Latinas are getting regular screening.

FURTHER CONSIDERATIONS

The Latino population represents a diverse community including Cuban, Puerto Rican, Mexican, and other Central and Latin Americans. Cancer statistics are almost always reported for Latinos as a whole. Therefore, the overall rate of breast cancer in Latinas may mask higher or lower rates in certain sub-populations. The length of time in the United States may also influence the likelihood of developing breast cancer so, although the numbers look lower overall, sub-groups of Latinas may have risks similar to White women.

More needs to be done to ensure that Latinas participate in regular mammography screening and receive the appropriate treatment for breast cancer in a timely fashion. Currently, barriers exist which keep Latinas from achieving survival rates on a par with White women. Although most Latinas get a least one mammogram, lack of knowledge that regular screening is necessary, absence of encouragement by physicians, and limited access to mammography screening services are problems faced by many Latinas.[1]

In order to continue to increase the rates of mammography screening and thus reduce the number of cancer deaths in Latinas, there must be outreach education efforts and culturally appropriate cancer control interventions delivered in Spanish.[2] In addition, as the Latino population is too often understudied and underserved, continued research in this population is critical.[3]

ADVOCACY GROUPS

COSSMHO
1501 16th St NW
Washington, DC 20036
(202) 387-5000

A national coalition of Hispanic health and human services organizations. Also conducts its own research on Latinos' experience with cancer services.

National Latina Health Organization
P.O. Box 7567
Oakland, CA 94601
(510) 534-1362

Education and health advocacy on health issues and reproductive rights for Latinas.

Hispanic Health Council
98 Cedar St.
Hartford, CT 06106
(203)527-0856

Research, advocacy and education.

NOTES

1. Hispanic American Women: Breast Cancer and Mammography Facts. *Cancer Facts*. National Cancer Institute. Update printed May, 1996.
2. "Latinos less likely to be screened for cancer". *Research Activities*. October/November 1994, p.7.
3. Ruiz, E & Caban, CE. Introduction: Cancer Research in Hispanic Populations. *Journal of National Cancer Institute Monographs, No. 18*. 1995, pp. ix–xi.

Breast Cancer and African American Women

INCIDENCE

The breast cancer incidence for African American women is lower than White women and higher than Latinas. In any one year, 95 out of every 100,000 African American women are diagnosed with breast cancer. In comparison, 112 out of every 100,000 White women, and 70 out of every 100,000 Latinas are diagnosed with breast cancer.[1] However, up to age 40 African American have a higher incidence than Whites.[2]

MORTALITY

Like the overall U.S. population, the site with the second highest cancer mortality rate for African American women is the breast The leading cancer killer among women is lung cancer.[3]

The breast cancer mortality rate for African American women is higher than for White women and Latinas. In any one year, 31 out of every 100,000 African American women die of breast cancer. In comparison, 27 out of every 100,000 White women, and 15 out of every 100,000 Latinas die of breast cancer.[1]

Between 1989 and 1992 there was approximately a 5% decrease in mortality rates for White women with breast cancer, but approximately a 2% increase for African American women.[4]

SURVIVAL

The five-year-breast cancer survival rate for African American women is lower than for White women and Latinas. The five-year survival is 69% for African Americans, 84% for White women and 70% for Latinas.[1]

There are several reasons for the lower survival rate in African American women:

1. Late diagnosis; i.e. African American women are more likely to be diagnosed after the cancer has spread.[5]
2. Poverty, i.e low income cancer patients are less likely to survive, even when diagnosed early.[5,6,7]
3. Undertreatment; African American women are less likely than White women to receive appropriate treatment. According to a study in the *American Journal of Public Health,* in younger as well as older patients, and in earlier as well as later stages, African American patients were more likely than White patients to be untreated and to be treated by non-surgical methods.[7]
4. Cancer nature; A recent study found that the actual tumor cells in African American women grow more rapidly, leading to more aggressive cancers at an earlier age. The differences seen in this study also led to breast cancer that was less responsive to hormone treatment.[8]

FURTHER CONSIDERATIONS

Mammography rates for African American women are lower than White women and Latinas, but are increasing steadily.[1] Several barriers to getting mammograms exist for African Americans such as office visit and screening procedure costs, physicians' failure to discuss mammography with women, misconceptions that screening is unnecessary, and/or lack of health insurance.[5] The biggest unmet need for African American women is early recognition of the disease.

There are many unanswered questions concerning African American women and breast cancer. Why is it more common in younger women? Do the reasons above fully explain the worse survival rate? Further research in this population is necessary to answer these questions. In addition, there must be increased access to appropriate prevention, detection, and treatments for African American woman.

ADVOCACY GROUPS

National Black Women's Health Project
600 Pennsylvania Ave S.E.
Suite 310
Washington, D.C. 20036
(205) 543-9319

A national grassroots advocacy organization with local chapters, and self-help groups.

African American Breast Cancer Alliance
P.O. Box 8981
Minneapolis; MN 55408
(612) 644-1224

A member supported advocacy and support group for women with breast cancer. Includes regional and national networks.

Notes

1. African American Women: Breast Cancer and Mammography Facts. *Cancer Facts*. National Cancer Institute, National Institutes of Health. Update printed May 1996.

2. Hankey, BF, et al. Trends in Breast Cancer in Younger Women in Contrast to Older Women. *Journal of the National Cancer Institute Monographs*. No.16. 1994. p. 7.

3. *Cancer Statistics Review*. 1994. National Center for Health Statistics.

4. *Health United States 1994*. National Center for Health Statistics 1995.

5. Wells, BL and Horm, JW. Stage at Diagnosis in Breast Cancer: Race and Socioeconomic Factors. *American Journal of Public Health*. Vol, 82, No 10, October 1992, pp. 1383–1384.

6. Eley, JW, & Hill, HA, et al. Racial Differences in Survival from Breast Cancer. *Journal of the American Medical Association*. Vol. 272, No. 12, September 1994, p. 952.

7. McWhorter, WP, & Mayer, WJ. Black/White Differences in type of Initial Breast Cancer Treatment and Implications for Survival. *American Journal of Public Health*. Vol. 77, No. 12, December 1987, pp. 1515–1516.

8. Siegel, R, et al. Survival of Black Women with Stage I and Stage II Breast Cancer is Inferior to Survival Among White Women When Treated the Same Way at a Single Institution. Proceedings of the Annual Meeting of the American Society of Oncology; 13:A75, 1994.

The National Women's Health Network, founded in 1976, is a non-profit organization which advocates for better federal health policies for women. The Network is financially supported by over 14,000 individual and 400 organizational members, and accepts no contributions from drug companies. In addition to policy work, the Network maintains a Women's Health Information Clearinghouse. For information about the Network, the list of health packets and publications available from the Clearinghouse, or information on becoming a member, please contact our office.

514 Tenth Street, N.W. Washington, D.C. 20004
(202) 347-1140 Clearinghouse (202) 628-7814

Fact Sheet: "Breast Cancer Genes"
Myths and Facts

by the Boston Women's Health Book Collective

All women have two copies of the so-called "breast cancer genes," BRCA-1 and BRCA-2. When functioning properly, these genes are thought to help suppress the growth of cancerous cells. If one copy of these tumor suppressor genes becomes damaged, the other copy can act as a "brake" on uncontrolled cell growth. Scientists have identified at least four other genes that may play a role in breast cancer risk.

Over 200 variations of the BRCA genes have been identified so far. Some of these appear to be linked to an increased risk of breast and ovarian cancer. A woman born with one damaged version of a BRCA gene has only one working set of "brakes" for uncontrolled cell growth. If her second BRCA gene becomes damaged by exposure to carcinogens, the woman can develop cancer. BRCA variants, in and of themselves, do not *cause* cancer. However, women who inherit certain variants appear to be more susceptible to environmental carcinogens.

Inherited mutations appear to play a role in only about 5% of breast and ovarian cancer cases. The remaining 95% do not involve inherited mutations.

It is now possible to test women to see if they have inherited an altered BRCA gene. Such testing offers few clear advantages:

- A positive test for a cancer-associated BRCA variant will not tell you if you are going to get breast cancer. It simply means that you have one of many possible factors which may increase your likelihood of getting cancer, and therefore may have a higher than "average" risk of developing this condition.
- A negative test for a BRCA variant does not mean that you will not get breast or ovarian cancer. It means that your risk is approximately the "average" lifetime risk for breast cancer. One out of every nine women in the United States will develop breast cancer during her lifetime.

- There is no known effective prevention for breast or ovarian cancer. The surgical removal of healthy breast and ovarian tissue is believed by some to lower a woman's risk of cancer, but it cannot eliminate it.

Getting tested can have many adverse effects:

- Testing positive can have devastating psychological effects. This can impact not only the individual being tested but her entire family, all of whom may share her genetic risk status.
- Positive test results can lead to discrimination. Healthy people who carry genes linked to risk of future disease are vulnerable to discrimination in insurance, employment and other arenas.
- Tests with limited predictive value may lead to women having unnecessary surgery, such as prophylactic mastectomies and oophorectomies.
- The overemphasis on genetic factors in cancer, when environmental carcinogens are known to make major contributions, takes attention away from environmental clean-up measures that could, in fact, reduce the incidence of cancer. Current research has identified links between cancer and a host of nongenetic factors, including organochlorides, estrogen and estrogen-like chemicals, pesticides, radiation, bovine growth hormone, diet and exercise. The "geneticization" of cancer creates a blame-the-victim mindset that obscures these social and environmental factors.

Until we have effective prevention strategies, tests for variants of so-called "cancer genes" benefit mainly the commercial companies that market them, who stand to make huge profits by exploiting women's justifiable fear of cancer.

For more information, contact: Boston Women's Health Book Collective (617) 625-0277 or Council for Responsible Genetics (617) 868-0870

Fact Sheet: Genetics, Health, and Human Rights

by the Boston Women's Health Book Collective

Genetics used to be considered a subspecialty of medicine. Now some individuals in the medical and biotechnology fields view medicine as a subspecialty of genetics. Because this dominance is a growing trend in medicine and medical research, the media report daily on the role of our genes in everything from disease susceptibility, to sexual orientation, to criminal behavior, to even such things as our lifelong tendency to be optimistic or pessimistic. The centuries-old "heredity vs. environment" debate has now swung sharply to heredity.

The Boston Women's Health Book Collective has joined others in criticizing this tendency toward the "geneticization" of our health and lives, toward "genism" and "genomania", terms that are used to convey an overzealousness to find genetic explanations for complex medical and social conditions. The public is receiving the message that genes are on a fixed trajectory and will produce inevitable results, instead of a message that underscores the inherent unpredictability of gene function. Even if a person is predisposed genetically to an illness or disease, usually other factors trigger the changes that set the disease process in motion. In only a small fraction of illness and disease can genetic effects be specified in a predictable way. The overemphasis on genes opens the door to "blaming the victim": if people become ill, the responsibility does not lie with the industries that poison our environment or the employers unwilling to invest in eliminating occupational health hazards. Rather, the locus of responsibility is shifted to the people who get sick because they have "bad genes." Yet, increasingly, research indicates that many, if not most, mutations to our genes result from environmental influences.

Because women continue to carry most of the burden of medical care decision-making as well as most of the caregiving responsibilities in their families, we believe women deserve high quality unbiased information about all genetic issues. Moreover, most of the controversial genetic testing thus far deals with conditions having the greatest impact on women: prenatal testing, tests for breast cancer and for Alzheimer's disease.

We believe that much of the planned research and marketing of genetic tests and gene therapies should not proceed in advance of a wider public discourse on issues such as the following:

- What public policies will best ensure that we will control who has access to our tissue samples and the genetic information scientists derive from it?
- How can we better preserve the confidentiality of general medical records so that genetic information is released only with the consent of the individual to whom it refers?
- How can we prevent genetic tests from being marketed and widely used before their usefulness and the ethics of their use have been established?
- How does the pursuit of genetic tests, therapies, and "enhancements" affect our attitudes toward disability and our tolerance for difference and vulnerability among us all? How can we prevent genetic research from being used to further stigmatize particular racial and ethnic groups?
- How can we best ensure that genetic counselors do not pressure individuals to be tested or to take particular actions based upon test results? How do we ensure that no genetic testing is done without informed consent and thorough pre- and post-test counseling?
- What public policies will best prevent the misuse of genetic information and resultant genetic discrimination in insurance, housing, employment, child custody, medical care, and adoption?
- What are the most ethical ways to obtain samples for genetic testing (e.g., from blood and tissue) and make them available for research? Can informed participation and informed consent be assured and, if so, how?*

These matters are human rights issues and debate about them must involve *all* of us, not only scientists, medical specialists and ethicists, but policy makers, religious groups, disability rights activists, social scientists, health care consumers, public health workers. We are, after all, much more than the sum of our genes.

Boston Women's Health Book Collective

May 1998

Contact Public Responsibility in Medicine and Research (PRIM&R), 132 Boylston Street, Boston MA 02166, for a copy of *Model Consent Forms and Related Information on Tissue Banking from Routine Biopsies,* compiled by the National Action Plan on Breast Cancer Tissue. Banking Working Group, with comments by the PRIM&R/ARENA Tissue Banking Working Group (December 1997)

An excellent source of further information on genetics is the *Council for Responsible Genetics,* 5 Upland Road, Cambridge MA 02140, which publishes position papers as well as the newsletter *Genewatch.*

Tamoxifen: Breast Cancer Prevention That's Hard to Swallow

by Rita Arditti

The recent announcement from the National Cancer Institute that tamoxifen prevents breast cancer in women at high risk has resulted in a veritable media frenzy. "Researchers Find the First Drug Known to Prevent Breast Cancer," (*The New York Times,* April 7); "Breast Cancer Breakthrough," (*New York Times* editorial, April 8); "Study Finds Breast Cancer Treatment Also Prevents It," (*Boston Globe,* April 6). Dr. Harold Varmus, director of the National Institute of Health, calls the study "a big deal." To this, we must ask: "A big deal for whom?"

Tamoxifen, an antiestrogen synthetic hormone, is one of the most widely prescribed drugs for prevention of breast cancer recurrence, and is used in treating postmenopausal women at practically all stages of breast cancer. The Breast Cancer Prevention Trial involved 13,388 women considered at high risk for breast cancer—based on personal history, family history or age. Half took tamoxifen while the other half were given a placebo. Tamoxifen cut the rate of breast cancer almost in half, according to the National Cancer Institute Press Office. The trial was stopped fourteen months short to allow the untreated women the "benefits"

of tamoxifen. British scientists criticized the decision to stop the trial because it will now be harder to establish the long-range effects of the treatment. Their skepticism is quite reasonable since there are already a number of serious problems emerging from this study.

Maryann Napoli, Associate Director of the Center for Medical Consumers in New York, has pointed out that a closer look at the data reveals that there were five deaths in the group taking the drug—three from breast cancer, two from pulmonary embolism—and five in the group taking the placebo—all from breast cancer. (See Napoli's letter to the editor, *New York Times,* April 13, 1998). *In other words, both groups had the same number of deaths.* The two women who died from pulmonary embolism did not develop breast cancer; they died from "side effects" of the drug. The study showed seventeen cases of blood clots in the lung for the treated group and six for the control, and thirty cases of blood clots in major veins for the treated versus nineteen in the control. Total: 47 blood clots versus 25, almost twice as many for those taking tamoxifen.

From *Sojourner: The Women's Forum,* July 1998, Vol. 23, No. 11, p. 32. Copyright © 1998 by Sojourner. Reprinted by permission.

Rita Arditti is one of the founding members of The Women's Community Cancer Project in Cambridge, MA. The project can be reached through the Women's Center, 46 Pleasant Street, Cambridge, MA 02139. (617)354-9888. She would like to thank Renée Shapiro for her editorial comments.

Uterine cancer is another main "side effect" of tamoxifen: 33 cases in the treated group versus 14 in the control. Apparently, these cases were treated successfully through hysterectomy, though there is evidence that the type of tumors that develop while a woman is taking tamoxifen are very aggressive. In light of this it is hard to swallow comments like the one by Dr. Judy Garber at Dana Farber Cancer Institute. She says, "The drug is proven to prevent breast cancer, and the endometrial cancer risk is manageable. It's the blood clot risk you're left with, and this may seem like the [least] of several evils for many women." (*Boston Globe,* April 13, 1998).

But blood clots and uterine cancer are only the most visible of the "side effects" of tamoxifen. In their book *Tamoxifen and Breast Cancer,* Michael W. DeGregorio, professor of medicine, and Valerie J. Wiebe, assistant professor of medicine and pharmacy at the University of Texas Health Science Center, San Antonio, devote a chapter to the side effects of tamoxifen. The most common side effect of tamoxifen is hot flashes. Other effects reported are menstrual irregularities, vaginal bleeding and vaginal dryness or itching; mild nausea with or without vomiting, loss of appetite, constipation, diarrhea, edema and weight gain. Tamoxifen has also been associated with depression or irritability and other psychological symptoms associated with menopause. For a small percentage of women, it has a suppressive effect on the bone marrow, leading to a decrease in the number of platelet and red and white blood cells.

Two more areas of concern are liver cancer and eye problems. In animal studies, rats fed low doses of tamoxifen developed liver tumors in approximately 11.5 percent of the cases, and at higher doses, 71.2 percent developed liver cancer. As DeGregorio and Wiebe point out, "although no direct link to liver cancer has been made, accounts of liver complications from tamoxifen are on the rise." As for eye problems, 6.3 percent of patients reported both corneal and retinal changes, which did not disappear when tamoxifen was discontinued.

In spite of these problems, it is estimated that 2.9 million healthy women would be "potentially eligible" for preventive treatment of tamoxifen. This includes all women over 60, and many younger women whose personal or family history suggests a high risk (even though no one knows how long the treatments should be continued or its effect on women of color who comprised only 3 percent of the women in the study.) At a cost of $80 to $100 for a monthly supply, this is unquestionably "a big deal" for Zeneca, the company based in Wilmington, Delaware who manufactures the drug under the brand name of Nolvadex. On the first day of the announcement of the trial results, the shares of Zeneca closed at $147 on the New York Stock Exchange, a gain of $9.75. Zeneca will now apply to the FDA to have the drug approved as preventive therapy for breast cancer. Zeneca also makes money owning and managing eleven cancer-treatment centers in the U.S., where they prescribe the drugs they make. On top of this, Zeneca is the primary sponsor of October as Breast Cancer Awareness Month, and has veto power on the materials produced. Not surprisingly, the literature of Breast Cancer Awareness Month never mentions the word "carcinogen" and it relentlessly emphasizes mammography as the "best protection" for women. Next October, we can expect tamoxifen to be included in the list of recommendations. Zeneca is also the producer of a carcinogenic herbicide, acetochlor, and has been involved in litigation stemming from environmental damage in California harbors.

The other corporation that stands to profit is Myriad Genetics, Inc., of Salt Lake City, Utah, which does the genetic tests for the mutated genes BRCA1 or BRCA2, which increase breast cancer risk. Blood samples from women in the study will now be tested for these genes. If it is found that tamoxifen lowers the risk, the demand for gene tests will increase. Unquestionably, another "big deal."

It is frightening to think that our most influential scientists and physicians doing cancer research have bought into the cancer industry's definition of breast cancer prevention. The whole concept of prevention has been distorted to fit the needs of greedy companies. We need to open up a national debate about what prevention really means. Otherwise, God help us all, this "big deal" will encourage the development of other "prevention" strategies in which, as in this case, exchanging breast cancer for other life-threatening problems will be considered a success.

Breast Cancer: The Environmental Connection

by Rita Arditti • Tatiana Schreiber

Today in the United States, we live in the midst of a cancer epidemic. One out of every three people will get some form of cancer and one out of four will die from it. Cancer is currently the second leading cause of death; by the year 2000, it will likely have become the primary cause of death. It is now more than two decades since the National Cancer Act was signed, yet the treatments offered to cancer patients are the same as those offered 50 years ago: surgery, radiation, and chemotherapy (or slash, burn, and poison, as they are called bitterly by both patients and increasingly disappointed professionals). And in spite of sporadic optimistic pronouncements from the cancer establishment, survival rates for the three main cancer killers—lung, breast, and colo-rectal cancer—have remained virtually unchanged.

In the '60s and '70s, environmental activists and a few scientists emphasized that cancer was linked to environmental contamination, and their concerns began to have an impact on public understanding of the disease. In the '80s and '90s, however, with an increasingly conservative political climate and concerted efforts on the part of industry to play down the importance of chemicals as a cause of cancer, we are presented with a new image of cancer. Now it is portrayed as an individual problem that can only be overcome with the help of experts and, then, only if one has the money and know-how to recruit them for one's personal survival efforts. This emphasis on personal responsibility and lifestyle factors has reached absurd proportions. People with cancer are asked why they "brought this disease on themselves" and why they don't work harder at "getting well."

While people with cancer should be encouraged not to fall into victim roles and to do everything possible to strengthen their immune systems (our primary line of defense against cancer), it seems that the sociopolitical and economic dimensions of cancer have been pushed completely out of the picture. "Blaming the victim" is a convenient way to avoid looking at the larger environmental and social issues that form individual experiences. Here we want to talk about environmental links to cancer in general and to breast cancer in particular, the kinds of research that should be going on, why they're not happening, and the political strategies needed to turn things around.

Extensive evidence exists to indicate that cancer is an environmental disease. Even the most conservative scientists agree that approximately 80 percent of all cancers are in some way related to environmental factors. Support for this view relies on four lines of evidence: (1) dramatic differences in the incidences of cancer between communities—incidences of cancer among people of a given age in different parts of the world can vary by a factor of ten to a hundred; (2) changes in the incidence of cancer (either lower or higher rates) in groups that migrate to a new country; (3) changes in the incidence of particular types of cancer with the passage of time; and (4) the actual identification of the specific causes of certain cancers (such as the case of beta-naphthylamine, responsible for an epidemic of bladder cancer among dye workers employed at du Pont factories). Other well-known environmentally linked cancers are lung cancer, linked to asbestos, arsenic, chromium, bischloromethyl ether, mustard gas, ionizing radiation, nickel, polycyclic hydrocarbons in soot, tar, oil, and of course, smoking; endometrial cancer, linked to estrogen use; thyroid cancer, often the result of childhood irradiation; and liver cancer, linked to exposure to vinyl chloride.

The inescapable conclusion is that if cancer is largely environmental in origin, it is largely preventable.

From *Sojourner: The Women's Forum,* (December, 1992). Copyright © 1992 by Sojourner, Inc. Reprinted by permission.

Rita Arditti is a biologist, a woman with breast cancer, and a founding member of The Women's Community Cancer Project. She is also an editor of *Issues in Reproductive and Genetic Engineering—A Journal of International Feminist Analysis.* Tatiana Schreiber is the editor of the *Resist* newsletter and a freelance journalist.

Our Environment Is a Health Hazard

"Environment" as we use it here includes not only air, water, and soil, but also our diets, medical procedures, and living and working conditions. That means that the food we eat, the water we drink, the air we breathe, the radiation to which we are exposed, where we live, what kind of work we do, and the stress that we suffer—these are responsible for at least 80 percent of all cancers. For instance, under current EPA regulations as many as 60 cancer-causing pesticides can legally be used to grow the most commonly eaten foods. Some of these foods are allowed to contain 20 or more carcinogens, making it impossible to measure how much of each substance a person actually consumes. As Rachel Carson wrote in *Silent Spring* in 1962, "This piling up of chemicals from many different sources creates a total exposure that cannot be measured. It is meaningless, therefore, to talk about the 'safety' of any specific amount of residues." In other words, our everyday food is an environmental hazard to our health.

Recently, a study on the trends in cancer mortality in industrialized countries has revealed that while stomach cancer has been steadily declining, brain and other central-nervous- system cancers, breast cancer, multiple myeloma, kidney cancer, non-Hodgkin's lymphoma, and melanoma have increased in persons aged 55 and older. Given this context, it is not extreme to suspect that breast cancer, which has reached epidemic proportions in the United States, may be linked to environmental ills. This year, estimates are that 180,000 women will develop breast cancer and 46,000 will die from it. In other words, in the coming year, nearly as many women will die from breast cancer as there were American lives lost in the entire Vietnam War. Cancer is the leading cause of death among women aged 35 to 54, with about a third of these deaths due to breast cancer. Breast cancer incidence data meet three of the four lines of reasoning linking it to the environment: (1) the incidence of breast cancer between communities can vary by a factor of seven; (2) the risk for breast cancer among populations that have migrated becomes that of their new residence within a generation, as is the case for Japanese women who have migrated to the United States; and (3) the incidence of breast cancer in the United States has swelled from one in twenty in 1940 to one in eight in the '90s.

A number of factors have been linked to breast cancer; a first blood relative with the disease, early onset of menstruation, late age at first full-term pregnancy, higher socioeconomic status, late menopause, being Jewish, etc. However, for the overwhelming majority (70 to 80 percent) of breast cancer patients, their illness is not clearly linked to any of these factors. Research suggests that the development of breast cancer probably depends on a complex interplay among environmental exposures, genetic predisposition to the disease, and hormonal activity.

Research on the actual identification of causal factors, however, is given low priority and proceeds at a snail's pace. We still don't know, for example, the effects of birth control pills and the hormone replacement therapy routinely offered to menopausal women. Hormonal treatments are fast becoming the method of choice for the treatment of infertility, while we know nothing about their long-range effects. And the standard addition of hormones in animal feed means that all women (and men) are exposed to hormone residues in meat. Since there is general consensus that estrogen somehow plays a role in the development of breast cancer, hormonal interventions (through food or drugs) are particularly worrisome.

A startling example of the lack of interest in the prevention of breast cancer is the saga of the proposed study on the supposed link between high-fat diets and breast cancer. The "Women's Health Trial," a fifteen-year study designed to provide conclusive data about the high fat-cancer link, was denied funding by the National Cancer Advisory Board despite having been revised to answer previous criticisms and despite feasibility studies indicating that a full-scale trial was worth launching. Fortunately, it now appears that the study will be part of the Women's Health Initiative, a $500-million effort that will look at women's health issues. This success story is a direct result of women's activism and pressures from women's health groups across the country.

But even if the high fat-breast cancer correlation is established, it is unlikely to fully explain how breast cancer develops. The breast is rich in adipose cells, and carcinogens that accumulate in these fat tissues may be responsible for inducing cancer rather than the fat itself or the fat alone. Environmental contamination of human breast milk with PCBs, PBBs and DDE (a metabolite of the pesticide DDT) is a widely acknowledged phenomenon. These fat-soluble substances are poorly metabolized and have a long half-life in human tissue. They may also interact with one another, creating an additive toxic effect, and they may carry what are called "incidental contaminants": compounds like dibenzofurans, dioxins, etc., each with its own toxic properties.

Among the established effects of these substances are: liver dysfunction, skin abnormalities, neurological and behavioral abnormalities, immunological aberrations, thyroid dysfunction, gastrointestinal disturbances, reproductive dysfunction, tumor growth, and enzyme induction. Serious concerns have been raised about the risks that this contamination entails for infants who are breast-fed. But what is outrageous in the discussion about human breast-milk poisoning is that little or no mention is made of the possible effects on the women themselves, particularly since it is known that most of these substances have *estrogenic* properties (that is, they behave like estrogen in the body). It is as if the women, whose breasts contain these carcinogens, do not exist. We witness the paradox of women being made invisible, even while their toxic breasts are put under the microscope.

The Pesticide Studies

Very recently, some scientists have at last begun to look at the chemical-breast cancer connection. In 1990, two Israeli scientists from Hebrew University's Hadassah School of Medicine, Elihu Richter and Jerry Westin, reported a surprising statistic. They found that Israel was the only country among 28 countries surveyed that registered a real drop in breast cancer mortality in the decade 1976 to 1986. This happened in the face of a worsening of all known risk factors, such as fat intake and age at first pregnancy. As Westin noted, "All and all, we expected a rise in breast cancer mortality of approximately 20 percent overall, and what we found was that there was an 8 percent drop, and in the youngest age group, the drop was 34 percent, as opposed to an expected 20 percent rise, so, if we put those two together, we are talking about a difference of about 50 percent, which is enormous."

Westin and Richter could not account for the drop solely in terms of demographic changes or improved medical intervention. Instead, they suspected it might have been related to a 1978 ban on three carcinogenic pesticides (benzene hexachloride, lindane, and DDT) that heavily contaminated milk and milk products in Israel. Prior to 1978, Westin said, "at least one of them [the three pesticides] was found in the milk here at a rate 100 times greater than it was in the U.S. in the same period, and in the worst case, nearly a thousand times greater." This observation led Westin and Richter to hypothesize that there might be a connection between the decrease in exposure following the ban and the decrease in breast cancer mortality. They believed the pesticides could have promoted enzymes that in turn increased the virulence of breast cancer in women. When the pesticides were removed from the diet, Westin and Richter speculated, there was a situation of much less virulent cancer and the mortality from breast cancer fell.

Westin and Richter are convinced that there is a critical need to increase awareness about environmental conditions and cancer. Health care clinicians, for example, could play an important role in the detection of potential exposures to toxic chemicals that might be missed in large studies. This is a refreshing view since it encourages individual physicians to ask questions about work environments, living quarters, and diet, the answers to which could provide important clues about the cancer-environment connection.

In the United States, only one study we know of has directly measured chemical residues in women who have breast cancer compared to those who do not. Dr. Mary Wolff, a chemist at New York's Mount Sinai School of Medicine, recently conducted a pilot study with Dr. Frank Falck (then at Hartford Hospital in Hartford, Connecticut) that was published in *The Archives of Environmental Health.* In this case-controlled study, Falck and Wolff found that several chemical residues from pesticides and PCBs were elevated in cases of malignant disease as compared to nonmalignant cases.

The study involved 25 women with breast cancer and the same number of women who had biopsies but did not have breast cancer. The results showed differences significant enough to interest the National Institute for Environmental Health Sciences, which will fund a larger study to look at the level of DDT and its metabolites in the blood samples of 15,000 women attending a breast cancer screening clinic in New York. A recent report just released by Greenpeace, entitled "Breast Cancer and the Environment: The Chlorine Connection," provides further evidence linking industrial chemicals to breast cancer.

In the United States, levels of pesticide residues in adipose tissue have been decreasing since the 1970s (following the banning of DDT and decreased use of other carcinogenic pesticides) while the breast cancer rate continues to rise. This observation would seem to contradict the pesticide hypothesis. However, it is important to remember that the chemicals could act differently at different exposure levels, they are unlikely to act alone, and the time of exposure may be important. For example, if a child is exposed during early adolescence, when breast tissue is growing rapidly, the result may be different than exposure later in life.

Radiation and Mammography

Another area that demands urgent investigation is the role of radiation in the development of breast cancer. It is widely accepted that ionizing radiation at high doses causes breast cancer, but low doses are generally regarded as safe. Questions remain, however, regarding the shape of the dose-response curve, the length of the latency period, and the importance of age at time of exposure. These questions are of great importance to women because of the emphasis on mammography for early detection. There is evidence that mammography screening reduces death from breast cancer in women aged 50 or older. However, Dr. Rosalie Bertell (director of the International Institute of Concern for Public Health, author of *No Immediate Danger: Prognosis for a Radioactive World* [1985] and well-known critic of the nuclear establishment) raises serious questions about mammography screening. In a paper entitled "Comments on Ontario Mammography Program," Bertell criticized a breast cancer screening program planned by the

Ontario Health Minister in 1989. Bertell argued that the program, which would potentially screen 300,000 women, was a plan to "reduce breast cancer death by increasing breast cancer incidence."

Bertell's critique of mammography suggests that the majority of cancers that would have occurred in the group could have been detected by other means. A recent Canadian mammography study on 90,000 women looked at cancer rates between 1980 and 1988. Preliminary results show that for women aged 40 to 49, mammograms have no benefits and may indeed harm them: 44 deaths were found in the group that received mammograms and 29 in the control group. The study also suggests that for women aged 50 to 69, many of the benefits attributed to mammography in earlier studies "may have been provided by the manual breast exams that accompanied the procedure and not by the mammography," as Bertell noted in her paper. Not surprisingly, the study has been mired in controversy. As study director Dr. Anthony Miller remarked, "I've come up with an answer that people are not prepared to accept."

According to Bertell, the present breast cancer epidemic is a direct result of "above ground weapons testing" done in Nevada between 1951 and 1963, when 200 nuclear bombs were set off and the fallout dispersed across the country. Because the latency period for breast cancer peaks at about 40 years, this is an entirely reasonable hypothesis.

Other studies have looked at the effect of "low-level" radiation on cancer development. A study investigating the incidence of leukemia in southeastern Massachusetts found a positive association with radiation released from the Pilgrim nuclear power plant. (The study was limited to cases first diagnosed between 1978 and 1986.) In adult cases diagnosed before 1984, the risk of leukemia was almost four times higher for individuals with the greatest potential for exposure to the emissions of the plant. Other types of cancer take a greater number of years to develop, and there is no reason to assume that excessive radiation emission was limited to the 1978-to-1986 time frame. In other words, as follow-up studies continue, other cancers (including breast cancer) may also show higher rates.

The Surveillance Theory

Current theory supports the concept that cancerous mutations are a common phenomenon in the body of normal individuals and that the immune system intervenes before mutated cells can multiply. Known as the "surveillance" theory of cancer, the basic premise is that cancer can develop when the immune system fails to eliminate mutant cells. Carcinogenic mutations can be induced by radiation or chemicals, for instance, and if immunological competence is reduced at a critical time, the mutated cells can thrive and grow.

Given the apparent importance of the immune system in protecting us from cancer, we ought to be concerned not only with eliminating carcinogens in our environment but also with making certain that our immune systems are not under attack. Recent evidence that ultraviolet radiation depresses the immune system is therefore particularly ominous. At a hearing on "Global Change Research: Ozone Depletion and Its Impacts," held in November 1991 by the Senate Committee on Commerce, Science, and Transportation, a panel of scientists reported that ozone depletion is even more serious than previously thought. According to the data, the ozone layer over the United States is thinning at a rate of 3 to 5 percent per decade, resulting in increased ultraviolet radiation that "will reduce the quantity and quality of crops, increase skin cancer, *suppress the immune system,* and disrupt marine ecosystems" [our emphasis]. (The report also states that a 10 percent decrease in ozone will lead to approximately 1.7 million additional cases of cataracts world-wide per year and at least 250,000 additional cases of skin cancer.) As the writers make chillingly clear, since this is happening literally over our heads, there is no place for us to run.

In addition, dioxin (an extremely toxic substance that has been building up steadily in the environment since the growth of the chlorinated-chemical industry following World War II) can produce alterations that disrupt the immune system. "Free radicals" created by exposure to low-level radiation can cause immune system abnormalities. In other words, our basic mechanisms of defense against cancer are being weakened by the chemical soup in which we are immersed.

It follows that an intelligent and long-range cancer-prevention strategy would make a clean environment its number one priority. Prevention, however, is given low priority in our national cancer agenda. In 1992, out of an almost $2 billion National Cancer Institute (NCI) budget, $132.7 million was spent on breast cancer research but only about 15 percent of that was for preventive research. Moreover, research on the cellular mechanism of cancer development, toward which much of the "prevention" effort goes, does not easily get translated into actual prevention strategies.

In his 1989 exposé of the cancer establishment, *The Cancer Industry,* Ralph Moss writes that until the late '60s, the cancer establishment presented the view that "cancer is . . . widely believed to consist of a hereditable, and therefore genetic," problem. That line of thinking is still with us but with added emphasis on the personal responsibility we each have for our cancers (smoking and diet) and little or no acknowledgement of the larger environmental context. In a chapter appropriately titled "Preventing Prevention," Moss provides an inkling of why this is so.

The close ties between industry and two of the most influential groups determining our national cancer agenda—the National Cancer Advisory Board and the President's Cancer Panel—are revealing. The chair of the President's Cancer Panel throughout most of the '80s, for example, was Armand Hammer, head of Occidental International Corporation. Among its subsidiaries is Hooker Chemical Company, implicated in the environmental disaster in Love Canal. In addition, Moss, formerly assistant director of public affairs at Memorial Sloan-Kettering Cancer Center (MSKCC), outlines the structure and affiliations of that institution's leadership. MSKCC is the world's largest private cancer center, and the picture that emerges borders on the surreal: in 1988, 32.7 percent of its board of overseers were tied to the oil, chemical and automobile industries; 34.6 percent were professional investors (bankers, stockbrokers, venture capitalists). Board members included top officials of drug companies—Squibb, Bristol-Myers, Merck—and influential members of the media—CBS, the *New York Times,* Warner's Communications, and *Reader's Digest*—as well as leaders of the $55-billion cigarette industry.

Moss's research leaves little doubt about the allegiances of the cancer establishment. Actual cancer prevention would require a massive reorganization of industry, hardly in the interest of the industrial and financial elites. Instead of preventing the generation of chemical and toxic waste, the strategy adopted by industry and government has been one of "management." But as Barry Commoner, director of the Center for the Biology of Natural Systems at Queens College in Brooklyn, New York, put it rather succinctly, "The best way to stop toxic chemicals from entering the environment is to not produce them."

Instead, the latest "prevention" strategy for breast cancer moves in a completely different direction. A trial has been approved that will test the effect of a breast cancer drug (an antiestrogen, tamoxifen) in a healthy population, with the hope that it will have a preventive effect. The trial will involve 16,000 women considered at high risk for breast cancer and will be divided into a control group and a tamoxifen group. The National Women's Health Network (a national public-interest organization dedicated solely to women and health) is unequivocal in its criticism of the trial. Adriane Fugh-Berman, a member of the Network board, wrote in its September/October 1991 newsletter, "In our view the trial is premature in its assumptions, weak in its hypothesis, questionable in its ethics and misguided in its public health ramifications." The criticisms center on the fact that tamoxifen causes liver cancer in rats and liver changes in all species tested and that a number of endometrial cancers have been reported among tamoxifen users. Fugh-Berman points out that approving the testing of a potent, hormonal drug in healthy women and calling that "prevention" sets a dangerous precedent. This drug-oriented trial symbolizes, in a nutshell, the paradoxes of

short-sighted cancer-prevention strategies: more drugs are used to counteract the effect of previous exposures to drugs, chemicals or other carcinogenic agents. It is a vicious circle and one that will not be easily broken.

Cancer, Poverty, Politics

Though it is often said that affluent women are at higher risk for breast cancer, this disease is actually on the rise (both incidence and mortality) among African-American women, hardly an "affluent" population overall. The African-American Breast Cancer Alliance of Minnesota, organized in October 1990, has noted this steady increase and the limited efforts that have been made to reach African Americans with information and prevention strategies. People of color often live in the most polluted areas of this country, where factories, incinerators, garbage, and toxic waste are part of the landscape. Native American nations are particularly targeted by waste-management companies that try to take advantage of the fact that "because of the sovereign relationship many reservations have with the federal government, they are not bound by the same environmental laws as the states around them."

Poverty and pollution go hand in hand. The 1988 Greenpeace report *Mortality and Toxics Along the Mississippi River* showed that the "total mortality rates and cancer mortality rates in the counties along the Mississippi River were significantly higher than in the rest of the nation's counties" and that "the areas of the river in which public health statistics are most troubling have populations which are disproportionately poor and black." These are also the areas that have the greatest number of toxic discharges. Louisiana has the dubious distinction of being the state with the most reported toxic releases—741.2 million pounds a year. Cancer rates in the Louisiana section of the "Chemical Corridor" (the highly industrialized stretch of river between Baton Rouge and New Orleans) are among the highest in the nation. Use of the Mississippi River as a drinking-water source has been linked to higher than average rates of cancer in Louisiana. The rates of cancer of the colon, bladder, kidney, rectum, and lung all exceed national averages. Louisiana Attorney General William J. Guste, Jr., has criticized state officials who claimed that people of color and the poor *naturally* have higher cancer rates. You can't "point out race and poverty as cancer factors," said Guste, "without asking if poor people or blacks . . . reside in less desirable areas more heavily impacted by industrial emissions."

It follows that African-American women, living in the most contaminated areas of this country, would indeed be showing a disproportionate increase in breast cancer incidence. However, widespread epidemiological studies to chart such a correlation have not been undertaken. For instance, given the evidence implicating pesticides in the development of breast cancer, studies of migrant (and other) farm workers who have been exposed to such chemicals would seem imperative.

Women's groups around the country have started organizing to fight the breast cancer epidemic. A National Breast Cancer Coalition was founded in 1991. Its agenda is threefold: to increase the funding for research, to organize, and to educate. All of the recently organized groups consider prevention a priority, and one of their tasks will undoubtedly entail defining what effective prevention really means. In Massachusetts, the Women's Community Cancer Project, which defines itself as a "grassroots organization created to facilitate changes in the current medical, social, and political approaches to cancer, particularly as they affect women," has developed a Women's Cancer Agenda to be presented to the federal government and the NCI. Several demands of the agenda address prevention and identification of the causes of cancer. The group has received endorsements of its agenda from over 50 organizations and individuals working in the areas of environmental health, women's rights, and health care reform and is continuing to gather support. This effort will provide a networking and organizing tool, bringing together different constituencies in an all-out effort to stop the cancer epidemic.

Cancer *is* and needs to be seen as a political issue. The women's health movement of the '70s made that strikingly clear and gave us a road map to the politics of women's health. In the '80s, AIDS activists have shown the power of direct action to influence research priorities and treatment deliveries. In the '90s, an effective cancer-prevention strategy demands that we challenge the present industrial practices of the corporate world, based solely on economic gains for the already powerful, and that we insist on an end to the toxic discharges that the government sanctions under the guise of "protecting our security." According to Lenny Siegel, research director of the Military Toxic Network, the Pentagon has produced more toxic waste in recent years—between 400,000 tons and 500,000 tons annually—than the five largest multinational chemical companies combined.

Indeed, if we want to stop not only breast cancer but all cancers, we need to think in global terms and to build a movement that will link together groups that previously worked at a respectful distance. At a worldwide level, the Women's World Congress for a Healthy Planet (attended by over 1500 women from 92 countries from many different backgrounds and perspectives) presented a position paper, Agenda 21, at the 1992 United Nations Earth Summit conference in Brazil. The paper articulates a women's position on the environment and sustainable development that stresses pollution prevention, economic justice, and an end to conflict resolution through war and weapons production, probably the greatest force in destroying the environment.

On February 4, 1992, a group of 65 scientists released a statement at a press conference in Washington, D.C., entitled "Losing the 'War against Cancer'—Need for Public Policy Reforms," which calls for an amendment to the National Cancer Act that would "re-orient the mission and priorities of the NCI to cancer causes and prevention." The seeds of this movement have been sown. It is now our challenge to nourish this movement with grassroots research, with demonstrations, and with demands that our society as a whole take responsibility for the environmental contamination that is killing us.

Author's note: Many thanks to the women of the Women's Community Cancer Project in Cambridge, Massachusetts, for their help and support. A longer version of this article with complete footnotes and references appeared in the Resist *newsletter (May/June 1992). Copies of the issue (which includes the Women's Cancer Agenda) are available from: Resist, One Summer St., Somerville, MA 02143. Send $1.00 for handling.*

Ten Years of Self-Help Achievement
Interview with Mary Lou Ballweg, President and Co-founder Endometriosis Association

by Carolyn Keith

The Endometriosis Association, headquartered in Milwaukee, WI, started 10 years ago with its first support group meeting of eight women with endometriosis. From that base, a highly successful self-help women's health organization has grown. The Association now has almost ten thousand paid members, chapters and support groups all across North America, a unique research registry and research program, and highly acclaimed educational materials.

CK: How is the concept of self-help expressed currently in the Association?

ML: This organization, which has grown immensely, is run by a majority of women with endometriosis at every level. From top to bottom, the organization is run by women with the disease. Every chapter is run by women with the disease and the groups are started by women with the disease. Every so often a physician will want to start a chapter, but we will always get it started by women and then connect them to the supportive physician.

The research program includes a data registry (the only data registry in the world on endometriosis) that relies on reports from women. A rather radical thing that we've done is to take information from "patients" and compile solid data that serve as the basis for our work and for articles published in scientific journals. Through the Association, women have made a difference in the research and in what's known about the disease. The medical establishment has accepted this information because we have been very professional about how we've presented it. But it is really rather radical to have that kind of information and research come from lay people and we faced a lot of questioning about that when we started.

Another aspect of self help that is critical is by having a disease *in* you, you can put it all together in a way that no physician can—you *feel* it, you have the motivation, you have all the information and experience all in one body.

Modern medicine is so super-specialized. Particularly for endometriosis, I don't think we're going to get answers unless we cross specialties. *We* don't have territory to protect if it relates to the disease. I think one of the best examples of this is the work we did linking endometriosis and candidiasis (systemic yeast infection). That linkage points to the immune system. Now a few of the research studies on endometriosis are starting to evolve from the immunological side of it, a process that is starting to tie it together a little. The women experiencing these problems aren't tied to the professional "Bibles" that say this is the only way it can be. They commit medical heresy every day. And medical heresy is what's needed to break through some of these walls. Also, lay people can sometimes do things that medical people can't do.

CK: Such as?

ML: Well, for example, Dr. Billy Crook, who wrote THE YEAST CONNECTION, was at headquarters recently. He was talking about how to get the information about candidiasis out and how to get medical credibility. We were talking about what he

Carolyn Keith was Health Education Coordinator at Bread & Roses Women's Health Clinic in 1980 when she and Mary Lou Ballweg started the Association. Carolyn is now involved in geriatric health concerns.

could do, what doctors could do, what lay people could do. I really pushed him to help start lay groups. Lay groups can form a national, regional or local network and either create business or take business away from physicians. The medical establishment may pay lip service to science, but they live day-to-day with their business and their pocketbooks.

We've seen it in city after city where we get groups going—the physicians really start to treat women with endo a lot better. It's consumer power. When they start listening, they learn, and it just moves everything along a lot faster. Then you start to see a few of the little breakthrough research studies. For endometriosis, the studies really are just beginning, but at least it's starting to happen and it wouldn't have happened without the Association. The medical establishment would have been more than happy to do another 30 years of hormones and surgeries; drug companies could make millions and millions on new hormonal drugs that shut down the system, but that wouldn't get us anywhere. With the Association, we can force a direction. We can also benefit from some of the millions that are made by those drug companies if we can propose projects that we need to get done that we don't have money for and say, "Look drug company, you're making millions on women with endo, will you help us do this outreach?" This, I know, is a controversial point.

CK: It's like accepting *Playboy* money.

ML: It's not like *Playboy* money because I think *Playboy* money is dirty money made off the backs of women by hurting women. In contrast, the pharmaceutical companies have indeed made life tolerable. Danazol, when it first came out, scared the wits out of all of us. But danazol forestalled hysterectomy for so many thousands of women that, while it's not the answer or the cure, it's better than what we had

---

FDA Approves Synarel

In mid-February, 1990, the FDA approved Synarel for treatment of endometriosis. It is the first GnRH drug approved for this condition. Synarel, which is administered as a nasal spray, acts to stop production of the hormones of the menstrual cycle. Although Synarel is not a cure for endometriosis, the Endometriosis Association welcomes FDA approval of the drug because it gives women another treatment option.

---

before. Now the new GnRH (gonadotropin-releasing hormone) drugs will help a lot of women by buying more time to keep them from hysterectomy and surgical castration. So, I think it's ok money. They made their money on the drug, but I like to see some of it go back to help women.

CK: So you've helped them to do that.

ML: Yes, I've helped them to do that. I was amazed when I added up the cost involved in our 1987 advertising campaign that was funded by a drug company. We advertised in 20 national magazines using full-page ads and several insertions. We reached many hundred thousand women and obviously educated many on endometriosis. That campaign alone cost more than all the funds that we've raised in the Association's operating budget in 10 years, over $1.3 million. So do we hurt women by taking that million plus? The project didn't mention their drug or their company, except for one line I added to the ad so that people wouldn't think that *we* had that kind of money because we depend on donations for other programs. I think it would have been really sad to miss that tremendous opportunity to educate all those women about the symptoms and maybe they'd get diagnosed earlier and they'd find the Association. But there are some people that would say, no, don't take any money like that.

CK: What do you see as the difference?

ML: First, our main operating budget comes from women with the disease and always has—over 80% from membership dues, literature sales, and donations from members. We use corporate contributions for special projects outside the main annual operating budget. Second, we propose projects, so these are things we want to do. Third, we maintain total control over the project and make that clear to the potential donor from the outset. In fact, I see us with far more control over our special projects than many nonprofits have after they've bent themselves to fit philanthropic proposal guidelines.

For instance, now we really have our hearts set on programs to reach black women and teen women with endo. We are just really tired of what's happening to these 15- and 16-year-olds with severe problems. They need help and nobody is helping them. It's going to take some fairly serious money. A drug company can see that a 15-year-old with endometriosis is perhaps their future market. That's the kind of project that we don't have the money for now, but maybe we can get. And it's our project. So if somebody has the money to give, and the money might even have been made from women with endometriosis, my word, why not use it.

While you're being pure, somebody else out there right now is screaming in pain or crawling to the bathroom. I think that's part of what makes a difference—that the Association is real women with real pain with real disease. We become practical.

CK: This started out as a support group—a self-help support group—wow, when did we do that?

ML: January 1980. Eight women met on January 14. By summer, I think we were up to 50 or 60 women. In August we got the yellow brochure ["What is Endometriosis?"] out. Then, we helped the women who found us by word-of-mouth or through feminist publications. Then they asked, "How do we do it out here in San Francisco or New York?" You sent out materials for starting chapters and then we had to develop guidelines for who's officially affiliated with us, how do we handle dues, etc. Pretty soon there was too much work and we had to get more staff, and more staff . . .

The need for the Association will probably continue for a long time, even if we are lucky enough to find a cure (which I don't think is going to be soon . . .). But even if we were that lucky, we'd have to work through the Association or with women who have a serious vested interest in this disease of the most female of functions. What's really at the heart of endometriosis and the awful attitudes about it and toward women with it are cultural taboos about menstruation and female sexuality and infertility and what it means to be a female.

Those kinds of attitudes come out every single day in the Association. Today on the way home I was reading a letter from a woman who has severe throbbing pain in her clitoris from the endometriosis. She has been insulted time and time again by physicians who, of course, have said kind of what you would expect: "It's because you don't have a sexually fulfilling relationship," or "You're hung up," or whatever. Endo is those kinds of experiences. The attitudes of people are really appalling. Men who think the only kind of sex is intercourse; women who think they're not women because they can't have babies; the reluctance to talk about normal menstruation, much less painful menstruation. A woman with endometriosis has to deal with all of this because her life often eventually comes to a screeching halt because of the disease. This woman is at the forefront and the cutting edge of changing attitudes. It's also critical to all women who don't have the disease that we do what we're doing because we're out here saying, "Look, to be female is not to have pain. To have pain with your periods is a disease." I think our medical establishment and main culture tell us that our normal bodily functions are goofed up just because we're female.

Endometriosis Still Underdiagnosed

from WomenWise

The Endometriosis Association has just announced new research results concerning women with endometriosis. These results were released at the 6th World Congress on Endometriosis in Quebec City, Canada.

The survey, carried out by the Endometriosis Association across the United States and Canada, has revealed that endometriosis is not being appropriately diagnosed and treated. Recognition and diagnosis by women and girls, as well as physicians, is still taking a combined average of nine years (4.67 years delay in seeking medical help and 4.61 years delay in physicians' diagnoses). From a sample of 4,000 respondents, almost half said that they had had to see a doctor five times or more before they were diagnosed or referred.

The survey asked women to indicate which symptoms they experienced. Pain at the time of menstruation was cited by 95 percent of 4,000 who replied, with fatigue being experienced by 87 percent. When asked how bad the pain was, seven out of ten respondents ranked it between moderate and severe with a further fifth saying that it could swing from mild to severe.

Commenting on the result, Mary Lou Ballweg, President of the Endometriosis Association, headquartered in Milwaukee, Wisconsin, said, "Many physicians believe that infertility is the main symptom of endometriosis. While it is very important, the pain that women endure is indescribable. The data we've collected show that pain at the time of the menstrual period and during ovulation is experienced by a majority of our membership."

Other common symptoms experienced by women with endometriosis are: diarrhea and painful bowel movements at the time of menstruation (85 percent), abdominal bloating (84 percent) and two-thirds mentioned heavy bleeding, pain with or after sex, nausea and stomach upset, and dizziness or headaches at the time of the menses.

From *WomenWise* (A Quarterly Publication of the Concord Feminist Health Center), Summer 1998, p. 5.

Women and HIV:
A Review of Current Issues, Trends, and Understandings

— *by Lise Alschuler, MD*

ABSTRACT: Human immunodeficiency virus (HIV) infection is emerging as a major cause of morbidity and mortality among women in the United States. African-American and Latina women are disproportionately represented among acquired immunodeficiency syndrome (AIDS) cases in women. The primary modes of transmission for women are heterosexual contact and intravenous drug use. The manifestations of HIV and AIDS in women are somewhat gender specific with gynecological manifestations being one of the major differences. Women with AIDS have shorter survival time than men with AIDS. Despite these differences, there is still a relative lack of research on women with HIV disease. More research is needed to improve the early diagnosis and treatment of women with HIV disease.

The proportion and actual number of women with human immunodeficiency virus (HIV) is rising worldwide and in the United States. Women represented 9% of the first 100,000 cases of AIDS reported between the years 1981 and 1990. Between October 1991 and September 1992, women comprised 13% of the 46,000 AIDS cases reported (5,980 cases).[1] As of December 1993, approximately 80,000 women were infected with HIV in the United States and 3 million women were infected with HIV worldwide.[2] Despite the alarming rise in the incidence of HIV infection in women, there is a great deficit in research concerning women and HIV infection. As a result, women have been placed at a disadvantage in terms of proper diagnosis and treatment. This is particularly ironic in that the majority of care givers to individuals with AIDS have been, and continue to be, women.[3]

While male homosexuals still account for the largest proportion of AIDS cases in the United States, African-American and Latina women have the highest percentage increase in incidence of AIDS cases.[1,3,4] It may well be that the lack of research on women with HIV and AIDS is because the majority of women affected by HIV are from disenfranchised populations without political or financial clout, namely women of color, partners and/or users of intravenous drugs. and professional sex workers. As the number of women with HIV continues to increase, it has become imperative to do more research. In the meantime. it is critical for the practicing physician to be well apprised of what is known about women and HIV.

The incidence of AIDS varies by racial and ethnic populations, by geographic regions, and by risk behaviors. Compared with Caucasian women, African-American women are 13 times more likely to develop AIDS, and Latinas are 8 times more likely to develop AIDS.[4] Said another way, of all cases of AIDS in women, 52% are African-American. 20% are Latina, and 27% are Caucasian.[5] Within the United States, most of the cases of AIDS in women occur in the Eastern states. In order of decreasing prevalence New York, the District of Columbia, New Jersey, Florida and Puerto Rico report the greatest number of cases of AIDS in women, although all states have reported AIDS cases in women.[1,4] In New York and New Jersey, AIDS is the leading cause of death among women ages 20 to 40.[5,6] There are several exposure categories for women to HIV. These include intravenous drug users, heterosexual transmission, and professional sex workers.

Intravenous drug use is associated with most AIDS cases in women in several ways. The Center for Disease Control in 1991 reported that 51% of all women with AIDS have used injection drugs.[5] Some of these women most likely contracted the virus through sharing contaminated needles. For this route of transmission, specific risk factors for HIV infection include the number of injections

From *Journal of Naturopathic Medicine*, Vol. 7, No. 1, Winter 1997, pp. 62–65. Copyright © 1997 by the Journal of Naturopathic Medicine. Reprinted by permission.

per month, type of drug injected (heroin vs. cocaine), the extent of needle sharing, income level, and ethnic background (African-American or Latina).[5] There appear to be no differences in risk or infection rate between female and male intravenous drug users (IDUs). A related category of HIV transmission to women is through sexual activity with HIV+ male IDUs. Many women with injection drug using partners use noninjected drugs, namely crack cocaine. Many female crack users trade sex for drugs and these sexual encounters tend to be unprotected and frequent. Crack use is a significant risk factor for HIV because of its association with high-risk sexual behavior (i.e., unprotected vaginal and anal sex). Additionally. crack use is associated with syphilis which, as a sexually transmitted disease, enhances HIV transmission.[7] Male-to-female transmission of HIV is more efficient than female-to-male transmission, thus these sexual encounters primarily place the women at risk. Women with genital ulcer disease, cervical ectopy, and frequent sexual encounters are at the greatest risk of infection.[1]

Heterosexual transmission of HIV is the most common category of transmission world-wide. Heterosexual contact with an HIV-infected person accounted for one third of all female and adolescent cases in the United States in 1991.[5] Latex condoms reduce the risk of transmission during intercourse; however, the usage of condoms varies greatly according to level of education, access to community resources, nature of the primary relationship, and racial origin. Poor, uneducated inner-city African-American and Latina women in abusive relationships or in relationships with IDUs are at the highest risk of not using safer sex practices, namely condoms.[5] Of note is that nonoxynol-9, a widely used spermicide, is not a good preventive measure against the transmission of HIV. While nonoxynol-9 does inhibit HIV growth *in vitro,* in women it increases the incidence of vaginal ulceration which facilitates HIV transmission.[1,5] In addition, oral contraceptives increase the transmission of HIV by either increasing estrogen levels (to be discussed later) or by decreasing the concomitant use of barrier methods of birth control.[6] Many studies indicate that female adolescents engage in high-risk sexual activity, including anal sex and infrequent use of condoms. This high-risk sexual behavior coupled with the increasing incidence of other sexually transmitted diseases make female adolescents particularly susceptible to HIV infection.[5]

Professional sex workers are at very high risk for contracting HIV. Certain behaviors increase the risk of transmission for these professional sex workers: frequency of sexual activity, multiple sex partners, high-risk sexual activity, injection drug use, crack use, and decreased use of safer sex practices.[5] Despite the popularized notion that sex workers are major transmitters of HIV, in reality, female sex workers face a greater risk of becoming infected themselves. Many of the studies on professional sex workers and HIV transmission have not delineated the differences in risk and incidence between different types of sex workers and thus the data are not very generalizable to this group as a whole. This is an area which needs further study.

The clinical manifestations of HIV infection and AIDS in women differ from those in men. Unfortunately, little is definitively known about why these differences exist. This lack of understanding is due primarily to the fact that research on AIDS has been done for the most part on men. Notwithstanding, the known differences between men and women are significant. Women with HIV appear to be more sick than men with HIV at the time of diagnosis, have more severe disease and women's overall survival is significantly shorter (20%) than that of men.[1,5,6] Female African-American IDUs with Pneumocystis carinii pneumonia (PCP) as the indicator disease have the shortest survival.[1,6] Several studies have examined the sex difference in the survival time of women and men with AIDS and have found no demonstrable biologic difference in the rate of disease progression between the sexes. Instead, the explanation offered in most of these studies for the shorter survival of women is the result of late diagnosis, delayed treatment and more limited access to care.[1,4,6] In addition, other risk factors such as intravenous drug use, age, race, and economic status are strongly correlated with survival time in women with HIV. Given the lack of awareness and education on the part of doctors about the prevalence and manifestation of HIV infection in women, coupled with societal denial about women being at risk for HIV infection, delayed diagnosis and treatment of HIV+ women are inevitable. Physician education and public awareness are essential in order to prolong survival of HIV+ women,

The clinical manifestations of HIV infection in women are somewhat unique to their gender. The pattern of opportunistic infections in women in the United States is more similar to that of IDUs than of homosexual men. Therefore, women are more likely to present with PCP than with Kaposi's sarcoma. In several small studies (of primarily white women who contracted HIV through heterosexual contact), *Candida* esophagitis was the most common AIDS-defining illness in women, followed by PCP. All AIDs-defining illnesses have been documented to occur in women with CD4 counts below 200/mm^3 (with a single exception of lymphoma).[1] Women with HIV also have a high rate of mucocutaneous disease in vaginal tissue. HIV+ women have a significantly higher frequency of vaginal candidiasis than HIV-women and often vaginal candidiasis appears before any other signs of immune dysfunction.[5] If a woman with HIV had at least four discrete episodes of *Candida* vaginitis per year and the frequency of episodes had at least doubled in the absence of other known predisposing factors, it is likely that the vaginal candidiasis is attributed to her HIV-induced immunosuppression. It is hypothesized that vaginal candidiasis may serve as a reservoir for systemic yeast and thus contributes to the high rates of oral and esophageal candidiasis which develop in more severe immunosuppression. In fact, HIV+ women with chronic vaginal candidiasis appear to progress to AIDS much more quickly (within 30 months) than HIV+ women without vaginal candidiasis. It is therefore imperative for doctors to identify vaginal candidiasis as a clinical manifestation of HIV as this condition has such great implications for women's diagnosis and treatment.

Other gynecological conditions which are prevalent in HIV+ women include pelvic inflammatory disease, cervical dysplasia and human papillomavirus infection. Women with HIV are 7–10 times more likely to develop squamous cell intraepithelial lesions (SIL) than women in general.[2] Cervical dysplasia appears to be most strongly associated with advanced HIV-induced immunosuppression, most specifically with decreased cell-mediated immunity (CD4 counts below 364/ mm^3).[1,2] HIV infection, particularly with CD4 counts below 221/ mm^3, increases the risk of high-grade, extensive, and multifocal cervical lesions.[2,4] It is thus recommended that women with HIV receive yearly, if not semiannual Pap smears with referral for colposcopy with any abnormal results. The high incidence of HPV infection in women with HIV underscores the importance of condom use as certain polyamines found in seminal fluid may activate latent HPV infections and SIL transformation. Finally, secondary amenorrhea is associated with advanced immunosuppression and wasting. The endocrine factors responsible for this amenorrhea are still unknown.

As was mentioned earlier, there are no known reasons for the differences in HIV manifestations between men and women, aside from the obvious gynecological signs and symptoms. There is, however, speculation on the reasons for these differences in immunosuppression. Estrogen and progesterone directly and indirectly affect target cells in the immune system. Natural killer cell activity, for instance, has been shown to be affected by levels of circulating estrogen and other cyclical hormones. T-cells have estrogen and androgen receptors which indicate that their activity is affected by these hormones. Estradiol may inhibit suppressor T-cell activity. Sex hormones also may help to regulate the biosynthesis and secretion of thymic hormones.[5]

Previously, it was thought that pregnancy, through hormonally mediated mechanisms, accelerated HIV disease. However, more recent, controlled studies have found no acceleration of HIV disease with pregnancy.[1,5] HIV infection during pregnancy seems to be correlated with increased episodes of bacterial pneumonia due to the immunosuppression of HIV disease. For reasons not understood, HIV infection is also associated with increased incidence of breech presentation leading to a greater number of cesarean sections.[1] Women with AIDS are more likely to have premature and low-birth weight infants than are HIV+ women without AIDS.[4] Because pregnancy lowers CD4 counts normally, it is considered standard practice to use prophylaxis against opportunistic infections in pregnant women whose CD4 counts fall below 200/mm^3. Zidovudine (AZT) is commonly prescribed. This is despite the fact that AZT crosses the placenta readily where its effects on the fetus are as yet incompletely understood. Other antiretroviral drugs, such as didansosine (ddI) and zalcitabine (ddC) have not yet been studied in pregnant women. It is of note that HIV infection does not appear to affect fertility. Women who know that they are HIV+ may still choose to become pregnant. Approximately 1/3 of the infants born to HIV infected mothers will themselves become infected perinatally.[6] It is important for the physician to monitor the health of these pregnant women as well as to give them educated counsel about their personal health risks, potential prophylaxis and therapy of opportunistic infections, and the health risks to their fetus.

Treatment for HIV infection in women is largely based on extrapolations from drug trials of men. Women are often excluded from drug trials because of their reproductive potential. Thus, women with HIV are given drug therapy regimens that have not been developed with the known gender differences that exist in drug metabolism, toxicity, and efficacy. In general, women with HIV receive the same treatments as do men with HIV, the standard regimen being antiretroviral drugs (i.e., AZT, ddI, ddC) with certain drugs added for prophylaxis against known opportunistic infections (i.e., trimethoprimsulfa-methoxazole, acyclovir). In addition, women may be given systemic prophylaxis against yeast infection with ketoconazole or fluconazole although resistance to these drugs is already being seen.[1]

A recent survey of the types of alternative/complementary therapies used by persons with HIV disease reaffirms the place of wholistic medicine in the treatment of people with HIV disease. In this survey, the top ten therapies utilized by persons with HIV disease from highest use to lowest use were: vitamins, relaxation. laughter and humor, spirituality (prayer), meditation, vitamin C tablets, nutritional therapy, orthomolecular therapy, massage, and yoga. Also included in the most frequently used therapies were acupuncture, herbs, various forms of body work, and homeopathy.[8] The role of the naturopathic physician in the treatment of women with HIV disease is one of education, health monitoring, and appropriate naturopathic therapies (refer to *Journal of*

Naturopathic Medicine, Vol. 3, No. 1, 1992 for a complete review of naturopathic treatment of HIV disease and AIDS).

A further area that deserves attention is the psychological impact of HIV disease on women. Again, very little psychological research has been done on women with HIV disease. What research has been done suggests that there are several areas that present as unique stressors to women with HIV disease. Notification of HIV seropositivity is, of course, a major stressor reported by women with HIV disease. Some women (35%) reported an increase in yeast infections, amenorrhea, fatigue and sleep disturbance as a result.[9] Another major stressor was the disclosure of their HIV status to their children and worries about the future care of their children. The issue of guardianship is a major stressor for women with HIV. Primary relationship issues, occupation security, economic hardships and social networking are other areas of major concern and adjustment for HIV+ women. It is imperative that physicians working with women with HIV disease be aware of their concerns. Physicians should encourage informed decision-making on the part of these women and should be familiar with community resources.

Women with HIV and AIDS represent a growing number of women seeking healthcare. As the prevalence of HIV disease continues to increase among women, naturopathic physicians will no longer have the luxury of ignorance regarding this condition in women. The health issues for women with HIV disease are somewhat gender specific and necessitate informed intervention.

Naturopathic therapies may play an essential role in promoting the health of women with HIV disease. Clearly more research is needed in this area as well as more collective clinical experience.

REFERENCES

1. Cohn, Jonathan Allen. Human Immuno-deficiency Virus And AIDS 1993 Update. J Nurse~Midwifery 1993; 38(2):65–81.
2. LoveJoy, Nancy and Joyce Anastasi. Squamous cell cervical lesions in women with and without AIDS. Cancer Nursing 1994;17(4):294–307.
3. Rosser, Sue. Perspectives AIDS and Women. AIDS Educ Prevent 1991; 3(3):230–40.
4. Legg, Jill. Women and HIV. J Am Board Fam Pract 1993; 6:367–77.
5. Ickovics, Jeanette and Judith Rodin. Women and AIDS in the United States: Epidemiology, Natural History, and Mediating Mechanisms. Health Psychology 1992; 11 (1): 1–16. Human Retrovir 1995; 9(4):415–21.
6. Williams, Ann. Women In the HIV Epidemic. Crit. Care Nurs Clin Nor Amer 1992; 4(3):437–44.
7. Tortu, Stephanie, et al. The Risk of HIV Infection In a National Sample of Women with Injection Drug-Using Partners. Am J Public Health 1994; 84(8): 1243–50.
8. Nokes, Kathleen, et al. Alternative/Complementary Therapies Used by Persons with HIV Disease. JANAC 1995; 6(4): 19–24.
9. Semple, Shirley, et al. Identification of Psychobiological Stressors Among HIV-Positive Women. Women Health 1993; 20(4):15–36.

Spermicides, Virucides, and HIV

by Jane Juffer

Throughout the world women, are being infected with HIV, the virus that causes AIDS, at staggering rates—as a result of heterosexual sex with infected men. According to a recent report from the World Health Organization, by the year 2000 most of the newly infected will be women. Yet health professionals still promote the condom as women's main means of protection from HIV and other sexually transmitted diseases (STDs), even when virucides that kill STD-causing viruses might prove more effective.

Laboratory tests show that the condom may interrupt viruses like HIV in as many as 99 percent of sexual encounters. But what works in the lab doesn't seem to work in the bedroom. In research comparing the effectiveness of protection by condoms and by spermicides, Dr. Michael Rosenberg, president of a private research organization called Health Decisions, found that in real life condom effectiveness drops to 50 percent—a protection rate comparable to spermicides.

Rosenberg evaluated 5,681 visits by women to an urban STD clinic for chlamydia, trichomoniasis, and gonorrhea, the three most common STDs in women. The study, which was recently published in the *American Journal of Public Health,* found that, compared to women who used no contraceptives, women who used the sponge had a 71 percent reduction in gonorrhea, a 74 percent decrease in trichomoniasis, and a 13 percent drop in chlamydia; with a diaphragm, reductions were 65 percent for gonorrhea, 71 percent for trichomoniasis, and 72 percent for chlamydia. For women whose male partners used a condom, the decreases were far lower: respectively, 34 percent, 30 percent, and 3 percent.

These figures suggest that condoms are less effective than diaphragms and sponges because they are used less, probably because of male resistance. This isn't a new finding for feminists. "AIDS prevention experts are singing a one-note song: condoms, condoms, condoms," says Vicki Legion, program coordinator for the Chicago Women's AIDS Project. "Rosenberg's study confirms that this doesn't play too well in the real lives of many women. Condoms put many of us in a cruel Catch-22: if you insist on condoms, you may get battered. If you don't, you might get infected with HIV."

While the diaphragm and sponge act as barriers that protect the cervix, thus inhibiting transmission of some STDs, researchers believe that the spermicides often used with them have the greatest potential in preventing HIV transmission. Barrier methods by themselves *may* inhibit HIV, says Rosenberg, but the bottom line is that much more research must be done on the mechanisms of heterosexual transmission—how and when women are infected via the reproductive tract—before barrier methods of contraception can be proven effective against HIV transmission. Does the virus attach itself to sperm to cause infection in the uterus? Does infection occur mainly on the vaginal surfaces or at the cervix?

An ideal means of protection for women would be a virucide (virus killer) against HIV that a woman could insert without her male partner's knowledge, and that would be effective whether inserted before or after intercourse, further increasing a woman's leverage. And it would not have to be discarded, but should dissolve.

Most of these criteria seem to be met in the form of a product now marketed as a contraceptive—the Vaginal Contraceptive Film, or VCF. The VCF is a small, thin square with a 28 percent concentration of nonoxynol-9 Inserted high into the vagina, close to the cervix, the film dissolves within minutes, remains active for about two hours, and washes away with body fluids.

Nonoxynol-9's effectiveness against HIV has been proven in laboratory tests on monkeys infected with simian immunodeficiency virus (SIV, a retrovirus

Jane Juffer, a free-lance writer, is currently attending the University of Illinois at Champaign/Urbana as a graduate student in English literature.

closely related to HIV). In a recent study funded by the National Institute of Child Health and Human Development, only six out of 12 female monkeys treated with a contraceptive gel containing nonoxynol-9 became infected through vaginal transmission, compared to all six untreated control monkeys.

Many questions about nonoxynol-9 remain unanswered, however. It's not known, for example, how the different vehicles for spermicides—gels, creams, and foams—affect their ability to prevent HIV transmission. Also, what concentration of nonoxynol-9 is necessary to kill HIV in the vagina? Can nonoxynol-9 be used after intercourse and still be effective in killing viruses? Perhaps most critical is the fact that nonoxynol-9 can irritate the vaginal lining: results of recent studies conflict on whether and at what point irritation occurs—and the possible impact this may have on HIV transmission.

Clearly, nonoxynol-9 merits considerable research into its potential as a female-controlled virucide. "What struck me most in reading about the recent international AIDS conference in Amsterdam is that people are looking around for something new," says Rosenberg. "We're overlooking something that's been around since the turn of the century but needs more study. We may already have something to protect ourselves—nonoxynol-9."

Funding, however, lags far behind the need; currently, for example, the Centers for Disease Control is not funding any efficacy studies on the female condom or on virucides. The National Institutes of Health is at least funding some studies of immediate relevance: in addition to a study on the effects of nonoxynol-9, NIH is spending $2.7 million over four years to investigate a spermicide-releasing diaphragm that is discarded after one use. NIH is also funding a project to test substances for spermicidal and virucidal potential; $285,000 has been spent in the last three years. Next year a $1.2 million study on spermicides and virucides will begin; let your congressional representatives know that this is not enough money to research such a potentially lifesaving substance.

The search for woman-controlled methods does not mean that women must take complete responsibility for prevention of STDs. Men must still be educated about their role in preventing HIV transmission, and women must still be empowered to negotiate condom use with their partners. But to recognize that condoms are an unlikely option for many women is to recognize that the need for women-controlled methods is—for an increasing number of women around the world—a matter of life and death.

With or Without the Dam Thing:
The Lesbian Safer Sex Debate

by Carol Camlin

I have a rare lesbian safer sex poster on my office wall that shows two young white women embracing, naked and wet, in a steamy public bath. One woman sits on a tiled ledge with her legs spread, hair tossed in her face, smiling blissfully. The other is on her knees, leaning into her lover's open thighs, her head arched back. The text, in lavender, reads: "Wet your appetite for safer sex."

As a lesbian HIV/AIDS educator at the AIDS Action Committee of Massachusetts, I pay keen attention to the few safer sex messages and images produced for lesbians by national and international HIV/AIDS service organizations. For one thing, this environment brimming with gay male erotic safer sex posters would make any healthy lesbian long for a few pictures of nude women. I also pay attention to keep abreast of the raging debate about lesbian sexual transmission of HIV—the so-called dam debate—among those who advocate either for or against the use of dental dams for oral sex (dental dams are small latex squares available at your local dental supply store: just masquerade as a dentist and ask for the 100-pak).

The lesbian safer-sex poster on my wall is different from gay male posters in one significant way. The scene evokes the eroticism of wetness, and seems to encourage comfort with bodily fluids. Wetness is sexy but, in the context of HIV, has come to seem dangerous. Although the poster would probably be a turn-on for most lesbians, I would imagine that The Terrence Higgins Trust (THT), the British AIDS service organization that produced the poster, has taken some flak for this one. The poster introduces the idea that there is such a thing as lesbian safer sex, without directly advocating the use of dental dams.

Carrying this message one step further, at the VIII International Conference in AIDS in July, THT unveiled a poster that directly advocates that lesbians *not* use dental dams. "Very low risk in oral sex," it advised, "so ditch those dental dams. Don't bother with gloves unless it turns you on." The poster immediately unleashed a

storm of protest. Dozens of ACT UP members (most of them men) zapped the THT display booth, chanting "Shame!," spray painting it and modifying the poster with messages like "This poster is killing lesbians."

The intense controversy surrounding woman to woman sexual transmission of HIV is largely due to the fact that a very little HIV-prevention education information is geared to lesbians, despite our involvement in all aspects of the epidemic.

How many lesbians either harbor exaggerated fears of HIV or assume they're at no risk of HIV infection (or any other sexually transmitted disease)? How many lesbians are tacitly restricting their sexual practices, and so their sexual pleasure, out of fear of the unknown? How many HIV-positive lesbians know what they can safely do with their HIV-negative girlfriends? How many HIV-negative lesbians worry about how to have sex with their HIV-positive girlfriends without putting them at risk of an immune-threatening infection? Why this dearth of information?

In her July 1992 *Herizons* article, "Damned If You Do, Damned If You Don't," Lesli Gaynor of the AIDS Committee of Toronto argues: "The exclusion of lesbians and lesbian sexuality from AIDS education is not only a reflection of homophobia within mainstream education, but also a sign of the systematic sexism that exists within the gay community."

Lesbians need and deserve to get the facts abut AIDS, but the rare attempts to define safer sex for lesbians have focused almost exclusively on the use of dental dams. As a result, many lesbians have a vague idea that they should be using these devices, yet as Nancy Solomon notes in her Spring 1992 *Out/Look* article, "Risky business", very few women do—including lesbians safe sex educators who issue public pronouncements about dental dams.

Given the lack of availability of dental dams and their sexual unattractiveness, is it any surprise that we're not using them? I've heard the "damn dams" described as "about as sexy as a pair of rubber pants for the diaper wearing set" in Jenifer Firestone's "Memoirs of a Safe Sex Slut" (in *Bad Attitude*) and cunnilingus with a dam described as "chewing on a rubber tire."

Most lesbian health educators acknowledge that the three-inch-by-three-inch dental dams are small and difficult to use. How do you know when your spit ends and her fluids begin, unless you're really alert? Some educators advocate plastic wrap as an option for oral sex, because it's convenient, and it's larger. "Also," as one plastic-wrap aficionado puts it, "you can see through it, and that's nice."

Still others question barrier use in the first place. Louise Rice, a lesbian health educator and nurse at the AIDS Action Committee observes in her August 1992 *Sojourner* article, "Rethinking Dental Dams": "Barrier protection against HIV in vaginal fluids has no proven efficacy. Dental dams provide false security for an activity (going down) that already carries a relatively low risk."

Instead of broadening the topic of lesbian safer sex, the dam debate has sometimes obscured a deeper and more detailed discussion about the range of behaviors and activities which put lesbians at highest risk for infection with HIV and other STDs. After all, cunnilingus is not *all* we do. Do we focus on the use of dental dams because that's all we know how to talk about? Do we avoid discussion about the behaviors which put us at highest risk because of deep-seated taboos within the lesbian community?

Most HIV-positive lesbians became infected by sharing injection drug needles, or having sex with men without a condom. Several studies have shown that at least one-third of lesbians in the 20 to 35 year-old age group have slept with men, even after coming out. Simply having a lesbian identity does not make you "immune" to HIV: Our community must come to terms with the facts that lesbians sometimes use IV drugs and sometimes have sex with men.

Although these two risk factors are primarily responsible for the incidence of HIV among lesbians, it is possible for HIV to be transmitted sexually from woman to woman. Even those who aren't lesbian latex zealots agree that we are not "God's Chosen People." Lesbian sexual transmission of HIV is very rare—but just how rare, exactly how it happens, and how to prevent it are all points of debate. The information available to lesbians about what constitutes safer sex for lesbians is ambiguous and diverse in opinion.

AIDS service organizations offer advice to lesbians ranging from "stock up on latex condoms or dams" to AIDS Committee of Toronto's provocative suggestion "a little more sex, a little more leather, a little more lace, a little LESS LATEX." Somewhere in the middle of this, a growing number of lesbian health educators argue that, well into the second decade of this epidemic,

enough is known about HIV transmission to suggest that HIV prevention education for lesbians need not include the "dental dams at all times under all circumstances" message. What exactly are the HIV transmission risks with woman to woman sex?

Let's review the facts. For someone to get infected, HIV not only has to get OUT of one person, via an infected body fluid, it also has to get INTO another person's bloodstream, via the mucous membranes or a break in the skin.

How the virus leaves the body: The highest concentration of HIV can be found in blood, and the next highest in semen. In vaginal fluid and pre-seminal fluid (or pre-cum, the fluid that men emit before ejaculation), the concentration is much lower. In some fluids such as tears or saliva, the concentration of HIV is so low or non-existent that there's no risk of infection.

The chance of infection via oral contact with vaginal fluid is very low, and it depends on the presence of blood products. However, several factors can increase the likelihood of the presence of HIV: menstrual blood, vaginal infections (such as yeast) and sexually transmitted diseases (such as herpes and chlamydia) can elevate levels of HIV in vaginal fluid, because all would contain white blood cells which harbor HIV. In later stages of HIV disease all bodily fluids contain higher concentrations of HIV. Also, the pH, or level of acidity, of the vaginal fluid can influence whether HIV is present. The pH of vaginal fluid is normally low, or acidic, and "inhospitable" to HIV (the pH of semen, on the other hand, is higher, or alkaline— and therefore more "hospitable" to HIV). Vaginal fluid is more alkaline during menstruation and ovulation.

How the virus enters the body: You can become infected with HIV if someone else's infected body fluid enters your bloodstream via breaks in the skin or via mucous membranes. Mucous membranes line the rectum, vagina and mouth (and in men also the urethra and glans—the tip of the penis); they're also found in the inside of your nose and eyelids. Some mucous membranes are thick and strong, and others are thin, and easier for the virus to pass through. The rectum is the most vulnerable because the walls of the rectum are very thin and there are tiny blood vessels at its surface which are easily ruptured during anal intercourse. The walls of the vagina are tougher and thicker, therefore less vulnerable to fissures and tears (with well-lubricated penetration and trimmed fingernails). The mucous membranes in the mouth are thicker than either the rectum or the vagina. It's therefore difficult for HIV to enter the bloodstream through your mouth. Moreover, saliva has a neutralizing effect on HIV, making it harmless when present in a low concentration, such as in vaginal fluid.

Reducing Your Risks: "Lesbians do everything from nibbling on each other's ears to fisting—and in between there are a lot of things that are safe and some things that aren't," notes Amelie Zurn, Director of Lesbian Services at the Whitman-Walker Clinic in D.C. "The point is, risk is relative . . . for some people, any risk at all is unacceptable. For other people, more risk is okay."

The key to safer sex is communication: defining your limits and talking to your partner about what you want. To assess your risks and decide what to do, communicate with your partner.

Get to know your vagina: "Vaginal fluids have not been studied enough," Louise Rice acknowledges, "but women are capable of doing the studying. Getting to know your vagina, your discharges and smells, and those of a partner, can alert you to changes and potential infections. Unrecognized and untreated infections are a concern for all women, not just those with HIV. When HIV is present, an infection can quickly become disabling."

Get to know your mouth: Remember, even if you go down on a woman and she is menstruating or has a vaginal infection, the virus still has to find its way into your bloodstream. You may want to use a barrier under those circumstances—but if you don't there are ways to make oral sex even safer than it is, without having to use a barrier.

If you have a cold sore, or bleeding gums, or a cut on your tongue, "wait until you've healed so that you don't have to waste time and needless worry," Lesli Gaynor of Toronto advises. "If you have a contagious mouth condition like herpes, it's only courteous to consider the other person's health."

Gaynor offers an additional tip for safe licking: "Don't brush [or floss] your teeth before oral sex—use mouthwash to get that just-brushed fresh feeling." If your partner is HIV-positive, you may want to use mouthwash as a matter of course, to protect her from germs in your mouth.

You also may want to go down on your partner BEFORE you penetrate her with your hand or a sex toy. This will reduce the chance of there being blood present in the vaginal fluid.

Gaynor also suggests, "Take a closer look at what you're about to eat. If there are sores or areas of concern, don't panic but avoid contact. Kiss the surrounding areas lovingly."

Rimming: Oral contact with the anus isn't a risk for HIV transmission unless the rectum contains blood (such as following "rough" anal penetration, and even then bleeding may not necessarily occur). But, you could contract another kind of infection via rimming, such as hepatitis A or amoebas. It's a good idea to use a barrier for rimming.

Fingerfucking or using a dildo: HIV can be transmitted if menstrual or other blood of an HIV-positive woman gets into the vagina or anus of her partner. The safest option is to use your own toy. Wash thoroughly after each use with soap and water. If you share toys, use a condom and put on a new condom (with plenty of water-based lubricant) before you share. Or, wash thoroughly before sharing.

Remember, **intact skin is a good barrier against HIV infection.** If you have open cuts on your fingers and she's menstruating or has a vaginal infection, use latex or vinyl gloves or finger cots when penetrating her. A message to all you "Lee-Press On" femmes: trim those finger nails if you're planning to fuck her! The lesbian fashion of trimmed, smooth fingernails is in place for good reason: you don't want to cut or tear the lining of the vagina.

If you or your partner is HIV-positive, latex or vinyl gloves serve the function of not exposing an HIV-positive woman to bacteria and other germs under the fingernails, and reducing the risk of a cut in your or her vagina which could allow the germs to pass through to the bloodstream.

Fisting: This can result in fissures or tears in the vaginal (or rectal) lining, which can result in both the presence of blood and access to the bloodstream. Fisting is an activity which can place both partners at risk, since tears may occur on the skin of the person doing the fisting. Use latex or vinyl gloves with plenty of water-based lubricant when fisting, and if you plan to go down on her, either do so before you penetrate her or use a barrier.

Piercing, cutting and other S/M activities: Let the above principles of HIV transmission, and common sense be your guide in assessing risks and taking precautions with S/M activities. Invest in your own favorite equipment: latex or rubber toys, leather goods or metal equipment. The surest and safest guide is to not share equipment at all. If, however, it's not possible for you to supply your own, every precaution should be taken by you and your partner to make sure that equipment is properly cleaned prior to any sexual scene. 1) wash your equipment thoroughly, 2) soak it for several hours in a solution of one-part bleach to ten-parts water, and 3) rinse it thoroughly several times to be sure that all the bleach has been removed. These guidelines are adapted from the brochure "AIDS-Safe S/M/," distributed by the AIDS Action Committee of Mass. For further information about S/M safety, see Pat Califia's *The Lesbian S/M Safety Manual: Basic Health and Safety for Woman-to-Woman S/M* Denver: Lace Publications, 1988.

Do I think cunnilingus is an effective way of spreading HIV? No . . . and the reason is that cunnilingus is not an effective way of spreading things which are much more infectious, like hepatitis B, which has 100,000 times more viral particles per cubic milliliter of blood than HIV. There has never been a single reported case of woman-to-woman transmission of hepatitis B via oral sex. In addition, given the number of lesbians infected with HIV, we would be seeing many, many cases of women getting infected via oral sex with other women—and we aren't

When HIV/AIDS educators talk to gay men about oral sex, most say, "Oral sex is very low risk. You can make it safer by not taking his come into your mouth. To be absolutely safe, you can use a condom." Very few gay men use condoms for oral sex, yet studies have shown that only about two dozen gay men worldwide, of the millions infected with HIV, have become infected via oral sex—and in those cases, almost all the men had taken ejaculate in the mouth, there were usually severe dental or gum problems, and often a high number of sexual partners (in the hundreds).

Dental dam advocates argue that data on lesbian transmission is fragmentary, since the Centers for Disease Control (CDC) doesn't include woman-to-woman transmission among the risk factors they normally track. Any well-informed AIDS activist knows that the CDC AIDS surveillance system is faulty, because it is based on the identity rather than the behavior of the person with AIDS. The sexual orientation of a person with AIDS does not explain how they became infected. The category "male homosexual/bisexual" doesn't tell us, for example, whether a man had insertive or receptive anal sex. The "heterosexual" category doesn't differentiate between those who became infected via anal or vaginal intercourse.

Although the right questions are not asked, the surveillance data is based on a hierarchy of transmission grounded in medical research and the real experience of people who've become infected with HIV. Sharing injection drug needles will put you in the "IV Drug User" category whether you are a gay or straight woman. Having unprotected intercourse with a man will put you in the "Heterosexual" category even though you identify as a lesbian. Both of those behaviors are much more likely to have caused your infection with HIV than going down on your girlfriend, because HIV is transmitted very efficiently and easily via blood to blood or semen to blood

contact. To know the scope of the epidemic in the lesbian community at large, we need among other things a national seroprevalence survey of self-identified lesbians.

Most lesbian health educators acknowledge that although lesbians with HIV haven't been studied well, several lesbian health studies do exist. In studies of hundreds of lesbians with AIDS, only four cases of woman-to-woman transmission of HIV via sex have been reported in the medical literature. In the first case, both partners reported oral, anal and a vaginal contact with blood during sex (*Annals of Internal Medicine,* vol. 105, no. 6). The second case involved a woman whose female partner, an injection drug user, was in the late stages of HIV disease (*Annals of Internal Medicine,* vol. 111, no. 11). In the final two cases the HIV-positive lesbians' sexual partners were HIV-negative, and they reported no IV drug use or sex with men (*The Lancet,* 7/87 and *AIDS Research,* vol. 1, 84). The problem with these last three cases is that it is not reported exactly how the women became infected. There are several other anecdotal, word-of-mouth reports of sexual transmission of HIV between women. We may never know the full story with those cases, but we need only return to what we know about HIV transmission to be able to assess risks and make decisions about what we want to do sexually.

HIV prevention education for gay men is usually very sex-positive. Why do we reserve all of our sexual conservatism for lesbians, by passing out dams and gloves and issuing blanket statements to lesbians such as "oral sex on a woman is risky" and "putting your fingers inside her can be risky"? Most HIV/AIDS educators wouldn't dream of telling a heterosexual man to wear a glove when putting his fingers in his girlfriend's vagina.

Many lesbian educators and activists are feeling that lesbians already have so much stacked against our sexual pleasure and freedom: internalized homophobia, racism and sexual abuse drain our self-esteem and sexual power; sexism and the puritan tradition subtly pervade how we think about sexuality and our bodies; our parents inculcated sexual shame in most of us, and that shame and guilt is only multiplied when we realize that we are queer.

Coming out can be an explosion of that shame into delight and power—and yet well-publicized phenomena such as "Lesbian Bed Death" and the general perception hat lesbians do it less than everybody else ("Bullshit!" some of us say; "Well quantity and quality are two separate things," other of us say) are signs that these various forms of oppression have taken their toll on our community.

The implicit question asked by many lesbian educators is: Do we want to be a part of what's keeping lesbians from getting it on and enjoying themselves, by exacerbating fears and encouraging lesbians to restrict themselves sexually? Absolutely not. We do need to continue to get the information out about what's risky and what's not.

"Every day, women make decisions about the risk of different activities," Louise Rice noted, "Most of these activities (smoking or driving a car, for example) carry a far greater risk than cunnilingus. Thousands of lesbians' lives could be saved if we were to devote half the attention to mammograms and breast self-awareness that has been focused on dental dams."

Having put out all of this provocative information, I'd like to suggest that we turn our political focus outward and turn our activism towards improving the lives of ALL women with AIDS—not just lesbians with AIDS. In the United States, women with AIDS make up only 4 percent of all clinical trials, although women make up 13 percent of all people with AIDS (and that's an underestimate of about 28 percent). Fourteen million women still don't have access to health insurance. The CDC case definition of AIDS still doesn't include life-threatening gynecological manifestations of AIDS. The number-one HIV transmission risk for women is IV-drug use: We need to make clean needles available and drug treatment accessible. All of these issues are lesbian health issues. And we can achieve victories on many of these fronts if we ACT UP louder and in greater numbers. Meantime, let's talk about sex—and have as much as we want.

Pinstripes to Pullovers: Learning to Live with Chronic Fatigue Syndrome

by Donna Kiefer

I sat at the wide conference table on the tenth floor of an office building in downtown Boston. Half a dozen other attorneys ringed the table. We were there on a bitter January day to settle the U.S. Environmental Protection Agency's multimillion-dollar lawsuit against one of New England's most flagrant polluters.

As the lead attorney, I had spent most of my first two years at the EPA, including many evenings and weekends, researching and preparing to file this suit. Now, a year and a half later, we were finally negotiating a settlement. I wore what I considered my most imposing suit, a charcoal pin-striped blend of wool and silk.

My life was at a high point. I had finally found my niche in the legal world. Part of a solid circle of friends, I was also close to my two brothers and sister, often babysit-ting my nieces. I had just come out as a lesbian, and my family and closest friends were generally accepting.

But amidst my pride, I was also aware of a deep exhaustion that, along with headaches, sore throats, and low-grade fevers, had beset me for two months. It seemed to be a persistent flu. Weeks later, when the symptoms showed no sign of abating, I consulted a specialist. She diagnosed me with a common virus and could not predict how long I would be sick, saying there was no treatment except rest. I took a two-month leave to recover, but the exhaustion, sore throats, and headaches persisted. Desperate for answers, I returned to the specialist. After performing an array of blood tests, she diagnosed me with Chronic Fatigue Immune Dysfunction Syndrome (CFIDS).

This left me feeling even more lost than before. Very little is known about CFIDS. I was told again: rest, rest, rest. Other than that, there were treatments intended to relieve symptoms. The only way to determine if a certain treatment might be helpful was to try it.

One of the first treatments I tried was acupuncture. A year after falling ill, I still had hopes of being cured—hopes fed by my acupuncturist, who assured me I would burst with energy within months. Three times a week, I drove 30 minutes each way in rush-hour traffic to lie on a gurney and let my body be punctured by very thin needles. As I lay there gazing up at the skylight, gentle flute music drifting over me, I did feel a bit more vital and clear-headed. But that vitality vanished within an hour of leaving my doctor's office. Four months and more than a thousand dollars later, I was not any healthier.

At least acupuncture did not make me sicker, which is more that I can say for blue-green algae. After hearing stories of people recovering from CFIDS with the help of algae, I plunked down hundreds of dollars, this time for an entire algae nutritional regimen. After a week, my fatigue and mental fog were worse than ever. The distributor assured me that this was a normal reaction, and would soon subside. Exhausted and skeptical though I was, I hung on. But after another three weeks, even the distributor had to acknowledge that the algae was not helping me.

Even more pressing than my frustration over treatment options were my fears about how the illness would affect my future. My main worry was whether I could continue working, but I also wondered whether I would ever be able to travel or swim again. I remember the look in my first doctor's eyes when I told her I was planning a trip to Peru. So sad, so remote. She shook her head and said I could not take such a trip. In her eyes, I saw a diminishment of my life beyond what I could imagine.

The course of CFIDS varies greatly. Some people recover, some cycle between periods of relatively good health and illness, and some gradually worsen over time. Others remain the same, while some improve gradually but never fully recover. There was no way of knowing which of these categories I would fall into.

The not knowing made so much of life a challenge. For instance, I had to decide what sort of accommodations to request from the EPA. First, I took the two-month break. Then, feeling better, I began working out of my home; I transferred my big case, taking work that was less time sensitive and required fewer meetings. But even with this new setup, my headaches, sore throats, and exhaustion worsened. Over the next ten months, to cope with these worsening symptoms, I was gradually forced to weaken my connection to the EPA, first cutting back on work, then taking extended leave. Finally, a year and a half after first falling ill, I had to admit that I would not be able to return to work as a lawyer. Not in the near future; perhaps never.

In a way, my resignation from the EPA came as a relief. I could stop fighting to keep my job and focus on guarding my health. But a whole new set of worries appeared. How would I support myself? Was I eligible for disability benefits?

When everything is in question, waking up in the morning feels like disappearing into a black hole. The healthy, athletic body I had once known, along with my job, my future as a lawyer, my ability to spend time with friends and family, and my very identity had all vanished. I started wondering what my purpose was. I could no longer contribute by suing polluters or by babysitting my nieces and giving support to friends and family.

Indeed, on many days I remained in sweat pants and a beat-up pullover sweater all day, struggling just to make breakfast or take a shower. After sleeping ten restless hours, I awoke feeling as though 50-pound weights were attached to my limbs. Just as disturbing to me as the utter exhaustion was the mental fog that enveloped me. I began to have trouble balancing my checkbook or remembering how to get to places that I had been to many times before. I would walk into the kitchen and discover the I had left the refrigerator door open. Many days I could not read even one newspaper article. I began to bounce checks, forgetting to deposit money into my account—something that had never happened to me before.

One day when this fog was particularly dense, I sank into the plush green armchair where I spent much of my time and picked up a paper clip. I held it between my thumb and forefinger, staring. I absolutely could not remember the name of this object. After a minute, the word "clip" came to me, but that only led to "clipper," and, finally, "nail clipper." I gave up. Only later that afternoon was I able to retrieve from my brain the words "paper clip."

While many of these concerns—loss of identity, uncertainty about the future, fear of financial ruin—are common to anyone with a disabling illness, ignorance about CFIDS made my situation especially difficult. Medical experts debated how serious an illness this was, and whether its origins were physiological or psychological. People often simplified these issues, saying those with CFIDS "are just depressed." The press further stigmatized the illness by christening it the "yuppie flu." That people with CFIDS often do not "look" sick and may have symptoms that wax and wane for no apparent reason makes it harder for others to take seriously.

The impact that this stigma had on me was powerful. I had internalized so much of the social doubt that if I were having a relatively "good" day—one in which I could cook a full meal for myself and read for more than two minutes—I would start to question whether I was indeed sick. Could I be imagining the severity of my symptoms?

Unfortunately, my self doubt was mirrored in those around me. When I met with my supervisor upon returning from my first leave he smiled from behind his desk, asking, "So, did you use this break to write the Great American Novel?" I was shocked at his misunderstanding of my condition. Yet, I also struggled with the question—could I have written that novel if I had really tried? At that moment, feeling relatively good, I forgot the days when I could not finish an article or recall the name of ordinary objects. My specialist also minimized the severity of my illness. One day after I had sat for more than an hour in her waiting room she confided that she was running late because a person with AIDS had died that day. "Now *that's* an illness you don't want to get," she said.

Since those first days of fear and uncertainty, my life has improved. I was granted disability benefits and began two treatments that have improved my energy level. One is a medication that helps me to get refreshing sleep. The other is mega-doses of vitamin B-12 that I inject to increase my stamina.

Just as important, I found greater means of coping with the illness. Much of that came through joining a support group for women with CFIDS. I immediately saw that these women were quite sick, although they too struggled with denial. Gradually I was able to build my belief in the severity of their conditions into the conviction that I also must be seriously ill. Eventually I learned to hold onto this conviction even when I was having a "good" day. I grew to like and respect all of these women. I saw that although their daily activities were limited by chronic illness, the meaning and value of their lives was not. This helped me to value my own life as it is, rather than measure it against the standard of what it had once been. I was even eventually able to let go of the need to know what my life would be like in the future. I began to see that no one—whether chronically ill or in robust health—can know what life holds in store.

Now, six years after falling ill, I volunteer with several activist groups, pulling together meetings and organizing files. While it is a far cry from negotiating multi-million-dollar lawsuits, it gives me the sense that I am making a contribution. I have also begun exploring creative writing. As I sit in jeans and pullover sweatshirt typing these words into my home computer, just a few feet away hangs the pinstriped suit that was once a symbol of my status in the world. I don't know if I'll ever wear it again, but I have learned that status, like good health, is ephemeral. I was born with one and attained the other, only to see them both stripped away.

I first reacted to my losses with sadness and anger, further fueled by the ignorance and insensitivity that I encountered. Yet, although I never would have chosen it, I have mostly made peace with my disability. It is a part of who I am, and I have accepted it in order to value my life and move forward. I have established new priorities; status is not among them. Instead I strive for honesty, compassion, and openness to each moment—qualities that come from the inside and cannot be taken from me.

Overcoming Obstacles

by Patricia A. Hanvey

It is common to encounter a course in college that you are able to relate to in some small way. However, it is much less common to take a course that almost completely outlines your entire life. Women's Studies 103, "Women & Their Bodies In Health & Disease", has been such a course for me. This course has given me the opportunity to explore many aspects of my life and also the knowledge and courage to challenge many prejudices of the medical field which my life is so closely intertwined with.

"Life is not easy", my father reminded me of this regularly before he passed away from cancer at the age of 58 and left me to take care of an alcoholic mother. I understood this and welcomed the challenge. However, being dealt a hand consisting of disability, chronic illness, sexism, poverty, and homophobia proved to be a challenge I never anticipated.

I gave up on college in the early 80's to pursue what I thought was a more worthwhile life. My dream was to become a police officer. Since I was not yet the required age of 21, I went into the next best thing until I could move into law enforcement. At age 18 I became one of the youngest paramedics in the field. I was also one of the most naive. It was my belief that if people performed their skill well that they would attain the respect and friendship of their peers. My eyes were soon opened to the contrary. In a turn-of-the-century firehouse, I was the sole female among a large group of firemen with ideas as old as the building in which we stood. A day never passed in which I wasn't reminded that this was a man's job and that I was intruding into a man's world! A female had no place there and, if I insisted on staying, I would pay the price. During the 3 years I worked the ambulance and waited to become a police officer, I endured everything from cold-shoulders to attempted sexual assaults.

My first opportunity to enter the law enforcement field happened in 1988. I was hired as a patrol officer by a small town in northwestern Indiana. The job consisted of routine police work. Serious violent crime was a rar-ity in this small community. My typical day consisted of dealing with domestic disputes, truancy, vandalism, and other common types of police calls. The majority of my time was spent patrolling the streets and performing traffic enforcement. The remaining amount of my time was spent fighting sexist attitudes that were even stronger than I had encountered as a paramedic. I faced this sexism both from within the department and also from the majority of the population I served who believed a woman's place was in the home. It was this antiquated ideology that eventually put an end to my career and nearly my life.

On a cool November morning, as I sat running radar, my dream turned into a nightmare. I observed a small two-door vehicle approaching at a high rate of speed. The car was weaving in and out of its lane and eventually crossed the centerline as it approached the intersection. I immediately began pursuing this car as it turned down the main road leading out of town. The vehicle finally pulled over in front of the town's only bar. I assumed this time would be like the many traffic stops I had made before, but I was not prepared for the events that followed.

At first, after placing the suspect into my squad car, the young man cooperated with my orders, but in the blink of an eye my life was turned upside down. The suspect, not yet handcuffed, struck me in the face nearly knocking me unconscious. He jumped out of my squad and began to run. I quickly composed myself and took chase after him. I tackled him hard into the gravel lot, only to lose grasp of him when my kneecap struck the ground and shattered. The suspect ran back to his car, but I was determined to stop him in spite of my injury.

The suspect had a spare set of keys and started his car seconds before I reached him. I grabbed the man's neck and arm in an attempt to pull him from his vehicle. Unfortunately, I did not realize he had his car in gear. He accelerated rapidly in reverse with my body pinned both in and under his car. From my waist up I was trapped between the suspect's body and the steering wheel and my legs were tucked under the car. Even though I was seriously injured, I still managed to pull myself completely into his car. During our hand-to-hand battle, one of the man's strongest reasons for putting up such a fight became clear to me. The man repeatedly shouted at me that there was no way in hell that he was letting a woman, much less a "goddamn dyke" take him to jail. This man did not see the uniform, the badge, or my authority. He simply saw a woman who was working somewhere she didn't belong. I was a woman out of her place trying to do a man's job. A chorus of howls accompanied his shouting from his friends exiting the nearby tavern. Over and over I heard them shout things that I choose not to repeat. The things they said consisted of remarks that made it clear to me that they shared their friend's ideas that a woman had no right to be anywhere but at home and under a man's control.

Despite the man's obvious advantage in size (but not necessarily strength), I knocked him unconscious and waited for my back up to arrive. Other officers finally arrived along with my department's chief. My chief stood next to me as I lay bleeding and in pain and all he could say was that this was exactly what he thought would happen; that maybe now the town would believe him that women "just don't have what it takes." A few minutes later the ambulance arrived and after immobilizing every inch of my body, transported me to the hospital.

After countless doctors poked and prodded at me, I learned my spine was fractured along with various other injuries to my ribs, both wrists, and kneecap. I was sent to a specialist at a teaching hospital in Chicago where I was placed in a body cast for eighteen months. I was told I might never walk again, much less ever be able to return to the police force.

I underwent several surgeries on my spine and years of rehabilitative therapy in an attempt to salvage what little function I had left. My condition improved beyond my doctors' expectations. However, it was, and still is, a horribly long road full of physical and emotional pain.

Throughout my medical treatment I began to see the many different issues facing women as health care consumers. My eyes were also opened to the fact that many members of the medical field carry the same prejudices as those that I have encountered in my personal and professional life. When I entered professional trades dominated by men, I was prepared to face sexist and even homophobic attitudes. However, dealing with these kinds of prejudices from a team of medical professionals, ultimately in charge of trying to help me stay alive, only makes my disabilities that much more painful to deal with.

I lost a great deal as a result of this injury and the disability that developed from it. Among the things I lost were my career, my income and the luxuries it afforded, and the freedom that mobility once provided me. However, the loss that hurt me most of all was the sense of control I used to feel. I began to feel as if I had no control over my own body. As a result, I felt that I had lost control over my entire life. I was now a poor, disabled, lesbian who felt utterly helpless. From this point on, my life was under the control of physicians, surgeons, and other health care providers. Those in charge, the physicians, surgeons, and even the residents were all male. They all asserted their authoritarian roles, and I, not knowing better, thought I had no right to object to anything they suggested. I felt as if I was their lab rat. The only members of my health care team that ever seemed concerned with how I felt were the nurses and therapists—all of whom were women—who provided care for me on a daily basis.

Losing the power to make decisions about my own health care was the first step in losing control of my body and ultimately my life. In between surgeries, my physicians ordered a non-stop barrage of diagnostic tests. Most of these test procedures were invasive and horribly painful. However, I never once understood that I had a right to refuse these tests or seek alternate treatments. On one occasion I was actually told by one of my surgeons that "You must have faith in me as if I was God . . . you should accept what I say blindly, like the word of God itself to be the absolute truth." It did not take long to discover that this was the prevailing attitude toward women as health care consumers. However, I knew no better and I accepted this as simply the way the system worked. As Mary A. Halas states in her article, "[t]he attitude with which women seek medical care within the male-dominated system is one of subservient dependence on all-knowing authority" (Halas, see chapter 1).

To complicate my situation even further, I began to develop symptoms unrelated to my spinal injury for which my doctors offered no explanation or comfort. As time went on, my symptoms became more severe and more numerous. I knew that there was something going wrong inside my body. It was a feeling I could not describe to my doctors,

A mixture of fear and a lack of knowledge concerning my own body left me without the ability to make my doctors understand. As women, it is the lack of information about our bodies and our submissive, unassertive relationships with our doctors that make it almost impossible to find out what is wrong with us and to discover what treatment options are available (Halas). I was not the only one at a loss for words. My doctors could offer no physical explanation for my problems.

My new symptoms coincided with my continued complaints that the spinal surgeries had not been successful in alleviating the pain as my doctors had promised. This led my doctors to take a new approach in my treatment. Suddenly I was being treated with a host of anti-depressants and other medications along with suggestions that I see a psychiatrist. The small amount of courage I managed to muster up to question my doctors led them to label me as a "problem patient" or a hypochondriac. My pain and new symptoms were no longer real in my doctors' eyes. I began to doubt myself, but I decided it was time to find a new doctor who would listen to me. However, I was told I was just "shopping for a doctor" who would agree with whatever I said.

After talking to friends and family members and researching countless physicians' backgrounds, I finally found a doctor who was genuinely concerned. Every test he ordered was explained in full detail and more importantly I was given the choice as to whether or not I wanted to go through with them. After almost 5 years of unanswered questions and unexplained symptoms, I finally began to feel as if I might be regaining control of my own body. However, the years of untreated symptoms had left me in poor physical health.

My new primary physician referred me to a surgeon, a specialist in pain management, who took over care of my back pain. I was horrified to learn that the surgeons I feared to question in the past had in fact damaged my spine far worse than my accident had. In an attempt to alleviate my pain, a hockey puck shaped morphine pump was placed in my lower abdomen with a catheter running backwards into my spinal cord. Small amounts of morphine are continuously bathing the injured area. Approximately every 45 days, I have the pump refilled through a large needle that pierces my abdomen into the pump. To this day I still have the pump, but the relief it provides is minimal at best. It does, however, provide me with a constant reminder of the consequences we must face if we blindly turn control of our bodies over to someone else.

My doctor tried diligently to find the cause of my problems before my health deteriorated further. At the time, I was suffering from several serious medical conditions such as: frequent pulmonary emboli (a serious condition in which a blood clot forms in one of the blood vessels and travels to the lung), pitting edema (severe swelling in the extremities that leaves a deep indentation, a "pit", when pressed), photosensitivity, skin ulcerations, fatigue, seizures, and a recurring facial rash. One of the more serious problems I suffered from and still

experience is recurrent renal insufficiency; my kidneys are not always keeping up with their expected workload.

My doctor and I knew that all these problems had to have a common link, but none of the tests had provided us with an answer yet. Finally, my doctor ordered a certain series of blood tests to check for the disease lupus. He explained lupus to me and, while I was terrified of having such a disease, I felt a sense of relief that I might finally have an answer, that all of this was not just "in my head" as other doctors had accused.

Lupus, more formally referred to as Systemic Lupus Erythematosus (SLE), belongs to the family of rheumatic diseases—diseases of the connective tissue. It is an autoimmune disease in which the body produces abnormal antibodies called autoantibodies. "Unlike normal antibodies, which are produced in response to and attack foreign substances such as viruses, autoantibodies attack normal body tissue" (Stehlin, 1989, par.4). Lupus can affect almost any part of the body causing serious damage. Lupus can affect the joints, muscles, skin, lungs, heart, kidneys, and even the brain.

It would be impossible to make a complete list of signs and symptoms that cover all the problems lupus patients experience. One of the reasons it is difficult to diagnose lupus is that the symptoms of this disease vary widely from patient to patient and can be similar to other diseases. However, physicians of the American Rheumatological Association have created the following list of indicators to help in distinguishing lupus from other conditions:

- A butterfly-shaped facial rash on the nose & cheeks
- A positive Anti-Nuclear Antibody (ANA) test
- Light sensitivity
- Mouth or nose ulcers
- Arthritis
- A false positive syphilis test
- Protein in the urine
- Inflammation of the tissue around the heart or lungs
- Low red or white blood cell or platelet count (Tanur, 1995, par.7)

The occurrence of any four of these signs could indicate the presence of lupus. Other characteristics and symptoms of lupus can be: disc-like lesions or other marks, whitening of the fingers after exposure to cold, hair loss, convulsions, fatigue, fever, muscle weakness, or joint pain (Boston Women's Health Book Collective [BWBHC], 1998, p. 603).

A major problem with trying to make a complete list of symptoms is that frequently the only complaint lupus patients have, especially in the early stage of the disease, is that we just don't 'feel right'. Far too often doctors rely on strict criteria to make their diagnosis and often overlook or flat-out dismiss the patient who comes to them without specific symptoms. Looking back at the beginning of my illness, I complained for over a 2 year period to different doctors, prior to any real symptoms emerging, that I knew something was wrong but couldn't quite pinpoint what is was. Before finding the doctor who diagnosed me as having lupus, my doctors treated me as if I was a psychiatric patient. I was treated with anti-depressants, tranquilizers, and numerous referrals to mental health practitioners. "Many physicians see women's physical complaints as trivial, neurotic disorders best treated with placebos or symptomatic therapy. Serious, treatable problems often progress to irreversible damage or death while a woman is trying to convince her doctor that her problems are not all in her head" (Halas). One doctor told me that my symptoms were *in my head and not my body* and that my behavior was typical of most women; I was simply being "high-strung and attention-seeking".

I hesitate to make any type of a list because symptoms are as different as those of us suffering with lupus are. We all experience this disease in different ways. I could make an endless list and still leave out some symptom(s) that other lupus patients may suffer. It is easy to create a list of physical symptoms lupus patients experience, but most people do not realize the problems we face in our everyday lives. Like so many others, I never know if I will wake up and face a new set of problems. I constantly have to put my life on hold. I never know when I will be able to attend school, whether I will be able to finish assignments, take exams on their given date and time, or even whether I will be able to walk from one classroom to the next. Some days I don't even know if I will be able to get out of bed. I never know from one day to the next if I can follow through on any of my plans. This not only affects me, but also affects loved-ones around me, primarily my long-time companion.

My lover understands the unpredictability of my disease and knows the pain I endure almost constantly. However, this disease is also painful for her. Day in and day out she sees me suffer from a wide variety of symptoms and feels helpless. She knows it is impossible for her to take my pain away. She is also frustrated with misdiagnoses and the lack of care I receive. This is a disease that affects millions of people, not just lupus patients, but anyone who loves and cares for them.

The statistics on lupus are staggering "According to a new nationwide marketing research study, almost 2,000,000 Americans suffer from the disease that is more common than AIDS and a host of other diseases such as cerebral palsy, multiple sclerosis, sickle cell anemia and cystic fibrosis" (Aikens, 1994, p. PG).

When people learn that I have lupus, they act genuinely concerned and some even ask *"how long do you have?"*. I try to explain to them that even though lupus can be very disabling, it isn't an automatic death sentence. In fact, 80%–90% of lupus patients live out normal life spans.

Lupus is not a universally fatal disease. Lupus does vary in intensity and degree, however, and there are people who have a mild case, there are those who have a moderate case and there are some who have a severe case of lupus, which tends to be more difficult to treat and bring under control. For people who have a severe flare-up, there is a greater chance that their lupus may be life-threatening. And we know that some people do die of this disease and because of that we have a tremendous amount of respect for the potential of this disease. (Lupus Foundation of America, 1999)

According to the Lupus Foundation of America, 90% of lupus patients are women (Geiger, 1998, par.6). The disease usually occurs during the childbearing years of 15 to 45. This rate is over eight times higher than the occurrence in similarly aged men. Lupus is also more common among African American, Asian, and Hispanic women than in white women, at a rate of almost 2 to 1. Many believe that it is for these reasons—that it is a disease more common among minorities and women in this country—that lupus is not given the attention it deserves in health and research circles (Aikens, 1994, p. PG).

Illnesses affecting women receive less attention from medical researchers than those affecting men do. The National Institutes of Health conducted an inventory of its total research budget in 1987 and found that only 13.5% was devoted to studying diseases unique to women. I fully believe that there would have been more progress toward finding a cure for my disease if lupus primarily affected men. I also believe that this holds true for all illnesses that affect women and other minorities.

Why are women so affected by lupus? There are several different theories as to why more women than men have this disease. One of the leading theories concerns the role of female hormones. Dr. Ellen Ginzler, chief of rheumatology at the SUNY Health Science Center in Brooklyn states that "We know that hormones play some role, some experts believe that estrogen puts the immune system into overdrive" (Geiger, 1998, par.7). In fact, researchers are discovering that all the sex hormones—estrogen, progesterone, testosterone, and prolactin have profound effects on the immune system. Many women, including myself, report flare-ups or worsening of existing lupus symptoms around the time of their menstrual cycle. Other researchers have been looking at the role of genetics. "The inheritance is not absolute, however. It can skip multiple generations, and so if a parent has the disease, there's no guarantee that any of the offspring will" (Stehlin, 1989, par.31). However, it is common for a lupus patient to have at least one family member with lupus or a similar disease. Other possible causes behind the higher prevalence in women can include physical and emotional stress, unidentified viruses, prescription drugs, or the lack of quality medical care.

Because of the wide variety of symptoms as I mentioned earlier, lupus is usually difficult to diagnose. It is also difficult because there is no single diagnostic test to determine whether or not a patient has lupus. The diagnosis is based on symptomology.

It is important to remember that one positive reaction does not qualify a patient as having lupus. Lupus is a very unpredictable disease. Test results may be positive one time and negative the next depending on whether the disease is in an active state or is in remission. Many doctors reach false conclusions because they rely on one set of test results. It is much more common for doctors to dismiss the patient's complaints, putting the patient in a dangerous predicament.

I was fortunate to have a doctor who understood how test results could fluctuate. My first test results were positive, but my doctor repeated these tests several times before reaching the diagnosis of lupus. While the tests usually yield positive results when the disease is in its active state, the lupus patient may not necessarily be experiencing noticeable symptoms during this time. In addition to the above tests, my doctor also obtained kidney and skin biopsies before making a diagnosis and beginning my treatment.

Treatment of lupus usually depends upon the degree to which the patient is experiencing symptoms. Most patients with mild symptoms involving the skin and joints respond well to aspirin and anti-inflammatory drugs. Other patients don't find relief from these medications and must take a variety of steroids or chemotherapy medications to control their symptoms. Many patients and their doctors are trying to get away from treatment using steroids and chemotherapy agents because of the serious side effects they can cause. The most common side effect from steroids is the development of a round, puffy, moon-shaped face. However, the biggest reason for concern is that steroids can cause bone cells to die, especially affecting the hips and shoulders, which can lead to the necessity of joint replacements. Both steroids and anti-cancer drugs suppress the immune system, which leaves the patient open to various infections that can be fatal. Another common treatment is the use of anti-malaria medications, which can cause irreversible blindness as a result of retinal damage.

Successful treatment consists of a great deal more from a doctor than just prescribing drugs and much more from the patient than simply taking them (Stehlin, 1989).

It is crucial that the patient and physician have a good relationship. Patients should be comfortable enough to express their complaints about both the disease and their treatment to the physician. Confidence in your doctor is extremely important, but you cannot leave your care completely in your doctor's hands. Things such as eating right, getting enough rest, and taking care of ourselves in general are vital to our health.

My treatment consisted of the use of steroids and anti-malaria drugs along with constant, close monitoring of my symptoms. However, after long conversations with my doctor, I chose to discontinue long-term treatment with these medications. I found the side effects to be as bad, if not worse, at times than the symptoms of the disease could be. My doctor believed that the patient had the absolute final word in regards to his or her treatment. However, not all of the physicians that I have encountered, both before this physician and after, have had such beliefs.

Approximately four years ago I moved. Since then, I have had to replay all my earlier struggles with the medical profession. My biggest problem has been my unsuccessful search for a physician who will truly listen to me and my complaints. Teams of doctors, in both internal medicine and rheumatology, have been less than responsive to the idea of an equal physician–patient relationship. I cannot recall how many times I have been talked over, talked down to, or ignored by my doctors here in Wisconsin. I have encountered the same prejudices and biases from the past such as sexism and homophobia on the part of my health care providers.

The sexism I face today has not changed over place or time. Just as my former doctors in Indiana and Chicago had done, the physicians I am now encountering have trivialized my complaints, often dismissing them as products of anxiety, depression, or just plain over-reacting. Even after presenting these doctors with literally volumes of my medical records that clearly show the pattern of my disease, these doctors insist on re-running their own diagnostic tests. Since I know that my disease requires close observation, I have agreed to many of the tests, but I refuse to be anyone's guinea pig ever again.

As I stated, test results for lupus can be positive one day and negative the next. However, my doctor based her current diagnosis on one single set of tests, concluding there was no evidence of lupus. This specialist wrote a letter to my primary physician stating "there is no indication that this patient is suffering from lupus". When I asked how she reached her conclusion, I was told that it was none of my business and that I had no right obtaining the letter that she had confidentially sent to my primary doctor. I confronted both of these physicians and told them I would no longer be using their services. This created somewhat of a problem since all the doctors and specialists I see are tied together through the hospital and clinics. From my own experience working in the medical field, I know how health care providers discuss patients "off the record" with one another. Since challenging these doctors, many of the other doctors I see have become cold towards me. Some of them have even become quite hostile toward me, accusing me once again of "doctor-shopping".

Another problem I have encountered among my health care providers is that of homophobia. "Surveys of the homosexual community suggest that medical practitioners may lack the knowledge of the issues salient in the lives of gay men and lesbians and inadvertently and sometimes purposely alienated their patients" (Schatz, 1996, par.1). Whether the products of ignorance, fear, or just plain hate, both my partner and I have experienced homophobic attitudes to varying degrees from my health care providers. As most patients with chronic illnesses would agree, the support of family and loved ones is crucial to maintaining good health. However, many health care providers and institutions fail to recognize our companions and lovers as "real" family, much less our spouses.

As a lesbian, I have experienced a wide range of difficulties with my health care providers. There have been numerous times when hospitals have refused to give my lover spousal or family visitation rights. On frequent occasions, my lover was not allowed to spend the night when other patients were allowed to have their spouse or other family member stay with them around the clock. I have also had doctors ask my lover to leave the room so they could examine me or perform a procedure. Many years ago when I was engaged to a man, I remember my doctors inviting my fiance to stay in the examining room even during a gynecological exam. I learned early on that things such as empowering my lover with medical power of attorney was the only way to prevent a biological family member from stepping in and overriding the wishes of my partner. Even though the domestic partner may be the primary caretaker and more knowledgeable of his or her partner's religious or ethical beliefs, doctors and hospitals often overlook their opinions for those of blood relatives (Schatz, 1996).

There are other problems that I have faced as a lesbian patient. Doctors tend to come to many premature, often erroneous, conclusions once they learn of my sexual orientation. Some of the outrageous attitudes I've experienced are as follows: doctors insisting I take a pregnancy test because "There isn't a woman alive who can abstain from *real sex*"; others have advised that I don't need mammograms or pap smears because I wasn't "truly sexually active"; and some have even insisted I submit to an HIV test before they would care for me because "homosexuals are the principal carriers of AIDS".

A 1996 USA Today article titled "HOMOPHOBIA Is A Health Hazard", reported a study in which 72% of lesbians surveyed reported experiencing "ostracism, rough treatment, and derogatory comments, as well as disrespect for their partners by their medical practitioners" after they revealed their sexual orientation (Schatz, 1996, par.23).

It is vital that homophobic attitudes within the health care system be eliminated. The homophobic attitudes of doctors, nurses, and medical students are perceived by their patients and negatively affect their experience of and quality of their care (Schatz, 1996).

Recognizing the importance of knowledge about diversity of sexual orientation in clinical practice is an important part of the solution. Physicians must be aware that as much as 6% of the patients they see-about 15,000,000 Americans are gay, lesbian, or bisexual, and that these individuals express part of the normal range of human sexuality. Such information must come from organized curricula in medical schools and/or residency training programs. (Schatz, 1996, par.33)

Dealing with a chronic illness or disability is hard enough without the added burdens from a health care system and society which refuses to let go of sexist and homophobic attitudes. I cannot change the attitudes of others, but I can change the way I personally deal with them. I will never give in or give up again! Understanding my rights as a health care consumer and as an equal and productive member of society has helped me overcome many of the obstacles put in my path by sexism, homophobia, and negative images of the disabled.

The most frustrating element of a disease such as lupus is the unknown, a feeling that you cannot control what will happen next. Even though I cannot control the next flare-up, I can control the treatment I receive *and* refuse. In spite of the fact that I am once again facing sexist and homophobic attitudes on the part of my health care providers, I will not relinquish the control it took me so long to regain. It is my body and my life and I have the final word on what happens to them both. It was not easy to reach this point in my life. It took a lot of mistakes, a great deal of pain, and many years for me to understand the desperate need to transform doctor-patient relationships in a way which would place the power into the hands of the health care consumers—the women. Every woman, regardless of race, class, sexual orientation, or disability has to learn that she has the power to control her life. By regaining control over what is done to my body, I have regained control over my life and so can each and every woman in this country.

REFERENCES

Aikens, C. (1994, Dec.1). Lupus: Little understood disease afflicts millions. *Oakland Post,* p. PG.

Boston Women's Health Book Collective (1998). *Our Bodies, Ourselves for the New Century.* Touchstone Books, Simon and Schuster.

Geiger, D. (1998, May 18). Facing Lupus [22 paragraphs]. *Newsday.* [Online]. *The Electric Library Online.* Available: http://www.elibrary.com [1999, Jan. 9].

Halas, M. (1994). Sexism in women's medical care, in N. Worcester and M.H. Whatley (Eds.), *Women's Health: Readings on Social, Economic, and Political Issues,* Kendall/Hunt., pp. 4–8. (See same article in chapter 1 of this 1999 edition of Worcester and Whatley.)

The Lupus Foundation of America (1999). *Commonly Asked Questions About Lupus.* <http://www.lupus.org/lupus-faq.html#22> [1999, Feb. 2].

Schatz, B., Nemrow, P. (1996, Nov.1). HOMOPHOBIA is a health hazard [43 paragraphs]. *USA Today Magazine.* [Online]. *The Electric Library Online.* Available: http://www.elibrary.com [1999, Jan.11].

Stehlin, D. (1989, Dec. 1). Living With Lupus [50 paragraphs]. *FDA Consumer,* pp. 8–13. [Online]. *The Electric Library Online.* Available: http://www.elibrary.com [1999, Jan.11].

Tanur, Marcia. (1995, March 1). Lupus signs and symptoms [9 paragraphs]. *Contemporary Women's Issues Database,* p.15H. [Online]. *The Electric Library Online.* Available: http://www.elibrary.com [1999, Jan.11].

Recurrent Headache: A Neglected Women's Health Problem

Gay L. Lipchik, PhD
Jeanetta C. Rains, PhD
Donald B. Penzien, PhD
Kenneth A. Holroyd, PhD
Fred D. Sheftell, MD

> Migraine gives some people mild hallucinations, temporarily blinds others, shows up not only as a headache but as a gastrointestinal disturbance, a painful sensitivity to all sensory stimuli, an abrupt overpowering fatigue, a stroke-like aphasia, and a crippling inability to make even the most routine cerebral associations. . . . The actual headache, when it comes, brings with it chills, sweating, nausea, a debility that seems to stretch the very limits of endurance. That no one dies of migraine seems, to someone deep into an attack, an ambiguous blessing. . . . "Why not take a couple of aspirin" the unafflicted will say from the doorway. . . . All of us who have migraine suffer not only from the attacks themselves but from this common conviction that we are perversely refusing to care for ourselves by taking a couple of aspirin—we are making ourselves sick—that we bring it on ourselves.
>
> —J. Didion, The White Album, 1979[1]

This is a vivid description of the migraine headaches that afflict almost nine million women more than 12 years of age.[2] Yet, recurrent headache disorders, specifically migraine and tension-type headaches, rarely are recognized as significant women's health problems. Headache disorders rarely are addressed in women's health texts or conferences and are overlooked in most federal research initiatives. For example, recently, the National Institutes of Health (NIH) has directed special attention in research agendas to disorders that affect women exclusively or disproportionately (eg, breast cancer, osteoporosis, eating disorders, and depression) or diseases that historically have presented a greater threat to males but are increasingly affecting women (eg, acquired immunodeficiency syndrome [AIDS] and cardiovascular disease). Notably, recurrent headache disorders were not included in the NIH agendas, perhaps because headache usually does not compromise life expectancy; however, recurrent headache disorders can be debilitating and have a major socioeconomic impact. In a recent investigation of headache and quality of life, the only chronic condition found to affect patient functioning as adversely as headaches was myocardial infarction; the only disease found to affect patient quality of life and functioning more adversely than headache was AIDS.[3] The following evidence argues that recurrent headache disorders deserve greater attention in women's health initiatives.

Epidemiologic studies conducted internationally indicate that on average, women are two to three times more likely than men to be disabled with some frequency by migraine headaches (18%-22% of women, 6–9% of men) or to experience disabling (daily or near daily) tension-type headaches (5% of women, 2% of men).[4-6] Migraine prevalence in women increases from puberty and peaks between the ages of 30 and 45, when migraine is 3.3 times more common in women than in men.[2] The gender difference in migraine prevalence is believed to be strongly related to hormonal influences; as many as 60% of female migraineurs experience migraine

Reprinted with permission from the Jacobs Institute of Women's Health (*Women's Health Issues*, 1998, Vol. 8, pp. 60–64).

around menses or ovulation.[7] It appears, however, that the difference in migraine prevalence among women and men is not explained entirely by hormonal influences, as migraine prevalence in women remains more than double that in men even after age 70.[2] The prevalence of tension-type headaches appears to follow a similar pattern to the prevalence of migraine, increasing steadily after age 12, peaking in middle age, and decreasing thereafter.

Not only do women experience more frequent headaches than men, they also report more severe headaches than men. For example, women report headaches of longer duration and higher headache pain intensity than men.[8] Women are more likely than men to experience nausea and vomiting, scalp tenderness, and neurologic symptoms such as a visual aura or parathesias with their headaches. These associated symptoms, vividly reflected in the epigraph to this article, contribute significantly to headache disability and diminished quality of life.

Recurrent headache is the seventh leading reason for seeking medical care, accounting for more than 18 million outpatient visits to physicians annually.[9] Women with recurrent headache disorders are twice as likely as men to consult a physician about their headaches and twice as likely as men to receive a prescription for their physical symptoms.[1] This places women at increased risk for developing complications associated with excessive use or abuse of analgesic medications such as drug-induced or rebound headache.

In the United States, migraine is associated independently with low household income[2,11] and low educational level.[11,12] Racial differences also have been reported, with a higher prevalence of migraine among African-Americans and Hispanic-Americans than whites.[12] The high prevalence of migraine in women with low incomes may be related to poor diet, limited access to medical care and/or poor medical care, and the stress of living in poverty.[13] On the other hand, women with migraines may have lower incomes because of the disruption in occupational and educational functioning caused by these headaches,[11,14] resulting in a downward socioeconomic drift. This latter hypothesis is supported by a recent investigation of unemployment among headache sufferers in the workforce. Women were two to three times more likely than men to report experiencing reduced employment owing to their headaches.[15] The reduced employment linked to recurrent headache disorders may help to explain the high prevalence of migraine found in low-income households in the United States.

Recurrent headache disorders have a significant impact on women's quality of life and on the economy. A recent study[15] found that greater than 80% of women with migraine report disability with an attack and that 8.7 million women rate this disability as moderate to severe.[16] In the United States alone, women with migraine spend more than 3 million days per month bedridden due to migraine.[11] Employed women with migraine suffer 18.8 million days per year of restricted activity,[11] with women who work during a migraine episode performing at about 40% effectiveness[2]. Housewives experience 38.5 million days per year of restricted activity and lost productivity due to migraine.[11] A recent Danish population study,[16] noteworthy for its careful diagnosis of headache, indicated that 820 work days were lost per year per 1,000 employees because of tension-type headache and that 270 work days were lost per year per 1,000 employees owing to migraine.[17] The data were not reported by gender, although it seems likely that employed women accounted for a substantial portion of the lost work days because of the higher prevalence of headache in women than in men.

Recurrent headache disorders also significantly disrupt family, social, and recreational activities. Almost 50% of headache sufferers report that their headaches interfere with family relations,[18] and almost 30% of headache sufferers report the discontinuation of normal activities, including social and recreational activities, as a result of their headaches.[4] Women who experience recurrent headaches are more than twice as likely as men who experience recurrent headaches to report that their headaches interfere with their family relations,[18,19] social life, and leisure activities.[18] Perhaps more disturbing is the recent finding[14] that the quality of life of headache sufferers is diminished during headache-free periods as well as during headache episodes.

The majority of women with headache disorders do not seek treatment, despite effective nonpharmacologic (psychological or behavioral) and pharmacologic therapies for recurrent headache.[20-22] As many as 40% of women who do seek treatment may not be diagnosed accurately or treated successfully. Much of the suffering described here could be reduced if more women sought treatment and were diagnosed accurately and treated appropriately. The low consultation rates may be related to the lack of awareness of effective treatments, poor access to medical care, and the lack of general acceptance of headache disorders as legitimate medical disorders.[23] For example, women are commonly told their headaches are all in their heads (implying that these are a problem of willpower), and they are stigmatized by other common headache myths such as "women with headaches have a problem with their personality," and they "don't need to" succumb to their headache problems.[23]

Public education about the biologic basis of headache disorders and the available effective treatments for headaches might encourage the recognition of headache disorders as legitimate medical illnesses and encourage women to seek treatment. Patient education materials are available from the American Council for Headache Education (ACHE) (ACHE; 875 Kingshighway, Suite 200, Woodbury, New Jersey, 08096; 1-800/255-2243). Medical specialists interested in the treatment of headache are often members of the American Association for the Study of Headache (AASH) (AASH; 875 Kingshighway, Suite 200, Woodbury, New Jersey, 08096; 1-800/255-2243) and can be located through the AASH member directory or through ACHE.

Population-based screenings to identify and bring into the healthcare system those women likely to benefit significantly from treatment have been recommended as another remedy for the problem.[24] Education of healthcare professionals concerning headache diagnosis and effective treatment with specific reference to women with recurrent headache disorders would increase the likelihood of an accurate diagnosis and successful treatment for those women who do seek treatment. Changes in the health care system to increase women's access to medical care may also be warranted, as recent data indicate that many women do not receive necessary health care because they are poor or lack adequate health insurance.[25] Lastly, we strongly encourage the inclusion of recurrent headache disorders into women's health research initiatives. Increased research attention focused on gender differences in the incidence, course, and treatment of headaches might illuminate the nature of chronic and recurrent pain. A deeper understanding of the biologic and psychosocial sources of this gender difference in headache prevalence might further our understanding of the pathogenesis of pain.

REFERENCES

1. Didion J. The white album. New York: Pocket Books, 1979:167.
2. Stewart WF, Lipton RB, Celentano DD, Reed ML. Prevalence of migraine headache in the United States: relation to age, income, race, and other sociodemographic factors. JAMA 1992;267:64-9.
3. Solomon GD, Skobieranda FG, Gragg LA. Quality of life and well-being of headache patients: measurement by the Medical Outcomes Study Instrument. Headache 1993;33:351-8.
4. Pryse-Phillips W, Findlay H, Tugwell P, Edmeads J, Murray TJ, Nelson RF. A Canadian population survey on the clinical, epidemiological and societal impact of migraine and tension-type headache. Can J Neurolog Sci 1992;19:333-9.
5. Rasmussen BK (1993). Epidemiology. In: Olesen J, Tfelt-Hansen P, Welch KMA (eds). The headaches. New York: Raven Press, 1993:439–443.
6. Rasmussen BK, Breslau N. Epidemiology. In: Olesen J, Tfelt-Hansen P, Welch KMA (eds). The headaches. New York: Raven Press, 1993:169-73.
7. Silberstein SD, Merriam GR. Estrogens, progestins, and headache. Neurology 1991;41:786–93.
8. Celentano DD, Linet MS, Stewart WF. Gender differences in the experience of headache. Soc Sci Med 1990;30:1289–95.
9. Ries PW. Current estimates from the National Health Interview Survey, United States, 1984. Series 10, No. 156. National Center for Health Statistics. Vital Health Stat. DHHS Publication No. (PHS) 86–1584, 1986.
10. Cooperstock R. Psychotropic drug use among women. Can Med Assoc 1976;115: 760–3.
11. Stang PE, Osterhaus JT. Impact of migraine in the United States: data from the National Health Interview Survey. Headache 1993;33:29-35.
12. Stang PE, Sternfield B, Sidney S. Migraine headache in a prepaid health plan: ascertainment, demographics, physiological, and behavioral factors. Headache 1996;36:69–76.
13. Stewart WF, Lipton RB. Societal impact of headache. In: Olesen J, Tfelt-Hansen P, Welch KMA (eds). The headaches. New York: Raven Press, 1993;29–34.
14. Osterhaus JT, Townsend RJ, Gandek B, Ware JE. Measuring the functional status and well-being of patients with migraine headache. Headache 1994;34:337–43.
15. Stang PE, Von Korff, M, Galer BS. Unemployment among primary care headache patients. Epidemiol Med. In press.
16. Stewart WF, Lipton RB, Celentano DD, Reed ML. The epidemiology of severe migraine headaches from a national survey: implications of projections to the United States population. Cephalalgia 1991;11(Suppl 11):87.
17. Rasmussen BK, Jensen R, Olesen J. Impact of headache on sickness absence and utilization of medical services: a Danish population study. J Epidemiol Community Health 1992;46:443–6.
18. Kryst S, Scherl E. A population-based survey of the social and personal impact of headache. Headache 1994;34:344–55.
19. Lacroix R, Barbaree HE. The impact of recurrent headaches on behavior lifestyle and health. Behav Res Ther 1990;28:235–42.
20. Holroyd KA, Penzien DB. Psychosocial interventions in the management of headache disorders 1: overview and effectiveness. Behav Med 1994;20:64–73.
21. Holroyd KA, Lipchik GL. Recurrent headache disorders. In: Gallant S, Puryear-Keita G, Royak-Schaler R, editors. Healthcare for women: psychological, social, and behavioral influences. Washington (DC): American Psychological Association Press. In press.
22. Rapoport AM, Sheftell FD, Headache disorders: a management guide for practitioners. Philadelphia: WB Saunders, 1996.

23. Rapoport AM, Sheftell FD. Headache relief for women. Boston: Little, Brown & Co., 1995.
24. Lipton RB, Amatniek JC, Ferrari MD, Gross M. Migraine: identifying and removing barriers to care. Neurology 1994;44(Supp 4):S63–8.
25. Chapin JL, Pereles SA. Women's access to the health care system. In: Horton JA (ed). The women's health data book: a profile of women's health in the United States. Elsevier Science Inc., 1995:129–51.

Gay L. Lipchik, PhD: Ohio University Headache Treatment and Research Project. Westerville, Ohio. Department of Psychology, Ohio University, Athens, Ohio.

Jeanetta C. Rains, PhD, Donald B. Penzien, PhD: Department of Psychiatry and Human Behavior. University of Mississippi Medical Center, Jackson, Mississippi

Kenneth A. Holroyd, PhD: Department of Psychology. Ohio University, Athens, Ohio.

Fred D. Sheftell, MD: Department of Psychiatry. New York Medical College, Vahalla, New York

WORKSHEET—CHAPTER 11

Politics of Disease

1. One of the most rapidly growing groups of people infected with HIV is that of adolescents, many of whom become infected through heterosexual intercourse.

   a. If you were to design an educational program for high school students to help prevent transmission of HIV, what specific information would you want to include?

   b. What obstacles might there be to presenting this information in the public schools? Discuss how you might present an argument for inclusion of the prevention program.

   c. Discuss any ideas you might have for overcoming adolescents' belief in their own invulnerability ("It can't happen to me") when teaching about HIV/AIDS.

2. Fill in the chart below, showing what is available in terms of prevention, detection, and treatment for each of the three cancers listed.

Cancer	Prevention	Detection	Treatment
Breast			
Cervical			
Endometrial			

3. Why do you think it is dangerous for there to be confusion about prevention vs. detection for cancers? How could health education and health policies emphasize *prevention*?

4. Identify and discuss a few common themes you found in the articles in this section on CFIDS, Lupus, endometriosis and recurrent headaches, about the relationship of women to the health care system.

CHAPTER 12

Violence Against Women

$\mathcal{M}$any women define violence—both their actual experiences with violence and their fear of violence—as their number one health issue. It is certainly an issue which affects both our mental and physical health. In fact, the level of violence a woman has experienced has been found to be a very powerful predictor of her use of medical services, more predictive than demographic variables, other life stressors, self-perceived health, or injurious health habits (I. Schwartz [1991] *American Journal of Preventive Medicine, 7*(6): 363-373). Many women who have suffered severe physical pain and life threatening injuries from violence have said that the emotional and psychological scars from abuse take years or decades longer to heal than the physical injuries.

This chapter looks at some of the many ways violence manifests itself in women's lives. Although each specific form of violence may be unique in its consequences and the knowledge needed to recognize it, respond to it, and prevent it, all forms of violence (against women) can be defined as issues of power and control where one person or a group takes power and control over another individual or group.

The continuum of family violence chart demonstrates the relationship of subtle forms of physical, verbal/emotional and sexual abuse, which society all too often tolerates and condones, to the forms more obviously recognized as serious and deadly. The more subtle forms can themselves have serious consequences and invariably lead to other means of control.

Women have not passively accepted violence as a part of our lives! Organizing against violence against women, and developing an analysis of how violence is based on and perpetuated by patriarchal structures which work to maintain power and control over groups of women in much the same way as individual men abuse women in intimate relationships, have been very visible parts of modern women's movements. For the last three decades, women have been putting much time, energy and resources into rape crisis centers, battered women's programs and incest survivors' groups. Although social change work is always slower than we imagine, in some ways the violence against women movements have had an almost "revolutionary" impact on the legal system, the criminal justice system, and the general public's awareness that this is a serious issue.

This chapter includes examples of the excellent information which is now produced and distributed by activist groups working to end violence in women's lives. The power and control wheel (developed by battered women and formerly battered women to describe the violence in their lives) is a key tool for educating people that domestic violence is not "just about hitting" but is about "an ongoing pattern where one person controls many or all aspects of another person's life." Clever abusers who never physically hit their partners may gain control by using the children, controlling finances, playing mind games, and isolating their partner from support systems, but they do not leave physical bruises or break the law so they may never get "caught." In contrast, the equality wheel (also developed by battered and formerly battered women) serves as an inspiring model of what we want to work for in creating healthy relationships, striving to equalize rather than use or abuse power.

The 1998 National/State Sexual Assault statistics sheets were developed by the Wisconsin Coalition Against Sexual Assault as a part of resource development in conjunction with a statewide project to work with schools on sexual assault prevention.

Some people are resistant to seeing violence against women as a part of wider societal issues of oppression. Much of the media coverage and individual attention given to violence against women depoliticizes the issues by individualizing violence (it just happens to happen between individuals and is not representative of or affected by bigger issues), blaming women, and looking for simplistic (band-aid type) answers rather than addressing fundamental issues. In "Acquaintance Rape: A Simple Misunderstanding?" Theo Lesczynski critiques how "communication theory" is used to depoliticize date rape. It is interesting to compare the problematic sexual double standard (men want sex but women aren't supposed to show they do) Lesczynski identifies with the messages to girls that Tolman and Higgins identify in "How Being a Good Girl Can Be Bad for Girls" (see chapter 8).

In the same way that we have examined hormones and other products sold to women, Judith Bonderman, in "Armed by Fear: Self-Defense, Handguns and Women's Health," exposes how the gun industry has played on women's fears of violence and the image of "independent, take-charge women" to sell women one more dangerous product. Instead of doing anything to address violence against women, Bonderman concludes, "gun ownership actually increases a woman's vulnerability to gun injuries in her home."

Violence against women affects women in *all* communities. Although activists have long been careful to emphasize this fact, more attention has recently been paid to going beyond the rhetoric to explore the unique issues faced by different groups of women. There is enormous pressure on women in some communities to hide the violence. In such communities, a woman may feel even more isolated and hopeless than in a community in which violence is acknowledged. It has been shown that battered women's programs see only a tiny percentage of all the women affected by violence and domestic violence service providers are increasingly aware that they do a better job of serving some groups of women than others. For example, even though many women with disabilities, older women, and lesbians are hurt by domestic violence, disproportionately few victims/survivors in these groups make contact with domestic violence programs. Urgent attention needs to be paid to the unique barriers different women face in trying to end the violence in their lives.

Four articles address domestic violence issues for specific groups. It is hoped that these articles will stimulate the reader to think about particular barriers to ending violence which other women face. "A More Hidden Crime: Adolescent Battered Women" identifies that, because of a number of factors, the ramifications of violence for young women are often magnified, but that there are few resources or options available to them. "Anishinabe Values/Social Law Regarding Wife Battering" helps us see that "wife battering among the Ojibwe people emerged as a result of dissolution of traditional lifeways, including spirituality, the structures of government, laws, economics, relationships, values, beliefs, morals, and philosophy that were in place in the pre-reservation era."

The article by Diana Courvant and Loree Cook-Daniels, "Trans and Intersex Survivors of Domestic Violence: Defining Terms, Barriers, and Responsibilities" (which includes a very helpful definition of terms) helps us think through the barriers to living safely which are at work for many trans and intersex people. A fundamental issue for domestic violence programs which is important for many survivors, that of gender-segregated services, is a major obstacle for this group of survivors. The authors outline many suggestions for how to improve services for trans and intersex survivors.

Demonstrating the problem that systems which make some women safer may not serve other women, "Not a Black and White Issue" addresses the fact that many women of color are revictimized by the police and criminal justice system. The article thoughtfully explores the difficult issue of Black women's organizing against violence against women when Black men are so disproportionately affected by violence themselves. It also introduces us to the African American Task Force on Violence

Against Women which plans to build community-controlled programs to help abused women. (Also see the section on domestic violence and Asian Pacific Island women, in chapter 4.)

Other articles in this chapter more specifically address the *new* issue of the health system's response to violence against women. Although women who were victims/survivors of violence have long identified violence as a major health issue and have been aware of how violence impacted on their mental and physical health, the health system has been notoriously poor at addressing violence issues and has often actually played a dangerous role in revictimizing survivors of violence. As articles in this chapter demonstrate, the good news is that the health system has now "discovered" that violence against women is an issue the health system must respond to. In "The Unique Role Health Workers Can Play in Recognizing and Responding to Battered Women," I (Nancy Worcester) outline the key issues I teach health practitioners about their *appropriate* roles. However, I see challenges ahead and getting the health system to see violence as a health issue may have been the easy part of the struggle; making sure the health system's response to battered women is appropriate and that it empowers women to find ways to end the violence in their lives may be even harder work. The dangers of medicalizing violence against women are addressed in "Health System Response to Battered Women: Our 'Successes' Are Creating New Challenges."

In "Surviving the Incest Industry," Louise Armstrong, one of the first incest survivors to break the silence about incest (many years ago), examines the dangers of one more women's health issue being medicalized and she describes what has gone drastically wrong with the medical response to incest. In the "capitalism-compatible incest industry" Armstrong sees that this political issue has been personalized so that personal growth of the survivor—not social change—becomes the answer, and in a trend which sounds distinctly like the very popular co-dependency concept (see chapter 5), the victim—not the abuser—is held responsible for violent behavior. In contrast to the individualistic "get the victim to adjust to a sick society" approach critiqued by Armstrong, Fiona Rummery's article in Chapter 4 describes how feminist therapy can provide incest survivors with appropriate supportive services to empower them to actively and consciously confront the legacy of their histories of abuse.

Many of the key issues described in the articles on health system response to violence are summarized in "The Medical Power and Control Wheel" and "The Empowerment (Advocacy) Wheel" at the end of the chapter. Building on the analysis of the battered women's movement, Amanda Cosgrove and Kevin Fullin, M.D., of the Kenosha, Wisconsin Hospital Based Domestic Violence Project have changed the power and control and equality wheels (pp. 529 + 530) into tools which health workers can use to determine whether their response to victims/survivors is abusing their power (medical power and control) or whether they are using their positions to advocate for women and help them end the violence in their lives.

Continuum of Family Violence
from Alaska Dept. of Public Safety

PHYSICAL → pushing punching slapping kicking throwing objects choking using weapons homicide/suicide → **DEATH**

VERBAL EMOTIONAL → name calling criticizing "you're no good" ignoring yelling isolation humiliation → **SUICIDE**

SEXUAL → unwanted touching sexual name calling unfaithfulness false accusations forced sex hurtful sex → **RAPE**

Without some kind of help, the violence usually gets worse. The end result can be death.

Power and Control Wheel

by the Domestic Abuse Intervention Project, Duluth MN

DOMESTIC ABUSE
INTERVENTION PROJECT
206 West Fourth Street
Duluth, Minnesota 55806
218-722-4134

Based on the "Power and Control Wheel" and the "Equality Wheel" by the Domestic Abuse Intervention Project. Reprinted by permission of the Domestic Abuse Intervention Project and the Domestic Violence Project, Inc.

Equality Wheel

by the Domestic Abuse Intervention Project, Duluth, MN

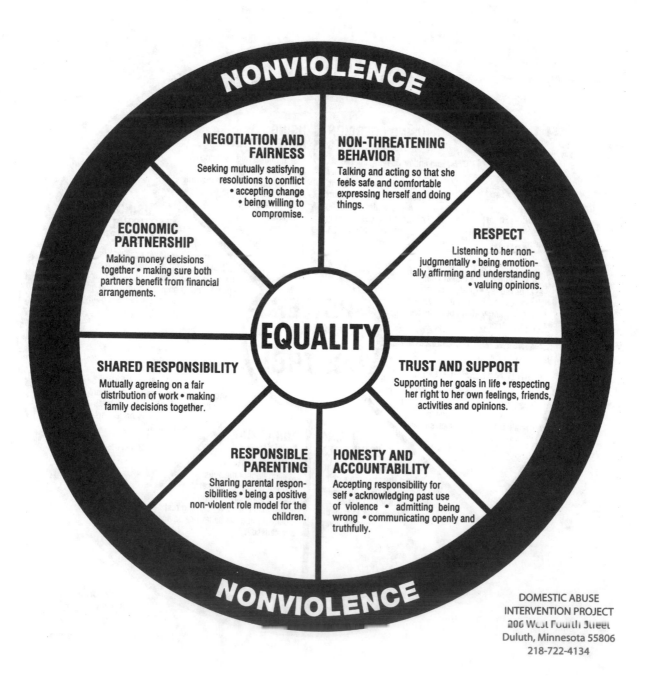

DOMESTIC ABUSE
INTERVENTION PROJECT
206 West Fourth Street
Duluth, Minnesota 55806
218-722-4134

Fact Sheet: National/State Sexual Assault Statistics

compiled by the Wisconsin Coalition Against Sexual Assault (1998)

Rate of Occurrence

- There were 6,020 sexual assaults reported in Wisconsin in 1996.
- 13 percent of American women, or 12.1 million total, have survived at least one forcible rape.
- It is estimated that as many as 1 in 5 to 1 in 8 men have been sexually abused as children.
- 84 percent of survivors of completed rapes do not report the crime to the police.
- Rape is the most underreported crime in the United States.

Teens

- In 1996, 77 percent of the sexual assault survivors in Wisconsin were juveniles. More than 70 percent were age 15 or younger.
- 38 percent of date rapes nationwide happen to girls between the ages of 14 and 17.
- 61 percent of all rape cases occur before survivors reach the age of 18.
- The average age of a sexual assault offender in Wisconsin was 25, an average of 10 years older than the survivor.

Tolerance

- In a survey of 11- to 14-year-olds, 47 percent of the girls and 65 percent of the boys said it was acceptable for a boy to rape a girl if they had been dating for more than six months.
- In a survey of high school students, 56 percent of the girls and 76 percent of the boys believed forced sex is acceptable under some circumstances.

- In a survey of 11- to 14-year-olds, 41 percent of the girls and 51 percent of the boys said forced sex was acceptable if the boy "spent a lot of money" on the girl.
- In a 1996 University of Wisconsin-La Crosse and University of Wisconsin-Madison study of 769 adolescent boys, 24 percent reported they engaged in unwanted touching, 15 percent reported using sexually coercive tactics with a girl and 14 percent reported they had already been sexually assaultive in some way.
- The 1996 UW-La Crosse and UW-Madison study of 769 adolescent boys indicates overall sexual aggression increases with grade level. In 7th grade, one-third of 769 boys reported engaging in some type of sexually, aggressive behavior. In 9th grade, the percentage rose to about 50 percent, and in 11th grade, six out of ten boys had been sexually aggressive at least once.

Scenario

- 62 percent of sexual assaults take place in either the survivor's or perpetrator's home.
- Weapons were used in 12 percent of all Wisconsin sexual assaults.
- 92 percent of all sexual assaults in Wisconsin were perpetrated by someone known to the survivor. Only eight percent were strangers.
- About 75 percent of the men and at least 55 percent of the women involved in acquaintance rapes had been drinking or taking drugs prior to the assault.
- 68 percent of rapes occur between the hours of 6 p.m. and 6 a.m.
- Sexual assaults occur more frequently in summer months in Wisconsin.

Consequences

- Rape survivors are 4.1 times more likely to have contemplated suicide and 13 times more likely to attempt suicide than noncrime victims.
- Six percent of all Wisconsin sexual assault survivors suffered minor injuries; one percent were seriously injured.
- Perpetrators convicted of sexual assault spend an average of 2.9 years behind bars, or approximately 49 percent of the average sexual assault sentence.
- A suspect was arrested in 58 percent of the sexual assaults reported statewide. Of those arrested, 90 percent were referred to criminal or juvenile court.
- Nearly 31 percent of all rape survivors develop Post-Traumatic Stress Disorder in their lifetimes. Post-Traumatic Stress Disorder dramatically increases women's risk for major alcohol and drug abuse problems.
- Persons convicted of a felony sex offense who have been released after serving their sentence are required to register annually with the Wisconsin Department of Corrections as a sex offender. They must update all information contained in the Sex Offender Registry within 10 days of a change. Following discharge, registered sex offenders are required to be on the registry for at least 15 years.
- Persons convicted of felony sexual assault must provide a DNA sample to the state crime laboratory.

Sources

Sexual Assaults in Wisconsin 1996, Wisconsin Office of Justice Assistance, Statistical Analysis Center;

Rape In America: Report to the Nation, 1992;

Warshaw, Robin, *I Never Called It Rape,* 1988;

Young People's Attitudes Toward Acquaintance Rape, John A. Humphrey and Jacqueline W. White, *Acquaintance Rape: The Hidden Crime,* In A. Parrot and L. Bechhofer (Eds.), 1991;

Kerns, Donell M. and Small, Stephen, *Adolescent Male Sexual Aggression: Incidence and Correlates,* a paper presented at the Society for Research on Adolescence, Boston, MS, March 1996;

Mendel, Matthew Parynik, *The Male Survivor: The Impact of Sexual Abuse,* 1995;

Violence Against Women, Bureau of Justice Statistics, U.S. Department of Justice, 1994;

Greenfield, Lawrence A., *Prison Sentences and Time served for Violence,* Bureau of Justice Statistics, U.S. Department of Justice, 1995;

Wisconsin State Statutes

Acquaintance Rape: A Simple Misunderstanding?

by Theo Lesczynski

The anti-rape movement has taken hold across the U.S., including UW Madison. Our community sees activism including annual Take Back the Night marches, services for survivors, educational prevention projects for men and women, and awareness campaigns. For the person who is raped, there are now many resources, including Rape Crisis Centers, which didn't exist twenty years ago. However, the anti-rape movement has come under attack because of some of the positions, and even information, it uses. More fundamentally, this backlash is in reaction to the way basic power and control issues are being exposed, which our society is often not ready to face.

One of the most important accomplishments of anti-rape activism is the awareness that sexual violence is widespread in our society. Study after study report that a substantial percentage of women experience sexual assault at some point in their lives. Further, the anti-rape movement has also highlighted the fact that the overwhelming majority of women (around 90%) who experience sexual assault report that the perpetrator was someone they knew. This awareness introduced words like "acquaintance rape" and "date rape" into our vocabulary for the first time, breaking the common assumption that all rapists are strangers who wait in bushes and alleys.

In 1985, Mary Koss conducted a study that is now a landmark. Of the college women that Koss surveyed, 27.1 percent reported being victims of rape, defined either as forced, nonconsensual sex (15.3) or attempted rape (11.8). The women reported their experience as highly negative, and many resisted verbally (84%) or physically (70%). Since then, other studies have found similar results and find that the incidence of sexual assault varies little across race and class. However, many critics of this feminist scholarship criticize Koss' and others' studies, saying that they exaggerate the prevalence of sexual violence. The most often made criticism of Koss' finding is that although the experiences that women reported met the legal definition of rape, only 41 percent of them labeled their experiences as rape or as a crime. Nearly half described their experience as a "miscommunication."

Why did so many rape survivors fail to describe their experience as rape? Feminists suggest that this is because most people have a different idea of rape than the legal definition. A typical "rape script" involves a stranger attack, but most rapes are perpetrated by an acquaintance. The prevalence of self-defense courses for women may indirectly reinforce the notion that rape is purely an act of physical force by a disturbed individual. The idea of an acquaintance assault may not fit with a woman's definition of rape. Rather than describe her experience as a rape, and take on all the baggage of that all too often victim-blaming label, women may be more likely to explain it as a misunderstanding.

Increasingly we are seeing that communication theory is serving to substantiate this vein of thought. One primary example is the best seller, "You Just Don't Understand," by Deborah Tannen in 1990. Tannen, a linguistics professor at Georgetown University, claims that she has found that men and women speak in different sociolinguistic dialects, which she labels "genderlects." Women's dialect is characterized by an emphasis on connection and relationship, while men's conversation reflects their concern for independence and status. Miscommunication occurs between men and women because they come from different, but equally valid cultures. Tannen's solution to improve understanding is for men and women to learn more about the "other culture." Similar best sellers like, "Men are From Mars, Women are From Venus," have further popularized such gender-difference theories.

Miscommunication theory gets applied to sexual assault and rape in a way that is troubling. This theory is used to argue that sexual violence is frequently the outcome of "miscommunication" between individuals. On the one hand, men are thought to view the world in a more sexually oriented way and interpret signals differently, either because it is in their biological programming or because they have been socialized that way. Theorists explain that a sexual double standard (men want sex, but women aren't supposed to show they do) allows men to ignore assertive rejections, assuming they are token, or to reinterpret them as seductive. On the other hand, women are said to have poor communication skills, and fail to clearly say no. Therefore, acquaintance rape is an "unfortunate breakdown in communication," and the solution is to improve communication between the sexes. Some writers, such as conservative feminist Camille Paglia, have attempted to further blur the line of consent, saying that a woman going into a man's room alone is, in effect, consent.

Miscommunication research has been critiqued on a number of different levels. Critics point out that men and women do not spend most of their time in single sex environments, and most of the time they do understand each other. Other critics assert that these theories make the issue apolitical. Genderlect theory claims that both styles of communication are equally valid, without examining the real differences in power and outcome or acknowledging sexism. Not only do "male" patterns of speech tend to be dominant, men have more power and privilege in society, holding the vast majority of elected offices and management positions.

Yet, judging from the popularity of miscommunication theory bestsellers like "You Just Don't Understand," the ideas are attractive to many men and women. Two British scholars suggest that miscommunication theory serves several purposes for women. First of all, say Frith and Kitzinger, it avoids blaming men. A Ms. Magazine survey found that 25% of women still considered their attacker a friend. By attributing their rape or assault to a misunderstanding, women may not have to sacrifice their relationships. Second, it gives women a sense of control. By accepting part of the blame (not saying no clearly, dancing suggestively), then women can believe that they can prevent future rape. Finally, they suggest that it obscures power relations that give men the right to ignore women's protests, to be less skilled at interpreting women's communication, and to believe that women are a "mystery."

There are other complications in the issues of acquaintance rape. Feminist scholars have pointed out that the sexual double standard means that, while men are praised for being "studs" when they have sex, women are often not supposed to express sexual desire. Examinations of teenage women's experiences show that when women are not expected to say "yes," sometimes when they say "no," and are ignored by men, even *they* feel confused about whether they adequately expressed their rejection.

If the issue of consent continues to be muddled for both men and women, then how can we work to end rape? Programs educating women, through assertiveness training, can be empowering and can avert attempted rape, but it seems clear that there needs to be more done to reach men. The idea of acquaintance rape as "miscommunication" needs to be debunked and seen as oversimplifying, depoliticizing the issue, and shifting blame to individual women.

SOURCES

Articles:

"Talk About Sexual Miscommunication", Hannah Frith and Celia Kitzinger, *Women's Studies International Forum*, v. 20 July/August 1997, p. 517–528.

"Preventing Acquaintance Rape Through Education." Lonsway, Kimberly A. *Psychology of Women Quarterly*, v. 20, no. 2, June 1996, p. 229–265.

"Women's Appraisals of Sexual-Assault Risk in Dating Situations." Cue, Kelly L. et. al. *Psychology of Women Quarterly*, v. 20, No. 4, Dec 1996, p. 487–504.

"Social Reactions, Coping Strategies, and Self-Blame Attributions in Adjustment to Sexual Assault," Ullman, 1996.

'Fraternities and Collegiate Rape Culture—why are some fraternities more dangerous places for women?," A. Ayres Boswell and Joan Z. Spade. *Gender and Society*, v. 10, no. 2, April 1996, p. 133–147.

"Review Essay: Selling the apolitical," Senta Troemel-Ploetz, *Discourse & Society*, 1992, vol. 2(4), p. 489–502.

"How Being a Good Girl Can Be Bad for Girls," Tolman and Higgins, in "Bad girls"/"good girls": Women, sex and power in the nineties, Maglin and Perry, eds, New Brunswick, NJ: Rutgers university Press, 1996.

Books:

Sexual Assault on Campus: the problem and the solution. Carol Bohmer and Andrea Parrot. New York: Lexington Books; Toronto: Maxwell Macmillan Canada; New York: Maxwell Macmillan International, c1993.

I Never Called It Rape, Warshaw.

Date Rape. Mary E. Williams, editor. Greenhaven Press, Inc., San Diego, California. 1998. (collection of essays on the debate about date rape; articles by Paglia, Wilson, Roiphe).

Transforming a Rape Culture. ed. Brownmiller.

Armed by Fear: Self-Defense Handguns and Women's Health

Judith Bonderman, JD, MPH
Director
Advocacy for Victims of Gun Violence Clinic
The Catholic University of America
Columbus School of Law
Washington, D.C.

Today's crime wave has women looking over their shoulders at every turn; mass murderers, rapists in ski masks, robbers at automatic teller machines, car jackers, drug dealers, and drive-by shooters strike with guns bigger than ever. With 17,790 firearm homicides in the United States in 1992 alone,[1] the epidemic of gun violence has become a public health issue and galvanized the nation politically. As a result, legislators passed some long-needed interventions such as Brady Law-mandated waiting periods, background checks on gun purchases, and bans on assault weapons. But at the same time, the firearm industry profits from the public fear of violence.

This article first describes the gun industry's exploitation of fear to create an enormous new female market. It then explores the real risk to women from firearm-related deaths and violent crime, and concludes that gun ownership actually increases a woman's vulnerability to gun injuries in her home, without conferring a demonstrable protective benefit.

The Advertised Risk: Fear of Strangers

Facing a decline in gun sales and a lagging National Rifle Association (NRA) membership, the gun industry badly needed a new target in the late 1980s. The industry began courting the image of the independent, take-charge woman of the '90s, just as cigarette and beer manufacturers had done in their promotions a few years earlier. Smith & Wesson's advertising department identified its potential first-time female gun buyer as 25 to 40 years old, professional, with a combined household median income of $55,000.[2]

"Firearms are one of the last bastions of male dominance," according to Christopher Dolnack, marketing manager for Smith & Wesson. "It's OK for women to be CEOs of companies and go into space as astronauts, so why shouldn't they own guns?"[3] Gun enthusiasts claimed that the LadySmith .357 double-action revolver had "come to represent the very concept of strong, capable, self-sufficient modern women who own guns."[4]

In women's magazines such as *Ladies' Home Journal,* Colt's Manufacturing Company recommended that mothers be armed to protect their loved ones, just as one might have a home fire extinguisher to use for a fire. The picture of a young mother tucking her precious child into bed carried the admonition, "Self protection is more than your right . . . It's your responsibility." Colt's suggested the new All American Model 2000, "holding 15 rounds of 9 mm ammunition, yet small enough to be easily handled."[5]

The National Rifle Association ran full-page advertisements that played to women's natural and real fear of being raped and their strong instinct to protect their children from intruders. The text equated fear of crime with fear of strangers, and scorned the criminal justice system for failing to protect the law-abiding public:

- **"He's followed you for two weeks, He'll rape you in two minutes. Who cares?** A sudden spray of shattered glass. Brutal blows from a shadow. Then terror and torture eternity can't heal."[6]

Reprinted with permission from the Jacobs Institute of Women's Health (*Women's Health Issues,* Vol. 5, No. 1, 1995, pp. 3–7).

- **"You were beaten to death last night. Who cares?** Your home turned into hell by a drugged-up thug. Your kids heard your screams."[7]
- **"Your mother just surprised two burglars who don't like surprises. Who cares?** The next few minutes of mindless cruelty will leave her broken, perhaps silenced forever."[8]

The NRA's current "Refuse To Be A Victim" campaign features a white woman in her mid-30s nervously leading her young daughter through a shadowy parking garage towards a lone minivan. The message is simple: Because criminals may be lurking anywhere and women cannot count on law enforcement, personal protection is the answer.

Although the mainstream women's magazines will no longer accept the more extreme scare-tactic advertising, newsstands offer new specialty magazines like *Women's Self Defense* and *Women and Guns*. They include graphic personal accounts by crime victims, offer information on gun-training courses, and market new firearm products and accessories, such as leather gun purses and pistol packs in fashion colors sold by companies like Lady B Safe, Bang-Bang Boutique, and Feminine Protection. According to the gun industry, these advertisements work: Gallup Polls commissioned by Smith & Wesson indicated a doubling of the number of women considering buying a firearm between 1983 and 1986. Estimated female gun ownership was 12 million in 1989;[2] the NRA claims 20 million females own guns today.[9] By some accounts, American women spent $608 million on guns in 1993.[10] The Lady-Smith sells for around $400. Other brands are competitively priced.

The Real Risk for Women: Domestic Violence

The gun industry's campaign targets working women and single mothers who think guns will tip the odds in their favor when they are violently attacked by a strange man or an intruder. Ironically, white females, so prominently featured in gun advertisements, are the least likely victims of violence by strangers, and the lowest risk group for firearm deaths. Based on data reported in national crime statistics from 1976 to 1987, the likelihood of a female being killed by a stranger was truly low: four per 1 million person years.[11] The 1992 firearm death rate (homicides, suicides, and unintentional shootings) for white women was 3.6 per 100,000 population, compared with 8.0 per 100,000 for black females, 21.3 per 100,000 for white males, and 63.9 per 100,000 for black males.[1]

Also contrary to the suggestions of the gun advertisements, the greatest threat to the more than 2 1/2 million women who experience violence each year comes from within their circle of relatives, acquaintances, and friends, not from strangers. From 1976 to 1987, more than twice as many American women were shot and killed by their husbands, ex-husbands, or boyfriends as were murdered by strangers.[11] Similarly, more than two-thirds of all nonfatal crimes of violence (rape, robbery, aggravated assault, and simple assault) against women were committed by spouses, family or acquaintances, according to a Department of Justice analysis of 400,000 interviews of crime victims from 1987 to 1991. The average annual rate of female nonfatal victimizations by intimates, family members, and acquaintances was 14.1 per 1,000, compared with 5.4 per 1,000 for incidents in which the offender was a stranger. Females were more than 10 times more likely than men to be victimized by a spouse, ex-spouse, boyfriend, or girlfriend. Only 5% of all violent victimizations against men were family related.[12]

Earlier Department of Justice studies of violent crime by strangers and nonstrangers had comparable findings. A 1987 report found that most of the violent crimes by strangers (70%) were committed against males, and most crimes by relatives (77%) were committed against females. This study also found that only 4% of stranger to stranger incidents (male or female) occurred inside the victim's home, compared with 18% of crimes by acquaintances and 58% of crimes by relatives.[13]

Will the gun kept in the home for self-defense against strangers protect against the much greater threat of domestic violence? Possibly. But women who own firearms will just as likely end up facing a greater danger from their intimate partners. A gun in the home is theoretically accessible to all who live there and can be used against its owner as well as by her. In a 1992 study, Linda Saltzman and colleagues at the Centers for Disease Control and Prevention looked at the risk of death and nonfatal injury during family and intimate assaults and found that firearm-associated family and intimate assaults were 12 times more likely to be fatal than those not associated with firearms.[14]

In a recent case-control study, Dr. Kellermann and colleagues at the Emory Center for Injury Prevention found that having a gun in the home was a significant risk factor for homicide. Households with guns were 7.8 times more likely to have a firearm homicide at the hands of a family member or intimate acquaintance than homes without guns. The use of illicit drugs and alcohol was also an important independent risk factor for homicide in the home, as was a history of prior domestic violence.[15]

The Real Risk for Women: Suicides and Unintentional Injuries

Keeping guns for self-protection may be counter-productive for other reasons as well.[16] Victims of crime are only a portion of the total universe of gun injuries. In 1992, firearms killed 37,776 people in the United States: 17,790 homicides (47%), 18,169 suicides (48%), and 1,409 unintentional shootings (4%).[1] An examination of the subset of gun deaths occurring in the home reveals an even higher percentage of suicides. Using 6 years (1978-1983) of medical examiner's files from the pre-dominantly urban, white population of King County, Wash., Kellermann and Reay analyzed a total of 743 firearm related deaths. Fifty-four percent of the deaths (398) occurred in the residence where the gun was kept. Of these, there were 333 cases of suicide (83.7%), 50 homicides (12.6%), 12 unintentional gunshot deaths (3%), and three unknown intent but self-inflicted gun-shot wounds. Seven of the homicides were committed in self-defense during a family dispute. Two other homi-cides were characterized as self-defense against burglars breaking into the home. These two cases were the only ones that involved a stranger."[17]

The high rate of suicide is particularly troubling in the context of guns and domestic violence. Spousal abuse and battering has been identified as a major risk factor for suicide attempts: one abused woman in ten at-tempts suicide, many more than once.[18] If these women have easy access to a firearm in the home, their suicidal attempts are more likely to be fatal.[19] Studies comparing the lethality of various suicide methods found death oc-curred in 92% of suicide attempts with a firearm com-pared with 11% of cases of a drug overdose,[20] and the leading method of suicide has changed in the last few decades, from drugs to guns.

Finally, having a handgun, loaded and ready for use against intruders, may be recklessly dangerous behavior when there are children in the home. Studies show a marked increase in the risk for suicide among adoles-cents when guns are available in the home.[21] And the fre-quency of headlines such as "Boy, 3, Kills Self with Mom's Gun"[22] is tragic. The National Center for Health Statistics reports that 551 children and teenagers died in unintentional shootings in 1991. Many more children are seriously injured by firearms. A substantial percentage of the guns used in these incidents are found by children in their homes.[23] An even larger number of home secu-rity guns end up stashed in the bushes on children's playgrounds or confiscated from bookbags and lockers by school security guards.

Benefits of Guns in the Home: Fact or Fancy?

The gun magazines gloss over the risks of gun own-ership, while their pages are full of "true crime stories" extolling the virtues of keeping a gun for self-defense. How deceptive is this advertising? Can a case be made that the benefits of guns for self-defense are so strong that they outweigh the many documented risks?

Although many gun advocates believe that an armed civilian population will deter crime, the claim remains as unsubstantiated today as it was 20 years ago.[24] First, there is no consensus on how frequently victims use guns against criminals. The estimates of defensive firearm use range from 1 million incidents per year (more than the 931,000 violent crimes committed with handguns), calculated by criminologist Gary Kleck, to 65,000 incidents per year (about 1% of all victims of vi-olence) according to a National Crime Victimization Survey conducted by the U.S. Department of Justice.[25]

Assuming that the real number is somewhere be-tween the extremes, little data indicate how often or under what circumstances defensive gun use is success-ful. But common sense tells us that the outcome in any particular case is totally unpredictable and depends on the circumstances of the crime, the intent of the of-fender, other people present at the scene, the firepower of the opposing weapons, the shooting skill level of the parties, and so on. In the 1993 Kellermann study on homicides in the home, 184 victims (43.8%) attempted in some way to resist the crime, and 21 of these (5.0%) attempted unsuccessfully to use a gun in self-defense. The authors found "no evidence of a protective benefit from gun ownership in any subgroup, including one re-stricted to cases of homicide that followed forced entry into the house."[15]

Conclusion

Using very sophisticated communications tech-niques, firearm manufacturers and the gun lobby are hyping women's understandable fear of stranger vio-lence. They design simple, heuristic messages to turn general anxiety into feelings of personal vulnerability. They offer a one-time behavior—buying a gun—as an easy solution.

This strategy may be brilliant marketing, but it is detrimental to the health and safety of women. By focus-ing on the demographic group least likely to be victimized by violent crime committed by strangers, the gun industry pays no regard to women's real safety. By bringing self-defense handguns into their homes, women move themselves and their families into a higher risk category for gun injuries, without any proven countervailing benefit. Only the gun industry wins.

REFERENCES

1. Kochanek KD, Hudson BL. Advance report of final mortality statistics, 1992. NCHS Monthly vital statistics report 1994;43(6):17–8.

2. Pogrebin LC. Pistols for the women of America. The Nation. 1989:666.

3. Horovitz B. Gun makers spark outcry as they target women buyers. The Los Angeles Times 1992 Sept 1; Sect. B:5.

4. Jones S. The Ladysmith story continues. Women and Guns 1992;4:12–13.

5. Colt's Manufacturing Co. Self protection is more than your right . . . it's your responsibility [advertisement] Ladies Home Journal 1992;July.

6. NRA. He's followed you for two weeks [advertisement]. Roll Call: The Newspaper of Congress 1988 Jan 31.

7. NRA. You were beaten to death last night [advertisement]. The Washington Post 1988 Jan 27; Sect. A:15.

8. NRA. Your mother just surprised two burglars who didn't like surprises [advertisement]. The New York Times 1988 Jan 26; Sect. A:13.

9. Sugarmann J, Rand K. Cease fire: a comprehensive strategy to reduce firearms violence. Washington (DC): Violence Policy Center, 1994:19.

10. Prufer D. On violence, a special report. Self 1994;Aug:155.

11. Kellermann AL, Mercy JA. Men, women and murder: gender-specific differences in rates of fatal violence and victimization. J Trauma 1992;33:1–5.

12. Bachman R. Violence against women. A national crime victimization survey report. Washington (DC): Bureau of Justice Statistics, U.S. Department of Justice; 1994 Jan. Report No.:NCJ-145325.

13. Timrots AD, Rand MR. Violent crime by strangers and nonstrangers. Washington (DC): Bureau of Justice Statistics Special Report. U.S. Department of Justice; 1987 Jan. Report No.: NCJ-103702.

14. Saltzman LE, Mercy JA, O'Carroll PW, Rosenberg ML, Rhodes PH. Weapon involvement and injury outcomes in family and intimate assaults. JAMA 1992;267:3043–7.

15. Kellermann AL, Rivara FP, Rushforth NB, Banton JG, et al. Gun ownership as a risk factor for homicide in the home. N Engl J Med 1993;329:1084–91.

16. Taubs G. Violence epidemiologists test the hazards of gun ownership. Science 1992;258:213–5.

17. Kellermann AL, Reay DT. Protection or peril? An analysis of firearm-related death in the home. N Engl J Med 1986;314:1557–60.

18. Stark E, Flitcraft AH. Spouse abuse. In: Rosenberg ML, Fenley MA (eds). Violence in America: a public health approach. New York: Oxford University Press, 1991:123–57.

19. Kellermann AL, Rivara FP, Somes G, et al. Suicide in the home in relation to gun ownership. N Engl J Med 1992;327:467–72.

20. Card JJ. Lethality of suicide methods and suicide risk: two distinct concepts. Omega Journal of Death and Dying 1974;5(1):37–45.

21. Brent DA, Perper JA, Allman CJ, Moritz GM, Wartella ME, Zelenak JP. The presence and accessibility of firearms in the homes of adolescent suicides. JAMA 1991;266:2989–95.

22. The Atlanta Journal/Atlanta Constitution 1993 Mar 8; Sect. B:2.

23. Wintemute GJ, Teret SP, Kraus JF, et al. When children shoot children, 88 unintended deaths in California. JAMA 1987;257:3107–9.

24. Yeager MG. How well does a handgun protect you and your family? Washington (DC): U.S. Conference of Mayors; 1976 Tech. Report No. 2.

25. McDowell D, Wiersema B. The incidence of civilian defensive firearm use. College Park (MD): Institute of Justice and Criminology, University of Maryland, Violence Research Group: 1992 Dec. Discussion Paper No. 10 (unpublished).

A More Hidden Crime:
Adolescent Battered Women

by Nancy Worcester

Domestic violence has often been referred to as our nation's most hidden crime. However, after 15 years of activism and the establishment of more than 1000 battered women's shelter programs around the country, the battered women's movement has made many people and community services aware of the fact that huge numbers of women are entrapped in relationships of ongoing abuse of power, control, and physical coercion. The FBI estimates that a woman is battered every 15–18 seconds in this country and that approximately one of every three women experiences some physical violence in her long-term relationship(s). The pervasiveness of the violence may be best represented by the statement that one of every five women probably experiences five or more serious battering incidents each year.

Just as there is finally a public consciousness of the magnitude of the problem of women being battered, we are discovering an even more hidden, perhaps even more prevalent crime—violence against adolescent women. It turns out that most of the understanding of the dynamics of power and control in intimate relationships gained from the battered women's movement applies as much to adolescent women in dating relationships as it does to adult women. Tragically, the ramifications of violence for younger women are often exaggerated by a number of factors, but there are far fewer resources and options available to adolescent than adult women who are trying to end the violence in their lives.

Working to prevent violence in young people's lives must be a highest priority for any of us committed to creating a better world for the next generation and to helping young women maximize on their full potential. The isolation and lowered self-esteem which are so often a *consequence* of violence will have exaggerated ramifications for a young woman if they cause her to limit or eliminate skill-building, career opportunities or educational opportunities which could affect the rest of her life. (It is important to emphasize that the isolation, lowered self-esteem, and unhealthy coping mechanisms which are often observed in abused women are predictable *consequences* of violence and are not the *cause* of the violence. Confusing a consequence of violence with a cause can lead to dangerous, victim-blaming misunderstandings of the violence.)

If a woman is experiencing violence in her dating relationship(s), it will almost certainly be related to many other issues in her life. Anyone working with adolescents will benefit from seeing the connections between violence and the issues they already address. Why she is not always able to show up for study group, why she "had to go" to a concert instead of studying the night before an important exam, why she is no longer best friends with "the nice girl who seemed to have such a positive influence on her" or why she "suddenly" started dressing in a way which always or never shows off her figure may be explained by knowing that a young woman is in a relationship where someone else is taking control over almost all aspects of her life. Health educators need to recognize that many women are beaten up if they try to insist that male partners wear a condom or abstain from sexual activity. Because battering so often starts or accelerates during pregnancy and because sexual assault and other forms of violence are so intimately connected, anyone who works with adolescent pregnancy or sexual assault issues needs to be aware of the connections.

Ironically, many women learn about motherhood and battering at exactly the same time. Retrospective studies show that 25% of battered women experienced their first physical abuse during a pregnancy and that 40–60% of battered women were abused during a pregnancy or during pregnancies. The consequences are a much higher rate of miscarriage, stillbirth, premature delivery, and low birth weight infants in battered than non-battered women. The problem may be even more exaggerated in pregnant teens. A study looking specifically at physical abuse during teen pregnancy found that 26% of pregnant teens reported they were involved with a man who physically hurt them and 40–60% said that the battering had begun or escalated since their boyfriends knew they were pregnant. This study also provides an urgent reminder that services are not addressing the issue of violence for adolescent women: 65% of pregnant teens had not talked to anyone about the abuse.[1]

Looking at the continuum of violence issues (The Power and Control and Equality Wheels by the Duluth Domestic Abuse Intervention Project (see pp. 529 & 530) and the Continuum of Family Violence Chart (see p. 528), by the Alaska Dept. of Public Safety are particularly useful), it becomes apparent how a range of forms of violence—physical, verbal, emotional, and sexual— are used by abusers to dominate their partners. The more subtle forms of sexual violence (unwanted touching, sexual name calling, unfaithfulness or threat of unfaithfulness, saying "no one else will ever love you", false accusations) are clearly emotionally as well as sexually controlling. These need to be identified as "violence issues" which are related to, and can escalate into, unwanted sex, unprotected sex, hurtful sex and other forms of sexual assault. Sexual violence is often the expression of violence which is the most painful for a woman to discuss. Emotional abuse is almost always present if there are other forms of abuse in a relationship but a clever abuser may achieve sufficient control by emotional abuse without ever resorting to other forms. Women consistently say that emotional abuse is the hardest form to identify (Is this really happening? Is this abuse? Am I making too much of this?) but recognize it as the form of abuse which has the most impact on their lives and their view of themselves. Many women who have been in life-threatening situations say, "The physical battering was nothing compared to the daily emotional abuse." Helping young women see the interconnectedness of verbal, emotional, physical, and sexual power and control issues may be the most useful information in empowering them to end *all* forms of violence in their lives.

By the time adolescents start experimenting with their own dating relationships, they have been bombarded with messages that violence against women is tolerated and even encouraged and that dominance, aggression, and abuse of power and control are appropriate masculine behaviors which are rewarded by society. Today's young people have been exposed to a tolerance and perpetuation of male violence which is unique to this generation. They grew up in the era when the average child was watching 24 hours of television a week

with children's programming averaging 15.5 violent acts per hour. By the time they reach 18, the average US adolescent has witnessed approximately 26,000 murders, in their own homes, via the tv screen.[2]

The role of television in sex-role socialization and the perpetuation of male violence has been grossly exaggerated for today's young people because changes in federal regulations, in the early 1980s, allowed the sale of toys directly connected to tv shows, removed regulations limiting the amount of advertising allowed on children's programming, and ruled that product-based shows were legal. The result was a totally new integration of the tv and toy industries. By 1986 all of the ten best selling toys had shows connected with them and by 1988, 80% of children's tv programming was produced by toy companies. Parallel marketing promoted definitions of masculinity and femininity as clearly defined as the distinct lines of boys' toys vs. girls' toys. Because of the new integration of tv and toys, today's young people did not learn to explore their own creativity or imagination in healthy ways but instead learned to "act out their scripts" as dominant and competitive *or* caring, helpless, and concentrating on appearance, either as GI Joe or Ghostbusters vs. Barbie or My Little Pony.[3]

With electronic video games, an even newer and unstudied phenomena, young people get to act out and be rewarded for playing their violent roles. The direct participation in "performing" the violence of video games is predicted to magnify whatever effect more passive tv viewing has on one's acceptance or perpetuation of violence. In a violence promoting and accepting culture, it is not surprising to find that *most* video games are very violent (a sampling of 120 machines in three arcades in Madison, Wisconsin, found that more than 70 involved either hand-to-hand combat or shooting to kill enemies) and that the most popular games in an arcade are the most violent.[4]

Consequently, *unlearning* the tolerance of violence and *learning* how to achieve violence-free, equal relationships are skills which are now as crucial to *teach* young people as reading, writing, math and the use of computers. The way people learn, in their earliest experimentation, to be in intimate relationships can set the pattern for what they expect in future relationships. It is a time when the highest standards should be set! Adolescents need to see models of healthy, equal, violence-free relationships, in order to aim for that in their own lives and *to be able to model that for their peers.*

At this stage, many teens do not have the knowledge or skills to prevent or react against violence in their own lives or in their friends' lives. In fact, exactly the opposite is much more likely. Many young women have said that even when they have told friends they were being hurt by their boyfriends, the response was that they were lucky to have boyfriends. There is enormous peer pressure not to break up. Many teens regard violence as a normal part of dating and have no idea they deserve better. Extreme possessiveness, jealousy, dominance, and not being "allowed" to break up get wrongly identified as desirable, positive signs of caring, love and commitment, rather than strong warning signs that they are in an unhealthy, potentially dangerous relationship.

Figuring out what to expect in relationships may be particularly confusing for anyone who grew up in a home where there was violence. Many young men only see abusing males (in reality and in the media) as role models. Many young women who told their mother about being hurt by their boyfriend, have heard, "you have to learn to take the bad and the good in a relationship to make it work."

Many teens who have grown-up in violent homes face the difficulty of trying to figure out how they want to be in their own young adult relationships while they are still learning (or not learning) to cope with being affected by the violence with which they grew up. The battered women's movement has very effectively identified that when a woman is battered, the children are almost always affected by the violence. Seventy-five percent of women who are battered in this country have children living at home. Children in homes where domestic violence occurs are physically abused or seriously neglected at a rate 1500% higher than the national average in the general population.[5] Even witnessing domestic violence can have a tremendous impact on young people and may result in symptoms very similar to those seen in people who have been abused.[6] Helping these young people learn healthy relationship skills can be particularly challenging as many teens do not recognize the impact the violence in their homes has had on them and many teens do not want to talk about witnessing or experiencing abuse.[7]

Particularly crucial to how we help young people learn relationship skills *and* acknowledge that violence in their lives may have already influenced their attitudes and behaviors is how we address the impact of the "intergenerational transmission of violence." There is a confusing body of work which examines how the cycle of violence can be passed on through the generations. We now know the old "dad beats mom, mom beats the children, and the children beat the pets" picture was much too simplistic and inaccurate. Increasingly, it is being shown that the person beating mom may also be the one beating the children and protecting the mother is often the best way to protect the children.[9] Although research is inconsistent in documenting the rates of intergenerational transmission of violence, there is a consistent trend which shows that boys who witness domestic violence as children are more likely to batter their female partners as adults than are men from nonviolent homes.

How we use this information can be a key factor in determining whether we help break the intergenerational transmission of violence or actually contribute to its perpetuation. Too much of the literature deals with this data as if were inevitable. Central to breaking the pattern is addressing and researching a different set of questions. *If* 30% of boys who witness violence become abusers, the question must be asked, "What can we learn from the 70% who witness violence but do not become abusers?" What factors help young people who have witnessed violence learn to resist violent behavior? Young people from violent homes who have experienced the ugliness of violence and have learned to value non-violent relationships can be exactly the people most committed to breaking the cycle of violence and can be incredibly effective peer leaders.

Most important, young people must *never* learn that violence is inevitable. Many dating violence resources (including some of the materials I highly recommend on other aspects) include information on the intergenerational transmission of violence without making it clear that the cycle can be broken. Information on warning signs of potential abusers almost always include "boys who grew up in violent homes". What does it feel like to see that information if you are a young man who witnessed violence at home? We must make certain that none of our materials or our messages ever contribute towards a young man feeling that he is destined to be violent.

Studies on dating violence consistently show that many teens in violent relationships have not talked to *any* adults about the violence in their lives. We need to start identifying the barriers which have made us so ineffective on this issue and acknowledge that we are only starting to have the language and tools for opening a dialogue on dating violence.

The good news is that a wide range of excellent resources, curricula, and videos have been produced on dating violence issues and violence-free relationships in recent years. It's a very exciting stage to be working on this issue because no one needs to "start from scratch". However, work needs to be done to make the excellent resources and services available to, and appropriate for, many more teens. Few of the resources address the issue in a way that has any meaning for lesbian, gay or bisexual teens or for young people of color. Many of the materials seem to have the underlying assumption that children grow up in homes where there is one male and one female adult. Special issues for teens with disabilities need to be addressed because of both the high rate of sexual assault of people with disabilities and the complexities of dating which arise from the myth that people with disabilities are "asexual". The obsession with body image and a very narrow definition of attractiveness can also be particularly cruel and abusive in adolescence.

"You deserve to be treated with respect."

"You are not alone if someone is hurting you. There are excellent resources to help you end the violence in your life."

These messages which we have been giving adult battered women for the last 15 years are now the same messages we have to give to much younger women.

REFERENCES

1. "Violence During Teen Pregnancy: Health Consequences for Mother and Child" by Judith McFarlane, in *Dating Violence,* edited by Barrie Levy, Seal Press, 1991, pp. 136–141.

2. *Boys Will Be Boys (Breaking the Link Between Masculinity and Violence)* by Myriam Miedzian, Doubleday, New York, 1991.

3. *Who's Calling the Shots? How to Respond Effectively to Children's Fascination with War Play and War Toys* by Nancy Carlsson-Paige and Diane E. Levin, New Society Publishers, Santa Cruz, CA, 1990.

4. "Decapitate Your Enemy for 50 Cents," "Most Violent Games Draw Most Attention," and "Researcher Says TV Programs Undoubtedly Affect Children" by Nathan Seppa, in *Wisconsin State Journal* January 3, 1993, pp. 1A & 7A.

5. National Women's Abuse Prevention Project, Washington, D.C.

6. A video of Susan Schechter speaking on "Battered Women and Abused Children: Interests in Common or Interest in Conflict?" is available from the WI. Domestic Violence Training Project. (See below.)

7. Ann Brickson, Briarpatch, Madison. WI.

8. "Exploring the Complexities of Working on Children's Issues" by Nancy Worcester, in *Wisconsin Coalition Against Domestic Violence Newsletter,* December 1988.

9. *Health Care Services for Battered Women and Their Abused Children* (manual about the AWAKE—Advocacy for Women and Their Kids in Emergencies Program), Boston's Children's Hospital, 300 Longwood Avenue, Boston, MA 02115 ($22), 1992.

A list of resources is available from the Wisconsin Domestic Violence Training Project, 313 Lowell Hall, 610 Langdon St., Madison WI 53703. Barrie Levy's books *In Love and In Danger* (A Teen's Guide to Breaking Free of Abusive Relationships), *Dating Violence—Young Women in Danger* and her curriculum, *Skills for Violence-Free Relationships* are particularly recommended.

Power and Control and Equality wall charts are available ($6 @) from the Minnesota Program Development, Inc. 206 W. 4th St., Duluth, MN 55806 and the "Continuum of Family Violence" is available in *Domestic Violence—A Guide for Health Care Professionals* ($10) from the New Jersey Department of Community Affairs, Domestic Violence Prevention Program (CN-0801), 101 S. Broad St., Trenton, NJ 08625-0801.

Anishinabe Values/Social Law Regarding Wife Battering

from Indigenous Woman

In pre-reservation life, there were explicit social laws to deal with the rare occurrence of wife battering. The Ojibwe term used to identify a wife batterer is "Metattiggwa Ish" meaning "he who fights his wife always," implying that he is irrational, petty, and jealous. Once a man battered his wife, she was free to make him leave her lodge if they lived among her people. He'd leave her lodge and from then on be known as a man whose wife had broken the household because of abuse. From then on, he could never "marry" again. When a "married" woman was abused by her husband, her brothers were obligated by social law to retaliate against him by not speaking to him, beating him or even killing him. If the couple lived among the man's relatives, his parents were obligated to get her away and return her to her people.

In a situation in which a household had been broken because of abuse, it was not known as a divorced family as it is today. It was viewed as a broken household and the woman was viewed as having self-respect in leaving the destructive relationship behind. In a broken household, the sons could go with the father, the daughters with the mother.

A man who battered his wife was considered irrational and thus could no longer lead a war party, a hunt or participate in either. He could not be trusted to behave properly and thus may bring harm to the other men involved. The wife batterer could no longer own a pipe. If he somehow did, no one would smoke it with him. He was thought of as contrary to Anishinabe law and lost many privileges of life and many roles in Ojibwe society and the societies within.

A man who killed his wife was considered as not Ojibwe anymore. He had broken a primary law of Anishinabe Society, that is an Ojibwe NEVER kills another Ojibwe. He became an enemy of the people. His name would never be spoken again. He would cease to exist. The children of this household would be given to another family so they would not be known as coming from a man who did not exist, and so they would not be known as the offspring of such a person.

The People: "The Relatives Living Together"

In pre-reservation Ojibwe society beliefs such as the preceding were handed down by ALL the people to the coming generations. For a clan/group to live in unity and cooperation, it was necessary for all to live according to the same beliefs, laws, and values. When people living together do not share the same beliefs, laws and values, there will be confusion as to what is considered proper behavior; individuals will not have a foundation from which to guide their behavior.

Reservation Ojibwe Society

The perspective can be taken that the daily occurrence of wife battering among the Ojibwe people emerged as a result of the dissolution of traditional lifeways, including spirituality, the structures of government, laws, economics, relationships, values, beliefs, morals, and philosophy that were in place in the pre-reservation era, prior to the coming of the white man.

Wife battering, as we have seen, was neither accepted nor tolerated among the Anishinabe people until after the freedom to live Ojibwe was subdued. Wife battering emerged simultaneously with the disintegration of Ojibwe ways of life and the beginning use of alcohol. The behavior of the Ojibwe people under the influence of alcohol is often totally contrary to Anishinabe values. It is especially contrary to the self discipline previously necessary to the development of Ojibwe character.

There is no single philosophy among the people in today's society regarding the social illness of wife battering. Many have forgotten or DID NOT RECEIVE THE TEACHINGS of the social laws surrounding it. In the old Ojibwe society, society itself was responsible for what took place within it; today that is not so. What is the evidence of that statement? The harmful, destructive, traumatic cycle of domestic violence that is befalling the Anishinabe Children of the Nation.

Today we have lost a lot of the traditions, values, ways of life, laws, language, teachings of the Elders, respect, humility as Anishinabe people because of the European mentality we have accepted. For the Anishinabe people to survive as a Nation, together we must turn back the pages of time. We must face reality, do an evaluation of ourselves as a people—why we were created to live in harmony with one another as Anishinabe people and to live in harmony with the Creator's creation.

Trans and Intersex Survivors of Domestic Violence: Defining Terms, Barriers, and Responsibilities

by Diana Courvant · Loree Cook-Daniels

In the early 1970's, as campaigns to raise awareness of domestic violence were first beginning in the United Kingdom and the United States, domestic violence was seen as a problem of male batterers and female survivors. Although this model still fits the vast majority of cases of domestic violence, it is no longer seen as fully describing the problem. In the 1980's, recognition spread of battering in lesbian relationships, and in the 1990's gay men awakened to battering within their own community. Therefore, over the course of the 25 years of the domestic violence survivors' movement, many communities have evolved programs to assist in meeting the needs of both male and female survivors, and developed intervention programs targeted to male and to female batterers. Within this framework, some few heterosexual men have also received survivor services.

However, even this expanded framework consistently neglects the growing class of survivors who transcend stereotypes of gender expression or physical sex. If these survivors have any interaction at all with supportive agencies, they nearly always confront staff or volunteers who lack even the necessary vocabulary to begin to understand the every day experience of these survivors. So let's begin with that vocabulary.

Defining Terms

Like the water surrounding the proverbial fish oblivious to it, all the various aspects of gender are invisible to most of us. Virtually all of us were given a *gender assignment*—boy or girl—by medical personnel at our birth, based on a visual inspection of our genitals (by using the genitals, doctors hope to match the gender assignment with the child's sex, the genetic or anatomical categories of male and female). Most of us grew into these gender assignments fairly smoothly, adopting them as our own *gender identity:* our personal view of our own gender. *Gender attribution* recognizes that what I think of myself isn't always what counts; this term refers to what someone assumes about my gender when they look at me. On the opposite side of the observer-observed dyad is *gender expression.* This is something I do (a behavior, the choice of clothing, etc.) that influences or is intended to influence another's perception of my gender. A *gender role* is the aggregate of a society's assumptions, expectations and mores for how a person of a particular gender is supposed to act. All of these terms are more likely to be heard in a therapist's office than a shelter, but knowing them can help one understand the complexities facing those who transcend stereotypes of gender expression or physical sex: those who are usually known as intersexual, transsexual, transvestite or cross-dressing, or transgendered persons.

An *intersex* or *intersexual* person has a body with external sexual characteristics typical of both male and female bodies. Nonetheless, in our society, children who are born intersexual are nearly always assigned a male or female gender role, although because of external sexual ambiguities, that assignment may not occur at birth. Intersexual children in the United States typically have their genitals surgically altered before age three to conform to gender assignment.

A *transsexual* is someone who lives full-time in the gender identity "opposite" the gender assignment they were given at birth. Currently in Western European and North American countries, transsexuals usually obtain medical intervention (hormones and surgeries) to alter their bodies to more closely conform physically to their gender identity. Some cultures have roles or institutions that allow what we would call transsexuals to live in their preferred gender identify, often without requiring them to seek medical intervention. Transsexuals may be either female-to-male (FtM) or male-to-female (MtF). They may be "post-operative" or "post-op," meaning they've had one or more surgeries to alter their body's sexual characteristics; "pre-op," meaning they have not yet had any or all such surgeries; or "non-op," a term that acknowledges that some transsexuals feel they can live out their gender identify without altering their bodies surgically.

Unlike transsexuals, *transvestites'* and *crossdressers'* gender assignment and gender identity match. However, they occasionally wear clothes that social custom says belong to the "opposite" gender role. While crossdressed, an individual might take on a name and/or mannerisms associated with that "opposite" gender role, although this is not always the case.

Transgender is a recently-coined term whose definition is still in some flux. Some people use it to refer to people who don't fit any of the above categories but whose gender identity also won't fit into the society's two given roles of male or female. Others include transsexuals and transvestites under the transgender, or *trans,* umbrella. For the remainder of this paper, this larger definition will be used.

Trans and Intersex Survivors

In preliminary data, the Gender, Violence, and Resource Access Survey of trans and intersex individuals found 50% of respondents had been raped or assaulted by a romantic partner, though only 62% of those raped or assaulted (31% of the total sample) identified themselves as survivors of domestic violence when explicitly asked. Of those who were raped or injured, 23% (12% of the total sample) required medical attention for injuries inflicted by a romantic partner. All of those who received treatment self-identified as survivors of domestic violence when asked.

Clearly, trans and intersex survivors exist. Like other domestic violence survivors, they need the help of service agencies, including shelters, to free themselves from abusive partners and to learn to recognize future abusive relationships before the abuse becomes extreme. Unfortunately, few ever manage to access these services openly. There are many reasons why so few trans and intersex survivors are served by the community that typically aids and advocates for survivors of domestic violence. The next section will discuss these barriers.

Barriers

Despite feminist strides, ours is still not a society that supports and rewards individuals who violate gender norms. Little boys are still kept in line with phrases like, "Don't be a sissy." Little girls and particularly older girls face fierce disapproval if they behave or dress too "boyishly." This early punishment for simply expressing gender identity leaves many scars, but the experiences that lead trans and intersexual domestic violence survivors to believe that it's normal for "people like me" to live with abuse only increase in magnitude as the trans or intersex survivor matures.

Perhaps the most damaging force is the one that teaches transgender and intersexual persons that "helping" institutions are often anything but, and may actually harm them. In Washington D.C., an MtF trans woman named Tyra Hunter, the victim of an accident, was allowed to die by paramedics and emergency room staff who discovered her trans status, then decided to mock her rather than provide aid. In the central United States, an FtM trans man named Brandon Teena was raped by two men who discovered his trans status. Upon reporting the rape to the local sheriff's department, the sheriff asked Brandon, "What are you?" and refused to investigate. Brandon's rapists returned to his house to kill him and two of his friends for reporting the rape. At an annual convention of the Society for the Scientific Study of Sexuality one doctor related the case of a girl child with a large clitoris sexually mutilated by her father, who was angered at the phallic proportions of his infant daughter's clitoris. Amazingly, this doctor completed the child's mutilation by performing a clitoridectomy and was using her story to justify surgery on infants in similar situations, rather than healing the child and calling attention to her abuse. Although these stories' power is anecdotal and not statistical, they and others like them are widely known and retold among trans and intersex individuals. Because of the extreme cruelty and casual indifference of authorities and institutions exemplified in these common stories, a trans or intersex survivor may fear an unknown service institution more than a familiar abuser.

A second level of fear trans and intersex survivors face when seeking help is the possibility that their trans or intersex status, if previously hidden, might become known and expose them to more violence, as in the Brandon Teena case. Exposure might also lead to the loss of a job, as very few jurisdictions provide employment discrimination protection to trans and intersexed persons, and stories of job loss or workplace harassment upon exposure are legion.

Should a trans or intersex survivor decide to brave these risks and seek help despite them, she or he faces other barriers. Some information suggests that trans and intersex survivors have frequently been multiply abused for years or decades. Often a trans or intersex survivor has a unique body and/or a unique vulnerability to the emotional aftermath of sexual violence; either can make difficult or impossible discussing this abuse with an unfamiliar victims' advocate.

Related to this problem is the shame and self-doubt that is endemic in these communities, due to the pressures trans and intersex persons have felt from their earliest years to deny their feelings and conform to others' expectations. Adding to this shame and self-doubt is the widespread perception that trans and intersex individuals are mentally ill. This popular stigma of mental illness is furthered by the existence of Gender Identity Disorder (GID) in the DSM-IV, the guidebook to diagnosis of mental illness and personality disorders, but this perception of mental illness is independent of the DSM-IV and is often strongly felt by those completely unfamiliar with the GID diagnosis. Abusers use this shame and self-doubt against their trans and intersex victims to undermine their victims' perceptions and to convince them that no one else will want them. Combined with stories of dating violence (such as that of Chanelle Picket, an MtF trans woman who was recently murdered by a date enraged at the revelation of her trans status) these "warnings" can convince trans and intersex survivors that they are lucky just to have a partner who doesn't kill them.

Finally, two other barriers that affect some trans and intersex survivors deserve attention. One is the barrier that children present. Although every domestic violence survivor with children worries about the safety and custody of those children, the problem is much greater for trans parents, who know that because of prejudice and ignorance about trans persons, courts are extremely unlikely to grant them custody no matter how abusive the other parent is.

The other barrier is the gender segregation of survivor services. Virtually all trans survivors go through a significant period when they are in legal or medical transition. Some intersex survivors have a unique body that prevents identification with either a male or a female gender. Some trans individuals, including such notable examples as authors Kate Bornstein and Leslie Feinberg, have a gender identity and gender expression that is neither male nor female, but mixes elements of both. For all of these people, turning to a gender-segregated service agency may be inconceivable.

Barriers Specific to MtF Individuals

For those MtF individuals not raised in abusive homes, childhood social education rarely includes any information about domestic violence. An MtF child whose parents are disturbed by the child's femininity may glorify violence or minimize the child's trauma from any peer violence in an attempt to encourage behaviour deemed masculine. As an adult survivor, this may be translated into feelings of guilt for not fighting back in violent situations, reinforcing the common perspective of survivors that they are responsible for their own abuse.

The vast majority of resources for survivors of domestic violence targets women. While this benefits the few MtF individuals who have completed medical, legal and social transitions, it typically excludes the majority. Unfortunately, the few who do have resources nominally available often find themselves feared as invaders if they attempt to access women-based services. In San Francisco, one shelter that had made the decision to welcome openly trans women experienced a case where such a survivor was turned away by a shelter supervisor hired after the initial training. Other MtF survivors may refuse to seek shelter or assistance from women-centered agencies out of a respect for the fears or discomfort of non-trans and non-intersex female survivors. Others may avoid seeking help from those agencies out of low self-esteem or feelings that others will not perceive them as "real" women.

Lastly, MtF survivors battered by women often fear that their stories will not be believed. The existing dominant framework of domestic violence can make this type of violence among the most unexpected. Often it is difficult for survivors' advocates to envision this abuse even though the advocates know that the most important tools for control an abuser possesses are not physical.

Barriers Specific to FtM Individuals

Because their gender identity (and probably also their gender expression) is male, FtM individuals cannot be served by agencies that only serve women. Even if an FtM is lucky enough to be in a place where survivor services are offered to men, he may find himself facing incredulous "helpers." Although many people have heard of Christine Jorgenson or Renee Richards, few realize that FtM's exist. FtM's are so "invisible" that even professionals who are well-versed in trans issues often are surprised at the community's growing contention that there are roughly equal numbers of FtM's and MtF's. An FtM survivor may also hesitate to access services for men out of fear that the other survivors may discover his trans status and ridicule him or worse.

Many FtM's lived within the Lesbian community prior to their transition, and oftentimes their partners still identity as Lesbian and keep ties to that community. Since Lesbian communities are often tightly-interwoven and heavily involved in anti-domestic violence work, an FtM battered by a female partner may well fear that if he seeks help the battery may become public, he will not be believed and/or advocates and community members will side with his partner's version of events. This close interplay between domestic violence workers and an FtM survivor's and/or Lesbian batterer's social network may also heighten an FtM's fears that accessing services will lead to public discussion of his trans status, thus exposing him to the discrimination and violence discussed above.

Barriers Specific to Intersex Individuals

Intersex children are often subjected to multiple genital surgeries in order to ensure that outward shape matches, as closely as possible, a cultural esthetic ideal. Typically, these children are not explained the reasons for these procedures and are made to feel that they have (or, indeed, are) an embarrassing secret. Since doctors still perform these surgeries with a primary goal of preventing psychological stress in the parents, it is not surprising that these children are rarely told the truth: that doctors fear their own parents will hate their bodies enough to mutilate them. It is also not surprising that many of them feel horribly ashamed.

When these children are given reasons for these surgeries and other procedures, they are frequently told that the treatment is necessary if the child wants to be loved as an adult. This message is a brutal double-edged sword: first, it tells the child that people will love or reject them based on their body. Second, it directly states that the child is physically inadequate to be loved. The intermittent affection of honeymoon periods mixed with violent explosions may seem the most loving a relationship for which an intersex adult can hope, if raised with these expectations.

As significant as these other barriers can be, invisibility is by far the most significant barrier. Few even are aware of the existence of intersex individuals in our communities. Large, governmental helping agencies that serve tens of thousands of clients each year may never have heard the word "intersex", much less be aware of a single individual case involving an intersex survivor. This ignorance exists despite the fact that intersexuality and surgical treatment of it in infants is much more common than surgical sex reassignment in adults. When an agency is made aware of intersexuality in a survivor, it may not consider that a factor worthy of special notice or attention. This flies in the face of the motivation for surgical alteration of intersex children: doctors repeatedly state that intersex individuals are at vastly heightened risk of abuse. Even after the May, 1997 breakthrough of this issue to the pages of prominent publications such as *The New York Times* and *Newsweek,* helping agencies have not heard this message, and intersex survivors—both adults and children—are nearly always forced to heal from their abuse alone.

Defining Responsibilities

Because trans and intersex individuals are victims of abuse, and because our society is complicit in creating conditions which perpetuate this abuse, we who have dedicated ourselves to helping survivors of domestic violence must include trans and intersex survivors as a part of that mission. Although the trans and intersex communities, where organized, can provide support to these individuals, we are the ones with domestic violence expertise and should retain primary responsibility for ensuring our services are accessible and responsive to these survivors.

Including trans and intersex survivors within our current mission entails three primary responsibilities. First, we must make certain that every community has a visible place to which survivors may turn, regardless of trans or intersex status. Second, we must not revictimize trans or intersex survivors. Third, we must follow up on our own efforts or referrals in order to ensure that our efforts are positive and effective. Fulfilling these responsibilities (they are never discharged) cannot be a passive resolution. Concrete action is required. An agency can begin by taking these steps:

- At minimum, every staff member and volunteer who works with survivors must be made aware that trans and intersex survivors exist and that the agency is committed to working on their behalf. This is the first step in ensuring that the cardinal rule of domestic violence assistance is implemented for trans and intersex survivors: welcome them, and believe their stories.

- If there are any organized trans or intersex communities in your area, contact them to make sure they know you exist and are prepared to at least counsel any of their members with a domestic violence problem. If possible, establish formal or informal training and consultation procedures with these groups to share expertise and promote referrals. These groups can also help you conduct outreach campaigns to trans and intersex persons.

- If you are the sole service provider in the community, ensure at least one staff member is trained in the unique barriers that trans or intersex survivors face and is empowered to anticipate and remove your agency's barriers to sensitively serving such survivors.

- If your area has multiple providers, use or develop a coalition to determine which agencies in each community will be responsible for providing which services. In larger communities, it may even be possible to define subsections of the trans and intersex communities and assign responsibility for serving each group to a different agency, if care is taken to ensure that no one "between the cracks" is left without options. Agencies in contact with survivors can then be made aware of where survivors should be referred and what questions must be answered before a proper referral can be made.

- This coalition should also publicly identify at least one specific resource that is openly welcoming of trans or intersex survivors. This resource might be an already existing hotline, or a separate number might be created either using regularly checked voice mail or automatic forwarding to an existing hotline or agency. Making a point of advertising the availability of this service tells frightened trans and intersex survivors that what they are experiencing is abuse and that other people feel they deserve better, a concept they may find more novel and life-changing than do many "more typical" domestic violence survivors.

- Once services are prepared to serve trans and intersex survivors, create a strategy of outreach to such survivors, including the addition of information about community resources for these survivors on written outreach materials targeting other communities.

- Finally, create a mechanism to follow up on referrals to other agencies and to make changes to coalition plans as new barriers or problems are identified.

Conclusion

Many of the barriers trans and intersex survivors face when trying to free themselves of domestic abuse are similar to those faced by all survivors: self-doubt, a belief that the known abuse is better than potential future unknown abuse, worry about the children and worry about finances. But because they have had to struggle to find pride in bodies and lives society labels "wrong" and because discrimination against them is so strong, trans and intersex survivors have many more hurdles to leap. One of these hurdles the domestic violence system itself created: a gender-segregated service system. We owe these survivors much more thought and effort to ensure that we do not either force them to stay in the hands of their abusers or revictimize them once they take that first step away.

RESOURCES

For more information about trans or intersex survivors, or for assistance in formulating policies or training staff and volunteers, contact the Survivor Project at:

10 NE Fargo # 2
Portland, OR 97212
(503)288-3191

Not a Black and White Issue
For Battered and Abused Latinas and Black Women, Dialing 911 May Be Risky Business

by E. Assata Wright

"I've never gone through what I went through that night," says Bebe Matan. I have no experience with cops and precincts. It's all a nightmare. That was the first time and the last time I call the police."

Matan's "nightmare" began on March 23 when she got into an argument with her husband, Deonarine. When the dispute escalated to physical violence—he allegedly slapped her—their son, Martin, interceded on his mother's behalf, and Bebe dialed 911. The Matan family and the New York City Police Department disagree on what happened after officers from the 102nd precinct arrived at the family's home in Queens. What is clear is that Officer Christopher Romanski shot the husband once in the abdomen and Deonarine died from his wound later that night. It is also clear that Bebe, 38 and a Guyana native, was probably abused twice that night; once by her husband, and then again by the criminal justice system she turned to for help.

Since the 1991 beating of Rodney King, several high-profile incidents, such as the alleged sodomizing and assault of Haitian Abner Louima, have put police brutality in the national spotlight. But it is the dozens of unpublicized, less notorious cases, like the Matan incident, that fuel the growing grass-roots movement against police misconduct. From national conferences on police brutality to anti-brutality marches, community activists are making this issue a top organizing priority. Even some Black and Hispanic officers are beginning to break ranks with their white colleagues and are calling for the dismissal of racist cops who brutalize Latinos and African-Americans.

The June 1994 death of Nicole Brown Simpson also helped to bring domestic violence to the forefront of public policy debates. Local organizing around this issue began in the early 1990s and later culminated in the Violence Against Women Act, which Congress passed as part of the 1994 Crime Law. The Act stiffened penalties for a number of violent crimes against women, including rape and assault, and allocated federal grant money to state and local government efforts that curb domestic violence through the criminal justice system. Since passage of the Crime Law, states have passed tougher domestic violence measures and have reorganized courts and police departments to better fight this problem. Absent from each debate, however, is how domestic violence and police brutality intersect—and sometimes collide—in the lives of Black women and Latinas.

It is estimated that more than 42,000 women in New York State (half of those in New York City alone) are abused each year. The recent changes in state and local domestic violence laws have put an emphasis on police and court intervention. But with mounting complaints of police brutality in several Black and Latina communities, abused women in these neighborhoods are put in a precarious position. To be protected from their abusers, they are encouraged to call the cops, but for women of color this means relying on the same police department they believe holds their communities in contempt.

"The Black women and Latinas we work with don't call the police because they are not always sure what the outcome will be. They believe they have to make a choice," says Shirley Traylor, executive director of Harlem Legal Services. "They believe if they call the police or invoke the intervention of the criminal justice system, the offender is very likely to be mistreated in some way. They feel they've exposed the offender to some larger danger and this has an impact on their decisions." As police brutality and domestic violence are elevated within the grassroots organizing and public policy arenas, they threaten to further overshadow battered women of color caught between the two movements.

From *On the Issues,* Vol. 7, No. 1, Winter 1998. Copyright © 1998 by Merle Hoffman Enterprises Ltd. Reprinted by permission.

E. Assata Wright is a freelance journalist based in Jersey City, New Jersey. Her work has appeared in *The Village Voice.*

The Poverty = Violence Controversy

Of the women who were killed by a husband or boyfriend, three-quarters were Black or Latina and two-thirds lived in New York's poorest neighborhoods. This finding led the Health Department and some researchers to conclude that poverty causes violence and that poor women of color are more likely to be victims of domestic violence than white women. Domestic violence advocates who work exclusively with Blacks and Latinas reject this controversial conclusion, which goes against the long-held assumption that abuse effects women of all races and classes more or less equally.

They agree, however, that domestic violence is exacerbated by poverty. Middle-class women have more of a possibility of leaving an abusive relationship by accessing a number of private resources available to those who can pay. Poor women, by contrast, are far more likely to rely on public resources, which would include the network of social service agencies, charity organizations, and the police. The agencies and charity groups, notoriously underfunded and understaffed, often cannot meet the needs of every woman who comes to them for help; many women are put on waiting lists or turned away. For the women who use these services actually leaving the abuser may not be immediately possible. Living with the batterer and using the police as the first line of defense may be the only option available.

Although they may be more hesitant to seek police protection, Latinas and Black women are at least as vulnerable to domestic abuse as white women. The New York City Department of Health released a report last March which found that between 1990 and 1994 there were 1,156 female homicide victims aged 16 and older. 52 percent of these victims were Black, 29 percent were Latina, and 16 percent were white.

The Health Department, which conducted the study by reviewing Medical Examiner's reports, had only cursory information on the victims' history with domestic violence, and not every murder was committed by a husband or boyfriend—some were committed during other disputes or robberies, for instance—but the report concluded that in murders with "identified motives, women were victims of intimate partner homicide more than any other homicide."

The study also reveals that strategies for addressing the problem of violence against women need to be different from those aimed at homicides committed against men, which the Health Department carefully noted. Furthermore, the report implies that strategies for addressing violence against women of color need to be different from those which target the needs of white women—a fact the department failed to comment on directly. "With only empirical data, the Health Department doesn't offer suggestions on where to go from here," says Gail Garfield of the African American Task Force on Violence Against Women. "What strategies, especially for the Black community, [have they] put in place, or plan to put in place, in response to the data?

The Health Department has yet to focus on the unique experiences of battered Black women, and so specific programs that take their needs into account have not been developed. In 1994, New York City implemented a one-strategy-fits-all approach to domestic violence that places a heavier emphasis on police and court intervention. New York State passed a domestic violence prevention act that same year. The new city and state policies and laws are consistent with federal guidelines outlined in the Violence Against Women Act.

Congress allocated $1.6 billion over six years to the Act, much of which will be passed on to state and local governments to fund their own domestic violence initiatives. One of the most striking aspects of the law is the link Congress made between funding eligibility and law enforcement. There are two pools of money available: state formula grants and discretionary grants. The Justice Department, which oversees the formula grant program, stipulates that states must use 25 percent of the money for law enforcement, 25 percent for prosecution programs, and 25 percent for nonprofit, non-governmental victim service programs. The remaining 25 percent is discretionary, and can be allocated to any or all of the 3 program areas. To receive discretionary grants as part of the Encourage Arrest Policies Program, applicants "must certify that their laws or official policies encourage or mandate the arrest of domestic violence offenders when there is probable cause or when a protection order has been violated."

The mandatory arrest policy is particularly problematic for Black women because, as Garfield points out, they are more likely to fight back and protect themselves when being abused. In cases where a woman hits her abuser, she can be arrested along with the attacker. This dual arrest policy has been highly controversial, in New York and elsewhere, and currently there is legislation pending in the state assembly which would curtail this practice.

The new state law gives battered women greater access to criminal courts and strengthened orders of protection. In the past, such orders were issued only in family court. The new law, however, makes it possible for a woman to get a protection order from a criminal court. Now, if the batterer violates the order, the woman can lodge a criminal complaint against him. Previously, if a batterer harassed a woman with threatening phone calls or letters he was charged with a misdemeanor and hardly ever given jail time. Abusers were charged with felonies only after they physically injured the woman. Additionally, a few offenses that were once considered misdemeanors are now classified as felonies, increasing the severity of their potential punishment. Offenses that were already considered felonies now carry longer sentences.

Advocates fear that these initiatives, although well-intentioned, are undercut by a failure to address racism in the criminal justice system, and as a result may have disastrous effects on Black and Latino communities in general, and in particular on battered women in those communities. Women know the impact of these sentencing policies could potentially be devastating, especially in a community like Harlem, where a disproportionately large number of men already have at least one felony conviction. In the aftermath of the federal Crime Law, mandatory sentencing measures, and "three strikes and you're out" legislation, offenders today will receive longer, stiffer penalties with each new conviction, and Blacks and Latinos know these laws hit their communities the hardest.

Traylor, whose clients have experienced "severe" abuse for years, notes that most Black women and Latinas who turn to Harlem Legal Services for assistance seek protection orders in family rather than criminal court for fear their husband or boyfriend will end up with a conviction. The women, she says, "are not at all sure they want the offender to be arrested and then face a jail term. They really want to know what we can do legally to help prevent the abuse." They are not interested in any available legal remedies that would include criminal prosecution. "Women have expressed those kinds of conflicts to me as well," says Byllye Avery, founder of the National Black Women's Health Project. "But that's when I say to women, 'You're not thinking about you. You're thinking about him. But is he thinking about you when you're being battered? See, that's us taking care of everybody else.'"

"Sure there are inequities in the law," Avery (whose late husband was a police officer) continues. "That's part of the reality. But what are you going to do? Keep them out of jail so they can continue to beat on you? Doing that is not going to make him stop." In fact, she says, it will only "give them permission to keep abusing you," and before long, abusers come to "expect" this kind of support from their victims.

In this context, many battered Black women and Latinas may protect the abuser from jail even if it means risking their own safety. In a 1996 report on police brutality in New York City, Amnesty International found that between 1993 and 1994 there was a "substantial" increase in the number of Blacks and Latinos who were shot or killed while in police custody. Advocates point out that while women want protection from their batterers, they don't want him beaten by cops, or worse, killed by them. At least four domestic violence calls to 911 over the past 18 months resulted in deadly confrontations between cops and the alleged batterer. Two nights before cops shot Deonarine Matan in Queens, Donald Davidson was killed by Bronx police who responded to a domestic dispute at the home of Davidson's daughter, Adrienne Matthews. In June 1996, Steve Excell was shot by police in Jamaica, Queens after he allegedly beat his wife, Sharon with an electrical cord. Bronx Officer Vincent Guidice was killed when he responded to a domestic dispute between Anthony Rivers and his girlfriend, Gloria Virgo.

There may be other repercussions to calling the cops. A woman may be conflicted about sending a man away if she has children with him or if he is the family's primary wage earner. The specters of the Single Black Mother and—if she is likely to need public assistance in the man's absence—the Welfare Queen weigh heavily on a woman's conscience. There could also be unintended consequences for the other members of the family. If there is evidence of illegal activity, drug use or dealing for example, the woman could be arrested herself and the children could be placed in foster care. The desire to keep the family together may supersede the need to be safe. "Well-meaning public policy can sometimes have an adverse effect, because it is not thought out in the context of how this may impact upon Black women's lives," says Garfield. "So, it can have the opposite effect of what it was intended to do."

Fortunately there is now an effort underway that will, if successful, ease this dilemma for Black women by giving them other alternatives. Under Garfield's leadership the African American Task Force on Violence Against Women received a $145,000 grant (one of a handful awarded to nonprofit organizations) from the Justice Department's Violence Against Women Grants Office to develop a "community-defined" response to physical and sexual abuse of women in Central Harlem. Working with residents, service providers, churches, elected leaders, and the private sector, the task force plans to build community-controlled programs that will help abused women and their families, and raise awareness about the problem. Garfield expects to have a set of recommendations ready to be implemented and tested within a year, and hopes these programs can serve as a model for other communities of color in New York and elsewhere across the country.

"We're not telling Black women, 'Don't call the police. Don't use criminal justice solutions.' But we want to figure out how we can create other solutions that might be more productive for us and our community," says Beth E. Richie, professor of public health at Hunter

College and a member of the task force. Currently, the group is surveying the community, through town meetings and focus groups, to learn what services and programs Harlem residents would like to see implemented or expanded. Because the task force is in the early stages of this survey process, Garfield says it would be premature to comment on what their alternative solutions might entail. Richie, however, says she expects that people will say the community needs more counseling services and programs for men who batter, in addition to more shelters.

One piece of the task force's strategy will be to get community groups and service providers to incorporate domestic violence education and prevention into their ongoing work. For example, "If a group is doing 'youth empowerment,' we'll ask them to make sure that includes girl safety," Richie says. "Since we know many battered women are living on the streets because they left abusive homes, we'll ask advocates for the homeless to deal with that issue as a part of their work"

Ultimately, Garfield, Richie, and their colleagues want violence to Black women to strike the same raw nerve within the community that police brutality hits, a task they know will be difficult. Police brutality—the not-too-distant relative of Southern lynchings—is consistent with the type of racially-motivated violence the community feels comfortable organizing against. Violence against women is rarely addressed unless it can also be placed in a racial context. The difficulty with this stance is that it changes the focus from brutality against women to black/white racism.

Ten years ago, Tawana Brawley received community attention and succor because she claimed she was raped by six white men. Other high-profile victims, whose accusations had more merit than Brawley's, have pointed the finger at Black men and received far less support from their community, which in these cases tends to doubt their claims of abuse, siding instead with the attacker. Boxer Mike Tyson and the late rapper Tupac Shakur—both convicted rapists—are widely regarded as victims of the criminal justice system and women who "were asking for it."

Then consider the case of Girl X, a nine-year-old black resident of Chicago's infamous Cabrini-Green housing project. Girl X was raped, beaten, strangled, blinded, and then forced to swallow gasoline in a stairwell last January. Although the child (whose real name has never been released) survived, she was unconscious for a month and may never regain her eyesight. Despite the hideous nature of the crime, community leaders remained silent for weeks following the incident and condemned the attack only after a local columnist publicly embarrassed them in print for their inaction. In the end, the community was moved less by girl X herself than by the lack of media attention she received in comparison

to JonBenet Ramsey, the white Colorado girl who was murdered in December 1996. In other words, the community chose to focus on racist media outside the community rather than the gender violence within it; racism was the issue, not sexism.

Incredibly, when convicted sex offender Patrick Sykes, 25, confessed to police he raped Girl X for "sexual gratification," some in the community said he was a victim. A radio station poll found that while Black women felt relieved after his arrest, men believed Sykes was innocent and his confession coerced by the police. The cumulative effect of cases like these is that Black women's experiences with violence are overshadowed by those of Black men. Similarly, the interests of battered women can be suppressed by community concern for incarcerated men. Traylor says she has seen this happen to her own clients.

"When the women go back to their community they are punished for raising their claims by their own family members and by the neighborhood. It's really the impact of racism on the community, and how it internalizes itself and plays itself out," she says. This punishment can take several forms. Some families may not offer material or emotional support when the woman tries to leave the relationship, refusing to give the woman a place to stay or to help with child care while she finds a job or new home. Even if relatives provide some material help, the women may be silenced by their families and told not to discuss the abuse.

The founders of the task force have already experienced the community's wrath firsthand. The organization grew out of the so-called "homecoming celebration" held for Mike Tyson after his 1995 release from prison. Calling themselves African Americans Against Violence, Garfield and other activists held a rally to oppose the celebration and raise awareness about the kind of abuse of which Tyson was accused. Opposition to the rally was bitter and came mostly from other Black women. Rally organizers realized the community has ignored this issue for so long that it could only be addressed through an ongoing, grassroots effort, and so the task force was launched. "We have to shift political consciousness to include the issues of women," Richie says. "It's consistent with the history of community self-determination to say, 'We've got to end violence against women. We've got to get empowerment zone money. We've got to figure out whether or not we want Barnes & Noble in Harlem. We've got to make sure some money for job corps comes back into our community. And our kids need summer jobs. *All* those things are part of the same ideology. We have to re immerse the rhetoric into something that's radical. And I think the Black community in Harlem is a wonderful laboratory for that because there are still folks there who talk about the need for community development."

The Unique Role Health Workers Can Play in Recognizing and Responding to Battered Women

by Nancy Worcester

"Battering appears to be the single most common cause of injury to women—more common than automobile accidents, muggings and rapes combined.[1]"

Many women identify violence in their lives, and their fear of violence, as the number one health issue they face. For health workers responding to battering, it is important to remember that battering is *much* more than the physical injuries. Violence serves as an excellent reminder that mental and physical health issues cannot be separated. For a woman being abused, physical violence is but one of the tools that her abuser uses to have power and control over many, or all, aspects of her life. Many formerly battered women who have even suffered life-threatening injuries say that the physical violence was nothing compared to the psychological and emotional abuse they endured.

Now that many states have mandatory arrest laws, battered women have been quick to remind us that stopping abuse in a home is much more complex than simply stopping the hitting. Women have noted that a result of abuser counselling can be that abusers learn they can no longer get away with hitting their partners. However, unless larger issues of power and control are also addressed, the abuser may learn to shift to psychological/emotional forms of abuse and the woman continues to be battered even if she is no longer physically injured.

A wide range of chronic health issues including headaches, backaches, sleep disorders, anxiety, abdominal complaints, eating disorders, depression and chronic pain are particularly common in battered women and are clearly related to the stress of living in a violent relationship.

You See Battered Women Everyday

The FBI estimates that a woman is beaten every 15–18 seconds in this country. Violence affects women of all social groups, ages, races, rural and urban environments, and affects both rich and poor and both heterosexual and lesbian women. Many health workers and health workers' partners live with violence as a part of their lives.

Battered women regularly call upon the health system even though health workers have a poor record of identifying them. Studies have shown that abused women have more health problems than non-abused women[2], so those who trust the health system and have insurance probably seek health care at disproportionately high rates. Studies have shown that 22–35 percent of all women who use emergency room services are battered women and because the same women may need to return time and time again, almost half of all injuries presented by women in emergency rooms may be a result of abuse.

Although health workers do not regularly ask about battering during pregnancy, it is more common then and has as serious consequences (increased rates of miscarriage, stillbirth, low birth weight babies, and risk of homicide) as the conditions routinely tested for in prenatal care. Retrospective studies of battered women have found that 40–60 percent were abused during pregnancy; 25 percent of battered women say they were beaten for the first time during a pregnancy. The problems may be even more exaggerated in pregnant teenagers. One study[3] found that 26 percent of pregnant teens were currently in a relationship with a man who was abusive;

many stated that the abuse had started when they discovered they were pregnant. Most alarming, 65 percent of the battered teens had not talked to *anyone* about the violence in their lives.

Health Workers Can Play a Key Role

Many battered women would like to tell someone about the violence in their lives and would greatly benefit from knowing that their situation is not unusual and that there are a range of excellent resources available to them. Understanding common patterns of domestic violence makes it obvious that health workers who do recognize battered women and empower them to explore their options can play a key role in helping women end the violence in their lives.

Isolation

Isolation is a primary weapon that one person can use to gain control over another person's life. Battered women describe how abusers gradually isolate them from their other social/emotional support networks so that eventually the abuser is the main person in the abused woman's life giving her information about her own value. Messages like "No one else will ever love you" and "You deserve to be beaten" become very powerful when a woman is not hearing any other messages. Understanding that isolation is a *consequence* (*not* a cause) of battering can help health workers recognize that what they say to battered women can be extremely important. Health workers aware of power imbalances in health worker-patient relationships can see why this can be exaggerated when the patient is an abused woman. A health worker who implies that the woman is "the problem" will reinforce the messages she gets at home; the health worker who says "You don't deserve to be hit" will be giving a crucial, different message.

The Cycle of Violence

The cycle of violence is a pattern that many battered women start to recognize in their lives. The battering incident seldom comes from "nowhere," but is the expected "explosion" from a period of increasing tension. Women describe the stress of living in the tension-building stage, the waiting for the straw that will finally provoke the battering, as so awful that some women remember when even a severe battering was almost a welcome "release" from the unbearable tension.

Particularly in the early years of abusive relationships, the battering incident is often immediately followed by a good stage which some women call the "honeymoon stage." The honeymoon stage is the wonderful stage we *all* want in relationships. Understanding the importance of the honeymoon stage in battering relationships can help us understand the complexities of these (and all!) relationships. This is the stage at which abusers say (and think they mean) that they are very sorry and it will never happen again. This is the stage when loving sex, extravagant presents, and a renewing of dreams and life long plans/goals can be very enticing.

If the battering is severe enough to cause injuries, the health worker, particularly emergency service providers, may see the woman immediately after the battering and before the "honeymoon stage." This is a key time to make sure the woman knows her options and resources, because she may be the most open to exploring alternatives to staying in a violent relationship. Once the "honeymoon stage" begins, the woman may be "hooked" into another cycle, convinced that if only she tries harder the violence will end.

Escalation

Unless there is intervention (and a sincere commitment from the abuser to learn totally new ways of communicating in the relationship), battering relationships tend to escalate over a period of time. The battering incidents become more frequent and often increase in severity. (Battered women describe the "honeymoon stage" as being less of a "hook" in long-term battering relationships than are the enormous social and economic pressures which keep them in relationships they know are unhealthy.) Because battered women may be seeing health workers long before they turn to other services, good medical records with clear notes, and even photographs, of injuries and chronic health problems that may be related to domestic violence are essential. These can help health workers who will see the records in the future, and the battered woman herself, to see the emerging pattern.

Revictimizing the Battered Woman

Even though health workers are not good at identifying battered women, studies have found that health workers do treat battered women differently than non battered women and that the treatment actually contributes to the consequences of battering.

Unless there is an understanding of battering, a woman who calls upon the health system regularly, with a range of symptoms and injuries, may be seen as a frustrating patient by health workers who pride themselves on being able to diagnose and treat specific conditions. Only 5-10 percent of battered women in emergency services are identified as such by physicians on their records. Instead, the ground-breaking work on this by Stark, Flitcraft and Frazier,[4] found that medical records included the labels "neurotic," "hysteric," "hypochondriac" or "a well-known patient with multiple vague complaints" for one in four battered women compared to one in 50 non-battered women. One in four battered women were given pain medications and/or minor tranquilizers compared to one in ten non-battered women. This "treatment" has the same effect as paying fire fighters to *push* people back into burning homes! Medication and victimizing labels reinforce the woman's feeling that she is the problem and may contribute to depression, drug and alcohol abuse, and the high rate of suicide attempts seen as a consequence of battering.

Empowering Battered Women

Excellent resources are now available for health workers spelling out specific ways to identify and respond to battered women and to help them end the violence in their lives. Responding more appropriately to battered women does not necessarily mean more work for the health care provider. It means *starting* to ask about violence ("Since so many women are hurt by their partners, we ask every patient with injuries like yours whether they've ever been hit/kicked/hurt by their partner.") and documenting it, making sure safety issues are addressed for a woman before she returns to the situation that caused the mental or physical injuries, giving women information about community resources, and *stopping* treating abused women by providing only labels and tranquilizers.

Battered women must be empowered to make their *own* decisions at their *own* pace. Outside intervention, certain behaviors, or trying to leave at the "wrong" time can escalate the violence. Thirty percent of women murdered in this country are killed by the men they had loved. Most of these murders occur when women are

> ### Hospital Protocols Now Required
>
> Effective January 1, 1992, all accredited hospitals are required to have protocols in place describing how they respond to battered women and how health professionals are trained on this issue. This is the ideal time for health workers and battered women's advocates to work together to make sure that protocols serve to empower battered women. There are over 1,000 programs in the U.S. specifically serving battered women. These "experts" can help a woman with the legal, safety, housing and support services she needs.

trying to get out of a relationship. Understanding the complexities of *leaving* battering relationships is central to serving battered women's needs.

Health workers will seldom know the impact of their responses to battered women. Saying "You don't deserve to be treated like this" or "Here is a list of community resources" may be the advice that saves more lives and does more for the mental health of patients than do other more "medical" skills.

References

1. "Domestic Violence Intervention Calls for More Than Treating Injuries" by Teri Randall, *Journal of the American Medical Association,* volume 264, no. 8, August 22–29, 1990, pp. 939–940.
2. "Abused Women and Chronic Pain" by Joel D. Harber, *American Journal of Nursing,* volume 85, September, 1985, pp. 1010–1012.
3. "Violence During Teen Pregnancy: Health Consequences for Mother and Child" by Judith McFarlane, pp. 136–141, in *Dating Violence* edited by Barrie Levy, Seal Press, 1991.
4. "Medicine and Patriarchal Violence: The Social Construction of a "Private' Event" by Evan Stark, Anne Flitcraft & William Frazier, *International Journal of Health Services,* volume 9, no.3, 1979, pp. 461–493.

Reprinted with permission from bulbul, *Feminist Connection,* Madison, WI. December, 1984.

Health System Response to Battered Women: Our "Successes" Are Creating New Challenges

by Nancy Worcester

*I*t is a time of celebration, contradictions, and enormous new challenges as the health system is finally, suddenly, "discovering" that violence against women is a mental and physical health issue.

It is a huge victory that domestic violence issues are now being taken seriously by the medical establishment. Without a doubt, if there is an *appropriate* response by health practitioners, many lives will be saved and the damaging effects of living in, or observing, years of domestic violence will be prevented or interrupted at earlier stages. Health workers' learning to say, "You don't deserve to be treated like this" or "Here is a list of local domestic violence services" is expertise which will save more lives and do more for patients' mental health than many more complicated medical or nursing skills.

How *appropriate* is the health system's response to domestic violence? The following situations are all ones which I have personally observed recently in communities near me, and they reflect both the extremely positive and the contradictory, potentially dangerous, patterns which are happening throughout the country as medical involvement in domestic violence becomes a "hot" issue:

- A menopausal woman is working with her physician to make decisions about osteoporosis screening and hormone use because she has a history of bone fractures. In the course of the examination, the physician asks a number of questions to determine whether the injuries are related to domestic violence and makes sure the woman knows about local domestic violence services. The woman thanks the doctor for asking these questions and giving her information which she will share with others, but confirms that this is not an issue for her personally.

- A woman makes a gynecological appointment with the same physician she saw a few months ago. The patient reminds the doctor that during her last visit the doctor had told her that domestic violence was a common problem and had asked whether bruises in various stages of healing (which were, in fact, related to gardening) were a result of someone hurting her. The patient now realizes that, although she has never been physically injured, she is being emotionally hurt by a very abusive partner. She returned to this doctor as the *one* person she knew who could help her find resources in the community to support her ending the violent relationship.

- A woman with a young child is isolated with no friends, family, or money. A brightly colored leaflet attracts her to a new, free women's health course, with free childcare, at the nearby community center. Within weeks, the woman has decided to leave town to escape her physically abusive husband. She stops by the community center to let people know that the domestic violence information and local referrals, covered in the health course, had literally saved her life.

- A group of Latinas are meeting for a Latina Health Course. When the issue of domestic violence is discussed, two women express anger that (in separate situations) white emergency room health practitioners recently asked both of them if their injuries were related to domestic violence. They feel they are only being asked this question because they are women of color.

- A woman is injured by her abusive partner and has to go to the hospital emergency room. Without the woman's permission, the physician decides to involve the police. This action causes an escalation of the violence. The woman's life is seriously threatened and she feels more trapped in the relationship than ever. The woman says she will never go to that hospital again.

- A city is proud of the new hospital-based domestic violence program which has opened and is receiving much positive media publicity. Very little attention is paid to the fact that the city's hospital-based sexual assault program was closed that same month.
- The medical auxiliary is meeting regularly and enthusiastically making all sorts of plans for the roles they can play (conference planning, training health workers, etc.) as the medical community becomes more responsive to domestic violence. Within the same hospital complex, the local battered women's shelter has just closed because of lack of financial support.
- A battered women's program is having to lay off several full-time employees because of a financial crisis. The half-time hospital-based domestic violence advocate will keep her job because she has "outside" funding specifically earmarked for domestic violence advocacy within a particular hospital.

Many of us have spent the last decade or more trying to get the health system to see that domestic violence is a major women's health issue.[2] That work has now paid off: domestic violence protocols are required for hospital accreditation, domestic violence curricula have been developed for professional training of most health practitioners, and many health system organizations have gotten the message that they need to be doing something about domestic violence. *But, getting the health system to see violence as a health issue may have been the easy part of the struggle; making sure that the health system's response to battered women is* appropriate *and that it empowers women to find ways to end the violence in their lives may be even harder work!*

Domestic violence is *not* a medical issue. It is a social, economic, and political issue which has health ramifications and which the health system can help detect and interrupt at an earlier stage. A goal of having the health system involved in a "community response to domestic violence" is for health practitioners to be a *bridge* to excellent services which can help people end the violence in their lives. With its present structure and philosophy, the medical model cannot take on domestic violence as just one more issue to be "treated."[3] In fact, it is frightening to think of the consequences for battered women if the health system's response to domestic violence is to medicalize and coopt one more women's health issue.[4] However, if we can work towards taking the empowerment model of the battered women's movement into the health care system, this could save many

battered women's lives and be a model for a health system response to other non-medical health issues.

Much of the following expertise, which has grown out of twenty years of the battered women's movement, will be crucial for health practitioners to incorporate into work with battered women if they are to play a role in empowering women to end the violence in their lives.

There is no one answer. The medical model basically works to identify a "problem," label it, and treat it with the identified "medical fix." This certainly saves lives when "the problem" can be identified and universally fixed with a particular antibiotic or surgical "solution." Health workers must learn to expect that they will seldom have the same instant gratification of knowing they have "fixed it" when they are dealing with domestic violence. The complexities of violence in women's lives are enormous. The dynamics, dangers, and "answers" differ for each woman, situation, and stage of a violent relationship. Understanding the complexities of surviving and/or leaving violent relationships—or by acknowledging that we don't understand all the complexities—is key to responding to battered women.

Domestic violence is an abuse of power and control in an intimate relationship. The clearest pattern to emerge in all physically or emotionally abusive relationships is that the abuser inappropriately controls many or all aspects of the other person's life. (Physical abuse can be seen as just one of many weapons of control. Clever abusers may never have to resort to using physical violence if they can gain the control they need through tactics such as isolation or erosion of self esteem.) A health worker who wants to be a part of the "solution" to issues of power and control in a battered woman's life needs to avoid being one more person trying to control the woman's life. Health workers have been trained to tell patients what to do and we even have a language of "compliance vs. non-compliance" to identify whether the patients behave as they "should." *Empowering* women to make their own decisions, at the pace which is safe for them, is crucial to serving battered women, but it may be challenging for health workers to develop this new skill.

It may be safer to stay in a violent relationship than to leave. The most dangerous times in most violent relationships are when there are changes in the dynamics between the abuser and the abused which the abuser perceives as weakening his control. Leaving relationships often escalates the violence for women and their loved ones and many women experience as much or more violence after they have left a relationship as they experienced in the relationship. Thirty to 40% of women murdered in this country are killed by men they had loved; most of these murders occur when women are trying to get out of the relationship.

Domestic violence provides a challenge to health workers to think through the many ramifications of their oath to "do no harm." Battered women have asked that health workers be trained to inform women that domestic violence is a crime and that victims have the right to call the police, but that health workers *not* call police without their permission. Not only is calling the police without permission the most common example of taking the power away from battered women, but such outside intervention can also cause the violence to escalate to more dangerous levels in many relationships. Battered women will not use the services of doctors or hospitals with a reputation for calling the police without their permission. Health workers need to check their own state's requirements for the reporting of domestic violence, but in most states there is not mandatory reporting for most domestic violence injuries. Indeed, if well-meaning but uninformed policy-makers propose mandatory reporting by health workers, they should be sent a copy of the useful policy paper, "Mandatory Reporting of Domestic Violence by Health Care Providers A Misguided Approach" by the Family Violence Prevention Funds.[5]

As a general rule, battered women are pretty good at assessing their own danger (their survival may have already depended on that) and will choose the most appropriate options for themselves and their children *if they are aware of all the options available to them.* The appropriate role for health practitioners is almost always to ask a woman about her safety and make sure she knows about options immediately available for crisis services (including housing) and longer term support available for the range of decisions she faces if she is going to try to end the violent relationship. Many women appreciate hearing about how to develop "safety plans" to help them prepare for future safety. One page model safety plans are available and a woman can be told that this safety planning, as well as support groups and free legal advice, are examples of the services available through her local domestic violence program even if she never plans to stay at the shelter. Health workers can play a crucial role in letting the widest range of women know that the local battered women's program does indeed provide services (including toll-free anonymous phone services) to "women just like her."

Definitions of "success" must be related to what health providers are doing about domestic violence. In the move towards writing measurable objectives for grant proposals or justifying more funding for the training of health workers, it is easy to get caught up in trying to prove success by claiming good intervention results in women leaving their abusers. This makes the dangerous assumption that the "right" answer is the same for everyone, overlooks the multiple complexities of safely

leaving a relationship and having the internal and external resources for "starting life all over" (sometimes literally on the run with a changed identity), and totally ignores that many battered women (particularly in the early years of a relationship) want the violence in their relationship to end but do not want the relationship itself to end.

Defining success as women leaving their abusers is not only inappropriate to the goal of empowering women to make their own decisions, but such a definition also contributes to the frustration of being a health worker trying to respond to domestic violence. Most health workers who appropriately ask about violence, document it in the patient's record, tell women they do not deserve this, and refer women to community services, will never know the impact of this intervention. On the other hand, most women who have managed to end the violence in their lives can remember the first person who ever said, "I'm worried about you. There are resources available," and planted the idea that they could change their lives, even if it were months, years, or decades before they could act upon that inspiration. Many battered women leave a violent relationship 5–7 times before they leave for the "final" time. Helping a woman leave the first time, the third time, or the fifth time, should be recognized as important parts of the process.

Health workers need to define success in terms of whether their roles are being played appropriately and effectively. Instead of measurable outcomes counting what battered women do, it's what the health workers are doing that should be counted. How many health workers in a setting have an understanding of the complexities of domestic violence? Are the appropriate personnel asking all women about violence, documenting it effectively, providing safety plan information, and referring to the most appropriate local agencies? Have local battered women's advocates been involved in evaluating the health service response to domestic violence?

Battering affects women of all classes, races, ages, professions, sexual identities, and affects both able-bodied women and women with disabilities (although options for getting out of relationships may be very different for different women). The goal needs to be that appropriate health practitioners are asking *all* women whether there is violence in their lives. This can be handled very effectively by including the questions with an explanation such as, "We are now aware that domestic violence is an issue for many women, so health care providers are asking *all* women a few questions and making sure they know about local domestic violence resources." For the woman who is not personally affected by the issue, it is an opportunity to learn about this epidemic. Having worked with thousands of health providers and battered women, I have never heard of anyone being offended by these questions if such an introductory statement is included. (In contrast, it is common to hear of women thanking their doctors for asking about this issue.)

Unless health providers explain that *all* women are being asked about domestic violence, it is easy for women who have previously experienced racism, classism, ageism, or homophobia in their health care interactions to assume this is more of the same. In the example above where two Latinas were asked about domestic violence, they had both called upon an emergency room where we had just done intensive domestic violence trainings, so I could assure them that the health workers there were asking *all* women about domestic violence. With this information, they felt very differently about what had happened and said, if they had known they were not being asked for racist reasons, they would have been open about discussing what was really happening in their lives, and they asked me to start training health workers to explain that they are asking *all* women!

This is the kind of information we can only know by constantly working to evaluate whether intervention in health settings is suitable for battered women. The most effective way to insure that the health system's response to domestic violence is appropriate, is to make sure that battered women's advocates and formerly battered women are closely involved with training health workers, are a part of health system task forces on domestic violence, and are a part of committees that design evaluation and forward planning processes.

It is also essential that health workers wanting to play a role in ending domestic violence identify that working to strengthen their battered women's programs is almost always a key issue. Health workers can only be effective in referring women to services to support ending the violence if those services are available! Local battered women's programs are almost universally underfunded in proportion to the amount of work they are trying to do. Long hours of crisis work are exhausting and committed workers are often put in the position of having to choose between life-saving services to battered women and their children, or taking care of administrative work. Services are often dependent upon volunteer work and donations. This all makes battered women's programs very vulnerable to changing financial and political climates.

Most importantly, health providers must be vigilant in never being a part of undermining the local battered women's program by promoting competing programs, applying for the same funding, etc. A basic question of "Will this help or hurt, strengthen or weaken, the domestic violence program?" can be a guiding principle. Extremely strong community programming for a wide range of domestic violence survivors can emerge when health workers actively look for ways to strengthen the battered women's program, by having health workers serve on the program's board, by working on team approaches to the community response to domestic violence, and setting up support groups at hospitals or clinics or hospital advocacy programs in close conjunction with the local domestic violence program.

Health workers and domestic violence programs *working closely together* will not only insure that the health system response to battered women is appropriate, it could also be the first step towards radically changing the way the health system learns to deal with non-medical health issues. This could be the best thing that ever happened to medicine!

FOOTNOTES

1. "The Unique Role Health Workers Can Play in Recognizing and Responding to Battered Women" by Nancy Worcester (National Women's Health Network's) *Network News,* 1992; March/April, 1, 4-5.

2. Examples of pioneering work: "Medicine and Patriarchal Violence: The Social Construction of a 'Private Event'," by Evan Stark, Anne Flitcraft & Willaim Frazier, *International Journal of Health Services,* volume 9, no. 3, 1979, pp. 461–493; *Nursing Care of Victims of Family Violence* by Jacqueline Campbell and Janice Humphreys, Reston Publishing Company, Reston, VA, 1984; *Guidelines for Mental Health Practitioners in Domestic Violence Cases* by Susan Schechter, National Coalition Against Domestic Violence, 1987.

3. Excellent analysis of these issues is covered in "Domestic Violence: Challenge to Medical Practice" by Carole Warshaw, *Journal of Women's Health,* volume 2, number 1, 1993, pp. 73-80, and in "Domestic Violence: How Physicians Can Respond" by Kevin J. Fullin and Amanda Cosgrove, *National Coalition Against Domestic Violence VOICE,* Winter, 1994, pp. 8–12.

4. The medicalization and cooptation of women's health issues in discussed in the following articles: "Medical Response to Women's Health Activists: Conflict, Accommodation and Cooptation" by Sheryl-Bert Ruzek in *Research in Sociology of Health Care, I,* 1980, 335-354; "The Response of the Health Care System to the Women's Health Movement: The Selling of Women's Health Centers' by Nancy Worcester and Mariamne H. Whatley in Sue V. Rosser's (1988) *Feminism Within the Science and Health Care Professions: Overcoming Resistance.* Oxford: Pergamon Press, 1988, pp. 117–30; "The Role of Technology in the Cooptation of the Women's Health Movement: The Case Study of Osteoporosis and Breast Cancer Screening" by Mariamne H. Whatley and Nancy Worcester in Kathryn Strother Ratcliff et al., *Healing Technology—Feminist Perspectives,* Ann Arbor, Michigan: University of Michigan Press, 1989, pp. 199–20; "The Selling of HRT: Playing on the Fear Factor" by Nancy Worcester and Mariamne H. Whatley, in *Feminist Review* (England), 1992, No. 41, summer, pp. 1–26.

5. "Mandatory Reporting of Domestic Violence by Health Care Providers: A Misguided Approach" by Ariella Hyman, is available from the Family Violence Prevention Fund, Building One, Suite 200, 1001 Potrero Ave., San Francisco, CA 94110, (415)821-4553.

Surviving the Incest Industry

by Louise Armstrong

Survivors of child sexual abuse spoke out about their experiences in order to expose this hidden aspect of male violence and destroy it. Louise Armstrong argues that their accounts have been reduced to fodder for a burgeoning 'incest industry' which individualises and medicalises survivors and marginalises feminist politics.

It is a dozen years since feminists first spoke out on the issue of incest, of repeated sexual violation of children by males—fathers, step-fathers, grandfathers, uncles. A dozen years later—survivors continue to speak out. Their writings, which I will call "I-story" books, have become a small sub-genre of the burgeoning incest literature (framed by books on healing yourself and, for professionals, books on healing others). When taken note of by the feminist press, "I-story" books tend to be dealt with gingerly, with delicacy, concerned to maintain a proper comportment in the face of anguish.

I will now proceed to be somewhat indelicate, to speak out—as it were—on speaking out.

Without in any way intending to diminish the genuine feeling which imbues these works or, in some cases, their literary qualities, I think the institutionalisation of speaking out on incest needs re-examination. I think we have been bamboozled.

Since I was among the first to break the silence, and since speaking out was one of the fundamentals of feminism, this may smack of the politically—not only incorrect, but outrageous. Since a central purpose of those speaking out is to help others know they are not alone, and since those who speak do so with great pain, this may smack of the callous. I do not think all that smacking applies. Bear with me.

What I want to show is that the context of speaking out has been altered so radically in these past dozen years that it changes the meaning of what is being said.

When we first exploded the news that this crime against children was routine and widespread, we did so within a feminist framework of the exposure of multiple, licensed violences against women and children: battering, rape, marital rape . . . Our analysis, our understanding, placed child sexual abuse squarely within this framework, identifying it as a historical permission, a male right: as normal, not deviant. The goal was to raise society's consciousness: to try for a consensus which—it seemed in that climate of feminist optimism—might now say, hey, let's revoke the license!

Oh, we did not expect the world to simply cry: 'good, glad you told us, we'll just cut that out'. But what we had learned, from talking, from listening, was so clearcut, so eminently *reasonable*—that men did not do this despite the fact they knew it was wrong, but because they believed it was their right— that it seemed possible the public would react at least to the embarrassing absurdity of so many fathers suddenly spotlighted playing doctor (and much worse) with their three-year-olds. Just because they wanted to. Just because they could. Ours was an exuberance that anticipated a healthy fight for which we felt properly armed.

From *Trouble and Strife* (Britain), No. 21, Summer 1991, pp. 29–32. Copyright © 1991 Louise Armstrong.

Louise Armstrong is the author of numerous books including *Kiss Daddy Goodnight,* and *Rocking the Cradle of Sexual Politics: What Happened When Women Said Incest.*

There was no fight. If we expected to be told to shut up, we were wrong. If we expected to be told we were wrong that abuse was so common, we were wrong. If we expected to be told we were wrong about the sexual politics—we were wrong as well.

On this last point, we were simply ignored.

The Message-Suppressors

It was not the forces of repression that were sent in to meet us. It was battalions of newly minted mental health professionals. And they were so sure we were *not* wrong about the incidence, and so sure we were *not* wrong about the entrenched license, that they were willing to stake their careers on it: to enter a new specialty, "incest expert". We had agitated the public. They believed that they had the balm to peddle which would calm them. Being professionals, they banked on the fact that their calm-balm would prevail over our call for social change. They were right.

Almost from the start, the media carried our stories—and their analysis. Minutes after first opening our mouths, our message was first muffled, then obliterated.

We spoke of male violence and deliberate socially accepted violation. They spoke of family dysfunction. We spoke of rage. They named rage a stage. We spoke of social change. They spoke of personal healing. We spoke of political battle. They spoke of our need to hug the child within.

If our speaking out was an effort to litter the landscape with our cry for reform, they were message-suppressors, sent in by the powers that be, the sanitation engineers. Overt argument would have lent vigour to the fight. Converting the issue to a non-issue, they spoke in pieties of the horrors of incest—all the while often crying for the human advance which would be represented by de-criminalising it. What they were after was medicalisation, making child-rape an individual emotional problem (the child's). This not only de-issued the issue, it gave birth to a lucrative incest industry—counselling programmes, prevention programmes (including a Spiderman comic so kiddies could know Spiderman had been "touched inappropriately" too)—all of which was terrifically capitalism-compatible.

We'd been dialing the cops. Who answered was a social worker. These new social police not only tidied up after us, they all but wiped out any trace that we had ever been there. The odd leaflet, the odd flyer, the odd piece in an increasingly limited feminist press were all that remained.

Now, having long since been quashed as a political issue, even incest-the-novelty-social-disease shows signs of going limp. (And this is one brilliance of the strategy of converting the personal-is-political into the political-as-personal: it palls so nicely.)

War on Women and Children

For a while there was some renewed vibrance as woman after woman, doing as she was told, believed her child's saying daddy'd raped her (or him), and sought protection—only to find herself vilified as vindictive and deprived of custody, often even of visitation. In the USA it is mothers who are regularly labelled as 'the real abusers'. Case after case described its arc across the horizon so predictably that it didn't seem even the shallowest of wit could fail to catch on to what was passing:

See Susie (or Johnny) tell. Now see mommy shocked. See mommy act: Pick up the phone, report the abuse, call her attorney, seek to protect the child, to end time spent with the alleged perpetrator.

Now see the court (the very court which would have convicted her of neglect had someone other than herself reported the abuse) react with disbelief. See daddy get access. See mommy take psychological tests. See daddy take them. See mommy's test label her hysterical. See daddy's anoint him as stable. See her anger called pathological. See his called righteous. See mommy lose custody. See mommy fight. See the court order her to be silent. See her argue. See mommy lose access. (And then, in America, see mommy take Susie and run. Run, mommy, run. Now see the FBI run after her . . .)

It did not seem possible that even the most stupid of the species could miss the fact that courts which would summarily remove a child from a mother for neglect based on *possible harm* were now consistently ruling for fathers in consideration of *possible error*. It did not seem possible to miss the idea that, while speaking out about abuse in the past did nothing to disturb the status quo, speaking out about abuse in the *present* was tantamount to a declaration of war. And the other guys had the army.

But the mainstream media continued insistently to term these cases "custody disputes". And the public, befuddled, looked on dimly. Interest waned.

Incest as Illness

The combination of medicalisation of the issues for survivors, alongside the open declaration of war on women and children in the present, is what I mean when I say the context of speaking out, of telling personal stories, has changed. This is what throws into question the idea a great many survivors embrace, that theirs is an "illness" from which they must "heal"; and that their speaking out about their "journeys" to "empowerment" in itself constitutes a political act. Each individual who has suffered socially sanctioned oppression feels individual pain from that oppression—may suffer "symptoms", emotional as well as practical. Whose purpose is served when the onus is on the oppressed to become well-adjusted (even as the oppression continues)? What goals are served by allowing the focus to be shifted to that pain, those symptoms which result? Absent emphasis on the root cause? All this does is to ensure business-as-usual—all the while converting a potentially uppity portion of the community into a new consumer group.

Medicalisation, personalisation of the *issue* of incest, has otherwise served to provide diversion. For a while multiple personalities (dubbed "multiples") kicked in, and suddenly—like would-be Miss Teenage Americas competing for Most Personality, survivors competed for The Most Personalities. That now appears to have topped out at ninety-two (with the book *When Rabbit Howls*). Multiples, I am told by counsellors, are out of fashion. So what will be next?

Retreats for survivors, often run by private for-profit psychiatric institutions charging exorbitant prices, have become a fad. Retreats? What we need are *attacks.*

"Gender neutrality" has triumphed. Equal emphasis on female offenders (who are statistically negligible in every study) obviates the fact that female sexual violence is *not* equally routine and equally normative within the culture. Worse than that. It means that to speak of sexual politics, of *male* violence, seems not only retrograde, but actually gauche and insulting and bigoted—so firmly is the subject now rooted in terms of the individual-psychological-emotional. And so we are now silenced by ourselves.

"Incested"—the conversion of a noun to a verb ("I was incested when I was five"). This struck me when I first heard it as truly horrific, deserving of ongoing remark. (Doesn't it sound like a rite of passage? I was baptized? I was confirmed?) But—it occasioned no remark.

Survivors, the "incested", continue to speak out.

Many of the "I-story" books now carry an introduction or endorsement by mental health professionals attesting that this is one brave woman's story of her journey through the stages of healing. Thus, the survivor is made into a case history, fodder for the professionals: pre-fabricated notions. Incest-as-illness has so successfully suffused the culture that the personal— illustrative of pathology—emerges truncated, stunted: personal. In effect, the stories illuminate not the need for social change, but only the need for personal growth. Childhood rape is presented as an opportunity: a challenge to your courage—to heal.

Detoxifying Feminism

In fact, the arc described by the issue of incest should provide, for feminists, a textbook case of the social system's newly refined techniques for detoxifying feminist protest. Unquestionably, the motives of survivors remain genuine—to help others. But placed side by side with the ongoing blatant threat that "abused children become abusers", the promise of `healing' bears an uncanny resemblance to that of salvation from hellfire and damnation.

Witness this: speak out today, and here are some of the twelve steps that may be provided for your recovery:

- Admit you are powerless over your early experience and that your life has become unmanageable.
- Come to believe that a power greater than yourself can restore you to sanity.
- Make a decision to turn your will and your life over to the care of God as you understand Her/Him.
- Admit to God, yourself and another human being the exact nature of your wrongs (yes, yours).
- Be entirely ready to have God remove these defects of character (yes, *yours*).
- Humbly ask Her/Him to remove your shortcomings.
- Make a list of all persons you have harmed and become willing to make amends to them all . . .

I ask you. If this were a 12-step designed by rapists, could they have improved on this programme of sin and redemption? (Sin, yours. Redemption task, yours.)

Why (one does not know whether to bang the table with one's fists or one's forehead)—*why* have so many survivors so readily bought into this "model" in which their childhood rape becomes the fuel driving an ongoing industry? Why have they been so ready to embrace the recommended teddy bear, rather than embracing their rage?

Many, many survivors came to consciousness after that brief light shone on the politics of incest. However all of their experience since then has taken place within the context of incest-as-illness. They have been courted by a cadre of helpers; given codewords and buzz phrases; had an emotional universe custom-designed, their feelings predicted and pre-articulated, their path delineated. In embracing their identity as "survivors" they are granted belonging in a community which celebrates the primacy of Feelings.

To be fair: they have been horribly threatened. Abused children become abusers. On your head be it. Take the cure, or else.

And—to be fair: the most perceptive of them must ask why, if feminists were so right, we made so little headway. And who better placed to know that when you challenge such a power-invested centre; attempting to storm, as it were, the very room where the king is diddling his daughter, the guards will do something nasty indeed to you should you get in. Those victimised as children by fathers must know more surely than any the threatened price of defiance.

Incest and Identity

But perhaps most importantly incest-as-illness offered survivors support—an item noticeably in short supply in the feminist movement in recent years. By the time incest arose as an issue, the women's movement had already become a loose collection of the single-issue identified: the battered women's contingent, the anti-pornography contingent, reproductive rights . . . It had already begun to splinter into a zillion often-antagonistic identity groups: Black, Jewish, Hispanic, lesbian, Marxist, socialist, communalist, spiritualist, vegetarian . . . Individuals were deriving their identities from these identifications. "Survivor" became a ticket, a passport, a membership card.

It was hardly survivors' faults that, in placing their primary identities in incest, they colluded with the medicalisers in their own clientisation.

And, of course, this ghettoising of the issue served to corroborate the more general feminist population's sense that the issue was off bounds for any but card-carrying victims.

Is the issue re-claimable as a feminist one? Can the greatest number of survivors yet be brought within a political base, and can their energies be converted to activism? I am told not by counsellors: that they are too weakened, and too emotionally fragile. I do not know this. I do not know anymore how much of the fragility is intrinsic and how much is fed by the prevailing wisdom.

I do suspect that nothing can change without concerted energy on the part of feminists as a whole, nor unless we can offer a satisfactory belonging and sense of community and purpose. What survivors are buying into presently is, after all, profoundly respectable. In a world in which people are volunteering wholesale to identify themselves as addicted to anything-you-name-it, to confess to an illness and subject themselves to a cure, those embracing incest as their illness seem positively wholesome (in the social sense).

The goals served by the illness model are deeply opposed to feminist goals. To fight on behalf of feminist goals is to focus attention on child-rape as a crime and on men and male power as the problem. The goal of most therapies is *forgiveness* of offenders. As with religious goals of enemy forgiveness. This is a beautiful way of containing the anger of an oppressed population by fostering an unholy delusion: that the oppressor gives a damn one way or the other; that your power to forgive is any kind of power at all.

Perhaps, ironically, a first step now is to speak out about all this. Perhaps now is the time to break the *real* silence.

Medical Power and Control Wheel and Medical Advocacy Wheel

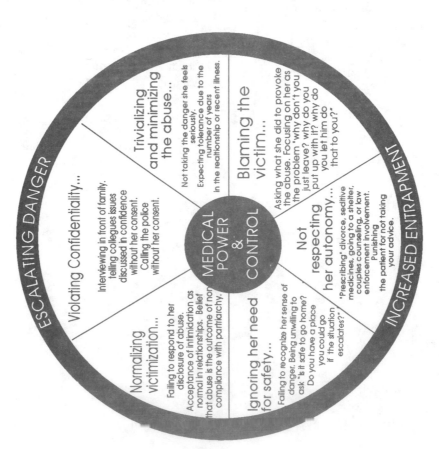

"The Medical Power and Control Wheel"

"The Empowerment Wheel"

Based on the "Power and Control Wheel" and the "Equality Wheel" by the Domestic Abuse Intervention Project. Developed by the Domestic Violence Project, Inc., 3556 7th Avenue, Kenosha, WI 53140, (414)656-8502. Reprinted by permission.

WORKSHEET—CHAPTER 12

Violence Against Women

I. Societal Responsibility for Violence Against Women

a. How do boys and men get the message that "it's ok", "it's socially acceptable" for men to be violent to-wards women? Give examples of ways in which boys and men are given this message. (Use examples from advertising, t.v., literature, movies, etc.)

b. For one day, in your own life, keep track of all the situations (t.v. shows, video games, cartoons, jokes, lectures, friends, language, etc.) in which violence is allowed or even encouraged.

c. Identify ways that gender-role socialization may play a part in violence against women.

II. Continuum of Violence

Sexual harassment at school or work, pornography, child sexual abuse, date rape, sexual assault, battering, and elder abuse are all part of a continuum of ways in which violence against women gets expressed.

Choose any two of the above mentioned forms of violence. Show ways in which these two forms of violence are similar, what they reflect about attitudes towards women, how they limit women's role in society, and why they are mental and physical health issues.

III. Identify ways in which domestic violence in lesbian relationships is the same and different from heterosexual domestic violence. (Think about what would be the same or different in a lesbian power and control wheel compared to the power and control wheel on page 529.)

IV. Identify some of the barriers the following women might face in trying to safely end the violence in their lives:

a poor woman _____

an undocumented woman from another country _____

a woman who is very ill _____

a woman whose abuser is ill _____

a very rich woman _____

a doctor's wife _____

a minister's wife _____

a Latina woman _____

an alcoholic_____

a 40 year old trying to get pregnant _____

V. Health workers recognize and respond to violence

Several articles in this chapter address the importance of health workers' response to violence.

a. Have you ever had a health worker ask you about violence issues? If you can remember the approach used (exact words, attitude, etc.), describe the situation and whether it felt appropriate to you.

b. If you were involved in training health workers to recognize and respond to violence, what specific recommendations would you give them?

CHAPTER 13

Body Image, Food and Nutrition

We are what we eat. This last section explores how social, cultural, and economic factors impact upon the basic physiological process of feeding our bodies. The relationship of women to food is as complex as any other phenomenon examined in this book.

"Nourishing Ourselves" pulls together many of the multi-layered interrelationships between women's roles as the world's food producers, how women's inferior status and internalized sexism may affect women's access to the very food they have produced, and the tragic short and long term individual and societal costs of females being undernourished. Placed within a global context, the similarities are drawn between malnutrition in poor countries/poor communities and in richer communities where societal pressure to be thin similarly deprives girls and women of the quality of diet they need for maximum mental and physical health. This leads to the ultimate question of whether the relationship to food is so different for women and men that it actually becomes a factor in determining gender differences.

The next articles concentrate on the ramifications, particularly for women, of learning to hate fatness in others and especially in ourselves. "Fatphobia" looks at one of the most prevalent, yet uncriticized, forms of prejudice in our society, and "Mental Health Issues Related to Dieting" discusses mental health consequences of this cultural obsession with trying to be thin.

Much healthier attitudes towards one's non-skinny body are expressed in "We'll Always Be Fat But Fat Can Be Fit." "The Great Weight Debate" builds on this healthier approach with Pat Lyons, a pioneer in the fitness for large women movement, asking us to participate in education and advocacy to reduce weight discrimination. Just as "Fatphobia" questions why people who would not think of laughing at sexist or racist jokes are still laughing at fat people, Lyons wonders why feminists have been so silent on this issue that hurts so many women.

Until quite recently, much of the research and writing on women, dieting, and eating disorders has been focused primarily on white middle class women. Individual women of color have often expressed frustration that such information did not reflect their experiences and have reminded us that if studies take place at health centers "which are not trusted by women of color," many women of color will be underrepresented in those studies! Becky Thompson has done cutting edge work examining how race, class, and heterosexism intersect with sexism to impact body image and "eating disorders" issues. Anyone interested in eating disorders will benefit from reading Becky Thompson's work. The chapter reprinted here is from her book, *A Hunger So Wide and So Deep (American Women Speak Out on Eating Problems),* and she also has a chapter in the highly recommended book, *Feminist Perspectives on Eating Disorders,* edited by Patricia Fallon, Melanie A. Katzman, and Susan C. Wooley. Becky Thompson's summary of her feminist research is complemented by the very personal perspective of Christy Haubegger in "I'm Not Fat, I'm Latina."

The worksheet, "The Continuum of Women and Food Relationships," is a study guide to thinking through how the so-called "eating disorders" are exaggerated manifestations of the ambivalent relationship many women have to their bodies and their food.

Nourishing Ourselves

by Nancy Worcester

What could be more ironic? Nourishing others is a fundamental part of women's lives but that very role itself limits the ability of women to take care of their own nutritional needs.

Women are the world's food producers and throughout the world, within a wide range of family units, women have responsibility for purchasing and/or preparing the daily food. Yet, both globally and within families, women are much more likely than men to be malnourished. Nearly universally, wherever there is a shortage of food or a limited supply of quality food, women's diets are inferior to men's quantitatively and qualitatively. Even when food supply is adequate or abundant, women's diets may be nutritionally inferior to men's.

It matters! At some level we all have a feel for how important a good diet is: "We are what we eat." If we feed our bodies the basic nutrients, the healthy body is amazingly clever at being able to take care of itself. An adequate diet is obviously important for *every* man, woman and child. However, both societally and individually, a terrible mistake is being made when women's diets are inferior to men's.

A woman's diet must be more "nutrient-concentrated" than a man's in order to be nutritionally adequate. Most women require considerably less energy than most men. For example, the US Food and Nutrition Board recommends an intake of 1600–2400 Calories per day for women age 23–50, compared to 2300–2700 Calories per day for the same age men. A US Food Consumption Survey showed that the average 23 year old woman consumes only two-thirds as many Calories as the average 23 year old man, 1600 compared to 2400.[1] However, women's requirements for many specific nutrients are identical or greater than men's. The ramifications for this are most serious for calcium and iron. US Food and Nutrition Board Recommended Daily Allowance (RDA)[2] for calcium is the same for men and women.

The RDA of 15 mg. of iron per day for reproductive aged women is 50% higher than the 10 mg. RDA for men.

Picture a woman and a man sitting down to consume their daily nutritional needs. The man's pile of food will be 50% bigger than the woman's but in the woman's smaller pile she will need to have the same amount of calcium and 50% more iron. Each bite the woman takes must contain 50% more calcium and twice as much iron! Put another way, even if a man does not have a particularly nutrient-rich diet, he will probably be able to meet his body's needs and he will even get away with consuming quite a few empty-calorie or low-quality foods whereas a woman's diet must be of a relatively higher quality. A man's diet can be nutritionally inferior to a woman's and still be adequate for his needs. The world and millions of individuals are paying a high price for the fact that women's diets are often inferior to men's.

Sex Differential in Food Distribution and Consumption

The trend to feed boys better than girls gets established early in life. In Kashmir, girls are breastfed for only 8–10 months but boys are allowed to suckle for three years or longer.[3] In Arabic Islam, girls are breastfed for only 1–1-1/2 years while it is common for a boy to be nursed until the age of 2–2-1/2.[4]

A recent Italian study also showed differences in the patterns of feeding baby boys and girls—girls are breastfed less often and for shorter periods; girls are weaned an average of three months earlier than boys. Additionally, it was observed that boys were more irritable and upset before feeding but went to sleep immediately after feeding. In contrast, the girls were less

"Nourishing Ourselves" by Nancy Worcester is an excerpt from *Women and Food,* being written for Pluto Press, London, England. Copyright © 1994 by Nancy Worcester.

aggressive in asking for food but settled down less easily after feeding.[5]

Throughout the world, men and boys get feeding priority. In many cases, men literally eat first and women and children get what food is left-over, such as in Bangladesh where the tradition of sequential feeding means adult men are served first, followed by male children, then adult women and female children. Ethiopian women and girls of all classes must prepare two meals, one for the males and a second, often containing no meat or other substantial protein, for the females.[6] Boys' better access to food based on a gender defined division of labour can get started early in life. For example, in Alor, Indonesia, very young boys are encouraged to do "masculine" work and food serves as an important incentive and reward for that work. Boys receive "masculine" meals as guests of adult men for whom they have performed some service. In contrast, young girls do less valued work like weeding and get a lower quality vegetable lunch.[7]

In whatever way a particular society works it out, there is a nearly universal pattern of men getting fed more and better. Most women recognize this pattern and can identify ways in which they feed their children and their partners better than themselves. Although this may mean nothing more serious than taking the burnt slice of toast or the least attractive piece of dessert for oneself, in times of shortage this pattern means that women are the most likely to be malnourished.

Family members may not even be aware of the sacrifices the woman is making. A British woman who fed her husband and her children even when she could not feed herself during the 1930s remembered, "Many a time I have had bread dripping [animal fat on bread] for my dinner before my husband came home and I said I had my dinner as I would not wait."[8] That pattern is becoming prevalent again as many families do not have enough food. How many women say they are on a diet when in fact they would love some of what they are serving up to their family?

Hilary Land's study of large families in Britain concluded, "It was very evident that the mother was the most likely to go without food for she was the most dependent on meals provided at home. . . It was clear that the father's needs were put first, then the children's and finally the mother's." Over half of the women had no cooked meal in the middle of the day. A quarter had no breakfast and nothing more than a sandwich for lunch. One in twelve women *never* had a cooked meal.[9]

Studies in both Britain and the US have shown that poor parents go without food in order to leave enough food for their children. A British survey found that children were generally better and more regularly fed than their parents. "Only" 15% of the children had fewer than three meals during the previous twenty-four hours in contrast to 75% of the parents having had fewer than three meals, 50% having had two meals and 25% having had only one meal in the twenty-four hour period.[10] A 1983 New York study interviewed people at various sites including emergency feeding centers, food stamp offices, health centers and community centers. When asked, "Do your children eat and sometimes you're unable to?", over one-third of all respondents answered yes and 70% of the parents interviewed at the emergency feeding sites said yes.[11] (These studies did not look for different impacts on mothers and fathers.)

The feminization of poverty means that women in singleheaded households are often the worst affected. A Northern Ireland survey of 700 lone parents found that food was the item on which economies were most likely to be made and inevitably the savings were made by the mother herself going without food.[12] An English woman living on Supplementary Benefits describes the stark "choice" between her needs and the children's:

> It has to be me cutting down on what I eat. It's the only way to find the extra money you need. The rest of it, they take it before you can get your hands on it really. So it's the food. It's the only thing I can cut because I use as little heating as I can and I don't smoke.[13]

Providing food for the children is such a worry for women who are the only parent that they may actually deprive themselves more than is necessary. Marsden's study of 116 lone mothers found that they hoarded food to be able to feed the children. He observed a stress reaction to living on low income in which the caregivers economized on their own food more than the size of their income required.[14]

Efforts specifically designed to improve women's diets are not successful if programmes are not planned around the recognition that women feed their families before they feed themselves and that men tend to get the high status foods. For example, a very ambitious 86 million dollar (US dollars) World Food Programme (WFP) project set up to improve the nutrition of pregnant and nursing mothers and their young children in Pakistan has had practically no nutritional impact. The major problem with the programme was that food was rationed so that each woman would receive an individual dietary supplement of 850 Calories per day, but, of course, the women shared the extra food with their families. The average family had six people so one-sixth of the supplement, less than 150 Calories a day, did not make a significant improvement in women's diets.

The acknowledgement that women do not give themselves priority in food allocation posed new problems for evaluators of the Pakistan WFP project:

> Another possibility that has been mentioned is to simply accept the realities of family structure and food habits in Pakistan and expand the rations given to the women so that they are enough to provide supplements to the entire family. Obviously, a major drawback to this approach is that the same amount of food would then supply fewer women because of the increased ration size and not nearly as many women would be drawn to the centers.[15]

Judit Katona-Apte, consultant to the World Food Programme (but apparently not terribly influential!), suggests that one way to make certain that women benefit from food aid is to provide foods which are nutritionally-rich but less desirable than traditional foods. In such situations, the high status traditional foods will be given to the men and the newer, less desirable but nutritional foods will be relegated to the members of low status in the household— the women and children![16]

The differential access to food is often exaggerated by food taboos, which have more impact on women that men. Food habits, including rituals and taboos are an integral part of defining cultures ("we" versus "others"). Food taboos serve the function of reinforcing social status differences between individuals and social groups and symbolize the place one has in society. Taboos characteristically involve the prohibition of the highest quality protein foods. Jelliffe and Jelliffe suggest that, "The reservation of the best foods for the males reflects the ancient situation where it was imperative that hunters be well fed." However, Trant's explanation seems more to the point, "Widespread prohibitions applied to women against the eating of flesh foods may have partly derived from the male wish to keep the foods for themselves."[17] Those Italian baby boys aggressively demanding their food are just perpetuating a very ancient pattern!

Overall, it seems that most permanent taboos and avoidances have little effect on the nutrition of individuals practicing them because the group's diet will have evolved so that other foods supply the nutrients found in prohibited foods. However, temporary avoidance, particularly at crucial periods of the life cycle can have grave consequences.

Such limited duration taboos particularly affect women because they occur at the most nutritionally sensitive periods. For example, hot and cold or yin and yang classifications of food are common throughout the world and are especially important in Latin America and parts of Asia. Although hot and cold and yin and yang are defined differently in diverse cultures, in all cultures practicing these classifications, the balancing concept is closely tied to women's reproductive cycles. So, however menstruation, pregnancy and lactation get defined, it will be particularly important that women avoid certain "unbalancing" foods during those times. The foods which must be avoided are often foods of high nutritional value. Some Puerto Rican women consider pregnancy to be a hot state so avoid hot foods and medications, including vitamin and iron supplements, to prevent babies from being born with a rash or red skin. Bangladeshi women must not eat meat, eggs, fish or hot curries for several days after childbirth because those foods are believed to cause indigestion. Women are expected to eat only rice, bread, tea and cumin seed for those nutritionally-demanding post-partum days.[18]

There are two more points to consider in looking at the impact of food taboos and avoidance on women's nutrition. First, food taboos, as a cultural construct, are a part of the values of the society which are taught to people as they grow up. People learn those taboos as patterns of behavior which are right, normal, best. Other ways of doing things are viewed as wrong, misguided, or irrational. Understanding and appreciating another culture will require getting to know the food habits and vice versa. Second, sound nutritional practices can, with thought and planning, be developed and reinforced within the context of most existing food patterns.

This relates to an important theme I am introducing here which I will then weave throughout this chapter. I am suggesting that our society's fear of fat and obsession with dieting play a role in limiting women's access to optimum nutrition similarly to the way food taboos can affect women's nutrient intake in more traditional cultures. Dieting certainly has more impact on women than men, reinforces social status differences, and leaves more food for others. As a cultural phenomenon, there can be no denying that women from many parts of the world would find the notion of purposefully restricting food intake to lose weight to be "wrong" or "misguided". Imagine trying to explain the pattern of American college women who intentionally skip meals to save calories for snacking and beer drinking at parties to Western Samoan women who exaggerate the amount they eat on diet surveys because, "The more they could say they had eaten . . . the more powerful that meant the village was in being able to amass lots of food."[20,21] When we hear that many nine year old girls are already on slimming diets, we must recognize dieting to be a part of the values which our society now teaches to young women. Because much dieting is erratic behavior, "a temporary drastic measure just to take off a few pounds" (repeatedly performed!), it is more similar to temporary taboos with the potential for grave consequences than to permanent taboos for which people have learned to compensate. Just as one can eat a nutritionally adequate or even nutritionally superior vegetarian or vegan diet if one knows animal products are going to be consciously avoided or unavailable, it is certainly possible to consume nutrient-rich low calorie or weight-maintenance diets. But, that is not how the dieting taboo is usually practiced in this society.

Nutritional Consequences of Sex Differentiation

Clearly there is no way to summarize the effects of sex differentiated nutrition. Nutritional vulnerabilities vary enormously from one part of the world to another, from one region to another, and between classes in the same small community. Malnutrition, of course, is not inevitable and is totally preventable. There is enough food and land available to feed the world's population if our governments considered that to be an important priority.[22] Factors such as cultural food preferences, storage and transport facilities, the soil the food is grown in and the value placed on equal food distribution within a community will have more influence on one's chances of being malnourished than whether one is a woman or a man. But, a pattern emerges which shows that universally malnutrition is far too common and that it affects girls and women more than boys and men.

Hunger affects whole regions and classes of people and sweeps men as well as women into its nets. It seldom happens that the male members of a family are well-fed or overfed while the females starve. The differentials are narrow, and the question is that of which sex first crosses the line between health and sickness. In general, those who skate closest to the margin of deprivation are the most powerless—the very young, the old, and, everywhere, the women.[23]

Nutritional studies do not always look for or find sex differences in nutritional deficiencies. However, when nutritional sex differences are found it is almost always in the direction of the higher occurrence being in females. *Women and Nutrition in Third World Countries*[24] summarizes hundreds of nutritional studies in poor countries and concludes:

Calorie intake is often low among women, although a few populations show adequate intake (Mexico, Tarahumaras, Korea) or excessive (Micronesia) ones. Deficiencies in caloric intake are common, regardless of physiological status . . . where intakes are reported by in-

come, low-income women appear to consume less than their middle and high income counterparts. Not only do women consistently eat less than men, in a number of studies, they consume, on average a smaller percentage of their recommended daily intake . . . Women often consume lower quality, vegetable protein while men receive the larger share of whatever animal protein is available . . . On the basis of quantity alone, women often consumed a smaller percentage of their protein requirements than did men.

The adequacy of vitamin intake varies greatly by culture. Riboflavin intakes are adequate in almost every country reviewed. The adequacy of vitamin A varies considerably, while most women (except those in Singapore, Iran, and the Tarahumara Indians) are deficient in their vitamin C intakes.

Calcium and iron are the two minerals most commonly studied and in a majority of the countries reviewed, women are seriously deficient in their intakes of both.

The particular ramifications of women's iron and calcium deficiencies will be recurring themes in this book.

Iron is vital to the oxygen-carrying capacity of the blood and muscles but iron deficiency anaemia is the most common nutrition problem in rich and poor countries and in rich and poor people. Iron is available in many foods including meats, eggs, vegetables (especially greens), cocoa powder, apricots, breads and cereals, but in light of the prevalence of iron deficiency, the United Nations Committee on Nutrition recommends that more priority be given to iron fortification and supplementation.[25]

Reproductive age women are particularly vulnerable to iron deficiency because iron lost through menstruation must be replaced and highly increased circulatory requirements of pregnancy must be supplied in addition to the body's other needs for iron. Iron deficiency anaemia's incapacitating physiological and psychological effects influence the lives of women three or four times as much as men in many parts of the world. In low income countries, about half of non-pregnant women and nearly two-thirds of pregnant women show signs of iron deficiency anaemia.[27] Bangladesh is the most extreme example where a national survey discovered abnormally low iron (measured as blood haemoglobin) levels in 95% of rural women.[28]

Serious anaemia increases the risks of difficulty and death in childbirth of these women. While the consequences of iron deficiency anaemia are usually less severe in richer countries, the debilitating condition is far too common. Anaemia was identified in 40% of pregnant women in New Mexico's Women, Infant, and Children (WIC) Program and in 33% of poor pregnant women in Minneapolis, Minnesota. Black children show consistently higher rates (often more that twice as high) of anaemia than white children, so the effects of anaemia are probably even more exaggerated for Black than white US women.[29]

The consequences of sex differentiated nutrition become most obvious at the vulnerable times just after weaning and during the childbearing years. These are the two stages of life at which the female to male sex ratios take a dive.[30]

Biologically, it seems females are stronger than males. In general, life expectancy in females is greater than that in males. More males than females are conceived (120–150 males: 100 females), seemingly to "prepare" for the male biological vulnerability. More male fetuses are spontaneously aborted or stillborn, so the male to female ratio is down to 103–105:100 at birth.[31] Fifty-four percent more males die of birth injuries, 18% more males die of congenital malformations, and males account for 54% of all infant deaths in the first year of life.

Given the apparent biological advantage of females, a fascinating exercise is to try to identify the biological versus social and political causes of sex differences in death rates. Obviously, the fact that 68% of the US deaths at age 21 are male is more related to societal messages about who should play with guns and drive fast cars than a biological difference. Whether the supposedly higher rate of coronary heart disease in middle aged men than in women is more related to different roles in society, women's higher oestrogen levels, or a difference of who gets diagnosed, is a much more complex debate. Wherever there is a higher death rate for males, there may be a combination of biological and social factors working. Higher death rates for females clearly indicate that there are social, political or economic conditions overriding the female biological advantage.

The most marked sex discrimination in nutrition occurs after disasters in which there is a food shortage. Although physiological differences between males and females suggest that figures would show an excess mortality among males, statistics which exist consistently show that it is females and especially girl children who are at highest risk.[32] In the economic disasters after flooding in West Bengal, girls under five had a 60 percent higher incidence of third-degree malnutrition than the same age boys.[33]

A number of studies in South Asia have shown dramatic differences in the food and health care available to girls and boys. Preferential treatment of boys begins at birth when the birth of a boy is almost always viewed as a splendid occasion. Attitudes to the birth of a baby girl are at best ambivalent. While explicit female infanticide is no longer commonly practiced, the withholding of food and health care resources from girls can be viewed as a modern day version of female infanticide. The end result is the same: female mortality exceeds male mortality by as much as 50 percent in the 1–4 year age groups in rural Bangladesh.

A detailed study of six rural Bangladeshi villages pinpoints how this happens.[34] Intrafamily food distribution surveys carried out by 130 families showed that energy and protein intakes were consistently higher for males than females in all age groups.

Protein consumption in males compared to females was 14% higher in 0–4 year olds, 22% higher in 5–14 year olds, 25% higher in 15–44 year olds, and 53% higher in males over 45. Malnutrition rates reflected the intrafamily distribution pattern. Of 882 children surveyed, 14.4 percent of girls were classified as severely malnourished compared to 5.1 percent of boys.

There is usually a distinct, almost synergistic relationship between malnutrition and infection. Malnutrition severely compromises the body's ability to resist infection, and resisting or succumbing to infection increases the body's nutritional needs, thus enhancing the degree of malnutrition. The effects of malnutrition will usually be exaggerated by this malnutrition—infection—increased malnutrition cycle and malnourished children can die from normally non-lethal diseases like measles.

Surprisingly, the six village rural Bangladesh study found rates of infection among female children were consistently lower than among males, although the differences were small and statistically insignificant. (More proof of the biological strength of little girls!) The tragedy was that girls were valued so much less than boys that health resources were made available to ill boys but not to ill girls *even when transport and health care was provided for free*. Despite nearly comparable incidence levels of diarrhea, boys exceeded girls at the treatment center by 66 percent: diarrhea treatment rates averaged 135.6 per 1000 for male children in comparison to 81.9 for female children.

Studies from India show even more starkly the consistent and systematic discrimination against females in the allocation of food and health care resources. Kwashiorkor (protein-calorie malnutrition) is four to five times more common among girls than boys. Though girls were more likely to be suffering from this life-threatening form of malnutrition, boys outnumbered girls at the hospital for treatment by a ratio of 50:1. When treated, children of both sexes responded equally well, but the mortality rate was considerably higher in girls due to both a lack of food and a lack of health care.[35,36]

Male-preferential distribution of food and other resources is certainly not a phenomenon only in poor households. Excess female to male mortality in 1–4 year olds is observed even among wealthy landowning families in Bangladesh, demonstrating that competition for scarce, insufficient resources does not explain all the disparity. It is not known whether this pattern is more marked in poor families when there is simply not enough for everyone so less valued members must be "sacrificed" for the sake of others or whether it is exaggerated in wealthier families where the social role of rich women is even more inferior in comparison to the status of rich men. In Bangladesh, excess female mortality is higher in rich households some years but other years excess mortality is higher in poor families.[37]

Intergenerational Consequences of Female Malnutrition

Malnutrition in girls and women can have long term and intergenerational repercussions, because of women's reproductive role. Any nutritional deficiency, such as rickets, which interferes with the physical development of little girls can cause problems, including maternal and infant death, decades later in pregnancy and childbirth.

The most profound and long term effect of women's malnutrition is demonstrated by the link between poor maternal height and weight and low birth weight babies. Low birth weight babies, defined as weighing less than 2500 grams (five and one-half pounds) at full gestation, have a much higher mortality rate and are more susceptible to illness throughout childhood than normal weight babies. A Sri Lankan study found an average maternal height of 150 cm (4'9") for low birth weight babies and a modal maternal height of 155 cm (5'1") for well-grown babies.[38] Poor maternal height and weight can be a reflection of the mother's own intrauterine growth retardation and inadequate childhood nutrition. Healthy diets for all potential mothers from pre-conception through pregnancy can be seen as a high societal priority when one realizes that *it takes at least two generations to eliminate the effect of stunted maternal growth on future generations of women and men.*

Reversing the effect of malnutrition brings new challenges. When a basic nutritionally-adequate diet for everyone becomes a national priority, young women with a family history of malnutrition will have access to a healthy diet after their own development has been stunted. In revolutionary China, as a consequence of major improvements in food production and distribution, birth weights rose dramatically within one generation. In order to maximize on its nutritional achievements, China's health services had to be able to cope with an increased rate of complicated deliveries as there was a generation of small mothers producing relatively large babies.[39]

While the relationship of women's malnutrition to generations of limited development may be most exaggerated in the poorest countries, it is certainly also an issue for wealthier countries. Some figures will help us follow through the impact of restricted nutrition on poor women in Britain and the U.S. but one has to be critical of categories of analysis. Not by accident, measures of social class such as wealth, income, education and job classification are seldom recorded on US records such as death certificates.[40] Britain is much better at recognizing/not hiding the importance of social class information but the information is more appropriate to men than to women. Women's social class is based on husband's occupation. Even when categorization is based on the woman's own job, as with unmarried heterosexual or lesbian women, women's jobs certainly do not sum up women's lives.[41]

In Britain, 41 percent of wives of professional men have a height of at least 165 cm (5'5") compared to only 26 percent of wives of manual workers. Similarly, in the US, women in low income families have an average height of 160.4 cm (5'3") compared to 163.4 cm (5'4") for women in higher income families.[42] Heights for US children have, on average, been increasing throughout the last century, but the average height for poor children lags behind that for nonpoor children by more than a generation. The average height of ten year olds from families above poverty level is now significantly higher than the average height of ten year olds living below poverty. (This is not a race difference, for the average height of Black children is slightly higher than that of white children of the same income.) Sweden has recently managed to eliminate growth differences between social classes and is probably the only country with this achievement.[43]

In Britain, low birth weight babies and stillbirths are nearly twice as common in poor families (social classes IV and V) as in wealthier families (classes I and II). In the US, infant mortality rate is thirty times higher in low birth weight babies than normal weight babies.[44] Infant mortality rate (IMR = the number of babies per thousand live births who die in the first year of life) is an invaluable tool for comparing the health status of groups because it is a figure which is calculated similarly all over the world and is an excellent reflection of maternal and infant nutrition, as well as general standard of living and access to preventative and curative health care. IMR is 50 percent higher for US whites living in poverty areas than for US whites living in nonpoverty areas and IMR is at least 2.5 times higher in poor than in wealthy families in the UK. The intersection of poverty and racism is obvious from national (US) figures showing IMR more than twice as high for Black babies as white babies. Blacks in poor areas have a far higher IMR than Blacks in nonpoor areas although Black IMR is higher than white IMR in both income areas.[45,46]

The potential for change with an improved standard of living, including an emphasis on nutrition and access to health care, is most striking when IMRs are compared for small geographical areas. The Physician Task Force on Hunger in America contrasts the New York City IMRs of 5.8 in the Sunset Park section of Brooklyn with the 25.6 rate for Central Harlem and the Houston, Texas IMRs of 10.0 in the Sunnyside areas versus 23.5 in the Riverside Health Center community.[47] When we see that two or four times as many babies are dying in one part of town than in another, little guessing is needed to figure out where the poor, malnourished people live in New York City or Houston.

Malnutrition: Cause and Effect on Women's Role in Society

It is women not men who are unequally distributing food within the family, giving men and boys more than their share of what is available for the household. Women depriving themselves and their daughters of life-sustaining nourishment is the ultimate example of internalized sexism. Men do not need to discriminate against women or carry out nasty plans to "keep women in their place" if women are sufficiently well socialized to their inferior role that they themselves perpetuate keeping women in inferior roles.

A profoundly intermeshing relationship exits between women's status in society and the responsibility for food production and distribution. Women's responsibility for domestic work, especially food production, is so undervalued that women internalize that low value and starve themselves literally or figuratively. Although millions of women and girls die each year as a result of malnutrition, that number is a mere fraction of the number of women and girls who cannot maximize on their full potential because of undernutrition and because their responsibilities for feeding others do not leave them food, time or energy to nourish and nurture themselves.

Women's role as food producer can actually restrict a woman's ability to feed herself and others. How often have we observed a woman who eats practically nothing herself after spending hours preparing a meal for others? How often have we seen a woman so busy serving others that she barely sits down herself? A woman's standards for feeding herself may be totally different than those she holds to for her family. For example, a (London) *Daily Mirror* survey showed that even though mothers of school-age children make sure their children have breakfast, a fifth of mothers do not take time to eat breakfast themselves.[48]

Charmian Kenner's interviews with English women who have survived times of economic hardship show how the family's dependence on mum's food can make mum so ill that she cannot feed them:

> There was a vicious circle in which sickness bred further sickness. Lacking food, women had less resistance to infections. And when a woman fell ill and especially needed better food nobody else could take over and stretch the budget. Some women did not even feel able to set aside valuable time to teach their children to help them.[49]

It is exactly the women who face the most demanding food preparation tasks who have the least time and energy for this work. The woman who can afford the latest food processor and microwave may also be able to afford to buy easy-to-cook or partially prepared nutritious foods when she is too busy to cook. The woman who has to work overtime to have money to buy beans may not be able to buy a pressure cooker to reduce cooking time. Before or after a long day, she may have to decide between spending several hours on food preparation and eating less nutritional foods.

In many agricultural communities, it is *because* women have put all their time and energy into growing and harvesting the food that they may not be able to take the final steps, often extremely time and energy consuming, of turning the raw products into an edible form so that they can feed themselves and others.

> One report speaks of African women "sitting about hungry with millet in their granaries and relish in the bush" because they were too exhausted to tackle the heavy, three-hour work of preparing the food for eating.[50]

The seasonal nature of agriculture exacerbates this. Peak periods for women's work in the fields are normally at planting, harvesting and post-harvesting processing times when the working day can average fifteen hours. This coincides with the food supply being scarcest, most expensive, least varied and least well prepared. As a consequence, it has been noted that in Gambia, pregnant women actually lose weight during the peak agricultural time and, in Thailand, there is a marked increase in miscarriages and an early termination of breastfeeding during the rice planting and harvesting seasons.[51,52]

The relationship between productivity and nutrition works in several ways. Not only does extreme work keep women from feeding themselves, but also undernutrition is clearly a factor limiting women's productivity. Intensity of work, the productive value of work activities selected, and labour time are all dimensions of productivity which have been shown to be affected by nutrition.

If women are not able to maximize on their productivity, food production is limited; several studies have identified women's labour input as the critical constraint on crop production. Although the value of women's productivity is universally and consistently *not* recognized, any signs of poor performance are definitely used to prolong women's low status.

The case of Sri Lankan women tea workers illustrates the cycle whereby low status affects diet, then malnutrition perpetuates low status. Tea workers' poor social and economic position is reflected by high morbidity and maternal mortality rates. Due to poor diets and hook worm manifestation, the women also have high rates of iron deficiency anaemia (measured as low haemoglobin levels). Studies found that this iron deficiency restricted work performance; a significant relationship was found between haemoglobin levels and various treadmill tests of physiological capacity. (Iron deficiency anaemia affects work intensity by decreasing the blood's oxygen transporting capacity.) After the women were given iron supplements for one month, significantly more tea got picked! These studies were of particular interest to the Sri Lankan government because tea has been the main asset for foreign exchange and the poor nutritional status of the female labour force was seen as having far reaching socio-economic consequence. Assuming women's increasing productivity was appropriately financially rewarded, one can see where something as seemingly simple as iron supplements can be an important step to improved economic status for some women.[53,54]

This specific example suggests an even bigger question: How much does the image and reality of the malnourished woman as weak, lethargic and not maximizing on her potential become the generalized description for "women" which then justifies and perpetuates women's inferior status?

Worldwide the high incidence of iron deficiency anemia has to be seen as a major, often unrecognized, component of women's low status. We know that this one nutrition issue affects as many as 95 percent of women in some communities and has profound physiological and psychological repercussions, including impaired work capacity, lassitude, lowered resistance to infection, and increased complications of pregnancy and childbirth. The Sri Lankan tea workers' example is worth remembering as a positive example of both how easily some consequences of iron deficiency can be reversed and the need to make sure our governments become better educated about what they have to gain from a well nourished female labour force.

A wide range of other nutrition problems also have an impact on women's status. As an illustration which has nearly universal ramifications, low Calorie diets serve as an important example of undernutrition which,

for very different reasons, can interfere with women maximizing on their potential and limiting their role in society in both rich and poor countries and for both rich and poor women. It is well known that low energy intakes restrict work potential and conversely that Calorie supplementation significantly increases work intensity and capacity.[55] The body, of course, has to work equally hard at coping with the limitations of a low Calorie diet whether that restriction is imposed because of a natural disaster food shortage or the fact that someone "chooses" to diet down to a smaller size. Research from poor countries indicates that the body does have adaptation mechanisms for adjusting to *permanently* restricted food intake but the body has a particularly chaotic job adjusting to great dietary fluctuations such as erratic food supply or yo-yo dieting.

What price do individuals and society pay for women's undernutrition caused by lifelong dieting? Hilde Bruch, psychiatrist respected for her groundbreaking work on eating disorders, describes "thin fat people" as people (usually women) who routinely eat less than their bodies require in order to stay at a weight which is artificially low for themselves. Very often these women are tense, irritable and unable to pursue educational and professional goals as a direct result of their chronic undernutrition. But, if they never allowed themselves to eat properly they do not recognize the signs that these limitations are due to undereating rather than personal weaknesses. Characteristic signs of malnutrition—fatigue, listlessness, irritability, difficulties in concentration and chronic depression—often escape correct professional diagnosis because the starved appearance (and especially average weight appearance in someone meant to be heavy) is a matter for praise rather than concern by our fatphobic society. "It has become customary to prescribe tranquilizers for such people; three square meals a day would be more logical treatment, but one that is equally unacceptable to physicians and patients because they share the conviction that being slim is good and healthy in itself."[56]

Is it possible that the relationship to food is sufficiently different between women and men that it helps determine gender differences in how women and men operate in the world? What if our scientific studies which "prove" that men are superior at performing certain tasks are actually measuring men's superior ability to fulfill their nutritional requirements rather than measuring task performing abilities? How would we even begin to start to think about or "measure" such things?

Claire Etaugh and Patricia Hill have started on some fascinating research to test their theory that gender differences in eating restraint (dieting) influence previously reported gender differences in cognitive restructuring tasks. Their initial study found that gender differences were in fact eliminated on one of two tasks when men and women were matched for eating restraint. On the other task, eating-restricted females performed the task more poorly than unrestricted females, thus exaggerating the male-female difference.[57] This work certainly confirms the need for eating restraint to be a factor which must be controlled in any study which attempts to measure gender differences. This research builds on previous work which showed that many differences found between fat and thin people are actually differences between restrained eaters (dieters) and non-restrained eaters (non-dieters). Even without further research, we know that some cognitive restructuring task gender differences disappear when dieting is controlled for and we know that dieting can result in poorer performance on a range of tests. What more proof do we need that dieting can prevent women from maximizing on their potential?

Although we have started to explore how the nearly universal pattern of men and boys getting fed more and better than women and girls can play a part in perpetuating women's inferior social and economic roles, it is hard to imagine all the many subtle and unnoticed ways in which this may manifest itself.

Hamilton, Popkin and Spicer suggest that nutritional status affects one's selection of work activities. Only well-nourished workers would be expected to qualify for the higher paying jobs if they are more physically or mentally demanding. Conversely, they suggest, individuals adapt to low energy intakes by being involved in less demanding occupations.[58]

Not surprisingly, most studies concentrate on nutrition-productivity relationships in men. Much less is known about the interaction of nutrition and productivity in women and, of course, even less is known about how nutrition affects women's roles outside the paid labour force. One study reported that supplementation of women's diets improves the mother-child interactions and enhances child development by providing women with greater energy and increasing their potential capacity for physical effort and active time for interaction with the children.[59] A study of Guatemalan peasants found that women who receive dietary supplements spent more leisure and market time in physically active tasks than women who did not receive supplements. Sixty-seven percent of the supplemented group were considered "fully active" compared to only five percent of the unsupplemented group.[60]

The long term and intergenerational costs of the malnutrition-low status relationship in girls is just starting to be recognized. It is now known that cognitive development is dependent on both adequate nutrition and intellectual stimulation. Ten year follow-up studies of children who were treated for severe protein-calorie malnutrition showed no significant difference in mental performance when compared to their siblings or controls. But, there was a strong correlation between their intellectual achievement and years of schooling. It was noted that malnourished children sometimes took a few years to recover from any mental consequences of early childhood malnutrition and that the normal curriculum might not be appropriate during that time. This finding has particular significance for girls since in many communities girls will have already been withdrawn from school before the recovery time and thus girls will be deprived of the educational opportunity even if they were lucky enough to be treated for malnutrition.[61]

Several studies have now demonstrated the crucial importance of female education as a factor contributing to lower child mortality even when family income is controlled.[62] These studies do not try to explain the complex mechanisms through which improved female education operates to reduce child mortality, but they help emphasize that women, their children, and society are deprived when women do not get to explore their educational potential.

The relationship of girls' undernutrition and girls' not being able to maximize on their mental development and educational capabilities obviously has enormous ramifications for what women can contribute to society, what women are expected or encouraged to do, and the recognition they are given for their achievements. We saw how a child's birth weight, and thus "good start in life", was influenced by the mother's height and weight which was affected by the grandmother's nutrition. We now see the vital link among childhood nutrition, female educational opportunities and child mortality. Although this may be two different ways of looking at similar information, it is also a reminder of how these social and economic factors work together and exaggerate each other.

Consequently, the low value of females can cause the mothers to feed boys better than girls so that boys are less apt to be malnourished and more likely to be capable of benefitting from, and having access to, educational opportunities. Boys will then be far more likely to be the "well-nourished workers to qualify for the higher paying, higher status, physically or mentally demanding jobs" than their undernourished sisters. In one generation, in one community, the pattern could be clear cut—the boys worked to their potential more than the girls and the boys have more status than their sisters. When the sisters have their own children, how equally will they distribute the food and will they be aware of the unequal distribution if they give more to their sons than their daughters? In the extreme Bangladesh example, women tended to deny unequal distribution except when male child preference was expressed in relation to marked food shortages or in reference to sex differentials with regard to food quality.[63]

Does this extreme but not exaggerated example give us clues to how this process may operate more subtly?

Having seen that cognitive development is dependent on both adequate nutrition and intellectual stimulation and having seen gender differences disappear (in one test) when men and women were matched for eating restraint, what significance is there in the fact that many nine year old girls are now dieting? We know the physical abilities of girls and boys are pretty evenly matched until age 10–12 when social pressure discourages young women from developing their physical potential. We know that many girls excel in maths at an early age but then internalize the "girls aren't good at maths" idea by adolescence. In what ways do these messages which limit young women from maximizing on their potential now get exaggerated by the pressure on them (and their mothers) not to let themselves get fat?

A young woman's nutritional needs are among the highest of her life when she is 11–14 years: an average 100 pound girl uses up 2400 Calories a day and needs a very vitamin and mineral concentrated diet. This is also one of life's most crucial times for making educational decisions which will influence future choices. If individuals or society wish to improve the role of women in society, this is the worst possible stage for young women to start practicing their lives as "thin fat people"!

REFERENCES

1. Judith Willis, "The Gender Gap at the Dinner Table", *FDA Consumer,* June, 1984, pp. 13–17.
2. 1989 RDA
3. Mary Roodkowsky, "Underdevelopment Means Double Jeopardy for Women", *Food Monitor,* September/October 1979, pp. 8–10.
4. Lisa Leghorn and Mary Roodkowsky, *Who Really Starve? Women and World Hunger,* New York: Friendship Press 1977, p. 20.
5. Colin Spencer, "Sex, Lies and Fed by Men", *Guardian,* November 4–5, 1989, p. 11.
6. Leghorn and Roodkowsky, *op. cit.*
7. E.M.Roenberg, "Demographic Effects of Sex Differential Nutrition" in N.W.Jerome, R.F.Kandel and G.H. Pelto (ed.) *Nutritional Anthropology—Contemporary Approaches to Diet and Culture,* Redgrave Publishing Co. 1980, pp. 181–203.
8. Charmian Kenner, *No Time for Women—Exploring Women's Health in the 1930s and Today,* London:Pandora 1985, p. 8.
9. Hilary Land, "Inequalities in Large Families: More of the Same or Different?" in Robert Chester and John Peel (ed.) *Equalities and Inequalities in Family Life,* New York: Academic Press 1977, pp. 163–175.
10. Hilary Graham, *Women, Health and the Family,* Brighton, Sussex: Wheatsheaf Books 1984, pp. 120–135.
11. Ruth Sidel, *Women and Children Last—The Plight of Poor Women in Affluent America,* New York: Viking 1986, p. 149.
12. E.Evason, *Just Me and the Kids: A Study of Single Parent Families in Northern Ireland,* Belfast: EOC 1980, p. 25, quoted in Graham, *op. cit.*
13. "Food for All?" *London Food News,* no.4-Autumn 1986, p.1.
14. D.Marsden, *Mothers Alone: Poverty and the Fatherless Family,* Harmondsworth, Middlesex: Penguin 1973, p. 43, quoted in Graham, *op.cit.*
15. Neil Gallagher, "Obstacles Curb Efforts to Improve Nutrition", *World Food Programme Journal,* no.3, July–September, 1987, pp. 19–22.
16. Judit Katona-Apte, "Women and Food Aid—A Developmental Perspective", *Food Policy,* August, 1986, pp. 216–222.
17. Paul Fieldhouse, *Food and Nutrition: Customs and Culture,* London: Croom Helm 1986, pp. 168–169.
18. *Ibid.,* pp. 41–54.
19. *Ibid.*
20. Betsy A. Lehman, "Fighting the Battle of Freshman Fat", *The Boston Globe,* September 25, 1989, pp. 23,25.
21. Joan Price, "Food Fixations and Body Biases—An Anthropologist Analyzes American Attitudes", *Radiance,* Summer 1989, pp. 46–47.
22. See for example the excellent resources of the Institute for Food and Development Policy, 1885 Mission Street, San Francisco, CA. 94103 (USA) or Oxfam, 274 Banbury Rd., Oxford OX2-7DZ (England).
23. Kathleen Newland, *The Sisterhood of Man,* London: W.W.Norton 1979, pp. 47–52.
24. Sahni Hamilton, Barry Popkin and Deborah Spicer, *Women and Nutrition in Third World Countries,* South Hadley, Massachusetts: Bergin and Garvey Publishers 1984, pp. 22–26.
25. United Nations Administrative Committee on Coordination—Subcommittee on Nutrition, *First Report on the World Nutrition Situation,* Rome, Italy: FAO Food Policy and Nutrition Division 1987, pp. 36–39.
26. UNICEF News Fact Sheet printed in Leghorn and Roodkowsky, *op. cit.*
27. Hamilton, Popkin and Spicer, *op. cit.* p. 55.
28. Shushum Bhatia, "Status and Survival", *World Health,* April, 1985, pp. 12–14.
29. Physician Task Force on Hunger in America, *Hunger in America—The Growing Epidemic,* Middletown, Connecticut: Wesleyan University Press 1985, pp. 119–120.
30. Newland, *op.cit.*
31. Ethel Sloane, *Biology of Women,* 2nd Edition, New York: John Wiley 1985, pp. 122–123.
32. J.P.W.Rivers, "Women and Children Last: An Essay on Sex Discrimination in Disasters", *Disasters,* 6(4), 1982, pp. 256–267.
33. Amartya Sen, "The Battle to Get Food", *New Society,* 13 October, 1983, pp. 54–57.
34. Lincoln C. Chen, Emdadul Huq and Stan D'Souza, "Sex Bias in the Family Allocation of Food and Health Care in Rural Bangladesh", *Population and Development Review,* vol. 7, no.1, March, 1981, pp. 55–70.
35. Newland, *op. cit.*
36. Bhatia, *op. cit.*
37. Chen, Huq and D'Souza, *op. cit.*

38. Priyani Soysa, "Women and Nutrition", *World Review of Nutrition and Dietetics,* vol.52, 1987, pp. 11–12.

39. Discussions with Chinese health workers and the All China Women's Federation, March 1978 and March 1983.

40. Victor W. Sidel and Ruth Sidel, *A Healthy State—An International Perspective on the Crisis in United States Medical Care,* New York:Pantheon 1977, p. 15.

41. Jeannette Mitchell, *What Is To Be Done About Illness and Health?* Harmondsworth, Middlesex:Penguin 1984, p. 22.

42. Soysa, *op. cit.*

43. Sidel and Sidel, *op. cit.,* p. 26,

44. Physician Task Force on Hunger in America, *op. cit.,* p. 99.

45. Melanie Tervalon, "Black Women's Reproductive Rights" in Nancy Worcester and Mariamne H. Whatley (ed.) *Women's Health: Readings on Social, Economic and Political Issues,* Dubuque, Iowa: Kendall/Hunt 1988, pp. 136–137.

46. Sidel and Sidel, *op. cit.,* p.17.

47. Physician Task Force on Hunger in America, *op. cit.,* p. 109.

48. Kenner, *op. cit.,* p. 10.

49. *Ibid.,* p. 8.

50. Ester, Boserup, *Women's Role in Economic Development,* London: George Allen and Unwin 1970, p. 165 quoted in Barbara Rogers, *The Domestication of Women—Discrimination in Developing Societies,* London:Tavistock 1981, p. 155.

51. Hamilton, Popkin and Spicer, *op. cit.* p.45.

52. Ellen McLean, "World Agricultural Policy and Its Effect on Women's Health", *Health Care for Women International,* vol.8, 1987, pp. 231–237.

53. Hamilton, Popkin and Spicer, *op. cit.,* pp. 20– 21.

54. Soysa, *op. cit.,* pp. 35–37.

55. Hamilton, Popkin and Spicer, *op. cit.*

56. Hilde Bruch, "Thin Fat People" in Jane Rachel Kaplan (ed.) *A Woman's Conflict—The Special Relationship Between Women and Food,* Englewood Cliffs, New Jersey:Prentice-Hall 1980, pp. 17–28.

57. Claire Etaugh and Patricia Hall, "Restrained Eating: Mediator of Gender Differences on Cognitive Restructuring Tasks?", *Sex Roles,* vol.20, nos.7/8, 1989, pp. 465–471.

58. Hamilton, Popkin and Spicer, *op. cit.*

59. *Ibid.*

60. *Ibid.*

61. Soysa, *op. cit.,* pp. 13–14.

62. Chen, Huq and D'Souza, *op. cit.*

63. *Ibid.*

Fatphobia

by Nancy Worcester

We learn not to like fat people, then we internalize that as anxiety of gaining weight ourselves or self-hatred if we are already overweight. Both English and American studies consistently show that excess body fat is the most stigmatized physical feature except skin color.[1,2] Fatphobia differs from racism in that being overweight is thought to be under voluntary control. Anti-fat attitudes are well established before a child reaches kindergarten. 'Even at that young age, children attribute negative characteristics to the heavy physique, do not want to be like that themselves, and choose a greater "personal space distance" between themselves and a heavy child than from other children.'[3]

The animosity towards fat people is such a fundamental part of our society, that people who have consciously worked on their other prejudices have not questioned their attitudes towards body weight. People who would not think of laughing at a sexist or racist joke, ridicule and make comments about fat people without recognizing that they are simply perpetuating another set of attitudes which negatively affect a whole group of people.

The pressure to look like the 'ideal' is so strong that we do not question the implications behind teaching that routinely instructs young women on how to make their bodies look 'as perfect as possible'. Home economics classes teach young women that horizontal stripes make one look wider, vertical stripes make one look thinner. I was so well socialized by such instruction that I still find it hard to be comfortable in horizontal stripes, unless, of course, they are strategically placed so as to make the chest look larger! Even after years of criticizing the pressure on women to look thin, instead of admiring a large woman who has the courage to wear the "wrong" stripes, I still find myself wondering, 'But, doesn't she know . . . ?'

Although the prejudice against fat people affects both men and women, its impact is most exaggerated on women and their lives. Women put on body fat more easily than men for a number of social and physiological reasons. Of course, every topic in this book is a part of the explanation. The physical abilities of females and males are identical until puberty, but by that time socialization in most western cultures discourages physical fitness in young women thus encouraging weight to be put on as fat rather than as muscle. (At the age of 25, body fat content averages 14% for men and 23% for women.[4]) Although both females and males have a mixture of the sex hormones estrogens and androgens, the average female tends to have higher levels of estrogens than androgens and this influences the deposition of fat. Times of hormonal changes, adolescence, going on oral contraceptive pills, pregnancy, and menopause, are all times when some women notice that they put on fat easily.

Women are judged by appearance far more than men and a much wider range of sizes and shapes is considered attractive in men. For example, a 1982 study of the most popular North American television programs, found that of male characters, less than one-fifth were slim and more than one-quarter were plump, whereas of the female characters, over two-thirds were slim and only one-tenth were plump.[5] Women, not men, are bombarded with information that the size and shape of their bodies is central to who they are and if it is less than perfect they should be working to try to change it. Comparing the most popular of men's and women's magazines, we see that articles and advertising relating to body weight and dieting appear 17 times more often in women's magazines.[6]

At any moment in history, the ideal female figure is quite precisely defined. Studies have shown that both men and women judge women's bodies by how closely they measure up to that supposed ideal. The more a woman deviates from that 'norm', the more her appearance will adversely affect her social life, her acceptance at college, her employment, and her status.

In both England and North America, obesity is more common in working class women than in women of higher socio-economic groups. With men, the relationship of class and body weight is not so well defined.[7,8]

It seems relevant to suggest that the relationship between social class and obesity is not as simple as just the fact that poor people have less access to healthy, non-fattening foods. It is *both* poor women and men who have less access to these foods so we would expect that the relationship of class to obesity to be more consistent for both women and men. I am not convinced that differences in manual labor provide an explanation. (It has been suggested that working class men offset a tendency to obesity by doing more physical labor than middle class men. This explanation does not take into account that middle class men have more access to leisure exercise opportunities and facilities than do working class men and that working class women are also more likely to be involved in physically active jobs than middle class women.)

Is it possible that in our society a woman's body build is a factor in *determining* her socio-economic status? Nearly twenty years ago, a paper on the stigma of obesity concluded that, 'Obesity, especially as far as girls is concerned, is not so much a mark of low social economic status as a condemnation to it.'[9] A study of 1660 adults in Manhattan observed that overweight women compared to non-obese women are far less likely to achieve a higher socio-economic status and are much more likely to have a lower socio-economic status than their parents.[10] This relationship was not found in men. A now classical study of the late 1960's found that non-obese women were more likely to be accepted for college than obese women even though the obese and non-obese women did not differ on intellectual ability or percentage who applied for college admission.

If obese adolescents have difficulty in attending college, a substantial proportion may experience a drop in social class, or fail to advance beyond present levels. Education, occupation, and income are social-class variables that are strongly interrelated. A vicious circle, therefore, may begin as a result of college admission discrimination, preventing the obese from rising in the social-class system.[11]

As long as women are valued and rewarded for their roles as sex objects, and the non-skinny woman is not seen as fitting this image, it is easy to see how the stigma of excess weight limits a woman's status through job discrimination, apparently less marriage to high-status men (sic!) and fewer social and economic opportunities. The discrimination against fat women should serve as a reminder to all of us that we need to change the basis upon which the worth of all women is determined by society. Tragically, instead of viewing fatphobia as *society's* problem, many women internalize the fear and intolerance of fat as their *individual* problem. Instead of trying to change the world, women end up trying to change themselves.

In this era, when inflation has assumed alarming proportions and the threat of nuclear war has become a serious danger, when violent crime is on the increase and unemployment a persistent social fact, 500 people are asked by pollsters what they fear the most in the world and 190 of them answer that their greatest fear is 'getting fat'.[12]

REFERENCES

1. S.J. Chetwynd, R.A. Stewart, and G.E. Powell, "Social Attitudes Towards the Obese Physique" in Alan Howard (ed.) *Recent Advances in Obesity Research: 1,* London: Newman Publishing 1975, pp. 223–225.
2. Susan C. Wooley and Orland W. Wooley, "Obesity and Women—I. A Closer Look at the Facts", *Women's Studies International Quarterly,* vol. 2, 1979a, pp. 69–79.
3. Orland W. Wooley, Susan C. Wooley, and Sue R. Dyrenforth, "Obesity and Women—II. A Neglected Feminist Topic", *Women's Studies International Quarterly,* vol. 2, 1979b, pp. 81–92.
4. Marion Nestle, *Nutrition in Clinical Practice,* Greenbrae, California: Jones Medical Publications 1985, p. 222.
5. Brett Silverstein, *Fed Up—The Food Forces That Make You Fat, Sick and Poor,* Boston: South End Press 1984, p. 107.
6. Silverstein, *op. cit.*
7. Wooley, 1979b, *op. cit.*
8. J. Yudkin, "Obesity and Society", *Biblthca Nutri Dieta,* vol. 26, 1978, p. 146.
9. W.J. Cahnman, "The Stigma of Obesity", *Sociological Quarterly,* vol. 9, 1968, pp. 283–299, quoted in Wooley, 1979b, *op. cit.*
10. P.B. Goldblatt, M.E. Moore, and A.J. Stunkard, "Social Factors in Obesity", *Journal of the American Medical Association,* vol. 192, 1965, pp. 1039–1044.
11. H. Canning and J. Mayer, "Obesity—Its Possible Effect on College Acceptance", *New England Journal of Medicine,* vol. 275, 1966, pp. 1172–1174.
12. *San Francisco Chronicle,* January 17, 1981, quoted in Kim Chernin, *Womansize—The Tyranny of Slenderness,* London: The Women's Press 1983, p. 23.

Mental Health Issues Related to Dieting

by Nancy Worcester

The assumption is that if anyone is overweight they must be trying to lose weight and if they are not trying to lose weight, they certainly should be. The slimming industry has sold us this assumption and it is time that we stop swallowing it. The dieting experience is pretty disastrous for many women. We need to be more aware of the mental hazards of slimming and figure out ways to be more supportive of women who choose not to lose weight.[1] The more that women discover that they can live in large bodies without having to torture themselves with endless slimming diets, the less pressure there will be on all women to carve themselves down to smaller sizes.

1. Women Feel Guilty if They Are Not Slimming

The most liberating gift many women can give themselves is the decision that they are not going to try to lose weight. Until that decision is made, it is tempting to put off everything else and meanwhile dislike oneself both because of the fat itself and because the fat becomes symbolic of an unfulfilled goal.

As long as someone is thinking about changing her body, she is not going to be putting energy into learning to like her body the way it is.

As long as someone is postponing accepting and liking her body, there is a tendency not to work at making that body healthy and fit. This is a part of a self-perpetuating cycle. The more 'out-of-shape' one is, the more dissatisfying (and hard!) it is to undertake even ordinary exercise, the less exercise the body has the worse it feels and fewer calories will be burned up. This, of course, contributes to the tendency to gain weight and feelings of sluggishness.

See 'We'll Always Be Fat But Fat Can Be Fit'[2] which takes a positive approach to accepting one's body weight and improving both mental and physical health.

2. Dieting Makes a Person More Aware of Food

We have all heard of someone who works through lunchtime without realizing they have not eaten or the person who loses weight because they are too busy to eat regularly.

One of the primary purposes of food advertising is simply to keep food on the mind so that the consumer is aware of her appetite. Secondly, of course, advertising aims to influence which particular product is on the mind.

In much the same way, the very act of dieting works to keep food on the mind. The constant preoccupation with not overeating (or more often, not eating normally) makes food take on a new significance. Thus, paradoxically, the most unmanageable time to restrict food consumption is when one is consciously attempting to limit food intake. Can you imagine committed dieters working through a lunchtime without realizing it or being so busy that they did not eat regularly?

Old studies claimed that a difference between fat people and thin people was that fat people ate according to external cues—set meal times, attractive foods, social situation—whereas thin people ate in response to internal cues such as hunger signals. Thus, this explanation implied, thin people were less likely to eat more than their bodies needed. This work is now being reinterpreted.[3] It seems that dieting is a major factor in determining whether one responds to external or internal signals. A dieter cannot respond to internal cues saying she is hungry because dieting creates a state of almost constant hunger. The old studies simply overlooked the fact that fat people are far more likely to be dieting than thin people. Instead of looking at the differences between fat and thin people, researchers were looking at the differences between dieters (restrained eaters) and non-dieters (non-restrained eaters). Dieting makes people unable to listen to their own body signals.

Dieting may be responsible for setting up a vicious cycle which increases the need for further dieting. Once a dieter's restraint is broken, the dieter can easily move in the opposite direction and 'overeat'. Depression and anxiety are emotions likely to break a dieter's restraint. Yet, dieting itself can cause anxiety, depression, and apathy.[4]

In attempting to change food habits, we are embarking upon changing one of our most conservative behaviors, something often intricately related to our inner sense of security. Food habits are the last patterns to change even when a person is living in a new environment and living a new lifestyle, e.g., immigrant food habits often more nearly resemble the diet of the homeland than of the new country even years after settling.

Additionally, changing one's pattern of food consumption presents a uniquely arduous challenge in that one has to deal with it daily, at regular intervals throughout the day. Difficult though it is, someone who is concerned about their smoking or drinking habits may choose to give up cigarettes or alcohol. Someone concerned about their eating habits does not have the option of giving up food.

These problems are all distinctly exaggerated for a woman responsible for others. She does not have the luxury of escaping from thoughts of food. While trying to ignore her own preoccupations with food/hunger, she will need to be making grocery lists, shopping in environments filled with visions and aromas of food, preparing food, serving food to others, and then cleaning up after the meals.

Such a seemingly unappetizing task as clearing up after a meal can be an immense challenge for the dieter. Keeping food intake records for nutrition classes, my students with young children have often discovered that a high percentage of their calorie intake comes from cleaning up the children's plates. They find themselves constantly torn between their lines not to waste food and their waistlines.

A major reason why women are somewhat less successful at losing weight than men is because their domestic responsibilities are so directly contradictory to the optimum conditions for dieting. Responsibility for food preparation is the worst imaginable antidote for the diet-induced obsession with food.

3. Dieting Often Fails

Few people would encourage a loved one, a friend, or a professional client to embark upon an activity which they knew was destined for failure. Yet, knowing that most dieting fails (probably 90%–98% in the long term), people in all types of capacities are constantly advising and cajoling each other to 'try to lose some weight', to check out the newest slimming gimmick, or to try the most recent bestselling diet.

While it may be an overstatement to say that it is sadistic to encourage someone else to diet, it is time to acknowledge that it is often irresponsible to influence someone else to diet. The act of encouraging dieting needs to carry with it the obligation to support the dieter practically and emotionally through the challenges of the dieting process and to nurture the dieter if the attempt to lose weight is not successful. How many people would be willing to commit themselves to something so risky and potentially demanding? There would be far less pressure on people to diet if such pressure had to be accompanied by appropriate supportive commitments.

No one likes failure in any aspect of their life. Too often failure at dieting can take on a significance unexpected and unrecognized by the dieter and her friends. Media bombardment of fictitious slimming success stories completely nullifies the fact that only one to ten percent of dieting is 'successful'. Therefore dieting gets experienced as 'something anyone should be able to do' and is not seen as a particularly ambitious goal. Failing at such a seemingly simplistic task can be especially disheartening.

Because of all the factors which influence body weight and the unpredictable ease with which one can or cannot lose weight, body weight is one of the most difficult areas of one's life to control. But, because body image is so central to a woman's self-image and confidence and is so related to her actual experiences in the world, a woman's inability to lose weight too often becomes symbolic for her of her failure to be in control of her own life.

4. Dieting May Be 'Successful'

If a woman is successful at losing weight, she will lose the advantages of being fat.

Advantages of being fat are imperceptible to most dieters. Yet having managed to lose weight, many women are shocked to discover that the expectations of a slim woman are different than those of a fat woman in this society. I have stopped being surprised by how regularly I meet women who have purposefully gained back weight because they found that 'sexual attractiveness' and not being taken seriously as thin women were so problematic. *Fat Is a Feminist Issue* has been immensely popular because it explores the meaning of being fat or thin in our society and enables women to discover why they may be subconsciously choosing to stay fat.

> My fat says 'screw you' to all who want me to be the perfect mom, sweetheart, maid, and whore. Take me for who I am, not for who I'm supposed to be. If you are really interested in me, you can wade through the layers and find out who *I* am.[5]

Food can be an invaluable tool for relieving tension, coping with stress, or rewarding oneself. Successful dieting inevitably means changing those food habits that one has developed over a number of years. Additionally, the stress of dieting itself may undermine even the most well established coping mechanisms. Ingenuity is necessary in providing oneself with healthy alternatives to the role that food has played in keeping life in balance.

Education against child abuse is increasingly suggesting that adults hit a pillow or eat something to relieve tension involved in some adult-child interactions. This is a questionable and simplistic approach to decreasing child abuse, but it is a reminder of the role that food can play in defusing tension which could lead to physical violence or verbal confrontation with a child or an adult. Eating, even if that means overeating, will often be the healthiest way of dealing with immediate distress. We need to be alert to the dangers of dieting blocking that outlet.

There is also an obvious problem with the inverse relationship between cigarette smoking and weight. Women have been encouraged to use cigarettes as a means of weight control since the American Tobacco Company introduced the slogan "Reach for a Lucky instead of a sweet" in 1928.[6] Probably because of the way cigarette smoking affects metabolic rate, most people gain some weight when they stop smoking. Fear of weight gain is a major reason why women are less successful than men at quitting smoking.[7] Thus, lung cancer has now surpassed breast cancer as the leading cause of death in middle-aged women (in the USA).[8] Women are paying with their lives for their success in keeping off a few pounds.

5. Suicide is Less Common in Obese

A most intriguing figure never gets explained. Hidden near the bottom of all the charts showing the differences in mortality for obese and non-obese are the figures for suicide. Suicide rates are noticeably lower in both obese men and women. If obese and non-obese committed suicide at the same rate, suicide rates for obese would be recorded as 100% of actual expected deaths. Instead, the figure is only 73% for obese women and 78% for obese men.[9]

There seems to be at least one mental health advantage of obesity that is overlooked and not understood.

REFERENCES

1. Many of the ideas in this section have grown out of discussions of *Fat Is a Feminist Issue* with students and women's groups. (Susie Orbach, *Fat Is a Feminist Issue,* London: Paddington Press, 1978.)
2. Carol Sternhell, "We'll Always Be Fat But Fat Can Be Fit", *Ms,* May, 1985, pp. 66–68 and 142–154.
3. William Bennett and Joel Gurin, *The Dieter's Dilemma,* New York: Basic Books, 1982, pp. 34–45.
4. Valerie S. Smead, "Anorexia Nervosa, Buliminarexia, and Bulimia: Labeled Pathology and the Western Female", *Women and Therapy,* vol. 2, no. 1, 1983, pp. 19–35.
5. Susie Orbach, *Fat Is a Feminist Issue,* London: Paddington Books, 1978, p. 21.
6. Bennett and Gurin, *op. cit.,* pp. 92–93.
7. Bobbie Jacobson, *The Ladykillers—Why Smoking Is a Feminist Issue,* London: Pluto Press, 1981, pp. 14–15.
8. *1986 Cancer Facts and Figures,* American Cancer Society, 90 Park Avenue, New York, N.Y. 10016.
9. Jean Mayer, "Obesity" in Robert S. Goodhart and Maurice E. Shils (ed.) Febiger Press, 1980, pp. 721–740.

We'll Always Be Fat But Fat Can Be Fit

by Carol Sternhell

Sometimes I think we've all gone crazy. Sometimes I feel like a feminist at a Right-to-Life conference, an atheist in Puritan New England, a socialist in the Reagan White House. Sometimes I fear that fat women have become our culture's last undefeated heretics, our greatest collective nightmare made all too-solid flesh. I worry—despite our new ethos of sexual freedom—that female bodies are as terrifying and repulsive as ever, as greatly in need of purification and mortification. Certainly these days, when I hear people talking about temptation and sin, guilt and shame, I know they're referring to food rather than sex. When my friend Janet calls me up and confesses "I was bad today," I don't wonder whether she committed adultery (how archaic that sounds!); I know she merely means she ate dessert. When posters quoting Mae West appeared recently on Manhattan buses ("When choosing between two evils, I always like to take the one I've never tried before"), I wasn't surprised to find her remark illustrated with a picture of two different ice cream sundaes. (As I recall, however, when Mae West talked about evil, she generally wasn't thinking of hot fudge.) Kim Chernin, in *The Obsession: Reflections on the Tyranny of Slenderness* (Harper & Row), compares the language of diet books to "The old fire-and-brimstone sermons, intended to frighten men and women away from the delights and pleasures of sexual experience of their bodies." The sins of the flesh have been redefined, but the message is the same; a tremendous fear that women's natural appetites, uncontrolled, will bring about destruction.

Everything in this world, for women, boils down to body size.

We all know the story—the ugly duckling transformed into swan after years of liquid protein, the virtuous but oppressed stepdaughter whose fairy godmother appears with a pumpkin and a lifetime membership in Weight Watchers. Our fantasies of transformation are desperate, thrilling; when women imagine changing our lives, we frequently begin with our weight. "I always feel as if real life will begin tomorrow, next week, sometime after the next diet," said one friend, a talented writer who has been cheerfully married for 12 years and a mother for five. "I know it's crazy, but I won't be happy until I lose these fifteen pounds." So far her efforts—like 98 percent of all diets—have been unsuccessful. A few years ago, when public opinion pollsters asked respondents to name their greatest fear, 38 percent said "getting fat." Even very slender women believe that their lives would be better if only they could take off five pounds, or three, or two. In a recent survey conducted for *Glamour* by Susan Wooley, an associate professor in the psychiatry department of the University of Cincinnati College of Medicine, 75 percent of the 33,000 women who replied said that they were "too fat," including, according to Wooley, "45 percent who in fact were underweight," by the conservative 1959 Metropolitan Life Insurance Company Height and Weight Table. (By the revised 1983 table, which set generally higher levels of up to 13 pounds for desirable weights, these women would be even more underweight.) Wooley, who is also codirector of the university's Eating Disorders Clinic, sees our contemporary obsession with weight in part as a perversion of feminism. "This striving for thinness is striving to have a more masculine-type body," she points out. "As we join men's worlds, we shouldn't be cashing in women's bodies. We have to reclaim the right to have female bodies and still be respected. Thinness has become the cultural symbol of competency—if we buy that symbol and foster it ourselves, that's a very self-mutilating stand to take."

Everything in this world, for women, boils down to body size.

Reprinted with permission from *Ms.* Magazine, May, 1985, pp. 66–68; 141–154.

Cinderella's unfortunate stepsisters cut off chunks of their feet in order to fit into the prince's slipper. He knew they were impostors when he saw their blood oozing insistently over the delicate glass. These days women merely wire their jaws, staple their stomachs, and cut off chunks of their intestines in their effort to win the prince. "Stomach stapling" operations—50,000 are reportedly performed each year, 80 to 95 percent of them on women—can have side effects, such as abdominal pain, severe malnutrition, nausea and vomiting, osteoporosis, brain damage, and possibly even cancer. "Weight-loss surgery, including intestinal bypass operations, has probably already killed well over a hundred times as many people as the toxic shock syndrome, and has caused more than ten times as many deaths as AIDS," notes Paul Ernsberger, a postdoctoral research fellow at Cornell University Medical College. "More Americans have died in the surgeons' War on Fat than died in the Vietnam War." Yet desperate fat women—veterans of Stillman and Atkins, Scarsdale and Beverly Hills, diet camps and amphetamines—gratefully welcome the surgeon's knife, perhaps dreaming of old fairy tales. "I sometimes wish I had cancer," said a large, pretty woman in her early twenties at a diet workshop I once attended in San Francisco. "I sometimes think I wouldn't mind dying, if only I could die thin."

Everything in this world, for women, boils down to body size.

I still remember those little girls drinking diet soda and waiting for the miracle. I was 14 years old and 145 pounds that summer, at Camp Stanley for overweight girls, but many of the campers were younger, chubby little kids who already knew their bodies were their shame. When some of us failed to lose weight even on the camp's low-calorie regime, we were put on a special plan: three scoops of cottage cheese a day and all the diet soda we could drink. I remember the hunger (I would roll my pillow up under my stomach at night, trying to fill the hollow so I could sleep), the dizziness, but also the exhilaration; I felt like a secular saint, virtuous, disembodied, utterly pure. We sat around, starving, and talked about food, food we recalled from our profligate pasts. We talked about the new lives we would inhabit in the fall, transmuted all into magical swans.

I lost 15 pounds that summer and felt quite swanlike for a while, particularly among my relatives, who often seemed to admire weight loss the way other families might esteem an Olympic medal. By Christmas, however, when a group of campers gathered for a mini-reunion, every one of us had recouped our loses, and then some. We talked about the new lives we would inhabit in the spring, after the next diet had made us swans.

After the next diet, of course, most of us were fatter than before. Not only do almost all diets fail; according to Kim Chernin, "ninety percent of those who have dieted 'successfully' gain back more than they ever lost." This is not because "overweight" people are weak-willed compulsives, unable to pull our faces out of the Haagen-Dazs. (The medical profession may still disagree, but the medical profession, remember, once advised women that our reproductive organs would shrivel if we made the mistake of obtaining a higher education.) In fact, observes Wooley, "On the whole fat people eat no more than thin people—often women who believe they're compulsive eaters are trying to deny the need to eat at all." The one thing fat women do more than other people is diet—and continual dieting, we now know, actually causes weight gain. "Repeated starvation can encourage fatness at the same time it destroys somebody's health," explains Ernsberger. "Cutting calories turns out to be the great fattener. The body—threatened with famine—overcompensates and creates new fat cells when normal eating is resumed. The cells may even double in number, and these new fat cells are forever. The body can now store more fat—the next diet will be harder."

A decade or so after my summer at Camp Stanley, I failed at a much more ambitious diet. This time I felt like a swan humiliatingly transformed into an ugly duckling. Even worse, I felt like a criminal; I was wearing my scarlet letter for all to see. My shame was intense—but as Wooley has remarked, "If shame could cure obesity, there wouldn't be a fat woman in the world."

During this period while attending graduate school in California, I sampled a variety of weight-loss groups. Two in particular were so disturbing that they made me question for the first time my own obsession with slimness. At the first, an Overeaters Anonymous meeting in Palo Alto, a depressed group of middle-aged people—mostly large and mostly women—sat on uncomfortable chairs in a chilly church basement and acknowledged that they were helplessly controlled by food. Only the aid of their "Higher Power" could save them, they agreed. At the height of the meeting one sad, gray-haired women got up to tell us that she "really was shit." She didn't understand why, now that she'd lost weight, her husband had left her, but she said she was sure it must be for the best because everything—of course—was part of her Higher Power's plan. She said again and again that without the guidance of her HP she was "a piece of shit," and many group members murmured that they were too.

Then, in a San Francisco workshop ironically titled "Fat Liberation"—a supposedly progressive approach to weight loss in which participants "got in touch" with their feelings about fat and food—a group of women, almost all slender (but feeling fat), sat in a circle and imagined meeting a fat person in the street. "You were huge, gigantic, obese," one women wrote, "a man or a woman, androgynous in fat. I feel uncomfortable around you, and guilty. I avoid looking at your body, I feel sorry for you, threatened—you don't have to look like that. Under the surface you have nothing. I follow you to a dark room; you go in alone and sit. I leave you sitting there in the dark. When I leave, I am happy, whistling." We then sat on the floor and told a pile of food that it couldn't scare us any more.

After this workshop I bought a new political button: "How Dare You Presume I'd Rather Be Thin?" I've never had the nerve to wear it.

Fat women are continually told to lose weight in order to improve our health—but, in fact, we are likely to damage our health while trying to lose weight. Women don't drink liquid protein, pour saccharin in our coffee, and staple our stomachs in order to be healthy; instead, women risk death in order to be thin. According to Dr. Faith Fitzgerald of the University of California at Davis, "Obesity, as we commonly use the term, may be more of an aesthetic and moral problem than one of physical health." Certainly our horrified revulsion at the sight of a fat body springs from deeper sources than a disinterested concern for that body's well-being. If it did, the billions of dollars poured into the diet industry each year would be transferred to an anti-smoking campaign.

"In general, the healthiest eaters we see are fat women," adds Susan Wooley. "Most would have to be on a starvation diet their whole lives to get them down to a weight the culture considers normal, and the physical and emotional effects of starvation are much worse than the effects of overweight."

Nevertheless, most Americans—including most medical professionals—believe that fatness and good health are antithetical. A panel convened by the National Institutes of Health recently proclaimed obesity a "killer" disease. The 14-member panel set the danger point at a level of 20 percent or more above "desirable" body weight, but said that even five to 10 pounds above recommended weights could pose increased health risks to those people susceptible to or suffering from diseases like high blood pressure, adult onset of diabetes, and some cancers. A woman of my height, five feet four, would be 20 percent overweight at about 160, 40 pounds less than I weigh. The health charge is disturbing. No one—however terrific, energetic, and attractive she may feel—wants to walk around with a "killer" disease.

According to Ernsberger, the NIH report is simply wrong. "Fatness is *not* associated with a higher death rate," he says. "In fact, in every given population examined, the thinnest people have the highest death rate." The new NIH panel "flatly contradicts" previous reports of the same data, the well-known Framingham Heart Study, he adds. "The fact is the very fattest women in

Framingham had a lower death rate than women who were at their 'correct' insurance table weights." The heaviest Framingham women, ranging from 40 percent to 172 percent over the 1959 tables, had lower mortality than both underweight women and women within a few pounds of their "desirable" weight. The *lowest* death rates, Ernsberger points out, occurred in women who were between 10 percent and 30 percent over the insurance tables. About 30 controlled studies correlating mortality and weight have reported similar findings. Dr. Ancel Keys of the University of Minnesota, a cardiovascular researcher, coordinated such studies in 16 different geographical areas with an emphasis on risk factors leading to heart attacks. He concluded that "in none of the areas of this study was overweight or obesity a major risk factor for death or the incidence of coronary heart disease."

"Cancer deaths actually decrease with increasing fatness," says Ernsberger. "Only one study, the study cited in the NIH report, showed an increase in cancer rates," he adds, "while five or six that I know of show a decrease with increasing fatness." The NIH panel chose to ignore the decreased overall cancer rate in obesity, mentioning only that a single type of cancer, uterine cancer, is more common in obese women.

Wooley concurs. "A person can definitely be fat and healthy," she says. "My reading of the literature tells me that for women there's a very sizable weight range in which extra weight does *not* constitute a risk in mortality." Wooley notes that some studies have shown that women can weigh up to 200 pounds, without increased mortality risks, and even after that point, she says, being overweight may be healthier than dieting.

Many of the health problems commonly associated with fatness are probably caused by fat people's incessant pursuit of thinness, Ernsberger points out. Thus the "yo-yo syndrome"—that deadly cycle of weight loss and weight regain—may cause hypertension; diet pills can also cause high blood pressure and amphetamine psychosis; low carbohydrate diets can raise cholesterol; and liquid protein diets have led to heart disease and sudden death. "We don't know how unhealthy overweight is in and of itself because most overweight people have been doing these things," Ernsberger comments.

Furthermore, fat people receive terrible health care, partly because doctors see them as "bad patients" and partly because the overweight person herself tends to give up in despair. "We've had it drummed into our heads that the *only* route to fitness is through weight loss," explains Nancy Summer, member of the board of directors of the National Association To Aid Fat Americans (NAAFA), a nationwide fat rights organization based in New York. Summer, a dynamic blond who weighs more than 300 pounds, swims twice a week on Long Island with a group of large women. "Many of us have developed an all-or-nothing attitude. If we can't be thin, we may as well not worry about nutrition or exercise—we are going to die young anyway. I think it's time we reject that concept."

The medical evidence may be contradictory—obesity "experts" may disagree—but the message to me as a self-accepting fat woman is fairly simple. People come in lots of different sizes, and our frantic struggle to squeeze—all of us—into the thinnest 10 percent of a once-normal bell-shaped curve is driving us all crazy (and at the same time making us fatter). Self-hatred and cultural stigmatization doesn't do anyone any good; indeed, many of the diseases frequently associated with overweight are stress-related illnesses. Even, if all the other things being equal, it is "healthier" to be thin, weight-reduction programs fail 98 percent of the time, according to Chernin. Therefore I have two choices: I can be fat and unhealthy or I can be fat and healthy. I can find a new miracle diet, or I can eat sensible food (fruit and veggies, fiber, not too much fat, sugar, or salt), avoid cigarettes, and get plenty of exercise.

I'll still be fat, but fat can be fit.

The six women flash brightly colored tights and leotards, shake to a driving rock beat, smile at their reflections in shiny mirrors, bend and stretch, tap some feet. It's just another Manhattan exercise class, but here all the women look like Rubens' models, ranging in size from perhaps 150 pounds to well over 200. At the Greater Woman, "New York's first exercise studio for the large woman," clients are expected to be at least 30 pounds over their "ideal" weight—some weigh nearly 300 pounds—but the program emphasizes fitness and self-esteem rather than weight loss.

"There's a great difference between fitness and skinniness," says Mary Sams, a family psychotherapist who heads the studio. "Women are told that fat is immoral, that everyone who is overweight is out of control, consuming massive amounts of food. That's garbage."

According to Sams, the purpose of Greater Woman "is not to get people to lose weight, but to help people become fit and healthy and change their feelings about themselves. A lot of women come here wanting to get thinner," she adds, "but three weeks into the program they're thinking entirely differently." Clients are likely to lose inches rather than pounds. "Over several months, their dress sizes may go down," says Greater Woman's nutritionist, Jeannette Harris, "but they don't see a decrease on the scale." "Fitness isn't a scale measurement," agrees Sams. "Our goal is to increase lean body mass and raise the metabolic rate." In order to accomplish this, the studio has developed exercise classes specifically tailored to the needs of larger women. "The only exercise that really increases metabolic rate is aerobics," explains Sams. "We have learned to choreograph aerobic dances that are very lively but don't involve pounding exercises, which put too much stress on the knees and back."

The class members I speak with seem genuinely enthusiastic, and sometimes amazed to find themselves moving about so vigorously. One, a psychiatric social worker who has lost 30 pounds in the last year, explains earnestly, "People don't come here to lose weight, just to feel human about their bodies."

Remember the old fairy tales, the ugly ducklings and crippled stepsisters and hungry little girls all waiting for their miracle? Well, it's not exactly the story I'd imagined, but my transformation finally took place. My chronicle has a happy ending, but it's an ending with a twist, for as Susan Wooley once remarked, "When it comes to weight, people can't accept a happy ending that leaves us different shapes and sizes. To me, a happy ending is when someone can accept her body as it is."

My fairy godmother showed up after all, but she didn't change my body: she changed my mind.

RESOURCES

Shadow on a Tightrope: Writings by Women on Fat Oppression, edited by Lisa Schoenfielder and Barb Wieser, foreword by Vivian Mayer (*Aunt Lute Book Company. Iowa City*). The best feminist collection I know of on the subject of fat. Includes much material from the original Fat Underground, a feminist fat liberation group that formed in Los Angeles in 1973.

The Obsession: Reflections on the Tyranny of Slenderness, by Kim Chernin (*Harper Colophon Book*). A subtle, well-written, and sometimes brilliant dissection of our cultures' frenzied pursuit of thinness, and its terror of female flesh.

The Dieter's Dilemma, by William Bennett, M.D., and Joel Gurin (*Basic Books*). A thoughtfully presented and scientific case against dieting as a means of weight control.

Such a Pretty Face: Being Fat in America, by Marcia Millman, with photographs by Naomi Bushman (*Norton*). A sociologist's investigation of what it is like "to live as a fat person in our society." Much of the material is drawn from interviews with fat people and from observations of organizations like NAAFA and Overeaters Anonymous.

Fat Is a Feminist Issue: a Self-Help Guide for Compulsive Eaters, by Susie Orbach (*Berkley*). Some feminists have found Orbach's discussion helpful, but it disturbs me because its emphasis is still on achieving thinness. Here fatness is seen not as a sin, but as a means of adapting to a sexist society. When women learn better ways of coping with sexism, Orbach believes, they will become slim. She also makes the mistake of confusing fatness with compulsive eating. They are two distinctly different conditions.

Big & Beautiful: How To Be Gorgeous on Your Own Grand Scale, by Ruthanne Olds (*Acropolis Books*). A fashion guide for women size 14 and up.

BBW: The World's First Fashion Magazine for the Large-Size Woman. Six-issue subscription is $13 from BBW (Suite 214. 5535 Balboa Blvd. Encino. Calif. 91316). A fashion magazine published six times a year. BBW stands for Big Beautiful Woman.

NAAFA—The National Association To Aid Fat Americans (P.O. Box 43. Bellerose. N.Y. 11426). The country's premier fat rights organization, active since 1969. Call 516–352–3120 or write for information. Sponsors both political action and social events.

The Greater Woman (111 East 65 St., N.Y., N.Y. 10128; telephone: 212–737–4889). Exercise classes for the larger woman.

The Great Weight Debate: Where Have All the Feminists Gone?

— *by Pat Lyons, RN MA*

"If shame could cure obesity there wouldn't be a fat woman in the world."
—Susan Wooley, PhD

At the persistent urging of a friend, a woman who has not been to a doctor in a long time works up her courage to go in for a routine Pap smear and pelvic exam. She is told by the doctor that she is too fat to receive a proper exam and to come back when she's lost weight. She tries, but she does not lose weight. Ten years go by. She does not go back for an exam. But if in the future she develops cancer, her weight will be blamed, not her biased, insensitive medical care treatment.

I met this woman in 1989 during a series of focus groups we conducted before starting the Great Shape Health and Fitness Program for Large Women at Kaiser Permanente. (*Network News,* May/June, 1992).1 wish I could say her treatment was an anomaly. But over a lifetime of listening to women agonize about their weight, and in ten years of specifically trying to improve quality health care and access for fat women, I have heard some version of this story over and over. Women of all sizes, but especially large women, delay or avoid medical care because of shame about their weight or to avoid a weight loss lecture (Olson, 1994). And yet the women's health community has been quite silent on the issue of weight prejudice. It is puzzling. But I'm hoping the latest action of the NIH to lower weight guidelines will finally be enough to galvanize every person who cares about women's health to stand up and say: enough already!

New National Institutes of Health Weight Guidelines: More Harm than Good

New weight guidelines issued on June 17th by the National Heart, Lung and Blood Institute of the NIH lower from 27 to 25 the BMI point at which weight is deemed unhealthy. (A 5'4" adult is now considered "overweight" and unhealthy at 145 pounds.) Overnight, 29 million more American—a total of 55% of the population—can now expect a weight loss lecture when they go for medical care. The guidelines being distributed to doctors nationwide urge doctors to tell their patients that "the most successful strategies for weight loss include calorie reduction, increased physical activity and behavior therapy," and to prescribe drugs and surgery when these strategies fail. (NIH, NHLBI, 1998) The guidelines present no new science whatsoever, nor has there been any research to contradict the 1993 NIH conclusions on the abysmal failure of that very advice for 95% of people who try to lose weight (NIH, 1993).

From *Network News,* September/October 1998, pp. 1, 4 & 5. Copyright © 1998 by Pat Lyons, RN, MA. Reprinted by permission.

Pat Lyons, RN, MA is co-author of Great Shape: The First Fitness Guide for Large Women (*Bull Publishing, 1990*) *and chapters in 3 other books, including* Feminist Perspectives on Eating Disorders (*Guilford Press, 1994*).

While the guidelines try to soften the blow by telling people they must only lose 10% of their weight, there is still no scientific evidence that people can succeed long term. While every patient could be encouraged to eat lots of fruits and vegetables and try to be more active to improve health, singling large people out for this advice to "prevent obesity" focuses the attention of both patient and provider on weight, not health. It also presumes that thinner people exercise, eat well and are healthy—which is hardly universally true. So if improving American's health is supposedly the goal of the new guidelines, let's get to the real issues at stake.

Lowering weight guidelines exposes 29 million additional Americans to weight discrimination, including the denial of health insurance. The guidelines create a potentially vast new market for weight loss treatment and diet drugs, without a whisper of concern about repeating the Redux/Fen-Phen diet pill debacle. Even Dr. Judith Stern, a long time advocate of the weight-loss at-any cost point of view and a member of the NIH Task Force on the Prevention and Treatment of Obesity, voted against the new guidelines and voiced criticism in the media: "They have misquoted the data . . . if they are going to do it scientifically, they should do it scientifically. I would not change public health policy on that . . . It is a slippery slope . . . there will be a big push to lower the BMI at which we treat with drugs, and that's not justified given the current drugs." (Squires, 1998)

The slippery slope of a medical model that relies on drugs is evident in a *New York Times* article on the new guidelines. The article features Deborah Gregory, a woman in her late 30's who "tries to eat a balanced diet, sleeps well and works an hour of exercise into her busy schedule almost every day." She considers herself fit and healthy and her weight has remained stable for 14 years. But because her weight is 227 pounds on her 5'11 frame, obesity researchers still aren't satisfied. Dr. Claude Bouchard of Laval University was quoted in the article, saying it was "marvelous" that she exercised "but at this weight she remains at great risk of having medical difficulties down the road. Good, solid, safe medication that would be capable of inducing weight loss of 25–30 pounds could help her dramatically, but for the moment we don't have that." (Villarosa, 1998)

Given the staggering profit potential embedded in this point of view—since people must stay on drugs forever or regain weight when they go off—the drug companies are, of course, in a diet drug development frenzy. The FDA has demonstrated little restraint in approving diet drugs. The ink was barely dry on the agreement for the withdrawal of Redux and Fenfluramine from the market, when the FDA turned around and approved Meridia—which can increase blood presure and be physically and psychologically addicting—despite it's being rejected by the FDA's own panel. I can almost hear the drug companies knocking on the FDA's door to change the prescribing rules. And did I mention that diet drug companies fund a great deal of obesity research?

If fourteen years at a stable weight and living an active, healthy lifestyle still requires a woman to risk potential side effects of lifelong drug use to be considered acceptable by the "experts," then what I want to know is—where are the those "just say no to drugs" people when we really need them? At a time when 80% of fourth grade girls are already dieting and five year olds are moaning about the size of their thighs, a public health policy that tells 55% of American women that we are unhealthy and should put weight loss at the top of our agenda is a prescription for heartbreak, not health. It is an outrage, and it is time to say so.

Speak Up: It's Time!

Although women's health newsletters and publications have been reluctant to publicly challenge the party line of obesity researchers, the *New England Journal of Medicine* has not. A January editorial—"Losing Weight—An Ill Fated New Year's Resolution"—issued an unprecedented call for action:

> Since many people cannot lose much weight no matter how hard they try, and promptly regain whatever they do lose . . . the $30–50 billion [spent] yearly, is wasted. . . . given the enomous social pressure to lose weight, one might suppose there is clear and overwhelming evidence of the risks of obesity and the benefits of weight loss. Unfortunately, the data linking overweight and death, as well as data showing the beneficial effects of weight loss, are limited, fragmentary and often ambiguous. . . . Until we have better data about the risks of being overweight and the benefits and risks of trying to lose weight, we should remember that the cure for obesity may be worse than the condition. (Kassirer J Angell M, 1998)

Journal editors also expressed concern over ever increasing rates of chronic dieting and eating disorders in girls, and cite metabolic and genetic research that confounds the simple notion that anyone can lose weight if they just eat less and exercise more. They advise physicians to "do their part to reduce discrimination against overweight people." If the NEJM can take this stand, surely women's health professionals can do so as well, especially since the new NIH guidelines completely ignore all of these issues.

The disease/pathology paradigm that insists that health can be determined by weight alone is outdated and harmful. Whether we look to research on the overriding effect of socioeconomics on health (Lantz et al, 1998) or in the mind-body medicine or social support literature, it is clear that weight is only one factor to consider in overall health and well-being, not THE factor. Even the fitness literature demonstrates that it is lifestyle that matters most, not weight. (Barlow, 1995)

I urge you to read the NEJM editorial and some of the 35 research articles they cite and at least discuss it with colleagues. I also invite you to join a national education and advocacy effort: *Free At Last: The Women's Body Sovereignty Project.* (see box). Everyone can do something. The most important thing is to stop being silent. A public health message that encourages women to live healthfully, whatever their size, is long overdue.

Whatever has kept so many feminists on the sidelines of the great weight debate—whether it is ignorance about the severity of the problem, shame or ambivalence about one's own weight, believing that weight is a trivial matter of appearance, or for whatever reason—it is time to come off the sidelines and get into the game. Educating ourselves, exposing bias, trusting our own experience, finding our voice and speaking up

is the essence of feminism. It is also the pathway to health, no matter what we weigh.

REFERENCES

Barlow C, Kohl H, Blair SN. Physical fitness, mortality and obesity. *Int. J Obesity,* 1995, Supp. 4, pp. S41–44.

Kassirer J., Angell M. Losing weight—an ill-fated new year's resolution. *N Eng J Med,* 1998; 338:52–54.

Lantz P et al. Socioeconomic factors, health behaviors and mortality. *JAMA,* 1998; 279;8, pp 1703–8.

National Institutes of Health, NHLBI Communications. *Frst federal obesity clinical guidelines released* June 17, 1998.

NIH Technology Assessment Panel. Methods for voluntary weight loss and control: technology assessment conference statement *Ann Int Med* 1993; 119 (7 pt 2) 764–770.

Olsen C., et al. Overweight women delay medical care. *Arch Fam Med* 1994; 3:888–92.

Squires S. New U.S. weight standard—millions more are fat. *Washington Post,* reprinted in *San Francisco Chronicle,* June 4, 1998.

Villarosa L. New fatness guidelines spur debate on fitness. *New York Times,* June 23, 1998.

Free At Last:
The Women's Body Sovereignty Project

ēsov-er-eign; having independent authority; ēsov-er-eign-ty: freedom from external control

Ways You Can Participate

S Stop making comments about weight—yours or other people's—especially in front of children.

O Observe how prejudice against fat seeps into discussions of weight and health.

V Volunteer your thoughts and feelings on the need for body acceptance and start a dialogue.

E Educate yourself on healthy alternatives to dieting/weight-loss focused medical care and info.

R Remember that prejudice has been learned. It can be unlearned. Have patience.

E Encourage and sponsor speakouts, workshops, professional training and conferences.

I "It's not OK to tell 'fat jokes' or ridicule fat people." Use this phrase as needed.

G Give yourself credit for taking on these issues. It will benefit people of all sizes, including you.

N News travels quickly through newsletters. Write about this topic. Review relevant books.

T Take time to nurture your body. Dance, play, rest, relax, eat & enjoy life just as you are.

Y YES! We want to hear from you—contact us for speakers, tell us about your activities . . .

Pat Lyons, RN, MA is Project Director and founder of CONNECTIONS Women's Health Consulting Network, the Project sponsor. CONNECTIONS is a diverse, national network of health professionals and educators dedicated to reducing weight discrimination in medical and mental health care by promoting body positive education and clinical services that support the well-being of people of all sizes. You can reach the Project at 416 Lester Ave., Oakland, C A 94606, (510) 763.7365, fax (510) 836.6227, plyons@earthlink.net.

Childhood Lessons: Culture, Race, Class, and Sexuality

by Becky Thompson

If there is one story that is an integral part of the folklore of growing up female, it is the chronicle of the onset of menstruation. These accounts are often embarrassing—a thirteen-year-old girl has to ask her father to tell her what to do, another is sure that people can tell from her face what is going on in her body—and many, like that of the young teenager who gets a red cake with red candles from her mother to celebrate her first period, are funny. Usually told only in the company of other women, these stories of a rite of passage are often filled with pain, ingenuity, and humor—and sometimes joy.

Equally revealing stories about the development of female identity in the United States spring from lessons girls learn about their body sizes and appetites. Whether they are fat or thin, Latina or Jewish (or both), lesbian or heterosexual, girls are barraged by complicated messages about their bodies, skin, hair, and faces. Not surprisingly, girls who do not fit the standard mold—who look like tomboys, whose skin is dark, who have nappy hair, who are chubby or just plain big, who develop early or develop late—are most aware of negative assessments, and their stories are commonly filled with shame and confusion.

Although there is no single message to girls about weight and food that crosses regional, religious, and cultural lines in the United States, early lessons about weight and appetite often leave indelible marks on their lives. Growing up on a working farm may protect a girl from the pressure to diet, but she may learn elsewhere that a big appetite is not acceptable for girls and women. While being raised in the Dominican Republic may help a young girl value women of all sizes, if she emigrates to the United States, the pressures to assimilate culturally and linguistically may make her especially determined to be thin.

Increasingly, one of the few experiences common to growing girls in the United States is the pressure to diet. This pressure not only reveals strictures about body size, it also telegraphs complicated notions about race, culture, and class. A girl's body may become the battleground where parents and other relatives play out their own anxieties. Just as stories about a first menstruation tell us about a family's social traditions and the extent to which the girl's body is respected within them, lessons about weight and eating habits tell us an enormous amount about culture, race, religion, and gender. It is through these familial and cultural lenses that young girls make judgements about their bodies and their appetites. The nuances in the socialization of girls show why—across race, class, and religion—they may become vulnerable to eating problems and demonstrate how many girls begin to use food to cope with trauma.

Growing up Latina

By the year 2020 the single largest minority group in the United States will be Latino people—including the descendants of people who were in what is now the United States before it was "discovered," people who fled El Salvador and Guatemala in the 1970s and 1980s, Puerto Rican people, and a host of others. Latinos share a history of struggling against colonialism and racism, and they share a common language. Other generalizations are often erroneous.

There is no single Latino ethic about body size and eating patterns. Even to profess that there is a common Puerto Rican explanation about women's body size would conflate significant generational and regional differences. The notion that Latinas as a group are somehow protected from or ignorant of cultural pressure to be thin simply does not hold up in the face of their diversity. Nor can it be said that any particular group of women is isolated from the culture of thinness; the mass media have permeated even the most remote corners of the United States. The pressures of assimilation and racism may make some Latinas especially vulnerable to strictures about weight.

The task, then, is to identify both how ethnic, racial, and socioeconomic heterogeneity among Latinos and Latinas influences their socialization and how these factors may make Latinas susceptible to developing eating problems. One of the Latina women I interviewed, Elsa, was raised by German governesses in an upper-class family in Argentina. Another, Julianna, was cared for by her grandmother in a middle-class family in the Dominican Republic. The other three are Puerto Rican women who grew up in the United States and whose backgrounds ranged from working- to upper-middle-class; among these women, the degree of assimilation varied markedly depending on whether Spanish was their first language, the degree of contact with other Latinas, and the extent to which they identified as Puerto Ricans.

What the Latina women learned about weight and size was influenced by nationality. Julianna, who grew up in a small town in the Dominican Republic, was taught that

> people don't think that fat is bad. You don't undermine fat people. You just don't. . . . The picture of a woman is not a woman who has a perfect body that you see on TV. A woman is beautiful because she is a virgin or because she is dedicated to her husband or because she takes care of her kids; because she works at home and does all the things that her husband and family want her to do. But not because she is skinny or fat.

In the Dominican Republic, female beauty is closely linked to being a good wife and mother and obeying gendered expectations about virginity and monogamy. Thinness is not a necessary criterion for beauty, regardless of a woman's class. By contrast, the Argentinian woman, Elsa, said that a woman's weight was the primary criterion for judging her worth. The diets and exercise her father enforced among his wife and daughters were "oppressive and Nazi-like." But judgments about weight varied with class and degree of urbanization:

> The only people who see being fat as a positive thing in Argentina are the very poor or the very rural people who still consider it a sign of wealth or health. But as soon as people move to the bigger cities and are exposed to the magazines and the media, dieting and figures become incredibly important.

None of the Puerto Rican women I talked with benefitted from the acceptance of size that the Dominican woman described. Laura, who lived in Puerto Rico with her family for four years when she was a child, recalls that "Latina women were almost expected to be more overweight. Latin women living in Puerto Rico were not uncomfortable with extra weight. To them it wasn't extra. It wasn't an issue." This didn't help Laura appreciate her own chunky size because her family's disdain for fat people was much more influential. Her father was British and her mother liked to "hang out with wealthy white women," both factors that impeded Laura's ability to adopt the Puerto Rican community's values.

Another Puerto Rican woman, Vera, who grew up in Chicago, was chunky as a child and learned that the people around her disapproved of her size. Vera remembers painful scenes at school and in clothing stores that taught her she should be embarrassed by her body size. Although she was an amazingly limber and energetic student in her ballet class, her mother took her out of it because Vera wasn't thin enough.

African-American Girls and Community Life

Rosalee grew up in Arkansas in a rural African-American community where, as she described it, "home grown and healthy" was the norm. She remembers that her uncles and other men liked a "healthy woman": as they used to say, "They didn't want a neck bone. They liked a picnic ham." Among the people in her community, skin color and hair were more important than weight in determining beauty. Unlike most of the other women I interviewed, Rosalee didn't think about dieting as a way to lose weight until she was a teenager. Because her family didn't always have money, "there were times when we hardly had food anyway so we tended to slim down. And then . . . when the money was rolling in . . . we celebrated. We ate and ate and ate." When poverty is a constant threat, Rosalee explained, "dieting just isn't a household word." This did not stop Rosalee from developing an eating problem when she was four years old as a response to sexual abuse and being a witness to beatings. Trauma, not size, was the primary factor.

Carolyn, a middle-class woman who grew up in an urban area, remembered that her African-American friends considered African-American women of varying weights to be desirable and beautiful. By contrast, among white people she knew, the only women who were considered pretty were petite. Both the white and the African-American men preferred white girls who were petite.

The women who went to schools in which there were only a few African-American students remember thinness as dominant. By contrast, those who went to racially mixed or predominantly African-American schools saw more acceptance of both big and thin women. One of the many hazards for black students who attend overwhelmingly white schools is pressure to adopt cultural values—including thinness—that may not reflect African-American values.[2]

The women who attended private, predominantly white schools were sent by parents who hoped to open up opportunities unavailable in public schools. As a consequence, both Nicole and Joselyn were isolated from other African-American children. Their parents discouraged them from socializing with neighborhood African-American children, who in turn labeled them arrogant, thus furthering their isolation. Both were teased by neighborhood children for being chubby and light-skinned. At school they were teased for being fat and were excluded by white people in ways both subtle and overt. Racist administrators and teachers granted the girls neither the attention nor the dignity they deserved. Joselyn, who attended Catholic schools, remembered both racial and religious intolerance: "Sister Margaret Anna told me that, basically, what a black person could aspire to at that time was to Christianize the cannibals in Africa." Neither Nicole nor Joselyn had a public context in which her racial identity was validated. As Nicole said, "By second or third grade I was saying I wished I was white because kids at school made fun of me. I remember . . . getting on the bus and a kid called me a brown cow." As the women were growing up, their weight and their race were used to ostracize them.

Intersection of Race and Class

Most of the African-American and Latina women were pressured to be thin by at least one and often all of their family members. For some, these pressures were particularly virulent because they were laced with racism. Rosalee, who grew up on a farm in the South, got contradictory messages about weight and size from her family. Like most of the African-Americans in her community, Rosalee's mother thought thin women were sickly and took her young daughters to the doctor because they weren't gaining enough weight. But her father told her she "had better not turn out fat like her mother." Rosalee and her mother often bore the brunt of his disdain as he routinely told them that African-American women were usually fatter and less beautiful than white women. Rosalee says:

I can remember fantasizing that "I wish I was white." . . . It seemed to be the thing to be

if you were going to be anything. You know, [white women] were considered beautiful. That was reinforced a lot by my father, who happened to have a strong liking for white women. Once he left the South and he got in the army and traveled around and had more freedom, he became very fond of them. In fact, he is married to one now. He just went really overboard. I found myself wanting to be like that.

Although she was not familiar with dieting as a child, she feared weight gain and her father's judgments. At puberty, she began to diet. Her father's sexism and prejudice against black women meant that she was raised with contradictory messages about weight. At the same time, she was learning about the dominant standard of beauty that emphasizes a fair complexion, blue eyes, and straight hair. About the lessons many black girls learn about straightening their hair and using lightening creams, Rosalee says:

It was almost as if you were chasing after an impossible dream. I can remember stories about parents pinching their children's noses so they don't get too big. I laugh about it when I am talking about it with other people but on the inside I don't laugh at all. There is nothing there to reinforce who you are, and the body image gets really confused.

Some of the Latinas' and African-Americans' relatives projected their own frustrations and racial prejudices onto the girls' bodies. Joselyn, an African-American woman, remembers her white grandmother telling her she would never be as pretty as her cousins because they had lighter skin. Her grandmother often humiliated Joselyn in front of others, making fun of Joselyn's body while she was naked and telling her she was fat. As a young child Joselyn began to think that although she couldn't change her skin color, she could at least try to be thin.

When Joselyn was young, her grandmother was the only family member who objected to her weight. Then her father also began to encourage his wife and daughter to be thin as the family's social status began to change. When Joselyn was very young, her family was what she called "aspiring to be middle class." For people of Joselyn's parents' generation, having chubby, healthy children was a sign the family was doing well. But, as the family moved up the social ladder, Joselyn's father began to insist that Joselyn be thin.

When my father's business began to bloom and my father was interacting more with white businessmen and seeing how they did business, suddenly thin became important. If you were a truly well-to-do family, then your family was slim and elegant.

Her grandmother's racism and her father's determined fight to be middle class converged, and Joselyn's body became the playing field for their conflicts. While Joselyn was pressured to diet, her father still served her large portions and bought treats for her and the neighborhood children. These contradictory messages confused her. Like many girls, Joselyn was told she was fat from the time she was very young, even though she wasn't. And, like many of the women I interviewed, Joselyn was put on diet pills and diets before puberty, beginning a cycle of dieting, compulsive eating, and bulimia. She remembers her father telling her, "You know you have a cute face, but from the body down you are shot to hell. You are built just like your old lady."

Another African-American woman also linked contradictory messages about food to her parents' internalized racism. As Nicole explains it, her mother operated under the "house-nigger mentality," in which she saw herself and her family as separate from and better than other African-American people. Her father shared this attitude, saying that being Cherokee made him different. Her parents sent Nicole to private schools and a "very white Anglican upper-class church" in which she was one of a few black children. According to Nicole, both parents "passed on their internalized racism in terms of judgments around hair or skin color or how a person talks or what is correct or proper."

Their commandments about food and body size were played out on Nicole's body in powerful ways. Nicole's father was from a working-class rural Southern family. Her mother, by contrast, was from a "petit bourgeois family," only one of three black families in a small New Hampshire town. While Nicole's father approved of her being, as he said, "solid," her mother restricted her eating to ensure that Nicole would grow up thin. Each meal, however, was a multicourse event. Like Joselyn, Nicole was taught that eating a lot was a dangerous but integral part of the family tradition:

> When I was growing up, I thought that breakfast was a four- or five-course meal the way you might think dinner is. I thought that breakfast involved fruit and maybe even juice and cereal and then the main course of breakfast, which was eggs and bacon and toast. On Sundays we had fancy breakfasts like fish and hominy grits and corn bread and muffins. So breakfast had at least three courses. That is how we ate. Dinner was mostly meat and potatoes and vegetables and bread. Then my father would cajole my mother into making dessert.

There were lots of rewards that all had to do with food, like going to Howard Johnson or Dunkin' Donuts.

At the same time, Nicole's mother put her on a diet when she was three and tortured her about her weight. Nicole became terrified of going to the doctor because she was weighed and lectured about her weight. Yet, after each appointment, her mother took her to Dunkin' Donuts for a powdered jelly doughnut. When her father did the grocery shopping, he bought Nicole treats, which her mother snatched and hid, accusing her father of trying to make her fat. When she was left alone, Nicole spent hours trying to find the food. In her mother's view, Nicole's weight and curly hair were what kept her from being perfect: her body became the contested territory onto which her parents' pain was projected.

The confusion about body size and class expectations that troubled some of the African-American women paralleled the experiences of two Puerto Rican women. Vera attributed her eating problems partly to the stress of assimilation as her family moved from poverty to the working class. When Vera was three, she was so thin that her mother took her to a doctor who prescribed appetite stimulants. By the time she was eight, though, she remembered her mother comparing her to other girls who stayed on diets or were thin. Vera attributed her mother's change of heart to pressure from family members:

> Even though our family went from poverty to working class, there were members of my extended family who thought they were better than everyone else. As I grew up, the conversation was, "Who is going to college? Who has a job working for Diamonds?" It was always this one-upmanship about who was making it better than who. The one-upmanship centered on being white, being successful, being middle class . . . and it was always, "Ay, Bendito [Oh, God] She is so fat! What happened?"

Vera's mother warned her that she would never make friends if she was fat. Her mother threatened to get a lock for the refrigerator door and left notes on it reminding Vera not to eat. While Vera's mother shamed her into dieting, she also felt ambivalent when Vera did not eat much. When Vera dieted, her mother would say, "You have to eat. You have to eat something. You can't starve yourself." The messages were always unclear.

Ruthie also remembers changes in the family ethic about size and eating that she attributes to assimilation with Anglo culture. In keeping with Puerto Rican tradition, Ruthie's mother considered chubby children a sign of health and well-being. According to Puerto Rican culture, Ruthie says, "if you are skinny, you are dying. What is wrong with you?" When Ruthie was ten to twelve years old, her mother made her take a food supplement and iron pills that were supposed to make her hungry. Ruthie did not like the supplement and felt fine about the size of her body. But how Ruthie looked was very important to her mother: "My mother used to get these dresses from Spain. She used to show everyone our closets. They were impeccable. Buster Brown shoes and dresses. She thought if I were skinny it would reflect badly on her." Ruthie questioned whether her mother cared about Ruthie or was actually worried about what the family and neighbors would say. When Ruthie became a teenager, her mother's attitude about weight changed:

> When I was little, it was not okay to be skinny. But then, at a certain age, it was not okay to be fat. She would say "Your sister would look great in a bikini and you wouldn't." I thought maybe this was because I felt fat. . . . Being thin had become something she valued. It was a roller coaster.

Ruthie attributed this change to her mother's acceptance of Anglo standards, which she tried to enforce on Ruthie's eating and body size.

The women's experiences dispel the notion that African-American and Latina women—as a group—are less exposed to or influenced by a culturally imposed thinness than white women. The African-American women who saw community acceptance of different size did not escape pressure to be thin from family members. While growing up in a rural area and attending predominantly black schools did protect two of the girls from pressures to diet, childhood traumas resulted in eating problems. For the women of color whose parent's internalized racism, an emphasis on thinness was particularly intense. Rosalee explains:

> For a black woman dealing with issues of self-esteem, if you don't get it from your family you [are punished] twice because you don't get self-esteem from society either. If you come from a dysfunctional or abusive family, there [are] just not a lot of places to go that will turn things around for you.

This reality underscores why some women of color may be more, rather than less, vulnerable than white women to eating problems.

White Girls in Their Families and Communities

As is true of the women of color, ethnic, religious, and national diversity among white women makes it difficult to generalize about a monolithic socialization process. With the exception of a Sephardic Jewish woman who grew up outside the United States, none of the white women I talked with escaped pressure to diet and be thin. Ethnic and religious identity, however, did influence their eating patterns and their attitudes about their bodies. Anti-Semitism and ethnic prejudice shaped the way some of the girls interpreted strictures about weight and eating. Like most of the women of color, the white women had little access to communities in which women of different sizes were valued. Messages that white girls received both in their homes and in their communities promoted dieting and thinness.

All of the American Jewish women I interviewed were taught that they needed to be thin. Although none were fat as children, all had parents who were afraid they would become fat and took what they saw as precautions. One family bought only enough food for one day at a time, reasoning that they would not overeat if no "extra" food was available. Two Jewish women who went to predominantly Protestant schools said belonging to a religious minority exacerbated pressures about body size. Both felt like outsiders because they were Jewish, and their Protestant classmates perceived them as talking, dressing, and looking different.

As for many of the Latinas and African-American women, the discrimination Jewish children experienced was most overt when they were in the minority. Sarah learned that some of her Protestant classmates thought that Jewish people had horns. Both Sarah and Gilda were called names and excluded from friendship groups. Gilda, who is a Sephardic Jew, remembers that when she began to attend school in the United States, other children spit on her and called her "kike":

> It was the craziest thing I have ever experienced. I hadn't experienced it from people I was told we were at war with [in North Africa]. If anything, the Arab women and mothers were more supportive. They would take us in.[3]

Children in the United States called her father the "Tasmanian devil" and made fun of her accent. The Jewish girls coped with discrimination by minimizing the ways they felt different from or inferior to others, including trying to hide their body sizes. Sarah explained that "in the school I attended, where I was only one of a handful of Jewish kids, I never felt like I fit in. I didn't have the right clothes, I didn't look the right way. I didn't come from the right family." When she was as young as eleven,

Sarah began to feel "that I had to lose weight or that something wasn't right." Although she wasn't fat, in her mind, she was.

Of the five Jewish women, Gilda—who grew up in North Africa and France before settling in the United States—was the only one exposed to a wholehearted acceptance of food. For Gilda's father, who was raised in North Africa, family meals were a central, celebrated aspect of maintaining North African and Jewish culture:

> First of all food and Friday night and Shabbes. Friday night for my father is a very important time. . . . We have a traditional [North African] meal with vegetables and different salads and [North African] spices. The whole flavor, the whole mood of the evening is not American at all. On holidays, Passover, we read the Haggadah in French, Arabic, Hebrew, and English. By page thirty, you are ready to die of hunger and exhaustion.

Eating together as a family was an important aspect of this tradition. Although Gilda learned that being a very thin child was not acceptable and that eating was a primary way her father celebrated his culture and religion, she remembered her mother always being on a diet, even though she was never more than slightly overweight. Gilda's father became angry with her when, as an adolescent, Gilda refused to eat with the family and did not keep kosher meals. Contradictory messages from her father and mother and differences between North African and U.S. standards caused confusion about weight and size.

The white women who were raised in Christian families were taught that being thin was crucial for females. Dawn, a middle-class white woman raised in a strict Catholic family, was taught from a young age that "a woman's worth was in her size." Antonia's ideas about eating and weight were deeply affected by her Italian-American ethnic identity. Like some of the Jewish women and women of color, Antonia felt like an outsider at school from kindergarten on, a feeling that was compounded by thinking she was overweight. At school she learned that to be accepted socially, she had to look and act like the "WASPs"—to have straight blond hair and be passive and quiet. She remembers that "I used to get called loud. I talked a lot. Very active. And I was very aggressive. I used to wrestle with the boys a lot. I stood out from other people." Because she was fat, she was often humiliated by other children at school. One of the boys called her "taters" (a big potato). At a high school prom fund-raiser—a "slave auction" where girls were auctioned off—"when it was my turn, no one was bidding. To this day, . . . I can't even really remember the actual sequence of events. It was just the most hu-

miliating thing in my life." When Antonia was eleven, her mother put her on a diet and a doctor prescribed amphetamines. During adolescence she tried to diet but her heart was not in it. In her mind, no amount of dieting would take away her assertive, emotional, and athletic ways, so what was the point in trying to lose weight anyway?

Grooming Girls to Be Heterosexual

While messages to girls about their bodies and appetites are shaped by race, class, ethnicity, and religion, no such diversity exists when it comes to learning about heterosexuality. In both subtle and overt ways, girls—across race, class, ethnicity, and religion—learn that being heterosexual is moral and inevitable. These expectations add up to what poet and writer Adrienne Rich has termed "compulsory heterosexuality" a largely invisible but enormously powerful force that orchestrates the range of what is considered acceptable female sexuality.[4] Elements of this enforced heterosexuality include pressure to marry and have children, male control of female sexuality, and an economic system that makes it difficult for many women to support themselves without marrying—plus prejudice and discrimination against gay men and lesbians and limitations on how emotionally close people of the same gender can be without facing reprisals. As girls reach their teenage years, they are punished if their friendships with other girls become intimate. They are also expected to show an interest in the opposite sex.[5] As Johnnetta Cole writes, women in the United States are "being measured against an objectified notion of female sexuality which is eternally young, never fat but 'well developed,' heterosexual, submissive to 'her man,' and capable of satisfying him sexually. It is striking how this ideal image cuts across racial, ethnic and class lines."[6]

The idea that heterosexuality is a necessary condition of "normal development" is often not overt or explicit unless girls begin to show signs of not being sufficiently heterosexual. For example, a Puerto Rican lesbian told me:

> My mother would say, there is nothing you can't do, if you want. But yet, in other subtle ways, she would encourage me to be a nurse. She wouldn't come right out and say, you can't be a doctor. She'd say I was supposed to be ladylike.

Being ladylike and having a traditionally female career was a prerequisite for marriage. Being thin was also integral to this heterosexual expectation.

All of the women I interviewed were taught that heterosexuality was essential. Many traced strictures about their bodies and appetites partly to this imperative. Implicit messages were commonly conveyed in the form of how girls were expected to look, how they were permitted to use their bodies athletically how they should dress, and how much they were allowed to eat. For many girls, these rules were most fiercely applied as they approached puberty. Tomboys who grew up riding bicycles, playing handball, and wrestling with boys were often summarily reprimanded as they approached puberty. As they were informed that they should start wearing dresses and go to the junior high dances, they were also encouraged to "eat like a lady" and pass up second helpings. In some families, boys were allowed to eat all they wanted while girls were not. The rationale for this double standard was that girls should be smaller than boys in order to be attractive to the opposite sex. Some girls remembered hating these restrictions. They missed being physically active, and they resented having to get by with less food.

As they approached their teen years, many were taught that having boyfriends depended upon being thin. One African-American woman remembers initiating her first self-imposed diet because her boyfriend liked thin women. All of his sisters encouraged it, too. When an Argentinean woman was eleven years old her mother told her, "You should really make an effort and diet. You won't be popular around the boys. You are going to have trouble finding a husband. You look terrible What a pity. You have a nice face but look at your figure." Laura, a Puerto Rican woman, remembers her mother and father both teaching her that she needed to lose weight or run the risk of being an "old maid." Integral to her socialization was the message that being successful heterosexually depended upon being thin:

> One day when I was eleven my parents and I were sitting on the beach in Puerto Rico. There was this blond woman walking down the beach with about ten men around her. She was in a bikini and my father and mother said, "She is not very attractive but she is thin. Look at all those men around her." They pointed out this other woman, who was heavy. She was by herself. She had a very beautiful face. They said, "See, she is beautiful. But she is not thin. She is by herself." It was right out front. That began at eleven years old. You are worthless unless you are thin.

The lessons about heterosexuality often went hand in hand with lessons about weight and dieting. Not surprisingly, those who questioned their heterosexuality at a young age were often best able to identify how these strictures reinforced each other. One of the characteristics of dominant ideology—including compulsory heterosexuality—is that it is understood as significant only when it is transgressed. This is also the power of dominant ideology, since it is often consciously felt only by those who contest it, who are encouraged—and sometimes forced—to accept it. For example, one woman who was not interested in boys during high school and had crushes on girls remembers that the "in group" of girls at school constantly talked about their boyfriends, diets, and losing weight. She partly wanted to be like them and thought that dieting would make her feel included in their friendship circle. Another woman's grandmother and mother taught her that "if you were thin, then all of your problems should be erased. You could be happily married, you could satisfy a man, anything you wanted could be yours if only you could be thin."

None of the girls grew up in homes where heterosexuality was questioned. This taken-for-granted aspect of their socialization meant that all the models for sexuality pivoted on attracting men; there were no alternatives. Consequently, there was no room for the idea that women's appetites and body sizes could be defined according to their own standards rather than norms based on rigid definitions of masculinity and feminity.

Whose Body Is This, Anyway?

Given the complex and sometimes contradictory messages that girls get as they are growing up, it is no wonder that many come of age distrusting their appetites and their bodies. The process highlights many feminist assertions about eating problems, and understanding the impact of gender discrimination takes us a long way toward seeing that many girls must reckon with the question, Whose body is this, anyway?

Girls are bombarded with complicated ideas about their bodies not just within their families; pressures in their communities, schools, and churches also play a vital role. Feminists rightfully recognize that it is impossible to understand girls' attitudes toward their bodies without scrutinizing what goes on both inside and outside their families. This comprehensive scope is especially important for a multiracial focus, since some women of color may get contradictory messages in their communities and in their homes.

Taking community pressures into consideration also counters the psychoanalytic tendency to reduce eating problems to psychic problems caused by mother-daughter dynamics. The psychoanalytic notion that a girl's anorexia is a "reaction to a hostile mother" or a manifestation of a child's unconscious ambivalence toward her mother is problematic when it is seen through a feminist, sociocultural lens.[7] Rather than placing blame solely on mothers, feminists explain that anorexia may be a girl's logical solution to a world in which women's bodies are treated like objects and ridiculed. While non-feminist theorists may root a girl's anorexia in unconscious conflcts with her mother, feminists argue that it is necessary to look at the entire family. Mothers are not the only ones implicated in encouraging girls to diet and distrust their appetites: fathers, siblings, and other relatives are often responsible as well. Fathers may ridicule girls as their bodies develop, tell them that they should not be "fat like their mother," demand that they diet, and link weight loss to the family's social success.

Whether they're African-American, Latina, or white, most girls grow up learning that being thin is valued—especially for women. All of the women I interviewed talked about being aware of this pressure at some point in their lives. They all experienced the physiological and psychological stress of dieting—which researchers have implicated in the onset of bulimia and anorexia.[8] Family pressure to curb their appetites, use diet pills, and diet did render many vulnerable to anorexia and bulimia. Many of the women were put on diets or were given diet pills before adolescence—perhaps disrupting their metabolisms and making it more rather than less difficult to lose weight. (We now know that persistent dieting can lower the resting metabolism, which can result in weight gain rather than loss.)[9] Diet pills also jeopardize physical strength and sleeping patterns. One woman had routinely cleaned her room in the middle of the night, not knowing that her insomnia was linked to the mescaline in her diet pills. It wasn't until she was in college and saw friends' frenetic activity when they were taking speed that she realized that her childhood hyperactivity was drug-induced. Another woman collapsed and had a seizure in reaction to diet pills. She was rushed to the hospital and prescribed a strong depressant. She remembers being "totally freaked out. I was shaking. I couldn't talk. It was like my tongue had swollen in my mouth and I was completely stoned. . . . That was . . . my first introduction to dieting." A third woman remembers feeling like she was going to pass out playing softball and running track because she had so little food in her body.

Many of the women responded to enforced dieting by sneaking or stealing food and then bingeing secretly. The woman who was hospitalized came home, ate an enormous amount of chicken, and slept for twenty-four hours because she hadn't slept in three weeks. The woman who worried about fainting at sports practice binged as a way of compensating for being deprived of food. Some of the women stole money from their mothers purses to buy food when they were as young as six and seven. In response to constant teasing about her weight, one woman remembers thinking, "I will show you. I can be as fat as I want. I will still have friends. I would go eat. Stuff myself. I would go get candy. Steal candy. Candy bars. Hide them in my pocket."

Many of the women say that they lost weight but eventually gained back more than they had lost. The presentation of dieting as an inevitable requirement of growing up female initiated a cycle of dieting, bingeing, and purging that, once it was begun, was hard to stop. Enforced dieting undermines a girl's bodily integrity—her ability to control what goes in and out of her body—by making it difficult for her to control her desire to binge. It whittles away her sense of being able to control how much or when she eats, which compromises her belief that she is in charge of her body.

Many of the women had a difficult time developing an accurate sense of their body size and shape as a result of their families' inaccurate and inconsistent assessments. Many who were put on diets would be considered "normal" according to insurance charts. Often what was identified as fat was actually their developing breasts and hips—suggesting that the psychoanalytic assumption that a girl develops eating problems as a result of her own fear of having an adult female body is in at least some cases unwarranted. In fact, *others'* fears of girls' growing bodies can serve as the catalyst for dieting and disruption of their normal processes of development.

Because the development of hips and breasts was misnamed as fat, the women often lost a realistic sense of their body sizes and shapes. Dawn says, "At age eleven or twelve, when I started to develop, I remember being fascinated. Loving my body. Standing in front of the mirror and looking. Posing with no clothes on. Loving the shape of my waist.'' During the same year, Dawn remembers, her mother turned to her and said, 'You have to be careful. You are starting to put on weight"; "I don't even think I weighed 105 pounds," says Dawn now. In response to this warning,

> I started lo realize that actually my hips were a little bigger than they should be. I had already been concerned around food because my sister has always been a little overweight. I got messages from very, very young that a woman's worth is in [her] size.

Stories of parents' confusing observations about their daughters' weight are common. Another woman, Vera, says:

> I was not a fat child. My mother had me believe I was. But I wasn't. I used to look at other girls and compare myself to them. I would think, I am not as thin as her, but I am not as fat as her.

As she tried to develop a realistic understanding of her body's contours, her mother continued to confuse her. Her mother told her that she was so fat she would have to wear a nurse's uniform to her eighth-grade graduation because a uniform store was the only place where they made white clothes big enough for her. The comment devastated her. Actually, though, her mother had already sent for a beautiful dress from Mexico—a size nine, certainly not large for a thirteen-year-old girl who had already been through puberty. She also remembers, when she was fifteen, walking down the street with her mother, who pointed to a woman who weighed 300 pounds:

> When she walked her behind went boom-boom-boom-boom. She was an incredibly obese person. My mother said, "You look just like her. Your body is exactly like hers." I can remember going home and standing in front of the mirror and looking and looking and looking. In my mind I was totally warped as to what I looked like. I was probably wearing [a size] eleven or thirteen. When I would lose a little weight I would wear a nine.

Another woman was told by all of her sisters and her mother that she was the fattest one of them all. She was the last to be served at each meal and was picked on for being overweight. She cried her way through most meals. It wasn't until she was an adult that she realized by looking at pictures that she was not a fat child and that, in fact, her mother was obese.

Dieting was the initial way many of the women had tried to cope with confusion about their body sizes. If they were not able to figure out if they were fat, many reasoned that it wouldn't hurt to diet. Paying close attention to their eating began as an attempt to assert some control over their bodies. At least initially, this helped avoid being teased about an "unacceptable" body size and allowed them to counteract what they were being blamed for.

Dieting often backfired. What began as a way to control eating frequently resulted in bingeing and, in some cases, purging. Other traumas exacerbated these cycles. Many of the women have had to adjust to major changes in their body sizes at least once and often many times during their lives. Extreme weight fluctuation not only can cause physical damage but also impairs a woman's ability to know her actual size. Sudden weight gain and loss leaves a woman little time to adjust to changes in her body dimensions.

American Dreams and Unsatisfied Hungers

The childhood lessons that African-American, Latina, and white women learn illuminate pressures about body size and appetites that have not yet been examined in research or focused on by the media. Jewish and black parents may assume that although they cannot protect their daughters from anti-Semitism and racism, encouraging thinness at least shields them from discrimination against fat people. An African-American or Latino parent who tells a child not to eat and then feeds her confuses the child as she learns to feed herself, yet the feeding may also indicate a cultural tradition of nurturing through food. When a Puerto Rican mother gives her five-year-old daughter a food supplement to make her gain weight, then ridicules her when she gains weight as an adolescent, pressures of assimilation may account for the mother's change of heart.

To understand why a girl's relatives want her to be thin, we need to know what forms of economic, racial, ethnic, and religious discrimination they have encountered. Underlying an attempt to make a girl thin is an often unspoken assumption that while the family might not be financially stable, or it cannot fully shield her from racism, or it does not speak English without an accent, her small size may make her life and theirs somewhat easier. Some African-American women and Latinas I interviewed related pressure to be thin to their parents' hopes to be middle class, and middle-class standing depended upon upholding this aesthetic. The dual strain of changing class expectations and racism may explain why some of the women of color linked an emphasis on thinness to class pressures while the white women did not. Class does not, by itself, determine whether or not the women were expected to be thin. Supposing that it does implies that poor women—both women of color and white women—are somehow culturally "out of the loop," an assumption that is both demeaning and inaccurate. But changes in class did fuel some parents' desire to control their daughters' appetites.

Pressures on parents do not justify their attempts to mold their daughters' bodies, but understanding why women across race and class develop eating problems requires clarifying what constitutes the "culture" in the culture-of-thinness model. Many people accept the notion that body size is, in fact, something that can be controlled, given enough self-discipline. This ideology makes dieting appear to be a logical strategy. When caretakers demand that their daughters be thin, some may do so believing that they have more control over weight than over other more complex and insidious forces that they have little power to change.

Doing justice to the social context in which eating problems arise also explains why the culture-of-thinness model needs to be considered along with other destructive social forces. Although thinness is an institutionally supported criterion for beauty, imperatives about age, color, and sexuality matter as well An often-cited 1980 study documents the emergence of the culture of thinness by showing a marked decrease in the weight of centerfold models in *Playboy* magazine and the winners of the Miss America Pageant between 1959 and 1978.[10] This study quantifies a relationship between the social emphasis on thinness and the increase in eating problems but does not point out that, until recently, women in *Playboy* and the Miss America Pageant have been almost exclusively white, young, and heterosexual. Although the study shows that both the magazine and the pageant support a tyranny of slenderness, an integrated analysis would also elucidate tyranny based on the glorification of whiteness, youth, heterosexuality, and able-bodiedness. An expansive understanding of socialization requires scrutiny of the power of racism and classism as they inform standards of appearance. While white skin will not protect a fat woman from weight discrimination, it does protect her from racial discrimination. The resilience of the stereotype of the fat black "mammy" shows the futility and damage of considering standards of beauty as simply gendered. Interpreting socialization inclusively shows the myriad pressures affecting girls' opinions of their bodies. This approach also paves the way for seeing why girls—across race, class, religion, and ethnicity—may turn to food as a reaction to injustice.

I'm Not Fat, I'm Latina

by Christy Haubegger

I recently read a newspaper article that reported that nearly 40 percent of Hispanic and African-American women are overweight. At least I'm in good company. Because according to even the most generous height and weight charts at the doctor's office, I'm a good 25 pounds overweight. And I'm still looking for the pantyhose chart that has me on it (according to Hanes, I don't exist). But I'm happy to report that in the Latino community, my community, I fit right in.

Latinas in this country live in two worlds. People who don't know us may think we're fat. At home, we're called *bien cuidadas* (well cared for).

I love to go dancing at Cesar's Latin Palace here in the Mission District of San Francisco. At this hot all-night salsa club, it's the curvier bodies like mine that turn heads. I'm the one on the dance floor all night while some of my thinner friends spend more time waiting along the walls. Come to think of it, I wouldn't trade my body for any of theirs.

But I didn't always feel this way. I remember being in high school and noticing that none of the magazines showed models in bathing suits with bodies like mine. Handsome movie heroes were never hoping to find a chubby damsel in distress. The fact that I had plenty of attention from Latino boys wasn't enough. Real self-esteem cannot come from male attention alone.

My turning point came a few years later. When I was in college, I made a trip to Mexico, and I brought back much more than sterling-silver bargains and colorful blankets.

I remember hiking through the awesome ruins of the Maya and the Aztecs, civilizations that created pyramids as large as the ones in Egypt. I loved walking through temple doorways whose clearance was only two inches above my head, and I realized that I must be a direct descendant of those ancient priestesses for whom those doorways had originally been built.

For the first time in my life, I was in a place where people like me were the beautiful ones. And I began to accept, and even like, the body that I have.

I know that medical experts say that Latinas are twice as likely as the rest of the population to be overweight. And yes, I know about the health problems that often accompany severe weight problems. But most of us are not in the danger zone; we're just bien cuidadas. Even the researchers who found that nearly 40 percent of us are overweight noted that there is a greater "cultural acceptance" of being overweight within Hispanic communities. But the article also commented on the cultural-acceptance factor as if it were something unfortunate, because it keeps Hispanic women from becoming healthier. I'm not so convinced that we're the ones with the problem.

If the medical experts were to try and get to the root of this so-called problem, they would probably find that it's part genetics, part enchiladas. Whether we're Cuban-American, Mexican-American, Puerto Rican or Dominican, food is a central part of Hispanic culture. While our food varies from fried plaintains to tamales, what doesn't change is its role in our lives. You feed people you care for, and so if you're well cared for, *bien cuidada,* you have been fed well.

I remember when I used to be envious of a Latina friend of mine who had always been on the skinny side. When I confided this to her a while ago, she laughed. It turns out that when she was growing up, she had always wanted to look more like me. She had trouble getting dates with Latinos in high school, the same boys that I dated. When she was little, the other kids in the neighborhood had even given her a cruel nickname: *la seca,* "the dry one." I'm glad I never had any of those problems.

Our community has always been accepting of us well-cared-for women. So why don't we feel beautiful? You only have to flip through a magazine or watch a movie to realize that beautiful for most of this country still means tall, blond and underfed. But now we know it's the magazines that are wrong. I, for one, am going to do what I can to make sure that *mis hijas,* my daughters, won't feel the way I did.

WORKSHEET—CHAPTER 13

Food and Body Image
The Continuum of Women and Food Relationships

This study guide is designed to help us see the similarities among a wide range of behaviors which get labeled as "eating disorders" and very related patterns which do not get labeled as "eating disorders."

The so called "eating disorders" feel less threatening to us if we can view them as extreme cases which have nothing to do with us. However, even if we look at how common the extremes are, we must already face the fact that eating disorders are very much a part of our lives.

It may be more helpful to understanding the ambivalent relationship many women (in most western countries) have to their bodies and their food if we look at a wide range of eating patterns as a part of a continuum. If anorexia, bulimia, and compulsive eating are seen as exaggerated manifestations of dieting, we may be better able to both understand how our society encourages "eating disorders" and the unnaturalness and unhealthiness of most dieting.

1. Make a list (collect examples from magazines, television, conversations, jokes) of messages women get about what they should look like. Make a list (collect examples from magazines, television, conversations, on-street advertising) of messages women get about delicious food available to them to eat or prepare.

    What is contradictory about these messages? How do women internalize these confused messages?

2. Read the definitions for all the eating disorders (pp. 607–608). Look for similarities between the different patterns.

    Being creative (!), think of a way to show the similarities between different patterns by connecting them with overlapping circles or lines. You may want to photocopy the page and do a "cut and paste" job. You may want to use several different colors to identify themes which keep occurring.

3. Reread definition #9 for "unnatural relationship to food and eating". Do you think this description of women for a body image study reflects *all* women or is peculiar only to women concerned with body image? Can you think of ten women you know who are not concerned about body image? Can you think of ten women you know who are not very conscious of food/weight/exercise issues?

4. Based on your own experiences and the two articles by Becky Thompson and Christy Haubegger, describe whether you think body image issues are the same or different for white women and women of color.

5. Describe how you think race, class, and heterosexism impact on body image issues.

6. Many girls and women are pressured to be thinner than they are genetically meant to be. Based on the articles in this chapter and your own observations, identify some of the consequences of this for individual women and society.

The Continuum of Women and Food Relationships

Starving[16]

Large for years[15]

Anorexia[1]

Subgroup of
weight preoccupied[2]

Weight
preoccupied[3]

Up and down dieters[14]

Anorexia-like symptoms[4]

Compulsive eater[13]

Chronic anorexia[5]

Dieter
ex-"normal eater"[12]

Recovered anorexic[6]

Bulimorexic[8]

Thin fat people[11]

Ex-anorexic difficulties resolved[7]

Used to living on
semi-starvation diet[10]

Unnatural relationship
to food and eating[9]

1. Anorexic—Try to avoid eating as far as possible. Often have a distorted view of their bodies seeing themselves as grotesque and enormous instead of thin. Tend to be extremely close mouthed about their eating but observe others closely. (Orbach, 1984, p.30)

2. Sub-group of weight pre-occupied women. This group scored high or higher than the anorexia nervosa group on all Eating Disorder Inventory (EDI) subscales. (The EDI is designed to assess the cognitive and behavioral dimensions characteristic of anorexia and to differentiate between patients with anorexia and those without the disorder.) "It is likely that at the very least, they suffer from a subclinical variant of the disorder." (Garner, 1984, pp. 255–266.)

3. Weight preoccupied women. This group was compared to women with anorexia by the EDI (see 2). Weight preoccupied women and anorexic women were comparable on body dissatisfaction, bulimia, perfectionism, and maturity fears subscales. The EDI subscales which best differentiated weight preoccupied women from anorexics were ineffectiveness and interreceptive awareness. (Garner, 1984, pp. 255–266)

4. Women with anorexia-like symptoms. College women who scored high on Garner and Garfinkel's Eating Attitudes Test. This group was similar to the anorexia group in the proportion of subjects reporting binge eating and self-induced vomiting. This group did not show distress on a psychiatric symptom checklist. "These findings indicate that food and weight preoccupations common in anorexia nervosa do occur on a continuum, but the milder expression was not associated with psychosocial impairment." (Thompson and Schwartz, 1982, quoted in Garner, 1984)

5. Chronic anorexic—anorexic makes a partial recovery, gains enough weight to keep her alive but maintains it at an artificially low level, sometimes for years. Her life continues to be utterly dominated by the desire to avoid food. (Lawrence, 1984, p. 108)

6. Recovered anorexic—sizeable proportion of ex-anorexics are able to live creative and independent lives but still retain some elements of their preoccupation with food and weight. (Lawrence, 1984, p. 108)

7. Ex-anorexic—difficulties resolved. "The woman is no longer vulnerable to further anorexic episodes and *is no more neurotic about food than anyone else.*" (Lawrence, 1984, p.109)

8. Bulimorexic—women often of average size, but weekly, daily, sometimes hourly, they binge on substantial amounts of food which they bring up. Very few feel comfortable talking about their way of coping. Feel purging after gorging is the only way to stay slim. (Orbach, 1984, p.30) Estimated 15–20% of USA college women have bulimia. Only 44% sought professional help. (Potts, 1984, p. 32–35)

9. Unnatural relationship to food and eating. For body image study, "I sought subjects with no history of psychiatric illness or eating disorder. It immediately became clear that it is a rare woman in this culture who is not eating disordered or who does not experience herself as struggling with food and weight issues. Of 114 women screened for this study 109 reported an unnatural relationship to food and eating. Of those selected as subjects—whose weights all fell within the normal range—only 1 woman was not actively waging a war against fat. This astonishing statistic suggests that weight and eating issues are inseparable from body image struggles in today's woman. "Although describing themselves as eating disordered . . . most women reported eating patterns typical of the culture as a whole, patterns that in men would never be labeled as pathological. These women are for the most part suffering not from eating disorders but from labeling disorders" (Hutchinson, 1982, p. 61)

10. Used to living on semi-starvation diet. Having grown up with the concept that thinness is identical with beauty and attractiveness . . . these women have grown used to living on a semi-starvation diet, never eating more than their bony figures show. Never having permitted themselves to eat adequately, they are unaware of how much their tension, bad disposition, irritability, even inability to pursue educational and professional goals is the direct result of chronic undernutrition. (Bruch, 1980, p. 19)

11. Thin fat people—people who stay reduced but who cannot relax. They seem as preoccupied with weight and dieting after they have become slim as before. (Bruch, 1980, p. 18)

12. "Diets turn 'normal eaters' into people who are afraid of food." (Orbach, 1984, p. 29)

13. Compulsive eating means eating without regard to physical cues signalling hunger or satisfaction. Feels out of control about what she eats. (Orbach, 1984, p. 29)

14. Women who go up and down the scale (maximum of 60 lbs), diet from time to time and binge irregularly. Open about talking about food problems. Feel that things would be better for them if they were thin. "The largest group of women." (Orbach, 1984, p. 30)

15. Women who have been large for years, who feel themselves to be fat, but are despairing about ever being able to lose weight. Experience their eating as chaotic. Discuss the topic openly. Feel things would be a lot better if they were slim. (Orbach)

16. Both starvation and dieting may produce many of the behaviors associated with anorexia. Both obese humans and starving organisms demonstrate thrifty metabolism, heightened preference for sweets and inhibition of satiety mechanisms. (Smead, 1983)

REFERENCES

Bruch, H., "Thin Fat People" in Kaplan, J.R. (ed) *A Woman's Conflict: The Special Relationship Between Women and Food,* Prentice Hall, New York, 1980.

Garner, D.M., Olmstead, M.P., Polivy, J., and Garfinkel, P.E., "Comparison Between Weight-Preoccupied Women and Anorexia Nervosa", *Psychosomatic Medicine,* Vol. 46, No. 3, 1984, pp. 255–266.

Hutchinson, M.G., "Transforming Body Image: Your Body, Friend or Foe?", *Women and Therapy,* Vol. 1, No. 3, 1982, pp. 59–67.

Lawrence, M., *The Anorexic Experience,* Women's Press, London, 1984.

Orbach, S., *Fat Is a Feminist Issue 2,* Hamlyn Paperback, London, 1984.

Potts, N.L., "Eating Disorders—The Secret Pattern of Binge/Purge", *American Journal of Nursing,* Vol. 84, No. 1, 1984, pp. 32–35.

Smead, V.S., "Anorexia Nervosa. Bulimarexia, and Bulimia: Labeled Pathology and the Western Female", *Women and Therapy,* Vol. 2, No. 1, 1983, pp. 19–35.

Resource Information

The following resources have been used in drawing together this collection of readings and are examples of the wide range of publications which now cover women's health issues.

NOTE: The following publications which produced articles reprinted here are no longer regularly published:

Bread and Roses

Changing Men

The Coalition for the Medical Rights of Women

Health/Pac Bulletin

Science for the People

Spare Rib

Abortion Access Project
552 Massachusetts Avenue, Suite 215
Cambridge, MA 02139
(617)661-1161

American Journal of Public Health
American Public Health Association
1015 15th Street, NW
Washington, D.C. 20005
(202)789-5600

The Boston Globe
135 Morrissey Blvd
PO Box 2378
Boston, MA 02107-2378
(617)929-2000
Website: *www.boston.com\globe*

Boston Women's Health Book Collective
PO Box 192
240A Elm Street
Somerville, MA 02144-0192
(617)625-0277

The Capital Times
1901 Fish Hatchery Road
Madison, WI 53713
(608)252-6480

Common Ground—Different Planes (The Wor of Color Partnership Program Newsletter)
100 Maryland Avenue, NE
Washington, D.C. 20002
(202)555-1212

COPE
Pulse Publications Inc.
Box 1700
Franklin, TN 37065-1700

Council on Interracial Books for Children
1841 Broadway, Room 500
New York, NY 10023

Domestic Abuse Intervention Project
202 East Superior Street
Duluth, MN 55802
(218)722-2781
Fax: (218)722-0779

Domestic Violence Hospital-Based Project
3556 7th Avenue
Kenosha, WI 53140
(414)656-8502

Essence Magazine
1500 Broadway
New York, NY 10036
Fax: (212)921-5173
e-mail: *info@essence.com*

FDA Consumer
Department HHS, FDA
5600 Fishers Lane, Room 15A19
Rockville, MD 20857
(301)827-7130

Feminist Review
c/o Routledge Journals
11 New Fetter Lane
London EC4P 4EE, England
(0171)583-9855

Frontiers: A Journal of Women's Studies
c/o Sue Armitage-Editor
Washington State University
Pullman, WA 99164-4032
(509)335-7268
Fax: (509)335-4377

Gender and Society
Sociologists for Women in Society
c/o Sage Publications
2455 Teller Road
Thousand Oaks, CA 91320
email: order@sagepub.com

Health Letter
Public Citizen Health Research Group
1600 20th Street, NW
Washington, D.C. 20009
Website: *www.citizen.org/hrg*

Health Values
PNG Publications
Box 4593
Star City, WV 26504-4593

Herizons (Women's News and Feminist Views)
Herizons, Inc.
PO Box 128
Winnipeg MBR3C 2G1, Canada
(204)774-6225

Indigenours Woman
Publication of the Indigenous Women's Network
PO Box 174
Lake Elmo, MN 55042-0174

Institute for Women's Policy Research
1400 20th Street, NW, Suite 104
Washington, D.C. 20036
(202)785-5100

International Journal of Childbirth Education
(Quarterly)
International Childbirth Education Association
Box 20048
Minneapolis, MN 55420-0048
(612)854-8660
Fax: (612)854-8772

Journal of the American Medical Women's Association
801 North Fairfax Street, Suite 400
Alexandria, VA 22314
(703)838-0500
Fax: (703)549-3864

The Journal of Naturopathic Medicine
American Association of Naturopathic Physicians
601 Valley Street, Suite 105
Seattle, WA 98109
(206)298-0126
Fax: (206)298-0129
Website: *www.naturopathic.org*

Journal of Women's Health
1651 Third Avenue
New York, NY 10128

Lilith Magazine
250 West 57th Street, Suite 2432
New York, NY 10107
(212) 757-0818/(888)254-5484
Fax: (212)757-5705

MS Magazine
Liberty Media for Women
20 Exchange Place, 22nd Floor
New York, NY 10005
(212)509-2092
Fax: (212)509-2407

The Nation
33 Irving Place
New York, NY 10003
(212)209-5400

National Coalition Against Domestic Violence
PO Box 18749
Denver, CO 80218-8749
(303)839-1852

National Latina Health Organization Newsletter
c/o National Latina Health Organization
PO Box 7567
Oakland, CA 94601-7567
(510) 534-1362
Fax: (510)534-1364
e-mail: *latinahlth@aol.com*

Network News (Newsletter of the National Women's
Health Network)
514 10th Street, NW, Suite 400
Washington, D.C. 20004
(202)347-1140

New Internationalist
PO Box 1143
Lewiston, NY 14092

On the Issues (The Progressive Woman's Quarterly)
Merle Hoffman Enterprises, Ltd.
97–77 Queens Blvd
Forest Hills, NY 11374-3317
Fax: (718)997-1206

The Progressive
409 East Main Street
Madison, WI 53703
(608)257-4626

Ragged Edge (The Disability Experience in America)
c/o Avocado Press
PO Box 145
Louisville, KY 40201-0145
e-mail: *editor@ragged-edge-mag.com*
on-line: *http://www.ragged-edge-mag.com*

Social Policy
Union Institute
25 West 43rd Street
New York, NY 10036

Sojourner (The Women's Forum)
42 Seaverns Avenue
Jamaica Plain, MA 02130
(617)524-0415

The Survivor Project
10 NE Fargo #2
Portland, OR 97212
(503)288-3191

Trouble and Strife
PO Box 8
Diss
Norfolk IP22 3XG, England
(0161)273-7535
United Council of UW Students
122 State Street, Suite 500
Madison, WI 53703
(608)263-3422

Wellesley College Center for Research on Women
Wellesley, MA 02181
(781)283-1000

Wisconsin Coalition Against Sexual Assault
123 East Main Street, 2nd Floor
Madison, WI 53703-3315
(608)257-1516

Wisconsin State Journal
1901 Fish Hatchery Road
Madison, WI 53713
(608)252-6100

Women's Health Issues and The Women's Health Data Book
Elsevier Science
Jacobs Institute of Women's Health
409 12th Street SW
Washington, D.C. 20024
(888)437-4636

Women's Health: Research on Gender, Behavior and Policy
Lawrence Erlbaum Associates
365 Broadway
Hillsdale, NJ 07642
(201)666-4110

Women's Institute for Childbearing Policy
c/o Jane Pincus
Box 72
Roxbury, VT 05669-0072

Women's Studies International Forum
Pergamon Press Inc.
Journals Division
660 White Plains Road
Tarrytown, NY 10491-5153

Women Wise
(Publication of Concord Feminist Health Center)
38 South Main Street
Concord, NH 03301
(603)225-2739

World Health Forum
World Health Organization
1211 Geneva 27
Switzerland